T0137173

IFIP Advances in Information and Communication Technology 307

IFIP – The International Federation for Information Processing

IFIP was founded in 1960 under the auspices of UNESCO, following the First World Computer Congress held in Paris the previous year. An umbrella organization for societies working in information processing, IFIP's aim is two-fold: to support information processing within its member countries and to encourage technology transfer to developing nations. As its mission statement clearly states,

> *IFIP's mission is to be the leading, truly international, apolitical organization which encourages and assists in the development, exploitation and application of information technology for the benefit of all people.*

IFIP is a non-profitmaking organization, run almost solely by 2500 volunteers. It operates through a number of technical committees, which organize events and publications. IFIP's events range from an international congress to local seminars, but the most important are:

- The IFIP World Computer Congress, held every second year;
- Open conferences;
- Working conferences.

The flagship event is the IFIP World Computer Congress, at which both invited and contributed papers are presented. Contributed papers are rigorously refereed and the rejection rate is high.

As with the Congress, participation in the open conferences is open to all and papers may be invited or submitted. Again, submitted papers are stringently refereed.

The working conferences are structured differently. They are usually run by a working group and attendance is small and by invitation only. Their purpose is to create an atmosphere conducive to innovation and development. Refereeing is less rigorous and papers are subjected to extensive group discussion.

Publications arising from IFIP events vary. The papers presented at the IFIP World Computer Congress and at open conferences are published as conference proceedings, while the results of the working conferences are often published as collections of selected and edited papers.

Any national society whose primary activity is in information may apply to become a full member of IFIP, although full membership is restricted to one society per country. Full members are entitled to vote at the annual General Assembly. National societies preferring a less committed involvement may apply for associate or corresponding membership. Associate members enjoy the same benefits as full members, but without voting rights. Corresponding members are not represented in IFIP bodies. Affiliated membership is open to non-national societies, and individual and honorary membership schemes are also offered.

Luis M. Camarinha-Matos
Iraklis Paraskakis   Hamideh Afsarmanesh (Eds.)

Leveraging Knowledge for Innovation in Collaborative Networks

10th IFIP WG 5.5 Working Conference
on Virtual Enterprises, PRO-VE 2009
Thessaloniki, Greece, October 7-9, 2009
Proceedings

 Springer

Volume Editors

Luis M. Camarinha-Matos
New University of Lisbon, Faculty of Sciences and Technology
Campus de Caparica, 2829-516 Monte Caparica, Portugal
E-mail: cam@uninova.pt

Iraklis Paraskakis
South East European Research Centre (SEERC)
Research Centre of the University of Sheffield and CITY College
24 Pr. Koromila Str., 54622 Thessaloniki, Greece
E-mail: iparaskakis@seerc.org

Hamideh Afsarmanesh
University of Amsterdam, Computer Science Department
Science Park 107, 1098 XG Amsterdam, The Netherlands
E-mail: h.afsarmanesh@uva.nl

Softcover re-print of the Hardcover 1st edition 2012

CR Subject Classification (1998): H.5.3, K.3.1, I.2.6, D.1.3, D.2.9

ISSN   1868-4238
ISBN-10   3-662-51937-0 Springer Berlin Heidelberg New York
ISBN-13   978-3-662-51937-0 Springer Berlin Heidelberg New York
ISBN-13   978-3-642-04568-4 (eBook) Springer Berlin Heidelberg New York
DOI   10.1007/978-3-642-04568-4

springer.com

© IFIP International Federation for Information Processing 2009
Softcover re-print of the Hardcover 1st edition 2009

Typesetting: Camera-ready by author, data conversion by Scientific Publishing Services, Chennai, India
Printed on acid-free paper   SPIN: 12755813   06/3180   5 4 3 2 1 0

Preface

Collaborative Networks

A Tool for Promoting Co-creation and Innovation

The collaborative networks paradigm offers powerful socio-organizational mechanisms, supported by advanced information and communication technologies for promoting innovation. This, in turn, leads to new products and services, growth of better customer relationships, establishing better project and process management, and building higher-performing consortia. By putting diverse entities that bring different perspectives, competencies, practices, and cultures, to work together, collaborative networks develop the right environment for the emergence of new ideas and more efficient, yet practical, solutions. This aspect is particularly important for small and medium enterprises which typically lack critical mass and can greatly benefit from participation in co-innovation networks. However, larger organizations also benefit from the challenges and the diversity found in collaborative ecosystems.

In terms of research, in addition to the trend identified in previous years toward a sounder consolidation of the theoretical foundation in this discipline, there is now a direction of developments more focused on modeling and reasoning about new collaboration patterns and their contribution to value creation. "Soft issues," including social capital, cultural aspects, ethics and value systems, trust, emotions, behavior, etc. continue to deserve particular attention in terms of modeling and reasoning. Exploitation of new application domains such as health care, education, and active aging for retired professionals also help identify new research challenges, both in terms of modeling and ICT support development.

PRO-VE 2009 held in Thessaloniki, Greece, was the 10th event in a series of successful conferences, including PRO-VE 1999 (held in Porto, Portugal), PRO-VE 2000 (held in Florianopolis, Brazil), PRO-VE 2002 (held in Sesimbra, Portugal), PRO-VE 2003 (held in Lugano, Switzerland), PRO-VE 2004 (held in Toulouse, France), PRO-VE 2005 (held in Valencia, Spain), PRO-VE 2006 (held in Helsinki, Finland), PRO-VE 2007 (Guimarães, Portugal), and PRO-VE 2008 (Poznan, Poland).

This book includes a number of selected papers from PRO-VE 2009, providing a comprehensive overview of recent advances in various CN domains and their applications. On this 10th anniversary of the conference, there was a special emphasis on the CN topics related to co-innovation and new collaboration patterns, performance management, competency modeling and management, VO breeding environments, partners' selection and e-procurement, soft issues and socio-technical aspects, collaborative work environments, and case studies and applications in industry and services, with particular emphasis on active aging and educational networks.

As in previous editions of PRO-VE, the book itself is the result of cooperative and highly distributed work among the authors of the articles and the International Program Committee members, representing a valuable tool for all those interested in innovation, emerging applications, research advances, and challenges of collaborative networks. We would like to thank all the authors both from academia/research and industry for their contributions. We appreciate the dedication of the PRO-VE Program Committee members, who helped with the selection of articles and contributed with valuable comments to improve their quality.

August 2009

Luís M. Camarinha-Matos
Iraklis Paraskakis
Hamideh Afsarmanesh

PRO-VE 2009 – 10th IFIP Working Conference on Virtual Enterprises

Thessaloniki, Greece, October 7–9, 2009

General Chair

Iraklis Paraskakis (Greece)

Program Committee Chair

Luis M. Camarinha-Matos (Portugal)

Program Committee

Witold Abramowicz (Poland)
António Abreu (Portugal)
Hamideh Afsarmanesh (The Netherlands)
Cesar Analide (Portugal)
Samuil Angelov (The Netherlands)
Dimitris Apostolou (Greece)
Américo Azevedo (Portugal)
Panagiotis Bamidis (Greece)
Eoin Banahan (UK)
Peter Bertok (Australia)
Xavier Boucher (France)
Jim Browne (Ireland)
Jorge Cardoso (Germany)
Wojciech Cellary (Poland)
Sophie D'Amours (Canada)
Alexandre Dolgui (France)
Guy Doumeingts (France)
Schahram Dustdar (Austria)
Elsa Estevez (Argentina)
Myrna Flores (Switzerland)
Rosanna Fornasiero (Italy)
Cesar Garita (Costa Rica)
Paul Grefen (The Netherlands)
Jairo Gutierrez (New Zealand)
Tarek Hassan (UK)
Tomasz Janowski (Canada)
Toshiya Kaihara (Japan)
Eleni Kaldoudi (Greece)
Iris Karvonen (Finland)

Alexandra Klen (Brazil)
Bernhard Koelmel (Germany)
Kurt Kosanke (Germany)
Adamantios Koumpis (Greece)
George Kovacs (Hungary)
John Krogstie (Norway)
Celson Lima (France)
Gregoris Mentzas (Greece)
István Mézgar (Hungary)
Arturo Molina (Mexico)
Mieczyslaw Muraszkiewicz (Poland)
Roumen Nikolov (Bulgaria)
Ovidiu Noran (Australia)
Paulo Novais (Portugal)
Adegboyega Ojo (Macau)
Eugénio Oliveira (Portugal)
Martin Ollus (Finland)
Angel Ortiz (Spain)
Luis Osório (Portugal)
Costas Pattichis (Cyprus)
Adam Pawlak (Poland)
Willy Picard (Poland)
Michel Pouly (Switzerland)
Goran Putnik (Portugal)
Ricardo Rabelo (Brazil)
Yacine Rezgui (UK)
Rainer Ruggaber (Germany)
Hans Schaffers (The Netherlands)
Raimar Scherer (Germany)

Weiming Shen (Canada)
Waleed W. Smari (USA)
Riitta Smeds (Finland)
António L. Soares (Portugal)
Jorge P. Sousa (Portugal)
Volker Stich (Germany)

Klaus-Dieter Thoben (Germany)
Lorna Uden (UK)
Antonio Volpentesta (Italy)
Lai Xu (Australia)
Peter Weiß (Germany)

Technical Sponsors

IFIP WG 5.5 COVE
Co-operation Infrastructure for Virtual
Enterprises and electronic business

Society of Collaborative Networks

Organizational Co-Sponsors

SOUTH-EAST

EUROPEAN

RESEARCH

CENTRE

UNINOVA
New University of Lisbon

Table of Contents

Part 1: Co-innovation in Collaborative Networks

Part 2: Collaboration Patterns

Part 3: Needs and Practices

Part 4: Collaboration in Supply Chains

Part 5: Teams and Collaboration

Part 6: VO Breeding Environments Modeling

Part 7: Modeling and Managing Competencies - I

Part 8: Modeling and Managing Competencies - II

Part 9: Knowledge Management in Collaboration

Part 10: Partners Selection

Part 11: e-Procurement and Collaborative Procurement

Part 12: Trust and Soft Issues in Collaboration

Part 13: Processes and Decision

Part 14: Management Aspects in Collaborative Networks

Part 15: Performance Management

Part 16: Agile Business Models

Part 17: Service-Based Systems

Part 18: Formal Models

Part 19: Socio-technical Issues in Collaboration

Part 20: Collaborative Work Environments

Part 21: Collaborative Networks for Active Ageing - I

Part 22: Collaborative Networks for Active Ageing - II

Part 23: Collaborative Networks for Active Ageing - III

Part 24: Collaborative Educational Networks - I

Part 25: Collaborative Educational Networks - II

Part 1

Co-innovation in Collaborative Networks

Networked Innovation in Innovation Networks:
A Home Appliances Case Study

Luis Berasategi, Joseba Arana, and Eduardo Castellano

IKERLAN Technological Research Centre
Pº J.M. Arizmendiarrieta, 2 0500, Arrasate-Mondragón, Gipuzkoa, Spain
{lberasategi,jmarana,ecastellano}@ikerlan.es

Abstract. Amongst different types of Collaborative Networked Organizations it is possible to highlight those created to develop and market product, process or business model innovation. In this type of innovation network, which has special characteristics, the challenge is to introduce effective networked innovation in the very same innovation network. This paper presents the main features of TALAI-SAREA © methodology that includes a reference model, a set of analysis tools and a method for implementing networked innovation in innovation networks.

Keywords: Innovation, Network, Model, Collaborative.

1 Introduction

Nowadays, it's quite difficult to think that internal competences and resources of an organization are just sufficient to respond to dynamic market requirements, so that the reason for collaboration [1] and [2]. In any case, with inter-organizational collaboration the need to adjust processes and tools, and achieve a level of trust needed for working together are factors that slow down and endanger, in many cases, the collaboration objectives themselves. Hence the need to constitute Virtual Breeding Environments (VBEs) that raise an organization's degree of preparedness for the agile launch of dynamic Virtual Organizations (VOs), where some VBE partners participate. The combination of these two concepts (VBEs and VOs), as part of the notion of Collaborative Networked Organizations (CNOs), is a powerful mechanism for establishing strategic alliances to create value [3].

There are many kinds of CNO, depending on the criteria selected. A good taxonomy is defined by Camarinha-Matos and Afsarmanesh [3] as a result of the ECOLEAD project. The criteria used in this taxonomy are based on orientation (long-term strategic/goal-oriented), driven aim (grasping opportunity/continuous production), and scope (organizations/professionals), amongst others. From the perspective of their objectives, different kinds of CNO can easily be identified according to their output: either creating new value (innovation), or translating this new value to the market (product/service supply).

In the current global and dynamic environment it seems clear that innovation must constitute a basic element for enhancing the competitiveness of European companies. Implementation of concepts developed under the CNO paradigm should also serve for

L.M. Camarinha-Matos et al. (Eds.): PRO-VE 2009, IFIP AICT 307, pp. 3–12, 2009.

the development of specific VBEs in the field of innovation, so-called "Innovation Networks" [4].

IKERLAN, based on its empirical knowledge in the field of innovation networks[1], has developed a methodology to help organizations analyze, design and deploy Networked Innovation. This methodology is called TALAI-SAREA © (Berasategi, 2009), and it contains a set of elements that, when treated holistically, allows a truly open networked innovation process to be implemented, one which contemplates the contributions of both organizations and individuals.

This paper presents the most relevant aspects contemplated by the methodology, and the principal key aspects to bear in mind.

2 State of the Art

The concept of innovation networks appears from at least Lundvall [5], but it is very recently, during the past few years, when this concept begins to be researched in volume. Roy Rothwell [6] in his work on innovation models already pointed to the fact that the nature of the innovation process evolves towards complex models that require high levels on integration, both on the intra and inter-organizational levels. Recently, Henry Chesbrough [7] complements the vision by coining the term 'Open Innovation' to describe the systematic integration of external inputs at different stages during the innovation process.

Although an unanimously accepted reference framework has not yet been achieved [8], important advances has been made by characterizing the networked innovation process. Kalthoff, Nonaka and Nueno [9] emphasis its informal nature and characterize it as multidimensional and multilevel, and Pyka [10] and Taatila et al. [11] examine its social aspects. These and other authors establish that innovation networks serve to promote creativity, increase the capacity for invention and act as a catalyst for innovation.

There have also been many attempts to categorize innovation networks. Dussauge et al. [12] carried out an initial classification according to field and strategic objectives, and Tidd [13] proposes identifying different types of innovation network according to two axes; radicalism of innovation, and partner similarity. But perhaps the most up to date classification and one that can shed the greatest light on the development of a networked innovation model is that based on criteria related to the sources of innovation. From this perspective, the literature distinguishes between three types of collaboration: (1) External collaborations with other organizations [14], [15] and

---

[1] IKERLAN's experience in the field of innovation networks arises mainly from its participation in a broad range of research and industrial projects. Some of the more representative are: (1) Research projects - TNEE (Thematic Network on Extended Enterprises). FP5. GTC3-2001-63019, K-FLOW (Advanced Methodologies and Tools for the Knowledge Management within the Extended Manufacturing Enterprise). FP5. G1RD-CT-2001-0066, ECOLEAD (European Collaborative Networked Organizations Leadership Initiative). FP6. IP 506958, REMPLANET (Resilient Multi-Plant Networks). FP7. 229333, LURRALDE (CON)ex (Promoting an Innovative Social Culture in the Basque Country for sustainable development). Basque Government 2007/09; (2) Industrial projects - Deployment of innovation networks in different domains: cycles (ORBEA), elevators (ORONA), white-appliances (FAGOR), gas&oil valves (AMPO), etc.

[16]; (2) Co-innovations through customers [17], [18], [19], [20], [21] and [22]; (3) Collaborations via Innomediaries; innovation market platforms [23] and [24].

From the perspective of managing innovation networks, the literature includes many approaches, in general more conceptual and descriptive in nature than experience based. Cooperation, coordination, creativity and chaos level are flagged as factors for success. On the other hand, García [25] centers his analysis on the importance of social networks, and Nooteboom [26] on the level of trust.

Particularly interesting from the perspective of empirical research is the work by Ojasalo [27], in which innovation network management patterns are analyzed. The results obtained serve to characterize innovation networks according to two axes, called "Rigid" and "Free".

In any case, and tackling the challenge of creating true networked innovation, there is still a long way to reach a holistic, systematic and integrating vision based on a networked innovation model. A model which embraces the different aspects to be managed taking into account the different collaboration types and with an eminently practical focus. This is the intention of the work presented in this paper.

3 Methodology

In developing the research we have based on previous studies identified in the literature, and a case study with a prestigious business group in the white appliance sector. This case study has been developed following an action research approach. Therefore, the research methodology adopted can be classified as a qualitative methodology [28].

Case studies are frequently used for exploratory and theory building research [29] and [30]. The selected case study, FAGOR Electrodomésticos, is mainly comprised of three companies: FAGOR Electrodomésticos S.Coop. located in Spain, FAGOR Brandt located in France, and FAGOR Mastercook located in Poland. Additionally, other subsidiaries participate in its innovation network within and without the electrical appliance sector.

The elements of the model, analysis methodology, and the transformation plan execution have profiled, and been enriched, within an action research type project [31], in order to improve understanding of social and cultural contexts within FAGOR's innovation network [32]. It is action research in the sense that IKERLAN is part of the process and the research directly influences its partner. But this is not a one-way process, the whole approach emphasizes co-creation [33].

4 TALAI-SAREA Model

4.1 General

IKERLAN, based both on its network research and its empirical knowledge, has developed its own methodology for helping organizations to analyze, design and set up Networked Innovation: it is called TALAI-SAREA - Advanced Techniques for Networked Innovation.

TALAI-SAREA contains: (1) its own reference model; (2) a set of analysis and synthesis tools for contrasting reality at the organization against the reference model, and; (3) the transformation plan necessary for each organization.

Six focus areas are defined in the model; the network of networks, the strategic orientation, the innovation factory, the collaboration space, the DNA of collaborative innovation and the innovation network scorecard (see Fig. 1).

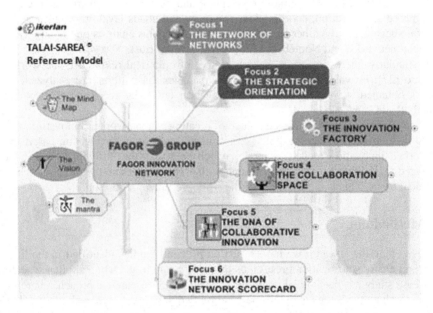

Fig. 1. Focus areas defined in TALAI-SAREA © model

The focus areas are axes for transformation where organizations that wish to innovate in a networked way must develop. The key aspects to develop within each focus area are identified (detailed for each focus point in the following points in this section). In many cases, the development of each key aspect can be configured as a subproject or workshop (we also call these "interventions").

The following are described for each aspect; objective, activities and actors implicated, content and form adopted by final result, set of methodologies and support tools and keys to success.

TALAI-SAREA seeks to develop integration as a key element of networked innovation:

- Holistic integration of activities (government, strategy, process, infrastructures and cultural) that require networked innovation.
- Integration of implicated organizations and bodies (internal and external).
- Persona integration (customers, workers, professionals, etc.) in open networks.

In the methodology, analysis of the situation of networked innovation in the organization leads to the identification and prioritization of key aspects to develop. The transformation plan within TALAI-SAREA implementation in FAGOR becomes a node project from which new interventions are developed (in the form of workshops and sub-projects), what orders, and integrates, other interventions currently under way. Such interventions are identified within the reference framework provided by the TALAI-SAREA model axes.

4.2 Focus 1: The Network of Networks

The network of networks describes the activities required by new organization to cease being isolated entities within a domestic space and become nodes within a global space. Interventions are included to:

> ✓ Design and form the network to assist designing networks of intra-organizational, inter-organizational nature and integrated within their corresponding regional and national innovation systems.
> ✓ The governance and orchestration of the network that identifies the activities required to organize and arrange activities between network members.
> ✓ The inclusion of the person (customers and non-customers, users, professionals, workers, etc.) in open networks during the innovation process.

Some of the key aspects are:

- Avoid hyperconnectivity and maintain ties outside the organization ("structural holes") [34].
- Adopt a light, efficient not excessively bureaucratized focus.
- Once the network is operational, don't stand still; continue orchestrating.
- Move from a Firm-Centric perspective to an individual (person) centric perspective and network [35].
- Adopt clear and shared IPR management strategies.
- Integrate the external open network activities with the internal innovation process.

4.3 Focus 2: The Strategic Orientation

The strategic orientation focus includes all interventions necessary to set a shared direction for activities in the innovation network system that are correctly aligned with strategy. Initially these activities are:

> ✓ The strategic positioning that identifies, according to markets and product typologies the best strategy (leader, follower, etc.) for networked organizations.
> ✓ The configuration of the innovation portfolio presents the correct mix of projects with different horizons for each product-market.
> ✓ The Roadmapping of the network focuses strategy on the innovation of products-services in concordance with: (a) the opportunities and threats in the environment, and; (b) the development, based on projects and collaborations, of technological competences.

Some issues of interest:

- Innovation is undoubtedly linked with strategy. The highest levels of involvement and leadership correspond to management teams.
- The creative process implicit in innovation is neither at odds nor restricted by strategic orientation. Furthermore, in the absence of infinite resources, strategy is needed to focus effort. Strategy is effective when the money invested in innovations projects is finally shared out.
- Strategy should not be an obstacle for an organization with a well-trained innovation culture going beyond initial goals and taking advantage of new opportunities in areas, a priori, not contemplated by strategy.
- The Roadmap is an excellent strategic definition and communication tool. Its content should be shared and sufficiently internalized by the members of the core network group.

4.4 Focus 3: The Innovation Factory

The innovation factory includes all interventions within the network innovation process under parameters of integration, efficiency and effectiveness when obtaining results. Such interventions are included in:

✓ The networked innovation process that describes the activities (innovation watch, identification of business opportunities, generation of innovative concepts and management of innovation portfolio) within a process of innovation in which multiple agents can participate from the network of networks.

✓ The innovation portfolio that describes the management activities for all the assets generated in the process (ideas, projects, products and innovative services).

Some of the key aspects are:

- Innovation is not just linked to the creation of "new things", like applying technology to products; on many occasions the best opportunities come from reconsidering other aspects: services, customer experience, value proposition, brand, etc.
- Although we know that innovation is also linked to chance and uncertainty we have wanted to use the name "the Innovation Factory" to reinforce the importance of articulating innovation according to parameters of efficiency and effectiveness when obtaining results.
- One of the greatest obstacles inherent in the innovation process is the slowness of the project development phase [36]. We must organize ourselves to develop innovations rapidly within a clear and shared process.
- The innovation process is not a linear process.
- It is important to manage all assets (opportunities, ideas, concepts and innovation projects) produced throughout the process.

4.5   Focus 4: The Collaboration Space

The collaboration space includes activities to construct the environment and infrastructure necessary to support the correct execution of network activities within the innovation process. This initially includes the following key aspects:

> ✓ The digital space that describes the characteristics and resources necessary for the virtual workspace in the ICT application.
> ✓ The physical space that describes the characteristics and resources necessary within the physical workspace.
> ✓ The social network, which describes the key aspects for designing a network between individuals that empowers interrelation, trust and obtaining results.

Some of the key aspects are:

- The approach should be light and focused on action, it not always being necessary to employ sophisticated IT systems for network operation.
- Useful, ready to use, applications are required, which seek interoperability with other systems already operating at the organizations.
- It is important to guarantee controlled security.
- Social networks must be actively managed. They are in large part one of the keys for obtaining high levels of network operation performance.
- The collaboration space must mix virtual interaction with face-to-face interaction, ensuring the necessary development of team feeling.

4.6   Focus 5: The DNA of Collaborative Innovation

The DNA of collaborative innovation contains interventions that lead to the conditioning and transformation of a culture favorable to networked innovation. Initially it includes the following key aspects:

> ✓ The network/community culture where basically the amplifiers and inhibitors of a network collaboration culture are analyzed.
> ✓ The innovation culture where were basically the amplifiers and inhibitors of a culture promote efficient and effective innovation.
> ✓ The cooperative culture where basically those amplification and inhibition aspects that in a cooperative culture may affect networked innovation.

Some of the key aspects are:

- The cornerstone of network working is the generation of trust between all network agents.
- Promote human relations.
- Share the same mind map, common language, but observing diversity.
- Manage uncertainly inherent in innovation and anxiety.
- Adopt an intra-entrepreneurial temperament in all members of the network of networks.
- Gather aspects that promote innovation that originate from the concept of cooperative organization, such as the sense of identity.

4.7 Focus 6: The Innovation Network Scorecard

The innovation network scorecard includes measurement and monitoring activities for network innovation systems. The activities revolve around the development of:

> ✓ The network scorecard, which gathers the evolution of critical indicators for governance and network orchestration, for the operation of the overall process and for the use of the collaboration space.
> ✓ The innovation scorecard to measure the amount and quality of knowledge assets generated during the process, and their impact on the business and activity of organizations.

Remember that:

- The innovation network scorecard is the best test for the proper operation of the innovation system as a whole.
- The number and quality of indicators used to construct scorecards must be selected carefully. The scorecard must contain little, but valuable information.

5 Conclusions

TALAI-SAREA obviously is not conceived as a closed model for universal application but basically as a practical approach that organizations could use to correctly guide the implementation of the Networked Innovation process. This approach takes into account innovation related practices and activities that many organizations already have, and require integration. Its main value comes from the orchestration of existing tools and practices in a holistic, systematic and integrating vision, taking into account different collaboration types.

From an Innovation Networks viewpoint, some differences with regards the generic model of VBE raise. The strategic alliance, in the case of Innovation Networks, is not only based on preparation for launching concrete initiatives (Virtual Organizations), but also on the following: (1) Clear and common strategy definition shared among partners; (2) Effective orchestration of different activities involved in the innovation process, also including the aforementioned strategic definition and innovation portfolio management, and; (3) The appropriate DNA that enhances the innovation collaboration culture. The challenge and opportunity, arises from the establishment of a true 'Networked Innovation' process inside the 'Innovation Network'.

References

1. Hagedoorn, J.: Inter-firm R&D partnerships: An overview of major trends and patterns since 1960. Research Policy 31, 477–492 (2002)
2. Hoffmann, V.E., Molina-Morales, F.X., Martinez-Fernandez, M.T.: Redes de empresas: uma proposta de tipologia para sua classificação. Encontro nacional dos programas de pós-graduação em administração, Curitiba 28 (2004)

3. Camarinha-Matos, L.M., Afsarmanesh, H.: Collaborative Networked: Reference Modeling. Springer, Heidelberg (2008)
4. Arana, J., Berasategi, L., Aranburu, I.: Collaborative Innovation Networks Management in the Elevation Sector. eChallenges Conference. The Hague (2007)
5. Lundvall, B.A.: Innovation as an interactive process: from user-producer interaction to nacional systems of innovation, pp. 349–369. Technical change and economic theory, London (1988)
6. Rothwell, R.: Successful industrial innovation: critical factors for the 1990s. R&D Management 22-3, 221–239 (1992)
7. Chesbrough, H.: Open Innovation: The New Imperative for Creating And Profiting from Technology. Harvard Business School Press (2003)
8. Oliver, A.L., Ebers, M.: Networking network studies: an analysis of conceptual configurations in the study of inter-organizational relationships. Organization Studies 19-4, 549–586 (1998)
9. Kalthoff, O., Nonaka, I., Nueno, P.: La luz y la sombra. La innovación en la empresa y sus formas de gestión. Deusto, Bilbao (1998)
10. Pyka, A.: Innovation networks in economics: From the incentive-based to the knowledge-based approaches. European Journal of Innovation Management 5-3, 152–163 (2002)
11. Taatila, V.P., Suomala, J., Siltala, R., Keskinen, S.: Framework to study the social innovation networks. European Journal of Innovation Management 9-3, 312–326 (2006)
12. Dussauge, P., Hart, S., Ramanantsoa, B.: Strategic Technology Management. John Wiley & Sons, London (1992)
13. Tidd, J.: A review of innovation models. Imperial Collage London (2006)
14. Gulati, R., Nohria, N., Zaheer, A.: Strategic networks. Strategic Management Journal 21-3, 203–215 (2000)
15. Contractor, F.J., Lorange, P.: Cooperative strategies and alliances. Emerald Group Publishing (2002)
16. Dilk, C., Gleich, R., Wald, A.: State and development of innovation networks. Management Decision 46-5, 691–701 (2008)
17. Cox, H., Mowatt, S.: Consumer-driven innovation networks and e-business management systems. Qualitative Market Research: An International Journal 7-1, 9–19 (2004)
18. Surowiecki, J.: The Wisdom of Crowds: Why the Many Are Smarter Than the Few and How Collective Wisdom Shapes Business. Economies, Societies and Nations. Abacus, London (2005)
19. Hippel, E.V.: Democratizing Innovation. MIT Press, Cambridge (2006)
20. Howe, J.: The Rise of Crowdsourcing. WIRED, 14 (2006)
21. Ogawa, S., Piller, F.T.: Collective Customer Commitment: Reducing the risks of new product development. MIT Sloan Management Review 47 (2006)
22. Tapscott, D.: Wikinomics: How Mass Collaboration Changes Everything. Portfolio Hardcover (2008)
23. Piller, F.T.: Interactive value creation with users and customers. Ideas for Innovative Leaders from the Peter Pribilla Foundation (2008)
24. Huston, L., Sakkab, N.: Connect and Develop: Inside Procter & Gamble's New Model for Innovation. Harvard Business Review (March 2006)
25. García, A.: Procesos de coordinación inter-empresa en la industria automotriz: un estudio de casos. Avance de tesis presentado en el Doctorado de Estudios Organizacionales, UAM-I (2003)
26. Nooteboom, B., et al.: Learning and innovation in organizations and economies. Oxford University Press, London (2000)

27. Ojasalo, J.: Key network management. Industrial Marketing Management 33, 195–204 (2004)
28. Myers, M.D.: Qualitative Research in Business & Management. Sage Publications, London (2009)
29. Eisenhardt, K.M.: Building Theories from Case Study Research. Academy of Management Review 14-4, 532–550 (1989)
30. Yin, R.K.: Case Study Research, Design and Methods, 3rd edn. Sage Publications, Newbury Park (2002)
31. Susman, G.I.: Action Research: A Sociotechnical Systems Perspective. In: Morgan, G. (ed.). Sage Publications, London (1983)
32. Rapoport, R.N.: Three Dilemmas in Action Research. Human Relations 23-6, 499–513 (1970)
33. Whyte, W.F. (ed.): Participatory Action Research. Sage Publications, New York (1991)
34. Burt, R.: Structural Holes: The Social Structure of Competition. Harvard University Press (1995)
35. Prahalad, C.K., Ramaswamy, V.: The Future of Competition: Co-Creating Unique Value with Customers. Harvard Business School Press (2004)
36. BW, BCG. The World's Most Innovative Companies. Business Week SPECIAL REPORT - INNOVATION (April 24, 2006),
http://www.businessweek.com/magazine/toc/06_17/
B39810617innovation.htm

Managing Distributed Innovation Processes in Virtual Organizations by Applying the Collaborative Network Relationship Analysis

Jens Eschenbächer, Marcus Seifert, and Klaus-Dieter Thoben

BIBA – Bremer Institut für Produktion und Logistik GmbH, Hochschulring 20,
28359 Bremen, Germany
esc@biba.uni-bremen.de

Abstract. Distributed innovation processes are considered as a new option to handle both the complexity and the speed in which new products and services need to be prepared. Indeed most research on innovation processes was focused on multinational companies with an intra-organisational perspective. The phenomena of innovation processes in networks – with an inter-organisational perspective - have been almost neglected. Collaborative networks present a perfect playground for such distributed innovation processes whereas the authors highlight in specific Virtual Organisation because of their dynamic behaviour. Research activities supporting distributed innovation processes in VO are rather new so that little knowledge about the management of such research is available. With the presentation of the collaborative network relationship analysis this gap will be addressed. It will be shown that a qualitative planning of collaboration intensities can support real business cases by proving knowledge and planning data.

Keywords: Distributed innovation processes, Virtual organizations, collaborative network relationship analysis.

1 Introduction

Companies are forced to shorten and improve their innovation cycles in order to stay competitive in the global market [1] and [2]. A good example for a short innovation cycle in a new market segment shows the introduction of the iPhone. Apple was able to create from the scratch a world-wide successful mobile phone. The success of the iPhone is based on an attractive design, the concept of being permanently online and a new and innovative user interface technology [3]. The question is how Apple was able to manage these challenges successfully without being active in the mobile phone industry before. The approach in this case was to integrate experienced partners with complementary core competencies into a collaborative network. The aim of this collaboration was to design a new and innovative product by sharing and combining previously isolated and distributed knowledge. This successful example demonstrates the potential impact of collaborative networks on innovation projects. As unpleasant side effect, collaboration within innovation projects always includes an increasing

L.M. Camarinha-Matos et al. (Eds.): PRO-VE 2009, IFIP AICT 307, pp. 13–22, 2009.

number of risks. Examples for those risks are the lack of synchronization due to the distribution of tasks and responsibilities, competing goals of the collaborating partners or the possible loss of intellectual property of certain partners.

Having the benefits on the one hand and the risks of distributed innovation processes on the other hand, the question is how to exploit the collaboration benefits while coping with the risks. The principle of the Collaborative Network as new organisational framework has been introduced by many authors [4], [5], [6] and [7]. As a special type of the Collaborative Network, the Virtual Organisation (VO) represents the task specific, short term alliance between independent companies. Due to its temporary character, the VO is the suitable collaboration type to create collaborative innovations based on identified business opportunities [8]. Here the analysis of collaborative relationships is a very important subject which needs further investigations.

The paper proposes an approach to plan and to maintain the individual relationships within a VO on an operational level, based on a quantitative characterization of these relationships. Specific attention will be paid to both the conceptual presentation and a basic mathematical representation of the approach. The application of the proposed approach, the so called "Collaborative Network Relationship Analysis (CNRA) will lead to an improved operational management of distributed innovation processes in Virtual Organizations. Finally, the CNRA is evaluated in an industrial case of a Virtual Organization in the automotive supplier industry.

2   Perspectives on Collaborative Network Relationship Analysis Supporting Innovation Processes

Innovation management can be seen from two perspectives: While the *strategic perspective* covers mainly innovation strategy and innovation organization (Gerpott 1999), the *operational perspective* deals with the design and management of innovations projects. A lot of research has been done to conduct innovation processes on the operational level. Approaches such as the Stage Gate method [9], the Innovation Funnel, Fuzzy Front end [10] or Process Diagram [11] have been introduced to maintain mainly innovation processes on an intra-organizational level. Distributed innovation processes in Collaborative Networks and especially in Virtual Organisations (VO) have been subject of several recent PHD thesis [12]. However the results are still in a nearly stage in comparison to the large amount of research analyzing intra-organisational innovation processes e.g. in multinational companies [13]. Additionally, most of this research is dedicated towards the optimization of the strategic perspective [14]. So far, an approach to better understand the operational issues of managing distributed innovation processes in VO is missing.

The operational management of distributed innovation processes in Virtual Organizations can separated in *early stage innovation phases* (focus on ideas management [15] and *late innovation phases* (focus on innovation project management [16]. Whereas the financial risks in the early phase are comparatively low, the management of distributed innovation processes becomes in later phases a decisive issue due to the increasing usage of resources and necessary investments. Consequently an approach is needed which both plans and controls the distributed innovation processes in the late phase.

Whereas the single site company as well as stabile Supply Chains or Extended Enterprises led by an OEM do have homogenous and synchronized goals and motives within an innovation project [12], in VOs the objectives and interest of the partners are normally very divergent and heterogeneous due to the independency of the partners. The distributed innovation processes in the Virtual Organization are based on the achievement of competing and synergetic objectives in the same time and the share of the related risks.

Consequently, the understanding and consideration of heterogeneous interests of the partners (nodes) within the VO as well as the harmonization of these interests when setting up the relationships (links) between the partners are essential success factors of innovation processes in VOs. The intensity of the bilateral relationships between the VO partners needs to be designed according to the specific collaboration needs of these partners during the entire innovation project.

3 Analysis of Collaborative Relationships

The analysis of collaborative network relationships has been introduced with the developments of the social network analysis [17]. The social network analysis was focusing on quantitative approaches analyzing nodes and edges. Recently qualitative approaches have been developed to supplement the quantitative approaches. In the following sections quantitative and qualitative approaches will be described and potential and limits will be illustrated.

3.1 Quantitative Approaches

The application area of the network analysis is very broad [18]. Especially the developments in the social network analysis led to many approaches (Wassermann and Fausst 1994) and a high number of tools [19]. Meanwhile business oriented study results are available focusing on the application of the methods of the network analysis in companies [20]. The authors were analyzing intra-organisational networks from the BASF corporate group. A recent study discusses the analysis of ICT aspects in the Siemens Corporation [21]. Ellmann has analysed two indicators out of many in the framework of the quantitative network analysis. Specifically she has studied the density and centrality of nodes within a network. Consequently the methods of the social network analysis arrived in the framework of business management. In general the quantitative network analysis is divided into three phases: data acquisition, data representation and data analysis [20]. Indeed there are different methods available to collect, structure and evaluate quantitative data [22].

The quantitative network analysis captures network structures by using mathematical calculations, which implies a very formalistic way of handling network relationships. In fact this has been the basis for a lot of criticism towards quantitative procedures of the network analysis [20]. Basically two points can be summarized:

- **Too Static:** Due to the different measurement of various characteristics, the procedures of network analysis are able to construct networks in deep according to their structure but content, and dynamics of relationships cannot be captured. Additionally, lacking consideration of context awareness seems to be a problem [23].

- **Difficult translation from experiences into numbers:** As a matter of fact the quantitative description necessary to operational qualitative characteristics by using indicators is to a certain extent impossible. Indeed an actor which is acting a long time already in the network can be a layman considering network analytic methods. But – and this is important – such a layman can most probably understand and translate the network behaviour due to his experience better than every network analyst.

The quantitative methods for network analysis can be used specifically in those situations in which already a lot of knowledge about the behavior of the network is available. This knowledge can be used within a precise analysis leading to concrete results. Additionally a narrow and precise research question should be formulated to make it understandable. In case of rough investigated research fields and non precise research questions the quantitative methods and not recommended. The research field should not have many explorative elements.

3.2 Qualitative Approaches

Indeed it is a question of the massive criticism towards the quantitative network research that qualitative network analysis is getting increasing attention. In comparison to quantitative approaches the usage of qualitative approaches is still in its beginning.

Qualitative methods for network analysis aim to transfer the layman theories of members of the virtual organisation about relationship constellations in the network analytical outward perspective. Exactly this transfer can be seen as the main objective of qualitative network research methods.

When it is made possible to interpret the actor's behavior in networks for outsiders in a transparent manner, then the network analysis touches ground, which were closed so far [23]. For this reason the qualitative network analysis can give direction for the network analytical research in general. Instruments which can capture and analyse both dynamic and temporal changes in the network can be seen as biggest conceptual challenge for research. The qualitative network research offers opportunities for doing this [18].

The qualitative network analysis can in the same manner as for the quantitative be divided in data acquisition, data representation and data analysis. The main difference lies in the kind of instruments and the respective questions. Naturally the qualitative network approaches are analyzing different instruments focusing less on mathematical accuracy but more on gathering and understands layman theories.

A nice overview about more qualitative tools for network analysis can also be found at [19]. Additionally, Hollstein [18] discusses the whole range of tools.

In order to achieve transparency by using qualitative research methods, the network researcher must enter the subsurface structure and the social reality of the network actors. This complex task gets even more difficult, because there is no common language between network actor and network researcher. While the network researcher is able to capture emotional and systematic characteristics of networks and transfer that to a comprehensive language, actors within the network might not understand this. Contrariwise it will be very difficult to translate layman theories into a network describing formal language. This is especially true because there is no commonly accepted network language which offers much room for interpretation [23].

The qualitative network analysis highlights context conditions such as trust and emerging standards. The analysis can be used as a form for exploring new issues such as innovation processes. Additional qualitative network analysis methods can be used for interpreting each actor, subjective perceptions and guided orientations [18]. However the results of the qualitative network analysis are always subjective because they are based on prognosis and estimates. In the case of this chapter both procedures are sued to investigate innovation processes.

4 Concept of the Collaborative Network Relationship Analysis (CNRA)

This chapter discusses the CNRA as qualitative approach to support the planning and maintenance of innovation processes.

4.1 Concept and Method

The concept of collaborative network analysis is based on some assumptions and basic conditions. The main assumption is that a group of companies have the intention to cooperate. In other words they are not carefully analyzing "make-or-buy" or deciding if collaboration is the right way to do the things. The SME have simply decided to collaborate in order to bring together resources, Knowledge and core competencies. The basis for the collaborative network analysis is the identification of the needed collaborative relationships. In a second step the collaboration intensity have to be specified. Another assumption is that the collaboration intensity varies substantially within the different tasks in cooperation. Thirdly it is necessary to forecast the needed interactions differentiated in 6 categories. Finally these issues have been supplemented by a model to analyze innovation processes (see Figure 1).

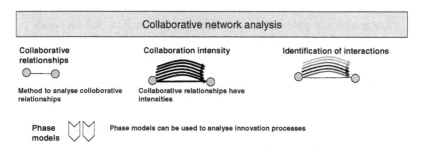

Fig. 1. Concept of the collaborative network analysis

Based on the concept of Figure 1 the collaborative relationships have to be forecasted and analyzed. The aim is to identify all three the relationships, the interactions within these relationships and the optimal collaboration intensity between the partners. Based on these conceptual ideas the collaborative network analysis method has been proposed which is shown in Figure 2.

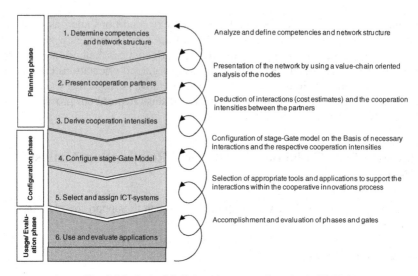

Fig. 2. Method of Collaborative network analysis (CNRA)

Basically the method differentiates three phases:

- Planning phase: in this phase the stage for cooperation is being set.
- Configuration phase: In this phase stage-gate model will be build on the basis of collaborative relationships and ICT system will be selected.
- Usage/Evaluation phase: In this phase the success of the forecasting results will be evaluated.

In the following the three sub-phases of the planning phase of the method is briefly described:

1. Determine competencies and network structure: First the necessary competencies and the network structure need to be identified. This is done based on the identification of collaborative relationships, their respective interactions with their divers' intensities.
2. Present cooperation partners: In this step a value chain model is being used to analysis the competencies of the nodes.
3. Derive cooperation intensities: In this step the deduction of cooperation intensities is taking place which finally led to the specification of cooperation intensities on the level of interactions.

In the following two sub-phases of the configuration phase of the method is briefly described:

1. Configure stage-gate model: In this step the stage gate model is build on the basis of collaborative relationships, intensities and interactions.
2. Select and assign ICT-systems: Select appropriate ICT-tools to support the innovation processes.

Finally the evaluation phase – sub-phase 6 – use and evaluate applications – analysis if the forecast and planning of the VO was successful or not. Here the focus is on the quality of the forecast of collaborative relationships and the forecast of ICT tools.

4.2 Derive Collaboration Intensity: Application in a Case Study

The ideas of collaborative relationships have been introduced in the previous section. In order to develop the collaboration intensity a five-step approach has been developed which links the needed information towards the identification. Figure 3 shows the developed approach to specify the collaborative relationships.

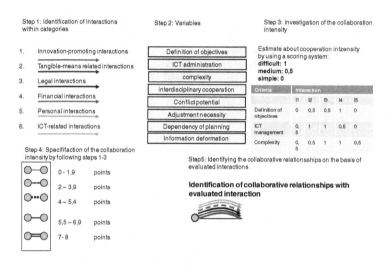

Fig. 3. Approach to specify the collaborative relationships

1. All identified interactions within the forecasted VO are collected. Additionally the interactions will be specified towards one of the six categories.
2. The variables are selected.
3. The variables are evaluated by using a simple method. An estimated about the collaboration intensity is investigated by a simple scoring system. This scoring provides ideas about the potential difficulty to conduct the interaction.
4. The collaboration intensity will be specified on the basis of the scoring result from the previous step.

Finally the collaborative relationships are specified by using the evaluated interactions.

4.3 Exemplary Usage of the CNRA Method

Based on the description of the previous section an example for the application of the CNRA method is presented here. In sub-phase 1 the competencies and the number of network partners have been investigated. Four partners collaborate within an innovation project. Altogether five competencies have been selected. The different partners do bring in such competencies in the collaboration. In the first place such competencies are based on interactions which are so far neither coupled nor further specified. The logical structure of the connections between the different competencies is shown in Figure 4. Here the interactions are not evaluated in a quantitative or qualitative manner. Finally Figure 4 presents the result of sub-phase 3 of the planning phase. Basically the approach has been applied to identify the type of interactions, the intensity of interactions as basis for and the interaction value chain. This Figure illustrates the forecasting approach clearly. The main objective is the identification of the needed competencies with the SME collaboration and to evaluate them. The color codes indicates the different interaction types.

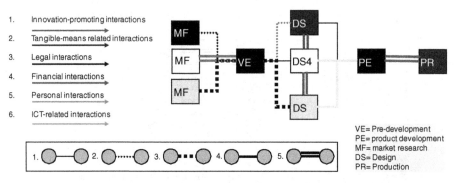

Fig. 4. Specification of collaboration intensity

The collaborative network analysis provides a detailed way to better understand and forecast collaborative relationships. From an application point of view the method focuses on an operational support for innovation project. The results provide a detailed overview about the concept of collaboration intensity on the level of edges between nodes.

5   Results and Conclusions

The method shall be used to support the forecasting innovation processes in VO. The CNRA focuses more on the forecasting of business developments. However both methods deliver ex ante suggestions of potential developments so they can be considered as explorative approaches. The results of the CNRA can be summarized as follows:

- Structural dimension: Short-term / mid-term planning of actors and their relationships; Network structure; Specification of necessary relationships, Roles of VO partners; Value chain structure
- Functional dimension: Design of distributed business process by using Porter Value chain model; Stage-Gate-Process; Collaboration intensity, Understanding of secondary value chain processes

In general the example illustrates a major improvement in their planning and forecasting activities by using the proposed approaches.

- More transparency about log, mid- and short term planning,
- Awareness about the usefulness about the usage of a VBW,
- Clear scenarios about potential developments of cooperation projects by using the CNRA an
- Better understanding about the evolution and metamorphosis of VBE and their respective partners.

It can be summarized that the proposed concepts do support VO in their ability to conduct planning and forecasting in an open, collaborative environment.

Acknowledgements. The authors thank the partners and the European Commission for support in the context of the COIN project under contract number EU-FP7-216256. For more information see http://www.coin-ip.eu/.

References

1. Gassmann, O., von Zedtwitz, M.: Trends and Determinants of Managing Virtual R&D Teams. R&D Management 33(3), 243–262 (2003)
2. Segarra, G.: The Advanced Information Technology Innovation Roadmap. Computers in Industry 40(11), 185–195 (1999)
3. Gassmann, O., Sutter, P.: Praxiswissen Innovationsmanagement. München, Carl Hanser Verlag (2008)
4. Camarinha-Matos, L.M., Afsarmanesh, H., Galeano, N., Molina, A.: Collaborative networked organizations – concepts and practice in manufacturing enterprises. Computers & Industrial Engineering, Article in Press (2009)
5. Schuh, G., Lenders, M., Bender, D.: Lean Innovation. Auf dem Weg zur Systematik. Industrie Management 25(1), S.23–S.27 (2009)
6. Chesbrough, H.W.: Open Innovation. The New Imperative for Creating and Profiting from Technology. Harvard Business School Press, Boston (2003)
7. Eschenbächer, J., Graser, F., Hahn, A.: Governing Smart Business Networks by Means of Distributed Innovation Management. In: Verwest, P.-H., van Heck, E., Preiss, K. (eds.) Smart Business Networks, Berlin Heidelberg New York, pp. 307–323 (2005)
8. Seifert, M.: Unterstützung der Konsortialbildung in Virtuellen Organisationen durch prospektives Performance Measurement. Dissertation an der Universität Bremen. Bremen (2007)
9. Cooper, R.G.: Third Generation New Product Processes. The Journal of Product Innovation Management 11(1), S.3–S.14 (1994)
10. O'Sullivan, D., Cormican, K.: A Collaborative Knowledge Management Tool for Product Innovation Management. International Journal of Technology Management 26(1), 53–67 (2003)
11. Cormican, K.T.: Product Innovation Management for Networked Organisations, Dissertation, National University of Ireland, Galway (2001)
12. Hagenhoff, S.: Innovationsmanagement für Kooperationen – Eine instrumentenorientierte Betrachtung. Göttingen (2008)
13. Christensen, C.-M.: The Innovators Solution: Creating and Sustaining Successful Growth. Havard Business School Press, Boston (2003)
14. Boutellier, R., Gassmann, O., Zedtwitz, M.: Managing Global Innovation – Uncovering the Secrets of Future Competitiveness. Springer, Heidelberg (2008)

15. Nyffenegger, F., Kobe, C.: IT-Unterstützung der frühen Phasen der Produkt-Innovation. Industrie Management 25, 45–49 (2009)
16. Herstatt, C., Verworn, B.: Management der frühen Innovationsphasen. 2. überarbeite und erweiterte Auflage, Wiesbaden, Gabler Verlag (2007)
17. Wassermann, S., Faust, K.: Social Network Analysis: Methods and Applications. Cambridge University Press, Cambridge (1994)
18. Hollstein, B.: Qualitative Netzwerkanalyse: Konzepte, Methoden, Anwendungen. In: Hollstein, B., Straus, F. (eds.) Wiesbaden. VS Verlag für Sozialwissenschaften (2006)
19. CASOS, http://www.casos.cs.cmu.edu/computational_tools/tools.html
20. Rank, O.N.: Formale und informelle Organisationsstrukturen: Eine Netzwerkanalyse des strategischen Planungs- und Entscheidungsprozesses multinationaler Unternehmen. Wiesbaden, Gabler (2003)
21. Ellmann, S.: Management komplexer internationaler Projekte: Netzstrukturen, Governance und Handlungsempfehlungen. PHD-thesis (2008) (to be published)
22. Eschenbächer, J.: Gestaltung von Innovationsprozessen in Virtuellen Organisation durch kooperationsbasierte Netzwerkanalyse, PHD-thesis (2008) (to be published)
23. Renz, T.: Management in internationalen Unternehmensnetzwerken. Wiesbaden, Betriebswirtschaftlicher Verlag Dr. Th. Gabler (1998)

A Balanced Scorecard for Open Innovation: Measuring the Impact of Industry-University Collaboration

Myrna Flores[1], Ahmed Al-Ashaab[2], and Andrea Magyar[2]

[1] Research and Networking, Processes and IT,
CEMEX Global Center for Technology and Innovation,
CEMEX Research Group AG, Römerstrasse 13 CH-2555 Brügg, Switzerland
[2] Decision Engineering Centre, SAS, Cranfield University, United Kingdom
myrnafatima.flores@cemex.com, a.al-ashaab@cranfield.ac.uk,
magyar.andy@gmail.com

Abstract. The Balanced Scorecard (BSC) can be considered as a strategic measurement tool. Since its first publication by Norton and Kaplan in the early 1990's, many companies have applied it to measure four key aspects of their organisations' performance: Financial, Customer, Internal Business Process, Learning and Growth. Although it is widely used in the business arena, this original BSC was not developed to assess the impact of collaborative research projects under an open innovation strategy, where the outputs of research and development (R&D) developed by collaborative projects undertaken by industry and universities should be measured in a different way. In fact, many companies are losing important opportunities to spur their R&D results by not being able to quantify the results of such collaborations. Therefore, this paper will propose a Scorecard to measure the outcomes of collaborative research. It is important to recall that this scorecard has been developed during a collaborative research project by CEMEX Research Group AG (Switzerland) and Cranfield University (UK). During such project, a survey was developed to carry out eleven face-to-face interviews in a sample of ten companies in UK, which provided important inputs to design such strategic scorecard. It was confirmed that a collaborative balanced scorecard is a very useful tool to measure, track and improve the impact of conducting collaborative projects with universities.

Keywords: Balanced Scorecard, Open Innovation, Industry-University Collaboration.

1 Introduction

The Balanced Scorecard (BSC) is a simple and useful measurement tool to track companies' performance [1]. It incorporates four main perspectives. Only one is related to the financial measures, which usually is the main concern of firms when measuring profitability and performance. Therefore, when the BSC was initially proposed, it integrated other three key elements to measure business success: customer satisfaction, internal business process and the ability to learn and grow. As a result, the traditional view to only measure the financial indicators of a firm was complemented in the BSC

L.M. Camarinha-Matos et al. (Eds.): PRO-VE 2009, IFIP AICT 307, pp. 23–32, 2009.
© IFIP International Federation for Information Processing 2009

to obtain the following four perspectives: 1) Financial, 2) Customer, 3) Internal Business Process, 4) Learning and Growth. The perspectives are the views of a company on particular vantage points which cover the main company's activities [2]. Those perspectives need to be assessed. This is possible due to the definition of the four elements proposed by Kaplan and Norton (1996) as shown in Figure 1: Objectives, Measures, Targets and Initiatives.

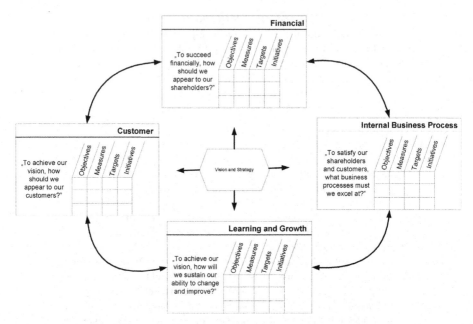

Fig. 1. The Balanced Scorecard as a Framework to translate strategy into action (Kaplan and Norton, 1996 [1])

The first element **"objectives"** focuses on clarifying and translating the company's vision into strategy. Companies need to define the aims and the achievements they want to reach in the future. This would allow creating a strategy that would enable them to reach their goals. The second element **"measures"** looks forward to communicating and linking the objectives with the results. Firms have to identify quantitative indicators for each objective. Therefore, the defined objectives and measures need to be distributed by means of newsletters, board meetings, companies' radios and electronic networks to make every worker aware of them. The third **"target"** element means planning and setting qualitative or quantitative goals. In other works, firms need to set numbered targets for each measured perspective. These targets may reflect the future aims in short or long term periods. The fourth and last element **"initiatives"** means using the strategic feedback and learning from past errors to improve. It relates to doing activities to facilitate reaching the targets [3].

When companies set out their future targets and plan them, they need to examine what they did during the last period in order to continuously improve. This supplies them with strategic feedback. Companies can then move forward with their business and decide for new initiatives or projects. Therefore, the Balanced Scorecard is used as a framework that emphasizes the importance of each of the four perspectives. It helps translating strategy into action [4]. Unfortunately, the traditional BSC is neither appropriate nor useful to measure the innovation outcomes when implementing an open innovation model when companies need to collaborate with external partners to develop new solutions [5], [6]. Therefore, this paper will present the outcomes of a collaborative research project where a novel Balanced Scorecard was designed to measure the outcomes of collaborative efforts with academia carried out in a particular area in CEMEX: Research and Networking in Processes and IT.

2 A Scorecard for Open Innovation: The Need to Measure Industry-University Collaborative Environments

It is important to highlight that the original BSC proposed by Norton and Kaplan was developed before the current growing trends to innovate and collaborate to be competitive in the global business environment. Therefore, the four proposed perspectives considered the firm as a closed entity and did not identified as strategic the current need from companies to be leaders at product and process innovations to remain competitive. Additionally, such first scorecard did not consider the fact that many new developments would be carried out along with external partners, such as universities or research institutions outside the firm boundaries.

R&D to achieve innovations is a very costly, risky and lengthy process. Nowadays, it is difficult and challenging for companies to innovate in short periods of time in an ever increasing global market where customers' needs change quickly and the products' life cycles get shorter. Some of these concepts have been lately spread by several authors. For instance, Chesbrough [7] defines the traditional innovation process as a Closed Innovation Model. The reason is that all innovation activities are located inside the company from the ideas creation, development process, sales and marketing. In this case, companies think that they are the best on their field; they have enough knowledge and resources inside their firm boundaries to develop such new solutions. According to Viskari [8], there are four erosion factors that cause problems in such closed innovation model: 1) availability and mobility of skilled people, 2) venture capital market, 3) external options for ideas sitting on the shelf and 4) capability of external suppliers.

Therefore, the closed innovation model cannot satisfy the fast changing demands of global customers in a changing society. Chesbrough [7] defines the Open Innovation model as the use of purposive inflows and outflows of knowledge to accelerate internal innovation, and expand the markets for external use of innovation. In other words, the new value chain is the assembly of all the processes and related activities that are important from the beginning to the final customers' product or service, as each of those activities add value during the process. Opening up can allow companies to tackle some issues such as: high costs involved in R&D, lack of skilled people and lack of knowledge inside the company.

In fact, many collaboration models have emerged to achieve more innovation outputs under collaborative environments, such as virtual organizations or living labs. As this is not a trivial matter, it should be considered a science where more research should be carried out to provide more tools and methodologies enabling more successful partnerships [9]. As a consequence, new models to measure collaboration outputs targeting value measurement systems have been also proposed [10].

In a nutshell, the Open Innovation concept strongly focuses on cooperation with others to achieve innovations, such as universities and research institutes. The main aim of corporate innovation with universities is to generate novel solutions improving business performance and also integrating new latent needs, such as sustainability. As a result, Chesbrough [11] defined six types of business models related to two aspects: Intellectual Property (IP) management and innovation process, as shown in Table 1. The adaptive business model, type 6, emphasizes the importance of the connection between the business model and the innovation process.

Table 1. Matrix of the Business Model Framework with the IP and innovation process (Source: Chesbrough, 2006 [11])

	Business model	**Innovation process**	**IP management**
Type 1	Undifferentiated	None	NA
Type 2	Differentiated	Ad hoc	Reactive
Type 3	Segmented	Planned	Defensive
Type 4	Externally aware	Externally supportive	Enabling asset
Type 5	Integrated innovative process into the business model	Connected to business model	Financial asset
Type 6	Adaptive (model is able to change by the market needs)	Identifies new business models	Strategic asset

Companies can apply an adaptive business model and collaborate with universities on different research projects in order to be more competitive in the market [12]. Collaborative research with universities is one of the main aspects for the development and dissemination of knowledge that helps accelerating the internal innovation process in firms [13]. The knowledge transfer between universities and companies allows the companies to survive on the quickly changing competitive market.

3   CEMEX – Cranfield University Research Project Objectives

As a result of the previously mentioned trends, there is a need to measure key elements besides the four perspectives proposed in the original BSC. Therefore, a collaborative research project between CEMEX and Cranfield University was defined and carried out to design a novel Balanced Scorecard to enable CEMEX measure the impact of collaborative projects with universities applying an Open Innovation model. Additionally, it was highlighted the need to assess how these collaborative projects, could also impact the economic, social and environmental axis of sustainable development. Hence, this CEMEX - Cranfield University collaborative research project had the following objectives:

1) To obtain best practices in regards to open innovation to measure collaborative research outputs based on a detailed literature review
2) To develop industrial case studies based on face to face interviews and a survey to design and validate a generic Collaborative Balanced Scorecard for Open Innovation, integrating new perspectives.

The Unit of Analysis to perform the data gathering and document such case studies, as a base to design the Open Innovation Scorecard was: **Industry-University collaborative research projects**. Therefore, the target was to define new perspectives and measures to design the Scorecard and analyze the result of such collaborations for innovation.

4 Research Methodology: Applying the Lead Collaborative Research Framework

The LEAD (Learn, Energize, Apply and Diffuse) framework developed in CEMEX to manage collaborative projects with external partners was applied as follows [14]:

1. LEARN
• Extensive literature review to capture the state-of-the-art about industrial opinions regarding their involvement in collaborative R&D projects with universities.
• The business application of the research's results, literature review on Key Performance Indicators (KPI), Scorecard and Open Innovation.

2. ENERGIZE
• Contact companies in UK to arrange interviews.
• Design, send and apply a structured questionnaire to obtain the lessons learned about their experiences and results when developing collaborative R&D projects with universities. In other words, how the research results were applied for business outcomes and how they were measured in terms of qualitative and quantities performance. Hence, with the help of the questionnaire, identify potential industrial's KPI's to measure the impact of collaborative R&D projects with Universities.
• Synthesize the industrial best practices to implement collaborative R&D out comes and measure the performance.
• Map the current literature of KPI against the industrial KPI from the questionnaire to measure the impact of collaborative research projects with universities.
• Propose a set of KPI (measures) to be integrated in the balanced scorecard for open innovation.

3. APPLY
• Design a matrix type of collaborative scorecard for open innovation to measure the impact on research results with universities on companies' performance with the help of literature and questionnaire results.
• Validate the collaborative balanced scorecard in two different companies.

• Based on Cranfield University results, develop a customised balanced scorecard for CEMEX to be applied in research and networking of Processes and IT.

4. DIFFUSE
• Disseminate the results internally in CEMEX and generic outcomes in international conferences and journals

5   Case Studies and Research Results

During the energize phase of the LEAD methodology, a questionnaire was designed to capture the industrial needs of collaborative R&D projects with universities. The firms' information enabled to design the Collaborative Balanced Scorecard for Open Innovation. Ten British companies from different sectors participated in this study. They are:

1. **Airbus:** One of the world's leading aircraft manufacturers
2. **Kodak:** Multinational for its imaging innovations in cameras and printers
3. **Skill2Learn:** SME doing serious business games
4. **Bookham:** Leading developer and manufacturer of optical solutions
5. **Smart Technology Limited**: Company that manufactures and develops products based on smart materials
6. **I-I-Ice Refrigeration**: Refrigeration and air conditioning
7. **SKF**: Leading global supplier of products and services related to rolling bearings, seals, mechatronics and lubrication systems
8. **Aerospace**: Global business providing integrated power systems for use on land, at sea and in the air
9. **Caltec:** Company that designs, develops and supplies equipment for improving production from oil and gas wells.
10. **Nissan Technical Centre:** Global car manufacturer.

The main findings of the face to face interviews were [15]:

1. Companies have different aims when applying Open Innovation models, but the most important aim is to create new technology, as shown in Figure 2.
2. Most of the companies believe that getting intellectual capital and developing knowledge relationships are the main benefits of collaborating with universities.
3. Another benefit was to generate more business by creating new products by collaborating with universities.
4. Most of the companies have always used peer review to measure research impact and have sometimes used return on investment, financial data analysis and number of patents to measure research impact. In contrast, most of the companies have never used the balanced scorecard or any other tool to measure collaborative research impact. The most common way to measure research impact is the number of publications and by developing satisfaction surveys.
5. The most important balance pairs are: Long/Short term objectives, followed by Financial/Non-Financial measures and by Lag/Lead indicators.

6. Most companies voted for the creation and dissemination of knowledge, worker efficiency and revenues as the three most important indicators to measure collaborative projects with universities or research institutes.
7. Competitiveness was selected by most of the companies as the most important perspective for collaborative research projects with universities and/or research institutes.

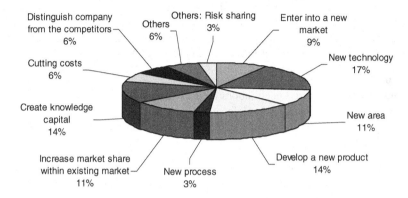

Fig. 2. Key aims of the collaborative research projects with universities based on face to face interviews to ten companies in UK

6 Proposed Scorecard for Open Innovation for Research and Networking – Processes and IT in CEMEX

After concluding the collaborative project with Cranfield University, based on the lessons learned of the 10 British Companies interviewed in the project, the following six BSC perspectives have been proposed by the Research and Networking area at Processes and IT Department [16] as follows:

1. Competitiveness: The ability to develop and implement new business models, tools, frameworks and methodologies for CEMEX to optimise its internal working practices and business processes performance.
2. Sustainable Development: Capacity to impact the environmental, social and economical concerns in each of the new collaborative projects with universities, integrating CEMEX key internal and external stakeholders.
3. Innovation: New value creation by developing new services, processes and intangible assets in CEMEX.
4. Strategic Partnerships: The development of new partnerships with external organisations, such as universities, consulting companies or associations in order to develop in a collaborative way new knowledge and innovation outputs.
5. Human Capital: Capacity to develop, share and diffuse new knowledge that can contribute to the company's growth and success. Support the formation of young scientists and researchers to then identify new talent for CEMEX while collaborating with students in universities.

6. Internal Business Processes: Processes that CEMEX requires in order to share and apply the collaborative research results during and after the conclusion of collaborative projects.

Each one of the proposed Balanced Scorecard's perspectives has objectives to achieve and there are certain relationships among them, for example creating new intellectual capital will increase new technology development in a firm. These cause and effect relationships among the objectives are shown in Figure 3. Some of the most relevant Key Performance Indicators (KPI's) as part of the "measures" element proposed to track and assess the performance of Open Innovation initiatives carried out by the Research and Networking area at Processes and IT in CEMEX [15] are:

1) Competitiveness
- Annual budget invested in collaborative Research and Development (R&D)
- Number of new business models or frameworks developed and implemented through collaborative projects per year to support the business and IT evolution in CEMEX

2) Sustainable Development
- Number of collaborative projects that improved environmentally or socially any region, community, or CEMEX facility
- Number of key internal and external stakeholders integrated in collaborative projects to improve sustainability concerns in the construction value chain
- Number of projects that developed new models, methods and/or standards to improve sustainability practices: health and safety, recycling methods, sustainable construction, etc
- Number of Knowledge Transfer Sessions organized to present Sustainability trends, novel technologies, etc

3) Innovation
- Number of intangibles per year as a result of collaborative projects with universities, in the form of patents, licenses, copyrights, trademarks, etc

4) Strategic Knowledge Partnerships
- Number of partnerships with which strategic collaborative projects are developed.
- Number of collaborative projects with universities per year
- Number of collaborative projects with consulting companies per year
- Number of successful proposals developed collaboratively to obtain external funding, such as the European Seventh Research Framework (FP7)
- Number of projects funded by external organisations
- Number of joint publications in scientific journals or conferences

5) Human Capital
- Number of new highly skilled employees per year hired in CEMEX as a result of collaborative projects, for instance students that participated in collaborative projects (attracting new talent)

- Number of CEMEX employees attending Knowledge Transfer Sessions (KTS) developed during and after collaborative projects
- Number of international conferences where CEMEX employees have attended to track trends and develop new projects

6) Internal Business Processes
- Number of new best practices developed and adopted in the company per year in each business process
- Number of improvements done to key End-to-End processes embedded in the CEMEX Business Process Architecture (BPA).
- Number of new tools, methodologies and methods developed to improve any internal business process to increase its efficiency as a result of a collaborative project with external partners

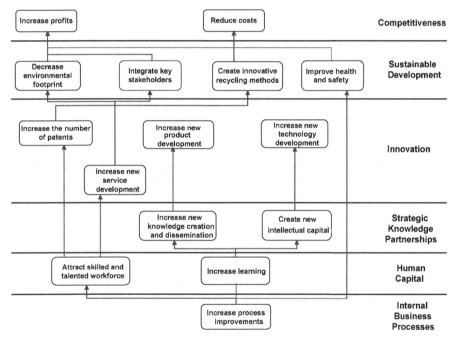

Fig. 3. Cause and effect relationships among the proposed Collaborative Balanced Scorecard objectives identified for CEMEX Research and Networking

7 Conclusions

A Balanced Scorecard to measure the impact of collaborative research projects was not available in the literature and is a current need for many companies to enable an open innovation model. Therefore, during this collaborative research project, a structured questionnaire was developed to obtain industrial requirements to design a novel scorecard that integrates the collaborative aspect with universities and other external partners.

Ten British companies from different sectors participated in this study. As a result, a generic collaborative scorecard for open innovation was designed. Based on this collaborative research outcome, CEMEX customised the findings to its specific strategic needs and defined different Key Performance Indicators (KPIs) in six perspectives to measure its current open innovation initiatives for Research and Networking in Processes and IT. This BSC for Open Innovation in CEMEX is still in the diffusion and implementation phases.

References

1. Kaplan, R., Norton, D.: Translating Strategy into Action: The Balanced Scorecard. Harvard Business School Press, Boston (1996)
2. Balanced Scorecard Institute: Balanced Scorecard Strategic Planning & Management Terminology (2008), http://www.balancedscorecard.org
3. NetMBA Business Knowledge Center, The Balanced Scorecard (2009), http://www.netmba.com/accounting/mgmt/balanced-scorecard
4. Niven, P.: Balanced Scorecard step-by-step: Maximizing Performance and Maintaining Results. John Wiley & Sons, Inc., Chichester (2002)
5. Voelpel, S.C., Leibold, M., Eckhoff, R.A.: The tyranny of the Balanced Scorecard in the innovation economy. Journal of Intellectual Capital 7(1), 43–60 (2006)
6. Gama, N., Mira da Silva, M., Ataíde, J.: Innovation Scorecard: A Balanced Scorecard for Measuring the Value Added by Innovation. In: Cunha, P.F., Maropoulos, P.G. (eds.) Digital Enterprise Technology Perspectives and Future Challenges. Springer, Heidelberg (2007)
7. Chesbrough, H.: Open innovation: the new imperative for creating and profiting from technology. Harvard Business School Press, Boston (2006a)
8. Viskari, S.: Managing Technologies in Research Organization: Framework for Research Surplus Portfolio, Research Report 176, Masters Thesis, Lappeenranta University of Technology, Lappeenranta (2006), http://www.openinnovation.eu
9. Camarinha-Matos, L., Afsarmanesh, H.: Collaborative networks: a new scientific discipline. Journal of Intelligent Manufacturing 16, 439–452 (2005)
10. Romero, D., Galeano, N., Molina, A.: Virtual Organisation Breeding Environments Value System and its Elements. Journal of Intelligent Manufacturing (2007), doi:10.1007/s10845-008-0179-0
11. Chesbrough, H.: Open Business Models, How to Thrive in the New Innovation Landscape. Harvard Business School Press, Boston (2006)
12. Flores, M.: Developing Collaborative Networks for Research and Innovation in Business Processes and IT Services. Internal CEMEX Research Group (CRG) Newsletter (2008)
13. Flores, M.: Industry - University Collaboration for Innovation and Regional Development: Evidence from Madras, Monterrey, Milan and Lausanne. PhD Thesis, Politecnico di Milano (2006)
14. Flores, M.: The LEAD Research Methodology to manage collaborative open innovation projects. CEMEX internal document (2008)
15. Magyar, A.: Measuring Impact of Research Projects on Company Performance. MSc Thesis, Cranfield University (2008)
16. Flores, M.: Developing a new Balanced Scorecard to measure collaborative research outputs. Internal CEMEX Research Group (CRG) Whitepaper (2009)

Co-creation and Co-innovation in a Collaborative Networked Environment

Edmilson Rampazzo Klen

GSIGMA – Intelligent Manufacturing Systems Group
UFSC – Federal University of Santa Catarina, Florianópolis-SC, Brazil
erklen@gsigma.ufsc.br

Abstract. Leveraged by the advances in communication and information Technologies, producers and consumers are developing a new behavior. Together with the new emerging collaborative manifestations this behavior may directly impact the way products are developed. This powerful combination indicates that consumers will be involved in a very early stage in product development processes supporting even more the creation and innovation of products. This new way of collaboration gives rise to a new collaborative networked environment based on co-creation and co-innovation. This work will present some evolutionary steps that point to the development of this environment where prosumer communities and virtual organizations interact and collaborate.

Keywords: Prosumer, Collaboration, Co-Criation, Co-Innovation.

1 Introduction

In the last recent years the globalized world has experienced its most amazing and rapid technological evolution. The repercussions and consequences of this (re-) evolution are many and can be seen and felt in the behavior of the enterprises and consumers. For enterprises, new organizational structures are taking place contributing even for the emergence of a new scientific discipline called Collaborative Networks. For consumers, a more active - and less reactive - role is gaining evidence and being directly influenced by the advances on information and communications technologies. The new web generation is participating in a silent movement of creation of prosumers[1].

As a consequence of this change in the behavior of the enterprises and consumers, a new space comes up with a high potential to be exploited. This space is called in this work as: products co-creation and co-innovation environment. It is an environment based on an innovation and creating value model, i.e., a model in which mostly collaborative activities take place.

In this sense this paper presents the surrounding and the evolution of the enterprises and the consumers (section 2) as well as analyses the requirements for the emergence of a collaborative production model where consumers are actively involved since the product design (section 3). In the sequence, having the innovation

---

[1] Prosumer is the result of the contraction of the words: producer + consumer, Toffler (1980).

L.M. Camarinha-Matos et al. (Eds.): PRO-VE 2009, IFIP AICT 307, pp. 33–40, 2009.

aspects on mind, the paper introduces the new actor of the proposed co-creation and co-innovation environment (section 4) and finalizes with some concluding remarks (section 5).

2   The Evolution of the Producers and the Consumers

Product is an item that ideally satisfies a market's want or need; a **consumer**, also called as client, or purchaser is the buyer or user of the paid products of an individual or organization; and a **generation** can be considered a stage or degree in a succession of natural descent and also stages of successive improvement in the development of a technology (WIKIPEDIA, 2009).

As production and its means evolve, the same happens with the generation of people to whom it serves (Fig. 1). This is mostly reflected by the evolution of the products themselves. But how about the interaction between producers and consumers? Did it also evolve? The next sub-sections present some aspects related to this question.

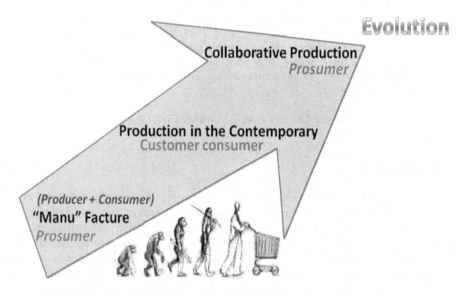

Fig. 1. Producers and consumers' evolution

2.1   "Manu" "Facturing" and the Prosumer

Prior to the eighteenth century "manu" "facturing" (in the real sense of the word, i.e., hand-made) was the only kind of production that was known. The artisans of technology of the Modern Age (1453 – 1789) were simultaneously responsible for product development and design, planning and manufacturing (PEREIRA-KLEN et al. 1993) as well as sales and after-sales activities. The available technology was very rudimentary. The producers at that time were often themselves their own consumers, that is, they produced for themselves.

During the Modern Age, and the times that preceded it, the majority of people ate what they produced. It was a "production for use". That is, people were neither producers nor consumers. They were what Toffler (1980) called *prosumers* (contraction of producer + consumer). There was, as Toffler said, a small quantity of production for exchange, i.e., for the market. But the production for use was predominant. And even when production was to exchange (or sale), the consumer had a great influence on the producer.

The events of the second half of the eighteenth century, as the Industrial Revolution, the independence of the United States and the French Revolution, helped to inaugurate the Contemporary Age. The increasing importance of trade and of capitalism at that time was one of the main reasons that contributed to separate the activities of the prosumers giving rise to what we now know as producers and consumers (TOFFLER, 1980).

2.2 Production in the Contemporary Age and the Consumers

Thanks to the invention of the steam engine there was an empowerment of the development of science and a considerable increase in the production through the manufacturing of clothing, shoes and other items. The ability to efficiently produce large quantities of products has improved as time passed by and with the studies that were being carried out. The studies of the Frenchman Perronet in 1760 and of the English mathematician Charles Babbage in 1820 on time and motion (CHANDLER and DALMS, 1980; BABBAGE, 1963) together with the classics "The wealth of Nations" (SMITH, 1776) and "Principles of Scientific Management" (TAYLOR, 1911) served as catalysts for the mass production.

At the beginning of the twentieth century Henry Ford, considered the creator of mass production, made use of assembly lines to allow the production of low unit-cost manufactured goods (ROCHA, 2003). This was an important trigger to the modern consumer culture we know nowadays. This means that with the born of the mass production, the consumer has also born.

Around 1950, Taiichi Ohno, went to the United States to study assembly lines of Ford. He soon realized that mass production in Japan would face major problems. Thus, in his return to Japan, along with his colleagues at Toyota, Ohno developed the Toyota Production System (GHINATO, 1996) that revolutionized, once again, the manufacturing models. This was the emergence of the world-wide known "Lean Manufacturing".

With the flexibility given to the idea of Ford, the "Lean Manufacturing" concept has gained notoriety in the west mainly at the end of the 1980s and at the beginning of the 1990s with the publication of the modern classic "The machine that changed the world" (WOMACK et al., 1990).

Still in the early 1990s, manufacturing gained new contours. It became "agile". The researchers who developed the term "agile manufacturing" (GOLDMAN, et al., 1991) were asked by the north-American Congress to conduct a study to define the bases of the industries of the next century (or the 21st century, in which we are currently today). The study should define how the US companies could become again internationally competitive, facing the new industrial potencies - mainly Japan.

In the report entitled "21st Century Manufacturing Strategy", the researchers foresaw an environment characterised by uncertainty and constant change. That is, they predicted challenges which needed to be faced in a different way. Thus the agile manufacturing emerged with the objective of developing agile properties (KIDD, 1994a and 1994b). This agility is then used to achieve competitive advantage and, therefore, to respond quickly to changes that occur in a turbulent market environment making use of the ability of people to use and exploit the fundamental resources of knowledge. Kidd defines agile manufacturing as the integration of organization, highly qualified people and advanced technologies to obtain cooperation and innovation in response to the need to supply customized and high quality products to consumers.

The decades of the 80s and 90s were very fruitful in terms of production models. This was also the time where mass customization was born. Despite being considered a relatively recent business strategy (VIGNA, 2007) the mass customization was envisaged in the middle of the eighties and emerged in the business environment in the middle of the nineties. The mass customization appeared to break some paradigms of the manufacturing reality: to offer customized products and/or services at a cost similar to that would be achieved by mass production.

Finally, it is worth to mention that consumers' society of the Contemporary Age was influenced by several factors. This consumers' generation has evolved to a similar extent as also did the marketing techniques, production technologies, financing methods as well as to the extent that the design has become even more important. Nevertheless the behavior of the Contemporary Age consumer in relation to companies of the same Age is predominantly passive. This means that the involvement of the *pre-internet* generation in the product life cycle is minimal or practically nonexistent. With the emergence of the internet and soon after with its popularization (something around 10 to 15 years ago), the behavior of consumers has changed. The consumer is now adopting a more collaborative behavior. And together with the advent of Web 2.0 they form the basis for the comeback of the prosumer, which is described in the next sub-section.

2.3   The Collaborative Production and the Comeback of the Prosumer

The evolution of the mass production paradigm to new ones is close related to technological development of productive systems and the advances of information technologies. The facilities offered by these technological improvements have a fundamental role in all this transition and evolution process.

Recently with the emergence of collaborative networks one more paradigm was broken and a new one arose. As a direct consequence of globalisation and the advances in the information and communication technologies companies had to adapt themselves and to change their way of doing business. The production became collaborative. Companies join into networks to share skills and resources in order to achieve common goals. And all that with the essential support of the new technologies (CAMARINHA-MATOS and AFSARMANESH, 2006).

The collaborative networking, also called *peering* by Tapscott and Williams (2006), is defined as a new way of producing goods and services through the use of the mass collaboration strength. In this sense, in the current society - triggered by technological advances - billions of people may cooperate and collaborate to carry out almost everything that requires human creativity, a PC and internet connection. Differently from the past, when the costs of production were high, people today can collaborative produce and share their creations at a very small cost. We are, now, in the era of co-creation and co-innovation. An era that is driven and leveraged by the power of the internet.

The companies need to understand this new web generation in order to remain competitive. They need to analyse and assess how co-creation, co-innovation and self-organized production may be introduced in their businesses. This new business and collaborative production model should be conceived within and outside the companies. The relationship among companies and the web generation needs to be more intense, interactive and dynamic in order to facilitate collaboration.

3   Prosumers and the CN Environment

Functional organization designs, which have served us so well for so long, together with matrix and partnership variants, are being rapidly marginalized. This is happening as increasing competitive intensity in many industry-market combinations drives consumers towards more aggressive and demanding buying behaviours (GATTORNA, 2006). Additionally the consumers are playing a more active role in recent times. This change in their behavior is directly influenced by the easy access and use of new tools based on information technologies and communication.

The new technologies also influence the companies and their way to produce. Paradigms are broken and new ones arise. The borders of the companies become tenuous and – in some moments – tend to disappear. The smart companies (TAPSCOTT and WILLIAMS, 2006) try to bring their consumers to their business networks and giving them leadership roles in the development of their next generation of products and services.

Consumers start behaving as prosumers and this silent movement gives rise to an environment based on an innovation and value creation model where collaborative activities predominate (Fig. 2). In this environment the exchange of ideas and views between the people via their social networks stimulate the creation of communities of prosumers. The interaction between these people generates valuable information for the productive sector and, with the support of the current available technologies, allows the involvement of the prosumers in the process of co-creation and co-innovation of products.

The prosumer community can be understood as an specific manifestation of Professional Virtual Community (PVC) (CAMARINHA-MATOS and AFSAR-MANESH, 2005). This community interacts in an integrated and active way with the virtual organization (VO) (CAMARINHA-MATOS and AFSARMANESH, 2004) which, in turn, is created from a VBE (CAMARINHA-MATOS and AFSAR-MANESH, 2004; SÁNCHEZ et al., 2005) in order to attend not only to the expectations of the consumers, but also – and most important – to the specifications of the prosumers. It is important to highlight that trust building (LOSS et al., 2007) is an important and essential component to leverage the co-creation and co-innovation.

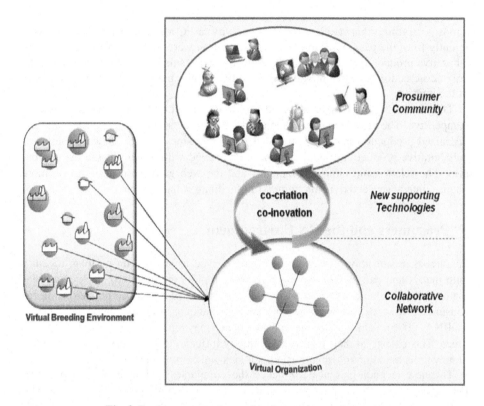

Fig. 2. Products co-creation and co-innovation environment

4 A New Actor

The new mass collaboration is changing the way in which companies and society make use of the knowledge and of the ability to innovate in order to create value. This closer and faster contact to the wishes and expectations of the new web generation will also require changes in way companies are managed. A more collaborative management model will be required. Governance principles and intellectual property rights will have to be re-analysed and re-assessed.

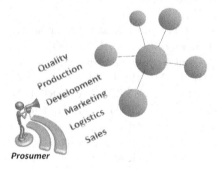

Fig. 3. Products co-creation and co-innovation environment

Prosumers have a stronger voice and a direct contact with the companies (Fig. 3). The companies have to prepare themselves to hear, to analyse and, when adequate, to implement the proposed suggestions and modifications in the products.

After all, according to Gattorna (2006): "If we are sensitive to customer needs and buying preferences, it will be obvious what we have to do, we won´t have to worry so much about our competitors – they´ll be worrying about us".

5 Conclusions

The work presented in this position paper analysed the evolution and the transformation of the production systems and the behavior of the consumers in the last 5 centuries. Starting with hand-made production and ending up in the recent years with a collaborative production model enabled by the advances of information and communication technologies. Starting with prosumers and ending up with prosumers again, but in a complete different environment. The new environment is not composed of artisans anymore. It is made up of companies and consumers. One working alongside the other and both co-creating a new generation of products.

This collaborative networked environment is challenging and new. Many aspects still have to be deeply and further studied. But if one considers what has already been done in the areas of ambient intelligence and cloud computing we realize that this co-creation and co-innovation environment is not so far away from us.

Acknowledgments. Special thanks to Alexandra Augusta Pereira-Klen for her contributions and valuable comments.

References

1. Babbage, C.: On The Economy of Machinery and Manufactures, 4^a ed. NY (1963)
2. Camarinha-Matos, L.M., Afsarmanesh, H.: Collaborative networks: Value creation in a knowledge society. In: Wang, K., Kovács, G.L., Wozny, M.J., Fang, M. (eds.) Knowledge Enterprise: Intelligent Strategies in Product Design, Manufacturing and Management, PROLAMAT. IFIP, vol. 207, pp. 26–40. Springer, Heidelberg (2006)
3. Camarinha-Matos, L.M., Afsarmanesh, H., Ollus, M.: Ecolead: A Holistic Approach to Creation and Management of Dynamic Virtual Organizations. In: Camarinha-Matos, L.M., Afsarmanesh, H., Ortiz, A. (eds.) Collaborative Networks and their Breeding Environments. Springer, Heidelberg (2005)
4. Camarinha-Matos, L.M., Afsarmanesh, H.: Collaborative Networked Organization. Kluwer Academic Publishers, Dordrecht (2004)
5. Chandler, A.D., Dalms, H.: Managerial Hierarchies: Comparative Perspectives on the Rise of the Modern Industrial Enterprise, Cambrige, Massachusett (1980)
6. Gattorna, J.: Living Supply Chains. Prentice-Hall, Englewood Cliffs (2006)
7. Ghinato, P.: Sistema Toyota de Produção – mais do que simplesmente Just-in-time (in Portuguese), CDD 658.562, 1^a ed., Editora EDUCS (1996)
8. Goldman, S.L., Nagel, R.N., Preiss, K., Dove, R.: 21st Century Manufacturing Enterprise Strategy, An industrial Led View, vol. 1 & 2. Iacocca Institute, Bethlehem (1991)
9. Kidd, P.: Agile Manufacturing: Forging New Frontiers. Addison-Wesley, Reading (1994a)

10. Kidd, P.: Agile Manufacturing: Key Issues. In: Advances in Agile Manufacturing – Integrating Technology, Organization and People. IOS Press, Amsterdam (1994b)
11. Loss, L., Schons, C.H., Neves, R.M., Delavy, I.L., Chudzikiewicz, I.S., Vogt, A.M.C.: Trust Building in Collaborative Networked Organizations Supported by Communities of Practice. In: IFIP TC 5 Working Group 5.5 Eighth IFIP Working Conference on Virtual Enterprises, Portugal, pp. 23–30. Springer, Heidelberg (2007)
12. Pereira-Klen, A.A., Vöge, M., Hirsch, B.E.: Experience with Implementation of a Shop Floor Monitoring and Control System in SMEs. In: Proceedings of the 2nd Int. Conference on Computer Integrated Manufacturing, Singapore, vol. 2 (1993)
13. Rocha, C.H.M.: Fordismo: Desenvolvimento e Crise. Revista Múltipla (in Portuguese), n°15, Editora UPIS (2003) ISSN 1414-6304
14. Sánchez, N.G., Zubiaga, D.A.G., González, J.A.I., Molina, A.: Virtual Breeding Environment: A First Approach to Understand Working and Sharing Principles. In: Proceedings of the first International Conference on Interoperability on Enterprise Software and Applications (2005)
15. Smith, A.: An Inquiry into the Nature and Causes of the Wealth of Nations. Penguin, Classics, London (1776)
16. Tapscott, D., Williams, A.D.: Wikinomics – Como a colaboração em massa pode mudar o seu negócio, Editora Nova Fronteira (2006) (in Portuguese) ISBN 978.85.209.1997-2
17. Taylor, F.W.: Principles of Scientific Management. Harper & Brothers, NY (1911)
18. Toffler, A.: The Third Wave. Bantam Books, USA (1980)
19. Vigna, C.M.: Capacitação das operações internas para a customização em massa: estudos de casos nas indústrias brasileiras. Dissertação de Mestrado em Engenharia de Produção – in portuguese, Escola Politécnica, USP-SP (2007)
20. Wikipedia.: The free Encyclopedia (03/2009),
    http://en.wikipedia.org/wiki/Generation,
    http://en.wikipedia.org/wiki/Generation,
    http://en.wikipedia.org/wiki/Generation
21. Womack, J.P., Jones, D.T., Roos, D.: The Machine that Changed the World. MIT, Ed. Rawson, NY (1990)

Part 2

Collaboration Patterns

A Cooperative Model to Improve Hospital Equipments and Drugs Management

Ilaria Baffo[1,2], Giuseppe Confessore[1], Giacomo Liotta[1], and Giuseppe Stecca[1]

[1] Istituto di Tecnologie Industriali e Automazione, Consiglio Nazionale delle Ricerche,
Area della Ricerca Roma 1, Strada della neve, Via Salaria Km 29,300,
00010 Montelibretti, Rome, Italy
[2] Dipartimento di Ingegneria dell'Impresa, Università di Roma "Tor Vergata",
Via del Politecnico 1, 00133, Rome, Italy
{Ilaria.Baffo,Giuseppe.Confessore,Giacomo.Liotta,
Giuseppe.Stecca}@itia.cnr.it

Abstract. The cost of services provided by public and private healthcare systems is nowadays becoming critical. This work tackles the criticalities of hospital equipments and drugs management by emphasizing its implications on the whole healthcare system efficiency. The work presents a multi-agent based model for decisional cooperation in order to address the problem of integration of departments, wards and personnel for improving equipments, and drugs management. The proposed model faces the challenge of (*i*) gaining the benefits deriving from successful collaborative models already used in industrial systems and (*ii*) transferring the most appropriate industrial management practices to healthcare systems.

Keywords: Multi Agent Systems, Healthcare Management Systems, Logistics.

1 Introduction

The cost of services provided by public and private healthcare systems is nowadays becoming critical. Since in several countries, hospital revenues are not more cost based, reduction in costs are becoming the critical point for the sustainability of all medical structures. Moreover, the great size of the hospital, while on one hand allows to exploit the economies of scale, on the other hand makes the internal dynamics of a hospital a complex non-linear structure [1] that is difficult to manage.

This work tackles the issues of hospital equipments, personnel and drugs management by emphasizing its implications on the whole healthcare system efficiency. The adopted approach is based on the assumption that the hospital is a complex system composed by a great number of entities and processes. Camarinha-Matos and Afsarmanesh [2] defined a collaborative network as a network consisting of autonomous, distributed, heterogeneous entities that collaborate to better achieve common or compatible goals. Following this definition, the application of a Multi Agent System (MAS) to collaborative network modeling turns out to be natural.

The MASs have been widely exploited in several application fields in order to govern the complexity through cooperation and decentralization of decisions when

L.M. Camarinha-Matos et al. (Eds.): PRO-VE 2009, IFIP AICT 307, pp. 43–50, 2009.

competitive requests and divergent objectives have to considered. In this work a MAS-based approach is adopted in order to offer a model able to manage the complexity of a healthcare system while:

- fostering technological innovations through information sharing and recovery;
- fostering organizational innovations for more efficient and effective distributed decisions whenever possible.

A MAS can be herein considered as the basic methodological factor for then deploying technological enablers (e.g., ICT) and managerial enablers (e.g., a cooperative decision system of the healthcare organization). The system is supposed to consist of several decisional and operational agents that can be related to departments or wards. Every agent is considered as a single decisional entity that influences the achievement of system's goals. The work presents a model of agents' cooperation for addressing the problem of departments, wards and personnel integration in order to improve the efficiency regarding drugs, equipments, and personnel management. The overall goal of the system is related to the need of providing, with a fixed budget and consequently a fixed set of resources, the highest level of customers served with high service level. In particular, the cooperative model for drugs management is based on cooperative actions for obtaining service effectiveness while reducing inventory costs through information sharing and coordination. According to Camarinha-Matos and Afsarmanesh [3] more than one modeling perspective must be integrated in order to properly design a Collaborative Networked Organization (CNO). We will describe architectural aspects presenting the agents and their roles in the CNO, component aspects describing technological aspects in terms of hardware/software needed in the CNO in order to fulfill the overall objective, functional aspects describing peculiar processes of the CNO.

The paper is organized as follows: Section 2 presents the main issues concerning healthcare management systems with respect to the management of equipments and drugs. The problem is described in Section 3. In Section 4 the agent-based cooperative model is presented and discussed. Conclusions follow.

2   Resource Management in Healthcare Systems

The efficiency of healthcare systems is influenced by increased demand for quality, technology investments and increased drug supplies [4]. The consequent trade-offs among effectiveness, efficiency and equity objectives have fostered the development of theory and applications concerning health economics and management science [4].

Since in several countries, hospital revenues are not any more cost based, cost reductions are becoming the critical point for the sustainability of all medical structures. For this reason some managers tried to apply some principles and techniques deriving from management science, for improving the efficiency and effectiveness of hospital facilities. In order to obtain cost savings, hospitals need to review their activities, to identify the costs associated with the activities and reduce them, to classify the activities in terms of added-value, and to decrease or eliminate not added-value activities [5]. By applying this methodology, called Activity Based Management (ABM), a lot of organizations focused their efforts to improve activities belonging to the logistic department. This department is a vital part of a hospital because it may have responsibilities for activities like purchasing, receiving, inventory management, management information systems, telemedicine, transportation, and home care services. Although these activities do not represent the core mission for the hospital, they take part into definition of service level offered by the organization. Consequently, it is important to examine the activities of this department to improve services and possibly reduce costs while adopting lean service processes. The internal dynamics of a hospital represents a complex non-linear structure [1]. Planning and management of hospital daily operations require a thorough understanding of the system with information for decision making [1].

Literature review confirms that several studies address management issues although many gaps need to be bridged, for instance with respect to integrated logistics of healthcare systems. De Angelis et al. [6] investigate the problem of assigning resources and servers (e.g., doctors, beds, instruments) to services. Akcali et al. [7] tackle the problem of optimizing hospital bed capacity planning through a network flow approach. Harper [1] proposes an integrated simulation tool (PROMPT, Patient and Resource Operational Management Planning Tool) for the planning and management of hospital resources such as beds, operating theatres, and needs for nurses, doctors and anaesthetists. Van Merode et al. [8] study the potential adoption of Enterprise Resource Planning (ERP) systems in hospitals while facing the issues of planning and control processes and determining ERP systems requirements. Liu et al. [9] and De Treville et al. [10] argue that efficiency and quality of healthcare management have been enhanced by the computerization of healthcare information. Several studies concern the information management, workflow (see [11]) and automation in healthcare systems. Thornett [12] discusses potential roles, introduction benefits and difficulties related to computer decision support systems within the practice in primary healthcare. It can be concluded that organizational innovations and enabling ICT-based solutions are essential conditions to reach the efficiency and effectiveness improvement in hospital operations management.

3 Problem Description

Thanks to the effort of an Italian research project's partners it was possible to analyze and synthesize the main problems related to drugs and equipment management within some Italian hospital structures. In particular, the study of the AS-IS processes and the survey on the employers showed several problems in the following processes: (*i*) central drugs management, (*ii*) drugs management in each ward, (*iii*) medical equipment management.

With regard to the first aspect, the problems arise from some lacks in the continuous monitoring of the central drugstore. When the responsible of the drugs is not present, the nurses, filling a paper register, are free to use the pharmacy. That approach could produce an inappropriate management of the drugs or errors in the related information records. Other problems come from the variability of the drugs in terms of codes and packaging. When a drug order is fulfilled, it is possible that the required drug it is not available. Consequently, it is substituted with an equivalent drug. It was observed that equivalent drugs are registered with different codes. This approach generates difficulties in the drugstore management. Regarding the drugs management in each ward, instead, the followings problems can describe the scenario analyzed by researchers, medical personnel and industrial managers:

- The stock levels of the wards drugstores can be out of control whether not recorded in the computer system of the hospital.
- The drug order fulfillment of the central drugstore could not properly take into account the stock levels of wards drugstores. Since information on the availability of medicines in the wards drugstores could not be recorded into the computer system, the nurses may need to check the availability by physical inspection in the wards.
- The decisions about the fulfilling of drugs are made by the nurses. Minimum supply concept is not used in the fulfilling process. The orders are often made without information about the stock availability. That approach can generate an over abundance of drugs. Furthermore, it was observed that the nurses tend to make large orders in order to increase their responsiveness capability.
- Problems arise in the management of medicinal products expiration dates with possible unreasonable costs of not usable drugs.
- With regard to the movements of medicinal products between the wards drugstores, it can happen that the nurses of a ward instead of replenishing the local drugstore by using the central pharmacy of the hospital, take the medicinal products from other wards drugstores. This procedure can imply that the nurses do not physically move throughout proper the hospital structure and consequently the drugs that have been taken could not be registered. It was observed that the movements of medicinal products can tend to generate conflicts between nurses of different wards.

Other problems coming from medical equipments management are:

- High cost of the management of hospital equipments. It has to be considered that the weekly movement of the required materials take 1.5 workdays of the store employee.
- The hospital equipments store is not managed by a computer system. The stock level is not exactly known. In order to find the equipment necessary for a patient it is often necessary for a nurse to move physically into the store where there is not a standard procedure to find the selected equipment but it needs to be founded by visual inspection.
- The localization of the equipments into the hospital structure is not defined. When something is not found in the equipments store, the nurse needs to check this stuff in all the hospital building.
- Tags are used to assign each instrument to each patient. The tag can be lost or it deteriorates too much, making it ineffective with the risk of loosing data of the patients.

Currently, several internal possible solutions are object of studies to improve the quality of the drug management. It seems that the most efficient manner to organize the system is to create a centralized unit, represented by the central drugstore, with higher control on the whole drugs and equipments management process.

4   Methodology: The Cooperative Model

This section proposes a model based on multi-agent theory in order to formalize the cooperative model under two dimensions: (*i*) organizational innovation for cooperative process   and (*ii*) technological framework supporting the cooperative process. Moreover, as Camarinha-Matos and Afsarmanesh [3] claim, the collaborative network requires the development of models, not only as a help to better understand the area, but also as the basis for the development of methods and tools for better decision-making [3]. The realized model will be illustrated through the description of the agents, the explanation of the collaborative decisional process and the technological architecture. Finally, a discussion on ongoing and foreseen applications is made.

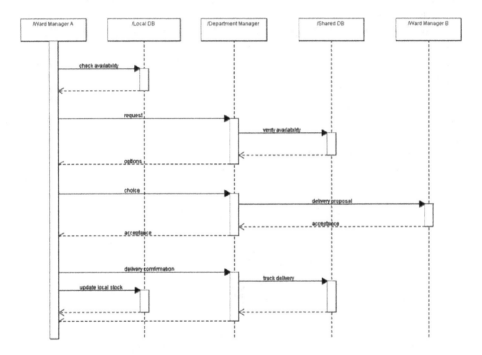

Fig. 1. UML sequence diagram for a general request

4.1   Description of Agents

The reengineered system should enable the collaboration among medical wards in the processes of material procurement and resource allocations. As described in Section 3, the lack of integrated information systems and the not formalized collaboration rules are the main obstacles to the development of a collaborative process. A model composed by a central manager and by medical ward managers is proposed. They act as interfaces of the central warehouse and the local ward warehouses. The *Department Manager* (DM) is a coordinator of resource allocation, and of material management processes. The *Ward Managers* (WM) represents the local decision maker for the ward and department objectives. The DM is a composition of three specialized decision makers: (*i*) Equipment manager, (*ii*) Drugs procurement manager, (*iii*) Human resource manager.

The DM is an enabler for centralized information and an enabler to collaboration among wards for drugs procurement, equipment allocation and human resource assignment.

4.2   Collaborative Decisional Process among Agents

The decisional process is general and foresees an interaction between WMs and DM each time that a request is generated by the WM.

As showed in Figure 1, a WM sends a procurement request to the DM. The DM verifies the central and the local warehouses. Then, it sends a set of procurement options to the WM who replies with its choice. If the choice is an inter-ward delivery (for instance from WM B), then this request is forwarded to the ward chosen. The process terminates with a delivery from WM B to WM A and a notification of the delivery to the DM.

4.3   Applications and Discussion

The architecture shown in Figure 2 supports the collaborative process and the information centralization in a hospital system. The information systems must be fully integrated in order to track deliveries and material consumption.

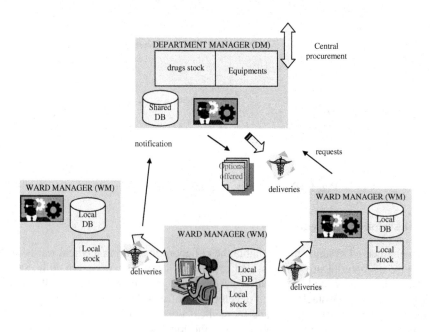

Fig. 2. System Architecture

Very promising technological enablers for effectively managing, even in real time, particular products or systems (equipment, medical devices, drugs) are the Radio Frequency Identification (RFId) technologies. The introduction in healthcare structures of a pervasive technology such as the RFId with complementary decision tools likely entails the redesign of key logistic processes as described in this work. On the other hand the presence of RFId technologies raises the complexity of the system. In fact, together with the introduction of RFId different critical issues must be resolved or managed such as privacy management and signal transmission interferences. The tracking points for deliveries and material consumption are detailed in the collaborative procurement procedures. In order to enable physical tracking and localization, RFId technology can be used in combination with automatic delivery devices. Automatic delivery devices impose the authentication and enable the tracking of the delivery. Moreover, introducing the prescription of the doctors in the hospital information system, it is possible to perform a crosscheck between the prescribed drugs and the drug quantities that have been taken from the stores. Overall, three main areas of application of the system have been identified: *(i)* drugs procurement, *(ii)* equipment management, *(iii)* human resource scheduling. The application to drugs procurement allows the improvement of the FIFO material management strategy and effective use of decentralized warehouses. When the requests arrive to DM, the drugs manager verifies the stocks and propose different delivery options based on the expiry dates, distance from the warehouses, lead-time of procurement from suppliers.

If an inter-ward delivery is chosen then it must be tracked. The ward from which the drug has been sourced will be supplied once the supplier procurement will arrive. The application to the equipment management foresees the localization and the tracking of the equipments uses. This information enables the correct allocation of the equipments. The utilization requests should allow to plan maintenance and substitution for assuring a high service level in term of equipment's availability . The application to Human resource scheduling foresees the use of a medical skills database for planning the deployment of medical teams. The Human resource manager should verify that every operation of medical personnel is tracked in terms of duration and used skills.

Through the adoption of the herein presented MAS-based approach for modelling the drugs and equipments management processes, it is expected in particular a better medicinal products inventory management while introducing process innovations and enabling technologies. The logistic department should then have a strategic role inside of a hospital due to the visibility on state and location of drugs, equipments, personnel, patients, etc.

5 Conclusion and Acknowledgments

In this paper a collaborative model for efficiency improvements in healthcare systems has been proposed. The proposed model faces the challenges of *(i)* gaining the benefits deriving from successful collaborative models already used in industrial systems and *(ii)* transferring the most appropriate industrial management practices to healthcare systems. The proposed approach could allow a better medicinal products inventory management. The drug expiration problems can be avoided and the costs significantly reduced. To develop the solution proposed in this paper the authors propose a MAS-based approach to model the drugs and equipments management processes. With this solution they propose an innovation of the processes based on re-design of operations and on the introduction of technological solutions. The logistic department acquires a strategic role inside of hospital because it can become the gathering point of all the hospital information related to state and location of drugs, equipments, personnel, patients, etc. Future research steps foresee an improvement of the model while possibly including performance indicators (e.g., time, costs and service level) in the analysis.

This work is partially supported by the Italian region "Lombardia" within the "Lean Healthcare" project that is in progress. The presented work is based on part of the project's outcomes. The project joins industrial managers and researchers with the aim to transfer the most known industrial management practices to healthcare systems. The authors would like to acknowledge the whole project's partnership, the hospital structures that have allowed the analysis of their internal processes, and the financing authority.

References

1. Harper, P.R.: A Framework for Operational Modelling of Hospital Resources. Health Care Manage. Sci. 5, 165–173 (2002)
2. Camarinha-Matos, L.M., Afsarmanesh, H.: Collaborative Networks: A New Scientific Discipline. J. Intell. Manuf. 16, 439–452 (2005)
3. Camarinha-Matos, L.M., Afsarmanesh, H.: A Comprehensive Modeling Framework for Collaborative Networked Organizations. J. Intell. Manuf. 18, 529–542 (2007)
4. Athanassopoulos, A., Gounaris, C.: Assessing the Technical and Allocative Efficiency of Hospital Operations in Greece and its Resource Allocation Implications. Eur. J. Oper. Res. 133, 416–431 (2001)
5. Aptel, O., Pourjalali, H.: Improving Activities and Decreasing Costs of Logistics in Hospitals. A Comparison of U.S. and French Hospitals. The International Journal of Accounting 36, 65–90 (2001)
6. De Angelis, V., Felici, G., Impelluso, P.: Integrating Simulation and Optimisation in Health Care Centre Management. Eur. J. Oper. Res. 150, 101–114 (2003)
7. Akcali, E., Coté, M.J., Lin, C.: A Network Flow Approach to Optimizing Hospital Bed Capacity Decisions. Health Care Manage. Sci. 9, 391–404 (2006)
8. Van Merode, G.G., Groothuis, S., Hasman, A.: Enterprise Resource Planning for Hospitals. Int. J. Med. Inform. 73, 493–501 (2004)
9. Liu, D.R., Wu, I.C., Hsieh, S.T.: Integrating SET and EDI for Secure Healthcare Commerce. Comp. Stand. Inter. 23, 367–381 (2001)
10. De Treville, S., Smith, I., Rolli, A., Arnold, V.: Applying Operations Management Logic and Tools to Save Lives: A Case Study of The World Health Organization's Global Drug Facility. J. Oper. Manag. 24, 397–406 (2006)
11. Dang, J., Hedayati, A., Hampel, K., Toklu, C.: An Ontological Knowledge Framework for Adaptive Medical Workflow. Journal of Biomedical Informatics 41, 829–836 (2008)
12. Thornett, A.M.: Computer Decision Support Systems in General Practice. Int. J. Inform. Manage. 21, 39–47 (2001)

Modeling Adaptable Business Service for Enterprise Collaboration

Khouloud Boukadi, Lucien Vincent, and Patrick Burlat

Division for Industrial Engineering and Computer Sciences, ENSM, Saint-Etienne, France
{Boukadi,Vincent,Burlat}@emse.fr

Abstract. Nowadays, a Service Oriented Architecture (SOA) seems to be one of the most promising paradigms for leveraging enterprise information systems. SOA creates opportunities for enterprises to provide value added service tailored for on demand enterprise collaboration. With the emergence and rapid development of Web services technologies, SOA is being paid increasing attention and has become widespread. In spite of the popularity of SOA, a standardized framework for modeling and implementing business services are still in progress. For the purpose of supporting these service-oriented solutions, we adopt a model driven development approach. This paper outlines the Contextual Service Oriented Modeling and Analysis (CSOMA) methodology and presents UML profiles for the PIM level service-oriented architectural modeling, as well as its corresponding meta-models. The proposed PIM (Platform Independent Model) describes the business SOA at a high level of abstraction regardless of techniques involved in the application employment. In addition, all essential service-specific concerns required for delivering quality and context-aware service are covered. Some of the advantages of this approach are that it is generic and thus not closely allied with Web service technology as well as specifically treating the service adaptability during the design stage.

Keywords: Service oriented architecture, model driven architecture, adaptable business service, context-aware.

1 Introduction

Service oriented architecture (SOA) plays an ever more important role in modern networked economies. SOA can reinforce business aspects with a flexible infrastructure thanks to independent, reusable automated business processes called services. This trend is a leading paradigm shift in enterprise structure from the traditional single entity to a collaboration of services. So from this perspective, enterprise collaboration can be seen as a conglomeration of outsourced business services on the Web, cooperating to achieve a shared goal. Although the hype surrounding SOA is widespread, the concept is still in its infancy with regards to actual implementations. Several problems have arisen. Some authors believe that technology and standards are crucial to achieve the aims of SOA but they are not sufficient on their own [1]. Issues like the lack of precise definitions for the SOA concepts involved and the enormous demand for process guidance and proven best practices in these projects are among the most frequently discussed in both industry and academia.

L.M. Camarinha-Matos et al. (Eds.): PRO-VE 2009, IFIP AICT 307, pp. 51–60, 2009.
© IFIP International Federation for Information Processing 2009

Previously, we discussed in [2] the importance of context-aware business services that fit dynamic enterprise collaboration and demonstrated that business services must have the capacity to adapt their own behavior by configuring appropriately to the situation in which they evolve. Following those conclusions, the main issue of the present endeavor is to propose a conceptual framework. This will consider adaptable business service as a base class modeling entity, to provide appropriate guidance for SOA modeling. We believe that in order for successful service-oriented development, SOA should be described at a high level of abstraction regardless of implementation details. Besides, business services need to be updated or altered in order to follow the rapid shifting trends or demands of e-commerce. These kinds of issues related to reusability, customizability and adaptability of the service development needs to be considered early in the service-system development. One of the current influential trends is Model-Driven Architecture (MDA). The ideas behind MDA can be used to facilitate and improve SOA development [3]. MDA is a framework for software development driven by the Object Management Group (OMG). Within MDA, models are considered as core class elements during system design and implementation. MDA is based on a separation of the development process in three abstraction levels, namely Computational Independent, Platform Independent and Platform Specific Models, respectively CIM, PIM and PSM [4].

The contribution of this paper is twofold. First, a Contextual Service Oriented Modeling and Analysis (CSOMA) is presented and framed into the MDA framework. Second, UML profiles for the PIM-level service-oriented architectural modelling, as well as its corresponding meta-models, are proposed. These UML profiles cover all essential service-specific concerns required for delivering quality and context-aware services.

The remainder of this paper is organized as follows. In Section 2, the Model Driven Architecture (MDA) and the service oriented architecture are outlined. The CSOMA is presented in Section 3. Then, in Section 4, our UML profiles defined to support the representation of adaptable business SOA concepts are presented. Section 5 details some related work for comparison. Finally, a conclusion and possible further research is discussed.

2   Background

2.1   Model Driven Architecture (MDA)

As defined by the Object Management Group, Model-Driven Architecture (MDA) is "a way of writing specifications, based on a platform-independent model. A complete MDA specification consists of a definitive platform-independent base UML model, one or more platform-specific models and interface definition sets, each describing how the base model is implemented on a different middleware platform" [4].

The core paradigm of MDA is model transformation. With MDA, system construction consists of a sequence of models and transformations among these models. The MDA approach separates the business and application logic by presenting the static and dynamic aspects of a system as a high level abstraction with the implementation details hidden. The abstraction is called the *platform-independent model* (PIM). The MDA also supports a *platform-specific model* (PSM), which contains enough implementation information that can convert it to particular source codes.

2.2 Service Oriented Architecture (SOA)

There are a multitude of definitions for SOA. Furthermore, they are not always pointing in the same direction and often discussing the subject at different levels of abstraction. However, many authors agree that SOA is not a product but rather an architectural style or concept. Some pertinent definitions will be presented below.

Thomas Erl defines an SOA as: "an **open**, **agile extensible**, **federated**, **composable architecture** comprised of autonomous, capable, vendor diverse, interoperable, discoverable and potentially reusable services" [5]. A business definition of the SOA is presented in [6]: "SOA is a conceptual business architecture where business functionality is made available to SOA users as shared, reusable services on an IT network. Services in an SOA are modules of business or application functionality with exposed interfaces, and are invoked by messages". The W3C minimally defines the SOA as "a set of components which can be invoked, and whose interface descriptions can be published and discovered" [7].

The three definitions presented above are on different granular levels. However, they are all cohesive. The definition of [5] and [6] has a wider perspective of SOA then [7], focusing more on architectural features. While the W3C provides a very technical definition that considers what can be done with a service but does not refer to the architecture nor give any additional information on how a service should be designed or configured.

3 MDA and Contextual Service Oriented Modeling and Analysis

The research work presented in this paper is part of our methodology: Contextual Service Oriented Modeling and Analysis (CSOMA) [8]. CSOMA is vendor-independent and provides a systematic approach and a well defined process to guide the design and development of an SOA. CSOMA is the result of applying two kinds of SOA practices: IT SOA and Adaptable Business SOA. IT SOA is based on standard methods to identify IT services. The intent of Business SOA is to offer services which will support business goals of the enterprise. CSOMA delivers a set of business services that suit enterprise collaboration.

One of the most important characteristics of CSOMA is its support of the MDA. As can be seen in Fig.1, CSOMA is organized into three layers aligned with the MDA layers. Each layer has specific architectural characteristics and addresses some particular concerns, as described below:

The CIM level for CSOMA: describes the business logic defined within enterprise's business models and business processes. These models constitute the basis for the business services identification and modeling. Examples of the CIM level include business motivation models, business process models and enterprise architecture, etc.

The PIM level for CSOMA: includes the PIM for Adaptable Business SOA and describes the business service models in a technology independent manner. These models are created by refining the business model identified in the CIM level. Each model defines new modeling elements which extend the UML meta-model [9]. The process describing the tasks associated to the generation of each business service model as well as the mapping rules among them is out of the scope of this paper.

The identified business services models are completed by designing and analyzing service variability among various clients and diverse service contexts. The aim is to design business services that are more than a functionality provided through the Web. Indeed, they must have the capacity to adapt their behavior by providing the appropriate function or capacity which accommodates the current situation. Recently, the aspect-oriented programming (AOP) has gained growing acceptance. AOP furnishes an abstraction and encapsulation mechanism with the purpose of enhancing separation of concerns [10]. This aspect based separation is applied to the service modeling process. In the PIM for Adaptable Business SOA, an aspect-oriented technique is used to help identify and model the crosscutting concerns and separate them from the services functions during the service modeling process. Hereafter, these aspects will be referred to as "Conceptual Aspects".

The PSM level for CSOMA: includes models relating to the Web services technology. The business services models should be mapped and applied over the Web service technology. Example of these models could be BPEL, Web services Models etc. Note: this topic is beyond the scope of this paper.

The focus in this paper is in the proposition of UML profiles for the PIM-level service-oriented architectural modeling.

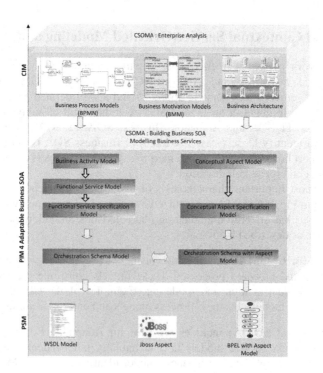

Fig. 1. CSOMA and MDA

4 UML Profiles for Adaptable Business Service Oriented Architecture

In this section we introduce our aforementioned UML profiles for their use in the definition of the adaptable business SOA at PIM-level. A UML profile extends the standard UML elements in order to precisely describe specific domain or application concepts [11]. Our Adaptable Business SOA UML profiles consist of two profiles:

– *Business service profile*: describes how to model a service including its description and interactions.
– *Conceptual Aspect profile*: extends the business service profile and describes how to model context-aware business services.

Next the concepts in the UML profiles using the associated meta-models will be described.

4.1 Concepts Involved in the Business Service Profile

Fig. 2 presents the business SOA meta-model using UML notations. When dealing with a business SOA, there are four different concepts for service: the business idea, as well as the service's description, interactions and adaptability. These four concepts are explained.

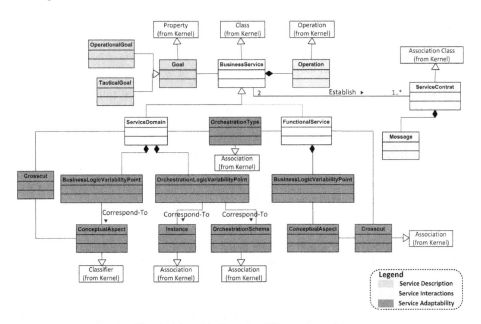

Fig. 1. Adaptable Business SOA meta-model

Business Service: is treated as core class modeling entity in our business SOA meta-model. The business services inside our CSOMA methodology play different roles. They can be classified according to their atomicity and scope. The business services can be atomic services called functional or composite services called service domains. Functional services are fine grained services exposing a set of business activities. Examples of functional services can be *computing price for delivery* or *delivering merchandise*. Service Domain orchestrates a set of functional services in order to provide high level of functioning as well as a comprehensible external view to the end user. Service domain will be published as a composite service, thus reducing the complexity of publishing, selecting and combining fine grained functional services. This composite structure is used as major building block for implementing on demand enterprise collaboration.

Service Description: business services have a set of operations (serviceOperations) and fulfill goals (Goal). We define service operations as atomic functions that are used to accomplish the service goal. A goal is 'an optative' statement, an intention that expresses what is wanted [12]. Goal can be expressed at different levels of abstraction starting from tactical to operational. Functional services relate to operational goals, i.e. goals that are achieved with tasks provided by the service. Services domains correspond to high level aims (tactical). For example, *take customer order* service domain fulfils an enterprise tactical goal which is "Use the Web to expose enterprise products". While a computing delivery price, which is a functional service, achieves a "Managing Customer Invoice" goal. This is an operational goal which can be fulfilled by the service operations. These two elements (operations and goals) constitute the service description at the PIM level.

Service Interactions: business services communicate and interact with each other through contracts. Within the SOA, service contract establishes the terms of engagement and interaction among the different architecture components. These interactions include service contract and messages flowing between services.

– Service Contracts: contracts established between services must reflect the services that are involved in the contract, the roles played, and several other properties such as, purpose or contract expiration time. Other authors like [13] treat the service contract as part of the service description itself. Even though the way to interact with a service depends generally on its operations shown in its interface, we propose that, by making the service contract an independent element of the model, the independence of the different relations that a service can establish with other services, each with its own restrictions and characteristics is assured.

– Messages: messages in SOA represent the communication exchanged between services. Each message is related to a service contract and has meaning to both the service and the consumer. Some authors suggest that the message format and its addresses such as HTTP or SMTP should be included in the model [14]. We consider that the format of a message is an issue that depends mostly on the implementation technology and so it should be modeled in the correspondent PSM-level models.

Business service adaptability: business services must have the capacity to alter their own behavior to accommodate the situations as they occur. To meet to this objective, service designers should model services with points that mark where the service can be customized depending on the customer and the environment context. We call these, variability points, similar to those variability points that are introduced in software product line engineering [15]. Depending on the business service itself (service domain or functional service), we identify two types of variability points. Functional service has a set of variability points which concern essentially its business logic. While a service domain has variability points concerning its business logic as well as its orchestration logic. Our hypothesis is that more the modeling of the business service is parameterized, more its adaptation is facilitated. At the design phase, the variability points, concerning the orchestration logic, deal with the creation of a set of orchestration schemas for a single service domain. When the service domain receives an incoming request, it selects a suitable schema. The selection of the orchestration schema takes into account the context of the incoming request. The variability of orchestration logic was the object of our research project in [16], so further details are provided there. In our present work, the variability points concerning the business logic, which are handled through Conceptual Aspects, are examined. These are explained in the next section.

4.2   Concepts Involved in the Conceptual Aspect Profile

We define Conceptual Aspect as a domain-specific concern for a business service which groups non functional requirements or designates a business rule or addresses an adaptability action in response to contextual information. According to our definition, three types of Conceptual Aspects can be distinguished:

The *Non-Functional Aspect* is used to classify the quality attributes for a service such as security, performance, availability and so on. Its objective is to provide a behavioral guideline on service or its element, as well as means to control one or several services. For example, a non-functional aspect for security enforces the control of access to services.

The *Business Rule Aspect* defines or constrains some concerns of the business. It is intended to control the behavior of the business. As its name suggests, this aspect encapsulates a rule that can be: constraint, action enabler, and computation or inference rules.

The *Context Enabler Aspect* is used to personalize the basic functions of services according to customer's context or preference. The Context Enabler aspects try to satisfy customer preferences and to improve convenience by altering the messages or operations in a service. For example, in a Delivery Service Domain, we can define an Aspect related to the calculation of extra fees when there is a context change that corresponds to a modification in the delivery date.

The Conceptual aspects need to be explicitly and coherently modeled, their design should not be scattered throughout the business service model. We propose to use Aspect Oriented Programming principles to model Conceptual Aspects. AOP introduces unit of modularity called Aspects containing different code fragments (*advice*), and location descriptions (*pointcuts*) to identify where to plug the code fragment. The points which can be selected by the *pointcuts* are called *join points* [17]. Fig.3 presents the meta-model of a Conceptual Aspect, which extends the one presented in Fig. 1. The advice is represented by the advice stereotype that can be applied to a service operation. Advice is linked to a business service by the <<crosscut >> association.

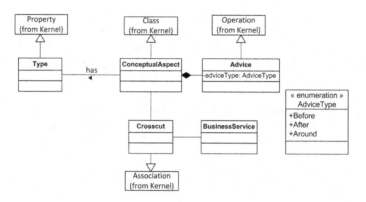

Fig. 2. Conceptual Aspect meta-model

5 Related Work

This section reviews some publications in literature in order to better illustrate the position as well as the novel aspects of our endeavors. There are many ongoing research efforts related to the model-driven development of SOA systems such as [18], [19]. Baresi et al. propose static SOA model and dynamic model in UML [20]. Nevertheless, these authors define the models into a transition system and specify a set of transformation rules to support the dynamic reconfiguration in SOA. This work differs in that it assumes that any SOA development is built upon service clients, providers and service discovering agents. Otherwise, the scope in which SOA can be used is constrained since it cannot be generalized to other execution platforms apart from the ones that follow their predesignated schemas.

Heckel et al. already proposed an excellent UML profile for SOA modeling that takes into account the MDA principles [18]. However, their UML profile defines only two kinds of services (provider and registry) and does not include any facility to model adaptive services.

MIDAS is a first rate model-driven methodology for Web information system development based on MDA principals [21]. The methodology does suggest some PIMs, PSMs and mapping rules between the models. The methodology uses the UML to represent the different models. At the PIM level, they propose a UML profile for SOA. Their work is one of the closest publications to the content presented in this article. However, the authors do not consider the service adaptability. To our knowledge, our paper is the first to adopt service adaptability at the PIM level.

IBM presents a UML 2.0 profile for software services [22]. The profile includes messages, specification of a service, manner in which services are composed into aggregate services, choreography view of services, and policy perspective. This similar research presents SOA concepts not so constrained to the Web service technology. However, once again this does not deal with our focus on the business service adaptability at the PIM level of the MDA.

6 Conclusion

Service oriented architecture presents a promising integration approach to enable inter-enterprise collaboration and deliver maximum reusability, agility and flexibility when facing changing conditions. However, its implementation in actual enterprise contexts is more challenging and requires particular attention, comprehensive guiding framework and strong design principles. In this paper, we highlight the importance of the application of the MDA principles to the SOA paradigm. We presented UML profiles for the design of PIM-level Business SOA. These profiles covers all concerns required for delivering high-quality and context-aware services. The modeled business services constitute the building blocks for on demand enterprise collaboration. As to future work, of course, an empirical study to validate and test the proposed approach will be at the centre of ongoing research. For other related endeavors, integrating or taking into account the behavior of business services and defining an appropriate specification for them appear to be a promising path as well.

References

1. Erradi, A., Anand, S., Kulkarni, N.: SOAF: An Architectural Framework for Service Definition and Realization. In: IEEE International Conference on Services Computing (SCC 2006), pp. 151–158 (2006)
2. Boukadi, K., Ghedira, C., Vincent, L.: An Aspect Oriented Approach for Context-Aware Service Domain Adapted to E-Business. In: Bellahsène, Z., Léonard, M. (eds.) CAiSE 2008. LNCS, vol. 5074, pp. 64–78. Springer, Heidelberg (2008)
3. Lopez-Sanz, M., Cuesta, C.E., Marcos, E.: Modelling of Service-Oriented Architectures with UML. Electronic Notes in Theoretical Computer Science 194(4), 23–37 (2008)
4. OMG, MDA guide version 1.0.1, proposed by the Object Management Group (2003)
5. Erl, T.: Service-Oriented Architecture (SOA): Concepts, Technology, and Design, p. 792. Prentice Hall, Englewood Cliffs (2005)
6. Marks, E.A., Bell, M.: Service-Oriented Architecture: A Planning and Implementation Guide for Business and Technology, 1st edn. Wiley, New Jersey (2006)
7. W3C, Web Services Glossary (2004), http://www.w3.org/TR/ws-gloss
8. Boukadi, K., Vincent, L., Burlat, P.: The Contextual Service Oriented Methodology (CSOMA) (2009), http://www.emse.fr/~boukadi/
9. UML, UML Superstructure 2.0, OMG Adopted Specification PTC/03-08-02 (2003), http://www.uml.org/
10. AOP, Aspect-Oriented Software Development (2007), http://www.aosd.net
11. OMG, Object Management Group, UML2.0 Super Structure Specification (October 2004)
12. Rolland, C., Kaabi, R.S.: An Intentional Perspective to Service Modeling and Discovery. In: Proceedings of 31st Annual International Computer Software and Applications Conference, COMPSAC 2007. IEEE Computer Society, Los Alamitos (2007)
13. Krafzig, D., Banke, K., Slama, D.: Enterprise SOA Service Oriented Architecture Best Practices. Prentice Hall PTR, Upper Saddle River (2004)
14. Amir, R., Zeid, A.: An UML Profile for Service Oriented Architectures. In: Companion to the 19th Annual ACM SIGPLAN Conference on Object-Oriented Programming, Systems, Languages, and Applications, OOPSLA 2004 (2004)

15. Jaring, M., Bosch, J.: Variability dependencies in product family engineering. In: Heidelberg, S.B. (ed.) Software Product-Family Engineering, pp. 81–97 (2004)
16. Boukadi, K., et al.: CWSC4EC:How to Employ Context, Web Service, and Community in Enterprise Collaboration. In: The 8th International Conference on New Technologies of Distributed Systems (NOTERE 2008), Lyon, France (2008)
17. Kiczales, G., Lamping, J., Mendhekar, A., Maeda, C., Lopes, C.V., Loingtier, J.-M., Irwin, J.: Aspect-oriented programming. In: Aksit, M., Matsuoka, S. (eds.) ECOOP 1997. LNCS, vol. 1241, pp. 220–242. Springer, Heidelberg (1997)
18. Heckel, R., et al.: Towards a UML Profile for Service-Oriented Architectures. In: Workshop on Model Driven Architecture: Foundations and Applications (MDAFA 2003), University of Twente, Enschede (June 2003)
19. Zhang, X.G.: Model Driven Data Service Development. In: IEEE International Conference on Networking, Sensing and Control, ICNSC 2008, China (2008)
20. Baresi, L., et al.: Modeling and validation of service-oriented architectures: Application vs. style. In: The 9th European Software Engineering Conference (ESEC/FSE 2003), Helsinki, Finland, September 1-5 (2003)
21. Cáceres, P., Marcos, E., Vela, B.: MDA-based approach for web information system development. In: Proceedings of Workshop in Software Model Engineering (2003)
22. Johnston, S.: UML profile for software services, in IBM DeveloperWorks (April 2005), http://www-128.ibm.com/developerworks/rational/library/05/419_soa

A Collaboration Pattern Model for Virtual Organisations

Nikos Papageorgiou[1], Yannis Verginadis[1], Dimitris Apostolou[2],
and Gregoris Mentzas[1]

[1] Institute of Communications and Computer Systems,
National Technical University of Athens
9 Iroon Polytechniou Str., Athens, Greece
npapag@mail.ntua.gr, jverg@mail.ntua.gr, gmentzas@mail.ntua.gr
[2] Informatics Department, University of Piraeus
80 Karaoli & Dimitriou Str., Piraeus, Athens, Greece
dapost@unipi.gr

Abstract. Collaboration, either inter or intra-organization is a critical business function that demands skills and knowledge spanning a wide range of domains including social, business and technical domains. Collaboration patterns can be a means to capture best practices about recurring collaborative problems and solutions. Many forms of patterns have been proposed addressing specific aspects of collaboration such as business interaction design and workflow. In this paper we propose a novel collaboration pattern model that aims to constitute a framework capable to describe recurring collaborative activities taking place in the context of virtual organisations.

Keywords: Collaboration model, collaboration patterns.

1 Introduction

Organisations increasingly seek to establish collaborations in order to expand their activities by forming Virtual Organisations (VOs). A VO constitutes a collaborative business environment with increased needs for modelling, executing and monitoring dynamic collaborations. In an effort to address these needs, we introduce the concept of patterns in VOs as a means for capturing and re-using recurring segments of work or parts of collaboration.

The concept of patterns is inspired by the way experts tackle work on a particular problem: It is unusual to tackle it by inventing a new solution that is completely different from existing ones. Instead, they often recall a similar problem they have already solved, and reuse the essence of its solution to solve the new problem. This kind of 'expert behaviour' is a natural way of coping with many kinds of problems [8]. The concept of design pattern was first introduced in the field of engineering by Christopher Alexander, a professor of Architecture in University of California, Berkley. His book, where he describes a language for architectural patterns [1], is seen as the prototype for patterns in many other domains, including Software Engineering [13] and Human Computer Interaction (HCI) [6].

L.M. Camarinha-Matos et al. (Eds.): PRO-VE 2009, IFIP AICT 307, pp. 61–68, 2009.

We focus on applying the concept of patterns in collaborative work taking place in the context of VOs. A common definition of collaboration is: people or organizations working jointly with others or together especially in an intellectual endeavour[1] that is creative in nature[2]. In the context of a VO, many challenges encountered, both in its day-to-day operations and in its strategic choices, are often addressed collaboratively by the participating partners. The overall aim of using collaboration patterns (CPats) in the VO domain is to enhance support of the networked enterprises by providing a means for capturing and reusing solutions to collaborative processes.

In this paper we set out to develop a CPat model that aims to constitute a framework capable to describe recurring collaborative activities taking place in the context of VOs. We base our work on existing research in patterns and on our analysis of requirements of specific case studies. In the next sections we present related work and we describe the proposed CPat model consisting of a pattern structure, a categorization scheme and a diagrammatic description for VO CPats.

2 Related Work

To our knowledge, the application of patterns in VO collaboration is a new research domain. In our effort to reuse related previous research we have investigated a widespread range of related fields. Starting from the field of communities of practice (CoP), we see that CPats have been proposed [9] as conceptual structures that capture socio-technical lessons learnt in optimizing collaboration processes.

In the field of workflow systems, workflow patterns can be viewed as patterns addressing the structured part of collaborative processes. A workflow is often defined as a collection of tasks, performed by systems or humans, organized to accomplish some business process [14]. Control flow [28], resource [25] and data patterns [24] are subcategories of workflow patterns. Similar research is that of business process patterns [20], [3]. Activity theory on the other hand, provides a framework that addresses the ad-hoc part of collaboration. Activity patterns have been proposed to "formalize the structure and content of an activity and the integration methods it depends on, thereby making it reusable as a template in future activities" [17]. The Unified Activity Modeling methodology [18] is based on activity theory and aims to design systems that utilize repetitive activities [15].

In the field of Collaboration Engineering (CE) which deals with the design, modelling and deployment of repeatable processes for recurring collaborative tasks [7], thinkLets aim to describe elementary, atomic group processes from a leader's point of view. CE processes consisting of thinkLets can provide ready-to-apply facilitation "recipes" that capture the best practices of highly experienced facilitators. CE researchers have codified a large number of patterns [7], [10], [19].

Patterns have also been used to support distributed software engineering processes [22]. Similarly, service interaction patterns [2] are applied to the service composition or lower layers (message handling and protocols) in service-based business process interconnections.

---

[1] Collaborate, Merriam-Webster's Online Dictionary, 2007.
[2] Collaboration, Oxford English Dictionary, Second Edition, (1989). (Eds.) J. A. Simpson & E. S. C. Weiner. Oxford: Oxford University Press.

A significant aspect of CPats is that of capturing knowledge exchanges taking place during collaborations. Pattern-based knowledge workflows can enable the automation of knowledge flows across an organization [26]. Patterns for knowledge management processes have also been suggested [23].

All previous mentioned research streams propose prescription-oriented patterns. Techniques stemming from Social Network Analysis have been proposed to identify and mine patterns of human interaction captured during the usage of collaborative systems. They aim to improve business processes by mining the deviations between a given model and its real world execution [12] or enable the automatic generation of abstract form of CPAts [4].

Alexander [1] suggests that, if a pattern author is not able to draw a picture, then the solution described is not a pattern. Although Alexander was referring to architectural design patterns, the necessity for a schematic representation of patterns exists also for all types of CPats. For instance, in the field of action patterns, EMOO diagrams have been proposed [5], a notation that is based on the MOO notation [16]; in workflow patterns, YAWL, a Petri-Net based graphical modelling language has been proposed [28]. Similarly, the BEMN notation has been proposed in the field of business events and event patterns [11] and the CIAN notation has been proposed in the area of interaction patterns for CSCW systems [21]. In all cases, the CPat diagram provides a schematic overview of the solution the CPat prescribes in order to facilitate the design process and reduce the likelihood of errors.

3 Collaboration Pattern Model

We define CPats as follows [29]:

"A collaboration pattern is a prescription which addresses a collaborative problem that may occur repeatedly in the environment. It describes the forms of collaboration and the proven solutions to a collaboration problem and appears as a recurring group of actions that enable efficiency in both the communication and the implementation of a successful solution. The collaboration pattern can be used as is in the same application domain or it can be abstracted and used as a primitive building block beyond its original domain."

From the CPat definition we deduce that CPats should prescribe a collaboration situation or problem as well as proven solutions to the problem. In addition to the concepts deduced from the definition, a CPat model should encapsulate some of the key findings of the related research in patterns, such as: (a) CPats can serve different objectives or functions and can be of different levels of abstraction; (b) CPats should trigger human and machine processes when certain events occur and condition hold [9]; (c) patterns may include a structure (in the form of a series of steps and the applicable user roles), content (describing the activities to be done), and methods for accessing IT resources to get things done [15]; (d) CPats should contain a diagrammatic description. In the remaining of this section we elaborate how these issues are represented explicitly in the proposed CPat model.

3.1 Collaboration Patterns Categorization

Related literature distinguishes two categorization approaches for patterns: according to their objective/function and according to their granularity. Virtual community patterns [9], CE patterns [7], workflow patterns [27], resource patterns [24], data patterns [24] and subcategories of knowledge-flow elementary patterns or knowledge-flow advanced patterns [26] are examples of pattern modelling approaches that use pattern categorization based on objective or function. Such a categorization is relevant for CPats because it allows e.g., identifying that two or more CPats present the same functional behaviour and hence both of them could be used in a specific situation.

In our CPat model, we propose a three-level categorization of CPats based on the VO objective or function they support. Specifically: (i) the *Strategic CPat* category contains CPats that facilitate strategic objectives of a VO which may refer e.g., to the actual VO formation, to the addition or removal of a new partner in the VO, to the structure of the VO, to actions that determine the VO goals, etc. (ii) the *Business CPat* category contains CPats that serve operational functions of the VOs (e.g. proposal preparation, conflict resolution, scheduling a meeting etc.), and (iii) the *Simple CPat* category which includes patterns that focus on elementary collaborative activities (e.g. completing a task) and are expected to propose a solution that involves a small number of simple activities.

3.2 Collaboration Patterns Structure

The CPat structure comprises all attributes needed for specifying what a specific CPat does, where it is applicable and under which circumstances it may be initiated. The CPat example provided in Table 1 model the structure of "Schedule a meeting", a recurring collaboration activity, which takes place in the context of a VO that consists of a number of pharmaceutical companies intending to develop a drug according to a

Table 1. VO Collaboration pattern model structure

Field	Description	Example
Name & No:	A name and a number for quick referencing.	*<Schedule a Meeting> - CPat 1*
Category:	Positioning in one of the proposed categories (Strategic/Business/Simple)	*Business Pattern*
Problem:	A description of the problem(s) the CPat has addressed before or it is expected to address in the future.	*Check the work progress for a specific deliverable*
VO lifecycle phase:	One or more VO lifecycle phases where it can be applicable (pre-creation, creation, operation or termination).	*VO Operation*
Application Area:	Declares the sector (e.g. Manufacturing) where it is applicable.	*Pharmaceutical Industry*
Pre-Conditions:	The list of the states and conditions that must be satisfied before the specific CPat can be considered applicable.	*(No. of collaborators > 3) AND (VO coordinator available) AND (Budget available)*

Table 1. (*continued*)

Triggers:	Events and event patterns that can trigger the execution of the CPat.	*(The last progress meeting was held 3 months ago) OR (Deliverable Derma1 delayed)*
Triggers of Exceptions:	Events that can raise an exception during the implementation of CPat.	*Deliverable Derma1 has just been sent.*
Roles:	Includes the collaboration roles that are to be involved in the CPat.	*VO Coordinator, WP leader, VO member*
Input Information:	Documents or data that will be used in terms of this CPat.	*Project's DoW , VO members' contact details*
Output Information:	Documents or data that will be produced in terms of this CPat.	*Meeting minutes document*
Duration:	The acceptable time frame in which the proposed by the CPat solution can be successfully implemented.	*2 Weeks (this can be a variable)*
Exception:	A description of an exception to the pattern (e.g. termination of the specific CPat and execution of another one).	*<Postpone Scheduled Meeting CPat>*
Post-Conditions:	Conditions and states that hold after the successful termination of the CPat.	*Meeting took place AND Agreed minutes stored in system.*
Related CPats:	- CPats that optionally can be executed in parallel or after its termination. - Alternative CPats that can be used instead of the described one. - Conflicting CPats that cannot be executed concurrently with the described one.	*-CPat that optionally: <Schedule conference call CPat> -CPat that can be executed subsequently: <Postpone Scheduled Meeting> -Alternative CPat : <Schedule an Online Meeting CPat>*
Solution:	Comprises prescriptions of solutions to the designated problem in the form of action lists, workflows or even instructions for tool usage. *Action list:* *-WP leader sends email to the coordinator* *-Coordinator notifies collaborators about the need of organizing a meeting* *-Use tool for agreeing on the date* *-WP leader stores meeting minutes*	*Usage of tools:* *- Engage with www.doodle.ch to find date based on collaborators' availabilities* *-Use a file server to store meeting minutes*

new set of drug administration regulations. According to this, a meeting needs to be scheduled either periodically (every 3 months) or upon the delay of a specific deliverable (triggers). At least 3 collaborators should be available along with the coordinator and the necessary budget (pre-conditions). When the aforementioned pre-conditions and triggers are satisfied, the specific CPat is applied and the solution it prescribes, in terms of action to be taken and tools to be used, can be followed. Specifically, the work package leader should be notified in order to send an e-mail to the VO coordinator asking him or her to notify the VO members about the need of organizing a meeting. Further, a web tool for agreeing on the meeting date is identified and possibly automatically configured (e.g., with partner names and possible meeting dates) and invoked. When the meeting takes place, the meeting minutes are stored. In case the delayed deliverable that triggered this meeting is submitted by the responsible partner before the actual meeting takes place, an exception event is triggered and the CPat is stopped; moreover, a CPat for postponing the meeting is invoked.

3.3 Collaboration Patterns Diagrammatic Description

We propose the Business Process Management Notation (BPMN) [30] as the notation for CPat diagrams. Figure 1 describes the BPMN diagrammatic description of the CPat "Schedule a Meeting" with a BPMN diagram. The requirements for the selected CPat graphical notation are imposed by the elements of the presented CPat model which, to our opinion, are adequately covered by BPMN because BPMN is typically used for business process modelling and has symbols that are able to model, beyond the collaborative process of the CPat solution, CPat triggers, pre and post-conditions, exceptions, input and output information. The capability of BPMN to model abstract processes is also very important. The abstract form of CPat diagrams can be used where the solution of a CPat should have the form of a loose action list and thus allow the CPat designer to decide about the rigidity of the solution that a specific CPat proposes.

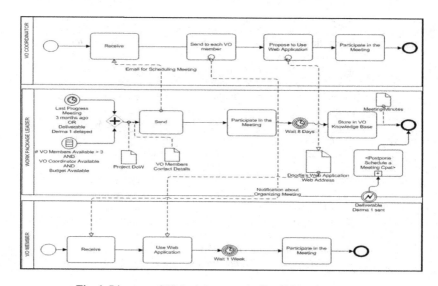

Fig. 1. Diagram of "Schedule a meeting" collaboration pattern

4   Conclusions and Future Work

To our knowledge, existing approaches address only isolated aspects of virtual enterprise collaboration with patterns (e.g. workflows, knowledge, ad-hoc activities). In this paper we have introduced the notion of collaboration patterns in virtual organisations. We have described a model which consists of a pattern structure and a diagrammatic description along with a complete example. This model will serve as a framework for VO CPats. With the proposed CPat model we aim to address the specific requirements of VO collaboration. We have found that the model adequately represents a number of CPats we have found in the literature and derived from case studies of the EU research project SYNERGY. The model will be used in the development of a VO collaboration platform following an event-driven architecture. The collaboration platform shall provide services for detecting and executing relevant CPats. The detection of a relevant CPat will be automatically performed upon events that match the CPat triggering conditions and provided additional conditions (problem, context, pre-conditions) hold. The execution of the CPat will be handled by appropriate collaboration and workflow services of the collaboration platform or even by humans, as prescribed in the CPat solution.

Acknowledgments. This work has been partially funded by the European Commission in project SYNERGY, Grant Agreement No. 216089.

References

1. Alexander, C., Ishikawa, S., et al.: A Pattern Language. Oxford University Press, New York (1977)
2. Barros, A.P., Dumas, M., et al.: Service Interaction Patterns: Towards a Reference Framework for Service-based Business Process Interconnection (2005)
3. Barros, O.H.: Business Information System Design Based on Process Pattern and Frameworks. Industrial Engineering Department, University of Chile (2004),
   http://www.BPtrends.com
4. Biuk-Aghai, R., Simoff, S.J., et al.: From Ad-hoc to Engineered Collaboration in Virtual Workspaces. In: Eleventh Americas Conference on Information Systems, Omaha, NE, USA (2005)
5. Biuk-Aghai, R.P.: An Information Model of Virtual Collaboration. In: Proceedings of the 2003 IEEE International Conference on Information Reuse and Integration, Las Vegas, Nevada, USA. IEEE SMC, Los Alamitos (2003)
6. Borchers, J.O.: A pattern approach to interaction design. AI & Society 15(4), 359–376 (2001)
7. Briggs, R.O.: Collaboration Engineering with ThinkLets to Pursue Sustained Success with Group Support Systems. Journal of Management Information Systems 19(4), 31–64 (2003)
8. Buschmann, F., Meunier, R., et al.: Pattern-oriented software architecture: a system of patterns. John Wiley & Sons, Inc., New York (1996)
9. de Moor, A.: Community Memory Activation with Collaboration Patterns. In: Proceedings of the 3rd International Community Informatics Conference (CIRN 2006), Prato Italy, p. 1 (2006)
10. de Vreede, G.J., Briggs, R.O.: Collaboration Engineering: Designing Repeatable Processes for High-Value Collaborative Tasks. In: Proceedings of the 38th Annual Hawaii International Conference on System Sciences (HICSS 2005)-Track (2005)
11. Decker, G., Grosskopf, A., et al.: A Graphical Notation for Modeling Complex Events in Business Processes (2007)
12. Dustdar, S., Hoffmann, T.: Interaction pattern detection in process oriented information systems. Data & Knowledge Engineering 62(1), 138–155 (2007)
13. Gamma, E., Helm, R., et al.: Design patterns: elements of reusable object-oriented software. Addison-Wesley, Reading (1995)

14. Georgakopoulos, D., Hornick, M., et al.: An overview of workflow management: From process modeling to workflow automation infrastructure. Distributed and Parallel Databases 3(2), 119–153 (1995)
15. Geyer, W., Muller, M.J., et al.: ActivityExplorer: Activity-Centric Collaboration from Research to Product. IBM Systems Journal 45(4), 713–738 (2006)
16. Hawryszkiewycz, I.T.: Analysis for Cooperative Business Processes. In: Proceedings of the Fifth Australian Workshop on Requirements Engineering (2000)
17. Hill, C., Yates, R., et al.: Beyond predictable workflows: Enhancing productivity in artful business processes. IBM Systems Journal 45(4), 663–682 (2006)
18. IBM. Unified Activity Management project (2005),
    `http://domino.research.ibm.com/comm/research_projects.nsf/`
    `pages/uam.index.html`
19. Kolfschoten, G.L., Briggs, R.O., et al.: A conceptual foundation of the thinkLet concept for Collaboration Engineering. International Journal of Human-Computer Studies 64(7), 611–621 (2006)
20. Malone, T.W., Crowston, K., et al.: Organizing Business Knowledge: The Mit Process Handbook. MIT Press, Cambridge (2003)
21. Molina, A.I., Redondo, M.Á., Ortega, M.: A Conceptual and Methodological Framework for Modeling Interactive Groupware Applications. In: Dimitriadis, Y.A., Zigurs, I., Gómez-Sánchez, E. (eds.) CRIWG 2006. LNCS, vol. 4154, pp. 413–420. Springer, Heidelberg (2006)
22. Norta, A., Hendrix, M., et al.: A Pattern Repository for Establishing Inter-organizational Business Processes, Beta, Research School for Operations Management and Logistics (2006)
23. Qureshi, S., Hlupic, V., Briggs, R.O.: On the Convergence of Knowledge Management and Groupware. In: de Vreede, G.-J., Guerrero, L.A., Marín Raventós, G., et al. (eds.) CRIWG 2004. LNCS, vol. 3198, pp. 25–33. Springer, Heidelberg (2004)
24. Russell, N., ter Hofstede, A.H.M., et al.: Workflow Data Patterns (2004)
25. Russell, N., ter Hofstede, A.H.M., et al.: Workflow Resource Patterns, Beta, Research School for Operations Management and Logistics (2005)
26. Sarnikar, S., Zhao, J.L.: Pattern-based knowledge workflow automation: concepts and issues. Information Systems and E-Business Management, 1–18 (2007)
27. van der Aalst, W.M.P., Hofstede, A.H.M., et al.: Business Process Management: A Survey. LNCS, pp. 1–12. Springer, Heidelberg (2003)
28. van der Aalst, W.M.P., ter Hofstede, A.H.M.: YAWL: yet another workflow language. Information Systems 30(4), 245–275 (2005)
29. Verginadis, Y., Apostolou, D., et al.: Collaboration Patterns in Event-Driven Environment for Virtual Organisations. In: Intelligent Event Processing – Association for the Advancement of Artificial Intelligence (AAAI), Spring Symposium 2009, Stanford, USA (2009)
30. White, S.A.: Business Process Modeling Notation (BPMN) Version 1.0. Business Process Management Initiative, BPMI. org (May 1, 2004)

Issues and Experiences in Logistics Collaboration

Nadia Lehoux[1], Jean-François Audy[1], Sophie D'Amours[1],
and Mikael Rönnqvist[2]

[1] FORAC,CIRRELT, Université Laval, Québec, Canada
[2] Norwegian School of Economics and Business Administration, Bergen, Norway
Nadia.Lehoux@cirrelt.ca, Jean-Francois.Audy@cirrelt.ca,
Sophie.Damours@gmc.ulaval.ca, Mikael.Ronnqvist@nhh.no

Abstract. Collaborative logistics is becoming more important in today's industry. This is driven by increased environmental concerns, improved efficiency through collaborative planning supporting resources sharing and new business models implementation. This paper explores collaborative logistics and reports on business applications within the forest products industry in Sweden and Canada. It first describes current opportunities in collaborative planning. It then discusses issues related to building the coalition as well as sharing resources and benefits. Three business cases are described and used to support the discussion around these main issues. Finally, different challenges are detailed, opening new paths for researchers in the field.

Keywords: Collaborative logistics, inter-firm collaborations, game theory.

1 Introduction

Logistics and transportation are activities that provide many opportunities for collaboration between companies. This collaboration, either through information or resource sharing, aims to reduce the cost of executing the logistics activities, improve service, enhance capacities as well as protect environment and mitigate climate change. Specifically, collaboration occurs when two or more entities form a coalition and exchange or share resources (including information), with the goal of making decisions or realizing activities that will generate benefits that they cannot (or only partially) generate individually. This can range from information exchange, joint planning, joint execution, up to strategic alliance (e.g. co-evolution) (D'Amours *et al.*, 2004). Collaborative logistics may involve different levels of resource and information sharing between two or many entities. It can be driven by a voluntary action or imposed by certain policies. It can also bring together business entities which are competitors, collaborators or supplier/customers. In addition, collaboration is related to some forms of interdependency. Frayret *et al.* (2004) have reviewed these forms. They are listed and briefly described in Table 1.

In this paper, we will discuss motivations and issues related to building a coalition of business entities aiming for collaborative logistics. We will also describe three case studies and express how, in different types of collaboration scheme, enterprises have addressed challenges related to coalition building and benefit sharing.

L.M. Camarinha-Matos et al. (Eds.): PRO-VE 2009, IFIP AICT 307, pp. 69–76, 2009.

Table 1. Forms of interdependency

Type of relation	Description
1. Pooled interdependence	Occurs when each part of a system renders a discrete contribution to the whole, while each part is supported by the whole
2. Producer-consumer relationship or sequential interdependence	Links two manufacturing activities for which the output of one is the input of the other
3. Reciprocal relationships	Concerns activities whose outputs are the reciprocal inputs of the other activity
4. Intensive interdependence	Relates to the intrinsic sophistication of activities that are imbedded
5. Task/sub-task interdependencies	Relates to the decomposition of tasks into sub-tasks
6. Simultaneity interdependence	Occurs when activities need to be performed, or not, at the same time, such as for meeting scheduling

2 Collaborative Logistics

Logistics deal with moving and storing products as they flow through the supply chain. Efficient logistics planning and execution can provide competitive advantages to the different entities of the supply chain. Moreover, collaboration in logistics based on information exchanged has been identified as one means of reducing the negative impacts of the bullwhip effect, known as the amplification of demand variation going upstream the supply chain (Lee *et al.*, 1997, Moyaux *et al.*, 2004). The supply chain entities such as carrier, producer, customer and third party logistics collaborate in different ways. In terms of transportation, they try to optimize the traveling time and load capacity usage. They share information to capture the benefit of a denser network, aiming to minimize transportation costs, in particular the backhauling costs (i.e. combining two transport orders to minimize the unloaded distance). The supply chain entities may also collaborate to increase responsiveness and reduce inventory holding costs. In such cases, they share demand and consumption information in a timely manner and use different approaches to synchronize efficiently their activities.

2.1 Strategic and Operational Collaboration in Logistics

Enterprises may face large transportation costs and aim to deploy new infrastructures that will provide them with a competitive advantage over others. Such shared infrastructure could be pipelines (e.g. crude oil and gas); terminals (e.g. forestry); warehouses (e.g. retailing) or transportation modes (integrating e.g. train, ship, truck in general transportation organizations). The location and the investment for such infrastructure are considered strategic for the entities involved. Other strategic collaboration relates to defining industry standards. This is the case when entities of a same industry collaborate to define business standards so as to improve the interoperability of their systems (e.g. PapiNet – a standard for information exchange in the forest products industry). Strategic collaboration can also imply a long term business contract and the exchange of demand and capacity information. At the strategic level, it is likely to see entities exchanging a "complete" model of their demand or capacity, permitting the coalition to compute the value of the collaboration and to propose a realistic sharing strategy (Montreuil *et al.*, 1999, Frisk *et al.*, 2006). On the other hand, operational collaboration requires low commitment. An example of such collaborations could be a web based platform inviting enterprises to share their transportation needs so as to find joint routes that will reduce their transportation costs. Applications can be found in the Swedish and Finnish forest industry. In Erikson and Rönnqvist (2003), a web-based transportation planning tool is described. Here, a backhauling solution is provided to all transport planners in several regions and companies in order to support manual planning of daily routes.

Collaboration can bring together two or more entities. In all cases, the need for each entity to improve its logistics is a prerequisite for the collaboration. In a many-to-many context, the design of proper collaboration mechanisms is more difficult, mainly because the exchanges are not bilateral as in a supplier-customer type of collaboration. Some entities may enter with a lot to provide and little to gain, while others will benefit greatly with little to offer.

While collaboration usually emerges from a coalition of voluntary entities that share information to improve their logistics, this may also be imposed by one of the leading entities of the supply chain. For example, WalMart move to set RFID systems with all major suppliers was done in order to increase the collaboration but it was imposed on the different entities. Other imposed schemes can be set by public policies. For example, natural resources can be managed by governmental authorities and the allocation rules may impose collaboration between many entities. This is the case in the forestry industry in Canada where the different entities are asked to find harvesting plans which meet the coalition members' needs (Beaudoin et al., 2007).

In a context where a supplier and a customer aim for more efficiency in their logistics, they can evaluate the possibility of exchanging more information and plan jointly their activities. Several responsibilities can also be shifted from one entity to another so the global efficiency of the coalition is improved. For example, under a Vendor Managed Inventory (VMI) agreement, the producer is responsible for managing the inventory of its customer. The customer provides the daily consumption to the producer so it can build a production-distribution plan that meets the fixed service level as well as optimizes the usage of its resources. The VMI approach has contributed positively to enhancing the logistics performance. Danese (2006) reported the benefits gained by the pharmaceutical giant GlaxoSmithKline. Another example of technique frequently implemented by companies is Continuous Replenishment (CR), where the replenishment is structured around a pre-scheduled reservation of capacity. In particular, the collaboration may set a one truck per day delivery to the customer. Then, the customer is responsible for setting the mix of products to be on the truck every day. This approach satisfies the needs of the customer over time and reduces the pressure on the producer. Finally, the Collaborative Planning, Forecasting and Replenishment (CPFR) business model aims to balance demand and production-distribution capacity up-front in order to define a win-win unique plan for both parties. Cederlund et al. (2007) reported reduction of 50% of transportation costs and 30% of inventory holding costs at Motorola.

However, bilateral collaboration may not reach equilibrium; collaborative entities may gain different benefits when using the different models. Often, one needs to share the benefits to motivate the others to participate in the collaboration.

3 Case Studies

In this section, we discuss three industrial case studies where the authors have been involved. The first case considers coordinated transportation planning in Sweden involving eight forest companies. The second case was conducted with four North American furniture manufactures aiming for co-distribution to the USA, while the third case is dealing with a bilateral collaboration between a pulp and paper producer and a wholesaler. These cases describe what can be done and raise aspects and considerations when testing and implementing theories in collaborative logistics in practice. They were based on a structured methodology adapted from Lehoux and D'Amours (2004). Table 2 provides a summary of the properties of the three cases.

Table 2. A brief summary of the case studies (LP: Linear Programming, MIP: Mixed Integer Programming)

Case	Total players	Industry	Logistics approach	Decision level	OR method	Stable equilibrium	Put into practice?
1	8	Wood supply	1	Tactical	LP	Yes - but not when implemented	Yes - by 3 players
2	4	Furniture	5	Operational	Heuristic	Yes - with cost allocation	Waiting
3	2	Paper	4	Operational	MIP	No - need incentives	Yes - CR

3.1 Wood Supply Collaboration in Sweden

This first case study is based on work done by the Forest Research Institute of Sweden with eight forest companies involved in transportation of logs from forest harvest areas to industries such as saw, pulp and paper mills (Frisk *et al.*, 2006). Transportation planning is an important part of the supply chain or wood flow chain in forestry. It often amounts to about a third of the raw material cost. There are often several forest companies operating in the same region and coordinated planning between two or more companies is rare. Wood bartering (or timber exchange) between forest companies to reduce transport cost is fairly common in Sweden. In wood bartering, two companies agree to deliver a specific volume to the others company's demand points. The company still plans its operations itself and there is no need to give away any sensitive information. Also, there is no need to provide information about the own savings to the other company.

In 2004 a group of eight forest companies in southern Sweden wanted to know the potential for coordinated transportation planning. Here, all companies viewed their supply and demand as common and a problem for one integrated artificial company could be done. This problem can be solved using the system FlowOpt (Forsberg *et al.*, 2005). The optimization model can be solved with a Linear Programming (LP) model. It turned out that the potential saving was as high as 14.2%. Some part comes from improved planning within each company and the part from collaboration was 8.7%. A very important question is how the savings or the cost should be distributed among the companies. Initially, the companies argued that the total cost should be based on their share of the overall volume. However, when we computed the relative savings, it was ranging from 0.2-20%. This difference was too high it was not possible to agree on. The reasons for this difference in relative savings are twofold. First, each company takes responsibility of their own supply and makes sure that it is delivered to the new destinations (coupling between supply and demand points). Secondly, the geographical distribution differs between companies and this affect the new distribution solution.

In order to come up with a sharing principle that the companies could agree on, several sharing principles based on economic models including Shapley value, the nucleolus, separable and non-separable costs, shadow prices and volume weights were tested and analyzed. As a part of the analysis, a new approach, called Equal Profit Method (EPM), was developed. The motivation was to get an allocation that provides an as equal relative profit as possible among the participants. In addition it satisfies core constraints from cooperative game theory and is a stable solution. This approach was acceptable among the forest companies. This was further extended in a two-stage process where the first identified volumes that make a contribution to the collaboration. Then the EPM was applied to these identified volumes.

As a result of the case study, three companies started in 2008 a collaboration where monthly coordinated planning was done. Before each month, each company provided the information about supply and demand to a third party, in this case the Forest Research Institute of Sweden. Then an integrated plan was done and the result was given back to the forest companies for their own detailed transportation planning. The sharing principle was based on having the same relative savings applied to each company own supply. In addition, there were some constraints making sure that each company is the main supplier for its own mills, and that pairwise exchange flows were the same. The latter is to avoid financial exchange between companies. Moreover, some core conditions were not included. With this revised model, it was not possible to guarantee a stable solution. The approach was tested during four months in 2008 and the potential savings were 5-15% each month.

3.2 Outbound Transportation Collaboration

The second case study refers to the potential collaboration between four furniture manufacturers in Canada. The aim was to optimize collectively the outbound transportation of their products to the USA. In Audy and D'Amours (2008), four different logistics scenarios were explored to establish the collaboration. Cost and delivery time reductions as well as gain in market geographic coverage were identified in each scenario. However, even though a scenario can provide substantial benefits for the group, each company needs to evaluate the scenario according to its own benefits. This individual evaluation can lead to a situation where the scenario with the highest cost-savings for the group (optimal cost-savings scenario) does not provide the individual highest cost-savings to some companies or worse, provides one or more negative benefits. As a result, without any modification, this optimal cost-savings scenario would be rejected in favour of another scenario that may not capture all the potential cost-savings and may exclude some of the companies.

Audy et al. (2008) integrated in the optimal cost-savings scenario the modifications which satisfy the conditions allowing its establishment by the whole group. However, by doing so, the result in cost reductions go from 21% to 12.9%. In other words, an additional cost of 8.1% was incurred in the collaborative plan to satisfy the heterogeneous requirements of some partners. Since some companies have more requirements than others and because the impact on cost increase between two requirements is almost never the same, this raises a new question: how the additional cost incurred to satisfy the special requirements should be shared between the companies? Using the solution concept of a cost allocation scheme called Alternative cost avoided method (see Tijs and Driessen, 1986), a new method was proposed and analyzed. This new method allows a share according to the impact of the requirements of each partner on the cost of the collaborative plan. Thus, the partner who increases the most the cost of the collaborative plan obtains the highest part of the additional cost incurred to satisfy the requirements of all partners. The previous costs allocated to each partner were then considered as a fix cost parameter in a sharing principle to determine the individual cost-savings of each company. The Equal Profit Method proposed by Frisk *et al.* (2006) was used as the sharing principle with two modifications: (i) to tackle the previous fix cost parameter and also two other fix cost parameters typical to the furniture industry, and (ii) to ensure a minimum cost-savings percentage for each partner.

As a result of the case study, a pilot project was initiated by companies with the support of their industrial association. As agreed by the four companies, one of them defined a business agreement to manage the collaboration in the pilot project. The definition of the business agreement was delayed for many reasons and then, one opportunistic company used the transportation rates inside the business agreement to put pressure on its carriers to reduce its own transportation rates. Since that, the project pilot was suspended but was not abandoned by the three other companies.

3.3 Collaboration Approaches in the Pulp and Paper Industry

The last case concerns a pulp and paper producer who decided to establish a partnership with one of its clients (Lehoux *et al.*, 2008). Since the production capacity was limited, the producer had to plan operations in order to satisfy the demand of the partner and the demand of other clients. The partner was a wholesaler, thus he bought products and sold them to consumers without transforming the merchandise. Even if each partner wanted to create a real partnership with mutual benefits, they made decisions based on their local costs rather than the global costs of the system. The producer planned operations in order to minimize production, distribution and inventory costs, while the wholesaler ordered products so as to minimize buying, ordering and inventory costs. For this context, the idea was to identify the collaboration model to use to ensure an efficient exchange of products and information as well as maximum benefits for the network and for each partner. Four potential approaches were first identified for the case study: a traditional system without any collaboration scheme, CR, VMI and CPFR. For each approach, decision models from the point of view of both the producer and the wholesaler were developed. Specifically, Mixed-Integer Linear Programs (MIP) were used to take into consideration the costs, revenues and constraints involved in using each approach. Afterwards, models were tested and compared so as to find the type of relationship the most profitable for the system. Results showed that CPFR generates the greatest total system profit because of an efficient optimization of both transportation and inventory costs (CPFR inventory cost up to 44% lower than inventory costs of other approaches). VMI is second best since the transportation cost is optimized. CR and the traditional system obtain the lowest total system profit.

After comparing each model using the system profit, the investigation was based on the profit of each partner. Specifically, the different types of relationship were compared to verify if the same approach could generate the highest profit for both the producer and the wholesaler. This analysis revealed that CPFR generates the greatest profit for the producer, while the CR technique is the most beneficial for the wholesaler. For this reason, a method for sharing benefits was defined so as to obtain a CPFR collaboration profitable for each partner. Results showed that if the producer shares a part of the transportation savings with the wholesaler, the profit of the wholesaler is higher than the profit obtained with CR, and the producer obtains a higher profit than the one generated by other approaches.

Actually, partners work together using a CR technique. But in the future, they aim to implement a form of CPFR. Therefore, as observed in the study, they will certainly have to share benefits if they want to establish a win-win relationship. Otherwise, it is possible that the wholesaler may prefer to work with someone else.

4 Concluding Remarks

This paper sought to review some critical issues in building and planning a coalition with the aim of conducting collaborative logistics. As shown throughout the paper, the interest for this domain is rising in the academic community as well as in industry.

Even though new ideas and methods are provided to support the different decisions, many problems are still very difficult to deal with. These problems often call for interdisciplinary solutions and collaborative network is emerging as a new discipline to study such collaborative issues (Camarinha-Matos and Afsarmanesh, 2005). For example, in the process of building a coalition, some entities may be strong competitors. In such a case, trust may play an important role in the decision process. Moreover, building a coalition involves taking into consideration implementation costs, risk, information needs, the share of costs/benefits and all the difficulties that could emerged from the collaboration.

Each of the cases discussed brings up interesting issues. The first case has identified different strategies for costs sharing. The need for a fair approach clearly illustrates the values of the companies involved. The second case raises issues in dealing with non tangible benefits as well as specific requirements and their impact on the collaborative cost structure. Finally, the third case describes a context where the only way to obtain a stable equilibrium is through the share of savings.

The case studies express a variety of strategies. However, all were studied on the basis of post-information. Great challenges still remain to support the day-to-day operations of such coalition, managing efficiently variations such as market changes or currency fluctuations. The changing context in which a coalition evolves may require a revision of the collaboration policies. When implementing theoretical models in practical collaborative logistics, it is also important to match these theories with practical issues and the planners' understanding, goals and restrictions.

References

1. Audy, J.-F., D'Amours, S.: Impact of benefit sharing among companies in the implantation of a collaborative transportation system – An application in the furniture industry. In: Camarinha-Matos, L., Picard, W. (eds.) IFIP International Federation for Information Processing, Springer, Heidelberg (2008)
2. Audy, J.-F., D'Amours, S., Rousseau, L.-M.: Cost allocation in the establishment of a collaborative transportation agreement-an application in the furniture industry. Working paper, CIRRELT, CIRRELT-2008-50 (2008)
3. Beaudoin, D., LeBel, L., Frayret, J.-M.: Tactical supply chain planning in the forest products industry through optimization and scenario-based analysis. Can. J. For. Res. 37(1), 128–140 (2007)
4. Camarinha-Matos, L.M., Afsarmanesh, H.: Collaborative networks: A new scientific discipline. J. Intellig. Manuf. 16(4-5), 439–452 (2005)
5. Cederlund, J.P., Kohli, R., Sherer, S.A., Yao, Y.: How Motorola put CPFR into action. Supply Chain Management Review, 28–35 (October 2007)
6. D'Amours, F., D'Amours, S., Frayret, J.-M.: Collaboration et outils collaboratifs pour la PME Manufacturière. Technical report, CEFRIO (2004)
7. Danese, P.: The extended VMI for coordinating the whole supply network. J. Manuf. Techn. Manag. 17(7), 888–907 (2006)
8. Eriksson, J., Rönnqvist, M.: Decision support system/tools: Transportation and route planning: Åkarweb – a web based planning system. In: Proceedings of the 2nd Forest Engineering Conference, Växjö, Sweden, May 12-15 (2003)
9. Frayret, J.-M., D'Amours, S., Montreuil, B.: Co-ordination and control in distributed and agent-based manufacturing systems. Prod. Plann. and Cont. 15(1), 1–13 (2004)
10. Forsberg, M., Frisk, M., Rönnqvist, M.: FlowOpt – a decision support tool for strategic and tactical transportation planning in forestry. Int. J. For. Eng. 16(2), 101–114 (2005)
11. Frisk, M., Jörnsten, K., Göthe-Lundgren, M., Rönnqvist, M.: Cost allocation in collaborative forest transportation. Working paper (2006) (to appear in EJOR)
12. Montreuil, B., Frayret, J.-M., D'Amours, S.: A Strategic Framework for Networked Manufacturing. Compt. in Indust. 42(2-3), 299–317 (1999)
13. Moyaux, T., Chaib-draa, B., D'Amours, S.: The impact of information sharing on the efficiency of an ordering approach in reducing the bullwhip effect. IEEE Trans. Syst. Man. & Cyb. (Part C) 37(3) (2007)
14. Lee, H.L., Padmanabhan, V., Whang, S.: Information Distortion in Supply Chain: the Bullwhip Effect. Manag. Science 43(4), 546–558 (1997)
15. Lehoux, N., D'Amours, S., Langevin, A.: Collaboration and decision models for a two-echelon supply chain: a case study in the pulp and paper industry. Working paper, CIRRELT, CIRRELT-2008-29 (2008) (to appear in JOL)
16. Lehoux, N., D'Amours, S.: La collaboration interentreprises dans le secteur alimentaire: l'Étude d'une relation entre manufacturier et distributeur. R. Franç. Gest. Indust. 23(2) (2004)
17. Tijs, S.H., Driessen, T.S.H.: Game theory and cost allocation problems. Manag. Science 32(8), 1015–1028 (1986)

Part 3

Needs and Practices

Analyzing Enterprise Networks Needs: Action Research from the Mechatronics Sector

Luca Cagnazzo[1], Paolo Taticchi[1], Gianni Bidini[1], and Enzo Baglieri[2]

[1] Department of Industrial Engineering, University of Perugia, Via Duranti 67, Perugia, Italy
luca.cagnazzo@unipg.it, paolo.taticchi@unipg.it,
gbid@mach.ing.unipg.it
[2] SDA Bocconi School of Management, Via Ferdinando Bocconi, 8, Milan, Italy
enzo.baglieri@sdabocconi.it

Abstract. New business models and theories are developing nowadays towards collaborative environments direction, and many new tools in sustaining companies involved in these organizations are emerging. Among them, a plethora of methodologies to analyze their needs are already developed for single companies. Few academic works are available about Enterprise Networks (ENs) need analysis. This paper presents the learning from an action research (AR) in the mechatronics sector: AR has been used in order to experience the issue of evaluating network needs and therefore define, develop, and test a complete framework for network evaluation. Reflection on the story in the light of the experience and the theory is presented, as well as extrapolation to a broader context and articulation of usable knowledge.

Keywords: Enterprise Network, SME, Network analysis.

1 Introduction

Today acceleration and complexity of technological changes, globalization of markets and demanding customers, make companies look for new ways to stay ahead of the competition. Particularly, in the case of Small & Medium Enterprises (SMEs), additional difficulties arise due to their small size, which must be borne in mind [1]. In this knowledge-based economy, the key factor for obtaining a competitive edge for SMEs lies in their capacity to acquire and absorb knowledge, to develop new products and processes, and to study the best business practices [2]. In order to do this, among other factors, it is important for SMEs to strengthen ties with other companies and organizations by creating inter-organizational networks. Cooperation with other companies of similar or bigger size is an alternative strategy that allows them to make use of the competitive edge of the associated companies, whether they are vertical or horizontal networks. In these new forms of collaboration among small companies, new forms of competence measurement and adequate methodologies for analyze the partner needs should be developed, in order to increase their competitiveness. For these reasons Action Research (AR) has been used in order to experience the issue of evaluating network needs and therefore define, develop, and test a complete framework for networks' evaluation. This paper is organized as follows. In the next section,

L.M. Camarinha-Matos et al. (Eds.): PRO-VE 2009, IFIP AICT 307, pp. 79–87, 2009.
© IFIP International Federation for Information Processing 2009

the research methodology adopted is presented. Consequently, the SME context is presented in respect of networking issues. Further, the methodology extrapolated from the AR is presented, by highlighting its applicability to a broader context. Then, the AR context and the activities are presented. Conclusion section ends.

2 Research Methodology

This kind of research can be characterized as being exploratory in nature and longitudinal; the project took 1 year to be completed. During this extended period of study the authors supported the network involved in the project from its inception, participating with the network enterprise owners and managers in the problem solving of evaluating network needs. Formal project management methods and a variety of data collection techniques were also utilized during this process, e.g. direct observation, surveys, interviews and customer oriented focus groups, as well as direct participation in meetings, marketing activities and product development projects. From this point of view our work might be further classified as AR as defined by [3] since in this approach "The action researcher is not an independent observer, but becomes a participant, and the process of change becomes the subject of research". [4] emphasizes the importance of this approach in building theory in complex situations, arguing that "the grounded, iterative, interventionist nature of AR ensures closeness to the full range of variables in setting where those variables may not all emerge at once" and that "AR requires us to be creative, because, it is usually conducted to develop a new approach or solution to a situation for which there is no existing prescription". [5] highlights eight major characteristics of AR:

1-Action researcher not limit to observe but take action; 2-AR involves two goals: problem solving and contribute to science; 3-AR require cooperation between the researchers and the client personnel; 4-AR aims at developing holistic understanding and recognition of complexity; 5-AR is fundamentally about the comprehension and investigation of change; 6-Ethical issues have to be understood since the close cooperation between the researchers and the client personnel; 7-AR includes all types of data gathering methods; 8-The action researcher should have a pre-understanding of the company business and environment.

3 Context: SMEs and Networking

SMEs have to make changes in the form of their organizations and of doing business in order to evolve and adapt themselves to a knowledge-based economy. These changes have to include the creation of inter-organizational cooperation. The most usual type of cooperation is an association between its own suppliers and clients or cooperation with other companies in the same sector or geographical region. Network analysis is an approach to the analysis of cooperation among companies, which has increased greatly in recent years, especially in the form of Virtual Organizations (VOs). The analysis of this type of organization gives three principal sources of value social structure, learning and generation of external economies in the network [6]. Research in cooperated systems has contributed to characterizing the following benefits for SMEs correlated to the relationship of cooperation among companies [7], [8],

[9], [10] and [11]: increment of the market share; improvement of efficiency in using the company's asset; improvement of the level of services offered to clients; time reduction in developing a new product; sharing and cost reduction correlated to the development of new product; reduction of the risk in relation to the failure in the development of a new product; improvement of the quality of product; improvement of the level of competence and acquaintances inside the company; possibility to take advantage in a more effective way of company economies; reduction of stocks; facilitating access to the market. Further motives for engaging in inter-organizational ties and co-operation include access to information, resources, markets and technologies [12]. On the other hand, networking of enterprises entails new organizational problems, such as the decentralization of decision-making process and the horizontal coordination between different business functions as well as, outside the firm, between complementary activity performed by suppliers and customers [13] and [14]. Different researchers have attempted to assess the impact of networking in enterprises performance [15] and [16]. Understanding the performances in terms of competences and attitudes of the partner network is a fundamental task for the environmental competitiveness. Although it is an important issue for these new forms of collaboration, few studies are available in literature.

4 Analyzing Enterprise Networks Needs

In this section, the methodology extrapolated from the AR is presented by highlighting its applicability to a broader context. The methodology proposed relies on two elements (an auto-evaluation questionnaire, an evaluation matrix) that are further explained.

4.1 The Questionnaire Structure

The methodology proposed consists in an auto-evaluation process based on a questionnaire which can be submitted to the network companies. Through the questionnaire, the analysts (in the AR the authors) can achieve the classification of firms in classes of affiliation through the parameterization of several critical aspects for the network competitiveness. Particularly, data collected from the questionnaire allow the analysts to classify and group the network companies in a 4x4 evaluation matrix, after a parameterization of the manipulated information. The matrix realized by the authors cross the "technical-productive managerial competences" with the "industrial technologies appropriateness" of the companies. The first dimension highlights the managerial competences in the company operations and underlines the gaps with the best practices. The second dimension points out the status of the technology use adopted by the companies. Thus, the matrix does not allow the analysts to know the entire system as a whole, but it represents a useful tool for having a picture of the companies' situation and to deeply analyse the managerial and technological conditions of the network companies. The questionnaire and the related auto evaluation model structure consist of two main sections (Figure 1-a).

4.2 The Dimensions of the Auto-evaluation Questionnaire

As introduced before, the Managerial Competences dimension and the Technological Appropriateness dimension, X and Y branches respectively in the tree in Figure 1-a, are investigated through an auto-evaluation questionnaire. Regarding the managerial competences and in particular the product/process coherence (X.1 branch of the tree), the authors evaluated the answers furnished by the companies of the network, following a methodology that confronts the product structures, in terms of mix and volumes, with the process structures (adapted from [17]), as shown in Figure 1-b. The products can be indeed realized in different ways, from a unique prototype (specialty) to standardized products (commodity) with obvious volume increasing. The productive processes can be instead defined from fragmentary to an high degree of continuity. The intersectional squares in the matrix can highlight physiological "status" of the analyzed companies or pathological "states" of inefficiency. In particular, the right upper part of the matrix represents cost-opportunity areas, since standardized products are realized with high flexible processes. Vice versa, the left lower area represents a situation in which non-standard productions are realized through high automated and standardized processes; this situation points out a clear inefficiency, since company doesn't benefit from the massive production. The positioning along the diagonal line corresponds to an high coherence between the product and the productive processes. Upper and lower positions identify non-coherence areas, corresponding to a 1-4 value score for the company and definable with the following scale: a 4 score for optimal values (along the diagonal), good values (3-squares), inappropriate values (2-sqaures) and a 1 score for critical values (1-squares). Regarding the second aspect of the Managerial Competences area, that is the operation management dimensions (X.2 branch of the tree), the analysis is conducted by the authors evaluating the second part of the questionnaire with a 1-4 answer score scale. For each operation area (quality, production, logistic, ICT), the answer scores have been parameterized on a new 1-4 value scale, that allows the authors to give an overall evaluation for each company on these areas. In this way the managerial competences have been measured for each of the investigated aspects. In order to assign an evaluating score to the "Technical-productive managerial competence" global section (X. branch of the tree in Figure 1-a), another parameterization on a 1-4 value score has been performed by the authors as average (taking in consideration particular weight values) between "Product-Process combination coherence" (X.1 branch) and "Operation management" (X.2 branch). The score attributed to the global "Technical-productive management competence" represents the value of the x-axis of the final matrix, presented in the next paragraph for the classification of the companies. Regarding the Technological appropriateness dimensions, and in particular the three industrial technological classes, the investigation has been conducted by the authors following a similar criterion of the previous dimension. For each of the analyzed aspects, the authors realized a 1-4 score evaluation on the specific technology role for the company competitiveness in the belonging business sector, the impact of the adopted technology on the customer perception and the technology innovation degree.

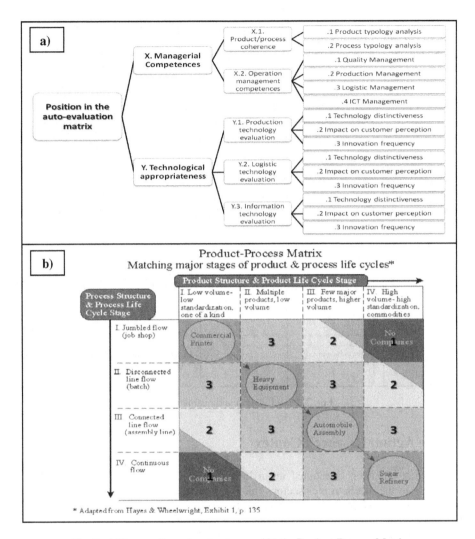

Fig. 1. a) The questionnaire structure and b) the Product-Process Matrix

4.3 The Evaluation Matrix

The model used for the auto-evaluation matrix is based on the balancing principal between management competences and technological potentialities. The aim of the two main sections is to classify the global technological appropriateness and managerial competences, with the 1-4 weight scale developed on the results of the questionnaire. The crossing between these two values can be summarized in a 4x4 matrix as reported in Figure 2. The orange zones in the matrix are the problematic areas in which the weaknesses in one of the two dimensions are symptoms of a low company competitiveness. The yellow zones are areas in which companies present good potentialities but they cannot use all of them since a mismatching between managerial competences and industrial technology appropriateness. The green zones identify non-critical situations for the companies, but they don't still represent a full excellence. The last quadrant on the bottom-right represents the best positioning in the market and the excellence benchmarking for all the other companies.

			Technical-Productive managerial competence			
			To be improved	Sufficient	Good	Excellent
			1	2	3	4
	To be improved	1	Weaknesses in both the technological area, both in the managerial area. Need of important actions on both the areas	Not technologically able to sustain the managerial progresses	Strong potentiality on managerial competences, but not distinctive technology	Excellent managerial competences in an inadequate technological context
	Sufficient	2	The technology can be improved, more priorities under the managerial area	The stability of the system is globally sufficient, but not much to guarantee a sustainable competitive advantage	Non-alignment between the managerial status and the technological level	Absolute priority on the technological area recover
	Good	3	Very good technology, problems related to a backward in managerial area	Adequate technology level and increasing margins that require an improvement on managerial competences	Strong potentiality, managerial and technology are at an adequate level. Nevertheless it is difficult to identify the distinctive element to increase the competitiveness	Good level of technology and excellent competences on managerial area, state of art to potentiate the entire system
	Excellent	4	Excellent technological capacities, but strongly limited by low managerial competences	Emphasis on technology mismatched with just sufficient managerial competences	State of art technologies, but certain investments on managerial competences should be pursued to use them	Continuous improvement is a philosophy to pursue, but at the moment the company should be taken as a benchmark from the other companies

Industrial technology appropriateness (left vertical axis label)

Fig. 2. Classification and evaluation matrix

5 The Action Research Context

The project has been conducted in an Italian network of 39 manufacturing SMEs, belonging to the mechatronics sector. This is a valuable sample of companies because it represents the main part of industries belonging to this particular sector in the Umbria region, in the central part of Italy. The network global turnover is 752 M€ and it has 4.490 total employees working within the 39 companies. The average dimension of the companies is 18 M€ turnover and 115 employees. In the 35% of the cases, the companies work on customer commitments; the remaining part of the sample has a more standardized product portfolio and in the 29% the normal ordering process is based on standard products catalogues. The companies of the network increased the selling growing rate of 11% in the last three years versus an average profitability before taxes of 5,8%. Under an economic-financial point of view, all the companies performances are in the average sector indicators. Referring to the internationalization process, its impact is the 33,8% of the total turnover. Research & Development (R&D) investments are contained: it is the 2,1% of total turnover with a number of 9,43 employees specifically dedicated to the R&D. These values are however higher than the national average. All the companies are deeply different for products, organizational adopted structure, technologies and governance. This apparent heterogeneity however allows the network to find new business solutions, developing new products and services, as well as to increase their competitiveness since the collaboration among them.

6 Action Research: Data Gathering and Analysis

6.1 Data Gathering

The project has been conducted in 2008. Data gathering has been performed through: a simple software tool to help the matrix fulfilment in the companies; and an electronic guide that helps companies in the correct use of the matrix.

Through the implementation of the matrix in the 39 companies of the case study network, final documents for each of them have been prepared, in which the own results of the analysis are presented, the needs of the firm are highlighted and preliminary solutions are discussed. A final document with aggregated data and cluster analysis, in which a picture of the network state is showed and further resolving problem actions discussed has been realized.

6.2 Data Analysis

Trough the research methodology explained in the previous paragraphs, authors present in this section the results of the analysis conducted within the network. In particular the classification of the partners through the evaluation matrix is caught out and the data analysis follows. The investigated companies show a strong industrial and technological identity, that allow them to cover the explicit weaknesses showed in the managerial profile. As shown in Figure 3, 23 of the 39 companies are characterized by a good technological profile (value 3), while just 14 show a good managerial competence level in the technical-productive area.

			Technical-Productive managerial competence			
			To be improved	Sufficient	Good	Excellent
			1	2	3	4
Industrial technology appropriateness	To be improved	1	1 company	2 companies	1 company	-
	Sufficient	2	3 companies	6 companies	3 companies	-
	Good	3	3 companies	10 companies	10 companies	-
	Excellent	4	-	-	-	-

Fig. 3. Evaluation matrix for the case study network

Moreover, 7 of the 39 companies are characterized by a critical situation related to the managerial profile and they need aids since their short term visions and competitive weaknesses. 10 of the 39 companies are collocated in the good performance quadrant and they attain both the matrix dimensions with a good degree of satisfaction. Under the managerial point of view, 32 of the 39 companies of the network highlight a productive system non-aligned with the product characteristics. This finding is pointed out through the data analysis from the product-process coherence matrix (Figure 1-b). In these cases the company timeliness in response to the rapid changing of the market demand has been mismatched with a quick productive system review. This phenomenon is comprehensible in a short term period, but very few companies are nowadays investing in order to heal the weaknesses of their operation management system in the next 3 year period. The most critic area is the logistic one, with 24 companies showing difficulties on this topic. This is due to a misunderstanding of the logistic role in the supply chain management; companies treat logistic just as strictly related to transport and shipping. Contrarily, the quality management is very well developed within the companies of the network, confirming the historical attention of Italian industry for this topic. Moreover, they very pay attention to the production management in general, as well as to the Human Resource Management (HRM) and to the organization intellectual capital. These peculiarities should be strengthened and kept hold for next years. Under the technological profile, the company analysis has highlighted some excellent situations regarding the core technologies, for maintaining and increasing the own competitiveness. However, in some occasions this attention at the technology role becomes an exasperated behavior that lead companies to frequently renew them, under a five year period. 16 companies highlight strong weaknesses under the logistic area in terms of technology, low hardware and software automation warehouse level. The recognizing, tracing, traceability, controlling and movement systems are often manual and obsolete. This is negative for the involved companies, since on the one hand this implies an heavy weak capacity to serve customers, on the other hand it decrease the economical performances of the companies, with excessive stock quantities and very low material rotation rates. 15 companies show to heavy undervalue the Information & Communication Technology (ICT) contributes for their own businesses. Hardware obsolete tools, inadequate infrastructures, non-appropriated low-price managerial software seem to be particularly critic topics as obstacles for the potential development of the single companies and of the network as a whole.

7 Conclusions

This paper, based on an AR, offered a structured methodology, based on auto-analysis, for evaluating the technological and managerial competences of enterprise networks. Through the use of a questionnaire, the methodology proposed offers the possibility to classify firms in class of affiliation through the parameterization of several investigated key performance indicators. The use of visualization matrixes permits to easily identify those network companies which lack particular technological or managerial competences, and therefore significant information is collected for the development of cluster improvement initiatives. The objective of the network investigation performed by the authors is the development, testing and strengthening of an auto-analysis model that can allow the users to investigate the technological and management competences of the collaborative environment and therefore identify the needs for a global competitiveness increasing. The usefulness of the auto evaluation tool is tangible under three different point of views: 1-For the enterprise that performs the auto evaluation activity, through which it increases the knowledge of its strengths and weaknesses, with the aim to start the appropriate improving actions; 2-For the entire network since it allows to continuously develop a benchmarking activity through a systematic approach, guaranteed by the rigour of the used methodology; 3-For all the stakeholders involved within and outside the network, because it permits to focalize the actions on sustaining innovation and improving the local industrial system performance, thank to the guide lines developed from the observed network data interpretation.

Future research will focus on building theory from this AR so as to validate the model proposed and enlarge the context of applicability.

References

1. Gilmore, A., Carson, D., Grant, K.: SME marketing in practice. Marketing Intelligence and Planning 19(1), 31–38 (2001)
2. Collison, C., Parcell, G.: Learning to Fly: Practical Lessons from One of the World's Leading Knowledge Companies, Capstone (2001)
3. Benbasat, I., Goldestein, D.K., Mead, M.: The case research strategy in studies of information systems. MIS Quarterly, 369–386 (September 1987)
4. Westbrook, R.: Action research: a new paradigm for research in production and operations management. International Journal of Operations and Production Management 15(12), 6–20 (1994)
5. Gummesson, E.: Qualitative methods in management research, 2nd edn. Sage, Thousand Oaks (2000)
6. Lazzarini, S.G., Chaddad, F.R., Cook, M.L.: Integrating Supply Chain and Network Analyses: The Study of Netchains. Journal on Chain and Network Science 1(1), 7–22 (2001)
7. Lewis, D.J.: Partnership for profit: structuring and managing strategic alliances. The Free Press, New York (1990)
8. Parker, H.: Inter-firm collaboration and new product development process. Industrial Management & Data Systems 100(6), 255–260 (2000)
9. McLaren, T., Head, M., Yuan, Y.: Supply Chain collaboration alternatives: understanding the expected costs and benefits. Internet Research: Electronic Networking Applications and Policy 2(4), 348–364 (2000)
10. Horvath, L.: Collaboration: the key to value creation in supply chain management. Supply Chain Management: An International Journal 6(5), 205–207 (2001)
11. Holton, J.A.: Building trust and collaboration in virtual team. Team Performance Management: An International Journal 7(3-4), 36–47 (2001)
12. Gulati, R., Nohria, N., Zaheer, A.: Strategic networks. Strategic Management Journal 21, 203–215 (2000)
13. Ghoshal, S., Bartlett, C.: The multinational corporation as an interorganizational network. Academy of Management Review 15, 603–625 (1990)
14. Ernst, D.: From partial to systemic globalization: international production networks in electronics industry. Berkley Roundtable on the International Economy (BRIE), Working Paper 98 (1997)
15. Easton, G., Quayle, M.: Single and Multiple Network Sourcing – Network Implications. In: Proceeding of 6th IMP Conference, Milan, pp. 474–488 (1990)
16. Puto, C., Patton, W., King, R.: Risk Handling Strategy in Industrial Vendor Selection Decisions. Journal of Marketing 49, 89–98 (Winter 1985)
17. Hayes, R.H., Wheelwright, S.C.: Link manufacturing process and product life cycles. Harvard Business Review, 133–140 (January-February 1979)

Comparing Notes: Collaborative Networks, Breeding Environments, and Organized Crime

Alejandro Hernández

Georgetown University School of Foreign Service, USA
ah342@georgetown.edu

Abstract. Collaborative network theory can be useful in refining current understanding of criminal networks and aid in understanding their evolution. Drug
trafficking organizations that operate in the region directly north of Colombia's
Valle del Cauca department and the "collection agencies" that operate in the
Colombian city of Cali have abandoned hierarchical organizational structures
and have become networked-based entities. Through the exposition of Camarinha-Matos and Afsarmanesh's business networking ideas, this chapter examines the similarities and differences between the application of collaborative
networks in licit enterprises, such as small and medium enterprises in Europe,
and how the networks might be used by illicit criminal enterprises in Colombia.

Keywords: Organized crime, Colombia, drug trafficking organizations, collection agencies, illicit criminal enterprises, collaborative networks.

1 Introduction

We should not underestimate the importance of national and transnational organized
crime networks. In its most recent analysis, the United States National Intelligence
Council noted that

> Concurrent with the shift in power among nation-states, the relative power of
> various non-state actors—including businesses, tribes, religious organizations,
> and criminal networks—will continue to increase. Several countries could even
> be "taken over" and run by criminal networks. In areas of Africa or South Asia,
> states as we know them might wither away, owing to inability of governments
> to provide for basic needs, including security [1].

In light of the National Intelligence Council's Global Trends 2025 report, Juan Carlos
Garzón's work on criminal networks in Colombia, detailed in his book Mafia & Co.,
comes at a particularly critical time for policy-makers. If states are to get the upper
hand on criminal networks, policy-makers need pertinent theoretical frameworks and
applied research to understand what they are combating. Together with that of Luis
Camarinha-Matos, Garzón's work on collaborative-networked organizations represents one such combination of theory and empirical research that can help us advance
our understanding of criminal networks.

L.M. Camarinha-Matos et al. (Eds.): PRO-VE 2009, IFIP AICT 307, pp. 88–95, 2009.

I utilize Camarinha-Matos' work on collaborative networking theory and breeding environments as a theoretical framework through which I examine the phenomenon of the "collection agencies" described below. I will draw out the differences, from the point of view of collaborative-networked organization theory, between Colombia's post-Norte Del Valle cartel trafficking structures, also covered in Garzón's work, and the sort of networks that the collection agencies represent. The paper demonstrates how collaborative network and breeding environment theory can be useful in developing a new understanding in relation to networked criminal organizations.

I set out to examine Camarinha-Matos and Afsarmanesh's work on business networking in the spirit of the enterprise theory of organized crime. Nikos Passas provides us with a definition of the enterprise theory.

> If the goods or services happen to be outlawed, then illegal enterprises will emerge to meet the demand. In this respect, there is no difference between conventional and criminal enterprises. Very often, all that changes when the business is illegal are some adjustments in modus operandi, technology and the social network that will be involved [2].

I attempt to draw parallels between the application of collaborative networks in licit enterprises and consider how the networks might be used by illicit ones. I begin by describing networks and apply the concept to Colombia's criminal networks. I then consider "collaborative networks" and "breeding environments", drawing on the business networking ideas of Camarhina-Matos and Afsarmanesh, and apply these to the Colombian case. I conclude that collaborative network theory can be useful in refining current understanding of criminal networks and aid in understanding their evolution.

2 Colombia's Criminal Networks

In Mafia & Co., Juan Carlos Garzón presents us with a somewhat frightening proposal regarding the evolution of organized crime.

> Es posible, que de la misma manera que acontece con los seres humanos, cuya esperanza de vida no ha dejado de crecer dese 1840, las organizaciones criminales perduren cada vez más en el tiempo, adaptándose a los cambios en las condiciones [de su entorno] [3].

Organized crime in Colombia seems to be presently undergoing one such adaptation. Garzón highlights a shift from rigid hierarchical organizational structures to more networked-based criminal organizations. He depicts a new kind of criminal organization, one where traditional hierarchical structures have been replaced with more horizontal configurations.

> De organizaciones pesadas, y si se quiere burocráticas, que buscan monopolizar las economías ilegales, se ha pasado progresivamente a la configuración de células que se especializan en una parte de la cadena de producción o en un mercado especifico [como en de la protección]. El líder que lo manejaba todo, ya no existe. Ahora se adoptan formas de dirigencia colegiadas, que coordinan una compleja red de facciones locales, que se articulan alrededor de transacciones constantemente cambiantes, según dicte la oportunidad del momento [3].

Garzón provides two pertinent examples of these newer, networked criminal organizations. I begin with the smaller criminal groups that came to replace the now defunct Norte Del Valle cartel, and then consider the phenomenon of the collection agencies in Cali.

The Norte Del Valle cartel, once one of the most powerful in Colombia, largely disintegrated following the death or capture of its former leaders [3]. The various factions of the defunct Norte Del Valle cartel have been atomized into smaller organizations, and each of these now specializes in one aspect of the drug production process that former cartel leadership used to control [3].

The new organizations receive product from others down the supply chain, process it, and sell it to the next organization in the chain. A separate group of organizations provides security for all those groups involved in the production and processing. The cooperation amongst them, intermittent as it may be, has allowed them to continue producing and profiting from the Norte Del Valle cartel's former business.

We can see a similar shift away from hierarchical criminal organizations in the example of the collection agency phenomenon in Colombia. Although "collection agency" might conjure up the mental image of a creditor's office, it turns out it that these entities are in fact

> Un conjunto de relaciones mediante las cuales son coordinadas distintas actividades criminales. [...] Las "oficinas de cobro" tienen una extensa red que logra establecer vínculos desde los carteles, bajando por las organizaciones sicariales, la delincuencia común, las pandillas [...] la "oficina de cobro" no debe de ser entendida como un lugar físico [3].

We can conceptualize the collection agencies as a networked organization that marshals the relevant criminal elements within a geographic area. The collection agencies in Cali link together the criminal community of the city, from the neighborhood gangs to the powerful assassin organizations. In some cases, they can exert such a large influence over the criminal underworld as to be able to impose a "tax" on the profits from all criminal activity within its area of influence [3]. Although it may not direct all criminal activity within the city, it clearly has influence over most of it. Garzón points out that collection agencies often maintain a group of assassins on their payroll to collect profits from a city's drug trade and enforce agreements among criminal elements within the city. Moreover, collection agencies can act as brokers, between the criminal underworld and citizens, to facilitate any assassination or other illicit service.

Whether through supply chains or linking the criminal elements of a city, the post Norte Del Valle cartel criminal organizations and the phenomenon of the collection agencies in Cali provide us with two clear examples of criminal organizations that rely more and more on networks. This begs the question; What can network theory tell us about these entities? Can we differentiate among them, and if so, how?

3   Collaborative Networks and Breeding Environments

Collaborative network and breeding environment theory holds the key to ascertaining the type of networks each of our two examples exemplify. Luis Camarinha-Matos and Hamideh Afsarmanesh's research on collaborative-networked organizations provides

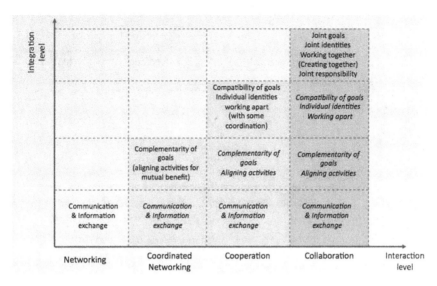

Fig. 1. Refining Concept of Collaboration As Advanced Interaction [4] [6]

useful, cutting-edge work on business networks. In this section, I present their ideas relevant to our interest in criminal organizations.

It is clear that the post Norte Del Valle cartel organizations and the phenomenon of the collection agencies represent some type of networked organization. Moreover, it seems that even though some of these organizations may compete with one another, or with other organizations, they also at points collaborate. In the case of the post Norte Del Valle cartel organizations, they collaborate in a drug production supply chain. Collaboration in relation to the collection agencies is somewhat different. The agencies themselves do not normally collaborate with other organizations, although they do create an environment that allows individuals under their purview to collaborate with one another. In both cases, the concept of collaboration is central to our understanding of the kinds of networks that these organizations represent. In order to better understand the concept of collaboration and its possible application to our understanding of Colombia's criminal networks, we will consider collaboration, a collaborative network, and a collaborative-networked organization.

Camarinha-Matos and Afsarmanesh define collaboration as

> *A process in which entities share information, resources and responsibilities to jointly plan, implement, and evaluate a program of activities to achieve a common goal. [...] [Collaboration] can be seen [...] as a process through which a group of entities enhance the capabilities of each other [...] Collaboration involves mutual engagement of participants to solve a problem together, which implies mutual trust and this takes time, effort, and dedication [4].*

Camarinha-Matos and Afsarmanesh differentiate the concept of collaboration from that of networking, coordinated networking and cooperation [fig. 1]. Collaboration must not only have a purpose; it must also involve "parties that mutually agree to collaborate [...] that know each other's capabilities [...] and that share a [common] goal" [5].

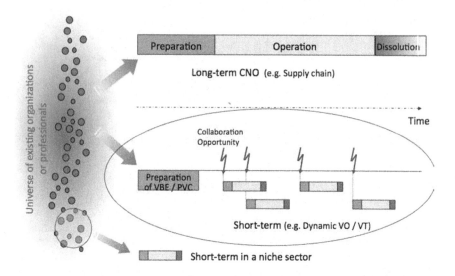

Fig. 2. Collaborative Networked Organization Formation Possibilities [6]

With collaboration defined we can consider a collaborative network. Camarinha-Matos and Afsarmanesh define a collaborative network [CN] as

> A network consisting of a variety of entities [e.g. organizations and people] that are largely autonomous, geographically distributed, and heterogeneous in terms of their operating environment, culture, social capital and goals, but that collaborate to better achieve common or compatible goals, and whose interactions are supported by a computer network [4].

Furthermore, if it implies "some kind of *organization* over the activities of [its] constituents," [4] a CN can come to represent a collaborative-networked organization [CNO]. We can define a CNO as

> *A collaborative network possessing some form of organization in terms of structure of membership, activities, definition of roles of the participants, and following a set of governance principles and rules* [4].

It is clear that the concept of a CNO imposes certain requirements upon the network. Moreover, collaboration, as it has been defined, remains at the core of the CNO. Camarinha-Matos makes it clear that developing the trust required to successfully establish and operate a CNO is not simple [5]. It takes time and resources. Knowing the capabilities of potential CNO partners can also present its own challenges. Given the costs and time involved in setting up a CNO, only those organizations that foresee long-term cooperation are likely to be willing to invest the capital and have the time necessary to establish one [Fig. 2] [5]. In such a case, the organizations involved would work towards the construction of what we can refer to as a long-term CNO [5].

In the past, European small and medium enterprises [SMEs], missed out on business opportunities that required collaboration with other SMEs because they did not have the resources or were simply not prepared to quickly set up CNOs with other SMEs [5]. In order to correct this situation, European SMEs have jointly developed frameworks that can aid them in the rapid creation of CNOs.

These frameworks can be referred to as long-term strategic networks, or breeding environments, and they emerged as the solution to the problems of SMEs in Europe. Camarinha-Matos and Afsarmanesh define these breeding environments as

> A strategic alliance established with the purpose of being prepared for participation in collaboration opportunities, and where in fact not collaboration but cooperation is practiced among their members. In other words, they are alliances aimed at offering the conditions and environment to support rapid and fluid configuration networks, when opportunities arise [4].

When organizations come together, not in a long-term CNO such as in the case of a supply chain, but in the short-term with the explicit purpose of pursuing a single business opportunity, we refer to them as virtual organizations [Fig. 2] [4]. An example of a virtual organization would be that of an "organization" formed when multiple SMEs joined together to respond to a business opportunity. Breeding environments designed specifically to support the creation of virtual organizations [VO], are called virtual breeding environments [VBEs]. And we can define a VBE as

> An association of organizations and a number of related supporting institutions, adhering to a base long-term cooperation agreement, and adoption of common operating principles and infrastructures, with the main goal of increasing their preparedness towards rapid configuration of temporary alliances for collaboration in potential Virtual Organizations. Namely, when a business opportunity is identified by one member [acting as a broker], a subset of VBE organizations can be selected to form a VO [4].

4 Comparing Notes

With these basic concepts from collaborative network theory, we can return to Colombia's criminal networks. First, let's examine the post Norte Del Valle cartel organizations. As we have previously mentioned, each organization that emerged as a result of the atomization of the cartel now plays a specialized role in a drug production supply chain. The overall structure of these organizations is analogous to a long-term CNO, the kind that a supply chain would embody. Even so, if we examine the differentiation between the concepts of cooperation and collaboration, it quickly becomes evident that the post Norte Del Valle cartel organizations don't fully adhere to our concept of collaboration [Fig. 1]. It is difficult to see how these organizations, each with an armed security apparatus under its disposal and with shifting alliances, would have joint identities and joint responsibility.

On the other hand, they do share compatible goals and work with some level of coordination as cooperation would require. Moreover, we can now establish that the post Norte Del Valle cartel organizations are simply networked. Although they might not fully embody a collaborative network, they certainly seem to demonstrate the attributes of a cooperative network, which would point to more robust integration than simple networking would represent.

The phenomenon of the collection agencies presents a more difficult task. At first glance, the collection agencies would seem to be analogous to a breeding environment in the sense that they establish an environment that facilitates cooperation amongst different criminal elements within Cali. Even so, they do not fully embody to the concept of breeding environments as we have defined it. It is clear that the different criminal factions of Cali did not create the collection agencies in order to facilitate collaboration amongst themselves. Rather, the collection agencies were first established by the cartels to create money-laundering fronts and extort the various criminal activities of Cali [3]. Therefore, the collection agencies have evolved into a hybrid between a traditional hierarchical and a networked organization. The armed wing of the organization, which enforces agreements between the agency and other organizations, is fully under the purview of whoever controls the collection agency at a given point in time [3].

Even so, the vast network of criminals that the collection agency links is not directly under the agency's control. Moreover, the agency also allows for the cooperation between citizens and criminals by acting as a broker when the former requires an illicit service. Thus, breeding environment theory can help us conceptualize the collection agency's role in facilitating cooperation amongst criminal elements and between these elements and the general population. On the other hand, it is difficult to establish that the collection agencies represent an illicit counterpart to breeding environments, as these are utilized by licit SMEs around the world.

5 Conclusions

As we have seen, at the moment Colombia's criminal networks and its various criminal organizations do not fully embody collaborative-networked organizational structures. Yet, if one grants the usefulness of collaborative network theory, there is a broader question that arises. Namely, if illicit enterprises differ from their licit relatives only in their modus operandi, social networks, and technology employed, could they adopt collaborative-networked structures and create breeding environments to capture a broader range of business opportunities, ensure their long-term survival, and successfully evade law enforcement? The possibility seems likely and would resolve the ongoing tension between a desire to monopolize criminal markets, and a tendency towards ever more fragmented and networked criminal organizations. One can foresee a scenario where a VBE would be the criminal monopoly, and the various member criminal organizations would collaborate to take on all the criminal business in a particular city or region. If its knowledge base and operational tools were safeguarded from law enforcement and distributed to new organizations as they joined, a VBE would be longer lasting than any of the particular criminal organizations involved in it. Therefore, it is possible that the next step in the evolution of criminal networks might be closely linked with CNOs and VBEs.

Most importantly, the present analysis demonstrates the usefulness of Camarinha-Matos and Afsarmanesh's business networking ideas to social scientists attempting to understand networked illicit enterprises. To those of us involved in the study of organized crime—but not necessarily fluent in the language of networking—the development of these business networking ideas and their accompanying reference models represent an important knowledge base. By drawing on the new organizational dynamics of SMEs in Europe, we can develop new ways to conceptualize these illicit enterprises and work towards the creation of new typologies of organized crime groups. Thus aiding national and transnational efforts in data collection and organization on illicit networked and other organized crime enterprises.

Acknowledgments. I am enormously grateful to Georgetown University professors John Bailey and Daniel Sabet for their support and encouragement. Lindsay King of the University of Pennsylvania graciously shared her expertise and aided in the editing process. I would also like to thank professor Luis Camarinha-Matos for providing his diagrams for the paper. They proved to be an invaluable tool for illustrating the links between collaborative network theory and organized crime.

References

1. Intelligence Council, Nat.: Global Trends 2025, p. 1. National Intelligence Council, Washington (2008)
2. Passas, N.: The Rise of Transnational Crime. In: Presented paper, International Conference on Responding to the Challenges of Transnational Crime (1998); Leong, A.: The Disruption of Intrnational Organized Crime: An Analysis of Legal and Non-Legal Strategies, p. 15. Ashgate, Burlington (2007)
3. Garzón, J.C.: Mafia & Co.: La Red Criminal en México, Brasil y Colombia, pp. 38–61. Planeta Colombiana, Bogotá (2008)
4. Camarinha-Matos, L., Afsarmanesh, H.: Collaborative Networks Reference Modeling, pp. 54–60. Springer, New York (2008)
5. Camarinha-Matos, L.: CNO Base Concepts: 1st ECOLEAD Summer School on Collaborative Networks, ECOLEAD Learning Environment. Video file, http://videolectures.net/ess06_matos_cbc
6. Camarinha-Matos, L., Afsarmanesh, H.: Collaborative Networks: Value Creation in Knowledge Society. Keynote paper, PROMALAT 2006, IFIP International Conference on Knowledge Enterprise—New Challenges (2006)

Mapping R&D within Multinational Networks: Evidence from the Electronics Industry

Paula Urze[1] and Maria João Manatos[2]

[1] FCT/UNL – Faculdade de Ciências e Tecnologia, Universidade Nova de Lisboa
[2] UNINOVA – Instituto de Desenvolvimento de Novas Tecnologias
pcu@fct.unl.pt, mjm@uninova.pt

Abstract. Based on the final results of the R&D.COM - Local R&D COMpetencies within Global Value Chains project, this paper aims at mapping the trajectories of delocalised R&D units within a multinational's global strategy and designing the knowledge flows within the global value chain. This analysis was performed using typologies proposed in the theoretical framework, which help us to have an overview of the network. The methodology is grounded on one extended case study that involves a local R&D unit (Portugal), a foreign R&D unit (Netherlands) and the headquarters (Norway) - developed on a multinational from the electronics industry. This case is an example of a multinational company where R&D is developed mainly in the headquarters but it is also delocalised to some subsidiaries with a certain level of autonomy.

Keywords: Multinational networks, I&D, Innovation, subsidiaries, knowledge transfer and autonomy.

1 Introduction

It seems undeniable that we face a different social and economic structure from the one which predominated in previous societies and that this new context is profoundly influenced by a dynamic of creation and dissemination of knowledge. In the emergent economy and society, the accumulation of knowledge becomes the main growth and development motivational strength.

The economies based on knowledge are, essentially, economies where the knowledge managing activity, in relation to the innovating process, has become decisive in the competition among economical actors (Murteira, 2004).

In this way, Castells (2005) tell us about an economy that is, simultaneously, informational, global and networked. According to the author, global economy designates an economy with the capacity to work as a unit in real time, in a planetary scale.

Actually, one of the central actors of this globalization process refers to the multinational companies (MNCs) that elaborate their strategy and organize their activity in a planetary scale. Thus, with the internationalization of companies – it can even be stated, today, the transnationalization – part of the functions considered strategic, as, for example, the R&D, have been targets for delocalisation (Sölvell et al, 2002).

Following this theoretical research line, this paper aims at mapping the trajectories of delocalised R&D units within a multinational's global strategy and designing the knowledge flows within the global value chain.

L.M. Camarinha-Matos et al. (Eds.): PRO-VE 2009, IFIP AICT 307, pp. 96–105, 2009.
© IFIP International Federation for Information Processing 2009

2   R&D in Multinational Networks: A New Approach in a New Context

2.1   From Hierarchical to Heterarchical Organizational Forms: The Trend to R&D Delocalization

In the last decades, the activity of multinationals enterprises (MNCs) has grown, not only in extension, but also on variety and intensity. These developments are commonly associated with the economy globalization process, more specifically with the increase of the interdependences outside borders between different markets.

In a growing way, companies tend to invest abroad, in order to explore resources and activities already in place, but more and more trying to create new activities and competencies (Cantwell et al., 2001).

If before, the multinationals were seen mainly in terms of their capacity to explore the advantages generated in the headquarters of the multinational, recently, this point of view has changed, emerging, increasingly, the potential to create knowledge by companies fitted in chains of global value.

This new perspective has been driven by structural changes in global economy, as well as by the tendency to the internationalization of R&D functions in multinational companies that we have been testifying. As a matter of fact, the internationalization of companies has contributed to the delocalization of an important part of strategic functions, as, for example, R&D.

According to this alternative perspective, an important source of competitive advantage to multinationals is the capacity of subsidiaries to generate innovations based in resources of the local environments where they are positioned (Frost, 2000: 21).

As wrote Cantwell and Mudambi (2005), from an historical point of view, multinationals use to locate R&D in subsidiaries in other countries especially with purpose of adapting the products to the countries where they were developed. In this way, the subsidiaries depended on the competencies of other companies and their role was mainly the exploration of those competencies (competence-exploiting). Recently, some subsidiaries acquired a more creative role, generating new technologies, innovation and new competencies. This transformation lead to an increase of the R&D destined to these subsidiaries creators of competencies (competence-creating).

As a matter of fact, the level and type of R&D developed in the subsidiaries, which determine subsidiaries to be creators of competences or, simply, explorers of competences are influenced by several factors (Cantwell and Mudambi, 2005): a) the place where the subsidiary is located and the relations that are established between the subsidiary and the local environment; b) the strategy of subsidiary acquisition by the MNC; c) the autonomy and strategic independence of the subsidiary.

This scenario, where subsidiaries can play an active role as developers of innovative processes is not compatible with the traditional view of MNCs as a clear hierarchical structure but with an horizontal and heterarchical form. In this sense, multinationals appear as flexible horizontal networks, characterized by processes of lateral decisions, where the headquarters are no longer the company brain, but instead, the whole company is faced as a brain (Schmidt et all, 2002: 45). It seems that hierarchy as the dominant organizing principle in MNCs is being supplanted by the emerging principle labelled heterarchy, which is associated with laterally/horizontally oriented MNCs[1].

In new the organizational form, first, the importance of autonomy in the organization as a stimulant to the creation, adoption and diffusion of knowledge and innovations contrasted with the traditional emphasis on efficiency an tight controls; and, second, the structure was radically transformed from hierarchy in which knowledge, resources and expertise are centralized into a network where they might be located anywhere but are able, by various communications systems, to be disseminated to any other subsidiary (Johnston, 2005: 38)[2].

2.2 Subsidiaries and Organizational Contexts: The Diversified Role and Autonomy

This new horizontal understanding of multinationals and of the subsidiaries' behaviour gives a great relevance to the subsidiaries' autonomy issue, which should be seen not only in the unidirectional and hierarchical relations context between headquarters and subsidiaries, but also in the subsidiaries development point of view (Cantwell and Mudambi, 2005 and Cantwell and Iammarino, 2003). Subsidiaries are not only instruments doing tasks imposed by headquarters, but also play an active part in the multinational network (Simões et al., 2002).

In this line of thought, Simões, Biscaya e Nevado (2002) carried out a study where they tried to identify the factors that determine the autonomy of subsidiaries. For the authors, they are, as in the study of Cantwell e Mudambi (2005) at three levels: at level of the subsidiary, at the level of the multinational network and at the level of the local economy.

In this perspective, the literature faces the subsidiaries as organizations with three faces. On one side, they are members of the multinational group, that supply them with resources (financial, knowledge and reputation) and with whom they develop connections and synergies. It is, therefore, a face turned to the group. On other side, the subsidiaries, more than belonging to multinational groups, are located in certain countries and develop relations with the local economy and with the economical agents established there, accessing the knowledge of other companies, recruiting local qualified personnel and cooperating with other local research centers. Thus, it is a second face, turned to the local economy. Finally, the subsidiaries have their own history and develop their own competences (Simões et al., 2002). This is therefore, a third face, turned to the subsidiary itself.

---

[1] Heterarchy is a new trend in multinational organizations, which it doesn't mean, however, that vertical and hierarchical organizations don't play an important role in economies s any more. What we are emphasizing is that the transformations in global economies are creating new strategic and organizational imperatives for companies worldwide, which lead to new organizational forms.

[2] The organizational knowledge management in MNCs and the network as a new pattern of organization are important issues in the new organizational context. The process of effectively creating, disseminating and leveraging a company's knowledge resources is vital to MNCs' competitiveness. At the same time, networks constitute what organizations must become if they want to be competitive in today's business environment (Johnston, 2005; Nohria, 1992).

Considering that subsidiaries are multidimensional organizations, which characteristics are a result of the combination between several factors, it is possible to identify types of subsidiaries. Simões (1992) propose a typology of subsidiaries, through which is possible to establish a relation between MNCs' strategies and subsidiaries' characteristics[3]. By its turn, Johnston (2005) adopts an integrated model of the headquarters-subsidiary relationship, where he develops a typology of subsidiaries tasks. These proposals, despite being very different in terms of theoretical bases, methodologies and goals, have some similarities. They contemplate from subsidiaries typically related with hierarchical organizational forms, which are high centrally controlled and low autonomy subsidiaries ("marketing satellite" or "distributors") to subsidiaries in line with the perspective of MNCs as heterarchical organizations, which enjoy independence and contribute to the development of knowledge and innovative processes and products ("strategic major" or "innovators").

In point of fact, there has been an increased emphasis on innovation and the creation of new products and services in MNCs. New product and innovation strategies have always been important to the MNC but the process of their generation was usually centralized in the headquarters. The new emerging strategy extends the MNC's innovative and entrepreneurial skills via the development of a multidimensional, distributed, integrated, flexible, interdependent, learning organization that generates locally leveraged and globally linked innovations (Bartlett and Ghoshal, 2002).

2.3 The Creation and Diffusion of Innovation and Knowledge: The Rise of a Network-Based Perspective

The development of knowledge and innovation in MNCs and, mainly, the way they are diffused, is central to corporate success.

Therefore, a crucial challenge for multinationals is to avoid that subsidiaries become isolated from other parts of the multinational and assure that competencies from the different units of the multinational are diffused throughout the group (Andersson et al, 2002: 116).

At the same time, the knowledge transfer process is related with the type of organizational form of the MNC and, consequently, with the "status" of the subsidiaries (as competencies explorers or creators). The knowledge flows and the "dynamic" of the transference itself, on an integrated and interdependent MNC are different from the ones developed in a vertical and centralised organization.   According to this, Mudambi (2002) develops a knowledge flows perspective, in which he identifies the flows between a source and a target, which occurs along a channel in a MNC. The author identifies four flows: from the subsidiary to parent, from location to subsidiary, from subsidiary to location and from parent to subsidiary.

In the same way as Mudambi's perspective (2002), the taxonomy of innovation processes proposed by Bartlett and Ghoshal (in Simões, 2008), provides an important instrument to assess the organizational context where the subsidiary develops its activities.

---

[3] The author alerts to the fact that this typology must be used with care, especially when applied to the links between corporate strategies and subsidiaries characteristics. There is not a one-to-one correspondence: a given strategy may lead to the setting-up of different types of subsidiaries, and a single firm may follow different strategies (Simões, 1992: 262).

In this manner, the knowledge management issue is closely related with innovation and, mainly, with the innovative capacity of the MNC, which can be centralized in the headquarters (considering a hierarchical perspective) or can be localized in the subsidiaries (considering a horizontal view), and consequently related with the capacity of diffusing innovations in the network.

They considered four basic types: central, local-for-local, locally leveraged and globally-linked. The first corresponds to the traditional perspective that new opportunities are identified in the MNC home country and lead to centrally developed innovations, which are then exploited internationally. This perspective, based on a hierarchical view, the innovative capacity is centralized. The second type is characterised by the development of innovations by subsidiaries just for local use, not being diffused in the multinational context. The last two types follow a network view. Locally leverage innovation processes enable the dissemination of the innovations developed by the subsidiaries in the multinational network. Finally, globally-linked processes are characterised by putting together the resources and capabilities of diverse worldwide units in the company, at both headquarters and subsidiary level, to create and implement innovations on a joint basis (Bartlett and Ghoshal in Simões, 2008: 10).

Taking into account the new concept of MNC, that we have been pointing out, its straightforward to understand that the two first types of innovation processes described, characterized by a vertical and hierarchical view of MNC and by an inefficient communication and transfer, in this specific case, of ideas and innovations, between the different units of the multinational and between them and the headquarters, doesn't allow that the company takes advantage of its units.

In this way, the hierarchical approach is gradually giving rise to a more network-based perspective of the MNC. This is not to say that hierarchical control no longer exists, it means that control mechanisms are changing and that more open control mechanisms, putting less emphasis on centralisation and promoting subsidiary involvement, are gaining room (Simões, 2008: 10).

3 The Case of a Multinational from the Electronics Industry

3.1 Methodological Steps

Concerning the methodological aspects, we used the case study method. The results presented are based on one extended case (that involves a local R&D unit (Portugal), a foreign R&D unit (Netherlands) and also the headquarters of the global chain (Norway) developed on a multinational from the electronics industry.

In the case studies two techniques were combined to carry out the empirical research: *in-locu* observation of the work processes and semi-directive interviews addressed to actors belonging to different departments and hierarchical levels.

In the extended case study three R&D units have been studied. In the first unit, the headquarters in Trontheim, 11 interviews have been conducted: a) From Top Management: CEO; vice president business development & compliance; vice-president R&D; Human Relations Manager. b) From Operation: System Development Manager, Head of Project Management, Service and Maintenance Manager and Project Engineering Manager. c) From R&D: two group managers. d) From Sales: Sales Regional Director. The second R&D unit, located in Beilen (Netherlands) has been recently acquired by KNetwork. In this company we conducted 6 interviews addressed to the General Manager, the Responsible for the R&D and the Automation and Computation Tooling. We interviewed the Responsible for the Data Entry, the Financial Manager and the Office Manager as well. In Portugal 5 interviews were conducted: General Manager, two Projects Development, the Office Manager and the Responsible for the Maintenance.

3.2 Mapping R&D in the Network: Understanding Trajectories, Patterns and Specificities

KNetwork is a MNC from the electronics industry. It is a global supplier of solutions and products for the Road User Charging and Traffic Surveillance offering solutions and products such as DSRC (tag) and OCR (image processing), with deliveries in Europe, Asia-Pacific, Middle East and North and South America. The company has 270 employees in 12 locations and representatives in 6 other countries.

Despite being present worldwide, it is a small MNC, which, on the one hand, has offices with a considerable number of people, a good degree of maturity and experience and, consequently, a high level of autonomy; but on the other hand, has in the majority of the countries, small offices, mainly dedicated to sales and maintenance.

The core R&D is centralized in the headquarters, and some subsidiaries develop local specifications to the products. However, the level of development done by the subsidiaries is different, so it is their autonomy and independence, which varies with factors like: the longevity and maturity of the subsidiary, the weight of the local market, the importance of local costumers or local relations, the local products and business, the local activities (from development to sales), the distance to the headquarters.

KNorway defines clear centralized management strategies, and doesn't want to lose control of its subsidiaries. In the words of the CEO: "I want that subsidiaries can have some autonomy and can decide for themselves but everyone has to follow the same strategy, and of course I never want to lose control."

There is also a strategy of new companies' acquisition with new competencies needed by KNorway. The strategy of KNorway is to be leader in its business area, and in order to achieve that, it had to acquire competencies and tools, which they didn't have, like the case of the video system, in which "KNetherlands was simply the best company." In this sense, KNetherlands became a completely different subsidiary, acting like an extension of the headquarters, and being the most important R&D unit after KNorway. According to the CEO of KNetherlands the great achievement for his company was "to take advantage from the big sales experience and also from the financial maturity from a very mature company." As a matter of fact, KNetherlands continues his R&D activity independently and have a very autonomous management, although both companies are following a path where practices are being standardized, and where KNetherlands is slowly becoming a special company with his individuality but part of a multinational network.

Therefore, KNetherlands is what we can call, according to Cantwell et all (2005), the competence creating subsidiary with the higher level of innovation creation. Other subsidiaries, like Australia, Portugal, Brazil and Malaysia are also competence-creating subsidiaries, mainly developing some local specifications, but in a lower level than Netherlands. The other subsidiaries don't have competence creating expertise because they are mainly sales officers, being classified as competence explorers.

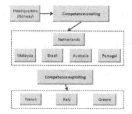

Fig. 1. Cantwell et al (2005) orientation of subsidiaries

As a matter of fact, the subsidiaries of the network have different tasks, levels of maturity, degrees of autonomy, capacities of innovation, and all these differences allow us to integrate them into typologies, which help us to have an overview of the network. We will consider the Simões (1992) subsidiaries typology and Johnston (2007) integrated model of headquarters-subsidiaries relationship.

KNetherlands is a type of subsidiary that enjoys a strategic independence, contributes with innovative processes and products and plays an important role within the network as well. That's why we can call it a strategic major and innovator subsidiary.

KPortugal, KAustralia, KBrasil and KMalaysia have been classified as product specialists, in the way that, despite not developing the entire product, they introduce specifications and particular configurations in it, originating some kind of product specialization. Nevertheless, if the first two subsidiaries can be called "contributors", the last ones will be designated as "adapters".

Portugal had since the beginning of its foundation a strategic importance for the company, due to the strong and special local costumer, to which Portugal developed specifications and develop the maintenance of the systems. But later this costumer "wanted to control of the systems, just buying components and integrate them in the systems". Even after the decreasing of this activity, Portugal continues to perform developments for this costumer, whereas they establish relations with other local costumers and started to collaborate in projects with KNorway. "Portuguese people are now participating in projects in Norway that having nothing to do with Portugal" (CEO). In this way, KPortugal always was, in different ways and stages, mainly on the first stage, a product specialist based on the local relations and, especially on the second stage, a contributor to the value chain, due to the projects developed with the headquarters and other subsidiaries. Remind us the manager of Kportugal that Portugal is not only a contributor to the network, but it is also "one of the subsidiaries that can influence the most the strategic decisions of the headquarters due to the important projects that are being developed there."

KAustralia was a very autonomous and strategic independent organization, very focused on the local market and on the relations with local costumers, being responsible for the development of local specifications. However, nowadays efforts have been made in order to integrate Australia in the multinational network, to establish a bi-directional relation between the headquarters and Australia, and to make Australia contribute to the headquarters and the other subsidiaries, being for this reason also a contributor to the network.

Brazil and Malaysia are what Johnston (2007) called "adapters", in the sense that they are subsidiaries that generated products adapted to the unique demands of the local market. Actually, Brazil is fundamentally a sales office with some development skills, making some local specifications, but this specifications don't have special contributes to other places of the network, maybe just in a small portion to some other South American countries.

In Malaysia the development that is made is locally based, because it is a special product just for Asian countries. "In Malaysia we have a center of excellence where we develop a manual toll system that only work in Asia" (vice president business development and compliance). Therefore, this local product is adapted to a local market, which can involve other local countries like Bangkok and Taiwan.

The other subsidiaries, like French, Italy and Greece, are classified as "marketing satellite", which the main objective is to sell products developed centrally, and consequently they act like sales and distribution units ("distributors").

Fig. 2. Simões (1992) subsidiaries typology and Johnston (2007) integrated model of headquarters-subsidiaries relationship

In summary, the main R&D is centralized in the headquarters and then diffused to the subsidiaries. In this sense, the major knowledge flow come from Norway and goes to the other subsidiaries. Despite this knowledge pattern being the predominant, we also observe that some subsidiaries, mainly KNetherlands, have a strong position in terms of creating and diffusing knowledge for the headquarters and for the other subsidiaries, being an example of a locally leveraged innovation process. There is a second particular case of a subsidiary (Portugal) that initially developed innovations based on local relations with a strong local costumer, and nowadays the creation and diffusion of innovation is done in a more global scale, resulting from the decrease of the local relations. However, the MNC seems to be developing a strategy where globally linked innovation processes are putting together the resources and capabilities of diverse worldwide units in the company, at both headquarters and subsidiary level, to create and implement innovations on a joint basis strategy.

The knowledge transfer is made, whenever is possible, through the presence of researchers or other workers in the place where the knowledge is and can be learnt. Usually, workers from other subsidiaries go to KNorway to learn some competencies, although workers from the headquarters could also go to other countries to teach locally, even though they can also learn some local knowledge. "What we usually do is to bring people here to work with us and to learn and then the come back with the knowledge, but it is important for us they come here because they have important local knowledge" (vice-president R&D).

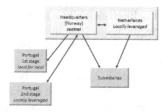

Fig. 3. Mudambi (2002) knowledge flows perspective and Bartlett and Ghoshal (2008) processes of innovation typology

In terms of organizational mechanisms, there is an intranet, an internal network with internal information of the MNC accessible to all the subsidiaries; a competencies system, useful to find out people from the group with certain competencies, which are needed for a specific project or work, which could lead to a cross use of resources. Nevertheless, the most common way to share and diffuse knowledge is the informal way. Notwithstanding, it is something that is being improved: "that is something we are working on (...) we want to have more interaction and communication with people all over the world" (vice-president R&D).

4   Conclusion

Summing-up, the study points to a multinational with a new vision on the business and on the network as well, justified by a recent new CEO. This new vision is based on the assumption that the network needs to be stronger; it means to reinforce the relationship among the subsidiaries but also with the headquarters. Another important point is related to the fact that the multinational wants to incorporated new competencies into the network, buying companies with specific knowledge. In fact, they used to subcontract these competencies but now their preference is not to be dependent, broadening what they could offer to the market. As far as R&D strategy is concerned, one can say that it is essentially centralised into the headquarters and now, also into one of the companies that has been recently acquired. In fact, they work as an extension of Norway, thus they have specific competencies central to the business strategy followed by the new President (CEO). The network is present in many countries but with different positions according to the level of the business and the costumers specificities. As analysed, they are trying to enter into new markets some of them considered quite difficult because of their specificities, such as EUA, or South African. One can say that some of the old markets are not so strong as they were in the past; on the other hand, they are trying to extend the variety of products in order to enter into the new markets with wider possibilities to the costumers. Finally, the headquarters' strategy is based on building a broader network of business relationships with stronger subsidiaries, thus it will be easier for them to assert their own identity.

Finally, it would be interesting to extend the number of case studies so that we can have a comparative perspective in terms of subsidiaries with similar characteristics, but situated in different latitudes around the world.

Acknowledgments

This work has been supported by the R&D.COM – *Local R&D Competencies in Global Value Chains* – project (POCI/SOC/60092/2004). A project funded by Foundation for Science and Technology, Ministry of Science, Technology and Higher Education.

References

1. Andersson, U., et al.: Subsidiary Absorptive Capacity, MNC Headquarters' Control Strategies and Transfer of Subsidiaries Competencies. In: Lundan, S. (ed.) Network Knowledge International Business, Cheltenham. Edward Elgar Publishing (2002)
2. Cantwell, J., Narula, R.: The Eclectic Paradigm in the Global Economy. International Journal of the Economic Business 8(2) (2001)
3. Cantwell, J., Iammarino, S.: Multinational Corporations and European Regional Systems of Innovation. Routledge, London (2003)
4. Cantwell, J., Mudambi, R.: MNE Competence-Creating Subsidiary Mandates. Strategic Management Journal 26 (2005)
5. Castells, M.: A era da informação: economia, sociedade e cultura, vol I. A sociedade em rede, Lisboa, Fundação Calouste Gulbenkian (2005)
6. Frost, T.: The Geographic Sources of Foreign Subsidiaries' Innovation. Strategic Management Journal 22 (2000)
7. Johnston, S.: Headquarters and Subsidiaries in Multinational Corporations: strategies, tasks and coordination. Palgrave MacMillan, New York (2005)
8. Murteira, M.: Economia do conhecimento, Lisboa, Quimera Editores (2004)
9. Schmidt, S., et al.: The MNC as a Network: a closer look at intra-organizational flows. In: Lundan, S. (ed.) Network Knowledge International Business, Cheltenham. Edward Elgar Publishing (2002)
10. Simões, V.C.: European Integration and the Pattern of FDI Inflow in Portugal in John Cantwell, Multinational Investment in Modern Europe – Strategic Interaction in the Integrated Community, Great Britain. Edward Elgar (1992)
11. Simões, V.C., et al.: Subsidiary Decision-Making Autonomy: Competences, Integration and Local Responsiveness. In: Lundan, S. (ed.) Network Knowledge International Business, Cheltenham. Edward Elgar Publishing (2002)
12. Simões, V.C.: Innovation initiatives by MNE subsidiaries: an integrated research framework. Paper presented in IV International Iberian Conference of Management – Burgos (2008)
13. Urze, P., Manatos, M.J.: Local R&D Competencies in Global Networks. Paper presented in I Fórum de Sociologia ISA, Barcelona (2008)

Part 4

Collaboration in Supply Chains

Developing a Taxonomy and Model to Transfer and Assess Best Practices for Supply Chain Management

Myrna Flores[1], Ana Mendoza[2], Victor Lavin[2], and Benito Flores[2]

[1] Research and Networking, Processes and IT,
CEMEX Global Center for Technology and Innovation,
CEMEX Research Group AG, Römerstrasse 13 CH-2555 Brügg, Switzerland
[2] Departamento de Ingeniería Industrial,
Universidad de Monterrey (UDEM), Mexico
myrnafatima.flores@cemex.com, toryana@hotmail.com,
victor.lavin@gmail.com, bflores@udem.edu.mx

Abstract. Supply Chain Management can be briefly defined as the orchestration of a network of entities such as suppliers, distributors and clients to achieve a common goal: delivering cost efficient products and services exceeding customers' expectations. Therefore, firms should consider all those End-to-End processes enabling an efficient integration and interoperability of partners collaborating in such Supply Chain when designing their Business Process Architecture (BPA). One key enabler to accomplish this goal is the identification, documentation and sharing of best practices. This paper describes the outcomes of a collaborative project carried out by CEMEX Research Group and the Universidad de Monterrey (UDEM), which focused on developing taxonomy to document best practices for the supply chain management together with a generic model to evaluate their level of implementation.

Keywords: Best Practices, Supply Chain Management, SCOR, Taxonomy.

1 Introduction

Today, competition plays one of the most important roles within the industrial sector as companies are struggling every day to position themselves in existing and new markets, providing their customers new or improved products or services with the best possible quality, lower costs and in a global way. In order to offer such products and services, reducing costs and improving delivery times, firms are forced to go beyond their boundaries; integrating customers and suppliers in their End-to-End (E2E) processes structure [1]. According to Hammer and Stanton [2], executives do not see anymore their organizations as sets of discrete units with well-defined boundaries. Instead, they see them as flexible groups of intertwined work and information flows that cut horizontally across business, ending at points of contact with suppliers and customers.

In order words, firms need to go beyond their own company and orchestrate the complete supply chain in a more effective way. This is where a Business Process Architecture (BPA) is needed to map, analyze, improve and monitor End-to-End

L.M. Camarinha-Matos et al. (Eds.): PRO-VE 2009, IFIP AICT 307, pp. 109–116, 2009.
© IFIP International Federation for Information Processing 2009

business processes to determine what improvements could be carried out and define new initiatives considering both suppliers and customers. The procedure is to identify opportunity areas, analyze their economic impact and then define and carry out improvement projects to increase profits for total customer satisfaction.

One critical enabler for the development and improvement of such E2E business processes are best practices. These latter can be defined as a proved method, procedure or activity that has provided the best possible outcomes or improvement when being applied to a specific process. For instance, two successful and very well known examples of best practices implementation are: a) the Toyota Way, which has been proved to be a best practice for lean production reducing waste, costs and increasing adding value activities [3] and b) Six Sigma which has proved not to be only a structured statistical methodology to improve and design of processes and products, but also a standard way to communicate and manage projects internally; bringing economic returns to companies such as Motorola and General Electric [4].

As a consequence, there is an increasing interest from both large and small organizations to develop, implement and continuously upgrade industrial best practices [5]. In fact, Arthur Anderson has created a "Global Best Practices" division, which performs "best practice" audits for companies to identify areas for improvement [6].

Thus, in order to identify, document and transfer such best practices, a five step methodology can be considered: 1) research for those proved industrial best practices, 2) select the ones that are best aligned to the firm strategy, 3) assess their potential business impact, 4) transfer them internally in a successful way and 5) measure their returns after implemented. In such a context, there is a need to identify, document, share, adapt, reuse and implement best practices in a systematic manner. Therefore, a collaborative research project between CEMEX Research Group (CRG) and the Universidad de Monterrey (UDEM) was defined to identify best practices that have proved to increase the supply chain performance and document them in a standard way to diffuse and implement them internally in CEMEX.

2   Research Methodology

The defined CEMEX – UDEM collaborative research project objectives were:

- Search, identify and select supply chain best practices, applying a process perspective. In this case the SCOR standard reference model was applied.
- Design a taxonomy to document the selected best practices.
- Document the selected best practices to share them in a global repository under construction (SMARTBRICKS) by the international DiFac project.
- Develop an evaluation model to map the implementation and improvement of supply chain best practices and define new initiatives.

The LEAD methodology, developed in CEMEX Research Group [7], which proposes four stages for collaborative research with external partners (Learn, Energize, Apply and Diffuse) was applied to manage this collaborative research project with UDEM as follows:

1) LEARN

- The research project objectives and research questions were defined. CEMEX and UDEM agreed on the objectives and expected deliverables and deadlines.
- An extensive literature review on supply chain and best practices was carried out. CEMEX suggested using the well known SCOR generic model to map best practices under a process perspective.

2) ENERGIZE

- An initial list of more than 100 supply chain best practices was identified under the three key processes of the SCOR model: Source, Make and Deliver and for Make to Stock (MTS) and Make to Order (MTO) manufacturing typologies.
- A survey questionnaire was designed to gather information from experiences from several companies in Monterrey to map recognized best practices in the supply chain.
- Face-to-face interviews were carried out to companies in Monterrey by UDEM's team

3) APPLY

- The interviews' and survey data was analyzed to identify the best practices which proved business results in the interviewed companies. Twenty best practices were selected and documented for the development of a best practices digital library in CEMEX
- A taxonomy to document and share supply chain best practices was designed.
- A model for best practices assessment was developed

4) DIFFUSE

- During this last phase, diffusion of results are carried out within CEMEX, in scientific journals and international conferences.

The deliverables of this collaborative research project are: 1) the design of a taxonomy to document best practices in the supply chain, 2) to create an evaluation model to assess the level of implementation of best practices in CEMEX and 3) the documentation of the selected best practices for the supply chain as the foundation to create an open repository or digital library where employees could have global access to learn about such best practices.

3 Identifying and Documenting Supply Chain Management (SCM) Best Practices: Towards A Standard Taxonomy

Supply Chain Management is the total manage of a network of facilities and distribution options in a partnership between a consumer, distributor and manufacturer with the purpose of transfer and exchange information and physical goods for the supplier's suppliers to their customer's customers ensuring the right goods in the most efficient manner, reached accurately wherever they are required in a company and beyond [8].

An excelling supply chain performance is essential to meet customers' requirements, therefore, it is important to provide CEMEX employees a tool to enable them to learn, use, implement and continuously update in a global, dynamic and collaborative way, supply chain practices. This latter can be possible by developing a digital library to diffuse and reuse documented best practices, facilitating workers to evolve into "knowledge workers" to learn and implement supply chain best practices in their daily activities.

3.1 Applying the SCOR Framework

The Supply Chain Operational Reference Model (SCOR) is defined as a process model combining elements of business process engineering, benchmarking, and best practice into a single framework [9]. It was designed to encompass the supply chain from the supplier's supplier to the customer's customer. It integrates business processes definitions, performance indicators and best practices. Under the SCOR model, best practices are defined as successful standard operating procedures for a given process. Business analysts observe and evaluate various companies and gather information on what works best. SCOR is based on three process types: Planning, Execution and Enable. The execution process is then divided into Source, Make, Deliver and Return [10]. One additional fact is that the Source, Make, Deliver processes have been documented by manufacturing typologies, in other words: Make to Stock (MTS), Make to Order (MTO) and Engineering to Order (ETO).

3.2 Identifying, Selecting and Documenting Supply Chain Best Practices

Fifteen filled-in surveys were obtained with the aim of confirming the theoretical study conducted to understand the relevance of best practices within the supply chain. The survey consisted of two main parts:

1) Discussion and analysis of best practices in the supply chain: This part of the survey aimed to obtain from supply chain experts, from different firms, the importance of best practices listed. Respondents were asked to carefully analyze, select and rank 20 best practices, from a list of 100 identified best practices in supply chain, that according to their work experience and knowledge can be considered as the most strategic to optimize the supply chain and which have provided economic returns in their company. Table 1 shows the twenty selected best practices by the experts.

2) Assessment of best practices within the processes of the SCOR model: In this second step, each expert was requested to assign a value to assess the impact of each of supply chain practice. Values were 7 (high), 5 (medium), 3 (low), 0 (none). The eight companies that responded to the survey in this research project were both local manufacturing and consulting firms in Monterrey (Mexico) with vast experience in supply chain management such as: TERNIUM, AHMSA, CEMEX, TRINITYRAIL, TEKSID, RIMSA, OPTIMA SERVICE and CONSULTORES ASOCIADOS INTEGRA.

3) Selection and documentation of the twenty best practices: Twenty top best practices were identified to optimize the supply chain performance based on the findings of the research (step 2). All these best practices were documented in detail.

Table 1. Twenty Best Practices identified in the Study

Number	BEST PRACTICES
1	Just in Time (JIT)
2	Benchmarking
3	KANBAN
4	Lean Production
5	Material Requirements Planning (MRP)
6	Total Quality Management (TQM)
7	Electronic Data Interchange (EDI)
8	Forecasting
9	ABC Classification
10	Enterprise Resource Planning (ERP)
11	International Organization for Standardization (ISO)
12	Outsourcing
13	Warehouse Management Systems (WMS)
14	Total Productive Maintenance (TPM)
15	Real time inventory control
16	Route optimization
17	Distribution Resource Planning (DRP)
18	Inventory, cycle counting
19	Manufacturing Resource Planning (MRP II)
20	Supplier qualification systems

3.3 Supply Chain Best Practice Taxonomy Design

To develop the taxonomy to define and document supply chain practices in a standard way, the following elements were taken into consideration:

- **Definition of best practice:** Description of the meaning of the practice and why the relevance of it within the supply chain.
- **Background of the best practice:** How and why the best practice emerged, who created it and for what purpose.
- **Components of best practice and their definitions:** The key factors of best practice, those elements that help the practice to achieve their objectives and have an optimal performance for the supply chain.
- **Implementation Methodology:** It describes the method of implementation of the best practice.
- **Benefits of implementing the best practice:** Advantages of its deployment, control and the proper handling of the best practice for the chain.
- **Limitations:** Restrictions and conditions for the implementation and scope of the practice.

Figure 1 presents and example of how the proposed taxonomy was applied to document one of the identified best practices: lean production.

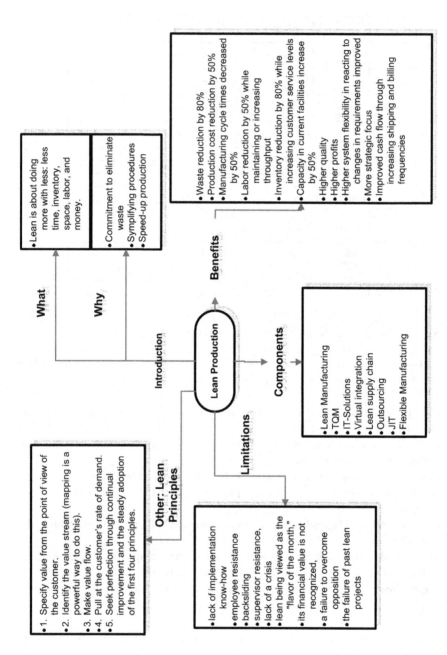

Fig. 1. Example of a documented Best Practice using the proposed Taxonomy

4 Best Practices Assessment and Evolution Model

To evaluate the level of best practices implementation, a Supply Chain's Best Practices Evaluation Model was developed as a tool to identify opportunity areas for improving the performance of the supply chain aligning them to the business strategy. The model consists of three stages:

1) **Assessment of the "AS IS" implementation level of best practices:** During this first step, the model focuses to assess the level of implementation of the different identified best practices. This assessment consists of six levels ranging from total ignorance of the practice, to a level of maturity of the practice within the process, i.e. a maximum level at which the practice has already given results and could be transferred to other entities. The six implementation levels are:

> LEVEL 1   WE DON'T KNOW THE PRACTICE
> LEVEL 2   WE KNOW THE DEFINITION AND THE OBJECTIVES OF THE PRACTICE
> LEVEL 3   WE KNOW HOW TO IMPLEMENT THE PRACTICE WITH A METHODOLOGY
> LEVEL 4   THE PRACTICE IS IN THE PROCESS OF IMPLEMENTATION
> LEVEL 5   WE HAVE IMPLEMENTED THE PRACTICE AND HAS PRODUCED RESULTS
> LEVEL 6   THE PRACTICE IS IMPLEMENTED WITH RESULTS AND HAS BEEN IMPROVED

2) **Identification of the level of relevance of best practices "TO-BE" within the supply chain:** At this stage of the model, the selected best practices are assessed from 1 to 4 level of strategic relevance in the supply chain being 1 the least important and 4 the most relevant.

3) **Developing an Implementation / Results Matrix to define key improvement initiatives:** During this third and last step, the results of the previous two stages were mapped within a chart in order to relate the level of implementation (x axis) with the strategic relevance of the practice (y axis). In order to support decision-making, the chart is divided into four quadrants (Figure 2):

• **Improve:** The practices located in this quadrant show that the level of implementation is still low and its relevance is high, therefore an opportunity area is detected to improve and speed up the implementation of such practice.

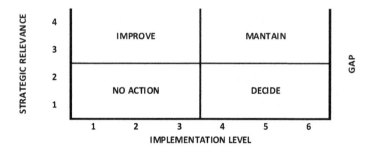

Fig. 2. Best Practices Assessment and Evolution Model

- **Maintain:** This quadrant contains those best practices that have been successfully implemented and that are still relevant, so they should be maintained.
- **Decide:** The practices classified in the third quadrant are of a high level of implementation and low relevance, so the organization should decide to act or not on improving the performance of such practice. In fact, this last quadrant shows those practices which have been implemented but represent a cost as they are not anymore relevant or strategic for the business.
- **No Action:** This last quadrant reflects that the assessed practice has a low implementation and is not relevant according to the strategy; therefore the model suggests not taking any action.

5 Conclusion

Companies need to evolve into fully integrated supply chains, based on the implementation of End-to-End processes. This project concluded successfully proposing a standard taxonomy to document supply chain best practices and a model to assess their implementation and evolution according to the business strategy. The documentation of such best practices will enable knowledge workers in CEMEX to learn and improve their competences managing in a better way supply chain processes integrating suppliers and customers.

References

1. Flores, M.: End-to-End Process Management, Towards a Process Centric Organization. In: Internal CEMEX Whitepaper (2008)
2. Hammer, M., Stanton, S.: How Enterprises Really Work. Harvard Business Review (1999)
3. Liker, J.K.: The Toyota Way, 14 Management Principles. Tata McGraw-Hill Publishing Company Limited (2004)
4. Pyzdek, T.: The Six Sigma Handbook, A Complete Guide for Greenbelts, Blackbelts, and Managers at All Levels. McGraw-Hill Professional Management (2003)
5. Bogan, C., English, M.: Benchmarking for Best Practices: Winning through innovative adaptation. McGraw-Hill, New York (1994)
6. Hiebeler, R., Kelly, T., Ketteman, C.: Best Practices: Building Your Business with Arthur Andersens' Global Best Practices. Simon & Schuster, New York (1998)
7. Flores, M.: The LEAD Research Methodology to manage collaborative open innovation projects, CEMEX internal document (2008)
8. Towill, D., Naim, M.: System Dynamics and Lean Supply Chains. In: 26th International Symposium on Automotive Technology and Automation, Aachen, Germany (1993)
9. Supply Chain Council, Supply Chain Operations Reference-model framework (1996), http://www.supply-chain.org/
10. Bolstorff, P., Rosenbaum, R.: Supply Chain Excellence: A Handbook for Dramatic Improvement using the SCOR Model. American Management Association, New York (2003)

Supply Chain Coordination in Hospitals

Nazaré Rego[1] and Jorge Pinho de Sousa[2]

[1] Department of Management, Escola de Economia e Gestão, Campus de Gualtar,
University of Minho, 4710-057 Braga, Portugal
nazare@eeg.uminho.pt
[2] INESC Porto / Faculty of Engineering, University of Porto, Campus da FEUP,
Rua Dr. Roberto Frias, 4200-465 Porto, Portugal
jsousa@inescporto.pt

Abstract. This paper presents an innovative approach to support the definition of strategies for the design of alternative configurations of hospital supply chains. This approach was developed around a hybrid Tabu Search / Variable Neighbourhood Search metaheuristic, that uses several neighbourhood structures. The flexibility of the procedure allows its application to supply chains with different topologies and atypical cost characteristics. A preliminary computational experience shows the approach potential in solving large scale supply chain configuration problems. The future incorporation of this approach in a broader Decision Support System (DSS) will provide a tool that can significantly contribute to an increase of healthcare supply chains efficiency and encourage the establishment of collaborative partnerships between their members.

Keywords: Supply chain configuration, health care, hospitals, metaheuristics, Tabu Search, VNS.

1 Introduction

In the last decades, we have seen a significant and persistent increase in the effort represented by healthcare expenditures in many countries' economies. Probably as a consequence of this trend, many researchers (e.g., [1]) and consultants (e.g., [2]) have been claiming that Supply Chain Management (SCM) principles should be applied to the healthcare industry, as a way to simultaneously achieve a considerable cost reduction and an improved service quality (for example, through increased service and materials availability and medical errors reduction). There were also many attempts to enhance the healthcare supply chain through cooperation among their members.

De Vries et al. [3] consider that a hospital can be seen as a *durable* (according to the classification proposed by [4]) virtual organization (VO), because: a) although the patients/clients have the perception that the service is provided by a single organization, there are many organizations (i.e., services/wards/specialties) that operate with a high level of autonomy; b) there is some degree of separation between the strategic decision level (where policies and investments are defined in a centralized way) and the operational decision level (where there is almost complete freedom on how to organize operations); c) it is easy to add a new specialty to the hospital or to close an

L.M. Camarinha-Matos et al. (Eds.): PRO-VE 2009, IFIP AICT 307, pp. 117–127, 2009.

existing one; d) there is (or it could/should exist) information sharing in the operational chain and between the operational and the strategic levels. This perspective is in accordance with the VO definition proposed by Norman et al. [5]: "VOs are composed of a number of semi-independent autonomous entities (representing different individuals, departments and organizations) each of which has a range of problem solving capabilities and resources at their disposal, ... that co-exist and sometimes compete with one another..."

In a similar way, the whole (internal and external) hospital supply network, including producers, distributors, and some neighbour hospitals, can also be viewed as a VO, whose nature will be more temporary than if only the internal chain is considered.

The work presented in this paper intends to contribute to the improvement of the logistic organization of healthcare services, through the development of an approach to support the formulation and implementation of their supply chain configuration strategies, with positive impacts on costs, on service quality and on the time and the place available to perform healthcare provision (to be gained by enhanced logistic activities). This approach was developed around a hybrid Tabu Search / Variable Neighbourhood Search metaheuristic that uses several neighbourhood structures.

The remainder of the paper is organized as follows. In Section 2 we emphasize the complexity of the healthcare supply chain and describe the most common cooperation experiences between its members, in Section 3 the developed approach is described, in Section 4 an illustrative example is presented, and finally in Section 5 we present some conclusions.

2 The Healthcare Supply Chain

2.1 Complexity

The healthcare supply chain is particularly complex when compared with those of other industries. The main reasons for this complexity are:

- it provides a great variety of services and products;
- it fulfils the needs of multiple and different internal and external clients - the patients [6], the hospitals and primary care centres, which are the final institutional clients [7], the persons in charge of material orders and supplier choice (these may be physicians, pharmacists, managers, etc.) [7], the professionals that treat the patients [6], and the payers of the healthcare service (in the case of a public provider, the State i.e., the tax payers) [6];
- it is highly dependent on the role physicians play in its management, as they perform the diagnosis and decide treatment paths, evaluate the demand of goods/services required by each patient, influence the length of time that each patient spends in the hospital (and this impacts the consumption of materials/services), and develop long run relationships with suppliers and preferences on specific materials and products, reflecting for example their education in specific medical schools [6];
- it involves very large costs, particularly concerning medical-surgical supplies and pharmaceuticals;

- it must assure a high service level, as the occurrence of stock-outs can damage the healthcare system image or, in extreme situations, threaten the patients' life;
- it is highly conditioned by existing legislation (e.g. reimbursement systems);
- it is managed through a complex line of command based on a sensitive balance of power relationships among diverse highly trained professional groups (managers, physicians, nurses, pharmacists, etc.) that work at autonomous units [3];
- besides the management of the flows and inventories of materials, it involves issues related to the availability of the appropriate facilities, equipments and human resources at the right time and place, and to the flows of people (personnel, patients and visitors) at the services and when providing domiciliary care.

Burns [7] emphasizes that hospitals and their (internal and external) supply networks are responsible for much of this complexity.

2.2 Cooperation in the Healthcare Supply Chain

The development of ICT has supported the creation of diversified cooperation experiences in the healthcare supply chain:

- group purchasing organizations – GPO (see [8-10]);
- resource sharing/pooling among neighbour healthcare providers (e.g., [11, 12]);
- outsourcing of product delivery in small quantities (enough to satisfy the consumption needs of a couple of days) directly to the wards and bypassing hospital store rooms, the so-called stockless system - see a description of the system in DeScioli [13]; Rivard-Royer et al. [14] analyze the implementation of a hybrid stockless system in the urology unit of one hospital; Nicholson et al. [15] compare analytically the stockless system with a traditional 3-echelon distribution scheme;
- Vendor Managed Inventory (VMI) systems - see a description of VMI in DeScioli [13]; Tsui et al. [16] evaluate the implementation of a VMI system on the pharmacy services of an Australian teaching hospital; Danese [17] studies a VMI implementation in the downstream and upstream supply network coordinated by GlaxoSmithKline to co-ordinate material and information flows among different suppliers, manufacturing and distribution plants;
- e-commerce and/or e-communication (namely, in the area of telemedicine) platforms - More and McGrath [18] evaluate the Australian healthcare industry e-communication project; Breen and Crawford [19] analyze the role of e-commerce in the acquisition of pharmaceutical products; Zheng et al. [20] analyze the links between e-adoption and the supply chain strategy; Korner et al. [21] present a successful case of a strategic partnership between 169 health academic institutions in the USA, whose collaboration involves internet-based knowledge, information and reporting tools management and sharing;

- many vertical and/or horizontal <u>concentration experiences</u> (see [22]), that were not directly motivated by logistical reasons but that necessarily impact supply chain management;
- integration initiatives at the care service level, often known as <u>integrated care</u>, concerning all patients or, more frequently, groups of patients with specific needs (e.g. elderly people or patients with chronic diseases like diabetes or AIDS) that require a set of differentiated care (consultations, domiciliary care, inpatient treatments, counseling, physiotherapy, etc.), provided by different entities, that were motivated by patient characteristics but that influence supply chain management - Kodner e Spreeuwenberg [23] clarify that the expression *integrated care* is used in relation to a group of distinct situations, and discuss the practical applications and the consequences of this type of integration.

Although the USA have been considered as pioneers in the implementation of most of these cooperation experiences, a survey performed by Aptel e Pourjalali [24] suggests that supply chain managers at Californian hospitals feel that the existent cooperation is still insufficient and that there is a need to reinforce partnerships with suppliers and other care providers.

Some obstacles to the total success of many of these cooperation experiences are related to communication, leadership or conflicting interests conciliation difficulties (see e.g., [18, 25]), or with suspicions about the fair distribution of costs and benefits of the collaboration processes (see e.g., [11]).

As the financial impact of the reversion of an unsuccessful cooperation process may outcome the initial costs of that process implementation [25], and the knowledge about the supply chain and about the consequences of the actions undertaken upon it may improve the willingness to think and discuss alternative actions to develop cooperation among supply chain members (see e.g., [26]), it is important to prepare potential cooperation processes by analyzing and negotiating possible forms of collaboration and their consequences to the group and to also to individual participants.

3   Developed Approach

3.1   The Model

Our model was inspired by the Ahuja et al. [27] formulation of the multi-stage, multi-level, multi-product production-distribution system planning problem, which is based on a representation of the problem through Graph Theory. The multi-period dimension of the problem is incorporated in the model through the replication of the supply chain with "inventory edges" connecting storage areas in subsequent periods. Figure 1 illustrates the application of this modeling logic to the planning of a very simple supply chain (two producers P_1 and P_2, one intermediary I_1, and two hospitals H_1 and H_2, with two points of care units U_{ij} each) during 3 periods.

The model structure, in terms of constraints and costs considered, incorporates the information collected through several interviews with managers responsible for the hospital supply departments. Therefore, the model considers fixed administrative costs for establishing commercial relationships between a supplier and a customer

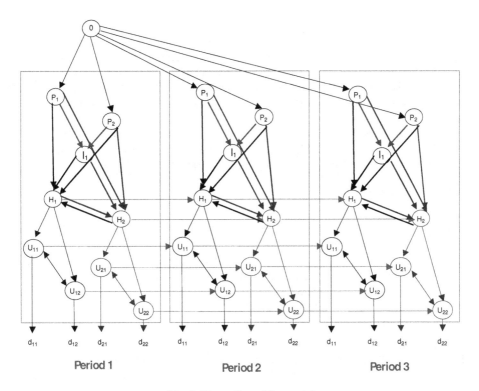

Fig. 1. Illustration of the model

Table 1. "Verbal" formulation of the model

Decision variables		
Quantities leaving entity i at period p, and arriving at entity j at period t (at supply edges: j ≠ i, t = p; at inventory edges: j = i, t = p + 1)		
Objective function		
Minimize	Total cost	= Acquisition cost + + Transportation cost + + Administrative cost + + Inventory carrying cost
Constraints		
Demand satisfaction (no stock-outs allowed) Flow conservation at the nodes (Supply-Chain members) Storage capacity (at hospital Distribution Center (DC) and point of care units) aggregating all items Producers supply capacity affecting all potential buyers Non-negativity and integrality of decision variables		

(e.g., costs of negotiation and contracts), fixed transportation costs, variable transportation costs, acquisition costs, including intermediary margins; and inventory carrying costs.

Due to the nature of the acquisition costs and inventory carrying costs considered, the model formulation cannot be based on the structure that is frequently found in the literature (some examples can be found in [28]), that associates the decision variables to the quantities that flow through the network edges. Therefore, as any item flowing through a specific edge, can have different costs, depending on the supply path followed to get to that point, we developed a formulation that associates the quantities supplied to the supply paths that have been used. Difficulties with supply capacity can occur episodically while the warehouse storage constraints are assumed to be constant along the whole planning horizon.

Table 1 presents the "verbal" formulation for the problem, assuming that all relevant data (costs, capacities, and other parameters) have been collected using appropriate estimation / forecasting methods and company-specific business analysis.

3.2 Solving the Model

General algorithmic strategy
The approach developed to solve the model consists in a hybrid algorithm based on Tabu Search (TS), a very well-known and broadly used metaheuristic that was first presented by Glover [29, 30], and VNS (Variable Neighborhood Search), developed by Hansen and Mladenovic [31]. This algorithm combines the search scheme of a Tabu Search, by incorporating a tabu list that forbids repetition of recent moves, with the diversification of VNS, by changing the neighborhood structure when the search seams unable to improve the current solution.

Initial solution
Feasibility was considered an important requirement of the initial solution, since the restrictive characteristics of the problem may complicate the attainment of a feasible solution during the search.

The adopted initial solution construction algorithm for the initial solution consists in a randomly generation procedure.

Objective function
The objective function implemented has two components: the original objective function of the problem (see Section 2.1) plus a function that penalizes unfeasibility. This includes a parameter that adjusts the penalization to the scale of the costs considered, and a dynamic parameter (updated every κ iterations) that is multiplied (divided) by 2 if the search stays in unfeasible (feasible) regions.

Neighbourhood structures
Due to the specific characteristics of the costs considered in our model, where the cost of sending a given quantity through one edge depends on the supply path that quantity travelled before, we could not employ the most usual and simple moves, such as insertion or swapping of elements. Therefore, we move to a neighbour solution by swapping supply paths. During the search process we allow the temporary occurrence of unfeasibility.

We developed 3 neighbourhood structures using (complete or partial) path substitution:

- NS1 selects the paths with minimum unit cost, ignoring the current solution structure (i.e., the selection does not take into account the fact that other paths of the current solution may use common edges of the path under analysis);

- NS2 selects the paths with minimum unit cost but considering the current solution structure; and
- NSR (random neighbourhood structure) selects a new path by randomly choosing the chain elements in a way that the capacity constraints are satisfied.

The algorithm combines these three neighbourhood structures by running each of them during a given number of iterations.

Table 2. Distributions used to generate data

fixed administrative cost	producer→GPO producer→hospital GPO →hospital Uniform[1000,1500]	producer→care unit GPO→care unit hospital→hospital or care unit of other hospital distribution identical to the one of the hospital where the care unit belongs			hospital→hospital Uniform [500,1000]
fixed transportation cost	producer→GPO producer→hospital GPO →hospital hospital→hospital Uniform [200, 500]	producer→care unit GPO→care unit hospital→hospital or care unit of other hospital distribution identical to the one of the hospital where the care unit belongs			hospital→care unit of the same hospital care unit →care unit of the same hospital Uniform [10,20]
variable transportation cost	producer→GPO GPO →hospital hospital→hospital Uniform [1,10]	producer→ hospital hospital→care unit of other hospital Uniform [5,10]	producer→care unit Uniform [10,15]	GPO→care unit Uniform [5,15]	hospital→care of the same hospital care unit → care unit of the same hospital Uniform [5,15]
acquisition cost	Base cost *Item1:* Uniform [100, 120]; *Item2:* Uniform [50, 70]	Quantity discount structure			
		Order quantity		Discount	
		[0, LS1]		0%	
		[LS1, LS2]		Uniform [0%, 5%]	
		[LS2, LS3]		Uniform [5%, 10%]	
		[LS3, +∞]		Uniform [10%, 20%]	
inventory carrying cost	Uniform [1/1000,3/1000]				
commercial margin	producer→GPO Uniform [-10%,-1%]	producer→care unit GPO→care unit hospital→hospital or care unit of other hospital Uniform [5%,10%]			GPO →hospital hospital→hospital Uniform [2%,7%]

Note: LS1 = 25% of total demand/no. of periods
LS2 = 50% of total demand/no. of periods
LS3 = 75% of total demand/no. of periods

Table 3. Analysis of the obtained solutions values (costs) (30 runs of the algorithm)

Minimum	1st quartile	Median	3rd quartile	Maximum	Average	Standard deviation	Variation coefficient
1.295.040	1.345.560	1.369.370	1.383.073	1.398.620	1.362.904	30.582	0,02244

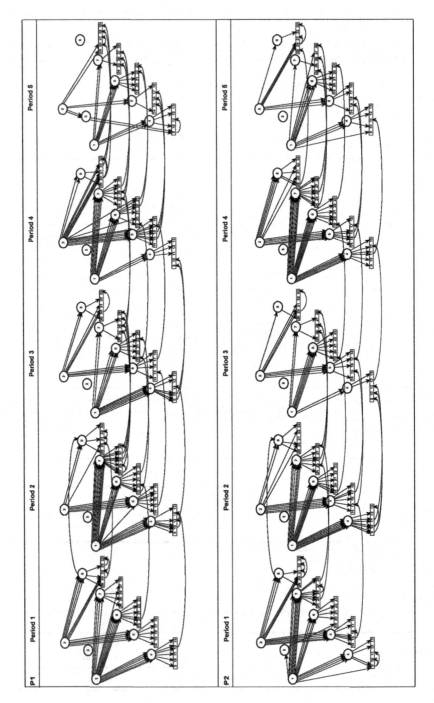

Fig. 2. Representation of one of the best solutions obtained

4   Illustrative Example

Assume we would like to configure a health care supply chain with 2 producers, 1 GPO, 5 hospitals and 5 point of care units per hospital (165 network nodes) for 2 items, during 5 periods. All possible supply connections, including lateral transshipments, are allowed. The point of care units were classified as units of high demand or units of low demand according to a binomial distribution with $p = 0,5$. Demand was simulated through a normal distribution: $N(\mu=100, \sigma=20)$ or $N(\mu=50, \sigma=20)$ for high or low units demand, respectively, and costs and constraints limits were also randomly generated (Table 2). Additionally, we considered a discount structure depending on the quantity ordered of the two items.

The developed algorithm was run 30 times for this test instance, and Table 3 summarizes the solution values obtained.

We have graphically represented one of the best solutions obtained in order to allow an easy assessment on how reasonable these solutions are (see Figure 2). This solution is formed by 255 supply paths that denote a concentration of the acquisitions of both items in one producer. This in accordance with our expectations due to the existence of quantity discounts. Because of the existence of fixed costs, there is a pattern in the supply and storage systems, that repeats itself along the 5 periods and for the 2 items.

5   Conclusions

The model proposed in this paper was designed strongly based on several interviews with managers responsible for the hospital supply departments. This model, along with the described resolution procedures, can be effectively used to design and evaluate alternative strategies for the configuration of hospital supply chains. Given the combinatorial nature of the problem and the dimension of real life instances, we have designed an approach based on metaheuristics. The flexibility of the developed algorithms allows their application to supply chains with different topologies and atypical cost characteristics.

Preliminary computational results show the potential of the developed approach in solving large scale, diversified supply chain configuration problems. We believe that the future incorporation of this approach in a broader Decision Support System (DSS) will provide a tool that can significantly contribute to an increase of healthcare supply chains efficiency and encourage the establishment of collaborative partnerships between their members. It may, in fact, be used to simulate, discuss and negotiate alternative supply chain coordination partnerships between neighbour hospitals and other supply chain members, as it allows the evaluation of alternative supply chain designs both in terms of the global network impact, and in terms of the costs and benefits of each supply chain member. The next stage of our research will be the application of these methodologies to real data obtained through case studies based on real hospital supply chains.

References

1. Ford, E.W., Scanlon, D.P.: Promise and problems with supply chain management approaches to health care purchasing. Health Care Management Review 32, 192–202 (2007)
2. Blamey, J.: Introdução à Logística Hospitalar - Tendências e Melhores Práticas (DHL Healthcare, experience within hospital logistics). Presentation at Reunião Temática "Programa do Medicamento e Melhores Práticas de Logística Hospitalar, Infarmed, Lisboa, November 9 (2007)
3. De Vries, G., Bertrand, J.W.M., Vissers, J.M.H.: Design requirements for health care production control systems. Production Planning & Control 10, 559–569 (1999)
4. Van Aken, J.E., Hop, L., Post, G.J.J.: The virtual organization: a special mode of strong interorganizational cooperation. In: Hitt, M.E., Ricart, J.E., Nixon, R.D. (eds.) Managing Strategically in an Interconnected World Wiley, Chichester (1998)
5. Norman, T.J., Preece, A., Chalmers, S., Jennings, N.R., Luck, M., Dang, V.D., Nguyen, T.D., Deora, V., Shao, J., Gray, W.A., Fiddian, N.J.: Agent-Based Formation of Virtual Organisations. International Journal of Knowledge Based Systems 17, 103–111 (2004)
6. Schneller, E.S., Smeltzer, L.R.: Strategic Management of the Health Care Supply Chain. Jossey-Bass, San Francisco (2006)
7. Burns, L.R.: How the Health Care Value Chain Operates. In: Burns, L.R. (ed.) The Health Care Value Chain: Producers, Purchasers, and Providers, pp. 41–56. Jossey-Bass, San Francisco (2002)
8. Schneller, E.S.: The value of group purchasing in the health care supply chain. School of Health Administration and Policy, Arizona State University College of Business, Tempe (2000)
9. Nollet, J., Beaulieu, M.: Should an organisation join a purchasing group? Supply Chain Management: An International Journal 10, 11–17 (2005)
10. Burns, L.R.: Role of Group Purchasing Organizations (GPOs). In: Burns, L.R. (ed.) The Health Care Value Chain - Producers, Purchasers, and Providers, pp. 59–125. Jossey-Bass, San Francisco (2002)
11. Pasin, F., Jobim, M., Cordeau, J.: An application of simulation to analyse resource sharing among health-care organisations. International Journal of Operations & Production Management 22, 381–393 (2002)
12. Beaulieu, M., Patenaude, G.: La gestion des approvisionnements en réseau: le cas du Centre hospitalier Notre-Dame de la Merci. Logistique & Management Numéro spécial, 59–64 (2004)
13. DeScioli, D.T.: Differentiating the Hospital Supply Chain for Enhanced Performance. Engineering Systems Division. Master of Engineering in Logistics. Massachusetts Institute of Technology, Boston (2005)
14. Rivard-Royer, H., Landry, S., Beaulieu, M.: Hybrid stockless: a case study. Lessons for health-care supply chain integration. International Journal of Operations & Production Management 22, 412–424 (2002)
15. Nicholson, L., Vakharia, A.J., Erengüç, S.S.: Outsourcing inventory management decisions in healthcare: Models and application. European Journal of Operational Research 154, 271–290 (2004)
16. Tsui, M., Wilson, D.I., Merry, H., Phulwani, K., Dooley, M.J.: Implementing a Hospital Vendor-Managed Inventory System. Journal of Pharmacy Practice and Research 38, 40–43 (2008)
17. Danese, P.: The extended VMI for coordinating the whole supply network. Journal of Manufacturing Technology Management 17, 888–907 (2006)

18. More, E., McGrath, M.: An Australian case in e-health communication and change. Journal of Management Development 21, 621–632 (2002)
19. Breen, L., Crawford, H.: Improving the pharmaceutical supply chain: Assessing the reality of e-quality through e-commerce application in hospital pharmacy. International Journal of Quality & Reliability Management 22, 572–590 (2005)
20. Zheng, J., Bakker, E., Knight, L., Gilhespy, H., Harland, C., Helen, W.: A strategic case for e-adoption in healthcare supply chains. International Journal of Information Management 26, 290–301 (2006)
21. Korner, E.J., Oinonen, M.J., Browne, R.C.: The Power of Collaboration: Using Internet-Based Tools to Facilitate Networking and Benchmarking within a Consortium of Academic Health Centers. Journal of Medical Systems 27, 47–56 (2003)
22. Bazzoli, G.J., Dynan, L., Burns, L.R., Yap, C.: Two decades of organizational change in health care: what have we learned? Medical Care Research and Review 61, 247 (2004)
23. Kodner, D.L., Spreeuwenberg, C.: Integrated care: meaning, logic, applications, and implications - a discussion paper. International Journal of Integrated Care 2, 1–6 (2002)
24. Aptel, O., Pourjalali, H.: Improving activities and decreasing costs of logistics in hospitals – A comparison of U.S. and French hospitals. The International Journal of Accounting 36, 65–90 (2001)
25. Burns, L.R., Pauly, M.V.: Integrated Delivery Networks: A detour on the road to integrated health care? Health Affairs 21, 128–143 (2002)
26. Van Donk, D.P.: Redesigning the supply of gasses in a hospital. Journal of Purchasing & Supply Management 9, 225–233 (2003)
27. Ahuja, R.K., Magnanti, T.L., Orlin, J.B.: Network flows - theory, algorithms and applications. Prentice Hall, New Jersey (1993)
28. Muriel, A., Simchi-Levi, D.: Supply Chain Design and Planning. In: Kok, A.G., Graves, S.C. (eds.) Supply Chain Management: Design, Coordination and Operation, vol. 11, pp. 17–94. Elsevier, Amsterdam (2003)
29. Glover, F.: Tabu Search - Part I. ORSA Journal on Computing 1, 190–206 (1989)
30. Glover, F.: Tabu Search - Part II. ORSA Journal on Computing 2, 4–32 (1990)
31. Mladenovic, N., Hansen, P.: Variable neighborhood search. Computers & Operations Research 24, 1097–1100 (1997)

A Supply Chain Architecture Based on Multi-agent Systems to Support Decentralized Collaborative Processes

Jorge E. Hernández, Raúl Poler, and Josefa Mula

CIGIP (Research Centre on Production Management and Engineering), Universidad Politécnica de Valencia. Escuela Politécnica Superior de Alcoy, Edificio Ferrándiz y Carbonell, 2, 03801 Alcoy (Alicante), Spain
{jeh,rpoler,fmula}@cigip.upv.es

Abstract. In a supply chain management context, the enterprise architecture concept to efficiently support the collaborative processes among the supply chain members involved has been evolving. Each supply chain has an organizational structure that describes the hierarchical relationships among its members, ranging from centralized to decentralized organizations. From a decentralized perspective, each supply chain member is able to identify collaborative and non collaborative partners and the kind of information to be exchanged to support negotiation processes. The same concepts of organizational structure and negotiation rules can be applied to a multi-agent system. This paper proposes a novel supply chain architecture to support decentralized collaborative processes in supply chains by considering a multi-agent-based system modeling approach.

Keywords: Enterprise architecture, Supply chain management, Multi-Agent Systems, Collaborative decision-making.

1 Introduction

Nowadays, market trends move toward a clean and natural business integration, which means that companies (according to both their current behaviour and own initiative) head toward establishing coordination/collaborative mechanisms in order to improve those aspects which, for example, are not as competitive as they used to be. Moreover, [3] consider that this integration may be achieved in terms of the knowledge that companies acquire from the environment, and vice versa. Therefore, as companies tend to work together by considering a specific matter, supply chain management (SCM) concepts emerge with a view to considering, in the first place, the perspective of each company and, in the second place, the perspective from the whole system (the supply chain). This management process involves planning at every decision-making level (strategic, tactical and operative [22]), and also aims to find the best possible supply chain (SC) configuration [13].

Thus at the tactical-operational planning level, the master planning (MP) task plays a crucial role (coordination problem). The coordination process of autonomous, yet interconnected, tactical-operational planning activities refers to collaborative planning (CP)

L.M. Camarinha-Matos et al. (Eds.): PRO-VE 2009, IFIP AICT 307, pp. 128–135, 2009.

in whatever follows [8]. This CP means that the decision-making process will be supported by the exchange of demand plans in order to timely conduct and set possible future problems related to, for example, the capacity availability or to the defined inventory level in order to meet any sudden changes in orders at all times. In this context and from a decentralized collaboration viewpoint, each node considers their collaborative and non collaborative partners (customers and suppliers) [18]. In this way, we may state from the study of [6] that information fields can be used as the basis to coordinate an organization, which can be seen as a collective agent composed of other individual collective agents that may encompass multiple embedded information fields. Moreover, [9] view a SC as a composed set of intelligent (software) agents (responsible for one or more activities and for the interaction with other related agents in planning and executing their responsibilities). In addition, [10] explains the relationship between inter-firm coordination mechanisms and the interdependence characteristics among the actors involved in implementation based on a multi-agent approach. In this context, and as will see in Section 2, most of the current contributions to support collaboration in supply chains consider a centralized approach to manage the information exchange process. Hence the contribution of this novel architecture is the reason for considering a decentralized information exchange process representation in a collaborative manner in which multi-agent system technology has been considered to support this enterprise architecture, which not only considers the related negotiation process among the SC nodes, but also the objectives and constraints from the upper SC level to lower N-tier supplier levels.

Therefore, this paper is set out as follows: Section 2 briefly reviews the relevant literature on architectures in the SC in a collaborative context. Section 3 shows the main elements of the proposed architecture using the Zachman enterprise framework in which an N-tier SC supplier configuration is considered. Finally, Section 4 provides the main conclusions of the paper and also establishes a brief description of our future work.

2 Background

In the SCM context, enterprise architectures have been considered to define and represent complex systems by considering, in many cases, the different points of view within the same problem or the configuration that may be considered. In addition and in relation to [7], [11], among others, there are three types of representations from a conceptual viewpoint: informal, semi-formal and formal. Therefore, the proposed architecture will be composed of all the necessary elements from a formal point of view (or representation), such us the conceptual, logical and physical elements. Hence a modeling language that is currently being widely considering is the UML [16], which has been enriched with the multi-agent-based model paradigm. Thus this subsection presents the most relevant literature in the SCM modeling field in order to carry out the architecture proposal of this paper. Further detailed information on this field can be found in [2] and [19] where full surveys and state of the arts can be seen.

In this context, one of the first SC architectures was presented by [1] which considers five main elements to support effective and coordinated operations (web clients, agents, directories, knowledge and an MIS broker). In the same way, [21] propose an architecture that collaboratively supports a recursive and multi-resolution process by considering multi-agents. Furthermore, this architecture proposed by [21] also considers three main layers which aim to support communication, manage the coordination and cooperation processes and categorize each agent within the system. Likewise, [4] propose an architecture that facilitates the organizational memory in SCs. To go about this, two layers are considered (storage and facilitation). Thus, these harmony mechanisms, as proposed by [4], are to be supported by agents, collaborators, transactors, objects and registry facilitators. In relation to this, [17] establish that virtual and/or extended enterprises should be considered to cooperatively support information exchange, material and services. In this same context, [14] propose a novel architecture to support the inter-enterprise functions/resources integration and collaboration under a networked context by considering the robustness of the multi-agent system which enables agents to exhibit hybrid (continuous and discrete) behaviours and interactions. Finally, another contribution in this field is that of [5] who present a decoupled federated architecture to support distributed simulation cloning, fault tolerance, inter-operability and grid-enabled architectures. Hence as the way in which the reviewed architectures have been proposed is generic, they can be presented as frameworks from which other architectures are developed in order to detect the main elements and relationships that may exist among them. Therefore the following section not only considers all the valuable architecture elements obtained from this section, but also the main existing frameworks in the literature, as well as the Zachman enterprise framework to support multi-agent-based architecture which takes into account the collaborative processes in the SC in a decentralized context, mainly regarding their multi-dimension perspective.

3   A Multi-agent-Based Architecture to Support the Collaborative Processes in Supply Chains

As we have seen in the last section, most of the authors suggest considering a framework to carry out the enterprise architecture development process. Moreover, the right selection of a framework will depend on the modeler's experience and how robust it can be in the environment to which is to be applied. In this context, the Zachman Framework [23] has been chosen to represent the main elements of the architecture based on multi-agent systems which will support the collaborative processes in the SC. In this context, an X node will represent the upper level (customer), a Y node the first-tier supplier and a Z node the supplier at the lower level (second- or N-tier supplier).

Moreover, the Zachman framework considers a total of thirty cells to represent different views of an enterprise architecture that primarily aims to identify aspects of the people involved in the process such as what, how, where, who, when and why, as well as those aspects related to the representation of processes such as: context, concepts, logic, physical, performance and content. In this way, only the five most representative cells are taken into account to represent the decentralized collaborative process in SCs with a view to favoring the simplicity of the representation and to not overextend the proposed architecture.

Therefore, the cells selected from the Zachman framework grid [20] have been chosen to collect and transmit the related information from the SC nodes which are intended to participate in a collaborative process as collaborative or non-collaborative nodes. The information flow takes place in this context, firstly at the upper level of the Zachman grid (Enterprise model/Why) to identify the main motivation (Model 1) and the collaborative process goals. Because they are supported by these flows, the related models are developed to obtain the business process (Model 2, Enterprise model/How), logical data (Model 3, System model/What), role (Model 4, System model/Who) and the control structure model (Model 5, Technology-constrained model/When). Thus, the following subsections show the model representation related to each selected cell by considering, on the one hand, the representation proposal of [15] and, on the other hand, the collaborative UML-based framework by [12].

Thus, the collaborative process, represented in the Figure 1 as BPMN diagram, is oriented to promote the exchange of information. In this context, the main purpose of the proposed architecture is to show the informational flows which supporta the collaboration among the SC nodes. In this sense, it is possible to say that the collaboration involve much type of processes, being ones of the more important the forecasting, planning and replenishment processes. These processes, under a collaborative context, will be related to the exchanging of the demand plans which, at the end, will imply to consider a tactical perspective in the decision-making process. In addition important to highlight is that, under a SCM context, there are many relevant processes in order to foster the collaboration such as forward and reverse logistic, requesting management, inventory control, key performance indicators among others. Thus, in order to explain in a conceptual and graphical manner the decentralized collaborative process (among the nodes of the SC), this architecture will be focused in the planning process as the main information (demand plans) exchange engine in order to support the decision-making process.

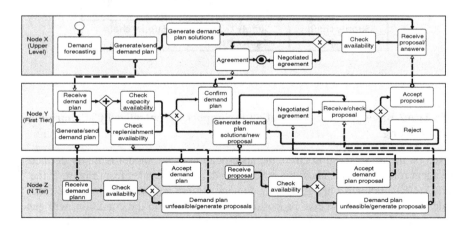

Fig. 1. Generic decentralized collaborative process (BPMN – Model 1)

Moreover from the perspective of every node, it is possible to state that the collaboration in the SC firstly considers the identification of the collaborative and non collaborative nodes. Therefore, the relationship among the collaborative nodes will be supported by the demand plan exchanging process (Figure 1), which will promote the negotiation of the unfeasible values in a collaborative manner. Hence by considering a a longer horizon plan, the capacity to react to some unexpected demand plan requirement will be improved (and example of this may be found in [13]) Thus by conspiring the advancement of orders or by making changes in the respective safety stock, the respective suppliers will be able to react to uncertainty in demand by avoiding excess orders or by maintaining a sufficient stock of materials to effectively and efficiently cope with changes in orders. Under the SC terms, the request may be accepted, negotiated or rejected. So the negotiation process takes place when the SC configuration is such that suppliers of suppliers will exist. Then the information exchange (inherent in the decision-making process) will involve several SC nodes which will, in turn, imply that the nodes will exchange information properly and timely to cover possible backlogs in the production planning process from the upper and lower SC tiers in a collaborative and decentralized manner (Figure 2).

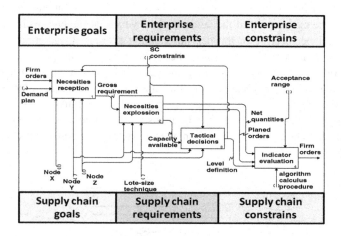

Fig. 2. Business process model (IDEF0 – Model 2)

3.1 Agent-Based Model Specification to Support Decentralized Collaborative Planning

Based on the previous subsection, the specification of the model is firstly defined by the agent role in the SC. Thus it is possible to define three roles from Figure 2: the "X node" role which will only generate a demand pattern and will receive offers; the "Y node" role which will receive proposals and, depending on the condition, will generate another demand at a lower level node that will be identified by the "Z node" role. Each agent, with their related roles (Figure 3), will interact and negotiate according to their own capacities with a view to solving order requirements.

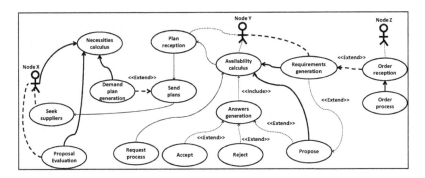

Fig. 3. Agent role interaction (UML Use Case – Model 3)

This interaction process is supported by the corresponding methods and attributes that each agent considers as they are instances of the agent class (Figure 4). Hence, from one side, the supply chain nodes consider (under a one-to-many relationship oriented) the related ontology's in order to support the planning process (delivery time, request, product and stock register). In addition, from the other side, each node considers their behaviours (under an agent-based model approach). Thus, as the decentralized collaboration and negotiation, the behaviours considered are supported by the FIPA-ACL-Protocol to model each agent class. In this context, the classes consider behaviours to support the related protocol communication and ontologies which promote the interoperability among them by considering the Knowledge Query and Manipulation Language (KQML) standard (Figure 5). Therefore, decentralized collaboration, which in many cases will require a negotiation process, is supported by (Figure 6) the ContractNet FIPA-Protocol (CFP) that has been implemented in ECLIPSE and validated through the SNIFFER agent of the JADE 3.6.1 platform (Figure 7).

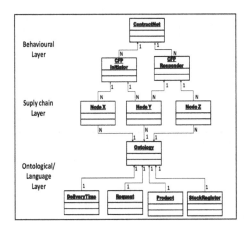

Fig. 4. UML class diagram (Model 4)   **Fig. 5.** CFP KQML code (extract)

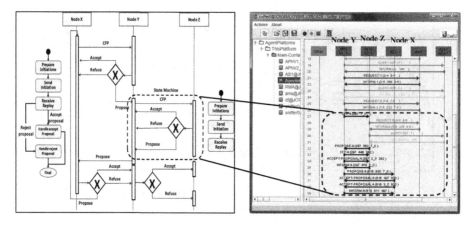

Fig. 6. Sequence and state UML diagram of decentralized SC collaboration (Model 5)

Fig. 7. Structure/negotiation validation through SNIFFER/JADE 3.6.1

4 Conclusions and Further Research

This paper has presented a novel architecture proposal based on multi-agent systems to support the decentralized collaboration process in SC networks which also considers the Zachman enterprise framework. Furthermore, we may conclude that agents are an appropriate tool for collaborative process modeling from a decentralized perspective which has been defined by considering the information coming from the collaborative and non-collaborative SC nodes. As further research objectives, we expect to (1) apply this architecture to study the collaboration in SC with another modeling approaches such us mathematical models, discrete event-based simulation, among others and (2) apply this architecture to a real SC.

Acknowledgments. This research has been supported partly by the EVOLUTION project (Ref. DPI2007-65501) which is funded by the Spanish Ministry of Science and Education and partly by the Universidad Politécnica de Valencia (Ref. PAID-05-08), www.cigip.upv.es/evolution.

References

1. Ba, S., Kalakota, R., Whinston, A.B.: Using client-broker-server architecture for Intranet decision support. Decision Support Systems 19, 171–192 (1997)
2. Bousqueta, F., Le Page, C.: Multi-agent simulations and ecosystem management: a review. Ecological Modelling 176(3-4), 313–332 (2004)
3. Camarinha-Matos, L.M., Afsarmanesh, H.: Collaborative networks: a new scientific discipline. Journal of Intelligent Manufacturing 16, 439–452 (2005)
4. Chang, J., Choi, B., Lee, H.: An organizational memory for facilitating knowledge: an application to e-business architecture. Expert Systems with Applications 26, 203–215 (2004)
5. Chen, D., Turner, S.J., Cai, W., Xiong, M.: A decoupled federate architecture for high level architecture-based distributed simulation. Journal of Parallel and Distributed Computing 68, 1487–1503 (2008)

6. Confessore, G., Galiano, G., Stecca, G.A.: Collaborative Model for Logistics Process Management. In: Camarinha-Matos, L.M., Afsarmanesh, H., Ollus, M. (eds.) 7th Working Conference on Virtual Enterprises (PRO-VE 2006), Network-Centric Collaboration and Supporting Frameworks, Helsinki, Finland, vol. 224, pp. 237–244 (2006)
7. Davis, A.M.: Software requirements: objects, functions and states. Prentice-Hall, Englewood Cliffs (1993)
8. Dudek, G., Stadtler, H.: Negotiation-based collaborative planning between supply chains partners. European Journal of Operational Research 163(3), 668–687 (2005)
9. Fung, R.Y.K., Chen, T.S.: A multiagent supply chain planning and coordination architecture. International Journal of Advanced Manufacturing Technology 25(7-8), 811–819 (2005)
10. Gomez-Gasquet, P., Franco, R.D., Rodríguez, R., Ortiz, A.: A Scheduler for extended supply chains based on combinatorial auctions. Journal of Operations and Logistics 2(1), V1–V12 (2009)
11. Hernández, J.E., Mula, J., Ferriols, F.J.: A reference model for conceptual modeling of production planning processes. Production Planning and Control 19(8), 725–734 (2008a)
12. Hernández, J.E., Poler, R., Mula, J., Peidro, D.: A collaborative knowledge management framework for supply chains: A UML-based model approach. Journal of Industrial Engineering and Management 1(2), 77–103 (2008b)
13. Hernández, J.E., Poler, R., Mula, J.: Modelling collaborative forecasting in decentralized supply chain networks with a multiagent system. In: Cordeiro, J., Filipe, J. (eds.) 11th International conference on Enterprise Information system, Milan, Italy, Portugal. AIDSS, pp. 372–375 (2009)
14. Melo, M.T., Nickel, S., Saldanha-da-Gama, F.: Facility location and supply chain management – A review. European Journal of Operational Research 196, 401–412 (2009)
15. Nahm, Y.E., Ishikawa, H.: A hybrid multi-agent system architecture for enterprise integration using computer networks. Robotics and Computer-Integrated Manufacturing 21, 217–234 (2005)
16. Noran, O.: An analysis of the Zachman framework for enterprise architecture from the GERAM perspective. Annual Reviews in Control 27, 163–183 (2003)
17. Odell, J., Parunak, H., Bauer, B.: Extending UML for agents. In: Wagner, G., Lesperance, Y., Yu, E. (eds.) Proceedings of the Agent-Oriented Information Systems Workshop at the 17th National conference on Artificial Intelligence, TX, pp. 3–17 (2000)
18. Ortiz, A., Franco, R.D., Alba, M.: V-Chain: Migrating From Extended To Virtual Enterprise Within An Automotive Supply Chain. In: PRO-VE 2003, Proceedings. Processes and Foundations for Virtual Organizations, pp. 145–152 (2003)
19. Poler, R., Hernandez, J.E., Mula, J., Lario, F.C.: Collaborative forecasting in networked manufacturing enterprises. Journal of Manufacturing Technology Management 19(4), 514–528 (2008)
20. Shen, W., Hao, Q., Yoon, H.J., Norrie, D.: Applications of agent-based systems in intelligent manufacturing: An updated review. Advanced Engineering Informatics 20, 415–431 (2006)
21. Sowa, J.F., Zachman, J.A.: Extending and formalizing the framework for information systems architecture. IBM Systems Journal 31(3), 590–616 (1992)
22. Ulieru, M., Norrie, D., Kremer, R., Shen, W.: A multi-resolution collaborative architecture for web-centric global manufacturing. Information Sciences 127, 3–21 (2000)
23. Vidal, C.J., Goetschalckx, M.: Strategic production–distribution models: A critical review with emphasis on global supply chain models. European Journal of Operational Research 98, 1–18 (1997)
24. Zachman, J.A.: Enterprise Architecture: The Issue of the Century. Database Programming and Design, 44–53 (1997)

Collaborative Manufacturing Management in Networked Supply Chains

Michel Pouly, Souleiman Naciri, and Sébastien Berthold

Ecole Polytechnique Fédérale de Lausanne (EPFL)
Laboratory for Production Management and Processes, Station 9,
1015 Lausanne, Switzerland
{michel.pouly,souleiman.naciri,sebastien.berthold}@epfl.ch

Abstract. ERP systems provide information management and analysis to industrial companies and support their planning activities. They are currently mostly based on theoretical values (averages) of parameters and not on the actual, real shop floor data, leading to disturbance of the planning algorithms. On the other hand, sharing data between manufacturers, suppliers and customers becomes very important to ensure reactivity towards markets variability. This paper proposes software solutions to address these requirements and methods to automatically capture the necessary corresponding shop floor information. In order to share data produced by different legacy systems along the collaborative networked supply chain, we propose to use the Generic Product Model developed by Hitachi to extract, translate and store heterogeneous ERP data.

Keywords: Collaborative networked supply chains, ERP, RFID, data sharing.

1 Introduction

The European manufacturing sector has experienced considerable changes in the last 15 years due to the reduction of the manufacturing depth. In the past, most industrial companies produced almost everything in house. Continuous pressure on the prices and the global competition forced them to focus on their core competences like engineering and final assembly as OEM manufacturers thus outsourcing almost the whole manufacturing operations.

Information is one of the most valuable resources for manufacturing companies and supply chains. Due to the huge amount of produced and exchanged data needed for the production activities, it is essential to identify the most useful ones and to focus only on the "strategic data" leading to potential improvements at the supply chain level and the "production data" leading to potential improvements at the company level.

The actual production management software (ERP, MES etc.) [1] does not rely on accurate and up-to-date shop floor data, as the classical manual collection is time consuming, error prone and not real time. Major improvements are expected from an automatic capture of shop floor data.

Numerous research works have outlined the benefits of information sharing throughout the supply chain [2]. Sharing data such as machine loads, sales previsions,

L.M. Camarinha-Matos et al. (Eds.): PRO-VE 2009, IFIP AICT 307, pp. 136–145, 2009.
© IFIP International Federation for Information Processing 2009

inventory positions etc. has proven to increase companies and supply chain key performance indicators like the fulfil rate and the product cycle time [3], and to decrease order fluctuations [4] that characterize the bullwhip effect. However, data sharing and integration remain a major concern as companies may use heterogeneous hardware and operating systems, data management software, data models, schemas and semantics [5], which hinder data sharing efficiency.

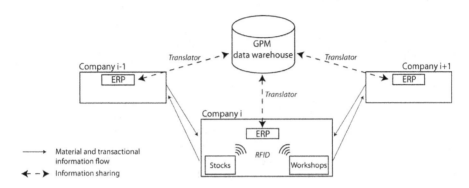

Fig. 1. Information acquisition and sharing within a collaborative networked supply chain

This paper addresses the data identification, collection and sharing processes by proposing corresponding methods and solutions based on the results of the IMS Di-FAC and VIPNET research projects [6].

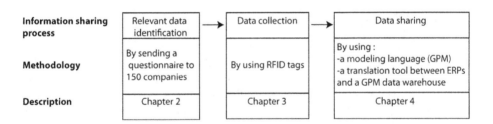

Fig. 2. Plan of the article

2 Industrial Requirements

A web based survey on 150 enterprises of the watch, medical appliances and mechanics sectors in the Western part of Switzerland showed the major requirements of companies working in collaborative supply chains [7]. Two thirds of the answering companies were small SME (less than 100 employees):

– 70% of them have already installed an ERP
– 84% of them have an Intranet solution
– 58% of them have their own IT department

Table 1. Industrial requirements

Requirements	Very important	Important
Orders follow-up along the supply chain	82%	9%
Stock information (WIP, raw material, components and finished goods inventory)	74%	17%
Availability to promise	70%	17%

2.1 Orders Follow-Up along the Supply Chain

The most important customers' expectation is to be accurately informed about the actualized real delivery schedules. In many cases, this information is important enough to motivate customers to select only suppliers able to provide this service. Actually, this information is not immediately available to the sales department clerks, who must investigate first and then call back. What is needed is an interface to seamlessly provide this information to the authorized supply chain collaborators for instance by linking a web portal to the legacy ERP systems. The actualized delivery schedules can be calculated by using the actual locations of the orders and the average actualized lead times of the remaining operations. The following shop floor data are required for this function:

- actual locations and amounts of WIP (Work in Progress) along the supply chain
- lead time for each operation
- starting/ending time of each operation

2.2 Stock Information

The second most important industrial requirement is the updated information about the stocks that include the raw material and purchased components, the parts along the manufacturing lines (WIP) and the finished goods. Inventory management is also important because it is the base to calculate the available to promise schedules that are the third most important requirement of the above-mentioned survey.

2.3 Availability to Promise Function

The main objective of any Customer Relationship Management (CRM) ERP module is to better satisfy customer needs in order to retain them and to attract new ones. Sales people often promise their customers unrealistic delivery schedules that cannot be met. The customers become dissatisfied and resulting delay penalty fees can cut the supplier's margin. Moreover, this fact is a great source of tension between the sales and manufacturing departments. In this paper, we propose a tool connected to the company's ERP to help sales people providing more realistic delivery schedules (see figure 3).

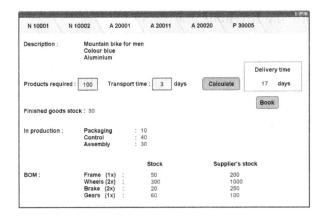

Fig. 3. Available to promise tool

This tool has multiple tabs corresponding to the different products sold by the company, each tab containing a product description, the number of available products in the finished goods stock (FGS), the number of products actually in production that are not yet reserved for a specific order, the number of each required component in the stock and in the supplier's stocks. The inputs are the number of required products and the transport time for the corresponding customer. The tool uses the following algorithm to compute the best possible actual available to promise schedule:

1. Test if the available FGS can cover the entered number of required products. If yes, the available to promise schedule is set to the corresponding transport time and the algorithm stops
2. If no, the number of available products is set to the value of FGS and the algorithm goes one step backwards in the manufacturing line starting from the end to check how much of the remaining needs can be covered by half-finished products in this processing step. Using the Bill of Materials (BOM) and the operation sequence, it calculates the corresponding lead times and adds them to the available to promise schedule
3. If the needs are still not fully covered, the algorithm continues another step backwards until the needs are covered. Finally, the transport time is added to the calculated available to promise schedule

The following shop floor data are needed for this function:

- WIP at each shop floor station
  - number of parts entering the station
  - number of parts leaving the station
- lead time for each operation
  - arriving time at the station
  - departure time from the station

The next chapter describes the possible methods to automatically capture the corresponding shop floor data.

3   Data Capturing Methods and Technologies

Different technologies can be used to automatically capture the shop floor data like image recognition, voice recognition and RFID (Radio Frequency Identification). After having compared these three technologies considering the implementation possibilities, the corresponding costs and the acceptance by workers, we selected the RFID as the most suitable one.

The four basic components of a typical RFID system are an antenna or coil, a reader, a transponder (RFID tag) and a middleware. Normally, antennas and readers are coupled and distributed around the working area. Each object to track has a tag attached to it. When a tag and a reader are in the same area, data can be exchanged in read only or read/write mode. The middleware is the software layer in charge of linking the RFID readers and the ERP.

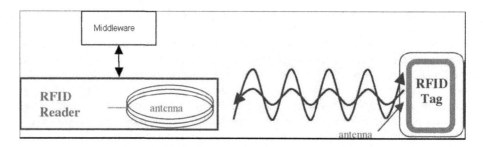

Fig. 4. Components of a RFID system

3.1   Example of RFID Implementation in the Shop Floor

Different implementations are possible using either fixed or mobile readers attached for instance to forklift trucks. We will present in the next section a possible implementation layout for a manufacturing station.

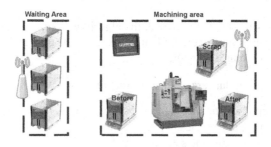

Fig. 5. Implementation for a manufacturing station

1. A pallet arriving at a station is stored in the corresponding waiting area where an RFID reader periodically reads all tags to identify the available pallets. This information is sent to the middleware.

2. The operator receives the next order on his screen with the data to identify the corresponding pallet(s) to bring to the machining area.

3. The operator puts the pallet on a scale before the machine. When the weight measured by the scale reaches a certain level, the scale sends a signal to the RFID reader of the machining area through the middleware to identify the pallet and make plausibility check against the order. The corresponding operation parameters are automatically downloaded from the ERP to the screen or directly into the CNC machine control. Furthermore, the code of the parts used after the manufacturing operation is written onto the tag attached to the pallet receiving the parts after the operation.

4. The operator takes the first part. At this time, the weight measured by the scale changes. The time between the first signal of the scale (weight reaches a certain level) and the second signal (weight changes) is recorded as setup time.

5. Then, with the weights of the three scales, it's possible to get the number of parts in each pallet (parts before operation, parts after operation and scrap) and even to know the machining time of each part.

6. When the operation is finished, the operator can enter on the screen the data that are not automatically recorded: labor time, resources used, consumables, additional data, etc. Then he removes the pallet of machined parts that can be brought to the next station. At this time, the corresponding scale measures a weight equal to zero and sends a signal to the middleware. This signal allows the time spent in the machining area to be known and to inform the ERP that the operation is completed.

7. The operator takes the empty pallet before the machine, puts it on the scale after the machine and gets the next order on the screen.

The following raw data are captured automatically in such a manufacturing station:

Table 2. Captured raw data and corresponding capturing method

Raw data	Capturing method
Arriving time in the waiting area	RFID reader, periodically
Departure time from the waiting area	RFID reader, periodically
Arriving time in the machining area	Scale (sends a signal to the middleware)
Departure time from the machining area	Scale (sends a signal to the middleware)
Number of parts entering the machining area	Scale (divides total weight by weight of one part)
Number of parts leaving the machining area	Scale (divides total weight by weight of one part)
Setup time	Scale (time between two signals, see point 4 of process description)
Starting time of operation	Scale (signal when weight changes)
Ending time of operation	Scale (signal when first pallet is empty)
Scrap	Scale (divides total weight by weight of one part)

4 Data Sharing along the Supply Chain

Once we have defined the technical means to collect shop floor data, we introduce a methodology and a tool to make collaborative networks partners able to share this data. To reach this goal, two major conditions must be met:

- a method to extract data from the different legacy ERP systems
- the possibility to store the data in a common data warehouse using a common language

4.1 Generic Product Model (GPM)

GPM was initially developed by the Hitachi group to store and keep nuclear power plants data (technical data, BOM and drawings) over a very long period of time even if the software that generated these data had disappeared meanwhile. GPM is a core model [8] that describes one to many relationships. It defines that objects are simply connected to objects via associations. These associations can be seen as verbs that link together a subject and one to several objects:

A valve "is classified as" piping components, "is classified as" stop valve, on/off valve etc. and "has property of" size, diameter, throughput etc.

4.2 GPM-XML

The GPM model is used to represent the relations between objects. However, computers cannot process it. To do so, GPM-XML has been developed. This language based on the W3C XML uses strings that make GPM-XML very close to natural language and therefore easily understandable by humans. XML also ensures data persistent storage through its adoption as a standard and its ease of understanding [9]. This point is very important, as it is one of the main objectives of GPM, to allow people to retrieve and visualize data that may have been produced decades ago.

The *association library* contains the whole set of GPM available associations that are used to connect objects together. It contains information about an association name, its meaning and its roles (which define the viewpoint from which the association is seen (subject or predicate)). The 19 existing GPM associations are based on EPISTLE, POSC/Caesar and USPI-NL. Among these associations, we can cite "is an instance of", "is assembled from", and "has property of". The *class library* is an XML file that gathers all the information about GPM associations and classes. A class is defined as the regrouping of several objects that have the same classification, semantics, names and attributes and that can be recognized as common by everybody [10]. GPM classes are object-oriented and inherit all the nature of their super class(es) [9]. Consequently, classes dealing with specific products' fields or views can be gathered in groups called "genres" as mechanical components, plant and system, production management and linked together using associations. *Instances* represent the allocations of classes and attributes for the purpose of the unique recognition and the designation of the attributes and relationships between other instances [9]. While classes describe concepts and groups of objects, instances represent real world objects. Instances are built from the association and class libraries using a translator as detailed later in this paper. Initially designed to model nuclear power plant data [11], new GPM classes have been created to handle management data as illustrated in following section.

4.3 Data Sharing Methodology

The management data we want to share are the data stored in ERP that are used to run companies and supply chain processes as planning, purchasing, production etc and the automatically captured shop floor data. To handle this type of data in the GPM data warehouse, the first step consists in mapping these data with GPM objects and related attributes. However, this task is not straightforward as we deal with alphanumerical data stored in tables that are eventually the result of other queries. As a consequence, apart from the case where we know the query and the underlying tables, it is often difficult to understand the nature and the meaning of the data that are displayed on ERP panels. Therefore, the only information users have to identify data is the name of the table and the label of the data. Knowing that these labels can have several meanings or even differ between companies and ERP, it appears very difficult to propose an automatic way to translate management data as it could be done for drawings and other technical data. Consequently, the mapping must be done in a semi-automatic way depending on the data we deal with. It means that it is the label of the data, and the knowledge of the person in charge of the mapping that will allow the creation of the mapping schemes.

Collaborative networked supply chains of SME are characterized by a large number of legacy ERP systems, and consequently a large variability of data formats and databases schemas. A common way of sharing information is through the Excel files database extractions that are proposed in the basic package of almost all ERP applications. Excel extractions make information sharing quite complex as the initially structured data contained in the ERP database is flattened in the Excel file, which can hinder extracted data understanding. The methodology detailed below explains how to give back a coherent GPM structure to flattened Excel files.

We focus in this paper on widespread products like watches that can be easily described using a Generic Bill of Materials (GBOM) [12], defined as "a Generic Bill of Material (GBOM) is designed to describe the components structure for a family of products in one data model. The specific Bill of Material for any particular product variant can then be generated on demand" [13]. Alternative methodology for customized products ERP data translation into GPM can be found in [14].

When users deal with data belonging to domains that haven't been explored yet, they may be confronted to some articles or features that are not represented by GPM classes and may have to build new classes. In the case of ERP management data, few relevant GPM classes were found in the initial class library. Consequently, a few classes covering the most common production management features (lead time, delivery time, inventory level, production cost, etc.) have been created. However, to produce a more consistent set of GPM management classes, GPM developers could use all the existing work related to business process modelling and ontologies.

4.4 Translator Development

Even if a reverse translator has also been developed to extract and convert GPM data into Excel files, we will focus on Excel to GPM translator development in the following section. The translation process for widespread products is described below:

1) Identification of relevant GPM classes and attributes for representing products GBOM (*),

2) Mapping between product structure (previous step) and Excel file. The mapping is made between GPM classes and attributes on one hand, and Excel file head of columns on the other hand as illustrated in figure 6. The mapping file is saved as an "association file" (*),

3) once a user wants to import an Excel file content into a GPM data warehouse, he or she must browse two files: the "association file" and the Excel file to upload. Then translation is made automatically and data is stored in GPM XML in the data warehouse.

(*) Refers to steps that are done just once. In concrete terms, Step 2 is made by dragging and dropping Excel head of columns on corresponding GPM objects or attributes.

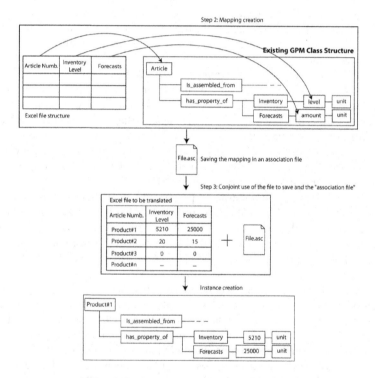

Fig. 6. Translator for widespread products

5   Conclusions

Collaboration within networked supply chains only makes sense if up to date information is shared between the different actors to be better informed about the corresponding real delivery schedules and lead times, the stocks all along the supply chain and the demand for products. Actually the large majority of the industrial SME don't have a correct view of their own shop floor activities. The automatic capture of shop floor data using RFID is an important step towards this goal as the actual manual capturing methods are time consuming, error prone and not real time.

In this paper, the focus is also placed on the translation and the storage of initially flat ERP management data that are characterized by a huge variability between companies. A methodology is proposed to make a semi-automatic mapping in order to translate in a friendly way (using drag and drop) unstructured and proprietary management data into a structured modelling language.

Acknowledgments. The authors would like to thank our industrial partners SAGE ProConcept SA and the Nuclear Power Plant Division of the Hitachi Group for their support and commitment and the Commission for Technology and Innovation (CTI) of the Swiss federal government, which funded this research.

References

1. Jacobs, G.P., Weston, F.C.: Enterprise resource planning (ERP) – a brief history. Journal of Operations Management 25(2), 357–363 (2007)
2. Cachon, G.P., Fisher, M.: Supply chain inventory management and the value of shared information. Management Science 46(8), 1032–1048 (2000)
3. Chen, M.C., Yang, T., Yen, C.T.: Investing the value of information sharing In multi-echelon supply chains. Quality and Quantity 41(3), 497–511 (2007)
4. Croson, R., Donohue, K.: Impact of pos data sharing on supply chain management: an experimental study. Production and Operations Management 12(1), 1–11 (2003)
5. Ziegler, P., Dittrich, K.R.: Three decades of data integration all problems solved? Building the Information Society 156, 3–12 (2004)
6. IMS DiFAC, http://www.difac.ch, IMS VIPNET, http://openknow.com/vipnet/index.htm
7. Berthold, S.: Integration of real time shop floor data into ERP software. EPFL Master thesis (2008)
8. Hitachi Group: "A GPM basics," Technical report (2004)
9. Hitachi Group: B - markup languages (gpm-xml), Technical report (2004)
10. Koizumi, Y., Seki, H., Yoon, T.: Data integration framework based on a generic product model. In: Tools and Methods of Competitive Engineering, vol. 1&2, pp. 891–902 (2004)
11. Mun, D., Hwang, J., Han, S., Seki, H., Yang, J.: Sharing product data of nuclear power plants across their lifecycles by utilizing a neutral model. Annals of Nuclear Energy 35(2), 175–186 (2008)
12. van Veen, E.A.: Modelling Product Structure by Generic Bill-of-Materials, pp. 139–188. Elsevier Science Inc., Amsterdam (1992)
13. Wu, P., Olsen, K.A., Saetre, P.: Visualizing the construction of generic Bills of Material. In: Chang, S.-K., Chen, Z., Lee, S.-Y. (eds.) VISUAL 2002. LNCS, vol. 2314, pp. 302–310. Springer, Heidelberg (2002)
14. Naciri, S., Pouly, M., Binggeli, J.-C., Glardon, R.: Using the Generic Product Model for storing and sharing ERP data. In: 13th International Conference on Computer Supported Cooperative Work in Design, CSCWD 2009, April 22-24, pp. 618–623 (2009)

Part **5**

Teams and Collaboration

Collaborative Capability of Teams in Network Organizations

Sebastian Ulbrich[1], Heide Troitzsch[1], Fred van den Anker[1], Adrian Plüss[2], and Charles Huber[2]

[1] UAS Northwestern Switzerland, School of Applied Psychology, Riggenbachstrasse 16, 4600 Olten, Switzerland
[2] UAS Northwestern Switzerland, School of Engineering, Promenade 26, 5200 Brugg, Switzerland
{Sebastian.Ulbrich,Heide.Troitzsch,Fred.vandenAnker, Adrian.Pluess,Charles.Huber}@fhnw.ch

Abstract. In this paper, we present a study on collaborative capability of teams in three network organizations in Austria and Switzerland. So far, collaborative capability was mostly conceptualized on organizational or individual level as a set of attributes that actors employ to collaborate successfully. We found that this view of collaborative capability has to be enlarged. Collaborative capability of teams is characterized by at least two components: an attribute-based perspective that focuses on capabilities of single actors or organizations, and a perspective on group dynamics, that describes how teams develop collaborative capability. We discuss our findings with regard to the different organizational settings of the networks analyzed and the current literature on collaborative capability and network organizations.

Keywords: Collaborative capability, network organizations, group dynamics.

1 Introduction

In recent years, collaborative capability was found to be a major contributor to firms' competitive advantage [1, 2]. Scholarly interest in the subject co-evolved with organizations' interest in implementing more flexible forms of collaboration both within and beyond organizational boundaries. Finally, network organizations as promising new forms of collaboration emerged [3, 4, 5].

Miles and Snow [3] point out, that these new dynamic forms of inter-firm collaboration are able to "[...] accommodate a vast amount of complexity while maximizing specialized competence [...]" (p.69). As flexible and voluntary forms of collaboration become important themes in business, the question how actors establish, develop, and maintain the ability to collaborate successfully is crucial. Today, there are many conceptualizations of collaborative capability on organizational and individual level, but organizational research is still lacking a detailed description of how managers translate collaborative capability into the social praxis of inter-firm collaboration [2]. Furthermore, there is still some necessity for research with regard to collaborative capability at the team level [6]. Thus, with this research we tackle the problem how teams in network organizations establish, develop, and maintain collaborative capability.

L.M. Camarinha-Matos et al. (Eds.): PRO-VE 2009, IFIP AICT 307, pp. 149–156, 2009.
© IFIP International Federation for Information Processing 2009

We studied the emergence and maintenance of collaborative capability of teams in three diverse network organizations in Austria and Switzerland focusing on attributes of single actors as well as the organizational framework and work requirements. Employing a process-based view on collaboration our focus lies on the dynamics of collaboration at an early stage of project work in network organizations.

2   Collaborative Capability – A Multifaceted Concept

A large body of research has grown around collaborative capability and related concepts. In an overview, Blomqvist and Levy [7] identify trust, communication, and commitment, as crucial factors for collaborative capability. Trust is the basis for effective communication among network partners, thus facilitating knowledge creation and innovation in networks [7]. Building relationships which are based on mutual trust seems to be one of the most important tasks in inter-firm collaboration [1, 8, 9, 10, 11, 12].

Vartiainen [13] found a strong emphasis on collective competences in a study on virtual organizations. Characteristics of the collective competences were clarity with regard to goals and operations, the establishment of a "bird's eye view" on the project, mutual trust, "l'esprit d'équipe" (team spirit), and commitment. On the level of actions, open and frequent interaction as well as working process compliance turned out to be important in virtual organizations. For Heimeriks and Schreiner [10], mutual trust is a crucial characteristic of high performance alliances. It comprises actors' willingness to act in benevolence to the relationship and not against it. Trust builds around partner's credibility, the mutual goodwill to act in benefit of the relationship, and a general predictability of the behavior of others.

Cullen et al. [9] describe the "soft side" of successful strategic alliance management to be closely related to the concepts of trust and commitment. According to the authors, trust in alliances is rooted in a rational and emotional base. Partners trust each other to meet their obligations and make promised contribution but also believe that an alliance partner will behave with goodwill towards the alliance and single partners. Commitment concerns the willingness of the partners to continue the relationship. It can be calculative or attitudinal. If partners are willing to care for the alliance, they will more likely allocate resources to the alliance [9]. Of course this kind of "caring" for a professional relationship is closely related to economic gains. As Sivadas and Dwyer [12] pointed out, partners enter into a strategic alliance to maximize their own gains. If gains are made at the expense of others, and are perceived as deceit, the relationship will be negatively affected. Effective communication can help solve the problem if an initial lack of trust is experienced.

We argue that the three main components of collaborative capability – trust, communication, and commitment – are closely interrelated and dependent on the economic success of the collaborative process. For example, Mohr and Spekman [14] found better communication quality and information sharing in successful partnerships. According to Blau [15], trust develops slowly through experiencing immediate returns from collaboration. In a longitudinal study on interfirm networks, Lorenzoni and Lipparini [16] found, an increase in trust and familiarity among partners reduced transaction and coordination costs.

To disentangle the complexity of the concept, but add yet another line of thought, a process-based approach to collaborative capability may be helpful. Actors, be it organizations or individuals, learn from collaboration experiences, thus having the chance to adapt their behavior in future collaborations accordingly. In consent with this line of argument, Kale et al. [17] define alliance capability as the firm's ability to learn from alliance experience and successfully apply insights to future alliances. From a perspective on organizational learning, this capability develops through recombining and integrating knowledge acquired from past actions. Effective actions will more likely be repeated in the future. As Anand and Khanna [18] pointed out that one of the most important factors of alliance success is previous experience with alliances. Kale et al. [17] argue that alliance experience helps firms to develop a relational capability.

From the literature on collaborative capability it is not clear whether capabilities that are beneficial to collaboration, for example to be able to communicate in a way that more likely builds trust relationships, are cause or consequence of successful collaboration. Moreover, if we consider a given set of organizational actors who collaborate for the first time, even if they are trustworthy, committed to the team, and communicate in an open manner – many potential pitfalls of collaboration may influence the process. Because collaboration success depends on the outcome of specific situations and organizational settings in which actors have to meet many challenges to fulfil work requirements, we propose to enlarge the perspective on collaborative capability.

2.1 A Process-Based Approach to Collaborative Capability

Many attribute-based concepts approach collaborative capability in hindsight, after it had been established among partners. However, there is empirical evidence that this perspective is somewhat skewed due to structural and historical self-selection effects. For example, in the field of Science and Technologies Studies it was found, that researchers tend to collaborate within their own groups [19, 20]. Furthermore, researchers' readiness for transdisciplinary collaboration in science tends to be higher among those who share a history of previous collaboration [21]. This historical perspective on collaboration unfolds two possible mechanisms. Firstly, actors with a history of collaboration seem to be more prone to collaborate with others in general. Secondly, actors tend to more likely choose those alters to engage in new projects with whom they already have collaborated successfully in the past. With regard to collaborative capability, these mechanisms support the argument that once a team has achieved to accomplish its goals through collaborating, actors are more likely to repeatedly collaborate in same or similar constellations in the future.

A positive outcome of collaboration feeds back as a potential input, thus strengthening a given relationship. We suggest that it is for this particular structuring of collaboration that both attributes of single actors and social dynamics are adjusted. Social dynamics of collaboration overlay individual attributes, such as engendering trust, mutual adjusting individual styles of communication, committing to subtasks, and coordinating activities. Each interaction episode adds to the shared history of collaboration. Following Dosi, Nelson and Winter [22], we argue that capability fills the gap between intention and outcome of activities, so it is important for actors who work together to reach a collective state in which tasks at hand can be effectively dealt with. In this study, we explored how actors establish collaborative capability and how it is put to the test by critical incidents that occurred in the process of working together in network projects.

3 Empirical Findings

Following an exploratory case study approach, we studied team collaboration in three network organizations in Austria and Switzerland by means of semi-structured interviews with executives of partnering firms as well as network managers. Table 1 gives an overview of the three network organizations. The inter-firm networks varied in size and industry sector, as well as in network typology [6, 23]. According to Sydow et al. [23], network organizations can be distinguished by their general purpose which can be product or process innovation (explorative type) or combining compatible resources in order to increase revenue, for example by reducing production costs or increasing market share (exploitative type) [24].

All three network organizations were set up to increase competitive advantage of their members but varied with regard to the means of how to achieve this. Whereas KC's main objective was to facilitate product and process innovation, thus initiating explorative projects, VB and SMT both aimed at reducing costs and optimize business processes, thus following an exploitative strategy. Whereas KC facilitated R&D projects with changing network partners, VB and SMT partners tended to collaborate with one another repeatedly. The latter strategy resulted in more cohesion and stability over time.

Table 1. Characteristics of participating network organizations

Network organization	KC	VB	SMT
Industry	Plastics	Construction	Metalworking
Number of network partners	400	60	7
Competitors in the network	Yes	Yes	No
Geographic propinquity	Yes	Yes	Yes
Cohesion of network	Low	Medium	High
Variability of relationships	Dynamic	Stable	Stable
Organizational design	Heterarchic	Hierarchic	Heterarchic
Main objective	Exploration	Exploitation	Exploitation

3.1 Partner Selection

On an organizational level, partner selection is an important prerequisite of successful collaboration, thus influencing the establishment of collaboration capability right from the start. Sivadas & Dwyer [12] suggest that complementary competences of partners will be beneficiary whereas competition among partners should be largely ruled out. In network organizations, direct competition acted detrimental to the establishment of collaborative capability, since network partners sought to increase their competitive advantage and to remain independent at the same time. We found that partners who shared economic interests with regard to the same technology, markets, or products, and pursued similar strategic goals would rather not collaborate.

Framing important factors for alliance capability and collaboration quality, Heimeriks and Schreiner [10] emphasize that compatibility and similarity of partners facilitate the successful combination of complementary assets. Combining resources is root to competitive advantage of collaborating firms. According to Lambe et al. [25], successful alliances manage their complementary resources and rather not build on competitive resources.

To identify a matching partner, knowledge about technological competences and market activities is required. Partner selection was found to be a crucial prerequisite for successful collaboration, especially with regard to competition and complementary technologies and knowledge. Network partners were selected because their core competences fit the requirements of the task. Firstly, this step required knowledge about the competences necessary to fulfil the task. Secondly, actors who initiated projects had to get to know other companies, in order to target them as potential partners.

Our results illustrate that this first step of partner selection was merely based on individual attributes of partners, such as technological specialties or expertise needed for the task at hand. Partner selection emphasizes the economic factors of collaboration. Here, network management was supportive in providing information about potential partners. In addition, network management actively brokered contacts between firms. Once potential partners got to know each other and initiated collaboration, network management restricted its supportive role to monitoring the process. Network managers intervened only if they were requested to do so by the partners, for example in case of conflicts. Neutrality of network management was stressed be an important requirement for successful collaboration in all three network organizations. Whereas actors' attributes such as expertise were crucial for partner selection, collaborative capability developed in the process.

3.2 Impact of Critical Incidents on Collaborative Capability of Teams

Table 2 presents some example episodes that were reported to us as critical at initial stages of collaboration. In early project phases initial trust in network partners and confidence in collaboration sucesss needed to be established. This required the negotiation of shared goals, as well as an open discussion of individual interests and expectations. To build trust in project teams, open discussion and presentation of expertise was crucial. Once this first step of knowledge sharing was achieved, confidence in collaboration success rose and influenced the commitment of the partners. The same effect was observed with external feedback on preliminary project results which influenced partners' collaborative capability positively. Thus, we found that initial trust has to be backed up by behavioral evidence for partners' willingness to collaborate, the quality of the contributions, and reciprocated investments.

Table 2. Influence of critical incidents on collaborative capabiliy

Network	Incident	Outcome	Mechanisms
KC	Kick off workshop at distrusted network partner	Presentation and open discussion of products and processes has lead to intensive knowledge sharing and joint problem solving	communication, trust, expertise, commitment
KC	Firms leave project due to differences of objectives and uncertainty of project outcome	Firms negotiate project goals, uncertainty is reduced by clarifying individual interests and expectations	communication, confidence
KC	Positive feedback on preliminary project results	Network partners increase investment in project. Uncertainty is reduced	Resource allocation, commitment
VB	Quick wins in low risk projects	Firms learn to build confidence in collaboration	confidence, trust cohesion
SMT	Firms simulate business collaboration, free riders leave the network when asked to contribute	Remaining executives encourage each other to continue and initiate successful project. Other firms join the network	resource allocation, reciprocity, confidence, cohesion

4 Concluding Remarks

Collaborative capability in network organizations is established as a mixture of the uncertain and the assertive somewhere between future promises of and past experiences with collaboration. Where partners were able to create an atmosphere of confidence in collaboration, which was assured by the perceived quality of single contributions, collaborative capability was built. In two of the three network organizations under study firms engaged in long-term relationships. KC as a project network [6], brought independent partners together for short range R&D projects. This is important to note, when discussing our findings. In KC collaborative capability had to be built faster, thus relying heavily on early assurance of success. Early success increased partners' investments on the one hand but was measured by initial investments on the other. The more partners committed to the project before a promising outcome was assured, it was more likely that commitment would be reciprocated.

Individual attributes of the organizations moderated the process from the start. We found allocation of financial and human resources of single firms to be crucial for collaboration success. Collaboration in network organization was also found to be dependent on whether executives took part in the process, which increased the overall commitment to the project. Once compatibility of firms was reached through partner selection, for example the combination of complementary resources required by the task at hand, social dynamics within teams became more important. This reflects the more general discussion about economic and relational factors of inter-firm collaboration and collaborative capability [7, 10]. As Blau [15] states: "Social exchange relations evolve in a slow process, starting with minor transactions in which little trust is required because little risk is involved and in which both partners can prove their trustworthiness, enabling them to expand their relation and engage in major transactions. Thus, the process of social exchange leads to the trust required for it in a self-governing fashion." (p. 454).

Since the process of building collaborative capability comprises mutual adaptation of partners, it is rather slow and time consuming. Therefore our finding, that partners tended to repeatedly collaborate with one another once they shared a history of successful collaboration is not surprising. This kind of "nurturing" of existing relationships occurred in the KC network, too, resulting in more cohesive networks and in some cases in the establishment of virtual enterprises. Dyer and Singh [26] argue that such processes of establishing structural cohesion lead to coevolving capabilities. From their perspective, partners gain competitive advantage from inter-firm relationships by recombination of resources and capabilities at early stages of collaboration. Over time, partners' competences coevolve and may become indivisible.

Acknowledgments. This research is supported by the Swiss National Science Foundation (SNF) DORE grant 13DPD3-117972. The authors would like to thank the Swiss National Science Foundation for its support.

References

1. Tyler, B.B.: The Complementarity of Cooperative and Technological Competencies. A Resource-based perspective. Journal of English Technology Management 18, 1–27 (2001)
2. Schreiner, M., Corsten, D.: Integrating Perspectives: A Multidimensional Construct of Collaborative Capability. In: Beyerlein, M.M., Johnson, D.A., Beyerlein, S.T. (eds.) Complex collaboration: Building the capabilities for working across boundaries. JAI Press, Asterdam (2004)
3. Miles, R.E., Snow, C.C.: Organizations: New Concepts for New Forms. California Management Review 28, 62–73 (1986)
4. Miles, R.E., Snow, C.C.: Organizational Strategy, Structure, and Process. Stanford University Press, Stanford (2003)
5. Powell, W.W.: Neither market nor hierarchy: Network forms of organization. In: Staw, B.M., Cummings, L.L. (eds.) Research in organizational behavior. JAI Press, Greenwich (1990)
6. Sydow, J.: Management von Netzwerkorganisationen - Zum Stand der Forschung. In: Sydow, J. (ed.) Management von Netzwerkorganisationen. Gabler, Wiesbaden (2006)
7. Blomqvist, K., Levy, J.: Collaboration Capability – A Focal Concept in Collaborative Knowledge Creation And Innovation in Networks. International Journal of Management Concepts and Philosophy 2, 31–48 (2006)
8. Curall, S.C., Judge, T.A.: Measuring trust between organizational boundary persons. Organizational Behavior and Decision Processes 64, 151–170 (1995)
9. Cullen, J.B., Johnson, J.L., Sakano, T.: Success through commitment and trust: the soft side of strategic alliance management. Journal of World Business 35, 223–240 (2000)

10. Heimeriks, K.H., Schreiner, M.: Alliance capability, collaboration quality, and alliance performance: an integrated framework. Eindhoven Center for Innovation Studies, Eindhoven (2002)
11. Niemelä, T.: Inter-Firm Co-Operation Capabilit. In: The Context Of Networking Family Firms: The Role Of Trust. Working paper, University of Jyväskylä (2003)
12. Sivadas, E., Dwyer, F.R.: An examination of organizational factors influencing new product success in internal and alliance-based processes. Journal of Marketing 1, 31–49 (2000)
13. Vartiainen, M., Kokko, N., Hakonen, M.: Competences in virtual organizations. In: Proceedings of the 3rd International Conference on Researching Work and Learning, pp. 209–219. Universtiy of Tampere, Tampere (2003)
14. Mohr, J., Spekman, R.: Characteristics of partnership success: partnership attributes, communication behavior, and conflict resolutions techniques. Strategic Management Journal 15, 135–152 (1994)
15. Blau, P.M.: Interaction: Social exchange. In: Sills, D.L. (ed.) The international encyclopedia of the social sciences. The Free Press and Macmillan, New York (1968)
16. Lorenzoni, G., Lipparini, A.: The leveraging of interfirm relationships as a distinctive organizational capability: a longitudinal study. Strategic Management Journal 20, 317–338 (1999)
17. Kale, P., Dyer, J.H., Singh, H.: Alliance capability, stock market response, and long-term alliance success: the role of the alliance function. Strategic Management Journal 23, 747–767 (2002)
18. Anand, B.N., Khanna, T.: Do firms learn to create value? The case of alliances. Strategic Management Journal 21, 295–315 (2000)
19. Zucker, L.G., Darby, M.R., Brewer, M.B., Peng, Y.: Collaboration Structure and Information Dilemmas in Biotechnology: Organizational Boundaries as Trust Production. In: Kramer, R.M., Tyler, T.R. (eds.) Trust in Organizations – Frontiers of Theory and Research. Sage, Thousand Oaks (1995)
20. Bozeman, B., Corley, E.: Scientists' collaboration strategies: implications for scientific and technical human capital. Research Policy 33, 599–616 (2004)
21. Stokols, D., Harvey, R., Gress, J., Fuqua, J., Phillips, K.: In Vivo Studies of Transdisciplinary Scientific Collaboration. Lessons Learned and Implications for Active Living Research. American Journal of Preventive Medicine 28, 202–213 (2005)
22. Dosi, G., Nelson, R.R., Winter, S.G.: The Nature and Dynamics of Organizational Capabilities. Oxford University Press, Oxford (2000)
23. Sydow, J., Duschek, S., Möllering, G., Rometsch, M.: Kompetenzentwicklung in Netzwerken: eine typologische Studie. Westdeutscher Verlag, Wiesbaden (2003)
24. March, J.G.: Exploration and Exploitation in Organizational Learning. Organization Science 2, 71–87 (1991)
25. Lambe, C.J., Spekman, R.E., Hunt, S.D.: Alliance Competence, Resources, and Alliance Success: Conceptualization, Measurement, and Initial Test. Journal of the Academy of Marketing Science 30, 141–158 (2002)
26. Dyer, J.H., Singh, H.: The Relational View: Cooperative Strategy and Sources of Interorganizational Competitive Advantage. Academy of Management Review 23, 660–679 (1998)

Knowledge Value Creation Characteristics of Virtual Teams: A Case Study in the Construction Sector

Chalee Vorakulpipat[1] and Yacine Rezgui[2]

[1] National Electronics and Computer Technology Center, 112 Thailand Science Park, Phahonyothin Rd., Klong 1, Klong Luang, Pathumthani 12120, Thailand
chalee.vorakulpipat@nectec.or.th
[2] School of Engineering, Cardiff University, Queen's Buildings, The Parade, Cardiff CF24 3AA, United Kingdom
RezguiY@cardiff.ac.uk

Abstract. Any knowledge environment aimed at virtual teams should promote identification, access, capture and retrieval of relevant knowledge anytime / anywhere, while nurturing the social activities that underpin the knowledge sharing and creation process. In fact, socio-cultural issues play a critical role in the successful implementation of Knowledge Management (KM), and constitute a milestone towards value creation. The findings indicate that Knowledge Management Systems (KMS) promote value creation when they embed and nurture the social conditions that bind and bond team members together. Furthermore, technology assets, human networks, social capital, intellectual capital, and change management are identified as essential ingredients that have the potential to ensure effective knowledge value creation.

Keywords: Knowledge management, value creation, virtual teams, construction sector.

1 Introduction

Construction is a knowledge intensive industry characterized by some unique work settings and virtual organization-like modus operandi (including fragmentation, non-collocation, and short-term partnering of teams on projects) that differentiate it from other industrial sectors [1, 2].

It is argued that team formation is influenced not only by the inherent characteristics of the sector, but also by an increasing sophistication and complexity of design and construction processes triggered by the need to address higher building performance and quality standards, as well as the continuous introduction of new techniques and materials. These characteristics require multi-disciplinary teams with specialized expertise that have the potential to create value out of their existing knowledge. Therefore, the support for the formation of ad-hoc virtual teams becomes essential. However, more empirical research is needed to understand the socio-technical features which influence knowledge value creation in the fragmented environment of the construction industry. This is the gap the paper is addressing. A multiple case study approach is employed involving several organizations across Europe.

L.M. Camarinha-Matos et al. (Eds.): PRO-VE 2009, IFIP AICT 307, pp. 157–167, 2009.
© IFIP International Federation for Information Processing 2009

The paper, first, presents the concept of knowledge value creation, and then the research methodology employed in this study. The research results are then given, followed by the discussion. Finally, the conclusions are drawn.

2 Knowledge Value Creation

The gaining popularity of Knowledge Management has been reinforced by the quest for innovation and value creation [3, 4]. In this context, KM is perceived as a framework for designing an organization's goals, structures, and processes so that the organization can use what it knows to learn and create value for its customers and community [5].

Innovation in construction is 'the act of introducing and using new ideas, technologies, products and/or processes aimed at solving problems, viewing things differently, improving efficiency and effectiveness, or enhancing standards of living' [6]. It is argued that construction project-based forms of enterprise are inadequately addressed in the innovation literature [7]. Project-based organization focuses on the production and/or delivery side of a firm's business [8], and is characterized by 'the coexistence of a continuing organization structure, typically based on functional departments with a temporary organizational structure based on project teams' [9]. Firms across a variety of industries are increasingly experimenting with project-based models of organization to accommodate and exploit fundamental changes in the nature and roles of markets and technologies [10, 11].

Knowledge value creation is grounded in the appropriate combination of technology assets, human networks, social capital, and intellectual capital, facilitated by change management [12, 13]. Alavi and Leidner [14] suggest that *technology* (in the form of knowledge management systems) is commonly used to sustain value creation. The concept of Community of Practice (CoP) [15] was introduced as an effective social activity to promote and nurture *human networks* which in turn motivate people to share and create knowledge. Any process within *human networks* resulting in the creation of social values is defined as *social capital*. In this context, the *social capital* of an organization emerges as an essential ingredient to help employees develop trust, respect, social cohesion, and understanding of others. Because *social capital* emphasizes on collectivism rather than individualism, distributed community members will be more inclined to connect and use electronic networks when they are motivated to share knowledge within these virtual spaces or KMS [16]. These may help foster *social capital* by providing the context and history of interaction and offering a motivational element (e.g. reward) to encourage people to share knowledge with each other [16]. The *intellectual capital* of an organization encompasses organizational learning, innovation, skills, competencies, expertise and capabilities [17]. Liebowitz and Suen [18] suggest a strong and positive relationship between the value creation capability and *intellectual capital* of an organization, pointing to factors such as training, R&D investment, employee satisfaction, and relationships development. Lastly, *change management* plays an increasingly important role in sustaining "leading edge" competitiveness for organizations in times of rapid change and increased competition [19-21], and the future has only two predictable features – 'change and resistance to change' and the very survival of organizations will depend upon their ability not only to adapt to, but also to master these challenges. Therefore, study of the change process is necessary to create the requisite organizational and societal values [22].

3 Methodology

The research involves a European consortium from Finland, France, Germany and UK comprising key research and industry players in the sector. The specific aim of the research is to explore the distinctive social and cultural features which influence the creation of knowledge values effectively in the organizational socio-cultural environment of the construction industry. Therefore, the following research question underpins the research: *"What are the distinctive social and cultural features which influence the creation of knowledge values in the organizational socio-cultural environment of the construction industry?"*. The methodology employed the principles of Action Research, a qualitative research method that uniquely associates research and practice through change and reflection [23]. A multiple case study approach is adopted involving four case study organizations (illustrated in Table 1).

Table 1. Case study organizations

Case Study	Profile	**Business Activity**	**Country**
Company A	SME	Engineering	France
Company B	Large Organization	Design & Construction	UK
Company C	Large Organization	Design & Construction	Germany
Company D	Large Organization	Design & Construction	Finland

Three main instruments were used to gather data required to address the research questions: participant observation, semi-structured interviews, and documentation. Participant observation involved the researchers being immersed in the work environment of the end-users; the interviews were conducted with 24 senior staff (holding the positions of business unit, IT and human resource managers) across the four organizations; documentation involved analyzing corporate and project documents. The aim of the interviews was to analyze the strategic positioning of each organization and its technological and organizational capabilities and competencies.

4 Findings

The interview results indicate an overall good awareness of the respondents in relation to the challenges faced by their organization. They have identified several main factors critical to their (organization) future growth and success. These have been categorized into four main areas listed in order of identified importance: Production (factors including costs, market knowledge and product development), Human Resources (factors such as knowledge sharing, training, and human resource management, including motivation and competence), Organization / Process (factors including teamwork, political decisions and customer relations), and Technology (factors including technology adoption: perceived limitations and future needs).

Many interviewees highlighted the need for a shared project knowledge base in a virtual team context. There is a strong belief that this would improve communication and cohesion amongst team members, and promote shared language and mental models across teams, leading to the development of trust and culture of knowledge sharing, which concurs with recent literature [24, 25].

A majority of the respondents highlighted the limitations of their current systems in supporting collaborative working, as these do not integrate seamlessly with the engineering applications used on a daily-basis, and provide therefore limited support to the practice. They have expressed concerns about the invasive nature of ICT and the need to adapt to continuous technology introduction on projects. This corroborates the interviewees' analysis on this issue: they have indicated that ICT require constant adaptation and re-configuration for new use and deployment, while offering limited growth path and scalability. In fact, gathered data suggest that team members on projects are affected more by the newness of the technology being used than by the newness of the team structure itself. The interviewees have pointed out that these problems of technology adoption can have a negative effect on individual satisfaction with the team experience and performance, as also reported in the literature [26, 27]. Conversely, when team members are able to deal with technology related challenges, high trust develops [28].

Also, a majority of respondents reported that they tend to be tied to a physical location (mainly their office) to do their jobs. For instance, the information available in the form of written specifications and drawings produced during the design stage is required by contractors to construct the building facility. However, access to this information from the Construction site tends to be limited due to the lack of availability of software / hardware resources and network facilities. Therefore, software is usually accessed from the office, and in very few instances on site. Support and maintenance is provided through many points of service representing the different ICT technology licensees.

A large majority of respondents have indicated the need for more adapted training. While specialized software training is available, respondents have highlighted the need for continuous training and learning so as to improve their level of ICT awareness and maturity. Gathered data suggests that adapted training can foster cohesiveness, team work, commitment to team goals, individual satisfaction, and higher perceived decision quality, as also highlighted in the literature [27, 29]. However, respondents did also report that short time scales, due to simultaneous involvement in projects, creates additional pressure, and leaves little time for training.

In terms of team setting, while gathered data suggests that the process involved in setting up a teamwork solution is complex and time-consuming, the team-building exercise is overall perceived as essential in order to establish a clear team structure and shared norms, as confirmed in related literature [25, 30]. Early face-to-face meetings during the team's launch phase tend to improve the team's project definition [31], to foster socialization, trust, and respect among team members [25, 32], and to enhance the effectiveness of subsequent electronic communications [33].

Several interviewees have reported the issue of clash of cultures on projects (due to their multi-national and multi-cultural dimension), and have expressed a need for the goals of the project to be shared and embraced collectively. In fact, differences in organizational affiliations can reduce shared understanding of context and can inhibit a team's ability to develop a shared sense of identity [34]. An important number of respondents expressed concerns about the bureaucratic and hierarchical culture in their organization, which is in several instances reproduced in teams. Issues related to motivation, trust and team cohesion have been raised. High motivation levels and job satisfaction are critical success factors in any organizational environment and even more important in a virtual environment. It was suggested that 'participatory' type of culture, with a flat structure, open communication channels, and participation and involvement in decision-making, enhances sharing of information and facilitates team cohesion, which in turn promotes trust. These are indeed important problems faced by virtual teams [35-38]. This, as reported in [26], contributes to improve employees' overall satisfaction and job effectiveness. Indeed people work together because they trust one another and successful virtual teams pay special attention to building trust throughout their lifecycle [37]. Interviewees pointed out that people generally tend to trust people rather than companies and that trust ultimately emerges where communicated information is reliable, people stand by their promises, and outcomes equal or exceed expectations. Teams with trust converge more easily [30], organize their work more quickly, and manage themselves better [37].

The interviewees reported that value creation is best reflected in their sustainability and health and safety initiatives. Sustainability goals can only be achieved if existing and new resources of knowledge and expertise inform construction activities. Some of this comes in the form of good practice and standards, but much comes from situated and contextual appreciations of sustainability goals and local practices developed within and across projects and organizational boundaries. In this respect, the participants felt strongly that knowledge sharing initiatives provide means to capture, represent, and disseminate sustainability information and experiences acquired on projects, and enable these to be nurtured within and across organizations and applied successfully in projects with real impacts. In response to the critical situation of health and safety on construction projects and the consequences in terms of image and reputation to the sector, the respondents reported the use of basic knowledge management solutions to record the number of recent incidents and then making these widely available and accessible through the company Intranet to all employees, including designers. The participants felt strongly that the capture, representation, and dissemination of health and safety measures create real values in terms of reduction of accidents on sites and improvement of the overall well being of staff and future users.

5 Discussion

It has been argued earlier (section 2) that technology assets, human networks, social capital, intellectual capital, and change management are important factors that underpin value creation activities [12, 13, 39]. This section answers the research question formulated earlier in the paper by articulating the findings around the above factors.

5.1 Human Networks

Interviewees have expressed concerns about the potential lack of face-to-face interactions during the virtual team lifecycle and in particular during the inception stage where the vision, mission, and goals can be communicated and shared. They have suggested the need to develop strong communication and collaboration protocols, including code of conduct, standards for availability and acknowledgement.

Team collaboration through face-to-face communication creates stronger social relationships while these are difficult to establish in virtual contexts due to the lack of emotional expressions. Therefore, team members in a virtual team are aware of the greater societal acceptance of face-to-face rather than virtual interaction. Virtual communication such as email may form bridges between people (e.g. across different geographical locations) but it does not bond team members enough together. Construction relies heavily on ad-hoc relationships between individuals and companies. This seems to influence the success of a project.

That is, collectivist or participatory culture is needed in a team to help create network ties. Therefore, the organization's knowledge values must be created through the network of relationships possessed by people in collectivist cultures. Strong social relationships and collectiveness are perceived as a critical factor to create more opportunities for team members to participate in problem-solving and decision making, and offer a range of different skills, abilities, knowledge, and experience to ensure that creative ideas are supported.

5.2 Social Capital

Much of valuable knowledge is tacit and nurtured in small social networks. It was suggested that a "participatory" type culture, with a flat structure, open communication channels, and participation and involvement in decision-making, enhances sharing of information and facilitates team cohesion, which in turn promotes respect and trust. This contributes to improving employees' overall satisfaction and job effectiveness.

A culture that recognizes tacit knowledge and social networks results in the promotion of open dialogue between staff allowing them to develop social links and share understandings, as outlined in Rezgui [12]. The need to share tacit knowledge by face-to-face social communication has emerged from the research, to foster social capital. This method is perceived to (a) break down barriers between employees and management, (b) establish stronger relationships among them, (c) allow employees to reduce personal barriers and gain confidence, and (d) practice and improve their knowledge sharing skills.

Social networks can be facilitated and nurtured by providing informal forums that can be assimilated into communities of practice. These are complemented with virtual spaces to share knowledge (including sensitive information) protected by a role access control system. The interviewees confirmed that employees need the creation of strong relationships and networks ties across projects and organizations and avoid any conflicts so that to maintain a good level of relationship between project members. In fact, it has been shown that human networks can only be effective if the social conditions that underpin collaboration are met (including trust). This is where conscientious behavior reveals important. This emphasizes the role that social capital plays in creating organizational value underpinned by strong human networks. A participatory culture helps develop trust, respect, and understanding for others at different levels in the construction sector. Clearly, a culture of confidence and trust in which people are willing to communicate is perceived to initiate KM.

5.3 Technology

The results suggest that controlled access to information and knowledge enhances trust in technology, an important factor in promoting a culture of knowledge sharing facilitated by ICT. Moreover, the results show that there is a lack of a clear vision and ICT strategy. The prevailing policy based on acquiring off-the-shelf solutions fails to deliver. These commercial solutions tend neither to accommodate existing practices nor build on existing corporate solutions.

The results show the concerns about lack of social-oriented communication and social events due to the tendency to completely rely on computer technology, which results in people feeling that they are usually "stuck" in front of their computers. This perception leads to KM fallacies or traps that directly influence the perceived functionality of IT applications for the support of KM initiatives [40]. As also reported in Huysman and Wulf [16], these fallacies relate to the tendency of organizations to concentrate too much on the IT role supporting KM practices, especially knowledge sharing, resulting in the "IT trap". It is important to recognize that IT is not independent from the social environment, as it is not the technology itself, but the way people use it that determines the role of IT in supporting knowledge management practices [16]. Therefore, the organization's success with the use of IT will not depend on IT skills, but the appropriate social context that can benefit from electronic communication technology [41]. This requires the use of socially embedded technologies or collaborative system such as KMS or groupware, influenced by the belief structures (perceived ease-of-use and perceived usefulness) of TAM [42]. It is suggested that collaboration through groupware is highly valued overall, and the functionality like discussion forum has been described as important in nurturing knowledge sharing within a social context, as confirmed in related literature [43, 44].

5.4 Intellectual Capital

Issues pertinent to organizational learning, innovation, skills, and best practices were raised. These also include improved competence management and sustained motivation through adapted training and incentive / reward systems. Whilst the organization has an overall good awareness of KM practices, there are some limitations that may have caused only a gradual improvement in KM over several years. These limitations revealed the following issues:

- Employees have expressed strong concerns about sharing their knowledge, arguing about confidentiality implications and Intellectual Property Rights (IPR) issues as they fear that their knowledge will be stolen or given away to others.
- Dominant bureaucratic (hierarchical) organizational structure in place is perceived to inhibit the development of skills and best practices amongst employees and managers who are of higher social rank, also leading to personal barriers.

The coding and sharing of best practice is one of the common initiatives employed to initiate organizational KM [14], and knowledge sharing can take place only once a corporate knowledge repository is made widely accessible to staff [45]. These have helped improve knowledge connectivity, access, and transfer across the construction sites.

An appropriate representation of the history of knowledge sharing activities may be useful since it allows human actors to better understand and refer to past interactions [16]. As reported in the results, the respondents promoted their idea about recording a number of recent incidents and making them available through the organization Intranet. Not only this, it is suggested that this explicit knowledge sharing method should be combined with the tacit knowledge sharing method. This concept is in line with the concept of how to augment collocated communication spaces with complex materials [46]. They present the Envisionment and Discovery Collaboratory (EDC), an environment in which participants collaboratively discuss issues of mutual interest. The EDC supports face-to-face discussion activities by bringing together individuals who share a common problem. Moreover, the EDC provides an additional systematic feature to store historic data. Computer recognition of physical representations is designed to allow the computer to reduce the effort of capturing and formalizing problem information. They perceive that face-to-face discussions without some capture mechanism may be rich interactions, but only participants around the table benefit, and when the discussion is over the interaction is lost.

5.5 Change Management

Change management may include technical and human issues. In terms of technical sides, interviewees expressed concerns about the invasive nature of ICT and the need to adapt to continuous technology introduction across projects in which they are involved, suggesting that project team members are affected more by the newness of the technology being used than of the team structure itself (which changes from one project to another). They pointed out that these problems of technology adoption can have a negative effect on individual satisfaction with the team experience and performance. Conversely, when team members are able to deal with technology related challenges, a culture of knowledge sharing is promoted. There is a poor software adoption culture as ICT solutions, including previously deployed KMS, tend to lack flexibility and scalability as the needs of the organization and users evolve.

In terms of human issues, the participants have acknowledged that knowledge value creation would imply new approaches to the management of human resources, information and knowledge within their organization. While the potential gains have been well articulated, concerns have been raised in that the necessary changes might be resisted. Therefore, to be effective, any KM program should be incorporated within a change management program that promotes a "participatory" type of culture while taking into account the team-based structure and discipline-oriented nature of the Construction industry.

Clearly, the research acknowledges the pivotal and strategic role that human networks, social capital, technology, and intellectual capital play in enhancing value creation in the construction sector. This has resulted in increased awareness, knowledge quality, and business intelligence, which have in turn triggered a value added dimension that did not exist prior to initiating the change processes.

6 Conclusion

It is vital that the construction sector migrates to a knowledge value creation culture where technology assets, human networks, social capital, intellectual capital, and change management must be blended successfully to ensure effective knowledge value creation. Understanding the social and cultural features, which influence knowledge value creation in the fragmented socio-cultural environment of the construction industry, is needed. As far as the research question is concerned, crucial cultural features emerging from the results include collectiveness and conscientiousness. *Collectiveness* represents collectivist culture and social relationship and *Conscientiousness* represents avoidance of uncertainty and risk and being patient with uncertain situations.

Firstly, the study shows that the organizations clearly support employees' opportunity to work in a team rather than to work individually. Collectivist or participatory culture is needed in a team to help create network ties. Therefore, the organization's knowledge values must be created through the network of relationships possessed by people in collectivist cultures. The cases confirm that strong social relationships and collectiveness are perceived as a critical factor to create more opportunities for team members to participate in problem-solving and decision making, and offer a range of different skills, abilities, knowledge, and experience to ensure that creative ideas are supported. a knowledge-based organization needs all of its employees to share a culture that promotes the virtues of knowledge acquisition and sharing, requiring a number of essential attributes, as pointed out by Rezgui [12]. The collective characteristic of a virtual team is exemplified by the dimension given to team working. However, it has been shown that human networks can only be effective if the social conditions that underpin collaboration are met (including trust). This emphasizes the role that social capital plays in creating organizational value underpinned by strong human networks. A participatory culture helps develop trust, respect, and understanding for others at different levels in the construction sector. Clearly, a culture of confidence and trust in which people are willing to communicate is perceived to initiate knowledge value creation.

Conscientiousness may encourage opportunities for creating relationships and network ties among teams. However, the research so far does not claim that social capital with conscientiousness is effective. It may create only the "opportunity" to bridge people (such as those who are from different geographical locations) together, but does not bond them together. Moreover, conscientiousness may help channel people in the organization to the same goals and mission. Nevertheless, it does not confirm that this is an organizational advantage as conscientious employees have never raised concerns, requests or comments explicitly, so that the management does not know the employees' needs.

To sum up, the research has explored and identified distinctive socio-cultural features influencing knowledge value creation of virtual teams in the construction industry. More research is needed to validate the above results and deepen the understanding of the socio-organizational factors affecting value creation in industry.

References

1. Rezgui, Y.: Review of Information and the State of the Art of Knowledge Management Practices in the Construction Industry. The Knowledge Engineering Review 16, 241–254 (2001)

2. Rezgui, Y.: Exploring Virtual Team-Working Effectiveness in the Construction Sector. Interacting with Computers 19, 96–112 (2007)
3. Aranda, D.A., Molina-Fernandez, L.M.: Determinants of Innovation through a Knowledge-based Theory Lens. Industrial Management & Data Systems 102, 289–296 (2002)
4. Huseby, M., Chou, S.T.: Applying a Knowledge-focused Management Philosophy to Immature Economies. Industrial Management & Data Systems 102, 17–25 (2003)
5. Choo, C.W.: Closing the Cognitive Gaps: How People Process Information. In: Marchand, D., Davenport, T., Dickson, T. (eds.) Mastering Information Management, pp. 245–253. FT-Prentice Hall, Harlow (2000)
6. CERF: Guidelines for Moving Innovations into Practice. In: CERF, Working Draft Guidelines for the CERF International Symposium and Innovative Technology Trade Show Washington, DC (2000)
7. Barrett, P., Sexton, M.: Innovation in Small, Project-Based Construction Firms. British Journal of Management 17, 331–346 (2006)
8. Artto, K.A.: Global Project Business and Dynamics of Change. Helsinki: TEKES/PMA (1998)
9. Grant, R.M.: Contemporary Strategic Analysis: Concepts, Techniques, Applications. Blackwell Publishers, Oxford (1997)
10. DeFillippi, R.J., Arthur, M.B.: Paradox in Project-Based Enterprise: The Case of Film Making. California Management Review 40, 1–15 (1998)
11. Kanter, R.M.: The Frontiers of Management. Harvard Business School Press (1997)
12. Rezgui, Y.: Knowledge Systems and Value Creation: An Action Research Investigation. Industrial Management & Data Systems 107, 166–182 (2007)
13. Vorakulpipat, C., Rezgui, Y.: Value Creation: The Future of Knowledge Management. Knowledge Engineering Review 23, 283–294 (2008)
14. Alavi, M., Leidner, D.: Review: Knowledge Management and Knowledge Management Systems: Conceptual Foundations and Research Issues. MIS Quarterly 25, 107–136 (2001)
15. Wenger, E., McDermott, R., Snyder, W.M.: Cultivating Communities of Practice: A Guide to Managing Knowledge. Harvard Business School Press, Cambridge (2002)
16. Huysman, M., Wulf, V.: IT to Support Knowledge Sharing in Communities, towards a Social Capital Analysis. Journal of Information Technology 21, 40–51 (2006)
17. Rastogi, P.N.: Knowledge Management and Intellectual Capital – The New Virtuous Reality of Competitiveness. Human Systems Management 19, 39–48 (2000)
18. Liebowitz, J., Suen, C.Y.: Developing Knowledge Management Metrics for Measuring Intellectual Capital. Journal of Intellectual Capital 1, 54–67 (2000)
19. McAdam, R., Galloway, A.: Enterprise Resource Planning and Organisational Innovation: A Management Perspective. Industrial Management & Data Systems 105, 280–290 (2005)
20. Wheatcroft, J.: Organizational change, the story so far. Industrial Management & Data Systems 100, 5–9 (2000)
21. Reddy, S.B., Reddy, R.: Competitive agility and the challenge of legacy information systems. Industrial Management & Data Systems 102, 5–16 (2002)
22. Christiansson, P.: Next Generation Knowledge Management Systems for the Construction Industry. In: CIB W78 Construction IT Bridging the Distance, Auckland (2003)
23. Avison, D., Lau, F., Myers, M., Nielsen, P.A.: Action research. Communications of the ACM 42, 94–97 (1999)
24. Crampton, C.: The Mutual Knowledge Problem and its Consequences for Dispersed Collaboration. Organization Science 12, 346–371 (2001)
25. Suchan, J., Hayzak, G.: The Communication Characteristics of Virtual Teams: A Case Study. IEEE Transactions on Professional Communications 44, 174–186 (2001)

26. Kayworth, T., Leidner, D.: The Global Virtual Manager: A Prescription for Success. European Management Journal 18, 183–194 (2000)
27. Van Ryssen, S., Hayes Godar, S.: Going International Without Going International: Multinational Virtual Teams. Journal of International Management 6, 49–60 (2000)
28. Jarvenpaa, S., Leidner, D.: Communication and Trust in Global Virtual Teams. Organization Science 10, 791–815 (1999)
29. Warkentin, M., Beranek, P.M.: Training to Improve Virtual Team Communication. Information Systems Journal 9, 271–289 (1999)
30. Sarker, S., Lau, F., Sahay, S.: Using an adapted grounded theory approach for inductive theory building about virtual team development. Database for Advances in Information Systems 32, 38–56 (2001)
31. Ramesh, V., Dennis, A.R.: The Object-Oriented Team: Lessons for Virtual Teams from Global Software Development. In: HICSS35, Hawaii (2002)
32. Maznevski, M., Chudoba, K.: Bridging Space Over Time: Global Virtual Team Dynamics and Effectiveness. Organization Science 11, 473–492 (2001)
33. Powell, T.C., Dent-Micallef, A.: Information Technology as Competitive Advantage: The Role of Human, Business, and Technology Resources. Strategic Management Journal 18, 375–405 (1999)
34. Espinosa, J.A., Cummings, J.N., Wilson, J.M., Pearce, B.M.: Team boundary issues across multiple global firms. Journal of Management Information Systems 19, 157–190 (2003)
35. Kezsbom, D.: Creating teamwork in virtual teams. Cost Engineering 42, 33–36 (2000)
36. Alexander, S.: Virtual teams going global. InfoWorld 46, 55–56 (2000)
37. Lipnack, J., Stamps, J.: Virtual Teams: People Working Across Boundaries with Technology, 2nd edn. Wiley, New York (2000)
38. Solomon, C.: Managing virtual teams. Workforce 80, 60–65 (2001)
39. Vorakulpipat, C., Rezgui, Y.: An Evolutionary and Interpretive Perspective to Knowledge Management. Journal of Knowledge Management 12, 17–34 (2008)
40. Huysman, M., de Wit, D.: Knowledge Sharing in Practice. Kluwer Academics, Dordrecht (2002)
41. Zack, M.H., McKenny, J.L.: Social Context and Interaction in Ongoing Computer-Supported Management Groups. In: Smith, D.E. (ed.) Knowledge, Groupware and the Internet. Butterworth-Heinemann, Boston (2000)
42. Davis, F.D.: Perceived Usefulness, Perceived Ease of Use, and User Acceptance of Information Technology. MIS Quarterly 13, 319–340 (1989)
43. Ellis, C.A., Gibbs, S.J., Rein, G.L.: Groupware: Some Issues and Experiences. Communications of the ACM 34, 38–58 (1991)
44. Poltrock, S., Grudin, J.: Groupware and Workflow: A Survey of Systems and Behavioral Issues. In: CHI 1995, ACM Conference on Human Factors in Computing Systems, Denver (1995)
45. Davenport, T., Prusak, L.: Working Knowledge: How Organizations Manage What They Know. Harvard Business School Press, Boston (1998)
46. Fischer, G., Scharff, E., Ye, Y.: Fostering Social Creativity by Increasing Social Capital. In: Huysman, M., Wulf, V. (eds.) Social Capital and Information Technology. MIT-Press, Cambridge (2004)

Social Protocols for Agile Virtual Teams

Willy Picard

Dept. of Information Technology, Poznan University of Economics,
Mansfelda 4, 60-854 Poznan, Poland
Willy.Picard@ue.poznan.pl

Abstract. Despite many works on collaborative networked organizations (CNOs), CSCW, groupware, workflow systems and social networks, computer support for virtual teams is still insufficient, especially support for agility, i.e. the capability of virtual team members to rapidly and cost efficiently adapt the way they interact to changes. In this paper, requirements for computer support for agile virtual teams are presented. Next, an extension of the concept of social protocol is proposed as a novel model supporting agile interactions within virtual teams. The extended concept of social protocol consists of an extended social network and a workflow model.

1 Introduction

Computer support for Human-to-Human (H2H) interactions has a long history in computer science: from early visionary ideas of Douglas Engelbart at the Stanford Research Institute's Augmentation Research Center on groupware in the 60's, through CSCW and workflows in the 80's, and with social network sites in the 2000's. However, computer support for agile H2H interactions is still insufficient in most collaborative situations.

Among various reasons for the weak support for H2H interactions, two reasons may be distinguished: first, many *social elements* are involved in the H2H interaction. An example of such a social element may be the roles played by humans during their interactions. Social elements are usually difficult to model, e.g. integrating hierarchical relations among collaborators to collaboration models. A second reason is the *adaptation* capabilities of humans which are not only far more advanced than adaptation capabilities of software entities, but also are not taken into account in existing models for collaboration processes.

The insufficient support for human-to-human interactions over a network is a strong limitation for a wide adoption of *professional virtual communities* (PVCs). As mentioned in [1], "professional virtual community represents the combination of concepts of virtual community and professional community. Virtual communities are defined as social systems of networks of individuals, who use computer technologies to mediate their relationships. Professional communities provide environments for professionals to share the body of knowledge of their professions [...]". According to Chituc and Azevedo [2], little attention has been paid to the social perspective on Collaborative Networks (CN) business environment, including obviously professional virtual communities in which social aspects are of high importance. Additionally, the

L.M. Camarinha-Matos et al. (Eds.): PRO-VE 2009, IFIP AICT 307, pp. 168–176, 2009.
© IFIP International Federation for Information Processing 2009

adaptation capabilities of humans have been the object of few works [3]. As a consequence, support for *agile virtual teams* (VT) is currently insufficient.

Virtual team agility (VTA) refers to the capabilities of a group of human beings, the VT members, to rapidly and cost efficiently adapt the way they interact to changes. Changes may occur:

- within the VT: e.g., a collaborator may be temporary unavailable or he/she may acquire new skills,
- in the environment of the VT: e.g., a breakdown of a machine may occur, weather conditions may prevent the realization of a given task.

In this paper, we present a model which provides support for agile VTs based on the concept of social protocols. In Section 2, requirements for a computer support for agile VTs are presented. Next, the concept of social protocols supporting agile VTs is detailed. The proposed solution is then discussed. Section 5 concludes the paper.

2 Requirements for Support for Agile Virtual Teams

2.1 A Model of the Social Environment

A first requirement for support for agile VTs is the modeling of the *social environment* within which interactions take place. Each VT consists of at least two members, each of them having her/his own social position. By social position, we mean a set of interdependencies with entities (generally individuals or organizations): e.g. a VT member has colleagues, works in a given company, and belongs to a family.

VTA implies a rapid adaptation of the VT to new conditions. The social environment is a core tool in the adaptation process as it provides information about available resources VT members are aware of:

- within the VT: e.g., if a VT member is temporary unavailable, another person in the social environment may substitute for the unavailable VT member,
- in the environment of the VT: e.g., if weather conditions prevent the realization of a given task, new VT members which were not initially involved in the realization of the cancelled task may be needed to overcome it.

A partial answer to the question of modeling a social environment may be found in popular in the last five years social network sites, such as LinkedIn [4], MySpace [5], Orkut [6], Facebook [7], to name a few. Boyd and Ellison [8] define social network sites as "web-based services that allow individuals to (1) construct a public or semi-public profile within a bounded system, (2) articulate a list of other users with whom they share a connection, and (3) view and traverse their list of connections and those made by others within the system." The second and third points of this definition illustrate a key feature of social network sites, i.e. social network sites allow users for an easy access to information about persons they know (friends, colleagues, family members) and potentially about contacts of these persons.

However, the model of social environment adopted in social network sites captures only interdependencies among individuals or organizations. The interdependencies with information systems, e.g. web services, are an important element of the landscape of interactions within VTs: while individuals represent the "who'" part of the interactions, information systems usually represent the "how" part. A VT member (the individual) performs some activity with the help of a tool (the information system). Therefore, we claim that a model of the social environment for interactions within VTs should integrate both interdependencies among VT members and interdependencies among VT members and information systems.

Such a model of social environment would allow VT members to react to new situations not only by changing the set of members but also by changing the set of tools. Additionally, such a model would allow VT members for agility with respect to changes related with information systems: e.g., if an information system is unavailable, VT members may seek for an alternative in their social environment.

It should be noticed that, while the social environment encompasses the professional virtual community (PVC), some elements of the social environment can be external to the PVC. During the adaptation process of VTs, the identification of required resources, either VT members or information systems, should not be limited to the PVC, as some valuable resource may come from personal relations of VT members, external to the PVC.

2.2 Structured Interactions within Virtual Teams

Supporting agile VTs requires guidance for VT members about tasks they may perform at a given moment of time. Such a guidance allows VT members for *focusing on appropriate tasks* that need to be fulfilled at a given moment of time, in a given collaboration situation, instead of facing all potential tasks that they may perform.

The tasks that a given VT member may perform depend also on the *role* he/she is playing within a given VT. Therefore support for VTA implies the mapping between VT members and roles they are playing within a given VT. Additionally, interactions within VTs are often structured according to collaborative patterns [9, 10]. In similar situations, in different VTs, members perform activities whom successiveness is identical among the various VTs: e.g., a brainstorming session consists of 5 phases:

1. the chairman presents the problem,
2. every participant presents his/her ideas,
3. the chairman classifies the ideas,
4. every participant may comment any idea,
5. the chairman summarizes the brainstorming session.

In the former example, each phase may be decomposed as a sequence of activities to be performed, with activities associated to roles. Interactions within VTs could therefore be structured with the help of a *process* and an *associated process model* specifying the sequences of activities, the association between activities and roles, and the mapping between VT members and roles.

Results of studies in workflow technology and process modeling [11 – 14] provide a strong foundation for support for structured interactions within VTs based on the concepts of workflow and process models.

2.3 Layered Interaction Models

The concept of process model presented in the former subsection as a mean to structure interaction within VTs has to be considered at three levels of abstraction:

- *abstract process model*: a process model is abstract if it defines the sequence of activities to be potentially performed by VT members playing a given role, without specifying neither the implementation of activities, nor the attribution of roles to VT members. As an example, an abstract process model for a brainstorming session may specify that, first, a chairman presents the brainstorming session problem, next, participants present their ideas. Neither the implementation of the presentation of the problem and participants' ideas, nor the VT members are defined in the abstract process model.
- *implemented process model*: a process model is implemented if it defines the implementation of activities defined in an associated abstract process model. As an example, an implemented process model based on the brainstorming abstract process model formerly presented may specify that the presentation of the brainstorming session problem will be implemented as an email to all par-ticipants, while the presentation of ideas will be performed as posts to a forum.
- *instantiated process model*: a process model is instantiated if the attribution of roles to VT members for a given implemented process model has been set. Additionally, an instantiated process model, referred also as *process instance*, keeps trace of the current state of the interactions within a given VT. As an example, *the* former implemented process model may be instantiated by specifying who plays the chairman role and who the participants are. Additionally, the process retains its current state which may for instance be "participants are presenting ideas".

The following analogy with object-oriented programming illustrates the three levels of abstraction presented above:

- abstract process models are similar to interfaces or abstract classes. An abstract process model does not rely, nor provide an implementation of activities, as an interface does not provide an implementation of methods;
- implemented process models are similar to classes. An implemented process model provides an implementation of activities, as a class provides an implementation of methods.
- instantiated process models are similar to objects. An instantiated process model rules the interactions according to a given implemented process model and has its own state, as an object behaves according to its class and has its own state.

The separation of these three levels of abstraction leads to *process model reuse*. By separating the logical structure of interactions from its implementation, an abstract process model may be reuse in various contexts, IT environments, VTs. The PVC may provide its members access to a library of abstract and implemented process models. As a consequence, VT members facing some unpredicted situation may identify an already defined abstract or implemented process model allowing them to solve their problem. Then, the VT may react rapidly by just (eventually implementing and) instantiating the process. The brainstorming process presented above is an example of an abstract or implemented process that may be reuse by various VTs in a given PVC to interact in an agile way.

2.4 Adaptability

Adaptability is a core requirement of support for VTA. Adaptability refers in this paper to the capability of a VT to modify *at run-time* the model ruling its interactions.

In typical workflow management systems, two parts may be distinguished: a *design time* part allows for definition of workflow schemas while the *run-time* part is responsible for execution of workflow instances. A main limitation of typical workflow management systems is the fact that once a workflow schema has been instantiated, the execution of the workflow instance must stick to the workflow schema till the end of the workflow instance execution.

PVCs are a typical case of environments in which there is a strong need for the possibility to modify a workflow instance at run-time. Such modifications are usually needed to deal with situations which have not been foreseen nor modeled in the associated workflow schema. Adaptability refers to the possibility to modify a running instantiated process model to new situations which have not been foreseen and modeled in the associated abstract/implemented process model.

3 Social Protocols

Computer support for VTA requires novel models to support requirements presented in Section 2. The solution presented in this paper is based on the concept of *social protocol*. This concept has been presented first in 2006 [15], based on the concept of *collaboration protocol* [3]. A generic extended version of the concept of social protocol, including elements related with the modeling of the social environment, has been formally presented in [16]. The application of extended social protocols to PVCs and VTs is presented in this section.

3.1 Abstract Social Protocols

An abstract social protocol, SP_a, consists of two parts:

- an *abstract social network*: a direct graph modeling interdependencies among *abstract resources*. An abstract social network models the social environment required for a particular collaboration pattern.
- an *abstract interaction protocol:* a direct graph modeling interdependencies among *abstract activities*. An abstract interaction protocol models the sequence of activities in a particular collaboration pattern.

An example of an abstract social protocol for brainstorming is presented in Fig. 1.

In an abstract social network, vertices represent abstract resources that may support or be actively involved in the collaboration process, such as a collaboration role or a class of information systems. Edges represents relations between resources associated with social interaction types, such as "works with", "has already collaborated with" among roles, or "is the owner", "uses" between a role and a class of information systems. Labels associated with edges are not predefined, as the concept of social protocol should be flexible enough to encompass new types of interdependencies among resources. Therefore, new labels may be freely created at design time.

In an abstract interaction protocol, vertices represent:

- abstract activities that may be performed during the collaboration process, such as "present the brainstorming problem" or "present an idea". Activities are associated with a given role, e.g. only the chairman may present the brainstorming problem;
- states in which the group may be at various moments of the collaboration process, e.g. the group may be "waiting for ideas".

Edges run between activities and states, never between activities nor between states. Edges capture the potential activities in a given state, or states after the execution of a given activity. One may recognize in abstract interaction protocols the concept of Petri nets, where states are places and activities/roles pairs are transitions.

3.2 Implemented Social Protocols

Similarly to the relation between implemented process models and abstract process models presented in Section 2.3, an implemented social protocol defines the implementation of abstract activities associated with an abstract social protocol.

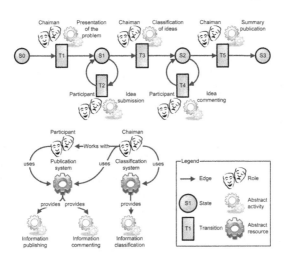

Fig. 1. An example of an abstract social protocol. At the top, the abstract interaction protocol of a brainstorming session. At the bottom, the abstract social network.

Therefore, an implemented social protocol consists of three parts:

- an abstract social protocol,
- a mapping of *abstract resources* associated to with abstract activities to *implemented resources*. For instance, the abstract resource "Publication system" of the former example may be mapped to a forum system on a given server.
- a mapping of *abstract activities* to *implemented activities*. For instance, the abstract activity "presentation of the problem" of the former example may be mapped to the URL of the form used to post information on the formerly mentioned forum system.

These two mappings may be built based on a pre-existing social environment defining interdependencies among resources (abstract and implemented). Additionally, the pre-existing social environment may be extended by the addition of missing resources. Therefore, on the one hand, the implementation procedure may take advantage of the social environment, on the other hand, the social network may benefit from the implementation procedure.

3.3 Social Processes

Similarly to the relation between instantiated process models and implemented process models presented in Section 2.3, a social process defines the implementation of abstract roles associated with an implemented social protocol, as well as keeps trace of the state of the interactions within the VT.

Therefore, a social process consists of three parts:

- an implemented social protocol,
- a mapping of *abstract resources* associated with roles to *collaborators*. For instance, the abstract resource "brainstorming chairman" is mapped to "John".
- a *marking* of active states.

The role-collaborator mapping may be built based on the pre-existing social environment. Additionally, the pre-existing social environment may be extended by the addition of missing resources, by the addition of collaborators. Therefore, on the one hand, the instantiation procedure may take advantage of the social environment, on the other hand, the social network may benefit from the instantiation procedure.

3.4 Meta-processes

The concept of *meta-process* is our answer to the adaptation requirement. During the execution of an instantiated social protocol, collaborators may identify a need for modification of the process instance they are involved in. As a consequence, collaborators need to interact to decide how the process should be changed. A meta-process is a social process associated with another social process π allowing collaborators of π to decide in a structured collaborative way how the process π should be modified. More information about meta-processes and adaption may be found in [16, 17].

4 Discussion

Some interesting works have been done in the field of electronic negotiations to model electronic negotiations with the help of negotiation protocols. In [18], it is stated in that, in the field of electronic negotiations, "the protocol is a formal model, often represented by a set of rules, which govern software processing, decision-making and communication tasks, and imposes restrictions on activities through the specification of permissible inputs and actions". One may notice the similarity with the concept of social protocol. The reason for this fact is that the model presented in this paper was originally coming from a work on protocols for electronic negotiations [15]. However, to our knowledge, none of the works concerning negotiation protocols provides support for the modeling of the social environment. Moreover, these works are by nature limited to the field of electronic negotiations which is just a subset of the field of interactions within VT.

As process modeling is concerned, many works have already been conducted in the research field of workflow modeling and workflow management systems. Many works [19 – 22] have focused on formal models and conditions under which a modification of an existing – and potentially running – workflow retains workflow validity, the ADEPT2 project [24] being probably the most advanced one. However, current works concerning workflow adaptation focus on interactions, and the importance of social aspects are not or insufficiently taken into account by these works.

Sadiq and al. [25] have proposed an interesting model for flexible workflows, where flexibility refers to "the ability of the workflow process to execute on the basis of a loosely, or partially specified model, where the full specification of the model is made at runtime, and may be unique to each instance." However, support for flexibility does not ensure support for adaptability, as flexibility, as proposed by Sadiq and al., implies that the workflow designer has specified at design time frames and boundaries to possible modifications of the workflow.

5   Conclusions

While many works are currently done on modeling collaboration processes in which software entities (agents, web services) are involved, modeling collaboration processes in which mainly humans are involved is an area that still requires much attention from the research community. Some of the main issues to be addressed are the social aspects of collaboration and the adaptation capabilities of humans. In this paper, the requirements of computer support for virtual team agility (VTA) are presented. Additionally, the concept of social protocol, combining social networks and workflow models, is proposed as a model supporting interactions within agile VT.

The main innovations presented in this paper are 1) the requirements for VTA, 2) the refinement of the concept of social protocol by the addition of a social network as a way to model the social environment, and 3) the three-layer view on social protocols – abstract, implemented, and instantiated – and the concept of meta-process.

A prototype is currently under implementation to validate the model presented in this paper. Among future works, methods to update the social network to reflect interactions within the VT performed in a given process are still to be proposed.

Acknowledgments. This work has been partially supported by the Polish Ministry of Science and Higher Education within the European Regional Development Fund, Grant No. POIG.01.03.01-00-008/08.

References

1. Camarinha-Matos, L.M., Afsarmanesh, H., Ollus, M.: ECOLEAD: A Holistic Approach to Creation and Management of Dynamic Virtual Organizations. In: 6th IFIP Working Conf. on Virtual Enterprises, pp. 3–16. Springer, Boston (2005)

2. Chituc, C.M., Azevedo, A.L.: Multi-Perspective Challenges on Collaborative Networks Business Environments. In: 6th IFIP Working Conf. on Virtual Enterprises, pp. 25–32. Springer, Boston (2005)
3. Picard, W.: Modeling Structured Non-monolithic Collaboration Processes. In: 6th IFIP Working Conf. on Virtual Enterprises, pp. 379–386. Springer, Boston (2005)
4. LinkedIn, http://www.linkedin.com/
5. MySpace, http://www.myspace.com/
6. Orkut, http://www.orkut.com/
7. Facebook, http://www.facebook.com/
8. Boyd, D.M., Ellison, N.B.: Social Network Sites: Definition, History, and Scholarship. J. of Computer-Mediated Communication 13(1), 210–230 (2007)
9. van der Aalst, W.M.P., van Hee, K.M., van der Toorn, R.A.: Component-Based Software Architectures: A Framework Based on Inheritance of Behavior. BETA Working Paper Series, WP 45, Eindhoven University of Technology, Eindhoven (2000)
10. Russell, N., ter Hofstede, A.H.M., Edmond, D., van der Aalst, W.M.P.: Workflow Resource Patterns. BETA Working Paper Series, WP 127, Eindhoven Univ. of Technology (2004)
11. Fisher, L.: BPM & Workflow Handbook. Future Strategies Inc. (2007)
12. Jeston, J., Nelis, J.: Business Process Management, Second Edition: Practical Guidelines to Successful Implementations. Butterworth-Heinemann (2008)
13. Harrison-Broninski, K.: Human Interactions. Meghan-Kiffer Press (2005)
14. van der Aalst, W.M.P., van Hee, K.: Workflow Management: Models, Methods, and Systems (Cooperative Information Systems). MIT Press, Cambridge (2004)
15. Picard, W.: Computer Support for Adaptive Human Collaboration with Negotiable Social Protocols. In: 9th Int. Conf. on Business Information Systems. LNI, vol. P-85, pp. 90–101. Gesellschaft fur Informatic (2006)
16. Picard, W.: Computer Support for Agile Human-to-Human Interactions with Social Protocols. In: 12th Int. Conf. on Business Information Systems. LNBIP, vol. 21, pp. 121–132 (2009)
17. Picard, W.: Support for adaptive collaboration in Professional Virtual Communities based on negotiations of social protocols. Int. J. Inf.Tech. and Mgmt. 8(3), 283–297 (2009)
18. Kersten, G.E., Strecker, S.E., Lawi, K.P.: Protocols for Electronic Negotiation Systems: Theoretical Foundations and Design Issue. In: 5th Conf. on Electronic Commerce and Web Technologies, pp. 106–115. IEEE Computer Society, Los Alamitos (2004)
19. van der Aalst, W.M.P.: The Application of Petri Nets to Workflow Management. J. of Circuits, Systems and Computers 8(1), 21–66 (1998)
20. van der Aalst, W.M.P., Basten, T., Verbeek, H.M.W., Verkoulen, P.A.C., Voorhoeve, M.: Adaptive Workflow: On the Interplay between Flexibility and Support. In: 1st Int. Conf. on Enterprise Information Systems, vol. 2, pp. 353–360. Kluwer Academic Publishers, Dordrecht (1999)
21. Sadiq, S.W., Orlowska, M.E.: Analyzing process models using graph reduction techniques. Information Systems 25(2), 117–134 (2000)
22. ter Hofstede, A.H.M., Orlowska, M.E., Rajapakse, J.: Verification Problems in Conceptual Workflow Specifications. Data Knowledge Engineering 24(3), 239–256 (1998)
23. Dadam, P., Reichert, M.: The ADEPT Project: A Decade of Research and Development for Robust and Flexible Process Support. Tech. Report. Fakultät fur Ingenieurwissenschaften und Informatik, Ulm (2009),
http://dbis.eprints.uni-ulm.de/487/1/Reichert_01_09-2.pdf
24. Sadiq, S.W., Orlowska, M.E., Sadiq, W.: Specification and validation of process constraints for flexible workflows. Information Systems 30(5), 349–378 (2005)

Analysis of Interpersonal Communication Processes in Digital Factory Environments

Jens Schütze[1], Heiko Baum[1], Martin Laue[2], and Egon Müller[1]

[1] Chemnitz University of Technology, Institute of Industrial Management and Factory Systems,
Department of Factory Planning and Factory Mangement
09107 Chemnitz, Germany
{jens.schuetze,heiko.baum,egon.mueller}@mb.tu-chemnitz.de
[2] Volkswagen AG, Department of Production Development (PKP-K/I)
38436 Wolfsburg, Germany
martin.laue@volkswagen.de

Abstract. The paper outlines the scope of influence of digital factory on the interpersonal communication process and the exemplary description of them. On the basis of a brief description about the theoretical basic concepts of the digital factory occurs the illustration of communicative features in digital factory. Practical coherences of interpersonal communication from a human oriented view were analyzed in Volkswagen AG in Wolfsburg in a pilot project. A modeling method was developed within the process analysis. This method makes it possible to visualize interpersonal communication and its human oriented attribute in a technically focused workflow. Due to the results of a developed inquiry about communication analysis and process models of modeling methods it was possible to build the processes in a suitable way for humans and to obtain a positive implication on the communication processes.

Keywords: Digital factory, Human communication, Business process modeling, Collaborative networks, Social network analysis.

1 Introduction

Most major carmakers, including Daimler AG, BMW AG, General Motors Corp., Ford Motor Co. and Toyota Motor Corp., investing billions of dollar in digital factory solutions. Using sophisticated design and manufacturing tools, engineers should be able to determine before production, whether a car part is going to fit into a vehicle as planned or whether a weld point can be placed as expected [1]. Improvement in all essential factory processes is a further anticipated benefit from the digital factory [2].

Volkswagen Group, which reported in the year 2008 sales totaling €113.8 billion, noticed recently an unwanted side effect of integrated digital concepts. While implementing digital manufacturing planning in their main plant in Wolfsburg (Germany) social aspects were left unconsidered. When Volkswagen implemented more and more digital factory applications the interpersonal communications were reduced. The fact was known and wanted, because the 'digital' communication (Communication between technical devices) is considered more accurate and less error-sensitive than

L.M. Camarinha-Matos et al. (Eds.): PRO-VE 2009, IFIP AICT 307, pp. 177–184, 2009.
© IFIP International Federation for Information Processing 2009

the 'analog' communication (Human communication, no matter if face-to-face or media-mediated). This approach was successful in many departments, but not completely. In some cases, the reduction of communication options led to coordination problems in certain business processes. Some major issues identified in communication processes were due to interruption and malfunctioning. It was not expected that interpersonal communications plays such an important role in a strong hierarchical environment. Volkswagen in Wolfsburg decided to start the research project 'HoSeKo' together with Chemnitz University of Technology to analyze the role of interpersonal communication processes in digital factory environments, to identify main influencing factors in order to develop best practice concepts and workflows.

2   Corresponding Base Concepts

Digital Factory. According to Guideline #4499 of the Association of German Engineers [3] the digital factory is the generic term for a large network of digital models, methods and tools (for e.g. simulation and 3D visualization) which are integrated through an unified data management. The digital factory's function is the planning, realization, supervision and permanent improvement of all essential factory processes and resources in association with the product. The key elements of the present digital factory approach in relation to communication are: (a) Reduction of interpersonal communication by automation. (b) Intuitive access to complex cases by multimedia support. By this 'a digital factory represents a persistent hybrid community where a rich virtualized environment demonstrating a variety of factory activities will facilitate the sharing of factory resources, manufacturing information and knowledge and help the simulation of collaborative design, planning, production and management among different participants and departments' [4].

Communication. Communication is a complex and polymorphic process. Even if it is commonly understood as 'a process by which information is exchanged between individuals through a common system of symbols, signs, or behavior' [5] there are at least 126 [6] or even 160 [7] different definitions of this term's existence. A number of models and theories attempt to explain this phenomenon [8]. The main object of communication is considered as understanding between individuals and collaboration.

Collaborative Network. The term of a Collaborative Network (CN) is usually defined as 'variety of entities (e.g. organizations and people) that are largely autonomous, geographically distributed, and heterogeneous in terms of their operating environment, culture and goal' [9]. Another commonly used definition ('Collaborative network is a set of participants who would like to work together in respond to one or multiple common goals and a set of relationships between the participants.' [10]) understands the CN term in a wider sense. Autonomy, geographical distribution and heterogeneity are no explicit prerequisites to form a CN. Based on the second point of view, individuals from a strong hierarchical environment such as a multi-national company could be perceived as CN too, if they 'work together in respond to one or multiple common goals' as long as the collaborative aspect is essential. The discussion about theoretical foundations and possible forms of CN is still going on [11, 12].

Social Network Analysis. Beginning of the 1950s social network analysis (SNA) has emerged as a key technique in several scientific areas, i.e. sociology, biology, information science, organization science and others [13]. SNA is usually being associated with certain metrics, like degree centrality, betweenness centrality, closeness centrality or eigenvalue. For analyzing qualitative aspects of networks, other methods are more appropriate.

3 Digital Factory and Communication

Digital factory tools are used as technical work equipment to process a task. By this they can play different roles in the communication process. On the base of the Lasswell formula of communication [14] different roles of the digital factory are possible:

Digital Factory as Actor. Digital factory systems can work as sender or receiver of communication. Communication is possible (a) among digital factory systems or (b) between digital factory systems and humans. In case (a) the compatibility of data formats between the used systems has to be ensured. In case (b) the most important factor is operation of Human-Machine Interface (HMI).

Digital Factory as Medium. Especially in the area of production planning Data Management Systems (DMS) and Workflow Management Systems (WfMS) are used as communication medium. DMS are primarily used for storage, documentation and exchange of data. A special case is Knowledge Management Systems (KMS), which offers support for creation, organization, capture, storage and dissemination of information. In contrast to what WfMS provides completely or partially automated support for workflows, in which information, data or documents are passed on from one employee to the other.

Digital Factory as Message. The use of digital factory systems can influence the message or how the message is understood by humans. One explanation could be the phenomenon described in Channel Reduction theory [15]. Moreover, the communication context (Situation, chosen communication channel, etc.) is influencing the message and leading to distortions.

4 Case Study: Production Planning Workflow

Concrete implications of the digital factory on the communication process as a medium of communication will be explained in greater detail using the example of Volkswagen. The example displays a workflow already implemented in the production planning. The workflow concept is supposed to help the organization to achieve its aims, such as the reduction of work proceeding time, an improved transparency and documentation with an enhancement of the proceeding quality.

Problem. The workflow described here supports automatically the coordination of any change requests within production planning prior to their transfer to the Production Development Department in the field of Research and Development (R&D).

Products cannot be modified anymore while running through the manufacturing process. The internal production plan execution is necessary to coordinate the implications of change requests of a trade on the manufacturing processes for the other trades. For this purpose, a production planner is sending his change request to his representatives of each trade via a workflow system. During a first phase, the representatives can comment on this change request in case they feel that their manufacturing processes will be concerned. During the second phase, the planner is sending the change requests to each trade again after considering all comments and impulses. At this point, the trades have the following three possibilities to classify themselves: (a) Not being concerned (b) Approving the change request or (c) Rejecting the change request. In case of a rejection, the planner has the possibility to re-send the change request into the workflow system, which means that the whole process will be taken up again. After all trades have either approved the change or have classified themselves as not being concerned, a person responsible of the project has to endorse the change request as well. However, his approval depends on specific premises being formerly settled, such as the amount of investments. After the internal agreement and the planner's approval, the change request will be sent to the Department of Production Development, which will decide about the production changes in the end.

This workflow system showed that a reduction in work proceeding time and an improvement of transparency could be reached. Moreover, managers and leaders are now updated about the current situation for change requests of certain products due to some monitoring data. All completed and hence documented plans to change a product provide valuable experience for future projects. However, there are still some problems regarding communication during this workflow process: Before the creator enters a change request into the workflow system, it is advisable to agree on the feasibility of the product change with the Department of Production Development responsible, as the change request can be rejected after the workflow run. An initial agreement could save the trades time and works, since they have to approve the change, too. Although, this agreement process was a common procedure prior to the introduction of the workflow, it is not regularized in the workflow and not practiced by some production planners anymore. This could be because the new production planners do not know anything about such agreement processes. This case shows clearly the lacking regularization of parallel communication processes in the workflow concept which are not identified as a core process. On the other hand, it displays the production planners' altered attitude towards work routine through the introduction of the workflow. The planner has the impression that his amount of work becomes less after the introduction of the workflow. The effort of one's own work influences the expectation and the perceived justice of the result. This, in turn, has an impact on one's satisfaction. Consequently, it is likely that one will not seem that dissatisfied about a possible rejection by the R&D. Thus, the planner does not seem as motivated as he used to be after the introduction of the workflow. The planner's aim to achieve a positive result and to exploit all necessary means seem to have become less important. If the parallel communication processes in the workflow had been regularized, the problem would have been to select the appropriate medium of communication for this process. The following case is supposed to illustrate this fact.

During a workflow process lack or conflict-laden communication between the production planner and the representatives of the trades may appear. Prior to the introduction of the workflow the planner had to agree with each trade when changing a product. All suggestions for each trade were considered and incorporated into the change request. For this, all representatives of the concerned trades met to agree on the change. It is quite salient that some impulses and comments given by the representatives of the trades from the first phase are not considered. Hence, the change request will be sent unchanged to the second phase where it is commonly rejected. Moreover, it can be observed that agreements conveyed medially are sometimes rather conflict-filled and not always held in a friendly way. A medial transmission enables the planner to decide anonymously. This communication via computer and the resulting anonymity can lead to an anti-social behavior. This latter fact is substantiated by territorial-minded employees. Territorial-mindedness describes the positive attitude towards co-workers of one's own department and the mistrustful and biased attitude towards co-workers of other departments. Moreover, as computer is a technical device, persons communicate without perceiving any sense in comparison to any personal conversation. Thus, computer-mediated communication can lead to a rather deficient and impersonal communication which makes statements and comments difficult to interpret. Generally-speaking, communicating via computer makes the conversation 'unreal' as one is talking to a machine. This can further support tendencies of estrangement and isolation between colleagues as well as an increasing inability to solve conflicts.

Solution. The biggest potentialities to improve interpersonal communication in digital factory are to influence the system development in the analytical phase. The analytical phase of the system development is divided into the conduction of a so called actual analysis and creation of the target concept. Some influencing factors on the communication process are embedded into the Man-Technology-Organization approach (MTO). The general target of the system development is to support a working task on a system-technological basis. Therefore, the targets adapt themselves towards the business objectives from a technical as well as organizational point of view. The aim of the workflow management is to reduce the time for information flow, to increase process transparency and to avoid the storage of redundant data. All the targets which are set by the process management and which can be reached by a system-technological support are the following: Process documentation, Creation of flexible processes in order to react quickly to organizational changes as well as Process standardization. Certain objectives like 'How to accomplish a task?' and 'How to support these on a system-technological basis?' are hardly considered in current system development processes. Tasks which are oriented towards human strengths do not have to oppose the business objectives. Employees' competences can be maintained, encouraged and better used by creating human-oriented tasks. The so called Contrastive Task Analysis [16] can be understood as a tool which aims at improving communication as well as using and encouraging human competences. The criteria of the Contrastive Task Analysis are to be considered when analyzing and setting up the task. The human-oriented system development aims at improving the communication between the employees to meet their needs and qualifications. The system further supports individual's personality so that they can fully develop their potentialities and competences. The digital factory as a Workflow Management System is supposed to face possible problems in the interpersonal communication process. Hence, it was suggested to influence the system development in the analytical phase by using the MTO approach. The following approaches aim at analysing and improving the communication. They can either be integrated into the Contrastive Task Analysis or conducted as independent measures.

The so called 'Task-Oriented Media Choice' is a method to find an adequate communication medium [17]. It could be integrated into the contrastive task analysis within the human criteria 'communication'. This method links the task-related demands to the appropriateness of a medium in terms of the criteria of accuracy/ability in documentation, rapidness/convenience, privacy and complexity. Thus, the media to be applied is determined by the degree of task structuring and the need of social presence. Hence, an e-mail would be suitable for messages which should be sent, documented and stored in an error-free way. Personal communication, on the other hand, is preferable when conveying complex issues, since Non-Verbal Communication can be easily understood. As a consequence, it is advisable to think about the usefulness of making all communicative task activities within system development automatic. It should be taken into account that complex and difficult contents are conveyed more easily while interacting personally in the workflow. Creating a trustful and an anxiety-free atmosphere in the organization should help to improve interpersonal relationships. At this point, it becomes quite clear how strong interpersonal relationships are intertwined within the organizational culture. Executives are able to influence the following aspects to a certain extent: positioning, strategy, structure, form and selection of personnel of the organization. These parameters could be analyzed in the Contrastive Task Analysis while framing the organizational unit.

However, the staff's communicative behavior is so far found more difficult to be described. Nevertheless, according to the analysis of the organizational culture as well as the personnel's motivation and attitudes, some behavioral suggestions can be drawn. Managers and their way of behaviors are assigned with a symbolic role here owing to their role model functioning. The executives and managers are also responsible for observing and dealing with co-worker's possible misbehavior. In this case, the manager could either talk to the employee or provide training courses to enhance communicational skills. In order to achieve a change in the employee's mind, the manager should appear trustworthy. He should have powers and be able to apply measures to reward or penalize the staffs. The employees of the various departments have to realize that certain differences between them and other departments do exist. They need to accept other person's attitudes in order to oppose territorial-mindedness and co-operational and communicational barriers. Therefore, it is advisable to create certain conditions for interdisciplinary teams, which leave an ample scope to achieve one's own aim in every field. If this is not the case, cooperation barriers resulting from competing interests will arise. Another important aspect is the protection of the employee's own identity which can be secured by clearly restricting the area of competence. The organization may also reward a successful communication between persons, which the interdisciplinary team can consider as a common challenge. Thus, if employees of different fields conduct some aspects of a task together, they will create a common base of experience, create mutual confidence and reach a better understanding.

Informational meetings are suitable qualification measures to support cooperation and communication across the different fields. These meetings should deal with issues related to cooperation by means of concrete situations. Such training courses ideally take place prior to a development process of a team or as a regular event. They can help to improve the communication between participants of different fields. Another crucial point is that, such a kick-off meeting can oppose anonymity. The participants would have the opportunity to meet each other and to represent their tasks and roles in this project. In line to this, the rules and norms related to the common cooperation and communication could be set up right at the beginning. The kick-off meeting serves to settle targets, to make fixed appointments to define responsibilities as well as to create a base for common teamwork. If all these aspects come into existence, quality effects in the interdisciplinary groups can be expected particularly with long-term, continuous team development processes.

5 Conclusions

It is fair to say that the consideration of interpersonal communication processes in digital factory environments is essential for collaborative work tasks. The largest potential for improvement can be located at the design or selection phase of the digital factory solutions.

The two most important analysis results of the workflow are: (a) Practically, a pure technically focused approach dominated. (b) Deficient visualization possibilities of such processes are available. The actual aspects of interpersonal communication and their exemplary image were not discussed practically till now. The solution of examining interpersonal communication was found through the inquiry developed in the project 'HoSeKo'. This inquiry analyzed the information flow, the relation quality and human criteria. In addition to that, a graphical modeling technique was created for the visualization of such processes. This visualization enables building important magnitudes that are analyzed in the inquiry in a suitable form. Furthermore, it was possible to submit those visualized processes of multi-personal discussion. The discussions were required for the localization of the improvement potentials. The specification of interpersonal communication in an IT-supported process of the digital factory should be given more attention from researchers in the future.

Acknowledgments. This paper is mainly based on work performed in the projects 'HoSeKo' (Joint research project between Volkswagen AG, Germany and Chemnitz University of Technology) and 'Me2Co' (Funded by the German Federal Ministry of Education and Research, Reference No. 01 IS C37).

References

1. Cunha, P.F., Maropoulos, P.G. (eds.): Digital Enterprise Technology: Perspectives and Future Challenges. Springer, New York (2007)
2. Neil, S.: The digital factory. Managing Automation 22(10), 20–27 (2007)

3. VDI4499, Digital factory: Fundamentals. VDI-Richtlinie 4499 [Guideline of the Association of German Engineers]. Blatt 1 [Part 1]. Ausg. deutsch/englisch [Issue German/English]. Düsseldorf: Beuth (2008)
4. Sacco, M., Redaelli, C., Constantinescu, C., Lawson, G., D'Cruz, M., Pappas, M.: DIFAC: Digital Factory for Human Oriented Production System. In: Jacko, J.A. (ed.) HCI 2007. LNCS, vol. 4553, pp. 1140–1149. Springer, Heidelberg (2007)
5. Merriam-Webster. Communication: Definition from the Mirriam-Webster Online Dictionary (2009),
   http://www.merriam-webster.com/dictionary/communication
   (retrieved on March 18, 2009)
6. Dance, F.E.X., Larson, C.E.: The Functions of Human Communication: A Theoretical Approach. Holt, Rinehart and Winston, New York (1976)
7. Merten, K.: Kommunikation: Eine Begriffs- und Prozeßanalyse [Communication: An Analysis of Term and Process]. Westdeutscher Verlag, Opladen (1977)
8. Schütze, J.: Modellierung von Kommunikationsprozessen in KMU-Netzwerken: Grundlagen und Ansätze [Modeling of Communication Processes in SME Networks: Fundamentals and Approaches]. Gabler, Wiesbaden (2009)
9. Camarinha-Matos, L.M., Afsarmanesh, H.: Collaborative Networks: A New Scientific Discipline. Journal of Intelligent Manufacturing 16(4), 439–452 (2005)
10. Rajsiri, V., Lorré, J.P., Bénaben, F., Pingaud, H.: Collaborative Process Definition using an Ontology-based Approach. In: Camarinha-Matos, L.M., Picard, W. (eds.) Pervasive Collaborative Networks. IFIP International Federation for Information Processing, vol. 283, pp. 205–212. Springer, Boston (2008)
11. Camarinha-Matos, L.M., Afsarmanesh, H.: Collaborative Networks: A new scientific Discipline. In: Camarinha-Matos, L.M., Afsarmanesh, H., Ollus, M. (eds.) Virtual Organizations: Systems and Practices, pp. 73–80. Springer Science + Business, Boston (2005)
12. Müller, E. (ed.): Competence-cell based Networks: Theories, Models, Methods and Tools. Springer, London (2009)
13. Freeman, L.C.: The development of social network analysis: A study in the sociology of science. Empirical Press, Vancouver (2004)
14. Lasswell, H.D.: The structure and function of communication in society. In: Bryson, L. (ed.) The communication of ideas: A series of addresses, pp. 37–52. Institute for Religious and Social Studies, New York (1948)
15. von Mettler-Meibom, B.: Kommunikation in der Mediengesellschaft. Tendenzen, Gefährdungen, Orientierungen [Communication in media society: Tendencies, dangers, orientations]. Ed. Sigma, Berlin (1994)
16. Dunckel, H., Pleiss, C. (eds.): Kontrastive Aufgabenanalyse: Grundlagen, Entwicklungen und Anwendungserfahrungen [Contrastive Task Analysis: Fundamentals, Developments and Experiences from Application]. vdf Hochschulverlag der ETH Zürich, Zürich (2007)
17. Reichwald, R., Kathrin, M.: Management und Technologie [Management and Technology]. In: von Rosenstiel, L., Regnet, E., Domsch, M. (eds.) Führung von Mitarbeitern: Handbuch für erfolgreiches Personalmanagement [Leading of Employees: Handbook for Successful Human Resource Management], 5th edn., Schäffer-Poschel, Stuttgart (2003)

Part **6**

VO Breeding Environments Modeling

Modeling Virtual Organization Architecture with the Virtual Organization Breeding Methodology

Zbigniew Paszkiewicz and Willy Picard

Department of Infromation Technology, Poznan University of Economics,
Mansfelda 4, 60-854 Poznań, Poland
{zpasz,picard}@kti.ue.poznan.pl

Abstract. While Enterprise Architecture Modeling (EAM) methodologies become more and more popular, an EAM methodology tailored to the needs of virtual organizations (VO) is still to be developed. Among the most popular EAM methodologies, TOGAF has been chosen as the basis for a new EAM methodology taking into account characteristics of VOs presented in this paper. In this new methodology, referred as Virtual Organization Breeding Methodology (VOBM), concepts developed within the ECOLEAD project, e.g. the concept of Virtual Breeding Environment (VBE) or the VO creation schema, serve as fundamental elements for development of VOBM. VOBM is a generic methodology that should be adapted to a given VBE. VOBM defines the structure of VBE and VO architectures in a service-oriented environment, as well as an architecture development method for virtual organizations (ADM4VO). Finally, a preliminary set of tools and methods for VOBM is given in this paper.

Keywords: Virtual organization creation, enterprise architecture modeling.

1 Introduction

The concept of Virtual Breeding Environment (VBE) has been proposed by the ECOLEAD project as "an association of organizations and their related supporting institutions, adhering to a base long term cooperation agreement, and adoption of Common operating principles and infrastructures, with the main goal of increasing their preparedness towards collaboration in potential Virtual Organizations (VO)" [1]. An important task of each VBE is the support of VO creation [2, 3]. While the various steps of the VO creation phase have been studied in the ECOLEAD project [4], a methodology allowing VBE members to model a VO is still to be proposed.

On the other hand, various methodologies addressing enterprise modeling, and more specifically enterprise architecture modeling (EAM), have been proposed in the past 20 years [TOGAF, FEAF, Zachman, MDA] as ways to ensure that the deployed IT infrastructure is aligned with the enterprise's business needs and goals. Methodologies such as TOGAF [5, 6] and FEAF [7] are well developed, mature and accepted by practitioners.

L.M. Camarinha-Matos et al. (Eds.): PRO-VE 2009, IFIP AICT 307, pp. 187–196, 2009.

However these methodologies miss important concepts identified in the ECOLEAD project, e.g. the concepts of VBE, VO composition, partners search and selection, definition of roles in VBE. Therefore, EAM methodologies have to be adapted to the specific characteristics of VBE to be useful for VO modeling.

Some works [8–10] have studied the benefits that VO modeling would give to VBE members. However, the results presented in formerly mentioned papers were mainly focused on expected benefits without a definition of the methodology allowing VBE members to build the VO models [8] or were not concentrated enough on VBE characteristics [9, 10]. Additionally, to our best knowledge, none of these works are based on widely accepted EAM methodologies.

Therefore, there is need for an EAM methodology tailored to the needs for VBEs and VOs. Such a methodology should be built on existing popular EAM methodologies, so that the learning curve of this newly developed methodology would be relatively small for EAM practitioners. The main contribution of this paper is such an EAM methodology, referred as the Virtual Organization Breeding Methodology (VOBM). VOBM is based on the TOGAF methodology, tailored to characteristics of VO and VBE architectures.

This paper is organized as follows. In section 2, enterprise architecture modeling and popular existing methodologies are presented. In section 3, the Virtual Organization Breeding Methodology is presented. Then, the Architecture Development Methodology for Virtual Organizations is detailed; Next, VOBM tools and methods are introduced. Finally, section 6 concludes the paper.

2 Enterprise Architecture Modeling

2.1 Overview of Enterprise Architecture Modeling

Enterprise architecture modeling (EAM) aims to provide a formal description of a given system: structure of components, their interrelationships, principles, guidelines, building blocks (applications, people, infrastructure, data etc.), to facilitate system evolution, evaluation, understanding and implementation. In particular, EAM focuses on business goals, strategy, organizational structure, business processes, human and technical resources, competences, information flows [5] Enterprise architecture is typically divided into four architectural domains: business, applications, data and technology [5], each domain having its set of models. This approach and its benefits have been described in [8].

Among EAM methodologies and frameworks the most popular ones [11] are The Open Architecture Group Framework (TOGAF) and the Federal Enterprise Architecture Framework (FEAF).

2.2 The Open Group Architecture Framework (TOGAF)

The Open Group Architecture Framework (TOGAF) is a mature and complex methodology for enterprise architecture modeling proposed by the Open Group [12]. The most important three parts in TOGAF are: the Architecture Development Method (ADM), the TOGAF Enterprise Continuum, and the TOGAF Resource Base. ADM is the core of TOGAF and provides a precise description of all EAM steps leading to an enterprise architecture. The TOGAF Enterprise Continuum is "a "virtual repository" of all the architecture assets - models, patterns, architecture descriptions, and other artifacts - that exist both within the enterprise and in the IT industry at large, which the enterprise considers itself to have available for the development of architectures for the enterprise" [5]. Finally, the TOGAF Resource Base is a set of tools and techniques available for use in applying TOGAF. A detailed description of TOGAF may be found in [5, 6].

An important aspect of TOGAF is that TOGAF is a generic architecture, i.e. it must be tailored to the need of a specific organization, mainly via the choice of appropriate tools and artifacts. Then, TOGAF is flexible enough to allow architects to use other enterprise frameworks, e.g. the Zachman Framework or Federal Enterprise Architecture Framework (FEAF), within TOGAF.

2.3 Federal Enterprise Architecture Framework (FEAF)

The U.S.A Federal CIO Council has defined in FEAF an enterprise architecture for federal agencies or cross-agencies systems. FEAF is based on the concept of federation of architectures as "independently developed, maintained and managed architectures that are subsequently integrated within a meta-architecture framework. Such a framework specifies principles for interoperability, migration and conformance. FEAF allows specific business units to have architectures developed and governed as standalone architecture projects" [5]. In fact it is not possible to develop organization-wide architectures and keep them integrated, well documented, and flexible. It is necessary to have a number of different architectures existing across an organization and focused on various aspects of the organization.

3   Overview of the Virtual Organization Breeding Methodology

Existing EAM methodologies are not tailored to the characteristics of VBEs. On the other hand, an EAM methodology is needed to guide the creation of VOs within the framework presented in the ECOLEAD project.

The solution proposed in this paper is an EAM methodology tailored to VBE and VO creation, referred in this paper as VOBM (Virtual Organization Breeding Methodology). VOBM is based mainly on TOGAF and the results of the ECOLEAD project, but it also takes advantage of concepts present in FEAF.

3.1   VOBM as a Generic Methodology

The aim of the development of VOBM is the definition of a generic methodology providing a set of standard methods and tools for VO modeling. Such a generic methodology then should be customized to the needs and characteristics of a specific VBE. For instance, the characteristics and purpose of a VBE in the construction sector may be significantly distinct to a VBE in the car industry. As a consequence, the shape of created VOs (and therefore their architecture models) will also probably differ from one VBE to another.

In the VOBM approach (*cf.* Fig. 1), the VBE manager is responsible for tailoring VOBM to the VBE he/she is managing. Therefore, every VBE should have specific virtual organization architecture modeling framework that would allow creation of virtual organization architectures. In this sense VOBM is a generic methodology. Definition and modeling of VO architecture is a responsibility of VO planners.

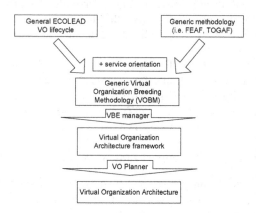

Fig. 1. Approach to specification of Virtual Organization Breeding Methodology

3.2 Architecture Domains in VOBM

TOGAF introduces four architecture domains: business, application, data and infrastructure and two service domains: business and information system services. The *business architecture* defines the business strategy, governance, organization, and key business processes. The *application architecture* provides a blueprint for the individual application systems to be deployed, their interactions, and their relationships to the core business processes of the organization. The *data architecture* describes the structure of an organization's logical and physical data assets and data management resources. Finally, the *technology architecture* describes the logical software and hardware capabilities that are required to support the deployment of business, data, and application services.

Additionally, two levels of services – business services and information system services – are distinguished in TOGAF. Business services are mainly provided at the business architecture domain, while information system services are mainly provided at application, data and infrastructure architecture domains.

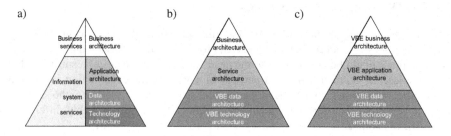

Fig. 2. Architecture domains: a) TOGAF b) VO c) VBE

These concepts may be applied to model not only the architecture(s) of organizations being members of the VBE, but also the architecture of the VBE itself. The VBE business architecture domain encompasses e.g. VBE members' role definitions, VBE internal processes. The VBE application architecture domain encompasses applications to be used in all phases of VBE and VO lifecycle, e.g. application supporting the registration of new VBE members or applications for conducting negotiations among potential VO partners. The VBE data architecture domain encompasses, e.g., standard format of documents, definition of data types. The VBE infrastructure architecture domain consists of shared infrastructure and IT solutions or Enterprise Service Bus (ESB) used by VBE for member integration.

VBE architecture domain formation should be a part of VBE instantiation methodology and is not a subject of VOBM. However, VOBM assumes that VBE is organized as formally presented.

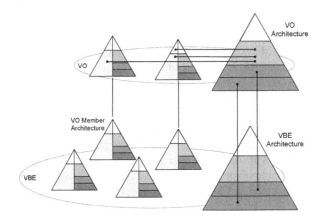

Fig. 3. Virtual Organization architecture development. The two lowest architecture domains are shared with the VBE; the service architecture domain integrates services from VO members.

The four architecture domain proposed by TOGAF should be adapted to VOs: while the concept of business architecture domain applies to VOs, the three remaining architecture domains should be adapted.

The application architecture domain usually does not apply to VOs, as VOs do not possess their own applications and processes but usually take advantage of applications and processes offered by VO members in a form of services [13]. Ideally, integration of partner services should take place at the highest possible level, i.e. business level. In practice, however, integration at the business level is usually not possible: the operation of a VO usually requires services not only on at the business but also information, data and infrastructure level. Therefore, in the VOBM, the application architecture domain is replaced by a service architecture domain which integrates business services and information system services of VO members.

In the VOBM, the data and infrastructure architecture domains of VOs have been tailored to characteristics of VBEs. VBE creates frames for VO creation and operation. These frames include shared standards of data exchanged among VBE members, as well as a common infrastructure. Therefore, in the VOBM, all VOs of a given VBE share the data and infrastructure architecture domains of the VBE.

The architecture domains of VBE members (.i.e. TOGAF architecture domains), VBEs (as defined in VOBM), and VOs (as defined in VOBM) are illustrated in Fig. 2. The composition of a VO architecture in the VOBM is illustrated in Fig. 3.

4   ADM for Virtual Organizations

A core element of the VOBM is the Architecture Development Method for Virtual Organizations (ADM4VO). ADM4VO is a tailored version of the Architecture Development Method (ADM) developed in TOGAF, adapted to the characteristics of VOs. In ADM4VO, a number of ADM components have been reviewed, modified, added or removed. While ADM consists of 10 phases, ADM4VO consists of only 6 phases as the following phases of TOGAF ADM have been left out:

- Preliminary phase: in ADM, this phase includes the choice of tools and methods to be used. In ADM4VO, these decisions are made by the VBE manager during the adaptation of VOBM to VBE needs.
- Information Systems Architecture and Technology Architecture phases: these phase have been replaced by the VO Service Architecture phase, as VOs do not possess their own systems and infrastructure, but compose processes and system using services provided by VO members.
- Migration planning and Implementation governance phases: these phases are strictly connected with the implementation of the modeled architecture, i.e. development and deployment of applications and infrastructure. Some aspects of this phase are included in VO Service Architecture phase.

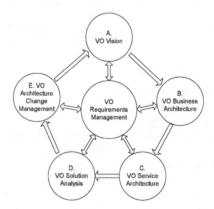

Fig. 4. Architecture Development Method for Virtual Organization (ADM4VO)

Two phases of ADM4VO – VO Architecture Change Management and Requirement Management – do not have an equivalent in ECOLEAD VO creation methodology, while existing in ADM. VO Architecture Change Management focuses on the adaptation of VO to changing environment/circumstances, on conditions under which the architecture, or parts of it, will be permitted to change. The VO Architecture Change Management phase should exploit advanced concepts of business process adoption, change and impact analysis.

The Requirements Management phase focuses on monitoring every VO architecture creation step and verifying the results of these steps against requirements, assumptions and results of the previous phases. For instance, if a set of services is identified during the Service Architecture phase as needed by the VO, but it appears as a result of the VO Solution Analysis phase that these services are not provided by any member of the VBE, then the Architecture Service assumptions have to be verified and changed, which may lead to changes in Business Architecture or even VO Vision. The Requirements Management phase provides a mechanism for back-loops within one architecture development cycle.

The goals of other phases are listed below:

Phase A: VO Architecture Vision
- Definition of relevant stakeholders, their concerns and objectives, key business requirements;
- Articulation of goals and requirements for VO and VO architecture.

Phase B: VO Business Architecture
- Development of a Target Business Architecture, describing the organizational, functional, process and information aspects of the business environment;
- Description of the Baseline Business Architecture and gap analysis between the Baseline and Target Business Architectures when a VO already exists and the aim of ADM4VO is to adopt it to changing environment.

Modeling can go far beyond simple business process modeling, taking advantage of already existing building blocks present in Architecture Repository (VBE bag of assets).. This phase includes also definition of VO requirements (needed competences and partners) on a basis of business process.

Phase C: VO Service Architecture
- Development of a Target Service Architecture describing the needed services, and competences of partners;
- Description of the Baseline Service Architecture and gap analysis between the Baseline and Target Service Architectures when a VO already exist and the aim of ADM4VO is to adopt it to changing environment,
- Choice of partners for cooperation, based on competencies, service description, and on information about social network
- This phase does not exist in TOGAF ADM. It has been developed for the need of VOBM. Phase C is an initial partner selection phase. The result of this phase is the composition of services offered by selected partners into complex business models developed in phase B.

Phase D: VO Solution Analysis
- Evaluation in terms of costs, benefits, potential problems etc. and selection among various possible implementations of business and service architectures,

The aim of this phase in ADM (very briefly described in TOGAF) is to evaluate in terms of costs and benefits various possibilities of organization architecture implementation. In ADM4VO, the idea of comparing many possible variants of VO (variants differ by selected partners, services, etc.) is similar, even if the concept of service plays a greater role than in ADM.

5   ADM for Virtual Organizations

An important element of each EAM methodology is the identification of methods and tools to be used in each phase. TOGAF EAM suggests methods that might be used in each phase but on the other hand it is stressed that TOGAF must be adapted to particular organization what includes the definition of other set of methods. In Table 1, a preliminary list of methods and tools has been established. It should be noted that this list is not exhaustive. For phases common for ADM and ADM4VO, methods and tools defined in TOGAF can be used. Similarly, tools and methods identified by the ECOLEAD project should be evaluated as regards VOBM. For phases specific to ADM4VO, e.g. the VO Service Architecture phase, new tools and methods still need to be identified and developed.

Table 1. Virtual Organization Breeding Methodology steps and methods outline

	VOBM phases	Methods
A	VO Vision	Business scenario method
		Methods for aligning goals with business process, partners and services for change and impact analysis
B.1	VO Business Architecture VO Business Modeling	Business process modeling method with iterative task decomposition
		Method of abstract business process definition
		Business process model storage and reuse
		Method for collaboration protocol selection for the particular collaboration opportunity
		Method of collaboration protocol to business process mapping
		KPIs and Social Network requirement definition methods
B.2	VO Business Architecture VO Requirements Definition	Models and methods of description of: VO requirements, services, partners competences.
C	VO Service Architecture	Service search method
		Partner and service selection
		Method for social network modeling and analysis
		Method for semi-automated service composition
D	VO Solution Analysis	Method for VO efficiency estimation
		Methods for service level agreement (SLA) negotiation
E	VO Change Management	VO and business process adaptation
		Change and impact analysis methods
F	VO Requirements Management	Change and impact analysis methods
		Key Performance Indicators for Virtual Organization
		VO requirements management methods

6 ADM for Virtual Organizations

The main contribution presented in this paper is a new EAM methodology – the Virtual Organization Breeding Methodology (VOBM) – which is tailored to the characteristics of VOs and concepts identified by the ECOLEAD project. VOBM is based on one of the most popular EAM methodologies, TOGAF, which ensures a relatively small learning curve for TOGAF practitioners.

As regards TOGAF, VOBM introduces Service Architecture in VO architecture domains, the VBE architecture, and modified development phases. As regards ECOLEAD, VOBM introduces Change and Requirements Management phases to support VO agility. Introduced changes are oriented to use SOA approach.

Among future works, a detailed specification of each phase of ADM4VO is still to be written. Additionally, both TOGAF and ECOLEAD provide a set of tools, artifact templates, and methods which should be evaluated as regards their potential use in VOBM.

Finally, within the context of the IT-SOA project [14], a service-oriented VBE is currently under development. This VBE will gather companies from the construction sector in the Great Poland region. During the IT-SOA project, the VOBM will be evaluated in a real business environment.

Acknowledgments. This work has been partially supported by the Polish Ministry of Science and Higher Education within the European Regional Development Fund, Grant No. POIG.01.03.01-00-008/08.

References

1. Camarinha-Matos, L.M., Afarmanesh, H., Galeano, N.: Characterization of Key Components, Features, and Operating Principles of the Virtual Breeding Environment. Deliverable 21.1. ECOLEAD (2004)
2. Camarinha-Matos, L.M., Afarmanesh, H., Galeano, N., Oliveira, A.I.: Specification of VO creation support tools. Deliverable 23.2. ECOLEAD (2006)
3. Camarinha-Matos, L.M., Oliveira, A.I.: Requirements and mechanisms for VO planning and launching. Deliverable 23.1. ECOLEAD (2005)
4. Eschenbaecher, J., Ferrada, F., Jansson, K., Karvonen, I., Klen, E., Loss, L., Negretto, U., Paganelli, P., Klen, A.P., Riikonen, H., Salkari, I.: Report on Methodologies, Processes and Services for VO Management. Deliverable 32.2. ECOLEAD (2005)
5. The Open Group: The Open Group Architecture Framework (TOGAF), version 8.1.1, Enterprise Edition (2007)
6. The Open Group, TOGAF Version 9, The Open Group Architecture Framework (TOGAF), http://www.opengroup.org/togaf/
7. US Office of Management and Budget: A Practical Guide To Federal Enterprise Architecture. Version 1.0. Chief Information Officer Council (2001)
8. Bernus, P., Nemes, L., Schmidt, G.: Handbook on enterprise architecture. Springer, Heidelberg (2003)
9. Katzy, B.R., Sung, G.: State-of the Art of Virtual Organization Modeling, Munich University (2007)

10. Petersen, S.A.: The Role of Enterprise modeling in virtual enterprises in Collaborative Networks and Their Breeding Environments. Pro-Ve proceedings. Springer, Heidelberg (2005)
11. Infosys: Infosys Enterprise Architecture Survey 2008 (2008), http://www.infosys.com/IT-Services/architecture-services/ea-survey/
12. The Open Group website, http://www.opengroup.org
13. Rabelo, R., Gesser, C., Tramontin, R., Gibert, P., Nagellen, T., Rodrigo, M., Ratti, R., Paganelli, P.: Reference Framework for a Collaborative Support ICT infrastructure. Deliverable D61.1a (Version 2). ECOLEAD (2005)
14. IT-SOA project, http://www.soa.edu.pl/

For a Methodology to Implement Virtual Breeding Environments – A Case Study in the Mold and Die Sector in Brazil

Fabiano Baldo and Ricardo J. Rabelo

Department of Automation and Systems, Federal University of Santa Catarina,
PO Box 476, Zip Code 88040-970,
Florianópolis, Brazil
baldo@gsigma.ufsc.br, rabelo@das.ufsc.br

Abstract. This paper addresses the general problem of how classical cluster of industries can become a Virtual Breeding Environment (VBE). Using reference frameworks and models, a methodology to support this evolution is being conceived and its preliminary results are presented. This work tackles a cluster of moulds and dies industries from Brazil as the basis for the research and propositions. In the future, this methodology intends to serve as a concrete mean to systematize the implementation of a variety of VBEs.

Keywords: Virtual Breeding Environment, Virtual Enterprise, VBE implementation methodology.

1 Introduction

The importance of strategic alliances of diverse types has been pointed out by many authors as a way to increase companies' competitiveness [1]. Their benefits mainly depend on the type of alliances, varying from lobbying and sharing common services to dynamic composition of geographically dispersed companies to attend unique business opportunities [2].

In Brazil, since late 1990s several governmental and industry support institutions have promoted the formation of strategic alliances over the country, typically in the form of clusters and of the so-called local productive arrangements. Despite of the considerable benefits brought up with this initiative, it has been realized that such forms of alliances are limited by nature to face relevant requirements of nowadays economy, as volatility of economic barriers, harder global competition and higher innovation needs [3]. However, the problem is to identify which kind of alliance evolution they should pursuit and, once defined, how they should perform this? It is important to highlight that most of the companies are Small and Medium Enterprises (SMEs), which use to have a sort of restrictions to lead a deep study upon this.

There are several types of alliances. Virtual organization Breeding Environments (VBEs) [4] have arisen as a tremendously promising form of strategic alliance for

L.M. Camarinha-Matos et al. (Eds.): PRO-VE 2009, IFIP AICT 307, pp. 197–206, 2009.
© IFIP International Federation for Information Processing 2009

reaching those requirements. A VBE can be generally defined as a long-term alliance of organizations aimed at offering the necessary conditions to support the rapid configuration of virtual organizations, strongly supported by ICT artifacts [5]. A number of references models, frameworks and prototypical software have been proposed to support such type of alliance, all of them with the potential to help companies in terms of providing theoretical foundations to evolve from e.g. a classical cluster to VBE. Nevertheless, while this helps answering the first part of the problem, this is not true at all for the second part: how to do that?

Actually, this is a complex issue as it embraces many technical (e.g. business processes, ICT and legal issues) and non-technical (e.g. organizations' cultures and working methods) perspectives, at several levels. In other words, there is not a simple and single answer to that. A first comprehensive attempt to answer this question, under a more technical-centric perspective, has been proposed by Romero et al. [5]. They have devised a methodology to create and to manage VBEs based on a reference framework for modeling collaborative networks (CNs). In spite of its great importance, the methodology's steps are too abstract to be ready and easily applied to real cases of VBEs.

Trying to leave this methodology more concrete, this paper presents ongoing results of an applied, qualitative and combined case study and exploratory research, which is being carried out close to a cluster of mould and die companies in the south of Brazil. In general, it corresponds to an instantiation of Romero's work in order to better guide cluster's managers to form a VBE type of alliance.

This paper is organized as follows. Section 2 gives an overview on relevant VBE modeling frameworks. Section 3 depicts the mentioned Brazilian cluster, highlighting its main shortcomings. Section 4 presents the VBE model created to represent the cluster towards a VBE. Section 5 introduces the VBE methodology that is being developed. Conclusion and future work are presented at the end.

2 VBE Modeling Frameworks

Several works have approached the problem related to VBEs, generating a number of supporting models. From the scientific foundation point of view, the conceptual framework proposed by Hamided and Camarinha-Matos [4] has been considered as the most prominent basis for most of the works on VBEs.

In this framework, a VBE is not seen as a static multi-organizational entity, but rather as one which has its dynamics so having a life cycle: VBE initiation, recruiting, creation, operation, evolution, dissolution and metamorphosis phase. According to this framework, a set of activities have to be done within each phase. This includes the establishment and setup of a common base ICT infrastructure, VBE foundation, management of competencies, registration of new members, recording of past performance and collaboration in virtual enterprises/organizations, selection and reorganization of information and knowledge, inheritance management, governance, among many other activities.

In order to frame all this into a single and comprehensive model, VBE modeling frameworks are required. Next paragraphs provide a general overview about the most relevant works on VBE modeling.

VERAM (*Virtual Enterprise Reference Architecture and Methodology*) [6] aimed at increasing the preparedness of entities involved in networks for efficient creation and operation of Virtual Enterprises (VE). VERAM facilitates the modeling process through the provision of guidelines on how to build the models and how to identify the common characteristics of VEs. Inspired in the CIMOSA enterprise framework [7], it includes a methodology (Virtual Enterprise Methodology – VEM) that describes how an organization should use the various components of the architectural framework during the VE engineering [8]. The VERAM model is divided in three main layers: 1) VE and networks Concepts; 2) VE Reference Architecture (VERA) [9] and; 3) VE Reference Architecture Components. Although not focused on VBE itself, it provided an important systematization of the process and organization of the framework's elements, which inspired other further works.

AmbianCE (*Environment for creation of Virtual Enterprises*) [3] is a framework developed to support the creation and operation of VBEs that are composed of SMEs. Adopting a bottom-up methodology, the cluster's companies have been firstly deeply analysed in order to design a more generic model of VBE. This cluster, called VIR-FEBRAS, is now established in the city of Caxias do Sul, in the south of Brazil. . AmbianCE provides an environment where *social capital, competence, use of ICT* and *knowledge reuse* are the key elements for supporting a collaborative work. AmbianCE framework is used by means of three steps, namely *AmbianCE Preparation, AmbianCE Structuring*, and *AmbianCE Acting*. It strongly relies on knowledge management and benchmarking. These three steps are executed cyclically as a mechanism to guarantee the continuous VBE evolution.

Romero et al. [5] have created a methodology as a controlled process, addressing systematically a set of steps, supported by different mechanisms and methods required to establish and to characterize the management as well as to operate a VBE along its entire lifecycle. Based on the VBE reference framework developed by Afsarmanesh et al. [4], this methodology corresponds to an instantiation of ARCON modeling framework (see next paragraph) specifically for CNs of VBE type. The provided systematization is very useful as it not only transforms that framework in a sequence of more concrete steps, but also gives some guarantee that VBEs are to be created following more solid scientific theoretical foundations. Actually, this methodology corresponds to the so-called *general* perspective of ARCON, from which particularizations of CNs can be derived. This means that it is naturally too general to be ready applied when a real VBE is going to be created. Following ARCON, another perspective should be considered, which is the so-called *specific* one. This means that another methodology should be created to derive specific VBEs from this general methodology. This is exactly what this paper is about, and that will be explained in sections 4 and 5.

ARCON (*A Reference Model for Collaborative Networks*) [2] can be considered as the most relevant modeling framework and reference model for CNs. Its basic rationale is the possibility to model generic and abstract representations for understanding the involved CN's entities and the relationship among them. ARCON intends to be used as the basis for deriving models for any manifestations of CNs. In very general terms, this is made applying three inter-related perspectives:

- Life Cycle: It captures the evolution of CN and the diversity during their entire life cycle: creation, operation, evolution, dissolution and metamorphosis.
- Environment Characteristics: It focuses on capturing the CN environment characteristics and includes the internal elements ("Endogenous Elements") and the external interactions ("Exogenous Interactions").
- Model Intents: It is related to the different intents for the modeling of CN features and addresses three possible modeling stages: *general*, *specific* and *implementation* modeling.

3   Mold and Die Cluster of Joinville City

Due to the special importance SMEs have in Brazilian economy, several initiatives have been carried out by governmental and industry related institutions to promote their organization in the form of clusters to enhance their competitiveness in the internal and external markets.

Nuferj (*Group of Moulds and Dies Industries of Joinville*) is one of these clusters and represents the one that is going to be prepared to become a VBE. Joinville, a very industrialized medium-sized city placed in the State of Santa Catarina, in the south of Brazil, has about 450 moulds and dies industries and it is considered the largest pole of Latin America in this sector. Nuferj was founded in 1993 and it currently has 50 permanent members. Several members are competitors of the others. Automobile and household appliance companies are its main clients.

Moulds and dies are very unique parts. Each one uses to be very much complex to manufacture. Considering the increasing and extreme hard world-wide competition, Nuferj's members are more than ever exposed to – in a global market of US 20 billion – the competitiveness variables of cost, delivery date and quality. If investments on high-precision and high-speed CNC machines and on sophisticated CAD/CAM software have been enough to keep them competitive, this is no longer true nowadays. Other benefits of the cluster formation, such as the exchange of experiences and lobbying, are clearly not enough as well. That is the reason why Nuferj has been looking for an alternative model which allows it and its members to better and more effectively prepare themselves for the new reality.

Considering the extensive list of potential benefits that an alliance like VBE can add to Nuferj, they are investigating how this can be done. In this sense, the work presented in this paper corresponds to a contribution to this, identifying the required elements to propose an initial but more concrete methodology for a VBE creation, derived for the Nuferj case.

4   Nuferj VBE Model

From the methodological point of view, the derivation activity being done in this research assumes two essential premises: i) ARCON is comprehensive enough to effectively gathers the elements of work of real CNs and, ii) Romero's methodology is comprehensive enough to effectively gathers the Nuferj's elements of work. The underlying research hypothesis is that a VBE can be more properly created and further managed if more solid methodologies are used since the beginning of the process. This corresponds to a top-down approach, which tries to avoid the problems with the bottom-up approach, where the creation of VBEs is totally realized in a *ad-hoc* and empirical manners, as happened in the investigated cases [10].

Therefore, taking into account ARCON reference model and Romero's methodology, a NuFerj VBE Model has been created. This model classifies every element necessary to design the NuFerj VBE, which in turn will guide the work towards its implementation. According to ARCON, the NuFerj VBE model is a Specific Model that has been derived from the General Model specified by Romero's methodology. Table 1 presents the NuFerj VBE Specific Model, considering all the characteristics and elements involved in the Endogenous and Exogenous subspaces [11]. They include Structural elements (e.g. the actors that would be involved in the Nuferj VBE as well the existing roles), Componential (e.g. the type of resources necessary to operate the VBE), Functional (the business processes necessary to support its operation), Behavioral (elements that regulate its operation), Market (elements that are involved in the relationship between the VBE and the market), Support (the supporting entities involved and supporting services), Societal (elements that are involved in the relationship between the VBE and the society in general) and Constituency (actions mainly related with the attraction and selection of new members).

5   Nuferj VBE Implementation Methodology

Olave and Amato Neto [12] have discussed about the requirements of designing, implementing and sustaining clusters. They have highlighted three crucial aspects that are determinant for a cluster success: trust among partners, technical competence and excellence, and fluid use of ICT tools in their processes and collaborations. Therefore, creating a VBE requires a number of pre-requisites that should be incorporated in an implementation methodology. The problem is that none of those aspects are implemented at Nuferj. In this sense, this section introduces the current results of the VBE implementation methodology that is being developed looking at Nuferj's profile. This methodology aims at identifying all the activities necessary to cope with the main aspects modeled in the NuFerj VBE Model (Table 1). When totally finished, this methodology intends to serve as a concrete and systematized guideline to implement a variety of VBEs. As already mentioned, so far it is being customized for Nuferj.

Figure 1 shows the current status of the VBE implementation methodology, i.e. how the reference methodology is being derived to implement the Nuferj VBE. The methodology organization follows the VBE reference framework proposed by Hamideh and Camarinha-Matos [4], when identifies which steps should be done within the VBE life cycle. Next paragraphs detail the proposed methodology phases.

VBE Creation (*Initiation & Recruiting*): this phase is mainly devoted to define the VBE mission and goals, its strategies in terms of marketing, political, economical issues, and the operating rules and duties. Although it may vary, a VBE usually begins with the so-called strategic members, whose selection can be accomplished by a sort of commission, depending on the local conditions.

Table 1. Nuferj VBE Model based-on ARCON Modeling Framework

VBE Endogenous Elements				VBE Exogenous Interactions			
Structural	Componential	Functional	Behavioral	Market	Support	Societal	Constituency

Active Entities
Actors:
• Primary-entities
  o Machining Industries
  o Steel and Insert Sellers
• Support-entities
  o Financial Institutions
  o Machining Industry Association (NuFerj)
  o Local Government
  o National Government
  o Research Agencies (CNPq, FINEP)
  o Educational Institutions (UFSC, UDESC, SENAI, SOCIESC)
Concepts
Roles:
• VBE Member(s)
• VE Support Provider
  o Opportunity Broker
  o VE Planner
• VBE Administrator
• VBE Support Provider
  o Service Provider
  o Support Institution
Relationships:
• Collaboration
• Exchange/sharing
Network:
• Size: around 200 members
• Topology: Network
• Participants: Only NuFerj members
	Passive Entities
	Physical Resources:
	• Machining Centers
	• Milling Machines
	• Drilling Machines
	• Screw Machines
	ICT Resources:
	• Hardware
	  o ICT-Infrastructure
	• Software
	  o CAD/CAM Systems
	  o Distributed DBMS
	  o Service-Oriented Architecture
	  o Financial Mgmt System
	  o Price Quotation System
	  o Production Mgmt System
	  o Business Intelligence Systems
	  o VBE Mgmt System
	Human Resources:
	• Mold and Die Designers
	• Mold and Die Producers
	• Opport. Broker Agents
	• Administrative Staff
	Info./Knowledge Resources:
	• VEs & VBE Members Profile & Competency Info
	  o Governance Info
	  o Support Institutions Info
	  • VE Inheritance Info
		Actions
		Fundamental Processes:
		• VBE Membership Mgmt
		• Members' Profiling & Competency Mgmt
		• Members Trust Mgmt
		• Performance Mgmt
		• Decision Support
		• VE Creation
		  o CO Identification
		  o Opportunity Management
		  o Opportunity Quotation
		  o VE Planning
		  o Partners Selection
		  o Agreements/Contracts Negotiation
		• VE Information Mgmt
		  o VE Registration
		  o VE Inheritance Mgmt
		Background Processes:
		• Strategic Mgmt
		• Marketing Mgmt
		• Financial Mgmt
		• Acquisition Mgmt
		• Resources Mgmt
		• Customer Relationship Mgmt
		• ICT Mgmt
		Concepts
		Methodologies:
		• VBE Instantiation
		• VBE Management
		• VE creation
			Concepts
			Prescriptive Behavior:
			• Cultural Principles:
			  o Regional Traditions
			  o Business Culture
			• Governance Principles:
			  ▪ Network Principles
			  ▪ Honesty and Integrity
			  ▪ Trust and Accountability
			  ▪ IPR Policies
			  o Code of Ethics
			  o Domain Specific Principles
			  ▪ Leadership role principles
			  ▪ Decision-making principles
			Obligatory Behavior:
			• Bylaws:
			  o Molds & Dies Policies
			  o Rights & Duties Policies
			  o Membership Policies
			  o Security Issues
			  o Internal Regulation Policy
			  o Conflict Resolution Policy
			  o Amendments to Bylaws
			  ▪ Internal Regulations:
			  o ICT User Guidelines
			Contracts & Agreements:
			• Adhesion Agreement
			• Agreement Amendments
			Constrains & Conditions:
			• Legal Constrains (Contracts)
			• Internal Normative Constrains
			Incentives & Sanctions:
			• Incentives Policies
				Network Identity
				Mission Statement:
				• VBE Mission / Vision
				• VBE Strategy / Goals
				References/Testimonials:
				• Collection of customers' testimonials
				Network Profile:
				  o NuFerj's Web Site
				  o Yellow pages, newspaper
				Market & Branding Strategy:
				• Marketing Strategy
				  o Seminars & Workshops
				  o National & International Fairs
				  o Advertisement Strategy
				  o Newspaper, technical magazines
				• Branding Strategy
				  o Create a Trademark
				Interaction Parties
				Market Interactions:
				• Customers:
				  o Strategic Customers: Automotive, Pipes
				  o Potential Customers: Foreign enterprises
				• Suppliers: Steel Sellers
				Interactions
				Transactions:
				• Bidding & Ordering
				• Contracting
					Network Identity
					Network Social Nature:
					• Profit-oriented VBE
					Interaction Parties
					Support Entities:
					• Certification Entities
					  o Inmetro, CERTI
					• Logistics Entities
					  o Ship, truck & airplane
					• Financial Entities:
					  o Banks (BNDES)
					  o Investors & Sponsors
					• Coaching Entities:
					  o VBE Coach: UFSC
					• Training Entities:
					  o VBE concepts: UFSC
					  o Molds Manufacture: SOCIESC, SENAI
					• Research Entities:
					  o Universities: UFSC, UNIVILLE
					  o Research Institutes: SOCIESC, SENAI
					Interactions
					Service Acquisition:
					• Financial Support
					• Quality Control Service
					• Technological Service
					• Training Action
					• Knowledge Transfer
					• Consulting Service
					Agreement Establishment:
					• Knowledge Transfer
						Network Identity
						Network Legal Identity:
						• Legal Status
						  o Legal Entity: NuFerj
						• Values & Principles: Free commerce, free competition
						Impacts:
						• Advertising VBE Competency Domain
						• VE Creation
						Interaction Parties
						Public Interactions:
						• Governmental Organizations:
						  o Development Agency
						  o City Hall, Parliament
						• Machining Industry Association (NuFerj)
						• Interest Groups
						  o Supporters: ACIJ, Ajorpeme
						Interactions
						Public Relations:
						• Political Relations
						  o Political lobby
						  o Seeking Support
						  o Promote strategic meetings
						• Information Transfer
						  o Students Fair
						  o Unemployed qualification
						• Social Relations
						  o Technical courses for high school students
						  o Patronage of poor students
							Network Identity
							Attracting
							Factors:
							• Attracting & Recruiting Strategy
							  o Direct invitation
							  o Near localization
							  o Incentives for essential partners
							Rules of Adhesion:
							• Follow the established rules
							• Be part of NuFerj
							• Have recognized competencies
							Interaction parties
							Potential Members:
							• Business entities:
							  o Mainly Machining Industries
							• Public Institutions:
							  o Provide support
							Interactions
							Sustainability
							Factors:
							• Members
							  o Searching:
							  o Personal Invitation
							  o Receiving application: Rigorous membership evaluation

Business processes, ICT infrastructure and governance structure definitions complete the list of activities in this phase. Its legal establishment is also done.

VBE Creation (*Foundation*): in this phase the main activities are concerned to recruiting the VBE members (the companies themselves) and the VBE supporting institutions (e.g. educational, financial, R&D institutions), whom a contract should be signed with. In the case of the VBE members, the envisaged competences should be firstly specified in order to ensure the right members will be invited. This does not mean that any of the mould and die company in Joinville region will be selected (although a VBE can comprise members from any region / country, only companies from Joinville are so far being considered). Every candidate should be empowered with basis knowledge on how to work in a/the VBE, which includes the aspect of trust (as most of the potential NuFerj VBE members are competitors). Once a given company is considered prepared to become a member, its roles are settled and its ICT infrastructure is prepared. Having all this prepared, the VBE can be launched.

VBE Operation: it is the phase which presents the largest number of activities. This phase is divided into two main subgroups: VBE Management and VE Creation. VBE management comprises the activities related to the full operation of the VBE and its main business processes. VE creation encompasses the activities devoted to the creation and initiation of new VEs once new collaboration opportunities are grasped (mostly) from the market. About the VBE management phase, in NurFerj the processes (and further systems) of Membership management and ICT infrastructure management should be firstly introduced. Profile and Competence Management activity comes as a sequence of the previous one. It includes the deployment of a system to register and to maintain the information related to the VBE members. A number of activities can start in parallel after this: Financial, Marketing, Performance, Acquisition, Trust, VE inheritance and Customer Relationship management. Acquisition management activity is critical for NuFerj as it is the one where the purchasing of raw material (mainly steel) is effectuated. This has a tremendous impact on the final cost of the mould or die, so it can represent winning or losing the business. Therefore, here is one concrete aspect where working collaboratively (i.e. buying together) can bring enormous business advantages.

About the VE creation phase, for NuFerj the Opportunity Identification management process/system is the first one to be deployed. This seems natural as it is responsible for brokering, fostering and gathering business opportunities to the VBE. The Opportunity Quotation management system/process is the next one to deploy. It is in charge of analyzing and making quotations for gathered clients' business opportunities. This is another critical activity in this sector as wrong quotations (not so abnormal regarding the complexity of this activity) can provoke very high financial losses. If the business opportunity is got, the necessary partners should be properly selected to compose the respective VE. The remaining activities are performed in sequence: Contract Negotiation management system/process (among the selected VE members, and between the VBE [or the company which got the business and that will usually act as the so-called VE coordinator] and the customer), VE Planning management system/process (to specify which partners will do what and when), VE Registration (to prepare the VBE's information repositories to store the information about the VE as well as to use this information for further inheritance management), and Launching management systems/processes (to coordinate the VE starting).

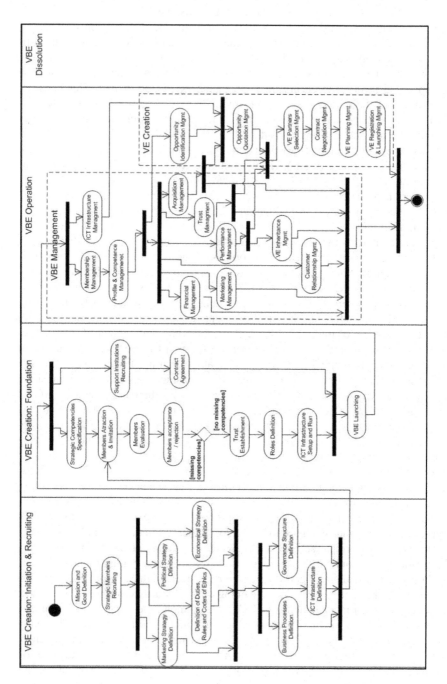

Fig. 1. NuFerj VBE Implementation Methodology

The methodology is essentially organized arranging the functional elements of the Nuferj VBE Model (Table 1) in a proper way considering the other model´s elements along the several functional processes. For example, in the first stage of the VBE Creation the behavioral elements should be taking into account to e.g. set up the governance structure. In the VBE Creation / Foundation stage the structural elements of the model should be considered when selecting the VBE members and setting up their roles. In the VBE Operation stage, the market elements have to be considered in the marketing management business processes, and so forth.

As the current focus of the methodology is on how to create and launch a VBE, the phases of VBE dissolution and metamorphosis have not been addressed yet.

It is important to point out that Romero´s methodology do not specify a strict sequence of actions, especially in VBE operation. This is natural as it is to be a reference methodology. As such, they only identify a set of general actions but that then need to be further adapted regarding the necessary particularities of the envisaged business environment / VBE. In this work, this has looked at Nuferj's environment. Other VBE can present different derivations.

6 Conclusions

This paper has presented the results of a methodology for implementing VBEs. It is a preliminary step towards a wider reference methodology for implementing VBEs. A cluster of mould and die industries has been used as a case study of this research.

A VBE model and methodology have been created, identifying the elements and processes required to create and launch a VBE. Although it is a bit generic, it provides a more detailed path when compared to other VBE methodologies, besides being applied to a real case.

It can be said that the developed methodology is compliant with the most relevant reference model for collaborative networks, which is ARCON modeling and reference framework. Although it is a very recent outcome and has not been deeply validated, its usage in practice showed feasible and comprehensive. In the interviews with Nuferj's representatives and in the methodology development, the necessity of all the identified elements has been confirmed.

The systematization provided by the methodology is very useful as it not only transforms a conceptual framework in a sequence of more concrete steps, but also it provides some guarantee that VBEs can be created following more solid scientific theoretical foundations, instead of purely *ad-hoc* recommendations.

Considering that the main purpose of this methodology is to implement VBEs, activities related to the dissolution and to the metamorphosis of such VBE have not been addressed yet.

As mentioned, the current version of the methodology has some limitations, which will be dealt with in the next phases of its development. Besides requiring a second stage of detailing in order to be even more concrete, the methodology does not cope yet with the temporality and complexity of the actions. For example, how long the establishment of trust among partners can take? How complex the mechanisms to empower partners can be, so that they can effectively be prepared to work in a VBE scenario? Other open points, which will be also focus in the continuation of this research, are related to the identification of the most critic actions (in terms of complexity and importance) as well as to the most sensible actions (in terms of VBE strategy and confidentiality against other competitors).

Only after this it is possible to go through the Implementation level of ARCON, instantiating all the models and tools (based on the devised and preliminary Specific level/model presented in this paper) to Nuferj and hence the creation of Nuferj VBE itself.

Acknowledgements. This work has been supported by Brazilian National Council for Scientific and Technological Development – CNPq. The authors thank Nuferj's managers, Mr. Alexandre Wanzuita and Mr. Christian Dihlmann, and the companies for the provided information.

References

1. Porter, M.E., Fuller, M.B.: Coalitions and global strategy. Competition in global industries 10, 315–343 (1986)
2. Camarinha-Matos, L.M., Afsarmanesh, H.: The ARCON Modeling Framework. In: Camarinha-Matos, L.M., Afsarmanesh, H. (eds.) Collaborative Networks: Reference Modeling, pp. 67–82. Springer, New York (2008)
3. Vallejos, R.V., Lima, C.P., Varvakis, G.: Towards the development of a framework to create a virtual organisation breeding environment in the mould and die sector. Journal of Intelligent Manufacturing 5, 587–597 (2007)
4. Afsarmanesh, H., Camarinha-Matos, L.M.: A Framework for Management of Virtual Organization Breeding Environments. In: Sixth IFIP Working Conference on Virtual Enterprises, pp. 35–48. Springer, Heidelberg (2005)
5. Romero, D., Galeano, N., Molina, A.: A Virtual Breeding Environment Reference Model and its Instantiation Methodology. In: Ninth IFIP Working Conference on Virtual Enterprises, pp. 15–24. Springer, Heidelberg (2008)
6. Zwegers, A., Tolle, M., Vesterager, J.: VERAM: Virtual Enterprise Reference Architecture and Methodology. VTT 1999, 17–38 (2003)
7. AMICE: CIMOSA - Open Systems Architecture for CIM, 2nd revised and extended edition. Research Report. ESPRIT Project (1993)
8. Zwegers, A., Hannus, M., Tølle, M.: Integration issues in virtual enterprises supported by an architectural framework. International IMS Project Forum - A common platform for cross-fertilization among IMS projects and promotion of the IMS program (2001)
9. Vesterager, J., Tolle, M., Bernus, P.: VERA: virtual enterprise reference architecture. VTT 1999, 39–52 (2003)
10. Galeano, N., Molina, A., Beeler, J., Monnier, F., et al.: VBE Pilot Demonstrators. In: Camarinha-Matos, L.M., Afsarmanesh, H., Ollus, M. (eds.) Methods and Tools for Collaborative Networked Organizations, pp. 405–430. Springer, New York (2008)
11. Camarinha-Matos, L.M., Afsarmanesh, H., Ermilova, E., Ferrada, F., et al.: ARCON Reference Models for Collaborative Networks. In: Camarinha-Matos, L.M., Afsarmanesh, H. (eds.) Collaborative Networks: Reference Modeling, pp. 83–112. Springer, New York (2008)
12. Olave, M.E.L., Amato Neto, J.: Redes de cooperação produtiva: uma estratégia de competitividade e sobrevivência para pequenas e médias empresas. Gestão & Produção, pp. 289–318 (2001)

Virtual Operations in Common Information Spaces: Boundary Objects and Practices

Demosthenes Akoumianakis, Giannis Milolidakis, Dimitrios Stefanakis,
Anargyros Akrivos, George Vellis, Dimitrios Kotsalis, Anargyros Plemenos,
and Nikolaos Vidakis

Department of Applied Information Technology & Multimedia
TEI-Crete, Heraklion, Crete, Greece
Tel.: +30 2810 379190
{da,epp382,epp966,epp2063,epp646,epp665,epp1128,
vidakis}@epp.teicrete.gr

Abstract. The paper presents a field study aimed at identifying and analyzing the role of boundary artifacts in cross-organization virtual communities of practice (CoP). Our analysis is informed by a recent case study in vacation package assembly (VPA), which is defined as the distributed collective practice carried out by members of a boundary-spanning virtual alliance inhabiting a 'common' information space (CIS). The CIS forms the virtuality through which members of the alliance engage in coordinative actions on boundary artifacts. The CIS implements the facilities required for constructing, negotiating and re-constructing these boundary artifacts so as to assemble personalized regional vacation packages for tourists. The results lead to several conclusions on the design of CIS as computational host of virtual communities of practice.

Keywords: Boundary objects, common information systems, virtual CoP.

1 Introduction

Building up collective experiences for improved knowledge-based work is important for geographically distributed organizations whose members are bound by a long or short-term common interest or goal, and who communicate and coordinate their work through information technology. In this vein, the present work aims to shed light to the design of tools for boundary-spanning virtual workgroups. In effect, we seek to advance an understanding of how cross-organization virtual alliances can be formed and facilitated by Common Information Spaces (CIS) (Bannon & Bødker, 1997). In this context, a particular set of challenges seems to relate to the dual role members of these virtual alliances are engaged in (Lave & Wenger, 1991) and the corresponding cognitive demands placed upon the CIS. Such duality arises from the fact that members of boundary-spanning virtual alliances are required, on the one hand to obey to their instituted 'local' practices and tools specific to their own business domain, and on the other hand to internalize and perform the 'shared' and 'collaborative' practice established and followed by the virtual alliance. As these constituent practices are frequently intertwined (i.e., local arrangements influence the members' collaborative

L.M. Camarinha-Matos et al. (Eds.): PRO-VE 2009, IFIP AICT 307, pp. 207–216, 2009.
© IFIP International Federation for Information Processing 2009

behavior and praxis and vice versa), the cognitive demands placed upon the partners are high, while the design of the information infrastructure is typically complex and cumbersome.

This paper examines some of these challenges using a case study which describes distributed collective practices of boundary-spanning virtual alliances engaged in the assembly of vacation packages – a particular type of information-based product. Our interest is on the design of CIS so as to allow vacation packages to transcend across boundaries set either by competence-based electronic neighborhoods of the virtual alliance (i.e., accommodation, transportation, entertainment, food and beverage) or external and dynamic conditions, largely defined by online behavior and purchasing patterns of prospective customers.

The rest of the paper is structured as follows. The next section presents the theoretical base of the present work and elaborates on two concepts, namely CIS and boundary objects. Then, we present a case study on vacation package assembly in a cross-organization virtual alliance setting. We identify boundary artifacts and present details of their interactive manifestation in a CIS. The paper is concluded with a summary of key contributions and a discussion of their implications upon designing boundary practices in CIS.

2 Theoretical Links

The term 'common' or 'shared' information spaces (CIS) was introduced in (Bannon & Bødker, 1997) to characterize information infrastructures which empower cooperating actors, engaged in interdependent activities of work, to coordinate their tasks so as to accomplish a collective objective. Subsequent refinements of the concept, mainly by CSCW scholars, have attempted either to establish links with communities of practice (Bossen, 2002) or to qualify parameters of CIS in terms of notions such as boundary objects (Star & Griesemer, 1989), intermediary objects (Boujut & Blanco, 2003), etc. Nevertheless, in the vast majority of cases CIS and their associated practices are examined in the context of single organizations. The more challenging problem of CIS crossing organizational boundaries – either through inter-organizational partnerships or external communities of practice – is seldom or loosely addressed (Dewhurst & Cegarra Navarro, 2004). As our current intention is to consider cross-organizational collaboration in boundary spanning domains, it is of paramount importance to devise a suitable frame of reference to understand and facilitate such collaboration. To this effect, the boundary object concept offers a useful construct serving as 'language' or protocol for engagement in shared practices.

Since the introduction of the boundary object concept (Star & Griesemer, 1989), researchers have explored the boundary role of a variety of artifacts such as diagrams, drawings, and blueprints (Bechky, 2003); workplace timelines and schedules such as Gantt and PERT charts in project-based work (Yakura, 2002); and digital documents (Murphy, 2001, Wegner, 1998; Brown & Duguid, 1996; Bossen, 2002). Moreover, several studies have analyzed the role of boundary objects in domains such as translation (Bowker & Star, 1999), micro-negotiations in CAD (Henderson, 1999), new product development (Carlile, 2002) as well as software development and HCI (Lutters & Seaman, 2004). Despite the wide recognition, the boundary object concept is not without its critiques. Recently, CSCW scholars have questioned prevailing conceptions of boundary objects and have emphasized the need for a broader connotation for boundary artifacts (Carlile, 2006; Lutters & Ackerman, 2007), extending the range of candidates to include information technologies such as document-centered groupware, organizational memory systems, social software and community management tools such as Blogs and Wikis.

Our current work shares common ground with these efforts as it aims to explore boundary artifacts as first class objects in CIS. By this account our intention is to shift the focus from the information processing characterizations of boundary artifacts (e.g., as repositories, diagrams, maps, etc) to the interaction affordances such artifacts should exhibit if they are to serve boundary practices in virtual space.

3 Case Study

The above research challenges are explored using a case study in building information-based vacation packages tightly coupled to a regional setting and offering added value to prospective visitors independently of pre-packaged holiday plan, choice of tour operator or destination management system. There are at least two possible perspectives on the added business value of these regional vacation packages – the first is derived from the packages' neutral role which makes it conceivable either as peripheral supplement to pre-packaged vacations or as a factor stimulating the ultimate choice of destination and/or pre-packaged solution; the second amounts to customers' increased capacity to exercise control and plan vacations in advance.

To gain insight to constructing vacation packages an exploratory survey was conducted utilizing interviews, on-site visits and scenarios to establish a context for design. As our intention was to unfold hidden or implicit elements of collaborative practices, interviews and on-site visits were tailored so as to feed envisioning of new (improved) practices. In turn, these were materialized using scenarios and rapid prototyping. Our survey was directed to tour operators, travel agencies and was complemented by documented codes of practice i.e., "Tour Operators Initiative". The findings led to insights on prevailing practices and the consolidation of an envisioned (virtual) practice.

3.1 Current Practices

Building vacation packages is instituted as a set of basic activities, such as defining package details and services, finding appropriate service providers, negotiating service details, finalizing agreements with service suppliers, promoting the package and package retailing. Some of these activities are administered individually (by one actor alone), while others entail a degree of cooperation and agreement between the involved parties. Moreover, depending on the nature of the vacation package, these activities may vary in scope and effort. For instance, package promotion subsumes different tasks for overseas vacation requiring special travel documents than domestic vacation where inland traveling is involved. As for the objects/artifacts of practice, a broad range was identified, including notebooks, drawing boards, schedules, etc, and a variety of IT tools facilitating communication (telephone, fax, e-mail, etc.), community support (i.e., portals and bulletin boards) as well as more advanced data-intensive operations (i.e., databases, repositories, reservation systems (CRS), customer relationship management (CRM) systems).

Our empirical evidence, as documented in the interviews, reveal that the above constrain both the types of vacation packages produced as well as the end users' testified willingness to exercise influence and plan vacations in advance. Moreover, although vacation package developers seem to recognize such constrains, they appear to be reluctant to introduce radical changes in the way the practice is conducted. These observations motivated the assessment of an envisioned practice designed to examine how a cross-organization virtual community of practice could cope with assembling rather than crafting vacation packages.

3.2 Envisioning Practices in Virtual Settings

Synthesizing the new practice entailed decisions on two primary constituents, namely the package development workflows (i.e., the practice domain) and community management. In terms of package development workflows, four distinct stages were identified, namely initiation, elaboration, deployment and tailoring, each hosting separate activities. Initiation amounts to the definition of the package, its duration and designation of the required services. Package elaboration entails negotiation and commitment of resources on behalf of the partners for the activities each can support. The deployment stage gathers all contributions and compiles them into a concrete offering which can be disseminated to prospective customers. Finally, the tailoring stage is concentrated on the package retailing which is geared to allowing customers to request further changes and modifications so as to suit own requirements.

The second constituent relates to the management of the cross-organization virtual alliance. For our purposes, the community of practice is conceived of as a mission-specific electronic squad. The mission is the development of the vacation package so as to meet designated constraints. The electronic squad is the cross-organization community of practice engaged in the vacation package development workflows. Three distinct roles are identified, namely the squad moderator, the squad member and the customer. This should be contrasted to the typical workgroup established in the traditional practice environment comprising the tour operator, the travel agent, the service providers and the end-customer. Moreover, as our squads are dynamic they follow a designated lifecycle. Our survey built upon existing sociological accounts rooted in dynamic group stabilization theories (Tuckman, 1965) to confirm four basic lifecycle stages, namely forming, storming, norming and performing.

The squad is formed once the package is defined in abstract terms. Squad reformation continues through the initiation workflow and up to the end of the elaboration workflow to allow candidates either to commit or opt out from a squad. At this point, the squad is stabilized and not likely to change until the end of the package creation lifecycle. The storming stage starts when initial activities are defined and the squad has taken its principal form. Storming is about reaching consensus on the specific mission and subsuming activities. The stage ends once all relevant issues have been addressed. Devising a common agenda with respect to the issues raised is the objective of the norming stage which is in partial overlap with the package elaboration workflow lasting until the end of the deployment workflow. Finally, the performing stage is in full temporal overlap with the package tailoring workflow.

4   Common Information Space and Sense-Making

This section describes components of the CIS which was designed to facilitate vacation package assembly as the distributed collective practice of an electronic squad. The emphasis is on the boundary artifacts used to make sense of the shared practice in virtual space and how such artifacts transcend different social worlds.

4.1   Boundary Artifacts

Vacation packages have two distinct properties – there are collective offerings with a prominent boundary function. Their 'collective' nature is derived from the fact that no single member of the virtual alliance can provide the package effectively and efficiently by account of own resources. On the other hand, their 'boundary' function is evident from the fact that vacation packages, as composite offerings as well as their constituent parts, should be recognizable by at least the following social groups: (a) different members of the cross-organization virtual alliance, each offering their own services such as accommodation, food & beverage, transportation, etc., and (b) end user communities with different interests and preferences in the optional service offerings of the vacation package. Thus, they should be designed so as to transcend institutional boundaries resulting from the cross-organizational nature of the alliance and the exogenous boundaries implicitly set by different target end user communities. Recalling the definition of a boundary object by Star and Griesemer (1989, p. 393), some of the necessary qualities of these objects are that they should (a) be relevant and meaningful to different social worlds (b) have different meanings in different social worlds and c) have a common enough structure to make them recognizable in different social worlds. In our work, a social world is a neighborhood whose services are demanded by a vacation package. Thus, there are two types of boundary objects satisfying the above requirements of plasticity, namely neighborhood offerings (or activities) considered as primitive boundary objects and package families constituting composite boundary objects.

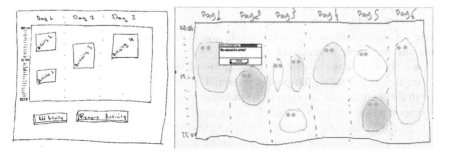

Fig. 1. Sketches of boundary objects with context information

In an attempt to derive suitable symbolic representations of these boundary objects and their tractable properties, which would lead to an appropriate interactive manifestation in virtual settings, we used sketches and mock-ups to assess meaning and interpretive capacity across social worlds. Figure 1 presents examples of low-fidelity mockups of summative views of vacation packages and their primitive constituent activities. Rectangles represent neighborhood offerings which have specified type and duration in the context of a vacation package (i.e., panel). Color coding and social awareness indicators may be used to enhance the interpretive flexibility across collaborative contexts. Subsequent efforts aimed to further detail interaction-specific properties of these boundary objects as they transcend computing platforms, contexts of use and institutional boundaries.

4.2 Spanning Internal Virtual Organization Boundaries

Since neighborhood offerings are the primary constituents of a package, they need to be associated with a suitable interaction object class whose physical properties afford the intended meaning and interpretation. Following design deliberations, it was deemed appropriate to interactively manifest activity objects as customized 'elastic' buttons (with a label, color and size manipulation), inheriting the two-state dialogue model of a conventional button. The visual appearance of 'elastic' buttons is different from the typical, two-state GUI button. Specifically, their color designates neighborhood type, while direct manipulation of size allows indication of duration of the corresponding activity. To facilitate their interpretive flexibility, elastic buttons can host labels and icons to designate some of their features or current state. Furthermore, when rendered and manipulated in synchronous collaborative sessions, their dialog is enhanced to convey interim feedback through color and size variation as well as nested buttons for accepting / rejecting the current state values. These features were implemented by augmenting the Java Swing (Akoumianakis 2009).

Elastic buttons obtain their designated meaning when bundled into a suitable container which binds them to a vacation package. Flexible activity panels serve this purpose by utilizing dedicated layout management functions to organize neighborhood offerings (i.e., elastic buttons) in a particular layout. We have constructed two alternative layouts to represent role-specific (i.e., the moderator's and squad members') views of a vacation package. As shown in Figure 2, the moderator's view (left-hand side instance) concentrates on neighborhoods, while the squad members' view emphasizes activity timelines within days. It is worth noticing the representation of activities spanning across several days. In the moderator's view, these are represented as a uniform elastic button, whereas in the squad members view there are populated as a series of elastic buttons with slight modification of appearance to convey continuity of the offering across several days.

Some silent features of the implementation of the two activity panels include (a) the fact that at all times the panels present instances of the same object, although through different layout managers, (b) moderators have access to and can manipulate all components of an activity panel, while squad member belonging to a neighborhood can only manipulate objects of that neighborhood and (c) each activity operates in its own locale allowing automatic tailoring to the context of use and computing devise.

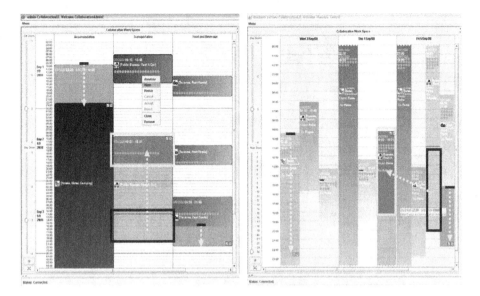

Fig. 2. Collaboration patterns in synchronous sessions

As vacation packages constitute 'collective' offerings their details are negotiated in the course of synchronous collaborative sessions. To this end, there are different versions of mutual awareness relevant, but due to space limitations we will briefly review the case of mutual awareness in synchronous collaboration sessions. A synchronous session is initiated by a moderator and allows members to negotiate aspects of a vacation package. The object of these negotiations is either part of or the entire package at a given point in time. However, as already mentioned, depending on their role different collaborators may view the same package differently and with different access rights. This requires object synchronization to ensure consistency of coordinative actions.

In the current implementation synchronization is achieved through managing distributed object replicas irrespective of their interactive manifestation. In Figure 2 the examples assume that the moderator (left screen) is the holder of the floor, thus the initiator of the collaborative tasks. The right screen depicts the effects of the initiator's actions on the collaborating partner's user interface The components marked in red and yellow represent start and end conditions respectively. The 'accept/reject' buttons are automatically introduced in the elastic buttons to indicate direction in the change of state. This allows collaborators, not only to make sense of current and proposed states, but also to express opinion and influence the ultimate details of the object of negotiation.

4.3 Spanning External Boundaries: The Customers' Social Worlds

Thus far we have examined how vacation packages span internal boundaries of the virtual workgroup as they are being constructed, negotiated and reconstructed. Nevertheless, the same objects once assembled are required to cross the boundary between

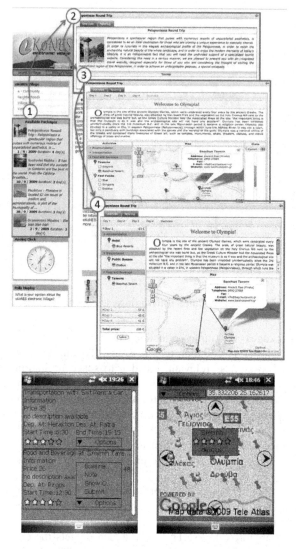

Fig. 3. Vacation packages in the customers' social world

the virtual workgroup and the customer base. To facilitate such crossing the assembly line undertakes to translate vacation packages in a language meaningful to the end users. The top image in Figure 3 depicts one type of such a translation illustrating how prospective users are informed of the package's availability (step 1) and prompted to consider making a personalized reservation (steps 2-4). The result of these interactions is fed back to the virtual workgroup, as request for tailoring, thus generating new cycles of meta-negotiations until a customized version of the package is derived. In a similar vein, while in vacation, customers may further reflect upon their experience with the package. The bottom images of Figure 3 depict how this is done using a mobile device. In the example the user has the ability to get an overall view of the services' details and their providers, as well as to add comments and rate the service quality. Such information is also fed back to the virtual work group facilitating meta-negotiations and perhaps improvements in subsequent versions of the package. Another useful provision in the mobile device context is derived by integrating the Google Maps services and the GPS of the device to allow users to find out the relative location of the supplier of a service on the map (i.e., the blue pin-like marker) and to become aware of the location of other customers (i.e., green pawn marks) that have registered in the same package family, thus strengthening ties between consumers of similar products.

5 Consolidation and Contributions

Guided by the need to understand the processes and mechanics of cooperation in cross-organization virtual alliances within the context of a virtual community of practice, the present work provides useful insights to fulfilling theoretical and engineering challenges. The theoretical challenge is concerned with understanding virtual practices and their constituent elements in online collaborative settings. On the other hand, the engineering challenge amounts to designing virtualities for social construction of boundary spanning knowledge and managing 'collective' artifacts. In terms of the theoretical challenge, the present work reveals that in virtual settings involving knowledge-based collaborative work, social interaction alone is not sufficient to reveal the constituents of practice in which collaborators engage in. In fact, a more thorough insight of the process, tools and the artifacts of work is required to make sense of what collaborators actually do and how the 'boundary' practice of the community intertwines with the collaborator's 'local' activities. The implication on engineering CIS is that they need to be designed so as to establish the 'place' for engaging in the practice the community is about. This extends current thinking on virtual CoP, which assumes that practice is revealed by analyzing the content of interactions in bulletin boards, threaded discussion forums and other types of community-support systems. Our experience indicates that, whatever practice may be unfolded through such systems, it will offer only partial insight to 'collaborative' praxis. A more informative account of what collaborators become engaged in requires re-framing practice beyond social interaction and into the activities subsumed by the boundary artifacts (i.e., the processes, objects and the tools) of cooperative work.

6 Summary and Conclusions

We have described the rationale of boundary artifacts as first class objects in a CIS devised to support vacation package assembly. Additionally, we have elaborated how these artifacts can be designed to exhibit plasticity and interpretive flexibility so as to facilitate sense making in virtual boundary-spanning settings. Collectively, the boundary objects, the tools for manipulating them and the shared workflow constitute the CIS for the designated practice of vacation package assembly. Recently completed and on-going virtual ethnographies of operating squads indicate a number of implications related both to the necessary quality attributes and the role of boundary objects in CIS (Akoumianakis, in print). Specifically, whereas for traditional boundary objects (e.g., drawings, forms and documents, repositories), interpretive flexibility, abstractness and plasticity suffice as necessary qualities, in the context of CIS boundary objects should additionally satisfy role-adaptability, replication, multiple view capability and view synchronization. As for the role of boundary objects in CIS, our work supports a notion of boundary artifacts as computer-mediated social practice vocabularies rather than mere translation devices.

References

Akoumianakis, D.: Managing Universal Accessibility Requirements in Software-intensive Projects. Software Process – Improvement & Practice 14, 3–29 (2009)

Akoumianakis, D.: Electronic community factories: The model and its application in the tourism sector. Accepted for publication in Electronic Commerce Research. Springer, Heidelberg (in print)

Bannon, L., Bødker, S.: Constructing Common Information Spaces. In: Hughes, J., Rodden, T., Prinz, W., Schmidt, K. (eds.) ECSCW 1997: Proceedings of the 5th European CSCW Conference, pp. 91–96. Kluwer Academic Publishers, Dordrecht (1997)

Bossen, C.: The Parameters of Common Information Spaces: the Heterogeneity of Cooperative Work at a Hospital Ward. In: CSCW 2002, New Orleans, Louisiana, USA, November 16-20 (2002)

Boujut, J.-F., Blanco, E.: Intermediary Objects as a Means to Foster Co-operation in Engineering Design. Computer Supported Cooperative Work 12, 205–219 (2003)

Bowker, G.C., Star, S.L.S.: Sorting things out: classification and its consequences. MIT Press, Cambridge (1999)

Brown, J.S., Duguid, P.: The social life of documents. First Monday 1(1) (1996), http://www.firstmonday.dk/issues/issue1/documents/

Carlile, P.R.: A Pragmatic View of Knowledge and Boundaries: Boundary Objects in New Product Development. Organization Science 13, 442–455 (2002)

Carlile, P.R.: Artifacts and Knowledge Negotiation Across Domains. In: Rafaeli, A., Pratt, M.G. (eds.) Artifacts and Organizations: Beyond Mere Symbolism. LEA, Mahwah (2006)

Dewhurst, F.W., Cegarra Navarro, J.G.: External communities of practice and relational capital. The Learning Organization 11(4/5), 322–331 (2004)

Henderson, K.: On Line and On Paper: Visual Representations, Visual Culture, and Computer Graphics in Design Engineering. MIT Press, Cambridge (1999)

Lave, J., Wenger, E.: Situated Learning: Legitimate Peripheral Participation. Cambridge University Press, Cambridge (1991)

Lutters, W., Ackerman, M.:) Beyond Boundary Objects: Collaborative Reuse in Aircraft Technical Support. Computer Supported Cooperative Work 16, 341–372 (2007)

Lutters, W.G., Seaman, C.B.: Software Maintenance and Support: Identifying Routine Work Artifacts as Boundary Objects Across Time (2004), IFIP 7.2, http://www.se-hci.org/bridging/chi2004/papers.html

Murphy, D.L.: Digital Documents in Organizational Communities of Practice: A First Look. In: 34th Hawaii International Conference on System Sciences. IEEE Computer Society, Los Alamitos (2001)

Star, S.L., Griesemer, J.: Institutional ecology, 'translations' and boundary objects. Social Studies of Science 19, 387–420 (1989)

Wegner, E.: Communities of Practice: Learning, Meaning and Identity. Cambridge University Press, Cambridge (1998)

Yakura, E.K.: Charting time: timelines as temporal boundary objects. Academy of Management Journal 45(5), 956–970 (2002)

An Alignment Model for Collaborative Value Networks

Carlos Bremer, Rodrigo Cambiaghi Azevedo, and Alexandra Pereira Klen

Axia Consulting, Av. Nações Unidas, 12551, 18°Andar, 04578-903,
São Paulo – SP, Brazil
{carlos.bremer,rodrigo.cambiaghi,
alexandra.klen}@axiaconsulting.com.br

Abstract. This paper presents parts of the work carried out in several global organizations through the development of strategic projects with high tactical and operational complexity. By investing in long-term relationships, strongly operating in the transformation of the competitive model and focusing on the value chain management, the main aim of these projects was the alignment of multiple value chains. The projects were led by the Axia[1] Transformation Methodology as well as by its Management Model and following the principles of Project Management. As a concrete result of the efforts made in the last years in the Brazilian market this work also introduces the Alignment Model which supports the transformation process that the companies undergo.

Keywords: Value Chain, Business Transformation, Alignment Model, Customer Segmentation, Axia Methodology.

1 Introduction

For a Collaborative Value Network to succeed one of the main challenges is to guarantee the alignment between customer value proposition and its subsequent value delivery. A careful analysis of some companies' businesses showed that they experience the same main problems: their choices and trade-offs are not converted into execution because their strategies are primarily deployed within departments thus breaking down the value generation flows disperse throughout the organization and consequently increasing the difficulty for decision makers to align themselves.

With this in mind, the key objectives of the discussions carried out in this work are twofold:

- To anticipate, react to and reduce value chain variabilities in the company delivery and value generation flow; and
- To integrate and align value proposition with value delivery.

This paper focuses therefore on presenting the research developed as well as the actions taken for achieving the above mentioned objectives.

The remaining part of this paper is organized as follows: section 2 provides an overview of the Axia Transformation Methodology which arose from the award-winning

---

[1] Axia in Greek means "Value".

L.M. Camarinha-Matos et al. (Eds.): PRO-VE 2009, IFIP AICT 307, pp. 217–224, 2009.

academic research of the SAP University Alliance Grant Awards. Its *prima facie* effectiveness allows fundamental dimensions to be wholly and simultaneously developed ensuring long-lasting transformation and excellence in competitiveness and value generation. Section 3 addresses the 7 processes of the Axia Management Reference Model and section 4 shows how the alignment projects are managed according to the Transformation Methodology. In this fourth section it is highlighted how the proposed 7 dimensions of business transformation allow the use of a holistic approach to critical factors of success throughout the course of developing the alignment projects, ensuring that the 6 phases of transformation meet the business objectives proposed. Section 5 depicts the Alignment Model and the main concepts that have guided its development. Finally, section 6 presents some conclusions and the next envisaged steps.

2   Fundamental Dimensions

The boom of ERP implementations in the late 90s brought alongside with it a vast level of unsuccessful rate; at least when analyzed through a perspective of the achieved value chain improvements. At that time, as members of an academic institution, we have launched a research question aiming to investigate the causes of the gap between the proposed value of an ERP and the value companies were achieving with its implementation. In January 2000, this research was granted with the SAP University Alliance Awards as the best applied research in Americas and its result is still today a core element of our methodological approach applied in global transformation projects.

In this research, we found out that ERP implementations were always driven by 3 business dimensions: processes, people and information technology. However, through an explorative approach, we have figured out that by applying this 3-dimensional perspective in the transformation, projects were leaving behind other vital aspects of a value chain "ecosystem". The research concluded that 7 dimensions drive any complex value chain transformation: vision, strategy, organization, key performance indicators (KPIs) plus the previous three dimensions; people, processes and technology. Till today, and according to the best knowledge of the authors, there is no similar methodology that considers all these 7 dimensions foreseen in the Axia transformation methodology. Figure 1 depicts the 7-dimensions transformation approach and in its sequence each dimension is outlined.

- Vision: in charge of aligning the value expected with proposed transformation among multiple stakeholders across the value chain;
- Strategy: sets and aligns across the organization the steps (e.g. projects, stages, sub-projects) required for the transformation;
- Organization: probably one of the most complex aspects during any value chain transformation, this dimension is responsible to design a new organizational structure better aligned with the future arrangement of the value chain;
- KPIs: it is in charge of setting the most appropriate indicators which will drive the new configuration of the value chain;
- People: deals with the organizational and individual knowledge and skills required for the future scenario;

- Technology: is the dimension that searches for the best IT solutions in order to support the new business challenges;
- Processes: the set of activities required for carrying out the new work system. This dimension links all previous ones and for this reason it is placed in a central position in Figure 1.

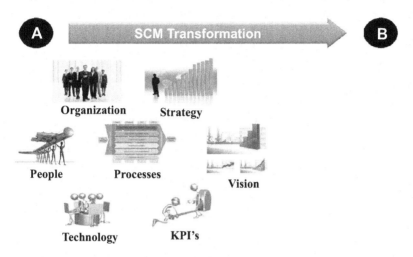

Fig. 1. Seven Dimensions of a Business Transformation

3 Management Processes Reference Model

Our academic background alongside with the hands-on experience on several global value chain transformations, allowed us to develop a reference model for managing complex value chains. This model aims to address the important decisions a company faces; from the strategy formulation down to its deployment, execution and follow up.

Fig. 2. Axia Management Model

Figure 2 illustrates the model which is composed of 7 core processes: strategic planning, integrated planning (S&OP), fulfillment management, order management, execution flow management, supply management and demand management. While the 5 former processes (strategic planning, S&OP, fulfillment management, order management, and execution flow management) are in charge of deploying and managing strategic drivers through tactical and operational flows, the supply and demand management processes are in charge of pursuing forward and reverse alignments with, respectively, customers and suppliers of a value chain (Bremer et al., 2009) enabling the alignment of the collaborative value network.

4 Transformation Methodology

The alignment projects are executed in 6 phases: initiation, visibility, proposition, design, implementation and value capture. The first 3 phases comprise what is called the "Supply Chain Challenges Identification". By applying the 7 fundamental business dimensions (Figure 3) a through ample and in-depth analysis is developed in the companies and a value chain diagnosis is provided together with an action plan that provides clear and concrete recommendations in order to promote value chain transformation. This diagnosis takes in average 12 weeks. The last 3 phases are carried out in the sequence.

The key achievements are usually identified during the phase of value capture. At this stage two kinds of results are perceived: the first one can be measured (very notable improvement in the performance of operations and financial results of the company, for instance); the second can be felt (collaborative value networks are made up of people, and the success of the value chain transformation depends directly on them).

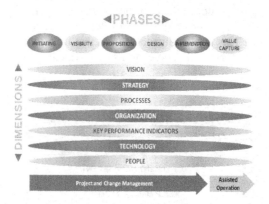

Fig. 3. Axia Transformation Methodology

5 Collaborative Value Networks

The breakthrough point in the alignment projects was the awareness that current segmentation approaches do not translate and align the value chain. The variabilities and the lack of confidence have to be faced considering that suppliers, producer and clients are part of a collaborative value network (CAMARINHA-MATOS and AF-SARMANESH, 2006) and that distributed and collaborative business processes are being managed in a dynamic way (PEREIRA-KLEN et al., 2001; PEREIRA-KLEN and KLEN, 2005; RABELO, PEREIRA-KLEN and KLEN, 2004). This means that value chains come in a number of different forms, and some companies use more than one for different parts of their businesses (GATTORNA, 2006). One chain may run lean to keep inventory costs low, whereas another may be more flexible to enable it to respond to new opportunities as they arise. The very important thing is that different value chains within a single organization must work together so that its global performance can be enhanced.

The challenge therefore was to work towards the development and implementation of a multiple value chain alignment strategy which in turn is based on the segmentation of suppliers and clients according to their dominant behavioural forces. To this end this work has adopted the segmentation model of Gattorna (2006) that takes in to consideration the buying behaviour of the clients (Figure 4) and has extended it also to the suppliers.

After realizing that the improvement of the value chain performance in the projects is a consequence of the dynamic alignment of the multiple value chains that co-exist in the companies, other challenges were identified.

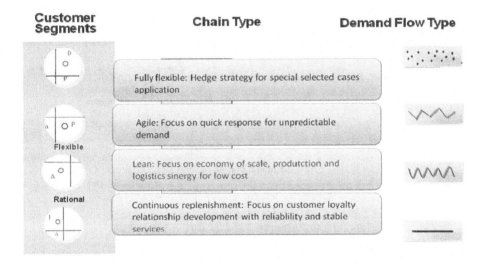

Fig. 4. Segmentation model (GATTORNA, 2006)

The first challenge is to make the companies aware that inside the organization people usually do not have a clear and single vision of the main questions. To clarify this situation in the companies an exercise is proposed and carried out with the executive and tactic managerial levels. In a workshop they should position their business according to what they believe that their competitive strategy is. To this end it is made use of a triadic model (based on a previous work developed by MIT, 2007) that considers: the operational efficiency, the customer intimacy and the products (Figure 5, top left). After the usual polarization of opinions of the insiders, the promotion of the alignment of the transformation strategy is stimulated and achieved.

The second challenge is to find an internal agreement about what metrics the companies want to be recognized for by their clients and the market as "best-in-class". To this end it is made use of the SCOR Performance Attributes (Figure 5, top right) defining a set of measurements and establishing internal targets for improvements in processes, functions, products, and so on.

The third challenge is to identify the profile of the companies as well as of their suppliers and clients, according to the segmentation model of Gattorna (Figure 5, bottom). Their behaviour might be classified according to 16 different possible combinations derived from the four dominant behavioural forces, namely:

- Producer (P): the force for action, results, speed and focus.
- Administrator (A): the opposing force to D, and represents stability, control, reliability, measurement, logic and efficiency.
- Developer (D): the force for creativity, change, innovation and flexibility.
- Integrator (I): the opposing force to P, and represents cooperation, cohesion, participation and harmony.

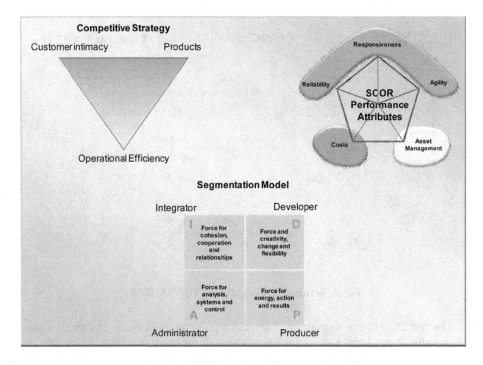

Fig. 5. Alignment challenges

In order to overcome the challenges and to care for a dynamic alignment of the multiple value chains, an alignment model has been developed (Figure 6). The model combines the triadic model of competitive strategy, the SCOR pentagon of the performance attributes and the "PADI" square of Gattorna. The model shows that companies that are more oriented to operational efficiency present a behavior that tend to be more "producer" (P) or "administrator" (A) usually putting more emphasis on indicators such as costs and asset management. At the same time, companies that have their center of gravity on customer intimacy present a behavior that is predominantly "integrator" (I) and the performance attributes that they mostly care for are reliability and responsiveness. Finally, the model shows that companies that strongly focus on their products behave as "developers" (D) and are more concerned about agility and responsiveness.

This model allows for a better comprehension of the companies situation and therefore speeds up the alignment process of the multiple value chains that flow simultaneously thorough the companies. This understanding and alignment are essential for an adequate and efficient management of collaborative value networks (CAMARINHA-MATOS, L. M.; AFSARMANESH, H.; OLLUS, M., 2005).

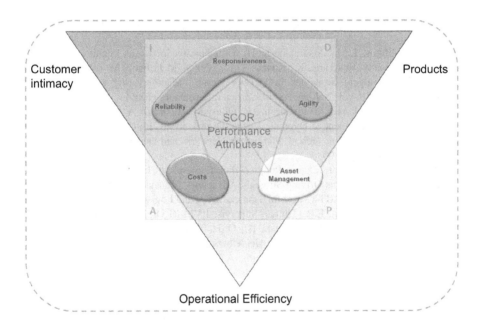

Fig. 6. Alignment Model

6 Conclusions

This paper summarizes the achievement of almost ten years of research and work. The whole approach has been maturing during all this time. The research question that was launched almost one decade ago was the trigger for the search for even more questions. We are now in the process of finding the answers. Some of them were already found. For collaborative value networks, for instance, we have realized that their management can be significantly improved if the multiple value chains that co-exist inside a single company can be aligned. And to this purpose an alignment model was proposed in order to support the transformation process of the companies.

The next planned steps include an analysis on how this alignment model could impact the virtual breeding environment and its members as well as the consideration by the model of performance attributes related to sustainability aspects.

Acknowledgments. Axia Alignment Model has emerged, matured and improved thanks to the joint work performed for and with our customers. The authors thank all Axia´s customers for their collaborative spirit as well as the contributions from the whole Axia team.

References

1. Bremer, C.F., Azevedo, R.C., Aravechia, C., Horta, L.C.: Supply Chain Alignment – Brazilian Style, in Dynamic Supply Chain Alignment - A New Business Model for Peak Performance in Enterprise Supply Chains Across All Geographies. Gower Publishing, London (2009)
2. Camarinha-Matos, L.M., Afsarmanesh, H.: Collaborative networks: Value creation in a knowledge society. In: Wang, K., Kovács, G.L., Wozny, M.J., Fang, M. (eds.) Knowledge Enterprise: Intelligent Strategies in Product Design, Manufacturing and Management, PROLAMAT. IFIP, vol. 207, pp. 26–40. Springer, Heidelberg (2006)
3. Camarinha-Matos, L.M., Afsarmanesh, H., Ollus, M.: Ecolead: A Holistic Approach to Creation and Management of Dynamic Virtual Organizations. In: Camarinha-Matos, L.M., Afsarmanesh, H., Ortiz, A. (eds.) Collaborative Networks and their Breeding Environments. Springer, Heidelberg (2005)
4. Gattorna, J.: Living Supply Chains. Prentice-Hall, Englewood Cliffs (2006)
5. Lapide, L.: Supply Chains Driving Strategic Advantage: Managing Dynamics and Innovating the Future January. MIT-Centre for Transportation and Logistics (2007)
6. Pereira-Klen, A.A., Klen, E.R.: Human Supervised Virtual Organization Management. In: Camarinha-Matos, L.M., Afsarmanesh, H., Ortiz, A. (eds.) Collaborative Networks and their Breeding Environments. Springer, Heidelberg (2005)
7. Pereira-Klen, A.A., Rabelo, R.J., Ferreira, A.C., Spinosa, L.M.: Managing Distributed Business processes in the Virtual Enterprises. Journal of Intelligent Manufacturing 12(2) (April 2001) ISSN 0956-5515
8. Rabelo, R.J., Pereira-Klen, A.A., Klen, E.R.: Effective Management of Dynamic and Multiple Supply Chains. International Journal of Networking and Virtual Organizations 2(3), 193–208 (2004)

Part 7

Modeling and Managing Competencies - I

Competence-Based Approach in Value Chain Processes

Rodrigo Cambiaghi Azevedo[1], Sophie D'Amours[1], and Mikael Rönnqvist[2]

[1] Université Laval, For@c Research Consortium, CIRRELT – Centre Interuniversitaire de
Recherche sur les Réseaux d'Entreprise, Quebec, QC, G1V 0A6, Canada
{Rodrigo.Cambiaghi,Sophie.DAmours}@cirrelt.ca
[2] Norwegian School of Economics and Business Administration,
NO-5045 – Bergen, Norway
Mikael.Ronnqvist@nhh.no

Abstract. There is a gap between competence theory and value chain processes frameworks. While individually considered as core elements in contemporary management thinking, the integration of the two concepts is still lacking. We claim that this integration would allow for the development of more robust business models by structuring value chain activities around aspects such as capabilities and skills, as well as individual and organizational knowledge. In this context, the objective of this article is to reduce this gap and consequently open a field for further improvements of value chain processes frameworks.

Keywords: Value Chain Management, Business Process, Competence.

1 Introduction

Value chain management and the competence-based approach are considered to be two distinct bodies of knowledge and have been intensely debated in academic and practical fields in recent years. The former, here considered as synonymous with supply chain management, is defined as a management philosophy where the coordination and optimization of material, information and financial flows happen not within a business unit, but among the involved parts of a collaborative network [15]. At the centre of this philosophy lays the concept of business process and this explains why academia and practitioners intensively debate the most suitable collection of processes when implementing value chain business models [8].

In an analogous fashion, the competence-based approach has emerged in recent decades as a basis for new insights into the nature of inter-firm competition and potential sources of competitive advantage [12]. Defining "competence" as the ability to sustain the coordinated deployment of assets in ways that help a firm achieve its goals, its study investigates the association between company internal characteristics and market value creation.

In spite of the importance of competence theory for contemporary management thinking, we observed that its wisdom has still not been explored in the field of value chain processes. This article aims to reduce this gap and consequently open a field for

L.M. Camarinha-Matos et al. (Eds.): PRO-VE 2009, IFIP AICT 307, pp. 227–234, 2009.

further improvements in terms of value chain processes frameworks. In order to do so, we organize this article as follows: first, we discuss value chain processes and this aims to identify where the competence-based approach might be applicable. Second, we depict a core processes framework for value chains networks. This framework forms the backbone for competences to support the achievement of the firm's goals. Third, competence theory is introduced and its construction around value chain management processes is proposed. Finally, the main findings of the research are outlined.

2   Classifying Value Chain Processes

Hammer [6] defines a business process as a collection of activities that takes one or more kinds of input and creates an output that is of value to the customer. Davenport and Short [4] reiterate this definition by affirming that business processes have two important characteristics: (a) they focus on their customer and (b) they cross organizational functions. More recently, the value chain management concept has expanded the second characteristic to include an inter-organizational approach among different elements of a value chain.

Some classifications of business processes can be found in the literature [1]. One of the most frequent classifications is associated with the purpose of the business process inside an organization or a value chain. Regarding this subject, Davenport [5] categorized business processes as operational or managerial. More recently, Mentzer *et al.* [11] have expanded this classification by proposing three main categories: (i) *core processes* that are needed to realize business goals by enabling goods and services to reach an external customer; (ii) *support processes* that are needed to make the core processes work as well as possible, but which are not critical to the success of the company; (iii) *management processes* which are broader knowledge domains used to control and coordinate the core and support processes.

A common feature in the literature is that core processes are defined as a set of a few processes vital for a company's survival. They present structured and continuous patterns of performance [1;5]. In contrast to core processes, management processes are considered unstructured and discontinuous, which in a certain way, means the term becomes an oxymoron [5].

The distinction between core and management processes is supported by the coordination theory proposed by Malone and Crowston [10]. According to the authors, this theory endeavors to address the growing interest in questions about how the activities of complex systems can be coordinated. The theory is founded on the idea of conceptual separation of two types of activities that are present within any process: activities that directly contribute to the output of the process and additional activities called coordination mechanisms, which must be carried out in order to manage various interdependencies among activities and resources. Figure 1 illustrates the three classifications of value chain processes. On it, management competences are depicted as sets of elements (e.g. activities, skills, capabilities) which are applied throughout core processes.

Management

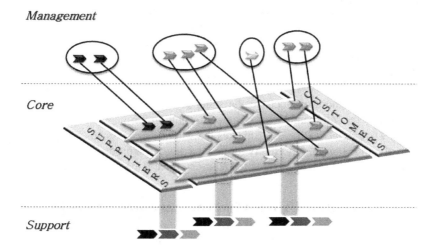

Core

Support

Fig. 1. Value Chain Processes Classification Framework

3 Value Chain Core Processes Framework

Following the above classification for value chain processes, Azevedo *et al.* [2] propose a core processes framework. Based on a content analysis of over 184 articles, the authors identify seven core processes for manufacturing companies located in the middle of a value chain. The processes are: strategic planning, sales and operations planning, value commitment, order fulfilment, inventory replenishment, product return and value development. Each process scope is introduced in the following:

- *Strategic Planning Process* – is the set of activities in charge of determining the direction and scope of an organization over the long term which achieves advantages for the organization through its configuration of resources within a changing environment, to meet the needs of markets and fulfil stakeholder expectations.
- *Sales & Operations Planning Process* – is the process responsible for the deployment of the company's strategic drivers into a set of aligned cross-departmental plans. While strategic planning is in charge of the company's direction and scope over the long term, the S&OP responsibilities lay throughout the tactical horizon.
- *Value Commitment Process* – is the process in charge of conducting the mutual discussion and arrangement of the terms of a sales order. To do so, it spans from the initial dialogue between the company and the customer when dealing with a request up to the moment when the customer inquiry is converted into an order for the vendor. This moment is represented in the framework by the Commitment Point (C.P.).
- *Order Fulfilment Process* – covers all related activities from the moment the order is received to the instant the customer obtains the product and the seller collects the agreed compensation. In other words, it encompasses all (order-driven) activities upwards to the Decoupling Point (D.P.).

- *Inventory Replenishment Process* – as the counterpart of the order fulfilment process, the responsibilities of the inventory replenishment process span from the update of the forecast as well as inventory consumption along the value chain network up to the moment when the material is replaced in its exact inventory position.
- *Product Return Process* – this core process begins when a customer decides to return one or more products to the seller and it ends with the disposal of the product by the seller and the provision of a solution for the customer.
- *Value Development Process* – invokes the whole series of steps from the generation of an idea or an opportunity to the launching of a product/service (or a combination of both) that adds value to end users, the company and the value chain.

4 Competence-Based Value Chain Management Processes

In this section we demonstrate how value chain processes are correlated to the competence theory. The following introduces the concept of organizational competence, which will allow us to propose and illustrate management processes as competences to be built and leveraged within organizations.

4.1 Competence-Based Approach

Conceptualizing and analyzing the competences of organizations has become a key focus of management thinking in recent decades. The term "competence" is defined as the ability to sustain the coordinated deployment of assets in ways that help a firm achieve its goals [14]. Therefore, its study relies on the investigation of the association between a company's internal characteristics and market value creation [7].

In order to avoid terminological confusion, Sanchez *et al.* [12] define the following key elements involved in the conceptualization of organizational competence:

- *Assets*: anything tangible or intangible the firm can use in its processes for creating, producing and offering its products (goods or services) to a market;
- *Capabilities*: repeatable patterns of action (activities) in the use of assets to create, produce and/or offer products to a market. Because capabilities are intangible assets that determine the use of tangible assets and other kinds of intangible assets, capabilities are considered to be an important category of assets.
- *Skills*: Special forms of capability usually embedded in individuals or teams that are useful in specialized situations or related to the use of a specialized asset.
- *Knowledge:* the set of beliefs held by an individual about casual relationships among phenomena. To the extent that a group of individuals within a firm has a shared set of beliefs about causality, that set of shared beliefs constitutes *organizational knowledge*. Since competence implies an intention to achieve some desired result (goal) through action, and since action-taking requires notions of cause and effect, knowledge and the application of knowledge through action are at the foundation of the concepts of skills, capabilities and (ultimately) competence.

Other elements related to the concept of competence are the *organizational systems* or also denominated *management routines* [9] or even *controls and incentives* [14].

Organizational systems are the conjunct of systems such as rules, norms, values, rewards, supervision etc. which govern the way a firm obtains and allocates resources to competence building and competence leveraging activities. Their role is one of monitoring and motivating the value-creating processes envisioned by a given strategy [14].

In addition, in order to support the identification and development of competences within organizations, Sanchez [14] discusses four core natures of any organizational competence: dynamic, systemic, cognitive and holistic.

- *Dynamic* nature: a central objective in competence theory and practice is the understanding of the co-evolutionary dynamics of environmental and organizational change and their roles in shaping organizational competences [13]. Therefore, a competence must include the ability to respond to the dynamic nature of an organization's external environment and of its own internal processes;
- *Systemic* nature: company competences must include an ability to manage the systemic nature of organizations and of their interactions with other organizations. The requirement of coordination of assets (tangible and intangible) addresses this dimension of competence, either just within the organization's boundaries (called *firm-specific assets*) or also beyond the boundaries of the firm (called *firm-addressable assets*);
- *Cognitive* nature: competence must include an ability to manage the cognitive processes of an organization. The requirement of deployment of assets – directing organizational assets to specific value-creating activities – addresses this dimension of competence;
- *Holistic* nature: it involves the requirement of goal achievement for the multiplicity of individual and institutional interests that intermingle in and are served through any organization. Thus, the definition of organizational competence recognizes the existence of multiple stakeholders and the importance of meeting expectations of all providers of essential resources in sustaining the value-creating processes of an organization.

4.2 Value Chain Management Processes as Management Competences

Here we present how value chain management processes should be supported by competence theory. In reality, we claim that management processes should be understood as management competences when processes-oriented business models are pursued. We justify this proposition based on two central arguments: first the misinterpretation caused by the wording "process" in the term "management process" and second, the alignment of the competence-based approach to what is expected from management processes. We state both arguments in further detail.

As previously mentioned, there is still a lot of ambiguity in the definition of management processes in the literature. Davenport [5] asserts that the reason for this ambiguity lies in the fact that the term "management process" results in a kind of oxymoron when the word "process" gives the sense of a collection of sequenced activities with clear inputs and outputs; in management functions this rationality is not clearly evident. In connection with this issue, Mentzer *et al.* [11] prefer defining management processes as broad knowledge domains.

In addition, envisaging management functions simply as sets of activities (e.g. demand management process) veils the importance of additional management aspects such as organizational systems (e.g. decision rules, values, and incentive structure), skills as well as individual and organizational knowledge. These aspects are of crucial importance when coordinating core and support processes towards the organization's strategic goals. By taking this perspective, the definition of management process becomes aligned with the four natures of a competence introduced by Sanchez [14]. By being in charge of translating and coordinating the company's changing environment by decisions throughout its core processes, management activities must present *dynamic* behaviour in order to cope with the complexity of the environment in which the company is situated. Management processes must also be *systemic* in order to be able to address internal elements of an organization or along the value chain. The *cognitive* aspects of management processes are in charge of defining and implementing the appropriate set of coordination activities throughout core and support processes in order to assure the objective of the management domain. Finally, management processes must also present *holistic* behaviours once they deal with different expectations of multiple stakeholders across the value chain.

Based on the above statements we suggest denominating "management processes" as "management competences" in the value chain processes literature in order to eliminate the ambiguity inherent in the former nomenclature as well as to allow further exploratory research that will hopefully capture more elements of the business environment within processes-based value chain frameworks.

4.3 An Illustrative Example of Value Chain Management Competence

Based on the debate presented, we illustrate how management processes might be addressed as competences within organizations. In order to do so, we selected the demand management competence as the object of our investigation. The selection of the demand management domain relies on its significant position in the agendas of academics and practitioners.

However, it is important to emphasize that the descriptions provided below do not intend to be assumed as a reference model for demand management competence. On the contrary, they simply aim to illustrate the competence deployment. This lack of confidence is related to the fact that competence building and competence leverage is conditional on market characteristics [9], which means that reference models for management competences should be proposed according to firms' environments contingent characteristics. As for this concern, Sanchez [14] asserts that "competence often appears to be contingent – i.e., to be capable of creating value in certain kinds of competitive contexts, but not necessarily in others."

Demand management is defined in the 11th edition of the APICS dictionary as the function of recognizing all demands for goods and services to support the marketplace. It involves prioritizing demand when supply is lacking. Proper demand management facilitates the planning and use of resources for profitable business results. Therefore, Table 1 presents some examples of demand management activities which may exist in different core processes of an organization. Although omitted here, activities flows are usually presented together with other related elements such as actors, resources (assets) and information [3].

Table 1. Illustrative example of activities of the demand management competence

Processes	Activities
Strategic Planning	Forecast long-term sales volume
	Forecast market conditions
Sales & Operations Planning	Forecast medium-term sales volumes
	Adjust demand according to supply restrictions
Value Commitment	Offer appropriate value to customers (e.g. delivery lead-time and prices)
	Prioritize commitments when supply is lacking
Inventory Replenishment	Adjust short-term forecasts

Once the activities have been identified, it makes the deployment of complementary competence perspectives essential to guarantee proper pursuit of the firm's goals. Table 2 illustrates fundamental organizational systems, skills and knowledge for two demand management activities.

Table 2. Example of a competence perspective for demand management activities

Activities	Org. Systems	Skills	Knowledge
Forecast medium-term sales volumes	Value: information transparency Rewards based on forecast accuracy	Planning skills Analytical skills	Statistics Customer and market behaviour
Prioritize commitments when supply is lacking	Rule: optimize profitability and service level	Optimization Strategic vision	Operations research Company strategy

5 Conclusions

This article has sought to open innovative debates concerning processes-oriented value chains. To accomplish this, it recovers the fundamental principles of competence theory in order to propose a more robust approach when dealing with management processes.

According to the findings presented, firms' business models are composed of core (and support) processes as well as management competences. While core processes are needed to realize business goals by enabling goods and services to reach external customers, management competences are in charge of setting the proper set of coordination activities, organizational systems, skills and knowledge through core and support processes in order to properly control and coordinate their use of assets towards firm's goals. This approach differs from the traditional proposition by assuming the unstructured and discontinuous behaviours of management activities as well as by integrating additional organizational aspects such as norms, rules, skills and knowledge into the management processes perspective.

In this way, we aim to eliminate the oxymoron caused by the term management process as well as to allow further explorative research which will hopefully capture more elements of the business environments within processes-based value chain frameworks. For instance, in the academic arena, we have been applying the proposed perspective of value chain processes in order to investigate the integration between the value chain and revenue management bodies of knowledge for commodity-type manufacturing environments.

References

1. Aguilar-Saven, R.S.: Business Process Modelling: Review and Framework. Int Journal Prod Econ. 90, 129–149 (2004)
2. Azevedo, R.C., D'Amours, S., Rönnqvist, M.: Core Supply Chain Management Business Processes – A literature-based framework proposition. In: The Third World Conference on Production and Operations Management, Tokyo, Japan (2008)
3. Boucher, X., Kühn, H., Janke, J.: Integrated Modelling and Simulation of Inter-Organizational Business Processes. In: 4e Conférence Francophone de Modélisation et SIMulation, Tousouse, France (2003)
4. Davenport, T.H., Short, J.E.: The new industrial engineering: information technology and business process redesign. Sloan Management Review 31-4, 11–27 (1990)
5. Davenport, T.H.: Process innovation, reengineering work through information technology. Harvard Business Review, Boston (1993)
6. Hammer, M.: Reengineering work: don't automate, obliterate. Harvard Business Review 68-4, 104–112 (1990)
7. Harmsen, H., Jensen, B.: Identifying the determinants of value creation in the market – A competence-based approach. Journal of Business Research 57, 533–547 (2004)
8. Lambert, D.M., Garcia-Dastugue, S.J., Croxton, K.L.: An evaluation of process-oriented supply chain management frameworks. Journal of Business Logistics 26-1, 25–49 (2005)
9. Lewis, M.A., Gregory, M.J.: Developing and Applying a Process Approach to Competence Analysis. In: Sanchez, R., Heene, A., Thomas, H. (eds.) Dynamics Competence-Based Competition – Theory and Practice in the New Strategic Management. Pergamon, Oxford (1996)
10. Malone, T.W., Crowston, K.: The Interdisciplinary Study of Coordination. ACM Computing Surveys 26-1, 87–119 (1994)
11. Mentzer, J.T., Myers, M.B., Stank, T.P.: Handbook of Global Supply Chain Management. Sage Publications, Thousand Oaks (2007)
12. Sanchez, R., Heene, A., Thomas, H.: Introduction: Towards the Theory and Practice of Competence-Based Competition. In: Sanchez, R., Heene, A., Thomas, H. (eds.) Dynamics Competence-Based Competition – Theory and Practice in the New Strategic Management. Pergamon, Oxford (1996)
13. Sanchez, R., Heene, A.: Reinventing Strategic Management: New Theory and Practice for Competence-based Competition. Eur. Manag. Journal 15-3, 303–317 (1997)
14. Sanchez, R.: Understanding competence-based management – Identifying and managing five modes of competence. Journal of Business Research 57, 518–532 (2004)
15. Stadtler, T.J., Kilger, C.: Supply Chain Management and Advanced Planning – concepts, models, software and case studies, 3rd edn. Springer, Heidelberg (2004)

Towards a Methodology for Managing Competencies in Virtual Teams – A Systemic Approach

Marinita Schumacher, Julie Stal-Le Cardinal, and Jean-Claude Bocquet

Ecole Centrale Paris, Industrial Engineering Department,
Grande Voie des Vignes, 92295 Chatenay Malabry Cedex, France
{marinita.schumacher,julie.le-cardinal,
jean-claude.bocquet}@ecp.fr

Abstract. Virtual instruments and tools are future trends in Engineering which are a response to the growing complexity of engineering tasks, the facility of communication and strong collaborations on the international market. Outsourcing, off-shoring, and the globalization of organisations' activities have resulted in the formation of virtual product development teams. Individuals who are working in virtual teams must be equipped with diversified competencies that provide a basis for virtual team building. Thanks to the systemic approach of the functional analysis our paper responds to the need of a methodology of competence management to build virtual teams that are active in virtual design projects in the area of New Product Development (NPD).

Keywords: Virtual teams, competence management, methodology, systemic approach, house of quality.

1 Introduction

An integral part of fostering new knowledge, continued innovation and technological progress are improvements of the NPD and project management process [16]. As prospective partners of design projects are spread out over countries, organisations need access to worldwide communication to aspire worldwide competitiveness. In view of the increasing de-centralisation and globalisation of work processes, many organisations have responded to their dynamic environments by introducing virtual teams [6]. These virtual teams have unique characteristics including geographic distance, language and cultural barriers [17]. We are following the definition of Griffith who declares that a virtual team consists of Individuals that act interdependently through technology to achieve a common goal [7].

The changing nature of teams has brought on a need to identify the competencies that are necessary to work effectively in a virtual team environment. Competence is seen as the basis of competitiveness, it enables a company to offer products and valued services to customers and to generate new innovative products and services. Indeed this "new" way of considering human resources requires a more precise formalisation of concepts like competence or skills, in order to be able to identify the competencies needed to work effectively in a virtual team environment and to link employees efficiently to tasks. We refer to North who declaims that competencies are

L.M. Camarinha-Matos et al. (Eds.): PRO-VE 2009, IFIP AICT 307, pp. 235–244, 2009.

substantiated in the moment of knowledge application, which means that competencies only exist when the knowledge meets a task [14].

Broadly speaking, competence management comprises identification, acquisition, development, distribution, preservation and use of competencies and is the way in which organisations manage the competencies of the organisation, teams and individuals [19]. In our research we are essentially focussing on gaps between existing competencies and required competencies for current or future needs. In this case competence management occurs in the moment where a task and its required competencies are linked to an Individual and his acquired competencies [19] According to Harzallah and Vernadat, this is one of the major benefits of a competence management system for virtual teams: Individuals can be matched with specific jobs or tasks [8]. Competence matching is invaluable in the field of NPD that comprises numerous knowledge intensive tasks, and thus the need for highly skilled employees. One of the strategic reasons for virtual teams is to combine different competencies of experts from different locations to take advantages of market opportunities. Due to costs, such experts are a rare resource which has to be applied in order to achieve innovative products and thereby to accomplish competitive advantages. Nevertheless Olsen et al. [15] point out that only little empirical work is done on specific competencies related to product development and although virtual collaborative environments and platforms are getting more and more popular in various domains such as R&D, problem-solving task forces, NPD, customer services etc., Horvarth and Tobin [11] distinguish that empirically-based prescriptions, guidelines and specifications for virtual team competencies are often missing. In our study we aim to respect the virtual aspect in NPD processes that claim other demands than traditional design projects in the area of NPD.

2 Objectives and Framework of Our Research

Our focus is set in providing a generic methodology of competence management for building virtual teams that are active in design projects in the area of NPD. This methodology should handle competencies in a virtual environment and should be adaptable to each specific organisational context. As distributed development projects can be difficult to control from a project management perspective, we aim to provide virtual teams whose competencies match the best with the requirements of design projects or by providing an individual who matches the best with a specific task to improve the NPD process.

The framework of this paper is organised into four stages: The following section 3 overviews in a first step our previous work based on the functional analysis, its objectives and main components that build the basis of our research. This section explains the systemic approach of the functional analysis that we choose to provide our methodology. In a second step we present the tool of the House of Quality that is part of the Quality Function Deployment [10]. The House of Quality and its adaption to our work is the focus of this study and bestride the results of section 4. Detected key functions of the functional analysis are analysed in terms of existing techniques and concepts of competence management and virtual team building. Finally, section 5 contains the concluding remarks and perspectives for future work.

3   A Systemic Approach

In order to reach our goal, a competence management methodology for virtual team building, we chose the holistic approach of the functional analysis to get information from a systemic point of view. We regard our methodology as a system that interacts with all its components. The functional analysis helps to emphasize the importance of all the properties of a given system that is considered as a whole. The system cannot be determined or explained by its components alone but only by the interdependencies of each component that interacts constantly with the others [21]. With this approach we aim to identify needs and requirements and show interrelations of the system and its properties to establish sustainable research results.

The functional analysis aids to gain a clear picture about functionalities and usability of a new product or services and assists in identifying main actors. Referring to the APTE® formalism for conducting a Value Analysis the functional analysis takes into consideration the various points of view of different research domains as well as the environmental aspects influencing a system [2].

3.1   Functional Analysis

Due to the systemic approach our "methodology of competence management for virtual team building" is considered a system that is described by functions. The functional analysis is performed to establish the system's functions, to define key functions related to the system and to control the distribution and maintenance of these functions in a systematic and useful manner [22].

We pursue the following steps that are presented in figure 1.

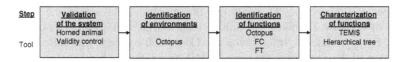

Fig. 1. Steps and tools of the functional analysis according to our study [18]

The specific results and their corresponding steps and tools are briefly described in this section. The tool of the horned animal helped us to get a first impression about the system itself, its target group, application areas and limits, the reason for its existence and its intention. After this step we passed a validity control to analyse the cause of the system, the objectives it aims for, and the risks of evolution or disappearance of the need. Through a tool that is called octopus we defined in a multidisciplinary brainstorming process 11 main environments and 40 sub-environments that permit us to take different concepts, critical terms and conditions into consideration. They are shown on the left side of following figure 2.

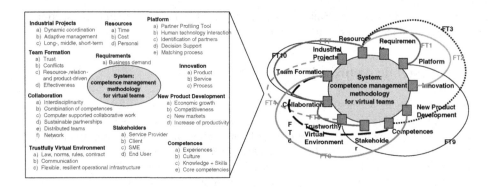

Fig. 2. Environments and extract of functions according to them [18]

The right side of the figure visualises an extract of the identification of functions according to the identified environments. In visual terms, the sub-clusters are not listed in this figure. We identified 243 transfer functions (FT) and 38 constraint functions (FC) by regarding each component of the system that interacts constantly with its environment. Transfer functions include at least two different environments that interact by the means of the system while constraint functions are generated by only one environment [2]. An example of FT and FC functions is shown in the following listing.

FT20   The system should be applicable to a wide range of organisations in the domain of NPD, to various application domains and to different design projects.

FC13   The system should provide that employees offer voluntary their individual competencies and their availability.

In a collaborative negotiation process we defined 40 key functions that represent main aspects of the system. They describe the optimum behaviour of the system and its terms of usability. Each key function is characterized with quantitative data in term of Time, Energy, Material, Information and Costs with a generic tool called TEMI$ in the last step of the functional analysis. TEMI$ supports the characterization of functions in a global way and help us to provide a definition of main quantitative aspects of the functions [18].

Based on the key findings, in the final step of our functional analysis the focus lays on the qualitative characterization of the functions. The importance of the key functions is measured in terms of percentages with the tool of the "hierarchical tree".

The tree structure provides a clear visibility of the large number of functions making up the system. It helps us to measure the importance of the functions in a qualitative way and to represent the system in a hierarchical form and to formulate substantiated qualitative recommendations. To determine the different basic categories of the top level of the hierarchical tree we referred to a model called CEISAR Enterprise Architecture Cube [4] [5].

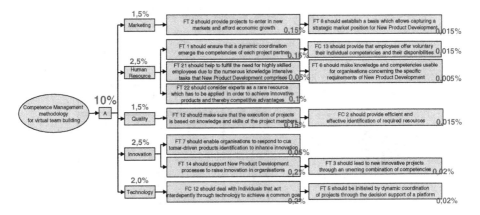

Fig. 4. Extract of branch A "I do" of the hierarchical tree according to our system [20]

We translated its eight mini-cubes to the foundation of our hierarchical tree and built eight categories A-F. Figure 5 gives a brief inside of the category A "I do" that is visualized as branch of the hierarchical tree according to the functions.

For reasons of visualisation this figure shows only the first and second level of functions. In the holistic figure of the hierarchical tree, all branches are treated and functions are broken down to several levels. The tree structure provides a clear visibility of the large number of functions making up the system. The hierarchical form delivers insights of the functions' importance. They depend on the specific needs of an organisation or also a particular design project without a real organisational structure which copes with the generic aspect of our methodology. It allows for the adaptation of not only each kind of organisation but also of each kind of design project. The percentages that are seen in figure 5 are just noted as examples. They depend on the purpose of the specific needs and have an important impact on the house of quality that is presented in the following section.

3.2 House of Quality

In a next step the detected key functions are analysed with a tool called "House of Quality" in terms of existing techniques and concepts of Competence Management and virtual team building. The House of Quality is a graphic tool for defining the relationship between customer requirements and the product capabilities that is a part of the Quality Function Deployment (QFD) [1]. QFD is a method to transform user demands into design quality and to set up the characteristics forming quality [10] Its ability to be adapted to the requirements of a particular problem makes it a very strong and reliable tool to use. It translates customer requirements called "Whats" and is based on our functions of the functional analysis, into a pertinent number of engineering targets, called "Hows". Its basic construction is made up of six major building blocks that compose the form of a house. These include customer requirements, technical requirements, a planning section, that deals with the importance of the costumers' requirements, a relationship matrix, a technical correlation matrix, and a

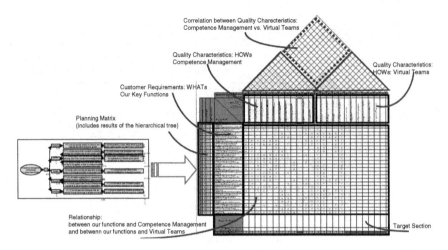

Fig. 5. House of Quality according to our system

technical priorities and targets section. The basic structure is a table with "Whats" on the left and "Hows" on the right site. The roof is composed as diagonal matrix of "Hows vs. Hows" and the body of the house builds a matrix of "Whats vs. Hows". Figure 6 gives an overview of the house of quality. It shows also the link between the hierarchical tree and the house of quality that is adapted to our study.

We use the tool of the House of Quality to deduce substantiated recommendations of our key functions that are detected by the functional analysis. Those essential functions are used as customers' requirements in this tool, visualised in figure 6 as "customer requirements". They describe what must be achieved to satisfy these demands. By putting them in relation with the technical requirements, the "Quality Characteristics", we try to get information about if they match their demand and to what degree. The main purpose of the relationship matrix is to establish a connection between the customer's product requirements and the performance measures designed to improve the product. The planning matrix shows the weighted importance of each requirement that our methodology is attempting to fulfil. Customer ratings are allocated to each requirement. In our case, the already analysed importance, presented as percentages of the hierarchical tree, will be incorporated into the planning matrix to get a coherent model. The customer ratings are combined with the weighted performance of each demand to produce an overall performance measure.

In this study we are concentrating on the relationship matrix and the correlation matrix. On the one hand we aim to find out strengths and weaknesses of the existent techniques and concepts due to the demand of the functions that could be adapted easily to our methodology. On the other hand through this approach we try to get information about those functions whose demands are apparently difficult to achieve. We intend to find out if the sum of our essential functions is satisfied by already existent techniques and concepts or if there are still solutions missing in the literature to satisfy our functions. With the help of the correlation matrix we try to get an idea if those quality characteristics have a specific rapport.

4   Results

Our detected key functions of the functional analysis are put in relation to the technical requirements that we have detected by analysing existent techniques and concepts of competence management and virtual team building.

We used concepts and techniques defined in different already well-developed methodologies. These techniques have then been critically analysed in the context of our functions and analysed in the relationship matrix in terms of meeting their demands. The concepts used for the House of Quality are based on mainly two sources, one that focuses on competence management, and one that concentrates on virtual team building. They are briefly explained in the following listing.

1. CRAI *(Competency Resource Aspect Individual)* approach that provides a formal representation of acquired and required individual competencies and define competencies in a generic way [3] [9].
2. Product Development 2.0 that provides a collaborative Web 2.0 environment for NPD that changes the structure of team interaction and collaboration from a "push" to a "pull" system [12] [13].

Following figure 7 gives an extract of the results of our house of quality. Competence management and virtual teams are each presented with an extract of five quality characteristics. They are analysed in terms of the relationship to the two beforehand described functions FT 20 and FC 13. Furthermore we are concentrating on the upper part of the house of quality to give a brief insight of the correlation between the quality characteristics of competence management and virtual teams.

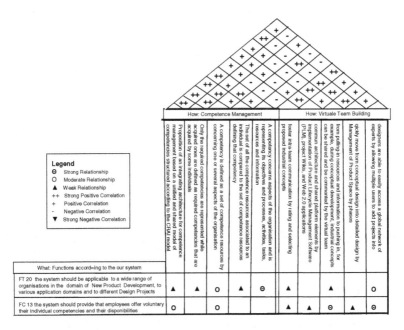

Fig. 6. Extract of Results according to our House of Quality

For reasons of visualisation this figure shows only a brief extract of our house of quality. We have analysed more than 50 different concepts and the list is not yet finished. The house of quality helps us to get a clear idea about which concepts are compatible and for which ones we have to find other solutions. On the one hand, the results of this critical analysis point out strengths and weaknesses of the existent techniques and concepts due to the demand of the functions that could be adapted easily to our methodology. On the other hand, this approach gives information about those functions whose demands are apparently difficult to achieve. Some functions are easily achievable, while others are complex and difficult to meet.

The structure of the house of quality seems especially useful for us as we are in the process of the initial decomposition and structuring of functional requirements. As a result of a successful analysis with this tool, we get substantiated information of our key functions that help us to interpret them and to provide guidelines for our methodology. A brief extract of those outcomes is seen in the following listing.

- The end of our dynamic system of methodology of competence management for virtual teams should be the realisation of the conception of the innovative product or service and not its industrialisation.
- Within the competence management methodology competence ontologies should be stored together with process descriptions and the process flows of the design projects. This competence approach should differentiate between competencies in terms of cognitive knowledge, procedural (methodical) knowledge on and social and competencies derived from activities.
- Moreover, competence should be described qualitatively and quantitatively. The qualitative evaluation differentiates the degree of expertise in "no competence", "basic competence", "independent work on the task" and "expert". Quantitative evaluation asks for the frequency of certain activities in a design process or in relation to a defined time frame.
- Characteristics of individual competencies as well as characteristics of the tasks and their activities for a new design are imprecise data that are hard to measure. Our methodology of competence management should be capable of dealing with this challenge.
- It should be connected on long term to the HR strategy of an organisation that could include assessment, recruitment, promotion, training, coaching, and evaluating processes.

Before having used this method, we did not have a clear picture of the different concepts that help to satisfy the specific functions of our system. In our example, the tool of the house of quality helped us to take our key functions in relation to existent concepts into consideration and to find substantiated guidelines. Furthermore, the correlation matrix helped us to analyse which quality characteristics are compatible to provide our methodology of competence management for virtual team building.

5 Outlook and Perspectives

In further research we aim to determine our "methodology for competence management for virtual team building" by proposing other techniques or concepts that satisfy all the functions of our system or at least the critical ones. We aim to find out if the sum of our essential functions is satisfied by already existent techniques and concepts or if there are still solutions missing in the literature to satisfy our functions. We will focus our work on the still missing solutions to cope the demand of those functions. Firstly, we used concepts defined in different already well-developed methodologies, secondly we aim to use concepts that we find in the practical field.

After determining which functions are most important to the organisation of a specific design project, the quality characteristics must be translated into particulate specifications. We aim to give more detailed recommendations for the specific quality characteristics. Nothing can be produced, serviced or maintained without detailed specifications or some set of given standards. That is the reason why our objective is to provide a catalogue of precise possibilities of HOWs. Another step will be to include the percentages of importance of the hierarchical tree to have a clear idea of the significance of each function.

In further research we aim to determine the formalisation of our "methodology for competence management for virtual team building". It should improve the NPD process by providing a virtual team whose competencies match the best to the requirements of design projects. In a proximate step our methodology must be applied to the industrial reality and especially to innovative organisations in the domain of new services, processes or product development. We intend to build virtual teams by matching individual competencies of potential team members to requirements of the design projects. It should be applicable to a wide range of organisations in the domain of NPD, to various application domains and to different design projects.

References

1. Akao, Y.: Quality Function Deployment. Productivity Press, Portland (1990)
2. Apte, La Méthode APTE (®) d' AV/AF, Petrelle (2000)
3. Berio, G., Hazallah, M.: Towards an integrating architecture for competence management. Computer in Industry 58, 199–209 (2007)
4. Ceisar, ECP - Center of Excellence in Enterprise Architecture, White Paper, Business Process Modeling (April 2008), http://www.ceisar.org (dated: 06/04/2008)
5. Ceisar, ECP - Center of Excellence in Enterprise Architecture, White Paper, Enterprise Modelling (April 2008), http://www.ceisar.org (dated: 29/04/2008)
6. Grenier, R., Metes, G.: Going virtual: Moving our organsiation in the 21st Century. Prentice Hall, Upper Saddle River (1995)
7. Griffith, T.L., Sawyer, J.E., Neale, M.A.: Virtualness and Knowledge in Teams: Managing the Love Triangle. Organizations, Individuals, and Information Technology, MIS Quarterly (27), 265–287 (2003)
8. Harzallah, M., Vernadat, F.: Human resource competency management in enterprise engineering. In: 14th IFAC World Congress of Information Control in Manufacturing, Beijing, China (1999)
9. Harzallah, M., Vernadat, F.: IT-based competency modeling and management: from theory to practice in enterprise engineering and operations. Computers in Industry 48, 157–179 (2002)
10. Hauser, J., Clausing, D.: House of Quality. Harvard Business Review (2009)

11. Horvarth, L., Tobin, T.J.: Twenty-first century teamwork: Defining competencies for virtual teams. Virtual Teams 8, 239–258 (2001)
12. Marion, J.T., Schumacher, M.: Moving New Venture NPD from Information Push to Pull Using Web 2.0. Submitted for International Conference on Engineering Design, ICED 2009, Stanford (2009)
13. Marion, T.J.: NPD Practices at Early-Stage Firms: A Pilot Study. Academy of Management 2008, Annual Meeting, paper 13663 (2008)
14. North, K.: Wissensorientierte Unternehmensführung - Wertschöpfung durch Wissen, 3rd edn. Gabler Verlag, Wiesbaden (2002)
15. Olsen, R.J., Harmsen, H., Friis, A.: Linking quality goals and product development competences. Food Quality and Preference 19, 33–42 (2008)
16. Ramesh, B., Tiwana, A.: Supporting Collaborative Process Knowledge Management in NPD Teams. Decision Support Systems 27, 213–235 (1999)
17. Rezgui, Y.: Exploring virtual team-working effectiveness in the construction sector. Interacting with Computers 19, 96–112 (2007)
18. Schumacher, M., Le Cardinal, J., Mekhilef, M.: A competence management methodology for virtual teams – A systemic approach to support innovation processes in SME's. In: International Design Conference: Design 2008, Dubrovnik (2008)
19. Schumacher, M., Le Cardinal, J., Mekhilef, M.: Competence management for virtual team building: A survey. In: International Conference on Integrated, Virtual and Interactive Engineering for fostering Industrial Innovation - IDMME 2008, Peking (2008)
20. Schumacher, M., Le Stal-Cardinal, J., Bocquet, J.C.: Towards a generic methodology of virtual team building adapted to specific needs of design projects, Cahier d'études et de recherche- ECP-2009-02 (2009)
21. Snodgrass, T.J.: Function Analysis – The Stepping Stones to Good Value, CVS at KASI. Muthiah, CVS (1986)
22. Yosida, K.: Functional analysis, 5th edn. Springer, Heidelberg (1978)

An Organization's Extended (Soft) Competencies Model

João Rosas[1], Patrícia Macedo[1,2], and Luis M. Camarinha-Matos[1]

[1] New University of Lisbon, Faculty of Sciences and Technology, Portugal
[2] Polytechnic Institute of Setubal, Portugal
jrosas@uninova.pt, pmacedo@est.ips.pt, cam@uninova.pt

Abstract. One of the steps usually undertaken in partnerships formation is the assessment of organizations' competencies. Typically considered competencies of a functional or technical nature, which provide specific outcomes can be considered as hard competencies. Yet, the very act of collaboration has its specific requirements, for which the involved organizations must be apt to exercise other type of competencies that affect their own performance and the partnership success. These competencies are more of a behavioral nature, and can be named as soft-competencies. This research aims at addressing the effects of the soft competencies on the performance of the hard ones. An extended competencies model is thus proposed, allowing the construction of adjusted competencies profiles, in which the competency levels are adjusted dynamically according to the requirements of collaboration opportunities.

Keywords: Soft Competencies, Hard Competencies, Collaboration.

1 Introduction

In partnership formation, a competencies' assessment is usually done in order to determine the suitability of potential partners and to establish which activities should be assigned to which organizations, in an effort to build the best network with an increased chance of achieving the desired goals. This competencies' assessment inform about the organizations capability to perform a number of related tasks, activities or processes. However, it usually happens that these competencies are typically tuned for working as a single entity in a regular market-like environment. Although accurate for such environment, considering just these competencies might not be enough in a collaboration context. This comes from the fact that a collaboration process has its specific requirements, to which organizations must be apt to comply, or otherwise their performance inside the partnership is affected. In order to comply with these collaboration-related requirements, it is necessary that organizations own other type of competencies. While the former competencies are more functional and technical, the later are of a more behavioral nature. As such, we can refer to hard and soft competencies.

This research aims at identifying the performance effects of the soft competencies on the hard ones, within a collaboration context. The duality between soft and hard competencies is observed from a behavioral perspective, which also considers the very values of an organization, its traits, and the activities performed at a more functional and technical level. A modeling approach is proposed combining both hard and

L.M. Camarinha-Matos et al. (Eds.): PRO-VE 2009, IFIP AICT 307, pp. 245–256, 2009.

soft competencies. The assumption is that considering these aspects in the partners' competencies assessment provides a broader and more accurate perception of partners' capabilities, and that such vision of capabilities allows an improved assignment of roles and activities inside networks. This assignment in turn leads to the formation of more effective consortiums.

In order to achieve these aims, a number of concepts are introduced, such as the Extended Competencies Model, the Adjusted Competency Model, and Adjusted Competency Level. An example illustrating how to use the proposed approach is presented afterwards.

2 Literature Review

The *Competencies profile* subject has been studied during the last decades, using diverse approaches and for distinct purposes. For instance, in Human Resource Management research, competencies are studied from the point of view of *Job Competencies* in which they are considered as technical skills to perform job activities. In the last decades, some authors initiated a new approach to competency management, introducing the importance of some behavioral characteristics for the proficiency of professional careers [1]. The term *"soft competencies"* was defined as "personal behaviors or attitudes". Diverse authors defended that soft-competencies are complementary to technical competencies, and that they are of great importance in human resource management [2] [3].

In [4] a model for competency management in organizations called "Core competency notion" is proposed in order to support strategic planning and provide means for achieving better synergies among the various organization's business units. Another contribution to this issue was provided by [5] proposing an extension of the core competency notion, where the concepts of resource and capabilities are included in the core-competency model. He proposed also, a method based on the discussion of eight structured questions that will help managers to identify the company's core competencies and capabilities in a systematic and methodical way.

In recent years, the collaborative networks community developed some work related to competency management in a collaborative context. Molina and Flores [6] proposed a core-competency model for the manufacturing clusters. The basic idea of this model is to match the tasks defined for a new Virtual Organization against the constituent skills provided by the cluster of organizations. Another model for competency analysis in collaborative context, called s-a-r-C model, was introduced by Boucher and Leburean [7]. This model supports the idea that competencies usually increase in networked organizations as a consequence of the interaction between tasks, human resources and material capabilities. Odenthal and Peters [8] further developed the concept of competency profiles in collaborative environments, proposing a method to generate target competency profiles in a Virtual Enterprise. These target profiles are based on the allocation of competencies to activities and where each set of activities correspond to a specific task. Recently Ermilova and Afsarmanesh [9] developed a competency model specific to competencies management in Virtual Organizations Breeding Environments (VBEs). This model is called the "4C-model" and considers four fundamental components of competency: "Capability", "Capacity", "Cost" and "Conspicuity".

Although the soft competencies concept has been addressed in related fields, our perception led us to conclude that, in spite of the potential value and benefits it could bring, the subject of soft versus hard competencies has so far received little attention in collaborative networks.

3 The Extended Competencies Model

Model specification. In order to establish an approach and adequate analysis, it is important to mention that the aim of this research is not to obtain a complete and detailed competencies model, but as mentioned before, to address the soft competencies performance effects. As such, the adopted approach is to define an abstract model, maintaining the compliance with existing models, but allowing the integration of the findings from this research.

The meaning of competency, according to the Cambridge dictionary, corresponds basically to the ability to do something successfully or efficiently [10]. In a similar way, an organization that is considered competent on a certain domain has got the necessary ability, knowledge, and skills to perform the corresponding tasks towards achieving specified goals [1].

Competencies can be either of hard or soft nature. In order to establish an adequate framework, this dual notion of competencies must be considered inside a behavioral space, in which the relevant organization's behaviors can be characterized. This space, as illustrated in Fig. 1, starts from the very values of an organization and spans to the activities and tasks performed at a technical and functional level.

Fig. 1. Organization's competencies in a continuous behavioral space

Value systems are related both to the purposes of an organization and its roles inside society. The behaviors developed by organizations should, in principle, be in accordance with their values, and their influences are propagated to the lower technical and functional behavioral levels[1]. Principles of ethics and code of conduct are also of great importance in collaborative networks [11, 12]. Next to the values, there are organization traits, which are also values, but with a more concrete connotation to organizations' behaviors. These traits can be perceived from the behavioral patterns that arise from the behaviors performed by organizations. For instance, an organization may be classified as reliable because it has performed in a very reliable way, and

---

[1] One can imagine a 'green' enterprise adopting renewable energies and performing recycling in its manufacturing system.

can be considered friendly if it reveals friendly attitudes. This organization could therefore be characterized as owning the traits of reliability and friendliness.

Soft competencies come next to traits. This "proximity" is related to the fact that soft competencies are more behavioral, as opposite to the hard ones, which are connected to a more functional level. The ability to develop soft competencies is in accordance to the mentioned organizations traits. For instance, if an organization is capable of building consensus on a conflicting situation, which is an example of a soft competency, that might be due to its empathy and openness, which are examples of traits. Going further through the considered behavioral space, we can find the hard competencies concept. Such type of competencies is associated to the specific skills, functions, activities, and knowledge, used to achieve specific goals and outcomes, establishing the association to the mentioned more technical and functional nature.

These concepts can be represented using a formal notation, starting from traits and covering all the concepts mapped in the mentioned behavioral space. For subsequent modeling, let us consider the set of organizations $O=\{o_1, o_2, o_3, ...\}$.

Definition 1 (Organization's Behaviors). The organization's behaviors can be represented by the set $B=\{b_1, b_2, b_3,...\}$, in which each behavior b_i represents a way an organization acts or conducts itself and toward others, or the way it behaves in response to a particular event, internal or external stimuli, or situation.

Definition 2 (Organization's Traits). A set $T = \{t_1, t_2, t_3, ...\}$ where each trait t_i represents a relatively stable predisposition to act in a certain way, and which can be used to describe or characterize the behavior of organizations (e.g. reliability, openness, and adaptability).

Definition 3 (Organization's Soft Competencies). A set $SC=\{sc_1, sc_2, sc_3, ...\}$, in which each element sc_i can be abstractly understood as a general aptitude to perform a behavior (e.g. the ability to exchange knowledge), which is beneficial for the achievement of the outcomes associated to the performance of a hard competency.

The following definition introduces the concept of hard competence, which is built upon the *4C* competence model described in [9].

Definition 4 (Organization's Hard Competency). Abstractly understood as an aptitude to act towards achieving specified outcomes or goals. It represents an organization's capability to run activities, tasks or processes, which allows achieving concrete outcomes or goals. Assuming a set of given hard competences $HC=\{hc_1, hc_2, hc_3...\}$, each of its elements can be defined as a tuple $hc_i=(C_{i,1}, C_{i,2}, C_{i,3}, C_{i,4})$, such that (taking the index 'i' out):

- C_1 represents the competence <u>capability</u> information in terms of the processes and activities an organization can perform.
- C_2 represents the competence <u>capacity</u> information, used to represent the free capacity of related resources, and to specify quantitative values of capabilities, such as a production rate (e.g. units/day).
- C_3 represents <u>cost</u> information of products/services that are related to the organization's capability C_1.

- C_4 represents <u>conspicuity</u> information, which is used as a mean to validate and certify the organizations' capabilities. This conspicuity information can take the form of certifications, licenses, or recommendation letters.

The following definition introduces the extended competency model concept, which results from the combination of an organization's traits, observed behaviors, and both the hard and soft competencies specified in the previous definitions.

Definition 5 (Organization's Extended Competencies model). Can be specified as a tuple SCP=(o_k, OT, OB, HCL, SCL), where:

- o_k – represents a given organization, such that $o_k \in O$.
- $OT = \{(t_i, v_i) \mid t_i \in T, v_i \in \{low, average, high\}\}$ are the organization's traits.
- $OB = \{(b_i, v_i) \mid b_i \in B, v_i \in \{low, average, high\}\}$ are observed organization's behaviors, associated to previously observed soft competencies manifestations.
- $HCL = \{(hc_i, l_i) \mid hc_i \in HC, l_i \in [0,100]\}$. The value of l_i represents the hc_i competency level. HC is the set of hard competencies (as in Definition 4).
- $SCL = \{(sc_i, l_i) \mid sc_i \in SC, l_i \in \{low, average, high\}\}$. The level l_i indicates the level of the soft competency sc_i, for the organization o_k.

The competency level in this definition can result from an aggregated evaluation of the hc_i information that is embedded in its *4C* elements described in definition 4. The scale of values for the soft, and even the hard competency levels might be of a qualitative type (e.g. 'low', 'average' or 'high' values), when it is difficult to evaluate such information in a crisp way. Taking this into consideration a corresponding relation $hcLevel: O \times HC \rightarrow [0,100]$ can be defined, which obtains an aggregated competency level value from the information embedded in the *4C* elements. In addition, the relation $scLevel: O \times SC \rightarrow \{low, average, high\}$ obtains the soft competency level for a given organization. The computation of these levels is further explained in the competencies assessment. A collaboration opportunity (CO) can be related to the competencies that are necessary for its fulfillment. These competencies are usually of the hard type, but the consideration of soft competencies is also necessary. For instance, certain activities associated to a hard competency might require intensive knowledge exchange. In this case, only partners that have such soft competency can assume these activities.

Definition 6 (Collaboration Opportunity Competencies Requirement). Can be specified as a tuple COCR=(co,RC) where:

- co is the identification of a specific collaboration opportunity.
- $RC=\{(hc_i, sc_j, q_{ij}) \mid hc_i \in HC, sc_j \in SC, q_j \in \{low, medium, high\}\}$, establishes that an hard competency hc_i requires a certain level q_{ij} of soft competency sc_j for its performance (e.g. the ability to exchange knowledge).

In addition, we can consider a relation $reqLevel: HC \times SC \times CO \rightarrow \{low, medium, high\}$, which obtains the soft competency level required by a hard competency needed in a given *CO*, and from the information characterizing that *CO*. The next concept corresponds to the definition of the adjusted competencies model.

Definition 7 (Organization's adjusted hard Competencies). Represents an organization's adjusted competence profile, in which the competence levels are evaluated, taking into consideration the information provided by the extended model (definition 5) and the requirements of a given collaboration opportunity (definition 6). An adjusted competency can be specified as a tuple ACP=(o, AHC, co) where

- o is a given organization, such that $o \in O$.
- co is a specific collaboration opportunity.
- $AHC=\{\{(hc_i, al_i) \mid hc_i \in HC, al_i \in [0,100]\}\}$. al_i represent the adjusted hard competency levels.

The distinction between the extended and the adjusted competences model is that the later is instantiated whenever there is a concrete CO establishing both hard and soft competencies requirements. In such a case, the adjusted model, through its adjusted competency levels, provides better information concerning an organization's effective capacity to use its hard competencies in such collaboration opportunity.

Competencies assessment. The assessment of competencies includes the evaluation of both soft and hard competencies. The information required for the soft competencies evaluation can be obtained from several sources (Fig. 2a), as explained below. These competencies are then used together with the organization's hard competencies and the collaboration opportunity in the calculation of the adjusted hard competency levels (Fig. 2b).

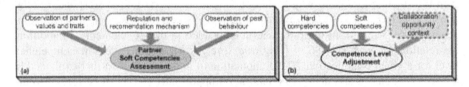

Fig. 2. (a) Soft-Competencies assessment, and (b) hard competencies levels adjustment

The hard competencies of an organization are information that is specified in the provided 4C elements. The rationality for this assumption is based on the fact that, whenever an organization wishes to join a consortium, it delivers a statement describing its best competencies, aiming at obtaining a favorable qualification.

Soft competencies assessment. For the soft competencies assessment, an adequate way to specify the competency values is required, due to the intrinsic subjectivity and underlying ambiguity that characterizes such type of concepts. For instance, it is not straightforward to provide a percentage value for a soft competency related to the ability to lead a consortium composed of autonomous and conflicting parties. One solution is to adopt a qualitative scale based on:

- Perception of organizations' traits. For instance, the capacity to build consensus on a conflicting situation depends on organization's traits, such as diplomacy and honesty.

- Receiving advice from a trustworthy partner, who informs about third parties competencies.
- Observation of past behavior, which was characterized as a successful manifestation of a soft competency.

The observation of past behavior is amongst the others the most reliable way to perceive soft competencies. If, for instance, a partner was observed to engage on knowledge sharing on a situation that provided positive outcomes, then it is likely that this partner is willing to engage in such a behavior again in the future. However, if the outcomes were not satisfactory, the partner might be less prone to repeat that behavior. The information concerning past behavior can be obtained, for instance, from a history repository of a *VBE*.

Definition 8 (Soft competencies assessment process). The process that takes an organization's traits, recommendations and observed behavior, in order to infer a level for a given soft competency. This process can be represented as:

$$\forall_o \forall_{sc} (observ(o, sc, L) \vee recommend(o, sc, L) \vee traits(o, sc, L) => scLevel(o, sc, L)) \quad (1)$$

The order in which each predicate appears is intended to model the fact that advisor's recommendations are more important than traits perception, and that observed behavior overlaps both recommendations and traits.

Hard competencies levels adjustment. As illustrated in Fig 2b, the hard competency levels adjustment takes as inputs the original soft and hard competency levels (from definition 5), and the requirements of a given CO, including its context, in order to obtain adjusted values for such levels, which provide a more accurate information about the partners performance for the actual CO. It is worth to mention the context, because there might be requirements that are exogenous to the collaboration opportunity (e.g., the necessity to deal with adverse market or to establish relationships with difficult partners).

Definition 9 (Adjusted hard Competency Level). Represents a value obtained with a function *adjLevel*: O×HC→ [0, 100], which for a given organization o_i, calculates the adjusted level for its competency hc_j, according to the soft competencies owned by the organization, and the ones required by a given collaboration opportunity *co*. The adjustment function can be specified as:

$$adjLevel(o, hc, co) = \underbrace{hcLevel(o, hc)}_{\text{Original level}} \times \underbrace{\frac{1}{\#(SC_{co,hc})} \times \sum_{n=1}^{\#(SC_{co,hc})} \left[\frac{scLevel(o, sc_n)}{reqLevel(co, sc_n, hc)} \right]}_{\text{Adjustment factor (}adjFactor\text{)}} \quad (2)$$

where:

- *hcLevel*, gives the original organization's hard competency level.
- $o=o_i$ and $hc=hc_j$ for a better function understanding.

- $SC_{hc,co}$ corresponds to the set of soft competencies that are required in the performance of hard competency hc, in the context of the actual CO. The expression $\#(SC_{hc,co})$ represents the size of this set.

The above expression that computes the adjustment factor is enough for providing the desired adjustment effect. But other expressions reflecting the situations' specificities could also be used. Nonetheless, this *adjLevel* function requires more generality in order to cope with known cases of collaborative networks. Let us see how this can be done considering the following collaboration-related soft competencies, namely the ability to: (1) perform tasks in a collaborative way, (2) share resources and knowledge, (3) lead a group of autonomous organizations, possibly with conflicting interests and goals, and (4) achieve consensus-based decision-making.

If we consider a single enterprise operating in the market, in which its interactions are mostly transactional, all that matters are hard competencies, with little consideration for collaboration-related soft competencies. This can be modeled as:

$$\#(SC_{co,hc})=0 \quad => \quad adjLevel(o,hc,co) = hcLevel(o,hc) \tag{3}$$

In an Extended Enterprises (EE) most of the business interactions are controlled by a dominant partner [13]. Nevertheless, the involved entities are autonomous, which requires a greater level of multilateral coordination. A VE/VO, in turn, is essentially constituted by autonomous organizations, which make decisions on a consensus basis [14], and the interactions are mostly collaborative. In this case, there is a higher need for collaboration-related soft competencies. The adjustment level for these two cases can be modeled as:

$$\#(SC_{co,hc})>0 \quad => \quad adjLevel(o,hc,co) = hcLevel(o,hc) \times adjFactor \tag{4}$$

In the case that an organization is invited to join a Virtual Organizations Breeding Environments (VBE), there is no concrete collaboration opportunity to fulfill, neither hard competences requirements to consider at that time. Here, the focus is predominantly put on the organization's soft competencies, being the main concern to assess its preparedness to participate in future partnerships. This can be modeled as:

$$\#(HC_{co})=0 \quad => \quad adjLevel(o, nil^2, nil) = adjFactor \tag{5}$$

These cases can be classified in a scale, in which they are ordered by their growing needs for soft competences, as illustrated in Fig. 3.

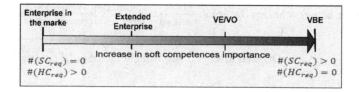

Fig. 3. Soft Competencies importance according to network type

---

[2] Nil corresponds to a non specified value.

Considering these cases, the resulting expression for the adjusted level calculation is given by:

$$adjLevel(o,hc,co) = \begin{cases} hcLevel(o,hc) \times adjFactor & \Leftarrow \quad \#(SC_{co,hc}) > 0 \\ hcLevel(o,hc) & \Leftarrow \quad \#(SC_{co,hc}) = 0 \\ adjFactor & \Leftarrow \quad \#(HC_{co}) = 0 \end{cases} \tag{6}$$

An example in next section illustrates how to use this concept.

4 Modeling Example

A Prolog implementation
In order to do some tests and verify the model and its usability, a translation of the above definitions into Prolog rules was made as illustrated in the diagram of Fig.4.

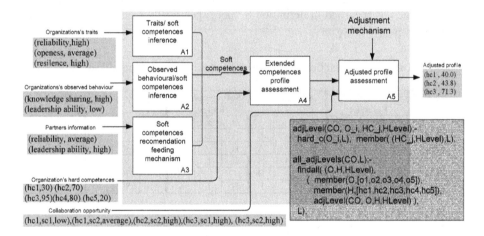

Fig. 4. Diagram for the Prolog version of the competences model

Each block in this diagram represents the assessment steps previously described. Typical inputs and outputs, instantiated from the above definitions are also illustrated.

An illustrative example
Let us consider a situation in which there is a possibility to engage in a collaboration opportunity. For this opportunity, a set of candidates are considered for the formation of a consortium. This CO is described in terms of required soft and hard competences, as illustrated in table 1. The values in this table are assumed to be obtained from the identification and characterization of the CO and its context. By context, we mean the exogenous factors that also imply soft requirements. For instance, this table states that performing hc_1 is not very demanding on knowledge or resources sharing (sc_1, sc_2), that hc_2 requires a partner with strong leadership quality (sc_3), and that hc_3 is a competency that requires both intensive knowledge and resources sharing.

Table 1. Requirements for a collaboration opportunity (L:low, A:average, H:high)

Collaboration opportunity context			
Required hard competencies	**Associated (and required)soft competencies**		
	sc_1	sc_2	sc_3
hc_1	L	A	-
hc_2	-	H	H
hc_3	H	H	-

A number of organizations have applied to participate in the given CO. Each organization is characterized by its soft and hard competencies, its traits, and its past behaviors, as illustrated in Table 2. In this example, it is established that when we say that a partner assumes a hard competency, it means that it assumes the responsibility to undertake the activities associated to this competency. The soft competencies considered in this example are in the set $SC=\{$ 'ability to share its resources', 'capacity to exchange knowledge', 'ability to lead a consortium'$\}$. The set considered for traits is $T=\{$ 'reliability', 'adaptability', 'resilience'$\}$. The soft competency levels are assumed to be obtained as specified in definition 8, more specifically from the organizations' traits and observed behavior.

Table 2. Extended Competency Profile for a set of organizations (Def. 5)

	Observed Behavior	Org. traits			Soft competencies levels			Hard competencies levels				
Org.	(sc, out)	t_1	t_2	t_3	sc_1	sc_2	sc_3	hc_1	hc_2	hc_3	hc_4	hc_5
O1	$(sc_1,H), (sc_3,L)$	H	A	L	H	L	A	30	70	95	80	20
O2	(sc_2,H)	H	-	A	H	-	L	70	80	50	50	90
O3	$(sc_1,H), (sc_2,L)$	L	A	H	L	L	A	100	50	30	70	70
O4	$(sc_2,H), (sc_3,L)$	H	-	H	-	-	H	80	70	60	30	40
O5	(sc_3,H)	H	L	L	H	L	-	50	80	30	70	50

The values for the hard competencies levels were obtained taking in consideration the organizations' competency statements showing the 4C information (definition 4 and 5), in relation to the critical competencies and resources that are necessary in the collaboration opportunity. The candidates provide that information when they apply for the collaboration opportunity, both to convince that they are qualified, and to be subsequently used in the process planning. The VO planner digests this information and translates it to the aggregated competency levels, illustrated in Table 2, allowing a straightforward comparison between the candidates.

Given the inputs provided in Tables 1 and 2, let us apply the equation specified in definition 9, in order to determine the adjusted profile of candidate o_1. Using the referred inputs, the corresponding adjusted levels are:

$$adjLevel(o_1,hc_1) = 30\% \times 1/2 \times (80/40 + 40/60)=40\%$$
$$adjLevel(o_1,hc_2) = 70\% \times 1/2 \times (40/80 + 60/80)=44\%$$
$$adjLevel(o_1,hc_3) = 95\% \times 1/2 \times (80/80 + 40/80)=71\%$$

Performing similarly for the remaining partners, we get the adjusted competency profiles illustrated in Fig. 5, which are next to the initial profiles taken from Table 2.

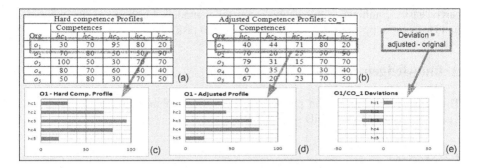

Fig. 5. (a) Original competency levels, and (b) the adjusted values c) o_1's initial profile, (d) the adjusted profile, and (e) the deviations

In order to evaluate partners, it is better to present this information as profile charts, as shown for partner o_1.

The initial hard competencies profile shows that partner o_1 would be very competent at performing hc_3. However, the information in Table 2 states that this partner is low scored at sharing knowledge. But the CO establishes that hc_3 requires intensive knowledge sharing (table 1). This means that, although being initially considered highly qualified in hc_3, this partner might in fact display poorer performance in the actual CO, due to its knowledge protection concerns. This fact is illustrated in Fig. 5d, which shows its adjusted profile stating a lower adjusted level for hc_3, incorporating the knowledge sharing concern. The values that are shown in Fig. 6e correspond to the difference between the adjusted and the original competency levels. Taking in consideration these deviations, this chart shows precisely that there is an inadequate (or negative) adjustment of this partner to the actual CO in terms of hc_3, caused by its concern to protect its knowledge. It also suggests that this partner should instead assume the competency hc_1, which might contradict the initial assumption that this partner was very good on hc_3, probably the very reason it was initially considered for the consortium. If nevertheless it is decided that partner o_1 will assume this competence, the remaining partners involved in the consortium should expect problematic interactions with this partner.

5 Conclusions

We have addressed the effects of the soft competencies on the performance of the hard ones. An extended partners' competencies abstract model, combining both type of competences was proposed. This model allows the adjustment of the hard competences levels, taking in consideration both soft and hard competencies required in a collaboration opportunity. These dynamically adjusted levels display a more accurate indication about the partners' performance of their competences in the given collaboration opportunities.

The Prolog implementation of the model, together with the illustrative example, shows this approach is useful and that its utilization is straightforward. This approach can be easily combined with existing competency models. Furthermore, its integration in a Decision Support System is not a complicated task.

Acknowledgements

This work was supported in part by the Portuguese "Fundação para a Ciência e a Tecnologia" through two PhD scholarships.

References

1. McClelland, D.: Testing for competence rather than for intelligence. American Psychologist 20, 321–333 (1973)
2. Dainty, A., Cheng, M.I., Moore, D.R.: A comparison of the behavioural competencies of client-focused and production-focused project managers in the construction sector. Project Management Journal 36, 39–48 (2005)
3. Dubois, D.: Competency-Based Performance: A Strategy for Organizational Change. HRD Press, Boston (1993)
4. Prahalad, C.K., Hamel, G.: The core competence of the corporation. Harvard Business Review 68, 79–90 (1990)
5. Javidan, M.: Core Competence: What does it mean in practice? Long Range Planning 31, 60–71 (1998)
6. Molina, A., Flores, M.: A Virtual Enterprise in Mexico: From Concepts to Practice. Journal of Intelligent and Robotics Systems 26, 289–302 (1999)
7. Boucher, X., Lebureau, E.: Coordination of Competencies Development within Networks of SMEs Collaborative Networks and Their Breeding Environments, vol. 186, pp. 57–66. Springer, Boston (2005)
8. Odenthal, B., Peters, M.: Competence Profiling in Virtual Companies. In: Network-Centric Collaboration and Supporting Frameworks, vol. 224, pp. 143–150. Springer, Boston (2006)
9. Ermilova, E., Afsarmanesh, H.: Competency Modeling Targeted on Promotion of Organizations Towards VO Involvement.: Pervasive Collaborartive Networks, pp. 3–14. Springer, Boston (2008)
10. Soanes, C., Stevenson, A. (eds.): Oxford Dictionary of English, Oxford, UK (2003)
11. Hall, B.: Values Shift: A Guide to Personal and Organizational Transformation. Twin Lights Publishers Rockport, MA (1995)
12. Macedo, P., Sapateiro, C., Filipe, J.: Distinct Approaches to Value Systems in Collaborative Networks Environments. In: Network-Centric Collaboration and Supporting Frameworks, vol. 224, pp. 111–120. Springer, Boston (2006)
13. Camarinha-Matos, L., Afsarmanesh, H.: Collaborative Networks -Value creation in a knowledge society. In: PROLAMAT 2006. Springer, Shanghai (2006)
14. Afsarmanesh, H., Camarinha-Matos, L.M., Ollus, M.: Ecolead and CNO Base Concepts. In: Methods and Tools for Collaborative Networked Organizations, pp. 4–31. Springer, Heidelberg (2008)

Part 8

Modeling and Managing Competencies - II

A Generic Framework of Performance Measurement in Networked Enterprises

Duk-Hyun Kim[1] and Cheolhan Kim[2]

[1] Sejong Cyber University, 111-1 Gunja-dong, Gwangjin-gu, Seoul 143-150, Korea
dhkim@sjcu.ac.kr
[2] Daejon University, 96-3 Yongun-dong, Dong-gu, Daejon 300-716, Korea
chkim@dju.ac.kr

Abstract. Performance measurement (PM) is essential for managing networked enterprises (NEs) because it greatly affects the effectiveness of collaboration among members of NE. PM in NE requires somewhat different approaches from PM in a single enterprise because of heterogeneity, dynamism, and complexity of NE's. This paper introduces a *generic framework of PM in NE* (we call it *NEPM*) based on the Balanced Scorecard (BSC) approach. In NEPM key performance indicators and cause-and-effect relationships among them are defined in a *generic strategy map*. NEPM could be applied to various types of NEs after specializing KPIs and relationships among them. Effectiveness of NEPM is shown through a case study of some Korean NEs.

Keywords: Performance Measurement, Networked Enterprise, Balanced Scorecard (BSC), Cause-and-Effect Relationships.

1 Introduction

Networked enterprise (NE) is an aggregation of private companies that work together for common goals; it is a kind of *Collaborative-Networked Organization* (CNO) [1]. Only to reduce the scope of our study we consider NE instead of CNO that includes non-profit organizations. NEs can be classified into three types: *hub-and-spoke* (e.g., extended enterprise with main contractor), *supply chain* (process-oriented), and *peer-to-peer* (e.g., project-oriented virtual enterprise) [2]. Regarding the degree and direction of integration we call them *vertical NE*, *horizontal NE*, and *ad-hoc NE*, respectively. Three types of NEs have somewhat different characteristics in duration, goals, products or services, processes, ICT infrastructure, *key performance indicators* (KPIs), etc. For example, coordination mechanisms of vertical NE and ad-hoc NE are different, i.e., the former is close to command-and-control whereas the latter relies on debate or managerial/technical leadership. A generic framework for various types of NE could reduce efforts to implement management and ICT systems of NE.

Performance measurement (PM) is 'a systematic approach using methods and tools to plan, measure, monitor, assess, reward, and control the performance of processes and organizations' [3]. With PM an organization could be more goal-oriented, strategy focused, productive, and continuously improved. PM is essential for managing NEs because it greatly affects the effectiveness of collaboration among members. PM

L.M. Camarinha-Matos et al. (Eds.): PRO-VE 2009, IFIP AICT 307, pp. 259–265, 2009.

in NE requires somewhat different approaches from PM in a single enterprise because of heterogeneity, dynamism, and complexity of NE. Researches on PM in NE are relatively few yet compared to PM in Supply Chain Management (SCM) [5, 6, 7]. VOPM in ECOLAD [3, 4] touches PM in CNO; but, for now, it focuses on virtual organizations, i.e., *ad-hoc NE*, only.

This paper introduces *a generic framework of PM in NE* (we call it *NEPM*) based on the Balanced Scorecard (BSC) approach [8]. NEPM consists of 28 *generic KPIs* and *cause-and-effect relationships* (*CAERs*) among them, which makes a *generic strategy map*. The generic strategy map could be specialized into a specific strategy map of an NE, e.g., ad-hoc NE (type) or 'K-consortium' (instance), after selecting some KPIs and CAERs among them. Derivation of CAERs is often missed in previous researches based on BSC [5], which usually results in misalignment of business strategy and PM implementations or mismatch of enablers and results.

In Section 2 we review related work on PM in SCM and NE. Section 3 introduces basic features, i.e., KPIs and CAERs of NEPM. Section 4 explains a case study of applying NEPM to some Korean NEs and section 5 draws conclusion.

2   Review of Related Work

2.1   Frameworks of Performance Measurement

Lots of PM frameworks have been developed. Examples include Supply Chain Council Organization Reference (SCOR) model, BSC, economic value added, the European Foundation of Quality Management (EFQM) Excellence model, Supply Chain Event Management (SCEM), etc [3]. SCOR is effective for PM in an enterprise, but it does not yet provide sufficient measures for inter-enterprise collaboration and has no formal linkage between KPIs in different perspectives, e.g., finance and internal process [3]. BSC has been widely used for PM in profit and non-profit organizations because it helps keep balance between different forces in an organization, i.e., long-term vs. short-term, internal vs. external, in-process vs. outcomes, and financial vs. non-financial measures. In this sense it categorizes KPIs into four perspectives: *learning/growth*, *internal process*, *customer*, and *finance*. A *strategy map* in BSC represents transformation of intangible assets (e.g., human capital, information and knowledge) into tangible assets including cash [8]. EFQM [9, 10] is one of Total Quality Management (TQM) frameworks. It consists of 9 criteria in 2 categories, i.e., leadership, people management, policy & strategy, resources, and processes in *enablers* category; people satisfaction, customer satisfaction, impact on society, and business results in *results* category. SCEM [6] is a tool-based approach that focuses on *visibility* of entities that can be simply defined as 4-tuple, *<entity, time, place, status>*.

BSC and EFQM are more adequate for *strategic-level* PM, whereas SCOR and SCEM are more adequate for *operational-level* PM. EFQM has more *generic* constructs than BSC, SCOR, and SCEM because it aims at TQM of whole company rather than partial functions or processes. SCEM is an efficient and effective approach for visibility of some entities when mistrust among members exists [3]. Because it requires only a few metrics that could be accepted by most NE members.

2.2 Performance Indicators and Causal Relationships

Performance measures or KPIs have been defined in most frameworks and by many researchers. For example, in SCOR 13 KPIs at strategy level and more than 200 KPIs at operational level are defined. In VOPM, KPIs are defined in 3 perspectives, i.e., finance, process, and collaboration [4], which means customer and learning/growth perspectives in BSC are omitted and collaboration is inserted instead. Gunasekaran et al. [7] suggest 46 metrics for SCM and classified them into SCOR processes (i.e., plan, source, make, deliver) and levels of management (i.e., strategic, tactical, operational). Bhagwat and Sharma [5] developed this framework and classified the metrics into 4 BSC perspectives. They stress the importance of building cause-and-effect relationships (CAERs) that enable managers to identify and control dependency between enablers and results. Matopoulos et al. [11] suggest a conceptual model for collaboration where they identify good indicators of collaboration, e.g., reduced inquiry time and inventory, increased quality and speed.

There have been many causal and factorial researches on interdependencies between enablers and results, but few findings are generally accepted yet. This is because it is not easy to formalize the semantics of interdependency that vary depending on viewpoints, focuses, and context of PM. Bou-Llusar et al. [9] review researches on CAERs among 9 criteria of EFQM. Examples of some meaningful findings are as follows.

- *Leadership* is the most important driver of system performance and affects *financial results* through *systems element. Information and analysis* is the second most important category (by Wilson and Collier).
- *Information management, human resource management,* and *customer focus* have significant effects on customer satisfaction and business results (by Pannirselvam and Schweikhart).

Besides EFQM, there have been some researches on interdependencies among performance measures. Most of them are not holistic but partial approaches that usually investigate the effects of several enabler variables to business results.

3   A Framework of Performance Measurement

3.1   Overview of the Framework, NEPM

NEPM is developed on the following rationale or assumptions.

- A PM framework helps create and design NEs, implement management/information systems, and share understanding of risk and benefit with all stakeholders.
- PM in NE should guarantee balance of different forces for all stakeholders of NE.
- In all types of NE, KPIs of collaboration among members are essential for NEPM.
  Basic features of NEPM can be summarized, as follows.
- NEPM is a result of integrating ideas and constructs of BSC, EFQM, and SCEM.
- NEPM comprises of the following concepts:
  (1) a set of *generic KPIs* in four perspectives of BSC;
  (2) a *generic strategy map* with *CAERs* among the generic KPIs.

• Generalization or specialization of NEPM could be accomplished by abstracting or augmenting KPIs and CAERs, which provides efficiency of design and execution of PM in NE to managers and practitioners.

3.2 Generic Key Performance Indicators of NEPM

Most of the generic KPIs of NEPM are developed on two previous frameworks: (1) the SCM metrics suggested by Gunasekaran et al. [7] and (2) the classification of those metrics into 4 BSC perspectives by Bhagwat and Sharma [5] (see the last column of Table 1). As the metrics of Gunasekaran's are result of theoretical and empirical analysis we adopt their key metrics to 28 KPIs of NEPM. However, because of some problems in the framework of Bhagwat and Sharma's we modify and extend it. One problem is that there is duplication of KPIs. For example, a KPI, i.e., 'buyer-supplier partnership level' appears 3 times in finance, customer, and learning/growth

Table 1. KPIs and Some Features in the NEPM

	KPIs in NEPM	SCOR proc.	SCOR level 1	Key Metrics for SCM
F1	*Procurement cost*	source	cost	Buyer-supplier partnership
F2	*Production cost*	make	cost	Manufacturing cost
F3	Transportation cost	deliver	cost	Total transportation cost
F4	*Marketing/sales cost*	deliver	cost	Buyer-supplier partnership
F5	*Customer service cost*	deliver	cost	Customer query time
F6	Return on investment	plan	assets	Rate of return on investment
F7	Total inventory cost	plan	cost	Total inventory cost
F8	*Total cash flow amount*	plan	assets	Total cash flow time
F9	Information carrying cost	plan	cost	Information carrying cost
C1	*Partner collaboration*	plan	agility	Buyer-supplier partnership
C2	*Product quality*	make	resp.	Flexibility of service systems
C3	Delivery reliability	deliver	rel.	Delivery reliability
C4	Delivery lead time	deliver	resp.	Delivery lead time
C5	*Customer response*	deliver	resp.	Customer query time
C6	*Information service*	plan	agility	Information carrying cost
P1	*Network cycle time*	plan	agility	Total supply chain cycle time
P2	Accuracy of forecasting	plan	rel.	Accuracy of forecasting
P3	Product development cycle time	make	resp.	Product develop. cycle time
P4	*Cash-to-cash cycle time*	plan	assets	Total cash flow time
P5	*Total inventory amount*	plan	assets	Total inventory cost
P6	Flexibility of service systems	plan	agility	Flexibility of service systems
P7	Capacity utilization	make	assets	Capacity utilization
L1	*Leadership*	plan	agility	Accuracy of forecasting
L2	*Policy & strategy*	plan	resp.	Buyer-supplier partnership
L3	*Human resources*	plan	rel.	Product develop. cycle time
L4	*Other resources (asset, finance, information)*	plan	rel.	Capacity utilization
L5	*Sourcing capability*	source	resp.	Supplier ability to quality
L6	*Delivery capability*	deliver	resp.	Flexibility of service systems

perspectives. This, we believe, will make practitioners confusing when apply the framework. Another problem is that some KPIs in learning/growth perspective, e.g., 'product development cycle time' and 'capacity utilization', are not adequate for representing *intangible asset of an organization* according to BSC. For the problem of duplication we rename KPIs; and some KPIs are also renamed to have clear meaning according to BSC. For the problem of inadequate KPIs in learning/growth we adopt enablers in EFQM, e.g., leadership, human resources, etc. In addition, we try to extend the frameworks of a supply chain to a network of enterprises.

Table 1 shows the resultant KPIs of NEPM (see column 2) that consist of 9 KPIs in *finance* (F1, .., F9), 6 in *customer* (C1, .., C6), 7 in *internal process* (P1, .., P7), 6 in *learning/growth* (L1, .., L6). (Due to the limitation of space meaning of every KPI is omitted here.) The generic KPIs could be classified into 4 SCOR process types, i.e., plan, source, make, and deliver (see column 3). They could be classified into 5 categories of SCOR 'level 1 strategic metrics', i.e., reliability (rel), responsiveness (resp), agility, cost, and assets (see column 4).

3.3   Generic Strategy Map of NEPM

CAERs among the generic KPIs are not completely identified yet. So, we define them relying on few research results mentioned in section 2.2 and on some hypothesis. Empirical research need to be executed to further develop or augment the CAERs as well as the KPIs. Figure 1 shows the resultant *generic strategy map*.

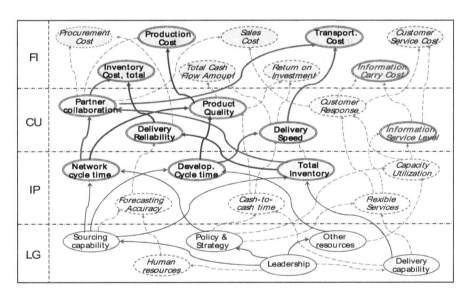

Fig. 1. The Generic Strategy Map & A Strategy Map of K-consortium

Due to the limitation of space two concepts, i.e., the generic strategy map and a specific strategy map of a NE called K-consortium, are overlapped in the figure. In the figure you see the generic KPIs (ellipse) in 4 perspectives, i.e., learning/ growth

(LG), internal process (IP), customer (CU), and finance (FI), and CAERs among them (curved lines). Other meanings will be explained in section 4.

4   An Illustrative Example

For verification of NEPM we applied it to 10 Korean NEs. Some of them belong to *vertical NE* of automotive and shipbuilding industry and the others belong to *horizontal NE* of textile and electronics industry. They perform process innovation projects using RFID technology, partly sponsored by Korean government since 2006. K-consortium belongs to automotive industry and consists of one vehicle maker as the leader, 4 suppliers of electronic/ mechanical/ optical parts, and one transportation company.

We obtained performance data for two years of execution from the final report of the project. K-consortium had less than 10 KPIs when the project began. It, of course, doesn't have a strategy map, yet. So, it's hard to monitor and improve collaborative efforts and to calculate the effects of introducing new technology. Based on the cost-benefit analysis K-consortium published we could identify its KPIs and implicit CAERs among them to draw a strategy map above. Note that it's a kind of reverse engineering to infer strategy and enablers from business results. If we are at planning stage of PM, after establishing vision and strategies, KPIs and CAERs are defined and then used to choose right resource allocation and courses of action.

In the strategy map 12 KPIs (double-lined ellipses) among 28 are identified in three perspectives (i.e., FI, CU, and IP) and CAERs among them (thick curved lines) also identified. Two KPIs, i.e., 'information carry cost' and 'information service' are identified, but CAERs that reach them are not identified, which means appropriate KPIs (say 'flexible services') are not measured, or some CAERs are missing or wrongly defined in the generic strategy map. In learning/growth perspective, 5 more KPIs (single-lined ellipse) and corresponding CAERs (thin curved lines) could be defined to allocate resources to appropriate actions at planning stage and could be identified to explain enablers (e.g., leadership, sourcing capability) of business results at evaluation stage.

Reviewing the results of applying NEPM to several Korean NEs we obtain many research questions that need to be investigated. Examples include: (1) relevance or relative importance of KPIs in each perspective, (2) definition of detailed metrics that will be actually measured for each KPI, (3) identification of more meaningful CAERs, (4) similarities and differences between different types of NEs, e.g., procurement-, engineering-, distribution-, and R&D-focused NE as well as NEs with different properties (e.g., size, age, product or service).

5   Conclusion

In this paper, we suggest a generic framework of performance measurement in Networked Enterprises (NEPM) based on the Balanced Scorecard (BSC) approach. NEPM consists of a set of *generic KPIs* and *cause-and-effect relationships* (CAERs) among them to make a *generic strategy map*. It includes 28 KPIs in four perspectives like BSC, i.e., learning/growth, internal process, customer, and finance. CAERs among the KPIs are identified on the basis of existing research, EFQM, and intuition of authors.

Although it may be a conceptual or theoretical model yet, NEPM has the following unique features: (1) the generic KPIs can provide network-centric view of PM to various stakeholders in NE, e.g., leading company, member company, supporting institutions, Virtual-organization Breeding Environment (VBE), etc; (2) NEPM considers total quality of management by adopting some constructs from EFQM such as 'leadership' and 'policy & strategy'; and (3) CAERs among KPIs enable managers to align strategy and implementation effectively at both planning and evaluation stage.

Comparing with VOPM in ECOLEAD project our approach is somewhat different in the following points: (1) NEPM focuses on vertical NE and horizontal NE while VOPM on ad-hoc NE; (2) NEPM considers relatively long-lasting NEs including VBE while VOPM does short-lived or impermanent NEs; (3) the KPIs of NEPM are balanced in four perspectives while that of VOPM are classified into three perspectives, i.e., finance, process, and collaboration excluding customer and learning/growth in BSC.

Further research will include the following issues: empirical analysis of PM in various Korean NEs through interviews and surveys, theoretical research on the effects of *enabler variables* to *result variables*, comparative analysis between Korean and EU NEs, etc.

References

1. Camarinha-Matos, L.M., Afsarmanesh, H., Ferrada, F., Klen, A., Ermilova, E.: Rough Reference Model for Collaborative Networks. ECOLEAD Deliverables D52.2 (2006)
2. Katzy, B., Loeh, H.: Virtual Enterprise Research State of the Art and Ways Forward. CeTIM Working Paper (2003)
3. Graser, F., Westphal, I., Eschenbaecher, J. (eds.): Roadmap on VOPM Challenges on Operational and Strategic Level. ECOLEAD Deliverables 31.1 (2005)
4. Westfahl, I. (ed.): VOPM Approach, Performance Metrics, and Measurement Process. ECOLEAD Deliverables 31.2 (2005)
5. Bhagwat, R., Sharma, M.K.: Performance Measurement of Supply Chain Management: A Balanced Scorecard Approach. Computers & Industrial Engineering 53, 43–62 (2007)
6. Francis, V.: Supply Chain Visibility: Lost in Translation? International J. of SCM 13(3), 180–184 (2008)
7. Gunasekaran, A., Patel, C., McGaughey, R.E.: A Framework for Supply Chain Performance Measurement. International J. of Production Economics 87, 333–347 (2004)
8. Kaplan, R.S., Norton, D.P.: The Strategy Map: Guide to Aligning Intangible Assets. Strategy & Leadership 32(5), 10–17 (2004)
9. Bou-Llusar, J.C., Escrig-Tena, A.B., Roca-Puig, V., Beltran-Martin, I.: An Empirical Assessment of the EFQM Excellence Model: Evaluation as a TQM Framework Relative to the MBNQA Model. J. of Operations Management 27, 1–22 (2009)
10. Conti, T.A.: A History and Review of the European Quality Award Model. The TQM Magazine 19(2), 112–128 (2007)
11. Matopoulos, M., Vlachopoulou, M., Manthou, V.: A Conceptual Model for Supply Chain Collaboration: Empirical Evidence from the Agri-food Industry. International J. of SCM 12(3), 177–186 (2007)

Transferability of Industrial Management Concepts to Healthcare Networks

Dario Antonelli[1], Agostino Villa[1], Bart MacCarthy[2], and D. Bellomo[3]

[1] Department of Production Systems & Economics, Politecnico di Torino, Italy
agostino.villa@polito.it, dario.antonelli@polito.it
[2] Operations Management Division, Nottingham University Business School, UK
bart.maccarthy@nottingham.ac.uk
[3] Azienda Sanitaria Locale ASL-AT, Asti, Italy
bellomo@asl.at.it

Abstract. The paper presents the preliminary results of a RTD project devoted to the transfer of concepts and methods, originally developed in the industrial area, to the subject of healthcare services where a profitable application is envisaged. The approach is based on drawing out the analogies between supply chains, composed by a network of resources connected by transport devices, and the local networks of healthcare services (family doctors, specialists, ambulatories, first aid centers, hospitals) to which patients are directed. The crucial task of efficiently and effectively managing a territorial network of healthcare service centers is modeled by using control theory concepts, and application conditions are discussed.

Keywords: We would like to encourage you to list your keywords in this section.

1 Introduction

Governments of developed countries are presently facing severe budget problems: among them, one of the most critical is the management of the national and regional healthcare systems, to assure a fair service level to the population under reasonable costs. Unless relevant adjustments will be applied, incidence of the healthcare costs on the GNPs will become explosive in a few years, thus forcing a reduction of the public covering of expenses.

With such a scenario, recent studies ([1] and [2]) expressed the necessity of a deep review not only of how to finance the healthcare costs, but mainly of how to plan the service capacity through suitable funding installments and to control the quality level of provided services. Then new tools and procedures for the management of healthcare services provided by local Healthcare Territorial Agencies (HTA) appear to be mandatory. Their utilization could allow a real management of the crucial nodes of the healthcare systems of any country because the reduction of costs does not be obtained at the population's expense. Till now management "protocols" able firstly to

L.M. Camarinha-Matos et al. (Eds.): PRO-VE 2009, IFIP AICT 307, pp. 266–273, 2009.

estimate, from the large data base of a HTA, the values of some Key Performance Indicators (KPIs) which could evaluate the service quality, efficiency and cost, secondly, to suggest criteria and procedures for the planning and control of the HTA operations, have not yet been established. To be more explicit, performance evaluation of individual services, like Emergency Rescue, Hospital Divisions, has been already applied but there is a lack of results referring to the performance evaluation of the whole health network. In the industrial sector, since many years, the attention has been focused on the performance of the entire Supply Chain more than to the local optimization of the individual processes.

This paper will utilize the experience acquired by the partners of the CODESNET[1] project in the field of the performance evaluation of SME networks, to the aim of analyzing the transferability of industrial management methods to the service planning and control in the healthcare sector. The scope is to investigate the possibility of transferring the industrial methods of network performance analysis to a different kind of network, a HTA made of a number of local healthcare service providers of different types, namely: hospitals, pharmacies, medical centres, panel doctors, diagnosis laboratories, etc. The main idea is the application of concepts of supply chain management, such as localization and networking, to a HTA. Here, localization means to delegate the administration of healthcare centres to administrative units on a local scale, provided that a common planning of expected service capacity and level has been centrally defined; networking refers to a comprehensive management of all the health related services in order to exploit the advantages of collaboration and information sharing.

New models for the management of HTA could apply the principles of optimal planning of the network capacity and of real-time (in practice, day-by-day) control through feedback by measuring appropriate KPIs. Dealing with the transferability of the mentioned industrial planning & control concepts and methods to healthcare sector, it must be noted that direct transfers are not always successful: systems, concepts and techniques often need specific interpretation, adaptation and adjustment for the different application domain. Special care must be used if the "subject" of the service is a person, having proper decisional autonomy, as in the case of a patient, even if such a decisional autonomy is often limited by a reduced knowledge of the service system itself. In this case there is the risk of a dynamic adaptation of the system measures to the chosen KPIs in order to increase the attractiveness of the service.

The paper begins with the description of the respective features of industrial supply chains on one side and healthcare service networks on the other. There is a "theoretical part" that outlines the main ideas of the transferability of management methods from industrial sector to the healthcare system by highlighting the analogies and the differences between the two networks. Eventually there is an "operative part", in order to outline main contents and potential usefulness of a _HTA Management Protocol_ for supporting the HTA manager and the local service controllers.

---

[1] CODESNET – COllaborative DEmand & Supply NETworks is a Coordination Action funded by the European Commission in the 7th FP, chaired by A. Villa (re: www.codesnet.polito.it).

2 Specific Characteristics of a Supply Chain

Health networks can be analyzed by similarity with the other industrial service networks. The most common industry network is the supply chain. For industrial supply chain it is intended a network of production and distribution services connected through agreements, which performs the functions of procurement of materials, transformation of them into intermediate and finished products, and finally distribution of final products to customers [3].

Supply chain management has been viewed as the decision-making structure to be developed to make possible a real interaction among firms operating concurrently. In terms of a conceptual model, a supply chain can be graphically represented such as a graph of production stages and markets, alternatively connected: it means that each node "production stage" can be only connected with nodes "market" both upstream and downstream [4] and [5]. Owing to its multi-stage structure, supply chain management is referred to as a typical large-scale management problem since each component firm can be viewed as an "agent", whose management decision should be planned through a *negotiation* with other agents, namely with its own *suppliers* (upstream) and *buyers* (downstream). Then the organization of a supply chain must solve the following two complementary problems [6]: (a) define efficient and effective negotiation procedures for each "market"; (b) define a common coordination strategy for all production stages, such to assign to each stage a reference plan assuring a global efficiency/effectiveness of the supply chain.

These two management problems must be solved in a coordinated way, such as to avoid conflicts between the coordination action (to be centrally planned) and the local negotiations among consecutive production/service stages.

3 Specific Characteristics of a Healthcare System

In a territorial healthcare system – as the HTA - three different *"agents"* are present:

1. the *HTA manager*, with the scope of planning the service capacity of the healthcare service centres in a specific local region;
2. the healthcare service *providers*, each one being committed to provide a given healthcare *service* within a HTA centre;
3. the set of *end-users* – the *patients* – each one asking for a given healthcare service, either autonomously or driven by a provider.

The following types of services are considered:

1. "hospital service", summarizing in this concept all different functions which could only be provided there upon request of a patient;
2. "intermediate service", such as local consulting, health status testing;
3. "input services", as family doctor and specialist.

The most important service structures composing the healthcare system can be represented as components of a network as the one sketched in Fig. 1.

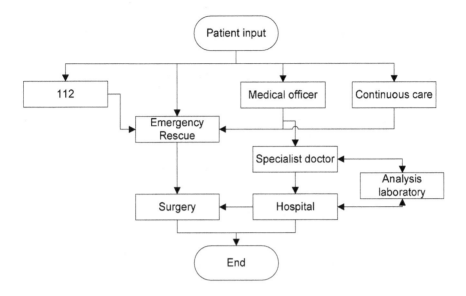

Fig. 1. A generalized network of healthcare services

The hospital plays the role of the main service (here considered in an aggregated form), which collects flows of patients coming from several upstream service, namely: day-hospital, local consulting services, considered as intermediate services of the network; family doctors (medical officers) and specialists, usually acting as the upstream services or input services for patients. Upstream services have to address their patients to the downstream ones, according to the service capacity values of these latter.

Differently from industrial supply chain, in a HTA it is important to take into account the geographical localization of service providers as the patients are spread on the territory. As an example, in Fig. 2, the distribution of accesses to the Asti hospital, in the northern Italy, shows that the attractiveness of the service 'hospital' is a complex combination of the quality of the service offered, the availability of efficient communication infrastructures and of the distance from the patient.

From a theoretical point of view, Fig. 1 gives an illustration of how services could be used in various sequences by patients, in industrial terminology the *"routing"*. It is assumed that *"precedence conditions"* exist among services, that means conditions which make necessary to ask for specific sequences of services often denoted *"healthcare protocols"* (that is the medical equivalent of the routing). The set of healthcare protocols at disposal in a HTA defines the graph of Fig. 1, where nodes are the services and each link represents the precedence conditions between two services. The flows of patients asking for that sequence of services are assigned by either monitoring or estimating the number of patients per unit time accessing both services, according to all "protocols" including the two services themselves.

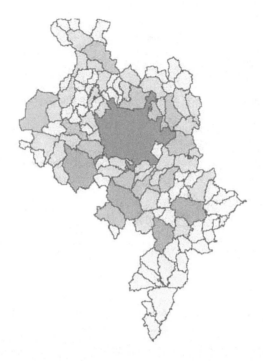

Fig. 2. Maps of attractiveness of the Asti hospital (darker area mean more accesses)

4 Analogies for Transferability

The scheme of healthcare service network of Fig. 1 and 2 presents several analogies with a supply chain model describing production operations. The following Table 1 gives evidence of these similarities between healthcare system functionality and production network operations.

The aim of this table is to illustrate correspondences both with regard to the "agents" acting inside the two systems, and their interactions, as well as their respective goals. The scope is to envisage the similarities but also to recognize the differences: these last ones will give the right suggestions for a correct transferability of models and tools from the two sectors.

By Table 1, indeed, evident similarities can be envisaged, but also a significant difference. The real goal of a patient is to find a service which could assure that a desired health status could be reached. This target can be reached by the *cooperative actions* of both the patient – who must be able to explain symptoms and ready to carefully follow prescriptions – and the service provider – who must be efficient in using right competence to make diagnosis. Cooperation, instead of the competition governing industrial interactions, and the territorial distribution of one type of agents (the potential patients) are the two milestones of healthcare systems: they call for a better specification of this sector itself.

Table 1. Similarities/differences between industrial and healthcare systems

Items	Industrial Network (SC)	HTA
Agents	(a) Supplier (b) Client	(a) Service provider (b) Patient
Agents' position in the process	concentrated-parameter process: agents are associated to nodes of the network.	mixed-parameter process: service providers are associated to HTA, patients are distributed on the territory.
Agents interactions	Negotiation to manage competition between the two types of agents	Cooperation to assure the most effective service.
Agents decisions	Each type of agent chooses the counterpart based on convenience	The patient chooses the service provider who seems to be more credible
Agents goals	To maximize agents' own profits.	The patient wants to reach a desired health status; the provider aims to assure a desired performance minimizing service costs.

5 Modeling Healthcare System by Use of Industrial Concepts

The similarities and the differences outlined in Table 1 allow to develop a model of the healthcare system – specifically referred to a HTA – by using industrial concepts. The model is generated by making reference to the classic functional diagram of a SC.

The model of the healthcare service network does not describe the HTA as a network of resources; then, it does not account for the management of the resources (that are the service centres) neither for the choice of specific resources made by patients.

To this extent, it is necessary to translate the main functionalities of the three agents into proper management decisions, namely:

i.   planning decisions adopted by the HTA network manager;
ii. decisions to assure the quality level of services and the service centre attractiveness, made by the service providers;
iii. decisions to choose the most credible provider and the most accessible service centre, done by the patients.

By using this classification of decision types, a model of the HTA management can be stated in terms of a block diagram (and related planning/control actions) directly derived from the industrial application of control theory – as represented in Fig. 3.

This figure gives a clear view of the application of concepts developed in the frame of Control Theory and frequently applied in industrial management, to the healthcare sector. The application indeed describes the interactions among the three agents of a HTA in terms of respective decisions concerning either the planning and local control of the offered services, or the choice of some service centres, and the service providers there operating.

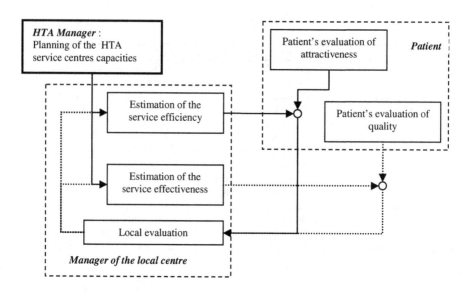

Fig. 3. A control diagram of the interactions among the three HTA agents

According to the above block diagram, the HTA manager has the task of programming the service capacities of the HTA centers, thus assuring a planned attractiveness and a sufficient quality level. To this aim, the HTA manager can use information concerning the population distribution in the HTA territory, and evaluate the expected flows of persons towards the centers (e.g. by gravity models and methods to subdivide a region into sections depending on the transport connections, as in Iwainsky et al, 1986).

Considering a local service center, the center manager has to transform the centralized plans into time-by-time controls. On one hand, it has to assure that the attractiveness of its own center be as high as possible, through a careful management of the incoming patients' flows (e.g., through scheduling of arrivals and services, by applying industrial scheduling tools as presented in [9]). On the other, it has to monitor the offered quality (e.g., by Quality Control tools, as in [10]). Both actions should be designed – and applied – by tacking into account that the local manager's decision is a typical feedback control, driven by information both on the currently offered service types and levels, and on the number of patients who decided to use this same service center.

The utilization of a service center by a patient depends on two main considerations (as in case of a "client" of an industrial service): first, the possibility of a fast utilization of the service; then, the a-priori evaluation of the service quality, usually based on the "credibility" of the provider and the information previously received on the efficiency of the center personnel. The industrial approach is based on the estimation of the patients flows over the network of service centers by formally modeling the preferences of patients (e.g., as in choosing among alternative products by a AHP procedure, as shown in [11]) and their dynamics over the service network (e.g., by queue theory models, as in [12]).

6 Conclusions

The presented block diagram of Fig. 3 gives a scheme of management for a territorial healthcare system concurrently based both on the goals of the central manager, efficiency and service capacity, and on the needs of the patients, service quality and effectiveness of the cure.

The real application of this scheme requires two main actions: first, to define central strategies easy to be understood also locally; second, to support local managers in their crucial task of understanding the patients desires and choices. The application of techniques successfully experienced in the industrial sector seems to be promising and has originated the RTD projects currently developed at Politecnico di Torino, funded by the Italian Ministry of University and Research (PRIN). The research is also supported by the Compagnia San Paolo of Torino – Italy.

References

1. Starfield, B., Leiyu, S.: Policy relevant determinants of health: an international perspective. Health Policy 60, 201–218 (2002)
2. Organizational Environment and Content Requirements for Health Promotion and Care Information, http://www.virtual.epm.br/material/healthcare/A03.pdf
3. Bergman, E.M., Feser, J.E.: Industrial and Regional Clusters: Concepts and Comparative Applications (1999), http://www.rri.wvu.edu/WebBook/BergmanFeser/
4. Akif, J.C., Blanc, S., Ducq, Y.: Comparison of methods and frameworks to evaluate the performance of supply chains. In: 4th IFIP Int. Workshop on Performance Measurement, Bordeaux, June 27-28 (2005)
5. Lin, C., Chow, W.S., Madu, C.N., Kuei, C.H., Yu, P.P.: A structural equation model of supply chain quality management and organizational performance. Int. J. of Production Economics 96, 355–365 (2005)
6. Villa, A., Antonelli, D.: A Road Map to the Development of European SME Networks – Towards Collaborative Innovation. Springer, London (2008)
7. Healthcare Informatics Alliance, http://www2.wmin.ac.uk/hscmg/pdf/ WestFocus_Talk_31-05-2006_Millard.pdf
8. AHRQ – Agency for Healthcare Research and Quality, http://www.qualityindicators.ahrq.gov/
9. Brandimarte, P., Villa, A.: Advanced Models for Manufacturing Systems Management. CRC Press, Boca Raton (1995)
10. MacCarthy, B.L., Wasusri, T.: A review of non-standard applications of statistical process control (SPC) charts. The International Journal of Quality & Reliability Management 19(3), 295–320 (2002)
11. Dyer, R.F., Forman, E.H.: An Analytic Approach to Marketing Decisions. Prentice Hall, Englewood Cliffs (1991)
12. Papadopoulos, H.T., Heavey, C., Browne, J.: Queueing Theory in Manufacturing Systems Analysis and Design. Chapman & Hall, London (1993)

People at Work: Modelling Human Performance in Shop Floor for Process Improvement in Manufacturing Enterprises

Siti Nurhaida Khalil, R.H. Weston, and J.O. Ajaefobi

MSI (Manufacturing System Integration Institute), Loughborough University
Leicestershire, UK, LE11 3TU
s.n.khalil@lboro.ac.uk, r.h.weston@lboro.ac.uk,
j.o.Ajaefobi@lboro.ac.uk

Abstract. Predicting actual human performance in manufacturing plants is difficult and not a straightforward task. This motivates further investigation of ways of modelling, measuring and predicting behaviours of people working in production systems. People can be modelled in terms of their competences in relation to the roles they play in realising enterprise activities. This research introduces a combined application of Enterprise Modelling (EM) and Simulation Modelling (SM) to investigate and understand how people systems can be matched to process-oriented roles in production situations. EM facilitates the development of static models of structural aspects of people system from both top-down and bottom-up points of view. It can also provide organisational models in terms of roles and role relationships. Developed versions of EMs can also explicitly define key attributes of current and possible future 'work contexts in which productions systems' are used. In this way any given EM can underpin the creation of multiple SMs that characterise important structural and dynamic aspects of production systems (in terms of human configuration, performance, flexibility, etc), and production throughput within specific contexts of use. The research methods are illustrated via the use of case studies in which roles that people play in the production systems of an international company were studied and modelled. The findings of related SM experiments have generated useful insights for industrialist and academics.

Keywords: Enterprise Modelling, Simulation Modelling, Competency.

1 Introduction

As designers and managers of Manufacturing Enterprises (MEs), assigned person's need, 'abilities' and 'tools' to help them systematically determine appropriate 'roles' for other groups of people, i.e. 'human systems' that can appropriately resource role sets determined by responsible designers and managers. But ME design and management is in general very complex, not least because competent human resources will be limited and costly and will themselves be complex. Recently there has been increased interest in the study of human systems and human systems integration with MEs. This

L.M. Camarinha-Matos et al. (Eds.): PRO-VE 2009, IFIP AICT 307, pp. 274–281, 2009.
© IFIP International Federation for Information Processing 2009

growing interest is beginning to lead to new strategies for coping with human system complexity (behavioural, psychological, culture, attributes etc).

Previous literature reviews show that ME's are subjected to increasing dynamic impacts arising in the business environment in which they operate. To address this kind of concern, manufacturing philosophies like Agile Manufacturing Group Technology [1] Reconfigurable Manufacturing Systems (RMS), Mass Customization & Postponement and Holonic Manufacture[2-4] have emerged to inform ME managers and designers about how to achieve increased flexibility and responsiveness. However, on general these philosophies are only supported by limited implementation tools to quantify relative benefits of choosing alternative philosophies; and more particularly in the context of this research paper, to relative quantify benefits of alternative ways of resourcing process oriented roles in accordance with selected philosophy. Also observed is that despite significant advance in best practice complex systems engineering, as yet in industry there is neither model nor coherent means of modeling organizational structures and related time based behaviors of the human and technical (machine and IT system) resources. On the other hand, various modeling techniques have been developed to characterize machines (and their competencies and behaviors) and these techniques are becoming commonly implemented using virtual engineering and simulation of NC and robot systems. But generally because ME modeling plant's human system is so complex their software support tools are somewhat special purpose model kinematic and ergonomic characteristics.

2 Paper Scope and Focus

This paper addresses the question: given a well-defined set of process-oriented roles how best should work roles be resourced? In this respect it is assumed that either (1) people or (2) some form of machine or IT system or (3) some combination of (1) and (2) will prove most effective; and that generally these kinds of 'active' resource'; will be constrained in terms of their availability short and long term. Also assumed is that (a) the nature of roles and (b) the works loads placed on the roles will determine the most effective match of 'role holders' to 'the defined set of process oriented role.' Furthermore it is assumed that because the work loads in MEs are typically determined by customers and related factors in the ME's environment then these workloads will frequently change. This provides a baseline rationale thus benefits manufacturing enterprise for better human resources allocation. This study includes the competency requirements for an operator should have to perform manufacturing processes and study for an improved systematic method, and supporting modeling tools needed to compare the match of different choices of candidate human and technical (active) resources to process oriented roles and their workloads; and also that the developed method and tools should enable short term planning of resource deployment as well as longer term strategic decision making.

Figure 1 illustrates the systematic modelling approach under development by the authors. The underlying idea is to create multi-perspective models using enterprise models (EM's) technique i.e. CIMOSA that can be computer executed in the form of simulation models (SMs); such that they provide a computer tool to inform 'ongoing planning' and 'longer term investment' decision making leading to effective use of human and technical resources. Here specific ME models related to perspective P1 are created using an EM technique which is geared toward specifying sets of ordered activities (or process models) that can be decomposed into explicitly defined roles. These roles and role relationships specify a process oriented relatively enduring structure for any ME being modelled. A second dynamic workload perspective P2 is derived from (a) analysis of historical patterns of work that previously have passed through the defined roles and/or (b) a forecast or prediction of likely future workloads. The third perspective P3 relates to candidate role holders in the form both of stereotypical and actual human and technical resources. Here modelling can be with respect to (i) known competencies (of people) and capabilities (of machines), (ii) capacities and/or performance levels (of both resource types) and (iii) psychological behaviours (of people).

This multi-perspective modelling approach is designed to enable: (I) independent change to the three perspectives P1, P2 and P3; (II) reuse of models of MEs in the form of process and enterprise models; and (III) ongoing systematic reuse of models belonging to those three viewpoints, as required in support of short, medium and longer term ME decision making.

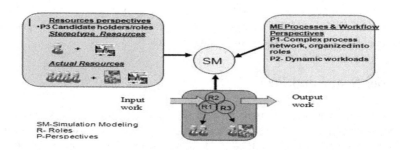

Fig. 1. Human System Modeling in ME

3 Modelling Concepts and Research Methodology

MSI researchers for some time have been using enterprise engineering and simulation modelling technique to aid decision making. Enterprise modelling is used primarily to (1) externalizing enterprise knowledge about case study MEs, and can add value to the enterprise by enabling knowledge sharing and (2) provide a process-oriented decomposition mechanism, so that high levels of complexity can be handled so that it becomes possible to break down the barriers in organization that hinder productivity by synergizing the enterprise to achieved better understandings about how business goals can be achieved in an efficient and productive way.

The enterprise modelling (EM) technique [5] used in this study is known as CI-MOSA (refer Figure 4). CIMOSA is an acronym derived from CIM Open System Architecture and this acronym was introduced by the AMICE consortium. In CI-MOSA the user representation and system representation, and related function information and control perspectives are decomposed. The associated decomposition and isolation of different modelling concepts and viewpoints enables an organization to be represented in a flexible fashion, so as to realise changing requirements for functional and facilities integration.

CIMOSA modelling enables ME decomposition into the following:

- **Domains (DM)**
- **Domain Processes (DP)**
- **Business Processes (BP)**

- **Enterprise Activities(EA)**
- **Functional Operators (FO)**
- **Functional Entities (FE)**

Graphical representation of CIMOSA models is shown in generic form in Figure 2.

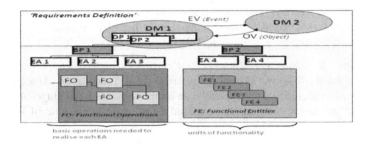

Fig. 2. CIMOSA static model

Case study modelling is also supported by simulation models (dynamic models) that are in part, derived from (and hence are consistent with) selected segments of the CIMOSA static model. EM using CIMOSA offers mechanism to systematically modelling common processes and relatively enduring structures that governs the way ME operates[6]. CIMOSA graphical models are static in the sense that they only encode relatively enduring properties of ME's and cannot be computer executed to show ME behaviours over time. The simulation models are capable of modelling queues, stochastic events, product flows, process routes, resource utilisation, breakdowns and absence and exception flows.

Enterprise and simulation modelling techniques can mutually support analysis of human system roles in a manufacturing enterprise. First EM enables modelling via systematic decomposition of processes into enterprise activities and second these models could be computer exercised, via a selected simulation tool to enable experiments to be carried out which predict behaviour outcomes if human systems are deployed in different ways. The simulation software used for this case study is Teknomatix Plant Simulation software, a discrete event, object-based simulation software that offers simple and user friendly application and also provides better flexibility to human system modelling as compared to other familiar software in MSI (Manufacturing System Integration Institute Loughborough University) such as Simul8 etc.

4 Choice of Study Domain

The Case Study chosen was an international based 'point of purchase' (POP) manufacturing company ABC. The 'produce and deliver' domain of the company is studied in this research where this includes all the activities involved in its production section including its assembly section. The majority of the parts are fabricated in the production plant i.e. in sections called 'Vacforming', 'Woodworking', 'Printing' and 'Injection Moulding'. But some are outsourced to external suppliers. The assembly work is currently carried out in two working units, namely: the batch assembly and lean cell assembly. Currently, on average, lean cells take over 20% of the overall assembly jobs. Lean Cells had recently been introduced to overcome the WIP problems, which were costing a high fraction of the company's stake. However key aspects of people working in both lean cell and batch assembly have not been studied in detail because the management assumed the assembly job can be performed by anyone without any training nor experience. In general assembly operators are temporary workers that are hired through an agency. This case study was conceived to investigate effects of workers performance based on their competency: here by batch and lean assembly lines are studied in terms of achievable Takt times and throughput.

Assumptions: Relationships connecting performance, speed and efficiency were assumed to be as follows. **P**(performance) is some function of **A**(accuracy) and **S**(speed); where accuracy may typically be expressed as a percentage of successful job completions and speed can be expressed as measure of the rate of job completions. Efficiency is expressed as workers ability to perform their work with accuracy. Also assumed is that **A** can be viewed as being a measure of the **C1** (competency) of an individual or a group or team of people. S can be viewed as being a measure of the **C2** (capacity) of an individual or a group or team of people.In many manufacturing situations it was also assumed that P=**C1** times **C2** = **A** (accuracy) multiplied by **S** (speed) that can be written as:

$$P = C1 \times C2 = A \times S \tag{1}$$

The justification: for these assumptions was that workers performance is actually the multiplication of worker's accuracy of working and speed of working. This is because the worker's performance increases when workers ability to perform their work with accuracy as well as by worker's ability to work at higher rate (speed). Thus performance is assumed to be a multiplication of C1 and C2 of workers working in a unit of process, or role or workstation. The enterprise model (EM) was built using CIMOSA decomposition and modelling constructs. This EM explicitly mapped the ordered set of activities of the network of business processes used by the case company to realise products. This state-of-the-art method leads to top-down abstraction of the processes and these can be seen in Figure 3 and Figure 4. The assembly functions form a more definitive focus for simulation modelling as the case company wanted to understand what assembly paradigms might best suit its production situations. The static models EM's were therefore transformed into equivalent dynamic models (i.e. simulation models to understand assembly process dynamics). The actual historical order rates of the company were used as input to the SM. In the SM, five simulation trials have been exercised for which relationships connecting worker's accuracy and worker's speed has been changed and tested systematically. These models have been run at slow speed for specific time to show the behavior of work movement through different entities of the systems with respect to time. The model is verified because it is similar to the real system behavior. The simulation model from both batch assembly line and lean assembly cell configurations are recorded in Figure 5.

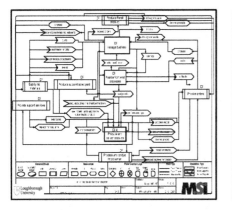

Fig. 3. Business Domain of ABC Company

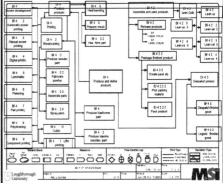

Fig. 4. Produce and Deliver activities

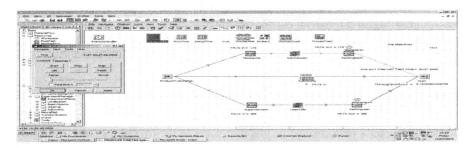

Fig. 5. Simulation Model

5   Results and Discussion

The results obtained from the simulation models are the used to populated graphs that show the relationships between worker's accuracy, worker's speed, takt time and production throughput. Graph 1 portrays relationships between worker's speed and throughput; Graph 2 co-relates takt time against throughput; Graph 3 shows the relationship between takt time, speed and accuracy; and Graph 4 depicts the relationship between throughput, speed and efficiency.

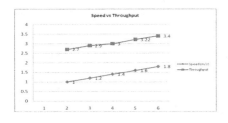

Graph 1. Worker's Speed vs Throughput

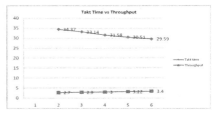

Graph 2. Takt Time vs Throughput

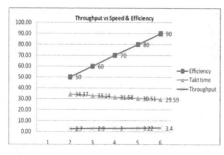
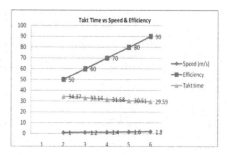

Graph 3. Throughput, Speed & Efficiency   **Graph 4.** Takt Time, Speed and Efficiency

The first graph shows positive relationship between speed and throughput. As the speed of the worker increases in the simulation model, the total production throughput increases. In Graph 2, as the efficiency and speed of the worker increases, the Takt time decreases. However the throughput increases. This can be explained as the time taken to produce one assembly is reduced when the worker's performance increases; thus resulting higher throughput in the assembly line. These graphs show that increase in C1 and C2, increases the throughput of the production line and therefore decreases the Takt time of the assembly line. Thus the relationship can be mathematically portrayed as follows:

Takt time (Tt) decreases as competency (C1) and capacity (C2) increases
Thus $Tt/(C1.C2) = \infty$, and therefore $Tt = C$ (2)

Hence the worker's performance is directly related to the overall takt time of the assembly line. Graph 3 and Graph 4 portrays that when speed and efficiency of workers increases, the production throughput increases and takt time decreases. Thus by improving worker's performance in the production line, process performance in the shop floor can improved. However, these parameters (accuracy and speed) are not the only factors that influenced the process performance in the shop floor, this also includes organization structure i.e. team, group, motivation, ergonomics and work organization etc.

6 Conclusion

This research illustrates how simulation models can be used to predict production systems performance in terms of people performance factors (competency and capacity). This is achieved by:

1. Linking the static modeling approach-time independent (EM) and dynamic modelling approach-time dependent (SM) tools. This enables prediction of the system behaviour systematically.
2. SM tool enable quantification of the effects of the observed issues i.e. competency on system performance thus objectively predicts the system behaviour.

3. The combination or EM and SM provides 'as-is' systems performance, also enables possible opportunity to evaluate different working scenarios that allows prediction of future system behaviour and performance.

Acknowledgement

The first author is currently pursuing her PhD in Loughborough University and sponsored by the Ministry of Higher Education Malaysia. She is also on study-leave from the Universiti Teknikal Malaysia Melaka (UTeM).

References

1. Yusuf, Y.Y., Adeleye, E.O.: A comparative study of lean and agile manufacturing with a related survey of current practices in the UK. International Journal of Production Research 40(17), 4545–4562 (2002)
2. Zhang, X., et al.: Design and implementation of a real-time holonic control system for manufacturing. Information Sciences 127(1-2), 23–44 (2000)
3. Gou, L., Luh, P.B., Kyoya, Y.: Holonic manufacturing scheduling: architecture, cooperation mechanism, and implementation. Computers in Industry 37(3), 213–231 (1998)
4. Rodriguez, S., Hilaire, V., Koukam, A.: Towards a holonic multiple aspect analysis and modeling approach for complex systems: Application to the simulation of industrial plants. Simulation Modelling Practice and Theory 15(5), 521–543 (2007)
5. Vernadat, F.: Enterprise modelling and integration (EMI): Current status and research perspectives. Annual Reviews in Control 29, 15–25 (2002)
6. Rahimifard, A., Weston, R.: The enhanced use of enterprise and simulation modelling techniques to support factory changeability. International Journal of Computer Integrated Manufacturing 20(4), 307–328 (2007)

Competence Ontology for Network Building

Kafil Hajlaoui, Xavier Boucher, Michel Beigbeder, and Jean Jacques Girardot

Ecole Nationale Supérieure des Mines de Saint Etienne G2I,
42023 Saint Etienne, France
{hajlaoui,boucher,mbeig,girardot}@emse.fr

Abstract. The overall objective of this research is to engineer a decision aid approach to support the identification of collaborative networks which could then constitute potential Virtual Breeding Environments. An interesting aspect of this approach is working with internet and thus considered an "open universe" of potential partners. In this perspective, the paper puts the focus on extracting essential facets of firm competences using an ontology approach. The method followed to construct the ontology is presented as well as a brief introduction on its use. This work is part of an on going project to produce cognitive aids to support decisions when seeking to form partnerships and establish VBEs.

Keywords: Information extraction, Ontology, Competence model, Enterprise networks.

1 Introduction

A lot of research work deals with the formalization of characteristic data concerning potential partners for networked organizations [3][13][4]. Most of these approaches are adapted to a semi-closed environment defined by a Virtual Breeding Environment (VBE). VBEs provide a collaborative environment, facilitating trustable exchanges of information to help the selection of partners when creating virtual organizations.

The research we refer to focuses on a complementary step: furnishing a decision aid support for identifying potential VBE. This is based on the hypothesis of an open environment of potential partners to build VBEs where any company can participate. Typically, this issue often appears when you have to analyse a regional business area to identify potential collaborative networks among firms. As a consequence, the identification of potential collaborative partners will be based on the use of public information, available through the public web sites of the companies. This assumption induces the use of specific information extraction mechanisms.

As in the coordination approach the information extraction procedure focuses on two key factors: the activity fields of the companies and their internal competences (see justification in [9]. This information on company activities and competences will be further used, at a second stage, to generate new knowledge on the potential structure of VBEs. The overall approach of such a decision aid has been already described in [10].

This communication concentrates on a competence ontology required to extract synthesized information on company proficiencies. Due to the aforementioned complexity

L.M. Camarinha-Matos et al. (Eds.): PRO-VE 2009, IFIP AICT 307, pp. 282–289, 2009.
© IFIP International Federation for Information Processing 2009

of this competence concept, a semantic oriented approach is required for the extraction. Ontology is used as a semantic resource to guide the extraction process applied to competences. One of the objectives of this paper is to explain the method used to engineer the ontology. Furthermore, its use, with syntaxic and semantic patterns which support the information extraction procedure, is underlined. These patterns can treat semantically and pragmatically the data available on company web sites. To reduce the ontological complexity, our research is limited to a sole enterprise activity domain: the mechanical industry.

In section 2, some essential references on competence modelling are provided as well as the basic competence model used as the starting point of the ontology. In section 3 the methodology utilized is described along with some ontological components. In section 4, we briefly introduce the use of this ontology for information extraction. Finally, our conclusions are presented.

2 Competence Modeling

The competence management is an important lever for business competiveness and for cooperation between firms. With an increasing production after the 90's, scientific literature published quite a large amount of research examining how to better characterise the notion of competence. Several competence modelling approaches have been

Table 1. Examples of references on competence models, from diverse sectors

Ref	field	Key points
[1]	Industrial management	CRAI model (Competence Resource Aspect Individual) for enterprise modelling. This semantic model represents the links between competence and other enterprise modelling constructs: the context, resources, individual and activity missions.
[12]	Industrial management	A formal model of competence is proposed to be integrated within an organization model for the management and development of competences. This supports a quantitative approach of competence assignment, applicable both to individual and collective competence
[4]	Computer Science	In the context of VO creation the authors present a generic model of competence based on the concepts of Capability, Capacity, and Conspicuity. This was created for the management of firm competence profiles, so as to make possible evaluation of competence profiles.
[11]	Computer Science	Firm competences are described by a set of qualifications, technologies and knowledge, but without referring to a more generic model of competence. Based on the use of a Multi-agent System, some user scenario are proposed to create business collaboration among companies, with a explicit view on their internal competences.
[14]	Management Science	An ontology formalises the concepts necessary to represent and manage the corporate memory of a company. This ontology is suggested as a support for competence management.
[15]	Management Science	The Resource Based View of the firm initially proposed by Wernerfelt has generated a large amount of scientific work. His theory provides notably a stable definition and articulation of the crucial concepts necessary to describe firm competences.

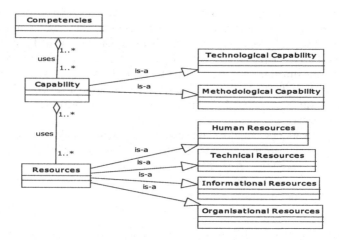

Fig. 1. Basic competence model

suggested, for the implementation of methods and tools for competence management. Table 1 provides some examples of contributions from three different scientific communities, which intend to manipulate the notion of competence using more or less formalized models. This table is not exhaustive, but already underlines the diversity of publications on this modeling issue.

Referring to a larger state of the art developed in our research, we present in figure 1 a basic model of competence used as a root to develop a more detailed competence ontology (see section 3). This model refers to the key notions of the Resources Based View for firms: the competences of a company emerge as a combination of internal capabilities. These capabilities are the result of the activation of different resources acquired by the company. To define further these key notions needed, we consider four basic types of resources: human, technological, informational, organisational resources. Furthermore, two basic types of firm capabilities are distinguished: methodological linked to the added value provided by the working methods used by a company to deliver its products or services; and technological referring to the creation of added value based on the use of technical resources and processes. This structure supplies a generic and abstract model used as a starting point to create an ontology.

3   Ontology Engineering

As mentioned in section one, the final information sought is a similarity indicia among the overall competences of individual companies. In that objective, our approach consists in extracting a set of "traces" concerning company competences. Consequently, the ontology required here is that of "competence traces", dealing with only sector of activity of the mechanical industry, as mentioned before. Of course, on a company web site there are a lot of separate phrases, referring to a large variety of concepts (human or technological resources, activities, processes, working methods...) which can be considered as "traces" of competences. Often the concepts behind these keywords or phrases are not straightforward but ambiguous. These reasons make it necessary to structure rigorously and carefully craft the ontology, making possible semantic treatments when necessary.

3.1 Methodologies for Ontology Engineering

The construction of an ontology is a complicated process, requiring the definition of rigorous principles or mechanisms to identify concepts and relationships. Several scientific research efforts have tried to create and formalise ontology engineering methods [7][5]. However, most of these advances are linked to some specific point of view. Importantly, there is still no convergence on the best practices on this issue.

The methodologies proposed to engineer an ontology, structure the transition from non formal knowledge towards a conceptual domain. Then, the formal model of this domain is transformed into an operational ontology. It is commonly accepted to follow these steps of conceptualisation, formalisation, operationalisation in this order. However, while the majority of the methods provide a well structured procedure, most of them still rely on intuitive criteria and on non-formal opinion of experts when modelling the concepts of a knowledge field.

To cope with the ambiguities mentioned earlier, we need to more rigorously conceptualise the notions related to firm competences. Therefore, we selected ARCHONTE methodology [2], which defines precise principles and cognitive mechanisms for each step formalisation of ontology. This method induces a clear definition of the meaning for each concept of the ontology, through a « semantic normalisation » mechanism. ARCHONTE is composed of three main steps illustrated in the following sections: normalisation, formalisation, operationalisation.

3.2 Building an "Ontology for Competence Traces"

3.2.1 Normalisation

The first normalisation step is to render explicit the concepts of the knowledge domain. These concepts should be expressed in the form of "cognitive constructs", which have a non-contextual meaning. This allows the arrangement of various constructs into semantically interpretable formulations. [2] proposed to identify such cognitive constructs by applying differentiation mechanisms among concepts. He suggested applying 4 semantic differentiation principles to clarify the difference between each "cognitive constructs" and its "parent" constructs[1].

Our objective is to engineer an ontology that deals with "competence traces". The normalisation procedure has been divided into three phases. The first automatically identifies candidate terms for the ontology. A corpus was extracted from mechanical industrial company web sites, with the indexation tool SMART[2] for this application.

---

[1] The 4 principles induce to formalize what is different or common among one concept and its paternal / fraternal notions.

[2] ftp://ftp.cs.cornell.edu/pub/smart/

Using this first identification of terms, the second phase uses informal domain expertise, asking several experts to provide an initial version of the potential organisation of the domain concepts (conceptual classes and their relationships). Here the experts' thoughts have "converged" to two approaches. First, a top-down method offers a generic conceptualisation of the notion of "competence traces". We show in Figure 2 that the results are a so called "generic ontology". Second, a bottom up approach which entails a pragmatic notion of competence traces, closely linked to the activity filed analysed (mechanical industry). This 2nd approach results in a enumerated part of the final ontology called the "domain ontology".

Finally, the third normalisation phase reduces ambiguities among the concepts identified and improve the formalisation of relationships among terms and their definitions. The differentiation principles proposed by Bachimont were applied.

3.2.2 Formalisation

The formalisation structures the various levels of the ontology, notably by defining additional properties to the "cognitive constructs" identified previously. The three main types are differentiated: metaphysical, structuring, and parataxic concepts. These 3 types correspond also to distinct generality levels, from the conceptual level of the ontology, to the more pragmatic.

The first level of the "competence traces" ontology is composed of very generic so-called "metaphysical concepts". For this level, the generic competence model mentioned in section 2 must be created. Two generic classes are defined which correspond to the types of company capabilities of interest: the classes "technological competence traces" and "methodological competence traces".

The structuring level covers a set of interrelated concepts which should make possible to provide an enumerative and conceptual description of the knowledge domain. Note: here, the "competence traces ontology" CTO is what we called just before the "generic ontology". CTO structures general conceptual classes of "competence traces". These concepts have the advantage being independent of the specific activity field addressed: CTO can be re-used for various company activity domains. As illustrated in figure 2, CTO details the 2 classes identified at the metaphysical level. The classes "technological trace capabilities" (as well as methodological competence traces) are specialised by a set of more detailed classes of "competence traces".

The third, parataxic level of the ontology is constituted by what we called in 3.2.1 the "domain ontology". The "competence trace" concepts at that level are directly linked to the application field (mechanical industry sector). When applying our approach to another industrial sector, it is interesting to underline that the structuring level of the ontology remains stable and only the parataxic level has to be modified. Furthermore, the concept classes of this "domain ontology" are characterised by sets of class instances. These instances correspond to specific terms of the domains, used as "competence trace *identifiers*". As explained in section 4, they are directly used to extract the pertinent information which is composed of the company competence traces. Figure 3 partially illustrates this domain ontology.

Operationalisation will not be described in detail for this paper. This does implement a computer version of the ontology for the application of inference mechanisms. We have employed the competence trace ontology using *OWL (Ontologie Web Language)*.

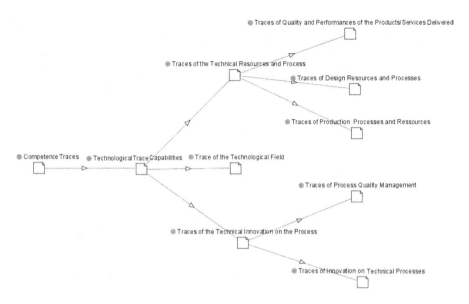

Fig. 2. "Structuring level" of the ontology for "Technological capabilities"

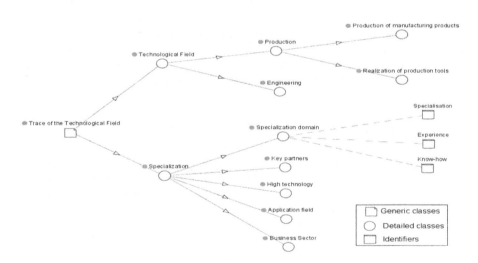

Fig. 3. "Parataxic level" of the ontology (mechanical industry)

4   Basic Principe of Utilization

As aforementioned, the class instances of the domain ontology are employed as information identifiers. Their role can detect the presence of a given competence trace concept in the web site of a company. A set of identifiers is associated with each conceptual class of the domain ontology to support this validation process. This is called the activation process of the ontology classes. Each company website generates a different activation of the overall ontology, which is interpreted as the competence trace of the company. To avoid ambiguities, the context of use of the identifiers on the web sites has to be considered in the activation process. The performance of the extraction system of competence traces rests on the activation quality of the ontology classes.

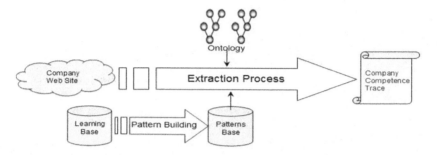

Fig. 4. Extraction process using Ontology and Patterns

To deal with this contextual analysis, a pattern-based approach is currently under development. The approaches by patterns are used in linguistics for associated structural regularities with semantic information [8][6]. Part of the web site corpus, has been used as a "learning base" to identify patterns. The objective is to identify structural regularities linked to the identifiers. Patterns consist in lexico-syntaxic expressions which formalise the context of use of these identifiers. In the extraction process of figure 4, patterns are typically used for two objectives:

- To avoid semantic ambiguity when detecting the so-called identifiers.
- To extract additional information on competences, not directly provided by identifiers.

In the learning step which consists in identifying and formalising patterns, a library with roughly 35 elaborated patterns supplemented with 100 unambiguous identifiers (without the necessity of patterns) has been constituted. A specific locating algorithm is under development, which uses these patterns to confirm the presence of identifiers.

Then, depending on the identifiers detected for a given web-site, an activation procedure will confirm or not the activation of each concept class of the competence trace ontology. This will provide the competence traces characterising a company. Afterwards, this information can be further interpreted in a decision aid procedure for establishing VBEs.

5 Discussion and Conclusion

The method followed to engineer a rigorous ontology on competence traces has been explained thoroughly. Future work will build upon this ontology and entail the development of a semantic activation process which requires formalising syntaxic patterns. This should be able to measure a similarity among competence traces extracted from various company web sites. This information should then be processed through a decision aid algorithm oriented on network building.

References

1. Berio, G., Harzallah, M.: Towards an Integrating Architecture for Competence Management, in Special Issue « Competence Management in Industrial Processes. In: Boucher, X., Bonjour, E., Matta, N. (guest eds.) Computers in Industry 58(2) (February 2007)
2. Bachimont, B., Isaac, A., Troncy, R.: Semantic commitment for designing ontologies: A proposal. In: Gómez-Pérez, A., Benjamins, V.R. (eds.) EKAW 2002. LNCS (LNAI), vol. 2473, pp. 114–121. Springer, Heidelberg (2002)
3. Camarinha-Matos, L.M., Afsarmanesh, H.: Elements of a base VE infrastructure. Computers in industry 51, 139–163 (2003)
4. Ermilova, E., Afsarmanesh, H.: Modeling and management of profiles and competences in VBEs. Journal of Intelligent Manufacturing 18, 561–586 (2007)
5. Frédéric, F.: PhD Thesis, Contribution à l'ingénierie des ontologies: une méthode et un outil d'opérationalisation. Université de Nantes, France (November 2004)
6. Finkelstein-Landau, M., Mori, E.: Extracting semantic relationships between terms: Supervised vs. unsupervised methods. In: Proc. of the Int. Workshop on OEGII, Dagstuhl Castle, Germany, pp. 71–80 (1999)
7. Grüninger, M., Fox, M.S.: The Role of Competence Questions in Enterprise Engineering. Paper presented at the IFIP WG 5.7 Workshop on Benchmarking. Theory and Practice, Trondheim, Norway (1994)
8. Hearst, M.A.: Automatic acquisition of hyponyms from large text corpora. In: Zampolli, A. (ed.) Computational Linguistics (CoLing 1992), Nantes, France, pp. 539–545 (1992)
9. Hajlaoui, k., Boucher, X., Mathieu, M.: Information Extraction procedure to support the constitution of Virtual Organisations. In: Research Challenges in Information Science, RCIS 2008, Marrakech (2008a)
10. Hajlaoui, K., Boucher, X., Mathieu, M.: Data Mining To Discover Enterprise Networks. In: 9th IFIP Working Conference on Virtual Entreprises (PRO-VE 2008) Poznan, Poland, September 8-10 (2008b)
11. Jirí, H., Vokrínek, J., Bíba, J., Becvár, P.: Competencies and profiles management for virtual organizations creation. In: Burkhard, H.-D., Lindemann, G., Verbrugge, R., Varga, L.Z. (eds.) CEEMAS 2007. LNCS (LNAI), vol. 4696, pp. 93–102. Springer, Heidelberg (2007)
12. Pepiot, G.: PhD Thesis, Modélisation des Entreprises sur la base des compétences, EPFL (2005)
13. Plisson, J., Ljubic, P., Mozetic, I., Lavrac, N.: An ontology for Virtual Organisation Breeding Environments. To appear in IEEE Trans. on Systems, Man, and Cybernetics (2007)
14. Yussopova, Y., Probst, A.R.: Business concepts ontology for an enterprise performance and competences management, in Special Issue « Competence Management in Industrial Processes ». Boucher, X., Bonjour, E., Matta, N. (guest eds.) Computers in Industry 58(2) (February 2007)
15. Wernerfelt, B.: A Resource-Based View of the Firm. Strategic Management Journal 5, 171–180 (1984)

Part **9**

Knowledge Management in Collaboration

Knowledge Management with Snapshots

Hilda Tellioğlu

Vienna University of Technology,
Institute of Design and Assessment of Technology,
Argentinierstrasse 8/187, 1040 Vienna, Austria
hilda.tellioglu@tuwien.ac.at

Abstract. This paper presents the concept of snapshots for knowledge management in distributed cooperative work environments. Snapshots are used to record important stages of collaborative project work, provide mechanisms for indexing, retrieval and visualization of relevant data for users in form of suggestions. They combine meta-level information with content and enable additional tagging and commenting. A prototype *SUGGEST!* has been developed to implement and evaluate the functionality and usability of such a knowledge management system.

Keywords: Knowledge management, information retrieval, snapshots.

1 Introduction

In a cooperative work environment, companies need to establish computer supported knowledge management. Project members have to find out easily who to contact, whom to ask certain questions and who to cooperate with in concrete projects. Experiences in previous projects need to be used to decide which company to collaborate with in future. Some of partner networks established are sustainable. Some are only temporal. In case of a real project setup, if one member of the network is not available, the most of the plans need to be modified. Sometimes a new partner must be found very fast.

Not only at the beginning of a project in globally networked settings, but also during ongoing projects, it is usually very difficult to capture, retrieve and manage information about people's knowhow, skills, availability and experiences. In most cases, the worth full information about past projects is not really existing or available. Several questions need to be answered: What did happen in a certain past project with a similar context? Who was involved in which part of a project? Who (internal or external) could cooperate without any problem? And so forth. Knowhow and experiences of past could help to avoid repeating mistakes done so far. Unfortunately there are still problems to support people in companies in organizing themselves and in creating their network due a specific project setting.

Although this problem is very well defined, there are no real solutions to it. Some attention has been given to technology development. Research in the area of semantic web has been done, e.g., about large-scale information extraction [1] [6] of entities and relationships from semi structured and natural-language Web sources [10] or about extracting valuable data from hidden Web sources by using a combination heuristics and probing with domain instances as well as by using supervised machine learning technique [7]. The main idea was to use Web as a comprehensive knowledge

L.M. Camarinha-Matos et al. (Eds.): PRO-VE 2009, IFIP AICT 307, pp. 293–300, 2009.
© IFIP International Federation for Information Processing 2009

base. Others used ontologies to manage multimedia knowledge [5]. Takahashi et al. [9] tried to support designers by providing a web-based knowledge database that selected the information mainly from news sites and reduced the useless information for design by applying a filter.

We found other research work focusing on concepts and theories. Speer et al. tried to acquire common sense knowledge by using a game based interface [8]. Chung and Hossain [2] developed a theoretical model based on social network theories and the social influence model to understand how knowledge professionals utilize technology for work and communication. They investigated task-level and communication-level ICT use.

Finally there is research on combining conceptual and functional level. Georgalas [3] advocated that knowledge repositories support strong mechanisms for the management of meta-level information and system specifications. They tried to integrate meta-level knowledge of systems and data at a conceptual level, before they integrate knowledge and software components at a functional level, analyzed in an environment called DELOS [4].

All these approaches are not really addressing the problem of knowledge management in organizations. It is still not possible to establish an easy-to-setup and easy-to-use system in organizations to capture, store, index, retrieve and visualize relevant project and product information in a lightweight. Only relevant data about and in projects need to be recorded and linked to each other. Additionally links can be tagged to provide another level of information about relations between people or artifacts or objects in the network of information captured.

In this paper the theory if knowledge management by means of snapshots is introduced to meet the requirements mentioned above. A snapshot freezes a moment in time, photographic or electronic. If a computer creates snapshots, you can time travel in your computer system. You can jump to a former state of the system. So, a snapshot can help capture properties and relations between components of a system. A snapshot can be used to establish knowledge management in an enterprise. We can record important stages of cooperative project work, provide mechanisms for indexing and tagging, in order to be able to retrieve them in the future. With a configurable visualization system users can make sense and use of this information.

This paper tries to design such a system, first theoretically and then prototypically. In an example, based on ethnographic research in automotive industries, it illustrates how to proceed in dealing with snapshots in a coordinative work environment. Requirements to a supporting system are described in a prototype by showing which information is needed to support creation, access and maintenance of a knowledge base for a work group.

In the next section we will describe the use case setting in which we gathered the requirements and data that we used in our prototype. In the section 3 we introduce the concept of snapshots for knowledge management, which follows the description of the prototype in section 4, before we conclude the paper.

2   Our Case

We carried out ethnographic studies in a European STREP project called MAPPER (Model-based Adaptive Product and Process Engineering) (IST-016527)[1] at three

---

[1] http://mapper.eu.org/

different industrial sites. One of them is KeyA that we refer in this paper to. KeyA is a company that produces car parts like gearshifts, head strains, and seat heating for automotive industry. It has several branches all over the world. The projects are multinational, involving different people from different branches depending, on the one hand, on people's skills and knowledge, and on the other hand, on the production facilities at the site. The geographically distributed way of project organization makes computer-supported communication and collaboration necessary. Meetings are arranged regularly to overcome the distance between distributed project members. Common information spaces have been established to enable central management of project documents. We could observe several meetings and carry out in-depth interviews with some of the key actors during four visits between 2005 and 2008.

Project members of all sites were used to participate regular and ad-hoc *meetings*. By means of teleconferencing facilities and sometimes screen sharing, single open issues were discussed by asking responsible persons the status of the work progress. In some meetings, suppliers or customers were present. The main artifacts used in all kinds of meetings were *to-do lists* that actually belonged only the project managers, who were the moderators of the meetings. Sometimes, *emails* were mentioned or quoted when there were misunderstandings, gaps of communication, uncertainty about the status of some issues. Emails provided different communication paths within and across distributed groups. They were used as information holders with attached documents like text files, presentation slides or spreadsheets related to the current project. They were also applied just for arranging, clarifying or negotiating open issues. Project members were actively using their emails, e.g., to search for information in their attachments, where the information in the email's body was used to identify the right document. Mailboxes were used to manage emails. No one would like to delete an email exchanged in a current project. Emails helped keeping track of data and document transfer between cooperating people. Documents created at KeyA were mainly *text files, spreadsheets* or *presentation slides*. Besides to-do lists, MS Power Point slides were the main project management instrument. For certain purposes project members were using other artifacts as well, like a groupware system to manage the emails and files on a common information space, a PLM system for managing product lifecycle, chat logs, product catalogues, product descriptions, test reports, etc. No configuration management environment has been established.

In our ethnographic study at KeyA[2] we could identify the need for organizational knowledge recovery what we illustrate here with two cases. Several questions about projects, persons and artifacts came up and could not be answered in a timely manner. In several meetings, there were questions about who to contact to carry out a certain activity or to prepare information to decide a certain step in the project, what the problem in a previous similar project was, who was involved in certain projects and problem cases, etc. In one case, it was not clear what really happened a couple of years ago in an ongoing project (P). They missed to send a document to the customer (C) and the same customer was now asking for it. Unfortunately, the project team has been changed, persons involved at that time were not present any more, no one had a clue who to ask or where to find the document the customer was waiting for. There were several meetings to plan a strategic solution to this problem and try to reduce the financial damage for the company. The second case is about missing information on

---

[2] The studies were carried out by Gianni Jacucci, Hilda Tellioğlu and Ina Wagner.

part id's needed in IMDS system in use within the automotive industry in compliance with a EU directive, which requires companies to provide a detailed specification of the materials used in their parts. The following excerpt describes some of the difficulties involved in information retrieval with and around IMDS:

A[3] checks her email – the first is a request from their office in Detroit concerning IMDS calculations – a colleague needs details for different heating wires. The email is about not finding the weight for all the wires and has an MS Excel sheet attached. A has a file on her drive – she talks about having to copy the files all the time and sending them back and forth, she opens a table, noting down numbers on a post-it. On her list there are two heating wires but colleague D looks for more – A sends him the ID for one of the wires and then tries to call the responsible for heating wires to ask her. A continues searching in another list and still cannot find the item. In the meantime A picks up another email, which is also about IMDS. A explains: "No one is able to give us the right ID for some parts – the problem is that we deliver one part directly to the car producer and one to the seat producer and each has their own part ID – each supplier to LL has different numbers and at LL they don't know which code we have". A then prints out the list sent by colleague D and goes to discuss it with the colleague next to her office. She returns with two new numbers to search for which she jotted down in pencil – these numbers also don't fit. A explains: "This is our own list, the one the girl made for us, and it is already a little bit old". A looks at the data sheet – there are two part numbers, one for the front seat (21153) and one for the rear seat (211618), "when they buy it – when we sell it, we have to use the customer IDs for these parts". A calls L who asked for this change, tries another ID – maybe the customer AA has forgotten to approve these numbers – she calls L again who promises to contact AA about this – A makes a note on the print-out of the email message so as to remember.

Here we can identify several problems: Suppliers, in particular small ones, have problems in providing detailed information about their parts, often it is not clear whom to contact on the supplier site. That is why A has problems to retrieve this information. Different stakeholders use different part numbering systems and the mapping problems between these have not been resolved. These makes the retrieval of information about part id's almost impossible. There is no process support provided by KeyA's IT infrastructure for A: A switches between her email, different lists, including print-outs of lists, her post-its, phone conversations, printing out lists, carrying them to another office to discuss the problem, and so forth.

These two cases illustrate the problem of knowledge management at KeyA. Our approach tries to avoid such situations. In the next section, we introduce the concept of snapshots to show how to approach to this problem of knowledge management in distributed work environments.

3   The Theory of Knowledge Management with Snapshots

The concept of a snapshot is based on the network of projects, persons and artifacts. Persons work in projects and cooperate with other persons inside or outside the

---

[3] "A" is a material specialist at KeyA. The product, company and person names are blanked.

company. Persons create artifacts, exchange them with others they cooperate, modify or remove them. During a project, artifacts evolve. They host content, changes made, debates carried out, questions asked, answers given, etc. Looking into artifacts give us insight into processes connected to *content*. Additionally, we need the *meta-level information* like who accessed which artifact when, what was the modification, was there additional communication about these changes, who did work with whom in which project when, etc. Meta-level information is the information about people and their actions by using several artifacts and by cooperating internally in their company or with external partners. It helps construct relations between projects, persons and artifacts. It builds up a network that can be captured as a snapshot. If we apply this model in an enterprise cooperating with other enterprises worldwide, the picture becomes very complicated (Fig. 1). Persons from different enterprises share some artifacts. Some persons have direct exchange, some communicate with others implicitly by means of an artifact, some artifacts are exchanged automatically when workflows have been established.

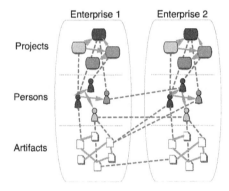

Fig. 1. Model of a snapshot consisting of a network of projects, persons and artifacts including content- and meta-level information in case of a cooperation between enterprises

On the one hand, one can see the importance of artifacts in this model. On the other hand, the meta-level information needs to be captured and related to content-level information stored as artifacts. In our case study, artifacts we studied were mostly not related to each other electronically. Only persons using them knew more or less where to find which information about a certain project. If persons left the company, there was no possibility to recall past events and decisions at all. This can be solved by introducing the prototype *SUGGEST!* that we describe in the next section.

4 The Prototype: *SUGGEST!*

Based on the study at KeyA, we created an example network with real data that we used in our prototype called *SUGGEST!* The prototype is used to create, access and visualize snapshots in form of useful suggestions for users. With this prototype we try to show the principle underlying this approach. The prototype gives us the possibility to examine the model of snapshots. Unfortunately, we could not really introduce *SUGGEST!* in KeyA and see its impact on work practices around knowledge management (as described in section 2), because the project has already been finished at the time of its availability. Still, *SUGGEST!* is the first prototype illustrating the application of a new concept, namely snapshots, in knowledge management.

SUGGEST! uses a data structure to store meta-level information and content (Fig. 2). Based on the entities of projects, people and artifacts, the data structure tries to link all entities to each other. The meta-level information excerpted from emails (Name=Subject, Content=Message Body, FromPerson, ToPerson), to-do lists (Name=Issue Name, Content=Issue Description, Deadline, Status, Responsible Person), documents' meta-information (Name=File Name, Content=Full text, Location, Type, Size) and of course also the explicit tagging and commenting are needed to create the context of data, to access the links between people, projects and artifacts in time.

Fig. 2. Data model used in *SUGGEST!* Associations are meant to be many to many

How are snapshots created? To feed the knowledge base with relevant content- and meta-level information, interfaces are needed. The meta-level information of emails containing the subject, from and to fields, the message body and the information about the attachments must be accessed by *SUGGEST!* to keep track of data exchange between project members and to identify email threads that enable to follow negotiations, problems or dense cooperation between people. To-do lists contain meta-level information as single issues, which needs to be accessed by *SUGGEST!* as well. The meta-level information of documents of any format is additionally needed to complete the picture.

A file or configuration management system delivers the name of the file, its location, the name of the creator or modifier of the file and the date of modification.

It is obvious that interfaces must be able to gather all relevant information at the background without disturbing people in their daily work. Within an enterprise, the necessary access to mail server, file and configuration management server must be provided. It must be clear that the data collected this way will not be made accessible directly. It will just be used to create snapshots, saved in the *SUGGEST!*'s relational database, and to create suggestions. This is an important privacy issue. In case of collaborations with externals like suppliers, an explicit agreement must be set up to avoid confidentiality problems and legal issues.

How is this knowledge base used? *SUGGEST!* must enable data capturing, storing, indexing, useful retrieving and visualizing of meta-level information connected with relevant content-level information. Considering the usability criteria and building up on people's habits the following simple interface has been designed (Fig. 3). If someone wants to consume data managed in *SUGGEST!*, he or she needs to formulate the query in a natural language like in our case "who has experience with seat heating?". Depending on the meta-level information saved in the system, *SUGGEST!* responds with a list of search results (of person, project and artifact data) providing a context for the suggestion. If these first suggestions are not efficient or useful enough, more suggestions can be required. In our cases, for the first request a query like "which documents were emailed to customer C in project P?" would deliver artifact information, and for the second case a query like "who knows the part id of heating wires?" person and product information, and a query like "are there emails exchanged about part id's of heating wires?" artifact information as suggestions.

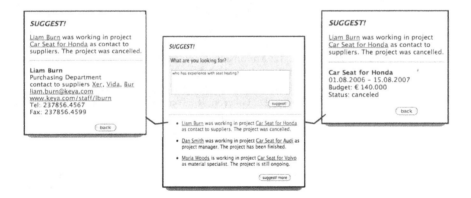

Fig. 3. An example query that delivers person and project data by *SUGGEST!Client*: The user request and the first list of suggestions matching the search criteria (middle), detailed information about person (left) and about project (right). User and project names have been changed. With "suggest! more" additional suggestions can be required.

5 Conclusions

This paper presents a new theory to knowledge management in organizations. It is based on the concept of snapshots that continuously capture properties of and relations between projects, people and artifacts in a cooperative distributed work environment. Based on an ethnographic case study, requirements to such systems are gathered and analyzed. A prototype called *SUGGEST!* has been developed to implement the idea of snapshots and to evaluate the functionality and usability of this knowledge base. *SUGGEST!* does not just collect all data available in an organization, it captures people's actions and exchange with others in concrete project teams. It is work in progress and needs to be developed further. It needs to be evaluated in a real work setting, as a running system and not as a prototype. More interfaces to legacy systems must be developed to build a wide range of possibilities for data capturing. In case of geographically distributed work, especially when externals like suppliers or third party companies are involved in projects, performance, integration, confidentiality and intellectual property issues must be addressed and solved. Still, we believe that snapshots are the correct approach for implementing a knowledge base for an organizational setting. We will continue on the development of *SUGGEST!* for further use and evaluation.

References

1. Agichtein, E.: Scaling information extraction to large document collections. IEEE Data Eng. Bull. 28(4) (2005)
2. Chung, K.S.K., Hossain, L.: Network structure, position, ties and ICT use in distributed knowledge-intensive work. In: Proceedings of the ACM 2008 Conference on Computer Supported Cooperative Work, pp. 545–554 (2008)
3. Georgalas, N.: A framework that uses repositories for information systems and knowledge integration. In: Proceedings of the 1999 IEEE Symposium on Application-Specific Systems and Software Engineering and Technology, ASSET, pp. 128–135 (1999)
4. Klimathianakis, P., Loucopoulos, P.: DELOS - A repository based environment for developing network centric applications. In: Olivé, À., Pastor, J.A. (eds.) CAiSE 1997. LNCS, vol. 1250. Springer, Heidelberg (1997)
5. Penta, A., Picariello, A., Tanca, L.: Multimedia knowledge management using ontologies. In: Proceeding of the 2nd ACM Workshop on Multimedia Semantics, pp. 24–31 (2008)
6. Sarawagi, S.: Information extraction. Foundations and Trends in Databases 2(1) (2008)
7. Senellart, P., Mittal, A., Muschick, D., Gilleron, R., Tommasi, M.: Automatic wrapper induction from hidden-web sources with domain knowledge. In: Proceeding of the 10th ACM Workshop on Web Information and Data Management, pp. 9–16 (2008)
8. Speer, R., Krishnamurthy, J., Havasi, C., Smith, D., Lieberman, H., Arnold, K.: An interface for targeted collection of common sense knowledge using a mixture model. In: Proceedings of the 13th International Conference on Intelligent User Interfaces, pp. 137–146 (2009)
9. Takahashi, K., Sugiyama, A., Shimomura, Y., Tateyama, T., Chiba, R., Yoshioka, M., Takeda, H.: Web-based knowledge database construction method for supporting design. In: Proceedings of the 10th International Conference on Information Integration and Web-based Applications & Services, pp. 575–578 (2008)
10. Weikum, G.: Harvesting, searching, and ranking knowledge on the web: Invited talk. In: Proceedings of the Second ACM International Conference on Web Search and Data Mining, pp. 3–4 (2009)

Short-Term Semantic Consensus: Towards Agile Ontology Specification for Collaborative Networks

Carla Pereira[1,2], Cristóvão Sousa[1,2], and António Lucas Soares[1,3]

[1] Instituto de Engenharia de Sistemas e Computadores do Porto
[2] Escola Superior de Tecnologia e Gestão de Felgueiras (IPP)
[3] Faculdade de Engenharia da Universidade do Porto
csp@inescporto.pt, cpsousa@inescporto.pt, als@fe.up.pt

Abstract. This paper presents our method to support the collaborative conceptualisation process focusing our strategy for building consensus in the context of collaborative networks. This new strategy comes from the application of the results and recommendations obtained in an experimental evaluation performed in the scope of a large European project in the area of industrial engineering. The usage of our strategy and the collaborative platform supporting semantic consensus building in the scope of the European research project H-Know is described.

Keywords: Conceptualization, social construction of meaning, ontology development, collaborative networks, conceptual blending, consensus building.

1 Introduction

Although there is an increasing number of semantic tools and resources available for the companies to use in everyday business activities, problems in establishing a common conceptualisation of a given reality arise in two flavours: (i) notwithstanding the evolution of semantic technologies, it is virtually impossible to establish a priori comprehensive and complete semantic artefacts that account for all the possible variations in business situations and contexts (which are more and more dynamic); (ii) in spite of all the standardization efforts, there is a kind of "social resistance" in accepting semantically oriented standards (viewed as "grand narratives" of a domain). A good example of this is the construction industry, where an enormous effort and money has been spent in standard terminologies, vocabularies, thesaurus, ontologies, etc. with results well behind the expected (Silva et al., 2006).

Cahier et al., 2005 argue about the role of a "socio-semantic web": "we need to go beyond the approaches that provide a high level of 'automation of the meaning'; instead, we need to address situations where human beings are highly required to stay in the process, interacting during the whole life-cycle of applications, for cognitive and cooperative reasons".

Even though the most used definition of ontology (Gruber, 1993) "An ontology is a formal, explicit specification of a shared conceptualisation", underlines the collaborative construction of conceptualisations in the scientific context, we agree that: "While different degrees of formalizations have been well investigated and are now found in various ontology-based technologies, the notion of a shared conceptualisation is neither

L.M. Camarinha-Matos et al. (Eds.): PRO-VE 2009, IFIP AICT 307, pp. 301–310, 2009.
© IFIP International Federation for Information Processing 2009

well-explored, nor well-understood, nor well-supported by most ontology engineering tools" (Staab, 2008). Current knowledge about the early phases of ontology construction is insufficient to support methods and techniques for a collaborative construction of a conceptualisation (Pereira and Soares, 2008). The conceptualisation phase is of utmost importance for the success of the ontology. But it is in this phase that a social presence is needed as it requires an actor to reliably predict how other members of the community will interpret the conceptual representation based on its limited description. By incorporating the notion of semantics into the information architecture, we thus transform the users of the system themselves into a critical part of the design. Our view is that ontology engineering needs a "socio-cognitive turn" in order to generate tools that are really effective in copying the complex, unstructured, and highly situational contexts that characterize a great deal of information and knowledge sharing in businesses collaboration. This line of research is therefore directed towards the application of cognitive semantic results in the creation of artefacts acting as socio-technical devices supporting the view that meaning socially constructed through collaboration and negotiation. The first line of this research work deals with the application and extension of the Conceptual Blending Theory (CBT) (Fauconnier and Turner, 1998) to the realm of collaborative semantic tools. The practical application of our approach is to support the co-construction of semantic artefacts by groups of social actors placed in organizational contexts interacting towards a set of common objectives. Simple examples of these artefacts are the creation of a common taxonomy (or ontology) for classifying and retrieving content from an inter-organizational portal, the creation of specific terminological accounts to serve as conceptual references in project tasks, or the specification of ontologies for systems interoperability.

In this paper some increments in our method to support the collaborative conceptualisation process are presented. These increments are consequence of the application of the results and recommendations obtained in an experimental evaluation already executed in the scope of a large European project in the area of industrial engineering (described in (Pereira et al., 2009)). The main contribution reported in this paper is the new approach to consensus building during a collaborative conceptualization process within the context of collaborative networks. The usage of this method in the scope of the European research project H-Know[1] is also explained.

2   A Method to Support the Conceptualisation Process

Our proposal to support a collaborative process of conceptualisation is grounded on cognitive semantics, specifically on the Conceptual Blending Theory (CBT) (Fauconnier and Turner, 1998). CBT representation gives rise to complex networks by linking two (or more) input spaces by means of a generic space. The generic space provides information that is abstract enough to be common to all the input spaces. Elements in the generic space are mapped onto counterparts in each of the input spaces, which motivate the identification of cross-space counterparts in the input spaces. A further

---

[1] H-KNOW is an European research project in the area of building rehabilitation, restoration and maintenance, particularly in the cultural heritage domain. The project objective is to develop an ICT solution, to support SME's collaborative networks in integrating collaboration, knowledge and learning in the RR&M field (http://h-know.eu).

space in this model of integration network is the blended space or blend. This is the space that contains a new or emergent structure: information that is not contained in both the inputs. The blend takes elements from both inputs, but goes further on providing additional structure that distinguishes the blend from either of its inputs. In CBT, there are three component processes that produce an emergent structure (Fauconnier and Turner, 1998): (1) composition; (2) completion; and (3) elaboration. Due to the lack of space and scope of this document, we advise interested readers to obtain more information about CBT in the following sources (Fauconnier and Turner, 1998) (Evans and Green, 2006) and (Pereira and Soares, 2008), whereas now we'll continue giving a brief description of our method.

The following is assumed as the initial state: (1) a collaborative network has been formed and its goals and mission are defined and understood by all members (that we call "strategic frame"); (2) a common ontology with certain goals and to be used in a given time-frame has to be developed; (3) each organization has a representative in a "network team" in charge of developing the ontology; the common conceptualisation regarding given domains, processes and tasks, is the first important collective task to undertake by this team; (4) a common conceptualisation is to be collaboratively created through explanation, discussion and negotiation. The proposed method establishes the following steps (see figure 1): (1) each organization has assigned one or more input spaces (only one input space per organization is considered here, for simplicity); (2) each organization represents its conceptualisation proposal through the input space; simultaneously, the organization shares the information and other knowledge sources (e.g., URLs, documents and other contents) which allow the correct understanding of the conceptualisation proposal; no specific knowledge representation technique is proposed, but it is important that it has a graphical nature (in the case study we are using concept maps (Canas et al., 2004) (Eskridge et al., 2006)); (3) by some manual or automated (or something in between) process, a generic conceptualisation is generated (generic space); the common conceptual structure in the generic space should be broad enough to be accepted by all the team members with minimum negotiation; (4) considering the "counterpart" elements (concepts of the input spaces subsumed by concepts of the generic space), the process of creating the blend space is started using selective projection; based on the input spaces, strategic frame, generic space and documentation available in the input spaces (called background information), the blend is "run" to obtain new conceptualisation proposals; (5) new conceptual structures proposed in the blend space are object of negotiation; the concepts for which consensus exists are represented in ("copied" to) the generic space; situations that justify "backward projection" to the input spaces and their modification are analyzed (this analysis will be performed by the users, after obtaining consensus) then the emergent blend structure is validated (confirm or eliminate new concepts that raise in the blend); (6) if input spaces modification takes place, the method should resume at step 4; however the creation of a new blend space, is not necessary; (7) when all participants manifest their agreement with the conceptualisation represented in the generic space, the method instance is finished.

Summarizing, at the end of the process the generic space contains the collective conceptualization. The blend was used during the negotiation process with the goal to improve, enrich and mainly help obtaining consensus (proposing new concepts, modifying, improving or eliminating concepts).

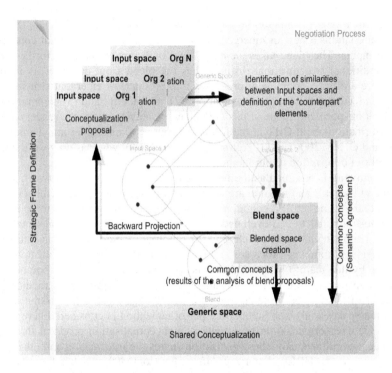

Fig. 1. Method to support collaborative conceptualization process

This method may also be used by each organization to support the creation of its own input space, which can result in the presence of multiple "blendings". It is important to reinforce that in this collaborative process, the validation/agreement achievement requires that each organization indexes to its input space, the sources of information which lead to the input spaces creation and justify the proposal content and structure. Whenever an organization introduces a new concept or association in their input space, it becomes a target for negotiation. At this moment the negotiation process is started. The network team evaluates the new entrance running the steps (3), (4), and (5). To ensure a successful negotiation process, which lead to a shared conceptualisation (accepted by all partners), is also very important to define an approach for obtaining consensus. In the next section we present a strategy for building consensus in the context of collaborative networks. There are some good practices that should be applied, but that need to be adjusted for each case.

3   Reaching Agreement during the Conceptualisation Process

We present below a strategy for building consensus in the context of collaborative networks, aligned with the fact that the process of building consensus is regarded collaborative right from the design, once the process design itself should involve all participants (Suskind, 1999). Before developing a specific consensus strategy, the following aspects should be considered: (1) the context in which the process will occur, that means that the main intervenient should be aware about the scope of the domain, otherwise some background information should be read; (2) to design the process, it is important to understand the organizational culture of each group of stakeholders. Organizational culture also influences the degree of formality required; (3) when several organizations are involved and their organizational cultures differ, it is important to recognize the specific needs of each group to avoid misunderstandings; (4) the language is also a factor to be considered when different cultural groups are represented; and (5) social and cultural factors. Participants must choose one approach or a combination of the following approaches (see (Susskind et al., 1999)): (i) conventional problem-solving approach; (ii) working with a single-text document; and (iii) taking a visioning approach. Figure 2 shows the phases for the process of building consensus in the context of collaborative networks. Our approach to reach a semantic agreement for the collective conceptualization is thus based on consensus building techniques and involves, besides the negotiation itself, a preparation and an evaluation phases (see figure 2 for the detailed steps).

For the preparation phases, the creation of the team and the governance model of the collaboration are the main tasks. Of particular importance are the selection of the type of participation, the mediation approach, the establishment of rules and responsibilities and the plan elaboration. As for the evaluation phase the most important aspect is to systematise and register the lessons learnt during the process.

In the consensus building phase, must be used a combination of the following two approaches to drive the process, "working with a single-text document" and "taking a visioning approach". The single-text approach involves introducing a working draft of an agreement early in the process for parties to discuss and revise. This approach provides a clear structure for discussions and a focal point to identify areas of agreement and disagreement. A subgroup of participants works to draft a preliminary proposal. This preliminary proposal is considered the best way to focus a consensus building dialogue. This proposal will be presented using concept maps building with CMapTools (http://cmap.ihmc.us/conceptmap.html) (this preliminary proposal is presented in the generic space, see figure 1).

Fig. 2. Consensus building approach

Brainstorming will be used to expand and improve the preliminary proposal and others proposals that arise during consensus building dialogue (presented in the input spaces of each organisation) as well as to encourage creative thinking. The exploration of several proposals should be accomplished using questions of the type "what if" and performing the steps 3, 4 and 5 of the method to support the collaborative conceptualisation process. The "taking a visioning approach" intend to focus participants' attention toward the future in the course of identifying options and seeking agreements. Conduct the process according to the following questions: What do you have?, What do we want? And "How do we get there? These questions allow the semantic team evaluates the strengths and weaknesses of the current conceptualisation proposal and to maintain the process more creative. To support the dissemination of information, a content management system should be used, that allows to notify the participants in the process, to distribute materials to participants during the process, allow the information sharing, keep all stakeholders updated about the group progress and keep a record of all items discussed. A set of documents such as: meeting minutes, agendas, schedules, working documents and background resources, are taken as important to share. If necessary, at this stage, the agenda and procedural rules can be modified.

4   A Collaborative Platform to Support Semantic Consensus Building

A part of our research work is dedicated to design of ITC tools supporting collaborative processes for the development of semantic artefacts according to a socio-semantic stance. For supporting the proposed CBT based methodology, two modules are considered: one supporting the semi-automated construction of the conceptual integration spaces (semBlend) and the other supporting negotiation and consensus reaching (semCons). Our strategy is to develop the semantic artefacts on top of existing collaboration and information management platforms, specifically content management systems (CMS) and wiki systems. In the case of the semCons module, the same platform that was implementing the H-Know project portal was used to implement the module: the Plone CMS. The development involved developing an information structure based on a message board and a workflow implementing the consensus reaching procedure (see figures 3 and 4).

Some remarks about this process follow:

Semantic team creation: (i) There are two different roles that the participants can assume (see figure 3): partner (any member of the project may take this role) and reviewer (each partner organization define a representative who will assume the role of reviewer; (ii) the representatives are part of the group responsible for making decisions; (iii) when the specificity of the conceptualisation increases the need to create different work groups will be evaluated again; (iv) a set of background information as a base to develop skills and the necessary knowledge required to the team was made available in the project portal.

Planning, responsibilities and roles: (i) The mediator is responsible for ensuring the proper participation of all and managing the conceptualisation; (ii) those who assumed the partner role, are expected to submit proposals and consult, periodically, the state of the process; for the participants engaged as reviewer, it is expected to review, periodically, the proposals submitted by partners and approve, reject or suggest changes. If the proposal is rejected or any change is proposed, the decision must be justified. Only the participants that propose the concept and the reviewers are able to see the candidate concepts. All participants can see the approved concepts. The "reviewers" are electronically notified when a new concept is proposed. A concept is declared as approved whenever at least 80% of the reviewers vote in favour. However, the ideal is that the concept is approved by unanimity. The reviewers can also propose some changes or clarifications of the concept meaning; in this case the concept is retracted. If a concept is rejected, it can be proposed for change or be rejected definitely. A partner can also dispose a concept. If the reviewers think that a concept is not useful or is no longer part of the common project language, its state would be archived. The replaced state means that the concept was being phased out and was being replaced by a newer concept. The new concept means the same thing as the original but is considered as more appropriated; (iv) the plan should not be too detailed but enough to stress the most important points, dates, etc.

Consensus building: The consensus workflow "execution"; a variety of techniques can be used although in this project we were limited (by the time available) to use the online message board as the main tool.

Evaluation and lessons learnt: Before closing the process, the final version of the conceptualization should circulate for all participants. At this moment should be organized a workshop to divulge the final result to all partners. The evaluation of strengths and weaknesses of the process will be performed based on experience obtained through our participation in the process and carrying out an online questionnaire to all participants.

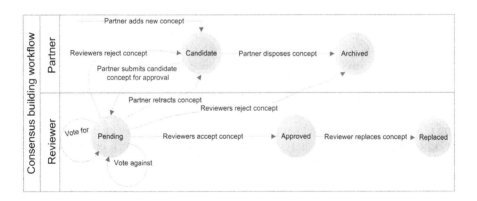

Fig. 3. Consensus building workflow

Fig. 4. Example of a concept page in Plone

5   Conclusions and Further Work

The approach described in this paper proposes a shift in the process of creation of semantic artefacts from a "semantic artefact engineering" perspective to a "actor-artefact co-evolution" one. Socio-semantics is the scientific umbrella to this approach, which is also inspired in cognitive semantics and social networking theories. A set of detailed case studies is under way, whereas action research was adopted as the privileged way to generate knowledge in socio-technical settings. In our process, is already possible to visualize the concept maps inside Plone canvas, which provides an excellent overview about the state of the conceptualisation process. Despite of being a static feature, a graphical representation is a great input for decision support on concepts. Yet, much more benefits can be withdrawn from the CmapTools versatility in knowledge representation of a shared conceptualisation. Concept mapping is a suitable mechanism to emerge that mental framework, which can be used to set up a content management system in a collaborative network environment. On pursuit of this believe, our research and work is targeted to join this two worlds (Concept Mapping and Collaborative Content Management Platforms), in a dynamic, flexible and collaborative environment, according to the architecture depicted in Figure 5.

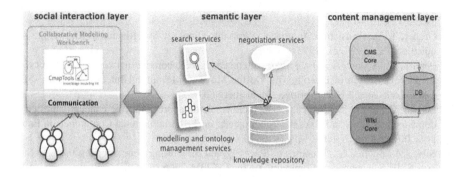

Fig. 5. Dynamic Collaborative Environment Architecture

Regarding the tools development part of our research, Service-Oriented Knowledge Management System is the objective of our future work. According to the Figure 5, the central mechanism of the architecture is the knowledge repository which provides an online location where the semantic team could locate, ideas, documents, tips, etc., from other members. This autonomous data access would make use of common terms representing organizational data. Semantic layer would be powered by a seta set of available services provided by semBlend and semCons modules on supporting to the CBT based methodology. The semantic layer is surrounded by other two layers, the Content management Layer and the Social Interaction Layer. The first, would give support, at the structuring information level, to the artefacts developed on the semantic level. At the Social Interaction Layer, we would have a collaborative workbench, making use of CmapTools, allowing the team to interpret a domain, create models about it and attach meaning via specification of semantic conceptual structures.

References

1. Cahier, J.-P., Zaher, L., Leboeuf, J.-P., Guittard, C.: Experimentation of a socially constructed "Topic Map" by the OSS community. In: Proceedings of the IJCAI 2005 workshop on KMOM, Edimbourg (2005)
2. Camarinha-Matos, L.: Collaborative networks in industry – Trends and foundations. In: Proc. of 3rd International CIRP Conference in Digital Enterprise Technology. Springer, Heidelberg (2006)
3. Canas, A., Hill, G., Carff, R., Suri, N., Lott, J., Eskridge, T.: T. Cmaptools: A knowledge modeling and sharing environment. Concept Maps: Theory, Methodology, Technology. In: Cañas, A.J., Novak, J.D. (eds.) Proc. of the first Int. Conference on Concept Mapping, Pamplona, Spain, vol. I, pp. 125–133 (2004)
4. Eskridge, T., Hayes, P., Hoffman, R., Warren, M.: Formalizing the informal: a confluence of concept mapping and the semantic web. In: Cañas, A.J., Novak, J.D. (eds.) Proc. of the Second Int. Conference on Concept Mapping, Costa Rica (2006)
5. Evans, V., Green, M.: Cognitive Linguistics: an introduction. Edinburgh University Press (2006)

6. Fauconnier, G., Turner, M.: Conceptual Integration Networks. Published in Cognitive Science 22(2), 133–187 (1998)
7. Gruber, T.: A Translation Approach to Portable Ontology Specifications. Knowledge Acquisition 5(2), 199–221 (1993)
8. Pereira, C., Soares, A.: Ontology development in collaborative networks as a process of social construction of meaning. In: On the Move to Meaningful Internet Systems: OTM 2008 Workshops. LNCS. Springer, Heidelberg (2008)
9. Pereira, C., Sousa, C., Soares, A.: A socio-semantic approach to the conceptualisation of domains, processes and tasks in large projects. In: 11th International Conference on Enterprise Information Systems, May 6-10 (2009)
10. Silva, M., Soares, A., Simões, D.: Selecting and Structuring Semantic Resources to Support SME'S Knowledge Communities. In: INCOM 2006, 12th IFAC Symposium on Information Control Problems in Manufacturing, St. Etienne, France (2006)
11. Staab, S.: On understanding the collaborative construction of conceptualisations. International and Interdisciplinary Conference Processing Text-Technological Resources at the Center for Interdisciplinary Research (ZiF - Zentrum für interdisziplinäre Forschung), March 13-15, Bielefeld University) (2008)
12. Susskind, L., Mckearnan, S., Thomas-Larmer, J.: The Consensus Building Handbook: A comprehensive Guide to Reaching Agreement. The Consensus Building Institute. Sage Publications, Thousand Oaks (1999)

Ontological View-Driven Semantic Integration in Collaborative Networks

Yunjiao Xue[1], Hamada H. Ghenniwa[1], and Weiming Shen[1,2]

[1] Department of Electrical and Computer Engineering,
The University of Western Ontario, London, Ontario, Canada
[2] Centre for Computer-assisted Construction Technologies,
National Research Council, London, Ontario, Canada
yxue24@uwo.ca, hghenniwa@eng.uwo.ca, weiming.shen@nrc.gc.ca

Abstract. In collaborative enterprise networks, semantic heterogeneity is an important factor that hinders collaboration of various information systems. Ontology-driven semantic integration is an important category of solutions for the semantic integration problem. However, in many domains, there are no explicit and formal ontologies available. This paper proposes to adopt ontological views to address such challenges. It investigates the theoretical foundation of ontologies and ontological views. It presents a framework as a solution, based on the theoretical foundation, including the architecture of a semantic integration enabled environment, the modeling and representation of ontological views, and the semantic equivalence relationship discovered from the ontological views.

Keywords: Semantic Integration, Ontology, Ontological View, Collaborative Network, Semantic Equivalence Relationship.

1 Introduction

In a collaborative enterprise network, various information systems must collaborate to support information exchange and information processing and to meet other requirements. Due to the nature of being independently designed and built, the information systems, even for the same domain, are often heterogeneous in terms of (1) their supporting infrastructures (hardware, operating systems, communication facilities, etc); (2) syntactic representations of information; (3) schematic designs of information models, and (4) semantics of information, which will significantly hinder the collaboration between these systems. There have already been plenty of solutions for the first three areas of concern [9]. The final one, also known as the *semantic integration* problem [7], is attracting more and more attention from today's research communities.

As a category of solutions for the semantic integration problem, schema matching [8] aims at finding semantic relationships between schema elements such as database tables and table columns. Schema matches can be discovered by analyzing the similarity of schema information, preservation of constraints, domain knowledge, and instance data. The limitation to this solution is the lack of a concept model.

Ontology-driven semantic integration is another category of solutions for the semantic integration problem [4]. The traditional solutions are based on available ontologies.

L.M. Camarinha-Matos et al. (Eds.): PRO-VE 2009, IFIP AICT 307, pp. 311–318, 2009.

The *ontology integration* can be applied to discover semantic correspondences among these ontologies [10]. However, in many domains, there are no pre-established explicit ontologies available.

This paper is dedicated to investigate the theoretical foundation of ontologies and ontological views, and analyze ontological view-driven solutions to address the semantic integration problem. The rest of the paper is organized as follows: Section 2 defines some fundamental concepts; Section 3 analyzes a hypothesis for this work; Section 4 discusses the framework for ontological view-driven semantic integration, and Section 5 concludes the paper.

2   Fundamental Concepts

2.1   Ontology and Ontological View

Research on *semantics* bases itself on computer-based information systems. Generally speaking, semantics refers to the intended meaning of a subject. In another words, the semantics of information in the information systems refers to the users' interpretation of the computer-based representation of the world [5]. It reflects the way that users relate computer-based representations to the real world. *Ontology* plays an important role in specifying the information semantics. An ontology is a formal and explicit specification of a conceptualization [3]. Simply, an ontology specifies the concepts and relationships between the concepts in a domain [1]. In the following we present a set of definitions based on [2] that are necessary to formally define ontology.

A *domain* D is a set of concepts, i.e., $D = \{C_1, C_2, ..., C_n\}$ where each C_i is a concept. A *domain space* is a structure <D, W>, where D is a domain and W is a set of maximal states of affairs of such a domain (also called *possible worlds*). Given a domain space <D, W>, a *conceptual relation* ρ^n of arity n is a function from a set W of possible worlds to the set of all n-ary relations on D, 2^{D^n}, $\rho^n: W \rightarrow 2^{D^n}$. A *conceptualization* of domain D is defined as an ordered triple $\mathbf{C} = <D, W, \mathfrak{R}>$, where $\mathfrak{R}$ is a set of conceptual relations on the domain space <D, W>.

For each possible world $w \in W$, the *intended structure* of w, according to a conceptualization $\mathbf{C} = <D, W, \mathfrak{R}>$, is the structure $\mathbf{S}_{wC} = <D, \mathbf{R}_{wC}>$, where $\mathbf{R}_{wC} = \{\rho(w) \mid \rho \in \mathfrak{R}\}$ is the set of extensions (relative to w) of the elements of $\mathfrak{R}$. We use $\mathbf{S}_C = \{\mathbf{S}_{wC} \mid w \in W\}$ to denote all the intended structures (or intended world structure) of $\mathbf{C}$.

A *logical language* $\mathbf{L}$ is a composition of a vocabulary V and a set of models of the language. V contains constant symbols and predicate symbols. A *model* of $\mathbf{L}$ is a structure <S, I>, where $S = <D, R>$ is a world structure and I: $V \rightarrow D \cup R$ is an interpretation function assigning elements of D to constant symbols of V, and elements of R to predicate symbols of V.

An *intensional interpretation* of a logical language $\mathbf{L}$ with a vocabulary V is a structure $<\mathbf{C}, \mathfrak{I}>$, where $\mathbf{C} = <D, W, \mathfrak{R}>$ is a conceptualization and $\mathfrak{I}: V \rightarrow D \cup \mathfrak{R}$ is a function assigning elements of D to constant symbols of V, and elements of $\mathfrak{R}$ to predicate symbols of V. This intensional interpretation is called *ontological commitment* for $\mathbf{L}$, denoted as $\mathbf{K} = <\mathbf{C}, \mathfrak{I}>$. We also say that $\mathbf{L}$ commits to $\mathbf{C}$ by means of $\mathbf{K}$, where $\mathbf{C}$ is the underlying conceptualization of $\mathbf{K}$. $\mathbf{K}$ constrains the intensional interpretation of **L**, i.e., the language is used in an intended way for a domain instead of an arbitrary way.

Given a language **L** with a vocabulary V and an ontological commitment **K** = <C, $\mathfrak{S}$> for **L**, a model <S, I> is *compatible* with **K** if: i) S∈ S$_C$; ii) for each constant symbol $c \in$ V, I(c) = $\mathfrak{S}$(c); iii) there exists a world w such that for each predicate symbol $p \in$ V, I maps the predicate into an admittable extension of $\mathfrak{S}$(p), i.e. there exists a conceptual relation ρ, such that $\mathfrak{S}(p) = \rho \wedge \rho(w) = I(p)$.

Given a language **L** and an ontological commitment **K**, the set **I$_K$(L)** of all models of **L** that are compatible with **K** is called the *set of intended models* of **L** according to **K**. Given a language **L** with an ontological commitment **K**, an *ontology* for **L** is a set of axioms designed in a way such that the set of its models approximates as best as possible the set of intended models of **L** according to **K**.

According to the above definition, an "ontology" is a designed artifact that is committed to a conceptualization according to an ontological commitment. It reflects a view on the conceptualization. Since the conceptualization can be viewed in various ways, there actually is not just one unique "ontology" for it. Instead, different views of the conceptualization may exist. We define the formal and explicit specification of each view as an *ontological view*. Accordingly, its intensional interpretation is called an *ontological commitment of view*. There can be multiple ontological views for a single conceptualization.

Different languages can be employed to specify the ontological views. Further, if two languages are employed for ontological views with partially overlapping intended models, it is possible for the corresponding ontological views to be semantically integrated. Formally, given an ontological view O with intended models **I$_K$(L)** and another ontological view O' with intended models **I$_{K'}$(L')**, O and O' are integrate-able (denoted by ◊) if and only if **I$_K$(L)** overlaps with **I$_{K'}$(L')**. That is,

$$(\mathbf{I_K(L)} \neq \mathbf{I_{K'}(L')}) \wedge (\mathbf{I_K(L)} \cap \mathbf{I_{K'}(L')} \neq \varnothing) \leftrightarrow (O \lozenge O').$$

2.2 Semantic Integration

Information systems are built based on *information models* which are explicit models specifying information in the systems, such as a database schema. Given a set of information models IM_1, IM_2, ..., IM_n, the semantic integration upon them includes two aspects:

(1) For any two elements e_i and e_j from IM_i and IM_j, if they refer to the same concept in terms of the domain of discourse, independent of the way they are represented, this fact can be discovered.

(2) For any element e_i from IM_i, if it is required to be communicated to IM_j (if applicable), it can be converted into another element (referring to the same concept) that is correct in both representation and semantics in IM_j such that IM_j can handle it in a semantically reasonable manner.

3 Hypothesis for Semantic Integration

Based on how information systems are built in a collaborative enterprise network, we can safely assume that there are explicit information models available and the models are committed to the intended models that overlap. The information models are not restricted to a particular language or paradigm, such as relational, XML, or Objected-Oriented (OO). Further, the modeling languages of the information models adopt symbols based on a natural language foundation such as English. The constant symbols such as English words refer to concepts under an ontological commitment.

An ontological view, as an explicitly represented model, can be created from an information model. The ontological views provide a common base that eliminates syntactical and schematic heterogeneities among information models, therefore the semantic integration can be conducted at the ontological view level.

Before we present the hypothesis of this research, we formally define the *semantically equivalent mapping* (or *equivalence mapping*) between languages:

Given a source language L_S with ontological commitment of view $K_S = <C, \Im_S>$ and vocabulary V_S, a target language L_T with ontological commitment of view $K_T = <C, \Im_T>$ and vocabulary V_T, the two languages share the same conceptualization $C = <D, W, \Re>$, a semantically equivalent mapping is a function from V_S to $V_{T,}$, m: $V_S \rightarrow V_T$, assigning symbols in V_T to the ones in V_S which share the same intensional interpretation, i.e., i) for constant symbols $c_S \in V_S$ and $c_T \in V_T$, $m(c_S) = c_T$ if and only if $\exists d \in D$, such that $\Im_S(c_S) = \Im_T(c_T) = d$ and ii) for predicate symbols $p_S \in V_S$ and $p_T \in V_T$, $m(p_S) = p_T$ if and only if $\exists \rho \in \Re$ such that $\Im_S(p_S) = \Im_T(p_T) = \rho$.

In this context, we base our research on the following hypothesis:

If the semantically equivalent relationships between concepts (specified by symbols in languages) in multiple ontological views can be discovered, then these ontological views, as well as the information models from which the ontological views are developed , can be semantically integrated.

To support this hypothesis, we introduce the following two propositions.

(1) A concept in a conceptualization can be externalized by a constant symbol in a language under an ontological commitment.

Prove: According to the definition of the intended model, given a language **L** with an ontological commitment **K**, the set $I_K(L)$ of all models of **L** that are compatible with **K** is defined as the set of intended models of **L** according to **K**. Therefore, for any two models m_1 and m_2 in $I_K(L)$, m_1 and m_2 are compatible with **K**. That is, for each constant symbol c in the vocabulary of **L**, there is $I_1(c) = \Im(c)$ for m_1 where I_1 is the interpretation function of m_1, and $I_2(c) = \Im(c)$ for m_2, where I_2 is the interpretation function of m_2, and $\Im$ is the interpretation function in **K**. That is, under the given ontological commitment **K,** a constant symbol c is always interpreted as a concept in the domain of discourse.

On the other hand, since **I** is a function in any model, it is guaranteed that c is interpreted as only one concept, say C, under **K**. In other words, it is an explicitness of concept C. Therefore, even C is implicit, c can be taken as its representative. Since c is explicit, it can be used for processing the concept that it represents.   □

(2) The semantically equivalent relationship between symbols under an ontological commitment implies the same concept reference.

Prove: Given symbols v_1 and v_2 from two ontological views such that v_1 maps to a concept C_1 in a conceptualization and v_2 also maps to a concept C_2 in the same conceptualization (Proposition 1), if v_1 and v_2 have a semantically equivalent relationship between them, then they have the same semantics, i.e., the same concept reference. Therefore, it can be concluded that C_1 and C_2 are actually the same concept in the conceptualization. Consequently, information models corresponding to v_1 and v_2 are semantically equivalent.   □

The first proposition indicates that each ontological view has a specific *representation* based on a language since the ontological view is an explicit model. The second proposition shows that the *semantic similarity* between representations of models can be used to approximate the semantically equivalent relationships between the models themselves. Semantic similarity is a metric upon explicitly represented models computed from either a linguistic or structural perspective. Such a metric implies that two models may have the same semantics because their representations are linguistically or structurally similar to each other.

4 A Framework for Ontological-View Driven Semantic Integration

We propose a framework to achieve ontological view-driven semantic integration in open environments. This framework includes three main aspects: the architecture of a semantic integration enabled environment, ontological view modeling and representation, and the semantic equivalence relationship discovery.

(1) Architecture of Semantic Integration Enabled Environment
We propose a novel architecture that extends the traditional data/information architecture into three layers (see Figure 1), including:

(a) A data management and integration layer. This layer provides abstraction for the binary digits and organizes the digits into various types of elemental data such as numbers, characters, and strings.
(b) An information management and integration layer. This layer associates data to information models, providing specifications to data and converting data into information.
(c) A semantic management and integration layer. This layer deals with the semantics of information, resolves semantic heterogeneities, and ensures that information with the same semantics is handled in semantically consistent ways. The management and integration of this layer are addressed by a set of semantic integration services.

(2) Ontological View Modeling and Representation
Many of the paradigms used to build information models, such as relational and OO, follow the *concept-property* construct, where a concept is modeled as a set of properties. In this work we believe it will be normal to adopt the *concept-property* construct for modeling ontological views. Therefore, we shall adopt a paradigm to support modeling concepts, properties, and relationships between concepts such as *isA* and *partOf*.
    FRAME [6] is adopted for modeling the ontological views. It is a knowledge modeling approach that provides a clear and explicit structure adequate for modeling

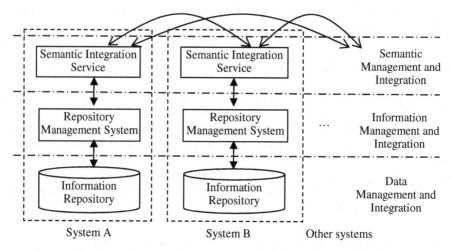

Fig. 1. Architecture of the semantic integration enabled environment

ontological views, particularly in describing the properties of concepts. A FRAME has a four-level structure, including FRAME (representing a concept), SLOT (capturing properties and relationships), FACET (capturing details of each SLOT), and DATA (providing specific information for instances of concepts). When modeling concepts, usually the DATA level is not used.

To specify the ontological views based on FRAME, we propose the FOSL (FRAME-based Ontological view Specification Language). FOSL is a logical language created from the following vocabulary:

(1) Constant symbols: the set of $FR \cup S \cup F \cup V$, where FR is a set of symbols referring to frames (concepts), S is a set of symbols referring to slots (properties), F is a set of symbols referring to facets, and V is a set of values that the facets can take.

(2) Predicate symbols: the following predicate symbols are considered:

a) A binary predicate *hasProperty* applied on $FR \times S$. *hasProperty(fr, s)* indicates that frame *fr* has a slot *s*.

b) A binary predicate *hasFacet* applied on $S \times F$. *hasFacet(s, f)* indicates that slot *s* has a facet *f*.

c) A binary predicate *hasValue* applied on $F \times V$. *hasValue(f, v)* indicates that facet *f* has a value *v*.

d) A binary predicate *isA* applied on $FR \times FR$. *isA(fr_1, fr_2)* indicates that frame fr_1 is a type of frame fr_2, i.e., the concept modeled by fr_1 is a specialization of the concept modeled by fr_2.

e) A binary predicate *partOf* applied on $FR \times FR$. *partOf(fr_1, fr_2)* indicates that frame fr_1 is a part of frame fr_2, i.e., the concept modeled by fr_1 is a part of the concept modeled by fr_2.

We adopt XML-based representation for FOSL. An ontological view can be modeled as a set of FRAMEs and represented in an XML document. The document is supported with multiple <concept> tags for concepts (FRAMEs) respectively. Under a <concept> tag the SLOTs are tagged as <relationship> or <property>. The FACETs of each SLOT are tagged as <facet> which is described by two attributes: *name* and *value*.

To create an ontological view from an information model, the concepts, properties, and relationships need to be extracted. Given that an information model M is specified by language $L_M = <S_M, I_M>$ with vocabulary V_M and the ontological view model is specified by language $L_O = <S_O, I_O>$ with vocabulary V_O, the creation of an ontological view is to find a mapping m between L_M and L_O such that $m(I_O) \subseteq I_M$. The mapping adopts a set of rules for each modeling paradigm to identify what constructs in the information model can be mapped to concepts, properties, facets of properties, and relationships, and then maps them into corresponding constructs in the FRAME model.

(3) Semantic Equivalence Relationship Discovery from Ontological Views
The semantic equivalence relationship is deduced from the *semantic similarity metric* between symbols. A semantic similarity metric is a combination $<A, t>$ where A is an approach to compute the similarity between symbols and t is a threshold. The approach A can be viewed as a function $A: S \times S \rightarrow R$ where S is the set of symbols and R is the set of real numbers. If $A(s_1, s_2) > t$, $s_1, s_2 \in S$, then it can be confidently believed that two symbols are semantically equivalent, i.e., s_1 and s_2 have a semantic equivalence relationship.

In the research of schema matching and ontology mapping, multiple approaches have been developed to discover the semantic relationships between elements of the schemas or ontologies [7, 8]. These approaches can be applied to ontological views.

(a) Linguistic (Syntactical) Matching
Linguistic matching utilizes the vocabulary of the modeling language to discover the semantic equivalence relationships. Linguistic matching works on symbols that are mapped to concepts under an ontological commitment.

In linguistic matching, the principle is that the more syntactically similar two symbols are, the more likely they map to the same concept, the same property, or the same facet. To increase the precision of the comparison, the symbols will often be normalized and compared, sometimes with the help of natural language dictionaries to determine the synonym when the symbols are syntactically different.

(b) Structural (Semantic) Matching
The structural matching utilizes the semantic structures captured by the FRAME model to discover the semantic equivalence relationships if syntactically matching cannot provide sufficient clues. The principle is: even two symbols are syntactically different, they can be semantically similar if the structures around them are similar. FRAME model's tree-like structure is utilized to support the inference that two symbols are semantically equivalent if their properties are very similar, even though they are syntactically different.

5 Conclusion

Understanding and integrating heterogeneous information have become more important and challenging in collaborative enterprise networks. Semantic integration, as an important factor for successful information integration, has become one of the most active research areas. It has received extensive interest and attention from both the academic and industrial communities.

Our work on semantic integration fits into the evolvement by extending the traditional ontology-driven approaches to an ontological view-driven approach to overcome the grand challenges that were not thoroughly addressed by the traditional approaches. The most significant advancement is the removal of the assumption about the availability of explicit ontologies. Besides this, our study embeds the support for semantic integration into existing systems and makes them semantic-sensitive. This extension will provide a new level of capabilities for the information systems to interoperate at the semantic level.

References

1. Crubzy, M., Pincus, Z., Musen, M.A.: Mediating Knowledge between Application Components. In: Proceedings of the Semantic Integration Workshop of the Second International Semantic Web Conference (ISWC 2003), Sanibel Island, Florida (2003)
2. Guarino, N.: Formal Ontology and Information Systems. In: Proceedings of FOIS 1998, pp. 3–15. IOS Press, Trento (1998)
3. Gruber, T.R.: Toward Principles for the Design of Ontologies Used for Knowledge Sharing. International Journal of Human-Computer Studies 43(5-6), 907–928 (1995)
4. Hakimpour, F., Timpf, S.: Using Ontologies for Resolution of Semantic Heterogeneity in GIS. In: Proceedings 4th AGILE Conference on Geographic Information Science, Brno, Czech Republic, pp. 385–395 (2001)
5. Meersman, R.: An Essay on the Role and Evolution of Data (base) Semantics. In: Proceedings of IFIP WG 2.6 Working Conference on Database Application Semantics, pp. 1–7. Chapman & Hall, Ltd., London (1995)
6. Minsky, M.: A Framework for Representing Knowledge. In: Winston, P.H. (ed.) The Psychology of Computer Vision, pp. 211–277. McGraw-Hill, New York (1975)
7. Noy, F.N.: Semantic Integration: A Survey of Ontology-based Approaches. SIGMOD Record, Special Issue on Semantic Integration 33(4), 65–70 (2004)
8. Rahm, E., Bernstein, P.A.: A Survey of Approaches to Automatic Schema Matching. The International Journal on Very Large Databases (VLDB) 10(4), 334–350 (2001)
9. Sheth, A.P.: Changing Focus on Interoperability in Information Systems: from System, Syntax, Structure to Semantics. In: Goodchild, M.F., Egenhofer, M., Fegeas, R., Kottman, C.A. (eds.) Interoperating Geographic Information System, vol. 47, pp. 5–29. Kluwer Academic Publishers, Norwell (1999)
10. Wache, H., Vogele, T., Visser, U., Stuckenschmidt, H., Schuster, G., Neumann, H., Hubner, S.: Ontology-based Integration of Information – A Survey of Existing Approaches. In: Proceedings of the IJCAI 2001 Workshop: Ontologies and Information Sharing, Seattle, Washington, USA, pp. 108–117 (2001)

Part 10

Partners Selection

Uncertainty in Partner Selection for Virtual Enterprises

José Crispim[1] and Jorge Pinho de Sousa[2]

[1] Department of Management, Escola de Economia e Gestão, Campus de Gualtar,
University of Minho, 4710-057 Braga, Portugal
crispim@eeg.uminho.pt
[2] INESC Porto / Faculty of Engineering, University of Porto, Campus da FEUP,
Rua Dr. Roberto Frias, 4200-465 Porto, Portugal
jsousa@inescporto.pt

Abstract. A virtual enterprise (VE) is a temporary organization that pools the core competencies of its member enterprises and exploits fast changing market opportunities. The success of such an organization is strongly dependent on its composition, and the selection of partners becomes therefore a crucial issue. This problem is particularly difficult because of the uncertainties related to information, market dynamics, customer expectations and technology speed up. In this paper we propose an integrated approach to rank alternative VE configurations in business environments with uncertainty, using an extension of the TOPSIS method for fuzzy data, improved through the use of a stochastic multiobjective tabu search meta-heuristic. Preliminary computational results clearly demonstrate the potential of this approach for practical application.

1 Introduction

The success of a Virtual Enterprise (VE) strongly depends on all of the participating organizations being capable of cooperating as a single unit. Therefore, an adequate selection of partners is surely very important to overcome the fragilities of this type of organization (e.g., lack of formal contracts and heterogeneity of companies), that are much related with trust [1].

Moreover problem solving with explicit consideration of uncertainty may have a very high impact on real world situations, as problems arising in practice are becoming increasingly complex and dynamic, due partially to the fast development of communications that makes the perception of changes more rapid, stochastic and difficult to forecast [2]. Stability cannot be considered a reasonable assumption any more as we do not have perfect information either in terms of the VE projects (some activities or activity features, like the processing time, or the resources capacity cannot be known with certainty) or in terms of the characteristics and behaviours of the companies that will perform those activities (e.g., market capacity entrance). Moreover, each company's performance is affected by the operations or decisions of the others, i.e., there is a propagation of uncertainty through the members of a supply chain, and in the business environment customers' needs and preferences, market forces, technologies, and even the original problem being solved may change [3].

L.M. Camarinha-Matos et al. (Eds.): PRO-VE 2009, IFIP AICT 307, pp. 321–330, 2009.

In many situations (like in partner selection) decisions have to be made in environments with high uncertainty. Actually, in dynamic environments, the context may change at any time, making a current VE no longer viable. In such a situation a new VE composition that better fits the prevailing circumstances has to be found.

In Stochastic Combinatorial Optimisation Problems, all or part of the information about the problem is unknown, but it is possible to assume some knowledge about its probability distribution. To our best knowledge, there is in the literature no explicit reference to stochastic versions of the partner selection problem in the context of virtual enterprises. An interesting and complete survey about supplier selection that can be found in Aissaoui et al. [4] reflects this situation. Nevertheless, various models are available to select supply chain partners with uncertainty and risk (see e.g., [5-8]). Uncertainty in the configuration of collaborative networks has also been object of study by analytical or multi-agents approaches but not in terms of stochastic models (see e.g., [9] or [10]).

In this work we propose the use of a multistage stochastic model that captures both the stochastic and dynamic elements of real world situations, as a way to deal with uncertainty. Unfortunately, realistic stochastic models often lead to optimisation problems impossible to solve due to their astronomical number of possible outcomes. Therefore some kind of approximation procedure has to be performed. Our approach is based on a scenario tree formulation and makes use of the flexible hybrid algorithm presented by Crispim and Sousa [11] adapted to deal with uncertainty. This algorithm combines multiobjective (tabu search) with a multiattribute (fuzzy TOPSIS) technique. The scenario reduction technique adopted aims at reducing the vast number of possible scenarios to a manageable scenarios subset, keeping the approximation as close as possible to the original.

The remainder of the paper is organized as follows. In Section 2 the problem is formulated as a scenario tree, in section 3 the method used to solve the problem is presented, in Section 4 an illustrative example is described and finally, in Section 5 some preliminary conclusions are presented.

2 Scenario Trees

The discretization of the problem formulated as a scenario tree is a standard approach to solve multistage stochastic programs. A scenario is a path starting at the root node and ending at a node of the last period T. Along time, in different stages, several uncertain events can occur. In this way a representation is obtained for a finite number of possible realizations of the future outcomes of a given variable x (Figure 1). At each stage we have as many nodes as different realizations of ξ. The stages do not necessarily refer to time periods, but they correspond to steps in the decision process [12]. A (conditional) probability $p_{ij} > 0$ (such that $\sum_j p_{ij} = 1$) is associated to each arc of the tree. Therefore, at each stage, decisions must be made for different probability values. In scenario-based multistage stochastic programs, for feasibility reasons, one assumes that the probability distribution is discrete, and concentrated on a finite number of points, or branches. We also assume that the probability distributions of the various stages are independent of each other.

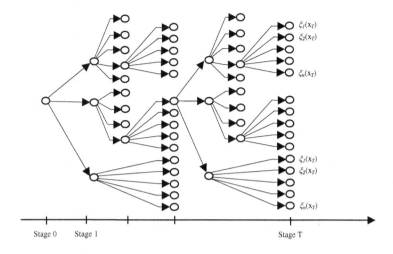

Fig. 1. Multistage problem formulation

It was found that uncertainties on demand quantity and timing are the two most common changes occurring in supply chain management [13].The scenario-baseapproach attempts to capture uncertainty by representing it in terms of a moderate number of discrete realizations of random quantities. We assume here that the values taken by random variables ξ_T are independent between stages.

Unfortunately, realistic models often lead to optimisation problems impossible to solve because of their size. According to Kim [14], in most large-scale stochastic programming problems, the total number of outcomes is huge and hence it is practically impossible to enumerate those outcomes. Therefore an approximation has to be done, i.e., a scenario tree is generated/aggregated/reduced (Figure 2).

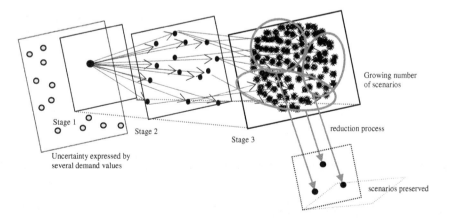

Fig. 2. Scenario tree generation/reduction

Scenario reduction techniques aim at reducing the vast number of possible scenarios to a manageable subset (with or without a predefined cardinality). In the literature the studies along this idea basically follow one of two different perspectives:

- partition of the simulated scenarios, for example through cluster analysis (e.g., [15]);
- aggregation methods, for example by merging nodes with similar states of the stochastic parameters [16].

The objective is to make the scenario tree practically manageable, with a loss of information as small as possible. To avoid having to deal with exponentially growing scenarios we have used a reduction scheme based on cluster analysis.

The cluster simulation method adopted is similar to those introduced by Gülpinar et al. [17] or Shen and Zhang [15]. The main idea is to partition the simulated scenarios into random clusters and select one scenario in each cluster taken as representative – this scenario is known as the "centroid" (Figure 2). Therefore, the centroids[1] of the various clusters should be (in some sense) far away from each other. In our work, since we do not know the number of clusters in advance, we have chosen an agglomerative "hierarchical clustering" approach. In this procedure, to start the process, we assume each data point has its own cluster, and with each step of the clustering process, these clusters are combined to form larger clusters, in an iterative way. "Similarity" among each cluster's members is measured through an Euclidian distance formula (see [18]).

These principles resulted in the design of a two phase scenario tree reduction procedure, as follows:

Phase 1: Simulation: randomly generate random variables (demand, production capacity and processing times) data through simulation.

Phase 2: Clustering: the generated data is grouped into clusters around a given number of centroids according to the hierarchical clustering scheme. Initially, we consider that the probability associated to the various clusters is the same and equals a given value - 1/#_of_clusters. After the clustering process, these probabilities have to be redistributed amongst the remaining scenarios (which correspond to the centroids). Therefore, we consider that the probability of each centroid is proportional to the number of elements in the respective cluster.

3 The Algorithm

The algorithm we have designed to cope with uncertainties in partner selection was firstly presented in Crispim and Sousa [11] and comprises two phases, namely: identifying good VE configurations, and then rank them according to a set of weights provided by the decision maker. In the first phase a multiobjective tabu search metaheuristic is used. As we take a multi-objective perspective, we are basically looking for a set of nondominated alternative solutions (the Pareto frontier).

---

[1] The centroid of a cluster is the average point in the multidimensional space defined by the scenarios, i.e., the cluster's centre of gravity.

A stochastic feasible solution (i.e., a potential VE configuration) is represented by a set of companies in the network, associated to the different project activities, along with the corresponding attribute values, considered in an uncertain environment.

In other words, a solution is a subset of potential candidates (that all together form a so-called Virtual Breeding Environment) that fulfils the requirements of the project, respecting a set of constraints (associated to competencies, capacities...) and resulting in values for the different, possibly conflicting objectives.

In order to evaluate the stochastic Pareto solutions we adopted the stochastic domination concept proposed by Medaglia et al. [19] with the exception that we use distances instead of probabilities. Let x and y be a pair of feasible solutions for the partner selection problem, we say y stochastically dominates x (i.e., $y \preccurlyeq x$) if and only if the following conditions hold:

i) $E[f_k(y, \omega)] \geq E[f_k(x, \omega)]$ and $D\{f_k(y, \omega) - T_k\} \leq D\{f_k(x, \omega) - T_k\}$,   for all k;

ii) there exists a k such that $E[f_k(y, \omega)] > E[f_k(x, \omega)]$ and $D\{f_k(y, \omega) - T_k\} > D\{f_k(x, \omega) - T_k\}$

where $E[f_k(x, \omega)]$ is the expected value of the kth objective and $D\{f_k(x, \omega) - T_k\}$ is the distance between $f_k(x, \omega)$ and the target value T_k specified by the DM. In our algorithm we propose T_k as the ideal value of the objective and, since we use fuzzy sets to express the information, T_k assumes the value of 1 in case of a benefit criterion or 0 in case of a cost criterion. Therefore, the differences to the deterministic version of the problem is in the way we evaluate each neighbourhood solution, as here a given number of samples is randomly determined to obtain the expected value of each objective, and the correspondent probability for each stochastic variable.

In the search (first) phase of the global procedure, we have introduced in the metaheuristic algorithm the directional search concept, with the aim of generating a good approximation of the set of Pareto solutions, hopefully not neglecting any region of the search space. This concept tries to incorporate some important features into the algorithm: the ability to generate all available non-dominated solutions and be relatively easy to implement and apply.

The algorithm starts by exploring all objective functions choosing a specific objective f_1, to be improved, when f_1 has not been improved for a certain (large) number of iterations. In this situation, in the next iteration, the search only makes use of objective f_1.

Since we admit the exploration of unfeasible solutions during the search (e.g., one potential VE formation may be unfeasible because of the lack of production capacity to satisfy the demand), we apply the same scheme to the constraints, i.e., in cases where the search has been performed in unfeasible regions of the solution space for too long, in the next iteration, the algorithm only accepts solutions that are feasible for the constraint with higher unfeasibility. To direct the search in such occasions we make use of two matrices, one for constraints and another for objectives. They are somehow similar to a tabu list, but they are used to force, and not to forbid, the search in a given direction..

For the second phase of the algorithm, we have designed a fuzzy TOPSIS approach that accepts different types of variables (numerical, interval, linguistic, etc.) to facilitate the Decision Maker preferences expression. For a more detailed description of this procedure see Crispim and Sousa [11].

The algorithm steps are as follows:

Step 0. ***Initialization:*** Initialize the tabu list (the list of moves that is forbidden for a given number of iteration) and the ND (non-dominated) solutions list.

Step 1. ***Select the current solution:*** Randomly (uniformly) select a single current solution from the set of ND solutions.

Step 2. ***Search the neighbourhood:*** Search all possible defined moves, according to the adopted neighbourhood structure.

    Step 2.1 ***Directional search***

- If the objective parameter is activated, make the correspondent objective function active, otherwise, all objective functions are activated.
- If the constraint parameter is activated, only feasible solutions with respect to the activated constraint are kept.

    Step 2.2 ***Choose***

- Calculate the expected value of the kth stochastic objective and the distance to the ideal value for each neighbour.
- Choose the non-tabu candidate solution with the best activated stochastic objective function(s) value(s) (or if it is tabu, but dominates any solution in the ND solutions list) as the best candidate solution.

Step 3. ***Stochastic scheme (applied in each stage)***

    Simulate a given number of scenarios for the stochastic variables (demand, processing time and production capacity) and compute the number of representative centroids and the respective occurrence probabilities.

Step 4. ***Update the ND solutions list and the tabu lists***

4   Illustrative Example

Suppose that we have 3 manufacturing stages for a given product in which some stochastic events can occur, namely variations in demand (with an impact on the capability of firms to respect production capacity constraints and on the production costs). This example will allow us to demonstrate how the approach reacts to uncertainty influencing the objective functions and the constraints. Figure 3 shows a scenario tree in which several realizations of the uncertain demand are considered at each of three distinct stages (events). These events in which uncertainty unfolds over the planning horizon can be, for example, market research reports (important in case of fluctuating markets or in case of innovative and technological products), publicity actions, new market entrances, new competitors, etc. The number of scenarios represented in Figure 3 is only used for illustrative purposes (as the total number of scenarios of the studied example is 512).

Making use of the data of the problem example proposed by Crispim and Sousa [11], namely: a project composed by 6 activities (Table 1) and a network composed by 100 (candidate) enterprises where 12 different activities that require 10 different resources has to be performed. These companies are characterized by: enterprise identification code (a number from 1 to 100); activity; interval time for the availability of resources; capacity; and 8 evaluation attributes (Table 2).

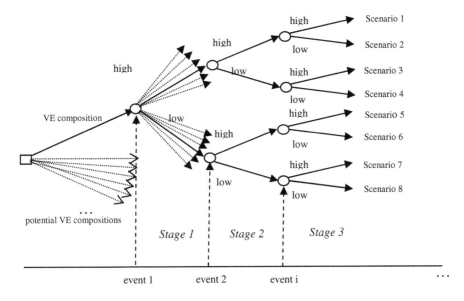

Fig. 3. Scenario tree

Table 1. Project data

Project						
Activities (code)	Resources	Precedent activities	Duration	Earliest start time	Latest start time	Quantity of resources
A	7	-	36	0	106	400
B	8	-	62	0	97	604
C	3	-	67	0	122	528
D	5	A	16	36	122	275
E	4	B	25	62	122	368
F	8	C,E,D	43	87	165	304

Table 2. Description of attributes

attributes (objectives)	c1	c2	c3	c4	c5	c6	c7	c8
type	linguistic	numerical	interval	interval	linguistic	numerical	numerical	linguistic
max (+) / min (-)	+	+	-	-	+	+	-	+
cardinality (for linguistic)	7	-	-	-	3	-	-	7
weight (%)	20	23	2	7	19	13	14	2

Impact of demand uncertainty on the constraints. As the final demand at each stage is unknown *a priori*, we will not be sure about each firm's capability to produce the required quantity. Therefore, for each company, we have calculated its probability of being capable of satisfying the required demand. For example, if the demand at a given stage is normally distributed with $N(\mu=2000, \sigma=200)$, the probability that a company with a production capacity of 2561 units is able to satisfy the demand is $\Phi\left(\frac{2561-2000}{200}\right) \approx 0,997$. For decision purposes, we have assumed that a solution is feasible if the probability of respecting the capacity constraints is higher or equal to 0,8 for all companies involved in the three stages considered. In a practical situation the DM would be able to define their own rules to distinguish between feasibility and unfeasibility.

Impact of demand uncertainty on the objective functions. At each stage we obtain several realizations (in our case several centroids for high demand and several centroids for low demand) through the clustering procedure presented above (Table 3). Once an acceptable clustering is found, it is necessary to represent each cluster by a single point to be used in the scenario tree. If the centre of the cluster does not correspond to any obtained point (e.g., in the case where the cluster of points is quite sparse), the centroid should be the closest point to the cluster centre. The probability of each centroid is proportional to the number of elements in the respective cluster. This process starts with the generation of a sample of size 100 from the normal distribution [20] based on the Central Limit Theorem (CLT). Moreover, we assume that the probability distributions at the three stages are independent.

Table 3. Centroids of the stochastic demand

	Stage 1		Stage 2		Stage 3	
	N(2000,200)		N(2500,250)		N(1500,150)	
	demand value	probability	demand value	probability	demand value	probability
high demand	2146	0,37	2245	0,26	1367	0,15
	2356	0,12	2834	0,18	1828	0,10
	1906	0,36	2537	0,56	1612	0,31
	1721	0,15			1487	0,34
					1233	0,10
	N(1000,100)		N(1500,150)		N(500,50)	
low demand	873	0,20	1698	0,15	436	0,23
	1046	0,26	1409	0,35	545	0,29
	973	0,37	1847	0,8	494	0,48
	1128	0,17	1550	0,32		
			1240	0,10		

In terms of production costs we are assuming the VBE companies benefit from a quantity discount depending on the demand level that follows a discrete uniform distribution.

The algorithm found 18 non-dominated solutions for the project, with capacity and time windows constraints. It should be noted that for activity D, only 5 companies have an adequate production capacity, this leading to the formation of a consortium between some of them. Table 4 shows the ranking and composition of the alternative configurations. These coalitions are those that prove to be more "robust" to face the demand uncertainty with impact on the objective function and on the constraints.

Table 4. Results

Rank	VE	$\bar{d}_i^+$	$\bar{d}_i^-$	$\tilde{R}_i$	Project activities					
					A	B	C	D	E	F
1	5	307.975	152.146	0.0470763	35	71	14	31	47	71
2	10	308.717	137.358	0.0425979	21	44	20	101	72	44
3	4	308.682	134.007	0.0416065	21	28	14	90	95	28
4	2	309.287	132.176	0.0409843	35	6	14	26	72	6
5	14	309.216	127.847	0.0397040	21	97	14	26	72	44
6	3	309.221	127.776	0.0396821	21	97	14	26	72	97
7	18	309.221	127.776	0.0396821	21	97	14	26	72	97
8	6	309.640	118.609	0.0368921	74	44	20	90	57	44
9	11	309.822	115.400	0.0359096	74	44	20	101	72	44
10	8	309.967	115.299	0.0358630	7	44	20	26	72	44
11	9	309.762	114.749	0.0357210	46	44	20	101	72	44
12	7	310.010	110.672	0.0344689	74	44	20	101	39	44
13	16	310.243	106.676	0.0332415	74	97	14	26	72	94
14	17	310.320	104.907	0.0327005	74	97	14	26	72	6
15	12	310.320	104.613	0.0326120	74	97	14	26	72	44
16	15	310.320	104.613	0.0326120	74	97	14	26	72	44
17	13	310.260	103.886	0.0323986	46	97	14	26	72	44
18	1	310.459	975.056	0.0304506	46	97	14	101	39	97

Note: The company n° 101 consists in one consortium formed by 7 individual companies (company n°s: 9, 13, 43, 49, 55, 68, 79)

5 Conclusions

The approach developed in this work creates a quite general and flexible research framework that can be used to analyse numerous partner selection scenarios. With this framework the decision maker is able to easily change the objectives and constraints in order to obtain a satisfactory solution, and allowing the use of a mix of variable types to express his/her preferences. All types of evaluation criteria can be used and, in a real situation, the decision maker should use criteria that are in accordance with the available (or obtainable) information.

The proposed algorithm includes an innovative multiobjective directional stochastic tabu search metaheuristic. The flexibility provided by this approach becomes even more important if we think in the uncertainty propagation within the network and/or in the specificity of the virtual environment. This efficient quantitative tool should be able to provide an adequate, useful support, in simulating and assessing different alternative solutions for the uncertain business environments associated to VE formation or re-organization.

References

1. Camarinha-Matos, L.M., Afsarmanesh, H.: A framework for virtual organization creation in a breeding environment. Annual Reviews in Control 31, 119–135 (2007)
2. Bianchi, L., Dorigo, M., Gambardella, L.M., Gutjahr, W.J.: Metaheuristics in stochastic combinatorial optimization: a survey. Technical Report IDSIA-08-06. Dalle Molle Institute for Artificial Intelligence, Manno, Switzerland (2006)

3. Molokken-Ostvold, K., Jorgensen, M.: A comparison of software project overruns - flexible versus sequential development models. IEEE Transactions on Software Engineering 31, 754–766 (2005)
4. Aissaoui, N., Haouari, M., Hassini, E.: Supplier selection and order lot sizing modeling: A review. Computers & Operations Research 34, 3516–3540 (2007)
5. Goetschalckx, M., Vidal, C.J., Dogan, K.: Modeling and design of global logistics systems: A review of integrated strategic and tactical models and design algorithms. European Journal of Operational Research 143, 1–18 (2002)
6. Paulraj, A., Chen, I.J.: Strategic supply management: theory and practice. International Journal of Integrated Supply Management 1, 457–477 (2005)
7. Ding, H., Benyoucef, L., Xie, X.: A simulation-based multi-objective genetic algorithm approach for networked enterprises optimization. Engineering Applications of Artificial Intelligence 19, 609–623 (2006)
8. Wu, D., Olson, D.L.: Supply chain risk, simulation, and vendor selection. International Journal of Production Economics 114, 646–655 (2008)
9. Ivanov, D., Kaeschel, J., Sokolov, B., Arkhipov, A.: A Conceptional Framework for Modeling Complex Adaptation of Collaborative Networks. In: Camarinha-Matos, L.M., Afsarmanesh, H., Ollus, M. (eds.) Network-Centric Collaboration and Supporting Frameworks, pp. 15–22. Springer, Boston (2006)
10. Tolkacheva, V., Ivanov, D., Arkhipov, A.: Assessment of Collaborative Networks Structural Stability. In: Camarinha-Matos, L.M., Afsarmanesh, H., Novais, P., Analide, C. (eds.) Establishing The Foundation of Collaborative Networks, pp. 75–82. Springer, Boston (2007)
11. Crispim, J.A., Sousa, J.P.: Partner selection in virtual enterprises. International Journal of Production Research (2008) (in press),
   http://dx.doi.org/10.1080/00207540802425369
12. Dupačová, J.: Applications of stochastic programming: Achievements and questions. European Journal of Operational Research 140, 281–290 (2002)
13. Das, S.K., Abdel-Malek, L.: Modeling the flexibility of order quantities and lead-times in supply chains. International Journal of Production Economics 85, 171–181 (2003)
14. Kim, J.: Event tree based sampling. Computers & Operations Research 33, 1184–1199 (2006)
15. Shen, R., Zhang, S.: Robust portfolio selection based on a multi-stage scenario tree. European Journal of Operational Research 191, 864–887 (2008)
16. Blomvall, J., Shapiro, A.: Solving multistage asset investment problems by the sample average approximation method. Mathematical Programming 108, 571–595 (2006)
17. Gülpinar, N., Rustem, B., Settergren, R.: Simulation and optimization approaches to scenario tree generation. Journal of Economic Dynamics and Control 28, 1291–1315 (2004)
18. Balopoulos, V., Hatzimichailidis, A.G., Papadopoulos, B.K.: Distance and similarity measures for fuzzy operators. Information Sciences 177, 2336–2348 (2007)
19. Medaglia, A.L., Graves, S.B., Ringuest, J.L.: A multiobjective evolutionary approach for linearly constrained project selection under uncertainty. European Journal of Operational Research 179, 869–894 (2007)
20. Tavares, L.V., Oliveira, R.C., Themido, I.H., Correia, F.N.: Investigação Operacional. McGraw-Hill, Lisboa (1996)

Supplier Selection in Virtual Enterprise Model of Manufacturing Supply Network

Toshiya Kaihara and Jayeola F. Opadiji

Kobe University, Graduate School of Engineering,
657-8501, Japan
{kaihara,femi}@cs.kobe-u.ac.jp

Abstract. The market-based approach to manufacturing supply network planning focuses on the competitive attitudes of various enterprises in the network to generate plans that seek to maximize the throughput of the network. It is this competitive behaviour of the member units that we explore in proposing a solution model for a supplier selection problem in convergent manufacturing supply networks. We present a formulation of autonomous units of the network as trading agents in a virtual enterprise network interacting to deliver value to market consumers and discuss the effect of internal and external trading parameters on the selection of suppliers by enterprise units.

Keywords: Virtual enterprise, supply network, supplier selection, multi-agent.

1 Introduction

Synergies forged by manufacturing enterprises in order to remain competitive in their market domain often result in the formation of complex supply networks. There are two major ways of analyzing such networks; based on either focusing on the functional units that make up the network or focusing on the interaction between these functional units. The first approach is referred to as function-based analysis while the second is called market based analysis (Vob, 2006). In the market-based analysis of supply network which we employ in this study, attention is paid to the competitive interaction among autonomous enterprises that make up the network. We consider a convergent manufacturing supply network in which every enterprise unit that makes up the network use a combination of input resources to produce their output. Each enterprise will therefore have to source its input from a number of possible suppliers in different markets. Resource contention and different purchasing overheads for all the autonomous units make the task of finding an optimal solution for the multiple supplier selection problems arduous. Introducing some other constraints such as the fill-or-kill constraint in combinatorial auctions make the job all the more difficult (Xia, 2005). Our approach uses a competitive market algorithm to obtain a satisfying solution to resource distribution problem in a convergent supply network. A satisfying solution presupposes a solution that satisfies all the constraints in the optimization

L.M. Camarinha-Matos et al. (Eds.): PRO-VE 2009, IFIP AICT 307, pp. 331–340, 2009.

model and suffices in relation to the objective function (Schwartz, 2002) (Fingar, 2004). The objective of this work is to provide a tactical planning framework for supplier selection in a supply network which will aid in balancing between competitive behaviour among autonomous enterprises and the ultimate goal of value delivery maximization in the network. Competitive interaction in the supply network is provided for in this model by means of $(k+1)$st auction algorithm which is a variant of the Vickery auction(Vickery, 1961) (Walsh, 2003). In order to enhance value delivery, the network is modeled as a Virtual Enterprise Network (VEN). The concept of a VEN assumes the existence of a supply network consisting of autonomous business units which interact in such a way as to form one giant enterprise with the goal of maximizing value delivery to consumers; their interaction is enabled by means of Information Technology infrastructure (Camarinha-Matos, 1999). We assume a set of enterprise agents that are individually rational and an auction mechanism that is incentive compatible; therefore, going by the impossibility theorem (Myerson, 1983), we can only obtain solutions that trade-off between budget balance and economic efficiency. Our goal at this stage of our work is to obtain solutions with no budget subsidies.

2 Supply Network Model

2.1 Supply Network

The supply network shown in figure 1 is a convergent manufacturing supply network with resource complementarity; the demand for a particular input resource by an enterprise unit affects the demand of other input resources by the same enterprise unit. As shown in the figure, the generalized supply network is made up of $(l+1)$ layers with layers 1 to l representing the production section of the supply network and layer C representing the consumption layer. In each of the production layers, there are multiple markets with each market containing enterprises that require inputs from a preceding layer to produce a resource unique to that market. It is possible for the number of markets in the layers to be different. The figure can be represented using a graph description as follows:

S = set of production enterprise

C = set of consumers

$H : (N, A)$

$N = T \cup G$ = nodes in graph H; $T:\{S,C\}$ = traders; G = goods

$A : \{a_i = \langle g,t \rangle_i \, or \langle t, g \rangle_i \mid t \in T; g \in G\}$ = set of directed arcs in graph H

$\langle g, s \rangle$ = resource g is an input to enterprise s

$\langle g, c \rangle$ = resource g is consumed by consumer c

$\langle s, g \rangle$ = resource g is produced by enterprise s

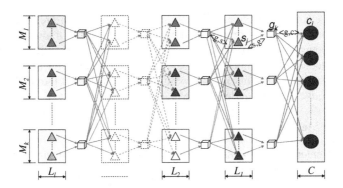

Fig. 1. Convergent supply network with alternative suppliers

2.2 Supplier Selection Problem

With the above graph description, the supply network planning problem can be defined with regards to allocation of resources across the network as

$$u((N^*, A^*)) = \max_{(N',A') \in (N,A)} (u((N', A')) \mid (N', A') \text{ is feasible}) \tag{1}$$

Given that

$$u((N', A')) = \sum_{c \in C} u_c((N', A')) - \sum_{s \in S} \pi_s((N', A')) \tag{2}$$

$$\text{s.t} \quad u_t \geq 0; \quad \forall \ t \in T \ \text{and} \ g \in G \tag{3}$$

u_t = value accrued to an enterprise and π_s = production cost of supplier s

Equation (1) is an objective function defining the goal of value maximization across the supply network. This objective function requires all participating traders to have feasible allocations in the network. The feasibility condition ensures budget balance in the network. Equation (2) the value accrued for a set of possible allocations across the network. Equation (3) represents the assumption of individual rationality among traders in the network which ensures that no trader incurs a deficit in value. With multiple units of every market resource expected to be traded, a scenario in which every trader computes his own optimal bid prices and bid quantities for market resources is assumed.

3 Market-Based Solution Approach

Considering the convergent supply network of figure 1, the network is divided into two parts. The first part is layer C consisting of all pure consumers in the network while the second part consists of all the production layers in the network. We assume the second part to be a Virtual Enterprise (VE). The idea of modeling this part of the network as a VE stems from the need to induce cooperation among individually rational competing enterprise units. This idea is plausible because of the increasing popularity of electronic auction markets via the internet which create virtual market places. This makes the outcome of trading dependent on the trading mechanism as much as it depends on the bidding tactics of participating traders. In this model, the VEN is divided into a number of virtual markets depending on the number of resources to be traded in the market. The trading mechanism and the bidding tactics of the two different classes of traders in the market are described next.

3.1 Trading Mechanism

The fact that enterprise units may have more than one possible supplier for an input type increases the complexity of the already difficult combinatorial problem. We therefore introduce the idea of average supplier overhead per unit input as known variables for each enterprise agent. These values help them make decisions on which supplier and what quantity of a particular market resource to bid for. The Trading mechanism chosen is based on simultaneous ascending price adjustment as used in (Walsh, 2003) where all consumer agents and agents in the market are only allowed to review their bids upward. However, unlike the *SAMP-SB* protocol used in that work, where bidding is asynchronous, here, the bidding process is synchronous; this is to reduce the communication overhead of the auction mechanism. The algorithm is listed below:

Algorithm

- *Step 1: Initialize all trading agents and virtual markets*
- *Step 2: Consumer agents send bids at current market price (Adjust bid if not winning)*
- *Step 3: Enterprise Agents inspect number of winning sales bid*
- *Step 4: Enterprise Agents check if there is enough inputs to meet winning sales bid (if not, adjust procurement bid upward and increment price for sales bid)*
- *Step 5: Auctions compute new market price for all resources and posts bid results privately using the (k+1)st price mechanism*
- *Step 6: If no bid revision for all agents auction clears else go to Step 2*
- *Step 7: Terminate Auction*

The $(k+1)$st price mechanism is used at *step 5* of the algorithm to compute the current market going price and how much quantity every of a resource every bidder will be allocated at that going price. The traders can then review their bids accordingly if their bidding tactics permit it. A market clearing point is reached when no trader is willing to review their bids at the current going price. The traders are then allocated the quantities of the resource they bid for at their bid prices. It is guaranteed that this algorithm will reach the point of market equilibrium but the equilibrium point may differ from the point of optimality. This difference is a function of the bidding tactics of the trading agents in the market. The advantage of the simultaneous ascending price trading mechanism is that it allows bidding to move in only a single direction thereby increasing the speed with which the system reaches equilibrium since bidders can not offer bid prices in both the positive and negative sides of the going price in the market.

3.2 Bidding Tactics of Traders

This section is devoted to formulations of bidding tactics of each of the agent types in the network.

Consumers
A pure consumer is assumed to be a trader whose main interest is to use its endowment of numeraire resource (money) to satisfy a private utility need. The total endowment of consumers represents the total amount of possible investment into the supply network over the planning phase. The bidding tactic of consumer agents in the market is defined as follows:

$$p_c(g_i) = p'(g_i) + \alpha_c \quad if \quad p(g_i) < p'(g_i) \tag{4}$$

$$For \qquad g_i = \arg \max_{g_i \in G} (\min(e_c^{g_i}, p_c(g_i))) \tag{5}$$

$$s.t. \quad (e_c^{g_i} - p_c(g_i)) \geq 0; \quad \forall \, i \in G; \tag{6}$$

Where

$p_c(g_i)$ = new bid price of consumer c for resource i
$p'(g_i)$ = current market price for resource i
g_i = bid quantity for resource i
α_c = price bid adjustment variable of consumer c
e_c^i = endowment of consumer c for resource i

Equation (4) is the price bidding tactic for the consumer agent. A consumer agent adjusts its bid price by a value α_c if its last bid price is not enough to make it win all the quantity of that input. It therefore bids above the current market price for that input. Equation (5) represents the quantity of an input a consumer agent will bid for at its current bid value. It bids such that it can get as much units as possible at the current bid price subject to its total valuation for that input. Equation (6) guarantees individual rationality on the part of the consumer agent.

Producers
Every production enterprise belongs to a virtual market in which it produces. They however require inputs from other markets. This makes them both consumers and producers in the supply network. Their bidding tactic is formulated as:

$$p_w^{i+1}(g_o) = \begin{cases} \max(A, B); & if \ p_w^i(g_k) < p'(g_k) \\ p'(g_o) & otherwise \end{cases} \tag{7}$$

$$A = (p_w^i(g_o) + \beta_w) \tag{8}$$

$$B = (\sum_{k=1}^{m_{l+1}} p_w^{i+1}(g_k) + c_k^w)$$ (9)

$$p_w^{i+1}(g_k) = \max(p'(g_k), p_w^i(g_k) + \alpha_k^w)$$ (10)

$$g_o = \arg\max_{g_o \in G_L \subset G}(p'(g_o))$$ (11)

$$g_k = \arg\max_{g_k \in G_{L-1} \subset G}((p'(g_k) + c_k^w)) \quad \forall \ k = 1,2...m_{l-1}$$ (12)

s.t.

$$(\sum_{k=1}^{m_{l-1}} p_w(g_k) + c_k^w) \leq p'(g_o)$$ (13)

$$g_k \leq \max(g_k(SPH))$$ (14)

$$g_o \leq \max(g_o(SPH))$$ (15)

where

SPH = strategic planning time span

$p_w^{i+1}(g_o)$ = new bid price for output resource of enterprise w

$p_w^{i+1}(g_k)$ = new bid price for input resource k of enterprise w

$p'(g_k)$ = current market price of input resource k

β_w = sales bid price adjustment variable of enterprise w

c_k^w = overhead cost of procuring resource k for enterprise w

α_k^w = input bid price adjustment variable of resource k for enterprise w

g_k = bid quantity of enterprise w for input resource k

g_o = output resource bid quantity of enterprise w

$\max(g_k(SPH))$ = procurement budget estimate for resource k over strategic planning horizon

m_{l+1} = total number of markets in input layer $(l + 1)$

Equation (7) is the price bidding function of an enterprise agent for its product (selling price). It updates this price whenever there is a change in the price of any of its inputs. Equation (8) is a producer's adjusted selling bid price while equation (9) is the adjusted selling price due to variation in the price of an input resource. The price bid for inputs is done in much the same way as in the case of a consumer agent as shown in equation (10). Equation (11) is the output quantity bid policy. Equation (12) is the quantity bid function for inputs and is determined by the number of units the enterprise agent is willing to sell at that point in time. The equation shows how an enterprise agent selects the suppliers of an input by considering the allocation that will minimize its average overhead cost, i.e. the most input at the cheapest cost. The constraint of equation (13) is the non-negative profit constraint while equation (14) is the input budget constraint imposed by the strategic plan and equation (15) is the output capacity constraint also imposed by the strategic plan of the enterprise.

4 Simulation Experiments

4.1 Hypothetical Network Simulation

Experimental simulation was conducted with a hypothetical target supply network (Opadiji and Kaihara, 2008) made up of four layers. The first layer is the consumer layer while each of the three remaining layers is a production layer which consists of more than one market. Figure 2 shows the layout of this hypothetical network. In this network, a resource combination ratio of unity across the network is assumed. This means that every production enterprise requires one unit of all of their inputs to be able to produce their outputs; this is strictly for simplicity and there is no loss of generalization. Also, the bidding process in the virtual enterprise network is assumed to be synchronous and enterprise units bid for resources in bundles rather than in single units.

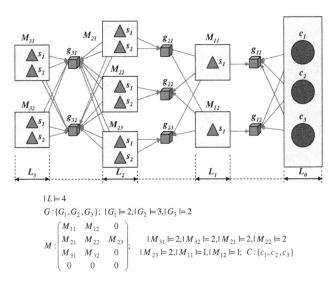

$|L| = 4$

$G : \{G_1, G_2, G_3\}; \ |G_1| = 2, |G_2| = 3, |G_3| = 2$

$$M : \begin{pmatrix} M_{11} & M_{12} & 0 \\ M_{21} & M_{22} & M_{23} \\ M_{31} & M_{32} & 0 \\ 0 & 0 & 0 \end{pmatrix}, \quad \begin{array}{l} |M_{31}| = 2, |M_{32}| = 2, |M_{21}| = 2, |M_{22}| = 2 \\ |M_{23}| = 2, |M_{11}| = 1, |M_{12}| = 1; \ C : \{c_1, c_2, c_3\} \end{array}$$

Fig. 2. Target convergent supply network

4.2 Simulation Results and Discussions

Initially, a production enterprise bids its maximum output with the hope of securing all the inputs it requires to meet the demand. However, as prices rise in its input markets and it has to bid higher for the inputs, it is possible for it not to be able to secure all its input at the current market price, therefore it drops bid in its output market to the size of the lowest amount of input units it is able to secure. This method prevents a producer from winning output bids without being able to secure enough inputs. Hence, the output of producers decrease in response to market states until the market clearing point is reached. Figure 3 shows changes in the output quantity bids of enterprise units in the supply network as trade progresses.

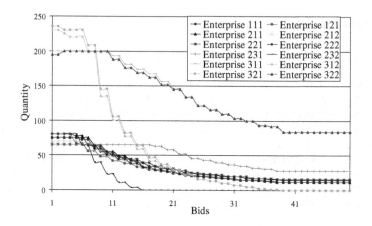

Fig. 3. Supply bids of production enterprises

The bidding tactics of enterprise units are such that they send bids to suppliers via the auction mechanism based on their perceived input and overhead cost as well as their maximum procurement budget for each supplier. If an enterprise needs more inputs than can be supplied by one supplier, it bids for the inputs from other suppliers in order of cost preference. After the market clears, suppliers of all market resources would have been selected and various supply quantities allocated to them by the auctioneers in the virtual enterprise network. Figures 4 and figure 5 show supply and demand allocations for members of the hypothetical supply network generated from simulation.

From figure 4, it is observed that some enterprise units have zero supply allocation. This is because the condition of the virtual markets as dictated by private bidding variables of each trader makes them uncompetitive at the present tactical planning horizon. It then means for example, that only *Enterprise* 31 of layer L_2 will supply all the units of market resource 3 of layer L_2 required by producers in layer L_1 because *Enterprise* 32 of the same layer has been eliminated from the allocation while both *Enterprise* 11 and *Enterprise* 12 will supply market resource 1 of layer L_2 because both remain competitive till market clearing. The same holds for all the order layers in the virtual enterprise.

In figure 5, the demand of all consuming traders in the supply network is shown; traders in layer L_3 are not included because they are assumed to be primary producers transforming resources from their natural state into outputs that can be used by used by enterprises in the next layer. In this figure it can also be observed that producers that are not selected for any supply allocation do not have any input allocated to them. This satisfies the individual rationality assumption in the auction mechanism. Figure 6 depicts link formation in the network.

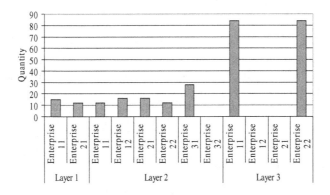

Fig. 4. Supply allocation of producers

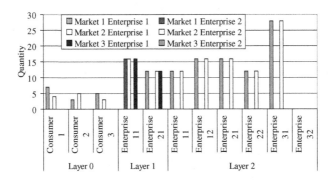

Fig. 5. Demand allocation of all traders

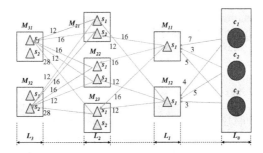

Fig. 6. Supplier selection and resource allocation

5 Conclusions

Supplier selection in a supply network is essentially a tactical level decision which requires compliance with the strategic procurement budgets of all the enterprises in the network. The increasing popularity of internet-based auctions makes it possible for autonomous enterprises to form virtual networks with low information latency that will help increase the flexibility of their value delivery system. Such virtual market places require robust mechanisms that will provide solutions acceptable to all participants where there is contention for resources. We have presented a market-based approach to solving the supplier selection problem in a typical convergent manufacturing supply network. This model obtains a satisficing solution which obtains budget balance at the expense of network efficiency. In this study, some parameters that affect the selection of suppliers by individual enterprise units were considered and the effects they have on the throughput which is a measure of network efficiency. However, a concrete algorithm on how to go about adjustment of some environmental variables using the many auctioneers in the market is still being researched. The complexity of this problem stems from the fact that there are many auctioneers in the virtual enterprise network; therefore a sort of cooperative interaction is required among them. The direction of future research activities will be towards finding correlations between the supplier selection parameters already defined and the effects of mediations by auctioneers on the network throughput and budget balance.

References

1. Camarinha-Matos, L.M.: The Virtual Enterprise Concept. Infrastructures for Virtual Enterprises, pp. 3–14. Kluwer, Dordrecht (1999)
2. Fingar, P., Belini, J.: The Real Time Enterprise. Meghan-Kiffer Press, Tampa Florida (2004)
3. Opadiji, J.F., Kaihara, T.: Optimal Resource Allocation in Supply Network with Competitive Market Concept. In: Proceedings of the 41st CIRP International Seminar on Manufacturing Systems, CD-ROM (2008)
4. Myerson, R.B., Satterthwaite, M.A.: Efficient Mechanism for Bilateral Trading. Journal of Economic Theory 29, 265–281 (1983)
5. Schwartz, B., et al.: Maximizing versus Satisficing: Happiness is a Matter of Choice. Journal of Personality and Psychology 83(5), 1178–1197 (2002)
6. Vickery, W.: Counterspeculations, Auctions, and Competitive Sealed Tenders. Journal of Finance 16, 8–37 (1961)
7. Vob, S., Woodruff, D.L.: Introduction to Computational Optimization Models for Production Planning in a Supply Chain, 2nd edn. Springer, Berlin (2006)
8. Walsh, W.E., Wellman, M.P.: Decentralized Supply Chain Formation: A Market Protocol and Competitive Equilibrium Analysis. Journal of Artificial Intelligence Research 19, 513–567 (2003)
9. Xia, M., Stallaert, J., Whinston, A.B.: Solving the Combinatorial Auction Problem. European Journal of Operations Research 164(1), 239–251 (2005)

Design and Implementation of a Multi-agent Framework for the Selection of Partners in Dynamic VEs*

Pedro Sanz Angulo and Juan José de Benito Martín

University of Valladolid, Industrial Engineering School,
Paseo del Cauce, 59, 47011 Valladolid, Spain
{psangulo,debenito}@eis.uva.es

Abstract. Many researchers agree that a key element in the VE succeed is the search, identification and selection of partners. This task is complex and is deeply influenced by the negotiation needs. This paper presents a simple but operational model of the selection process, in which partners are selected from a VE Breeding Environment. This model is the core of the multiagent platform that we have developed specifically for the selection of partners in the DVE context, which we also present in this paper.

Keywords: Dynamic Virtual Enterprise, VE Breeding Environments, Selection of Partners, Multiagent Technology, Expert System.

1 Introduction

In order to survive in the present context, companies must be able to permanently satisfy the desires of their customers, improving productive efficiency and adapting continuously to a global, competitive and dynamic environment [1]. However, added value creation for customers has become an increasingly complex process which requires the mix of different kinds of resources and expertise that companies do not necessarily have [2]. Companies are forced to cooperate, sometimes even with their direct competitors, which has led to the introduction of many organizational concepts and structures, highlighting among them the Dynamic Virtual Enterprise model.

There are many benefits associated to this business model: a faster access to new markets and new business opportunities; partners can overcome challenges, achieve business goals, access to resources (skills, know-how ,...), etc., which usually are outside the scope of a single firm; increases the utilization of assets, improves customer service and product quality, reduces risks, costs, etc., allows to achieve economies of scale, SMEs achieve international presence, etc.

However, to achive its large-scale implementation we need to overcome several obstacles, especially those arising from the selection of partners. This is undoubtedly

---

* This work stems from the participation of the authors in a research project funded by Junta de Castilla y León (Spain), title "The Information and Communication Technologies in the Organizational Networks Creation: Application in the Field of Child Abuse Prevention".

L.M. Camarinha-Matos et al. (Eds.): PRO-VE 2009, IFIP AICT 307, pp. 341–348, 2009.

the main reason why many researchers in different areas of knowledge have focused their efforts in this direction in last years. Therefore, it is necessary to offer innovative solutions that meet the demands of the DVE in an efficient way.

Based on these considerations, this paper presents an operational and innovative model of the selection process. This model is the core of the multiagent platform we have developed, and which we also present here, for this purpose.

2 Basic Considerations

DVE is an organizational model where a set of organizations, institutions or individuals (legally independent and geographically dispersed) develop a cooperation environment aimed at achieving a specific objective [1]. This environment allows the manufacture of products of higher quality and tailored to the needs of the market, incurring in a lower cost, a risk-sharing and a lower time to market, resulting in an improved response to the customers' requirements. In short, the goal is to create a best-of-everything organization [3] through the coalition of the complementary strengths of each member.

A DVE often evolves through four stages [4]: creation, operation, evolution and dissolution. Both in the creation and reconfiguration phases, the key element is the search, identification and selection of partners [4-6, etc.]. This task is complex and it is determined by the negotiation needs. It consumes, in addition, large amounts of time and resources which translates into a flexibility loss. The formation of a DVE requires, among other things, adequate information about potential partners, a certain degree of mutual trust, infrastructure to interoperate, common business practices and operational rules, etc. Ultimately, it depends on the potential partners are prepared to participate in such collaboration.

Guarantee this basic set of requirements could be a difficult challenge to achieve when temporal relations are considered. However, this does not happen with long-term collaborations that are not limited to a single business opportunity. Based on this idea a new organizational form has emerged to combine the advantages of DVE with those derived from long-term relationships. These new structures, known as VE Breeding Environments (VBE), are clubs of organizations prepared to work in long term relations and from which temporary coalitions emerge dynamically able to respond to different business opportunities [7].

3 The Model for the Selection of Partners

Based on the study of the different approaches existing in the literature to face the selection of partners in virtual architectures [5,8-10, etc.], we have created a generic and simple model with a multi-approach orientation which supports the advantages of the existing solutions and mitigates their weaknesses, a model that allows the formation of dynamic VEs could be a more effective and efficient process.

To achieve this goal, each involved actor can select the service providers in two different ways, as shown in Fig. 1.

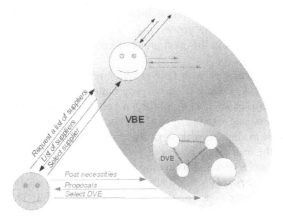

Fig. 1. Selection process model

First, when an entity needs a service it can ask the VBE the list of suppliers, and select one through a negotiation process that takes into account multiple criteria, both objective and subjective. On the other hand, it can also post its needs and expect a DVE (or sub-DVE) to be formed spontaneously in order to provide the requested service in an aggregate way. In both cases, the formation of the DVE is transparent with regard to the service requesting entity.

Allowing this simple choice our model makes possible the formation of DVEs that fit the different models and planning structures found in the literature and, in addition, any other possible combination. The model allows us the creation of any imaginable type of Dynamic VE and with the level of control we need in each moment (Fig. 2).

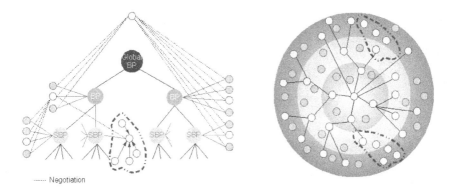

Fig. 2. Possible example of a DVE constituted from our model

4   The Multi-agent Platform

To support the partner selection process in these virtual environments, any software tool has to permit a flexible network reconfiguration using, in turn, the optimal set of available resources, both human and material, financial, etc. To achieve this purpose, and after an elaborate planning process, we decided to employ a technology that is producing excellent results in different areas of knowledge where it has been applied: the multi-agent systems.

Specifically, we have work with Jade as implementation tool. Jade is a FIPA compliant agent framework, widely used by programmers and researchers, which has a great number of qualities such as flexibility, a good management of the platform and the exchange of messages, extensibility of the code, allows to create distributed applications on different machines easily, extensive documentation, etc. Furthermore, it is free software and the user group is very active.

Starting with this election and following the steps in the methodology proposed by Nikraz, Caire and Bahri [11] specifically for Jade, we have analyzed, designed and finally developed a framework for the multiagent application. This framework will serve as a basis for developing multiagent tools tailor made for each specific application domain.

The analysis phase aims to clarify the problem without any concerns about the solution [11]. Based on both the functionality of the platform and the main use cases of the platform, and following an iterative process of refinement, we identified the main types of agents (and their responsibilities), users, resources and relationships, (Fig. 3) as well as the physical layout of each agent.

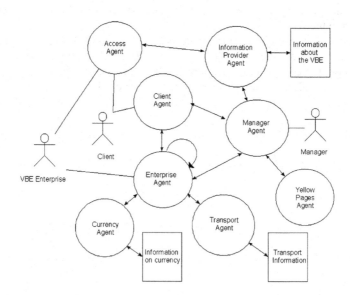

Fig. 3. Agent diagram for the multiagent platform

After analysis it comes the design phase which aims to specify the solution. The adopted methodology considers Jade [12] as implementation platform, focusing specifically on the constructs provided by it (classes, concepts, behaviors, etc.), which is an important advantage. This allows us to reach a level of detail that is enough to achieve a direct transition to the development phase without having to adapt the results of the design phase to the selected agent platform, and with the possibility of a significant amount of code being generated by an automatic tool. Obviously, this decision provides a significant improvement in time and also a clearer vision of how to move forward on implementation.

Now, in this phase, we bear in mind all the responsibilities related to an acquaintance relation with another agent, leading to an interaction table for each agent type (all roles of the identified interaction protocol are implemented as JADE behaviors). Besides, the MessageTemplate objects are also specified to be used in these behaviors to receive incoming messages (Table 1).

Table 1. Interaction table extract for the enterprise agent

Interaction	Resp	IP	Rol	With	Template
Negotiate with the provider agent	15	Contract net	I	Enterprise Agent	Conv-ID, Perf=CFP Prot=CFP, InReplyTo
Negotiate with the requesting agent	16	Contract net	R	Enterprise or Client Agent	Conv-ID, Perf=CFP Prot=CFP, InReplyTo

As regards the agent interactions with external resources, there are four active resources: these are the XML documents[1] with information about VBE members, the business processes, currency exchange and finally the necessary information to calculate the transportation cost or the distance between two locations. Based on the transducer approach the methodology suggests, we have used four different transducer elements with the necessary methods to have access and manage the information through DOM code. This action results in numerous advantages for the future: modularity, easy modification, reuse, etc.

Moreover, in our scenario there are four agents who need to interact with the users of the system: the enterprise agent, the client agent, the access agent and the manager agent. To make this user-agent interaction easier we have created a local graphical user interface (GUI) based on Swing for each one of these agents. Moreover, and given that agents and graphic elements are operating in different threads, we have used the jade.core.GuiAgent class specifically built for this purpose.

About ontologies, it is necessary to define an ontology for the application domain, the photovoltaic modules installation, which we have called the "main ontology": this ontology describes the business process architecture for the considered domain. However, we also use another set of ontologies associated with the different types of information we need for the operation of the platform. Specifically, we have created an ontology for the management which considers both users and their characteristics, their relations, the requested information, etc., and one for each auxiliary service we have defined (an ontology for the currency exchange and one for the transportation calculations).

---

[1] Since the necessary resources are XML documents, we have used an *ad hoc* content language through the XMLCodec codec developed by the Team JADE [12].

After analysis and design we developed the framework of our multiagent tool, the DVEBreeder platform. For this work we have used different software applications and plugins which are shown in Fig. 4.

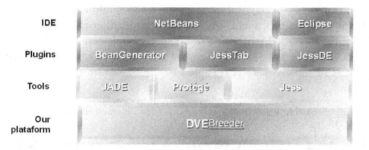

Fig. 4. Development tools overview

Taking into account all these considerations and the Jade peculiarities, we have created a distributed multiagent platform (Fig. 5). This platform consists of a main container in which the manager agent and the service agents reside (in addition to the AMS and DF agents of Jade) and several remote containers where we can find the access agents and those agents representing the platform users (client or enterprise).

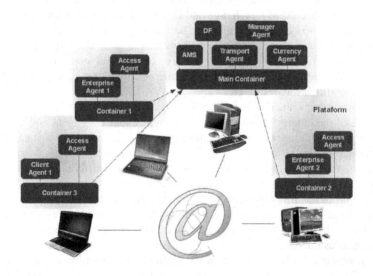

Fig. 5. The platform distributed architecture

Finally, we have built an open and modular GUI for each of these agents. This allows us a quick and easy customization to any business domain. In Fig. 6 some agent GUIs of the DVEBreeder platform are shown.

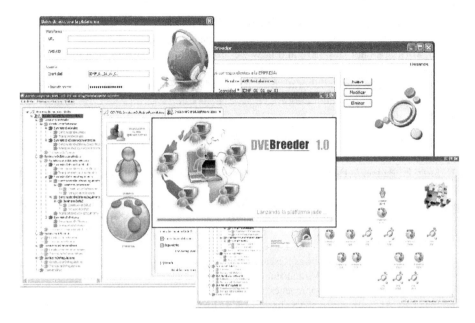

Fig. 6. Some DVEBreeder platform snapshots

As mentioned above, we have worked on the formation of DVE oriented on the installation of photovoltaic modules. In this platform agents make their decisions based on a system of rules and facts implemented by Jess, a rule engine and scripting environment written entirely in Sun's Java language by Ernest Friedman-Hill [13]. By studying different scenarios we have validated both the platform and the initial operational model. Furthermore, we have proved that the coalition of multiagent technology and expert systems is a correct approach to addressing the selection of partners in the DVE context.

5   Conclusions

Companies must begin to adapt their structures to a new business model, the Dynamic Virtual Enterprise paradigm, if they want to ensure their survival in the present complex context. However, there are still some challenges to be overcome for the DVE becomes a reality on a large scale. One of such challenges is the right selection of partners because of its high relevance in the final product or service and, consequently, in the success of the DVE.

In an attempt to overcome these difficulties, in this paper we have presented a simple but innovative and comprehensive model to select the most appropriate partners regardless of the control level. Based on this model we have developed the framework of a distributed multiagent application capable of responding to the selection process needs.

Through the personalization of this platform we can deal with the creation process of any kind of Dynamic VE. Indeed, we have developed a multiagent platform for the formation of DVE aimed at the installation of photovoltaic modules in which agents make their decisions based on a set of rules and facts implemented by Jess.

Our work does not stop here and now we are working on customizing this platform to the real and specific case of the DVO creation aimed at child abuse prevention. For this work we have the collaboration of REA [14], a spanish regional association for the Defense of Children and Youth.

References

1. Sanz, P.: Partner Selection in Dynamic Virtual Enterprises. Ph.D thesis. University of Valladolid (2008)
2. Beer, M., Eisenstat, R.A., Spector, B.: Why Change Programs don't Produce Change. Harvard Business Review 68(6), 158–166 (1990)
3. Adams, W.M., Wallas, R.M., Sengupta, A.: Collaborative Commerce: The Agile Virtual Enterprise Model. Pushing the Digital Frontier: Insights into the Changing Lands of E-Business. Penn State eBusiness Research Center, 242–262 (2001)
4. Camarinha-Matos, L.M.: Virtual Enterprise Modeling and Support Infrastructures: Applying Multi-agent System Approaches. In: Luck, M., Mařík, V., Štěpánková, O., Trappl, R. (eds.) ACAI 2001 and EASSS 2001. LNCS (LNAI), vol. 2086, pp. 335–364. Springer, Heidelberg (2001)
5. Petersen, S.A.: An Agent-based Approach to Support the Formation of Virtual Enterprises. Ph.D thesis. Norwegian University of Science & Technology (2003)
6. Fischer, M., Jähna, H., Teich, T.: Optimizing the Selection of Partners in Production Networks. Robotics and Computer-Integrated Manufacturing 20, 593–601 (2004)
7. Afsarmanesh, H.: (coord.). Key Components, Features, and Operating Principles of the Virtual Breeding Environment. ECOLEAD Deliverables (2005)
8. Rocha, A., Oliveira, E.: An electronic market architecture for the formation of virtual enterprises. In: Infrastructures for Virtual Enterprises, pp. 421–432. Kluwer, B.V., Dordrecht (1999)
9. Ouzounis, E.K.: An Agent-Based Platform for the Management of Dynamic Virtual Enterprises. Ph.D thesis. Universität Berlin (2001)
10. Rabelo, R., Camarinha-Matos, L.M., Vallejos, R.: Agent-based Brokerage for Virtual Enterprise Creation in the Moulds Industry. In: E-business and Virtual Enterprises, pp. 281–290. Kluwer Academic Publishers, Dordrecht (2000)
11. Nikraz, M., Caire, G., Bahri, P.A.: A Methodology for the Analysis and Design of Multi-Agent Systems Using JADE. International Journal of Computer Systems Science and Engineering 21(2) (2006)
12. Jade – Java Agent Development Framework,
    http://jade.tilab.com/index.html
13. Jess – the Rule Engine for the JavaTM Platform, http://www.jessrules.com/
14. REA – Asociación Castellano Leonesa para la Defensa de la Infancia y la Juventud,
    http://www.asociacionrea.org/

Part 11

e-Procurement and Collaborative Procurement

Collaborative Procurement within Enterprise Networks: A Literature Review, a Reference Framework and a Case Study

Luca Cagnazzo, Paolo Taticchi, Gianni Bidini, and Mohamed Sameh

Department of Industrial Engineering, University of Perugia,
Via Duranti 67, Perugia, Italy
luca.cagnazzo@unipg.it,
paolo.taticchi@unipg.it,
gbid@mach.ing.unipg.it

Abstract. Collaboration among companies is nowadays a success leverage from those involved, especially for SMEs. The networking advantages are several and among them, reducing costs is a critical one. Costs reduction due to the possibility of Collaborative Procurement (CP) among partners is one of the most important achievements in a network. While the literature available offers good bases for managing single contractor procurement issues, little research addresses the case of CP within Enterprise Networks (ENs). This paper explore the mentioned issue and proposes a general framework for managing CP in ENs, those with the Virtual Development Office (VDO) structure. The findings from the application of the framework proposed in an Italian network are highlighted so as to provide preliminary results and drive future research.

Keywords: Enterprise Network, Collaborative Procurement, SME, Virtual Development Office, Case Study.

1 Introduction

Several forms of structured collaborative organizations are growing up in the last decade, with different degree of formal relationships. Industrial clusters, districts, Virtual Organizations (VOs), Virtual Enterprises (VEs), Virtual Breeding Environment (VBE) [1], Collaborative Networks (CNs), are samples of collaborative enterprise networks. The most important advantages of these typologies of stable collaborations can be reassumed in developing new products/services, sharing new knowledge and risks, being part of critical mass and reducing costs [2], [3] and [4]. For the last purpose, one of the most important action within a collaborative environment is the Collaborative Procurement (CP) among partners, since through global purchasing with common suppliers it is notably possible to reduce costs and risks, as well as increase the contractual influence since the achievement of a sufficient critical mass. The article is organized as follows. In Section 2 we discuss the CP concepts, followed by a literature review on this topic in Section 3 that highlights the evolutions of the CP concept during the last decades. In section 4 we illustrate the particular network model, the Virtual Development Model

L.M. Camarinha-Matos et al. (Eds.): PRO-VE 2009, IFIP AICT 307, pp. 351–360, 2009.
© IFIP International Federation for Information Processing 2009

(VDO), in which the new CP framework has been adopted: the case study is indeed discussed in Section 5, considering the GPT (Gruppo Poligrafico Tiberino) success case as the first Italian network adopting the VDO structure. Concluding remarks and further developments are presented in Section 6.

2 Collaborative Procurement Concept

CP has so far been loosely defined in the existing literature. It is referred to as horizontal cooperative purchasing, group purchasing, collaborative purchasing, collective purchasing, joint purchasing, consortium purchasing, shared purchasing, bundled purchasing, etc. And this list goes on to about a hundred terms [5]. As a concept, the CP covers a very wide spectrum of possible definition, related to the systems in which it is applied, the involved actors, the relationship among subjects, etc. However a basilar definition is: CP is an effective way for more than one client, contractor, consultant or supplier to join together to procure works, services, materials or goods, share expertise, promote efficiency and deliver value for particular advantages in the delivery of a project, series of projects or service objectives [6]. In the literature, several general types of cooperation for CP are distinguished. A main distinction is between horizontal CP, i.e. buyer-buyer or seller-seller cooperation, and vertical CP, i.e. buyer-seller cooperation [7]. When referring to horizontal CP, concepts apply such as shared service centers, horizontal alliances, and horizontal cooperative purchasing. When referring to vertical cooperation, concepts apply such as co-makership, vertical alliances, and public-private partnerships. In this paper, we focus on horizontal CP, in terms of buyer-buyer actors (companies belonging to the same network). The main advantages of CP are more or less similar to advantages of coordinated or centralized purchasing in a single organization. The advantages follow from factors such as economies of scale [8], a reduced number of transactions between suppliers and buyers [9], improved relationships with suppliers and other organizations in the purchasing group, and stronger negotiation positions. Reported disadvantages of CP follow from factors such as an increased complexity of the purchasing process and loss of flexibility and control. However, the advantages of cooperative purchasing outweigh the disadvantages for many situations in the public and private sector [5].

3 Literature Review

A brief history of the CP concept can be developed starting from the early 1970s, when purchasing was viewed as having a passive role in the business organization [10]. This view was supported at that time by many strategists who stated that purchasing could be described as an administrative rather than a strategic function. There were, however, some people, for example, [11] and [12], who stressed in their articles the need to include purchasing in corporate planning. According to [13] the 1980s were a period of shifting attitudes towards the role of purchasing in corporate strategy. As a function, purchasing was claimed to be capable of being a source of competitive advantage for the business. [14] proposed that purchasing can contribute to corporate strategy in four different ways: monitor supply market, interpret the meaning of these trends for the firm, identify the materials and services required to support company and strategic business unit strategies and develop supply options. [15] discussed the contribution of purchasing in terms of strategic resources and the need to manage key materials in relation to product/market objectives of the particular businesses. In the end of 1980s [16] captured the spirit of the pursuit of world-class manufacturing and the need for continuous improvement in terms of cost reduction and improvements in quality, delivery, getting new products to market faster and customer responsiveness. The research focus during the 1990s appears to have shifted towards integration, and the means by which the procurement can work to become recognized as a more significant contributor to the company's success [13]. Over the past few years, there has been an outstanding shift in the way many companies approach buyer-seller relationships. Recent years have seen an increased interest and involvement in buyer-seller partnerships, which tend to be longer term, ongoing, and based on a sharing of the risk of the relationship outcomes [17]. [18] coined the term "lean production" to emphasize both minimal use of input resources for greatly increased output and the fact that the complete system requires coordination of all internal customers and suppliers with their external counterparts. [19] enhanced that idea in his book "Beyond Partnership".

From '90s the literature has exponentially investigated this topic; in particular the long tradition of CP has led to two outcomes. On the one hand, there seems to be a lot of literature mentioning purchasing groups or purchasing consortia. On the other hand, research on cooperative purchasing is still in its infancy [20].

Most sources on CP are found in textbooks and professional publications are often descriptive. Thus, especially compared to vertical buyer-seller cooperation, horizontal buyer-buyer cooperation has not been a major research area until now [21]. Academic research that has been done on CP has contributed to describing and analyzing several CP topics under different settings and circumstances. The existing research findings are categorized as follows:

- Advantages and disadvantages of cooperative purchasing [22], [23] and [24];
- Coordination structures of purchasing groups [25] and [26];
- Critical success factors, drivers, and preconditions for cooperative purchasing [27], [28], and [29];
- Development of purchasing groups over time [30], [31] and [32] ;
- Formation of purchasing groups in electronic marketplaces [33] and [34].

The academic sources described above do cover relevant topics. Still, some gaps exist in the CP literature. We found gaps in the research method used, as little large-scale empirical research exists. Moreover literature on CP within stable enterprise networks is practically inexistence. For this reason, new researches, methodologies, reference framework and application of the developed theories through case studies should be built up.

4 The VDO Model

The Virtual Development Office (VDO) model has been developed within the Italian research project MIGEN[1], during which the University of Perugia supported the development of an enterprise network from its first steps. The aim of the project was to define a conceptual organizational model for enterprise networks, in order to increase the competitiveness of the SMEs involved. The approach proposed is based on the creation of an independent subject, the VDO, GPT in the case study, which acts as a leading actor, and it has the role of creating, coordinating and managing a community of enterprises [35]. Particularly, it should be the market intelligence of the network, continuously catching business opportunities in the market and positioning the network on it. Moreover, the VDO is the permanent interface to public institutions, financial institutions and research centres. A proactive collaboration with such subjects is a leverage factor in today business. The VDO activities presented above are "external" to the network. However, the VDO also has a crucial role inside the network life. First of all, it has the role of maintaining and consolidating the trust of companies involved in the network by generating and promoting a long-term alliance. By acting as a central player on respect of the "business ecosystem", it promotes both the willing of cooperation, both the readiness to collaborate each time a business opportunity, which for a network can be defined as a "collaboration opportunity" (CO) arises. From a value chain point of view, particularly interesting is the creation of the Virtual Enterprise (VE) or Virtual Organization (VO) for specific business opportunities, since the processes that constitute the value chain, i.e. those activities that represent the value proposition of the network and lead to customer satisfaction will be split amongst the members of the network that are participating in the collaborative opportunity.

5 The EASM Framework

This section presents the CP framework, named EASM (Exploring, Analyzing, Selecting, Managing) that has been developed for VDO based networks, and tested in the GPT (Gruppo Poligrafico Tiberino) network case study. A representation of the proposed framework is provided in Figure 1. The VDO has the initial task of Exploring the network, in order to catch potential Collaborative Procurement Opportunities (CPOs) for the partners. During the Exploring phase the VDO explores the most common purchased products by the network companies, and gives a classification of them, with different weights, in terms of costs, volumes, possible buyers, etc. Tools that can support this phase are questionnaires, surveys, interviews, an so on. This action allows the VDO from one side to deeply know the network companies needs, from the other to realize an initial study on the most consumed items or services. The second phase of the CP framework is the "Analyzing" one. During this phase the VDO carefully evaluates the investigated potential CPOs, in order to select those with most potential benefit for the network and possibility of success.

---

[1] MIGEN (the name comes from the Italian acronym for Innovative Models for Enterprises Network Management) is a research project supported by Italian government with the PRIN (Research Project of National Interest) program. The project involved the Universities of Perugia, Florence and Genoa and it focused on the development of specific models and tools for managing networks of enterprises.

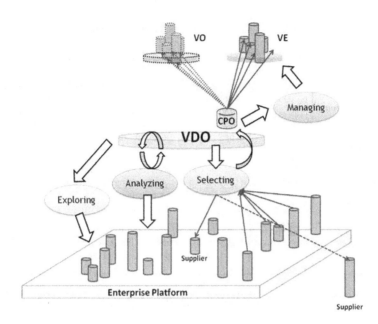

Fig. 1. The EASM Collaborative Procurement Framework for VDO based networks

A validation of the weights correlated to the potential POs is performed by the VDO, in order to avoid incorrect evaluations of these indicators that can lead to financial, economic, structural and competitive losses. Moreover, in this phase the VDO performs an analysis of the potential supplier (that can be internal or external to the network), through supply-chain management and buyer-seller relationship optimization criteria; and it evaluates the cost of the desired products/services, by comparing them with the actual costs of single buyers (companies). Additionally, the VDO individuates the strengths and weaknesses of each potential CPO, and it define a set of indicators that consider economic, financial, trust and reputational indexes. Thus, in this phase the VDO selects only the most highest ranked CPOs and excludes the others with lower evaluation. In the Selecting phase, the VDO selects the companies of the network that can be involved in each of the identified CPOs, as well as the supplier(s) for the CP. In the current phase the VDO realizes the Virtual Enterprise (VE) or the Virtual Organiza-tion (VO) (depending if also institutions are involved in the opportunity) for each se-lected CPO. The VE/VO are the groups of companies selected by the VDO that will benefit of the CPOs advantages. The last phase, the Managing one, is characterized by the management of the VE/VO by the VDO during the projects. In this phase the VDO has the important role of coordinating the CP processes, maintaining trust among part-ners, guaranteeing intellectual property rights, optimizing the supply-chain furniture. The VDO can eventually modify the VE/VO actor participation and change the VE/VO structure and parameters, in order to assure increasing benefits for the entire network. The EASM model has been realize by the authors following the Critical Success Factors (CSFs) for implementing a CP approach expressed in the literature during the last dec-ades. In particular a discussion of the model based on the CSFs is proposed in Table 1. The application of the model to the case study is presented in the next paragraph.

Table 1. CSFs for CP and evaluation of the EASM framework

CSFs	References in literature	EASM framework managed by the VDO
1) Commitment and internal support	[36], [30], [27], [37], [38] and [39]	1. All member contributes are comparable in terms of resources and efforts; 2. All members have internal support; 3. All members rarely change representatives; 4. The VDO acts as a leader; 5. In total, sufficient efforts and activities are contributed to be able to run the group successfully;
2) Communication	[40], [41], [42] and [39]	6. VDO communicates and keeps each other up-to-date regarding current projects; 7. VDO communicates and keeps each other up-to-date regarding new potential projects;
3) Allocation of gains and costs	[43]	8. Fair allocation of gains and costs;
4) Formality of the group	[6], [44], [45], [30], [37] , [31] and [39]	9. VDO is a formal structured stable network; 10. VDO make engagements regarding important decision moments; 11. VDO reports important performances of the group periodically;
5) Interorganizational trust	[46], [36], [47], [48], [37] and [49]	12. All members are honest and loyal due to the affiliation at the VDO network; 13. All members like each other personally; 14. All members meet one's commitments;
6) Knowledge on how to cooperate	[37] and [31]	15. All members contribute unique knowledge;
7) Organization	[25]	16. All members have a similar influence on the group activities and decisions; 17. Voluntary participation;
8) Uniformity of the members	[50], [41] and [51]	18. All members have similar objectives to participate in the group; 19. All members have similar organizational cultures; 20. All members have similar procedures.

6 The Case Study

The EASM CP framework has been tested in an Italian network of 20 companies belonging to the printing and packaging sector, namely the Gruppo Poligrafico Tiberino (GPT). Through the Exploring phase authors investigated the most common products/services purchased in the network. Since the manufacturing nature of the partners, several products/services belonging to the manufacturing sector have been individuated through the use of a questionnaire, such as for example pallets, cardboard, paper, transports, software applications, services, etc..

The Exploring and Analyzing phase, where classifications and multi-criteria evaluation were performed as suggested in paragraph 5, resulted in the identification of 3 potential CPOs: pallets, cardboard and paper. These choices are justified since the purchasing of these products within the network covered very high volumes, as shown in Table 2. During the Analyzing phase the best suppliers were identified and the VEs/VOs could have been built up in the Selecting phase. Table 2 summarizes the three CPOs actually performed in GPT, by highlighting the total volumes in terms of number of products and monetary value, the average cost of purchasing and the average saving in terms of money percentage.

Table 2. CPOs information

CPOs	Volumes				Average money saving	
	No. Prod. Per year	Total amount	Average price/product	Percentage	Total amount per year
Pallet	90.550 pz	602 K€/year	6,64€/pz	22,78%	137 K€
Cardboard boxes	2.641.500 pz	1,4 M€/year	0,53€/pz	11,80%	165,2 K€
Paper	3000 tons	3 M€/year	1000 €/tons	5,67%	170,1 K€

As shown in Table 2, an average cost reduction has been realized through a CP action in GPT: 472,3 K€ is the total amount saved in 2008 by GPT. This money saving is due to an increasing contractual power of the companies with the suppliers.

Companies that were before buying raw materials from different sellers, can now benefit of best prices, since the very high requested volumes. Table 2 shows high values of average money saving percentage for each CPO; this is an important result, since the identified CPOs involve low value-added products. Thus, direct costs have significantly been reduced by the application of the EASM framework, achieving the most important Collaborative Procurement objective.

7 Conclusions

This paper has investigated the leading topic of Collaborative Procurement within enterprise networks. After the definition of what "collaborative procurement" is, the literature available has been critically reviewed so as to highlight consolidate knowledge and lacks. Based on the learning from the literature, the authors presented a CP framework, EASM, that has been developed for an innovative typology of business networks, namely the Virtual Development Office (VDO) networks. The model proposed offers a step by step methodology for implementing CP initiatives within networks, and extend its applicability more generally to all networks having a central hub.

Future research will focus on multiple field test of the model, so as to identify criticalities of application and optimizing therefore the methodology based on feedbacks. Moreover, the applicability to other typology of business networks should be evaluated.

References

1. Camarinha-Matos, L.M., Afsarmanesh, H.: Elements of a base VE infrastructure. Journal of Computers in Industry 51(2), 139–163 (2003)
2. MacCarthy, T., Golicic, S.: Implementing collaborative forecasting to improve supply chain performances. International Journal of Physical Distribution & Logistic Management 32(6), 431–454 (2002)
3. McLaren, T., Head, M.: Supply Chain collaboration alternatives: understanding the expected costs and benefits. Internet Research: Electronic Networking Applications and Policy 2(4), 348–364 (2000)

4. Horvath, L.: Collaboration: the key to value creation in supply chain management. Supply Chain Management: An International Journal 6(5), 205–217 (2001)
5. Schotanus, F., Telgen, J.: Developing a typology of organisational forms of cooperative purchasing. Journal of Purchasing & Supply Management 13, 53–68 (2007)
6. Bakker, E., Walker, H., Harland, C.: Organizing for collaborative procurement: An initial conceptual framework. In: Thai, K., Piga, G. (eds.) Advancing public procurement: Practices, innovation and knowledge-sharing, pp. 14–44. PrAcademics Press, Boca Raton (2006)
7. Hendrick, T.E.: Purchasing consortiums: Horizontal alliances among firms buying common goods and services: What? Who? Why? How? Tempe: Center for Advanced Purchasing Studies (1997)
8. Rozemeijer, F.: Creating corporate advantage in purchasing. Ph.D. dissertation, Eindhoven (the Netherlands): Technical University of Eindhoven (2000)
9. Tella, E., Virolainen, V.M.: Motives behind purchasing consortia. International Journal of Production Economics, 93–94, 161–168 (2005)
10. Ammer, D.S.: Is your purchasing department a good buy? Harvard Business Review, 136–159 (1974)
11. Farmer, S.H.: The impact of supply markets on corporate planning. Long Range Planning, 10–16 (1972)
12. Kisser, G.E.: Elements of purchasing strategy. Journal of Purchasing and Materials Management, 3–7 (1976)
13. Ellram, L.M., Carr, A.S.: Strategic purchasing: a history and review of the literature. International Journal of Purchasing and Materials Management 11 (1994)
14. Browning, J.M., Zahriskie, N.B., Huellmantel, A.B.: Strategic purchasing planning. Journal of Purchasing and Materials Management 19, 24 (1983)
15. Spekman, R.E.: Competitive procurement strategies. Building strength and reducing vulnerability. Long Range Planning 18(1), 94–99 (1985)
16. Morgan, J.P.: Are you aggressive enough for the 1990s. Purchasing, 50–57 (1989)
17. Ellram, L.M.: Partnering pitfalls and success factors. International Journal of Purchasing and Materials Management 36 (1995)
18. Womack, J., Jones, D., Rooa, D.: The Machine that Changed the World. Macmillan Publishing Company, New York (1990)
19. Lamming, R.C.: Beyond Partnership: Strategies for Innovation and Lean Supply. Prentice-Hall, Englewood cliffs (1993)
20. Essig, M.: Purchasing consortia as symbiotic relationships. European Journal of Purchasing and Supply Management 6(1), 13–22 (2000)
21. Ellram, L.M.: A managerial guideline for the development and implementation of purchasing partnerships. International Journal of Purchasing and Materials Management 27(3), 2–8 (1991)
22. Ball, D., Pye, J.: Library purchasing consortia: The UK periodicals supply market. Learned Publishing 13(1), 25–35 (2000)
23. Evans, R.G.: Public health insurance: The collective purchase of individual care. Health Policy 7(2), 115–134 (1987)
24. Nollet, J., Beaulieu, M.: Should an organization join a purchasing group? Supply Chain Management 10(1), 11–17 (2005)
25. Enthoven, A.C.: On the ideal market structure for third-party purchasing of health care. Social Science and Medicine 39(10), 1413–1424 (1994)
26. Galaskiewicz, J.: Interorganizational relations. Annual Review of Sociology 11, 281–304 (1985)

27. Doucette, W.R.: Influences on member commitment to group purchasing organizations. Journal of Business Research 40(3), 183–189 (1997)
28. Exworthy, M., Peckham, S.: The contribution of coterminosity to joint purchasing in health and social care. Health and Place 4(3), 233–243 (1998)
29. Huber, B., Sweeney, E., Smyth, A.: Purchasing consortia and electronic markets: A procurement direction in integrated supply chain management. Electronic Markets 14(4), 284–294 (2004)
30. D'Aunno, T.A., Zuckerman, H.S.: A life-cycle model of organizational federations: the case of hospitals. Acadamy of Management Review 12(3), 534–545 (1987)
31. Johnson, P.F.: The pattern of evolution in public sector purchasing consortia. International Journal of Logistics: Research and Applications 2(1), 57–73 (1999)
32. Nollet, J., Beaulieu, M.: The development of group purchasing: an empirical study in the healthcare sector. Journal of Purchasing and Supply Management 9(1), 3–10 (2003)
33. Granot, D., Sošić, G.: Formation of alliances in internet-based supply exchanges. Management Science 51(1), 92–105 (2005)
34. Yuan, S.T., Lin, Y.H.: Credit based group negotiation for aggregate sell/buy in e-markets. Electronic Commerce Research and Applications 3(1), 74–94 (2004)
35. Botarelli, M., Taticchi, P., Cagnazzo, L.: The Virtual Development Office framework for business Networks: a case study from the Umbrian packaging district. In: Pervasive Collaborative Networks. IFIP International Federation for Information Processing, vol. 283, pp. 611–618 (2008)
36. Bakker, E., Walker, H., Harland, C., Warrington, J.: The effect of collaborative purchasing structures on managing cooperation. In: IPSERA conference proceedings, San Diego, United States (2006)
37. Hoffmann, W., Schlosser, R.: Success factors of strategic alliances in small and medium-sized enterprises, an empirical study. Longe Range Planning 34(3), 357–381 (2001)
38. Kanter, R.M.: Collaborative advantage. Harvard Business Review 72(4), 96–108 (1994)
39. Niederkofler, M.: The evolution of strategic alliances: Opportunities for managerial influence. Journal of Business Venturing 6(4), 237–257 (1991)
40. Anderson, J.C., Narus, J.A.: A model of distributor firm and manufacturer firmworking partnerships. Journal of Marketing 54(1), 42–58 (1990)
41. Laing, A., Cotton, S.: Patterns of inter-organizational purchasing: Evolution of consortia-based purchasing amongst GP fundholders. European Journal of Purchasing and Supply Management 3(2), 83–91 (1997)
42. Mohr, J., Spekman, R.: Characteristics of partnership success: Partnership attributes, communication behavior, and conflict resolution techniques. Strategic Management Journal 15(2), 135–152 (1994)
43. Heijboer, G.: Mathematical and statistical analysis of initial purchasing decisions. Ph.D. dissertation, Enschede (the Netherlands): University of Twente (2003)
44. Corsten, D., Zagler, M.: Purchasing consortia and internet technology. In: IPSERA conference proceedings, Belfast and Dublin, pp. 975–986 (1999)
45. Das, T.K., Teng, B.S.: Alliance constellations: A social exchange perspective. The Academy of Management Review 27(3), 445–456 (2002)
46. Aulakh, P.S., Kotabe, M., Sahay, A.: Trust and performance in cross border marketing partnerships: A behavioral approach. Journal of International Business Studies 27(5), 1005–1032 (1996)
47. Browning, L.D., Beyer, J.M., Shetler, J.C.: Building cooperation in a competitive industry: SEMATECH and the semiconductor industry. Academy of Management Journal 38(1), 113–151 (1995)

48. Das, T.K., Teng, B.S.: Trust, control, and risk in strategic alliances: An integrated framework. Organization Studies 22(2), 251–283 (2001)
49. Gulati, R.: Does familiarity breed trust? The implications of repeated ties for contractual choice in alliances. Academy of Management Journal 38(1), 85–112 (1995)
50. Woolthuis, K.R.: Sleeping with the enemy: trust, dependence and contract in interorganizational relationships. Ph.D. dissertation, Enschede (the Netherlands): University of Twente (1999)
51. Polychronakis, Y., Syntetos, A.: 'Soft' supplier management related issues: An empirical investigation. International Journal of Production Economics 106, 431–449 (2007)

eProcurement for Industrial Maintenance Services

Maik Herfurth, Axel Meinhardt, Jörg Schumacher, and Peter Weiß

FZI Research Center for Information Technology, Haid-und-Neu-Straße 10-14,
D-76131 Karlsruhe, Germany
{herfurth,meinhardt,schumach,weiss}@fzi.de

Abstract. E-procurement solutions can deliver great cost-saving potential for purchasing. But services have not generally been considered as a part of these cost-saving measures. The process of service procurement is often argued to be more complex and less standardized than material procurement. In this paper we propose solutions and standards for service procurement.

Keywords: Service Procurement, Service Specification, Service Classification, eProcurement.

1 Introduction

The paper looks at interoperability issues in the context of e-procurement for industrial maintenance services and asset management. The maintenance of industry facilities and assets challenges currently industry. The components of e-procurement are: back-end-system of buyer, e-proprocurement-system of buyer, electronic catalogs for service specifications and back-end-system of seller. E-Procurement can be further subdivided into e-ordering and e-sourcing in correspondence with its support to operational procurement and strategic procurement. More precisely, e-ordering is aimed at the realization of faster, easier and decentralized operational procurement processes at least possible cost which echoes the fact that e-ordering concentrates on reduction of procurement process costs. Today's, addressed industry domain is lacking shared e-business standards which allow classification of product data, customer data, material data, etc.. Known standards are UNSPSC [19] and eCl@ss [18] which intend to improve electronic data exchange between business partners. Corporate data management and master data management along the value chain are thus hot topics in industry today [14]. We will identify that standardization and harmonization of e-business solutions require harmonized business processes, good data quality and precise definitions of interfaces.

2 Objectives

Industrial services compass a high volume at industrial companies, mostly up to 50 per cent of total procurement volume. Therefore service processes cause actually high costs in most companies. But because of the high complexity of service products, there weren't a lot of attempts to achieve cost saving with electronic business transfer

L.M. Camarinha-Matos et al. (Eds.): PRO-VE 2009, IFIP AICT 307, pp. 361–368, 2009.

in this area. For the procurement of services, e-business processes are barely distinct and standardized as with pure material products. There is no standardized electronic trading by means of a catalogue like for material. Integrative, systematic e-business procedures and interfaces are missing to execute the electronic data exchange of services inclusive used material between customers and suppliers in a standardized way. The paper derives requirements for service procurement from a real life scenario of supply chains for industrial maintenance services at hand. We look at supply chains of small service providers which offer industrial maintenance services to large often globally operating companies. It is analyzed, how procurement for services can be described and automated using e-business standards and harmonized descriptions. Incipiently, basic concepts, definitions, historical backgrounds and examples of relevant subject areas are introduced. This includes in particular the general procurement, characteristics of services, ways to model a business and technical aspects. Furthermore, requirements for describing the organization of a business, the work process, the emerging data and the implementation in information technology are presented.

3 State-of-the-Art

This section provides a brief overview of state-of-the-art and related work. We outline existing challenges and limitations as well as shortfalls of current applications, solutions and approaches of service procurement. The reader gets acquainted with basic definitions and core concepts.

E-procurement supports the strategic- and operational procurement with electronic means to optimize the purchasing process taking into account the key indexes of process cost and process results [12]. The procurement process can be divided into strategic procurement and operational procurement according to different procurement tasks. Strategic procurement encompasses those, which undertake the function of forming general procurement conditions and configurations in order to create premises for operational procurement and to improve the operating efficiency of procurement from a centralized perspective. Operational procurement comprehends contrarily concrete transaction processing and places its emphasis on satisfying needs on specific objects in time rather than contributing to the procurement strategy. Service Procurement implicates its own challenges to be looked into in the remainder.

3.1 eBusiness and Industrial Maintenance

Industrial Maintenance is "the combination of all technical, administrative and managerial actions during the life cycle of an item intended to retain it in, or restore it to, a state in which it can perform the required function" [13]. Industrial maintenance belongs to the category of indirect products. Indirect procurement can be further divided into two kinds: ORM (Office Products and Travel Services) and MOR (Maintenance, Repair and Operating) [23]. The former refers to goods and services required in the administrative area to keep routine operation of company. The latter includes besides the overhaul and maintenance items also materials for research and development. In the remainder we shall look in particular at the latter, procurement of indirect services and related products. A variety of standards address areas related to e-procurement, like identification, classification, categorization, communication and process management. Most of those approaches focus on information about physical products. Eprocurement processes as service procurement processes can be seen and classified in two different objectives: the public (external) processes and the private (internal) processes. The public processes are characterized by their type of collaboration with different stakeholders. They are performed outside of the borders of the organization. The participants in these processes are suppliers in a supply chain scenario, partners in a virtual enterprise scenario and customers in a B2B scenario. Private processes are characterized by its internal focus within an enterprise. They are performed within a company by its organization. In our scenario we focus on suppliers of industrial maintenance service processes and customers from the industry. Related work can be found in [1] [2] [3] [4] [5] [7] [8] [9] [10] [11]. Products and Services Categorization Standards (PSCS) are flourishing as they seem to offer to overcome organizational and IT system barriers. PSCS are reflecting domain consensus about how products or services can be grouped and described.

3.2 Service Procurement

For manufacturing companies, the procurement has an important role. Every Euro which can be saved with the purchasing of goods and services, doesn't have to be generated as additional earning. The savings of procurement will be reflected directly in the success of the company. But for the procurement of services, it is a different picture: in catalogue systems and service specifications, there is only a summarized position for services along with the wide structure for articles. This entails a lack of transparency of costs for the services. But the expenditure for services is rising: services for cleaning service, facility management as well as maintenance and reparation. The consequences are raising expenses for service for the whole company. Besides material procurement, service procurement is the most requested good. In our days material procurement and ebusiness collaborate closely and a lot of software solution like ERP systems are on the market to provide ebusiness solutions. The standardization of material and goods reached a high grade. Since the capacity of service is continuously growing, the demand after standardized services is getting stronger and also ebusiness solution for service procurement. Service procurement is subject to certain problems and conditions. There are no equalized general purchasing conditions for services, no standards because of their complexity. In case that contents of delivered services are hybrid, combining material with service delivery (such as maintenance and repair of assets), the complexity of cases even increases.

4 Research Approach

The following section explains the elements of our approach and how we expect to solve identified problems and overcome existing barriers of service procurement. Our analysis of requirements for electronic description and transaction of service procurement is based on real use cases based on different service procurements scenarios. We analyzed and defined 12 different service procurement use case between large industry clients and small and medium sized companies as service providers. For the definition of requirements, we analyzed the supply chain and the internal and external processes and master data to derive a common understanding of a standard process and interfaces.

4.1 Definition of Industrial Services

To find solutions for the challenges in our research approach, we have to achieve specific goals and milestones. One of the most important issues is the definition and characterization of services. Services types have to be analyzed, structurized and classified. As a result of our pre analysis of services in the maintenance area we can define now by factors the characteristics of services and their execution. The first factor is the *performance*. The performance of the service can either be *immaterial and material* (combined) or only *immaterial*. The second factor *transaction of the specification* can be described by its subcomponents *attributes and information*. Other important factors are the *calculation, combinations of systems and rules* and the *documentation*. By using these factors we can classify all the different types of services to specify them. Also the transaction of services can be described by specific factors. As an important factor, the *type of a service* can be seen. The type can be either an *individual single intervention* or depending on a *frame contract*. As a factor the services can be distinguished by their *area of application* which can either be the *industrial maintenance area* or the *disposal area*. The factor *transaction types* defines the variants of the transaction of a service. The factor *trigger* defines the subcomponents *maintenance strategy* and the *parameter value* which correspond together. *Maintenance strategy* specifies the kind of the maintenance type in terms of the strategy and it can be defined more carefully by the *parameter value*. The *assignment*, the *placing* and the *transaction of industrial services* can be described by its *internal* or *external* handling. Other factors and criteria are the *acceptance*, the *accounting*, the *combination of systems and rules*, the *warranty*, the *documentation* and the *partners and permits*. The characterization of the description and transaction of industrial services by these factors support the classification of industrial services.

4.2 Data Model for the Description and Specification of Services

In order to describe and specify the structure of services in a formal way, we are going to define data models for the specific factors of services. The definition of data models are the pre-stage to transform the data model into a formal description based on XML, so-called ebus-XML. The structure defines the characteristics of services and specifies the transaction of services within a workflow of services processes. Figure 1 shows our predefined data model for the specification of services units. The approach allows specifying and maintaining complex service specifications which in practice comprise in average more than 15,000 positions. Another strand to be looked into is the standardization of service specifications inside large, multinational enterprises.

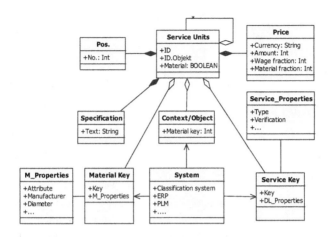

Fig. 1. Data Model for the specification of a Service Unit

In order to execute ebusiness processes for the procurement of industrial maintenance services, maintenance services have to be classified and structured to fulfill the requirements for electronic data exchange. A standardized description of service data lead to their classification among most accepted existing standards such as eCl@ss or UNSPC [18] [19] [20] [21]. For the procurement of material different kind of standards are already existing. Therefore an exact classification and description is implemented and master data for the procurement of services can be derived in a high quality for the purpose of ebusiness transactions.

4.3 Reference Process for the Transaction of Industrial Services

At the same time the execution of services has to be analyzed to understand the type of service. The specification and characteristics of services correspond closely to the transaction of them. By analyzing the different kind of transactions in this domain we defined a reference meta process for the procurement of services. The reference process concludes all the use case descriptions and analysis based on our research. By using our own defined meta language, we defined the reference process on different layers for different level of abstraction. The process describes the performance of e-procurement of services and visualizes the views of the service provider and the service customer. On a high abstract level, we defined the most important milestones within the process. On a second abstraction layer we model the individual characteristics of the procurement process of different services (see Figure 2). Based on the reference process we develop a configuration framework for services based on different characteristics of services. It defines the execution of services depending on different factors. Sub-processes can be called and combined in different ways. Along the flexible configuration of the execution of ebusiness service processes, the processes have to be implemented into an IT architecture. As a solution we use a centralized solution based on a catalogue system and an ERP system to connect the service providers and the service customers. Because of the nature of services and its need of interaction and communication between the customer and the service provider, an interactive

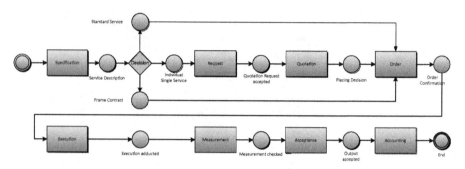

Fig. 2. Standardized service processing and transaction

shopping basket will be realized in order to reduce the communication cycles and to lower the transaction costs. The execution of sub-processes will be realized by a service oriented architecture (SOA). Depending on rules and logic, services can be called and triggered to perform.

5   Results

E-procurement of services can be described by four dimensions: (1) service, (2) characteristics of services, (3) IT solution and (4) electronic execution of service processes. Standardized descriptions lead to a deep integration with a high flexibility of service descriptions and are a precondition of flexible configurations of services. Therefore the IT solution in combination with the factors service and the characteristics of services build the fundamental basis for the electronic transaction of service processes. For the individual standardized execution of service procurement processes a Meta reference process have to be defined for the different kind of service procurement execution types. The Meta reference process can be configured depending on the factors describing the services and the service procurement processes based on its characteristics its description and execution.

After our analysis we can conclude that ebusiness of service processes in general can be formalized by certain dimensions. The description of services and the electronic transaction of services are based on these four dimensions (see Figure 3). These four factors define the relation and interdependence of the nature of services for its electronic transaction.

(1) Service. The service itself has to be described by a standardised description of services. With these formal descriptions, catalogue structures and performance specifications can be derived. With this structure, a profound integration of services with high flexibility can be reached and used for added value networks and collaboration networks.

(2) Description of Services. Specific factors can be used for the specification and description of services. These factors are properties of services and specify the typical behaviour and the kind of service. These factors are used to specify the services as well as to define the execution of services.

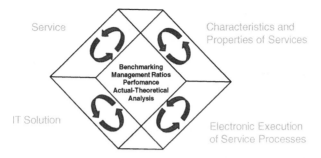

Fig. 3. Inducing intelligence in cross-organizational service procurement processes

(3) IT Solution. The IT system solution supports the definition and description of services to allow for their execution meaning the electronic description and execution of service master data. The IT solution provides a structure for catalogues and for performance specifications combined with a centralized portal solution.

(4) Service Processes. Service processes can be derived and executed based on the IT Solution, the service and the service description. The execution of service processes goes along with a meta process as a reference process for the service description and execution. A service process can be seen as an instance of the meta process, specified depending on its properties and configured by sub-processes based on the SOA.

6 Summary and Conclusions

E-procurement solutions can deliver great cost-saving potential for purchasing. But services have not generally been considered as a part of these cost-saving measures. The reasons at hand are manifold. Lack of standardized service descriptions and thereof resulting lack of transparency of services ("make or buy"-decisions are costly and vague) are most prioritized Service procurement requires collaborative business processes and a common view on exchanged business objects and data. Data quality is a major issue as it determines finally effectiveness and efficiency of IT systems and applications. Our test bed will allow a proof concept and a continuous evaluation of proposed IT solution and related results closely with the users. Further issues to be looked into are change management and methods for comparison of internal services with external service offerings. New concepts and paradigms as Service Oriented Architectures (SOA) and a need of integrated IT applications (within companies for analytical business applications such as data warehouses, business intelligence applications) require new ways of governance and e-business standards (such as classification systems) to achieve data quality in supply chains. Moving toward flexible SOA architectures often faces difficulties in information management and integration challenges.

References

1. Verbeek, H.M.W., Hirnschall, A., van der Aalst, W.M.P.: XRL/Flower: Supporting Inter-Organizational Workflows Using XML/Petri-net technology (2002)
2. van der Aalst, W.M.P.: loosely Coupled interorganizational Workflow: modelling and Analyzing Workflows Crossing Organizational Boundaries. Information and Management 37(2), 67–75 (2000)

3. van der Aalst, W.M.P.: Process-oriented Architectures for Electronic Commerce and Inter-organizational Workflow. Information Systems 24(8), 639–671 (2000)
4. Grefen, P., Aberer, K., Hoffner, Y., Ludwig, H.: CrossFlow: Cross-organizational Work-flow Management in Dynamic Virtual Enterprises. International Journal of Computer Systems, Science and Engineering 15(5), 277–290 (2001)
5. Lazcano, A., Alonso, G., Schuldt, H., Schuler, C.: The WISE Approach to Electronic Commerce. International Journal of Computer Systems, Science and Engineering 15(5), 345–357 (2001)
6. Yan, H., Bejan, A.: Modelling workflow within distributed systems. In: Proceedings of International CSCW Conference (2001)
7. Bons, R.W.H., Lee, R.M., Wagenaar, R.W.: Designing trustworthy interorganizational trade procedures for open electronic commerce. International Journal of Electronic Commerce 2, 61–83 (1998)
8. Frank, L., Wolfgang, D.: Modelling inter-organizational processes with process model fragments. In: Proceedings of the Workshop Informatik (1999)
9. van der Aaalst, W.M.P., Anyanwu, K.: Inheritance of Interorganizational Workflows to Enable Business-to-Business E-commerce. In: Proceedings of the Second International Conference on Telecommunications and Electronic Commerce (1999)
10. Lin, D.: Compatibility Analysis of Local Process Views in Interorganizational Workflow. In: 9th IEEE International Conference on E-Commerce (2007)
11. Larsen, M.H., Klischewski, R.: Process Ownership Challenges in IT-Enabled Transformation of Interorganizational Business Processes. In: Proceedings of the 37th Hawaii International Conference on System Sciences (2004)
12. Stoll, P.P.: E-Procurement-Grundlagen: Standards und Situation am Markt. 1. Auflage, Wiesbaden (2007)
13. Maintenance – Maintenance terminology; European standard: German and English version prEN 13306:2008; DIN EN 13306:2001-09 (2008), http://www.din.de
14. Master Data Management: Consensus-Driven Data Definitions for Cross-Application Consistency, Philip Russom, TDWI (The Data Warehouse Institute) (October 2006)
15. Bartels, A.: Services Procurement Grows Despite Obstacles, third document in ePurchasing Market, Forrester (2007)
16. Kock, N., D'Arcy, J.: Resolving the e-collaboration paradox: The competing influences of media naturalness and compensatory adaptio. Information Management and Consulting, Special Issue on Electronic Collaboration 17(4), P72–P78 (2002)
17. Kock, N., Nosek, J.: Expanding the Boundaries of E-Collaboration. IEEE Transactions on professional communication 48(1), P1–P10 (2005)
18. ECl@ss: International Standard for the Classification and Description of Products and Services (2009), http://www.eclass.eu/
19. UNSPSC (2009), http://www.unspsc.org
20. eOTD (2009), http://www.eotd.org
21. RosettaNet Technical Dictionary (2009), http://www.rosettanet.org
22. eBusInstand, 2009: Service procurement for industrial maintenance (2009), http://www.ebusinstand.de
23. Neef, D.: E-Procurement: from Strategy to Implementation, 1. Auflage, London (2001)

Guide to a Strategic Procurement Planning Approach on Regulated Commodity Markets

Marcus Seifert and Thorsten Wüst

Hochschulring 20, 28359 Bremen, Germany
sf@biba.uni-bremen.de

Abstract. The access of Virtual Organizations to raw materials normally requires external resources. In many cases, the market for raw materials is regulated and the VO principles of trust, customer orientation etc. are not applicable. In consequence, the VO needs to provide reliable solutions for the customer while being dependent on the access to the required raw materials. The objective of the proposed paper is to present a guide to a strategic procurement planning for the manufacturing industry on regulated commodity markets. This guide can be used to evaluate specific sourcing options. The main goal of this guide is to identify the negative effects of market regulation at an early stage and reduce them by developing strategic alternatives. The successful application of this guide is demonstrated by the practical example of the refractory industry and one of their commodities, refractory grade bauxite.

Keywords: Raw materials, regulated markets, virtual organizations, converters.

1 Introduction

Today's business environment is a global one. The ever-faster globalization and the increasingly open worldwide marketplace provide a wide variety of suppliers and potential partners to establish order specific, customer driven networks. In this environment companies reach their individual attractiveness as business partner through reducing their manufacturing penetration and focusing on their core competencies [1]. The single company/entity in the network, the virtual organization, is getting leaner. The virtual organization on the other hand is getting more flexible [2] in order to fulfill the customer demands. To achieve this goal, the single, lean and efficient, companies have to work closer together and develop a working relationship to succeed and be competitive. In general, it is not possible anymore for a single entity to achieve market success nowadays. Market success is a collaborative issue, risks and benefits shall be distributed among the participating partners. The chance to reach the goal of fulfilling customer needs depends largely on the companies' capability to commit to the appropriate partners for a specific product line-up and to design these relations in the most effective way [3]. The strength and competitiveness of these relationships is mostly based on factors like reliability, responsiveness, resilience [4], [5], reliance and trust [2]. Responsiveness describes the need for agile cooperation in virtual organizations and towards customers, whereas reliability, reliance and trust point out the need for a trustful relationship facing the uncertainties of a complex and turbulent

L.M. Camarinha-Matos et al. (Eds.): PRO-VE 2009, IFIP AICT 307, pp. 369–378, 2009.
© IFIP International Federation for Information Processing 2009

business environment. The same challenges increase the need for resilience to build strong and competitive structures. In this era of "Supply Chain Competition" [5] complex constructs of interrelated partners try to attract global customers [5], [6].

The outward boundaries of a collaborative network are hard to define. But at least two entities with interfaces to the outside business environment can be identified: one towards the consumer and one towards the supply side, the converter, who has to run the commodity procurement to provide the network with the right resources. Raw material suppliers themselves are mostly not part of the network. This article focuses on the converter, as he is the first stage of value creation inside the collaborative network and has to take care of the supply of necessary raw materials for the whole production process. All value added processes of the collaborative network begin with the procurement [7], [8] of raw materials. Without a reliable access to the needed raw materials, the customer needs cannot be fully fulfilled and the competitiveness of the whole collaborative network is in danger.

United to achieve the common purpose of customer orientation and the ability to react quickly to market needs, theoretical and applied science developed various approaches to integrate production structures [9], [10]. The latest papers on partnership-design are often based on the collaboration approach as the whole concept of virtual organizations/collaborative networks are based on that. Collaboration bases on the assumption that companies' involved have a desire to be reliable partners trusting each other and to agree on a common goal and that there is the possibility to successfully reach that goal. Hence, they recommend methods and tools, which support and boost a cooperative target achievement [11], [12]. The converter, on the one hand is part of such a vitual organization/collaborative network and as such, is committed to the goals of the virtual organization to achieve customers satisfaction. On the other hand, the converter he has to deal with parties, who have no stake in the collaborative network themselves and are not committed to the goals of the virtual organization. These outside parties, mostly raw material producers, do not care much about the principles like reliability, trust and reliance which are so important for the relationship of the partners inside the network. They primarily focus on their own progress and profits. As the whole virtual organization depends largely on a secure, reliable and steady supply with specific raw materials the question is, how the virtual organization can fulfill the common goal of satisfying customer expectations under these circumstances? The converters, as the link between the virtual organization and the outside parties with no stake in the network, have to deal with these uncooperative raw material producers on the one hand and with cooperative partners who expect a trustful and reliable relationship on the other hand. So the widely discussed tools focusing on a cooperative target achievement, are not or just partly applicable in such a case. Therefore, there is a need to describe the problems of the parties of the network who have to interface with uncooperative players in addition to the various available frameworks focusing on cooperative thinking partners. This topic is of increasing importance, as the supply of various raw materials will become more restricted, in terms of availability, price and many more.

2   Commodity Markets and Regulations

In order to understand the procurement processes for raw materials, knowledge of commodity markets and their driving mechanisms is necessary. It has to be noticed, that there is no commodity market in general, depending on the individual raw material the basic market conditions may strongly vary. Raw materials have an inner value and are not unique; they can be easily substituted among each other [13]. In general, availability of some specific raw materials plays a decisive role for the economic power of a community [14]. The worldwide raw material deposits are limited and they are not equally allocated around the globe. Increased worldwide usage of various raw materials, like copper, iron ore and bauxite [15] add to the limited availability. The spreading of the deposits is a major reason for the global nature of the commodity markets, as suppliers and customers are often stationed different continents. Therefore, raw materials are mostly traded worldwide with global pricing. This price is influenced by various factors. One of these factors is stock jobbing [16]. Others, like substitution- and recycling-processes are directly connected to supply and demand, as these factors increse or decrease the global availability. Furthermore, price developments depend on currency fluctuations, as raw materials are largely priced in US$, and the geographical location [17], first influencing the prices due to logistic costs and, maybe even more important, local customs like corruption and security situation. Characteristic for the commodity market is also the size and market power of the raw material producers. The need for huge capital investments and the potential economies-of-scale led to a consolidation process among the major players [14]. Thus, the market power of the commodity suppliers is elevated by their size and their control of the deposits. Hence, the few available options for alternative sourcing becomes even more constricted [18], [19].

With this background knowledge about commodity markets and their basic mechanisms, there can be certain regulatory mechanisms identified. A narrow definition of regulation is the direct interference of a government in the free market conditions [20], [21]. In this article the regulation concept is interpreted wider and the essential points will be structured in natural and artificial categories. In this scenario, natural

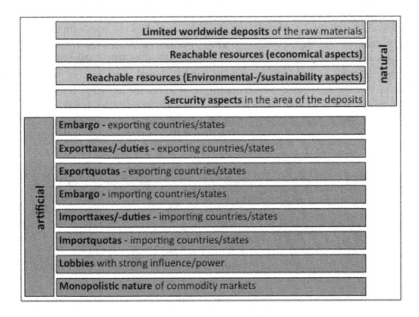

Fig. 1. Regulations with strong influence on the commodity market

regulations compromises regulatory mechanisms, which cannot be directly influenced to reach a certain goal. Whereas, artificial regulations include practices to influence the market conditions or the free trade on purpose with a specific goal in mind. The mapping of the different regulations to the two categories can be retraced in figure 1.

The **natural regulations** are interconnected, as exploitation of the limited world-wide resources is additionally limited by economical and sustainability considerations. Furthermore, as a major part of the deposits is located in political unstable areas or areas with a high corruption and/or crime rate, where security considerations can be also seen as a natural regulation factor with some artificial fractions. The **artificial regulations** on the other side are mostly based on decisions of the importing or exporting country/state in order to protect their own economy, for strategic considerations or even as a punishment for others. Even so organizations like the World Trade Organization (WTO) limit the administrative discretion, there are various regulative laws and rules in place. Furthermore, non- or part-governmental groups actively influence the market in many ways too. And, as mentioned before, the monopolistic nature of the commodity market with just a few players having control over the majority of the deposits can regulate the market by an increase or decrease of the worldwide production.

3   Assessment of Improvement Possibilities

The procurement processes of the converter, as the interface of the integrated supply network to the uncooperative raw material producers, are strongly influenced by the regulations on the commodity market. Due to these regulations and the often unpredictable and unstable supply, the converter has a hard time fulfilling expectations of its fellow partners further down the integrated network. These Expectations can include providing flexible and reliable high quality supplies [5] at a competitive price in the right quantity the right time [16]. Most production processes of the network are based on a reliable and steady supply from the converter. When the converter cannot fulfill this demand because of the difficult procurement situation on the commodity market, he will get in trouble with its partners, who are mostly large companies with a strong buying power. In this situation, the converter faces an unsteady, unpredictable situation with uncooperative players on the supply side and powerful partners with high expectations on flexibility and reliability on the customer side (see figure 2).

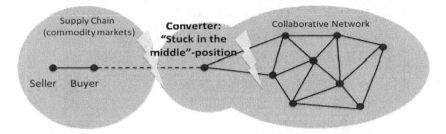

Fig. 2. Stuck in the middle position of the converter between raw material suppliers outside and customers inside the virtual organisation

The whole virtual organization, especially the converter, has to improve its procurement processes to satisfy its customer needs inside the collaborative network. In order to define strategic procurement strategies to strengthen the position of the virtual organisation, it is necessary to assess the current situation individually. The assessment of the individual procurement situation is based on four factors, which allow describing the performance qualitatively as a starting point for a later selection of promising actions. The factors of choice match the special requirements of a regulated commodity market and are supposed to be crucial measures for the performance [22]. They are based on procurement requirements, which are generally seen as premises in a working collaborative network, but are still essential in the area of raw materials procurement.

Figure 3 shows the four factors, security of supply, continuity, logistics and communication, and their interconnections including a brief explanation to each of them. The factor communication stands out, as it can have alleviative or cumulative implications on the performance of each of the other factors due to its generic nature. Once the assessment of the current procurement situation is completed and the result is available in a qualitative form (+/0/-) for each factor, the next step is to identify promising procurement strategies, which suit the result best. First, the possible approaches have to be cumulated.

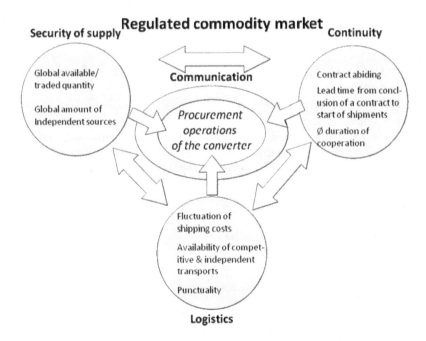

Fig. 3. Factors to assess the qualitative performance of the virtual organisation's procurement processes

A good way to generate various approaches is to check best practice methods from other industries or known creative methods like brainstorming within a group of experts. The assumed impact of every one of these approaches on the four factors, based on the individual situation, has to be estimated. The resulting list of the approaches and the need for improvement, gathered during the assessment, can be matched now. That way the approaches with the most impact on the identified critical areas can be found and elaborated in detail.

Figure 4 gives an overview and a framework of the presented model:

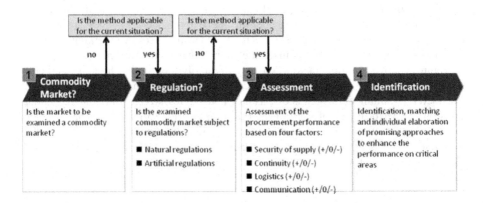

Fig. 4. Enhance the procurement performance of VOs facing raw material suppliers

4   Practical Example: Procurement Situation for Refractory Grade Bauxite

In order to demonstrate the application of the presented model, the framework will be used to analyze the procurement situation of a refractories manufacturer in the field of refractory grade bauxite. The collaborative network involved is a very demanding one. The refractory manufacturers secure the supply of high quality refractories to for example the steel industry. The steel industry then produces high quality steel for the

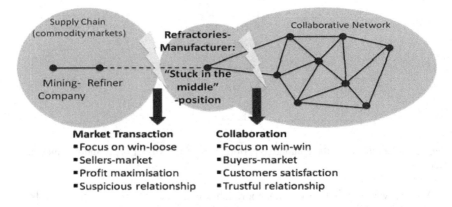

Fig. 5. Challenges faced by refractories manufacturers (converters) stuck in the middle between raw material suppliers outside and customers inside the virtual organisation

automotive industry, known as a very demanding industry in terms of expectation in deadlines and quality. Without a reliable, steady supply of high quality raw materials for the converter, here the refractories manufacturer, the whole virtual organization faces major problems through all stages of the manufacturing process.

As described, does the situation in the market for refractory grade bauxite contain all above discussed challenges, which are summarized in figure 5. This example will be analyzed according to the presented framework (see figure 4) in the following:

Commodity Market and Regulation: The raw material refractory grade bauxite is a specific quality of bauxite and is the basic material for industrial refractories. These refractories are used by various industries, like the iron- and steel-industry, which is the major consumer. The raw material supply of refractory grade bauxite is regulated in many different ways, both natural and artificial, what makes it a good and coherent example. Especially, since the regulations directly influenced the price development and the availability of certain qualities.

The market for refractory grade bauxite is regulated by all the presented natural regulations. The natural occurrences are limited to three locations worldwide, China, Guyana and Brazil, but just the Guyana and China deposits are currently exploited. As if not enough, the deposits in Guyana are exploited by governmentally owned Chinese companies. That is the direct link to the artificial regulations in place. China introduced various export-taxes, -duties and –quotas and the global customers have no alternative due to the monopolistic structures of the market. Bottom line is, the converter has to face an unsteady, unstable supply with increasing prices and on the other hand, with the big steel producers, powerful and demanding customers. The first two requirements of the framework, being a commodity market with regulations are fulfilled here. In the following the critical areas with a need for improvement will be identified using the introduced model. Later on, some examples of promising approaches will be presented.

Assessment: The factor security of supply rates very low in this case, as there is practically just one source for the raw material worldwide and the globally traded volume is considerably below the global demand. A similar negative performance can be noted for the factor continuity. Contracts are often not fulfilled and they are mostly signed shortly before the shipment. The result of the factor logistics is also negative, as the shipping rates vary heavily and the upstream processes are unreliable too. The last factor communications completes the negative performance evaluation as the cultural differences and language barriers add to the problems.

Identification: The result of the assessments indicates that an improvement in every area is needed. So in the end, an identification of a mix of different approaches targeting the specific needs for improvement is indicated. Examples for such approaches are the exploitation of alternative deposits outside of the area of influence of China, advanced materials preparation techniques in order to have a wider choice of supply qualities and a close cooperation between the new raw material producer of the alternative source. These are just examples of how promising approaches may look like, but there is no limitation on the creativity to target the challenges on improving the critical performance issues.

5 Conclusions

The global need for raw materials is increasing erratically as developing economies, like the BRIC-countries, are demanding their share [15], [23]. This trend will increase further in the future and more and more raw materials will be involved. This represents an eminent thread for almost all producing companies. Even so, virtual organizations are supposed to include all stages of a manufacturing process, in the case of basic supply with raw materials it might not be possible to convince raw material producers of the advantages for him to join the virtual organization with the common goal to satisfy customers expectations. In such a case the success and competitiveness of the whole virtual organization depends on a possibly very opportunistic party with strong selling power.

In that situation, the procurement of raw materials becomes the key factor for success for every producing virtual organisation. The commodity market distinguishes itself in various parts from other markets. A major attribute is the global nature, the unwillingness of the suppliers to integrate into collaborative structures and the many regulations. These attributes are all limiting the free trade and endangering the ones who do rely on a reliable and steady supply. Especially the role of the converter and how it handles its procurement process under these circumstances is in the focus of this article. The converter, as a part of an integrated and collaborative virtual organisation has to interact directly with the uncooperative and powerful raw material producers whilst, at the same time, satisfying its partners expectations and needs. Hence, the success of the whole collaborative network depends on the performance of the procurement processes of the converter and how well it handles the thread of natural and artificial regulations. Every virtual organization has to evaluate the possible future thread concerning limited worldwide supply of raw materials and increased dependencies of raw material producers.

In order to identify an easy to use way for affected firms to face the challenge, this article describes a framework including a model to identify first the critical areas with a strong need for improvement and approaches to sustainably enhance the procurement performance. The procurement situation of refractory grade bauxite, the basic raw material for various refractories, represents an ideal example for a commodity market with strict regulations in place. At the same time, the converter, in this case the producer of refractories for the iron and steel industry faces powerful customers with high expectations, its cooperation partners, the steel companies (see practial example). The execution of the presented framework and the identified approaches to enhance the performance of the procurement situation highlight the effectiveness and the applicability of the model.

The occurrence of the limited global natural resources and the increasing demand is of great importance for every producing company, every country/government and, in the end, every single customer worldwide. With this background further research is needed to identify raw materials, which are facing the described challenges in short notice. Furthermore, the implications on society and economy of single countries as well as on the relationship between countries have to be explored in detail. Last but not least, transferability of these concepts to other industries, with strong regulations, for example military technology, can be examined.

References

1. Hamel, G., Prahalad, C.K.: The Core Competence of the Corporation. Harvard Business Review 1990(33), S.79–S.91(1990)
2. Batt, J.P., Purchase, S.: Managing collaboration within networks and relationships. Industrial Marketing Management 2004(33), 169–174 (2004)
3. Seifert, M.: Unterstützung der Konsortialbildung in Virtuellen Organisationen durch prospektives Performance Measurement, Universität Bremen (2007)
4. Beckmann, H.: Supply Chain Management: Strategien und Entwicklungstendenzen in Spitzenunternehmen. Springer, Berlin (2003)
5. Christopher, M.: Logistics and Supply Chain Management – Creating Value-Adding Networks. FT Prentice Hall, Harlow (2005)
6. Katz, J.P., Pagell, M.D., Bloodgood, J.M.: Strategies of supply communities. Supply Chain Management: An International Journal 8(4), S.291–S.302 (2003)
7. Arnold, U.: Beschaffungsmanagement. Schäffer-Poeschel Verlag, Stuttgart (1997)
8. Kleinaltenkamp, M., Plinke, W.: Technischer Vertrieb: Grundlagen des Business-to-Business Marketing. Springer, Berlin (2000)
9. Camarinha-Matos, Luis, M., Afsarmanesh, H., Ollus, M.: Virtual Organisations – Systems and Practices. Springer, Heidelberg (2005)
10. Scholz, C.: Die virtuelle Organisation als Strukturkonzept der Zukunft?, Diskussionsbeitrag Nr. 30 des Lehrstuhls für Betriebswirtschaftslehre, insbesondere Organisation, Personal- und Informationsmanagement, Universität des Saarlandes, Saarbrücken (1994)
11. ECOLEAD: European Collaborative Organisations LEADership Initiative; Ecolead is an integrated project in the European Commission Sixth Framework Programme Proposal Number: IP 506958
12. COIN: Enterprise Collaboration and Interoperability, COIN is an integrated project in the European Commission Seventh Framework Programme - EU FP7 Project 216256
13. Rogers, J.: Rohstoffe – der attraktivste Markt der Welt: Wie jeder von Öl, Kaffe und Co. profitieren kann. FinanzBuch Verlag, München (2005)
14. Maull, H.W.: Strategische Rohstoffe – Risiken für die Wirtschaftliche Sicherheit des Westens. Oldenbourg Verlag, München (1988)
15. Buhr, A., Graf, W., Power, L.M., Amthauer, K.: Almatis global product concept for the refractory industry (2005),
    `http://www.almatis.com/download/technical-papers/`
    `UNITECR05-180.pdf` (retrieved September 27, 2008)
16. Koppelmann, S.: Beschaffungsmanagement – Grundlagen und Anwendung. Die Beschaffungsfunktion als Effizienzquelle. In: Festel, G., Hassan, A., Leker, J., Bamelis, P. (Hrsg.) Betriebswirtschaftslehre für Chemiker – Eine praxisorientierte Einführung, pp. S.225–S.236. Springer, Berlin (2001)
17. Berndt, R.: Global Management. Springer, Berlin (1996)
18. Bozon, I.J.H., Campbell, W.J., Lindstrand, M.: Global trends in energy. The McKinsey Quaterly 2007(1), S.1–S.5 (2007)
19. Church, R.: Getting into a supply chain state of mind (2006),
    `http://www.mmsmag.co.za/articledetail.aspx?id=250`
    (retrieved September 19, 2008)
20. Finsinger, J.: Wettbewerb und Regulierung. Verlag V. Florentz, München (1991)

21. Lange, K.M.: Duden Wirtschaft von A bis Z: Grundlagenwissen für Schule und Studium, Beruf und Alltag (Gebundene Ausgabe). Bibliographisches Institut., Mannheim (2007)
22. Gunasekaran, A., Patel, C., McGaughey, R.E.: A framework for supply chain performance measurement. International Journal of Production Economics 2004(87), S.333–S.347 (2004)
23. Specht, D., Braunisch, D.: Sekundärrohstofflogistik – Konzepte und Anwendungen. Zeitschrift für wirtschaftlichen Fabrikbetrieb 103(12), S.875–S.879 (2008)

Part **12**

Trust and Soft Issues in Collaboration

On Hard and Soft Models to Analyze Trust Life Cycle for Mediating Collaboration

Simon S. Msanjila and Hamideh Afsarmanesh

Informatics Institute, University of Amsterdam, Science Park 107,
1098 XG, Amsterdam, The Netherlands
{s.s.msanjila,h.afsarmanesh}@uva.nl

Abstract. Mediating short-term collaboration among organizations is very challenging in today's open world due to: the increasing intensity of market competition on acquisition of opportunities, the demand for the large amount of resources and the large number of different competencies, and the continuous increasing scarcity of resources, among others. One approach for organizations to reduce the severity of these challenges is joining their initiatives through collaborations. However, each organization has interests and goals that might be different and contradicting with those of other partners. Consequently, establishing fruitful collaboration is challenging and a proper approach to mediate collaboration among organizations is needed to support resolving emerging disputes during their interactions. Creating trust among organizations encourages them to quickly join their efforts to respond to these challenges and thus commit to the established collaboration. This paper addresses trust as a way to mediate collaboration among organizations. It addresses aspects related to soft-models and hard-models of trust and presents the application of these models in analyzing trust subjectively and objectively respectively. The paper finally introduces stages of life cycle of trust among organizations.

Keywords: Inter-organizational trust, trust life cycle, models of trust.

1 Introduction

Designing comprehensive trust models and mechanisms to address challenges related to mediating business oriented collaboration among organizations has become a fundamental focus of research on trust. Despite recent achievements from research addressing modeling of trust, there are still insufficient generic and customizable models, mechanisms and tools to support emerging requirements on trust analysis. Most available solutions supporting trust analysis are limited to: a specific application case (e.g. multi-agent systems), known actors (organizations or individuals), or domain of study (e.g. health domain). These solutions are also limited to some specific set of trust criteria applied to their development.

Business collaborations among organizations are usually objective specific and short-term in nature [5]. Developing bespoke solutions, such as models, mechanisms, tools, etc., to support analysis of trust among organizations for the purpose of mediating their collaboration is quite challenging. It is more challenging to analyze inter-organizational

L.M. Camarinha-Matos et al. (Eds.): PRO-VE 2009, IFIP AICT 307, pp. 381–392, 2009.

trust in virtual collaboration where organizations do not know each physically and inter-act through computer networks. A key catalyst to this challenge is the unclear picture of future business objectives that are usually dependent on market opportunities [4]. There is a need to develop customizable trust solutions to mediate collaboration among actors for every business objective.

This paper characterizes trust for mediating collaborations among organizations. It presents aspects of hard-models and soft-models of trust relationships and then ap-plies these concepts in characterizing life cycle of trust among organizations.

2   Nature and Dimension of Trust

Nature of trust: The following are some characteristics of trust that have been identi-fied for relationships between organizations:

Nature aspect	Description
Multi-level	Trust level is not an absolute value that can be measured once and applied in all cases. Each measured trust level depends on many factors such as involved organizations, available data, purpose of the assessment of the trust level, set of trust criteria, etc.
Multi-criteria	Trust is addressed as a multi-criteria subject. Every case requiring trust establishment is different and will need specific set of trust criteria to assess trust level of actors.
Cultural-rooted	Trust is closely tied to the norms, values and beliefs in the society. In addition to trust objective, the cultural practices and believes may influence perceptions of trust and preference on criteria that can be applied to assess trust level of organizations.
Communication based	Trust is the outcome of moral communication behaviors, such as providing accurate information, demonstrating sincere and openness, etc.
Dynamic	Trust perception and preferences are not static rather they change depending on different factors such as involved other organizations, goals of the collaboration, etc.
Multi dimensional	There are several dimensions of trust that characterize the dynamic nature of trustworthiness of trustees as addressed below.

Dimension of trust: Dimension of trust refers to the characteristics which indicate the dynamic nature of trustworthiness. Dimensions of trust are operational aspects of trust that when properly addressed may contribute to enhance their trustworthiness of organizations. Following are some dimensions of trust:

Dimension	Description
Integrity	The belief that organizations are fair in all decision that are made through or by them.
Reliability	The belief that organizations will do what they promise to do and act consistently.
Openness and Honesty	This dimension addresses the amount and accuracy of information that is shared among organizations, and how sincerely and appropriately it is communicated to others.
Vulnerability	The organizations' willingness to participate in relationships and commit transactions. Vulnerable is due to the belief that another organization is competent, open, honest, concerned, reliable, and identified with common goals, norms, and values.
Popularity / branding	Popularity and branding measure the extent to which organizations address common goals, norms, values and beliefs associated with the involved society culture and values. This dimension indicates how connected the actor feels to the (seen by the) society.
Influence mutuality	The degree to which organizations agree on who has rightful power to influence one another. For the stable trust relationships the actors must be able to influence each other.
Satisfaction	The extent to which one organization feels favorably toward the other as expected in the relationship. A satisfying relationship is one in which the benefits outweigh the costs.
Commitment	The extent to which one organization believes the trust relationship is worth to maintain and promote. Two sub-dimensions of commitment are continuance: which refers to a certain line of action, and affective: which is an emotional orientation.

3 Inter-personal and Inter-organizational Trust

As a subject, trust has gained increased attention and has been examined in both research and practice. It has been widely studied, most importantly as a component of relationships among organizations as well as among individuals. Below we describe and distinguish inter-personal and inter-organizational trust.

Inter-personal trust: Challenges related to inter-personal trust date far back and correspond with the beginnings of human life. Researchers have indicated that trust is important in smoothening inter-personal relationships [8]. Inter-personal trust has been practiced mostly in social relations and it is usually subjective in nature. Subjective trust is the most adopted and practiced form of trust for smoothening interactions among individuals. Subjective trust is created on the basis of qualitative data and is opinion-based. Some fundamental sources of information for creating subjective trust among individuals include experience and knowledge of trustors on trustees, recommendations of third parties on trustees, trustees' reputations, etc.

Inter-organizational trust: A key challenge on the establishment of collaboration among organizations is the selection of trustworthy partners for the purpose of fulfilling opportunities. Due to sensitivity nature of business goals the inter-organizational trust is rationally analyzed and supported with formal reasoning.

Traditionally, trust among organizations was only established "bi-laterally" and subjectively based on reputation and recommendation from others. In large collaborative networks [10], applying traditional approaches for creating bilateral trust among organizations is difficult, mostly due to the following reasons: (1) It is hardly feasible for trustors to collect reputation data or peer's opinions about the trustworthiness of trustees, with whom they had never interacted before. (2) It is hardly feasible to (rationally) reason on the trustworthiness of actors based on subjective data. Therefore, subjective trust (opinion-based) is too risky when applied alone and rational trust (fact-based) is required to be created among organizations to act as a foundation for evolution of trust during the goal oriented collaborations.

Rational trust is created on the basis of quantitative data and is fact-based. The main source of trust-related data is the organizational performance which is accumulated in the past from different activities in which it participated, both in collaboration with other partners, and as an individual organization. Rational approaches for assessing the level of trust in organizations employ formal mechanisms, such as mathematical equations, which in turn provide some formal reasoning of the resulting level of trust [11].

Inter-organizational trust vs. inter-personal trust: A fundamental difference between inter-personal trust and inter-organizational trust relate to their antecedents. Some antecedents of inter-organizational trust are known, such as the *shared values, the previous interactions,* and *the practiced behaviors* [10], and are aimed at preparing organizations towards trusting each other. As stated above inter-personal trust is very subjective in nature and dependent on individual's opinions. It is not yet clear what antecedents does an individual need to meet to be trusted by others.

Some other fundamental aspects applied in this paper to distinguish between inter-personal trust and inter-organizational trust include: *trust criteria, models of trust relationships, and mechanisms for assessing trust level* as addressed below.

+ **Trust criteria:** One important aspect of characterizing trust is the identification of trust criteria for various actors. Trust criteria for organizations are fact-based in nature and in our research are characterized to express organizational performance data [11]. Inter-personal trust is measured based on opinions, rating, voting and other types of subjective or probabilistic measures [13].

+ **Models of trust relationships:** Considering the key role trust plays in mediating collaboration among actors, an understanding of concepts relating to inter-actor trust relationships must be properly addressed. In [12] we examined the need of modeling trust relationships between organizations. Models of trust relationships between organizations are hard in nature applying fact-based elements, e.g. those related to their performance. Models of trust relationships between individuals are soft in nature and they represent subjective data related to trust (Section 4).

+ **Mechanisms for assessing trust level:** As discussed earlier, inter-personal trust is mostly regarded as a subjective aspect and its measurements have been frequently based on the probability perceived by a trustor that a trustee can do something [6]. However, a probability-based assessment works well when trust is regarded as a subjective aspect. It is easier to count opinions that supported the positive reputation of trustees and thus use these counts to calculate their trustworthiness as probability values. In such practices, the need to formally reason about results of the assessment is not necessary. Today, rational mechanisms for assessing the level of trust in organizations are needed to support making formal reasoning on the results. Assessing level of trust in organizations is fundamental to successfully establishing their trust relationships. Designing *rational (fact-based) mechanisms* for assessing the level of trust in organizations is of particular importance to enhance accuracy of computed trust level. In [10] we proposed a mathematical approach for formulating mechanisms to assess the trust level of an organization. Thus mechanisms are formal and support rational reasoning on the results.

4 Soft Models and Hard Models of Trust

Development of models of trust has attracted concentrated efforts from researchers and many variants of trust models have been developed. As these proposed models are built on different underlying concepts, a need is evident for systematic approach to categorize, evaluate and improve these models in order to apply them effectively.

We categorize models of trust as *hard-models*, *soft-models and semi-soft-models*. Hard-models of trust are designed to support the management of trust among organizations on basis of fact-based data, such as their performance data. Soft-models of trust are designed to support the management of trust among organizations on the basis of subjective data such as reputation, opinions, etc. Semi-soft-models of trust capture some aspects of both rational and subjective trust analyzes.

Hard-models of trust have been developed and applied to support management of trust in some specific cases. In research addressing security of distributed systems, hard-models of trust are developed to support the management of trust among communicating systems. These models can only detect and analyze trust based on data delivered through crypto-based mechanisms [9]. Furthermore, in security studies of systems, hard-models of trust are applied to develop mechanisms that can be used to analyze trust applying data related to violations of security assumptions, security performances, vulnerability, etc. In our previous work on inter-organizational trust we have proposed hard-models of trust based on mathematical equations [11]. Models are applied to formulate mechanisms for assessing the level of trust in organizations considering measurable criteria and a formal reasoning on results is supported.

Therefore, a number of different kinds of hard-models of trust are already developed for specific application cases. Hard-models do not consider the aspects of all stages of trust life cycle which is characterized with some soft aspects of trust as further addressed in Section 6. Thus there is a lack of conceptualized hard-models of trust that are comprehensive enough to adequately apply in any emerging objectives and can be customized to meet interests of any kind of organizations. Although hard-models of trust provide a base or foundation for designing other models for higher stages which consists of qualitative elements (soft-models of trust) there is a need for looking into the possibility of integrating the two types of models.

Soft-models of trust capture the trust relationships between organizations that are based on observable evidences about trustee's behavior, either through direct experience (witness reputation) or indirect experience (certified reputation). Hence soft-models of trust use social control mechanisms, namely, based on how actors socially recommend each other. Analysis approaches for soft-built trust include: probability measurements based on positive and negative opinions, logical operations to analyze trust transitivity, prediction analysis in relation to risks, etc. Existing models of trust for inter-personal interactions can be classified as soft-models [7].

While each type of models is able to provide a different focus on addressing trust issues in collaborative networks, both types also come with some drawbacks. Hard-models of trust are difficult to apply in real life as they demand a complete set of data for all considered criteria. Soft-models of trust suffer from the lack of traceability and the problem of trust saturation which can leave actors vulnerable to cheat attacks.

Some attempts have been made by researchers to develop models which can capture a few aspects of both had-models and soft-models of trust, here referred to as *semi-soft-models* of trust. A causal model as inspired in the discipline of systems engineering supports analysis of causal influence among measurable factors (hard-model aspects) but allows some qualitative reasoning to be made on the nature of influences (soft-model aspects). For example, as shown in Fig. 1 while factors "cash capital" and "capital" are both measured quantitatively with numbers the influence of cash capital on capital is qualitatively assumed as positive.

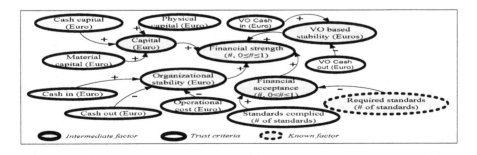

Fig. 1. Semi-soft-model of trust for the organizational economical perspective

Causal models as semi-soft-models of trust can also be transformed to hard-models of trust in form of mathematical equations. On the basis of assumptions as inspired by the discipline of systems engineering the formulation of mathematical equations (hard-models of trust) applying causal models (semi-soft-models of trust) is thoroughly addressed in [11]. The formulated equations are then applied in designing mechanisms for assessing the level of trust in an organization. For example, the equations for capital (CA) and financial acceptance (FA) can be represented as follows [11]:

$$CA = CC + PC + MC \text{ and } FA = \frac{SC}{RS}$$

Where CC represents cash capital, PC represents physical capita, MC represents material capital, SC represents standards complied, and RS represents required standards.

5 Mediating Organizations' Collaboration

The term mediation is applied in various disciplines carrying different meaning but what is common is the facilitative role it plays. In law, mediation refers to a form of "alternative dispute resolution" or "appropriate dispute resolution", which aims to assist two (or more) disputants in reaching an agreement [3]. As practiced in law, several different styles of mediation exist such as *evaluative, facilitative, and transformative*. Evaluative mediation does have somewhat of an advisory role in that its practitioners evaluate the strengths and weaknesses of each side's arguments should they go to court. Facilitative mediation acts as an interface to facilitate the flow and exchange of information for the disputants and therefore, enhance their communication. Transformative mediation looks at conflict as a crisis in communication and seeks to help resolve the conflict thereby allowing people to feel empowered in themselves and better about each other. In computer science, mediation is viewed as a *facilitative instrument* supporting the flow of information among nodes through the use of computer networks. It is an information request answered by providers, such as search engines, based on the analysis of the content of each information objects within a data collection such as a digital library, WWW, etc. [14].

Mediating collaboration among organizations needs to be looked at considering a variety of aspects from which a number of different alternatives can be preferred. Commonly, in business practice, contracts have been used as a fundamental approach to mediate and support collaboration among organizations. Contracts can be made between the collaborating partners (*direct contracts*) or through a third party (*insured contracts*). Contracts consist of "get out" clause such as penalties. Organizations sometimes end their commitment when they feel that possible risks are higher than expected gains and thus it is worthy to pay the penalties and quit the collaboration. Creating trust among organizations to mediate their collaboration has emerged as a potential approach to enhance commitment in the network towards achieving the common goals. Trusted organizations feel the burden of meeting their promises to sustain their trust due to the fact that trust cannot be traded.

Creating trust among organizations to mediate their collaboration focuses on avoiding possible future disputes related to their interactions by ensuring that each involved partner possesses the acceptable trust level. When the trust level of all involved partners is above the threshold, there is a high chance that their collaboration will be smooth and effective. The evaluation of trust level of partners is objectively performed and the computation applies mechanisms implemented based on hard-models of trust. As such, the avoidance of future disputes among organizations by rationally evaluating their trust level corresponds to the evaluative role of mediation as inspired in the discipline of law.

However, if disputes among organizations occur during their collaboration, such as those related to conflicts caused by issues like the lack of commitment, the failure to achieve promised goals, etc., then promoting and enhancing trust among partners can be applied to resolve such disputes. As such, the role supported by promoting and enhancing trust among organizations is similar to the two aspects of mediation -the facilitative and the transformative - inspired in law and/or computer science. The first aspect is related to finding proper channels to act as interface between organizations to exchange the information needed to sustain their trust (facilitative mediation). The second aspect is related to supporting each organization to decide on suitable information to communicate to other organizations (transformative mediation).

Therefore, management of trust to mediate collaboration among organizations must address the three fundamental aspects of mediation of: (1) *Evaluative:* Support the measurement of trust level of organizations, (2) *Facilitative:* Support the provision of information for creation of trust among organizations and establishment of their trust relationships, and (3) *Transformative:* Provide methodologies to maintain and sustain trust among organizations during the collaboration.

6 Stages of Trust Life Cycle

Trust between organizations evolves (grow, remain uniform or deteriorate) with time from its birth (creations) and keeps evolving with time while organizations know, learn and experience each other through collaboration. Also, trust among organizations and in particular, those aiming at achieving common goals through collaboration, has been observed as objective specific and need to be built on the foundation of fact-based data and thus must start with a rational analysis. With time trust of organizations will evolve to incorporate opinion-based analysis applying recommendations and reputation data (soft-built trust) (See Fig. 2).

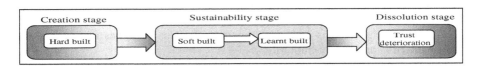

Fig. 2. Trust life cycle stages

And with relatively long-time some learning based analyzes of trust will also be incorporated in the trust life. Thus trust analysis needs to consider the notion of time and must address the evolution of trust level of organizations. Previous studies have indicated that requirements for collaboration among organizations differ depending on the life stage of the collaborative networks [1]. It has been shown that collaborative networks undergo three life stages namely: creation, operation and dissolution or metamorphosis [2]. Since trust among organizations is created to smoothen their collaboration we have characterized trust life cycle in three stages similarly to those of collaborative networks, namely: *creation, sustainability and dissolution*.

6.1 Creation Stage

This stage is initiated when organizations which do not know or know little about each other realize the need for trusting each other and thus start looking for fact-based data to analyze trust of others. The stage is experienced once, and in particular for those organizations that have never collaborated in the past. Thus to create trust among organizations, comprehensive rational data is needed and must be thoroughly analyzed which leads to the so-called "hard built trust". Only hard-built trust can be realized at this stage and acts as foundation for other next stages. The measurement of trust level, in this stage, reflects *the evaluative aspect of mediation* for collaboration.

Hard-built trust is established based on solid and measurable data. Formal mechanisms are needed to both measure the trust level and support reasoning on the computed results [11]. Hard-models of trust need to be developed to support establishment of hard-built trust. Using these models, it is possible to develop potential mechanisms and services to support processes related to trust management, such as assessment of the levels of trust in organizations [12].

Considering today's businesses that need organizations to virtually collaborate to serve a single customer, the inter-organizational trust creation must be based on facts. Measurable trust criteria and formal mechanisms must be applied to ensure that the analysis results are as accurate as possible and can be supported with some formal reasoning [11]. Therefore, the next stage – the sustainability stage - of trust life cycle should be initiated only when the involved organizations have proved beyond reasonable doubt that they have met the base trust level which is assessed based on mechanisms established using hard-models of trust.

6.2 Sustainability Stage

Sustainability stage inherits the success of the trust creation stage. This stage starts when organizations are convinced with provided rational data related to trust. Thus, as shown in Fig. 3, the computed trust level of each organization is either equal or higher than the base trust level. In this stage of trust life cycle, organizations focus on enhancing the trust to each other through looking at everyone's behavior (soft trust) and learning their achievements with time (learnt-trust). This stage has two sub-stages: "soft-built trust" and "learnt-built trust".

Soft built trust is created based on semi-rational data or subjective data, mostly captured from the analysis of behavior and initiatives of organizations during the post "hard built trust". At this sub-stage, organizations are convinced with the provided fact-based data, but they want to softly analyze responses and behaviors of others when hard-built trust is put into practice. This kind of trust is experienced when organizations want to learn about others and predict their possible behavior or commitment in near future.

Learnt-built trust is achieved through relatively long period of collaboration which is enough to thoroughly learn the activeness and long-time achievements of trustees.

This sub-stage is mostly focused on learning about trustees and trying to compare their achievements to the expectation which was predicted during the soft-built trust establishment. While collaborating, a number of changes, such as market conditions, might influence the behavior of organizations. Thus learnt-built trust allows the trustors to analyze the response of trustees to such changes. In this case, some sort of soft-built trust might again occur to re-predict possible future behavior. The sustainability stage incorporates both the *facilitative and transformative aspects of mediation* of collaboration. The establishment of soft-built trust and learnt-built trust which is based on the intensity of observation on organizations reflects the facilitative aspect of the mediation of collaboration. The support for and analysis of evolution of trust of organizations during the sustainability stage reflects the transformative aspect of the mediation of collaboration. Sustainability of trust can occur following one of the four disjoint possible scenarios of evolution of trust level as shown in Fig. 3.

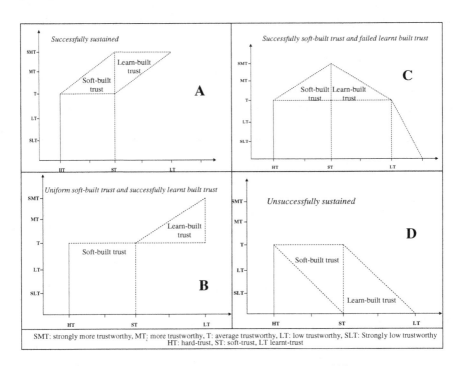

Fig. 3. Scenarios of trust evolution during the sustainability stage

Scenario A – Trust between organizations is successfully sustained: In this scenario, the level of trust in organizations keeps growing during the entire sustainability stage. This scenario occurs when the hard-built trust is realized and the trust level of organizations keeps on growing during the soft-built trust sub-stage. Thus at this point in time the organizations are convinced on the validity of hard-built trust and the positive predicted behavior of organizations is correct which means they can start collaborations. Furthermore, the trust level of organizations also keeps growing during the learnt-built trust sub-stage and thus it continues becoming stronger due to the positive results from the organizations' learning of each other. This is experienced, when organizations are effectively performing collaborative activities and are optimally achieving compatible/common goals. Thus organizations' experience and learning are positive, and they enhance trust in each other.

Scenario B – Uniform soft-built trust and successfully learnt-built trust: In this scenario the trust level of organizations remains uniform during the soft-built trust sub-stage, but it grows during the learnt-built trust sub-stage. Thus the same situation as explained in scenario "A" for the learnt-built trust sub-stage is experienced here.

Scenario C – Successfully soft-built trust and failed learnt-built trust: This scenario may occur when the trust level of organizations keeps growing during the soft-built trust sub-stage as explained in scenario "A" above. However, as the transition to learnt-built trust sub-stage starts, some failures emerge (such as failure to show the promised competencies) which lead to insufficient commitment of organizations in collaborations. Consequently, trust starts to deteriorate due to negative results from the learning process. This situation leads to dissolution stage.

Scenario D – Unsuccessfully sustained: This scenario may occur when organizations fail to realize soft-built trust. It may occur, for example, when organizations' behavior does not match with their trust level which was computed during the trust creation stage by using fact-data (hard-built trust). For instance, although organizations have strong trustworthiness, they can show poor behavior and indicated lack of proper initiatives to realize collaborative goals. In particular, this situation can occur when organizations indicated by using their fact-based data that they are capable of doing something but failed to prove during the negotiation, such as failing to show evidence of validity of their data trust related. Sometimes, trust among organizations may remain unchanged during the soft-built trust sub-stage. However, during the transition to learnt-built trust sub-stage some failures might be immediately experienced (such as failure to show the promised competencies). For example, if inadequate initiative is observed during the learning sub-stage and negatively affect the possible future collaboration then levels of trust in organizations may start to deteriorate. If the deterioration of trust continues to the point that the levels of trust in organizations become less than the base trust level then the dissolution stage starts.

6.3 Dissolution Stage

This stage occurs when organizations cannot trust each other enough to continue collaborating. Depending on the intensity of collaboration achieved in the past, during the dissolution stage a number of consequences might need to be inherited or divided between them. For example, distributing between them the incurred loss or achieved profit. In some cases a third party might be involved to smooth the dissolution process, such as acting as an insurer to both conflicting parties. In this case, assets that cannot be distributed among the organizations, such as accumulated knowledge, can be transferred to the third party where all organizations can have fair access, compensation, etc. At the end of this stage, organizations terminate their collaboration and starts searching for new partners or looking for other options. As it is practiced in daily life, during the dissolution stage the fault trustees might attempt to re-create their trust to their trustors. This might include, for example, the provision of some new fact-based data or reputation data. The provision of the data by the fault trustees aims at persuading the trustors to reconsider or recomputed their trustworthiness. As such, if accepted by the trustors then the mechanisms discussed in the creation phase shall be used for manipulation of fact-based data. If only reputation data is available then the trustor organization might reconsider using the mechanisms discussed in sustainability stage but if and only if the trustor is convinced on the trustee's hard-built trust.

6.4 Similarities and Differences between Trust Aspects in the Three Stages

The base characteristic of trust during the creation stage (hard-built trust) is the rational nature. The analysis is based on fact-data and applies rational mechanisms and approaches. As such, measurable trust criteria are used and some automated systems as well as services are needed to support the required computations. The characteristics of rational trust are summarized in Fig. 4.

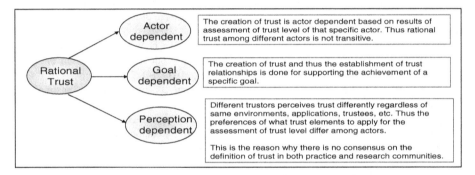

Fig. 4. Base concepts of rational trust among actors

The base characteristic of trust during the sustainability stage is its evolution with time. When soft-built trust and learnt-built trust are realized trust during this stage becomes transitive when applied to the similar applications or tasks. This means since the hard-built trust was realized during the creation stage, such as during the establishment and initiation of their trust relationships based on the results of the rational assessment of their trust level, and thus each organization can softly trust another organization based on the opinions or acquired reputation of other organizations. Opinions may refer to how trustees have been behaving in the previous interactions and how possible the trust in the trustees might evolve in the future.

7 Conclusion

Collaboration involves the mutual engagement of organizations to together address a challenge such as acquiring and responding to a business opportunity, which requires commitment, and it takes time, effort, and dedication. For this to be realized, trust among organizations needs to be properly managed to mediate their collaboration during the entire period. In this paper, we have addressed the characterization of aspects related to hard-models and soft-models of trust among organizations. We have applied these concepts to introduce and describe the life cycle of trust among organizations. We have also presented the application of trust in mediating collaboration among organizations.

References

1. Smith, T.F., Waterman, M.S.: Identification of Common Molecular Subsequences. J. Mol. Biol. 147, 195–197 (1981)
2. Afsarmanesh, H., Camarinha-Matos, L.M.: On the classification and management of virtual organization breeding environments. The International Journal of Information Technology and Management – IJITM 8(1), 1741–5179 (2009)
3. Afsarmanesh, H., Camarinha-Matos, L.M.: A framework for management of virtual organizations breeding environments. In: Proceedings of 6th PRO-VE 2005 - Collaborative Networks and their Breeding Environments, Spain, pp. 35–48. Springer, Heidelberg (2005)
4. Billikopf, G.: Party-direct mediation: Helping others resolve differences, 2nd edn. University of California (2009)
5. Camarinha-Matos, L.M., Afsarmanesh, H.: Collaborative networks in industry and services: research scope and challenges. In: COA 2007 – 8th IFAC Symposium on Cost-Oriented Automation, Habana, Cuba, vol. 8, part 1, p. 10 (1-16) (2007)
6. Camarinha-Matos, L.M., Afsarmanesh, H.: Collaborative networks: Value creation in a knowledge society. In: Proceedings of PROLAMAT 2006, IFIP International Conference on Knowledge Enterprise - New Challenges. Springer, China (2006)
7. Gambetta, D.: Trust: Making and Breaking Cooperative Relations. Basil Blackwell, Malden (1988)
8. Grandison, T., Sloman, M.: A survey of trust in internet applications. IEEE Communication Surveys, fourth quarter (2000)
9. Gulati, R., Singh, H.: The architecture of cooperation: managing coordination costs and appropriation concerns in strategic alliances. Admin. Science Quarterly 43, 781–814 (1998)
10. Lin, C., Varadharajan, V.: A Hybrid Trust Model for Enhancing Security in Distributed Systems. In: Proceedings of International conference on availability, reliability and security (ARES 2007), Vienna, pp. 35–42 (2007) ISBN 0-7695-2775-2
11. Msanjila, S.S., Afsarmanesh, H.: A Multi-Model Approach to Analyze Inter-organizational Trust. In: Collaborative Networks reference modeling, pp. 195–216. Springer, New York (2008)
12. Msanjila, S.S., Afsarmanesh, H.: Trust Analysis and Assessment in Virtual Organizations Breeding Environments. The International Journal of Production Research, 1253–1295 (2007) ISBN 0020-7543
13. Msanjila, S.S., Afsarmanesh, H.: Modeling trust relationships in Collaborative Networked Organizations. International Journal of Technology Transfer and Commercialization 6(1), 40–55 (2007)
14. Mezgar, I.: Trust building for enhancing collaboration in VOs. Network-Centric Collaboration and Supporting Frameworks, 173–180 (2006)
15. Neuhold, E., Niederee, C., Frommholz, I., Stewart, A., Mehta, B.: The role of context for information mediation. In: The proceeding of International Workshop on Ubiquitous Data Management, Tokyo, Japan, pp. 3–5 (2005)

Trust Building in Virtual Communities

István Mezgár[1,2]

[1] Computer and Automation Research Institute,
Hungarian Academy of Science,
Budapest, Hungary
mezgar@sztaki.hu
[2] Department of Manufacturing Science and Technology,
Budapest University of Technology and Economics

Abstract. By using different types of communication networks various groups of people can come together according to their private or business interest forming a Virtual Community. In these communities cooperation and collaboration plays an important role. As trust is the base of all human interactions this fact is even more valid in case of virtual communities. According to different experiments the level of trust in virtual communities is highly influenced by the way/mode of communication and by the duration of contact. The paper discusses the ways of trust building focusing on communication technologies and security aspects in virtual communities.

Keywords: Communication technology, trust, virtual community.

1 Introduction

Today can be talked about a communication technology explosion as information processing and communication technologies and tools are developing so rapid. The new technologies widen the world for the individuals to reach other human beings independently where they are on the globe. Various groups of people can come together according to their private or business interest forming a Virtual Community (VC). On the other side these technologies deeply modify traditional forms of social connections, communication and cultural habits as well. These modifications can be observed in particular in hierarchies, social rules, norms, conventions, familiarity and reputation.

A very important element of human contacts is trust. In a networked society, trust is the atmosphere, the medium in which actors are moving [1]. Trust can bridge cultural-, geographical-, organizational distances of members and individuals as well. Trust is the base of cooperation, the normal behavior of the human being in the society. In this new communication environment new methods and techniques of trust building has to be developed, as the conventional rules of face-to-face approach cannot be applied. According to different experiments the level of trust is highly influenced by the way/mode of communication [2] and by the duration of contact [3].

The paper deals with trust building among partners of virtual communities, with a special focus on the role of communication technologies. An overview is presented

L.M. Camarinha-Matos et al. (Eds.): PRO-VE 2009, IFIP AICT 307, pp. 393–400, 2009.

how security, user identification/authentication technologies (e.g. biometrics) can influence the trust building process. Finally some practical patterns are given that raise the efficiency of trust building.

2 Main Characteristics of Virtual Communities

Originally personal computers were totally disconnected from each other. The first big step was when all those computers (and the people behind them) got connected to the Internet and after reaching a critical mass digital networks were changing social groups into the Virtual Community.

According to Howard Rheingold, a virtual community is a community of people sharing common interests, ideas, and feelings over the Internet or other collaborative networks. In his book, *The Virtual Community* [4] he defines virtual communities as „social aggregations that emerge from the Internet when enough people carry on public discussions long enough and with sufficient human feeling to form webs of personal relationships in cyberspace". Cyberspace is the total interconnectedness of human beings through computers and telecommunication without regard to their geographical place. Today the convergence of mobile communication and computing is going on and this change in technology brings a change in the way communities come together and express themselves.

The classical definition of Rheingold describes the "clear" type of virtual community. Today there are additional forms of communities that are called also as virtual communities, in spite of the pretty big differences in their goals and technologies. Based on the types of the members (private individuals, professional individuals, organizations), on the goals of the community (private, social, business), the form of cooperation (free, formal), and on the type of participation (voluntary, voluntary organized, formally organized) three different basic types of Virtual Communities can be distinguished:

1. Community/network of independent intellectual workers (IIW)
2. Virtual Organizations (VO) – formalized cooperation of different remote business units.
3. (Voluntary) Virtual Communities – random connection among individuals or group of people.
   a). Working voluntary for a common goal of a community
   b). Collaborate in a certain field of hobby, discuss a topic without special responsibility.

A virtual community requires social capital to succeed in its goals. Social capital is the "ability to collaborate effectively," [5] and it includes three important factors: structure, trust, and common goals.

– Structure refers to human relations within the virtual community. Usually there is no real social hierarchy among the members of the virtual community. The rules are explained by the social norms for the community.
– Trust is a social construct. In order to increase social capital, there must be trust between members of the community. This may require individual members to refrain from taking actions that may benefit them in the short-term, for the sake of the

long-term benefit for the entire community. Establishing trust on the Internet is a difficult task, because of the anonymity and possible deception of members regarding their identities and information. Because of this difficulty in establishing trust, many individuals approach virtual communities with caution and suspicion.

– Common goals are the third factor of social capital. The basic goal is to create an online community of people.

To be a successful virtual community, there must be high social capital, meaning there must be low structure, high trust, and common goals. All the three classes and their subclasses of Virtual Communities can be organized independently of nationality and distance.

3 Media for Virtual Communities

3.1 Basic Wired Communication Technologies

Before the Web, virtual communities existed on bulletin board services (BBS). Today the main tool/technology for VCs is the Web. Among the first websites for virtual community were the Geocities (1994), and the Tripod (1995).

In general, there are two kinds of communication among virtual community members: message postings and real-time chat. Usenet newsgroups are an example of the former. For real-time chat, Internet Relay Chat (IRC) is a system used by many Web sites realizing virtual communities. Virtual communities are integrating Web 2.0 technologies with the community, so they can be described as Community 2.0.

Another mode of forming little virtual communities is the „weblog". The weblog is the frequent, chronological publication of personal thoughts and Web links. It is a mixture of what is happening in a person's life and what is happening on the Web, a kind of hybrid diary/guide site that can be read by other people free.

3.2 Mobile Technology in Virtual Communities

The mobility and the openness of virtual communities are continuously evolving. In the early 90s, the emerging digital networks were changing social groups in the Virtual Community; today we can live through what happens when the society, the economy and the networked communication goes mobile. The application of mobile equipment of different kinds is dramatically increasing. The combination of wired and wireless networks result that the members of the society have very broad possibilities to form VC, to build connection among the different cultures.

Rheingold, in his book „Smart Mobs: The Next Social Revolution" [6] described how efficient mobile communications (cellular phones, personal digital assistants, and wireless-paging and Internet-access devices) will allow people to connect with anyone, anywhere, anytime, and how they're already shaping communities around the world. Rheingold calls such group actors "smart mobs," and this expression has become already an important phenomenon.

Mobility is basic for the modern society - wireless technologies make faster the VC formation and operation in private life, in work, in entertainment and in civic organizations. The real impact of mobile communications will come not from the technology itself but as in case with other technological revolutions, from how people use it, resist it, adapt to it, and ultimately use it to transform themselves, their communities, and their social and cultural environment.

Mobility can be achieved by using different types of wireless networks as Satellite Communication, Wireless Wide Area Networks (WWAN – different types of mobile phone systems - GSM, UMTS and iMode), Wireless Local Area Networks (WLAN, such as WiFi –IEEE standard 802.11a/b/g/n), Wireless Metropolitan Area Network (WMAN) and Wireless Personal Area (or Pico) Network (WPAN – e.g. Bluetooth, IrDA2). These networks can be connected/integrated, according to the actual needs, developing very complex and powerful networks for VCs So the user can be reached really at any place through a type of wireless connection.

The most efficient wireless equipment for personal use are the mobile phones, Personal Digital Assistants (PDA) and the netbooks. When these "wireless terminals" are able to support, identification, authentication and authorization of users, confidentiality and seamless communication using various kinds of contents - including text, voice and video streams, etc. – they can be called as Personal Trusted Device (PTD). Using PTD for trust building can make authentication and confidentiality easier, more reliable that support the operation of virtual communities in a great extent.

An important service type of mobile phones is the MMS (Multimedia Messaging Service) that is an evolution of SMS (Short Message Service) and EMS (Enhanced Messaging Service). The multimedia element differentiates MMS from other messaging offers by integrating the ability to send and receive photos, images, video clips and polyphonic sound by camera phones. This message type is significant in forming virtual communities and also in trust building. The use of Internet-ready phones (VoIP) is challenging social customs, human relationships as people shift more of their attention and resources to the cell-phone. One recent trend is "moblogging," or mobile weblogging. Weblogging means reading/writing blogs in real time: this is what happens when you fuse digital cameras and text-entry functionality with a way to publish it to the Web.

4 Definition and Forms of Trust

In electronic environments, in digital communication B.J. Fogg and Hsiang Tseng [7] focus on trust among individuals mediated by technology, writing that trust indicates a positive belief about the perceived reliability of, dependability of, and confidence in a person, object (such as computers, networks, and software), or process (such as credit card transactions and airline e-ticket reservations). There are many additional definitions of trust, all professional fields where trust is important have developed its own definition [8]. Trust appears in different forms, according [9] trust has four main forms; Intrapersonal trust, Interpersonal trust, System trust and Object trust.

5 Trust Building in Virtual Communities

5.1 Fields/Technologies of Trust-Building

In building trust two main approaches can be distinguished; information technology approach and human centered approach, based on culture, and morality. A structured overview of trust elements and their hierarchy can be found in [10] differentiating the basic classes of structural-, managerial/behavioral-, social-, financial/economical- and technological trust. Information technology approach means that security has to increase by different architectures, protocols, certifications, cryptography, authentication procedures and standards and this increased security generates the trust of users.

It would be a mistake to think that applying only the human-centered approach would generate trust, the technological part has to be added as well (e.g. biometrical identification), so mainly the structured integration of the two approaches can result the expected level of trust.

Technical side of Trust

Approaching security from the side of trust, security is the set of different services, mechanism and software and hardware tools for generating trust with pure technology. More generally security is a condition that results from the establishment and maintenance of protective measures that ensure a state of inviolability from hostile acts or influences.

The building blocks, elements of security are the security services and the security mechanisms. The security services are, access control, authentication, confidentiality, integrity, and non-repudiation. Security mechanisms are e.g. encryption, digital signatures and checksums/hash algorithms. The main factor of trust is confidentiality that can be achieved by technologies that convert/hide the data, text into a form that cannot be interpreted by unauthorized persons. Identification is the process when a network element recognizes a valid user's identity. Authentication is the process of verifying the claimed identity of a user. Information used to verify the claimed identity of a user can be based on a password, PIN, smart card, biometrics, etc. Authentication information should be kept confidential.

Human side of trust-building process

The human side of trust is more complicated. From this aspect user interface has the main role, i.e. the menu structure, the messages send for the user by the system. In case the user feels that is easy to use, it is transparent, he/she can control the system (even with low level computer knowledge) i.e. the system is „user friendly", through this he can be convinced that he is using a trustworthy system. The more a user feels in control of an interactive system, the more the user will trust the site, the program, the system [11].

Trust is a dynamic process and it alters based on experience. Trusting process begins when an individual perceives indications that suggest a person may be worthy of trust [12]. These indications can include behaviors such as manners, professionalism and sensitivity and these forms are designed to represent trustworthiness.

5.2   Important Factors of Trust Building

In an experiment introduced in [2] four media types were compared: chat (text), phone conference, videoconference and face-to- face. Chat was significantly worse than each of the other three conditions, but audio and video did as well as face-to-face in overall cooperation, and were a definite improvement over text-chat only CMC.

The process of building trust is slow; trust is formed gradually, it takes quite a lot of time and repeated positive experiences [13]. On-line trust can be described as a kind of human relationship.

Trust is depending on the time span of cooperation and the type of connection as well. It can be stated that there are differences in trust building process in short-term and long-term relationships. In case of short-term relationships trust must be achieved quickly, and then maintain with no, or rare face-to-face interaction.

In long-term relationships trust building is influenced e.g. by using more communication channels and trust formation may assume a higher priority [3].

Other researches show if people meet before using computer-mediated communication (CMC), they trust each other easier. Using chat rooms and forums to get acquainted is nearly as good as meeting, and "even just seeing a picture is better than nothing" [14].

5.3 Generating Trust by Human-Computer Interfaces

As a communication/information system term a user interface (UI) is the point of communication between two or more processes, persons, or other physical entities. Interfaces are the key points for gaining the trust of the user/customer. They are the first connection point between the user and the system, identification and authentication (e.g. password/biometric input) of users take place at this point, so they have to be designed very carefully. When applying a reliable UI (menu structure that gives the feeling of control; secure authentication technique (biometry)) these technologies generate trust in user both to the system and partially to the other users (the partners also have to get through the same strict authentication, so they are really the person whom they states). The "reminder part" of trust in the partners can be built based on the content of communication.

Researchers test different new types of interfaces. Multimodal systems [15] process two or more combined user input modes— such as speech, manual gestures, gaze, and head and body movements— in a coordinated manner with multimedia system output. This class of systems represents a new direction for computing, and a paradigm shift away from conventional interfaces to the collaborative multimodal interfaces.

Remembering and entering passwords is a general problem, which is why everything should have seamless biometric identification built in. Researchers are working on different approaches that can make easy and convenient the reliable application of PTDs. Some examples; individuals can be identified from the faint sounds made deep inside the human ear. This could mean, users would be able to confirm their identity for computer logins simply by lifting a phone to their ear or putting on a set of headphones [16].

In case of an other approach the phone looks for a specific pattern of movements as the person brings it up to her/his ear when it has a built-in gesture based system using an accelerometer. These movements depend on characteristics like arm length, muscle structure, and patterns such as holding methods and other habits. These acceleration data makes possible the authentication. [17].

5.4 Practical Behavioral Patterns for Trust Building in VC

Members of VCs may trust other people or the system as long as they fulfill their expectations. When they do not, trust can evaporate quickly and take a much longer time to rebuild. To avoid loosing trust in the following some basic rules can be given for building connections in virtual space:

– Frequent and short communications help the dialogue process and trust building.
– Make your expectations clear -that helps the other party the ability to give a definitive response.
– Make small commitments and meet them.
– Make clear what is driving you to behave in certain ways.
– Be polite and thank every little service of the partner.
– Socialize - Informal conversation and identification of shared interests beyond the actual tasks, helps builds closer, personal connections.
– Demonstrate interest and commitment to the other person.
– Members of community organize meetings (if it is possible) to get in personal contact.

6   Conclusions

Today virtual communities are formed more frequently as the communication technology makes possible to join for more and more people. Internet and WEB technologies are developing very quick and new technologies as different types of wireless communication make even faster the evolution of cyberspace.

The number of users has reached the critical mass and that means these technologies have impact on the society, their influence change the behavior and culture of society. As trust is a social construct it is the base of virtual communities as well, especially in case of mobile technologies. Trust is the key problem as it has been proven in many studies that people don't use services in which they don't trust.

Those concepts, methods, technologies and tools that raise the level of trust among the collaborating partners or among the infocom systems and human beings (e.g. multimodal interfaces, new authentication technologies) have to be developed systematically. It is vital to introduce these technologies into the operation of virtual organizations, even by slightly changing their culture or organization structures.

References

1. Castelfranchi, C., Tan, Y.-H. (eds.): Trust and Deception in Virtual Societies. Kluwer Academic Publishers, Dordrecht (2001)
2. Bos, N.D., Olson, J.S., Gergle, D., Olson, G.M., Wright, Z.: Effects of four computer-mediated channels on trust development. In: Proceedings of CHI 2002. ACM Press, New York (2002)
3. Rocco, E., Finholt, T.A., Hofer, E.C., Herbsleb, J.D.: Out of sight, short of trust. Presentation at the Founding Conference of the European Academy of Management. Barcelona, Spain (April 2001)
4. Rheingold, H.: The Virtual Community, p. 325. Addison-Wesley, Reading (1993)
5. Blanchard, A.: Virtual communities and social capital. In: David Garson, G. (ed.) Social Dimensions of Information Technology: Issues for the New Millenium, pp. 6–21. Idea Group, Hershey (2000)

6. Rheingold, H.: Smart Mobs: The Next Social Revolution, p. 288. Perseus, Cambridge (2002)
7. Fogg, B., Tseng, H.: The elements of computer credibility. In: Proceedings of CHI 1999, Pittsburgh, May 15-20, pp. 80–87. ACM Press, New York (1999)
8. Harrison, D., McKnight, N., Chervany, L.: The Meanings of Trust" University of Minnesota Management Information Systems Research Center (MISRC), Working Paper. 96-04 (1996)
9. Luhman, N.: Trust and power. Wiley, Chichester (1979)
10. Msanjila, S.S., Afsarmanesh, H.: On Architectural Design of TrustMan Applying HICI Analysis The case of technological perspective. Journal of Software 3(4), 17–30 (2008)
11. Herrmann, T., Wulf, V., Hartmann, A.: Requirements for a Human-centered Design of Groupware. In: Shapiro, D., Tauber, M., Traunmüller, R. (eds.) Design of Computer Supported Cooperative Work and Groupware Systems, pp. 77–100. Elsevier, Amsterdam (1996)
12. Grabner-Krauter, S., Kaluscha, E.A.: Empirical research in on-line trust; a review and critical assessment. Int. J. Human-Computer Studies 58, 783–812 (2003)
13. Cheskin: eCommerce Trust, A joint research study with Studio Archetype/Sapient and Cheskin (January 1999),
    http://www.cheskin.com/p/ar.asp?mlid=7&arid=10&art=0
14. Zheng, J., Veinott, E., Bos, N., Olson, J.S., Gary, O.G.M.: Trust without touch: jumpstarting long-distance trust with initial social activities. In: Proceedings of the SIGCHI conference on Human factors in computing systems, Minneapolis, Minnesota, USA, pp. 141–146 (2002) ISBN:1-58113-453-3
15. Oviatt, S.: Multimodal Interfaces. In: Jacko, J., Sears, A. (eds.) Handbook of Human-Computer Interaction, ch. 14. Lawrence Erlbaum, New Jersey (2002)
16. Marks, P.: Our ears may have built-in passwords. New Scientist Magazine 2703, 16–17 (2009)
17. KDDI Gesture-based verification structure (2009),
    http://www.interweb.in/review-gadgets/
    37545-kddi-gesture-based-verification-structure.html
    (retrieved May 12, 2009)

Value Co-creation and Co-innovation: Linking Networked Organisations and Customer Communities

David Romero and Arturo Molina

Tecnológico de Monterrey, Campus Monterrey & Ciudad de México, México
david.romero.diaz@gmail.com, armolina@itesm.mx

Abstract. Strategic networks such as Collaborative Networked Organisations (CNOs) and Virtual Customer Communities (VCCs) show a high potential as drivers of value co-creation and collaborative innovation in today's Networking Era. Both look at the network structures as a source of jointly value creation and open innovation through access to new skills, knowledge, markets and technologies by sharing risk and integrating complementary competencies. This collaborative endeavour has proven to be able to enhance the adaptability and flexibility of CNOs and VCCs value creating systems in order to react in response to external drivers such as collaborative (business) opportunities. This paper presents a reference framework for creating interface networks, also known as 'experience-centric networks', as enablers for linking networked organisations and customer communities in order to support the establishment of user-driven and collaborative innovation networks.

Keywords: Collaborative Networked Organisation, Customer Communities, Value Co-creation, Co-Innovation, Open Innovation, User-Driven Innovation.

1 Introduction

In today's global economy, organisations are collaborating more and more, thus organisations are engaging in new forms of highly collaborative mechanisms and networked structures capable of providing a competitive advantage by combining the best skills or core competencies and resources of two or more organisations, plus customer knowledge regarding a product (good or service) to co-create a value proposition more compelling and relevant for the consumers' needs and expectations.

In this sense, *collaborative networks* represent a promising paradigm together with *customer communities* to emphasis on core competencies, personalisation and innovation, supported by collaborative mechanisms, in order to allow the consumer to stamp a product with his/her own applications, preferences and configurations, and therefore co-create value in a collaborative endeavour.

Collaborative Networked Organisations (CNOs) show a high potential as drivers of value co-creation, allowing organisations to access new knowledge, sharing risk and resources, joining complementary skills and capacities, which allow them to focus on their core competencies. In addition, CNOs induce innovation and thus co-create new sources of value by confrontation of ideas and practices, combination of resources and technologies, and creation of synergies [1].

L.M. Camarinha-Matos et al. (Eds.): PRO-VE 2009, IFIP AICT 307, pp. 401–412, 2009.

On the other hand, *Virtual Customer Communities (VCCs)* show a promising (business) value as "social networks" capable of leveraging all aspects of a product, from product design and marketing communication to creating the overall brand experience. VCCs can support mass-customisation strategies by allowing customers to become co-designers of their own products [2]; sales and marketing initiatives through viral marketing strategies [3]; and branding strategies through connecting customers around the lifestyles associated with their products [4].

In this context, CNOs working together with VCCs can be seen as a cooperative process of value co-creation and open innovation, through which a group of entities enhance the capabilities of each other by sharing risk, resources, responsibilities and rewards to co-produce a unique value proposition for each consumer and stakeholder.

2   An Experience-Centric Network Reference Framework

Conventional ways of gaining competitive advantages like cost, quality and response-time will not go away, but in order to compete successfully in the future companies will require building new capabilities to co-create value through *experiences*[1] together with their customers, rather than based-on the traditional product-centric approach [5]. Building new capabilities to compete in the future implies the design and development of innovative *experience environments* supported by collaboration ICT-infrastructures enabling the interaction between customers' communities and networked organisations, which allows the co-creation of value, and therefore shifts the bases of competition from products to experiences.

Creating *experience-centric networks* (interface networks)[2] requires crafting highly interactive and collaborative *experience environments* (e-platforms), and multiple *experience gateways* (interfaces), that work as communication spaces and channels for firm-customer interaction, allowing the consumer to shape his/her own personal *experiences* in a ubiquitous context in a fast, simple, opportune and secure way.

Following paragraphs will depict a *reference framework* as a synthetic structure of guidelines for describing a set of concepts, methods and technologies necessary for creating successful *experience-centric networks* and their supporting *experience environments* (see Fig. 1).

2.1   Value Co-creation Strategy Definition

Strategy helps organisations to be prepared for competing in the future. A strategy definition allows organisations to identify new opportunities to bring value to their customers and stakeholders.

A *value co-creation strategy* refers to the description of the manner in which a network of organisations intents to gain competitive advantage by involving their customers and business allies in a jointly value creation process.

---

[1] Experience(s) – Interactions between customer and producer for personalizing/shaping a product (good or service) based upon the customer's specific needs and situations (e.g. context).

[2] Interface Network – A meta-network compromising a network of enterprises (designers, manufactures, brokers, etc.) merged with a network of (lead) customers, which is supported by an adequate collaboration platform and infrastructure, creating a synergetic innovation ecosystem.

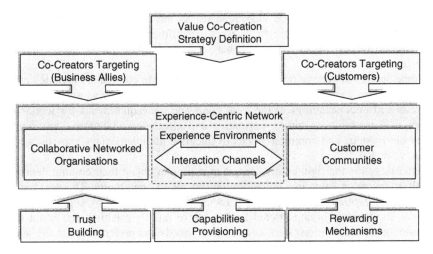

Fig. 1. Experience-Centric Network Reference Framework

A *value co-creation strategy* describes the actions aimed at configuring a value creation system as a set of people, organisations and technology acting as a symbiotic business ecosystem in which organisations and customers interact in dynamic and reciprocal relations towards their commitment in the process of co-producing value offerings: goods, services and *experiences*, in a mutually beneficial producer-customer relationship [6].

Furthermore, a *strategy* is adaptable by nature rather than a rigid set of instructions of how creating value for a target market. Hence, business models as definers of the value creation priorities in an organisation should be continuously reviewed in response to actual and possible changes in the perceived market conditions and evolve the enterprise strategy as the business environment and customers' needs change.

In *value co-creation* context, strategies and business models are continuously shaped over time in a discovering process of new sources of value and new opportunities and ways for co-creating it by/for the customers and stakeholders in the short- and long-term. Therefore, *strategy definition* will be a process of continuous discovery, active learning and adaptation within an agile business ecosystem capable of accessing new competencies, rapidly re-allocating resources and leveraging the organisational capabilities and capacities to compete based-on *experiences*.

2.2 Co-creators Targeting

Selecting the right criteria to target the right co-creators is a major task in the process of constructing effective co-creation partnerships with customers and business allies. Therefore, when selecting the most suitable co-creators two things are important to bear in mind: Not all *customers* can be good co-creators. This role depends on their complementary competencies understood as their knowledge, skills, expertise and behaviours in the *experience co-creation domain,* plus their enthusiastic attitudes to enhance existing product to match customers' requirements or co-create new ones that will serve to the new consumers' necessities. Furthermore, not all *business allies* can be good co-creators. This role also depends on the organisations' complementary competencies understood as their processes capabilities and resources capacities that are required to co-produce a product that serve as recipients to deliver *co-creation experiences*.

Some aspects to keep in mind when targeting the right co-creators include defining the kind of partnership to be established, making clear its aims as a set of common interests and understandings of the joint goals and the requirements for working together in a trustable cognitive, normative and affective collaborative environment based-on dialogue and common values to integrate complementary expertises to co-create value [7].

After targeting the right co-creators, then is time to obtain their commitment to act jointly to co-create value in a collaboration (business) opportunity. The next two elements of the *reference framework* will focus on this challenge by suggesting *CNOs creation* as dynamic organisational forms able to rapidly establish and adapt to the changing market conditions such as customers' needs and preferences [1] [8]; and the *CCs creation* as experience sharing and users communities aimed to inform and allow consumers to discuss about the quality and drawbacks of products prior to making a purchase, and after the purchase is made, help them to use at best their products by making them aware of all their potentialities and if necessary assisting them to solve their problems [9].

2.3 Collaborative Networked Organisation Creation

In today's society, value creation has become far more dependent on intangibles such as knowledge, relationships and branding, and very soon on *experiences*. Thus, characteristics such as flexibility, agility and adaptability have become the new key success factors to deliver customer value, which has also become increasingly complex, dynamic, and dependent upon consumers' expectations. Therefore, the possibility of rapidly configuring a group of organisations into a goal-oriented network, like the classical 'Virtual Organisation', triggered by a value co-creation opportunity and specially tailored to satisfy the customer's specific requirements it is frequently mentioned as an expression of agility in customer value delivery.

Virtual Organisations (VOs) represent temporary alliances of organisations driven by the objective of grasping a single collaboration opportunity and dissolve once their mission/goal has been accomplished. Its temporary nature has proven to better fit with the market dynamics and the variable duration of today's business opportunities, and its VO partners' competencies integration approach to better respond to the customers' specific needs and requirements [8].

Nevertheless, the effective creation of truly dynamic VOs, which are appropriate for catching-up with customers' continuously changing preferences, since customer value is contextual, requires the pre-existence of suitable *VO Breeding Environments (VBEs)* meant for preparing organisations to rapidly get involved in collaboration opportunity-based VOs [8].

Once a *collaborative network* has the conditions provided by a VBE to support the rapid and fluid configuration of VOs when a co-creation opportunity arises, the possibility of creating or redesigning a value creation system on-demand as a co-operative venture among business allies will emerge from the *breeding environment* with the capability and capacity to address each co-creation opportunity with a tailored value creation system that fits exactly with the customer specific requirements. In this sense, each co-creation opportunity will denote a *VO creation process* with its corresponding custom-made value creation system within a VBE, integrating the skills or core competencies and resources of the business allies (VO partners) involved for adequately supporting a co-creation opportunity together with the customer involvement and its specific needs. Under these conditions and according to the VO lifecycle (creation/operation/dissolution) each value creation system will be organisationally and technically integrated to co-create value for a specific customer and just for the period of existence of the co-creation opportunity which is being responded at the moment [10] [8].

The possibility of systematically integrating VO partners' skills and resources in a short-term coalition to serve to the customers' specific requirements represents a new source of sustainable competitive advantage in a changing global market of evolving and emerging customer needs.

2.4 Customer Communities Creation

Promoting the creation of *Virtual Customer Communities (VCCs)* provides companies with new interaction channels to co-create value through customer relationship management, by incorporating enthusiastic consumers that would be difficult to reach without the support of information and communities technologies [11].

VCCs represent valuable forums in which products, plus customer service, can be discussed, analysed, criticized and potentially improved. VCCs stand for real living laboratories in where multiple users (consumers) of the same or different products can come together to discuss the quality and satisfaction level of their current products, or comment about ideas for new ones, outside of the commercial negotiation. The social interaction among customers in this kind of virtual communities represents potentially insightful information, and a great possibility to foster companies' inter-relationships with their consumers [12].

10 best practices for building and facilitating VCCs according to Communispace Corporation [13] are: (1) Invite the right customers, keep the communities private and small, and categorize customers to uncover interests, passions and willingness to participate - avoiding using simply demographic criteria; (2) View community members as advisors to the company, not as a market research panel; (3) Find the social glue by focusing on topics of shared interest and relevance for the community, rather on just company's interests; (4) Work at building the community by creating activities (e.g. rituals/traditions) that help customers to feel comfortable in participating; (5) Be a genuine, open and encourage community's facilitator by reinforcing proactive behaviour; (6) "Just plain ask", the best way is to just ask, simply and straight-forwardly; (7) Pay even more attention to what members initiate, the best insights often come from discussions started by members - "listen more than ask"; (8) Don't squelch the negative, the best lessons come from hearing about those things that annoy, disappoint or outrage customers, so encourage members to give the good, bad and the ugly; (9) Don't ask members for too much too often or they will become fatigued; and (10) Make sure the community is built on multiple underlying technologies and methodologies so that

people aren't stuck just answering surveys or posting to message boards (e.g. live-chats, visual profiles, upload advertisements, video-diaries, etc.).

Furthermore, VCCs represent part of the knowledge revolution in where vast complement of knowledge and understanding can be tapped from customers, and combined with skilled and experienced knowledge workers (e.g. engineers as co-creators) in a greater customer intimacy and synergetic win-win situations (e.g. co-creation opportunities) to improve products by collaborating in a jointly value creation process to co-create products specially tailored to fit customers' desires. Therefore, any company capable of creating and sustaining *customer communities* related to its products and overall marketing strategy can expect to drive higher revenues, deeper customer loyalty and a real competitive advantage in today's economy [12].

Managing value co-creation in *customer communities* remains as one of the key research areas requiring that value managers, on both consumer and producer sides, understand the *value co-creation strategies* that drive, sustain and support *experience environments,* and thus comprehend which are the process and competencies that customers employ to render value according to its necessities, so companies will be able to create the capabilities to support those value co-creation processes in *experience-centric networks* [14].

2.5   Trust Building

Stability and success of *experience-centric networks* requires the right balance of trust among organisations and customers [15]. Trust is the glue that holds and links organisations and customers together, making possible the process of value co-creation. Trust is the atmosphere and the medium in which customers and organisations are dialoguing. It is also the base of cooperation among customers and organisations, and it is the main requirement in *experience-centric networks* in order for them to exist [16]. Thus, trust represents a bilateral process that requires mutual commitment between organisations and customers when attempting to keep their promises (e.g. building credibility). Some strategies identified by Jarvenpaa et al [17] suggest that trust building in virtual environments can be facilitated with: (1) proactive style of actions, (2) work-focused interactions, (3) optimistic team-spirit, (4) dynamic leadership, clear roles and objectives, (5) frequent interactions, and (6) immediate feedback. Hence, trust in virtual environments relies on virtual interaction and meeting to commitments.

In the co-creation paradigm, *trust building* can be supported through Prahalad's & Ramaswamy's [5] [18] DART building blocks: Dialogue, Access, Risk-assessment and Transparency. Therefore, in a value co-creation process it is clear that engaging customers directly in the co-creation of value involves *risks* for both, customer and producer, so keeping this in mind *dialogue* will be the element that encourages not just knowledge sharing, but even more importantly, shared understanding between companies' and customers' concerns. Additionally, *dialogue* also gives consumers an opportunity to interject their view of the outcomes of value into the process of value co-creation. Moreover, giving customers *access* to knowledge, tools and expertise helps them to construct their own experience outcomes, and this also challenges the notion that ownership is the only way for consumers to *experience value* by focusing on *access* to experiences at multiple experience gateways (interaction points), as opposed to mere ownership. Furthermore, since *risks* are involved for both sides, *risk assessment* assumes that if consumers become co-creators of value, they will demand more information about potential risks related to product developments, but they will also have to bear more responsibility for dealing with those risks. Thus, *transparency* of information in the interaction processes will be necessary for customers to participate effectively in a co-creation mode, and to build trust between organisations and consumers.

DART building blocks must be enabled by technical and social infrastructures (e.g. e-platforms & virtual communities) that allow consumers to co-create experiences they value and represent business value for organisations.

2.6 Interaction Channels Building

Experience gateways represent the creation of multiple customer interaction channels (e.g. Web-based and traditional ones), including *experience rooms* (e.g. sand-boxes)[3], aimed at providing consumers with an end-to-end experience across all the systems, people and organisations in a value network, and through all interaction points (channels) that a customer uses to create and shape his/her own personal experiences with their product providers by having access to a co-creation toolkit [19] to construct their own experience outcomes by co-design and co-developing their own products. Moreover, it is important to recall at this point that 'value co-creation' is contextual, and therefore customers' interactions are the key essentials in the value co-creation process with their product providers.

Furthermore, supporting multiple interaction channels, and at the same time avoid losing customers' value co-creation context when they move from one interaction channel to another, will require a new generation of customer contact centers (e.g. call-centers, help-desks) known as *customer interaction hubs* capable of processing distributed and heterogeneous sources of information, regardless of the multiple communication channels available to manage a customer unified and contextual profile to deliver a unique customer experiences of value [20].

Customer interaction hubs are emerging ICT-infrastructures able to support customer interactions across multiple channels and provide a uniform response to the customers demands at any point of the value co-creation process; allowing organisations to choose the right approach and method for responding to a customer requirement based-on a common view of his/her experience context. The end-result will be the right response with the right information to the customer, achieving a higher customer satisfaction level [20].

Some recommendations when building and managing *customer interaction channels* are: (1) Provide multiple interaction channels to the customers to allow them to choose which channels are more convenient for them in order to participate in different value co-creation processes; (2) Design each *experience gateway* considering the DART building blocks; (3) Manage *experience quality management* across all interaction channels - "it is about an integral experience"; (4) Ensure best practices to standardize the quality of customer service across all interaction channels and co-creator agents; (5) Enable intelligent cross-communication to turn the customer hub

---

[3] Experience Room – An interactive environment where customers "play" with products and shape them.

into a real experience environment; and (6) Consider multiple customers' choices from a simple transaction process (e.g. a purchase) to the overall co-creation experience through the interactive personalization of products [5] [18] [20].

One question that could arise when building interaction channels for the customers is where should an organisation create these *experience gateways,* and a possible response to this strategic question is suggested by Ramaswamy & Gouillart [21], who recommend the use of "interaction maps" aimed at discovering key interaction points where companies can devise new or better interactions for improving dialogue, access to knowledge, mutual understanding of risks and transparency in the value co-creation process with their customers. These *interaction maps* can be represented in a formal way by using *UML 2.0 interactive diagrams* such as a *sequence diagram* displaying the time sequence of the entities participating in an interactive process, or even better, a *collaboration diagram* displaying an interaction process organised around the entities and their links to each another. Using this kind of UML interactive diagrams, organisations may capture the behaviour of a single co-creation use case by visualizing the collaboration between entities in a value creation system to accomplish their value co-creation goal.

Another formal approach to map firm-customer interactions could be through a Business Process Modelling (BPM) approach as a way of providing organisations with the capability to understand their interactive/collaborative business processes in a graphical notation and comprehend better the organisational collaborative performance in each co-creation process with the customers and business allies.

Other possibility could be the use of simple cross-functional diagrams that can also serve to the process of mapping firm-customer interactions.

Experience environments will require the integration of multiple *experience gateways* as enablers of customer interaction with the node organisation and its network to co-create unique and personalized experiences of value [5].

2.7 Capabilities Provisioning

An *experience-centric network* can be understood as a solution generator capable of associating organisations core competencies and resources into *collaborative networks* on one side, and on the other side collect enough consumers' knowledge from *customer communities* to understand how to satisfy the personal consumers' requirements. Therefore, CNOs and CCs creation represent one of the most suitable ways for providing a group of organisations and consumers with the right capabilities and training to efficiently co-create value within *experience environments.*

CNOs allow the integration of organisations in networked structures (e.g. VOs) that represent tailored on-demand value creation systems with the capabilities to adapt and rapidly reconfigure resources and accommodate them to satisfy the consumers' demands within *experience environments,* which can deliver personalized products that complain with customers' specific needs.

Properly designed value creation systems will allow *CNOs* to perform value co-creation processes for satisfying consumers' specific requirements in a fast and efficient way thanks to the advantages and benefits of collaboration.

On the other hand, CCs can provide organisations with the information to recognize with enough time which will be the new required capabilities to satisfy consumers' needs and aspirations in the near future, so networked organisations (e.g. a VBE) can recruit new business allies that can contribute to the emergence of new competencies to support proactive interaction between consumers and producers in the conjoined personalization of products.

By integrating CNOs and CCs into *experience-centric networks,* both entities will be able to actively select the competencies required for co-creating *personalized experiences* in *experience environments.* These, with the technical and social infrastructures to align different business and consumer value co-creation processes with the agility and flexibility required to capture the time frame of co-creation opportunities (e.g. collaboration // business // opportunity).

Lastly, sustainable competitive advantages and business success in the emerging *experience economy* will depend on organisational networks capability to speed-up, innovate and focus on core competencies of their business allies to meet the consumers' specific requirements and demands, capture new markets and beat the competition by creating unique experiences with profitable business grow.

Furthermore, value will no longer be developed inside organisations, but from the interaction with consumers and business allies in *experience gateways,* allowing the co-design and delivering of personalized products. Thus, innovation and commercialization of technologies, goods and services will not be an organisational process, rather a value co-creation process with customers and business allies in the rising *experience economy* [5].

2.8 Rewarding Mechanisms

Co-creation may tap into the intellectual capital of customers; therefore companies should acknowledge their consumers and incentive them for their contributions, especially for those ideas that represent real economic benefits for the organisation. Companies should also keep in mind that rewarding consumers (e.g. free trials, samples of products, prizes for the best customer innovations) is one of the best mechanisms to keep alive proactive behaviour during the value co-creation processes [22] [23].

Considering the above, if companies want to keep the ideas flowing from their customers and their communities, they should show pre-emptive generosity, taking into consideration the consumers' contributions that are more significant for value co-creation, and reward customers by sharing intellectual property with them when they engage in a value co-creation processes (e.g. co-development, co-design, etc.) or simply share royalties in exchange for their ideas [22] [23].

Ultimately, a value co-creation process moves along to a joint product development, where individual contributions to value co-creation become more difficult to determine, and for this reason, ownership of Intellectual Property (IP) becomes quite troublesome. Therefore, new research in IP management is required, especially in the field of customer involvement in value co-creation processes.

The result of the following set of guidelines described by the *reference framework* presented in this paper represents the first steps towards formalizing a methodology for the creation of *experience-centric networks* (see Fig. 2).

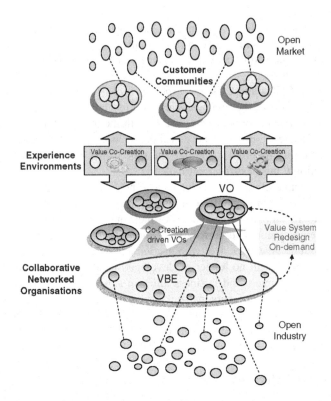

Fig. 2. Experience-Centric Network Scenario

3   Conclusions

Value co-creation has shift the traditional idea of value creation, in where customers were seen as "destroying the value which organisations create for them", while in alternative the new value creation paradigm views customers "actively co-creating and re-creating value with organisations" [24]. Thus, all these changes are setting the stage for an expanded role for customers, in new experience environments, where customers are no longer passive recipients of products; instead customers are now active partners co-creating value with organisations.

Furthermore, the current trend of *customer involvement* will continue maturing in the following years, changing the customer role from a pure consumer of products to a partner in the value creation process, and as a result organisational structures and business models will migrate into new strategic alliances and collaborative models based-on open business models that will support the creation and operation of adequate collaboration e-platforms for value co-creation. A lot of research remains to be done towards closing the interaction gaps that represent big obstacles for an effective involvement of customers in communities and organisations in collaborative networks to create the synergy necessary to integrate both sides in *experience-centric networks* capable of satisfying customers' needs, wants, and aspirations, and at the same time organisations' revenue goals.

As a conclusion, mass-customization, personalization, customer integration and open innovation trends will continue as early-strategies of value co-creation between organisations and customers, but as mentioned by Prahalad & Ramaswamy [5]: "The future will belong to those companies that continuously generate new knowledge from customers' experiences, and identify and enable new co-creation opportunities to support compelling *experience environments*".

Acknowledgments. The research presented in this document is a contribution for the ECOLEAD Project, funded by the European Community, FP6 IP 506958, for the "Rapid Product Realization for Developing Markets Using Emerging Technologies" Research Chair, ITESM, Campus Monterrey, and for the "Technological Innovation" Research Chair, ITESM, Campus Ciudad de México.

References

1. Camarinha-Matos, L.M., Afsarmanesh, H.: Collaborative Networks: Value Creation in a Knowledge Society. In: Wang, K., et al. (eds.) Knowledge Enterprise. IFIP, vol. 207, pp. 26–40. Springer, New York (2006)
2. Piller, F., Schubert, P., Koch, M., Möslein, K.: Overcoming Mass Confusion: Collaborative Customer Co-Design in Online Communities. Journal of Computer-Mediated Communication 10(4) (2005)
3. Subramani, M.R., Rajagopalan, B.: Knowledge-Sharing and Influence in Online Social Networks via Viral Marketing. Communications of the ACM 46(12), 300–307 (2003)
4. Andersen, H.: Relationship Marketing and Brand Involvement of Professionals Through Web-enhanced Brand Communities. Journal of Industrial Marketing Management 34(1), 39–51 (2005)
5. Prahalad, C.K., Ramaswamy, V.: The Future of Competition: Co-creating Unique Value with Customers. Harvard Business School Press (2004)
6. Normann, R., Ramirez, R.: From Value Chain to Value Constellation: Designing Interactive Strategy. Harvard Business Review 71(4), 65–77 (1993)
7. Ståhle, P., Laento, K.: Strategic Partnership: Key to Continuous Renewal. In: WSOY, Economy, Helsinki, p. 165 (2000)
8. Camarinha-Matos, L.M., Afsarmanesh, H.: A Framework for Virtual Organization Creation in a Breeding Environment. International Journal Annual Reviews in Control 31, 119–135 (2007)
9. Curien, N., Fauchart, E., Laffond, G., Moreau, F.: Internet and Digital Economics: Principles, Methods and Applications. In: Trousseau, E., Curien, N. (eds.) Online Consumer Communities: Escaping the Tragedy of the Digital Commons, pp. 201–219. Cambridge University Press, Cambridge (2007)
10. Katzy, B., Obozinski, V.: Value System Redesign. ACM SIGROUP Bulletin 19(3), 48–50 (1998)
11. Tzu-Ying, C., Jen-Fan, L.: A Comparative Study of Online User Communities Involvement in Product Innovation and Development. In: 13th International Conference on Management of Technology (2004)
12. Manville, B.: Knowledge Networks - Innovation through Communities of Practices. In: Hildreth, P., Kimble, C. (eds.) Building Customer Communities of Practice for Business Value: Success Factors Profiled from Saba Software and Other Case Studies, pp. 106–123. Idea Group Publishing (2004)

13. Communispace Corporation, Making Social Networking Work for Marketing: Communispace Shares 10 Best Practices for Online Customer Communities, in Press Releases by Swaysland, J. and Kelly, L. (2004)
14. Möller, K., Rajala, R., Westerlund, M.: Service Myopia? - A New Recipe for Client-Provider Value Creation. In: The Berkeley-Tekes Service Innovation Conference (2007)
15. Msanjila, S.S., Afsarmanesh, H.: Modelling Trust Relationships in Collaborative Networked Organizations. The International Journal of Technology Transfer and Commercialisation 6(1), 40–55 (2007)
16. Mezgár, I.: Trust Building for enhancing Collaboration in Virtual Organisations. In: Camarinha-Matos, L.M., Afsarmanesh, H., Ollus, M. (eds.) Network-Centric Collaboration and Supporting Frameworks. IFIP, vol. 224, pp. 173–180. Springer, Boston (2006)
17. Jarvenpaa, S.L., Knoll, K., Leidner, D.E.: Is there any body out there? Antecedents of Trust in Global Virtual Teams. Journal of Management Information Systems 14(4), 29–64 (1998)
18. Ramaswamy, V.: Co-Creating Experiences of Value with Customers: Building Experience Co-Creation Platforms Enhances Value Creation and Fosters Innovation. Platforms for Enterprise Agility: Business Innovation through Technology, SETLabs Briefings 4(1), 25–36 (2006)
19. Thomke, S., Von Hippel, E.: Customers as Innovators: A New Way to Create Value. Harvard Business Review 80(4) (2002)
20. eGain, Delivering Innovative Customer Interaction Hub Solutions, in Customer Inter@ction Solutions Magazine (2007)
21. Ramaswamy, V., Gouillart, F.: The Process of Experience Co-Creation. In: Experience Co-creation Partnership Workshop Proceedings (2007)
22. Trendwatching - Global Consumer Trends, Ideas and Insight, Customer-Made, in Trends Reports (2006)
23. Von Hippel, E.: Democratizing Innovation: The Evolving Phenomena of User Innovation. Journal für Betriebswirtschaft 55, 63–78 (2005)
24. Ramirez, R.: Value Co-Production: Intellectual Origins and Implications for Practice and Research. Strategic Management Journal 20(1), 49–65 (1999)

Part 13

Processes and Decision

Supporting Cross-Organizational Process Control

Samuil Angelov[1], Jochem Vonk[1], Krishnamurthy Vidyasankar[2], and Paul Grefen[1]

[1] School of Industrial Engineering, Eindhoven University of Technology
{s.angelov,j.vonk,p.w.p.j.grefen}@tue.nl
[2] Department of Computer Science, Memorial University of Newfoundland
vidya@mun.ca

Abstract. E-contracts express the rights and obligations of parties through a formal, digital representation of the contract provisions. In process intensive relationships, e-contracts contain business processes that a party promises to perform for the counter party, optionally allowing monitoring of the execution of the promised processes. In this paper, we describe an approach in which the counter party is allowed to control the process execution. This approach will lead to more flexible and efficient business relations which are essential in the context of modern, highly dynamic and complex collaborations among companies. We present a specification of the process controls available to the consumer and their support in the private process specification of the provider.

1 Introduction

Traditionally, the agreement for business collaboration is specified in a contract. Nowadays, to stay competitive, companies engage in highly dynamic and complex business collaborations. This dynamism and complexity requires improvement of the efficiency and effectiveness of business collaborations, which has led to the usage of information technology to support the contracting process and to the transformation of paper contracts into electronic contracts [1]. E-contracts contain the terms and conditions of the collaboration agreed by the parties in a digital, machine interpretable format. In process intensive collaborations (e.g., service delivery), e-contracts specify explicitly the processes agreed by the parties. Explicit, formal process specification allows dynamic coupling of the systems of providers and consumers for the duration of the collaboration.

With the advances in information technology, process providers started offering the possibility for consumers to monitor the process execution, thereby allowing them to quickly react and adapt their processes to the context [2]. To further improve their services, providers can offer the consumers (limited) control over the execution of the agreed processes. The benefits for the consumer are obtaining a more flexible, potentially more efficient and effective service [3]. For the provider, this opportunity can mean obtaining a competitive advantage over similar services offered by others.

In this paper, we present an approach for supporting process control in process intensive business collaborations. We identify control primitives that are valuable for a process consumer and which a provider can offer. We discuss how these primitives can be supported internally by the provider. The approach is illustrated with an example from the healthcare domain.

L.M. Camarinha-Matos et al. (Eds.): PRO-VE 2009, IFIP AICT 307, pp. 415–422, 2009.

2 Research Background

In business collaborations, in order to allow counterparties to be aware of the activities that will be performed by the party and to monitor the states of these activities during the business collaboration, providers share relevant parts of their processes with consumers. However, private processes should not be directly disclosed as they may reveal company sensitive information or may contain activities that will be irrelevant for the counterparty.

In [4], a three level framework for process specification is proposed, distinguishing external, conceptual, and internal process levels. At the conceptual level, the process specification is technology independent, specifying the process that will be performed by the party. Process specifications at the external level contain the activities that will be disclosed to an external party. At the internal level, the process specification reflects changes to the conceptual process specification that are driven by the specific technology used by the company. In this paper, we abstract from the technological side and consider process specifications defined at the conceptual and external levels.

Activities on the external level are derived by hiding and aggregating activities from the conceptual level. An external activity contains all conceptual activities between the starting conceptual activity and ending conceptual activity for this external activity and each conceptual activity is part of one external activity (see [5] for a detailed description of the rules for deriving an external level process specification based on a conceptual process specification).

3 Specification and Support of Process Control

We call an activity at the external level a Visibility point (VP). A VP provides information about the activity and the states of the activity during the process execution. The process provider may allow the consumer to exert certain control on a VP. We call VPs in which the consumer may exert control Interference Points (IPs). The control primitives that are offered to the process consumer are called Interference options (I-options). Different I-options may be available at different IPs. A request from the service consumer for the exertion of an I-option is called an I-request.

3.1 Specification of I-Options

Process control by a service consumer at the external level has been briefly addressed in [3]. This publication was a main source of inspiration for our initial work on the definition of I-options. Additionally, we investigated existing work on business process flexibility [6]. Flexibility of a process indicates the adaptability of a process to changes in the environment during its execution. The changes can be caused for instance by an I-request. After elaborating and extending the results from [3] and adapting the results from [6] to the context of cross-organizational collaborations, we have defined the list of I-options presented in Table 1.

We distinguish two types of I-options, i.e., *state* and *structural*. State I-options affect the execution state of an activity. Structural I-options are used to control the execution path of the process specification (shown in italic in Table 1).

Table 1. List of the I-options

I-option	Comments
DELAY/PROCEED	The start of execution of an activity is delayed/continued.
START	The execution of an activity is started.
PAUSE/CONTINUE	The execution of a started activity is paused/resumed.
SKIP	The execution of a non-started activity is skipped.
CANCEL	The execution of a started activity is terminated. Partial results from the execution of the activity remain.
RESET	The execution of a started activity is stopped and the activity is put back in its pre-start state without undoing any of the work that has been performed.
UNDO	The execution of a started activity is stopped, what has been done is undone, and the activity is put back in its pre-start state.
RETRY	An activity that has ended is put back in its pre-start state. Results from previous executions are not undone.
CHOICE	From a set of activities, the consumer chooses an activity(s) that will be executed.
ORDER	From a set of activities, the consumer selects the order of execution of the activities.

Each I-option is parameterized upon invocation. A parameter common for all I-options is the activity(s) to which the I-option is applied. Other possible parameters are time (e.g., for DELAY, PAUSE), sequence (for ORDER), etc. Based on the basic I-options defined in Table 1, complex I-options (combinations of several I-options) can be defined. Several complex I-option examples are listed in Table 2.

Table 2. Sample list of complex I-options

Complex I-options	Constituent I-options	Comments
REDO	UNDO+START	A started activity is stopped, undone, and started again.
RESTART	RESET+START	A started activity is stopped and is restarted.
TERMINATE	UNDO+SKIP	A started activity is stopped and undone. The control flow is passed to the next activity.
POSTPONE	DELAY+PROCEED	The execution of an activity is postponed and is subsequently started.

A state I-option leads to a change in the state of a VP. In Fig. 1, we present the state model of a VP and the state I-options that trigger the state changes. The model serves three purposes. First, we use it to clarify the I-options and illustrate their impact on the activity states. Second, we use it for the definition of the requirements on the support of the I-options at the conceptual level (see Section 3.2). Third, the model will serve as a main tool for the definition and system support of I-options where clear rules for the availability of I-options are required (see Section 3.3).

A state change of a VP caused by a state I-request should be reflected with the corresponding state change in the conceptual process (e.g., when a VP is paused, the corresponding conceptual activity(s) should be paused as well). However, the execution of

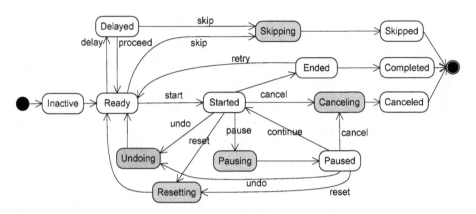

Fig. 1. The state model for the visibility points

an I-request at the conceptual level may require time. Thus, an activity at the external level must have states that represent these times of transition assuring consistency between the external and conceptual process levels. We call these transition states "ING" states, e.g., PAUSING, and show them in grey in Fig. 1. The transitions that do not have an "ING" state take place synchronously at the external and conceptual levels (see Section 3.2).

3.2 Support of the I-Options at the Conceptual Level

I-options require appropriate support at the conceptual level. The complexity of the solution for the I-options support depends on the activity state model that is used at the conceptual level. The support for an I-option will be trivial if each conceptual activity implements a state model that supports all non-"ING" states as shown in Fig. 1. However, typically, the activity state model supported at the conceptual level would be more limited (see e.g., [7]), which complicates the support for the I-options. Currently, no commonly agreed upon activity state model exists, so we use the most limited activity state model, which considers a conceptual activity as an isolated (i.e., non-interruptible) activity. Thus, a conceptual activity has three states, i.e., INAC-TIVE, STARTED, COMPLETED.

Our approach for defining the support at the conceptual level in the case of isolated activities is based on the introduction of "wait" states for the support of "state" I-options. A "wait" state has two functions. First, it is used to provide time to the consumer to invoke an I-option (as transitions between activities occur instantaneously). Second, it is used as an "activity" that "pauses" the conceptual level process execution (as activities are non-interruptible).

To explain the support for the I-options, we use x_i to denote the ith activity at the external level, and $c_{i1},...,c_{in}$ to denote the first and the last conceptual activities in the block of activities mapped to x_i. Note that in case of parallel execution of several first (last) activities, the first (last) conceptual activity c_{i1} (c_{in}) represents a set of concurrently executing activities. The support of complex I-options at the conceptual level is not discussed as it can be directly derived on the basis of the support defined for the I-option primitives.

DELAY(x_i), PROCEED(x_i), START(x_i): The support of these I-options requires the introduction of a "wait" state before c_{i1}. The consumer is given some time to exert the DELAY control. If the control is exerted, the wait state is entered until a PROCEED is requested. Otherwise, the execution proceeds with the execution of c_{i1}.

PAUSE(x_i), CONTINUE(x_i): These I-options require the introduction of a "wait" state at one or more places in the conceptual process model, in which the process can be paused. The external activity is in state PAUSING until this state is reached.

SKIP(x_i): The invocation of this I-option requires a "split" construct before c_{i1} and a "merge" construct after c_{in} (the WCP-4 and WCP-5 patterns[1]). During the transition period, x_i is in state SKIPPING. The transition can be direct or certain activities might have to be executed during the skipping. A "wait" state preceding the split must be introduced to represent the READY state of x_i during which the consumer has the time to apply the SKIP (see Fig. 2).

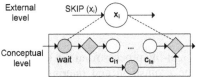

Fig. 2. Support of "SKIP"   **Fig. 3.** Support of "RETRY"

CANCEL(x_i): The invocation of this I-option requires the implementation of a cancellation construct on the conceptual level (WCP-19). The cancellation construct can be provided at several points between c_{i1} ... c_{in} allowing several points for internal reaction to a CANCEL. During a cancellation, x_i is in state CANCELLING.

RESET(x_i): Similar to the cancel I-option, a "split" is necessary at the conceptual level to "implement" this I-option. The control flow after the reset is passed to c_{i1}. During the transition between the started and ready states, activity x_i is in RESETTING state.

UNDO(x_i): Two approaches can be used to support the undo I-option. The first solution is comparable to the handling of the reset I-option and consists of explicit conceptual level undo point(s) at which activities will undo the work done. The second approach makes use of transaction management support, e.g., atomicity and compensation techniques (see [9] for an overview).

RETRY(x_i): To support the invocation of the RETRY I-option, a loop construct around c_{i1}, .., c_{in} has to be defined (WPC-21). The loop construct is preceded by a "wait" state (see Fig. 3). This activity represents the ENDED state of x_i.

CHOICE(x_i,...,x_j), ORDER(x_i,...,x_j): The invocation of these I-options requires the implementation of an exclusive choice construct (WCP-4 and WCP-6) or of a partial- or free-order construct (WCP-17 and WCP-40), respectively.

In cases of parallelism at the conceptual level, the I-option will be effectuated when each parallel running branch reaches a state that supports the I-option. If such a state cannot be reached the I-option cannot be carried out.

---

[1] In [8], workflow control patterns are presented under the abbreviation WCP, followed by their number.

3.3   Specification and System Support of I-Options

A process designer first defines the conceptual process specification. After applying aggregation and customization techniques [5] the external specification is derived. Based on the company policy, the process designer will define a set of I-options for the external level and if necessary will make adaptations on the conceptual specification that guarantee the support of the I-options.

A consumer may invoke an I-option whenever it is available. Several, mutually exclusive I-options can be available for the same activity (e.g., SKIP(x_i) and DELAY(x_i)). Different approaches to handle multiple, potentially inconsistent I-requests are possible: allowing multiple invocations and checking them for consistency (queuing of invocations), accepting one invocation and ignoring subsequent invocations, etc. The system providing control to the consumer should handle this. The state model shown in Fig. 1 is a first step in the support of I-options availability.

4   An Example Case

In this section, we illustrate our approach using a real-life process from the healthcare domain: teleradiology. This process concerns the acquisition and interpretation of medical scans of patients, and results in a report that a medical specialist, who ordered the scan, can use to base his diagnosis and treatment on.

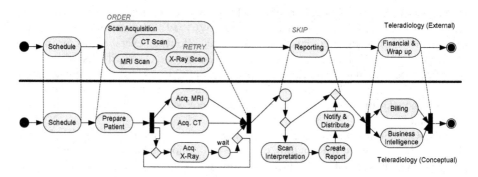

Fig. 4. Teleradiology example

Figure 4 shows a simplified teleradiology process (extensively described in [10]). The process starts by scheduling the patient. At the scheduled time, the required scans are acquired, after which an interpretation report is created and distributed to the service client. The process ends after financing has been handled. The dashed lines represent the mapping of external activities to conceptual activities, e.g., the 'reporting' activity actually consists of three conceptual activities.

As can be seen in the figure, three I-Options are specified for the teleradiology service: ORDER, RETRY, and SKIP. The scan acquisition activities are performed in sequence as the patient needs to be physically present. Using the I-option, the consumer can state the order of their execution. The conceptual process indicates that the three activities can be performed in any order defined with the I-request.

The consumer receives a copy of the scan after it has been made. The 'retry' I-option for the 'X-Ray Scan' activity allows consumers who are not satisfied with the result of the X-ray scan acquisition to request the X-ray scan to be taken again.

If the service consumer determines that the scans he has received are providing enough information, the 'reporting' activity could be skipped and process execution would be continued with the 'Financial & wrap up' activity. Financial consequences of exerting an I-option should be included in the e-contract.

5 Related Work

The control over a process in a service was initially explored in the CrossFlow project [3]. The CrossFlow approach was, however, rather ad hoc and a limited set of controls were devised. Mapping control primitives from the contract-level process to the internal process was determined by the possibilities of the underlying WfMS. Part of the work in process flexibility is concerned with controlling process executions [6]. However, it is only focused on intra-organizational processes. In this paper, relevant flexibility possibilities have been extended and adapted for the collaborative settings.

E-contracting research deals with the process of establishment and enactment of electronic contracts and determining their content to support digital collaborations between parties [1], [2], [11]. The work presented in this paper complements the research in e-contracting by extending e-contracts with the allowed I-options.

Collaboration types range from simple service outsourcing to forming complex, dynamic business networks. Web services are a de facto standard to offer services to parties [12], [13]. Web services, however, are black-box services that do not expose the process contained within. In [14], an extension is presented, which 'opens up' web services through different interfaces, one of which is the control interface to allow for process control to the service consumer. However, details on how to effectuate this control are not given.

6 Conclusions and Future Work

In this paper, we define a set of interference options, called I-options that can be given to a consumer organization to exert control over the process performed by a provider organization in the business relationship. To support these I-options on the internal process, we present a mapping from the external process to the private conceptual process. The approach is illustrated with a real-life scenario from the healthcare domain. The mapping from conceptual to internal process specification is system specific and is therefore considered outside the scope of this paper. Through the I-options offered, a provider organization has an additional mechanism to distinguish its services from those of other service providers. For a service consumer, I-requests offer an increased flexibility in service executions.

We note that the I-options can be defined also on a process level. For example, a process may be delayed, canceled, restarted. A subset of the I-options can be applied also on parts of the process. We shall address the support of I-options on processes and process parts in our future work.

Analogous to process execution control, a service provider may offer control over the usage and production of resources at activities. Example resource controls are selection of resources and selection of resource parameters (resource time allocation, resource quality). We see this as an interesting direction for future work.

References

1. Angelov, S., Grefen, P.: The Business Case for B2B E-contracting. In: 6th international conference on Electronic commerce, pp. 31–40. ACM Press, New York (2004)
2. Xu, L.: Monitoring Multi-Party Contracts for E-business. PhD thesis, University of Tilburg (2004)
3. Grefen, P., Aberer, K., Hoffner, Y., Ludwig, H.: CrossFlow: Cross-Organizational Workflow Management in Dynamic Virtual Enterprises. Int. J. of Computer Systems Science and Engineering 15(5), 277–290 (2000)
4. Grefen, P., Ludwig, H., Angelov, S.: A Three-Level Framework for Process and Data Management of Complex E-services. Int. J. of Coop. Inf. Systems 12(4), 487–531 (2003)
5. Eshuis, R., Grefen, P.: Constructing Customized Process Views. Data & Knowledge Engineering 64(2), 419–438 (2008)
6. Schonenberg, M., Mans, R., Russel, N., Mulyar, N., Aalst, W.: Process Flexibility: A Survey of Contemporary Approaches. In: Dietz, J., Albani, A., Barjis, J. (eds.) Advances in Enterprise Engineering. LNBIP, vol. 10, pp. 16–30. Springer, Berlin (2008)
7. Hollingsworth, D.: The Workflow Reference Model. TC00-1003, Workflow Management Coalition (1995)
8. Russel, N., Hofstede, A., Aalst, W., Mulyar, N.: Workflow Control-Flow Patterns: A Revised View. BPM Center Reports, BPM-06-22, BPM Center (2006)
9. Wang, T., Vonk, J., Kratz, B., Grefen, P.: A Survey on the History of Transaction Management: from Flat to Grid Transactions. Distributed and Parallel Databases 23(2), 235–270 (2008)
10. Vonk, J., Wang, T., Grefen, P., Swennenhuis, M.: An Analysis of Contractual and Transactional Aspects of a Teleradiology Process. Beta Working Papers, WP 263, Eindhoven Univ. of Technology (2008)
11. Milosevic, Z., Dromey, R.: On Expressing and Monitoring Behaviour in Contracts. In: 6th EDOC Conference, pp. 3–14. IEEE Computer Society, Washington (2002)
12. Alonso, G., Casati, F., Kuno, H., Machiraju, V.: Web Services: Concepts, Architectures and Application. Springer, Heidelberg (2004)
13. Papazoglou, M.: Web Services: Principles and Technology. Prentice-Hall, Englewood Cliffs (2007)
14. Grefen, P., Ludwig, H., Dan, A., Angelov, S.: An Analysis of Web Services Support for Dynamic Business Process Outsourcing. IST 48(11), 1115–1134 (2006)

A Service for Robust Decision Downloading in Collaborative Networks

Heiko Thimm[1] and Karsten Boye Rasmussen[2]

[1] Pforzheim University, School of Engineering, Tiefenbronner Str. 65
D-75015 Pforzheim, Germany
heiko.thimm@hs-pforzheim.de
[2] University of Southern Denmark, Department Marketing and Management,
Campusvej 55 DK-5230 Odense, Denmark
kbr@sam.sdu.dk

Abstract. Theory and observations about the positive influence of robust decision downloading among the employees within single companies can be related to the context of Collaborative Networks were a moderator makes decisions on behalf of the network. Especially, configuration decisions that generate a Virtual Enterprise arranged from the network members must be downloaded robustly within the network. Otherwise, the network collaboration climate can be damaged since in such decisions the network is separated in members that are included and others that are excluded from participation in the Virtual Enterprise. We present an information technological service that generates and downloads explanations from data about the network and about configuration decisions within the network. Through this service robust decision downloading can be performed effectively and with little time effort by moderators thus contributing to a successful network.

Keywords: Collaborative Network, Virtual Enterprise, Collaboration Platform, Network Moderator, Data Analysis, Decision Downloading.

1 Introduction

The term *decision downloading* refers to the communication of a decision to those who have not been involved in the decision-making process [4]. So-called *robust decision downloading* is considered to be the most appropriate mode of decision downloading. Robust downloaders discuss how and why the decision was made, what alternatives were considered, how it fits in with the organizational mission, and how it impacts the organization and employees. Less effective downloaders discuss some or only few of the above issues. Robust decision downloading has a number of positive implications for individual employees including features such as a stronger support of and commitment to the organization, a higher identity with the organization, and the employee perception that the organization is well managed and headed in the right direction [4]. It is a hypothesis of our research that these findings are to a large extent valid to decision making in Collaborative Networks too. We assume that the members of such networks, i.e. companies of typically smaller and medium size, can be compared to the

L.M. Camarinha-Matos et al. (Eds.): PRO-VE 2009, IFIP AICT 307, pp. 423–432, 2009.

individual employees in the classical decision downloading context. We especially investigate the influence of the decision making practice on the network collaboration climate in Collaborative Networks with a human moderator managing the network. By the engagement of a moderator the more time consuming multi-person decision processes can be substituted by the more agile single-person decision processes [11] in which the moderator makes decisions on behalf of the network. We look at networks were the moderator makes decisions concerning configuration acting as an elected manager of the Collaborative Network. Especially are we considering configuration decisions where companies are selected from the network for building a *Virtual Enterprise (VE)* for the handling of a business opportunity. We refer to these decisions as *VE creation decisions*.

Although there is no direct proof of our above described hypothesis available we view robust decision downloading as a major obligation for moderators in parallel with the obligation for managers towards employees. In the long run an inappropriate decision downloading can damage the network collaboration climate. This threat for the network can arise easily in particular from an inappropriate downloading of sensitive decisions. We regard VE creation decisions and other decisions that directly influence the economic situation of the individual network members as sensitive decisions.

We understand that due to the restricted amount of time that is available for moderators to deal with the large spectrum of different moderator tasks there is a strong demand for an effective automation of robust decision downloading in Collaborative Networks. In this article we address this need for automation by proposing a novel information technology based service for robust decision downloading. This service complements an earlier developed decision support service specialized on the configuration of VEs [12]. Both services are based on complex data analyses. The data available for the decision support service together with data about moderator sessions recorded in a machine processible format in a corresponding log is analyzed and decision explanations are generated. These explanations consist of different "views" that together provide the decision background as demanded for robust decision downloading. The views contain quantitative data retrieved from a comprehensive data repository that is specialized for VE creation decisions.

The remainder of the article is organized as follows. In Section two VE creation decisions are analyzed from a decision making point of view. In Section three, we present the conceptual framework of our proposed service for decision downloading. Also a typical application scenario for our services is given and the envisaged benefits are discussed. Section four gives an overview of a corresponding prototype. Related work is discussed in Section five. Section six presents our intended future work and concluding remarks.

2   VE Creation from a Decision Making Perspective

In the following sections we investigate processes in Collaborative Networks that are concerned with the forming of VEs. We especially focus on moderated Company Networks where a moderator is in charge of the selection of proper companies for a VE and related communication measures to inform the network. In our investigation general requirements for corresponding information technology based services are identified that are addressed in a later section.

2.1 Partner Selection for VE Creation

The process of handling an external request for information or offer by a network can be divided in three steps. In step one the request is received from the market by the network. In step two negotiations between the requestor and the network as well as further network-internal processing steps are performed. If a signed order contract between the requestor and the network is achieved a third step is completed. It is a characteristic of Collaborative Networks that in this third step the order is fulfilled as a collaborative task by a subset of the network members that form a Virtual Enterprise (VE). In order to be successful on the market a network is required to find for each request an appropriate VE under consideration of the company's profiles and competences, resource utilization states and other company specific criteria as well as criteria that relate to the network as a whole. Thus, the creation of a VE imposes to the network a complex multi-criteria decision problem [12] were hard and soft selection criteria from the perspective of a single network member but also the perspective of the network as a whole need to be reflected. Not only that the number of selection criteria is increasing with the size of the network, the number and complexity of the offered products, and the number of interdependencies between the network members such as overlapping competences between companies. Their relevance for the VE creation is also changing over time as a result of market changes but also changes with respect to the relations among the network members.

Because of the high degree of complexity of the VE creation task IT based solutions that allow to complete this task in a single person effort have been proposed [1, 2, 10]. The common premise of these approaches is that Collaborative Networks are coordinated and managed by an elected human moderator who as a manager performs the VE creation task on behalf of the entire network by effectively applying the descriptions supplied by the network members.

2.2 On the Need for Robust Downloading of VE Creation Decisions

The hypothesis of robust decision downloading will place it in the human nature that employees (or members of Collaborative Networks) will feel uncomfortable if decision downloading does not meet the above mentioned criteria for robust decision downloading. We consider this to be especially valid for decisions that influence the company's viability exemplified in the economic situation affected by such decisions as the VE creation decisions. Each individual VE creation decision is based on a separation of the network members into a group of members that will benefit from the decision – they will be assigned to work on a business and thus attracted by a revenue opportunity – and another group that will not benefit. The group of non-benefiters can be further divided into network members that for more obvious reasons have not become a member of the VE. For example, they might not offer any service or product needed for the fulfillment of the business opportunity. However, the group of non-benefiters can also consist of companies that offer exactly the services and products needed and that still have not been considered for the VE for some additional reasons. For example, they might have been participating in many previous VEs or their membership in the VE might be prevented due to an exclusion constraint of another more important member needed for the VE. Understanding the reasons for this decision can require complicated decision analysis including a projection into a future status of the network as a whole.

It can be expected that robust decision downloading is especially important for this specific subset of non-benefiters in order to obtain their acceptance for the VE creation decision. Since it can be assumed that this subset of non-benefiters is changing from decision to decision over the time many of the network members will make some non-benefiter experience. If the non-benefiters are not supported in overcoming this uncomfortable experience by a robust decision downloading the network collaboration climate can severely suffer in the long run.

3   A Decision Support and Downloading Service for VE Creation

Decision Support Service. Figure 1 contains a conceptual view of the proposed decision support service. The usage scheme of this service for the creation of VEs consists of three phases. In the first phase, the request is screened and decomposed into request components. The service supports this task by allowing the moderator to browse through products and services of the companies. The resulting request components determine the kind of products and services needed from the network for the handling of the request. In the second phase, a corresponding search profile for the demanded VE is specified which states a set of criteria for selecting companies and evaluating possible VE alternatives. In order to allow for convenient specification of a search profile a corresponding interactive template is presented to the moderator. In the third phase, the possible VE alternatives are scored reflecting the fit to the criteria given in the search profile. The scoring result is presented to the moderator in the form of a ranked list of VE alternatives that meet the search profile. The list might be empty if step one has included services and products that are not available and the list might be limited to the top priorities if a large number of alternatives are scored.

Through the use of the proposed support service moderators may achieve what is generally regarded as "informed decision making" [6]. That is, by iterating over the above described phases several times with different versions of search profiles the moderator can obtain deep insights into the decision problem space and explore corresponding VE alternatives. The decision security will increase with more and more iterations until the final decision can be made.

In order to allow for an informed decision making the service makes use of a comprehensive information base that contains the product and service offerings of the members of the company network and also their company profiles, competences, and collaboration preferences. The information base also stores the collaboration history of the company network, i.e. records describing previous VEs including information about the corresponding requests and the resulting collaboration experience. Moreover, the information base contains indicators that describe the economic status of the company network such as cash balance, order backlog, resource utilization, and inventory state.

Decision Downloading Service. By using the decision support service the moderator can conveniently find a proper VE alternative that is in turn brought into being. IT support for the workflow in dynamic virtual enterprises has been studied earlier [7]. The decision downloading service described in the following is targeting another

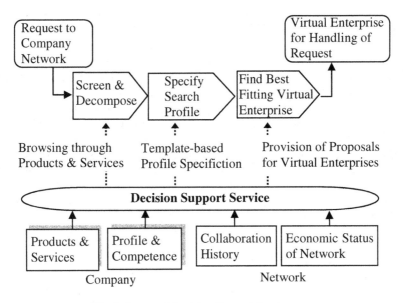

Fig. 1. Proposed Decision Support Service

moderator activity that too has to be performed after it has been decided for a final VE alternative. It is the goal of this service to perform a robust downloading of the moderator's VE creation decision to the network members where the main target group are the network members that are not selected as part of the VE. For the other network members the decision downloading has a more informative character. Through the downloading service moderators can perform the downloading task efficiently within very limited time without compromising on the richness and user-friendliness of the information that is conveyed. Once the moderator has decided for a particular VE alternative that has been generated by the decision support service the decision downloading service can be instructed to automatically generate and distribute the corresponding explanations within the network. There exist various options for the technical implementation of a distribution mechanism for the explanations such as email newsletters, intranet publishing, and provisioning of explanations in a dedicated online content repository.

The explanations are generated in three steps based on the content of the information base and further data recorded during moderator sessions with the decision support service. In a first step the relevant decision justification information is automatically derived from the individual decision-specific criteria, global policies and strategies defined for the network, and corresponding information about the current global status of the network. In a second step this information is augmented by further context specific background information to make it easier for users to perform a decision diagnosis and to gain understanding about the decision justification. The data are partly contributed by the decision support service that records data for each moderator session including search profiles, intermediate internal processing results, bookkeeping data, and the final ranking of alternative VE creation proposals. In a third step the decision downloading service generates decision explanations in the form of data views that are easy to read and understand by humans. By these data views we mean pre-computed views that include quantitative data retrieved from the underlying data collection describing attributes of the network companies.

Views. At the current stage of our research we consider three different types of views. The *Search Profile View* presents the search profile of the request as decomposed and specified by the moderator. This view gives insights into the needed products and services and the decision criteria that have been considered for the generation of the VE alternatives. The *Search Result and Criteria Evaluation View* contains the VE alternative for which the moderator has decided finally. This view is intended to clarify to the company representatives the reasons for the final decision and in particular the arguments why their company is a part of the VE or in the opposite case why their company is not part of the VE. The information being presented includes among others the total score and single scores of the chosen VE compared to mean score values of the VE alternatives in terms of the set of relevant decision criteria. The *Decision Impact View* is based on a projection of quantitative data in the future. Through this view one can learn about future network states from an economic and collaboration point of view as they will result from an order fulfilment by the selected VE. The network states are described in terms of corresponding quantitative indicators such as revenue, resource utilization, inventory state, and collaboration specific indicators. The description is intended to clarify both the consequences of the given VE creation decision for the network as a whole and for the single members of the network. The latter is given in the form of anonymous indicators such as mean number of participations in VEs, mean revenue that companies have obtained as contributor in VEs, mean duration between consecutive VEs that a company is participating in, mean revenue distribution over the network members.

Envisaged Application Scenarios and Benefits. In the following we will describe a fictive example of a small scale company network. The typical application scenarios addressed by our services will share the characteristics of the example except for a bigger size and larger network complexity. We suppose a company network specialized on the production of passenger seats for planes, ships, trains, and busses. Furthermore, we suppose that the moderator needs to select members to form a VE to handle a request for quotation from a shipyard asking for an offer for 400 passenger seats with an integrated infotainment system. From a corresponding process description for the production of the requested seats the moderator can identify or decompose that the following set of activities is needed for the order fulfilment: (1) production of metal seat frames, (2) production of seat upholsteries, (3) production of circuit systems, (4) production of monitors, (5) production of harnesses, (6) final assembly of seats.

The moderator uses the decision support service in order to efficiently explore an appropriate VE – ultimately finding the best fitting VE - among the set of possible alternatives. An initial search profile is accordingly specified which will lead to a list of possible VE configuration alternatives with corresponding scores. The scores reflect the goodness of fit of the VE configuration alternatives with respect to the selection criteria and constraints declared in the search profile. Typically, a moderator will perform several iterations with accordingly modified search profiles until it is finally decided for a configuration alternative that has been proposed by the decision support service.

In order to complete the obligation to appropriately download the chosen VE configuration decision the moderator submits the final decision to the downloading service by a corresponding selection operation on the presented result list. Given this activation event the downloading service analyses data recorded during the use of the decision support service and further company and network specific indicators. These analyses lead to decision explanations that are made available as stored documents in a specific repository where they can be accessed by the network members. The members will receive notification emails that contain general data about the decision situation and individualized access information that allows retrieval of the explanation documents.

Through the downloading service moderators can effectively and efficiently perform robust decision downloading. The network members benefit from the service by being supplied with purposefully and consistently prepared decision explanations giving them reliable clarity about reasons for VE creation decisions. Note that without such a service there is the risk that the provisioning as well as the content of the explanations can be biased by human factors. We expect that a decision making practice in Collaborative Networks which is based on the proposed service will contribute to a positive collaboration climate.

4 Prototype

A first standalone prototype of our proposed services for Collaborative Networks is currently being implemented. Figure 2 shows the major components of the prototype for which we apply the typical technologies of web-based multi-tier software architectures in combination with the JAVA programming language and other JAVA technologies. The XML standard is used as data interchange format between the system components. For example, session logs, search profiles, search results, and decision explanations are exchanged as XML documents. The prototype offers to moderators a web browser-based front end and another front end for network members specialized on information visualization. The components of the prototype store and maintain data in a common data base which can be logically divided into the four repositories shown in Figure 2. The *Company Network Directory* (CND) contains descriptions of the companies in terms of their product and service offerings and also their competencies and technical abilities. The *VE Creation Log* contains recorded sessions in which VE proposals have been generated by the system according to search profiles. The third data repository contains as the name indicates data about the economic status of the network and about collaborative processes and business transactions as completed within the network in reality. Decision explanations are administered in the *Decision Views Repository*.

The *Collaboration Proposal Generator* takes the search profile of the moderator and completes a sophisticated orchestration algorithm. A resulting ranked list of VE alternatives is delivered back to the moderator. During such a moderator session the Collaboration Proposal Generator records data about search profiles, processing steps of the orchestration algorithm together with intermediate results, and proposed VE

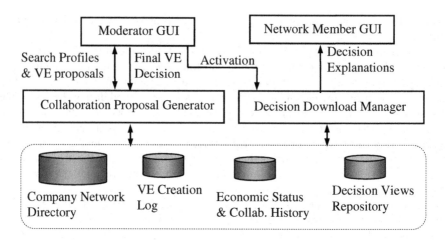

Fig. 2. Architecture of Prototype

alternatives. These data are stored in the VE Creation log for the purpose of automatically generating decision explanations. The *Decision Download Manager* is called interactively from the moderator GUI when a final decision for a VE alternative is available. The chosen alternative is selected first in the ranked list of alternatives presented to the moderator. This selection is recorded in the VE Creation log and the Decision Download Manager is activated when the moderator has confirmed the selection. The Decision Download Manager then retrieves information from the database to generate the corresponding decision explanations. The generated explanations are made available in the Decision Views Repository where they may be accessed by the network members. In addition to such a direct access, the decision explanations can also be published on the network's intranet. The members are automatically notified by the Download Manager through email messages.

5 Related Work

The configuration of Virtual Enterprises from the members of a Collaborative Network has been intensively investigated, for example in the ECOLEAD Project [3]. In many of these studies Virtual Enterprises are the result of a decision or negotiation process in which a multitude of different decision criteria are considered. Because of the complexity of decision criteria it is often difficult to understand the rationales behind such decisions for those uninvolved in the decision making process while the decision makers often believe that the long labored decision needs no explanation [4]. So far not a lot of attention has been paid to the question of how decisions in general and configuration decisions in particular should be communicated in the Collaborative Network. Investigations regarding decision making practices in Collaborative Networks and the impact on the network collaboration climate are only rarely available [9]. This is a surprising fact since decision making and communication in companies as single enterprises and the impact of the outcome and the communication on the individual employee perception of justice or fairness in the company has for long been an area of intense research in the concept of "organizational justice" [5, 8]. "Organizational justice" as a perception can be subdivided into or being dependent upon types of justice as "distributive justice", "procedural justice", and "interactional justice" [5]. The distributive concept of justice concerns the fairness of the output given the input. The extend of input from a given company might be more transcendent to all companies as well as to the single company itself due to the use of an information service. Secondly, the "procedural justice" that is covering the fairness in the process will certainly be demonstrated by the proposed service. The software cannot obtain any bias that is not presented as arguments and parameters in the logic of the system. The service will demonstrate how the companies have presented themselves as well as demonstrate the iterative logic in finding the most adequate outcome. The concept of "interactional justice" is about how people are treated with dignity and respect. The procedural aspect mentioned before can be said through the transparent and unbiased system to provide and signify dignity and respect for the individual company. We thus consider these concepts and findings of research on organizational justice as also being relevant for the companies forming Collaborative Networks. We intend to explore this research field in the future for example by simulation studies based on the core models for our moderator services and the prototype.

6 Future Work and Conclusions

A great deal of work still lies ahead in elaborating further the introduced decision downloading service. We will especially investigate information visualization concepts [13] with the goal to develop an approach that fits to the specific needs of effective visualization of decision explanations. This will also include solutions allowing the network members to customize the visual presentation of decision explanations to their individual needs. Another more long term goal will be the study of the service's effectiveness with respect to the upkeep of a positive collaboration climate in the Collaborative Network. We intend to experiment with the service on the basis of simulation of the central model. Live tests and first experience with the implementation of the model will necessarily lead to further investigation into the different data views and fact-based indicators that should be contained in decision explanations.

We understand that the network collaboration climate is a crucial success factor of Collaborative Networks and that the decision making practice of the network has a strong influence on this. Without proper IT support it will be extremely difficult for moderators to perform robust decision downloading which is understood as the ideal downloading mode. The article has presented a first approach to such a moderator service for automated robust downloading of VE creation decisions.

References

1. Bittencourt, F., Rabelo, R.J.: A Systematic Approach for VE Partners Selection Using the Scor Model and the AHP Method. In: Proc. IFIP TC5 Working Conf. on Virtual Enterprises, Valencia, pp. 99–108. Springer, Heidelberg (2005)
2. Camarinha-Matos, L.M.: ICT Infrastructures for VO. In: Camarinha-Matos, L.M., Afsarmanesh, H., Ollus, M. (eds.) Virtual Organisations: Systems and Practices, pp. 83–104. Springer, New York (2005)

3. Camarinha-Matos, L.M., Afsarmanesh, H.: Collaborative networks: a new scientific discipline. Journal of Intelligent Manufacturing 16, 439–452 (2005)
4. Clampitt, P., Williams, M.: Decision Downloading. MIT Sloan Mgmt. Review (January 2007)
5. Colquitt, J.A., Conlon, D.E., Wesson, M.J., Porter, C.O.L.H., Yee, K., Ng, K.Y.: Justice at the Millennium: A Meta-Analytic Review of 25 Years of Organizational Justice Research. Journal of Applied Psychology 86(3), 425–445 (2001)
6. Dave, G.: Informed decision making. J. of Information Science (51/1), 169–173 (1995)
7. Grefen, P., Aberer, K., Hoffner, Y., Ludwig, H.: CrossFlow: Cross-Organizational Workflow Management in Dynamic Virtual Enterprises. Int. Journ. of Computer Systems Science & Engineering 15(5), 277–290 (2000)
8. Greenberg, J.: A Taxonomy of Organizational Justice Theories. The Academy of Management Review 12(1), 9–22 (1987)
9. Noran, O.: A Decision Support Framework for Collaborative Networks. In: 8th IFIP Working Conference on Virtual Enterprises (PRO-VE 2007), Guimãraes, Portugal, pp. 83–90 (2007)
10. Shen, W., Kremer, R., Ulieru, M., Norrie, D.: A Collaborative Agent-Based Infrastructure for Internet-enabled Collaborative Enterprises. Int. Journal of Production Research 41(8), 1621–1638 (2003)
11. Sherer, S.A.: Critical Success Factors for Manufacturing Networks as Perceived by Network Coordinators. Journal of Small Business Management 41(4), 325–345 (2003)
12. Thimm, H., Thimm, K., Rasmussen, K.: Supporting Moderators of Company Networks by an Optimization Service for Orchestration. In: 16th European Conference on Information Systems (ECIS), Galway, Ireland, June 9-11, p. 12 (2008) ISBN 978-95553159-2-3
13. Zhu, B., Chen, H.: Information Visualization for Decision Making. In: Handbook on Decision Support Systems, vol. 2, pp. 699–772. Springer, Heidelberg (2008)

A Practice-Based Analysis of an Online Strategy Game

Giannis Milolidakis[1], Chris Kimble[2], and Demosthenes Akoumianakis[1]

[1] Technological Education Institution of Crete, Greece
[2] Euromed Management, Marseille, France
epp382@epp.teiher.gr, chris.kimble@euromed-management.com,
da@epp.teiher.gr

Abstract. In this paper, we will analyze a massively multiplayer online game in an attempt to identify the elements of practice that enable social interaction and cooperation within the game's virtual world. Communities of Practice and Activity Theory offer the theoretical lens for identifying and understanding what constitutes practice within the community and how such practice is manifest and transmitted during game play. Our analysis suggests that in contrast to prevalent perceptions of practice as being textually mediated, in virtual settings it is framed as much in social interactions as in processes, artifacts and the tools constituting the 'linguistic' domain of the game or the practice the gaming community is about.

Keywords: Online gaming, practice, social interaction, virtual worlds.

1 Introduction

In the early 1990s there was an upsurge of interest in on-line communities, stimulated in part by Howard Rheingold's book "The Virtual Community" [1] and in part by the growth of electronic networks such as the WELL (Whole Earth 'Lectronic Link). Multiplayer on-line games such as MUDS (Multiple User DungeonS) and MOOs (MUDS Object Oriented) were a focus of great deal of interest at the time. Now online multiplayer games are again attracting renewed attention. Although the earliest work in this area was concerned with issues of identity [2], later work began to focus on how on-line interaction takes place more generally and stressed the role played by social relationships [3]. More recent analyses of Massively Multiplayer Online Games [4] also makes use of social interaction and relationship building.

In this paper, we will continue this theme and analyze behavior in on-line games from a practice-oriented perspective informed by concepts from Communities of Practice [5], Networks of Practice [6] and Activity Theory [7]. In particular, we will examine the tools, processes and artifacts that allow the players to achieve their shared goals. Our analysis will centre on how the notion of practice is framed within the game and the ways in which this enables the players to interact, co-operate and compete. To this effect, we will employ what is sometimes termed virtual ethnography [8], to investigate the type, nature and scope of prevailing gaming practices and how they are framed and manifested during game play.

L.M. Camarinha-Matos et al. (Eds.): PRO-VE 2009, IFIP AICT 307, pp. 433–440, 2009.

The rest of the paper is structured as follows. The next section establishes the theoretical links of the present work by briefly addressing relevant concepts from the literature. Then, we present our research methodology and case study. Based on this the next section will discuss on-line gaming behavior from a practice oriented perspective. The paper concludes by summarizing key contributions.

2   CoPs and NoPs

The concept of a Community of Practice originated with Lave and Wenger [9] and was quickly adopted by other authors such as Brown and Duguid [10]. However, in much of this early work the notion of practice was left undefined beyond noting that practice is socially constructed and intimately connected to learning. Vann and Bowker [11] describe this early view as "*an epistemology of practice that entails a set of claims about how people learn and how knowledge is shared among social actors*". In his later work, Wenger developed the connection between practice and meaning arguing, "*Practice is about meaning as an experience of everyday life*" [5]. He explains that for the claims processors in his study, their 'practice' was something they had developed in order to make sense of their job. He also expanded the notion of what constitutes practice by introducing the idea that constellations of connected Communities of Practice could exist within a single organization. Later, Brown and Duguid [6] expanded this further by introducing the concept of Networks of Practice (NoPs) to describe groups of people who are geographically separate but who share similar interests or activities. NoPs share many of the features of CoPs but are organized at a more individual level and are based on personal rather than communal social networks. Using Granovetter's work on the strength of social ties, Brown and Duguid characterize NoPs as being linked by weak social ties.

The main difference between the two is that CoPs usually consist of people who know each other; they are primarily face-to-face communities that work closely together to accomplish their goals [12]. NoPs, on the other hand consist of people who may never get to know each other, but collaborate and transfer knowledge through the use of shared tools such as intranets [13]. Although they may develop similar identities, these are less tightly coupled to a NoP than would be the case with a CoP.

3   Activity Theory and Virtual Worlds

Activity Theory is a branch of Psychology that has a rich history of its own [7]; here we will simply highlight the points that are relevant to our own work. Briefly, Activity Theory argues that tools mediate human activity; when people interact to achieve some goal, they do so using tools. In Activity Theory, these tools are seen as an externalization of the internal knowledge of the toolmaker. As the knowledge of the toolmaker is 'embedded' in the tool, and as the tool mediates the activity, Activity Theory has become widely used in areas where a designer wishes to intentionally 'create' some activity, such as Human Computer Interaction [14].

Activity Theory is not a determinist theory: tools are remade and recast with use and new tools are created to deal with new situations. It does not argue that because knowledge is built into a tool in some way, and because a tool is sharable, then the knowledge used to create the tool also becomes sharable. The argument is more that tools condition certain patterns of actions and that by their repeated use these patterns become part of the accepted practice of the people who use the tools. This argument is more easily sustained in the world of CoPs and physical artifacts; when we move to the world of NoPs and 'virtual reality' however, the distinctions between the tool and patterns of action it conditions become harder to define. For example, in place-based social gatherings it is not possible for one person to deploy simultaneous multiple identities, whereas in virtual spaces tools to manage multiple identities are common-place [15]. Thus, the practice of identity management in traditional settings is not simply reproduced in virtual space but is extended by the tools used to create that space. Similarly, civil inattention, the process by which we demonstrate awareness of one another in physical places [16], has no direct equivalent in virtual space, although awareness can be enhanced in other ways [17].

In light of the above, an obvious question to ask is what is actually happening in virtual spaces and how is practice encoded, enacted and transmitted online. The literature tends to focus on elements of practice framed in social interactions. Although this is valid, it fails to explain why certain offline practices are not reconstructed online or how it is that certain online practices do not have offline counterparts [13]. If practice is not simply reproduced online, but extended and enriched through digital media, then insights into this should improve our understanding of online behavior and offer a more appropriate unit of analysis for framing online practice.

4   Case Study

Travian is a massive multiplayer online strategic war game created by Travian Games GmbH. Such games are relevant to the present work due to their inherent social connectivity, which classifies them both as interfaces to virtual spaces and community-support systems. Typically, communities are formed in the course of games to provide members with entertainment and/or online socialization using a dedicated repertoire of resources. Travian supports a 2D graphical environment and a messaging through which gamers can cooperatively attain individual and collective objectives, including private and public communication, diplomatic acts such as creation of alliances, declaration of war and the basic activities of warfare such as invasion, etc. The players' rewards, apart from entertainment, include socialization and the acquisition of a reputation within a community of online gamers [4].

The idea is that every new player becomes a major of a little village trying to attract (virtual) population by constructing and upgrading buildings and resource fields. New villages can be found or captured by players' joining alliances and coordinating their efforts. Winner of the game becomes the first alliance that will create a village containing a special building called "The World Wonder" and upgrade it to the highest level (i.e. 100). A village containing a "The World Wonder" needs enormous quantities of resources and a huge defense army to protect it against other alliances trying to destroy it. Achieving such a goal requires support of many players and consequently, it is nearly impossible for a single player to win.

4.1 Methods

Two game characters were created in one of the many worlds (servers) of Travian as part of our virtual ethnography. One of the characters was less socially active than the other and did not have such an intense presence in the virtual world. Sufficient time was spent online to support the second character in an effort to join in a high standard and demanding alliance to team-up with experienced players and take part in non-trivial activities. Through daily participation in the virtual world and interaction with co-gamers, the active character established close relations to other players enabling liaisons with other game worlds through accessing characters from other servers. Our virtual ethnography was conducted with the first author being fully immersed in the game and observing how third-party game characters deal with their duties in the different settings (i.e. different worlds, different alliances). In a period of 11 months, a large file was compiled containing data about conversations in private and public chat rooms and forums or in the small discussion boards and chats. It is worth mentioning that at the end of the 11 month period, the "social" character owned 25 villages with more than 20 thousands of population in contrast to the 5 villages and the 4 thousands of population of the less social character.

4.2 Research Questions

Our analysis of the data, as presented below, aims to provide insight to two basic research questions: (a) what are the online practices underlying the socially intensive character's engagement (b) how are these practices manifested and intertwined during game play? Prior to the conducting the virtual ethnography, our working hypothesis was that practice is not necessarily framed only as social interaction, but may be embedded into artifacts, tools and processes through which collaborators create a history of co-engagement in the game's domain. Such co-engagement and its evolutionary nature may be used to explain why offline gaming practice is not merely reconstructed online, but frequently extended and expanded.

5 Practice-Based Analysis of In-Game Behavior

Activity theorists consider practice as subsuming activity [7]. Activity becomes meaningful for a designated practice through objects whose symbolic manifestation and relational properties are clearly defined and labeled. Moreover, activities are built on knowledge, skills or competences of those performing them. It is therefore important to relate practice to knowledge as expressed in communication acts or embodied into routines, procedures or patterns of use. Then, virtual practice in online gaming communities should be framed as much in communication acts – typically manifested as social interaction – as in the virtuality through which the virtual world is made sense of.

For Travian communities, social interaction is manifested primarily during game play as text messaging, posting or replying on a post. Members use tools to join/leave communities, express opinion, request support and negotiate options and strategies. For example, in order to join an alliance, messages must be sent from / to the leaders of the alliance asking for invitation. When the game world is in its early stages, the only criterion for finding good players to join in an alliance is the game statistics boards. The dialogue below gives an example of such interaction.

> DeathWing says: Good morning, would u like to join my alliance? We are impressed by your evolution.
> DESTRO says: thanks for your invitation but I don't have embassy yet. I let you know {Embassy: a building required to join an alliance}
> DeathWing says: ok then, I'm waiting msg from you when you are ready

This type of online socializing takes place outside the game board (i.e., the interactive manifestation of the game's virtual world) and frequently, without using the build-in communication mechanisms. In fact, high standard and demanding alliances make use of external tools, such as VOIP systems, external forums and blogs to communicate. Nevertheless, social interaction is strongly intertwined with game play. Specifically, making sense of online discussions will inevitably require knowledge of game's status and vice versa. For instance, consider the following narrative that presents a group message sent to all the members of an alliance.

> Butterfly: Send 100 defend troops to the village (107 | -43) by midnight. Also send your hourly production to overcome the damages of the last attack {hourly production: the production of all villages of a player in an hour}

The message was sent using the build-in messaging system requiring from every player to send troops and resources to a specified village that was probably under attack. Players not familiar with the game may not immediately understand what is at stake. Consequently, narrative-based social interaction pre-supposes common ground on terms such as 'defend troops', 'hourly production', etc., which are tightly linked with the online game practice and its evolution. Eventually, such an intertwining between online game practices and social interaction leads to making sense of and co-engaging in the game's virtual space. Nevertheless, each type of practice is shaped and served by different artifacts. Online game practice tends to explore visual, spatial and textural representations, while social interaction is textually mediated.

Travian uses visual artifacts to allow players to make sense of the virtual world and to convey social awareness. Specifically, a village, which occupies a square tile in the game map (Figure 1-a), provides the conceptual object for understanding the virtual world and inviting micro-negotiations between the players. As the notion of the village needs to be compatible with its physical counterpart, its virtual embodiment is depicted as a place-based territory inhabited by villagers. Specific functions of the village are manifested through visual artifacts. Resource fields (Figure 1-b) and buildings (Figure 1-c) define the economy and give extra capabilities to a village.

The player, through the process of upgrading the structural components of a village, increases the population of his/ her village and is able to use extra features of the game (i.e. training new types of troops). It is important to note that the choice of visual forms and their tractable information-processing properties determine the range of activities in which the user engages in and give meaning to otherwise banal actions such as mouse clicks, keystrokes and interaction sequences. For example, in order to create a new building a number of activities must be performed. The player selects an empty building spot (round tiles in the center of Figure 1-c) to raise it. A list of available buildings appears in the screen and then the player can select the desired building. Buildings take some time to complete but when they are ready, the player can upgrade them. By selecting a building of the village, a screen will appear providing information about the building, giving access to the capabilities of that building and allowing the upgrade.

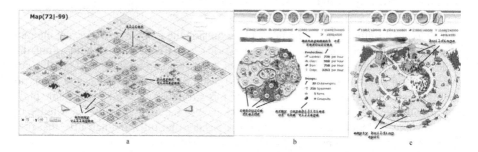

Fig. 1. a) Virtual world map b) Village overview, c) Village inner view

Another use of the visual artifacts offered by the game is to support social awareness. The game's map is used to represent who and what is around one player's village. In turn, this is used to determine tactics and drive social interactions. For example, depending on the setting (i.e., choice of tribes) the player explores the game map to identify possible enemies and / or allies. For a player with a big offensive army, other players with big offensive armies in the neighborhood are possible treats. This is because in order to keep and run such a big army a player needs to steal resources from other players nearby. Impediments to a player's development may occur when several other players seek to steal resources in the same area. On the other hand, such a player may take under his protection other players having defensive armies in order to get the extra protection from them. This, of course, influences the construction of alliances and who will be invited and included in them. Consequently, players with large armies find it difficult to coexist in the same alliance.

For a player it is important to know what exists near them; this becomes more important as the game world evolves in time and more collaborative duties need to be supported. The distinction of the allies in the game map is facilitated using colored tiles to represent the villages (see Figure 1-a). If a player wants to conquer a village then he / she must browse the game map to find out his / her nearby allies and ask for their help. An illustrative example is offered below.

Galactica says: Hi diamiano. Can u help me conquering the village of player XXX at (71l-87)?
Damiano says: Yes why not? Do u want to conquer the village tonight?

Once commitment of a sufficient number of players is obtained, the group is invited to join in a discussion group in order to cooperate and achieve the target. A typical discussion concentrates on resource types, troop size, distance from target, etc., and takes place between participants who know enough each other and have a history of co-engagement in the alliance.

> Galactica says: Hi guys. As you know, I want to conquer the village at (71I-87). How many available chiefs you have? {Chiefs: type of troops needed to conquer a village}
> Alinaki says: hi, I have 1 available and the necessary cp. {cp: culture points, needed in order to conquer a village}
> Galactica says: ok I also have 3{chiefs}... we need 2{chiefs} more
> Damiano says: I have 2 chiefs available now and one more later tonight
> Galactica says: ok 2{chiefs} will do the job
> Galactica says: please give your exact travel times to the village (71I-87) {a village is defined by its coordinates on the game map}

In the extract below, the group discusses the tactical approaches for attacking and misleading their opponents. This entails coordinative assessment of a shared object of reference, namely the map, which offers social awareness by presenting the villages (friendly or not) taking part in this campaign.

> Galactica says: I'm suggesting fake attacks to nearby villages {fake attack: an attack with one soldier}
> Galactica says: that is (77, -65) (77, -62) (71, -64) (76, -66)
> Alinaki says: ok
> Damiano says: one strike or multiple ones?
> Galactica says: multiple waves {multiple waves cause more damage to the enemy}
> Damiano says: ok

After negotiating and agreeing on the strategy, every player is aware of their respective duties in a specified time frame.

> Galactica says: I will hit first on 23:59. Alinaki will hit on 00:00 and damiano some time real close after alinaki's hit. Is everyone ok with that?
> Alinaki says: ok np
> Damiano says: no problem for me too

Generalizing this workflow, we observe that players in their effort to accomplish their target formulate small groups, establish common ground by sharing information, negotiate options, devise plans for action and finally execute the plan. Through this process, gamers make sense of the virtual world, negotiate their tactics and reconstruct their individual and social standings.

6 Conclusions

Our analysis leads to several conclusions. Firstly, online gaming practices seem to subsume activities of peripheral domains of relevance such as online identity management, social networking and orchestration practices. Secondly, gaming practice is framed as much in social interaction as in the artifacts and tools embedded in and interactively manifested through the game. Both these are intertwined to determine making of sense, as well as the gamers' individual and collective behavior. Finally, online practice does not entail mere reproduction of offline gaming patterns. Several extensions were observed resulting from the digital medium and the gamers' history of co-engagement. The later point implies that the game's artifacts embody elements of practice to which users become accustomed because of their participation in the game. Thus, these artifacts and tools that are used to process them serve as the 'artificial' language for engagement in the linguistic domain of the game (i.e., gaming practice the community is about). The distinct characteristic of such language is that it should bridge the gap between the community and the virtual space, rather than the gap between humans and machines, as typically conceived by HCI researchers.

References

1. Rheingold, H.: The Virtual Community: Homesteading on the Electronic Frontier. Addison Wesley, Reading (1993)
2. Bruckman, A.S.: Gender Swapping on The Internet. In: Leiner, B. (ed.) International Networking Conference INET 1993, San Francisco (1993)
3. Conkar, T., Noyes, J.M., Kimble, C.: CLIMATE: A Framework for Developing Holistic Requirements Analysis in Virtual Environments. Interacting with Computers 11, 387–403 (1999)
4. Jakobsson, M., Taylor, T.L.: The Sopranos meets EverQuest: social networking in massively multiplayer online games. In: Proceedings of the 2003 Digital Arts and Culture (DAC), Melbourne, Australia, pp. 81–90 (2003)
5. Wenger, E.: Communities of Practice: Learning, Meaning, and Identity. Cambridge University Press, New York (1998)
6. Brown, J.S., Duguid, P.: The Social Life of Information. Harvard Business School Press, Boston (2000)
7. Engeström, Y., Miettinen, R., Punamäki, R.-L. (eds.): Perspectives on Activity Theory. Cambridge University Press, Cambridge (1999)
8. Hine, C.: Virtual Ethnography. SAGE Publications Ltd., Thousand Oaks (2000)
9. Lave, J., Wenger, E.: Situated Learning: Legitimate Peripheral Participation. Cambridge University Press, Cambridge (1991)
10. Brown, J.S., Duguid, P.: Organizational Learning and Communities of Practice: Toward a Unified View of Working, Learning, and Innovation. Organization Science 2, 40–57 (1991)
11. Vann, K., Bowker, G.C.: Instrumentalizing the truth of practice. Social Epistemology 15, 247–262 (2001)
12. Kimble, C., Hildreth, P.: Dualities, Distributed Communities of Practice and Knowledge Management. Journal of Knowledge Management 9, 102–113 (2005)
13. Vaast, E.: What Goes Online Comes Offline: Knowledge Management System Use in a Soft Bureaucracy. Organization Studies 28, 283–306 (2007)
14. Nardi, B.A.: Context and Consciousness: Activity Theory and Human-Computer Interaction. MIT Press, Cambridge (1996)
15. Jung, Y., Jin, S.A., McLaughlin, M.: Multiple Layers of Conjoint Action: Players' Identity Management in Role-Playing Blogs. In: Annual meeting of the NCA 93rd Annual Convention, Chicago (2007)
16. Goffman, E.: Behaviour in Public Places. Notes on the Social Organization of Gatherings. Free Press, New York (1966)
17. Dourish, P., Bly, S.: Portholes: supporting awareness in a distributed work group. In: CHI 1992: Proceedings of the SIGCHI conference on Human factors in computing systems, p. 547. ACM Press, New York (1992)

An Anticipative Effects-Driven Approach for Analyzing Interoperability in Collaborative Processes

Nicolas Daclin and Vincent Chapurlat

LGI2P – Laboratoire de Génie Informatique et d'Ingénierie de la Production
Site EERIE de l'Ecole des Mines d'Alès, Parc Scientifique G. Besse
30035 Nîmes cedex, France
{nicolas.daclin,vincent.chapurlat}@ema.fr

Abstract. Partners involved into a collaborative process must satisfy interoperability requirements in order to fulfil adequately their mission all along the process. Indeed, interoperability is now considered as a key factor of success when sharing data, services, knowledge, skills, and resources. However, although the main desired effects (to respect a cost, to produce n products, to respect a quality ratio...) of this process are generally reached, some others effects (unpredictable, undesirable...) may be also induced and can lead in some cases, to a worsening of these desired effects that process has to perform. This paper presents and illustrates an Anticipative Effects-Driven Approach to check interoperability rules in collaborative process model.

Keywords: Interoperability, anticipative effects-driven approach, collaborative processes.

1 Introduction

Numerous initiatives [1; 2], developed from the last years and dealing with enterprises interoperability, have shown that ability for several partners to be interoperable is a key factor of the partnership's success. Moreover, considered for a long time only as a problem of computer sciences [3], these initiatives have demonstrated that enterprises interoperability is now considered as crucial in enterprise [4], relevant in research area [5] and can take place at different levels [6] (*e.g.* business, process, services...). In the limited frame of interoperability in process, partners are interoperable if they are able to share data, services, skills, resources. Thus, developing interoperability become crucial in order to ensure the success of the whole process and therefore to ensure a given level of performance, efficiency, reactivity and agility of this process. The waited effect of a considered process is to fulfil a given mission (to develop a new product, to find solutions facing a customer problem...) and to reach performance objectives in terms of costs, duration, and quality of service/product (*i.e.* adequacy between product/service, partners' needs and customer demand). However, this process can be affected by a lack of interoperability from a partner with others during the process runtime. As a consequence, allowing partners to know their potential to interoperate prior to the execution

L.M. Camarinha-Matos et al. (Eds.): PRO-VE 2009, IFIP AICT 307, pp. 441–448, 2009.
© IFIP International Federation for Information Processing 2009

could help (1) partners to anticipate a worsening of the achievement of process's objectives and thus (2) to adapt the process as far as possible. In this case it is about to analyze each effect that a partner can induce on the process in terms of interoperability. The purpose of this communication is to present the principles and to illustrate an Anticipative Effect-Driven Approach that allows partners to build an appropriate process and then to better control this one in the context of collaboration.

2 Interoperability Analysis

Generally speaking, interoperability represents the ability for two or more systems to operate together (or in conjunction). In the context of networked enterprise, interoperability takes place at various levels of the enterprise and has to consider various barriers as presented in the interoperability framework given in [7]. This one allows identifying and structuring the different fields in which interoperability must be analysed and improved. The goal is to develop relevant knowledge and solutions to remove, at least, one interoperability barrier at one enterprise level. Thus, this paper focuses on the analysis of interoperability in collaborative processes [8]. It is defined as the capability and the capacity of numerous resources, flows, processes, organization units (*i.e.* teams, departments) in enterprises, to work together with limited risks and without lost of performance, integrity, stability and autonomy. In this context, interoperability analysis has to be seen under two hypotheses: (1) Interoperability concerns each partner considered separately. The interest, in this case, is to know if this pointed out partner is able (or not, or in some measure yet) to perform a required service in time, a required ability at the right place and so on independently from other partners of the collaborative process. (2) Interoperability concerns all the possible interactions, their nature and dynamic all along the process runtime. The analysis of interoperability must focus first on interactions between activities of the process and second between partners themselves. Activities have to be synchronized and controlled, including the structure of the process (parallelism, sequence, mutual exclusion between activities…). As a consequence, interoperability - precisely interoperability in processes - can be seen as a set of requirements that partners will have to respect. Thus, this research work focuses on the questions: "How is it possible to define interoperability problematic? How is it possible to detect when and how some possible worsening effects due to lack of interoperability can occur? How is it possible to anticipate them?". The objective is to bring to partners, involved in the process execution, the knowledge about the potential effects that they can generate. In this case, partners will have the possibility either to validate the process and to start its execution or to improve it by providing alternatives. To do that, interoperability requirements have to be conceptualized and analyzing rules have to be implemented in order to detect if these requirements are fulfilled to avoid interoperability problems. Moreover, ensuring interoperability in process implies to define a modeling language and tool or to enrich existing ones according to interoperability requirements concept. Several modeling tool are effectively available but none allow an analysis of the possible effects and especially effects due to a lack of interoperability.

3 AEDA Principles

The proposed approach, named Anticipative Effect-Driven Approach (AEDA), allows to model, to analyse and to assess the interoperability according to the two hypotheses presented above. It is based on existing approaches developed in other fields of application (military, civil crisis response...). With regard to the approaches that take an interest on the assessment of effects that a system can produce before its implementation, the Failure Mode and Effects Analysis (FMEA) [9] is the most widely spread and used. Some extensions of this method, such as Process-FMEA, have been developed since. In this case, the objectives of the P-FMEA is to establish a set of "potential failure modes" and "effects of failure" that can occur during the process runtime in order to take corrective action before the process implementation. However this kind of method is essentially based on a brainstorming procedure and applied every time that a process has to be implemented. Others approach such as the Effect-Based Operation [10] consists to characterize and to evaluate the possible effects of actions which are supposed to reach a final outcome. In opposition to the FMEA, EBO is not based on the research of potential failure and effects that an action in a process can generate, but on the research of the outcome that actions have to achieve. In the case of collaborative processes facing to interoperability problems, these approaches remain interesting in their principles that consist to observe and to analyse the effects resulting from the execution of the process. They must be however enriched and conceptually rethought in order to match with the requirements presented before *i.e.* to characterize from a generic manner, to detect and above all to anticipate interoperability problems. As a consequence, the AEDA approach has to provide: (1) A set of modeling concepts and relations between concepts allowing partners to describe their characteristics and their role in the collaborative process in order to become able to reply to the questions such as: "Am I able to perform effectively and efficiently a task? and, if a failure is highlighted, in which measure this one can affects the entire collaborative process?". (2) A set of (as possible) generic interoperability requirements that have to be respected all along a collaborative process. The goal is to help partners to analyze their role, capacities and abilities within the process. (3) A mechanism for characterizing and detecting on the process model what, where and how can be the potential effects induced when a problem of interoperability occurs.

3.1 Modeling Concepts

As mentioned before, several concepts are required to implement the approach. The first ones are related to the process domain and coming from systemic domain, system engineering domain, enterprise modelling domain. They are justified to model properly the different configurations and characteristics of the collaborative process. Basically, processes are sequences of activities modelled from their start to their end. Activities transform and input state into an output state, use a set of resources (human and/or material as well) and are controlled. Thus, to make sure that an activity will be perform in a good way, some knowledge about the triplet resource, control and the activity itself are needed to be collected and implemented. To do that, the frame of reference time space and shape [11] can allow this collect about any elements involved in the process. Indeed, by the adaptation of this frame it is possible to position an activity, a resource and a control in this frame. This knowledge, represented in the form of attributes that characterize the considered element can be independent of any domain of application - *e.g.* resource capacity, availability, pre-emption... [12] - or specific to domain *e.g.* an activity can required a certain level of protection from its resources...It is based on this enrichment, that interoperability requirements can be developed and allow, thereafter, to reason about the possible effects about their achievement or not.

3.2 Interoperability Requirements Modelling

The others concepts required in the AEDA approach are related to (1) the design of interoperability requirement and (2) the effect characterization. The first one has to allow defining all the requirement a partner has to respect in the process. The second one enables to evaluate in which way the collaborative process may be affected if this set of requirements if not satisfied. According to the property concept proposed by [13], each interoperability requirement is modelled by a set of properties. A property is a causal temporized and constrained relation between two predicates called respectively cause or *Condition* and effect or *Conclusion*. Cause and effect are described by using variables *or attributes* and predicates *or functions* extracted from the collaborative process model. These variables characterize each element involved into the process (resource, flow, activity, etc.), taking into consideration the frame of reference time shape and space (TSS). It allows defining and formalizing physical attributes which characterizes any element, from a quantitative or qualitative manner, evolving in the time, in the space or in its shape. Any element may be "a part of" or "interacts" with another element. In this case, the evolution of each element affects and modifies the referential of the surrounding elements. Thus, defining which elements evolve in a given referential allows to know the impact of these elements on their environment. In order to refine the characterization of an element in terms of time shape and space, these ones are decomposed into sub attributes. The time attribute is defined by the sub-attributes called date and duration. The space attribute is defined by the sub-attribute called location in a defined space. The shape attribute is defined by the sub-attributes such as capacity, dimension, vulnerability (improvement or degradation of the object), quantity, *etc.*. The causal relation describes the nature of the link between the condition and the conclusion (implication, equivalence or influence) and details what are the temporal constraints on which this relation is established. An example of property is illustrated in natural language and by using TSS and predicates in table 1.

Table 1. Example of property

Cause	Relation	Effect (conclusion)
Exists a in Activities, forall x in Partner, [requiredAptitudes(a) in aptitudes(x) and location(x) = location(x) and availability(a) = true]	$\Rightarrow$ [forall t]	[x in elligibleResourcesOf (a)]

The set of property provides a support of reasoning allowing verifying the collaborative process model in respect of the interoperability requirements. However, if a given property is not satisfied by the model, it is also necessary to evaluate finely the real impact of this lack *i.e.* to characterize what can be the resulting effect on the process runtime.

3.3 Effect Characterization

An effect can be defined as a situation that can be expected, undesired, dreaded and results from an interaction. An effect results always and only from an interaction between one object, defined as the source, and one or several objects, defined as the destination. It can be simply modeled by the possible variation (or dependence) between one or several TSS attributes of the destination under the action of the source. An effect can be (1) predictable *i.e.* assessable and observable indicators exist either on the source object or the destination object(s); (2) potential *i.e.* a logic relationship between the cause and the effect exist and; (3) unpredictable or emergent, this kind of effect is not taken into consideration by the approach. An effect can be defined as direct or indirect taking into account the causal relation between situations which have induced the effect. The goal is now to characterize the nature of an effect by determining if it is [14]: Harmful, this effect is produced when the source induces a deterioration of the characteristics of the destination. These kinds of effects have to be annihilated. Good, this effect is produced when the source induces a variation of the characteristics of the destination as expected. These kinds of effects have to be maintained. Excessive, this effect is produced when the source induces a variation of the characteristics of the destination beyond this expected. In this case the effect has to be reduced. Insufficient, this effect is produced when the source induces a variation of the characteristics of the destination less than expected. The effect must be improved in order to become efficient. Furthermore, an effect is then modelled as property. For example, the property defined as: *Forall a in Activities, Forall element in input(a) [requestTSSInput(a) in TSS(element)]* ⇒ *[effect(a, element) := good]* means that if the TSS attributes requested by a given activity in input contains the TSS attributes of the element considered to be processed then the effect of the activity on the element is considered as good and this for all the activities of the collaborative process. This property can be decomposed into sub properties specifying the way to interpret the variation of effect value taking into account more precisely a given subset of TSS attributes of the activity and/or of the element. Thus, the following property: *Forall a in Activities, forall aptitude in requestedAptitude(a), forall partner in elligibleResourcesOf (a) [requestedCapacity(aptitude,a) < capacity (partner)]* ⇒ *[effect (partner, a):= insufficient and elligibleResourcesOf (a):= elligibleResourcesOf (a)-partner]* means that if an activity requires precisely a given capacity (evaluation i.e. quantification or qualification of a given aptitude taking into account a common scale of measure) then each partner selected as a potential resource must provide this capacity in order to be qualified, otherwise the effect of t element has a sub attribute quantity less than to the sub-attribute quantity describing the expected quantity of element by the activity *i.e.* the quantity of inputs from this partner on a is considered as insufficient.

4   AEDA in Use

All the concepts related the characterization of (1) the elements involved in the process and (2) effects resulting from its execution are synthesized in Figure 1.

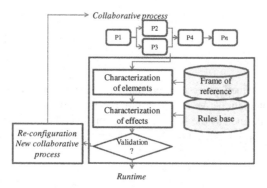

Fig. 1. The structure of the Anticipative Effects-Driven Approach

The first step consists to characterize the elements involved in the collaborative process. In this phase, the objective is to collect a maximum of information about the different activities, the resources that have to perform activities and controls. This characterization is based on the use of the TSS concept: each attribute of each element is detailed. Then the nature of the potential effects (harmful, good, insufficient, excessive and absent) induced by the collaborative process has to be determined. This step is performed thanks to the referential of interoperability requirements and effect characterization properties. At the end of this step the collaborative process is either validated or rejected. If the process is approved, the partners validate its planning and/or perform some adjustments and start its execution. If the process is rejected, this one can be re-configured or fully redeveloped. The new configuration is one more time submitted to the approach in order to detect other effects. Currently, the approach is developed in the French research project, dealing specifically with the interoperability of systems in crisis situation, ISYCRI (Interoperability of Systems in CRIsis situation, ANR-06-CSOSG). In order to illustrate the interest of the here presented approach, a specific collaborative process coming from a case study (NRBC exercise managed by the Prefecture of the Tarn in France, 27th February 2004) is used [15]. This scenario starts with the description of the crisis situation. The scenario which has been chosen is the following: *"At 10 AM, on 27th February 2004, the police is informed that an accident among a tanker truck (unknown substance) and a wagon containing chemical products is occurred. The policemen are sent on the scene and the employees of the railway station fall unconscious while several children of the neighboring kindergarten feel sick"*. A first collaborative process is created in order to face up the crisis. It consists in the execution of different activities both in parallel and in sequence. The execution of each activity required a given actor (or resource). Thus, the objective of the anticipative effect-driven approach is to validate the given collaborative process before its execution. Figure 2 shows the collaborative process that has to be implemented.

The first step is to collect, as far as possible, a maximum of knowledge related to element involved in the process *i.e.* about the different activities and the resource requested to perform them. Then, based on this knowledge collected, the potential effects that could occur in the process have o be determined. Let consider the interaction between the human resource "Red Cross" that have to perform the service "set medical post". If set medical post required an end date, it implies that the resource

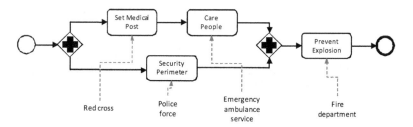

Fig. 2. Example of NRBC crisis management process

over the service at the required end date. If this requirement is effectively verified, then the effect of Red Cross on the service can be characterized as good. Conversely, if the requirement is not verified, it is question to know in which measure this requirement is violated. Does the end date will be superior or less than the expected end date? In the first case the effect will be characterize as insufficient in the second, as excessive. Then what is the effect on the first activity on the next one (care people), does its execution will be delayed or not? Thus the anticipative effect driven approach try to evaluate this set of effect all along the collaborative process and prior to its execution. Obviously, a complete process analysis has to be performed in order to characterize each effect and to provide a maximum of information to the partners. In order to do that in an automatic way, an application is currently developed ("E.D.A. for Process Analysis". under Eclipse Graphical Modeling Framework) allowing (1) to model the collaborative process and (2) to model and to check the effects characterization between elements.

5   Conclusion

This paper presents an approach to help partner to increase their organizational interoperability at process level. Currently, the anticipative effect-driven approach is developed specifically in the context of crisis management. This one has to allow an adaptation and a validation of collaborative process by anticipating potential effects that could occur during the runtime phase. This adaptation and this validation has to lead to an improvement of the interaction between objects involved in the crisis in order to perform a collaborative process perfectly adapted to cope to the crisis. The concepts of the approach are clearly identified and a referential of property is currently developed in order to characterize the nature of the effects. Future work is concerned by the development of analyses rules that have to propose alternatives to managers and the development of the resolution algorithm that has to allow the building of new collaborative process.

References

1. Interoperability Research for Networked Enterprises Applications and Software (INTEROP Network of Excellence). Annex 1 – Description of Work (2003)
2. Advanced Technologies for Interoperability of Heterogeneous Enterprise Networks and their Applications (ATHENA). Integrated Project Proposal – Description of work (2003)

3. IEEE. A compilation of IEEE standard computer glossaries. Standard computer dictionary (1990)
4. Chen, D., Dassisti, M.: Elveaeter. Enterprise Interoperability Framework and knowledge corpus – Final report. Interop deliverable Domain Interoperability, DI.3 (2007)
5. European Community Report (ECR) Unleashing the Potential of the European Knowledge Economy, Value Proposition for Enterprise Interoperability, Final Version (Version 4.0) (2008)
6. Enterprise Interoperability Research Roadmap (EIRR), Version 4.0, Cabral, R., Doumeingts, G., Li, M.S., Popplewell, K. (eds.) (July 31, 2006)
7. Chen, D., Daclin, N.: Framework for enterprise interoperability. In: 2nd IFAC Workshop on Enterprise Integration, Interoperability and Networking (EI2N), Bordeaux, France, March 20-24 (2006)
8. Chapurlat, V., Vallespir, B., Pingaud, H.: An approach for evaluating enterprise organizational interoperability based on enterprise model checking techniques. In: Proceedings of the 17th IFAC World Congress 2008, Seoul, Korea (2008)
9. IEC 60812. Analysis techniques for system reliability – Procedure for failure model and effects analysis (FMEA). Edition 2.0 (2006)
10. Lowe, D., Ng, S.: Effects-based operations: language, meaning and the effects-based approach. In: Proceedings of Command and Control Research and Technology Symposium-The power of information age and technologies, San Diego, USA (2004)
11. Le Moigne, J.-L.: La théorie du système générale – théorie de la modélisation. Presse Universitaire de France (1977) (in French)
12. Vernadat, F.B.: Enterprise Integration Modeling and Integration: Principles and Applications. Capman & Hall, London (1996)
13. Chapurlat, V., Kamsu-Foguem, B., Prunet, F.: A formal verification framework and associated tools for Enterprise Modeling: Application to UEML. Computers in Industry 57, 153–166 (2005)
14. Mann, D.: Hands on systematic innovation. CREAX Press Editor (2002)
15. Truptil, S., Bénaben, F., Couget, P., Lauras, M., Chapurlat, V., Pingaud, H.: Interoperability of Information in crisis management: crisis modeling and metamodeling. In: Proceedings of the 4th International Conference on Interoperability for Enterprise Software and Applications (I-ESA 2008), Berlin, Germany (2008)

Part **14**

Management Aspects in Collaborative Networks

On Services for Collaborative Project Management

Martin Ollus, Kim Jansson, Iris Karvonen, Mikko Uoti, and Heli Riikonen

VTT Technical Research Centre of Finland, Industrial Systems
Vuorimiehentie 5,
P O Box 1000, 02044 VTT, Finland
{Martin.Ollus,Kim.Jansson,Iris.Karvonen,Mikko.Uoti,
Heli.Riikonen}@vtt.fi

Abstract. This paper presents an approach for collaborative project management. The focus is on the support of collaboration, communication and trust. Several project management tools exist for monitoring and control the performance of project tasks. However, support of important intangible assets is more difficult to find. In the paper a leadership approach is identified as a management means and the use of new IT technology, especially social media for support of leadership in project management is discussed.

Keywords: Project management, Distribution, Networking, Collaboration, Collaborative projects, Social Media, Software Services.

1 Introduction

Today, many business activities are performed as collaboration in networks. Dispersed partners come together to perform a specific task. Also projects consist of partners from a wide variety of organizations collaborating towards a common goal, despite of different background, culture and business behavior. The success of the project depends heavily on the collaborative performance. Project management consists to a large extent of the support and guidance for collaboration. In a distributed environment, the project management needs support from services for monitoring status and performance and for implementation of own actions.

A collaborative and distributed project has common features with a Virtual Organization, for which the operation and management support has been of interest in research recently [1]. This paper deals with the alignment of the partners' activities towards a common aim through "shared working practices" and "delegated and participatory project execution". It presents previous results achieved for management of distributed organizations (Virtual Organizations) and further development of these ones towards collaborative project management and leadership support.

The paper is structured as follows. First, we introduce some basic concepts and definitions in chapter 2 and the characteristics of collaborative project management, especially focusing on intangible assets of collaboration. In chapter 3, available IT support and the use of social media approaches for supporting collaboration in project management is discussed briefly. Chapter 4 outlines the application of services based on the combination of leadership management supported by social media based tools.

L.M. Camarinha-Matos et al. (Eds.): PRO-VE 2009, IFIP AICT 307, pp. 451–462, 2009.

2 Collaborative Project Management

2.1 Concepts

An early definition of **management** was given by Mary Parker Follett in the early twentieth century: "the art of getting things done through people" [2]. Other definitions consider the management to deal with "directing and controlling a group of one or more people or entities for the purpose of coordinating and harmonizing them towards accomplishing a goal". The management can consist of several dimensions, like human, financial, technological, resources etc.

Project Management is the discipline of planning, organizing, and managing resources to bring a successful completion of specific project goals and objectives. The primary challenge of project management is to achieve all of the project goals and objectives while adhering to classic project constraints—usually scope, quality, time and budget. The secondary—and more ambitious—challenge is to optimize the allocation and integration of inputs necessary to meet pre-defined objectives.

The Project Management Institute (www.pmi.org) has made a considerable work in collecting the Project Management Body of Knowledge (**PMBOK**®). The **PMBOK**® **Guide**, one of the results, is an internationally recognized standard (IEEE Std 1490-2003) that provides the fundamentals of project management, as they apply to a wide range of projects. The PMBOK® Guide is process-based. It describes work as being accomplished by processes. The approach is consistent with other management standards such as ISO 9000 and the Software Engineering Institute's CMMI.

Another recognized body supporting the advancement of project management is The International Project Management Association, IPMA (http://www.ipma.ch), which is a world leading non-profit making project management organization. It certifies project managers, awards successful project teams and researchers, and provides a number of project management publications. IPMA also arranges the yearly World Congress on project management. IPMA E&T Board has collected recommended literature in the project management area. Some publications also cover collaborative project management [3, 4, 5].

The discipline of project management is well established and much good and relevant material is available. However, the focus is mainly on the management of project within a single enterprise and not for the management of dynamic collaborative projects. Despite of this fact, the large body of knowledge in the area can be used and extended to the complex domain of dynamic collaborative project management.

2.2 Collaborative Project Management

The term collaboration has been defined e.g. by Camarinha-Matos and Afsarmanesh as "a process in which entities share information, resources and responsibilities to jointly plan, implement, and evaluate a program of activities to achieve a common goal" [6]. The concept is derived from the Latin "collaborare" meaning "to work together" and refers to mutual engagement of participants to achieve the aims, indicating a close integration between the parties. Collaborative Project Management can be interpreted in two ways

- Management of Collaborative Projects,
- Collaborative Management of Projects

Collaborative Management of Projects includes shared project management, which means delegation of management responsibility and some extent of self organization. The management may in many cases be non-hierarchical and participative with results based assessment of progress.

Management of Collaborative Projects mainly refers to the management of projects in networked and distributed environments. The processes are distributed with participants and organizations in different locations, countries and cultures. The management can be either central or collaborative. Figure 1 illustrates the interpretations of the concepts.

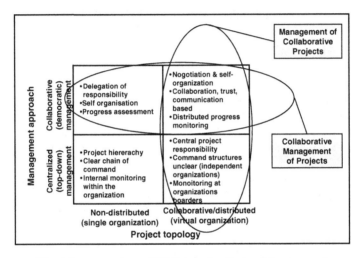

Fig. 1. Interpretations of "Collaborative Project Management"

So far, the management of collaborative projects has mainly focused on monitoring the progress of the activity and its performance. Based on the perceived measurements, the management is assumed to take suitable measure for coordinating the activities. Very little focus has been on the methods and tools to support the decision making. However, the management of inter-organizational activities is a complex task, which could be supported formally and systematically.

Also the management of inter-organizational activities has mainly been considered as transactions at the interfaces between the participating organizations. The focus has been on standardization of the information exchange in order to allow communication even between enterprise systems. Very little emphasis has been on the interactions between people and business processes. However, the collaboration is performed by people in the processes of their organizations.

In the Figure 2, the domain of collaborative management is illustrated from the perspective of management and interaction levels. Collaboration among organizations has in many cases focused on exchange of information between partners and the level of interaction has been transaction based. Further enhancement of the collaboration

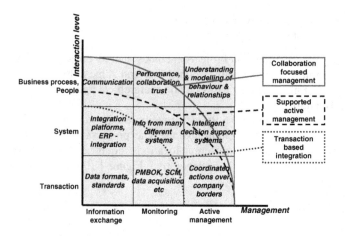

Fig. 2. Some dimensions of "Collaborative Project Management"

has resulted in system integration and solutions for interoperability between different IT systems. To support management, approaches for progress measurement have also been developed. However, the focus has been on monitoring the progress. This type of solutions is shown in the Figure 2 as "transaction based integration".

The active project management can be supported for coordinated actions over company borders, if it is supported by efficient information collection systems from the participating organizations, including monitoring of past events. In addition, intelligent decision support systems can aid for the decision making by providing proactive alarms on emerging or occurred problems. Also simulation based evaluation of different possible management actions can be performed. Approaches and solutions for this type of "supported active management" were developed and evaluated e.g. in the ECOLEAD project [1, 6, 7, 8]. The solutions give real time monitoring, alarm and decision support for the relevant stakeholders [9]. In these solutions, the focus has been on the management aspects. Implicitly, there was the assumption of a manger with the final responsibility for the task or delivery, even if the stakeholders have access to relevant information about the status of the activities. In these cases, the main management challenges are found to come from the temporary nature with distribution of operations in independent but interdependent organizations with their own aim, behavior and culture [10, 11].

Collaborative organization culture means community, which consists of relationships between people. Values underlie organizational culture that drives organizational towards knowledge sharing [12]. So far, monitoring and information exchange have taken place as transactions mostly between intra-company systems within the supply chain. In order to enhance interaction and collaboration between business processes and people, the focus needs to shift to also include understanding and monitoring of more intangible assets, like communication, collaboration performance and trust as indicated in the Figure 2 by the area for "collaboration focused management". This approach is seen as the next step for developing the management of collaborative projects.

The right upper corner in the Figure 2 requires strong modeling efforts and involvement of several different disciplines. This area also needs the understanding and concepts to be developed in the suggested area of "collaboration focused management".

Management focusing on business processes and relationships has to be performed through creating trust and a collaborative atmosphere, by considering risks and still relying on incomplete information. In the Figure 3, the collaborative management is illustrated. Management actions are introduced via the involved people, their communication and collaboration abilities to impact together with their mutual trust on the project performance in fulfilling the customers needs.

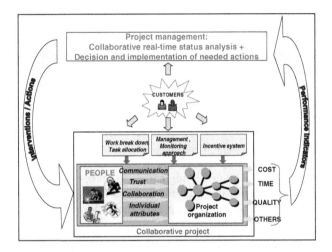

Fig. 3. Collaboration management means supporting people in their collaborative activities

In collaborative project management, decisions are made in a decentralized and democratic manner. The intangible assets and collaboration ability are even more emphasized. The coordination activities focus on the fulfillment of the customers needs and they are shown in the work break down structure with schedules and milestones. However, needed management interventions and actions aim either at enhancement of collaboration performance or reallocation of tasks.

2.3   Intangible Assets in Collaborative Project Management

Trust. The mutual engagement in collaboration also implies mutual trust. According to Grudzewski et al, trust is determined by the organizational culture, which is a critical factor to support collaboration [13]. In order to build trust, we need socialized individualism, universalism in work processes and operational rules, equality, scientific attitude to problem solving, law level of avoiding the uncertainty, clearness of activities [13, 14]. Handy has defined some statements related to trust [15]:

- Trust is not blind.
- Trust needs boundaries, because unlimited trust is unrealistic
- Trust-based organizations are reengineering their work.
- Trust demands learning

- Trust needs bonding
- Trust needs touch.

In business activities, like common projects, the inter-organizational trust also contains a rational dimension in addition to personal trust among people. Msanjila and Afsarmanesh have classified the so called fact based trust into the following categories [16]:

- Technological aspects
- Structural aspects
- Economical aspects contain the key counts of economical aspects for creating trust among organizations
- Social aspects
- Managerial aspects

Trust is a critical factor for efficient and effective communication, collaboration and knowledge creation, playing an important role in creating competitive advantage and reducing governance costs. Trust also enables open communication, information sharing, and conflict management [17].

Trust, including trust building, has become a major concern in the e-Business environment. Trust is seen as the coordinating mechanism which binds relationship together. It provides the necessary flexibility, lower transaction costs and reduces the complexity of relationship [18]. Trust management covers the activities of creating systems and methods. They allow relying parties to make assessments and decisions regarding the dependability of potential transactions involving risk. They also allow players and system owners to correctly represent their own reliability.

Leadership. Kouzes and Posner define leadership: "Leadership is ultimately about creating a way for people to contribute to making something extraordinary happen" [19]. They further describe the term, stressing that leadership can be learned.

Although there many definitions of leadership exist in the literature, most of them emphasize the support of others in the accomplishment of common objectives. Consequently, a main task of leadership is to define aims and to create a collaborative and inspiring atmosphere. A decentralized management style is usually adopted. In such an environment, culture means values, attitudes, and, understanding. A clear understanding of roles, both management's and employees', is essential, so also the organization of resources. The engagement of all participants is vital [12].

Monitoring the achievements and performance is an integrated part of collaborative actions, also leadership. The basic for performance in collaborative activities is the ability to forge relationships, the ability to communicate, and the ability for self-motivation, i.e. networking. Mental models are internal elements, including beliefs, reactions, and internal views. Also awareness of surrounding environment and the own context are internal elements of performance management. The intention of the organization and collaborative culture is to support and develop the performance, meaning enhancing the community, which consists of relationships between individuals.

Leaders may have different styles. House and Podsakoff identified 10 different leadership styles [20]. Although management and leadership sometimes are regarded as synonyms, there have also been attempts to understand their differences [21]. One could generalize that leadership focuses mainly on the activities and the processes, when management focuses more on concrete performance measures. Naturally, both approaches can lead to the wanted aims. In collaborative activities, like collaborative project management, a leadership approach creating trust and a collaborating atmosphere seams more preferable to a traditional management approach, which more relies on the authority of the manager. The basic idea of leadership is team working and customer orientation [12].

3 IT Support

3.1 Social Media and Project Management

As described in chapter 2, project management is inevitably a social effort involving all relevant actors. This social aspect has to be emphasized when considering collaborative project management, where already the management itself is a social effort. Social capable IT tools and software could support the project work and management. In this chapter, some applications of social media are introduced and their possible use for project management briefly elaborated.

The term **Enterprise 2.0**, originally introduced by Andrew P. McAfee [22], is sometimes used to describe the collaborative nature of an enterprise, consisting of both social and networked changes to the organization, as well as implementing social software as enterprise tools. The software adaptation basically means the introduction and implementation of Web 2.0 technologies within the enterprise; including rich internet applications, providing software as a service, and using the web as a general platform. McAfee introduces six fundamental components of Enterprise 2.0 technologies to describe the qualities of the paradigm, using the acronym SLATES (search, links, authoring, tags, extensions, and signals).

Social networking capabilities can help organizations in capturing unstructured tacit knowledge. The main challenge still remains on how to differentiate meaningful and re-usable knowledge from the other content also captured in tools like blogs, online communities, and wikis. As blogs and wikis are collaboration tools, they are useful for sharing unstructured information associated with ad hoc or ongoing projects and processes. They are not good for structured informational retrieval. Business processes often rely on access to structured but distributed data and documents. Social technologies can address such complexities, share and aggregate the information, eventually enhancing enterprise-wide search. Employees often seek information, which is held internally in a variety of formats and locations, including databases, document management systems, and other repositories. Search ability is an integral feature of social technologies [23].

The unstructured information provided by social technologies is particularly useful in business processes that are not strictly pre-defined, but where people work together in an adaptive way to innovate solutions.

While introducing several positive outcomes in adapting Enterprise 2.0 technologies, McAfee also illustrates two major remaining threats. The workers may not use the adapted technologies. The employees may use the system as intended, but producing unintended outcomes.

For compact and lightweight projects, the concept of **Agile Project Management** (APM) has been introduced. It has been developed from the needs of, and therefore especially implemented in, software development projects.

Traditional project management involves very disciplined and deliberate planning and control methods utilizing methodologies such as Waterfall and Capability Maturity Model (CMM), which are well-suited for long-term projects, but may actually slow down short-cycle projects. Today, business processes are more complex, interconnected, interdependent, and interrelated than earlier. In complex networks, they even reject the traditional organizational structures. The Agile Project Management methodologies are expected to respond to the needs of an agile and volatile business environment, being less complicated, iterative and incremental processes where all project stakeholders actively work together.

The main characteristics of APM are that projects are conducted collaboratively, in a small co-located team. The work is accomplished through a series of sessions, and the documentation produced is minimized as the project team relies almost exclusively on informal internal communication [24].

Developed for the software industry, the principles APM may not necessarily always apply for other industries.

Project Management 2.0 (PM2.0), or Social Project Management, is an evolution of project management practices and software built on Web 2.0 technologies and applications. Such applications include blogs, wikis and other collaborative and social software, and share characteristics like open APIs (Application Programming Interface), service oriented design and the ability to upload data and media, the ability to collaborate, share and communicate [25].

In the literature, PM2.0 is often associated with Agile Project Management or more collaborative style of project management. While PM2.0 is more about the collaborative tools, APM is more about lightweight project management practices – together they are complementary, but will as such offer no great differences to traditional project management.

Table 1. Comparison of project management approaches

Traditional Project Management	Project Management 2.0
Centralization of control	Decentralization of control
Top-down planning	Bottom-up planning
Authoritarian, strictly controlled environment	Collaborative environment
Implied structure, pre-defined structure and tasks	Emergent structures, tasking
Limited / restricted access to the plan	Organized / unlimited access to the plan
Local access to information, strict user restrictions	Universal access to information, very few restrictions
Limited communications within team, separate tools	Enhanced communications within team, e.g. shared project e-mails, chats
Separate projects	Holistic approach, resource pools
Often complex tools	Easy to use tools
Rigidity of tools	Flexibility of tools

Traditional project management places the manager in the centre of the project work. The manager collects all the information from the team, processes it and communicates to the upper management. It is hard to bring the project plan to life due to the fact that all the information on the project is passing a single person – the project manager [24].

The new generation of PM2.0 tools enables the creation of a collaborative space, giving each team member access to the full information on the project. Project progress is also visible to everyone on the team. The project manager has a visionary role choosing the direction for the project development. The tasking and structures evolve organically [25].

People and businesses are supposed to accomplish more with PM2.0 than with traditional project management tools. Insight and collaboration drive the project, instead of the management system. In Table 1, a summary of the key differences between Project Management 2.0 and traditional project management are given.

3.2 On-Line Presence

Widely viewed, virtual presence means being present via intermediate technologies, usually radio, telephone, television, or the internet. In addition, it can denote apparent physical appearance, such as voice, face, and body language. More narrowly, the term has been considered to denote presence on World Wide Web locations. People who browse a web site have been considered to be virtually present at web locations.

Recently, the term has developed further to mean more active presence in on-line social networks, meaning true social presence. A good example has been the emergence of businesses and state agencies in virtual worlds like Second Life.

3.3 Software Solutions for Project Management

Project management software is a term commonly used to cover software targeted to aid the project managers in managing their projects. This type of software can include functions for scheduling, budgeting, resource allocation, quality management, communication and documentation, as well as for administration of projects.

Most of the traditional PM solutions have focused on scheduling (tasks, durations and dependencies) and resource management (resources, availability, workload and criticality), providing functions for both planning and follow-up, in some cases also for multi-project management. Often the enterprise software suites have the functionalities for project management among their functions.

Two of the common commercial alternatives for project management software are Microsoft Project and dotProject. For viable collaborative project management, further innovations are needed. Such an innovative approach in developing support for project managers is to include "Web 2.0" applications into collaborative Project Management. This includes e.g. ability to

- Build on project partners distributed contribution to learning
- Collect rich user experience and shared intelligence
- Create and interact with content rather than just consume information

4 Applications and Further Development

Services for Collaborative Project Management have been studied e.g. in the COIN project (http://www.coin-ip.eu/) and requirements for development have been collected. The requirements definition is based on the analysis of the operations in several industrial companies. One of them is a global market leader in the process industry. The company provides engineering and project implementation services for investment projects worldwide, maintenance engineering and local services to process plants. According to the company outlook, future success in Europe will build on the combination of two paradigms:

- Fully automated and IT supported engineering process
- Totally networked and efficient global operation

The fully automated and IT supported engineering process means extreme and wide usage of emerging ICT technology resulting in radical breakthrough in efficiency, automated operations in design and project implementation with efficient tools and methods.

Totally networked and efficient global operations take full advantage of the efficient usage of core competencies in networked organizations. The work is distributed between the most competent and cost-efficient project partners. Agreed and shared work processes and operational procedure support social and participative project execution. To support the above mentioned paradigms, the following topics are selected for further development:

- Shared working practices – Project Alignment
- Delegated and participatory project execution – Communication through tasks

Project alignment is the process of ensuring that key stakeholders share a common understanding of the project work processes, operational procedures, objectives and plans. Alignment is not just a matter of agreement on certain project working habits, norms and styles. The achievement of a good level of alignment often requires participation in a learning process.

To build and increase the project alignment level, there is a need to analyze and measure the working and experience level at the project partners. Based on the alignment capabilities a suitable learning environment can be established. Consequently, the measurement of partner's alignment status and an interactive learning environment are the two building blocks in boosting project alignment.

The Participative Project Alignment Booster, with components to be implemented as web-services and currently under development, will contain the following services:

- Participative definition of maturity model and best practices.
- Project specific work process and operating instructions.
- Identification of alignment training needs
- Project interactive e-learning space

The paradigm of totally networked and efficient global operation requires support for delegated and participatory project execution – Communication through tasks. The approach of totally networked and efficient global operation takes advantage of efficient usage of the core competencies of networked organizations. Agreed and shared operational procedure support social and participative project execution. The basic underlying principle is that the work is broken down to a detailed task level. The planning of tasks on the lowest level is accomplished by the person actually performing the work. In that way, the defined task sizes, work content and duration will be fully understandable and realistic estimations about their performance can be done.

Acknowledgements. The paper is based on work performed in the Integrated project ECOLEAD funded by the European Community under the Framework programme 6 (IP 506958) and the Integrated project COIN funded by the European Community under the Framework programme 7 (Grant Agreement Number 216256).

References

1. Camarinha-Matos, L.M., Afsarmanesh, H., Ollus, M. (eds.): Methods and Tools for Collaborative Networked Organizations. Springer, New York (2008)
2. Graham, P. (ed.): Mary Parker Follett: Prophet of Management. Harvard Business School Press (1995) ISBN: 0-87584-736-6
3. Caupin, G., Knoepfel, H., Koch, G., Pannenbäcker, K., Pérez-Polo, F., Seabury, C.: ICP. IPM Competence Baseline. Version 3.0. IPMA International Project Management Association (2006) ISBN: 0-9553213-0-1
4. Project Management Institute: A Guide to the Project Management Body of Knowledge (PMBOK® Guide) - Third Edition, ISBN10: 193069945X, ISBN13: 9781930699458
5. APM Body of Knowledge. 5th Edition Paperback (2006) ISBN: 1-903494-13-3
6. Camarinha-Matos, L.M., Afsarmanesh, H. (eds.): Collaborative Networks: Reference Modeling. Springer, New York (2008)
7. Jansson, K., Karvonen, I., Ollus, M., Paganelli, P., Stewens, R., Negretto, U.: Real Time Virtual Organisations Management. In: Cunningham, P., Cunningham, M. (eds.) Innovation and the Knowledge Economy - Issues, Applications, Case Studies. IOS Press, Amsterdam (2005)
8. Jansson, K., Karvonen, I., Ollus, M., Negretto, U.: Governance and management of virtual organizations. In: Camarinha-Matos, L.M., Afsarmanesh, H., Ollus, M. (eds.) Methods and Tools for Collaborative Networked Organizations. Springer, Heidelberg (2008)
9. Negretto, U., Hodík, J., Král, L., Mulder, W., Ollus, M., Pondrelli, L., Westphal, I.: VO-Management Solutions; VO Management e-Services. In: Camarinha-Matos, L.M., Afsarmanesh, H., Ollus, M. (eds.) Methods and Tools for Collaborative Networked Organizations. Springer, Heidelberg (2008)
10. Ollus, M., Jansson, K., Karvonen, I.: On the Management of Collaborative Networked Organizations. In: Cunningham, P., Cunningham, M. (eds.) Conference Proceedings from IST-Africa 2006. IIMC International Information Management Corporation (2006)
11. Ollus, M., Jansson, K., Karvonen, I.: On the management of collaborative SME networks. In: The proceedings of COA 2007 – 8th IFAC Symposium on Cost-Oriented Automation, Habana, Cuba (2007)
12. Aarrevaara, T.: Johdatus organisaatioteoriaan ja johtamiseen (In Finnish: Introduction to organizational theory and management) (2000)
13. Grudzewski, W.M., Hejduk, I.K., Sankowska, A., Wantuchowicz, M.: Cultural determinants of creating modern organisations – the role of trust. In: PRO-VE 2008. 9th IFIP Working Conference on Virtual Enterprises, pp. 323–332 (2008)

14. Abuelmaatti, A., Rezgui, Y.: Virtual team wotking: Current issues and directions for the future. In: PRO-VE 2008. 9th IFIP Working Conference on Virtual Enterprises, pp. 351–360 (2008)
15. Handy C.: Trust and Virtual Organization. Harward Business Review (May-June 1995)
16. Msanjila, S., Afsarmanesh, H.: Inter-Organizational Trust in VBEs. In: Camarinha-Matos, L.M., Afsarmanesh, H., Ollus, M. (eds.) Methods and Tools for Collaborative Networked Organizations. Springer, New York (2008)
17. Afsarmanesh, H., Camarinha-Matos, L.M.: A Framework for Management of Virtual Organization Breeding Environments. In: PRO-VE 2005, pp. 35–48 (2005)
18. Ren, Z., Hassan, T.M., Cater, C.D.: Trust building for SMEs through an e-Engineering Hub. In: PRO-VE 2005. 6th IFIP Working Conference on Virtual Enterprises, pp. 157–166 (2005)
19. Kouzes, J.M., Posner, B.Z.: The Leadership Challenge, 4th edn. (2008) ISBN: 978-0-7879-8491-5
20. House, R., Podsakoff, P.M.: Leadership Effectiveness: Past Perspectives and Future Directions for Research. In: Greenberg, J. (ed.) Organizational Behavior: The State of the Science. Erlbaum, Hillsdale (1994)
21. Bennis, W.: On Becoming A Leader. Random Century (1989) ISBN 0-7126-9890-6
22. McAfee, A.P.: Enterprise 2.0: The Dawn of Emergent Collaboration. MIT Sloan Management Review 47(3), 21 (Spring 2006)
23. Stenmark, D.: How intranets differ from the web: organisational culture's effect on technology. In: Proceedings of ECIS 2005, Regensburg, Germany, May 26-28 (2005)
24. Haas, K.P.: The Blending of Traditional and Agile Project Management. PM World Today IX(V) (May 2007),
    http://www.pmforum.org/library/tips/2007/PDFs/Haas-5-07.PDF
25. Filev, A.: Bridging the Three Gaps in Project Management. Writing on Project Management 2.0 blog at Wrike (March 25, 2008),
    http://www.wrike.com/projectmanagement/03/25/2008/
    Bridging-the-Three-Gaps-in-Project-Management
26. Lynch, C.: Project Management 2.0. Project Management Planet (September 21, 2007),
    http://www.projectmanagerplanet.com/leadership/article.php/
    37010312007

Managing Decisions on Changes in the Virtual Enterprise Evolution

Marcus Vinicius Drissen-Silva[1] and Ricardo José Rabelo[2]

[1] Postgrad. Program of Electrical Engineering, Federal University of Santa Catarina, Brazil
[2] Department of Automation and Systems, Federal University of Santa Catarina, Brazil
GSIGMA – Intelligent Manufacturing Systems Group
drissen@das.ufsc.br, rabelo@das.ufsc.br

Abstract. VE evolution deals with problems that happen during the VE operation and that put on risk planned results. This requires the application of problem-solving mechanisms to guarantee the construction of a new but feasible VE plan. Grounded on Project Management and Decision Support Systems foundations, this paper proposes a distributed collaborative decision support system to manage the VE evolution. Its main rationale is that VE's members are autonomous and hence that all the affected partners should discuss about the necessary changes on the current VE's plan. In the proposed approach, this discussion is guided by a decision protocol, and the impact of decisions can be evaluated. Results of a first prototype implementation are presented and discussed, with a special focus on the part which regulates the argumentation, voting and comparison of possible solutions.

Keywords: Collaborative discussion, Decentralized Decision-making, Project Management, Management of Changes, Virtual Enterprises.

1 Introduction

Collaboration between companies is an increasing business strategy to face the global competition. Collaborative Networks (CN) offer conditions to companies to reduce expenses, increase capacity, broaden markets and improve themselves with knowledge acquired in business [1]. There are several manifestations of CN. This paper focuses on CNs of type Virtual Enterprises (VE).

A VE is seen as a dynamic, temporary cluster of autonomous enterprises that collaborate with each other to attend a given business opportunity or to cope with a specific need, where partners share risks, costs and benefits, and whose operation is achieved by a coordinated sharing of skills, resources, information and knowledge, mostly supported by computer networks [2], offering services abroad as if it were a single organization [1].

A VE is typically organized in a number of phases known as VE lifecycle: creation, operation, evolution and dissolution phases [3]. In very general terms, the creation phase comprises VE planning and partner's selection; the operation phase comprises the execution and monitoring of the planned activities; the evolution phase comprises the handling of problems detected in the operation phase; and the dissolution phase comprises all issues associated to the VE ending. This paper focuses on the

L.M. Camarinha-Matos et al. (Eds.): PRO-VE 2009, IFIP AICT 307, pp. 463–475, 2009.

VE evolution phase. It also assumed that companies belong to a VBE (Virtual Organization Breeding Environment) [4], so having common operating principles, rules and the required basis of trust among them.

In the evolution phase, managers have to deal with the need of changes in the current VE's plan, considering the different type of problems that may happen along its execution. Examples of problems include: anticipation or delay in item's delivery; low partner's performance; tasks not properly accomplished; changes in the product's specification; and logistics problems.

Unlikely other types of CNs, like supply chains or extended enterprises, the managing of the VE evolution implies the consideration of relevant additional aspects [5]: partners are totally autonomous so decisions cannot be imposed by a single company; they have different cultures and use different organizational practices; the decision process should be transparent regarding governance aspects; the information necessary to help solving the problem should be disclosed and shared taking into account temporary and current access rights; enterprises are often involved in several VEs simultaneously, where some of them are inter-related. Besides that, a VE is something very much unique, which means that the way a problem was solved in a given previous VE is not necessarily valid for another VE.

Therefore, managing the evolution of a VE requires an ample spectrum of issues that make decision-making extremely complex. As most of VE members are composed of SMEs, whose limitations are very known, this difficulty is even harder.

In this sense, this paper presents some results of an ongoing work which aims at developing a collaborative, flexible and human-centered decision support framework to help VE members in the management of problems that cause changes in the VE execution, considering those mentioned requirements.

This paper is organized as follows: Section 1 presented a general analysis of the requirements for VE management and the evolution phase. Section 2 discusses the distributed approach for management the VE evolution as well as points out some of the involved requirements. Section 3 introduces the proposed framework. Section 4 presents some current results of the framework. Section 5 provides a preliminary assessment and the next short-term steps.

2   Managing the VE Evolution

VE management "designates arrangement, allocation and coordination of the resources and their tasks, as well as their inter-organizational premises, to the VE goals, respecting time, cost and quality" [6]. This general definition can embrace diverse perspectives of analysis on how such management can be concretely done.

One can note that developing a comprehensive and flexible environment that can cope with all the mentioned requirements for the management of the VE evolution phase is indeed challenging, both in terms of managerial methods and models, and from the IT point of view. Some authors have approached this problem (including the operation phase) in different ways. For example, Rabelo and Pereira-Klen [7] have introduced a fixed decision protocol to deal with changes in the VE. Hodík and Stach [8] have developed a multi-agent-based decision support system to simulate the impact of decisions. Negretto et al. [9] have created a distributed supervision system to monitor the VE plan. Noran [10] has developed a decision support framework to help managers in the partners' selection in the VO creation.

Besides leaving only to the VE coordinator all the rights to access information and to take decisions, these works seem to be not so suitable to cope with two key requirements of VE evolution: the decentralization of decision-making and partners' autonomy. Considering the new requirements arisen with the VE concept, it seems unrealistic to apply a centralized approach where only one company can decide and impose to the others a solution for a problem. Finding a solution for a problem in this scenario is very complex as this involve many particular details and require several constraints analysis and relaxations. Thus, it is even dangerous to leave the decision only to the VE coordinator as the ultimate goal comprehends reaching a feasible and realistic solution, and not just another theoretical VE plan. Instead, partners should discuss about the problem, and the solution should emerge from this respecting their autonomies, leading to a decentralized and distributed scenario for decision-making.

Distributed decision-making is not a new research topic, and many works have been developed along the last decade concerning this matter, especially in the form of distributed decision support systems [11]. Despite its theoretical adequacy, one of the critical and practical problems of this approach is that it intrinsically imposes the need for having several discussions on the network, which use to be not so efficient, it is easy to lose the focus, and it depends too much of the quality of the communication and security infrastructures. On the other hand, this seems to be an intrinsic price to pay.

This paper presents a distributed approach to tackle the VE evolution requirements but where those problems are mitigated. In order to better understand the approach's rationale, it tries to implement the following vision:

"Partners, although being distributed and autonomous, belong to a VBE so they share common operating principles. One of them is that they trust on each other and they should collaborate towards reaching a globally feasible solution for a problem in the VEs they are involved in. They should discuss about it through the Internet, making use of an open distributed decision-making environment. The discussions should be structured and guided in order to keep the focus on the problem and to have a potentially better decision. This structure should be connected to the affected business processes (context), and not treated as an isolated event. It should be also flexible and adaptive regarding the usual uniqueness of the problem and of the VE so that partners can have some freedom to exchange ideas while they evaluate possibilities against their availabilities. This evaluation should be made via an easy access to common managerial software tools in order to facilitate SME managers' actions. After this, they should have means to evaluate the impact of their decisions before acting. All this should be supported by adequate ICT infrastructures, which can also provide the necessary security in the communications and access to information."

This vision imposes, however, a new set of (functional) requirements:

- *Partners' discussion*: this is related to endowing partners with a collaborative environment where they can exchange information towards the problem resolution. Groupware tools [12] have been largely used nowadays to support multiple users working on related tasks in local and remote networks. This can also involve supporting tools for argumentation, like HERMES [13], methods to help finding consensus on topics of discussion, like DELPHI [14], and integrated and secure web-based groupware services devoted to CNs, like the one developed by Woelfel *et al.* (described by Rabelo *et al.* [15]).

- *Methodological guidance:* the use of a methodology has the aim of preventing partners from dealing with the problem without any guidance, making them losing time and resources, which in turn can hazard the VE's business. An approach for that is to see a VE as a *project*, making use of project management reference models, like PMBOK [16] or ECM - Engineering Change Management [17].

- *Modular and flexible execution of decision protocols:* decision protocols can be seen as an instrument to: i) systemize a set of actions where there is a strong human intervention, ii) standardize and iii) enhance their execution efficiency [7]. The idea is to provide a base protocol where flexible configurations can be made considering the particularities of each VE.

- *Performance measurement and monitoring:* This issue looks to the current situation of the production system to further offer conditions for VE partners measuring their own performance as well as checking their capacity to get more confidence when deciding. This can involve traditional models/techniques, as BSC - Balanced Scorecard [18], SCOR - Supply Chain Operation Reference [19], and OLAP - *On-line Analytical Processing* [20], as well as the definition of the most adequate performance indicators that should be applied to the given case and members, as proposed in Baldo *et al.* [21].

- *Performance evaluation:* the goal of this aspect in the context of VE evolution management is to provide partners with techniques that help them to evaluate the impact of their decisions at their companies along the discussion process. At the same time, it allows the VE coordinator to evaluate the global solution before validating the final decision. These techniques can be based on analytical modeling, simulation, or direct measurement [22].

- *Knowledge Inheritance Mechanisms:* VE inheritance is considered as a process of transmitting the information and the knowledge acquired in the past experiences for future collaborative organizations [23]. The role of inheritance mechanisms is to help managers to improve their decisions when considering the lessons learned in the past.

- *Business Auditing:* auditing is crucial to keep the trust in the whole decision environment alive. When managers get together to discuss about a given problem, they exchange opinions, share data and take decisions. In this way, it is necessary to integrate information for further auditing (especially considering contractual non-conformity), giving the necessary transparency to the process [24].

- *ICT Infrastructure:* Information and Communication Technology (ICT) Infrastructures are a mean to support the main transactions among partners in a CN. Actually, this is one of the conditions to work as such [15]. In the context of VE evolution and decision-making, a secure ICT infrastructure is responsible for supporting all the mentioned functionalities.

In way to instantiate the presented vision and transforming these new requirements into more concrete artifacts and integrated framework, the purpose of this work is to provide a supporting framework and methodology that can systematize, guide and assist VE managers in the discussions about a specific problem towards its resolution, within the VE evolution phase. This methodology is represented by a decision protocol. It corresponds to decision blocks, grouped in a macro sequence of actions, which are instantiated according to the various specificities of each VBE, VE and types of problems, considering the set of requirements previously mentioned. Next section depicts this proposal.

3 Decision Support Framework

Previous section has presented the main aspects needed to support decision on changes in the VE evolution according to the authors' vision. In order to cope with this, a framework has been conceived. This framework gathers such aspects and groups them into four pillars: *Human, Organizational, Knowledge* and *Technological*. The essential rationale of these four pillars is to enable (empowered) *humans* to discuss and to decide about a problem related to a given *organizational* process, applying a set of *organizational* procedures and methods, using information and *knowledge* available in the VBE's data repositories, all this supported by a sort of ICT (*technological*) tools and infrastructures [5]. The discussion is framed by a decision protocol and it is carried out within a distributed and collaborative decision support environment. The decision protocol is the mechanism which links the four pillars according to each problem in the VE evolution. Figure 1 shows the framework.

Fig. 1. Framework for VE Evolution Management

The *Human* pillar represents people, i.e. the VE companies' managers who use their tacit knowledge and collaborative attitude to help solving the problem come from the VE operation. The *Organizational* pillar comprises intra and inter-enterprises processes, ontologies, working methods, techniques and procedures that should be involved in the envisaged distributed and collaborative decision-making process. The *Knowledge* pillar comprises explicit information and knowledge available in the VBE's data repositories. The *Technological* pillar refers to all kind of ICT tools, platforms and security artifacts available to help managers in the access to the organizational working methods.

3.1 Framework Architecture

The four framework's pillars are operated through three concrete elements: the decision protocol, the distributed and collaborative decision support computing environment, and the ICT Toolbox. They all form the Distributed Collaborative Decision Support System for the Management of VE Evolution (DDSS-VE). Based on the classification proposed by Turban and Aronson [26], DDSS-VE can be classified as a negotiation-based, decentralized, partially hierarchical, semi-structured, multi-participant and team-based system.

Figure 2 presents the framework's architecture, also illustrating the relation of the elements with the pillars.

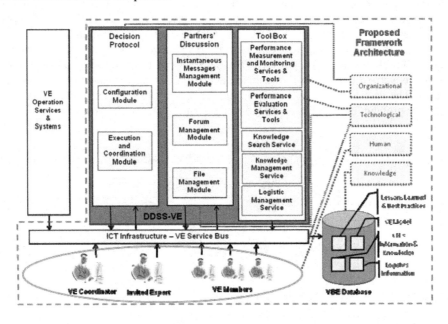

Fig. 2. Framework Architecture

VE operation services & systems represent the activities responsible for monitoring and detecting problems in the current VE's plan. Once a problem is detected, the control flow is then passed to the DDSS-VE in order to manage the problem resolution. There are three main modules involved in the DDSS-VE architecture. The *Decision Protocol* is responsible for guiding and coordinating the discussions among partners, also considering the set of (configured) particularities of the VE. The *Discussion Environment* is responsible for supporting the discussion itself among the VE partners (VE Coordinator, the VE members and, optionally, helped by an invited expert). It is composed of an instant message module (a *Chat*), a forum module and a file exchange module, where partners can discuss, argument and exchange information during the problem resolution. The *Tool Box* contains a set of tools and software services to help partners in the discussions and evaluations. It is composed of performance monitoring and evaluation tools and other supporting services. ICT infrastructure acts as the bus that integrates all these modules, tools and services as well as that grants access to the VBE database. These three modules are more detailed in the next sections.

Decision Protocol

The decision protocol is a sequence of steps which defines the activities that have to be executed in given situations within a given context to solve a problem. Its rationale was mentioned in section 2, and it is detailed explained in Drissen-Silva and Rabelo [5]. Conceptually, it should indicate what has to be done, why, by whom, where, when, how, and with which resources. In this work, it is the most important element as it governs the whole process.

This protocol intends to help managers in the decision-making process, showing them what have to be done in a proper moment. Figure 3 shows the proposed decision protocol. It is strongly based on the ECM reference model's phases [17] and O'Neill's model [25], but adapted to the VE evolution context. All steps are modeled as business processes using BPMN (Business Process Modeling Notation), which offers the required protocol's flexibility for being adapted to each different scenario and VE topology or objective. By means of a Business Process Management (BPM) tool, process execution (i.e. the protocol steps) can be monitored.

A problem is not solved at once. It requires the resolution of many sub-problems, which in turn can demand diverse rounds of exchange of information, computer-aided analysis and managers' opinions. The process ends when a considered good solution is achieved. After this, the control flow goes back to the VE Operation. The discussions and decisions are stored for future evaluation and eventual auditing. In the case no solutions are found out, the situation is sent to the tactic and strategic levels (which are out of scope of the proposed model) in order to, for example, renegotiate the delivery date with the customer.

Partner's Discussion Environment

After the problem has been detected, DDSS-VE starts the protocol steps (Figure 3), within the Need of Change Identification phase. The affected partners are identified and can be invited to participate in the collaborative discussion and decision-making. In the Change Proposal phase, the discussion is supported by services that combine the HERMES system's approach with Delphi method (see section 2). The part inspired in HERMES aims to organize partners' arguments in a concise structure, using an appropriate semantic, communicating their suggestions but in a organized way, including an association of weights to the most important arguments. This aims at finding a consensus about the problem resolution. The part inspired in Delphi aims at avoiding direct confrontations among participants, which could generate counterproductive discussions. All the arguments are gathered by the VE Coordinator who, at the first moment, acts as the moderator, selecting, deleting, changing or suggesting changes in the received arguments before they can become available to the others.

The Toolbox. Traditionally, SMEs have many difficulties to access, use and maintain software, mainly due to its costs and to the required staff to maintain it. The proposed architecture has been conceived to work under the *on-demand* approach, where

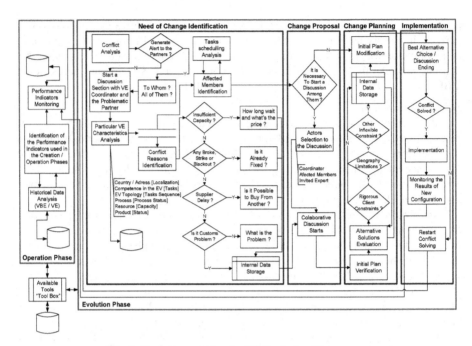

Fig. 3. Basis Protocol for the VE Evolution Management

software services and tools are accessed remotely and only when necessary. Rabelo et al. [15] have developed a secure ICT infrastructure devoted to CNs where the access to it is totally made in the form of services, following the SOA (Service Oriented Architecture) paradigm. The current version of this infrastructure only covers the VE creation [27] and operation phases [9]. The DDSS-VE intends to act as a service for the VE evolution within a wider and comprehensive framework for VE management. Other supporting software, like simulators and spread sheets, are to be accessed under the ASP (Application Service Provider) model. ICT Toolbox is therefore a logical repository of common tools that are accessed via the ICT infrastructure / Internet, facilitating members' acceptance and use of management methods. This however does not cover the existing local tools used by each member at their companies.

4 Prototype Implementation

This section presents current results of the implementation of the DDSS-VE framework, which is now concentrated on the Partners' Discussion Environment part. So far it assumes the existence of some of the architecture's elements, namely the VBE database, the ICT infrastructure, and some basic Toolbox's services. Within a controlled testing environment, the problems detected in the VE operation phase are manually introduced and the discussions are simulated in a distributed scenario using a number of PCs. The implementation of supporting simulation tools is not yet done, with the prototype currently assuming that members have this support.

In this first implementation phase, the goal has been to combine HERMES system and Delphi method, and to adapt them to the desired decision philosophy. In other words, it aimed at facing the partners' autonomy and transparency requirements as well as the need for a more structured way of deciding. The main adaptations include:

- The creation of a moderator (role), who is responsible to evaluate and to make available the arguments sent by members. Depending on the case, the moderator can be the own VE coordinator.
- The comparison of two different arguments using different *connectors* (better than; worse than; equal to; as bad as; as good as). Each comparison assigns negative and/or positive points to each argument, depending on the connector.
- Voting. Partners can vote pro or against to each argument.

4.1 Usage Scenario

In order to evaluate the current implementation stage of the DDSS-VE, a VE scenario has been created. This hypothetic VE would be responsible to develop a new helmet style for racing, involving four partners from different countries.

Fig. 4. Some snapshots of the Partner's Discussion Environment

Considering the decision protocol showed in figure 3, it is assumed that the phase "Need of Change Identification" has been passed (as the current implementation does not focus on it). The steps below and figure 4 illustrate in a general way (due to size restrictions) how the protocol would conduct the conflict resolution from the phase "Change Proposal" on. All this have been implemented in a web portal, on top of *Liferay* web application server (www.liferay.com). In this example, the VE Coordinator (*Ms. Cindy*) has concluded that it is necessary to start a discussion with two members (*Mr. Marcus* and *Ms. Maiara*) due to a problem detected in the specification of the first lot. After starting the collaborative discussion, the protocol gets in the "Changing Planning" phase and ends (in terms of current implementation stage) when the best alternative has been chosen, in the "Implementation" phase:

1. *Starting the discussion (to be conducted via the DDSS-VE):*
    * *The protocol ask some questions to delineate the better attitude for each case (e. g. if it is a rigorous client constraint that avoids from choosing another supplier);*
    * *Each participant will use some tools to preview which different scenarios could be acceptable to reschedule the activities that have to be done, choosing the best one, and publishing it as a suggestion for the problem resolution:*
        a. *Ms. Cindy posts the first suggestion: 'Buy from another supplier' (Figure 4a);*
        b. *Each partner can vote pro or against it (bottom Figure 4a);*
        c. *Each suggestion can be compared with other suggestions using 'COMPARE' button (Figure 4a). Figure 4b presents the list of suggestions and the possible logical connectors. For example, a comparison using 'is better than' as the connector assigns +1 point to the best suggestion and -1 to the worst;*
        d. *Figure 4c shows a tree (associated to the detected problem: helmet strip allotment) with the three posted suggestions (plus authors) and four comparisons among them. One of them is not yet evaluated as it is 'waiting for moderation';*
    * *The moderator (Ms. Cindy) evaluates the different suggestions and the comparisons, mainly to see if there is some confrontation among the participants. In this case, there is no confrontation as there is not any additional text below the text between quotes in the box, which is the initial moderator's suggestion to solve the problem:*
        a. *Figure 4d shows the Moderator's view. She can modify and/or simply approve Mr. Marcus' opinion ("RE: buy from another supplier is as good as ...") about her initial proposal (expressed between quotes: 'buy from another supplier') and send them to the group;*
        b. *Figure 4e represents the vision seen by the other two members before Mr. Marcus' opinion approval. Thus, they only see 'message waiting for moderation';*
    * *In what the final voting result is concerned:*
        a. *It is possible to see the number of votes of each suggestion, which is +3 in relation to the Ms. Cindy's one (Figure 4a), also meaning that the three consulted members (including the VE coordinator) have agreed on it.*
        b. *Figure 4c shows a signaled number beside each suggestion expressing the final sum of voting with the weights of comparisons. In this case, 'Buy from another supplier' has more positions in favor (+5): 3 from direct voting and 2 from two comparisons.*

2. *Once agreed, the most suitable solution is settled on the VE plan and partners (re)start to work based on it. This means that VE evolution is ended and the VE management goes back to the operation phase.*

5 Conclusions

This paper has presented a framework to support a collaborative discussion among VE members for solving problems during the VE evolution phase. It is essentially composed of a decision protocol, a distributed and collaborative decision support system, and of ICT supporting tools and communication infrastructure. It has been designed to cope with the VE requirements, mainly in what members' autonomy and decision transparency is concerned.

Developed based on project management methodologies, discussions are guided and assisted by the system but preserving and counting on the members' experience and knowledge in order to reach a suitable/feasible solution for the given problem.

Current implementation results have preliminary showed that the proposed mechanisms for supporting partners' autonomy, Internet-based decentralized decision-making, voting and transparency have worked out in a controlled environment. During the discussions, selected partners can have access to the problem, can freely exchange opinions about how to solve it, and can express their preferences via voting. This guarantees that the solution emerges from the collaboration and trust among partners.

This is an ongoing work. This paper has depicted the framework and the implementation of one of its parts, which is the discussion environment. Next short-term steps refer to: i) the implementation of the decision protocol part and; ii) its integration with the available toolbox's services (mainly the ones that will help in the evaluation of the changes impact on each local member).

Acknowledgments. This work has been supported by CNPq – The Brazilian Council for Research and Scientific Development (www.cnpq.br). The authors would like to thanks Ms. Cindy Dalfovo for the software implementation activities of this work.

References

1. Camarinha-Matos, L.M., Afsarmanesh, H., Ollus, M.: ECOLEAD: A Holistic Approach to Creation and Management of Dynamic Virtual Organizations. In: Camarinha-Matos, L.M., Afsarmanesh, H., Ortiz, A. (eds.) Collab. Networks and Their Breeding Environments, pp. 3–16. Springer, Heidelberg (2005)
2. Rabelo, R.J., Pereira-Klen, A.A., Klen, E.R.: Effective management of dynamic supply chains. Int. J. Networking and Virtual Organisations 2(3), 193–208 (2004)
3. Camarinha-Matos, L.M., Afsarmanesh, H.: The Virtual Enterprises Concept. In: Camarinha-Matos, L.M., Afsarmanesh, H. (eds.) Infrastructures for Virtual Enterprises: networking industrial enterprises, pp. 3–14. Kluwer Academic Publishers, US (1999)
4. Afsarmanesh, H., Camarinha-Matos, L.M.: A Framework for Management of Virtual Organization Breeding Environments. In: Proceedings 6th IFIP Working Conf. on Virtual Enterprises, pp. 35–48. Kluwer Acad. Publishers, Dordrecht (2005)

5. Drissen-Silva, M.V., Rabelo, R.J.: A Collaborative Decision Support Framework for Managing the Evolution of Virtual Enterprises. International Journal of Production Research 47(17), 4833–4854 (2009)
6. Jansson, K., Eschenbaecher, J.: Challenges in Virtual Organisations Management – Report on methods for distributed business process management. Tech. Report D32.1. European Collaborative networked Organizations LEADership initiative. FP6 IP 506958 (2005)
7. Rabelo, R.J., Pereira-Klen, A.A.: A Multi-agent System for Smart Co-ordination of Dynamic Supply Chains. In: Proceedings PRO-VE 2002, pp. 312–319 (2002)
8. Hodík, J., Stach, J.: Virtual Organization Simulation for Operational Management. In: 2008 IEEE CSM Int. Conf. on Distributed Human-Machine Systems, Czech Technical University in Prague (2008) ISBN 978-80-01-04027
9. Negretto, H., Hodik, J., Mulder, W., Ollus, M., Pondrelli, P., Westphal, I.: VO Management Solutions: VO management e-services. In: Camarinha-Matos, L.M., Afsarmanesh, H., Ollus, M. (eds.) Methods and Tools for Collab. Netwoked Org., pp. 257–274. Springer, Heidelberg (2008)
10. Noran, O.: A Decision Support Framework for Collaborative Networks. In: Camarinha-Matos, L.M., Afsarmanesh, H., Novaes, P. (eds.) Establishing the Foundation of Collaborative Networks, pp. 83–90. Springer, Heidelberg (2007)
11. Bostrom, R., Anson, R., Clawson, V.: Group facilitation and group support systems. Group Support Systems: New Perspectives. Macmillan, Basingstoke (2003)
12. Wulf, V., Pipek, V., Won, M.: Component-based tailorability: Enabling highly flexible software applications. Int. Journal Human-Computer Studies 66(1), 1–22 (2008)
13. Karacapilidis, N., Papadias, D.: Computer supported argumentation and collaborative decision making: the HERMES system. Information Systems 26(4), 259–277 (2001)
14. Dalkey, N.C., Helmer, O.: An experimental application of the Delphi method to the case of experts. Management Science 9, 458–467 (1963)
15. Rabelo, R.J., Castro, M.R., Conconi, A., Sesana, M.: The ECOLEAD Plug & Play Collaborative Business Infrastructure, in Methods and Tools for Collab. In: Camarinha-Matos, L.M., Afsarmanesh, H., Ollus, M. (eds.) Networked Org., pp. 371–394. Springer, Heidelberg (2008)
16. PMBOK.: A Guide to the Project Management Body of Knowledge. PMI Standards Committee (2004)
17. Tavčar, J., Duhovnik, J.: Engineering change management in individual and mass production. Robotics and Computer-Integrated Manufacturing 21(3), 205–215 (2005)
18. Kaplan, R.S., Norton, D.P.: The Strategy in Action, Rio de Janeiro: Campus (1997)
19. SUPPLY_CHAIN_COUNCIL.: Supply Chain Operations Reference Model - SCOR Version 7.0 Overview (2005)
20. Moon, S.W., Kim, J.S., Kwon, K.N.: Effectiveness of OLAP-based cost data management in construction cost estimate. Automation in Construction 16(3), 336–344 (2007)
21. Baldo, F., Rabelo, R.J., Vallejos, R.V.: Modeling Performance Indicators' Selection Process for VO Partners' Suggestions. In: Proceedings BASYS 2008 – 8th IFIP Int. Conf. on Information Technology for Balance Automation Systems, pp. 67–76. Springer, Heidelberg (2008)
22. Jain, R.: The Art of Computer Systems Performance Analysis: Techniques for Experimental Design, Measurement, Simulation and Modeling. J. Wiley & Sons, Inc., Chichester (1991)
23. Loss, L., Pereira-Klen, A.A., Rabelo, R.J.: Virtual Organization Management: An Approach Based on Inheritance Information. In: Global Conference on Sustainable Product Development and Life Cycle Engineering, São Carlos, SP, Brazil, October 3-6 (2006)

24. Gil, A.L.: Business Auditing. Governmental Auditing – Contingences versus Quality, 2nd edn. São Paulo, Atlas (2002) (in Portuguese)
25. O'Neill, H.: Decision Support in the Extended Enterprise, Ph.D. Thesis, Cranfield University, The CIM Institute (1995)
26. Turban, E., Aronson, J.: Decision support systems and intelligent systems. A Simon and Schuster Company, Upper Saddle River (1998)
27. Afsarmanesh, H., Msanjila, S., Erminova, E., Wiesner, S., Woelfel, W., Seifert, M.: VBE Management System. In: Camarinha-Matos, L.M., Afsarmanesh, H., Ollus, M. (eds.) Methods and Tools for Collaborative Networked Organizations, pp. 119–154. Springer, Heidelberg (2008)

An SSM-Based Approach to Implement a Dynamic Performance Management System

Roberto da Piedade Francisco and Américo Azevedo

INESC Porto & Faculdade de Engenharia da Universidade do Porto,
Rua Doutor Roberto Frias S/N
4200-465 Porto, Portugal
{roberto.piedade,ala}@fe.up.pt

Abstract. This paper underlines how the use of Soft Systems Methodology (SSM) for an efficient planning, implementation and monitoring of a dynamic performance management system supported by a conceptual scheme that enables a conscious and prepared implementation, can provide instances of performance of a collaborative network, and also promote alignment among the partners. A systematic way to implement it and a review on two practical applications in Brazilian collaborative networks of SMEs are also presented.

Keywords: Collaborative Networks, Soft Systems Methodology, Performance Management.

1 Introduction

The establishment of Collaborative Networks (CN) aims at reducing uncertainty and increasing competitiveness. This subject is increasingly acknowledged by academics and practitioners as a new paradigm that involves interoperation of distinct organisational systems that search for effectiveness, aggregating skills and resources of network's participants. Monitoring the CN's performance is advisable in order to understand how it is possible to manage this new environment and thus assist decision-makers in achieving the goals that motivated the creation of the CN.

The line of thought in this ongoing research implies that in dynamic environments, an organisation must obtain performance measurement outcomes and use them to obtain the results of operations, and to create actions that solve problems through available systematic practices in order to find an appropriate management tools.

This paper intends to highlight some issues regarding performance management in collaborative networks and encourage the use of the Soft Systems Methodology (SSM) in order to apply an action research to build a Performance Management System (PMS). After the introduction of relevant aspects, this document is organized as follows: the second section presents some definitions and explanations on performance management. In the third section an overview about SSM is provided. Then, the fourth section addresses the conceptual approach to support the creation of a dynamic Collaborative Network Performance Management System (CNPMS), and finally some conclusions are presented in fifth section.

L.M. Camarinha-Matos et al. (Eds.): PRO-VE 2009, IFIP AICT 307, pp. 476–483, 2009.
© IFIP International Federation for Information Processing 2009

2 Performance Management

Performance management systems are yet an important management decision support tool that represents a prerequisite to assure effective network operations towards operational excellence. Nevertheless, defining an appropriate set of categories of performance measures that meet the needs of a particular network represents a critical step towards the establishing of an effective performance management system. In order to contribute to support the CN decision-makers it is necessary to know how to define, configure, and implement an effective CNPMS.

2.1 Measurement and Management of Performance

Busi & Bititci [1] argue that the measure of performance is just the practical and technical instrument of performance management, which is something broader. Measuring performance helps monitor performance and identify processes and/or areas that need attention. According to Amaratunga & Baldry [1], performance management is defined as "the use of performance measurement information to effect positive change in organisational culture, systems and processes by helping to set agreed-upon performance goals, allocating and prioritising resources, informing managers to either confirm or change current policy or programme directions to meet those goals". The authors explore these baselines in order to facilitate the transition from performance measurement to performance management.

Lardenoij, Raaij & Weele [2] define performance measurement (referring Neely) as the "process of quantifying the efficiency and effectiveness of actions in order to compare results against expectations with the intent to motivate, guide and improve decision making", and define performance measurement system as "the set of metrics used to quantify the efficiency and effectiveness of actions, and the corresponding guidelines for linking these metrics to strategy and improvement". For an organization to make effective use of the performance measurement outcomes, it should be able to make the transition from measurement to management.

There are some specific performance management systems used in CNs that are found, applied by practitioners and adapted to each specific application, such as SCOR model [3], GPM-SME [4], PMS-EVE [5], and others specifically about virtual organizations, such as VOPM [6]. At the same time, there are some conceptual models such as a SCOR based model [7] and CNPMS [8]. Each of the models consists of gathering some concepts in order to build a framework that can support decision-makers so that they can achieve the specifics purposes or strategies and identify new challenges.

According to Supply-Chain Council [3], the Supply Chain Operations Reference-model (SCOR model) it is "a unique framework that links business process, metrics, best practices and technology features into a unified structure to support communication among supply chain partners and to improve the effectiveness of supply chain management and related supply chain improvement activities". This model tries to understand the enterprises' processes and the necessary reconfiguration, evaluating the performance of the internal processes and redefining the targets. At the same time, it proposes best practices to improve performance and imposes an alignment standard to features and functionality.

3 Soft Systems Methodology (SSM): An Overview

The SSM is a systematic way of using a structured approach that basically intends to understand a problem, build a conceptual model, find feasible and desirable changes and implement them.

3.1 SSM as a Learning Process

Proposed by Checkland [9], the SSM was developed in order to handle organizational problems. It is used in order to respond to symptoms caused by underlying problems, or when that problem is not yet understood [10].

According to Graelm, Graelm & Erdmann [11], a methodology is often confused with a method or technique when there is a situation that should be described or solved. Methods describe what to do and their results are previously defined expectations. Furthermore, methodologies are considerations that require structured approaches and analyses. It helps decision-makers understand the problems of the real world by comparing the perception of people, through the construction of theoretical models in order to facilitate the learning process.

Ferrari et al. [12] explain that SSM it is "a methodology that tries to analyze, under a systematic focus, a real organizational problem, extracting from this analysis actions for the improvement of the real world".

3.2 SSM as a Systematic Practice Approach

In order to better understand the complexities involving the existing organizations, there is a tendency to change the traditional systemic approach, or "hard-systems", in which the control of physical systems is based on predefined goals, for a "soft systems" that emphasizes the features found in complex systems of human relations.

Ferrari et al. [12] point out that "systemic practices are applications of systemic thought to start and to guide the actions of the real world". In this context, it is necessary find an adequate systematic practice to solve problems.

According to Checkland [9], the SSM contains a reasonable explanation for a scientific application and it is divided into seven distinct stages (see Figure 1):

1. The problem situation is structured and the key players as well the processes are defined in order to start the analysis or review;
2. The organizational structure and processes, as well the specific management and hardware technologies, are reviewed using techniques that can illustrate the problem situation and select the information to support the analysis;
3. Relevant systems are addressed using root definitions in order to express the central purpose of the chosen activity system and also using the CATWOE technique where some elements are used in order to understand the analysis of root definition sentences, and then originates transformations;
4. Conceptual models are built in order to be a model of human thought pattern that strictly conforms to the root definition using a minimum set of activities that can be drawn by applying system thinking;
5. Compares conceptual models with reality. Back to the real world, thinking on the adopted line. The conceptual models (stage 4) must be compared with real world expressions (stage 2);

6. Implement 'feasible and desirable' developments or/and changes that must be identified and discussed so that they can be put in action in the next stage;
7. Action to improve the problem situation in order to prepare solutions and define how to implement them in step 6.

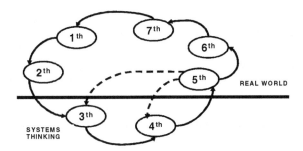

Fig. 1. The seven-stage of Soft Systems Methodology model

According to Bergvall-Kareborn et al. [13], the CATWOE technique is a combination of intuition, experience and willingness to deal with formal systems thinking. The main objective is to understand properly the meaning of CATWOE elements and their inter-relationship in order to improve the analysis. These elements are: customer, actor, transformation process, weltanschauung (world view), owner, and environmental constraints.

4   On the Design of PMS for Collaborative Network Environment

The PMS is still an important tool to support decision making. In fact, it is a prerequisite to ensure effective operations among partners. At the same time, it can help organizations provide instances of performance, and simultaneously lead to the alignment of CNs' participants.

Indeed, the emerging model of collaborative business requires appropriate infrastructure and technology support, as well as solutions in performance management that can ensure the alignment of strategic objectives among business partners in a collaborative networked business environment. So, it is extremely important that the CN is able to develop a structured way to design its PMS. This is a prudent way of finding appropriate management tools in addition to solutions for appropriate performance measurement. Thus, it seems that the use of SSM can develop an adequate methodology in order to find the necessary requirements for the definition of a performance management framework, as well as methods to implement it in practical applications.

4.1   Using SSM Approach to Implement a PMS

The purpose of using this methodology is to analyze how it is possible to configure and implement an effective PMS in a CN. Practical applications presented below showed that, when the construction of PMS framework occurs, there is a need to use scientifically consistent systematic, enabling and feasible solutions on trustworthy aspects regarding the definition of indicators, strategies and common goals, monitoring results, among others.

The implementation of a PMS in a CN is the problem situation that we must deal with. The use of the SSM enables a simple, adaptable and flexible methodology so that the decision-makers of the CN can use a sequence of steps (systematic) and thus bring together the interests and participation of each party in the design and implementation of CNPMS.

Thus, following the SSM assumptions, on the steps to create CNPMS are defined as follows:

1. Know the strategies and inter-operations of CN, and also the skills and expertise of partners in performance measurement and management;
2. Undertake effective analysis about the benefits for each partner of the CN, in accordance with their strategic objectives and purposes;
3. Choose a set of indicators that can translate the strategic and measurable objectives, and then consider an appropriate structure for the CNPMS;
4. Continuously check whether the alignment is maintained through performance feedback after the assessment of decision-makers;
5. Continuously monitor the performance of CN and check if the current results are compatible with those originally proposed;
6. In the event of poor performance or difficulty in achieving the goals and strategies, the processes of inter-operations must be reconfigured;
7. Check in time if the intentions and opportunities that promote the creation of the NC are still valid.

4.2 PMS Framework

According to Busi & Bititci [1], through a compilation of Adair *et. al*, Amaratunga & Baldry and Wagooner *et. al* works, support performance management systems should include the following "key elements":

- A structured methodology to design the PMS;
- A structured management-process for using performance measurement information to help make decisions, set performance goals, allocate resources, inform management, and report successes;
- A set of requirements specifications of the necessary electronic tools for the gathering, processing and analysis of data;
- Theoretical guidelines on how to manage through performance management systems are used to apply the information and knowledge arising from performance measurement systems; and
- A review process to ensure that measures are constantly updated to reflect changes in strategy and/or market conditions.

The framework proposed by Azevedo & Francisco [8] is based on two main layers (see Figure 2): data and information layer, and functionality layer.

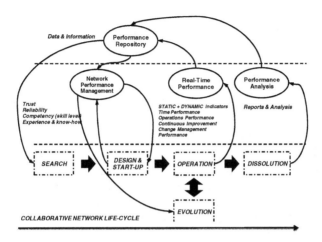

Fig. 2. Collaborative Network Performance Management System (CNPMS)

The first layer is related to data acquisition and repository management. The view of a performance repository of partners intends to provide trustworthy information about reliability, competences (skill level), experience and know-how. It is possible to achieve a time gain in the Search and in the Design phases.

The second layer comprises three main performance functionalities: network performance management to support the Design & Start-up phase, and also the Evolution Phase; real-time performance management to measure the outputs, solve emerging problems and formulate improvements during the Operation and Evolution phases, and performance analyses in order to get to know and understand the performance and knowledge reached during the life-cycle. To appropriately manage the Operation phase, there is a set of indicators in a specific chosen PMS framework through static and dynamic indicators that enable the improvement of the time factor (agility), operation performance, and provide sustainability for a continuous improvement and change management. This matter also has an implication on the Evolution phase. The static indicators provide the results of the operations, and the dynamic indicators can be set to create actions that enable problem solving.

Then, it is realized a performance analysis in order to understand if the CN has reached it goals and also to obtain a memory regarding their performance and to draw knowledge from the analysis itself. This is mandatory in the Dissolution phase.

4.3 Practical Applications

An explanatory case study was used to validate and prove the proposed system applied in two Brazilian collaborative networks in SMEs. The results encouraged the authors to further develop the system.

Application 1. LogVale Logistics is a small company that offers logistics operations management, seeking to decrease cost solutions for their customers. In 2007, the authors conducted an experiment where they implemented the CNPMS model in order to carry out an action research. In the beginning, there was particular concern with issues of trust, relationships and interoperability, which were considered to be the problem situations. The base of the CN is set up by this logistics company, which supplies products for a sales company of motorcycle (Motovale), assisted by a consulting company (Profit Able) and ICT services (E-Solution) acting as a general network topology that considers the proposition of Afsarmanesh, Marik & Camarinha-Matos [14] about a temporary partnership that is established in order to explore market opportunities on the short term.

The three initial steps (see 4.1) of the conceptual schema have been implemented in view of the need to prove (partially) the viability of the methodology. The aspects related to the strategy and skills were reviewed. The partners realized the benefits that could stem from the scope of its strategic objectives and were motivated to integrate operations. Thus, the internal processes and the inter-operations have been properly defined and integrated. After the implementation of the scheme, managers could verify the alignment among partners, improve the CNPMS and reconfigure processes and inter-operations that registered low performance. Thus, it was possible to validate the original purposes. Currently (2009), the CN is in its Dissolution phase. Step 6 and 7 are still being analyzed.

Application 2. In 2009, the companies Cepalgo Films (plastic films), Cepalgo Embalagens (plastic packs), and GSA (candy and snacks) intends to observe the interoperation among them working in a networked environment as a chain topology. This partnership was consolidated because the companies are controlled by the same stakeholders. Nevertheless, each one of them has their specific products and commercializes them to other clients, each one in their respective area. The Cepalgo Films produces co-extrusion plastic films and supplies about 50% (internal production) to Cepalgo Embalagens. On the other hand, this company supplies about 40% to GSA. The network strategy is to reduce that dependency more and more and look beyond the company's boundaries. Each one has autonomy (budget, infrastructure, market) despite not having a collaborative production planning and, therefore, there are no gains in synergy. The two initial steps are concluded yet.

Considering the proposition of Afsarmanesh, Marik & Camarinha-Matos [14], the network topology is a dynamic project-based partnership without a dominant participant. The problem situation that has to be solved is: how can we improve the logistics performance, as well as the quality of products, processes and people?

5   Conclusions

The strategic alignment among partners in environments with short time horizons, in networks that exploit business opportunities that are limited in time, is an essential reason for companies to use performance evaluation tools and for them to know the degree of compliance/non-compliance with objectives.

Thus, the use of tools for assessment of overall performance can help to achieve operational excellence in dynamic business networks, particularly when the involved partners are heterogeneous concerning management approaches, business culture, etc.

The use of SSM was satisfactory for the implementation of the framework and also for setting and re-setting of performance indicators. In fact, it is appropriate to use some methodology in order to create and manage a dynamic performance. It is valid for use on collaborative networks in order to enable to ensure a platform that will facilitate the effectiveness of the strategy.

References

1. Busi, M., Bititci, U.S.: Collaborative Performance Management: Present Gaps and Future Research. International Journal of Productivity and Performance Management 55(1), 7–25 (2006)
2. Lardenoij, E.J.H., Raaji, E.M., Weele, A.J.: Performance Management Models and Purchasing: Relevance Still Lost. In: Researches in Purchasing and Supply Management. Proceedings, 14th IPSERA Conference, Archamps, pp. 687–697 (2005)
3. Supply Chain Council (SCC): Supply-Chain Operations Reference-Model SCOR: version 9 Overview, http://www.supply-chain.org/resources/scor
4. Alba, M., Diez, L., Olmos, E., Rodríguez, R.: Global Performance Management for Small and Medium-sized Enterprises (GMP-SME). In: Camarinha-Matos, L.M., Afsarmanesh, H. (eds.) Collaborative Networks and their Breeding Environments. Springer, New York (2005)
5. Saiz, J.J.A., Rodríguez, R.R., Bas, A.O.: A Performance Measurement System for Virtual and Extended Enterprises. In: Camarinha-Matos, L.M., Afsarmanesh, H. (eds.) Collaborative Networks and their Breeding Environments. Springer, New York (2005)
6. Seifert, M., Wiesner, S., Thoben, K.-D.: Prospective Performance Measurement in Virtual Organisations. In: Camarinha-Matos, L.M., Afsarmanesh, H. (eds.) Collaborative Networks: Reference modeling. Springer, New York (2008)
7. Westphal, I., Thoben, K.-D., Seifert, M.: Measuring Collaboration Performance in Virtual Organisations. Establishing the Foundation of Collaborative Networks. Springer, New York (2007)
8. Azevedo, A.L., Francisco, R.P.: Dynamic Performance Management in Business Networks Environment. Digital Enterprises Technology. Springer, New York (2007)
9. Checkland, P., Scholes, J.: Soft Systems Methodology in action. Wiley, Chichester (1990)
10. Eva, M.: Soft Systems Methodology. Association of Chartered Certified Accountants, http://www.accaglobal.com/students/publications
11. Graelm, F.R., Graelm, K.S., Erdmann, R.H.: Soft Systems Methodology: an Urban Planning Application. In: Proceedings, 6th SIMPOI. FGV, São Paulo (2003)
12. Ferrari, F.M., Fares, C.B., Martinelli, D.P.: The Systemic Approach of SSM: the Case of a Brazilian Company. Systemic Practice and Action Research 15(1), 51–66 (2002)
13. Bergvall-Kareborn, B., Mirijamdotter, A., Basden, A.: Basic Principles of SSM Modeling: an Examination of CATWOE from a Soft Perspective. Systemic Practice and Action Research 17(2), 55–73 (2004)
14. Camarinha-Matos, L.M., Afsarmanesh, H. (eds.): Collaborative Networked Organisations: A Research Agenda for Emerging Business Models. Springer, New York (2004)

Part 15

Performance Management

Performance Based Maintenance Scheduling for Building Service Components

Karsten Menzel[1], Ena Tobin[1], Kenneth N. Brown[2], and Mateo Burillo[2]

[1] University College Cork, Iruse
k.menzel@ucc.ie, e.c.tobin@student.ucc.ie
[2] Cork Constraint Computation Centre, Department of Computer Science,
University College Cork, Ireland

Abstract. This paper discusses Performance Based Maintenance Scheduling as an enabler for Optimised Building Operation in terms of cost, energy usage, and user comfort, and the role of collaborative networks in achieving these optimal conditions. We finally explain what categories of constraints need to be considered to organize performance based maintenance scheduling in a holistic and integrated manner.

Keywords: Performance Based Maintenance, ITOBO.

1 Introduction

Performance based maintenance is a meeting point between scheduled and reactive maintenance. It allows for faults which were not foreseen at the time of scheduling to be dealt with before they become a failure, i.e. before reactive maintenance is needed. Also performance based maintenance has added benefit over reactive maintenance due to the fact that cost allocation can be carried out for performance based but not for reactive maintenance. How to achieve this allocation of costs will be discussed briefly, with respect to the information needed to do so, in the following paper.

This paper deals with performance based maintenance so it is necessary to have a facility management model which describes this type of maintenance. For performance based maintenance scheduling one must ensure for easy information transfer, information regarding component status, historical information and operation guideline information. Consider a Public Private Partnership (PPP) contract agreement, i.e. when a construction company is responsible for carrying out the maintenance works in a building for a specific amount of time (e.g. 10 years). The company may be based abroad and may have multiple contracts with locally based service companies. To allow for performance based maintenance scheduling it will be necessary for each of the appropriate entities in the organisation to have access to the necessary data and if possible within the contract rules, to share maintenance trends which have been noticed by individual companies in previous work with the network.

L.M. Camarinha-Matos et al. (Eds.): PRO-VE 2009, IFIP AICT 307, pp. 487–494, 2009.

2 Models for Facility Management

This chapter reviews models for Facility Management (FM) being utilized presently to ensure the enactment of maintenance activities. The following is a description of the most widely used models in the Anglo-American world as described in "Facility Management Towards Best Practice" (Barrett & Baldry, 2003):

Office Manager Model – In this model FM is not usually a distinct function within the organization. Instead it is undertaken by someone as part of their general duties such as office manager

Single Site Model - This model applies to organisations that are large enough to have a separate FM-department but are located at just one site. It also applies to organisations who own the buildings that they occupy.

Localised Sites Model - This model applies to organizations having buildings on multiple sites.

Multiple Sites Model - this model is generally applicable to large organisations that operate across widely separated geographic regions. Operational issues are dealt with at regional level.

International Model- this model is similar to Multiple Sites model but applies to large international organisations.

The following table summaries the above mentioned models:

Table 1. Facility Management Models summary

Model Type	Size	Coverage	Decision Making: Headquarter	Decision Making: On site
Single Site	1 site	One site	All – on site	All – on site
Local Site	≥1 site	Site in same metropolitan area	Technical assist., problems, budgets	Simple operational decisions
Multiple Site	Many sites	National geographically separated sites	Set Policy, Guidance to regional HQ	Operation matters
International	Many sites	Multi-national geographically separated sites	Set Policy, Guidance to regional HQ	Operation matters

3 Prerequisites and Current Deficits

The first assumption in this paper is that the use of wireless sensors and meters to monitor and control building services and energy consumption is increasing. This is due to a reduction in the cost of such devices and the decreasing installation costs based on the lack of wires. This leads to an increase in available (bulk) data.

The second assumption is that an integrated tool for holistic information modeling allowing the holistic, multidimensional management and analysis of building performance data in relation to the buildings energy usage will be available. Our colleagues here at University College Cork, under a project entitled ITOBO (Information and Communication Technology for Sustainable and Optimised Building) develop such a tool based on Data Warehouse (DW) technology. This tool supports complex queries and advanced features for aggregating, analyzing, and comparing data. It is also used to discover trends and patterns in data (Ahmed et al, 2009).

DW technology has been introduced to the construction management domain to improve the management of historical data (Ahmed & Nunoo 1999), (Lee & Lee 2002). So it is a natural progression for this technology to now be used in the building management sector especially as the availability of building documentation will lead to efficiency in this sector but however, few efforts have been made to explore the impacts of DW technology on building performance management supporting the creation of sophisticated data aggregation and analysis tools. By introducing collaborative networks into the scenario, it will become possible to ensure valid data and assumptions when aggregating the data and creating the analysis tools.

To facilitate our research with real example data the ERI building, a 4500 m² "Living Laboratory" located on the campus of University College Cork, Ireland, is used as Living Laboratory. The building has a wireless sensor network installed along with a wired BMS system. It is equipped with multiple types of solar panels, geothermal heat pumps and an under floor heating system. Building Performance Data is provided by 180 (wired) sensors. Additionally, a test bed for wireless sensors and actuators has been installed since April 2008 in three phases. Sensors include humidity, temperature, CO^2, and lighting sensors. Meters include devices to measure electricity, mains water, cold water, gas, lighting energy consumption, boiler heat, solar heat and under floor heat.

In the case of our example, aggregated performance data can be generated from the sensed and metered fact data and the dimensional data derived from Building Information Models which include information to structure the fact data (e.g. per location, per time, per user, etc.). Therefore, different stakeholders can retrieve customized information about the building performance. However, in future research further problems need to be addressed, such as how the maintenance and calibration for the sensors are organized. The need for "on site" inspection for these sensors should be on the lowest frequency possible. Secondly, manufacturer's data for HVAC components is very conservative so if this data is used in a diagnostic tool it will give a level of required maintenance which is too frequent. The next difficulty comes in the form of existing companies. Large companies which have worked in the FM-sector for some time will have discovered trends in building service components. For example, they may have noticed that when x amount of vibration is recorded by a sensor on a fan motor then the fan is close to failure. This knowledge is only gained by experience. However, this large company may be unwilling to share this knowledge as it gives them an edge over their smaller competitors.

4 Maintenance Planning Models

Currently, there is a lot of space for improvement in the manner in which buildings are maintained. Performance based maintenance will allow for a reduction in reactive and scheduled maintenance which is necessary in built artifacts. First we will discuss the two most widely used maintenance types, reactive and scheduled maintenance:

Scheduled maintenance includes preventative maintenance activities such as lubrication, visual inspection and testing. It also includes predictive maintenance activities such as obtaining checking filters, taking vibration measurements and drawing lubricant samples for analysis. In short routine maintenance is comprised of nearly all of what is referred to as preventative/predictive maintenance. In case of FM scheduled maintenance has an element of wasteful expenditure. Take for example, an Air Handling Unit (AHU), every six months the filters are cleaned. This is a scheduled event and it takes place without fail. However, depending on the environmental conditions and the intensity of usage the filters need either only is cleaned yearly or in case of extreme use cases 6 times a year. In this case scheduled maintenance will impede the users comfort and will result in unnecessary spending, due to over and under maintenance scheduling.

Reactive Maintenance requires immediate action to address breakdowns and other suddenly developing conditions. Traditionally reactive maintenance consumes excessive maintenance resources. Although an absolute necessity, it is a totally reactive function. Proper attention to the routine work and timely backlog relief will minimize the demand for reactive maintenance, (Kister, Hawkins, 2006). In case of FM reactive maintenance results, firstly, in a diminished level of user comfort due to the waiting time for the maintenance to be detected appropriately and consequently scheduled and also due to the unavoidable disturbance which is prominent during reactive (emergency response) maintenance. Secondly as this type of maintenance may require certain skills or stock at a minimal time delay this also invariably results in higher expenditure.

In case of performance based maintenance scheduling the following scenario is proposed, with respect to the situation described for scheduled maintenance: pressure sensors would be installed at either side of the filters, a vibration senor would be installed on the fan motor and room temperature and humidity sensors would be installed in the conditioned space. Sensed data would be sent to the data warehouse regularly, the data warehouse would analyse the data and discrepancies in the performance profiles (based on historical data and a predicted outcome) would trigger relevant maintenance activities. As a summary of this section, scheduled maintenance has the disadvantages of large cost overheads and unnecessary downtime. Reactive maintenance has no facility to determine costs and includes unexpected downtime. Performance based maintenance has the ability to reduce and control cost overheads and also to eliminate unnecessary downtime.

5 Collaborative Networks

"*A CN is constituted by a variety of entities that are largely autonomous, geographically distributed and heterogeneous in terms of their: operating environment, culture, social capital and goals. Nevertheless these entities collaborate to better achieve common or compatible goals and whose interactions are supported by computer networks.*" (Camarinha – Matos LM, 2005).

In the FM-industry of today, due to outsourcing, technical advancements and contract conditions, CN are constantly being introduced by large since buildings include components of the structural domain, mechanical domain and electrical domain, etc. To maintain all these components, a large variety of skills are necessary. This is an advantage for performance based maintenance.

There are two types of FM-company structures; the first is the in-house structure. This is when all the necessary skilled staff is employed by the company. When a problem occurs the appropriately skilled person will undertake the task. The second structure is the outsourcing company. This is when a company maintains a core number of skilled staff and when a problem occurs which needs the attention of a skill which is not available within the company's staff; the task is outsourced to a specialized company. For each of these two types, performance based maintenance can be used but to ensure cost effectiveness, it is necessary for both types to available of infrastructures set up by other sectors, i.e. document sharing, data sharing. Therefore collaborative networks are a necessity for viable performance based maintenance.

According to Camarinha – Matos "*A collaborative network is characterized by four variables: the external interactions amoung autonomous entities, roles of these entities, the main components that define the proper interactions of these entities, and the value system that regulates the evolution of the collaborative association and the emerging collective behaviour.*" (Camarinha – Matos LM, 2005). For performance based maintenance scheduling the individual components are specified in Table 2 below.

Table 2. Collaborative Network Variables

Type	External Interactions	Role of entities	Main components	Value system
Performance Based Maintenance Scheduling	Periodic virtual meetings, Email notifications	FM provider, Maintenance Provider, Bldg. Owner, Tenants	Invent. Mgmt. & Mainten. Web Interface, Inventory &Task DB	Mandatory regulations, codes, etc. determine contract cond

The overall components for a maintenance scheduling system are: (1) a wireless sensor network to monitor the performance of building service components, (2) the data warehouse which will store and analysis the performance data recorded, (3) the Maintenance task database, and (4) the web-based user interfaces which will allow to view data trends, check stock of spare parts, track maintenance activities, view purchase orders, etc. The main components for a performance based maintenance scheduling methodology – with an emphasis on topics (3) and (4) - their purposes and interactions will be described in more details in the following paragraphs.

6 Maintenance Process Management

The first component discussed is a maintenance template management system, consisting of process models for different maintenance tasks. Each building service component will have their appropriate maintenance tasks recorded in this template system. Each of these tasks templates details the position of the component with regard to the overall building service system, the sequence of actions which needs to be performed, the estimated time for each action, and the required resources (e.g. spare parts, tools, etc.). In our case the template management system will be complied using the ARIS methodology. This methodology was chosen due to its ability to allow for good decomposition and synthesis of complex value chains and the ability to drill down from value chain level to extended Process Chain Level.

More about this methodology can be found in ARIS - Business Process Modeling (Scheer A.W, 2000). By using this methodology it is possible to attach documents and codes to the process models. The responsible actors will also be detailed in these models through the use of organizational units. This will allow the maintenance support system to determine the employee skills type required to carry out a particular task. The task template can be evaluated by the predictive maintenance scheduling components and finally be attached to the work schedule forwarded to the individual member of the collaborative network.

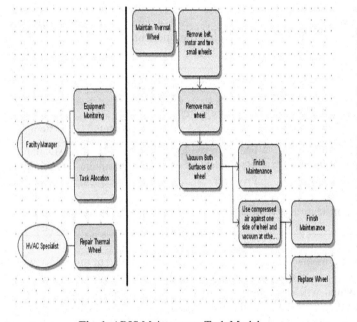

The ARIS diagram on the left is for the main wheel section of a thermal wheel component. This component is used for two purposes, as a heat exchanger and as humidity control device.

Fig. 1. ARIS Maintenance Task Model

We envisage triggering fault reports automatically through data analysis of building performance data in the Data Warehouse briefly described in section 3. Since the dimensional data of the DW will contain the multiple dimensions, such as building services system hierarchies, location hierarchies, etc. each fault report could specify the component by tracing the component through a building service component list and recording its position. This will allow the component to be isolated in terms of it whole system down to its own unique purpose and will allow for the exact determination of the maintenance task needed from the ARIS processes.

As performance based maintenance is dependant on past experience and past data trends, it will be possible to update these maintenance task with additional data as a building operational period progresses. As a building may incur a change in functionality over time and as a result the maintenance tasks may vary from original definition. The functionality of a collaborative network is paramount to ensure the transfer of knowledge with regard to such changes.

7 Constraints for Maintenance Scheduling

Performance based maintenance scheduling has to consider various constraints, such as (1) availability of staff, (2) availability of parts, (3) temporal constraints on tasks, (4) building use patterns, (5) criticality of repairs. Criticality of repairs is where the scheduling connects to the aims of performance based maintenance. We assume that we have diagnosis information which tells us the effect the part of the system is having on the performance of the building. The following paragraph describes two components created to deal with the above constraints.

The space management component checks the accessibility of locations, such as rooms, floors, zones to perform a maintenance tasks. It will serve the facility managers or the building operators of the building management company. The facility managers will use it to check the accessibility of rooms and that they need to access to carry out individual maintenance tasks. If rooms are available they will be booked and the maintenance will be scheduled. The tool helps to solve accessibility constraints within the Collaborative Network. The inventory control component checks the availability of spare parts and tools which are needed to perform maintenance tasks. It will serve the building technicians, the building operators and also the purchasing and accounting departments of the building management company. The operators and technicians will use it to book stock that they need to carry out individual maintenance tasks. If there is no available stock, the user will be able to check if a delivery is already scheduled and if not then the user will have the option to order the stock needed. There are a series of constraints that help the technicians pin point the appropriate stock that they need. It begins with the technician defining the location where the task will be carried out and then the type of stock needed the quantity and the time period when it will be needed. The accounting department will also be able to utilize the information gathered in order to analyse the financial constraints. The interfaces for this purpose have no been included here but they would display the history of stock usage and the suppliers most used, etc.

The competency management component checks the accessibility of staff with required skill sets and expertise within the Collaborative Network. It will serve the facility managers and the sub-contractors. The facility managers will use it to check the availability of subcontractors. Subcontractors will use the tools to offer available resources and skills to the Collaborative Network. The tool helps to solve competency constraints within the Collaborative Network.

8 Conclusions and Acknowledgements

The integration of complex renewable energy systems, such as solar panels, geothermal heat pumps etc. increases the complexity of required maintenance activities and the need to access more "specialized skills and competencies". Both, this need for more specialized knowledge and changing business models for Facility Management create a need for the introduction of Collaborative Network scenarios in the FM sector.

In our paper we propose a scenario and a methodology for integrated information management to support a new paradigm for maintenance management – performance based maintenance scheduling. We argue that the availability of wireless sensing and metering devices complemented by advanced data management and analysis tools will enable the introduction of predictive maintenance in the FM-sector and contribute to the more efficient operation of buildings.

The work presented in this paper is jointly supported by Science Foundation Ireland (grant-number 07.SRC.I1170) and five industry partners. Further information is available at http://zuse.ucc.ie/itobo.

References

1. Ahmed, A., Menzel, K., Ploennigs, J., Cahill, B.: Aspects of multi-dimensional Building Performance Data Management. In: Proceeding of EG-ICE, Berlin (July 2009) (to be published)
2. Ahmed, I., Nunoo, C.: Data Warehousing in the Construction Industry: Organizing and Processing Data for Decision Making. 8DBMC, pp. 2395–2406. NRC Research Press, Vancouver (1999)
3. Barrett, P., Baldry, D.: Facility Management towards best practice. Blackwell Publishing, Malden (2003)
4. Camarinha-Matos, L.M.: Collaborative networks: a new scientific discipline. Journal of Intelligent Manufacturing 16, 439–452 (2005)
5. Kister, T.C., Hawkins, B.: Maintenance Planning and Scheduling Handbook. Elsevier Inc., Amsterdam (2006)
6. Lane, P.: Data Warehousing Guide, 119g Release 1 (11.1), Oracle Data Base, Oracle (2007)
7. Lee, J., Lee, H.: Principles and Strategies for applying Data Warehouse Technology to Construction Industry. In: ECPPM, eWork and eBusiness in Architecture, Engineering and Construction, pp. 341–353. Swets & Zeitlinger, Slovenia (2002)
8. Scheer, A.-W.: ARIS - Business Process Modeling. Springer, Heidelberg (2000)

An Approach to Measuring the Performance of a Large-Scale Collaboration

Ronald C. Beckett

Centre for Industry and Innovation Studies (CInIS),
College of Business, University of Western Sydney, Australia
r.beckett@uws.edu.au

Abstract. Large-scale collaborations such as business networks and clusters are being promoted worldwide, but some OECD studies suggest that measuring the performance of such collaborations can be problematic. In this paper a grounded theory approach leads to the proposition that important attributes of a large-scale collaboration are its dimensions, maturity and relative heterogeneity of participants; whilst critical outcomes from a large-scale collaboration initiative are balanced housekeeping/beneficial transactions and improved market access/competitiveness. This proposition is used to demonstrate business process frameworks for characterizing and measuring the performance of such collaborations.

Keywords: Performance Measurement, Virtual Organisations, Clusters.

1 Introduction

Around the world, governments are stimulating large-scale collaborations such as business networks and clusters to improve the competitiveness of regions. The intention is to encourage networking between actors, to stimulate networks of activities and to build on clusters of resources, facilitating innovation and enhanced market access. In researching the dynamics of markets, the IMP group [1] has found it useful to characterize markets as intersecting networks of actors, resources and activities (ARA theory). In considering the research question *"Can we identify a simple way of measuring the performance of a large-scale collaboration?"* we draw on some literature on virtual enterprises and clusters and combine it with observations about multi-partner collaborations and the ARA theory literature.

2 Some Observations from Prior Case Studies and the Literature

We are taking a grounded theory approach in this research, combining observations from nine case studies we have described elsewhere with observations from the literature to identify categories of observations and some related properties using an ARA theory framework in the context of our research question.

L.M. Camarinha-Matos et al. (Eds.): PRO-VE 2009, IFIP AICT 307, pp. 495–504, 2009.
© IFIP International Federation for Information Processing 2009

The nine cases represented a cross-section of different kinds of collaboration. Three kinds of actors were involved. Firstly; sponsors (7/9 had some form of government support, 5/9 involved industry associations). Secondly; facilitators (5/9 were facilitated by some kind of industry association, 2/9 by individuals and in 2/9 cases a separate administration group was formed). Finally, contributors (generally SMEs, but in two cases micro businesses were the dominant group). Camarinha-Matos and Afsarmanesh [2] have observed a number of characteristic contributor roles associated with collaboration operations: focal firms, technology providers, local networks, communities of practice and supporting firms. These were all observed in the nine cases, although not all were necessarily present in a particular case.

Four kinds of joint activities were identified: activities that required collaboration to build scale (3/9 cases), activities that required collaboration to build scope (5/9 cases) activities supporting enhanced innovation through collaboration (4/9 cases), activities to enhance market access through collaboration (7/9 cases).

Three kinds of resource sharing were observed: firstly, access to a combination of somewhat unique physical assets (e.g. special production machinery or experimental equipment) and financial resources (e.g. government grants) (7/9 cases). Secondly, access to intellectual assets (both technological know-how and business know-how) (6/9 cases). Finally, participation in events that enhanced social capital (e.g. sharing access to personal networks, building networking skills) (9/9 cases).

Some selected examples of different perspectives found in the literature follow. A recent OECD report on clusters [3] suggested that measurement of performance was difficult, and not even attempted in many cases. Where measurement was attempted, there were commonly two separate kinds of measure. The first, and most common, assessed *the operation of the collaboration* – who got involved, what kinds of things were happening and was it developing and operating to plan. The second, and least common, considered *the impact of collaborating*. In the latter case, data collection could become a significant task, and being able to confidently appropriate particular benefits to the collaboration could be problematic [4]. Government sponsored programs were stimulated by one or more of three different policy areas: regional development, innovation and industry sector capability development, with economic growth being a common objective.

In studying the outcomes of a mid 1990's Australian Government initiative that encouraged small firms to form about 80 business networks, Marceau [5] noted firstly, that most did not persist after Government support was curtailed, and secondly, that the commercial outcome was more influenced by their success in engaging with the market than by their internal working arrangements.

Taken together with other references, this leads us to the list of categories and properties shown in Table 1, which we have characterised as either attributes (something about the collaboration) or critical success factors (something related to its likely impact). The outcome is a proposition that *the important **attributes** of a large-scale collaboration are dimensions, maturity and heterogeneity of participants; whilst **outcomes from** a large-scale collaboration are improved market access / competitiveness and balanced housekeeping and beneficial transactions.* In the following sections of this paper these two factors will be used in combination with other theories to first characterise a large-scale collaboration, then propose a performance measurement approach.

Table 1. Some Categories and their Properties Emerging from the Grounded Theory Approach to Collaboration Characterization and Performance Measurement

Performance Measurement Categories	Properties of the Category
Attribute - Dimensions (Size and scope of participant organizations influences the dominant nature of engagement)	- Geographical scope, relative concentration of firms, variety of products in different but related industries, range of value adding activities, growth potential, (e.g. [6, 7]) - Number of firms involved, size of firms and revenue, spending on innovation (e.g. [4])
Attribute - Maturity (emergent firms and emergent collaborations require additional support)	- Life-cycle of collaboration perspective (e.g. [8]) - Experience in collaborating perspective (e.g. [9]) - Maturity of collaborating firms (e.g. [10])
Attribute - Heterogeneous participants (Need to enact key roles and balance contributions)	- Collaboration managers need to enact key roles (e.g. [11]) - Roles of participants need to be understood – e.g. focal firm, technology provider, supporting firm - {2} - Need to balance similarity and complementarity attributes of participants (e.g. [12, 13]
Critical Success Factor - Market Access & Competitiveness (No access, no outcome)	- Able to effectively engage with markets (e.g. [5]) - Able to be competitive, at least regionally (e.g. [7, 14]) - Able to adapt to changing circumstances (e.g.[15]) – cluster absorptive capacity (e.g. [16])
Critical Success Factor - Transactions (Transactions are the life-blood of collaborations – no transactions, no outcomes, and they may have negative or positive effects. In a commercial enterprise revenue exceeds costs to yield a profit. We apply the same principle to value-adding and non-value adding transactions)	- Collaboration housekeeping transaction are required, but have a negative value, which must be offset by beneficial transactions (e.g. [17]) - Social transactions build social capital that facilitates other kinds of transactions and learning (e.g. via a breeding network – [2]) - Stimulating knowledge generation and knowledge flows creates knowledge capital that may be used to enhance competitiveness (e.g. [18]; via a community of practice - [2] - Economic transactions enhance profitability and build economic capital (e.g. via a virtual enterprise - [5; 19))

3 Characterising a Large-Scale Collaboration

Large-scale collaborations are characterized by actor-centric personal networking, sharing access to a network of resources, and supplementing a firm's traditional network of activities with additional networks of cooperative activities. Accessing markets traditionally involves working with networks of actors (customers and suppliers), networks of resources within and external to a firm (suppliers) and activities associated with the value chain, as observed by the IMP Group [1]. In Table 2 an approach to characterizing the performance of a large-scale collaboration is described by combining the categories from Table 1 with an ARA perspective.

Table 2. Characterizing the performance of a large-scale collaboration

Performance Measurement Categories	Measures of performance		
	Actors	Resources	Activities
Attribute - Dimensions (Size and scope of participant organizations influences the dominant nature of engagement)	- Number of firms involved, *size of firms and revenue*	- Geographical scope, relative concentration of firms, - variety of products in different but related industries - *Growth potential*	- *Scope of participant value adding activities,* - *Participant spending on innovation*
Attribute - Maturity (Emergent firms and emergent collaborations need additional support)	- Relative business maturity of participating firms - *Experience in collaborating*	- Relative maturity of participating firms knowledge base - Relative maturity of participating firms physical resources	- *Life-cycle view of collaboration* – Maturity stage reached in breeding network and spin-offs, projects
Attribute - Heterogeneous participants (Need to enact key roles and balance contributions)	- *Ownership of and commitment to the collaboration at multiple levels* - Diversity of participant professions	- *Balanced similarity and complementarity attributes of participant activities and resources*	- Need to enact key administration roles e.g. relationship and task management - Roles of participants need to be understood – e.g. focal firm, technology provider, supporting firm
Critical Success Factor - Market Access & Competitiveness (No access, no outcome)	- *Able to be competitive, at least regionally*	- Able to adapt resources to changing circumstances – Cluster absorptive capacity	- *Processes to effectively engage with markets*
Critical Success Factor - Transactions (Transactions are the lifeblood of collaborations – no transactions, no outcomes, and they may have negative or positive effects)	- Kinds of social capital built (competence / contract / goodwill based trust; bonding / bridging / linking relationships) - Kinds of knowledge capital built (technical / market, tacit / codified)	- *A clear cost-benefit in relation to the investment in cluster resources and ways that the participant foundation resources are used more effectively through collaboration* - Circumstances for sharing physical and knowledge resources	- Housekeeping transactions that add value - Social transactions that build trust and linkages - Knowledge generation transactions and knowledge flows - *Economic transactions enhance profitability and build economic capital*

Hofmann [20] suggested that a stakeholder value-added approach be taken to considering network performance. Different stakeholders are likely to see a particular collaboration in different ways. An OECD report [3] on competitive regional clusters stated that "A cluster member is presumably more interested in the overall cluster's competitive position than in the cost-effectiveness of a particular public policy action. A cluster initiative manager may be most interested in success at bringing actors together in joint activities and the development of stronger economic and social relationships. A politician may need to know how many jobs were created or how much the region's economy has improved". The political perspective will also depend on the administering policy area (regional development policy / science & innovation policy / industry sector development policy).

A Canadian study [4] primarily concerned with science-driven clusters put the individual firm and its performance in a central position, with influences from customers, competitors and supporting organizations plus a number of environmental factors. The argument is that impact is primarily driven by firm performance in its market context. Environmental factors such as natural resources may have some direct influence on outcomes, but environmental factors (such as establishing a large-scale collaboration) more often have an indirect influence on outcomes through the firm. This is the view taken in constructing Table 2, where some items are highlighted in *italics* to suggest those considered by the author to have the greatest impact.

In assessing a particular collaboration, the existence or otherwise of some of the features suggested in Table 2 and some quantification of these features will build an understanding of it's particular strengths and weaknesses, leading to ideas for improvement. Not addressing one of these features may be a fatal flaw.

4 Measuring the Impact of a Large-Scale Collaboration

To consider the impact of a large-scale collaboration we view it as a supplementary business ecosystem that is a light over-lay on the participant's normal (networked) business environment. Business activity arising through the cluster will generally provide some, but not all of a firm's total business. In this context, using a systems perspective [21] we characterise this overlay as follows:

- The collaboration is a business process having models of action and internal processes [22] seeking to provide benefits for the participants and the broader community and having some subsystems related to its own operations and some subsystems related to participant operations. Some process activities may be short term and some may be long term.
- Inputs to the process are the collaboration vision and intentions [22] plus business opportunities. Deficiencies in either of them will compromise the process
- Outputs from the process may be measured in terms of economic capital, knowledge capital and social capital, enhanced capability, lessons learned, and broader community benefits such as job creation. There may be spillover benefits to non-participants. If there are no outputs the process has failed
- Rules / constraints in terms of government policy, the business environment, competitive pressures and a customer perspective [22] condition process operations as well as less formal conditions like trust and equity [23]
- Resources to make the process work include cluster facilitation resources and participant capabilities [22]

Combining these ideas with some of the features identified in Table 2, and using a mapping tool [21], a business process representation of a large-scale collaboration was constructed, as shown in Figure 1.

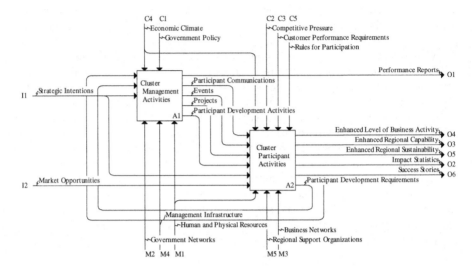

Fig. 1. A Representation of a Large-scale Collaboration as a Business System

A number of researchers (e.g. [24]) have noted that there may be a significant time lag between an input and an observable output, for example while absorptive capacity is built [16]. In addition, as a collaboration is an overlay on a participant's normal activities, it may be difficult to attribute outcomes to and spillovers from participation. Some researchers have compared the performance of collaboration participants with a control group, sometimes reporting a superior rate of growth, sometimes reporting no effect. One difficulty here is knowing whether the participating firms are the more innovative ones anyway. Swedish experience [24, 3] suggests that annual internal reviews plus an external review every three years may be appropriate. Evaluation should have a number of elements: firstly, identification of objectives and the relevant policy framework; secondly, selection of evaluation criteria; thirdly, monitoring over the life of the collaboration, fourthly a formal evaluation process, and finally, feedback and implementation of lessons learned.

Neely [25] has undertaken a comprehensive review of more than 30 years of research into business performance measurement. Whilst annual financial reporting has been the historical norm, a balanced scorecard [26] approach using key performance indicators to link strategy and measurement has been popular over the last 20 years. More recently, Kaplan [27] has suggested that achieving the vision should take precedence over financial measures in not-for- profit enterprises

Combining the collaboration-as-a-business system view with the suggestions above and some presented earlier, a set of key performance indicators appropriate to a long term breeding network environment is proposed in table 3. For shorter term collaborations where a virtual enterprise may be established for a specific project, successful completion of the project may be an adequate measure of collaboration performance, but this would not identify any gains in social or knowledge capital and lessons learned. Capturing these things in an annual survey as part of the collaboration management strategy may surface such outcomes.

Table 3. Some Illustrative Key Performance Indicators

KPI Type	KPI	Measure
Process	Cluster management operations according to plan	Annual internal review
	Events held	Annual reporting of number, type and attendance
	Projects established	Annual reporting of number started, finished and in progress with comment on issues and opportunities
	Individual firm services provided	Annual reporting of firms assisted and outcomes from the CRM system
	Member activities	Annual reporting of participation rates and firm profiles plus outstanding member activities and achievements
Input	Clear cluster vision and statement of intentions developed in conjunction with stakeholders	Annual reporting of progress against intentions, Review every three years
	Identification of business opportunities	Annual reporting of significant opportunities available to the cluster
Outputs	Economic benefits	From an annual member survey
	Member capability enhancements	From an annual member survey
	Knowledge flows	Annual reporting of lessons learned
	Collaborations established	From an annual member survey
	Jobs created	From an annual member survey
	Spillover benefits	Anecdotal evidence noted in annual report
Rules / constraints	Alignment with Government policy	Review every three years
	Business environment	Impact statement in annual report
	Competitive pressures	Impact statement in annual report
Resources	Cluster management resources	Annual report reviewing resources used, opportunities for improvement and the level of resourcing
	Cluster member resources	Annual report summarizing member cash and in-kind contributions

5   Illustrative Application of the Concepts

In February 2009 The University of Western Sydney Centre for Industry and Innovation Studies conducted an external review of the Western Sydney Information Technology Cluster (WSITC) that had been operating since 2001. The process involved a review of relevant documents and some literature on clusters plus direct interaction with the cluster managers and participants. A brief on-line member survey yielded fourty-seven responses, there were interviews with eight member firms, two focus group meetings were held, one with government participants, and the other with member participants.

Using ideas from Tables 2 and 3 to characterise the collaboration, the outcome was as follows:

- Dimensions – there are about 230 full members (still increasing by about 30 members each year) with a combined annual turnover of about $A700m plus

100 associate members. 70% are located inside of a 20km diameter circle. 60% of the member firms have less than five employees, and there are no large firms in the cluster. Most member firms are focused on IT applications rather than new technology development. About 60% own some form of intellectual property. About one-third of both the micro-firm and the SME firms plan to grow over the next five years.

- Maturity – the majority of the participants are either still growing their core business or learning more about exporting. Member firms do not tend to be continuously engaged, participating more during growth periods. A breeding network is well established, but there are relatively few projects.
- Heterogeneous participants – The 100 associate member enterprises provide a variety of education, business, market and technology support services, and this helps the developing member firms. The member firm clientele is commonly spread over seven different market sectors. Balancing similarity and complementarity seems to be an issue.
- Market access and competitiveness – strong growth in export activity since the cluster was established suggests that some firms are competitive, but the smaller firms have difficulty in accessing larger government projects. Absorptive capacity is an issue for some member firms, due to both knowledge and resource limitations.
- Transactions – considerable social capital and knowledge capital has been built. There is limited evidence of economic transactions between or in conjunction with member firms. Government funded housekeeping transaction management undertaken is appreciated by the members
- Process (from Table 3) - The cluster is achieving its original objectives. A significant number of cluster events are held each year, but there a few spin-off projects. About 60 % of the members attend two or three events each year, whilst the remainder did not attend any in 2008.
- Inputs - There is a statement of intentions that is currently under review, and some business opportunities are identified for members.
- Outputs - In our member survey, about 27% of micro-firms and 33% of SMEs reported revenue enhancement associated with the WSITC, but approximately double that reported other benefits to their business arising from participation. We interpret this as meaning that whilst some firms are getting direct benefits from the WSITC, the dominant benefit is back in the firm's primary business eco-system. There was clear evidence of member capability enhancement attributed to cluster participation, a significant number of jobs created, and some evidence of spillover benefits to cluster client firms.
- Rules/constraints – There was evidence of alignment with government policy and significant competitive market pressure
- Resources – members were satisfied with the cluster management resources, and many member and associate member firms were making in-kind contributions.

6 Concluding Remarks

We began with the research question *"Can we identify a simple way of measuring the performance of a large-scale collaboration?"* The suggested answer is - firstly establish a way to simply characterize such collaborations. Our proposition is that *the important attributes of a large-scale collaboration are dimensions, maturity and heterogeneity of participants; whilst outcomes from a large-scale collaboration are improved market access / competitiveness and balanced housekeeping and beneficial transactions.* Secondly, view operation of a large-scale collaboration as a business process that can be modeled, and using the characterization guidelines and this model, suggest some key performance Indicators. Finally, using this framework, go and talk to the participants. Using this approach in the illustrative case briefly presented in the paper, benefits that the government sponsors were not aware of were identified, as were many opportunities for improvement that had not been discussed. The data collected also supported some comparison with other clusters.

References

1. IMP (2009), http://www.impgroup.org/about.php (last accessed February 27, 2009)
2. Camarinha-Matos, L.M., Afsarmanesh, H.: The Emerging Discipline of Collaborative Networks. In: Camarinha-Matos, L.M. (ed.) Virtual Enterprises and Collaborative Networks, pp. 3–16. Kluwer Academic Publishers, Dordrecht (2004)
3. OECD. Competitive Regional Clusters – National policy Approaches, Organisation for Economic Co-operation and Development (2007) ISBN 978-92-64-03182
4. Cassidy, E., Davis, C., Arthurs, D., Wolfe, D.: Measuring the National Research council's Technology Cluster Initiatives. Presented at the CRIC Cluster Conference, Beyond Cluster – Current Practices and Future Strategies, Ballarat, Australian June 30-July 1 (2005)
5. Marceau, J.: Networks of Innovation, Networks of Production and Networks of Marketing: Collaboration and Competition in the Biomedical and Toolmaking Industries in Australia. Creativity and Innovation Management 8(1) (1999)
6. Enright, M.J.: Survey on the characteristics of regional clusters – initial results, Working Paper, Institute of Economic Policy and Business Strategy, Competitiveness Program, University of Hong Kong (2000)
7. Laitinen, E.K.: Financial statement analysis of a network of SMEs: towards measurement of network performance. International Journal of Networking and Virtual Organisations 3(3), 258–282 (2006)
8. ISO 1507. Requirements for enterprise reference architectures and methodologies. Annex A – GERAM: Generalized Enterprise Reference Architecture and Methodologies, Integration definition for function modelling (IDEF 0) US Federal Information Processing Standard publication 183 (1993)
9. Beckett, R.C.: Building Social Capital in the Australian Toolmaking Industry. In: Proc. 2nd meeting of IMP group in Asia, Building social capital in networks, Phuket, Thailand, December 12-14 (2005) ISBN 1 74067 425 1
10. Fornahl, D., Menzel, M.-P.: Co-development of firm founding and regional clusters. In: Proc. Clusters, Regional Districts and Firms: The Challenges of Globalization, Modena, Italy, September 12-13 (2003)

11. Lipnack, J., Stamps, J.: Virtual Teams – People Working Across Boundaries with Technology. John Wiley & Sons, New York (2000)
12. Biggiero, L., Sammarra, A.: Similarity and complementarity in inter-organisational networks. In: APROS (Asia-Pacific Researcher in Organisation Studies), Hong Kong Baptist University, December 3-5 (2001)
13. Inganas, M., Hacklin, F., Pluss, A., Marxt, C.: Knowledge management with a focus on the innovation process in collaborative networking companies. International Journal of Networking and Virtual Organisations 3(3) (2006)
14. Chapple, K.: Building Institutions from the Region Up: Regional Workforce Development Collaboratives, Working Paper 2005-01, Institute for Urban and Regional Development, University of California, Berkeley, CA (2005)
15. Seifert, M., Eschenbaecher, J.: Predictive performance measurement in virtual organizations. In: Emerging Solutions for Future Manufacturing Systems, pp. 299–306. Springer, Boston (2005)
16. Giuliani, E.: Cluster Absorptive Capability: An evolutionary approach for industrial clusters in developing countries. In: Proc. DRUID Summer Conference Industrial Dynamics of the New and Old Economy – who is enhancing whom? Copenhagen, June 6-8 (2002)
17. Beckett, R.C.: The Evolution of Some Collaborative Marketing Networks of SME's. In: 22nd Industrial Marketing & Purchasing (IMP) Conference, Milan, Italy, September 7-9 (2006)
18. Okkonen, J.: Performance of Virtual Organisations. In: Frontiers of e-Business research 2001, University of Tampere, e-Business Research Centre, Finland (2001) ISBN 951-44-5307-7
19. Camarinha-Matos, L.M., Abreu, A.: Performance indicators based on collaboration benefits. In: Collaborative Networks and their Breeding environments, pp. 273–282. Springer, New York (2005)
20. Hofmann, E.: Quantifying and setting off network performance. International Journal of Networking and Virtual Organisations 3(3), 317–339 (2006)
21. AIØWIN Automated Function Modelling for Windows, Knowledge Based Systems Inc.
22. Varamaki, E., Kohtamaki, M., Sorama, K., Wingren, T., Versalainen, J., Helo, P., Tuominen, T., Pahkala, T., Tenhunen, J.: A framework for a network-level performance measurement system in SME networks. International Journal of Networking and Virtual Organisations 5(3/4), 415–435 (2008)
23. Saiz, J.J.A., Rodriguez, R., Bas, A.O.: Performance measurement system for virtual and extended enterprise. In: Collaborative networks and their breeding environments, pp. 285–292. Springer, Boston (2005)
24. IKED, The Cluster Policies Whitebook" The International Organisation for Knowledge Economy and Enterprise Development, Sweden, 247 pages (2004) ISBN 91-85281-03-4
25. Neely, A.: The evolution of performance measurement research. International Journal of Operations and Production Management 25(12), 1264–1277 (2005)
26. Kaplan, R., Norton, D.: The balanced scorecard – measures that drive performance. Harvard Business Review, 71–79 (January-February 1992)
27. Kaplan, R.S.: Strategic performance measurement and management in nonprofit organizations. Nonprofit Management & Leadership 11(3), 353–370 (2001)

Reference Model for Performance Management in Service-Oriented Virtual Organization Breeding Environments

Zbigniew Paszkiewicz and Willy Picard

Department of Infromation Technology, Poznan University of Economics,
Mansfelda 4, 60-854 Poznań, Poland
{zpasz,picard}@kti.ue.poznan.pl

Abstract. Performance management (PM) is a key function of virtual organization (VO) management. A large set of PM indicators has been proposed and evaluated within the context of virtual breeding environments (VBEs). However, it is currently difficult to describe and select suitable PM indicators because of the lack of a common vocabulary and taxonomies of PM indicators. Therefore, there is a need for a framework unifying concepts in the domain of VO PM. In this paper, a reference model for VO PM is presented in the context of service-oriented VBEs. In the proposed reference model, both a set of terms that could be used to describe key performance indicators, and a set of taxonomies reflecting various aspects of PM are proposed. The proposed reference model is a first attempt and a work in progress that should not be supposed exhaustive.

Keywords: Virtual organization, performance measurement, key performance indicators.

1 Introduction

The concept of *Virtual Breeding Environment* (VBE) has been proposed by the ECOLEAD project as "an association of organizations and their related supporting institutions, adhering to a base long term cooperation agreement, and adoption of common operating principles and infrastructures, with the main goal of increasing their preparedness towards collaboration in potential *Virtual Organizations (VO)*" [1]. The main aims of VBE are the establishment of trust for organization to collaborate in VOs, the reduction of cost and time to search and find suitable partners of VOs, the assistance in VO creation, re-configuration, reaching agreement [1]. In ECOLEAD *Virtual organization* is defined in the following manner: "an *operational structure* consisting of *different organizational entities* and created for a *specific business purpose*, to address a *specific business opportunity*" [2].

Among various important aspects of VBE management and VO Management (VOM) identified by the ECOLEAD project, the concept of *VO Performance Measurement (PM)* has be defined as a "systematic approach to plan and conduct the collection and monitoring of data for performance indicators. The Performance Measurement is focused on the process of data collection. The input are defined

L.M. Camarinha-Matos et al. (Eds.): PRO-VE 2009, IFIP AICT 307, pp. 505–513, 2009.
© IFIP International Federation for Information Processing 2009

Performance Indicators (PI) including targets. For these PIs appropriate methods and tools of measuring have to be developed and planed. The collected data is then prepared into indicators. As a result performance measurement produces reports that could be used for further analyses and interpretation to assess the performance and to derive measures for improvement" [3].

Measuring the performance of distributed organization is a difficult task. Many works have justified the need for PM and have analyzed existing approaches in the management science as regards potential adaptation to VO [3–5]. However the studied approaches usually concentrate on specific aspects of organization operation, e.g. logistics, accomplishment of strategic goals, financial aspects. As a consequence, measuring the performance of a whole VO, and not only some aspects of it, still requires a more global approach. Additionally, to our best knowledge, no systematic classification of existing indicators exists, and therefore, it is difficult to describe and select suitable indicators and sources of data for their calculation.

Therefore, there is a need for a VO-specific *Reference Model (RM)* for VO PM. The goal of such a reference model should be two-fold: on the one hand, the reference model should define a set of common terms that could be used to describe key performance indicators (KPIs). On the second hand, the reference model should define various taxonomies of KPIs, each taxonomy focusing on various aspects of PM.

In this paper, a first attempt of a Reference Model for VO PM is presented. This paper is organized as follows. In Section 2, the concept of Service-Oriented VBEs (SOVOBE) is introduced, as our reference model focuses on such a type of VBE. Then, the importance of the concept of KPIs in context of SOVOBE is explained. In Section 4, a Reference Model for VO PM is proposed. Finally, Section 5 concludes the paper.

2 Service-Oriented VBE

2.1 SOA and CNOs

While the concept of VBE is currently rather accepted in the Collaborative Network Organization (CNO) research community, there is currently no consensus about the architecture and implementation of VBEs.

However, the Service-Oriented Architecture (SOA) has been suggested as a valuable approach for the architecture and implementations of VBEs in [6]. The definition of SOA by the OASIS group [7] is the following one: "Service Oriented Architecture (SOA) is a paradigm for organizing and utilizing distributed capabilities that may be under the control of different ownership domains. [...] in SOA, services are the mechanism by which needs and capabilities are brought together." This definition emphasizes some characteristics of SOA common to CNOs: CNOs may be seen as structures aiming at "organizing and utilizing distributed capabilities under the control of different ownership domains".

2.2 Main Elements of SOVOBEs

In this paper, only service-oriented virtual organization breeding environments (SOVOBE) are taken into account. In a SOVOBE, VBE and VO operations are based on services performed by people, organizations and information systems, composed in complex business processes.

Additionally, in this paper, it is assumed that a *social network* is supporting the SOVOBE by providing information about relations among people, organizations, information systems, and business processes.

A social network is a graph of *nodes* (sometimes referred as *actors*), which may be connected by *relations* (sometimes referred as *ties*, *links*, or *edges*). Social Network Analysis (SNA) is the study of these relations [8] and may be used to analyze the structure of SOVOBEs.

An important aspect of SNA is the fact that it focused on the how the structure of relationships affects actors, instead of treating actors as the discrete units of analysis. SNA is backed by social sciences and mathematical theories like graph theory and matrix algebra [9], which makes it applicable to analytical approaches and empirical methods. SNA uses various concepts to evaluate different network properties.

3   KPIs in SOVOBE

3.1   KPIs and SLAs in SOVOBE

Key Performance Indicator (KPI) has been defined in the ECOLEAD project as "a performance indicator which represents essential or critical components of the overall performance. Not every performance indicator is vital for the overall success of a company. To focus attention and resources the indicators with the highest impact on performance are chosen as key performance indicators. [...] An *indicator* is a variable which is feasible to assess the state of an object in scope. Indicators could be as well quantitative as qualitative measures. They can not only consist of a single measure but also be aggregated or calculated out of several measures" [3].

A similar concept has been proposed in SOA: *Service Level Agreement (SLA)*. A SLA is a part of a service contract where the level of service is formally defined. A SLA usually refers to a single service and a single organizational unit that is responsible for provision of this service.

The difference between KPIs and SLAs in SOVOBE is related with the scope of these concepts.

Table 1. Scope of SLAs and KPIs in SOVOBE

SLA	KPI
Service	-
Process	Composition of services within a process
Partner	Composition of services within a partner
	Composition of processes within a partner
VO	Composition of processes within VO
	Composition of partners within VO
VBE	Composition of VO within VBE

The scope of interest of SLAs and KPIs in SOVOBE is presented in Table 1. KPIs concentrate on compositions of elements of SOVOBE. For instance, the subject of a KPI is not a performance of a single service but a composition of services. Similarly, a KPI does not measure the performance of a single process, but of a composition of processes. On the other hand, composition of services may be perceived from process point of view – process as a composition of services – or partner point of view – partner as a composition of services that are provided by him. In turn, process may be analyzed in context of one partner – process a partner takes part in – or VO – processes that VO operation is based on. Finally VO is a composition of partners and VBE is a composition of VO. Again, it is important to stress, that KPIs defined on a level of single SOVOBE element (i.e. partner) do not refer to the element itself but to collection of its components.

3.2 Anticipation and Monitoring in CNOs

KPIs may be used through almost entire CNO life cycle. Especially, they are useful in CNO creation and operational phase. The possible set of KPIs that might be used in mentioned phases is the same, but the approach to the measurement changes.

Anticipation. During CNO creation, the aim of PM is to *anticipate* the CNO overall performance. A set of KPIs, together with expected values, are defining performance requirements for the CNO to be created. Then by comparing expected values of KPIs to calculated values for a chosen potential CNO realization, a CNO planner may identify strengths and weaknesses of the chosen potential CNO realization.

Monitoring. During CNO operation, constant monitoring of KPIs may take place. While anticipation is active, monitoring is passive. The performance of existing composition of artifacts is evaluated using KPIs and the result of the evaluation is compared with performance requirements. If there are any deviations from the accepted level of performance of a partner, process or a whole network, CNO can take actions to replace service, partner, process, information system or change business goal.

4   A Reference Model for KPIs in SOVOBE

The OASIS group have defined the concept of reference model as follows: "A reference model is an abstract *framework* for understanding significant relationships among the entities of some environment. It enables the development of specific reference or concrete architectures using consistent standards or specifications supporting that environment. A reference model consists of a minimal set of *unifying concepts, axioms* and relationships within a particular problem domain, and is *independent* of specific standards, technologies, implementations, or other concrete details" [7].

The main contribution of this paper is a reference model for KPIs in SOVOBE. In this section, both a set of terms that could be used to describe KPIs, and a set of taxonomies reflecting various aspects of PM are proposed. The proposed reference model is a first attempt and a work in progress that should not be supposed exhaustive.

4.1   Data Source

A significant issue related with KPIs is the accessibility of data. Some KPIs can be computed using publicly available data stored in SOVOBE, e.g. history of collaboration, description of services, opinion of services. However, the calculation of other KPIs requires access to data stored in partners' internal databases, usually not accessible for technical or organizational reasons (organization may not allow public access to certain piece of data, nonetheless this access may be granted as a result of negotiations). A potential solution to this problem consists in accessing the data via services. Such a solution implies an agreement among partners on conditions of providing additional services. This agreement might be reached during the process of partner selection and negotiation. These additional services may be composed in a *control process* that will be probably synchronized with the main *operational process* ruling partners' interaction.

Therefore, the following KPI subcategories presented in Table 2 may be distinguished:

Table 2. KPI Data source

	Category name	Description	Example
1.	Collaboration-based	Based on a data strictly connected with provision of services needed for operational process	
1.1	Subjective	Coming form a subjective opinion of one of parties involved in collaboration	
1.1.1	Service consumer opinion	Data provided by a service consumer, based on his perception of reality	Perceived time of partner's response
1.1.2	Service provider opinion	Data provided by service provider	Partner guarantees referring failure rate of services
1.2	Objective	Not dependent on opinion of parties involved in collaboration	
1.2.1	Continuous monitoring of collaboration	Data provided by monitoring of service use and process progress	Current time of partner response, current partner's reliability
1.2.2	Bag of assets	Data stored in VBE or VO	
1.2.2.1	History of collaboration	Data restored form the history of partners' performance and collaboration within VBE	Number of VOs a partner participated in, partner's average failure rate
1.2.2.2	Description of services	Quantitative values hold in service description	Formally declared time of response
1.2.2.3	Description of competences	Quantitative values hold in description of partner and competences	Number of services offered by partner
1.2.2.4	Contracts and SLA	Agreed conditions of cooperation	Real cost of the service in a particular process
1.2.3	Social network	Data modeled in SN, data coming from third parties that are not directly involved in evaluated collaboration process	Experience of the partner, acknowledgement of the partner

Table 2. (*continued*)

	Category name	Description	Example
2.	Non-collaboration-based	Based on additionally negotiated data not required in a operational process	
2.1	Control process	Data accessible within control process	Personal data of partner's subcontractors

The proposed subcategories are not exclusive, as the calculation of a KPI may require various sources.

4.2 Subject of Measurement

As mentioned in Section 2, it is possible to distinguish following elements of a SOVOBE: service, process, partner, VO, and VBE. As described in section 3.1 single services are not a subject of measurement by KPIs. Table 3 presents subcategories referring to consecutive elements.

Table 3. KPI subject of measurement

	Category name	Description	Example
1.	Process	Composition of services	Total cost of the process calculated on a basis of service costs
2.	Partner	Composition of services and processes	Partner's reliability calculated on a basis of average failure rate of services provided by partner
3.	Virtual Organization	Composition of processes and partners	Number of partners involved in more than one VO
4.	Virtual Breeding Environment	Composition of VOs	Average number of partners in VO

The proposed subcategories are not exclusive, as the calculation of a KPI may concerns various subjects. A KPI could determine the importance of a particular partner the ratio of a number of services provided by a partner to a total number of services used in a process.

4.3 Scope

KPIs may be defined at various level of granularity. The most typical case is to define a KPI for a given VO, with the KPI measuring performance aspects related with the specific characteristics of particular VO. However, some KPIs may be defined at the VBE level and be shared by all VOs, with KPI measuring performance aspects related with the specific characteristics of particular VBE [10].

KPIs defined at the VBE level would allow e.g. VO comparison, uniform validation of quality of created networks of cooperation, imposition of best practices and validation of conformation to these practices.

Table 4. KPI scope

	Category name	Description
1.	Global	KPIs obligatory for all VOs despite the VBE
2.	Standard	KPIs obligatory for all VO within a given VBE
3.	Custom	KPIs defined for a particular VO within particular VBE

Identified KPI scopes are presented in Table 4.

4.4 Performance of Collaboration

In SOVOBE, performance of collaboration is conditioned by *structure of the network* and by quality of SOVOBE elements. KPIs referring to the structure of collaboration are called *structural indicators* and their definition and analysis is based on SNA. Structure of the network represents relations among artifacts. Structure is modeled in

Table 5. KPI for performance of collaboration

	Category name	Description	Example
1.	Structural	Referring to a structure of collaboration network	
1.1	Service structure	Referring to a structure of collaboration (service composition) directly influencing operational process	Number of service provided by a partner for the network, degree of VO overlapping
1.2	General structure	Referring to critical for VO aspects different to a structure of collaboration i.e. partners' experience, competences, acknowledgment etc.	Level of trust, number of VO an organization is involved, level of experience
2.	Operational	Referring to the quality and non-functional requirements of partners', processes, and of-fered services	
2.1	Effectiveness	Reliability of the service and ability to meet expectations	Failure rate
2.2	Flexibility	Maximal additional capacity that could be provided to the VO	Possible additional production volume in comparison with contracted (%)
2.3	Substitutability	Ease of replacement of an SOVOBE element	Number of partners with the same competences
2.4	Efficiency	Usage of resources	Number of involved partners in a process
2.5	Responsiveness	Time of response	Time to fulfill the request
2.6	Cost	Cost of operation	Cost of VO process, cost of VO service
2.7	Productivity	Volume of requests that could be fulfilled	Number of offered services, number of products offered by VO

a social network. Among all multiple views and aspects of the network structure for performance analysis, it is useful to distinguish the structure of services. *Structure of services* is a structure of a graph representing composition, dependencies, and complexity of services. Relations among services directly influence fulfillment of an operational process and influence the operation of VO and VBE.

A second important aspect in performance measurement is a quality of SOVOBE elements and non-functional requirements that can be defined for them. KPIs measuring the use and operations are referred as *operational indicators*. Operational indicators are presented e.g. in the ISO 9126 standard [11] and in the ECOLEAD project [3]. A taxonomy of KPIs related with the performance of collaboration is presented in Table 5.

5   Conclusions

The main contribution presented in this paper is a definition of a Reference Model for KPIs in SOVOBEs. The proposed reference model is based on results of the ECOLEAD project [3–5] concerning performance management. The proposed Reference model aims at providing the CNO community with a vocabulary and a set of taxonomies useful to describe KPIs. However, the Reference Model presented in this paper is a work in progress and it may not be assumed that it is exhaustive.

Among future works, the reference model should be extended by practitioners that may confront the proposed reference model with the needs of CNO members in terms of performance management. It would also be interesting to confront the proposed reference model with the reference model for Collaborative Networks ARCON proposed by Camarinha-Matos et al. [2].

Finally, within the context of the IT-SOA project [12], a service-oriented VBE is currently under development. This VBE will gather companies from the construction sector in the Great Poland region. During the IT-SOA project, the Key Performance Indicators will be defined in a real business environment, based on an extended version of the presented Reference Model.

Acknowledgments. This work has been partially supported by the Polish Ministry of Science and Higher Education within the European Regional Development Fund, Grant No. POIG.01.03.01-00-008/08.

References

1. Camarinha-Matos, L.M., Afsarmanesh, H., Galeano, N.: Characterization of Key Components, Features, and Operating Principles of the Virtual Breeding Environment. Deliverable 21.1. ECOLEAD (2004)
2. Camarinha-Matos, L.M., Afsarmanesh, H., Ermilova, E., Ferrada, F., Abreu, A.: A reference model for Collaborative Networks. ECOLEAD deliverable 52.3 (2007)
3. Graser, F., Westphal, I., Eschenbaecher, J.: Roadmap on VOPM Challenges on Operational and Strategic Level. ECOLEAD deliverable 31.1 (2005)
4. Negretto, U.: Report on Methodologies, Processes and Services for VO Management. ECOLEAD Deliverable 32.2 (2005)

5. Westphal, I., Eschenbächer, J., Negretto, U., Jansson, K., Salkari, I., Paganelli, P., Borst, I.: VOPM approach, performance metrics and measurement process. ECOLEAD Deliverable 31.2 (2005)

6. Rabelo, R., Gesser, C., Tramontin, R., Gibert, P., Nagellen, T., Rodrigo, M., Ratti, R., Paganelli, P.: Reference Framework for a Collaborative Support ICT infrastructure. Deliverable D61.1a (Version 2). ECOLEAD (2005)

7. OASIS: Reference Model for Service Oriented Architecture 1.0. OASIS Standard (2006)

8. Baroudi, Olson, Ives: An Empirical Study of the Impact of User Involvement on System Usage and Information Satisfaction. CACM 29(3), 232–238 (1986)

9. Borgatti, S.: What is social network analysis? (1999), http://www.analytictech.com/networks/whatis.htm

10. Galeano, N., Romero, D.: Characterization of VBE Value Systems and Metrics. ECOLEAD deliverable 21.4a (2006)

11. International Organization for Standardization ISO/IEC 9126-1 (2001), http://www.iso.org/iso/iso_catalogue/catalogue_tc/catalogue_detail.htm?csnumber=22749

12. IT-SOA project, http://www.soa.edu.pl/

Part 16

Agile Business Models

Thinking Outside the Box:
Agile Business Models for CNOs

Leandro Loss and Servane Crave

Orange Labs R&D
905, rue Albert Einstein, 06921, Sophia Antipolis Cedex, France
{leandro.loss,servane.crave}@orange-ftgroup.com

Abstract. This paper introduces the idea of an agile Business Model for CNOs grounded on a new model of innovation based on the effects of globalization and of Knowledge Economy. The agile Business Model considers the resources that are spread out and available worldwide as well as the need for each customer to receive a unique customer experience. It aims at reinforcing in the context of the Knowledge Economy the different business models approaches developed so far. The paper also identifies the levers and the barriers of Agile Business Models Innovation in CNOs.

Keywords: Collaborative Networks, Agile Business Models, Customer Experience.

1 Introduction

Collaborative Networked Organizations (CNOs) (Camarinha-Matos and Afsarmanesh, 2005) are assessed as organizational forms with an appropriate compliance in a context of globalization and turbulent markets. This adaptability is due to their fast and reliable arrangement capacities with regards to the collaboration opportunities that occur or that they are able to detect.

One can observe that CNOs have been well described and documented thanks to real case studies (in Aeronautics, Automotive networks) and trends of research explored in European projects, such as ECOLEAD (theoretical and technological foundations for CNOs), ATHENA and INTEROP (interoperability issues and seamless business interactions across organizational boundaries). However, the CNO field of research is not yet complete; rather it still presents many issues to be further explored. One of these fields is related to the BM studies.

In Marketing, BMs have become in the last decade a fashionable term to describe the way an organization is going to address the market. In Organizational Sciences, it is presented as a conceptual tool composed of several interrelated building blocks which aim at defining the product/service, the revenue model, the value proposition, the distribution channel, that a single organization offers to one or several segments of customers (Osterwalder, 2004). It is of evidence that CNOs already make use of BMs when they are elaborating their strategy. However, proven BMs approaches like Chesbrough et al. (2002) and Osterwalder (2004) are rather static in the sense that

L.M. Camarinha-Matos et al. (Eds.): PRO-VE 2009, IFIP AICT 307, pp. 517–526, 2009.

they are designed for a single organization with a linear value chain, within a stable and predictable competitive landscape. Romero et al. (2006) attempted to cope with this issue through a multi perspective approach regarding BMs for CNOs focusing on two different features: the Value Proposition and the nature of the shareholders[1] & stakeholders[2]. Romero et al. (2006) is a noticeable asset but it could be enhanced in order to support CNOs in a context of globalization and increased uncertainty.

The aforementioned BM approaches face difficulties to capture the necessary shift in the new ways of working of CNOs' stakeholders, mainly regarding innovation aspects. Consequently, an agile BM strategy is required for CNOs. This paper proposes to ground it on a new model of innovation which finds its roots in a context where resources are spread out worldwide and where each customer will receive a unique experience. Prahalad et al. (2008) have extensively developed the idea of R=G (access to high-quality resources at low cost) and N=1 (the focus is on the individual consumer). These concepts are mobilized in this paper in order to create an agile Business Model for CNO's. This research work also includes the identification of innovation levers and barriers when defining BMs for CNOs.

The paper is organized as follows: section 2 presents the CNOs approach as a sound alternative in markets dominated by globalization and turbulence. Section 3 presents a joint perspective of the BM approaches introduced by Osterwalder (2004), Romero et al. (2006), and of empirical tools used to support BMs elaboration. Section 4 presents the levers that lead to innovation in BMs as well as the related uncertainties. To conclude, section 5 brings the final remarks of this work and opens new research avenues.

2   CNOs: An Alternative for Turbulent Markets

Since mid-2007 the economic world has been facing the so called "credit crunch". This phenomenon started with the lack of trust by investors in the value of securitized mortgages[3] in the USA. After that the crisis has deepened and affected the stock markets all around the world (with very few exceptions). Many financial institutions have collapsed or were nationalized being under federal regulations. Countries that have not been in recession (negative real economic growth) for many years are now also facing this problem. Both US Federal Reserve and the European Union countries have made efforts to minimize the problems caused by this unprecedented crisis.

On the one hand, recession is often synonymous of factories closing-down and employees' layoffs. On the other hand, as stated by Papadakis et al. (1999) and Stevenson and Jarillo (1990), periods of crisis can also be seen as moments for entrepreneurial growth, where organizations should be looking for new opportunities, rather than defending existing resources.

---

[1] A "shareholder" is an individual or company that legally owns one or more shares of stock in a joint stock company. A company's shareholders collectively own that company.

[2] A "stakeholder" is a person, group, organization, or system who affects or can be affected by an organization's actions.

[3] Securitized mortgages involve the pooling and repacking of cash flow producing financial assets into securities that are then sold to investors (Raynes et al., 2003).

One option to better explore opportunities and react to turbulent markets, mainly for Small and Medium sized Enterprises (SMEs), is to work collaboratively in strategic alliances. Lendrum (1997) defines a strategic alliance as a formal relationship that rises up from two or more participants in order to pursue a set of agreed goals or to meet a critical business. Oliver (1990) reviewed the literature on inter-organizational relations and argues that the core idea is that organizations working together are **stronger than when working only by themselves or isolated**. According to Loss et al. (2008), strategic alliances are also viewed as a form of Collaborative Networked Organization (CNOs).

Camarinha-Matos and Afsarmanesh (2006) argue that CNOs provide access to new/wider markets and novel knowledge, where risks and resources are shared and where skills and capacities can be complementary orchestrated. Therefore entities being part of a CNO may focus on their core competencies while keeping high level of agility. New organizational forms also lead to innovation, and thus creation of new value by confrontation of ideas and practices, combination of resources and technologies, and creation of synergies (Camarinha-Matos and Afsaramanesh, 2006).

CNOs are per nature dynamic and adaptive organizational forms, but they also need to be continuously aware of the non-stable and unpredictable competitive landscape. With a view to better explore market opportunities and improve their competitiveness, CNOs Managers shall not anymore rely only on the traditional BMs. They shall, therefore, look for dynamic supporting tools that allow the elaboration of new and innovative approaches in order to conquest new markets. It means to better adapt themselves to changes.

3   Current Business Models Approaches

According to Chesbrough and Rosenbloom (2002) the key to release value from a service or a technology is a successful Business Model. It means that the business model perspective takes into consideration the ways in which services and/or technologies can be valuable. The functions of a business model, according to these authors, are:

- Identify a *market segment*. The users to whom the technology is useful and for what purpose;
- Articulate the *value proposition*. The value created for users by the offering based on the technology;
- Define the structure of the *value chain* within the firm required to create and distribute the offering;
- Estimate the *cost structure* and *profit potential* of producing the offering, given the value proposition and value chain structure chosen;
- Describe the position of the firm within the *value network* linking suppliers and customers, including identification of potential complements and competitors;
- Formulate the *competitive strategy* by which the innovating organization will gain and hold advantage over rivals.

As a result BM is seen as the linking element from technical inputs to economic outputs (Fig. 1).

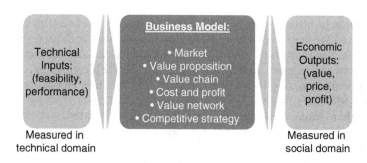

Fig. 1. Business Model Mediates Between the Technical and Economic Domains. Source: Chesbrough and Rosenbloom (2002).

It is understood that business models should embrace a wider perspective that also includes possible partnerships, customer requirements, revenue shares and other elements. Osterwalder (2004) defines Business Models as:

> "...a conceptual tool that contains a set of elements and their relationships and allows a company's logic of earning money. It is a description of the value a company offers to one or several segments of customers and the architecture of the firm and its network of partners for creating marketing and delivering this value and relationship capital, in order to generate profitable and sustainable revenue streams".

Looking for a formal way to accurately describe the business model of a firm, Osterwalder (2004) identified four main pillars seen as the basis of a BM: **product** (what?), **customer interface** (who?), **infrastructure management** (how?), and **financial aspects** (how much?). These four areas were broken down in nine interrelated building blocks: value proposition, under the pillar *product*; target customer, distribution channel, and relationship, under the pillar *customer interface*; value configuration, capability, and partnership, under the pillar *infrastructure management*; and cost structure and revenue model, under the pillar *financial aspects*. Romero et al. (2006) extended Osterwalder's work to CNOs introducing the idea of *multi-value proposition* and *configuration* to match the nature of CNOs. For supporting development of new services in the ICT sector. Plantin et al., (2008), have developed an exhaustive check-list of all relevant actions when developing a Business model including: *ecosystem analysis* - understanding the scope of the relevant field of economic activity; *breakthrough anticipation* - possible events that can change a value chain; *competitive analysis* - identifies the various competitors; *pre-segmentation* and *segmentation* - main strengths and weaknesses of the value perceived by the customer; *business analysis* - identification of the main values, key success factors, know-how, and critical resources; *fields of innovation* and *value creation*; *market analysis* - characterization of the target market in both qualitative and quantitative ways; *value chain* - understand the logic of a of activities performed; *supply strategy* - describe the services in order to make them intelligible; *value proposition*; and *SWOT analysis*.

Fig. 2 shows a graphical representation that merges the model for BM introduced by Ostervalder (2004) and improved by Romero et al. (2006). Additionally, the empirical-based marketing approaches that support the elaboration of BMs (Plantin et al., 2008) are also included. This graphical representation is in accordance with Chesbrough and Rosenbloom (2002) proposition where the BM is placed as a bridging element that links technical inputs (infrastructure management) and economical outputs (customer interface and financial aspects).

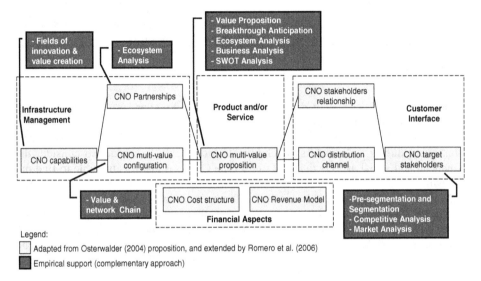

Fig. 2. Complementary tools and techniques applied to the approach proposed by Osterlwalder (2004) and extended to CNOs by Romero et al., (2006)

Nevertheless, the current approaches to develop BMs appear to be on a different wavelength from the current market landscape: especially when looking at new market dynamics caused by globalization, rising up of services in all activity sectors as well as open innovation processes. It is argued that new dynamics for BMs are required. As a result, next section introduces the concept of agile Business Models.

4   Fostering Agile Business Models

The motivation for this new perspective is spurred on the evolution from a *value chain* (Porter, 1985) where products definitions and customers' needs are stable and well defined (Li et al., 2008) to a *value network*. The latter embraces any web of relationships that generates tangible and intangible value *through complex dynamics between two or more individuals, groups or organizations* (Allee, 2002).

As it was mentioned before, the current BMs used by CNOs operate in a rather linear "one-way flow". It implies that customers or end-users are not included in the dynamics of product/service life cycle management (from ideation to market). As a result, their involvement to the CNO's BM is to a certain extent passive. Table 1

Table 1. Key features of Current BMs and Agile BMs

Current BMs (as-is)	Agile BMs (to-be)
Static	Dynamic
Financial aspects	Financial and social aspects
Profit	Profit / sustainability / effect of commoditization
Linear and Value chain	Value network / Digital ecosystems
Value analysis and creation	Value creation and capture
Product	Increased development of services / Services on top of the products
Customer interfaces	Customer empowerment
One to Many / One to one	Many to one

presents a holistic perspective about how conventional and/or current BMs in CNOs are traditionally focused (as-is) and how agile BMs are meant to be designed (to-be).

It is argued that an agile BM should be dynamic – to take into account the events that occur during and after its development. An agile BM should also consider the financial and social aspects that will impact the CNO, so that it is possible to find out in which spheres of the social activities the CNO business might have influence. CNOs should also look for profit but without forgetting the sustainability require-ments. Another relevant aspect is to be aware of the transformation of some goods and services into commodities: this shift in value has for sure an impact for CNOs in the sense that the competition will not be anymore on quality on these all of one kind products or services. This implies a search for additional differentiation features or a complete redefinition of the BM.

Indeed, the way of seeing the market (linear) needs to be reviewed. The evolution from a traditional value chain to a value network and digital ecosystems is essential: CNOs need to create an ecosystem promoting and enabling the sharing of ideas, knowledge and capabilities, as well as the evolution among services and solutions (Nachira et al., 2007). Another important aspect is that the development of a manufac-tured product is no longer enough. Services should be further developed and included on top of the products in order to create value to and with the customer. One example is the success of the Iphone which achieved a paramount breakthrough in the mobile landscape: it is of evidence that the device is stunningly beautiful which makes it attractive for all generations. But the genuine key success factor is the Apple Applica-tion Store with more than 25.000 applications and by March 2009, more than 500 million downloads. Service on top of the product is seen as a way to develop *cus-tomer loyalty*, i.e. in the Apple's case to lock-in customers on a single and unique application store which can not be overlooked and that no one can compete!

Finally, even if it is always of importance to capture and understand the customers' needs and requirements, this approach needs to be renewed. An interaction space is required where customers could participate through interactions with the CNO to product/service ideation or design. This can be achieved through changes suggestions, evaluation of new products/services. It implies to gather information and to analyze it, as well as to open communication channels to the customers. According to Prahalad et al. (2008), the behavior of individual customers and broad patterns of change must be understood. It has a direct impact on the infrastructure management, actors involved, financial aspects, quality of products and services.

Table 2 introduces what the authors have identified as levers and uncertainties for building agile business models in CNOs. The objective of this exercise is to find means to go beyond the concepts being used nowadays and to link them to a BM approach. These levers and uncertainties features are divided in three different categories: Organizational, Social, and Technological.

Table 2. Levers and uncertainties features for Agile Business Models

	Organizational	Social	Technological
Levers	Business processes in accordance to the Business Models Open Innovation (crowdsourcing)	Collective intelligence User empowerment (knowledge workers and value co-creation)	XaaS (SOA, web services) Web X.0, P2P Data analysis (analytics)
Uncertainties	Organizational culture Quality and maintenance	Trust aspects Intellectual Property Rights Sustainability	Costs / time consuming implementation Return of Investments for SMEs

On the **Organizational** side, it is argued that the (distributed) business processes should be developed in accordance with what is pointed out by the BM. It means that via the implementation of the strategies through their business processes, CNOs could be more agile and in a position to better react to new business opportunities. Another lever for an agile BM is the implementation of Open Innovation concept (Chesbrough, 2003), i.e. a subtle blend of internal and external innovation based on the subsequent acknowledgement: R&D can seldom, if ever, be only internally developed implying that R&D can be externally bought if this strategy brings advances to the BM.

However, impediments might occur due to the strength of the organizational culture. People inside the organization may not be used to this new open way of working: seeking the punctual help of an external expert for one specific opportunity can be interpreted as a threat by workers of the organization, or the process may not be modeled accurately causing bottlenecks to the CNO operation. Issues as quality and maintenance are also sensible to emergent approaches because they change the way the activities are performed.

Regarding the *Social* perspective, one may consider as a lever the power of collective intelligence in the Knowledge Economy (Brown and Hugh, 2001) as an important input which may modify the BM design. Individuals such as knowledge workers or active customers can provide content that may lead to changes in the BM. Collective intelligence rises up from the collaboration and competition, also called *"coopetition"* of many individuals, not necessarily being part of the CNO. CNOs may benefit from it for value creation and value co-creation (Prahalad et al., 2008).

Despite the importance of collective intelligence and user empowerment for value co-creation, issues like trust, intellectual property rights, and sustainability shall be carefully taken into consideration by CNOs. A clear definition of a value system model can provide support these issues.

The latest perspective addressed in this table is the **Technological** one, which is seen as a horizontal building block that provides tools to support the organizational and social aspects of BMs. An agile BM shall then rely on a horizontal building block composed of an ICT base and of an analytic model. An analytic model aims to support innovation via the analysis of both structured and unstructured data in order to use and/or allocate resources according to the users' requirements (Prahalad et al., 2008). Analytics are then focused on the needs of single individuals (N=1) through global resources (R=G) and the decisions are based on information gathered from Web 2.0 expressions such as blogs, chat rooms, micro-blogs, and social networks in order to collect the customer's preferences and trends. Likewise, (distributed) business processes, supported by Service Oriented Architecture (SOA), can be swiftly reengineered and compliant with changes. The concept of XaaS (X as a Service), where X can be understood as "anything" also supports an agile BM. Application interaction in multi-levels among users, organizations and even machines bring a higher level of agility to CNOs. Web 2.0 tools can also support an agile business model by collecting information. It facilitates the communication among CNO partners and clients by providing collaboration tools and interoperability for information sharing.

The uncertainties related to the technological perspective involve the costs of providing this kind of structure, even when using already developed tools (Rabelo and Gusmeroli, 2008) and the time necessary in order to implement these solutions. Furthermore, it is not yet clear to SMEs how to measure the return of investments in technology.

Fig. 3 shows the interaction of the levers in the three dimensions aforementioned. It also considers the approach presented in Fig. 2. The approach presented in Fig. 3

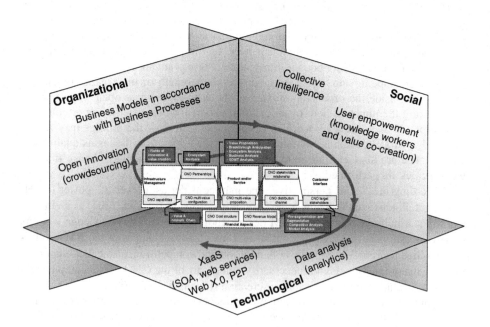

Fig. 3. Interaction of elements in Agile Business Models for CNOs

intends to complement and update the existing ones. It aims at opening CNO's managers to the richness and changes provided by globalization and the Knowledge Economy. It also shows that the three dimensions are interrelated and require to be worked out in a holistic and integrated manner. For instance, Collective Intelligence (Social), Open Innovation (Organizational) and Analytics (Technological) need to be strongly coupled when these features are addressed. If one of these features is not integrated in the approach when defining a BM, a potential failure due to imbalance will occur. On the contrary, a harmonious combination of them will allow BMs to become more dynamic and will provide them agility to react to market uncertainties.

5   Final Considerations

This work brought to light the concept of an agile BM for CNOs. The paper started emphasizing how CNOs can be seen as an alternative in turbulent markets and periods of crisis. In the sequence the importance of BMs for the CNOs was presented. Reference to the conceptualization of BMs (model proposed by Chesbrough and Rosenboon, 2002) and the investigation of the evolution from a framework for BMs focused on one single enterprise (Osterwalder, 2004) to an attempt to a CNO BM (Romero et al., 2006) has been achieved to frame the scope and the advances proposed by the authors.

It was verified that despite the model presented by Romero et al., (2006) proposed a solid contribution to BMs in CNOs, it missed an agile perspective that may provide dynamicity for BMs in CNOs. Based on these observations, key features of current approaches for BMs and agile BMs were introduced. The levers and uncertainties that can affect an agile BM were also presented. These levers and uncertainties were split into three categories (Organizational, Social, and Technological) in order to cover a wider perspective.

With this agile business model approach, the authors aim to give insights and inspiration to further investigate the fundamentals of future BMs where complexity and adaptability will prevail. The next steps of this research work shall be dedicated to an exhaustive investigation of the levers and uncertainties with a field research to further articulate and illustrate in a mock-up organization, social, and technological dimensions.

Acknowledgments

The authors would like to thank Mrs. Sylvie Plantin, from Orange Labs R&D, for her valuable comments.

References

1. Allee, V.: A Value Network Approach for Modelling and Measuring Intangibles. In: Proceedings Transparent Enterprise, Madrid (November 2002)
2. Brown, P., Hugh, L.: Capitalism and social progress: the future of society in a global economy. In: Brown, Lauder (eds.) Collective intelligence, Palgrave (2001)
3. Camarinha-Matos, L.M., Afsarmanesh, H.: Collaborative networks: a new scientific discipline. Journal of Intelligent Manufacturing 16, 439–452 (2005)

4. Camarinha-Matos, L.M., Afsarmanesh, H.: Collaborative networks: value creation in a knowledge society. In: Wang, K., Kovács, G.L., Wozny, M.J., Fang, M. (eds.) PROLAMAT. IFIP, vol. 207, pp. 26–40. Springer, Heidelberg (2006)
5. Chesbrough, H., Rosenbloom, R.S.: The Role of the Business Model in Capturing Value from Innovation: Evidence from Xerox Corporation's Technology Spin-off Companies. Industrial and Corporate Change 11(3), 529–555 (2002)
6. Chesbrough, H.: Open Innovation: The New Imperative for Creating and Profiting from Technology. Harvard Business School Press, Boston (2003)
7. Lendrum, T.: The Strategic Partnering Handbook, A Practice Guide for Managers. McGraw-Hill, Nook Company, New York (1997)
8. Li, M., Crave, S., Grilo, A., van den Berg, R.: Unleashing the Potential of the European Knowledge Economy: Value Proposition for Enterprise Interoperability. European Commission – Informations Society and Media. Office for Official Publications of European Communities, Luxemburg (2008)
9. Loss, L., Pereira-Klen, A.A., Rabelo, R.J.: Value Creation Elements in Learning Collaborative Networked. In: Camarinha-Matos, L.M., Picard, W. (eds.) Pervasive Collaborative Networks. IFIP International Federation for Information Processing, vol. 283, pp. 75–84. Springer, Boston (2008)
10. Nachira, F., Dini, P., Nicolai, A., Le Louarn, M., Lèon, L.R.: Digital Business Ecosystems. Office for Official Publications of the European Communities, Luxembourg (2007) ISBN 92-79-01817-5
11. Oliver, C.: Determinants of inter-organizational relationships: integration and future direction. Academy of Management Review 15(2) (1990)
12. Osterwalder, A.: The Business Model Ontology – a proposition in a design science approach. PhD Thesis. Lausanne University, Switzerland (2004)
13. Papadakis, V.M., Kaloghirou, Y., Iatrelli, M.: Decision making from crisis to opportunity. Bus. Strategic Rev. 10(1), 29–37 (1999)
14. Plantin, et al: Orange Labs R&D internal methodology for building business models (2008)
15. Porter, M.E.: Competitive advantage: creating and sustaining superior performance. Free Press, New York (1985)
16. Prahalad, C.K., Krishnan, M.S.: The New Age of Innovation: Driving Co-created Value Through Global Networks. McGraw-Hill Professional, New York (2008)
17. Rabelo, R.J., Gusmeroli, S.: The ECOLEAD Business Infrastructure for Netwirked Organizations. In: Camarinha-Matos, L.M., Picard, W. (eds.) Pervasive Collaborative Networks. IFIP International Federation for Information Processing, vol. 283, pp. 451–462. Springer, Boston (2008)
18. Romero, D., Galeano, N., Giraldo, J., Molina, A.: Towards the Definition of Business Models and Governance Rules for Virtual Breeding Environments. In: Camarinha-Matos, L.M., Afsarmanesh, H., Ollys, M. (eds.) Network-Centric Collaboration and Supporting Frameworks. International Federation for Information Processing (IFIP), vol. 224, pp. 103–110. Springer, New York (2006)
19. Stevenson, H., Jarillo, J.C.: A paradigm of entrepreneurship: Entrepreneurial management. Strategic Management J. 11, 17–27 (1990)

How to Increase Value in the Footwear Supply Chain

Rosanna Fornasiero[1,*], Mauro Tescaro[2], Enrico Scarso[3], and Giorgio Gottardi[3]

[1] ITIA-CNR, Via Bassini 15, 20133 Milan, Italy
[2] Politecnico Calzaturiero s.c.a.r.l., Via Venezia, 62, 30100 Vigonza (Pd), Italy
[3] DTG-Università di Padova, Stradella S. Nicola, 3, 36100 Vicenza, Italy
rosanna.fornasiero@itia.cnr.it,
{enrico.scarso,giorgio.gottardi}@unipd.it

Abstract. The Lean approach has been implemented in many different sectors as a methodology to improve industrial performance at company level. In the latest years this approach has been further developed in literature and in practice to integrate the principles of agility, adaptability and the mass customization paradigm where product and services have to be designed together to meet specific requirements, and where value originated by the supply chain enhance the value of single company thanks to the use of ICT and remote control. In this paper we analyze the Beyond-Lean paradigm and propose a path for companies in the footwear sector to improve their performance based on high-value-added products and processes. A detailed process analysis based on Value Stream Mapping is used to define criticalities and suggest improvements paths both at technological and organizational level.

Keywords: Lean production, Supply Chain, Beyond Lean paradigm.

1 Introduction

Innovative Lean principles have to be defined to attain high flexibility and efficiency, addressing radically new ways to organize production. New methods of organization and flexible equipments are needed to produce very differentiated products, to obtain reduced work in progress, short response time and low production cost. The Lean approach originally proposed in [15] and that bases on increasing the value created by reducing all types of "waste" can be applied in very demanding environment like consumable products. In this case it is important to go beyond the original dimension of Lean, i.e. time reduction, and to take into consideration also constraints of quality and service which are extremely important nowadays to differentiate European products from others.

This paper analyses some relevant issues emerging for Italian firms operating in the footwear industry in a specialized regional cluster. The research has been made possible thanks to a Project funded by the Veneto Region conducted by A.c.r.i.b. (Association of the shoe producers of the Riviera del Brenta district in Veneto Region) with the support of Politecnico Calzaturiero. In the footwear district of Riviera

---

* Corresponding author.

L.M. Camarinha-Matos et al. (Eds.): PRO-VE 2009, IFIP AICT 307, pp. 527–536, 2009.
© IFIP International Federation for Information Processing 2009

del Brenta, the creation of value is guaranteed by strong inter-firm relationships and is based on the formation of temporary Virtual Enterprises according to seasonal production. Production process is very much parcelized across different companies.

In the first part of the work the analysis of the most important actors in the supply chain has been carried out based on data and information collected from footwear producers who are the main tier of the chain. Their suppliers have been investigated as well to understand how problems in communication can affect the performance of the whole system. The supply chain structure has been analysed applying the Value Stream Mapping methodology that allows to discover the most important logistic inefficiencies and to identify the organizational drivers for improving the whole system.

The result of the research consists in a Future State proposition that contains many different opportunities that can bring the supply chain to a new scenario where performance indicators are based not only on time reduction but also on service and quality level both from suppliers and customers. It will be shown how the design and production processes, which are very much modularized, can be improved with the application of the principles of the lean and beyond-lean production.

A practical and affordable framework is proposed to allow a large number of SMEs in the footwear sector to adopt new, flexible and Lean production systems to improve their and their Virtual Enterprise performance.

2   State of the Art

2.1   Lean Production and beyond

Lean manufacturing can be considered itself an approach to face turbulent environment since it permits to give quick response to the market changes.

Agile and adaptive manufacturing approaches have arisen at the beginning of the last decade as ways to improve the competitiveness of the companies. Adaptive and Agile production is characterized by the integration of the suppliers and customers in the value chain from the design to the production, the marketing and the support services. The focus is not only on time reduction, but also on the provision of high quality and services. Moreover the focus has to go beyond the individual enterprise and involve the whole value chain. Actually, it is not only a matter of improving in a static way the performance of the company as a stand alone entity but it is necessary to consider the creation of a Virtual Enterprise as a coordinated entity which creates value in a dynamic way [16], [17].

There are many works applying different dimensions of the adaptive and agile paradigm like for example in [1], [2] and [3] not only from the point of view of relationship management but also of technology improvements (implementation of flexibly production systems, adoption of ICT tools, system integration) and people enhancement (competences management, training at all level).

In the latest years the European Commission has promoted the creation of some Technological Platforms among which Manu*future* (European Platform for High Adding Value in Manufacturing Industries) with the aim to support the manufacturing sector through strategies shared by the most important stakeholders like the implementation of adaptive production systems answering to the changes of the market where machines communicate and are integrated all together and they are easy reconfigurable and they can hold multiple tasks [4], [5], or the implementation of ICT systems to develop the virtual dimension of the factory for co-design and co-planning production. Organizational systems for networked companies are necessary to optimise the operations along the processes and monitor performance.

Moreover producing according to the "Beyond Lean" paradigm means to integrate sustainability goals and promote human resources and use of innovative technologies along the product and process life cycle. It is not only a matter of reducing production costs but also to maximize the value creation along the Value Chain moving the focus from the physical good to product and service solutions.

Suppliers and customers have to work in real time synchronizing their activities. The number of actors (number of tiers) involved in the value chain is larger than in the past because not only traditional suppliers but also advanced technology suppliers are to be considered. Logistics and materials handling are critical factors and have seen the establishment of companies highly specialized on these activities making longer the supply chain. Third party logistics providers typically specialize in integrated operation, warehousing and transportation services that can be scaled and customized to final user's needs based on market conditions and the demands and delivery service requirements for their products and materials.

2.2 Applications to the Fashion Sector

The fashion sector (limited in this study to apparel and footwear companies) is characterized by volatile product demand and need of quick planning and production. Companies need to re-define completely new models every 4-6 months using a long supply chain where for each tier level many actors have to collaborate together.

In literature there are not many studies on the application of the Lean and Beyond Lean approach to consumables and in particular to the footwear industry. As a matter of fact, these methodologies have been originally developed for the automotive and the durable equipments; therefore to implement it in the fashion sector needs a "customisation" mainly due to the different company dimension (large vs small), the type of product (durable vs consumable), and the kind of value chain (hierarchical vs. non-hierarchical).

Some works have dealt with the textile and apparel industry which has similar features to the footwear sector for the typology of demand, number of models to be produced, need to develop product by size etc (see for example [8]). Other works have analyzed the application of technological solutions or organizational solutions to the footwear sector but without making explicit reference to the lean or beyond-lean principles and without giving an overall view on how suggested innovation can bring companies to success from a lean point of view [14].

Recently there have been many papers discussing technological innovation in the footwear sector both in terms of automation and in terms of monitoring and real time control [6], [7] especially with reference to the mass customization paradigm. Rarely this kind of innovation is explicitly part of a strategic vision on the innovation with a Lean or Beyond Lean approach, and the organizational impact and overall performance of the company is not considered.

Lastly, some other works examine the characteristics of the apparel and textile sector to apply the Lean and the Agile paradigm to allow the value chain to answer rapidly to the changes of the market and reduce the lead time [8]. It is worth remembering that the value chain in the apparel sector as in the footwear sector is relatively long, and it includes many actors that may change during the year according to the specific production needs.

3   As-Is Model

3.1   Value Stream Mapping

The analysis of the business processes focused on value created along the Virtual Enterprise in the Footwear sector can be carried out through the implementation of the Value Stream Mapping (VSM) methodology. VSM is based on the evaluation with the company staff of the most important performance indicators like: cycle time for each step, number of people, amount of scraps, batch dimension, WIP, waiting time. The evaluation of these dimensions permits to identify the most important criticalities. VSM allows to separate value adding from non-value adding activities along the production of a typology of product [9].

Many examples are given in literature on the application of VSM to different industrial sectors [10]; [11]; [12]; the application proposed here is based on the analysis of collaboration of many different actors of the Supply Chain. It is not only analysis of internal processes but also relations with suppliers.

In the footwear industry the manufacturing of most products requires the involvement of many departments and partners both up- and down-stream in the value chain creating time by time a virtual enterprise according to the models to be produced. In fact, shoe production can be characterized by the involvement of 20-25 companies, from the designer to the suppliers and the distributors. The result of the VSM is that to deliver a pair of shoes it is necessary a lead time of 140 days out of a cycle time of 4 hours! And this is not uncommon because from previous studies it emerges, for example, that to produce beverage cans there occurs a lead time of more than 300 days with a cycle time of 3 hours [13], or that in many cases the value adding activities are only 10% of the whole [14]. To reduce the non value-adding activities, which are not strictly necessary for the batch under production, it is not sufficient to optimise each Supply Chain actor without considering the system as a whole. On the contrary, application of an integrated system of analysis and evaluation allows to focus on the whole value chain and on the value flow along the chain, from the customer order to the suppliers to the distributors.

3.2   VSM Applied to the Footwear Sector

During the development of the project we analysed the most important actors of the Value Chain: shoe producers and suppliers (in particular sole and heel suppliers). For each of them, VSM has been designed on the most important processes like R&D, industrialization and production. Also the development and industrialization processes need the involvement of all the suppliers because these phases are given in outsourcing to them for the related part to be developed. For each map, critical points (numbered flash frames) have been identified. For convenience and for space limitations, here we report only one of the maps developed during the study.

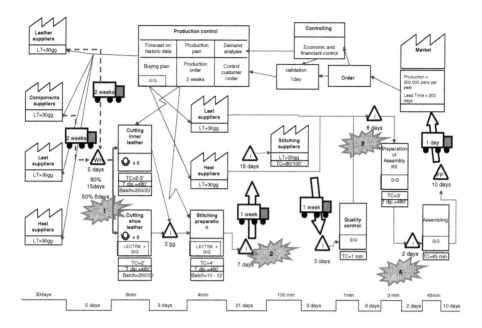

Fig. 1. VSM of the supply and production processes

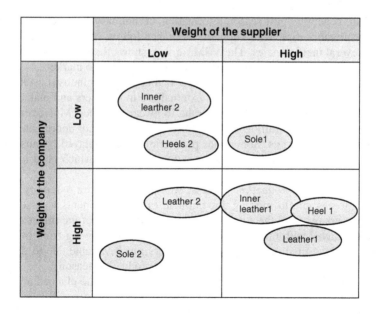

Fig. 2. An example of reciprocity matrix

In order to verify the reliability of the data collected during the VSM analysis it was necessary also to collect data directly from the ERP systems of the companies. What turned out was that most of the companies do not use any performance indicator system to evaluate their internal and external processes. Usually evaluation of each season performance is based only on amount of sold shoes but no detailed evaluation is done about the reason of increasing or decreasing sales.

Our analysis was based on data retrieved from the ERP systems for the production of a whole season and all related sales. Suppliers' reciprocity matrix has also been analysed to understand the relevance of each supplier in terms of materials volume compared to the relevance of the company itself. An example of the reciprocity matrix is given below. According to the chosen dimensions (amount of orders per season compared to the total revenue of the supplier and to the total purchasing of the company), it is possible to see the company under analysis establishes different kind of relationships with the suppliers. In the case of the most important suppliers of heels, leather and inner leather the company has a strong partnership based on strong commitment between the parts. They work at the same level with non-hierarchical relationship. In the case of the second supplier of sole and leather the contractual strength of the shoe company is stronger than the supplier itself.

3.3 Criticalities

The analysis of all the collected maps and data highlights some criticalities for each of the main processes both internally at company level and at supply chain level.

In the R&D process, information to be shared among the companies is not yet formalized and, generally, past season information are not easy to be retrieved. Most of the time, communication with suppliers does not follow shared protocols and this produces several inefficiencies. The VSM, in fact, shows that reiterative process with the suppliers is necessary very often, thus enlarging the time-to market.

Industrialization of the shoe models is too much tied to industrialization of the components (heels, sole, last), which is externalised to suppliers and makes the process very slow and difficult to control by the footwear producer. Moreover supplying process and industrialization of models is sequential and is not coordinated with the arrival of the raw materials. Sometimes production is also delayed because there are some parts of the shoe which are not yet industrialized and which need to be developed by size.

For what concerns production process, waiting time before assembly process is around 2-3 weeks due to missing appointment of all components to assembly. The arrival of the uppers from the stitching phase (which is most of the time externalised) is not synchronised with other materials and components arriving from other suppliers. Moreover lead time of stitching phase is very much variable due to the fact that working load is not kept homogeneous during the production season.

As regards the supply process, large differences between the planned and effective delivering time from the suppliers has emerged, which make it difficult to manage and synchronise arrival of components for a certain production model. This implies that there is large difference between production planning and delivery time of suppliers. Also there is too much WIP along the production process, especially in the phase of preparing assembly kit when all materials and components arrive from internal departments and from suppliers.

For the suppliers, like for example the heel producer, beside the difficulties of communication due to the lacking of a standard with the shoe producers (each shoe producer send its own information on shoe models and sometimes the same shoe producer does not use the same code system for all its models), they have also a problem with production process. The set up time is very long (15min) compared to the production of each single piece (some seconds) and to have the possibility to reduce the set up time can be very value adding. Moreover missing tools for production planning since heel producer collects orders from all shoe producers and the company produces keeping some unused capability to have flexibly during the peak demand.

4   To-Be Model: How to Increase Value

The peculiarities of the Riviera del Brenta footwear industry, which allow local companies to be competitive, are linked to the capability to design and produce high quality products and to provide high value service in a value chain of many small companies cooperating together. This is the reason why important worldwide griffes have chosen to produce their shoes in this cluster. But to stay competitive the Riviera del Brenta companies need to maintain the excellent qualitative level of their shoes and relevant services and to improve the performance of the Supply Chain in an even more demanding competitive environment. There is, in fact, the need of more frequent changes in the range of products, and most of the customers are asking for small batches.

The proposed to-be scenario is based on improvements to be implemented at different levels, step by step. Each intervention need to be further developed and designed on the needs of the companies. The integration of more than one intervention can have stronger impact and overdraw the overall impact. In particular we can state the following actions:

- Standardization of some parts of the shoe components: each shoe component can be divided in modules and some modules of heel, sole and some assembly layers are not influenced by the shoe style and can remain the same during the shoe development. It is important that shoe producers, together with the suppliers, standardize these modules and make quicker the development process. The normalization of what is not influence by shoe style permits to dedicate more time to the other shoe components.
- Parallelization of some R&D activities: thanks to the possibility of sharing CAD files and standard modules with the other actors of the Virtual Enterprise like suppliers of soles, heels, lasts it will be possible to define the set of information to be exchanged during development phase between shoe producer and suppliers so that the supplier has standard set of information and some activities can be done in parallel.
- Another important action is based on the introduction of a tool for the prioritisation of the production of the individual shoe models according to two drivers: lead time of production, and lead time of industrialization. Since every season has an average of 300-400 models to be industrialized and produced it is important to create categories of models according to the complexity of production,

complexity of supplying (certain materials – especially leather – may need longer delivery time than other due to type of leather or type of operations requested on the leather itself).

- For what concerns production processes, synchronization of materials and components delivery for the assembly of the shoe. In the footwear sector it is difficult to get rid of the "push" model in favour of the pure "pull" one. It can be useful to implement a system to synchronize the arrival of the materials to reduce waiting time before assemble, to reduce lead time and to reduce urgency. This means that it is necessary to control better the driver of production which is, in most of the case, the delivering of the uppers. Since the upper has the longer delivering time, the delivery of the other components (heels, sole, lasts, etc) should be organized according to uppers arrival.

Moreover the definition of a methodology to plan production with real time control of the supply chain can be the way to easily plan production reducing the number of urgency. The introduction of a real time monitoring system in some cases can be anticipated by the introduction of a visual system (kanban style) to allow companies (both producers and suppliers) to know day by day the order status. Another important action is the management of suppliers with anticipation of orders which means that at the beginning of each season a part of supplier production capacity is booked. During the production period, specific orders are released and no delays are expected. Bonus-malus conditions can be established with the suppliers so to guarantee both benefits in case of delivering on time and penalties in case of late or too early delivery. The definition of a delivery programme and organization of products pick up is important to improve delivering. The support of third party logistics can be organized by the SMEs belonging to the cluster in order to reduce logistics costs and keeping high the service.

5 Conclusion

Research on the field shows that there is the need to improve footwear Supply Chain performance in a consistent way. It emerges clear from the collected data that companies performance can be step up with different actions, from the technological to the organizational one according to a structured path. Some of these improvements are thought to be rapidly implemented and are thought to be low cost in order to overcome current difficulties integrating actions in a value chain mainly composed of SMEs.

In the analysed industrial footwear cluster, companies are already working according to the model of the extended enterprise to coordinate activities. Some of these actions are already under implementation in some companies but are not formalized and not part of an overall and shared strategy. For this reason there are always many urgencies to hold on. The matter is to define structured paths and to implement the actions proposed in a coordinated way without allowing modifications to the plans. Each shoe producer can play the role of catalyst for its Supply Chain and propose improvements for the benefit of all tiers.

Acknowledgement

The work described in this paper has been conducted as part of the regional project "Nuovi modelli organizzativi e logistici per la competitività nella filiera del Metadistretto Calzaturiero Veneto" funded by Veneto Region under the 2008 program for Industrial Clusters Innovation. We would like in particular to acknowledge Politecnico Calzaturiero for the support in contacting companies and providing information of the district, GMA Consulting for the technical work undertaken together during the project and companies of the Metadistretto Calzaturiero Veneto directly involved in the analysis.

References

1. Gunasekaran, A.: Agile Manufacturing: a framework for research and development. International Journal of Production Economics 62, 87–105 (1999)
2. Ashall, D., Parkinson, B.: Leaning towards agile. Manufacturing Engineer (February 2002)
3. Sharifi, H., Colquhoun, G., Barclay, I., Dann, Z.: Agile manufacturing: a management and operational framework. In: Proceedings of the Institution of Mechanical Engineers, vol. 215-B, pp. 857–869 (2001)
4. Westkamper, E.: Strategic Development of Factories under the influence of emergent technologies. Annals of CIRP 56-1, 419–4225 (2007)
5. Jovane, F., Westkämper, E., Williams, D.: The Manufuture Road: towards Competitive and Sustainable High-Adding-Value Manufacturing. Springer, Heidelberg (2008)
6. Carpanzano, E., Cataldo, E.: A Modular Design and Simulation Based Verification of the Logic Control Code for an Agile Shoe Manufacturing System. In: Proc. Industrial Simulation Conference, ISC 2003, EUROSIS, Valencia, Spain, June 9-11 (2003)
7. Boer, C.R., Dulio, S.: Mass Customization and Footwear: Myth, Salvation or Reality. Springer, Heidelberg (2007)
8. Bruce, M., Daly, L., Towers, N.: Lean or agile: a solution for supply chain management in the textiles and clothing industry? International J. of Operations and production management 24(2), 151–170 (2004)
9. Rother, M., Shook, J.: Learning To See: Value Stream Mapping to Add Value and Eliminate MUDA. The Lean Enterprise Institute (2003)
10. Setht, D., Gupta, V.: Application of value stream mapping for lean operations and cycle time reduction: an Indian case study. Prodution Planning & Control 16(I), 44–59 (2005)
11. Braglia, M., Carmignani, G., Zammori, F.: A new value stream mapping approach for complex production systems. International Journal of Production Research 44(18-19), 3929–3952 (2006)
12. Abdulmalek, F.A., Rajgopal, J.: Analyzing the benefits of lean manufacturing and value stream mapping via simulation: A process sector case study. International Journal of Production Economics 107, 223–236 (2007)
13. Jones, D.T., Hines, P., Rich, N.: "Lean logistics". International Journal of Physical Distribution & Logistics Management 27(3/4), 153–173 (1997)
14. Bertolini, M., Bottari, E., Rizzi, A., Bevilacqua, M.: Lead time reduction through ICT application in the footwear industry: a case study. International Journal of Production Economics 110, 198–212 (2007)
15. Womack, J.P., Jones, D.P.: Lean Thinking – Come creare valore e bandire gli sprechi. Guerini e Associati (2000)

16. Avai, A., Boer, C.R., Fornasiero, R., Carotenuto, P., Confessore, G.: A decentralized performance measurement system for Supply Chain. In: Camarinha-Matos, L.M. (ed.) Collaborative Business Ecosystems and Virtual Enterprises, pp. 814–828. Kluwer Academic Publishers, Dordrecht (2002)
17. Achanga, P., Shahab, E., Roy, R., Nelder, G.: Critical success factors for lean implementation within SMEs. Journal of Manufacturing Tecnology Management 17(4), 460–471 (2006)

Waste Management Using Request-Based Virtual Organizations

Stamatia Ann Katriou[1], Garyfallos Fragidis[2], Ioannis Ignatiadis[3],
Evangelos Tolias[1], and Adamantios Koumpis[1]

[1] ALTEC S.A.
M.Kalou 6, Thessaloniki 54629, Greece
{kann,tolv,akou}@altec.gr
[2] Technological Educational Institute of Serres
Terma Magnisias, Serres 62124, Greece
garyf@teiser.gr
[3] Kingston University, Faculty of Computing,
Information Systems and Mathematics Surrey KT1 2EE, UK
jignatiadis@gmail.com

Abstract. Waste management is on top of the political agenda globally as a high priority environmental issue, with billions spent on it each year. This paper proposes an approach for the disposal, transportation, recycling and reuse of waste. This approach incorporates the notion of Request Based Virtual Organizations (RBVOs) using a Service Oriented Architecture (SOA) and an ontology that serves the definition of waste management requirements. The populated ontology is utilized by a Multi-Agent System which performs negotiations and forms RBVOs. The proposed approach could be used by governments and companies searching for a means to perform such activities in an effective and efficient manner.

Keywords: Waste management, RBVO, SOA, Agents.

1 Introduction

According to The Economist's 2009 'Special Report on Waste', the average Westerner produces over 500kg of municipal waste a year. In addition, both developed and developing countries generate vast quantities of construction and demolition debris, industrial effluent, mine tailings, sewage residue and agricultural waste. Rich countries spend some $120 billion a year disposing of their municipal waste alone and another $150 billion on industrial waste, according to CyclOpe, a French research institute. The amount of waste that countries produce tends to grow in tandem with their economies, and especially with the rate of urbanization. So waste firms see a rich future in places such as China, India and Brazil, which at present spend only about $5 billion a year collecting and treating their municipal waste. Concern about global warming should also provide a boost for the waste business [1].

Waste is not just a substance that needs to be disposed. It is also a potential resource: it can be burned to generate energy; new technologies turn it into fertilizer,

L.M. Camarinha-Matos et al. (Eds.): PRO-VE 2009, IFIP AICT 307, pp. 537–544, 2009.

chemicals or fuel; paper, plastic, aluminum, etc can be recycled. Much waste can also be reused [1].

However, there is no centralized collaboration system supporting the management of waste. Companies and municipalities wishing to recycle or find other ways of disposing of their waste need to locate appropriate firms which can support them, i.e. from a simple transport company, which can take their waste to the appropriate place, to specialized recycling companies or firms that could reuse the waste.

In this paper we propose an approach based on which a system could be developed to be used by governments, companies and other organizations that are searching for a means to dispose of, transport, recycle, and reuse their waste in an efficient and cost effective manner. In order to do this they need to find and collaborate with appropriate combinations of firms.

In Section 2 we present an overview of the approach and its main concepts. Section 3 deals with the overall proposed system and its architecture, followed by a section which describes the potential use of such a system. Finally, there is a discussion which looks at the possible expansion and broader use of the system.

2 The Approach

From a functional point of view, our approach is designed bearing in mind the needs of a municipality, or a contracting company, in finding the appropriate combination of firms who can help dispose of its waste in an environmentally friendly and cost effective manner. The same approach holds for any business company that wants to recycle its waste. This is a difficult task, in general, because a variety of business actors are required to be involved and coordinated, each of which undertakes a specific and highly specialized task that needs to be performed in an accurate way and according to the general standards set. A participating actor performing his tasks in an ineffective and inefficient way could lead to a huge negative impact on the environment, the community and the reputation of the organization in charge.

As the green movement expands, the importance of finding appropriate partners for waste management becomes more acute. To provide a means for locating these partners, from a technological point of view, our approach is based on the concept of Request Based Virtual Organizations (RBVOs), a more sophisticated form of Virtual Organization (VO).

2.1 The Concept of RBVOs

A VO is usually described as a network among organizations and/or individuals [2]. Therefore, it appears as a single unified organization. The benefits of VOs (cost, transaction, process and strategic) are well-documented in the literature [3-5]. However, the static nature of VOs fails to address the growing demands to locate products, services and business partners. In Government to Business (G2B) or Business to Business (B2B) contexts the above problems are more profound, due to the large potential number of collaborative partners with diverse capabilities and the lack of standardization of service description [6]. Request Based Virtual Organizations (RBVOs) overcome this by enabling the discovery and matching of appropriate business partners.

RBVOs are short-living entities that are formed to respond to business opportunities offered by electronic commerce. An RBVO is comprised of a cluster of partnering organizations that have totally replaced their vertical integration into a virtual one [7].

According to Svriskas and Roberts, the key features of a RBVO as opposed to the "classic" VO are:

- A possibility for an enterprise to discover potential business partners upon demand and advertise itself in a standard way.
- Short-lived ad-hoc virtual formations of collaborating partners.
- Highly dynamic involvement of an enterprise in different e-business activities, serving different defined and advertised roles, at the same time, if needed.

In addition, RBVOs also inherit many of the features of a "classic" VO, i.e.

- A cluster of geographically dispersed organizations either within regions or inter regionally.
- A range of relationships from transactional to collaborative that vary dynamically over time in response to market opportunities.
- Lower transaction costs for geographically dispersed transactions [2].

Quotes from a large number of sellers can provide a good overview of price. However, overcoming ignorance of product quality and other supplier capabilities may be more difficult. RBVOs are coupled with the concept of sector specific Service Level Agreements (SLA) to address the issue. In its most basic form, a SLA is a contract or agreement that formalizes a business relationship, or part of the relationship, between two parties [2, 8].

Vokrinek et al. have designed an RBVO protocol which supports a flexible formation of RBVOs taking into account the use of SLAs with an emphasis on reflecting the conditions of real competitive environments. The protocol consists of three phases: (i) potential partner search, (ii) negotiation of SLAs and RBVO establishment and (iii) RBVO execution and dissolution [9].

Organizations participating in RBVO formations can reduce the costs of market search, and benefit from more effective monitoring schemes thus lowering transactional costs. Improved information flows can also facilitate improved planning and more coordinated actions to reduce uncertainty [7].

3 The Proposed System

There are many ways to implement RBVOs, but utilizing a community of Intelligent Agents (Multi-Agent System) has shown to be a most effective method [10]. In this way, the organization and functioning of the RBVO's activities are served by the Multi-Agent system that is developed to orchestrate and automate procedures and operations of RBVOs.

For the proposed system, a Service Oriented Architecture (SOA) is used. The SOA paradigm enables the linking of business and computational resources - mainly organizations, applications and data on demand [11]. SOA is seen to be essential for delivering business agility and IT flexibility [12]. The advantages of SOA can be obtained for a conglomeration of companies coming together to exploit complementary skills and competencies synergistically. Although there is no shortage of platforms for firms to collaborate online within particular industries or across industries, the advantages of adopting a SOA approach for such platforms need to be taken into consideration. This is due to the adaptability and easy reconfigurability that SOA offers which matches heterogeneous RBVO's business requirements [10]. In addition, SOA has also been shown to interoperate with agent technologies [13-14], which are used in the architecture described below.

3.1 Architecture

Figure 1 presents the architecture of the proposed system.

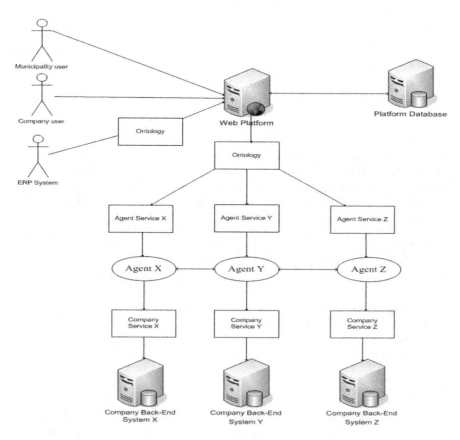

Fig. 1. System Architecture

The system is comprised of the following components:

- Web platform: A portal from which the user has access to the partner search functionality.
- Directory service: A data store with login information and user profiles which should be accessed via a web service.

- Ontology: A high level representation of waste related information which can be used to encapsulate the user's requirements regarding the types and amounts of substances that need to be disposed or recycled.
- Agent Services: A web service that enables the submission of a Collaboration Request to the Agent and the acquisition of the list of the proposed RBVOs.
- Agent: An independent distributed instance which interacts with other Agents and represents a potential collaborator.
- Company Services: A set of simple web services that enable the municipality's/company's Agent to access its Information/Enterprise Resource Planning (ERP) system or private repository, i.e. Company Back-End System.
- Company Back-End System: Contains private information of the company such as the municipality's/company's profile, requests for collaboration, contracts and recycling capacity it currently has available.

4 Usage of the System

4.1 A Usage Scenario

Let us assume that a municipality official wishes to find a new cost effective way to dispose of cardboard, used batteries, canteen food waste, plastic bottles, old computers and mixed rubble. To take advantage of the proposed system, the first step would be to register as a user and have an instance of an Agent set up to represent the municipality. This registration process would be required not only for municipalities and organizations who wish to find partners for waste management, but also for the companies offering these services in order for them to be represented in the system's network by their Agents.

After logging into the system, this new user needs to complete a web form in which the type of waste which requires management is defined. The waste is categorized as sorted or mixed. For each type of waste the corresponding amount (i.e. approximate weight/volume) should be provided. Also, the location, language in which the service is required, time constraints and any other specifications would be defined in this form.

Once completed, the form can be submitted as a request to find a combination of companies within the system's network which can complete the tasks. An ontology would be populated with the information which has been provided and then would be forwarded to the Agent Service.

Should the user wish to complete the aforementioned form on a frequent basis, manual insertion of values might become tiresome. For this reason a custom script could be incorporated as a means of automatically populating the ontology from specified values in the municipality's information system. (In the case of a company, the ontology could be linked to its ERP system).

After the Agent Service has received the populated ontology, this information would be forwarded to the user's Agent. The Agent in turn would send the specifications to the other Agents registered in the system. Each Agent filters the incoming specifications to see if any of the required tasks are of interest to the firm it represents. A set of negotiations, based on each firm's private constraints and on offered prices, would be performed between the Agents, resulting in a list of suitable RBVOs. The list would finally be returned to the user who would be presented with all the possible combinations of appropriate organizations which could perform the defined tasks.

The user, in this case the municipality official, can now select the preferred combination of firms (RBVO), either based on price, time constraints or other criteria. Of course, once selected, contracts would need to be signed - possibly in the form of SLAs - in order for collaboration to begin.

The sequence of the above described scenario is presented in Fig. 2.

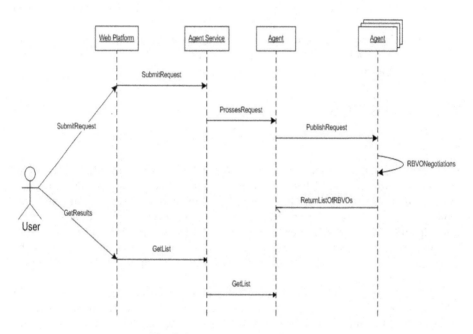

Fig. 2. Sequence of RBVO formation

4.2   Utilizing the Agents

The scope of Agent contribution can be formulated as Agent-based negotiation towards RBVO formation by using dynamic semi-private knowledge (i.e. Company Back-End System). As stated in the PANDA project [10], the Agents represent individual actors participating in the RBVO formation processes taking into account individual private constraints, preferences that are hidden to other actors and minimizing the disclosure of such private information. In their negotiations, agents can be guided by user-defined business rules. Agents need to decide which of these rules are applicable in each type of negotiation. Flexibility is essential when adapting and prioritizing these rules as the negotiations progress. Such rules can be set by each user to guide his/her Agent, and can be implemented using a rules engine.

Indicative user-defined business rules for the negotiation between Agents could include:

- Tolerance on price -x% to +y%.
- Prepared to wait x days to get a better price.
- Prepared to pay more for the tasks to be finished sooner.
- Prepared to pay more for 'greener' outcomes.
- Wishes only to consider partners in the same region/country as the user.
- Do not want to participate in projects less than x Euros.

5 Discussion

To improve waste management, it is vital that companies are able to collaborate with each other in the widest way possible and this system could open doors to previously unforeseen collaboration potentials. Examples of waste management companies that could be sought through the system range from simple waste disposal firms to more complex ones specialized in transport and disposal systems for dangerous substances.

The system could be used to encourage start-up firms in the waste cycle process, enabling them to find companies with small waste loads and progressing to expanding their client base as their equipment and resources grow. Such start-ups might include innovative bio-fertilizer firms who could recycle human and animal waste. Such schemes are popular in modern China and using an RBVO system would promote their expansion.

The architecture of the system could be expanded to consider more eco-friendly ways of managing waste and other resources of the company. An 'Eco' score built into the system might spur firms to improve their style of waste disposal. The system could rate the RBVOs based on each firm's Eco considerations. For example, emissions of CO_2 could be used as a basis for recommendations of the best ways of transporting the companies' waste to appropriate areas. This would require each waste management firm which registers in the system to complete its profile by providing eco-related details of its disposal methods. In cases of transport, distances would have to be calculated via a service such as Google Maps in order for emissions to be estimated.

The system could also be expanded to be a type of waste monitoring system because at present, nobody knows how much waste the world generates or what it does with this [1]. For this purpose active government support would be required.

6 Summary

This paper presents an approach and a brief outline of a proposed system for decision support on selecting a combination of firms to enable cost effective, ecologically sound and efficient waste management of a municipality's or a company's waste. A SOA based system which uses a Multi-Agent community to create RBVOs, enabling easy adaptability and reconfigurability, has been illustrated. Improving the options available online for assisting the management of waste is an essential step in minimizing global pollution.

References

1. McBride, E.: A special report on waste. The Economist (2009)
2. Svirskas, A., Roberts, B.: Towards business quality of service in virtual organisations through service level agreements and ebXML. In: 10th ISPE International Conference on Concurrent Engineering: Research and Applications. Madeira, Portugal (2003)
3. Bovet, D., Martha, J.: Value Nets: Breaking the Supply Chain to Unlock Hidden Profits. John Wiley, Chichester (2000)
4. Saabeel, W., Verduijn, T.M., Hagdorn, L., Kumar, K.: A Model of Virtual Organization: A Structure And Process Perspective. Electronic Journal of Organizational Virtualness 4(1) (2002)
5. Goldman, S.L., Nagel, R.N., Preiss, K.: Agile Competitors And Virtual Organizations: Strategies For Enriching The Customer. Van Nostrand Reinhold, International Thomson Publishing, New York (1995)
6. Roberts, B., Svirskas, A., Ward, J.: Implementation Options for Virtual Organizations: A Peer to Peer (P2P) Approach. In: Putnik, G., Cunha, M.M. (eds.) From: Virtual enterprise integration: technological and organizational perspectives. Idea Group Inc., IGI (2005)
7. Roberts, B., Svirskas, A., Matthews, B.: Request Based Virtual Organizations (RBVO): An Implementation Scenario. In: PRO-VE 2005: 6th IFIP Working Conference on Virtual Enterprises, Valencia, Spain (2005)
8. Trienekens, J.J.M., Bouman, J.J., van der Zwan, M.: Specification of Service Level Agreements: Problems, Principles and Practices. Software Quality Journal 12, 43–57 (2004)
9. Vokrinek, J., Biba, J., Hodik, J., Vybihal, J., Volf, P.: RBVO Formation Protocol. In: IEEE/WIC/ACM International Conferences on Web Intelligence and Intelligent Agent Technology Workshops, pp. 454–457 (2007)
10. Tektonidis, D., Ignatiadis, I., Katriou, S.A., Koumpis, A.: PANDA: Enabling RBVOs for the ERP/CRM industry using a Service Oriented Approach. In: The 5th International Conference on Information Technology and Applications, ICITA (2008)
11. Bloomberg, J., Schmelzer, R.: Service Orient or Be Doomed!: How Service Orientation Will Change Your Business. Wiley, Hoboken (2006)
12. Tews, R.: Beyond IT: The business value of SOA. AIIM E-DOC 21, 14–17 (2007)
13. Maamar, Z., Mostefaoui, S.K., Yahyaoui, H.: Toward an Agent-Based and Context-Oriented Approach for Web Services Composition. IEEE Transactions on Knowledge and Data Engineering 17(5), 686–697 (2005)
14. Maximilien, E.M., Singh, M.P.: Multiagent System for Dynamic Web Services Selection. Service-Oriented Computing and Agent-Based Engineering (SOCABE), Utrecht, The Netherlands (2005)

Part **17**

Service-Based Systems

Supporting Structural and Functional Collaborative Networked Organizations Modeling with Service Entities

Rubén Darío Franco, Ángel Ortiz Bas, Guillermo Prats,
and Rosa Navarro Varela

CIGIP Research Centre on Production Management and Engineering,
Edificio 8G, Acceso D, Planta 4,
CP 46022, Valencia, Spain
{dfranco,aortiz,gprats,ronava}@cigip.upv.es

Abstract. This work focuses on the Service Entities definition as an approach that may help to support structural and functional Collaborative Networked Organizations (CNO) modeling, when VOs are engineered inside Virtual Breeding Environments Management Systems (VMS). Manbree is an undergoing development which is intended to provide an integrated framework for CNO modeling and execution based on that approach and it is briefly described at the final section.

Keywords: Collaborative Networked Organizations, Enterprise Modeling, Service Oriented Architecture, Virtual Breeding Environment Management System.

1 Introduction

Collaboration among geographically dispersed entities, organizations or individuals, is increasing due to the facilities given by Information and Communication Technologies (ICT). Those technologies allow Virtual Breeding Environments enhance the effectiveness and rapidness of Virtual Organizations creation and operation.

But in order to realize such vision, it is necessary to design and implement a new kind of systems which can be able of managing both VBE and VO Life Cycles in a consistent and integrated way. The so-called VBE Management Systems are expected to fully support the creation, operation and dissolution of Virtual Organizations, by defining a set of reference models (at structural, functional or behavioral level, to name few of them) that must be adopted by VBE/VO participants when they are willing to be involved in collaboration opportunities.

By adopting such VBE-MS Reference Models, VBE/VO participants agree on common engineering and operating principles. Consequently, for really achieving such VBE/VO alignment, reference modeling plays a preponderant, if no critical, role. When exist, VO Reference Models provides reliable procedures for engineering those environments and more flexible operational structures can be easily deployed.

The research questions this paper raises are: how VBE and VO reference models must be supported by a VBE-Management System? How do they really may enable

L.M. Camarinha-Matos et al. (Eds.): PRO-VE 2009, IFIP AICT 307, pp. 547–554, 2009.

faster VO deployments? Which kind of architectural approach may be helpful for this purpose and how participants may take advantage of it?

As we consider that model-driven approaches may help to find suitable approaches in answering such questions, along this paper the concept of Service Entities, as a modeling construct which may facilitate both structural and functional Collaborative Networked Organizations modeling, is introduced. Additionally, based on this approach, a supporting tool will be briefly described.

The paper has been structured as follows. In Section 2, a shortly introduction to basic concepts is given and motivation of this work is stated. In Section 3, Services Entities concept and its life cycle are briefly described. In Section 4, main ManBree's functionalities are shown, mostly from the structural and functional modeling of CNOs. Finally, Section 5, next steps are envisioned.

2 Concepts and Motivation

Collaboration between partners is a preferred way to ensure optimal resource balance and to get perdurable benefits [1]. As it has been defined, Virtual Breeding Environments [2] are intended to harmonize the preparedness level of involved organizations while, at the same time, a collaborative infrastructure is deployed in order to deal with interoperability problems at different levels: communications, data, services, processes or business [3].

In VBEs, the main idea is to restrict the number of potential participants by drawing a border to the open universe and allowing some partners to come inside. Those partners have to agree on common operating principles: business semantics, strategies or goals, distributed business processes management practices or even common ICT tools. Being inside the border reduces uncertainty between partners, basic to share information and to reach their common objectives. Rapidness and flexibility in VO preparation and launching are requirements that any VBE management system must accomplish.

2.1 Virtual Organizations Model Driven Engineering

Along this text, we will refer to the VO Engineering process, with a broader scope but in a similar sense as it has been used in [4] to define Enterprise Engineering and which aims to: *"define, structure, design and implement [inter]enterprise operations as communication networks of business processes, which comprise all their related business knowledge, operational information, resources and organisation relations"*. Additionally, we argue that at VBE/VO level, such engineering process is driven by a set of reference models defined into the VBE and used/refined at VO level.

VBE Reference Models influence the VO Engineering process by providing a set of common constructs for modeling its processes, services or data. Consequently, VBE reference models will play a key role in dealing with interoperability concerns either at business, processes, services or data modeling level respectively. Complementarily, when potential VBE (or temporal VO) participants are looking for being involved into potential collaboration opportunities, as pre-requisite they must get a valid "VBE Membership". By doing so, they are implicitly agreeing on VO particular reference models (and VBE ones), depending on their intended scope.

But we consider that there exists a decoupling point between both reference modeling approaches. In terms of structural and, mainly, functional modeling, few or none correspondence can be established between VBE and VO reference models. From the structural point of view, VBE memberships ensure that VO members can be properly identified and characterized. A registered VBE participant can be involved in several VO instances since it has a unique identity.

However, from the functional perspective, requirements for a VBE/VO member only appear at VO engineering level and they frequently lack of consistency among several VO instances, even if they are belonging to the same VBE. For example, a VBE member offering a single business service may be required to support as many ad-hoc interfaces as VO memberships it may have. This approach would cause most of interoperability problems to appear, mainly when those potential partners need to overcome existing semantic gaps at either process, services or data levels.

In dealing with those modeling needs, a comprehensive modeling framework, for CNOs has been proposed by Camarinha-Matos and Afsarmanesh [5]. ARCON is intended to support most of CNO modeling needs, by considering both an internal and external perspectives. From its internal perspective and covering the whole CNO lifecycle, four interrelated near-orthogonal views have been identified, namely: structural, componential, functional and behavioral dimensions.

As it has been stated earlier [6,7], proper modeling constructs are also required when engineering for both VBE and VO environments. Modeling constructs are required for any modeling approach but this is a development that still must be introduced in ARCON. Next section introduces Service Entities which, in our consideration, are a promising approach in supporting some of those needs.

3   Service Entities (SE)

3.1   Concept

Service Entities (SE) are proposed as modelling constructs for CNOs, for both the Structural and Functional dimensions. As they have been defined, a single Service Entity **[8]** is the result of logically tying together:

- A finite set of business services which jointly defines the expected behaviour of those conceptual entities involved into the domain being modelled and,
- A finite set of attributes which will allow characterize and distinguish between them.

Depending on the modelling scope, SEs are classified into: Abstract Service Entities (ASE) and Concrete Service Entity and (CSE).

- An Abstract Service Entity is generic building block used to represent different 'types' of entities that are present in the problem domain, mostly at VBE level. ASEs are not associated with any specific instance of entities they are defining.
  They only represent the **abstract definition of the attributes and also the specifications of the electronic business interfaces which are being defined for them.** An example of a modelled ASE would be an abstract entity

"bank" for which two services (interfaces) have been defined: bank account validation and account balance sheet.

– Concrete Service Entity: since they are expected to be real entities of the problem domain, CSE are instances of their corresponding ASE. Instantiating an ASE means to provide meaningful values to its attributes and specific implementation for the service interfaces (i.e. bank account validation and account balance sheet). At modelling level, this means to create an open repository where CSEs can be searched, discovered and used to create and launch VO scenarios.

3.2 Service Entities Life Cycle

As defined, Service Entities will also have their own lifecycle. In Figure 1, it is possible to identify some of their main activities.

At their first stage, ASE must be modelled into the VBE Engineering Environment (Figure 1, Step 1). At this stage, and as in the object orientation paradigm, ASE may be refined or generalized as needed. In this way, each specific VBE will count with a repository of ASE that will be used during the instantiation process (Figure 1, Step 2). During the instantiation process, CSE are registered in an Open Repository which can be, later on, accessed from the VO Engineering Environment. This instantiation process provides the membership applicants with the service interfaces that they ought to locally deploy and integrate at level.

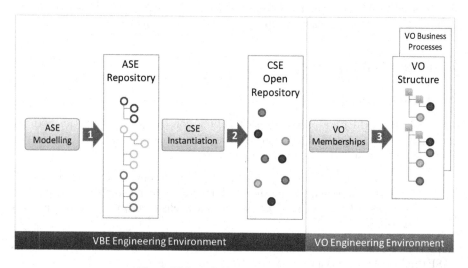

Fig. 1. Main activities of the SE lifecycle

From now on, they are prepared to be involved into as many VOs as they can be granted to be (Figure 1, step 3). The SE approach may provide some added-value for CNO modelers. To the **structural dimension** they provide:

– A mechanism that can be used for representing abstract VBE members' profiling and capabilities in terms of business services and interfaces.

- VBE memberships can be supported on ASE definitions and, consequently, identity and credentials validation would run smoothly.
- VO structure may be arranged from the CSE repository and the VO Manager counts with a trusted and uniquely identified set of partners.
- VO engineering process may also include ASE definitions in order to support, for instance, dynamic negotiation and contracting.

Complementarily, from the **functional dimension**, SEs provide:

- A set of functional services which can be used as building blocks for VO Process Modeling.
- Each CSE can be reached by means of their homogeneous service interfaces, which may simplify the development of new VO applications.
- As they preserve the commonly agreed services interfaces, each potential VBE/VO member may decide how to link their own internally deployed systems (legacy or not) in order to provide the VO requested functionality.

4 Manbree Modeling Environment

ManBree is a Virtual Breeding Environment Management System where VBE, VO and SE life cycles are supported (as shown in Figure 2). During the VBE Operational phase, VO and SE life cycles may take place simultaneously while they are feeding each other: a SE may be involved in a VO as a member or even become a full VO Manager. In turn, VOs requires SEs involvement either in a static or dynamic way in order to model their structure and operations.

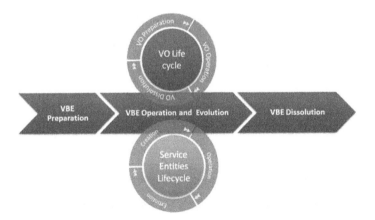

Fig. 2. ManBree Life Cycles support

4.2 Manbree Main Functionalities

ManBree's functionality supports three main macro-processes, namely: VBE Management, VO Management and Service Entities Management.

In terms of VBE and VO Management functionalities, ManBree partly implements functionalities identified in Ecolead for a full VBS [9]. **In Manbree implementation, a distinguishing feature is its support to the Service Entities Life Cycle, which is fully integrated both into the VBE and VO Engineering Environments** by means of an Abstract Service Entities Modeling component and the Scenarios Modeling component respectively (see Figure 4, below).

In terms of **Service Entities Management life cycle**, supported functionalities (see Figure 3) include:

- *Creation phase:* At this stage, a potential Manbree member asks for its SE instantiation into a Concrete Service Entity. The instantiation procedure includes a VBE Membership application and full access to its respective ASE definition (attributes and service interfaces to be implemented)
- *Operational phase:* at this stage, a just created CSE may receive offers, or even apply, for different VOs, either temporary or permanently. CSE operational phase also implies: both automated and non-automated service provisioning in supporting collaborative process execution, performance measurement indicators provisioning, and knowledge management procedures, among others.
- *Dissolution phase:* when a CSE is going to be deleted, its performance profile is updated.

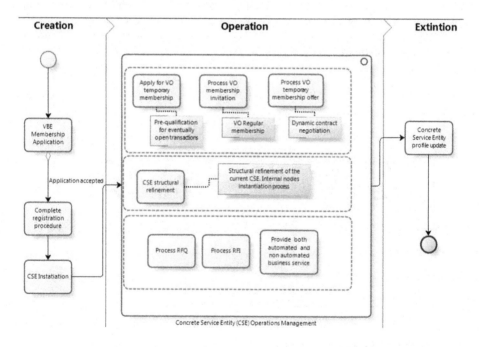

Fig. 3. Manbree Service Entities life cycle support

Figure 4 is a screenshot of the Manbree Scenarios (VOs) Engineering component. As it can be seen, the Structural view of the scenario has been modeled by using ASE and CSE definition. The Functional View is also built up by means of previously engineered services belonging to those entities.

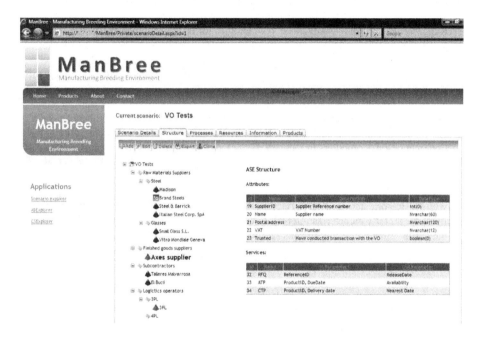

Fig. 4. SE-based Structural View of Manbree VO Engineering

5 Conclusions

The paper contribution has focused on introducing Service Entities as constructs that may support structural and functional CNO modeling when engineering VO inside a VBE-MS. By means of proper ASE definitions at VBE level, the instantiation procedure is able to provide concrete entities to the VO Manager. By using both ASE service definitions and CSE service implementations, the VO manager may create both structural and functional VO models.

Since this is an undergoing initiative, additional features will be incorporated into Manbree soon. Currently, VBE, VO and SE modeling needs are already being supported; next development will include evolving such VO structural and functional models into operational tools where distributed processes can be properly managed.

In doing so, Manbree currently supports collaborative processes modeling by using a XPDL-based editor which will enable us to get executable representations of VO processes to be moved into an Open Source BPMS (Business Process Management System).

References

1. Jagdev, H.S., Thoben, K.: Anatomy of enterprise collaborations. Production Planning & Control 12, 437–451 (2001)
2. Camarinha-Matos, L.M., Afsarmanesh, H.: Collaborative networks: a new scientific discipline. Journal of Intelligent Manufacturing 16, 439–452 (2005)
3. Ruggaber, R.: ATHENA-Advanced Technologies for Interoperability of Heterogeneous Enterprise Networks and their Applications. In: Interoperability of Enterprise Software and Applications, pp. 460–463. Springer, London (2006)
4. Kosanke, K., Vernadat, F., Zelm, M.: CIMOSA: enterprise engineering and integration. Computers in Industry 40, 83–97 (1999)
5. Camarinha-Matos, L., Afsarmanesh, H.: A comprehensive modeling framework for collaborative networked organizations. Journal of Intelligent Manufacturing 18, 529–542 (2007)
6. Ni, Q., Lu, W.F., Yarlagadda, P.K., Ming, X.: A collaborative engine for enterprise application integration. Computers in Industry 57, 640–652 (2006)
7. Kosanke, K., Vernadat, F., Zelm, M.: CIMOSA: enterprise engineering and integration. Computers in Industry 40, 83–97 (1999)
8. Franco, R., Ortiz Bas, Á., Lario Esteban, F.: Modeling extended manufacturing processes with service-oriented entities. Service Business 3, 31–50 (2009)
9. Ecolead, D21.1 Characterization of Key Components, Features and Operating Principles of the Virtual Breeding Environments (2005),
   http://www.ve-forum.org/projects/284/Deliverables/
   d21_1_vbe.pdf

Interoperability in Collaborative Processes: Requirements Characterisation and Proof Approach

Matthieu Roque and Vincent Chapurlat

LGI2P- Laboratoire de Génie Informatique et d'Ingénierie de Production
Site EERIE de L'Ecole des Mines d'Alès, Parc Scientifique Georges Besse 30035
Nîmes cedex 1, France
{Matthieu.Roque,Vincent.Chapurlat}@ema.fr

Abstract. Interoperability problems which can occur during the collaboration between several enterprises can endanger this collaboration. Consequently, it is necessary to become able to anticipate these problems. The proposed approach in this paper is based on the specification of properties, representing interoperability requirements, and their analysis on enterprise models. Due to the conceptual limits of existing modeling languages, formalizing these requirements and intending to translate them under the form of properties need to add conceptual enrichments to these languages. Finally, the analysis of the properties on enriched enterprise models, by formal checking techniques, aims to provide tools allowing to reasoning on enterprise models in order to detect interoperability problems, from an anticipative manner.

Keywords: Enterprise modeling, interoperability, model checking.

1 Introduction

The interoperability concept is started from a pure software problem in the middle of 90's where it is defined as *"the ability of two or more systems or components to exchange information and to use the information that has been exchanged"* [1]. Then, even if some efforts have been made to develop enterprise interoperability concepts, especially in Europe under various projects from FP5 and FP6, there is still no an overall satisfactory solution on interoperability. For example, [2] defines interoperability as *"the ability of a system or a product to work with other systems or products without special effort from the customer or user"*. Interoperability is then analyzed by considering simultaneously different levels of detail of the pointed out enterprise (business, process, service and data), three kinds of barriers (conceptual, technological and organizational) i.e. three kinds of 'incompatibility' or 'mismatch' obstructing sharing and exchanging data and three different approaches (integrated, unified, federated). These three dimensions represent the interoperability framework. According to this, the classification of some related works and solutions for interoperability issues become possible. A lot of research and development works have been done concerning the conceptual barrier such as UEML [3] or PSL [4]. The goal is then to provide solutions to solve syntax and semantic problems. In the same way, [5] proposes and interesting approach in order to design a Mediation Information System

L.M. Camarinha-Matos et al. (Eds.): PRO-VE 2009, IFIP AICT 307, pp. 555–562, 2009.

dedicated to deal with exchanged data, shared services and collaborative processes. This approach covers the technological and organizational barrier but considering only information system point of view. Other approaches are focused on the definition of maturity interoperability models. Let us cite for example LCIM [6], LISI [7], OIM [8] or EIMM [9] in order to evaluate the level of maturity of enterprises concerning their abilities to collaborate with other enterprises. However, they do not propose tools to measure and to evaluate interoperability itself. To solve this problem [10] proposes three kinds of enterprise interoperability measurements: interoperability potentiality, interoperability compatibility and interoperability performance. However, all these works do not provide a relevant solution in order to detect interoperability problems from an anticipative manner taking into account the different enterprise objects and their relationships within a network in which various enterprises must work together. Moreover, they do not allow identifying, in a formal way, what are the causes of interoperability problems. Thus, the research work presented in this paper aims to provide concepts and formal supports for reasoning on enterprise models in order to formalize and to detect interoperability problems as proposed in another domain by [11]. According to interoperability framework presented before, we focus, in this paper, on organizational interoperability problems by considering the Data and Service level. However, the Data level is extended in order to consider other natures of exchanged objects i.e. material, energy, financial, information or human objects. The interoperability approaches are not considered here because the goal of this work is only to detect where interoperability problems can occur by identifying their causes and not to provide solution to solve them.

Finally, the paper is structured respecting the following proposed approach:

Enterprise and Interoperability modeling: Formalization of concepts, existing modeling language conceptual enrichment and property modeling.
Enterprise model re-writing: From enriched model of collaborative process to formal model allowing reasoning mechanisms.
Checking technique and mechanisms: Proving properties in order to check the interoperability requirements.

2 Formalization of Interoperability Requirement

Interoperability is a crucial requirement having to be verified by systems when being in relationship (cooperation, collaboration, exchange) with other systems in order to assume a common mission. In this case, considered systems are enterprises or parts of enterprises which have to interact in a collaborative and common process with other enterprises or parts of enterprises in order, for example, to design a new product, to produce and integrate different part of a given product, etc. Formalizing what kind of relationships can exist in this area allows us to define more precisely this interoperability requirement. Thus, the relationship may be punctual or may exist during more or less long periods. Thus, all along the relationship life cycle, systems must being able to: (1) continue to fulfill their own missions, respecting the common mission and (2) remain independent of other systems and thus able to resume its autonomy when relationship will stop. In another words, the relationship must be totally reversible i.e. differs to the integration [2]. In the following, any enterprise, process, activity of an enterprise in relation with another one will be simply considered as a processor inspired by [12]. A processor is a point where an object carried by a flow (concretizing the relationship) is processed i.e. transformed. Indeed, one or several object's characteristics (time – duration, delay, ... –, space – position, speed, acceleration,... – or form – geometry, color, ... –) change during a processor execution under the action of entities considered as resources of the processor and respecting some constraints and rules. Moreover, any of these processors use resources (human actor, organizational unit, machine, tool, or software application) as means necessary to transform the inputs into outputs. According to the system modeling framework called SA-GACE [13], three types of relationships between two processors can be considered: transaction, coupling and interaction. Each relationship induces a set of requirements (functional and not functional [11] in order to assume that concerned processors are interoperable when it is needed. All these requirements have then to be checked in order to detect and to avoid interoperability problems. So, enterprise parts (processor, resources, flows, etc.) and interoperability requirements must be modeled. The next part intents to formalize the interoperability requirement corresponding to relationship typology.

Transaction is the basic relationship and only focuses on the flow of exchanged objects between two processors (supplier to customer).The flow can carry material, energy, financial, information or human objects. The customer processor can use this flow as an input to process or as a resource which support its execution. Transaction concerning objects of nature information induce, for example, the well known problems of the syntactic and semantic (form) of the exchanged information. It can also be related to the organizational aspects (time, form and/or space) i.e. the rules indicating how the different entities in the enterprise are structured and organized in order to fulfill the processor mission. For example, "is the actor in charge of a given processor must dispose of the required and updated information (about environment context, other processors and abilities for controlling the processor execution)?".

Coupling represents a reciprocal influence of a processor P1 named then controller processor to another processor P2 named operating processor: the controller processor P1 controls or constraints the execution of the operating processor P2 which have to provide reporting information and data to P1 as a feedback loop. This relationship corresponds typically to the link between decision and operating systems in system theory. The interoperability requirements are then, in addition to the ones of the transaction (based on form, state and time attributes), more related to the objectives or constraints provided by the controller processor to the operating processor. Thus, for example, the "production objectives" have to be clearly defined and well understood by all the resources involved in the processor "Reach production objectives" which receive the production objectives. Moreover, these production objectives have to be reachable in order to not induced interoperability problems between the two processors. Concerning the feedback loop, the requirements are the same ones of the transaction.

Interaction represents an influence of a processor to another processor requiring an intermediate processor which plays the role of interface between the two processors. This interface remains required because some change of one or more attributes of time, space and / or form of the object carried by the flow cannot be done by one of the two connected processors. However the interface processor cannot be controlled by one of the two processors. For example, the interface processor can be a service provided by external entity and the enterprise cannot intervene during its execution. An interaction is then defined as a 3-uple {Event, Processor, Condition} where:

Event: Event from which occurrence is required to execute the intermediate processor corresponding to an interruption of the normal running of the processor e.g. a machine failure or simply the end of the processor,

Processor: Description of the intermediate processor as an input/output function,

Condition: Condition under which the processor has fulfilled its mission. In case of the condition is not valid, the processor cannot provide its output and this can generates a hazard which can produce or not another interaction.

So, interaction can have a stochastic behavior taking into account the event occurrence, the condition validity but also of external constraints. In this case, interoperability requirements focus essentially on the intermediate processor. Indeed, neither of the two processors can have an influence on the behavior of the intermediate processor. The requirements consist then to prove that the processors are simultaneously aware about the possible risks associated to the fluctuations of interface processor behavior and able to adapt their own behavior, structure or functioning modes in order to anticipate these risks occurrences. In other words, are the processors able to find alternative in case of dysfunction of interface processor? The relationships between processors and this interface processor can be considered as a kind of Transaction relationship. So, the interoperability requirements concerning transaction have then to be checked to detect other interoperability problems.

3   From Interoperability Formalisation to Property

The requirement formalization consists on a representation under the form of a causal and constrained relation between two sets. This relation is called a property [11] defined by *as a requirement or a characteristic that have to be checked on each model of a pointed out system*. The first set models the condition called here the cause under which the requirement has to be checked. The second set describes the resulting situation of the studied part of the collaborative process i.e. the condition called here the effect under which the requirement have to be checked. The relation can be a logical (implication, equivalence or influence), temporized of not taking into account the requirement. If cause and effect are verified by the collaborative process, then the requirement is itself respected. This indicates that no prejudice can be induced to the collaborative process behavior regarding this requirement. Last, any effect can be considered as a new cause of other problem, so the interoperability requirements can be defined by using a recursive approach. For example, if given partners (i.e. part of enterprises) intents to be involved during a given activity A, they have to check all the abilities required by this activity A. In this case, if all partners check a set of abilities, they must be able to find internal resources able and available for supporting really the activity. At this stage, each interoperability requirement is formalized by (a set of) properties by experts from the domain. First, these properties are expressed by using natural. The Fig. 1 illustrates some other properties which can be written. However, due to the conceptual limits of existing modeling languages, formalizing all the requirements need to add conceptual enrichments to the enterprise modeling languages.

Thus, the meta-model of a modeling language (enriched BPMN language [14]), allowing to represent a model of the collaborative process to interoperability analysis issue, has been developed (not presented here). It has been implemented by using Graphical Modeling Framework of the Eclipse Platform [15]. This allows first to provide a modeling tool which is used in order to represent the collaborative process and enterprise models, second to develop the property proof mechanisms presented in the next part. Then, each property is translated into a formal language. Conceptual graphs are chosen [16]. A conceptual graph is a finite, connected, directed bipartite graph. It is defined as a graph with only two kinds of nodes: the concepts and the relations. The translation is performed by using interpretation mechanisms (considering the concepts and relations extracted from the modeling language which are described later in this paper). These ones are now under development and use the tool COGITANT [17].

Property 1	Each activity which provides an information or a product to another activity have to receive an acknowledgment receipt. [18]
Property 2	All shared information have to be periodically updated.
Property 3	The person who has the responsibility to update information has to be clearly defined.
Property 4	Partners of the collaboration have to be able to continue to achieve their own objectives.
Property 5	Partners have to remain independent of other partners and thus be able to resume its autonomy when relationship will stop (the relationship must be totally reversible).

Fig. 1. Example of properties

4 Enterprise Model and Properties Re-writing

The approach proposes to re-write enterprise models based with our enriched BPMN language in others models based on a formal language. The objective is to obtain models without sense ambiguity in order to check formal properties describing interoperability requirements. Thus, the enriched enterprise model is translated into Conceptual Graphs by using formal rules. The re-writing procedure starts from the meta-model of the enriched BPMN language, established in UML. This UML diagram is analyzed and formalized in order to provide all the needed concepts and relations of the Conceptual Graph. All concepts are obtained by considering all the modeling entities which will be used in the checking task. Thus, each class of the meta-model (but also its attributes) is translated into concepts. Then, the relations are obtained by translating each association between classes into a relation between concepts. Then, the defined concepts and relations (described in hierarchical structures called concepts and relations lattices) allow transforming the enterprise network model build with the enriched BPMN language into a conceptual graph. To do this transformation, each marker (which refers to specific instances of concepts) has to be extracted from the model in order to produce a unique conceptual graph G. Thus, G gathers all the knowledge described in the model. Moreover, according to the concepts and relations lattices which have been defined, it is also possible to re-write the properties written in natural language, in a formal way. The Fig. 2 illustrates the re-writing of the property 1 which has been presented in the chapter 3.

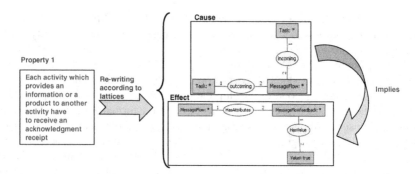

Fig. 2. Example of property re-writing

5 Checking Technique and Mechanisms

The checking technique is inspired by [19] which use analysis mechanisms allowed by conceptual graphs. These analysis mechanisms are:

Projection: This involves comparing the obtained conceptual graph coming from the translation of the model with another one translating the property. If the projection fails, then the modeled property cannot be verified and the causes are highlighted.

Constraint: A property describes what the links and/or constraints are between facts. In this case, the property is translated on a positive or negative conceptual graph constraint. A positive constraint between two facts A and B must be interpreted as: "If A is true, then B must also be true". Conversely, a negative constraint must be interpreted as: "If A is true then B must be false".

Dynamic and static rules: A property is directly modeled as a property composed of a cause and an effect. If the graph corresponding to the causes match with a part of the conceptual graph translating the system models, then the effect must be checked in the same way.

The Fig. 3 illustrates two examples of property proofs by using the projection mechanism. The Fig. 3a represents the studied model built by using our modeling tool. This model describes the exchange of data between two partners in order to find a common available day for organizing a meeting. The Fig. 3b illustrates a part of this model translated in conceptual graph taking into account the exchange of data between the activity "contact partner" and the activity "To check availability". The concepts and relations which are in black are the ones which allow to verify (by using the projection mechanism) the property 1 (defined in the chapter 3). Then, the responsible of the activity "To check availability" has to check his availability by accessing to his enterprise online agenda (linked to a common database concerning all employees of the enterprise). This agenda is normally updated regularly. The objective of the proof of the property 2 (illustrated in the Fig. 3c) is to check if the data in the agenda corresponds effectively to the last updated version. Thus, as for the property 1, the concepts and relations which are in black are the ones which allow to verify this property. These two properties concerns requirement of the transaction relationship as defined in the chapter 2.

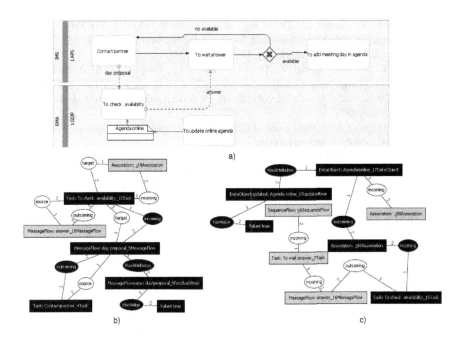

Fig. 3. Example of projection

6 Conclusions and Perspectives

This article presents the first results of our research. A formal model of interoperability requirement in collaborative processes context is introduced. A set of modeling and formal proof mechanisms is then described in order to analyze from a static point of view the network model. The main perspectives of this work are the following. First, a reference properties data base and rewriting mechanisms have to be developed in order to help actors to analyze more rapidly the collaborative processes and then become able to anticipate interoperability problems. Second, rewriting mechanisms from model and properties database have to be implanted in order to be interfaced with model checkers such as UPPAAL. Third, other works in progress intents to make the gap between network model and an enriched multi agents system allowing to simulate the behavior of the different parts of the enterprises involved in the collaborative process. The goal these two last works is then to assume dynamic properties can be then checked.

References

1. IEEE, A compilation of IEEE standard computer glossaries: standard computer dictionary, New York (1990)
2. INTEROP, Enterprise Interoperability-Framework and knowledge corpus - Final report, INTEROP NoE, FP6 – Contract n° 508011, Deliverable DI.3 (May 21, 2007)
3. Berio, G.: UEML 2.0, Deliverable 5.1, INTEROP project UE-IST-508011 (2005)

4. Schlenoff, C., Gruninger, M., Tissot, F., Valois, J., Lubell, J., Lee, J.: The Process Specification Language (PSL): Overview and Version 1.0 Specification, NISTIR 6459, National Institute of Standards and Technology, Gaithersburg, MD (2000)
5. Bénaben, F., Touzi, J., Rajsiri, V., Truptil, S., Lorré, J.P., Pingaud, H.: Mediation Information System Design in a Collaborative SOA Context through a MDD Approach. In: MDISIS 2008: Model Driven Interoperability for Sustainable Information System, Montpellier, France (2008)
6. Tolk, A., Muguira, J.A.: The Levels of Conceptual Interoperability Model. In: Fall Simulation Interoperability Worshop (2003)
7. C4ISR, Levels of Information Systems Interoperability (LISI), Architecture Working Group, United States of America, Department of Defence (1998)
8. Clark, T., Jones, R.: Organisational Interoperability Maturity Model for C2, Australian Department of Defence (1999)
9. ATHENA, Framework for the establishment and management methodology, Integrated Project ATHENA, deliverable A1.4 (2005)
10. Daclin, N.: Contribution au développement d'une méthodologie pour l'interopérabilité des entreprises (in French), PhD Thesis, University Bordeaux1 (December 2007)
11. Aloui, S., Chapurlat, V., Penalva, J.-M.: Linking interoperability and risk assessment: A methodological approach for socio-technical systems. In: Dolgui, A., Morel, G., Pereira, C. (eds.) Proceedings of INCOM 2006, 12th IFAC Symposium on Information Control Problems in Manufacturing, Information control: a complex challenge for the 21st century, Saint Etienne, France, hal-00354778 (2006) ISBN: 978-0-08-044654-7
12. Le Moigne, J.L.: La modélisation des systèmes complexes, Paris, Bordas, Dunot (1990)
13. Penalva, J.-M.: La modélisation par les systèmes en situation complexe (in French), PhD thesis. Paris Sud university (1997)
14. BPMN, Business Process Modeling Notation, V1.2 (2009), http://www.bpmn.org/
15. GMF, Graphical Modelling Framework (2008),
    http://www.eclipse.org/modeling/gmf/
16. Chein, M., Mugnier, M.-L.: Conceptual graphs: fundamental notions. Revue d'intelligence artificielle 6(4) (1992)
17. Cogitant, CoGITaNT Version 5.2.0: Reference Manual (2009),
    http://cogitant.sourceforge.net
18. Blanc, S.: Contribution à la caractérisation et à l'évaluation de l'interopérabilité pour les entreprises collaboratives (in French), PhD Thesis, University Bordeaux1 (December 2006)
19. Chapurlat, V., Aloui, S.: How to detect risks with a formal approach? From property specification to risk emergence. In: Proceedings of Modeling, Simulation, Verification and Validation of Enterprise Information Systems (MSVVEIS), Paphos, Cyprus (2006)

Services Systems to Leverage Innovators' Knowledge: The Telecoms Industry Case

Florie Bugeaud[1,2] and Eddie Soulier[1]

[1] University of Technology of Troyes – ICD/Tech-CICO FRE CNRS 2848,
12 rue Marie Curie – BP2060, 10010 Troyes Cedex, France
firstname.name@utt.fr
[2] Orange Labs, 38-40 rue du Général Leclerc, 92794 Issy-les-Moulineaux
florie.bugeaud@orange-ftgroup.com

Abstract. Today, telecoms operators have to prove their innovation capacity. They address corporate customers which are involved in collaborative value networks. They implement a process of new services research in order to create adapted solutions. This process is linked to a collaborative and complex practice between diverse innovators. However there is no structured method to leverage this community's knowledge. Based on the SSME[1] discussions, we suggest enriching the telecoms innovation approaches by the representation and the simulation of "services systems". This paper also proposes the development of a collaborative tool to support this suggestion and the innovators' practices. Our approach is currently tested on a specific telecom service in the e-health domain which presents an interesting business ecosystem.

Keywords: SSME, Service System, Innovation, Knowledge.

1 Introduction

The telecoms industry is a major actor in the innovation of services. It addresses corporate customers which are more and more involved in value networks. This engagement with business partners stems from the transformation from an organizational view (integrated model) to a market view (specialized and distributed model). It corresponds to the outsourcing logic and brings flexibility and agility. Moreover, this opening creates a broader range of market opportunities [1]. Telecoms operators have to take into account these complete value networks in order to propose them adapted and innovative services. Albeit the literature is comprehensive about the products innovation, there is not a lot of works on the design of innovative services. The lack of a structured method and the dispersal of the actors limit the innovators' reasoning of design. This reasoning is linked to a collaborative and complex practice underlying the process of innovative services research. According to Precup and al. [2] "the cross fertilisation of thoughts and ideas and knowledge generation is without doubt one of the key success factors to promote a culture of innovation". Indeed, the knowledge sharing and co-creation during the service design is an essential factor to improve the

---

[1] "Services Science Management and Engineering": initiated by IBM and some universities.

L.M. Camarinha-Matos et al. (Eds.): PRO-VE 2009, IFIP AICT 307, pp. 563–570, 2009.
© IFIP International Federation for Information Processing 2009

creativity. It is thus necessary to bring a structured framework and a shared representation in order to support the innovators' work. The SSME discipline proposes an interdisciplinary approach gathering all the synergies around the notion of "service". This paper pursues the ongoing discussions of SSME [3]. It suggests conceiving the service as a "Service System" and it studies the knowledge models allowing its emergence. One of the difficulties is linked to the service modeling because it does not have a specific formalization. The design reasoning of innovators is based on two spaces: the concepts and the knowledge (C-K theory [4]). Our works represent the distributed character of the telecoms innovators thanks to a social network [5]. They use the usual mechanisms of social networks to spread the design reasoning of innovators through their own social network. Our mechanism is based on the diffusion of forms and the use of tagged knowledge in order to co-create our models. Finally, our approach is currently tested on a specific telecom service in the e-health domain (the remote monitoring of diabetic patients) whose business ecosystem is complex and demanding. This application of our hypotheses and models will be the object of more specific publications.

This paper is organized as follow. The section 2 presents the context of the services innovation in telecoms operators. The section 3 introduces the identification of services and the modeling of services systems. The section 4 describes the main functionalities of the proposed tool (co-creation of models through the diffusion of forms, enrichment of a Services Systems repository, simulation/animation of the Service System, connection between the tags of the existing telecoms offer and the tags of the Service System). The section 5 concludes this paper.

2   Services Innovation in the Telecoms Industry

2.1   The Value Network of the Corporate Customers

In today's challenging global market, telecoms operators need to innovate in order to support the value creation of their corporate customer. The evolution of Information and Communication Technologies (TIC) has brought new ways to design and to deliver services. Moreover a lot of economic, organizational and sociologic evolutions have brought new issues. Telecoms operators try to remain competitive and to answer the evolution of their customers' requirements and organization. Their corporate customers are more and more involved in value networks. Indeed, we are currently living a transformation from an organizational view to a market view. This hypothesis criticizes the integrated model in favor of a specialized and distributed model. It considers companies as sets of business components involved in a value network. These components are "strategic areas" stemming from the junction of the value chain and the strategic segments (classical approach) or "business components" which are autonomous and logical groupings of people, technologies and resources whose objective is to deliver value (cf. Component Business Modeling methodology from IBM). Each company is specialized on a specific business domain and uses its partners' services when it is necessary. It corresponds to the outsourcing logic and it brings flexibility and agility.

For example, telecoms operators are more and more interested in services sectors such as the healthcare sector. They address the whole business ecosystem of the e-health field (Fig. 1) and propose new offers including telecoms products (telephony, networks), solutions (e.g. collaborative work, mobility) and pure services (e.g. project management, consulting). This requires having a complete view of the value network in which these actors are business partners.

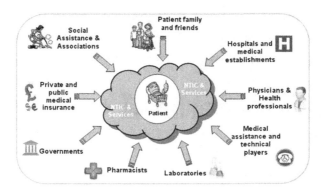

Fig. 1. The e-health business ecosystem: example of a complex and demanding business ecosystem which is addressed as a whole by the telecoms operators

2.2   The Design Process and Design Reasoning in Telecoms

In the telecoms industry, the design process is generally shared between four main departments (marketing, research and development, exploration centre, technologic centre) and three key moments (research, development, market entry) (Fig. 2). Their innovators come from several disciplines (marketing, usages experts, ergonomics, engineers, etc.). They initiate a sub-process upstream of the design process (at T-1 in Fig. 2) in order to research ideas of innovative telecoms services. The ideas or concepts go through three phases: evaluation, maturation and transfer (Fig. 2). Each phase is overseen by a decision committee. A reading committee makes a first selection of concepts and determines the actions plan. An anticipation committee selects the major enriched concepts and validates their transfer towards the design process at T0. This process usually includes the analysis of the sector, practices and business processes of the targeted corporate customer, and the detection of opportunities. Nevertheless, the global "service orientation" (growth of the tertiary sector and evolution of companies) has brought new issues. It is necessary to adapt the methods of telecoms operators to take into account the services specificities.

In addition, the success of this new services research process is based on the design reasoning and the interactions between the telecoms innovators. This reasoning is an analytic and cognitive process. The shared information and arguments give rise to a collaborative and complex practice in a specific community. These innovators work as a virtual team in a network environment such as the designers involved in a collaborative creativity of products concepts [6]. The emergence of a new concept or idea of service starts the design process. It needs and develops their individual and collective knowledge. Nevertheless, their actual collaboration is insufficient to reach the necessary sharing and co-creation of knowledge. There are two reasons. The former is that these innovators often prefer to share information into their personal network. The latter is that there is no structured method and that the existing modeling environments are not adapted. It is thus important to bring them a method and an associated tool to help them to collaborate and to share their knowledge.

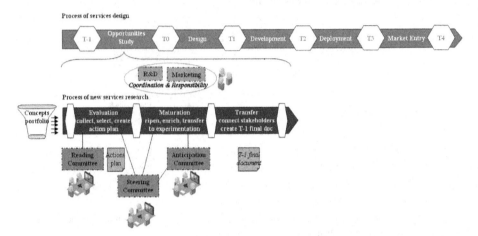

Fig. 2. The innovation processes in the telecoms industry: main milestones, stages, actors and deliverables

3   Service as a Service System

3.1   Identification of Services

The notion of "service" [7] remains hazy because of its several dimensions and characteristics such as its intangibility, its heterogeneity, the interactions between customers and providers, the coproduction by all the stakeholders, etc. The SSME field has proposed a notion of service which is more abstract than the one usually find in the literature. Indeed, the implementation dimension is predominant. It defines the service as a reusable technical functionality. Our works pursue the ongoing discussions of SSME. We distinguish three approaches to identify these services:

- a top-down approach based on business components or strategic domains,
- an intermediary approach based on the requirements and business goals,
- a bottom-up approach based on existing tools, applications, technologies…

The notion of "service" regroups static and dynamic aspects. In order to express this complexity, some researchers of the SSME discipline propose the term "Service System" [8]. They define it as "a value-coproduction configuration of people, technology, other internal and external service systems, and shared information". We conceive the "Service System" through the "Service Concept" and the "Service Delivery System" (Fig. 3). Indeed in the field of innovation, it is necessary to conceive at the same time the concept of service, the targeted customers' segment and the system for its functioning [9].

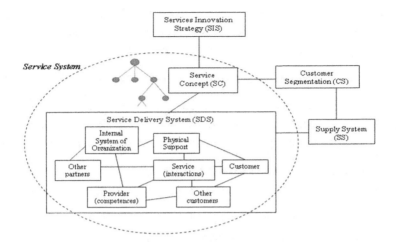

Fig. 3. The Service System: main elements

3.2 Service System: The Service Concept (SC)

Even if they focus on "products concepts", Volpentesta and al. [6] suggest that:

- the "concept development" is the first phase of the product development process,
- the "concept design" is relative to the work done by designers (task clarification, hypothesis formulation, solution searching) in order to determine an architecture,
- the design participants come from different disciplines and generate the "seeds of innovation" (i.e. the ideas for a new product concept) in a collaborative way.

In the same spirit, but within the context of services innovation, the "Service Concept" (SC) corresponds to the idea or object of the innovation for a targeted customer or activity sector. In 1989, Scheuing and Johnson defined a "concept" as "a description of a potential new service" [9]. For example, in the telecom industry there are the services of mobility, connectivity, security, cooperation or geolocalisation. We can also note some examples of a "Customers Segmentation": SMEs in the sustainable development, banks, insurance companies or hospitals. The initial SC can be broken down into sub-concepts which can be themselves broken down in an iterative way. This can be called a functional breakdown [10] with basic services and peripheral services. The SC presents a tree based structure [4] [9]. This design tree needs and develops the innovators' knowledge. It helps them to progress in the exploration of relevant concepts that may become designed and sold objects.

3.3 Service System: The Service Delivery System (SDS)

The "Service Delivery System" (SDS) is the hypothetic functioning of the "Service Concept" (SC). The SDS is linked to the notion of "servuction" which has been proposed by Eiglier and Langeard in 1987. It includes the customer, the physical support, the providers' employees (which are in front of the customer), its internal system of organization and the service as the result of interactions. Our works add to these elements the nature of the service target or medium (material, knowledge, information, relation) [10], the other customers and partners of the services provider. A SDS is thus composed of several facets which depend on six mains views: strategy, provider, customer, services interactions, information systems and technologies. The initial servuction model considers the back-office of the services providers as a black box. Nevertheless, this back-office comes from their internal system of organization and it is a key element for the service furniture and support. The usual distinction between back-office and front-office is insufficient in the case of services. We can distinguish two other spaces: the back-stage and the on-stage. The line between them depends on the visibility and the implication of the customer who access a part of the provider's front-office. Another distinction is linked to the results of the Service System: the output and the outcome. The former is a short-term result or immediate effect. The latter is a more long-term result or useful effect.

4 Supporting Tool for the Community of Innovators

4.1 Diffusion of Forms in a Social Network

The process of new services research needs the sharing of more or less tacit and individual knowledge between innovators. It also needs a shared representation of the Service System which has to be imagined. We have decided to represent the distributed telecoms innovators thanks to a social network [5]. The proposed web-based tool uses a method (Fig. 4) inspired from the usual mechanisms of social networks. It aims at facilitating the exchanges between innovators and stimulating their work. In an asynchronous and distributed way, the steps are:

- breakdown of the Service System models into several forms (always available),
- proposition of a research theme by an innovator or a group of innovators,
- diffusion of the forms in the social network according to the profiles,
- enrichment and registration of these forms by the targeted innovators who accept to participate to the Service System description,
- enrichment of the Services Systems repository based on the registered forms,
- generation of the Service System models and consolidation of the repository.

It is also possible to make some request in the Services Systems repository. Finally, this tool can also be used in a direct access by an innovator or a working group (e.g. during a brainstorming) to model the Service System. This working environment is based on a wiki in order to ease innovators' interactions (see the ANR ISICIL[2] and the SweetWiki in which the use of semantic web technologies is investigated to support and ease the lifecycle of the wiki [11]).

4.2 Connection with the Existing Services and Knowledge through Tags

Tags are keywords or descriptive terms. The process of tagging is a powerful tool to organize objects for the purposes of recovery, sharing and discovery them, when

---

[2] Information Semantic Integration through Communities of Intelligence online (http://isicil.inria.fr/)

combined with search technology [12]. The existing expertise and knowledge (K) and the existing telecoms services are already tagged. The addition of tags on the designed new Service System during its description brings an interesting help. Indeed, these tags are key elements for the connection between the existing telecoms supply system, services and know-how, and the current concept (C) (C-K theory [4]) of Service System. The proposed tool allows this automatic connection. Indeed it supports the emergence of ideas by the detection of possible adaptations of existing services to a new requirement. It proposes this kind of suggestions to the innovators which can decide if such adaptations are pertinent.

4.3 Animation, Annotation and Validation of the Service System

Some existing solutions allow the generation of an ergonomic expression of processes. They model and simulate these processes and their associated micro-world. This kind of tool is useful for the communication, the usages illustration and the validation of a hypothetic functioning. That is why it seems interesting to propose the generation of an animation of the Service System after the consolidation of the repository (Fig. 4). The result is a pretty realistic animated scene. This virtualized Service System (and its context) can help innovators to have a common representation stemming from their individual and collective contributions. They can discuss and exchange some commentaries and annotations based on this animation. After some hypothetic modifications of the models or forms (to obtain a more pertinent simulation/animation), they validate the Service System and transfer it to the design team (towards T0 as it has been described in the section 2.2).

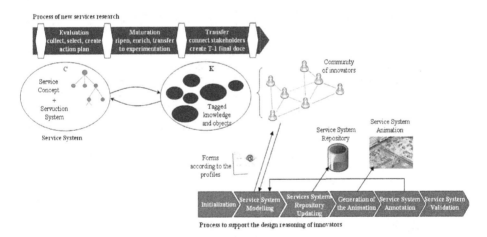

Fig. 4. A collaborative method and tool to support the innovators reasoning

5   Conclusion

The current tools and approaches to generate ideas for innovation are mainly based on the process modeling. Moreover they are focused on integrated companies and do not really take into account the entire business ecosystem involved. Our works propose to take into account the Service System as a whole in order to improve these tools and approaches. The proposed methodology aims at the identification and characterization of the "Service Concept" and the "Service Delivery System". It allows the leveraging and sharing of innovators' knowledge in order to obtain a shared representation. Innovators expand their knowledge, annotate and validate a new idea of Service System. Its animation helps them to visualize its hypothetic functioning. Finally the enriched repository brings available information for further services.

The next stages of our works concern the improvement of the Service System formalisms in order to take into account the collaboration, information and interaction issues. Moreover, because the e-health is a priority sector for telecommunications operators and an interesting field to test our hypotheses and models, we apply our approach to the remote monitoring of diabetic patients.

References

1. Rajsiri, V., Lorré, J.-P., Bénaben, F., Pingaud, H.: Collaborative process definition using an ontology-based approach. In: Camarinha-Matos, L., Picard, W. (eds.) Pervasive Collaborative Networks. IFIP, vol. 283, pp. 205–212. Springer, Boston (2008)
2. Precup, L., Mulligan, D., O'Sullivan, D.: Collaborative tool to support knowledge sharing and innovation in an R&D Project. In: International Conference of Concurrent Engineering, Espoo, Finland (2003)
3. Glushko, R.J.: Designing a service science discipline with discipline. IBM Systems Journal (2008)
4. Hatchuel, A., Weil, B.: A new approach of innovative design: an introduction to C-K theory. In: ICED, Stockholm (2003)
5. Newman, M.: The Structure and Function of Complex Networks. SIAM Review 45, 167 (2003)
6. Volpentesta, A.P., Muzzupappa, M., Ammirato, S.: Critical thinking and concept design generation in a collaborative network. In: Camarinha-Matos, L., Picard, W. (eds.) Pervasive Collaborative Networks. IFIP, vol. 283, pp. 157–164. Springer, Boston (2008)
7. Gadrey, J.: The characterization of goods and services: an alternative approach. Review of Income and Wealth 43(3) (2000)
8. Spohrer, J., Maglio, P., Bailey, J., Gruhl, D.: Steps Towards a Science of Service Systems. IEEE Computer 40, 71–77 (2007)
9. Lenfle, S.: Innovation in services: the contributions of design theory. In: 11th IPDMC Conference Trinity College. Dublin (2004)
10. Gallouj, F., Weinstein, O.: Innovation in services. Research Policy 26, 537–556 (1997)
11. Buffa, M., Crova, G., Gandon, F., Lecompte, C., Passeron, J.: SweetWiki: Semantic WEb Enabled Technologies in Wiki. In: 1st Workshop on Semantic Wikis, 3rd ESWC, Montenegro (2006)
12. Xu, Z., Fu, Y., Mao, J., Su, D.: Towards the Semantic Web: Collaborative Tag Suggestions. In: Proceedings of the Collaborative Web Tagging Workshop, WWW 2006, Edinburgh (2006)

Part **18**

Formal Models

Formal Grammars for Product Data Management on Distributed Manufacturing Systems

Rui M. Sousa, Paulo J. Martins, and Rui M. Lima

Department of Production and Systems, School of Engineering, University of Minho,
Campus de Azurém, 4800 058 Guimarães, Portugal
{rms,pmartins,rml}@dps.uminho.pt

Abstract. This work shows how formal grammars with attributes can be advantageously used to deal with two fundamental aspects of product data management - product diversity management and generation of specific product data based on clients' specification – in the context of distributed manufacturing systems, while networks of geographically distant collaborative entities. This contribution will constitute a new component for an existing model, developed by the authors, for dynamic production planning and control which includes the interoperability with industrial equipment. The proposed approach is centered on attributed formal grammars, allowing the formalization of the data representation for each family of products and also of some of the inherent processing (e.g. generation of specific products' bill-of-materials).

Keywords: Formal grammars, product data management, bill-of-materials, distributed manufacturing systems.

1 Introduction

Over the last years, the markets' tendency to frequently demand differentiated products with high quality and low prices has become even more accentuated. This tendency has direct implications over two aspects: the products themselves and the correspondent production systems.

Products are no longer strictly defined by the companies, being, instead, defined in some extent by the customers (e.g. Nike's customers can specify online their own sport shoes). Therefore, products' diversity is experiencing a dramatic increase, causing serious problems to the traditional product data management (PDM) systems (where, frequently, each product has its own bill-of-materials) due to the huge volume of information involved. From the PDM perspective, this paper does not intend to develop new models to overcome the problem of products' high diversity. Among other approaches, namely MBOM - modular bill-of-materials [1] and BOMO – bill-of-materials and operations [2], the GBOM - generic bill-of-materials [3] is a relatively recent concept, with recognized effectiveness, specifically designed to deal with that problem. Based precisely on the GBOM concept, the main objective of this paper is the formalization, using attributed formal grammars, of generic product data representation and of some of the inherent processing, namely the generation of specific product data.

L.M. Camarinha-Matos et al. (Eds.): PRO-VE 2009, IFIP AICT 307, pp. 573–580, 2009.

Reference [4] use graph grammars to model families of products accordingly to the modular product architecture [5] which also addresses the problem of product family design itself. A detailed state-of-the art review on product family design can be found in [6]. The present paper does not intend to cope with this design problem but rather to deal with existent families of products. Besides the rigour and absence of ambiguities that characterizes the formal approaches, the use of formal grammars reduces the gap between specification and implementation due to particular equivalences between formal grammars and automata [7].

Traditional production systems are also facing serious problems as they are not adequate to produce small quantities of a large diversity of products and, besides, to do that very quickly, with high quality and low price. A significant number of traditional production systems achieve reduced cycle times and low costs only for large quantities of an extremely reduced diversity of products (eventually unitary), i.e. they are oriented to mass production. To overcome this problem, paradigms like mass customization production [8] and customer oriented production [9] have been introduced. When based on these paradigms, systems are expected to respond to customers' specific demand (low quantities and high diversity) keeping the advantages of mass production (reduced cycle times and low costs). In structural/organizational terms, and to overcome the traditional "monolithic" companies, the so-called distributed manufacturing systems (while networks of separate collaborative entities) are expected to dynamically identify and select the resources (which can be geographically distant from each other) that can better respond to a given market opportunity. From the production systems perspective, it is expected that the previously referred formalization, will contribute to the improvement of a concrete distributed production planning and control (PPC) model [10, 11]. In this model, the distributed system for production of a specific product is composed of a network of autonomous processing elements directly related with the bill of materials of that product. It is assumed that each of these elements has the capacity and ability to deliver a product's component. Furthermore, the proposed mechanism for selection of processing elements could dynamically originate different networks for identical products. Therefore it is expected that the ability to cope with high diversity of products will contribute to the improvement of the referred distributed production planning and control (PPC) model.

The previous paragraphs show that the present work is included in an embracing project which involves a number of research areas, namely: formal approaches in manufacturing systems design, product data management, production planning and control, and, industrial automation. This diversity constitutes an additional challenge to the investigation team.

The paper is structured in five sections. After this initial section, a very brief introduction to PDM is provided in section 2, emphasizing the importance of the generic bill-of-materials concept. Formal grammars and correspondent equivalent automata are described in section 3 which also includes the description of the attributed formal grammar concept. On section 4 a specific attributed formal grammar for generic product data representation and processing is developed and an example of its application is provided. Finally, on section 5, some conclusions are outlined, including perspectives of future work.

2 Product Data Management

Product data management (PDM) is one of the most important functional areas of production planning and control (PPC) systems. PDM should provide mechanisms not only to represent product data, but also to make that information available to other functional areas (e.g. commercial management, master scheduling planning, materials requirement planning and products' budgeting).

One of the most important mechanisms involved in PDM is the bill-of-materials (BOM). In general terms the basic BOM represents the structure of components of a specific product. Typically the observed increase on the products' diversity happens because clients have the possibility to select values for some characteristics of the products (e.g. the colour of the sport shoes). Hence, instead of specifying a BOM for each specific product (implying thus huge volumes of information with high levels of redundancy), the specification of a single BOM for each family of products is much more effective from the information management point of view. That is precisely the main purpose of the generic bill-of-materials (GBOM) [3]. The specification of a GBOM for a given family of products includes the definition of a set of parameters which represent relevant characteristics of that family. Later, the instantiation of those parameters with specific values allows the transformation of the GBOM into a BOM of a specific member of the family. Inspired in an example from [3], Fig. 1 represents a basic chair and the correspondent GBOM.

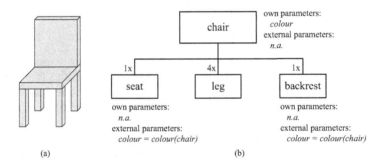

Fig. 1. (a) Chair, (b) Chair's GBOM (adapted from [3])

In this simple example the customer can choose the colour of the chair and that choice directly determines the colour of both seat and backrest, but has no effect on the legs. For both seat and backrest, colour is an external parameter whose value is inherited from the chair. For the chair, colour is an own parameter and thus should be directly instantiated.

The formalization of this kind of structures brings rigour and absence of ambiguities, but those are not the only reasons to formalize. The formal concept used in this work – the formal attributed grammar – provides mechanisms to model not only the tree structure with correspondent parameters and inheritance relations, but also synthesis relations (sections 3 and 4). The synthesis relations here proposed are not identifiable in the GBOM model [3]. Additionally, as already referred in the previous section, this particular kind of formalization reduces the gap between specification and implementation.

3 Formal Grammars

Basically a formal grammar uses an alphabet (with two types of symbols: terminal and non-terminal), and a set of rewriting rules (productions), to generate words (constituted by terminal symbols) that are subsequently used to represent aspects of a given area (e.g. manufacturing systems general area). The formal grammar concept is defined by several authors [12, 13, 14], but all those definitions are similar and based on Chomsky's definition [15]. Due to notation's adequacy the following definition, presented in [16], is here used: A formal grammar G is a four-tuple $G=(V_T, V_N, S, R)$ where V_T is a finite set of terminal symbols, V_N a finite set of non-terminal symbols ($V_T \cap V_N = \phi$), S is the initial symbol ($S \in V_N$) and R is a finite set of productions.

The existence of a production $\alpha \to \beta$ in R means that grammar G allows the substitution of the string α by the string β. To illustrate the process of derivation of a word consider the grammar $G=(V_T, V_N, S, R)$ where $V_T = \{m_1, m_2, m_3, \mapsto\}$, $V_N = \{S\}$ and $R=\{S \to m_i, S \to m_i \mapsto S\}$. To avoid the repeated use of the same index i both rules are subjected to an application condition $1 \leq i \leq 3 \wedge o_i = 0$ where $o = (o_1, o_2, o_3)$ is the so called occurrence vector. A possible derivation is $S \Rightarrow m_1 \mapsto S \Rightarrow m_1 \mapsto m_2 \mapsto S \Rightarrow m_1 \mapsto m_2 \mapsto m_3$. A derivation ends when the word only contains terminal symbols (i.e. no more productions can be applied).This particular derivation has three steps and the sequence of applied productions is $(2,2,1)$. The word $m_1 \mapsto m_2 \mapsto m_3$ can be graphically interpreted (Fig. 2).

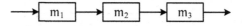

Fig. 2. Interpretation of word $m_1 \mapsto m_2 \mapsto m_3$

Based on the productions' type, the Chomsky's hierarchy identifies four classes of formal grammars: unrestricted, context-sensitive, context-free and regular. Moreover these grammars are equivalent, respectively, to the following four types of automata: Turing machine (TM), linear bounded (LBA), pushdown (PDA) and finite state (FSA). A detailed analysis on this subject can be found in [7]. The importance of these equivalences resides mainly on implementation (contrarily to formal grammars, automata are easy to implement). These grammars are syntactic mechanisms and to attain semantic aspects, attributed grammars were introduced.

An attributed formal grammar G_a is a triple $G_a=(G,A,P)$ where G is a context-free grammar, A is a finite set of attributes and P is a finite set of assertions. Basically in an attributed grammar any symbol (terminal or non-terminal) may have a set of attributes and every production may have a set of assertions which represent the relations between attributes. With these features, formal grammars become suitable for the PDM area (section 4). In fact each element of a BOM will be represented by a terminal symbol, those elements' parameters are represented by attributes associated to the correspondent terminal symbols and the relations between parameters of different elements are represented by assertions. Assertions allow the representation of not only the inheritance relations referred in section 3, but also of synthesis relations (e.g. the value of a given parameter of a given element is obtained from the values of parameters of other elements below in the hierarchy).

4 Formal Grammar for PDM

This section introduces an attributed formal grammar, denoted as G_l, able to represent the GBOM for families of products and also to process the involved parameters leading thus to the generation of the BOM for each specific product.

The attributed formal grammar $G_l=(G,A,P)$ includes: (i) a context-free grammar $G=(V_T,V_N,S,R)$ where $V_T = \{c_1, ..., c_n, \downarrow_1, ..., \downarrow_n ,],[\}$ with $n \in N$, $V_N = \{S, A\}$ and $R=\{S \rightarrow c_i, S \rightarrow c_i[A], A \rightarrow \downarrow_i c_i[A], A \rightarrow AA, A \rightarrow \downarrow_i c_i\}$, (ii) a finite set of attributes A, and, (iii) a finite set of assertions P. While G is a syntactic mechanism, A and P are already associated to semantics and thus their definition is dependent of each family of products. Productions 1, 2, 3 and 5 must have an application condition to avoid the repeated use of the same index i. That condition is $1 \leq i \leq n \wedge o_i=0$ where $o=(o_1, ..., o_n)$ is the occurrence vector. Two possible derivations performed by G are: $S \Rightarrow c_1[A] \Rightarrow c_1[AA] \Rightarrow c_1[AAA] \Rightarrow c_1[\downarrow_2 c_2 AA] \Rightarrow c_1[\downarrow_2 c_2 \downarrow_3 c_3 A] \Rightarrow c_1[\downarrow_2 c_2 \downarrow_3 c_3 \downarrow_4 c_4]$ and $S \Rightarrow c_1[A] \Rightarrow c_1[AA] \Rightarrow c_1[AAA] \Rightarrow c_1[\downarrow_2 c_2[A]AA] \Rightarrow c_1[\downarrow_2 c_2[\downarrow_3 c_3]AA] \Rightarrow c_1[\downarrow_2 c_2[\downarrow_3 c_3] \downarrow_4 c_4 A] \Rightarrow c_1[\downarrow_2 c_2[\downarrow_3 c_3] \downarrow_4 c_4 \downarrow_5 c_5]$. The derivation sequences are $(2,4,4,5,5,5)$ and $(2,4,4,3,5,5,5)$, respectively. The generated words, i.e. $c_1[\downarrow_2 c_2 \downarrow_3 c_3 \downarrow_4 c_4]$ and $c_1[\downarrow_2 c_2[\downarrow_3 c_3] \downarrow_4 c_4 \downarrow_5 c_5]$, may have the graphical interpretation represented on Fig. 3.

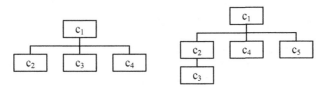

Fig. 3. Interpretation of words $c_1[\downarrow_2 c_2 \downarrow_3 c_3 \downarrow_4 c_4]$ and $c_1[\downarrow_2 c_2[\downarrow_3 c_3] \downarrow_4 c_4 \downarrow_5 c_5]$

Symbol c_i represents the element i of the structure and $\downarrow_i$ represents the relation between c_i and its parent. Thus, using this interpretation, grammar G is able to represent any structure similar to those represented on Fig. 3 and, obviously, this class of structures can be used to represent BOM. The pushdown automaton (PDA) T equivalent to G can be specified by the state diagram represented on Fig. 4.

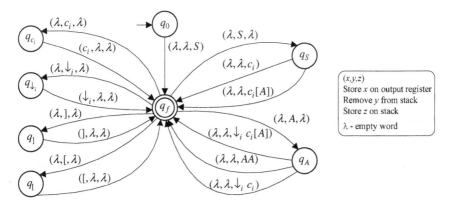

Fig. 4. State diagram of the PDA T equivalent to grammar G

The GBOM example (chair's family) presented on section 2 (Fig. 1) will now be extended with more parameters in order to demonstrate the application of G_1. The first step is the definition of the structure. The analyst will conduct the process, which is based on the PDA T (Fig. 4), indicating the product and its components (and correspondent quantities), until the desired structure is achieved (Fig. 5).

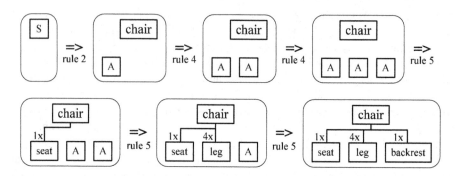

Fig. 5. Derivation process for chair's family GBOM

In this particular case the derivation sequence recorded at the end of the structure definition is $(2,4,4,5,5,5)$. Note that the analyst is not aware of this sequence – it is just an internal representation used by the PDA T.

In the next step the analyst indicates the parameters (Table 1) for each element (i.e. he indicates the set A of attributes for each symbol c_i and $\downarrow_i$ of G_1).

Table 1. Parameters for the chair's family GBOM

Symbol	Description	EIP	ESP	OP
c_1	chair		cost	totalHeight, width, depth, seatHeight
c_2	seat	width, depth		cost
c_3	leg	height		cost
c_4	backrest	height, width		cost
$\downarrow_2$	c_2-c_1 rel.			quantity
$\downarrow_3$	c_3-c_1 rel.			quantity
$\downarrow_4$	c_4-c_1 rel.			quantity

Parameters can be: external inherited (EIP), external synthesized (ESP) or own parameters (OP). Finally the analyst should indicate how the parameters are related to each other (i.e. he indicates the set P of assertions for each production of G1 derivation sequence). Thus, on the first derivation step (rule $S \rightarrow c_1[A]$) the OP assertions are *totalHeight(chair)="user input"*, *width(chair)="user input"*, *depth(chair)= "user input"* and *seatHeight(chair)= "user input"*, meaning that the referred parameters' values should be defined by the user. The only ESP assertion is *cost(chair)= quantity(seat)*cost(seat)+quantity(leg)*cost(leg)+quantity(backrest)* cost(backrest)*. On the second and third derivation steps (rule $A \rightarrow AA$) no assertions are necessary as the symbol involved has no parameters. On the fourth derivation step (rule $A \rightarrow \downarrow_2 c_2$) the EIP assertions are *width(seat)=width(chair)* and *depth(seat)=depth(chair)*, meaning that both EIP inherit their value from the chair. The OP assertions are *cost(seat)=seatCostTable[width(seat)*depth(seat)]*, and thus the cost of a seat is defined to be dependent of its dimensions, and *quantity(seat)=1*. For next step (rule $A \rightarrow \downarrow_3 c_3$) the only EIP assertion is *height(leg)=seatHeight(chair)* and the OP assertions are *cost(leg)=legCostTable[height(leg)]*, and *quantity(leg)=4*. For the last derivation step (rule $A \rightarrow \downarrow_4 c_4$) the EIP assertions are *height(backrest)=totalHeight(chair) - seatHeight(chair)* and *width(backrest)= width (chair)*, and the OP assertions are *cost(backrest)=backrestCostTable[height (backrest)*width(backrest)]*.

At this point, if the cost's tables are instantiated, G_1 is able to generate the BOM for any particular product of the chair's family. After the "user input" parameters have been instantiated (OP parameters of the chair), the automaton T (Fig. 4) starts the derivation sequence *(2,4,4,5,5,5)*, and, as the sequence proceeds, calculates all the EIP and OP (using the correspondent assertions). Then it calculates all the ESP (only one in this case: *cost(chair)*) going through the derivation sequence in the opposite direction *(5,5,5,4,4,2)* and using the correspondent assertions (note that this mechanism of going through the sequence in one and in another direction is one of the features of the attributed formal grammars, here effectively used). In other words, the client chooses the dimensions he wants for the chair (totalHeight, width, depth and seatHeight) and the system calculates the dimensions of each component (seat, leg and backrest) and the cost of the chair.

The previous example has shown that the developed grammar G_1 has achieved the intended purposes: capability to represent generic product data and to generate specific product data (only at the moment it becomes necessary).

5 Conclusions

The main objective of this work was achieved: the formalization, based on the attributed formal grammar concept, of the generic bill-of-materials (GBOM) model. The developed G_1 grammar formally describes the generic structure of the product's family, the parameters of each element of that structure (product/subassembly /component) and the relations that exist between parameters of different elements (inheritance and synthesis). The inclusion of synthesis relations is a contribution of this work as the original GBOM model does not mention them. Synthesis relations allow the modeling of situations where the value for a given parameter of a given element must be obtained from the values of parameters of other elements from lower hierarchical levels. Thus, G_1 is able to represent the GBOM for almost any family of products and to generate the BOM for any specific product of that family. Additionally, the equivalent pushdown automaton T (Fig. 4) provides a specification of the G_1 core, more close to the implementation stage. Note that neither the analysts nor the users have to know the formal grammar concept.

The developed formalization contributes to the improvement of the distributed production planning and control (PPC) model referred in the paper's introduction, because in that model there is, for each product, a direct relation between autonomous processing elements and BOM's elements.

In terms of future work the next task will be the update of the distributed PPC system's prototype (the automaton T will provide the core for the software module). However the developed formalization may also be applied to other manufacturing paradigms. Another possible improvement involves G_l itself - for now only one parameter (quantity) was associated to symbol $\downarrow_i$ (which represents the relation between component c_i and its parent). Other parameters can be added allowing G_l to deal with, for example, information about the operations necessary to assemble c_i.

References

1. Orlicky, J.A., Plossl, G.W., Wight, O.W.: Structuring the Bill-Of-Materials for MRP. Product Inventory Management 13(4) (1972)
2. Jiao, J., Tseng, M.M., Ma, Q., Zou, Y.: Generic Bill-of-Materials-and-Operations for High-Variety Production Management. Concurrent Engineering: Research and Applications 8(4), 297–322 (2000)
3. Hegge, H.M.H., Wortmann, J.C.: Generic Bill-Of-Material: a New Product Model. International Journal of Production Economics 23(1-3), 117–128 (1991)
4. Du, X., Jiao, J., Tseng, M.M.: Graph Grammar Based Product Family Modeling. Concurrent Engineering: Research and Application 10(2), 113–128 (2002)
5. Ulrich, K.: The Role of Product Architecture in the Manufacturing Firm. Research Policy 24(3), 419–440 (1995)
6. Jiao, J., Simpson, T.W., Siddique, Z.: Product Family Design and Platform-based Product Development: a State-of-the-art Review. Journal of Intelligent Manufacturing 18, 5–29 (2006)
7. Sousa, R.: Contribution to a Formal Theory of Production Systems. PhD thesis (portuguese language), Production and Systems Department, University of Minho (2003)
8. Gilmore, J.H., Pine, B.J.: The Four Faces of Mass Customization. Harvard Business Review 75(1), 32–49 (1997)
9. Mousavi, A., Adl, P., Rakowski, R.T., Gunasekaran, A.: Design of a Production Planning System Using Customer Oriented Design and Resource Utilisation (CODARU). The International Journal of Advanced Manufacturing Technology 17(11), 805–809 (2001)
10. Lima, R., Sousa, R., Martins, P.: Distributed Production Planning and Control Agent-based System. International Journal of Production Research 44, 3693–3709 (2006)
11. Lima, R., Sousa, R.: Agent-based Prototype for Interoperation of Production Planning and Control and Manufacturing Automation. In: 12th IEEE Conference on Emerging Technologies and Factory Automation (2007)
12. Denning, P.J., Dennis, J.B., Qualitz, J.E.: Machines Languages and Computation. Prentice-Hall Inc., Englewood Cliffs (1978)
13. Mikolajczak, B.: Algebraic and Structural Automata Theory. North-Holland, Amsterdam (1991)
14. Révész, G.E.: Introduction to Formal Languages. Dover Publications Inc. (1991)
15. Chomsky, N.: On Certain Properties of Grammars. Information and Control 2, 137–167 (1959)
16. Sousa, R., Putnik, G.: A Formal Theory of BM Virtual Enterprises Structures. In: Camarinha-Matos, L. (ed.) Emerging Solutions for Future Manufacturing Systems, pp. 315–322. Springer, Heidelberg (2004)

Information Flow Control for Cooperation Support in Virtual Enterprises

Peter Bertok[1], Abdelkamel Tari[2], and Saadia Kedjar[3]

[1] School of Computer Science and IT, RMIT University, Melbourne, Australia
[2] Laboratory of Applied Mathematics (LMA), University of Bejaia, Algeria
[3] Departement of Computing, University of Bejaia, Algeria

Abstract. Cooperation requires sharing data, but enforcing access restrictions across enterprises is a challenge. Different sites have different policies and use a variety of access control methods that are tailored to the individual enterprises' needs. Mapping one set of rules into another may require complex computations, possibly with a separate method for each pair of sites. This paper proposes an information flow control model for enforcing access restrictions across a virtual enterprise. Labels are assigned to data structures to ensure uniform treatment across the enterprise, and dynamic label checking provides flexibility during operation. A set of rules are presented to facilitate data manipulation so that they do not lead to information leak. The proposed solution particularly suits web-based environments and web services operations.

Keywords: Virtual enterprise, access control, information flow control.

1 Introduction

Preserving data security in a virtual enterprise is vital, as trust between the partners is limited. The loose coupling between sites facilitates cooperation, but also means that common mechanisms are kept at a minimum level and security policies of one site may be quite different from those at another site. Data needs to be exchanged and accessed at different sites for proper functioning of the virtual enterprise, but at the same time strict rules need to be enforced to prevent information leak to unauthorised entities. This paper presents a framework to share information between partners of a virtual enterprise while enforcing data security and privacy.

To facilitate integration with individual systems at virtual enterprise (VE) sites, we propose the use of role-based access control (RBAC) [9], as it is a proven method for VEs [8, 10]. By assigning access constraints to roles rather than to individuals, we can bridge the gap between different representations of actors by participants of the VE at different sites. Subjects are assigned roles before accessing objects, and the role of the subject determines the set of privileges a subject has on an object. Each object has a security label that describes its owners' access control policies with relation to reading and writing, and access restrictions are enforced by information flow control. Our model was designed primarily for web-based environments and web services.

L.M. Camarinha-Matos et al. (Eds.): PRO-VE 2009, IFIP AICT 307, pp. 581–590, 2009.

The structure of the paper is as follows. First we provide a brief description of information flow control, then we describe the basic components of our model. It is followed by the details of the model and a brief overview of the implementation, before the paper is concluded.

2 Background

2.1 Information Flow Control (IFC)

Access control mechanisms are designed to control immediate access to objects, without considering implicit information flow. For example, if user A has no read access to an object but user B has, then user B can forward the content of the object to user A, and the result is information declassification. Similarly, if A is not allowed to write the object but user B is, A can pass information to B for writing.

Information flow control (IFC) addresses such problems, as unauthorised operations can immediately be detected and declassification can be avoided. An information flow is secure if it does not lead to unauthorised disclosure or destruction of information.

Information flow control has a fairly long history. A very general treatment of information flow security models was given by McLean [6] and Millen [7]; while Wittbold and Johnson [12] applied standard information theory concepts to concrete but simple examples. Gray [5] attempted to bridge the gap between general but abstract and concrete, specific but limited solutions, and proposed a general state-machine model. Effective implementations, however, were not presented.

More recently, Tari et al [11] proposed IFC for web services. The model proposed here extends that model and has a wider scope. We also improve applicability by introducing additional operations, such as write and controlled declassification.

3 The Proposed Method

3.1 Outline

Our IFC model is based on dynamic label checking [11]. Data structures have security labels attached to them to describe data sensitivity, and data can be accessed only via special modules that use the labels to enforce access restrictions. The modules can be part of the VE infrastructure.

We propose a set of operations on the security labels, and define accessibility of results when data items are manipulated. The operations on the labels are designed to maintain security of the data items, and can be associated with any operations on the actual data itself. Our focus is on read and write operations, and we also consider controlled declassification under well-defined circumstances to help completion of operation sequences (transactions).

3.2 IFC Components

The model considers passive entities called objects that can be manipulated via different operations, and active entities called subjects who can perform those operations.

Data items are objects, and subjects can be owners, readers and writers of those objects. Each object can have a number of owners, readers and writers. An owner of an object may trust some of the other owners of the same object. Each owner can nominate readers and writers of the object, as well as potential declassification recipients. Accordingly, we define the following *sets of subjects* for each object q.

> Owner set Oq: all subjects that own this object. For example medical data owned by the patient and by doctors.

> Effective Readers set ERq: the intersection of all owners' Reader sets, i.e. subjects who have been granted read access to the object by all owners $ERq = \bigcap_{oi \in Oq} Rq,oi$

> Joint Reader set JRq: union of the Effective Reader set and all owners of the object, i.e. subjects who can read the object
> $JRq = Oq \cup ERq$

> Effective Writer set EWq: the intersection of all owners' Writer sets, i.e. subjects who have been granted write access to the object by all owners
> $EWq = \bigcap_{oi \in Oq} Wq,oi$

> Joint Writer set: union of the Effective Writer set and all owners of the object, i.e. subjects who can write the object
> $JWq = Oq \cup EWq$

> Trusted Owner TOq: an owner of the object who is trusted by at least one other owner of the object

> Effective Owner EOq: who is trusted by all other owners of the object.

> Effective declassification set for reading $EDRq$: subjects for whom reading declassification can occur $EDRq = \bigcap_{oi \in EOq} DRq,oi$

> Effective declassification set for writing $EDWq$: subjects for whom writing declassification can occur $EDWq = \bigcap_{oi \in EOq} DWq,oi$

We assign *security labels* to objects. These labels contain access control policies of all owners of the object, and they are used to control how the information contained in this object can be disseminated and modified. A label is a set of components where each component represents an owner's policy on the object.

$$L(q) = \{K_1, K_2, ..., K_i, ..., K_c\}$$

A component has six elements:

$$K = \{K_o, TO_{q,Ko}, R_{q,Ko}, W_{q,Ko}, DR_{q,Ko}, DW_{q,Ko}\}$$

where:

- K_o is an owner of object q, i.e. $K_o \in O_q$
- $TO_{q,Ko}$ is the trusted owner set defined by K_o
- $R_{q,Ko}$ is the reader set defined by K_o
- $W_{q,Ko}$ is the writer set defined by K_o

- $DR_{q,Ko}$ is declassification policy set for reading, such as

  $$DR_{q, Ko} = \{\delta_1, \delta_2, ..., \delta_p\}.$$

  Each component δ contains two parts:

  $\delta_{init} \in R_{q,o}$ the subject to whom the declassification will appear.

  $\delta_{inter} \subseteq R - R_{q,o}$ the subset of intermediate subjects (roles) that carry out the declassification, such that $\{\delta_{init}\} \cap \delta_{inter} = \varnothing$

- $DW_{q,Ko}$ is declassification policies set for writing, such as

  $$DW_{q, o} = \{\delta_1, \delta_2, ..., \delta_p\}.$$

  Each component δ contains two parts :

  $\delta_{init} \in W_{q,o}$ the role to whom the declassification will appear.

  $\delta_{inter} \subseteq R - W_{q,o}$ the subset of intermediate roles that carry out the declassification, such that $\{\delta_{init}\} \cap \delta_{inter} = \varnothing$

3.3 IFC Rules

A set of rules manage access to objects in the system and to their labels, and maintain data confidentiality and integrity. Permissions-to-roles assignments are represented by the function MapPR, its arguments being the permissions and the object.

Table 1. *Data access permissions.* Data can be accessed only by subjects who are authorized to perform the requested operation.

Rule	Interpretation
Rule 1 MapPR (read, q) = $\{r / r \in JR_q\}$	A role can read the object q if and only if the role belongs to the joint reader set of q
Rule 2 MapPR (write, q) = $\{r / r \in JW_q\}$	A role can read object q if and only if the role belongs to the joint writer set of q
Rule 3 MapPR (delete, q) = $\{r / r \in O_q \wedge |O_q| = 1\}$	A role can delete object q if and only if it is the single owner of q

Table 2. *Label access permissions.* Labels can be manipulated only by authorized subjects, who maintain the integrity of the labels and thereby the integrity of the whole system.

Rules	Interpretation
Rule 4 MapPR ({read, write, add, delete}, K. $R_{q,Ko}$) = $\{K_o\}$	Only the owner of a component in a label can read, write, add and delete an element of the reader set of that component.
Rule 5 MapPR ({read, write, add, delete}, K. $W_{q,Ko}$) = $\{K_o\}$	Only the owner of a component in a label can read, write, add and delete an element of the writer set of that component.

Table 2. (*continued*)

Rule 6 MapPR ({read, write, add, delete }, K. $TO_{q,Ko}$) = {K_o}	Only the owner of a component in a label can read, write, add and delete an element of the trusted owner set of that component.
Rule 7 MapPR ({read, write, add, delete }, K. $DR_{q,Ko}$) = {K_o}	Only the owner of a component in a label can read, write, add and delete an element of the read declassification set of that component.
Rule 8 MapPR ({read, write, add, delete }, K. $DW_{q,Ko}$) = {K_o}	Only the owner of a component in a label can read, write, add and delete an element of the write declassification set of that component.
Rule 9 MapPR (add, K.O_q) = {r / $r \in EO_q$} MapPR (delete, K. O_q.o) = {r / $r \in EO_q \wedge o \notin EO_q$}	Only the effective owners of an object can extend the set of the owners of the object and can delete an owner. The owner to be deleted must not be an effective owner.

Table 3. *Declassification rules.* These rules allow the normal execution of transactions even if an intermediate subject is not authorized to read or write an object; they can be used if and only if the initiator of this transaction is an effective reader or writer respectively.

Rules	Interpretation
Rule 10 (r_1, ε) $\in$ EDR_q $\wedge$ r_1 $\in$ ER_q $\Rightarrow$ add (ε) to ER_q	If (r_1, ε) is a component of the EDR_q set and r_1 is an effective reader, then we can add the reader set ε to the ER_q set
Rule 11 (r_1, ε) $\in$ EDW_q $\wedge$ r_1 $\in$ EW_q $\Rightarrow$ add (ε) to EW_q	If (r_1, ε) is a component of the EDW_q set and r_1 is an effective writer then we can add the writer set ε to the EW_q set

Table 4. *The rule of the safe information flow*

Rule 12	An information flow is safe, if it does not lead to information disclosure, and the confidentiality of information contained in the source object is guaranteed. In other words, the number of authorized readers will not increase as a result of the information flow. non-authorized writing an object, and the integrity of the recipient object will be maintained. This means that the number of authorized writers will not increase as a result of the information flow.

Operations on Labels. When performing operations on one or more objects, a result object with a new, derived label is produced. The operations on the labels can be associated with any operation on the objects themselves. In this section, we describe operations for deriving a new label. We define *join* operations, and introduce the operator "_" to join labels.

For all label joins, let q_1, q_2, $q_3 \in Q$, $L(q_1)$, $L(q_2)$ and $L(q_3)$ be the labels of q_1, q_2 and q_3 respectively and $L(x)$ a new label. Let us suppose that there is an operation on q_1 and q_2 that produces q_3, i.e. $q_3 = q_1 \, Op \, q_2$.

Assigning join (_^{a}). This operation is tailored to object assignment. Instead of inheriting all characteristics of one object, the result is a combination of both objects.

In the assignment operation the label of the destination object first takes over that of the destination object, and then the trusted owner, reader and read declassification sets are further enlarged, by adding effective owners, readers and read declassification sets of the source object. The write and declassification write sets are reduced in a similar fashion.

$$
\begin{aligned}
&\text{If } L(x) = L(q_1) \_^a L(q_2) \text{ then:}\\
&\quad O_x = O_{q1} \cup (O_{q2} \cap JR_{q1})\\
&\quad \forall o_i \in O_x \backslash O_{q1} \ (o_i \in O_x \text{ and } o_i \notin O_{q1}) \text{ and } \forall o_j \in O_{q1}\\
&\qquad R_{x,oi} = ER_{q1} \cup R_{q2,oi} \, ; \qquad\qquad R_{x,oj} = R_{q1,oj}\\
&\qquad W_{x,oi} = W_{q2,oi} \, ; \qquad\qquad\qquad W_{x,oj} = W_{q1,oj} \cap JW_{q2}\\
&\qquad TO_{x,oi} = EO_{q1} \cup TO_{q2,oi} \, ; \quad TO_{x,oj} = TO_{q1,oj}\\
&\qquad DR_{x,oi} = EDR_{q1} \cup DR_{q2,oi} \, ; \quad DR_{x,oj} = DR_{q1,oj}\\
&\qquad DW_{x,oi} = DW_{q2,oi} \, ; \qquad\qquad DW_{x,oj} = DW_{q1,oj} \cap EDW_{q2}\\
&\quad L(q_3) \leftarrow L(x)
\end{aligned}
$$

Restrictive join (_^{r}). This operation is appropriate when dealing with sensitive data. The resulting label will first take the properties of the source label, then the owner, reader and writer sets are reduced by removing those that do not have a similar role in the destination label. If no common owners exist, permissions are preserved through a new owner that represents the system itself.

$$
\begin{aligned}
&\text{If } L(x) = L(q1) \_^r L(q2) \text{ then:}\\
&\quad O_x = O_{q1} \cap O_{q2}\\
&\quad \text{if } O_x \neq \varnothing \text{ then } \forall o_i \in O_x\\
&\qquad R_{x,oi} = R_{q1,oi} \cap R_{q2,oi}\\
&\qquad W_{x,oi} = W_{q1,oi} \cap W_{q2,oi}\\
&\qquad TO_{x,oi} = TO_{q1,oi} \cap TO_{q2,oi}\\
&\qquad DR_{x,oi} = DR_{q1,oi} \cap DR_{q2,oi}\\
&\qquad DW_{x,oi} = DW_{q1,oi} \cap DW_{q2,oi}\\
&\quad \text{else } O_x \leftarrow System\\
&\qquad R_x = JR_{q1} \cap JR_{q2}\\
&\qquad W_x = JW_{q1} \cap JW_{q2}\\
&\qquad DR_x = EDR_{q1} \cap EDR_{q2}\\
&\qquad DW_x = EDW_{q1} \cap EDW_{q2}\\
&\quad L(q_3) \leftarrow L(x)
\end{aligned}
$$

Fusing join ($\_^f$). This join is similar to the restrictive join but is slightly less restrictive, because it keeps more owners in the new label. It calculates the label of the object containing the result of the operation as follows.

If $L(x) = L(q_1) \_^f L(q_2)$ then:
$$O_x = (O_{q1} \cup O_{q2}) \cap (JR_{q1} \cap JR_{q2})$$
$$\forall o_i \in O_x \text{ and } o_i \in O_{q1} \cap O_{q2}$$
$$R_{x,oi} = R_{q1,oi} \cap R_{q2,oi}$$
$$W_{x,oi} = W_{q1,oi} \cap W_{q2,oi}$$
$$TO_{x,oi} = TO_{q1,oi} \cap TO_{q2,oi}$$
$$DR_{x,oi} = DR_{q1,oi} \cap DR_{q2,oi}$$
$$DW_{x,oi} = DW_{q1,oi} \cap DW_{q2,oi}$$
$$L(q_3) \leftarrow L(x)$$

Declassification join ($\_^d$). During the execution of a transaction, if a step cannot be carried out because a participant does not have access to an object, the whole transaction will be aborted. Allowing the operation to proceed by temporarily declassifying the object can solve this problem, but strict rules have to be introduced to avoid total loss of security.

The proposed solution is adding an intermediate subject to the effective reader set of the requested object, if the initiator of this transaction is already an effective reader of the object. For writing, we add the intermediate subject to the effective writers, if the originator is already an effective writer. Declassification can proceed only if all effective owners agree to it by nominating subjects in their declassification sets.

When reading is performed, the declassified information must not be saved or used later. That can be ensured by setting the label of the object receiving the declassified information to empty ($\varnothing$). In case of writing, the label of the written object should not become less restrictive as a result. When the declassification read or write is finished, the intermediate principal will be removed from the effective reader or writer set respectively.

4 Implementation

4.1 Dynamic Label Checking

The labels are evaluated run-time, i.e. flow control is implemented dynamically. Object access is via special information flow control modules that check the labels of objects against the requester's credentials; no direct access is allowed. The IFC modules implement the rules and operations described above, and perform the necessary actions. The basic structure of the system is shown in Figure 1.

The system operates in conjunction with local policies that may be implemented statically. The integrated system provides uniform access to all objects. A web-based environment facilitates the deployment of IFC modules, they can be inserted between requesters and objects transparently.

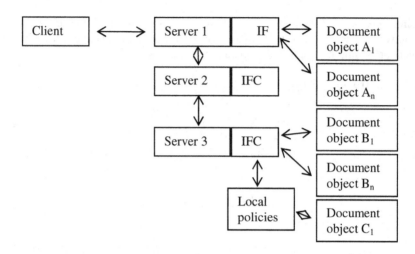

Fig. 1. System Architecture

5   Related Work

Several attempts have been made to secure documents in virtual enterprise environments. An early model suggested a federated process framework to coordinate access to shared data [1]. Cooperation on the process level enabled multiple acts, including iteration and re-attempting operations, to be conveniently performed on one hand, but resulted in a very complex system on the other.

Extending basic access control mechanisms across enterprises offered a simpler approach. An example of this is securing workflows with centrally controlled read access to documents [4]. The solution defines trusted virtual domains for individual workflows, which are under the control of a security kernel. The underlying security mechanism is encryption that provides durable protection, even in case of off-line access. A cornerstone of the method is encryption key management, but no solution is presented for that in the paper, although some notes refer to its complexity. The paper mentions that simple solutions such as key revocation or re-encryption of documents are unwieldy. More complex solutions, such a time-dependent keys or group keys are not considered in the paper, perhaps because of the computational load involved. The aims of the method are similar to ours in protecting objects (workflows) across different domains. However, our approach is more comprehensive because of introducing and handling object ownership and rights management as opposed to simple right enforcement, while we also deal with write operations not only with read.

A formal approach to the problem of authorizations in workflows for virtual enterprises was proposed in [8]. Their solution is more theoretical than that of [4], but still has the same constraints.

Object management on the virtual enterprise level requires a global approach; as an extension of local rights management may not be sufficient to address the complexities of the task. The web and its service-oriented paradigm offer a number of advantages, among them an established infrastructure with appropriate support. Such a solution utilizing role-based access control is described in [10]. It defines workspaces as online web environments shared by a cohesive set of actors, where access to information/data is controlled via services that support the business processes. Workspace membership helps the formation of communities of geographically dispersed actors, while their collaboration is controlled by the services that enforce security / confidentiality. The method complements our solution, as it provides a model for upper-level management of data sharing in a virtual enterprise, while it relies on the underlying mechanisms provided by the implementation platform to describe and enforce the security requirements.

Other high-level approaches include ontology-based knowledge sharing [2,3] that look at the assignment of user rights, and can be built on top of our model.

6 Conclusion

An information flow control model was proposed in this paper, to facilitate operations on and preserve confidentiality and integrity of objects. The model is tailored to environments where users at different sites with different access models need to work with shared, common objects.

The solution is based on security labels attached to objects. Owners of objects can nominate readers, writers of their objects, as well as express their consent to declassify the objects to specific subjects. Each owner also has a list of other owners of the object whom they trust.

We defined operations on labels, which can be associated with different procedures on the objects themselves, for example assignment and merging. Specific label operations also permit limited declassification of objects under controlled circumstances. The operations have been proven to preserve object security; however, space limitations do not allow the inclusion of proofs here.

References

1. Bae, K., Kim, J., Huh, S.: Federated process framework in a virtual enterprise using an object-oriented database and extensible markup language. Journal of Database Management (January 2003),
   http://www.accessmylibrary.com/coms2/
   summary_0286-22108914_ITM
2. Chen, T.Y., Chen, Y.M., Chu, H.C., Chen, C.C.: Knowledge access control policy language model for virtual enterprises. In: IEEE International Conference on Industrial Engineering and Engineering Management, December 2-4, pp. 1903–1907 (2007)
3. Chen, T.Y.: Knowledge sharing in virtual enterprises via an ontology-based access control approach. Computers in Industry 59, 502–519 (2008)
4. Gasmi, Y., Sadeghi, A., Stewin, P., Unger, M., Winandy, M., Husseiki, R., Stüble, C.: Flexible and Secure Enterprise Rights Management Based on Trusted Virtual Domains. In: ACM STC 2008, Fairfax, VA (2008)
5. Gray III, J.W.: Toward a Mathematical Foundation for Information Flow Security. In: IEEE Symposium on Security and Privacy, pp. 21–35 (1991)
6. McLean, J.: Security Models and Information Flow. In: IEEE Symposium on Security and Privacy, pp. 180–189 (1990)

7. Millen, J.K.: Covert channels capacity. In: Proceedings of the 1987 IEEE Computer Society Symposium on Security and Privacy, Oakland, CA (1987)
8. Qing, L., Huan, Z.: Research on Dynamic Authorization in Workflow of Virtual Enterprise. In: International Conference on Wireless Communications, Networking and Mobile Computing, WiCom 2007, September 21-25, pp. 6068–6070 (2007)
9. Osborn, S., Sandhu, R., Munawer, Q.: Configuring role-based access control to enforce mandatory and discretionary access control policies. ACM Transactions on Information and System Security (TISSEC) 3(2), 85–106 (2000)
10. Rezgui, Y.: Role-based Service Oriented implementation of a Virtual Enterprise: a Case Study in the Construction Sector. Computers in Industry 58, 74–86 (2007)
11. Tari, Z., Bertok, P., Simic, D.: A Dynamic Label Checking Approach for Information Flow Control in Web Services. International Journal of Web Services 1, 1–28 (2006)
12. Wittbold, J.T., Johnson, D.M.: Information flow in nondeterministic systems. In: Proceedings of the 1990 IEEE Computer Society Symposium on Security and Privacy, Oakland, CA (1990)

ICoNOs MM: The IT-Enabled Collaborative Networked Organizations Maturity Model

Roberto Santana Tapia*

Department of Computer Science
University of Twente
P.O. Box 217, 7500 AE Enschede, The Netherlands
r.santanatapia@utwente.nl

Abstract. The focus of this paper is to introduce a comprehensive model for assessing and improving maturity of business-IT alignment (B-ITa) in collaborative networked organizations (CNOs): the ICoNOs MM. This two dimensional maturity model (MM) addresses five levels of maturity as well as four domains to which these levels apply: partnering structure, information system (IS) architecture, process architecture and coordination. The model can be used to benchmark and support continuous improvement of B-ITa process areas in CNOs.

1 Introduction

B-ITa has been a concern in practice for several decades and has been studied by researchers for more than 15 years [1]. However, despite years of research, B-ITa still ranks as a major modern-day area of concern for both business practitioners and researchers. Interest in B-ITa is stimulated by cases of organizations that have successfully aligned their IT to gain competitive advantage [2, 3] and to improve organizational performance [4].

There is a considerable literature on B-ITa in single organizations. Within this broad scope of literature, a number of authors have stressed the importance to assess B-ITa in order to plan B-ITa improvement actions [5, 6, 7, 8]. In support of this, these authors have developed MMs. MMs describe the development of a specific domain over time. Based on maturity assessments, organizations know whether a specific area is sufficiently refined and documented so that the activities in such area now have the potential to achieve its desired outcomes.

However, B-ITa in CNOs has hardly been studied. Yet, the problem is important because improved B-ITa entails a more efficient use of IT in the CNOs supporting the integration of ISs and processes across organizational boundaries. CNOs form the core of a new discipline [9] that focuses on the structure, behavior, and dynamics of networks of independent organizations that collaborate to better achieve common goals. We define a CNO to be any "mix-and-match" network of profit-and-loss responsible organizational units, or of independent organizations, connected by IT, that

---

* Supported by the Netherlands Organization for Scientific Research under contract number 638.003.407 (Value-Based Business-IT Alignment).

L.M. Camarinha-Matos et al. (Eds.): PRO-VE 2009, IFIP AICT 307, pp. 591–599, 2009.

work together to jointly accomplish tasks, reach common goals and serve customers over a period of time [10].

In several case studies [11, 12, 13, 14], we have witnessed that achieving B-ITa in CNOs is more complex than in single organizations because in such settings, B-ITa is driven by goals of different independent organizations commonly with no centralized decision-making processes. In our research, we have developed a MM that specifically addresses the processes needed for achieving alignment between business and IT in CNOs: the ICoNOs MM. This MM presents a roll up of recommendations – e.g., coordination mechanisms, implementation strategies and organizational changes, in the form of process areas, specific goals and specific practices. The ICoNOs MM has been designed and validated based on results of conceptual and empirical research activities. These research activities, and their results, have been progressively made public in several publications as presented in Table 1.

Table 1. Research activities and publications

	Activity	Publication
Goals and research approach		[15]
Initial attempts to identify the domains	Focus group	[16]
	Case study	
MM design challenges and solutions	Literature survey	[17]
Domains validation and B-ITa principles	Case studies	[11, 12]
First version of the process areas	Literature survey	[18]
Process areas validation and B-ITa best practices	Case study	[13, 14]
Specific goals and practices of the partnering structure and the coordination domains		[19]

2 Model Dimensions

The ICoNOs MM is two-dimensional: the first dimension represents the number of discrete levels of maturity, whereas the second dimension represents the domains to which the levels apply. Domains are sets of process areas that share common knowledge of aspects within the scope of the MM (in our case, a domain is a group of processes which need to be performed by CNOs in their efforts for improving B-ITa – we call them 'B-ITa domains').

2.1 The B-ITa Levels

To maintain adherence to the CMMI (http://www.sei.cmu.edu/cmmi/), which is an internationally well-known MM, we decided to base the levels of the ICoNOs MM on it. Since our MM is a continuous MM in architecture [17], it is expected that our model incorporates six levels of maturity – as the CMMI does in its continuous representation. However, because we want to offer a roadmap to approach B-ITa process improvement (i.e., series of maturity levels) focusing on a set of B-ITa process areas that provide CNOs with specific practices characterized by each maturity level, we decided to include only five levels of maturity in the ICoNOs MM (as in the staged representation of the CMMI). That is, when using the ICoNOs MM, process improvement results are summarized in a single maturity level number in each of the B-ITa domains that the model includes. In our model, levels are used to describe an improvement path recommended for a CNO that wants to improve processes to achieve B-ITa. To reach a particular level, a CNO must satisfy all the set of process areas that are targeted for improvement in a particular B-ITa domain. The levels are:

- **Level 1: Incomplete.** At maturity level 1, processes related to a particular B-ITa domain are usually not performed or partially performed. It means such a particular domain is not explicitly considered when a CNO strives for B-ITa. Therefore, this level contains no processes in the ICoNOs MM.
- **Level 2: Isolated.** At maturity level 2, processes are the basic infrastructure in place to support a particular B-ITa domain. They (i) are planned and executed in accordance with a policy; (ii) employ skilled people who have adequate resources to produce controlled outputs; (iii) are monitored, controlled, and reviewed. However, such processes are isolated initiatives that are not managed from the entire CNO perspective.
- **Level 3: Standardized.** At maturity level 3, processes are directed to make improvements in the standardization and management of a particular B-ITa domain. Processes are performed from a CNO perspective (i.e., they are cooperative initiatives). They are well characterized and understood, and are described in standards, procedures, tools, and methods.
- **Level 4: Quantitatively Managed.** At maturity level 4, processes use statistical and other quantitative techniques. Quantitative objectives for quality and process performance are established and used as criteria in managing the process. Quality and process performance is understood in statistical terms and is managed throughout the life of the process.
- **Level 5: Optimized.** At maturity level 5, processes are improved based on an understanding of the common causes of variations inherent in the process. The focus of an optimized process is on continuously optimizing the range of process performance through both incremental and innovative improvements.

2.2 The B-ITa Domains

After conducting case studies in real-life CNOs to identify and validate the B-ITa domains, the ICoNOs MM includes the following four B-ITa domains:

Partnering structure, defined as the cross-organizational work division, organizational structure, and roles and responsibilities definition that indicate where and how the work gets done and who is involved. It helps to organize the collaborative work in the CNO.

IS architecture, defined as the fundamental organization of the information management function of the participating organizations embodied in the information systems, i.e., software applications, that realize this function, their relationships to each other and to the environment, and the principles guiding its design and evolution – based on IEEE 1471 [20]. It must be noted that, in our work, we distinguish IS architecture from IT architecture. For us, IT architecture consists of the (i) the implementation platform, i.e., the collection of standard general-purpose software needed to run the IS architecture. It ranges from operating systems, middleware, network software to database management software; and the (ii) physical network, i.e., the physical resources that run software applications. This includes computers, cables, and user interface devices to support the running of the IS architecture.

Process architecture, defined as the choreography of all processes needed to reach the shared goals of the participating organizations. These processes are both primary business processes of the CNO and processes needed for information exchange.

Coordination, defined as the mechanisms to manage the interaction and work among the participating organizations taking into account the dependencies and the shared resources among the processes.

Talking about B-ITa commonly leads one to think in aspects related to technology (IS architecture) and processes (process architecture). However, this is a misunderstanding when talking about B-ITa in CNOs. In collaborative B-ITa projects, beside those 'easily perceived' aspects, coordination and partnering structure are vital for assuring the success of such projects [19]. These two B-ITa domains are general domains in the sense that they are not directly related to B-ITa but they help to create an environment where B-ITa improvements can be easily achieved. If coordination and partnering structure are not considered in collaborative B-ITa projects, B-ITa efforts could turn more complex than they already are. In our case studies, we have found that these two domains affect B-ITa in CNOs. The case of IBM and its joint development alliance consortium (which includes Siemens, Samsung, Infineon, and STMicroelectronics), to develop semiconductor technologies (http://www.ibm.com), also supports our findings. As consortia often do it, this consortium conceded to one participating organization (IBM) the right to organize the consortium and to determine the behaviors of the other participants within a given context to coordinate their actions, to speak on everybody's behalf and to exert leadership, i.e., to use authority.

3   The ICoNOs MM

Table 2 presents the ICoNOs MM. The first column in the table represents the B-ITa levels. The cells of the ICoNOs MM contain B-ITa process areas grouped in domains. A process area is a group of practices in a domain which, when implemented collectively, satisfy goals considered important for making an improvement in that domain (e.g., a process area in the IS architecture domain is 'IS portfolio management'). We make the explicit note that, when finalizing the development of the ICoNOs MM, we have changed the position of some of the process areas presented in the previous version of the MM [18]. We found that some of the process areas are strongly related to each other. We then decided to re-arrange de position of them, so that some of the original process areas are now goals of, or practices in, another process area.

Similarly to CMMI, these process areas have specific and generic goals, which the activities in each process area are supposed to achieve. Specific goals describe characteristics that must be present to satisfy a particular process area. That is, they are specific for this area. In contrast, generic goals apply to all process areas, although their instantiation for each process area can differ. For example, a CMMI generic goal is

Table 2. The ICoNOs MM

	Partnering structure		IS architecture	
5			Inter-organizational IS arch. optimization	IoAO
			Risk analysis and mitigation	RAM
4	Metric-based roles exploration	MRE	Quantitative IS portfolio management	QPM
3	Governance structure and compliance	GSC	IS requirements management	IsRM
	Service level agreements definition	SLA	IS capabilities definition	IsCD
			IS portfolio management	IsPM
2	Business model definition	BMD	Current IS architecture description	CSA
1				

	Process architecture		Coordination	
5	Inter-organizational process optimization	IoPO		
4	Organizational process performance	OPP	Quantitative coordination relation analysis	QRA
	Event logs formal consistency	EFC		
3	Organizational process focus planning	PFP	Standardization	STD
	Target process architecture formulation	TPA	Communication-oriented coordination	COC
2	Current process architecture description	CPD	Informal communication adjustment	InCA
			Direct supervision	DTS
1				

'the process is institutionalized as a defined process'. This goal can be applied to all processes. Our ICoNOs MM incorporates the generic goals of CMMI and, therefore, we do not elaborate on them. The specific and generic goals are respectively decomposed in specific and generic practices. Practices describe what a CNO may implement to achieve the goals. These practices are expected and not mandatory. This means that one can implement alternative practices in substitution for the specific and generic practices that the MM includes. The only condition is that the goals must be satisfied, to perform a process, to reach a specific maturity level.

We conducted an exhaustive literature review in order to define the specific goals and the specific practices for each of the B-ITa process areas. However, due to space constraints, in this section, we only list the specific goals and the specific practices of the B-ITa process areas included in the domains of IS architecture and process architecture. The list of specific goals and specific practices of the other two domains can be found in [19]. We only introduce the specific goals and specific practices included in levels two and three because in these levels is where CNOs can make the most significant improvements. In the following, the acronyms SG and SP stand for specific goal and specific practice, respectively.

- **Current IS architecture description (CSA).** The main purpose of the CSA is to create a snapshot of the existing ISs and data, assessing what the current status of the CNO is concerning ISs.

    SG1 Characterize the existing software applications.
    SP1.1 Make an inventory of the current ISs of the entire CNO.
    SP1.2 Describe what the ISs do (not how they do it) and their status.

SG2 Build the software application model.
　SP2.1 Define the stakeholders (owners/users) of the ISs.
　SP2.2 Identify the organizational units supported.
　SP2.3 Identify the processes supported.
　SP2.4 Illustrate how data flows throughout the ISs.
　SP2.5 Describe the precedent and successor ISs.
SG3 Define the IS standards and principles.

- **IS capabilities definition (IsCD).** The main purpose of the IsCD is to define the ability of the CNO to operate efficiently by using ISs to achieve congruence with the business environment where it works and to improve its performance.

  SG1 Analyze the IT and business skills of the participants in the CNO.
  SG2 Identify the motivating values of the participants.
  SG3 Define the IS capabilities of the CNO considering the previous two SGs.

- **IS portfolio management (IsPM).** The main purpose of the IsPM is to create the right mix of ISs investments to properly use limited resources while providing the maximum business benefit.

  SG1 Define the target IS architecture.
  　SP1.1 Identify improvements and adjustments based on the requirements.
  　SP1.2 Build the target IS model.
  　SP1.3 Verify and validate the target IS architecture (gap analysis).
  　SP1.4 Define the new investments on ISs.
  SG2 Define insights and facts for decision making.
  　SP2.1 Define key application metrics.
  　SP2.2 Conduct risk analysis.
  SG3 Develop a plan to obtain all participants' buy-in.

- **IS requirements management (IsRM).** The main purpose of the IsRM is to manage the changing IS requirements during their engineering process and the development of the required ISs.

  SG1 Obtain an understanding of IS requirements.
  　SP1.1 Identify and record requirements.
  　SP1.2 Assess the impact of requirements.
  　SP1.3 Determine requirements priorities.
  SG2 Obtain commitment to requirements of all participants.
  SG3 Define policies for requirements management.
  SG4 Use a database to manage requirements.

- **Current process architecture description (CPD).** The main purpose of the CPD is to create a snapshot of the existing processes, and maintaining a repository of measures and assets.

  SG1 Characterize the existing processes.
  　SP1.1 Make an inventory of the current relevant processes.
  　SP1.2 Build a process model.

SG2 Establish the CNO's measurement repository.
    SP2.1 Determine the needs for storing, retrieving and analyzing measurements.
    SP2.2 Define and agree upon a common set of process measures.
    SP2.3 Design and implement the measurement repository.
    SP2.4 Make the contents of the repository available for use by the CNO.
SG3 Establish the CNO's process asset library.
    SP3.1 Design and implement the organization's process asset library.
    SP3.2 Specify the criteria for including items in the library.
    SP3.3 Specify the procedures for storing and retrieving items.
    SP3.4 Have the selected items entered into the library.
    SP3.5 Make the items available for use by the CNO.

- **Organizational process focus planning (PFP).** The main purpose of the PFP is to plan, implement, and deploy process improvements based on the strengths and weaknesses of the CNO's processes and assets.

    SG1 Determine process improvement opportunities.
        SP1.1 Establish the CNO process needs.
        SP1.2 Appraise the CNO's processes.
        SP1.3 Identify the CNO's process improvements.
    SG2 Plan and implement process improvements.
        SP2.1 Establish process action plans.
        SP2.2 Implement process action plans.
    SG3 Deploy CNO process assets and incorporate lessons learnt.
        SP3.1 Deploy CNO process assets.
        SP3.2 Monitor implementation.
        SP3.3 Incorporate lessons learnt into the CNO process assets.

- **Target process architecture formulation (TPA).** The main purpose of the TPA is to evaluate, select and design processes needed to support the desired to-be state of the process architecture.

    SG1 Establish general tailoring guidelines.
    SG2 Identify external interfaces.
    SG3 Gather information about services/products offerings.
    SG4 Define the mayor activities to support the services/products offerings.
    SG5 Build a target process model.

4 Conclusion

In this paper, we have presented a MM for assessing the maturity of B-ITa in CNOs: the ICoNOs MM. This model is a promising attempt to properly understand the B-ITa domains involved in collaborative B-ITa in terms of process maturity.

Although the ICoNOs MM is almost finalized, we stress that the model needs to be further revised, and eventually modified. At this moment, we have finalized a pilot assessment in a CNO composed by three Dutch universities, where we used the ICoNOs MM to appraise the maturity of its B-ITa. After the assessment, we asked to the participants in the CNO how they perceived the assessment process, the model, and the results. This is helping us to prove the usability of the ICoNOs MM in a real-life context, and to eventually produce an improved version of the model.

References

1. Chan, Y., Reich, B.: IT alignment: What have we learned? Journal of Inf. Tech. 22(4), 297–315 (2007)
2. Kearns, G.S., Lederer, A.L.: The effect of strategic alignment on the use of IS-based resources for competitive advantage. Journal of Strategic Inf. Systems 9(4), 265–293 (2000)
3. Powell, T.: Organizational alignment as competitive advantage. Strategic Management Journal 13(2), 119–134 (1992)
4. Floyd, S.W., Wooldridge, B.: Path analysis of the relationship between competitive strategy, information technology, and financial performance. Journal of Mngmt. Inf. Systs. 7(1), 47–64 (1990)
5. de Koning, D., van der Marck, P.: IT Zonder Hoofdpijn: Een Leidraad voor het Verbeteren van de Bedrijfsprestaties. Prentice Hall, Englewood Cliffs (2002) (in Dutch)
6. Duffy, J.: Maturity models: Blueprints for e-volution. Strategy & Leadership 29(6), 19–26 (2001)
7. Luftman, J.N.: Assessing IT-business alignment. Inf. Systems. Mngmt. 20(4), 9–15 (2003)
8. Sanchez Ortiz, A.: Testing a model of the relationships among organizational performance, IT-business alignment and IT governance. PhD thesis, University of North Texas, Denton, Texas, USA (2003)
9. Camarinha-Matos, L.M., Afsarmanesh, H.: The emerging discipline of collaborative networks. In: Virtual Enterprises and Collaborative Networks. Kluwer Academic Pub., Dordrecht (2004)
10. Santana Tapia, R.: What is a networked business? Technical Report TR-CTIT-06-23a, University of Twente, Enschede, The Netherlands (2006)
11. Santana Tapia, R., van Eck, P., Daneva, M.: Validating the domains of an interorganizational business-IT alignment assessment instrument. Technical Report TR-CTIT-08-53 University of Twente, Enschede, The Netherlands (2008)
12. Santana Tapia, R., Daneva, M., van Eck, P., Castro Cárdenas, N., van Oene, L.: Business-IT alignment domains and principles for networked organizations: A qualitative multiple case study. In: OTM 2008, Part II, pp. 241–252. Springer, Heidelberg (2008)
13. Santana Tapia, R., van Oene, L.: Some empirical evidence on business-IT alignment processes in the public sector: A case study report. Technical Report TR-CTIT-08-46 University of Twente, Enschede, The Netherlands (2008)
14. Santana Tapia, R.: Converging on business-IT alignment best practices: Lessons learned from a Dutch cross-governmental partnership. To appear in the 15th International Conference on Concurrent Enterprising (2009)
15. Santana Tapia, R.: A value-based maturity model for IT alignment in networked businesses. In: Workshops and Doctoral Consortium of the 18th Int. Conf. on Advanced Information Systems Engineering (CAISE 2006), pp. 1201–1208. Presses Universitaires de Namur (2006)

16. Santana Tapia, R., Daneva, M., van Eck, P.: Validating adequacy and suitability of business-IT alignment criteria in an inter-enterprise maturity model. In: The 11th IEEE Int. EDOC Enterprise Computing Conference, pp. 202–213. IEEE Computer Society Press, Los Alamitos (2007)
17. Santana Tapia, R., Daneva, M., van Eck, P.: Developing an inter-enterprise alignment maturity model: Research challenges and solutions. In: The 1st International Conference on Research Challenges on Information Science (RCIS 2007), pp. 51–59 (2007)
18. Santana Tapia, R., Daneva, M., van Eck, P., Wieringa, R.: Towards a business-IT alignment maturity model for collaborative networked organizations. In: The International Workshop on Enterprise Interoperability (IWEI 2008), CTIT, pp. 70–81 (2008)
19. Santana Tapia, R.: Coordination and partnering structure are vital domains in collaborative business-IT alignment: Elaborating on the ICoNOs MM. To appear in the 2009 IFIP/IEEE International Symposium on Integrated Network Mngmt. – Workshops Proceedings (2009)
20. Maier, M.W., Emery, D., Hilliard, R.: Software architecture: Introducing IEEE standard 1471. Computer 34(4), 107–109 (2001)

Part 19

Socio-technical Issues in Collaboration

A Socio-technical Approach for
Transient SME Alliances

Yacine Rezgui

School of Engineering, Cardiff University, Queen's Buildings,
The Parade, Cardiff CF24 3AA, Wales, UK
RezguiY@cardiff.ac.uk

Abstract. The paper discusses technical requirements to promote the adoption of alliance modes of operation by SMEs in the construction sector. These requirements have provided a basis for specifying a set of functionality to support the collaboration and cooperation needs of SMEs. While service-oriented architectures and semantic web services provide the middleware technology to implement the identified functionality, a number of key technical limitations have been identified, including lack of support for the dynamic and non-functional characteristics of SME alliances distributed business processes, lack of execution monitoring functionality to manage running business processes, and lack of support for semantic reasoning to enable SME business process service composition. The paper examines these issues and provides key directions for supporting SME alliances effectively.

Keywords: SME, Alliance, Construction, Service Oriented Architecture.

1 Introduction

The past two decades have seen a change in all industries and businesses from organizations that are rigid to a more sub-contracting and partnering way of working, with a strong tendency to outsource production and ideas development [1,2]. In this context, Construction SMEs face a number of challenging issues [3, 2]:

- They tend to follow conventional business models that provide traditional products and services against cost competitiveness. There is little room for value added business services that differentiate SMEs.
- They are small independent organizations but many are highly dependent on larger industry players for their work. This can disadvantage SMEs since they can be regarded as only "piece-workers" to do tasks with little opportunity to add value.
- They tend only to be present in a project during their part of the activity and this discontinuity of involvement is a particular challenge for the industry in relation to the adoption of the right business models and modes of project operation.

The paper argues that the adoption of alliance modes of operations would (a) help create opportunities that are not found in traditional organizations; and (b) promote innovation with the potential for SMEs to respond to complex business environments.

L.M. Camarinha-Matos et al. (Eds.): PRO-VE 2009, IFIP AICT 307, pp. 603–613, 2009.

While the technological infrastructure necessary to support virtual business operations is now readily available [4, 5, 6, 7], the paper argues that SMEs require collaborative solutions sensitive to socio-cultural and organizational issues that underpin long-term ventures. This forms the research gap that the present paper is addressing.

First, the paper reviews current developments in virtual teams, service-oriented architectures, and collaborative solutions in the construction sector. The specification of the technological solution to support SME alliances is then given. This is followed by a discussion of existing limitations that hinder full adoption of the proposed service-oriented solution. Finally, recommendations for future work are given.

2 Related Work

A number of concepts related to virtual teams have been reported in the literature, including: Virtual Enterprise (VE), virtual corporation, virtual organization, and alliance. While virtual organization and virtual corporation tend to refer to the same concept [7], Goranson [8] draws important differences between the virtual enterprise and virtual organization (or corporation), noting that the term 'corporation' suggests that there is an inherent vision of corporate identity. Enterprise conveys the meaning that the shared focus is the project at hand. Corporation implies a conventional organization whose control is centralized. Hence, the virtual enterprise is unified by its mission and distributed goals, not its control system [7]. An alliance sits in between a virtual enterprise and a virtual organization, as it has a corporate dimension but resembles the virtual enterprise in the way business is conducted.

Alliance arrangements rely on team working. A team is defined by (a) its unity of purpose, (b) its identity as a social structure, and (c) its members' shared responsibility for outcomes [4]. The distinctive characteristics of virtual teams include the fact that they are geographically, organizationally, and /or time, dispersed collections of individuals who rely primarily on ICTs to accomplish one or more organizational tasks [5]. They tend to be assembled to respond to specific business needs or customer demands [6].

Moreover, an alliance is defined as a grouping of partners built around a number of principles underpinned by the following key features [9]:

- A business model that provides sound controls whilst facilitating flexibility and innovation at the appropriate times. Legal, contractual and cultural diversity issues taken fully into account.
- A set of clearly defined but customizable roles.
- A total lifecycle process driven philosophy where the intervention of each SME in the alliance complements and provides added value across the supply chain while delivering customized services and / or products to customers' and clients'.
- A performance driven and environmental friendly approach to addressing clients' and customers' requirements.
- Technology and ICT mechanisms, underpinned by a sound legal and contractual framework, to support the operation and collaboration needs of the alliance (though appropriate to alliance, partner and project circumstances and needs).

Rezgui and Miles [9] argue that an alliance of independent peer organizations requires a "management" hub through an alliance broker. This would ensure (a) co-ordination of alliance strategic direction, (b) marketing the alliance, (c) handling contractual and advising on legal issues, (d) negotiating common resources (e.g. insurance and equipment), and (e) managing business opportunities. The latter is initially a bridge-head to customers that enquire but becomes the communication channel between the alliance and the appropriate partners for the particular opportunity, including their selection from the cluster of partners in the alliance. It is perceived as a brokering role. The broker will ensure that an integrated approach to addressing construction industry key challenges, including energy savings, is adopted. Such an approach co-ordinates technical and policy solutions, integrating engineering approaches with architecture, considering design decisions within the realities of building operation.

From a technological (software) perspective, the involvement in long-term partnerships with other SMEs in the context of alliances requires a shift from a software focused integration approach to a total lifecycle process integration philosophy where data / information / knowledge flows seamlessly. In this context, SMEs require focused, pragmatic, and easy to use solutions. Existing solutions tend to be technology (ICT) driven and are less sensitive to the socio-cultural and organizational issues that underpin long-term collaborative ventures.

SME characteristics and needs have to be factored into any collaborative platform for the concept of alliance to work. This platform must be able to transcend traditional methods based mainly on stable / static business models to facilitate dynamic alliances. Hence, there is a need to develop collaborative solutions addressing the needs of long-lasting alliances as opposed to existing solutions that suit the needs of large organizations collaborating with sub-contractors. Obviously, the two approaches are not mutually exclusive, but the former needs to be more sensitive to SME needs. A detailed discussion of SME socio-technical needs can be found in [9].

Web services have emerged as the most promising technology to provide the middleware platform to support effectively complex business operations [10, 11, 12, 13]. For many years, the goal towards which much research effort has been directed, concerns Service-oriented process implementations (or their ICT equivalent - business oriented service orchestrations) [14, 15] being able to transparently adapt to environment changes, including customer requirements, with minimal user intervention. As Leymann [16] notes, in current approaches, business process planning and implementation takes place during design-time when the architecture and the design of the software system are planned. The components to be used are chosen, linked together, and finally compiled and deployed. This approach is effectively the current state of the art in web services business process modeling practice and is successfully used and as long as the web service environment (business partners and service components) does not, or only rarely, changes.

However, if other businesses provide newer services, or other services replace older services, it is likely that inconsistencies may occur. In this case, an inevitable consequence is that the software architecture must be changed in order to accommodate new services (and their bindings to other services) or in the worst case, the process definition and design of the system needs to be changed. In fact, ACID (atomicity, consistency, integrity, and durability) properties of web service transactions are difficult to ensure [17]. In this context, static composition of services may be seen as restrictive, as components should ideally be able to automatically adapt to this kind of unpredictable change.

3 Functionality Specification for Transient SME Alliances

Based on the above, a number of technical and process requirements have been identified to support SME alliances [9]. Three categories of functionality emerge (Figure 1), namely:

Functionality to support alliance operations management:

> ➢ Alliance formation and membership management: SME member identification, registration, profile definition, and membership validation / acceptance and management.
> ➢ Alliance nurturing and long-term management: functionality to support social networking within the alliance, promoting trust and shared responsibility management, supporting negotiation and conflict resolution, and functionality to support financial incentives and reward management.
> ➢ Alliance creation and operations management: functionality for roles and responsibilities such as participation in decision-making, SME safeguards regarding information & knowledge, resource scheduling in an alliance, and arrangements for cost-effective software use in SME alliances.

Functionality to support alliance business management:

> ➢ Customer relationship management: integrated, socially-oriented approach to managing customers.
> ➢ Business Opportunity Management: functionality to exploit business niches in the surrounding local, regional, and international business environment, and identify / nurture business opportunities.
> ➢ Alliance branding and marketing: functionality to sustain a vibrant and positive (with a focus on sustainability and social corporate responsibility issues) outfacing image of the alliance.
> ➢ Broker / Customer management: functionality supporting the SME Broker in channels of communication inside the alliance Virtual Factory and outside to customers, regulators, suppliers etc.

Functionality to support Alliance Capability, Learning, and Innovation Management

> ➢ Functionality to support and nurture knowledge sharing and creation, including best practice.
> ➢ Functionality to support awareness raising through push and / or pull mechanisms (dissemination / advertisement / broadcasting of SME information days, brochures, newsletters, etc.).
> ➢ Innovation management environments including legal, IPR, contractual and cultural diversity issues.
> ➢ Functionality to identify SME Learning and Training needs.
> ➢ Functionality for SME learning and training needs learning / training modules definition.

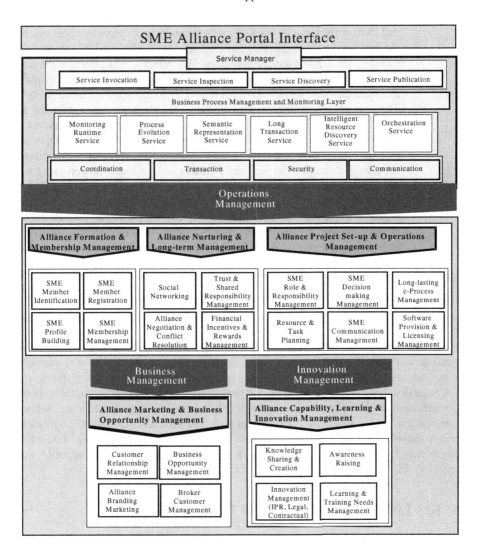

Fig. 1. The SME Alliance Portal Architecture

The proposed functionality is delivered using a service-oriented architecture. This is based on a set of loosely coupled components available as services, delivered using an Application Service Provider (ASP) like model [15]. Two main roles emerge in this model:

> ➤ Alliance ePlatform Infrastructure Provider and Manager (Alliance ASP): This has the responsibility of managing the service infrastructure (e.g. servers, computer resources, etc.) and allocating shared workspace environments to potential Alliance clients to host their projects. This involves hosting the core infrastructure through the provision of and access to both core services

and third party services (TPS). Core services refer to services necessary for the basic operation and management of services, including TPS that are provided by third party service providers. The Alliance ASP, through the core services, has the capability to host multiple alliance projects and to make available different services (both core and TPS) to various alliance projects. They can also play the role of application integrators, providing help and assistance to migrate legacy applications and legacy systems to web services.

> Third party service providers (TPSP): These represent various companies, including software houses, interested in making their software application(s) accessible through a service-based middleware solution hosted and managed by the Alliance ASP. These companies have their services published within the ASP UDDI (Universal Description, Discovery, and Integration) registry. Typically, these services would fulfill a particular purpose for an alliance project. Examples of services offered by TPSP include structural dimensioning services, HVAC simulation service, procurement service, and facility management (FM) service.

However, a number of key issues emerge from the literature as essential to support effectively web services, including: Coordination (to manage interaction between services and coordination of sequences of operations, to ensure correctness and consistency); Transaction (to manage short-duration / atomic and long running business activities); Context (to adjust execution and output to provide the client with a customized and personalized behavior: may contain information such as a consumer's name, address, and current location, the type of client device, including hard- and software that the consumer is using, or preferences regarding the communication); Conversation modeling (to facilitate service discovery and dynamic binding, service composition model validation, service composition skeleton generation, analysis of compositions and conversations and conversation model generation); Execution monitoring (involves either centralized or distributed execution of composite web services). These limitations are discussed in the following section.

4   Key Limitations and Proposed Research Directions

Existing web service technology is ill suited to support the dynamic and changing nature of service environments. Key limitations emerge and have been reported, which hinder full exploitation of web services as a promising middleware technology, including:

- Existing service description and Web Service flow languages do not support effectively the dynamics and non-functional characteristics of distributed business processes. The current Business Process Execution Language (BPEL) version as described in [16] does not support run-time alterations to address unforeseen problems, such as the replacement or addition of a Web Service. In order to manage this uncertainty, BPEL processes need to have the ability to be extended to meet unforeseen post-deployment requirements and user needs.

- Web service flow engines, such as the ones implemented to support BPEL, lack execution monitoring functionality to manage the running process. These can help debug processes during development stage, with monitoring, and may even be driven by agents at production stage. It is possible, for example, to embed, without modifying the engine implementation, a planner on the top of the latter. From events triggered by a monitor, this planner can take actions to avoid any disruption and to adjust the process. Such a tool can be useful particularly for long running processes.
- Web service composition methodologies have a focus on syntactic integration and therefore do not support automatic composition of web services. Semantic integration is crucial for web services as it allows them to (a) represent and reason about the task that a web service performs, (b) explicitly express and reason about business relations and rules, (c) understand the meaning of exchanged messages, (d) represent and reason about preconditions that are required to use the service and the effects of having invoked the service, and (e) allow intelligent composition of web services to achieve a more complex service.

The following sub-sections discuss potential research directions, with a focus on (a) business process description and management, (b) service discovery, (c) service composition, (d) service semantic compatibility management.

4.1 Business Process Description and Management

From a practice (industry) perspective, business processes are modeled as one-off exercise and assume that processes are static. If the requirements of the process change, then the entire specification is updated. The available business process description languages, such as BPEL, allow programmers to describe and implement complex web services as distributed processes and to compose them in a general way. However, the definition of new processes that interact with existing ones must be done manually, and this can be a technically demanding, time consuming, and error prone task. Additionally, in the current BPEL environment it is not possible at runtime, to add an unforeseen web service into the process, to replace Web services, or to hot-fix processes. The process needs to be stopped in order that it can be updated / extended.

4.2 Service Discovery

Mechanisms to easily locate services which meet the process requirements are necessary for both the service provider and the service requester. On the one hand, from the service provider standpoint, improved service reachability implies higher service use potential. On the other hand, the service requester needs to be able to find the most suitable services with respect to existing requirements. Publication, discovery and selection are based on a Service Directory, such as Universal Discovery Description and Integration [17]. The role of such a tool is to provide methods, which (a) can be used by the service provider to publish the provided services and (b) can be used by the service requester to look for the services, which satisfy his requirements.

However, even if UDDI allows browsing of the service registry through different indexes, it does not provide:

> an effective content-based service discovery
> a match with respect to the context in which the service operates
> a quality evaluation of the retrieved services

4.3 Service Composition

There are theoretically two main paradigms which can be used to model business processes or build workflows by means of web services. These are either manual or automatic composition. In the manual approach, human users who know the domain well (e.g., domain ontology) select suitable web services and assemble them into a cohesive workflow. Although users may use graphical user interface based software to facilitate the composition, in essence, it is a labor-intensive and error-prone task and thus is not seen as appropriate or efficient for large-scale composition problems.

However, in the automatic composition approach, it is assumed that software programs know if two web services can be connected or not (i.e., via syntactic matching of web services parameters or possibly via semantic matching). Major Web and Semantic Web services composition languages include: BPEL4WS, BPML, WSCI, WS-CDL and DAML-S. These standards all support the imperative elements of service composition, e.g. exception handling and compensation and all possess the capability to compose more complex structures and activities.

Business collaborations require the enforcement of business agreement on quality of service (QoS). However these languages do not all address this. BPEL has gained the widest support from industry and most major software vendors have pledged BPEL support in their products. Current web service composition frameworks include eFlow [18], MAIS, MOEM, SELF-SERV [19], OntoMat-Service [20], SHOP2 [21], WebTransact [22] and StarWSCoP [23].

The current state of the development effort is generally centered on attempts to create service composition platforms, since the current state of research lacks additional specifications concerning quality of service extensions in Web Services Description Language (WSDL), to name a simple but crucial example, and some platforms have developed their own proprietary data structures for extending WSDL.

4.4 Service Semantic Compatibility Management

Since individual web services are created in isolation, a key disadvantage is that there are often many issues related to the use of abbreviations, different formats, or typographical errors embedded within their vocabularies. For example, two terms with different spellings or abbreviations may have the same semantic meaning and are thus inter-changeable. Diverse matching schemes have been developed to address these semantic resolution problems, including through the use of ontologies [24]. In general, matching approaches generally fall into three categories:

> Exact matching using syntactic equivalence.
> Approximate match using distance functions (e.g. TF-IDF, Jaccard, SoftTF-IDF, Jaro, or Levenstein distance).
> Semantic matching using ontologies [25].

Research within the Semantic Web Community proposes a top-down, unambiguous description of service capability, e.g. in DAML-S, which allows for the automation of web services tasks such as discovery and composition through reasoning.

5 Conclusion

The paper has identified a set of functionality as well as key limitations in the area of dynamic web service based process modeling and execution to support alliance modes of operation of SMEs in the Construction sector. A call is made to further research in this area, including, on the one hand, developing solutions for transient SME alliances, and on the other, developing adapted solutions that support run-time adaptable and extensible service-based e-processes.

As argued above, the use of web service technologies is hampered by the static nature of the languages used to model business processes, which cannot easily adapt and allow for changes in processes and service components.

Therefore, some essential support features for designing and developing composite services are required. These include execution-monitoring capabilities to manage and trace service execution, dynamic service selection, quality of service (QoS) modelling and evaluation, dynamic transaction and coordination support, and the ability to dynamically model service flows.

The paper therefore argues that there would be great value in investigating the extension of BPEL environments towards more flexibility, agility and self-adaptability not only regarding the discovery and activation of services, but mainly in the context of long-lasting business processes, whose life span is much longer than the typical life span of a service provider or business partner. The networked enterprise software must be adapted to accommodate new features in the context of changing requirements. As BPEL is an extensible language (new instructions can be added to take account of user's evolving and changing needs), its engine should be extensible to integrate new behaviors for user-specific instructions (including instructions to replace an existing service in accordance with run-time criteria and context).

Future research should strive to illustrate how these applications with aspect weaving capabilities could be dynamically adapted to allow for unforeseen features. Aspects should be considered and employed at three levels:

> ➢ In the context of semantic analyzers.
> ➢ Within a BPEL engine that orchestrates Web Services.
> ➢ Within BPEL processes themselves.

Each level should use its own tailored Domain-Specific Aspect Language (DSAL) that should be easier to manipulate than a general purpose one (close to the programming language) with the pointcuts being independent from the implementation.

Research should create advances by addressing new requirements to the classical service-oriented approach, in particular:

> ➢ The ability to both abstract service characteristics from their operating environment and in some cases select services on the basis of their contextual features.

> ➤ The ability to select services both through interactive interfaces and through sophisticated matching algorithms.

Further research should strive to make advances by improving service semantic compatibility resolution and matching using ontologies (e.g., RDF and OWL). The latter should take a pivotal role in the process by checking semantic relatedness between data structures and / or concepts used by each partner service. It is essential in this context to handle uncertainty in the underlying reasoning by drawing on fuzzy concept research. Fuzzy concept techniques should offer the means to address these uncertainty aspects and should constitute real advances in the field of semantic service composition.

It is hoped that the paper has provided useful insights into the area of service-based business process execution research, and that this will trigger further research with promising potential.

References

[1] Dick, J., Payne, D.: Regional Sectoral Support: A review of the construction industry, SMEs and regional innovation strategies across Europe. International Journal of Strategic Property Management 9, 55–63 (2005)

[2] Abulma'thi, A., Rezgui, Y.: Virtual Organizations in Practice: A European Perspective. In: 14th Americas Conference on Information Systems (AMCIS 2008), Toronto, Ontario, August 14-17 (2008)

[3] Rezgui, Y., Zarli, A.: Paving the way to digital construction: a strategic roadmap. Journal of Construction Engineering and Management (Journal of the American Society of Civil Engineers) 132(12), 767–776 (2006)

[4] Powell, A., Piccoli, G., Ives, B.: Virtual teams: a review of current literature and directions for future research. The Database for Advances in Information Systems 35(1), 6–36 (2004)

[5] Jarvenpaa, S., Leidner, D.: Communication and trust in global virtual teams. Organization Science 10(6), 791–815 (1999)

[6] Lipnack, J., Stamps, J.: Virtual Teams: People Working Across Boundaries with Technology, 2nd edn. Wiley, New York (2000)

[7] Camarninha-Matos, L., Afsarmanesh, H., Ollus, M. (eds.): Virtual organizations: systems and practice. Springer Science, New York (2005)

[8] Goranson, H.T.: The Agile Virtual Enterprise: Cases, Metrics, Tools, Quorum Books, Westport, CT (1999)

[9] Rezgui, Y., Miles, J.C.: Transforming SME strategies via innovative transient knowledge-based alliances in the Construction Sector. In: INDIN 2009, 7th IEEE Conference on Industrial Informatics, Cardiff, June 24-26 (2009)

[10] Stal, M.: Web services: beyond component-based computing. Commun. ACM 45(10), 71–76 (2002)

[11] Zeng, L., Benatallah, B., Ngu, A.H.H., Dumas, M., Kalagnanam, J., Chang, H.: QoS-Aware Middleware for Web Services Composition. IEEE Transactions on Software Engineering 30(5), 311–327 (2004)

[12] Rezgui, Y.: Role-Based Service-Oriented Implementation of a Virtual Enterprise: A Case Study in the Construction Sector. Computers in Industry 58(1), 74–86 (2007)

[13] Rezgui, Y., Medjdoub, B.: A Service Infrastructure To Support Ubiquitous Engineering Practices. In: Establishing the foundation of collaborative networks, pp. 627–636. Springer, Heidelberg (2007)

[14] McIlraith, S.A., Son, T.C., Zeng, H.: Semantic Web Services. IEEE Intelligent Systems 16(2), 46–53 (2001)

[15] Papazoglou, M.P.: Service-oriented computing: concepts, characteristics and directions. In: WISE 2003. Proceedings of the Fourth International Conference on Web Information Systems Engineering, pp. 3–12 (2003)

[16] Leymann, F., Roller, D., Schmidt, M.-T.: Web services and business process management. IBM Systems Journal 41(2), 198–211 (2002)

[17] Menascé, D.A.: QoS Issues in Web Services. IEEE Internet Computing 6(6), 72–75 (2002)

[18] Rezgui, Y.: Exploring Virtual Team-Working Effectiveness in the Construction Sector. Interacting with Computers 19(1), 96–112 (2007)

[19] OASIS, BPEL specification,
http://www.oasis-open.org/committees/
tc_home.php?wg_abbrev=wsbpel (last accessed 05/04/09)

[20] OASIS, UDDI specification,
http://www.oasis-open.org/committees/
tc_home.php?wg_abbrev=uddi-spec (last accessed 05/04/09)

[21] Casati, F., Ilnicki, S., Jin, L., Vasudev Krishnamoorthy, V., Shan, M.-C.: Adaptive and Dynamic Service Composition in eFlow, HP (2000),
http://www.hpl.hp.com/techreports/2000/HPL-2000-39.pdf
(last accessed 04/04/09)

[22] Benatallah, B., Sheng, Q.Z., Dumas, M.: The Self-Serv environment for Web services composition. IEEE Internet Computing 7(1), 40–48 (2003)

[23] Onto-Mat website,
http://www.aifb.uni-karlsruhe.de/mailman/listinfo/ontomat
(last accessed 04/04/09)

[24] Nau, D., Au, T.-C., Ilghami, O., Kuter, U., Murdock, J.W., Wu, D., Yaman, F.: SHOP2: An HTN Planning System. Journal of Artificial Intelligence Research 20, 379–404 (2003)

[25] Pires, P.F., Benevides, R.F.M., Mattoso, M.: WebTransact: A Framework for Specifying and Coordinating Reliable Web Service Compositions. Technical Report ES-578/02 PESC/Coppe Federal University of Rio de Janeiro (2002),
http://www.cos.ufrj.br/~pires/webTransact.html
(last accessed 04/04/09)

[26] Sun, H., Wang, X., Zhou, B., Zou, P.: Research and Implementation of Dynamic Web Services Composition. In: Zhou, X., Xu, M., Jähnichen, S., Cao, J. (eds.) APPT 2003. LNCS, vol. 2834, pp. 457–466. Springer, Heidelberg (2003)

[27] Barresi, S., Rezgui, Y., Celson, L., Meziane, F.: Architecture to Support Semantic Resources Interoperability. In: Proceedings of the ACM workshop on Interoperability of Heterogeneous Information Systems (IHIS 2005), Germany. ACM Press, New York (2005)

[28] Rezgui, Y., Nefti-Meziani, S.: Ontology-Based Dynamic Composition of Services Using Semantic Relatedness and Categorisation Techniques. In: Proceedings of the 9th International Conference on Enterprise Information Systems (ICEIS), Funchal, Madeira - Portugal, June 12-16 (2007)

Social Requirements
for Virtual Organization Breeding Environments

Jan Świerzowicz and Willy Picard

Department of Information Technology, Poznan University of Economics,
Mansfelda 4, 60-854 Poznań, Poland
{jswierz,picard}@kti.ue.poznan.pl

Abstract. The creation of Virtual Breeding Environments (VBE) is a topic
which has received too little attention: in most former works, the existence of
the VBE is either assumed, or is considered as the result of the voluntary, participatory gathering of a set of candidate companies. In this paper, the creation
of a VBE by a third authority is considered: chambers of commerce, as organizations whose goal is to promote and facilitate business interests and activity in
the community, could be good candidates for exogenous VBE creators. During
VBE planning, there is a need to specify social requirements for the VBE. In
this paper, SNA metrics are proposed as a way for a VBE planner to express
social requirements for a VBE to be created. Additionally, a set of social requirements for VO planners, VO brokers, and VBE members are proposed.

Keywords: Social Requirements, Social Network Analysis, Virtual Breeding
Environment, Virtual Organization.

1 Introduction

A large variety of Collaborative Networks (CN) has emerged lately as a result of the
challenges faced by both the business and scientific worlds [1]. Sanchez [2] defines
Virtual Organization (VO) as a set of independent organizations that share resources
and skills to achieve its mission or goal. The concept of VO Breeding Environment
(VBE) has been proposed by the ECOLEAD project as a way to foster the creation of
VOs [3]. A VBE is a pool of institutions that have both the potential and the will to
cooperate with each other through the establishment of a "base" long-term cooperation
agreement and interoperable infrastructure. When a business opportunity is identified by
one member (acting as a broker), a subset of these organization can be selected and thus
forming a VO [2].

In most former works, the existence of the Virtual Breeding Environment is either
assumed, or is considered as the result of the voluntary, participatory gathering of a
set of candidate companies. In this paper, the creation of a VBE by a third authority is
considered. Organizations such as Chambers of Commerce (CoC) seem to be good
candidates as institutions that may be involved in VBE creation process. CoCs usually
bring together companies working in the same industry (often in the same geographical area). According to World Chambers Network [4], there are over 14,000 registered Chambers of Commerce and Industry (CCI) which in turn represent over 40

L.M. Camarinha-Matos et al. (Eds.): PRO-VE 2009, IFIP AICT 307, pp. 614–622, 2009.

million member businesses worldwide. CoC, as organizations whose goal is to promote and facilitate business interests and activity in the community, could be good candidates for exogenous VBE creators.

Creation of VBEs, similarly to creation of VOs, requires strategic and management decision-making processes substantially different from those in traditional organizations [5]. Various aspects have to be addressed during VBE planning, from technological, organizational, economic, to legislative, psychological, and cultural ones [6]. Having in mind these aspects, the three components of CNs identified by Bifulco and Sanotoro [7] for the case of PVCs should be addressed by the planner: a VBE planner should determine a set of requirements based on business (e.g. income of potential member), knowledge (e.g. ERP used by potential member) and social aspects (e.g. number of organizations that potential member collaborates with). It should be notice that modeling these requirements requires both models and methodologies to define the needs and goals of the VBE planner. To our best knowledge, no model for social requirements for a VBE to be created currently exists.

In this paper, SNA metrics are proposed as a way for a VBE planner to express social requirements for a VBE to be created. The paper is organized as follows. In section 2, the concept of social requirements is briefly introduced, along with common SNA metrics and a short example. In section 3, an approach to social requirements used for VBE planning is presented. Section 4 concludes the paper.

2 Social Requirements

2.1 Social Network Analysis

A social network is a graph of nodes (sometimes referred as actors), which may be connected by relations (sometimes referred as ties, links, or edges). Social Network Analysis (SNA) is the study of these relations [8].

An important aspect of SNA is the fact that it focused on the how the structure of relationships affects actors, instead of treating actors as the discrete units of analysis. SNA is backed by social sciences and strong mathematical theories like graph theory and matrix algebra [9], which makes it applicable to analytical approaches and empirical methods. SNA uses various concepts to evaluate different network properties.

Recently, numerous networking tools have been made available to individuals and organizations mainly to help establishing and maintaining virtual communities. The common characteristic to all of them is that members build and maintain their own social networks, which are, then, connected to other networks through hubs (individuals that are members of two ore more networks) [5].

2.2 SNA Common Metrics

There are several types of measures for assessment of properties for a particular node, a group of nodes, or the whole network [10]. The most common metrics for SNA are [11–13]:

- **Size** – the size of the network is the number of nodes in a given structure,
- **Average path length** – the average of distances between all pairs of nodes,

- **Density** – the proportion of ties in a network relative to the total number possible relations,
- **Degree** – the number of ties of an actor,
- **Closeness** – the inverse of the sum of the shortest distances between each individual and every other person in the network,
- **Eccentricity** – the maximum of the shortest paths to other nodes in the network; indicates how far given node is from the furthest one in the network,
- **Neighborhood size** – the number of other actors to whom a given actor is adjacent, i.e. has a direct path,
- **Reciprocated ties density** – the ratio of the number of ties that are bidirectional to the neighborhood size.

2.3 Social Requirements as Reversed SNA

Social Network Analysis may used to examine a given network by evaluating some of its properties. Social requirements may be considered as the reverse approach: social requirements may be used to define some properties of a network and their associated expected values, that may then be used to check if an existing network satisfies these social requirements. It should be noticed that social requirements are usually at a higher level of abstraction than SNA metrics, and therefore, a "translation" phase between social requirements and SNA metrics is usually required.

To illustrate the concept of social requirements, let assume that a wholesaler entering the market is planning the structure of his social network. In table 1, the social requirements she/he defined during her/his network planning are presented, together with associated SNA metrics and expected values.

Table 1. Social Requirements of wholesaler (example)

Social requirement	SNA metrics	Expected value
I want three distributors	Size of the network	=4 (including main actor)
Distributors must be my direct friends	Shortest path between main actor and a member	=1
Distributors must not know each other directly	Shortest path between any member	>1
Distributors must have at least one business partner except me	Neighborhood size	>1

Social business connections of the wholesaler are presented in Fig. 1, with 9 different actors connected to the actor A representing the wholesaler. The social requirements presented in table 1 define the structure of networks that would socially satisfy the wholesaler. The network consisting of actors A, F, J, I does not satisfy the wholesaler, as actor J does not meet the last requirement (his neighborhood size equals 1). On the contrary, the network consisting of actors A, F, C, and E is acceptable, as all social requirements are met in this case.

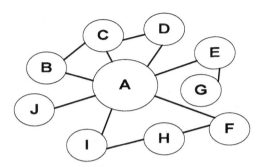

Fig. 1. An example of social network: the wholesaler is the A node

It should be note that the set of networks satisfying a set of social requirements may be empty (if the social requirements are too strict), may contain one network or many networks (if the social requirements are too vague).

3   Social Requirements for VBEs

3.1   Generic Social Requirements for VBEs

Social requirements described in the former section may be an important part of VBE planning, especially during the planning of social aspects of the VBE. One should notice that, while each VBE requires an individual approach, there is a set of social requirements that are common to all VBEs, such as:

- **Size** – every VBE planner must specify at least minimal size, with 3 being the common minimal size of all VBEs. In some cases, it may be worth defining a maximal size for the planned VBE;
- **Density** – one of the main assumptions of the VBE is that the partner are interconnected (density must be at least at the level of 50%);
- **Eccentricity** – cannot be too high, whilst agile VO forming requires fast and least (if at all) mediated communication.

3.2   VBE Roles and Social Requirements

Social requirements may not only be defined in a generic manner as presented in the former subsection, but may also encompass the characteristics of various VBE roles formerly identified by the ECOLEAD project [3]:

- **VBE Member:** the basic role played by those organizations that are registered at the VBE and are ready to participate in the VBE activities. As regards social requirements, a VBE member cannot be a passive/isolated actor in a network, i.e. a VBE member should be at least either a sender or a receiver of information. Such a social requirement may be "translated" in terms of SNA metrics as a constraint on its density

The inbound density or outbound density of a VBE member should be higher than 50%.

- **VO Planer:** a role performed by a VBE actor that in face of a new collaboration opportunity, identifies the necessary competencies and capacities, selects an appropriate set of partners, and structures the new VO. As regards social requirements, a VO planner should have a good knowledge of the members of the VBE, i.e. a VO planner should have a higher level of connectivity than average VBE member. Such social requirements may be translated in terms of SNA metrics as constraints on its inbound and outbound degrees and reciprocity density.

Inbound degrees, outbound degrees and the reciprocity density of a VO planner should be higher than the average of other VBE members.

- **VO Broker:** a role performed by a VBE actor that identifies and acquires new collaboration opportunities. As regards social requirements, a VO broker collects information. Such social requirements may be translated in terms of SNA metrics as constraints on its inbound and outbound degrees.

Inbound degrees, outbound degrees of a VO broker should be higher than the average of other VBE members.

3.3 Example of Social Requirements for VBE

To illustrate the formerly presented approach, let imagine a Chamber of Commerce that gathers 10 steel manufacturers. CoC wonders whether it makes sense to create a VBE among these manufacturers, and if so what companies should participate. Following on that, a VBE planner from the CoC defines the following social requirements for the VBE to be potentially created:

Table 2. Social requirements for steel manufacturers' VBE

Requirement	Measure	Value
The VBE should have at least 5 members	Size	≥ 5
Members must be interconnected	Density of the network	> 50%
At least half of the members must have a collaboration history	Reciprocated ties	> 50%
There must be at least one VO broker	Inbound density	> 80%
There must be at least one VO planner	Inbound density and Outbound density;	> 70%
	Reciprocated density	> 80%

The relations among manufacturers are modeled as a network, presented in Fig. 2, which is based on [11].

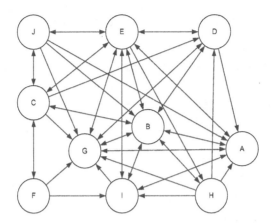

Fig. 2. Steel manufacturers' social network

Table 3. Steel manufacturers' social network matrix

	A	B	C	D	E	F	G	H	I	J
A	X	1	0	0	1	0	1	0	1	0
B	1	X	1	1	1	0	1	1	1	0
C	0	1	X	1	1	1	1	0	0	1
D	1	1	0	X	1	0	1	0	0	0
E	1	1	1	1	X	0	1	1	1	1
F	0	0	1	1	1	X	1	0	1	0
G	0	1	0	1	1	0	X	0	0	0
H	1	1	0	1	1	0	1	X	1	0
I	0	1	0	0	1	0	1	0	X	0
J	1	1	1	0	1	0	1	0	0	X

The graph presented in Fig. 2 may be represented by the matrix in Table 3, where columns correspond to inbound ties (sender of information), and rows correspond to outbound ties (receiver of the information), note that self-ties are ignored. To simplify computations only binary measures are taken into consideration, i.e. the intensity of information flow is not taken into account, just the fact that a relation exists (represented in matrix by "1") or not (represented in matrix by "0").

Let check if the whole network satisfies the social requirements defined for the steel manufacturers' VBE.

The first requirement concerning the size is obviously satisfied as the required size is 5 while there are 10 manufacturers.

The second requirement concerns the density of the network which is expected to be more than 50%. Since there are 10 actors in a network, there are 90 possible connections, i.e. $n \times (n-1)$, where n is the size of the network. The actual number of ties is 51 which means that the density of the network equals 56%. The second requirement is therefore satisfied.

The third requirement concerns the collaboration history of VBE potential members, with a number of reciprocated ties expected to be greater than 50% of the number of ties of the whole network. With 51 being the total number of ties and 19 reciprocated ties, the number of reciprocated ties is $(19 \times 2) / 51 = 75\%$. The third requirement is therefore satisfied.

The forth and fifth requirements concerns the existence of at least one VO broker and one VO planer in the VBE. These requirements are related with inbound and outbound densities, as well as to reciprocated ties for a given manufacturer. Outbound density is a measure of the contribution to the network (i.e. an actor sends information to most actors), while inbound density is a measure of use of the network by an actor (i.e. an actor receives information from other actors). Table 4 presents values for each actor.

Table 4. Outbound, inbound and reciprocated densities for steel manufacturers

Actor	Outbound density	Inbound density	Reciprocated density
A	0,44	0,78	4 (58%)
B	0,78	0,89	7 (88%)
C	0,67	0,44	4 (67%)
D	0,44	0,56	3 (50%)
E	0,89	0,89	8 (100%)
F	0,33	0,11	1 (33%)
G	0,33	1,00	4 (44%)
H	0,67	0,22	2 (33%)
I	0,33	0,56	3 (50%)
J	0,56	0,22	2 (40%)

About outbound density, actor E sends information to all but actor F, and its outbound density – 89% – is highest in the network. As a consequence, actor E has the highest potential to be influential. Actors B and E are the two only actors with an outbound density higher than 70% (cf. the fifth requirement).

About inbound density, the actors A, B, E, and G have inbound densities higher than 70% (cf. the forth requirement). All these actors but actor A have inbound densities higher than 80% (cf. the fifth requirement). As a consequence, actors B, E and G are potential candidates to the role of VO brokers. Therefore the forth requirement is satisfied.

From their outbound and inbound densities, only the manufacturer B and E are potential VO planner, under condition that their reciprocated density is greater than 80 % (cf. the fifth requirement). This condition is satisfied for actors B and E. Therefore the fifth requirement is satisfied.

As a conclusion, all five requirements for the steel manufacturers are satisfied. Additionally, the social requirements concerning VO planers and VO brokers defined in section 3.2 are more lenient than the forth and fifth requirements. Therefore, the social requirements related with VBE roles for VO planers and VO brokers defined in section 3.2 are satisfied.

But the social requirements concerning VBE members defined in section 3.2 are not satisfied by actor F. The number of ties of actor F is 4 (1 inbound and 3 outbound), while the number of potential ties of actor F is twice the number of remaining actors, i.e. 18 (9 inbound and 9 outbound). Therefore, the outbound density of actor F equals 3 / 9 = 33% and inbound density equals 1 / 9 =11%. Neither of these results exceeds 50%, therefore density requirement for VBE members defined in section 3.2. is not satisfied for actor F.

As a conclusion, the steel manufacturers' social network presented in Figure 2 satisfies the social requirements defined in table 2, but some actors do not satisfy social requirements concerning VBE roles. Therefore, the considered social network should not be casted into a VBE.

A further step could be the removal of actors that do not satisfy social requirements for VBE roles, e.g. actor A. Next, it should be checked if the resulting social network satisfies all social requirements.

4   Conclusions

The main contribution presented in this paper is twofold: first, the idea of exogenous VBE creation is proposed; second, the concept of social requirements for VBEs is introduced. The VBE creation process has currently been the subject of little work as it is usually assumed that either the VBE exists or that the VBE is the result of the participatory gathering of voluntary companies, eventually asking outside institutions for support [14].

Second, to our best knowledge, the use of SNA as a basis for modeling social requirements for VBEs is a novel approach to VBE modeling. Using Social Network Analysis methods to examine abovementioned requirements enables quantitative specification of characteristics of VBE often described in qualitative way.

Among future works, the concepts presented in this paper should be formally defined. Next, a methodology to translate social requirements into appropriate SNA metrics is still to be proposed. Finally, algorithms for the identification, within a given network of organizations, of sub-networks that fulfill a given set of social requirements need to be developed.

Acknowledgments. This work has been partially supported by the Polish Ministry of Science and Higher Education within the European Regional Development Fund, Grant No. POIG.01.03.01-00-008/08.

References

1. Camarinha-Matos, L.M., Afsarmanesh, H.: The Emerging Discipline of Collaborative Networks in Enterprises and Collaborative Networks. Kluwer Academic Publisher, Dordrecht (2004)
2. Sánchez, N.G., Zubiaga, D., González, J., Molina, A.: Virtual Breeding Environment: A First Approach to Understand Working and Sharing Principles. At: INTEROP-ESA 2005, Geneva, Switzerland (2005)

3. ECOLEAD: Characterization of Key Components, Features, and Operating Principles of the Virtual Breeding Environment. Deliverable 21.1 (2005)
4. World Chambers Network,
   http://www.worldchambers.com/WCN_about_WCN.asp
   (retrieved March 2009)
5. Lavrac, N., Ljubic, P., Urbancic, T., Papa, G., Jermol, M., Bollhalter, S.: Trust Modeling for Networked Organizations Using Reputation and Collaboration Estimates. IEEE Transactions on Systems, Man, and Cybernetics 37(3) (2007)
6. McKenzie, J., van Winkelen, C.: Exploring E-collaboration space. Presented at the Henley Knowledge Manage. Forum Conf., Henley on Thames, UK (2001)
7. Bifulco, A., Santoro, R.: A Conceptual Framework for Professional Virtual 3.-Communities Collaborative Networks and Their Breeding Environments. In: Sixth IFIP Working Conference on Virtual Enterprises, Valencia, Spain, September 2005, pp. 26–28 (2005)
8. Baroudi, J., Olson, M., Ives, B.: An Empirical Study of the Impact of User Involvement on System Usage and Information Satisfaction. CACM 29(3), 232–238 (1986)
9. Borgatti, S.: What is social network analysis? (1999),
   http://www.analytictech.com/networks/whatis.htm
10. Gencer, M., Gunduz, C., Tunalioglu, V.: CL-SNA: Social Network Analysis with Lisp, Draft Paper (2007), http://cs.bilgi.edu.tr/~mgencer/pub/ILC2007.pdf
11. Hanneman, R.A.: Introduction to Social Network Methods. University of California, Riverside (2001), http://faculty.ucr.edu/~hanneman/
12. Wasserman, S., Faust, K.: Social Networks Analysis: Methods and Applications. Cambridge University Press, Cambridge (1994)
13. Moody, J., White, D.: Structural Cohesion and Embeddedness: A Hierarchical Concept of Social Groups. American Sociological Review 67, 103–127 (2000)
14. Flores, M., Boer, C., Huber, C., Plüss, A., Schoch, R., Pouly, M.: The Role Of Universities Developing New Collaborative Environments; Analysing The Virtuelle Fabrik, Swiss Microtech and the Tenet Group. In: Proc. of the 8th IFIP Working Conference on Virtual Enterprises, Guimarães, Portugal, September 10-12 (2007)

Discovering Collaboration and Knowledge Management Practices for the Future Digital Factory

Myrna Flores[1], Tomas Vera[2], and Christopher Tucci[2]

[1] Research and Networking, Processes and IT,
CEMEX Global Center for Technology and Innovation,
CEMEX Research Group AG, Römerstrasse 13 CH-2555 Brügg, Switzerland
[2] École Polytechnique Fédérale de Lausanne (EPFL),
College of Management, Chair in Corporate Strategy & Innovation (CSI)
myrnafatima.flores@cemex.com, tomasvera@gmail.com,
christopher.tucci@epfl.ch

Abstract. Recently there has been an explosion of new technologies and tools such as wikis, blogs, tags, Facebook, among many others, that are commonly identified under Web 2.0 and which promise a new digital business ecosystem fed by formal/informal and internal/external relationships and interactions. Although Web 2.0 is very promising to enable such collective knowledge creation, technology by itself is not the only ingredient. It is also required to define the right strategy, governance, culture, processes, training, incentives among others, before implementing such innovative open spaces for collaboration and knowledge sharing. Therefore, the objective of this paper is to present a Knowledge Management (KM) Framework and a Maturity Model developed by a CEMEX and EPFL collaborative research project to discover the AS-IS collaboration practices in CEMEX before the implementation of the SMARTBRICKS Web 2.0 prototype for Business Process Management (BPM), currently under development by the Intelligent Manufacturing Systems (IMS) Swiss Digital Factory (DiFac) project.

Keywords: Collaboration Best Practices, Web 2.0, Knowledge Management Framework, Digital Factory.

1 Introduction

The Intelligent Manufacturing System (IMS) Digital Factory (DiFac) collaborative research project aims to develop a strategic planning design tool that is capable of supporting the construction of a digital factory. The Swiss IMS DIFAC project covers the workpackage dealing with the Enterprise Resource Planning (ERP), proposing a new Industrial Engineering System that should not only integrate information and knowledge from the production process but the complete Product Life Cycle [1].

To accomplish this objective, research targets the testing, implementation and diffusion of novel ICT technologies such as Semantic Web, RFID and discrete event simulation. CEMEX Research Group (CRG) is partner of the Swiss DIFAC project and leads Workpackage 1, which aims to develop a Web 2.0/Semantic Web prototype

L.M. Camarinha-Matos et al. (Eds.): PRO-VE 2009, IFIP AICT 307, pp. 623–632, 2009.

called SMARTBRICKS, currently under development, in collaboration with the University of Applied Sciences of Southern Switzerland (SUPSI). This new tool will enable CEMEX employees to share information and knowledge by exploiting Web 2.0 and semantic web technologies for Business Process Management (BPM). In other words, BPM specialists will evolve from "passive consumers" of business processes contents to "active contents developers" and accelerate BPM best practices global diffusion and sharing [2].

Although SMARTBRICKS is a very promising tool to enhance collaboration in BPM within CEMEX, it is also important to consider the organizational, cultural and change management elements for its successful implementation. Therefore a collaborative research project was defined and carried out by CEMEX Research Group and the College of Management of the École Polytechnique Fédérale de Lausanne (EPFL) to develop a Knowledge Management Framework and Maturity Model to assess current collaboration strengths and opportunities in CEMEX before implementing SMARTBRICKS. Therefore, the following sections will briefly explain the research outcomes of such CEMEX – EPFL collaborative project developed from September 2008 to February 2009.

2   Research Methodology

This CEMEX – EPFL collaborative research project had the following objectives:

1) To design a Generic Knowledge Management (KM) framework with its corresponding maturity level and
2) To discover current collaboration best practices in CEMEX applying the proposed KM Framework and maturity model through the development, deployment and analysis of an e-survey to potential users of the SMARTBRICKS tool from Processes and IT in CEMEX.

The LEAD methodology, developed in CEMEX Research Group [3], which proposes four stages to manage research projects with external partners (Learn, Energize, Apply and Diffuse) was applied in this collaborative research project with EPFL as follows:

1) LEARN
- The research project objectives were defined. CEMEX and EPFL agreed on the expected deliverables and deadlines.
- Extensive literature review on knowledge management, existing maturity models and Web 2.0 was carried out. Initially, relevant papers on the topic were provided by CEMEX to EPFL's project team. This latter complemented the literature review during the first two months.
- A glossary was developed to define all the important concepts linked to the project. Such document was continuously updated during the complete project.

2) ENERGIZE
- An initial Knowledge Management (KM) framework was proposed by EPFL. Afterwards, based on a several brainstorming sessions and CEMEX suggestions and requirements, a second and multilayered KM Framework was created by CEMEX and EPFL teams.

- EPFL and CEMEX designed a questionnaire based on the agreed final KM Framework for its validation and to discover current KM practices.
- A sample of 60 employees working in Processes and IT in CEMEX was identified and invited to fill in the questionnaire in the form of an e-survey.
- An e-survey developed in SurveyMonkey and was filled in by 21 persons of the selected sample from the Processes and IT department within CEMEX to discover such AS-IS collaboration best practices and identify opportunity areas.
- A Knowledge Management Maturity Assessment Model was developed

3) APPLY
- The e-survey data was analyzed and applying the proposed maturity model, it was possible to map the key strengths and weaknesses and obtain an overall understanding in which level is currently CEMEX in terms of collaboration practices for knowledge management.

4) DIFFUSE
- During this last phase, diffusion of results are carried out within CEMEX, in scientific journals and international conferences

3 Knowledge Management (KM) Foundations

Back in 1959, Peter Drucker coined the term "knowledge worker" as one who develops and uses new knowledge in the workplace [4]. Even if the concept was developed already five decades ago, only in the last years organizations have started to recognize "knowledge" as a strategic intangible asset. In this context, firms require to understand how useful knowledge can be successfully shared, stored, reproduced and re-used in a collective way for processes optimization.

For many, knowledge has become one of the most important resources a company disposes [5]. Researchers in knowledge management contend that any firm's competitive advantage depends on what it knows, how it uses what it knows, and how fast it can know something new [6]. But although creating knowledge is an important activity, knowledge has to be harnessed and leveraged to be useful. Learning occurs when knowledge in one part of an organization is transferred effectively to other parties and re-used to solve problems or to provide new and creative insights. Therefore knowledge sharing and reusing is what a "Learning Organization" is all about and is the vision of the future Digital Factory. In fact, Senge [7] defined a learning organization as a place where people continually expand their capacity to create the results they truly desire, where new and expansive patterns of thinking are nurtured, where collective aspiration is set free, and where people are continually learning to learn together.

But what is Knowledge and Knowledge Management (KM)? There is not one unique definition for either of them. Following Kogut and Zander [8], knowledge could be understood as recipe that specifies how to carry out activities. Devenport and Prusak [9] define knowledge "as a fluid mix of framed experiences, values, contextual information and expert insight that provides a framework for evaluating and incorporating new experiences and information. It originates and is applied in the minds of knowers. In organizations, it often becomes embedded not only in documents or repositories, but also in organizational routines, processes, practices and norms".

In regards to the Knowledge-based theory of the firm, it was developed by Winter [10], Kogut and Zander [8], [11], Nonaka [12], Nonaka and Takeuchi [13], Grant [14], and many other authors have contributed for its diffusion and continuous evolution. Wiig [15] states that KM is the management of corporate knowledge that can improve a range of organizational performance characteristics by enabling an enterprise to be more "intelligent active". Marshall [16] referred to KM as the harnessing of "intellectual capital" within the organization. According to Seemann et. al [17], Knowledge Management can be thought of as the deliberate design of processes, tools, structures, etc, with the intent to increase, renew, share, or improve the use of knowledge represented in any of the three elements (structural, human and social) of intellectual capital. For CISCO [18], Knowledge Management refers to a range of practices used by organizations to identify, create, represent, and distribute knowledge for reuse, awareness and learning across the organization.

One key element for successful Knowledge Management initiatives within a company is the definition and implementation of a knowledge management (KM) strategy and at the same time its diffusion is a requirement to make it possible to promote best practices, encourage employees to share their knowledge and collaborate, instigate managers to value those who do, and thus, finally increase and improve this valuable intangible asset. In fact, Zack [19], after doing research about KM in more than 25 firms has concluded that the most important context for guiding knowledge management is its firm's strategy. A few years later [20], Zack added that "once the role between strategy and knowledge is defined, the other aspects of strategic management such as resources allocation and organization design, among others, can be configured to bolster knowledge strengths and reduce knowledge weaknesses". As one interesting example, Hansen et. al [21], have identified two main strategies followed by business consulting firms: codification and personalization. The first one focuses on the codification of knowledge in repositories for it to be reused, while the second one in based on the development of new know-how and enabling it to be shared based on peer-to-peer interactions. The authors argue that firms can develop their strategy based on the customers they serve, the economics of its business and the people it hires.

4   Assessing Existing Knowledge Management Frameworks and Maturity Models

Although it is quite diffused that Knowledge Management can provide productivity returns, still many organizations struggle to identify which is the best possible path to implement a Knowledge Management strategy. Several consulting experts and academics have provided different models to enable the implementation of a KM strategy.

A model is a simplified representation of reality, developed with a specific goal; a maturity model follows the evolution of an entity from its early beginnings to a final status, be it one of declination and death or an ideal one of excellence and continuous improvement. Maturity models are usually structured on stages that have to be overcome one at a time, by fulfilling a set of requisites, or may allow for continuous improvement. Most of them have proved to be useful to measure the current maturity of the process employed, evaluate the current status of the field practices, set an objective for process design endeavors, guide the evolution of organizational change, and allow comparisons or benchmarking with similar efforts of other units or companies [22]. In order to develop a new Knowledge Management Framework for the future Digital Factory, this section will briefly explain the state of the art analysis of recently developed KM models and maturity models.

Gartner [23] has proposed a 5 level maturity model for collaboration ranging from no maturity to pervasive use of collaboration tools. According to a Gartner's research project carried out in 2007, most companies are around Level 2, where collaboration process maturity is emerging but still very new. Companies at this stage have realized that the basic tools are not enough; they are experimenting with new tools in order to make collaboration easier. However, only early adopters do any collaborative work, if at all. What Gartner provides is a model to support organizations to self-assess themselves and identify their maturity level. Even if the model is very complete, its weakness relies that it mainly focuses on IT collaboration tools and their adoption company wide. As a consequence, this maturity model is not enough to completely asses a company's standing point on collaboration as a whole, considering also soft aspects as the firm KM strategy, the organizational culture, recognition, etc.

On the other hand, SAP business analysts have developed a model that allows measuring knowledge management and collaboration practices in a more general manner. SAP provides a 5 level model [24], from initial to leader, but in contrast with the Gartner model, the SAP model is a more complete maturity assessment model, as it not only evaluates collaboration tools, but also states six different key areas that can be analyzed: People, Governance, Process, Content, Infrastructure and Tools/Techniques. The People improvement path, according to SAP, involves decreasing emphasis on only individual contributions but instead growing reliance on leveraging knowledge generated by communities; also increasing the recognition that the knowledge life cycle is woven into the fabric of daily work. While the Governance improvement path means increasing support for a culture that encourages knowledge sharing and validation of best practices. The "Process improvement path" involves improving content management and increasing the use of a collaborative environment in all communities, both internal and external. While the "Content path" means growing recognition of the importance of global reuse of knowledge assets. Finally, Infrastructure and Tools/Techniques paths deal with IT, as in the Gartner model.

McKinsey, on the other hand, states that Knowledge Management is not about managing knowledge but rather creating an environment that promotes and facilitates knowledge transfer [25]. As a consequence, the firm has implemented a four element model, where each element is multiplicative; in the sense that not delivering on any of them causes the knowledge transfer environment to fail. The four elements of the McKinsey model are: Clear Objectives, Knowledge Assets, Conducive Culture and Systems & Infrastructure. Clear objectives means having concrete goals as to the business impact KM has to have in the company, e.g. economic results. Knowledge assets deals with the knowledge process itself, and if which contents are regarded as valuable assets by the company. A conductive culture is achieved through proper training, support and rewards for transferring knowledge between people. They highlight the importance of this element that is often ignored, while giving more attention to systems and infrastructure. In fact, most people often think only of the IT infrastructure when talking about KM. This model assigns a very high importance to culture, reducing SAP's proposed six key areas into a more manageable quantity. On the other hand, this KM model is not designed to evaluate collaboration maturity.

Besides these three previously described frameworks proposed by Gartner, SAP and McKinsey, other identified KM frameworks and maturity models are: KPMG [26], Infosys [27], Siemens [28], APQC [29], EFQM [30], among others [31], [32], [33], [34].

5   Towards a Knowledge Management Framework and Maturity Model to Enable the Web 2.0 Future Digital Factory

As a result of the previous analysis of existing KM frameworks and maturity models, there is a current need to create a new KM framework that includes all the key elements that can enable knowledge sharing and incorporate new Web 2.0 functionalities for Business Process Management (BPM). Therefore, the proposed KM framework targets the identification and assessment of collaboration practices to obtain the readiness level of the company before the SMARTBRICKS prototype implementation. It consists of several layers, built upon the central goals, and governed by the overall KM Strategy. This framework is shown in Figure 1.

Based on the proposed framework, a maturity model was also developed to assign maturity steps in each of the framework's elements, against which the present standing of the company can be evaluated. The final goal of this model is to provide a simple tool to assess the company's current maturity level in collaboration and knowledge management issues. It is important to assess maturity in order to identify strengths and weaknesses in order to establish a baseline to define objectives for improvement. This section will briefly describe the five levels of the proposed knowledge management self assessment tool as follows:

Level 1 – Initial: The organization doesn't have a strategy for KM. Each department, or even each individual works in his own fashion, there are no common tools or platforms and sharing is very limited, if existent at all. There are no established goals and there is no acknowledgement of the Knowledge Management (KM) Process. Even if some tools might be present, such as basic tools or infrastructure (phone, email system) they are not companywide and follow no clear strategy. Also, there is no expressed vision or clear objectives.

Level 2 – Basic: The company considers collaboration simply as communication; thus providing basic communication support. At this point, the company lacks clear goals concerning KM, though it might already have a vision of where it would like to be in the future. Tools and infrastructure are the items where the most emphasis has been made, at this maturity level. The knowledge process exists intrinsically, but it is not communicated to all employees, particularly the storage and sharing ones. Concerning support structures, there is no organizational design to improve knowledge transfer; rewarding systems are not in place and there is no time provided to allow employees to share documents, experiences, etc. However, at this stage, the basic infrastructure and tools are in place. Supervisors and employees are aware of the need of sharing information, but knowledge content is created individually, and there is no strong culture of collaboration, beyond superficial meetings.

Level 3 – Emerging: The company has started to realize how important KM is to remain competitive and increase its productivity and innovation outputs. It has already developed some companywide initiatives, especially in the Knowledge Enablers layer. The organization is experimenting on the many collaboration items and is trying to develop richer and more diverse forms of knowledge transfer. It has moved beyond basic communication, and is already doing some planning, contributing and creating collaboratively. The company realizes the necessity of properly storing the information. Even though the knowledge process is carried out, it is basically for explicit knowledge; little is being done to store and share the implicit knowledge of the individuals, beyond meetings with partial and incomplete minutes. There is some basic organizational design towards a more collaborative environment, but more effort has to be put into developing cross-functional work-groups. There are companywide available central repositories for information but of a basic nature, such as file servers. The company is already providing some integrated access to the knowledge repositories and is also starting to experiment with Web 2.0 tools, and some might be available for users. The collaboration culture is emerging, some colleagues collaborate and there are more standardized protocols, especially for explicit knowledge. The company already has a clearer vision of where it wants to be concerning KM, there might also be some objectives. But no expected Business Impact has been analyzed, nor and Key Indicators been defined. There is no proper alignment of the various enablers towards the global KM Vision, since most of these processes are still being experimented with.

Level 4 – Expanding: The KM governance is formalized and understood by all employees in the company; a department is dedicated to the successful development of the KM initiative. Infrastructure and tools are carefully designed with collaboration as a goal, rather than as an experiment. Enablers have been optimized, and they are starting to be aligned with the overall KM strategy. Cross-functional tasks and teams are already being implemented. The company has significantly decreased its hierarchical nature. The Knowledge Management process has now been fully integrated companywide, at least for the explicit knowledge. Also, it has begun to be used to properly capture the more volatile implicit and tacit knowledge. Content is no longer created individually, but in a collective manner, by communities. A wide range of tools are available to search and explore the wide knowledge databases of the company. Information is properly organized, and therefore easy to access. Also, thanks to the implementation of Web 2.0 tools, such as tagging, finding the relevant information has become easier than ever. Infrastructure is mature. A collaboration-based rewarding system is in place although it is in an early stage. Employees, thanks to proper training, are developing the necessary skills and competencies to properly share and transfer knowledge. The collaboration culture is acknowledged as an influencing factor, and therefore as an enabler. The KM Strategy has been now properly laid out. The desired business impact of the KM Strategy has been established as well as the key indicators to measure the business impact. The company is beginning to align the various elements to its KM strategic views.

Level 5 – Pervasive: The Knowledge Process is not only integrated inside the company, but also with external partners, such as suppliers, clients, consulting firms and Universities. The company has realized that knowledge is a strategic asset. Implicit, as well as explicit knowledge is successfully acquired, extracted, stored, shared and updates by everyone. Knowledge Enablers are not only optimized but are now fully aligned with the overall KM strategy. Processes are built around collaboration; a rewarding system is now fine-tuned and steadily encouraging collaboration. Every tool available to employees has been optimized and even social networking applications are being fully used, information is shared freely between colleagues and employees have completely integrated collaboration to their everyday work. A collaborative culture is fully internalized. The KM Strategy is already in place and is continuously maintained and updated according to changes in the company's internal and external environment. The KM Strategy has had a business impact which can be measured and felt throughout the company. All Knowledge Enablers are aligned properly to the global strategy.

Fig. 1. Knowledge Management (KM) Framework for the Web 2.0 Digital Factory

6   Conclusions

A Knowledge Management framework and Maturity Self-assessment tool have been developed as a result of a CEMEX – EPFL collaborative research project. These latter have been applied in CEMEX to discover current collaboration and knowledge management practices to enable the future implementation of the SMARTBRICKS Web 2.0/Semantic Web tool currently under development by the Swiss DiFac project. For more information about the Digital Factory (DiFac), Intelligent Manufacturing Systems (IMS) Swiss project, please visit: www.difac.ch

Acknowledgments. The authors would like to thank the Swiss Innovation Promotion Agency – CTI International for the funding provided to the IMS Swiss Digital Factory (DiFac) Project. Gratitude is also given to Lorenzo Sommaruga and Junior Bontognali from the University of Applied Sciences of Southern Switzerland (SUPSI) for their effort to develop the SMARTBRICKS tool and for all their support during the IMS Swiss DiFac project. Special gratitude is also given to Ana Beatriz Dominguez Organero for the project's website development and communication activities carried out during the project.

References

1. Flores, M., Boër, C., Sommaruga, L., Salvadè, A., Lanini, M.: The Swiss IMS Digital Factory (DIFAC) project; implementing ICT technologies for sustainable innovation. In: Proceedings of the IFAC Workshop on Manufacturing Modelling, Management and Control (2007)
2. Flores, M., Sommaruga, L.: SMARTBRICKS: Developing an Intelligent Web tool for Business Process Management. In: International Conference of Concurrent Enterprising (ICE) Conference Proceedings, IMS Digital Factory (DiFac) Workshop, Leiden Holland (2009)
3. Flores, M.: The LEAD Research Methodology to manage collaborative open innovation projects. CEMEX internal document (2008)
4. Drucker, P.: The Coming of the New Organization. Harvard Business Review on Knowledge Management, pp. 1–19. Harvard Business School Press (1998)
5. Sveiby, K.E.: The New Organizational Wealth: Managing and Measuring Knowledge-Based Assets. Berrett-Koehler, San Francisco (1997)
6. Goh, S.C.: Managing effective knowledge transfer: an integrative framework and some practice implications. Journal of Knowledge Management 6(1), 23–30 (2002)
7. Senge, P.: The Fifth Discipline. Doubleday, New York (2006)
8. Kogut, B., Zander, U.: What Firms do? Coordination, Identity and Learning. Organization science (5), 502–523 (1996)
9. Devenport, T.H., Prusak, L.: Working Knowledge. Harvard Business School Press, Boston (1998)
10. Winter, S.G.: Knowledge and competences as strategic assets. In: Teece, D.J. (ed.) The Competitive challenge: Strategies for industrial Innovation and renewal. Ballinger, Cambridge (1987)
11. Kogut, B., Zander, U.: Knowledge of the firm, combinative capabilities, and the replication of technology. Organization Science 3, 383–397 (1992)
12. Nonaka, I.: The dynamic theory of organizational knowledge creation. Organization Science 5(1), 14–37 (1994)
13. Nonaka, I., Takeuchi, H.: The Knowledge-Creating Company. Oxford University Press, Oxford (1995)

14. Grant, R.M.: Toward a Knowledge-based Theory of the firm. Strategic Management Journal, Winter Special Issue, 109–122 (1996)
15. Wiig, K.M.: Knowledge Management Foundations. Schema Press, Texas (1993)
16. Marshall, L.: Facilitating knowledge management and knowledge sharing: new opportunities for information professionals. Online 21(5), 92–99 (1997)
17. Seemann, P., DeLong, D., Stucky, S., Guthrie, E.: Building Intangible Assets: A Strategic Framework for Investing in Intellectual Capital. In: Second International Conference on the Practical Applications of Knowledge Management (PAKeM 1999), April 21-23 (1999)
18. CISCO, Knowledge Management – Ciscowiki, http://supportwiki.cisco.com
19. Zack, M.H.: Developing a Knowledge Strategy. California Management Review 41, 125–145 (Spring 1999)
20. Zack, M.H.: Rethinking the Knowledge Based Organization. MIT Sloan Management Review (Spring 2003)
21. Hansen, M.T., Nohria, N., Tierney, T.: What's Your Strategy for Managing Knowledge? Harvard Business Review (April 1999)
22. Trejo, J.M., Rodriguez, E.: A guided approach to Quality Improvement of Knowledge Management Practices. In: Proceedings of I-Know Conference, Graz, Austria (2006)
23. Gartner: Gartner's Maturity Model to Improve Enterprise Collaboration (2007)
24. SAP: A knowledge management maturity model for a global field services organization (2007)
25. Morosini, P., Denöel, E.: Knowledge Sharing at McKinsey & Co., IMD Video (2001)
26. KPMG: Consulting, Knowledge Management Research Report (2000)
27. Infosys: Kochikar, V.P.: The Knowledge Management Maturity Model: A Staged Framework for Leveraging Knowledge. In: KMWorld 2000, Santa Clara, CA (2000)
28. Langen, M.: Knowledge Management Maturity KMMM® in Siemens AG. In: APQC Conference 2000 (2000)
29. O'Dell, C.: APQC Road Map to Knowledge Management Results: Stages of Implementation™ (2000)
30. European Foundation For Quality Management: The EFQM Framework for Knowledge Management, European Foundation For Quality Management, Brussels (2005)
31. Natarajan, G., Ganesh, U.: Unleashing the Knowledge Force, Harnessing Knowledge for Building Global Companies. Tata McGraw Hill, New York (2007)
32. Hung, Y.H., Chou, T.S.C.: On constructing a knowledge management pyramid model. In: IEEE International Conference on Information Reuse and Integration (2005)
33. Haggie, K., Kingston, J.: Choosing Your Knowledge Management Strategy. Journal of Knowledge Management Practice (June 2003)
34. O'Dell, C., Grayson, C.J.: If only we knew what we know: identification and transfer of internal best practices. California Management Review 40(3), 154–174 (1998)

Part 20

Collaborative Work Environments

Collaborative Environments to Support Professional Communities: A Living Lab Approach

Hans Schaffers[1], Steffen Budweg[2], Rudolf Ruland[2], and Kjetil Kristensen[1]

[1] ESoCE Net, Via Cortina d'Ampezzo, 164, 00135 Roma, Italy
{hschaffers,kristensen}@esoce.net
[2] Fraunhofer FIT, Schloss Birlinghofen, 53754 St. Augustin, Germany
{steffen.budweg,rudolf.ruland}@fit.fraunhofer.de

Abstract. The living labs approach within ECOSPACE focuses on early user community building and active user involvement in the process of developing, testing and evaluating new collaboration concepts and tools. This paper reports about implementing and evaluating the living labs approach to facilitate innovation in collaborative work environments to enhance professional communities. The living lab approach is considered as a strategy for innovation, change and adoption. The perspective of socio-technical systems is used to understand and explain the change-catalyzing role of the living lab approach.

Keywords: Collaboration, Professionals, Living labs, Workspaces, Community.

1 Introduction

Collaboration across teams, organizations and communities has become normal practice. The ECOSPACE Integrated Project (www.ip-ecospace.org) explores a model of collaborative working focusing on the needs of eProfessionals. An eProfessional is a professional knowledge worker who, enabled by a variety of cooperation technologies, works together with other professionals within groups, communities and organisations in order to carry out tasks and achieve common goals. Such collaboration often starts spontaneously, for example when an expert is searching for other experts to form a team in order to develop an innovative project proposal. Often, professional workers are engaged in multiple settings of collaboration, in parallel and in different projects, and are using different collaboration platforms and tools. The complexities and difficulties that arise from such dynamic collaborative situations are targeted by ECOSPACE.

Based on current forms of eProfessional working found in practice, ECOSPACE developed detailed scenarios of eProfessional working and explored different forms of collaboration enabled by advanced ICTs. A service-oriented reference architecture was developed to guide the development and integration of collaboration tools and to focus on interoperability across the different shared workspaces of professional workers. Such interoperability is enabled by collaboration middleware and services. A portfolio of collaboration tools has been developed to facilitate creative and knowledge intensive tasks. Instant collaboration is supported by the integration of asynchronous and synchronous collaboration tools, resulting in augmented social networks and rich virtual collaboration.

L.M. Camarinha-Matos et al. (Eds.): PRO-VE 2009, IFIP AICT 307, pp. 635–642, 2009.
© IFIP International Federation for Information Processing 2009

ECOSPACE launched an eProfessional living lab to experiment and evaluate innovative forms of collaborative working in three domains: media and publishing, complex projects, and professional communities of innovation. A living lab is an environment of user-driven open innovation experiments and evaluations [1]. Emphasis in this paper is on how the living lab accommodated change and adoption in the professional communities' collaboration environment.

2 Developing the Living Lab Facility

The ECOSPACE eProfessional living lab covers three different, distributed but interconnected experimentation settings based on the BSCW platform, a widespread web-based groupware system [2]: 1) the AMI@Work community; 2) the Frascati living lab community, and 3) the 14Plus living lab. A socio-technical systems change perspective on the collaborative work environment of professional workers allowed us to view these settings as socio-technical systems, exhibiting characteristics in terms of interactions between entities originally proposed by [3]: actors, tasks, technologies (collaborative support) and structures (organisation). This perspective provides a useful framework to understand the process of adoption and change related to information systems. In [4], a socio-technical information system change model is discussed which focuses on two types of systems: the "building system" and, a concept stemming from [5], the "work system". ECOSPACE adopted such concepts to understand the processes of change, adoption and resistance which are implied in innovation and adoption of new ways of working and new collaboration tools in professional communities. Besides the collaborative work environment system (CWE) which is evolving from the living lab innovation process, we distinguish the system of building the collaborative work environment as a separate socio-technical system in order to understand the interactions between both systems [4]. Additionally we examine the professional community system (Table 1).

Table 1. Three interacting socio-technical systems in the ECOSPACE living lab

System	Actors	Task	Technology	Structure
Living lab CWE system	Users, developers, researchers	Create technology for innovation projects	Collaboration tools, services, architecture	Cyclic, spiral development; roadmap
Living lab building system	Developers, local stakeholders	Create innovation environment conditions	Living lab methodologies, distributed infrastructure	Stakeholder communities
Professional community system	Members of the community (users)	Collaboration, creating projects	Collaborative working environment	Community organisation

We shortly introduce the three living lab settings and tools (see [1] for details). The AMI@Work community (www.ami-communities.eu) empowered by BSCW is a European-wide community of innovators active in project development with more than 3000 members. The CO-LLABS thematic network was chosen to experiment a series of tools meant to support thematic networks: besides the BSCW system, these included group blogging, integrated document upload and notification, multimedia conferencing, teambuilding, workspace synchronization and cross-workspace semantic querying using the SIOC Xplore widget (http://www.ami-communities.eu/wiki/ECOSPACE/SIOC).

The Frascati living lab community is a regionally based initiative led by ESA-ESRIN (European Space Agency Centre for Earth Observation) and focuses on business incubation using technologies in the domain of space and geographical information. Besides ESA-ESRIN, it is supported by research institutes, innovation agencies, universities and small businesses. We experimented various collaboration tools aiming to support the living lab community as well as specific projects within the community, among others portal services, community blogging, integrated document upload and notification services, multimedia conferencing, expert finding and team building, and workspace synchronisation.

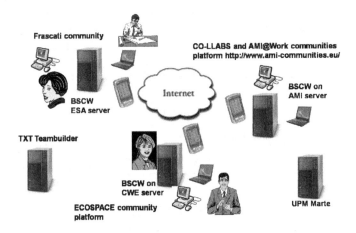

Fig. 1. Professional Communities living lab technical infrastructure

The 14Plus project supports collaboration in the German region of North Rhine-Westphalia between organizations promoting social and employment integration of young people above 14 years, cross-linking schools, craft industries and local community partners. A series of collaboration services have been experimented with and integrated into the BSCW system, e.g. single sign-on authentication, group blogging, tagging, portal modules with widgets, a wiki portal, and presence support.

The over-all living lab infrastructure comprises a number of different elements: the distributed networked living lab environment (Fig. 1), the local user communities which have been built up to establish user experimentation environments, methods and tools to organize, monitor and evaluate experiments, and the ECOSPACE tools development facility which creates and tests collaboration tools to be experimented in the living labs. The key approach has been to match user needs stemming from the living lab user communities and collaboration tools offered by the software partners. A tool implementation roadmap approach, adapting innovations to evolving user needs during project lifetime has been used to develop, test, introduce, train, use and validate the collaboration tools in the community settings. Researchers, users and developers worked together as much as possible to establish cycles of innovation.This deliberate approach might be called "action research" [6]. In itself, the launch and development of the living lab interacts with the innovation experiments carried out.

3 Collaborative Workspace Innovations: Examples

We experimented a series of collaboration tools in the three settings, emphasizing changing collaborative working practices. Lying at the basis of our experiments was a scenario framework proposing a set of new collaborative practices for eProfessionals. Scenarios emerged from confronting user and developer ideas, and were enriched by the experiments and user interactions, These practices include: setting up communities and providing access, sharing news and ideas, generating ideas, initiating community discussions, setting up personal workspaces, searching experts and forming teams, cross-workspace knowledge discovery and document sharing, and asynchronous and synchronous collaboration. These practices are enabled by the collaborative platform enhanced by selected and experimented services and tools. As an example we shortly present the approach and results of the 14Plus project. Table 2 presents an overview of 14Plus tool experiments and target groups during 2006-2008.

Table 2. 14Plus technology introductions

Date	Cooperation support	Base technology	Target group
2006-11	Project workspace	BSCW platform	Project management, community members
2006-11	Integrated Project Wiki	BSCW – Wiki	Project management, community members
2007-03	Project Blog	BSCW Blog	Project management
2007-03	Presence Awareness	BSCW platform	Project management, community members
2007-03	Event Notification	RSS	Project management, community members
2007-06	Tagging	Blog & BSCW	Project members
2007-10	Extended Logging	BSCW platform	Living Lab building system experts
2008-01	Objects visualisation	SwapIT	Project management
2008-04	Collaborative Task Management	CTM	Project management
2008-07	BSCW Presence	BSCW	Project management
2008-08	Activity Folder	BSCW	Living Lab Champions
2008-11	BSCW Widgets	Flash/JavaScript, Widget platform	Living Lab Champions

The setting of the 14Plus living lab is characterized by several challenges. The distribution of project partners over several locations in different regions required either intensive travel or remote communication and collaboration. Different work settings of project partners (e.g. schools, public administration, and businesses) result into different working times and difficulties to be available for synchronous communication. In order to cope with these challenges, the 14Plus innovation strategy followed a cyclic pattern of introductions, demonstrations, training, use and evaluations, supported by adoption and dissemination activities. Basic services were introduced first to create a support base, more complex services followed later on (the same approach has been pursued in the other settings). Table 3 presents examples of changes in the style and process of collaboration as a result of the living labs work.

Table 3. Workplace change indicators for 14Plus

Setting / Challenge	Communication & Cooperation support available / used		Workplace changes / improvements
	Before Ecospace	With Ecospace support	
Distribution of project partners over several locations in different regions	Limited to use of telephone, regular mail, basic eMail and/or intensive travel	Adoption of CWE platform and additional communication channels; Awareness Support	Overcoming / minimizing time-space barriers; efficient meeting support
Different work-settings of project partners including different work-times and availabilities	Asynchronous communication limited to traditional mail, basic e-mail; No support for availability / presence awareness	Additional synchronous & asynchronous communication media, support for handovers, presence awareness; flexible work-times	Facilitation of ad-hoc cooperation; lessening time-space barriers; support for different work styles
Availability of Group communication channels	Limited to Meetings or e-mail	Multiple Group Communications Channels	Efficient & appropriate communication support; Push- and Pull Media;
Project document repository with remote access for all members	Not available	Integrated CWE and project workspace	Access from distributed work places to main materials for work

The successful adoption and appropriation of new technology support introduced to support the project's innovation capability required careful interplay between the different systems and stakeholders involved. Two examples can illustrate the related co-evolution: First, within the initial three months of the introduction of the baseline CWE workspace and collaboration platform, more than 450 documents were created. This change resulted in new requirements and needs towards the living lab technology for maintaining structure and overview of the large project repository, iteratively leading to the development and introduction of increased support for awareness and change monitoring. Secondly, new members joining the network during the later evolution of the project increased the need for guidance and starting points for the long evolved cooperation structure. Both social and technical measures were implemented, including the establishment of local facilitators and champions serving as guides as well as the extension of the project's wiki system offering new users a specific entry point. With the wiki becoming an alternate starting point, widgets were then introduced to include presence and awareness support from the baseline system to support end-users with an integrated view.

We experimented the required integration of multiple technological systems in different ways, including the development of an interface to share workspaces across two CWE systems (BSCW and Business Collaborator; BC), by using the related concepts of *Shadow Folder* and *Semantic Folder*. Our scenario for this approach was as follows. Two companies collaborate: Turners Photography Studio, a photography company; uses the BC platform, and Baker Publication Design, a publications company that specializes in designing brochures; uses the BSCW platform. These two companies have been commissioned to produce a brochure, entitled European Cities. The photographers of Turners travel to Prague, Valencia, Rome, and Paris, taking photos and uploading them to a BC folder as they go. This BC Folder is connected as a *Shadow Folder* to the BCSW system of Baker. Via the *Shadow Folder*, Baker's publisher can access the photos and incorporate them immediately into the brochure. For a final review, the brochure is uploaded to a BSCW folder, which is connected as a *Semantic Folder* in Turners BC system. Here, the photographers may view the finished prototype, and representatives from both organisations can work in their own CWE, improving usability and efficiency. Additionally, we have been exploring a CWE interoperability architecture, based on SIOC (Semantically-Interlinked Online Communities), providing a middleware to enable multiple, independent CWE platforms and third-party applications to share and correlate data (Fig. 2).

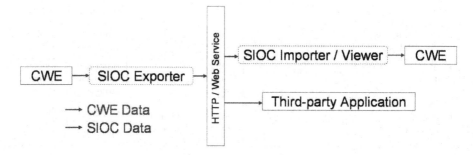

Fig. 2. Interoperability architecture

Firstly CWE data is exported as SIOC data. Then the SIOC data is imported by other CWEs or by third-party applications. Finally the SIOC data is utilized accordingly, including e.g. 1) SIOC Exporter; based on conceptual mapping, SIOC exporters translate platform-specific data into SIOC RDF data, 2) Workspace Synchronization Web Service; the workspace synchronization web service exposes the content of a CWE workspace as SIOC data to external systems. CWE items (documents, folders) may then be accessed, added, deleted, renamed, or replaced remotely via these services, and 3) SIOC Importer/Viewer; Importing remote SIOC data into a CWE allows a user to view data from a remote SIOC RDF source as if it was a local folder in the CWE. The SIOC Importer/Viewer reverts the SIOC data into CWE platform-specific data, based on conceptual mapping.

4 Living Lab Innovation and Workplace Change

Living labs are mechanisms for socio-technical systems change. ECOSPACE pursues the view of living labs as innovation projects, resulting in concrete innovations.

Whereas this is a valid and practical view, which might become clear from the examples presented in section 3, there is more to living labs. Living lab actors including researchers, users, developers and stakeholders engage in social relationships. To fulfil its potential, the living lab as an innovation system should be balanced with the system of initiating and building the living lab conditions, and with the dynamically changing characteristics of the wider professional community which is involved in living labs innovation. All three systems could potentially reinforce each other to support the development of a broad, self-sustainable innovation facility. We interpret our findings and results in terms of three interacting socio-technical systems as in Table 1: the living lab building system, the CWE innovation system, and the professional community system. Fig. 3 summarizes the interactions.

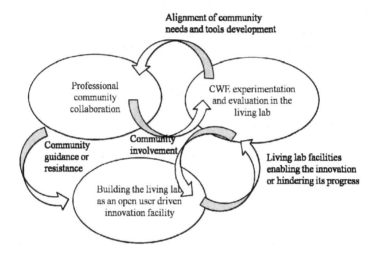

Fig. 3. The living lab as socio-technical system of learning and adaptation

The **living lab building system** is a dominant activity in the beginning of the project. However it strongly interacts with the professional community system, as community guidance and actually "ownership" is required in order to avoid negligence or even active resistance. The **CWE innovation system** in which the professional community normally should participate, regularly progresses through phases of preparation, limited prototyping and experimentation, wider scale experimentation and evaluation, and full-scale co-creation. Alignment of tools proposed by software developers and requested in the living lab is a critical process. Only if this alignment succeeds – which is essentially a human interaction process, conditioned by trust – there will be a basis for appropriation of the tools in the actual workplace. The **professional community system** evolves in close relation to the innovations in the CWE innovation system.

5 Conclusions

Our research shows that careful co-development of the living lab system, the CWE innovation system and the professional community system is required for living labs to fulfil the role as successful self-sustainable innovation facilities. In particular, the interplay and interfaces between these three systems must be carefully managed.

Change issues in socio-technological systems also play an important role in many facets of living lab related technology development and deployment, especially within the development models and processes (e.g. software design methodologies), change management during the development processes (e.g. management of requirements and releases) as well as the flexibility of the technological systems and tools provided (e.g. customisation and appropriation flexibility). Technology development within Living Lab activities brings multiple challenges, such as balancing openness and closure of the development process over time, balancing requirements and functionality implementation between local demands and broader target audiences, and balancing as-early-as-possible continuous user involvement and real-life usage with the required level of maturity for new tools released for productive use.

Ceating successful innovations in an open community setting is a complex undertaking that requires careful coordination of a number of different stakeholders and roles across the innovation lifecycle: Clear responsibilities and ownership is a critical success factor, and the level of ambition should be coherent with the resources available to avoid further fragmentation and situations where initiated activities are not completed, undermining the reputation of living labs as a systemic approach. Without clear leadership and proper clarification of ownership of the required support activities, there is a risk that valuable initiatives fail because phase-specific activities critical for the outcomes are missing or executed with poor quality.

References

1. Schaffers, H., Budweg, S., Kristensen, K., Ruland, R.: A living lab for enhancing collaboration in professional communities. Submitted to the ICE 2009 conference, Leiden (2009)
2. Appelt, W.: WWW based collaboration with the BSCW system. In: Pavelka, J., Tel, J., Bartosek, M. (eds.) SOFSEM 1999. LNCS, vol. 1725, p. 66. Springer, Heidelberg (1999)
3. Leavitt, H.J.: Applied organization change in industry: structural, technical and human approaches. In: March, J.G. (ed.) Handbook of Organizations, Chicago, Rand McNally, pp. 55–71 (1965)
4. Lyytinen, K., Newman, M.: Explaining information systems change: a punctuated sociotechnical change model. European Journal of Information Systems 17, 589–613 (2008)
5. Alter, S.: The work system method for understanding information systems and information systems research. Communications of the Association for Information Systems 9, 90–104 (2002)
6. Baskerville, R.: Investigating information systems with action research, Communications of the Association for Information Systems 2, Article 19 (1999),
   http://cais.isworld.org

Extracting and Utilizing Social Networks from Log Files of Shared Workspaces

Peyman Nasirifard, Vassilios Peristeras, Conor Hayes, and Stefan Decker

Digital Enterprise Research Institute,
National University of Ireland, Galway
IDA Business Park, Lower Dangan, Galway, Ireland
firstname.lastname@deri.org

Abstract[1]. Log files of online shared workspaces contain rich information that can be further analyzed. In this paper, log-file information is used to extract object-centric and user-centric social networks. The object-centric social networks are used as a means for assigning concept-based expertise elements to users based on the documents that they created, revised or read. The user-centric social networks are derived from users working on common documents. Weights, called the Cooperation Index, are assigned to links between users in a user-centric social network, which indicates how closely two people have collaborated together, based on their history. We also present a set of tools that was developed to realize our approach.

1 Introduction and Background

Online shared workspaces (e.g., BSCW[2], Business Collaborator[3], and Microsoft SharePoint) provide necessary tools and technologies for users to share various objects, synchronize them and collaborate together. When people collaborate within shared workspaces, they leave some fingerprints. These fingerprints may vary from events that happen on a document (e.g., read, revise, delete) to inviting a new member to the shared workspace. Most shared workspaces log these fingerprints and are able to export them in different formats. These log files contain valuable information and reflect the behaviors of users.

From one perspective, online social networks can be divided into two main groups[4]: object-centric and user-centric (i.e., ego-centric). In object-centric social networks, an object (e.g., document, video, music) connects people together, whereas in user-centric social networks, users are directly connected to each other. In this paper, we present an approach to use log files of online shared workspaces for extracting social networks

---

[1] An earlier version of this work was published in the paper [Nasirifard, P., Peristeras, V.: Expertise Extracting Within Online Shared Workspaces. In: Proceedings of the WebSci'09: Society On-Line (2009)].
[2] http://www.bscw.de/
[3] http://www.groupbc.com/
[4] http://www.zengestrom.com/blog/2005/04/why_some_social.html

L.M. Camarinha-Matos et al. (Eds.): PRO-VE 2009, IFIP AICT 307, pp. 643–650, 2009.
© IFIP International Federation for Information Processing 2009

among users. We use the extracted object-centric social network for assigning expertise. As well as using the extracted expertise as a dynamic approach for building inter- and intra-organization level expertise profiles, it can be also used to build teams that require specific expertise. We approach the hidden user-centric social network as a weighted graph. We call these weights Cooperation Indices. Cooperation Index is a factor that determines how closely two people work together and it can be used as a light-weight recommendation system in access-control mechanisms or for finding proxies.

In this paper, we also present the prototypes that we have developed: Holmes extracts the user-centric social network and calculates Cooperation Indices from log files of the BSCW shared workspace and Expert Finder extracts and assigns expertise elements to users of the BSCW shared workspace.

Before explaining our approach and demonstrating the tools, we present a brief overview of Semantic Web technologies. The Semantic Web [1] is an effort to ease interoperability among applications by providing standards for data representation and exchange (e.g., ontologies). The Resource Description Framework (RDF), which provides the grammar for the Semantic Web, is an important factor to enable this approach. RDF is a data model and supports the notion of subject-predicate-object; an RDF Triple. Recently, some shared workspaces (e.g., BSCW, BC) have started to export data in RDF. We decided to use the RDF data model in our approach. This eases the extension of our approach to different shared workspaces, as they are or will be RDF-aware. Moreover, using RDF enables other application developers to use our data and results in their own applications and/or mash-ups. A query language is required to query the RDF data. There exists some query languages for RDF, the most well-known being SPARQL[5] which was recently released as a W3C Recommendation. SPARQL is used in our work.

2 Related Work

For extracting social networks, we use a closed world called online shared workspaces, where various users (of a single or multiple projects) are able to share documents and collaborate together. In particular, we use the log files of shared workspaces, where all document-based events are stored.

Studying the relationships among people in a subset of the open environment (e.g., an online community, forums, mailing lists) or in a closed world (e.g., email), where the access to data is restricted to a specific person or a group of people, has attracted some researchers. Culotta et al. [2] present a system that extracts the users' social network by identifying unique people from email messages and finding their homepages and filling out the fields of a contact address book. Adamic et al. [3] present social network analysis of the Club Nexus online community. Xobni[6], which is a Microsoft Outlook plugin, is a search and navigation tool for Outlook inbox. It is able to follow the email discussions and generate the social network of email senders and receivers. Chang et al. [11] used blogs as a means for social learning and analysis.

---

[5] http://www.w3.org/TR/rdf-sparql-query/
[6] http://www.xobni.com/

Nurmela et al. [4] studied the log file of a groupware environment and demonstrated how the social network analysis approach can be used as a method to evaluate the social level structures and processes of a group studying in a Computer Supported Cooperative Learning (CSCL) environment. De Choudhury et al. [5] use social context to predict the information flow and introduce some parameters that play important roles in information flow. Demsar et al. [13] present coFinder, which crawls the Web for finding potential collaboration opportunities.

Finding experts and expertise have been also studied in many domains and platforms such as emails [6], Wikipedia [7], mailing lists [8], online communities [9], question-answering services [10], etc. There are many use cases for finding appropriate experts (e.g., recommendation systems for scientific and industrial activities). Our approach uses log files of online shared workspaces for extracting expertise.

3 Extracting and Using Social Networks

In this section, we present our model for extracting (object-centric and) user-centric social networks from log files of shared workspaces.

3.1 Object-Centric Social Networks

As stated in [12], a log file is composed of several log records and in each record, we assume that user ID, event name and object ID exist as minimum. User ID is the unique identification of a person that performs an event on an object that is also uniquely identifiable. For example, a log record in natural language can be *Person with ID 123 revised the document with ID 456*. In addition, log records can contain more information, such as description of the records, temporal aspects (e.g., timestamps) of log records, etc.

Building an object-centric social network from log file is quite straightforward. We translate the log records into RDF triples and store them in RDF store. In order to do this, we map the main elements of the log records to RDF concepts. The user ID of a record is mapped to RDF subject; the event is mapped to RDF predicate and the object ID is mapped to RDF object.

We approach the log file or extracted RDF triples in a document-centric perspective, which results in virtual clouds containing a document in the middle and several users around the document, who have performed various events on that document, as illustrated in Fig. 1. We use dynamic SPARQL queries for building such clouds from RDF repository. A document-centric perspective of a log file does not make sense, unless it is used for a useful use case.

3.2 Using Object-Centric Social Networks

As object-centric social networks, these document-centric clouds may be used as a means for extracting *expertise*. We define *expertise* as a piece of knowledge that has been acquired by a person in the past. We extract and assign expertise in three steps. For more information, refer to [12].

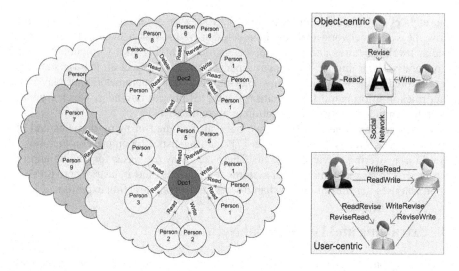

Fig. 1. Document-centric perspective of log file

Fig. 2. From object-centric to user-centric social network

3.3 User-Centric Social Networks

At this point we need to create a user-centric perspective, i.e., social relationships among users, where actions on objects (e.g., documents) connect people together. To obtain the desired user-centric social network, we remove the objects and connect people directly together based on the events that the users performed on a specific object. In other words, we combine the RDF predicates in order to build a user-centric social network, where people are directly connected together. Fig. 2 shows the overall approach of building a user-centric social network using an object-centric one.

The relationships between people are defined by a combination of events on objects. Generally, real-life social relationships are transitive. We noticed that we may also make the event-based relationships transitive by enabling users to traverse across document-centric clouds. Thus, the depth of event-based relationships is also important (i.e., moving from one cloud to another one). As an example, if user A has created a document which has been revised by user B and user B has read another document which has been deleted by user C, the depth of possible relationship between user A and user B (CreateEvent;ReviseEvent[7] is one, whereas the depth of the possible relationship between user A and user C is two (CreateEvent;ReviseEvent;ReadEvent;DeleteEvent), as two different documents were in the middle which were connected via user B. Note that all relationships are unidirectional. We do not store the user-centric social network in the RDF repository as these are built on-the-fly using SPARQL.

3.4 Assigning Weights to User-Centric Social Network

The extracted user-centric social network needs to be weighted. We call each weight of the user-centric social network a Cooperation Index; an index that determines how

---

[7] We use semicolon (;) as a separator between events.

closely two people work together. The higher the index is, the greater the collaboration history between two people. To calculate the index, we assign user-defined weights to the relationships between people and we sum up the frequency of relationships with consideration of weights. Due to space limitations, we do not present formal definitions, but just a use case scenario.

In the following, we provide an example for calculating Cooperation Index (for depth one). In our example, we have two users: Alice and Bob. They work together using the BSCW shared workspace and they take part in some document-based events (e.g., read, create) which then BSCW exports in CSV format. For simplicity, we just considered 8 records of the log file. Listing 1 shows this piece of log file. Of course, the greater the number of entries, the more accurate the Cooperation Index will be.

Listing 1. A piece of a sample log file

```
2007-03-10 17:17:55;337777;CreateEvent;11;D1;2;Bob;
2007-03-11 17:19:15;333481;CreateEvent;13;D3;1;Alice;
2007-03-16 09:13:22;335481;ReadEvent;13;D3;2;Bob;
2007-03-17 12:17:56;385481;ReviseEvent;13;D3;2;Bob;
2007-03-17 13:17:45;337431;ReadEvent;12;D2;2;Bob;
2007-03-17 14:19:35;332581;ReviseEvent;12;D2;1;Alice;
2007-03-17 16:10:25;346541;ReadEvent;12;D2;1;Alice;
2007-03-18 13:25:15;312431;ReviseEvent;11;D1;1;Alice;
```

Each log record/entry starts with temporal information; followed by event ID, event name, object ID, object name, user ID and user name. For simplicity, we did not present other elements of the actual BSCW log records.

Suppose that Alice wants to calculate her Cooperation Index at depth one with Bob. To do so, we should calculate the possible relationships between Alice and Bob taking into account the documents in the middle. In the following, such relationships are presented:

- Relationship regarding to D1: *ReviseEvent;CreateEvent*
- Relationships regarding to D2: *ReadEvent;ReadEvent* and *ReviseEvent; ReadEvent*
- Relationships regarding to D3: *CreateEvent;ReadEvent* and *CreateEvent; ReviseEvent*

In the next step, we should set user-defined weights for the relationships. Here users can decide what types of relationship are more important depending on the context of the specific common project or collaboration. In other words, it is the user that decides what types of relationship should have more effect and influence on calculation. In our example, Alice assigns the following weights to her possible relationships with others:

- CreateEvent;ReviseEvent = 0.4
- ReviseEvent;CreateEvent = 0.2
- ReviseEvent;ReviseEvent = 0.4

Due to space limitation, we did not present the relationships with the weight zero. Now, based on the relationships between Alice and Bob and also the weights assigned by her, we calculate the Cooperation Index by counting the frequency of the relationships between Alice and Bob for depth one with consideration of weights. We reach the value 0.6 for this Cooperation Index.

4 Prototypes

We have developed several prototypes to realize our approaches. The prototypes are based on a Service-Oriented Architecture (SOA). In SOA, business processes are packaged as services and are accessible via end points to end users. We used Apache CXF[8] in order to develop Web services. The User Interface (UI) of the prototypes is powered by JSP. We used OpenRDF[9] Sesame 2.0 as RDF store. The tools use the data provided by the Ecospace[10] project. 183 users were extracted from the log file.

As stated in [12], **Expert Finder** is a simple prototype for extracting and assigning expertise elements to users of BSCW shared workspace. Fig. 3 demonstrates some snapshots of Expert Finder. The prototype is accessible online[11].

Fig. 3. Some snapshots of Expert Finder   **Fig. 4.** Some snapshots of Holmes

Holmes extracts the user-centric social network from log files and calculates Cooperation Indices between users. Fig. 4 demonstrates some snapshots of Holmes. Ecospace users are able to select their user names from a select box, assign desired weights to their relationships and calculate the Cooperation Indices with the rest. To reduce the overhead for users, we assigned predefined weights to all relationships. In our case, *CreateEvent;ReviseEvent* and *ReviseEvent;CreateEvent* have bigger weights. The Holmes prototype is accessible online[12].

---

[8] http://cxf.apache.org/
[9] http://www.openrdf.org/
[10] Ecospace is a European Integrated Project (IP) in the area of Collaborative Working Environment (CWE). For more information refer to http://www.ip-ecospace.org/
[11] http://purl.oclc.org/projects/expertui
[12] http://purl.oclc.org/projects/holmes

5 Discussions and Evaluations

Using a query-based approach (i.e., SPARQL) enabled us to extract some interesting facts from existing log records. For example, by counting all triples that contain a certain user as a RDF subject and with the consideration of document-centric approach for social networks, it can be inferred who has read the most amount of documents during the life cycle of the project, who has revised the most, who has deleted the most, etc. These statistical results can be used to determine the most active persons during the time period of a project. The *active* person can be defined as a person, who carries out more document events than others taking into account the time intervals.

Besides statistical results, one of the interesting outputs was a dynamic approach for visualizing the social networks of users, based on document-events. To do so, we built a simple mash-up from RDF triples generated by queries to NetDraw[13] input format. NetDraw is a free social-network visualizer tool, which accepts plain text files as input. Due to space limitations, we do not present the snapshots.

We conducted a simple experimental evaluation for expert finding approach. The result can be found at [12]. We also conducted a simple experimental evaluation for Cooperation Index approach. We asked 12 participants of the Ecospace project to have a look at their extracted social networks. All of them confirmed that the presented results were relevant to them. They had also some suggestions: Currently, for calculating the Cooperation Index, we considered four main document events (i.e., Create, Revise, Delete, and Read) and only relationships at a depth of one. These events can be simply extended to cover more document events as well as deeper depths. One important issue that may arise with more types of events and deeper depths is to combine events and assign weights to them, which in some cases can bring overhead for users. In a more complex model for calculating Cooperation Indices, different weights can be posed to documents based on their importance for the collaboration process. So, some documents may have bigger weights assigned by their creators and this could be then taken into account when calculating the Cooperation Indices.

6 Conclusion and Future Work

In this paper, we presented an approach for extracting and utilizing social networks from log files of shared workspaces. We used the extracted social network for two main use cases: Finding expertise and calculating Cooperation Index, which can be seen as a weighted user-centric social network. Cooperation Index is a benchmark that determines how close two people collaborate together. We demonstrated also our prototypes (Holmes and Expert Finder).

Besides the points mentioned by the evaluators, we plan to benefit from temporal aspects of log files to enable users to calculate the Cooperation Indices within a specific time period. Currently, the Cooperation Indices are calculated during the life cycle of the project.

---

[13] http://www.analytictech.com/

Acknowledgments. The authors thank Alexander Schutz and Marco Zuniga. The work presented in this paper has been funded in part by SFI under Grant No. SFI/08/CE/I1380 (Lion-2) and the EU under Grant No. FP6-IST-5-35208 (Ecospace).

References

1. Berners-Lee, T., Hendler, J., Lassila, O.: The Semantic Web, A new form of Web content that is meaningful to computers will unleash a revolution of new possibilities. Scientific American (May 2001)
2. Culotta, A., Bekkerman, R., McCallum, A.: Extracting social networks and contact information from email and the Web. In: First Conference on Email and Anti-Spam (2004)
3. Adamic, L.A., Buyukkokten, O., Adar, E.: A social network caught in the Web. First Monday 8(6) (2003)
4. Nurmela, K., Lehtinen, E., Palonen, T.: Evaluating CSCL log files by social network analysis. In: CSCL 1999: Proceedings of the conference on Computer support for collaborative learning. International Society of the Learning Sciences (1999)
5. De Choudhury, M., Sundaram, H., John, A., Seligmann, D.: Dynamic prediction of communication flow using social context. In: HT 2008: Proceedings of the nineteenth ACM conference on Hypertext and hypermedia, pp. 49–54. ACM, New York (2008)
6. Balog, K., De Rijke, M.: Finding experts and their details in e-mail corpora. In: WWW 2006: Proceedings of the 15th international conference on World Wide Web (2006)
7. Demartini, G.: Finding experts using Wikipedia. In: Proceedings of the 2nd International ISWC+ASWC Workshop on Finding Experts on the Web with Semantics (2007)
8. Chen, H., Shen, H., Xiong, J., Tan, S., Cheng, X.: Social network structure behind the mailing lists. ICT-IIIS at TREC 2006 Expert Finding Track. In: Fifteenth Text Retrieval Conference, TREC (2006)
9. Zhang, J., Ackerman, M.S., Adamic, L.: Expertise networks in online communities: structure and algorithms. In: Proceedings of the 16th international conference on World Wide Web, New York, NY, USA, pp. 221–230 (2007)
10. Liu, X., Croft, W.B., Koll, M.: Finding experts in community-based question-answering services. In: CIKM 2005: Proceedings of the 14th ACM international conference on Information and knowledge management, New York, NY, USA, pp. 315–316 (2005)
11. Chang, Y., Chang, Y., Hsu, S., Chen, C.: Social network analysis to blog-based online community. In: ICCIT 2007: Proceedings of the 2007 International Conference on Convergence Information Technology (2007)
12. Nasirifard, P., Peristeras, V.: Expertise extracting within online shared workspaces. In: Proceedings of the WebSci 2009: Society On-Line (2009)
13. Demsar, D., Mozetic, I., Lavrac, N.: Collaboration opportunity finder. In: Virtual Enterprises and Collaborative Networks, pp. 179–186. Springer, Heidelberg (2007)

Supporting the Change of Cooperation Patterns by Integrated Collaboration Tools

Wolfgang Prinz[1], Nils Jeners[1], Rudolf Ruland[1], and Matteo Villa[2]

[1] Fraunhofer FIT, Schloss Birlinghoven, 53754 Sankt Augustin, Germany
{Wolfgang.Prinz,Nils.Jeners,Rudolf.Ruland}@fit.fraunhofer.de
[2] TXT e-Solutions S.p.A., Via Frigia 27, 20100 Milano, Italy
Matteo.Villa@txt.it

Abstract. Although a number of new collaboration systems emerged of the last years, it is remarkable that email is still the most used collaboration application. However, this messaging based pattern of organizing collaboration causes a lot of problems like information and attachment overload and versioning problems. This paper discusses some of these problems as well as reasons why users are reluctant to switch to alternative cooperation means like document sharing in virtual project environments. Based on these observations we present tools developed with the EU funded Ecospace project that address these issue. These tools simplify the sharing process by combining and integrating sharing functionality with messaging, thus reducing the functional and cognitive distance between both environments.

Keywords: CSCW, Collaboration, Sharing, Architecture, Interoperability.

1 Introduction and Motivation

Many cooperation support applications exist, but email is still the primary medium for electronic cooperation within and between organizations. Furthermore we can observe that email is often used for purposes that can be easier supported by other applications. However when we look for reasons to explain this misuse of email or the non-use of the more specialized systems instead of email, we can find a few simple reasons:

- Simplicity and usability: It is much easier to click the forward button to distribute an email or a document attachment than to start another application.
- Loss of context: If the user decides to start or use another application for his cooperation process the first step is to select the right process or group for his cooperation goal. This takes often several actions, i.e. finding and browsing to the right group or shared location, while typing the email address of a distribution list is much simpler.
- Lack of interoperability: Actually email is probably the most interoperable communication media. It works very reliably within and between organizations, while other systems like application sharing, shared workspaces and virtual project offices are almost not interoperable between different products.

L.M. Camarinha-Matos et al. (Eds.): PRO-VE 2009, IFIP AICT 307, pp. 651–658, 2009.
© IFIP International Federation for Information Processing 2009

- Lack of desktop presence: Email, together with a web-browser is the most present application on the user's desktop. Most other applications are started only on de-mand. Thus everything that does not appear in the email client is too far away from the user's attention and it thus not recognized.

The following table provides further examples of email usage and associated problems:

Table 1. Email use and misuse

Cooperation process using email	Associated Problem	Specific application for this process
Exchange of a document as an email attachment between two people or through a distribution list	Multiple copies in all users email inboxes, versioning problem, information overload via distribution list	Shared folder of shared workspace systems.
Lengthly email discussions with multiple replies and threads	Email overload, loss of context	Discussion forums, Blogs
Status emails explaining the fulfillment of a task or the creation or modification of a document	Email overload, loss of context between task and email	RSS feeds, awareness tools
Availability emails, asking for the presence and availability of a user	Use of an asynchronous media to support a synchronous task, email overload	Presence systems

Beside an identification of problems the table also indicates cooperation applications and services that may be more suitable for a specific cooperation process. In the remaining of this paper we will present further approaches that have been developed in the context of the Ecospace[1] project to address these problems in the context of a cooperative activity [1].

2 From Messaging to Sharing

Information and communication overload is caused by the fact that information that should actually be shared is distributed by a communication media like email. Instead of storing relevant information in a dedicated location, users tend to forward and distribute that information via a distribution list. As a consequence this information is copied to all recipients. Often this leads to multiple replies in which various versions of a document are exchanged, resulting in a situation in which nobody actually knows about the location and version of the current document.

An important reason for this behavior is the fact that it is much simpler to forward a document by email than to store it in a shared repository such as a shared workspace or virtual project system. For example, storing a document that has been received as an attachment by email in a shared workspace requires the following steps: Saving the attached document as a local file, starting the application or opening the appropriate web-site, navigation to the relevant project workspace, uploading the local file into

---

[1] Ecospace is an Integrated Project (No. 035208), partly funded by the EC.

the workspace. Compared to these steps the forwarding action is much simpler. This observation indicates that we need tools that support a paradigm shift from messaging to sharing. The following sections describe tools to simplify information sharing.

2.1 Smart Sharing Support

In recent years shared workspace systems [2] have become a widespread tool for the support of flexible and weakly structured cooperation in teams and communities. Typical examples for such systems are BSCW [3], Groove [4], or MS-Sharepoint [5]. Application areas for these systems are manifold such as the coordination of lectures, intra- and inter-organisational projects, or communities.

A shared workspace normally contains different types of information such as documents, pictures, URL collections, threaded discussions, or member profiles. The content of each workspace is represented as information objects arranged in a folder hierarchy. Since shared workspace systems do not impose a fixed structure on the workspace organization, each workspace can be organized according to the needs and requirements of the cooperating team. Most preferred structures for workspace organization are project structures (work packages, meetings) or organizational structures (departments, projects). Often structures that reflect both criteria are applied. However, the aim and intention of these structures is often not immediately visible to the users who share a workspace. Although workspace or folder descriptions can be used to describe the purpose of each workspace, users are often confused about the hierarchy, resulting in the effect that they have problems in finding the adequate folder to which they can upload a new document or where they can find the appropriate information. Although the users cooperate through a shared workspace, they often fail to develop a common understanding [6] or common conventions [7]. As a consequence they often complain about the complexity of a shared workspace and moreover they tend to turn back to email attachments for the sharing of documents, which contradicts the approach of a shared.

The shared workspace organizer [8] has been our first approach to address that problem. This approach makes use of the fact, that workspaces associate meta-information with each object (e.g. document owner, document mime type, creation date, version information, etc). The shared workspace organizer (SWO) uses that information in combination with a text analysis of all shared workspaces to propose suitable upload locations. After a user selects a local document the SWO suggests suitable upload locations based on a comparison of the document content with the indexed content of the shared workspace. Then the user could either select one of the suggested locations or he could use them for further navigation to the right place. In any case the SWO simplifies the upload of documents to a shared environment. The drawback of this solution is that it is mainly applicable to text documents and that it requires a continuous text mining and update of the shared workspace content. This consideration as well as experiments with a document context management tool [9] led to the development of a much simpler tool to support the smart upload of documents to a shared environment.

The smart upload tool is based on an extension of the standard document attributes by a context attribute that contains the original location of the document within the shared workspace. This context attribute is added by the shared workspace system and it contains information about the document location and the last modification date. This information is represented in XML as part of the new MS-Office document format that supports the extension of office documents by user defined attributes. The smart upload tool appears as an icon on the user's desktop. Whenever a user drags an object onto that icon, the upload tool analysis the document for the context information. If a document contains that meta-data it is interpreted and the document is stored at its original location in the shared workspace. If the tool detects that the document has been edited after the user downloaded the document from the shared workspace, it informs that user about a possible version conflict. The user can then decide to create a new version or to cancel the upload to solve the conflict manually.

This tool addresses primarily the *simplicity* problem identified above: it reduces the upload process that usually involves several navigation steps to a simple drag and drop action.

2.2 Sharing Instead of Forwarding Attachments

The Sharing Support[2] tool further supports the paradigm shift from messaging to sharing. The tool itself is realized as an MS-Outlook plug-in that creates a new toolbar within the Outlook environment, which allows users to select one or more e-mail attachments for being saved in a shared environment and to provide additional context information. Instead of forwarding the email to a distribution list he can activate the "ECOSPACE Share" button. This results in pop-up window in which the user is able to choose the location of the shared folders and to add or modify meta-data (sender, receiver, subject, date, body, and comments) from the email.

Once metadata and location have been set, the plug-in will upload the documents to the corresponding BSCW shared repository using a set of pre-defined web-services [10]. The metadata is stored as attributes of the document, thus keeping the context of the document preserved.

This tool addresses two of the problems identified above: *simplicity* by integration of the sharing functionality into the messaging environment and *loss of context* by preserving the email context as metadata in the shared document attributes.

3 Cooperation Interoperability beyond Email

Shared Workspace platforms support a wide variety of collaboration functionalities such as document management, versioning, project blogging, shared todo lists or calendars. In many organizations SW platforms providing these functionalities are already implemented. However, cooperation processes occur not only within a single organization but more and more between various organizations that are involved in common projects. In this kind of situation a strategy of using a single SW platform cannot be applied for the following reasons:

- Cooperating organizations have already different shared workspace technologies in use. Furthermore, it often happens that different departments or divisions within a single big organization use different shared workspace platforms.

---

[2] http://www.ami-communities.eu/wiki/ECOSPACE_Newsletter_No_4#Sharing_Support.

- Access policies or licenses restrictions make it impossible to open the local shared workspace platform to external users.
- Partners are unable to agree on which SW platform to select.
- Users are reluctant to learn another SW platform while they have already one in use.

For users who are involved in several cross-organizational cooperation projects, this strategy of using one SW platform per project would imply that they have to learn as many different cooperation platforms as selected by the projects they are involved in. However, users are absolutely not motivated to invest much time in learning different tools that provide almost the same services, as they feel like wasting their time. This kind of particular situation is explaining why often users turn back to the most simple cooperation tool they know the best such as email attachment to "share" a document (though, in this case it is more about "sending a document" than really "sharing a document"). For sure, as the emailing protocol is a standard it gives the freedom to organizations and users to select the email server and client they prefer which is a very good illustration of the power of standardization.

Consequently, it would be really great if SW platforms could have a good level of interoperability enabling users to access posted objects on other SW platforms from their own SW client whatever is the SW server.

Interoperability between SW platforms is addressed by the ECOSPACE Collaborative Working Environments (CWE) reference architecture. The most important components in this CWE reference architecture are the identification of basic services for each collaboration service and the definition of an exchange/communication protocol enabling the representation and interpretation of the workspace object meta-data from different SW platforms. Each SW application implements standardized basic services enabling:

- Access (read/write) to workspace objects,
- Retrieval of the workspace organization (i.e. the folder structure) and user information;
- Exchange of objects' meta-data through the use of the SIOC (Semantically-Interlinked Online Communities) format [11].

According to this interoperability approach, each SW service is now offering the same web services to access and modify objects' meta-data. Access to this information is provided by new interface components in each shared workspace user interface. These components provide access to the workspaces of remote systems in a transparent way and in the same look and feel as if they were local workspaces while they are external.

The following use case is an illustration of interoperability among 3 different Shared Workspace platforms (BSCW, Business Collaborator and SharePoint). Three companies are starting a joint project and they wish to use their own available SW platform (BSCW, Business Collaborator or SharePoint) for both their own developed objects and joint developed objects. Company A uses BSCW, company B uses Business Collaborator and Company C uses SharePoint. In a first step, each company creates a project workspace in their own SW platform. Afterwards, they reciprocally invite participants from the cooperating organizations as external users to their own project workspace. Finally, they exchange the web service address (the access path to their local workspace). The way this access path is used in the respective SW platform depends on the local implementation. The implementation for BSCW is described below.

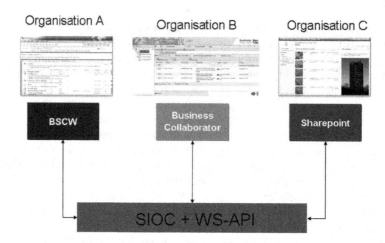

Fig. 1. Shared Workspace Interoperability based on the SIOC format and Web-Services API

A user in BSCW creates a new folder which is a "shadow" folder type by providing the access path to the external folder, located into another SW platform, as well as the authentication information to access the remote SW platform. This shadow folder is created as a "sub-folder" of the local project workspace which is the "top" folder. When a user opens this shadow folder then a special background color indicates that the information provided in this folder is not stored into the local SW platform but accessed from a remote SW server. Furthermore, the shadow folder provides the same look and feel that users are used to have on their own SW platform. It means that users can access the external objects information that are actually stored into another SW platform in a very transparent way without to have to learn other SW platforms.

Obviously the functionalities offered by this shadow folder type are limited to the necessary set of services required to access and modify objects. In this implementation example, the current limitation is that other advanced functionalities provided by some SW platforms (i.e. rating, annotating, tagging) cannot be used. Therefore, future work should address this issue by the development of a more advanced protocol that enables also the exchange of service capabilities between the different SW platforms.

This concept addresses the *interoperability* problem identified above: it provides a references architecture in combination with the definition of web-services and protocols to enable transparent access between different shared workspace systems.

4 Modularization of Cooperation Services

Current cooperation solutions are very often still monolithic entities. Although they often provide a user interface that can be adapted to the user's needs, they cannot be completely reconfigured or re-assembled by the user. This is in contrast to the self-service and customization mentality of the users who are used to configure their working environment by downloading and installing the appropriate tools.

Applying a reference architecture [12], including the definition of basic cooperation services, we can open the door towards an individually configurable cooperation solution. This is achieved by realizing a set of interaction widgets to support basic collaboration services. It means that users can configure their cooperation environment by the selection of those collaboration services that are most appropriate for their specific tasks. This motivation has lead to the development of a set of CWE widgets that correspond to basic collaboration functions.

Fig. 2. Comparison of a monolithic user interface and a widget based collaboration portal

Figure 2 is presenting, in the left part, a screenshot of BSCW user interface and in the right part an example of a widget based application which is a portal page in iGoogle that includes different widgets for basic collaborative services. Using that portal page to combine different cooperation widgets any project participant can personalize his private activity space and information visualization to support his collaborative activities in accessing different services of the Shared Workspace platform.

This widget approach for a cooperation environment addresses the *desktop presence* problem identified above: it enables users to add different cooperation functionalities as widgets to their desktop, thus staying aware of the ongoing activities in the related cooperation processes.

5 Summary and Conclusion

This paper presents different approaches to overcome current cooperation problems that originate in the use and misuse of email as the primary communication media. At the beginning we have identified four main problems and for each problem a possible solution has been presented:

Simplicity and usability as well as **loss of context** is addressed by simple sharing tools that reduce the overhead of navigation within a shared workspace to simple drag and drop operations. **Lack of interoperability** is addressed by a shared workspace interoperability approach based on a reference architecture including shared workspaces and a SIOC based exchange protocol. **Lack of desktop presence** can be overcome by the approach to widgetize a complex cooperation environment to enable users to configure their own environment as their desktop.

We believe that these concepts can provide a first step towards a change of cooperation patterns from messaging to sharing, thus reducing communication overload and complexity.

References

1. Harrison, B.L., Cozzi, A., Moran, T.P.: Roles and relationships for unified activity management. In: Proceedings of the 2005 international ACM GROUP conference, Sanibel Island, Florida, USA, pp. 236–245. ACM Press, New York (2005)
2. Hans Schaffers, T.B., Pallot, M., Prinz, W. (ed.): The Future Workplace - Perspectives on Mobile and Collaborative Working. Telematica Instituut, The Netherlands, p. 112 (2006)
3. Appelt, W.: WWW Based Collaboration with the BSCW System. In: Bartosek, M., Tel, G., Pavelka, J. (eds.) SOFSEM 1999. LNCS, vol. 1725, p. 66. Springer, Heidelberg (1999)
4. Groove-Networks, Groove (2005)
5. Microsoft, Microsoft Sharepoint (2005)
6. Bannon, L., Bødker, S.: Constructing Common Information Spaces. In: ECSCW 1997: Fifth European Conference on Computer Supported Cooperative Work, Lancaster, UK. Kluwer Academic Publishers, Dordrecht (1997)
7. Prinz, W., Mark, G., Pankoke-Babatz, U.: Designing Groupware for Congruency in Use. In: CSCW 1998: ACM Conference on Computer Supported Cooperative Work, Seattle. ACM Press, New York (1998)
8. Prinz, W., Zaman, B.: Proactive Support for the Organization of Shared Workspaces Using Activity Patterns and Content Analysis. In: GROUP 2005: 2005 International ACM SIG-GROUP Conference on Supporting Group Work, Sanibel Island, Florida, USA. ACM Press, New York (2005)
9. Vonrueden, M., Prinz, W.: Distributed Document Contexts in Cooperation Systems. In: Kokinov, B., Richardson, D.C., Roth-Berghofer, T.R., Vieu, L. (eds.) CONTEXT 2007. LNCS, vol. 4635, pp. 507–516. Springer, Heidelberg (2007)
10. Prinz, W., et al.: ECOSPACE – Towards an Integrated Collaboration Space for eProfessionals. In: CollaborateCom 2006, Atlanta. IEEE Press, Los Alamitos (2006)
11. Breslin, J., Decker, S.: The Future of Social Networks on the Internet: The Need for Semantics. IEEE Internet Computing 11(6), 86–90 (2007)
12. Peristeras, V., et al.: Towards a Reference Architecture for Collaborative Work Environments. International Journal of e-Collaboration (to appear, 2009)

Virtual Enterprises for Integrated Energy Service Provision

Luke Allan and Karsten Menzel

University College Cork, IRUSE, Ireland
{l.allan,k.menzel}@ucc.ie

Abstract. Holistic Energy Service Provision has the potential to provide new business opportunities for Facility Management Companies, Building Managers, Energy Providers, Maintenance Providers and many other stakeholders currently working in the area of building design, construction, building operation, energy management, maintenance, etc. since customers wish to get access to all services related to energy supply, energy consumption and building services maintenance through a "one-stop-shop".

Our paper describes how the concept of Virtual Enterprises/Virtual Organizations could be applied in the area of Energy Service Provision. The paper describes the context, the relevant stakeholders, required novel IT-services and finally the concept of "Extended Energy Profiles" to allow easy and standardised exchange of Energy Information amongst potential partners in an "Energy Service Company" established on the VO-paradigm.

Keywords: Virtual Enterprise, Service Provider.

1 Introduction

According to the "World Energy Assessment" delivered by United Nations Development Programme UNPD (cf. UNDP 2004), the global average growth rate of energy use of primary energy is about 1,5% per year. If this rate is preserved throughout the coming years, the total energy use will double between 2000 and 2040, and triple by 2060. This growth rate can no longer be supported. Most importantly, we must reduce our dependence on fossil fuels because their usage leads to CO_2 emissions contributing to global warming. A substantial part of the energy (approx. 40%) is used to operate buildings. Therefore, the challenges for the construction sector are (i) to improve the energy-efficiency of buildings and (ii) to provide solutions which enable the optimal usage of renewable energy sources.

Sustainable energy and carbon neutrality are now major management issues for building owners and operators. Organisations in the area of Total Energy and Facility Management need to become Virtual because of the increased complexity of the required technical solutions. Virtual Enterprises may be created to investigate and utilise alternative forms of energy sources such as solar, geothermal, biomass, wind but to name a few. These sources of energy can be tied into an existing system provided for by the national grid.

L.M. Camarinha-Matos et al. (Eds.): PRO-VE 2009, IFIP AICT 307, pp. 659–666, 2009.

2 Infrastructure for Energy Service Provision

Technologies for distributed energy generation provide an 'early action' approach to greenhouse-gas reductions because they are available now. They can be introduced into present-day BMS with moderate special network technology or market developments. Distributed energy refers to clean local generation and demand management at customer sites.

Domestic energy management is supported by Intelligent Building Management Systems (iBMS). They are being developed to help manage appliances efficiently, integrate renewable generation, and inform customers about options and consequences of different energy choices. Locally distributed controllers are part of iBMS. These controllers confer with the building occupants, to find out individual preferences, and accommodate these. They are also used to effectively manage the operation of (renewable) energy generation at the building or in a nearby district.

Mini-grids might combine heating, ventilation, air-conditioning, and refrigeration appliances; and receive energy generated from different sources; i.e. certain communities in an area of limited size can be independent of national energy grids, or achieve specific energy requirements while remaining grid-connected, by adopting local generation sources and new management and control technologies.

Smart Grids or Neighbourhood Management Systems (NMS) are based on the assumption that each house (or customer) has a controller that communicates with all major appliances, and with controllers in nearby houses in the network. The controllers also communicate with the electricity company, to find out when peaks in demand are expected.

All the infrastructure components described above are part of so called smart neighbourhoods where houses work together to ensure that they operate as efficiently as possible to minimise power drawn from the main grid, especially during times of peak demand. This means, home energy management will be coordinated across multiple households for aggregated benefits.

2.1 The Need for Virtual Enterprises

Over time changes have forced organisations and companies to review not only how they do business with others but also how they themselves are structured in order to become more competitive and profitable. Changes in technology, information systems, globalisation, economies and legal requirements have all played a part in how organisations act in today's world. In response to these changes companies have been forced to review and change their structures in order to not only comply but also to carry on as a viable business. Becoming part of a Virtual Enterprise within a Virtual Organisation will become the norm in order to service in an ever increasing competitive and technical world.

In terms of Energy Services the purpose of the Virtual Enterprise is to provide a new solution to a new scenario – the utilisation of independent energy services. This will mean that the Energy Services Virtual Enterprise will be based on the ability to create co-operation and to realise the value of business opportunities between the Energy Services partners. Energy Services also includes additional services such as inspection, maintenance, monitoring, decision support and retrofit. Katzy et al 1999 propose three goals of a Virtual Enterprise.

Applying these in the context of this paper the first goal is to create value from changing opportunities within the environment of the Virtual Enterprise. The Virtual Enterprise involving the Energy Services partners will show a distinct difference from the traditional monopolistic government owned energy provision. With the co-operation of the partners the Virtual Enterprise will be able to benefit from the changing opportunities within their environment.

For the second goal the Virtual Enterprise will also present an alternative way to the traditional form in so far as differentiating and integrating energy service provision under dynamic conditions. This will allow the providers to seize new opportunities rapidly through structured cooperation between providers.

In the third goal the Virtual Enterprise will be defined from its manoeuvres rather than its command structure and from the operations rather than from the organisation.

In the case of IT-supported Energy Service Provision (ESP) this will mean that the services of the Facilities Manager will co-operate with independent energy providers and users. Reasons are increased complexity triggered by additional components such as solar and geothermal power which may require local knowledge and expertise. Virtual Enterprises can be seen as a subset of these Virtual Organisations.

A further benefit from utilising Virtual Enterprises would be in the sphere of NMS whereby energy might be provided from a number of energy sources and managed through one central organisation, either the facilities manager or the Energy Service Company (ESCO). This would allow the various stakeholders to join forces and offer new value-added services for energy management.

3 Stakeholders for Energy Service Provision

Many decision makers are involved in producing and delivering various forms of energy, with different decision protocols, different time and space horizons, and different areas of concern. Utilities, regulators, and consumers need to know how to better use energy related information, since they all share the goal of maintaining service reliability while meeting necessary revenue or cost goals.

3.1 End Users – Occupants and Owners of Buildings

Occupants and owners of either residential or office buildings create an energy demand according to their energy usage profile. They have the closest control of the energy consumption. Therefore it is essential that energy management services can be delivered remotely and cost-efficiently in a mass market.

Furthermore building occupants are one valuable source to evaluate user comfort based on the performance of building systems and components. Measuring and documenting the user satisfaction with environmental factors such as air quality, thermal comfort, or lighting means this data could be used to determine and evaluate service level agreements with Facility Management and Energy Service Providers.

With increasing energy prices and increasing numbers and complexity of "consuming systems" (e.g. heating, lighting) and "producing" systems (e.g. solar panels, heat pumps) End Users and Owners of buildings have an increasing demand for expert Energy Management Services since the operation of such complex systems can no longer be managed by the user itself.

3.2 Energy Providers / Operators of Generation Facilities in NMS

The increased integration of renewable energy sources into Energy Grids leads to the fact that the grid operation becomes much more complex. Detailed information about the supply capacity of the individual (renewable) energy sources is essential to balance the grid operation and the overall capacity of the grid. Vice versa a more precise prediction of the energy demand is required to assist the grid operators in managing the different "generation sources" in the most sustainable way. This can create a position whereby energy providers may be able to purchase or trade-off in relation to the acquisition of the information produced through the use of iBMS.

As a major stakeholder the Energy Provider has much to gain from being part of the ICT Integration for ESP since they can facilitate more accurate information about user's needs and consequentially provide value added services to better support operation and maintenance of buildings.

3.3 Total Facilities Management Providers and Energy Service Companies

The provision of Facilities Management Services includes Energy Management and other forms of technical and infrastructural building management. Currently, Facilities Management Systems are insufficiently integrated with BMS. Therefore, the integrated planning of inspection and maintenance activities is not easily achievable. The availability of standardised data exchange formats and mechanisms would be of great help to improve the interoperability of the available systems, such as Building Information Modelling Tools (BIM), Building Management Systems and Computer Aided Facility Management Systems.

Furthermore, the information provided from energy audits would also allow the Facility Management Providers to make predictions depending on the course of action for retrofit and renovation determined by the Building Owner/Occupier/User as a result of that audit. Consultancy services to improve the energy efficient operation of buildings could be offered to users and owners of buildings.

Currently, so called Energy Service Companies are established to provide energy delivery from multiple sources, energy management, building operation, and equipment maintenance as a "one stop shop" to customers. Within this paper we consider these ESCO-scenarios as part of "Total Facilities Management" concepts

4 Novel IT Service and New Business Model for Energy Service Provision

The development of advanced IT-services for improved ESP addresses many challenges. The introduction of advanced BMS will lead to more energy efficient operation of buildings; the application of NMS will support the easy and efficient integration of renewable energy sources into existing energy networks. These IT-solutions will generate more data which document User Comfort and the Performance of systems and specify User Demands and available Supply Capacity from renewable energy sources. Energy Information could be used by Energy Providers, Facility Managers, Energy Experts and other stakeholders to offer so called Value Added Services to Owners and

Occupants of buildings. Therefore, new business models in the energy sector are required to close the gap between the interests (cf. Kettonen 2007) of the different stakeholders in the energy sector, to enable the integrated usage of Energy Information, to support the development of 'Value Added Services', and finally to offer these services in new, innovative ways to clients (Osterwalder 2005). Novel IT services are required to support these new business models for ESP.

4.1 Energy Profiling

Like other commodities, energy prices are tied to supply and demand, making it critical to forecast energy requirements to better quantify future needs.

Currently, utilities use energy profiling to predict future energy requirements. Load profiles, an estimate of average energy patterns for a group of customers based on load research sample data, are used to shape a cumulative meter reading from 15 minutes to 60 minutes intervals. The profiles are regressions made up of calendar, weather and daylight variables. New technology, like automated meter reading will make more granular data available and allow utility providers to:

* Achieve more accurate profiles by conducting more in-depth statistical analysis on individual customers and customer groups
* Complete more frequent updates on profiles or even to create more profile groups by utilizing actual historical data as opposed to "shaped" data.

4.2 Energy Information as 'Tradable' Good

In chapter 5 of this paper we argue that the introduction of additional energy profiles is required to support the exchange of relevant information for ESP in a standardised way (cf Gokce 2009). Advanced analytics and novel information technologies, such as Service Oriented Architectures, can enable the various stakeholders to reduce cost for information provided and exchanged, increase customer retention, and efficiently manage supply contract risk.

4.3 Demand Prediction

Demand, or load, modelling is a key planning tool. Under competition, and with increased consumer involvement in the market, demand side management (DSM) alternatives will also alter demand models as prices change with load and as consumers plan their own consumption more consciously, with their own energy profiles and demand models. This complex interaction of social and physical variables has the potential to produce significant nonlinear dynamics in local and regional demand for energy, such as electricity, gas, steam, or hot water. Energy Technology researchers are trialing intelligent, self-learning, interconnected controllers to manage energy demand and reduce greenhouse gas emissions by homes and businesses.

4.4 Supply Forecast

Some energy customers meet portions of energy demand with local co-generation. The economic and reliable operation of the renewable energy sources is especially demanding of accurate supply and demand forecasts and related tools for planning and operations management. Knowledge of accurate, location-specific weather, climate, and energy market information is necessary to model the supply capacity. Since retail energy prices vary with load, and other parameters, this calculation can be very complex.

Grid management involves many entities, and stakeholders with differing expertise all need the high quality information in forecasts and effective tools and decision support systems to integrate data, plan, and communicate their actions. New tools for supply forecast should combine the modelling and visualisation of the physical energy infrastructure with abstract notions of system performance. Emerging tools like probabilistic grid flow models seem to be well suited to integrate certain kinds of demand and supply forecasts.

When co-generation of heat (cold) is combined with distributed generation installation, the importance of the weather becomes crucial to economic performance. Optimal operation of the distributed generation depends, at a minimum, on accurate 1 to 2-day weather forecasts. These relationships must be studied and new tools for decision-making refined and developed.

4.5 Simulation as Part of iBMS

Models based on specific demographic, appliance, local generation, and social research data help to forecast the system behaviour of networks with large amounts of managed demand and local generation. Simulation tools use these models to provide the means to answer questions about scalability of large demand-side systems and the services they may provide to networks, retailers, and new businesses. The goal is optimal management of energy demand and consumption, taking into account individual consumer preferences such as: (1) comfort – for thermal comfort and (2) energy costs – ensuring that energy services are commercially viable and affordable.

5 Extended Energy Profiles for ESP

The problem of interoperability is usually addressed by specifying standardised information models. Energy Information is described partially in multiple standards, such as in BIM (e.g. IFC 2.x3), or BMS (e.g. using BACnet). However, most of these standards are very complex and not easily understandable. Therefore, we propose to define a format for the specification of "packages" or "containers" to support the exchange of Energy Information during the various phases of the building life cycle. These "packages" or "containers" should be called "Energy Profiles." Table 1 summarises the function of Energy Profiles to specify energy demand, energy supply capacity, required set of Performance Criteria, a certain level of User Comfort, and – if required – a set of proposed upgrades/improvements. Table 1 below gives an overview how energy profiles support certain functions of dedicated stakeholders.

Figure 1 illustrates the relationship amongst VE-stakeholders, functions performed under their responsibility, and energy profiles supporting or specified by these functions. The emphasis is on building operation and on performing real-time energy simulation using sensed and metered performance data ("as-is" Performance Profile).

Table 1. Proposed "Extended Energy Profiles"

Supply Profile	initial	This profile is used by the energy provider to inform a customer about the available supply capacity & energy tariffs. Optionally, the profile could contain information about available options in terms of Energy Mix.
	calibrated	
Demand Profile	ideal	This profile is used by end users to inform the energy provider about intended energy consumption and to optionally specify its preferred "Energy Mix".
	as is	
Consumption Profile	n.a.	This profile results from a negotiation process. It is used by the end user to inform the energy provider about the amount of energy to be consumed/purchased.
	customised	
Performance Profile	ideal	This profile is used by the Designer/MEP-Engineer to inform the Facility Mgr. /Bldg. Operator about the Performance Metrics of a Building & its Energy Systems.
	as is	
Control Profile	initial	This profile is used by the Facility Manager to inform the Building Operator about the "Control Scenario" of a Building and its Energy Systems.
	calibrated	
Maintenance Profile	initial	This profile is used by the Facility Mgr. to inform the Building Owner and Maintenance Staff about required maintenance activities.
	customised	
Retrofit Profile	initial	This profile is used by the Facility Mgr. to inform the Energy Expert about required replacement of Building Services Systems or proposed renovation activities.
	n.a.	

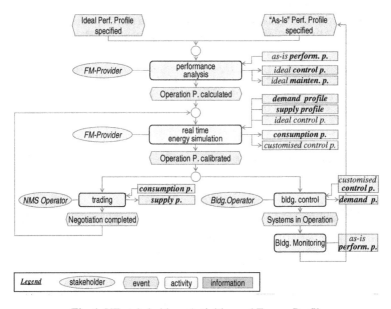

Fig. 1. VE-stakeholders, Activities and Energy Profiles

6   Conclusions and Acknowledgements

By representing the sequence of activities using the ARIS-methodology (Architecture of Information Systems) it becomes possible to easily specify the relationship between "business function", "stakeholder", and "Energy Profile" (see figure 1 above). The clear, consistent, and holistic specification of these relationships is a key pre-requisite for the set-up of supporting IT-infrastructure for Virtual Organisations supporting the "trade" of relevant information required for ESP. These specifications are currently under development at University College Cork, Ireland as part of the EU-FP7 project intUBE (further details at http://zuse.ucc.ie/intube and http://www.intube.eu/). The work presented in this paper is supported by European Union (ICT-2007.6.3 ICT for Environmental Management & Energy Efficiency).

References

1. Ahmed, I., Nunoo, C.: Data Warehousing in the Construction Industry: Organizing and Processing Data for Decision Making. 8DBMC, pp. 2395–2406. NRC Research Press, Vancouver (1999)
2. Barrett, P., Baldry, D.: Facility Management towards best practice. Blackwell Publishing, Malden (2003)
3. Camarinha – Matos, L.M.: Collaborative networks: a new scientific discipline. Journal of Intelligent Manufacturing 16, 439–452 (2005)
4. Kister, T.C., Hawkins, B.: Maintenance Planning and Scheduling Handbook. Elsevier Inc., Amsterdam (2006)
5. Lane, P.: Data Warehousing Guide, 119g Release 1 (11.1), Oracle Data Base, Oracle (2007)
6. Lee, J., Lee, H.: Principles and Strategies for applying Data Warehouse Technology to Construction Industry. In: ECPPM, eWork and eBusiness in Architecture, Engineering and Construction, pp. 341–353. Swets & Zeitlinger, Slovenia (2002)
7. Scheer, A.-W.: ARIS - Business Process Modeling. Springer, Heidelberg (2000)

Part 21

Collaborative Networks for Active Ageing - I

The Need for a Strategic R&D Roadmap for Active Ageing

Luis Camarinha-Matos[1] and Hamideh Afsarmanesh[2]

[1] Faculty of Sciences and Technology, New University of Lisbon,
Quinta da Torre, 2829-516, Monte Capatica, Portugal
cam@uninova.pt
[2] Informatics Institute, University of Amsterdam, Science Park 107,
1098 XG Amsterdam, The Netherlands
h.afsarmanesh@uva.nl

Abstract. The application of the collaborative networks paradigm, combined with a new generation of collaboration-support platforms, can offer a promising approach to active ageing and better use of the talents of senior professionals. This paper introduces a roadmapping initiative focused on elaboration of a new vision for extending professional active life. To support this vision, a strategic research plan for the development of a new collaborative ecosystem, covering the social, organizational, and technological perspectives, is being designed.

Keywords: Roadmapping, professional active life, active ageing.

1 Introduction

There is a growing recognition that the elderly population should not be seen as a burden on the society but instead an asset that needs to be properly considered [7]. In particular the senior professionals possess a number of skills and accumulated experience that need to be better used in value creation activities. And yet the way society is organized does not offer many opportunities to older people.

Recognizing this situation, the World Health Organization has been advocating the need for proactive strategies for the ageing population. Kofi Annan, while secretary-general of the United Nations, stated that "by promoting [older persons'] active participation in society and development, we can ensure that their invaluable gifts and experience are put to good use. Older persons who can work and want to should have the opportunity to do so" [9]. It is also well known that by keeping an active life people can remain healthier. As such, the concept of active ageing was developed.

The critical challenge for the society in respect to the "**active ageing / ageing well**" process [10] is to identify new organizational structures, approaches, and mechanisms so that elderly citizens do not feel excluded, and have the chance to use their knowledge and expertise to contribute to the communities where they live.

On the other hand, as the older population increases and the growth in the middle-aged population slow down, older adults are becoming an increasingly important labor source. They typically bring maturity, dependability, and years of relevant experience to the workplace. Nowadays with more people remaining in good health at

L.M. Camarinha-Matos et al. (Eds.): PRO-VE 2009, IFIP AICT 307, pp. 669–681, 2009.

older ages and increasingly more jobs not involving physical strength, more old adults are able to continue working than ever before. Retirement will indeed no longer represent the end of working period, but rather a career and lifestyle transition, where the retiree in principle has multiple options -- such as continuing to work (though perhaps at a different pace), returning to school for additional training or education, changing career, venturing into entrepreneurship, becoming more involved in volunteer work, or simply enjoying leisure and travel possibilities – thus a mix of working, learning, relaxing, and trying new things can be foreseen.

In addition to the traditional initiatives focused mostly on socialization and entertainment activities for elderly, a number of new organizational forms and mechanisms are emerging, focused on providing ways to help senior professionals remaining active, in professional terms, after retirement. Although with different involvement and commitment levels from retirees, such initiatives try to make use of their valuable knowledge, wisdom, and experience, namely through consulting and mentoring activities. ICT and particularly collaborative technologies, can play an important facilitator role in this area. There is a need to provide support in the form of "ready-made 2nd generation affective and socio-economically integrated communities" to which the elderly professional can join. Moreover, there is a need to provide the opportunity for elderly professionals to choose a balanced proportion between their value creating and the leisure activities, as well as the opportunity to modify the balance in their portfolio of activities over time. In order to elaborate a strategic R&D plan in this direction a 2-year European initiative – ePAL (extending Professional Active Life) project – was launched in 2008 [4].

2 Towards a Strategic Roadmap

Most R&D efforts regarding ICT and ageing, both past and present, have adopted a reactive strategy while trying to mitigate the problems "after" the elderly reach a critical phase in their physical and mental capabilities. ePAL however adopts a proactive strategy, identifying measures of a more "preventive" nature. The hypothesis followed in ePAL is that collaborative

| 1 Characterize and consolidate the baseline |
| 2 Perceive trends and design scenarios |
| 3 Elaborate first vision statement and instantiations |
| 4   Fill the gap: from Where we are – to – Where we wish to go |
| 5 Propose a plan of actions |
| 6 Verify the planned actions |
| 7 Plan the timing and other characterization of actions |
| 8 Finalize the definition of the roadmap chart |
| 9 Perform consultation and refinement |
| 10 Perform roadmap consolidation. |

Fig. 1. Roadmapping method

networks provide an adequate framework for the implementation of effective support to active ageing. In this context and bearing in mind that one of the main goals is to keep the elderly engaged and socially active in society, an organized collaborative network is a fundamental instrument. After retirement, most of the social and professional bonds are rapidly broken. An organised Professional Virtual Community for seniors is a vital instrument for keeping their involvement in society.

Need for a roadmap. The potential of ICT to support better ageing and individuals' well-being has been widely recognized, which has led to many R&D projects during the last decade. For instance, in the Framework Program 7 of the European Commission there is a research line devoted to ICT and ageing. And yet, the sensitivity of the area, the dependency on the "parallel" introduction of new organizational models and creation of a new culture in society, the lessons learned with the limited success of existing associations of senior professional, the risk of continuously developing technology that is not taken-up by target users, among others suggest the need for a careful analysis and a new approach towards what concerns new developments. It is thus clearly very important at this point in time to design a strategic R&D roadmap focused on active ageing. In ePAL a 10-step roadmapping process is adopted (Fig. 1). These steps result from a consolidation of experiences in previous roadmapping initiatives for collaborative networks, namely THINKcreative and VOmap [3].

ePAL aims at establishing a strategic **research roadmap towards a 2nd generation support system for active ageing**. ePAL aims to explore innovative ways to facilitate the development of the active ageing process and to ensure an improved transition for the elderly citizens as they cope with the onset of age. For this purpose, **a strategic RTD roadmap**, focused on novel collaborative solutions and ensuring a balanced post-retirement life-style is pursued in ePAL. It mainly defines the needed strategy and the action plan-assisted philosophy, to support both the dynamism in behavior/emotion as well as the elderly's desire to involve in professional interaction in socio-economic system.

Table 1. Studied associations of senior professions

Organization	Country
AGIRabcd	France
APCS	Portugal
ASECAT	Colombia
ASEP	Austria
BSC-I	Belgium
COGAMA	Spain
CONFEMAC	Spain
CONJUPES	Spain
ECTI	France
EGEE	France
FRAE	Spain
ISES	Italy
JUBIQUÉ	Spain
KOS	Poland
NESTOR	Finland
OTECI	France
PUM	Netherlands
REACH	UK
RSVP	UK
SECOT	Spain
SEN@ER	Spain
SENA	Belgium
SENIORES	Italy
SES	Germany
SFPA	Slovenia
SHARE	Portugal
SWB	Denmark
UDP	Spain
Vis VITALIS	Poland

3   Current Situation

Preliminary analysis. As part of the baseline characterization phase of the roadmapping process, an extensive analysis of the existing associations of senior professionals was conducted. Table 1 shows the list of those that either took part in the survey or participated in our workshops.

These associations are mostly composed of "professional elite" (people with a high education and that had high positions in the socio-economic system before retirement). In most cases, these people have reasonable pensions (although varying from region to region) and therefore can afford to do voluntary (unpaid) activities. However, the number of people involved in such mechanisms is not very high. On the other hand, considering the current difficulties of the social security systems all over Europe, most governments are trying to implement new formula for pension calculation which in practice means a reduction of the pension. In such context, it is foreseeable that more retirees will have fewer resources than needed to satisfy their standards of life and thus need to continue being involved in value creation activities.

Most participating organizations, in spite of their ambitious mission statements, operate on a relatively passive basis, basically "expecting the client or the business opportunity to show up". As a consequence, they do not have many projects. A frequent complaint we encountered is that they do not have enough work for all their members. And yet, many SMEs and start-ups world-wide that cannot afford to pay market prices for consultancy and coaching, could greatly benefit from the accumulated knowledge and experience of senior professionals. But there is a clear difficulty to reach the potential clients due to the lack of proper brokerage mechanisms or support of intermediary entities.

In addition to these associations, various other mechanisms and practices towards active ageing can be found. Examples include the maintenance of some links to the former employer [8] (as in the case of jubilee professors), free-lancing, time bank, etc. Free-lancing is a typical option for those that wish to continue involved in some form of remunerated activity. Nevertheless it represents an individual initiative, requiring some degree of entrepreneurial spirit that not retirees are able to exercise. It also requires some preparation for which training is not easily available. Most of these professionals have developed their careers in the context of an organization and are not prepared to start doing a consultant work.

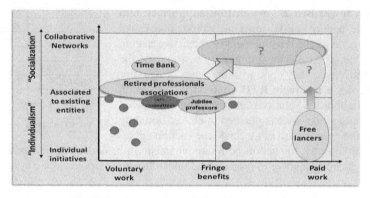

Fig. 2. Panorama of approaches in active ageing

In addition to the need to move from voluntary (only) activities to (some options of) paid work, it is also important to find new forms of "socialization", a critical issue after retirement for which collaborative networks can be an answer. Fig. 2 illustrates this situation and trends.

Multi-disciplinary area. The design of a new collaborative ecosystem to support active ageing and facilitating the integration of seniors with the socio-economic system requires the development of advanced ICT platforms and tools, and a sound theoretical foundation which requires the contribution of multiple disciplines (e.g. Collaborative networks, Behavior modeling, Causal reasoning and soft computing, Affective computing / emotion-oriented systems, Machine learning).

Another way of rephrasing the ePAL hypothesis is that an effective approach to prolonging the active life of elderly and their involvement in the economic and societal system involves the following key elements:

- *Organizational architecture element that includes the organization and support for operation of an affection-based virtual community of senior professionals as well as the organization of "business liaison" units that allow keeping them involved in the economic system.*
- *Theoretical foundation to cope with deeper understanding of the principles and laws regarding the evolution of people's behavioral pattern after retirement and their corresponding needs.*
- *Advanced ICT support (infrastructure and services), providing a platform to support active ageing (balancing professional, cultural, and leisure activities).*

Given the current state of the art, and the fact that different necessary scientific areas do not have a sound tradition of working together, it is quite risky to make big investments in focused R&D activities before a more strategic planning is made towards a **roadmap** for a research agenda.

Technology baseline. The current situation regarding technological support for a new model of active ageing for senior professionals can be summarized as in Table 2.

Table 2. Technological baseline

Theoretical foundation for technological developments
- Good progress was achieved on conceptual models for collaborative networks (CN) during recent years, including reference models (e.g. ARCON), CN taxonomy, VBE generic ontology, understanding of the VO creation process, etc. [1], [2].
- Achieved research results in the area of collaborative networks mostly address challenges related to collaboration among organizations, e.g., the results from the ECOLEAD project. Considering the ePAL scenario, these results need to be adapted and extended to meet the requirements and challenges related to collaboration among senior professionals.
- More research is needed on "soft issues", including trust management, collaboration readiness assessment, value systems alignment, credit assignment, emotional health of the network, etc.

Advanced collaboration support services, including (virtual) teams' formation and management
- Various advanced prototypes have been developed for management systems for VO Breeding Environments and Professional Virtual Communities, including tools for VO / VT creation have been developed, but still with limited use in real businesses.
- Generic tools in the areas of CSCW and social networking (including chats, forums, emails, VoIP, etc) are becoming widely available.

Support for user-generated knowledge content
- Configurable document management platforms supporting multiple users & different roles, over the net are becoming available (e.g. JOOMLA) but still offering limited flexibility.
- Various successful experiments (and supporting platforms) for "mass creation" of generic multimedia content (videos, photos, podcasts, etc.) are available (e.g. YouTube, Flicker, blogs). This is also creating a "culture" of content sharing. However, when it comes to supporting the generation of business related content (processes, drawings, and other technical data) the possibilities are much more limited and there are also many interoperability problems.
- This area also raises many unsolved issues e.g. IPR, ethical principles, ownership and protection.

Table 2. (*continued*)

"Configure yourself" based philosophy infrastructure
- Some preliminary attempts to let the user configure his/her user interface and customize his/her desired functionalities/services, through composing / assembling the system's components have started to appear (still in a rudimentary form) in some Internet systems (e.g. Face-Book, i-Google). Sustainable development of this concept requires the creation of libraries of components and proper interoperable reference architectures.

Easily adaptable and customizable user interfaces
- The growing number of application features and the desire to optimize usage of screen space raise the need to allow users or applications to customize the interfaces. Adaptive interfaces that can change their appearance based on some algorithm, such as a least-recently used criterion (e.g. the Microsoft XP/ Vista desktop icons, Portlet technology, etc.) start to appear.
- One of the simplest forms of user interface customization is the notion of skins and themes available in some applications and user interface toolkits (e.g. Microsoft OP themes, iGoogle). Other efforts are being directed towards automatic adaptation to different output channels.
- Together with the "configure yourself" approach, this area is likely to have fast developments in the coming years.

Tools supporting the process of value creation
- Preliminary conceptualization of value systems and benefit analysis for collaborative networks is emerging, but no practical support tools are available yet.
- Most existing value systems focus on providing guidelines related to optimizing and/or sharing organization's or individual's gains, and typically related to financial gains. For active ageing scenarios, new value systems and related supporting tools need to be developed.
- There is a lack of sound models and tools for IPR and risk management in CNs, which are fundamental in promoting value creation.

Affective computing and context aware enriched environments
- Affective computing is a new and very active research field. So far most efforts have been put in the perception/recognition of emotions (e.g. biosensors, digital cameras, speech treatment) and expression of emotions through complex media (e.g. robots, avatars, music). However, results are still at an early stage. Other research activities in affective neuroscience and psychology indicate that human affects and emotional experiences play a significant and useful role in human learning and decision-making.
- It is becoming clear that the utilization of emotions to regulate virtual environments (to motivate, engage or create trust) is a promising approach, but no developments yet exist in this direction. In the ePAL context, new directions for affective computing can be opened such as identification of the emotional state of the network (collective emotion), use of affective principles to smooth collaboration, development of self-healing mechanisms in case of conflicts, development of emotional models focused on elderly, etc. But all these areas are practically untouched.

Contractual and cooperation agreements, including negotiation support
- Some contract models / frameworks were developed for specific domains (e.g. civil construction) but this is still a research issue. Various prototypes and models of negotiation, namely following a multi-agent -systems approach, have been proposed, but are still far from practical use.
- There are also some conceptual and prototypical developments on e-institutions such as e-notary, including safety infrastructures, but still with poor integration with collaboration environments. For the support of electronic contracts and negotiation some facilitating tools have been suggested such as "Contract wizards".

Marketing and brokerage services
- Intensive developments around Service Oriented Architectures turned this approach and associated technologies a "popular" stream in systems integration, service publishing and access. Various standards try to facilitate the interoperability issues. However, the usage of this technology still requires good technical skills.

Table 2. (*continued*)

- Considering the universe of SMEs and senior professionals, further developments are needed, namely in the following directions: (i) Facilitating the technology usage by people not very skilled in SOA, (ii) Developing new conceptual and technological approaches to introduce a "pro-active" component in the software services. E.g. more dynamic services marketing / brokerage (how to make services provided by senior professionals known to the universe of potential clients). A combination of principles from SOA, Multi-agent systems, and blackboard architectures might provide some background in this direction, (iii) Elaboration of libraries of template services oriented to consultancy activities (and particularly to the kind of consultancy services to be provided by senior professionals).

Networking models for elderly communities' involvement with the socio-economic system
- In addition to the free-lancing activities, several (virtual) communities try to organize groups of retired professionals and promote their active ageing.
- One fundamental role for the establishment of collaborations among senior professionals is related to the intermediation of the interactions between individual senior professionals and clients for their services. The intermediary organizations can be either brokers or regulatory bodies. There is still a lack of clear understanding on how this role can be handled and who (or which organization) is responsible. Thus models and tools need to be developed to guide and support the needed interactions related to this role.
- These communities try to promote the involvement in the socio-economic system but currently face a number of limitations: (i) Most actions are carried out by single individuals (no real notion of collaborative network / team work); (ii) Very limited brokerage functionality; (iii) Poor integration with the other stakeholders of the socio-economic system, thus the associations are not really known by potential customers; (iv) Very little use of collaborative technologies is made as these communities only have access to basic tools.

Security and ethical / privacy support
- A large panoply of mechanisms and tools for safe communications (including cryptography), user identification and authentication (including biometric systems), access / visibility rights definition and control have been developed.
- Most base building blocks in this area are available, but their integration and configuration according to the specific needs of each application scenario is still a difficult issue.
- When considering the ePAL scenarios, in which it is necessary to combine leisure / social with professional activities, there is a need to design proper reference architectures that cope with these specific contexts.

The above characteristics set the baseline for the actual preparation of a roadmap towards a new vision of active ageing and the development of a new generation of support technology.

4   A New Vision for Active Ageing

A fundamental prerequisite for developing a vision for the desired future of this area is to identify both: the key drivers (i.e. the main driving forces in the market and society) and their related trends (i.e. the main happenings in the market and society) regarding the

Fig. 3. Key drivers for ePAL environment

ePAL environment. In our research, to comprehensively cover the most important aspects related to a desired vision for ePAL, we have identified three main perspectives that are required to be addressed, namely the technological, the social and the organizational perspectives (Fig. 3). Under these perspectives the main trends were identified and analyzed in terms of their potential positive or negative influence regarding active ageing [5].

Complementarily, building **scenarios** is a tool to provide actors with essential understanding, orientation, context, direction, and some degree of consensus in planning research developments and implementations. In relation to ePAL's vision for future, a number of scenarios were elaborated in order to support understanding of different future possibilities regarding the enhancing of active life of senior professionals, as well as possible actions to take and which events are probable to occur in future.

Based on extensive analysis and elaboration, a first vision statement for ePAL is

Core ideology:

Building a strong and cohesive social fabric to embody active senior professionals, as an important part of the European silver economy

Envisioned future:

In the coming decade, a comprehensive paradigm will emerge in response to Europe's ageing population and its inevitable skill shortage, that extends the balanced active life of senior professionals, facilitating the use of their talents and expertise, and thus facilitating value creation from these mature assets, for the benefit of both Europe's economy as well as the European society as a whole.

Main desired facets:

- Well founded reference model of the environment, specifying its:
  - endogenous *(structural, componential, functional, and behavioural)* and exogenous *(market, support, societal, constituency)* elements, and their interlinks
- Well established technological infrastructure, support tools/services
- Support for social responsibility and adaptation of suitable ethical code
- Established organizational infrastructure, supporting economic and societal involvement through government policies and actions
- Established national/international regulations for involvement of senior professionals in market/society and related legal frameworks

Fig. 4. 1st desired ePAL vision

proposed, as shown in Fig. 4. In order to facilitate the analysis of needs, it is effective to instantiate the vision statement according to the social, organizational, and technological perspectives (example in Fig. 5 for the technological perspective).

Taking into account the desired vision and the current baseline, a detailed gap analysis was then performed, comparing that state of today's market and society against the state planned by the vision for creating a balanced active life for senior professionals. This

In the coming decade, the ICT collaboration platforms and tools will be developed as an easy to use enabler of new approaches for continuation of the active involvement of elderly people in the socio-economic system. As such novel infrastructures and intelligent functionalities will act as a catalyst of new organizational forms, supporting effective management of geographically disperse communities of retired professionals, and facilitating the active participation in the socio-economic activities, as an extension of the human capabilities towards fitted participation.

Main desired facets:
V1. Advanced collaboration support services, including (virtual) teams' formation and management
V2. Development of collaboration ontology supporting variety of stakeholders
V3. Support for user-generated knowledge content
V4. "Configure yourself" based philosophy infrastructure
V5. Easily adaptable and customizable user interfaces
V6. Affective computing and context aware enriched environments
V7. Support for establishment of trust among stakeholders
V8. Tools supporting the process of value creation
V9. Novel contractual &cooperation agreements, including negotiation support
V10. Advanced marketing and brokerage services
V11. New networking models for elderly communities' involvement with the socio-economic system
V12. Security and ethical / privacy support

Fig. 5. 1st ePAL Vision instantiation – Technological perspective

analysis focuses on Strengths and Limitations, the most relevant elements facilitating or constraining the elaboration of a plan of actions. Table 3 shows the identified elements for the technological perspective. Similar tables were developed for the other two perspectives [6].

Table 3. Example of gap analysis for the technological perspective

Strengths
S1 Good progress in conceptual models for collaborative networks (but mostly focused on industry cases)
S2 There is already an understanding of the needed management functionalities for VO breeding environments and professional virtual communities
S3 Various partial models and advanced prototypes (e.g. negotiation, trust promotion, value systems) have been developed to support collaborative environments
S4 ICT infrastructures exist across Europe to provide the basic communication building blocks that will be needed to implement the ePAL vision.
Limitations
L1 Lack of consolidated theoretical base in areas such as reference modeling for active ageing support systems
L2 Lack of effective and integrated ICT support for collaboration (till large fragmentation of functionalities).
L3 ICT research in this area too much focused on the "last phases of life", reducing the needed attention to active ageing support.
L4 Fast proliferation of new tools and functionalities without a holistic approach, an obstacle for adoption by seniors.
L5 Increasing trend to focus on techno-centric approach for ICT R&D, which hinders proper understanding of the critical issues of the socio-technical systems needed to support active ageing.

	V1	V2	V3	V4	V5	V6	V7	V8	V9	V10
S1	+	+			+	+			+	
S2		+				+	+	+	+	
S3		+				+	+			+
S4		+	+	+						
L1							-		-	-
L2		-	-		-				-	-
L3	-	-				-	-	-	-	
L4		-	-	-	-				-	
L5	-					-	-	-	-	-

Positive Influence
| ▇ + | High | | + | Moderate |

Negative Influence
| ▇ - | High | | - | Moderate |

Fig. 6. Gap analysis - Influence map

The identified gaps can be expressed through the generation of an "Influence map" to represent both the positive and negative influences of the baseline Strengths/ Limitations on the achievement of the vision (example in Fig. 6). A qualitative scale (e.g. as High and Moderate) is adopted to express the influences.

5 Some Organizational Issues

One important aspect when designing a roadmap to extend professional life of individuals is to consider the organizational forms that can best support the main objective of keeping seniors involved in the socio-economic system.

An association of retired professionals can represent a special form of a professional virtual community. The establishment and management of such associations can benefit from well researched and developed concepts and tools for professional virtual communities. These communities are business oriented entities, mostly focusing on supporting their members to jointly optimize individual financial gains. The focus of traditional associations of retired professional is not necessarily the enhancing of financial gains of members as they might have a pension. The main aim of retired people that join such associations is to remain professionally active and thus involved in the society. They are mostly willing to share and exchange their knowledge and experience to those individuals or organizations that need them.

There are two challenges which are facing retired people when they do want to provide their knowledge and experience to beneficiaries as described below:

- *Finding opportunities to apply their knowledge and experience – beneficiaries, willing to accept their offers – is quite challenging. As mentioned by many associations, it is difficult for retirees to individually acquire opportunities in the society that are also being targeted by other formal service providers, such as consultancy and other organizations.*
- *Some acquired opportunities cannot be responded by one retiree alone, the normal practice in traditional associations. For example, SMEs which need consultancy on a subject, require more than one kind of expertise.*

To address these challenges a new kind of networked environment constituting seniors– **Community of Active Senior Professional (CASP)** can be envisioned:

CASP constitutes a long term association of senior professional individuals that are largely autonomous, geographically distributed, and potentially heterogeneous in terms of their: capabilities, offered capacities, culture, system of values, etc., but sharing their main compatible and/or common goals of increasing their active professional life in the society and/or market, through co-working with others in Teams of Senior Professionals (TSPs) supported by computer networks, under the slogan of: "Together Everyone Achieves More!".

TSP is a dynamically configured collaborative network of individuals configured and established within the CASP in response to opportunities in the society and market that are in need of their wisdom and/or knowledge assets that they can offer, which as a consequence supports the retired professionals remaining professionally active.

As mentioned above, the effective involvement of seniors in the socio-economic system needs to consider other entities (Fig. 7). Thus ePAL proposes a tri-partite network, involving, besides seniors, the intermediary entities and the recipients of the services provided by seniors, to benefit from tangible/intangible assets generated in CASP.

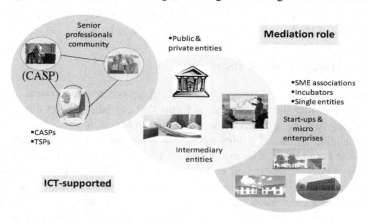

Fig. 7. A tri-partite ecosystem

Intermediaries: Organizations or people which act as mediators or agents between CASP (or individual TSPs) and recipients.

Recipients: These can range from individual persons, groups of people, entrepreneurs and start-ups, SMEs, or large organizations. Recipients include the categories of clients and beneficiaries.

There are further two categories of intermediaries depending on their objectives, i.e. the brokers and supporters:

- *Brokers are organizations or people whose principal objective is that of making it possible for senior professionals to be able to supply their services (experience and knowledge) to the market and society. These entities play an important role in extending professional active life of seniors.*
- *Supporters are organizations that have as their principal objective the maintenance of an active life for the elderly and improvements in their quality of life, providing a range of services that allow the elderly to provide a service in a more structured manner. These types of organization basically offer three types of support: financial support, service support, and ICT support.*

Each one of these groups might have distinct organizational forms. For instance, recipients can be organized around SME Associations, start-up incubators, etc. Therefore, an effective organizational form to cope with the requirements of the stated vision is a multi-level collaborative network involving three groups of stakeholders and their specific organizational forms.

6 Plan of Actions

Next challenge is to elaborate a plan of research actions and their suggested timing to lead us from current baseline to the desired vision, taking into account the gap analysis

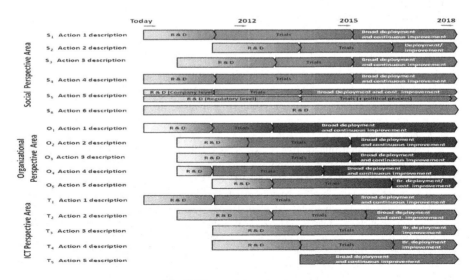

Fig. 8. The roadmap structure

results. As illustrated in Fig. 8, the roadmap includes a number of actions for each perspective. An example of action according to the technological perspective is:

"Develop affective-based and context aware ICT collaboration platforms for communities of senior professionals"

Furthermore, for each action, it also gives a qualitative indication of the efforts needed in R&D, take-up and deployment. The last step will be the consolidation and consensus building phase. The steps performed so far have been conducted in close interaction with dozens of stakeholders and experts in different domains, but a final consolidation is needed when all pieces of the roadmap will be assembled.

7 Conclusion

Extending active professional life of senior people became an important need as the expectancy of a longer healthy life increases. Such extension is likely to: (i) Facilitate active ageing, keeping elderly involved in and contributing to society; (ii) Generate additional income to help them keep their standard of living.

ICT can be an important enabler in facilitating the creation of collaborative networks involving not only communities of seniors, but also potential recipients of their services and intermediary entities in a multi-level network.

Given the lessons from early experiences and the sensitivity of the area, future RTD needs to be supported by carefully designed roadmaps. First results from ePAL give important insights in developing such roadmap. Ongoing activities are now addressing the finalization of the roadmap and consensus building process.

Acknowledgements. This work was funded in part be the European Commission through the ePAL project. The authors also thank the contribution of their partners in the project.

References

1. Afsarmanesh, H., Camarinha-Matos, L.M.: The ARCON modeling framework. In: Collaborative networks reference modeling, pp. 67–82. Springer, New York (2008)
2. Camarinha-Matos, L.M., Afsarmanesh, H.: On reference models for collaborative networked organizations. Int. Journal Production Research 46(9), 2453–2469 (2008)
3. Camarinha-Matos, L.M., Afsarmanesh, H.: A roadmapping methodology for strategic research on VO. In: Collaborative Networked Organizations – A research agenda for emerging business models, cap. 7.1. Springer, Heidelberg (2004)
4. Camarinha-Matos, L.M., Afsarmanesh, H.: Collaborative mechanisms for a new perspective on active ageing. In: Proceedings of DEST 2009 - 3rd IEEE Int. Conference on Digital Ecosystems and Technologies, Istanbul, Turkey, June 1-3 (2009)
5. Afsarmanesh, H., Camarinha-Matos, L.M., Msanjila, S.: A well-conceived vision for extending professional life of seniors. In: Proceedings of PRO-VE 2009 conference (September 2009) (to appear)

6. Leonard, W., Afsarmanesh, H., Msanjila, S.S., Playfoot, J.: Exploring the Gap for Effective Extension of Professional Active Life in Europe. In: Proceedings of PRO-VE 2009 conference (September 2009) (to appear)
7. HSBC Insurance, The future of retirement – The new old age (May 2007), `http://www.hsbc.com/1/PA_1_1_S5/content/assets/retirement/gender_perspective_eurasia_africa_1.pdf`
8. IPWEA, Guide to Retaining the Current Workforce, IPWEA National Skills Shortage Project, Institute of Public Works Engineering Australia (July 2006), `http://www.ipwea.org.au/skills/upload/NSSP1_Retaining_Current_Workforce.pdf`
9. United Nations. Statement of Kofi Annan, in Report of the Second World Assembly on Ageing, New York, Madrid April 8-12 (2002), `http://daccessdds.un.org/doc/UNDOC/GEN/N02/397/51/PDF/N0239751.pdf?OpenElement`
10. WHO, Active Aging: A Policy Framework, WHO/NMH/NPH/02.8, World Health Organisation report (2002)

A Well-Conceived Vision for Extending Professional Life of Seniors

Hamideh Afsarmanesh[1], Luis M. Camarinha-Matos[2], and Simon S. Msanjila[1]

[1] Informatics Institute, University of Amsterdam, Science Park 107,
1098 XG, Amsterdam, The Netherlands
{h.afsarmanesh,s.s.msanjila}@uva.nl
[2] Faculty of Sciences and Technology, New University of Lisbon,
Quinta da Torre, 2829-516, Monte Capatica, Portugal
cam@uninova.pt

Abstract. A fundamental challenge related to enhancing the active life of senior professionals is to identify ways to assist promoting the role of elder people within the continuously ageing European society. One approach to achieve this purpose is to establish a support environment which shall provide fundamental assistance to senior professionals to fully use their expertise and experience to continue delivering professional services to the society. A well conceived vision need to be established to guide the society towards achieving this goal. This paper presents the first vision statement and its instantiations for enhancing the active life of senior professionals in the European society. It first proposes an approach for building the vision.

Keywords: Visioning, multi-perspective vision, professional active life.

1 Introduction

The main concerns about population in the twentieth century were around the *growth of population* and the consequences on *resource scarcity*. However, the forecasts for the 21st century introduced some other new concerns, primarily focused on the *ageing population* and the *overloaded pension systems*. In several parts of the world the decline in birth rate seems to have reduced some of the severity of the problems related to scarcity of natural resources. Nevertheless, the main concern today related to the population, which is becoming even more serious in developed countries such as those located in Europe and North America, is the rapidly ageing population.

As the Europe's population ages the number of those who are of working age (defined as 15-64) becomes smaller in relation to those of 'non-working' age who are usually referred to as economic "dependants" [10]. The challenge of coping with this trend is now dominating Europe's attitude to population policy and if relevant measures are not put in place for this problem then the following example problems might occur in the European society:

Economical difficulties: Severe economical difficulties will rise for the pension system in Europe, in relation to supporting the life of this large group of retired people.

L.M. Camarinha-Matos et al. (Eds.): PRO-VE 2009, IFIP AICT 307, pp. 682–694, 2009.

Traditionally, the life of elder people was supported through pension systems, which relied on the taxes paid by the workers active at the time. Today, but more steeply in the coming decades, the pension systems are becoming overloaded, as on one hand the number of people who shall receive benefits increases, while on the other hand the labour force and thus the number of tax payers gradually decreases.

Lack of human resources: Harsh economical challenges will be faced increasingly at the workplace by the lack of qualified human resources, since every year a very large group of ageing population retires. One recent promising approach to address the challenge of dealing with the ageing population in Europe looks into the possibility of extending the involvement of senior professionals who are willing to do so in the ongoing activities in market and society.

A number of approaches and initiatives are now applied to support elders remaining professionally active and thus continue their participation in daily activities and by so doing contributing to addressing the above problems. The participation of elder professionals is either in individual manner or in some sort of communities. Applying the concepts of collaboration as inspired in the discipline of collaborative networks [1], the communities of senior professionals are established either as long-term strategic alliances (Community of Active Senior Professionals - **CASPs**) that are configured to enhance preparedness of senior professionals (**SPs**) towards actively participating in daily activities or as short-term networks (Teams of Senior Professionals - **TSPs**) that are configured to respond to a specific opportunity. Although there are a number of initiatives in Europe that are aiming at supporting seniors to remain professionally active, there is still no common focus regarding the future participation of seniors in societal activities. A well-conceived vision capturing fundamental aspects on future active life of elder people needs to be constructed.

This paper presents a systematic visioning approach and presents a vision which is built using the proposed approach and aimed at supporting extending Professional Active Life (ePAL) of elder people in Europe. The vision is instantiated into three perspectives of technological, organizational and social.

2 Base Concepts Related to Vision

Visioning is an important aspect for leadership, strategy implementation and change [8]. The application of *vision* in defining and shaping the future direction of an organization or a society is increasingly becoming popular in today's world. A vision defines *a desired future,* while strongly interconnected with the framework that underlies the organizations or societies [3]. It is a deeply held picture of where a person, a group of people, an organization, or a society, wants to reach in the future.

A vision, a compelling view of a future yet to be, creates meaning and purpose which catapults both the people and the society to high levels of achievement [5]. We create meaning in our lives by pursuing our future visions, and we refine our visions based on the meaning we are discovering through our experience. A vision is the most inspiring future the society can imagine. Because of this, the society can never truly achieve its vision. It works toward that vision. The societies' visions communicate to others who they are and who they want to become and not what they have achieved. A vision for a society shall provide the following: (1) Compelling image of the future,

(2) Credible and attractive view of what is potentially feasible for the society, (3) Unifying guides to what the society wishes to and can become, and (4) Inspirational focal point for the spirit of the society and its members.

A well-conceived vision consists of two major components, namely, the *core ideology* and the *envisioned future* [4]. *Core ideology* is the first primary component of the vision framework which consists of two parts: *core values* and *core purpose*. *Core values* are the essential and enduring tenets of an organization or a society - a small set of timeless guiding principles that require no external justification. Core values have intrinsic value and importance to those inside the organization or society. *Core purpose* however points to certain fundamental reason for society to exist. An effective purpose reflects the importance that people attach to daily activities of the organization or society. *Envisioned future* is the 2nd primary component of the vision framework which consists of 2 parts: a *long-term audacious goal* and a *vivid description* of what it will be like when goals are achieved.

Visioning process is one of the least straightforward, yet most important, concepts that enable influencing the future, and building successful organizations and societies. The cornerstone of a vision is a clear image of how the society will satisfy important stakeholders' needs. It is important that the vision is built from what stakeholders perceive to satisfy their needs not what the providers (government, non-government organizations, regulatory bodies, etc.) think will satisfy them. This requires an extensive interaction with all stakeholders in the society in order to perceive the needs from stakeholders' perspective. It should be noted that visioning differs from the common estimation practice related to understanding the possible future situations – *forecasting*. Forecasting is the process of performing an estimation of unknown situations related to certain aspect of the society. Nevertheless, while formulating a vision and when it is needed to estimate some possible future situation, forecasting can be used as a tool in visioning process, such as in understanding the societal drivers and trends as well as possible future scenarios (see further in section 3).

2.1   Related Visions for ePAL Environment

A number of initiatives such as research projects have been carried out in Europe addressing different aspects related to ageing well. Most of these initiatives see SPs as recipient of services from the market and ineligible to continue participating in societal activities. As a result, there is a lack of models or regulations guiding elders' participation in value creation activities. Consequently, the European society has been loosing or misusing the massive knowledge and experience possessed by these elders especially those who were involved in professional employments. Furthermore, after retirement most SPs feel lonely, isolated and useless to the society although they are sure that they possess both the knowledge and experience that their society is in need.

Senior professionals have been trying to remain active in the European society by volunteering to perform certain activities. Such volunteering has been realized either by individual initiatives or through certain associations of senior professionals. At present, a number of associations are established for senior professionals in some regions of Europe. They aim at supporting individuals and teams of individuals either to provide services which are lacking in the market or to address specific beneficiaries not dealt with by normal market actors, and thus there is no competition or conflict with business organizations. They also aim at providing services to some categories of organizations, e.g. those that cannot afford buying such services in the market.

To coordinate its activities towards aimed future, each of these associations has either explicitly or implicitly (in form of policies or mission) stated a vision. Below we present four example statements that are expressed by associations of senior professionals as their vision or mission (source: www.epal.eu.com)

SEN@ER – *Silver Economy Network of European Regions*: perceives that it is needed to consider demographic change and the ageing of European society as both a challenge and an opportunity for economic growth and improving competitiveness. Its vision states: *"Increased social inclusion of and improved quality of life for older people, employment and job creation in the regions increase of competitiveness"*.

PUM – *Netherlands Senior Experts*: addresses service provision in developing countries, founded on the base of free knowledge and experience offered by its SPs: *"Practical and business-like: helping small and medium-sized businesses stand on their own two feet is more effective than theorizing and moralizing"*.

ASEP – *Austrian Senior Experts Pool*: Under the umbrella of *"Net of experts"*, ASEP believes that nowadays the *"retirement phase"* is being addressed and treated as a separate phase of life. The engagement of elderly people within the family and within honorary voluntary jobs (activities) gives this phase of life a greater meaning. Members of ASEP aim at passing their experience, knowledge and competence free of charge to the community while realizing the concept of a 3rd phase of life, which is characterized by health, activity and service to the community.

ASECAT – *Asociación de Expertos para la Cooperación y Asesoría*: With the slogan *"be voluntary"*, the ASECAT association, using the knowledge and experience of its professional seniors, gives voluntary advice, assistance and administrative services to entrepreneurs and businesses with lower incomes. Its main objective is to contribute to the society in generating value, improving the conditions of life, and promoting the socio-economic development.

As it can be observed from the above statements these visions guide associations towards providing services on voluntary basis. As a result, few SPs are motivated to join such associations. Thus a number of aspects need to be addressed and included in a vision that shall guide the European society towards a better active life of elder people and better sharing of benefits for their participation in value creation activities.

3   Systematic Building of the ePAL Vision

There are two schools of thought when it comes to developing a vision for the society to address a particular aspect of a society in order to transform it to a better desired future situation. On the one hand vision building is believed to be the responsibility of the leadership of societies to develop and articulate a powerful vision. On the other hand, it is advocated that all 'stakeholders should together support what a society wants to achieve in future. Therefore, according to this second school, vision should be co-created by its stakeholders across the society.

In this paper, we perceive that none of these schools of thought are completely wrong or completely right for developing a vision for a part of the society! There is a case for the role of leadership in developing and articulating a vision. However, also all stakeholders must be involved to tune and re-define the vision by incorporating their interests and to commit themselves on providing support towards achieving the envisioned future [9]. It is challenging to properly involving both stakeholders and leaders in a coordinated manner while formulating a well-conceived vision for the ePAL. Another challenge is related to the identification of fundamental aspects that need to be included in the vision. A well-conceived vision can hardly be formulated in random and ad hoc manner. Therefore, there is a need for having a systematic approach to guide all steps that must be performed and the stakeholders that must be involved in such process.

We propose an approach for building a vision with involvement of stakeholders at different stages, providing a general step-wise guidance for the process of building a vision for an environment. To enhance the clarity of presentation of the proposed approach in some steps we provide examples related to vision construction for ePAL environment. The approach has five steps as shown in Fig. 1, namely: (1) *Discussion and generation of visionary ideas for the environment*, (2) *Elaboration of 1st vision*, (3) *Testing and validating the elaborated vision*, (4) *Consensus building through consulting and workshop*, (5) *Documenting and finalizing the vision*.

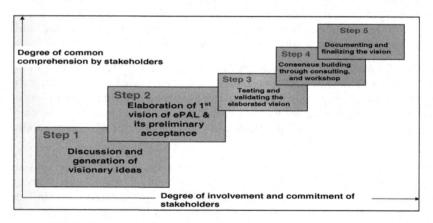

Fig. 1. Generic steps for building a vision, involving main stakeholders

The first two steps are the main steps in this process, performing the large analysis of many aspects and elements of the ePAL environment (Step 1), and analyzing all collected results to extract and build the 1st vision of ePAL and reaching preliminary expert consensus on the vision (Step 2).

Step 1: Discussion and generation of visionary ideas. This step starts when the need for building a vision is realized and that some aspects of the society require systematic changes to reflect on the future life of the society. For example, this step is triggered by identification of a crisis or immediate need in the society and where its possible solutions demand changes within the society.

A variety of people, such as decision makers and leaders, experts, research community, etc., are involved in the discussion of what elements must be addressed and/or included in the vision for the targeted environment. VOmap project has developed a so-called *"vision ideas building process"* [2] which is applied here. This process guides the identification of the main elements that must be addressed to build a comprehensive vision of an environment or a society, such as the vision for guiding the enhancement of active life of senior professionals (Fig. 2). The process is modelled in the style of IDEF0, addressing inputs (from left), resources and mechanisms used (from below), constraints (from above), and output (on the right).

As indicated in Fig. 2, in step 1 the process of generating preliminary vision's ideas for ePAL environment is influenced by three different types of elements/aspects, namely: (1) **Input materials**: Refer to existing materials that can be sources of fundamental ideas related to the ePAL vision. To build the ePAL vision some input materials that were considered and analyzed include: state of the art in literature, results of related projects, related vision and mission statements, (2) **Constraints**: Refer to practices that are relevant to the ePAL environment in the European society which unless properly considered and addressed by the vision may have the potential to prevent, restrict, or dictate the actions that may need to be taken to realize the vision. Example constraints that are addressed while generating vision's ideas include: laws, rules and regulations; society indicators; some practice related disruptions (such as emergence of new technologies), etc. and (3) **Resources and mechanisms**: Refer to the available knowledge, competencies and capabilities that can be applied to generate, analyze, and organize vision's ideas for ePAL environment. During the process of generating vision's ideas the resources and mechanisms are to be provided by the following: the research consortium (i.e. ePAL consortium), visionaries and experts in related areas, stakeholders, etc.

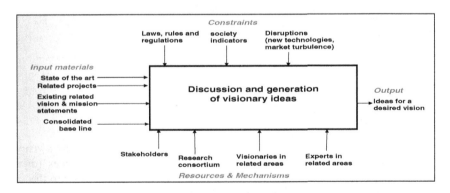

Fig. 2. Elements that need to be addressed while building ePAL vision

A number of different types of stakeholders were involved, namely through participation in a number of workshops and seminars, in the process of generating vision's ideas for ePAL environment to provide the consortium with necessary resources and mechanisms. Involved stakeholders included: (1) Representatives of communities of senior professionals, (2) Experts from different disciplines addressing enhancement of life of senior professionals, (3) Representatives of active labour forces in different market domains, (4) Representatives of employer organizations, (5) Visionaries in related areas, and (6) Individual senior professionals. The output of this step is a set of general visionary ideas, related to the ePAL environment, and achieving a deep understanding of this area.

Step 2: Elaboration of 1ˢᵗ vision. In this step the aim is the identification and generation of the main elements related to the vision statement for the environment, based on the knowledge and experience available/gained within the ePAL consortium, the acquired understanding of the baseline and the visionary ideas generated in Step 1. This phase is extremely important - where the 1ˢᵗ vision statement is established based on the analysis of the main drivers and trends, and through developing and analysing a number of scenarios (Fig. 3). Lessons learned from these studies are the constituting elements for the 1ˢᵗ vision. As shown in Fig. 3, there are two fundamental processes in this step whose results are important inputs to the elaboration of the 1ˢᵗ vision. It is necessary to establish and analyze drivers and trends to understand what is currently happening in the society. It is also necessary to build scenarios to understand the possible evolutions of the drivers and trends that can occur in the near future if a certain situation will have to be realized. The results of the two tasks provide an input to identifying main elements to be incorporated in the vision.

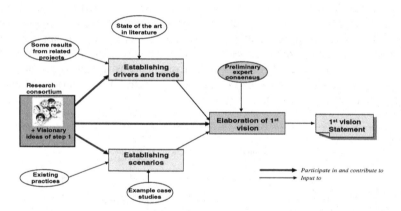

Fig. 3. Presenting and elaborating the vision ideas

Establishing drivers and trends: a fundamental prerequisite for developing a vision is to identify both drivers and trends. Drivers refer to the main influences (driving forces) which guide the running and changes of the society. Trends refer to the main happenings related to each driver. Thus trends indicate how each driver will influence the changes in the market or society. The analysis of drivers and trends enables the visionaries and researchers to identify fundamental areas or perspectives that need to be properly covered by the vision. Through extensive baseline study on achieved research results and existing practices related to ePAL we have observed that vision's ideas can be classified into three perspectives of technological, social, and organizational. As shown in Fig. 4, the categorization of main drivers is matched to these perspectives and a number of sub-drivers are identified. Furthermore, for each sub-driver a number of trends are characterized.

Establishing scenarios: Building scenarios serves as a tool to provide actors with essential understanding, orientation, context, direction, and some degree of consensus in planning research developments and implementations. In relation to ePAL's vision for future, scenarios are used to support understanding of different future possibilities regarding the enhancing of active life of senior professionals, as well as possible actions to take and which events are probable to occur in future. Table 1 summarizes example scenarios established for the ePAL environment.

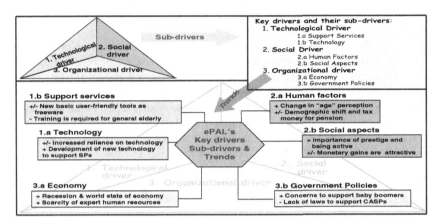

Fig. 4. Drivers and trends for ePAL environment

Table 1. Example scenarios for ePAL environment

Scenario Category	Main focus
Associations of retired professionals: voluntary work	Focusing on the need for communities of active senior professionals to enhance chances of the involvement of senior professionals in daily activities as volunteers within their own societies or in other regions. These scenarios address the establishment, management and operation of the elderly communities. They also characterize the nature of activities of the communities and roles of senior professionals in performing those activities.
Associations of retired professionals: brokerage and launching	Focusing on the role of brokerage of opportunities that can be responded by senior professionals either individually or through communities of active senior professionals. These scenarios characterize the roles related to brokering of opportunities, namely: direct brokerage where senior professionals are involved in capturing an opportunity or indirect brokerage where a third party is involved in capturing an opportunity.
Service markets	Focusing on potential markets, mostly technology enabled markets, which are typically feasible for senior professionals to deliver their services. These scenarios also address the categorization of clients into those who can pay and those who cannot pay for the services provided by seniors.
Tri-partite collaboration forms	Focusing on different roles that need to be performed by different parties to realize the establishment and operation of communities of active senior professionals. As such these scenarios first characterize different stakeholders of the ePAL and then define the roles of each category of actors.
Keeping the link to former employer	Focusing on existing practices regarding keeping communication with the former employers and how it enhances the professional activeness of senior professionals.
Second job	Focusing on the need for establishing some form of payments for the involvement of senior professionals in market and society activities.

From the results of the above two processes - identification of the drivers and trends related to the ePAL vision, and building of scenarios for potential cases, both the potential of the ePAL as well as its main constituents and limitations become evident.

One outcome of this extensive analysis is that we reached a good understanding of what which is necessary to properly "model" this environment. The achieved understanding is in relation to characterization of actors and their roles, as well as behaviour of stakeholders of the ePAL as influenced with both internal factors (membership, by-laws, value systems, etc.) and external factors (market regulations, government policies, intermediary roles, etc.)

Based on the results of the characterization of main elements of ePAL through building scenarios, analysis of trends and drivers, and study of baseline as well as based on the experience of the research consortium which was gained while performing the above processes, we were able to define the main elements of the 1st vision for the ePAL. We defined the vision by matching these results to the definition and components of a vision as described in section 2.1. Thus the main output of this step is therefore the elaborated 1st vision statement for ePAL. The next three steps are summarized in table below.

Step 3: Testing and validating the elaborated vision. Validating the vision is an important step focused on making sure that the society will be moving in the right direction once it implements this vision. In this step, representatives from each group of stakeholders must be involved in assessing the vision and providing improvement and extension suggestions. The focus is analyzing whether the vision is: (1) capturing the current objectives of the society, (2) properly addressing future potential objectives of the society, and (3) feasible for the society to achieve such future objectives, considering current trends, drivers and strategies.
Step 4: Consensus building through consulting and workshop. It is a decision making process that includes all stakeholders to together make a general agreement and commitment on a joint initiative. It is the most powerful decision process as stakeholders together agree to the final decision. In order for the vision to get full support from stakeholders in the society it first needs their acceptance. Building consensus on the proposed vision can apply the following approaches: (1) organizing workshops of representatives of stakeholders' groups, (2) generating questionnaires and other kind of surveys, (3) arranging round tables involving decision makers, and (4) performing online discussions and forums.
Step 5: Documenting and finalizing the vision. This step focuses on improving the vision statement by applying and incorporating feedbacks from the consensus building actions (Step 4). The final vision statement is documented to be ready for directing research regarding the gap analysis and defining actions for their realization and implementation in the society.

4   ePAL Vision for European Society

Establishment of ePAL vision. Following the approach presented in Section 3 and also based on the analysis of the current practices and the related literature (consolidated baseline), the drivers and trends in market and society, and the plausible scenarios of future, we have elaborated and formulated the 1st desired vision for ePAL, as shown in Fig. 5.

This vision statement provides a direction where the European society shall strive to follow, in order to achieve a balanced life for senior professionals who either need or desire to remain active in the society. It addresses providing opportunities and support for senior professionals who are willing to get involved in socio-economic activities. On the other hand, it suggests the main areas needing attention from other stakeholders in order to reach this desired state, such as (1) research institutions to provide innovative and new ideas in areas which require more R&D, (2) regulatory bodies (e.g. governments, law chambers, judiciaries) to provide a regulatory and legal infrastructure for the involvement of senior professionals in markets, (3) intermediaries (e.g. non-profit organizations, etc.) to support the brokerage of opportunities for senior professionals, etc.

Clearly enough, the creation of a desired vision for ePAL for the next decade is not a one shot action rather it is a live and interactive process. To develop the 1st vision statement for the ePAL environment we have followed a systematic approach, as presented throughout this paper. In the same manner, for the challenging task of **defining the vision statement** itself, we applied the classification proposed by Cumming [4] for defining a well-conceived vision, as addressed earlier in Section 2.1. We therefore piece by piece define the needed **conceptual elements** for the *well-conceived vision for ePAL environment.*

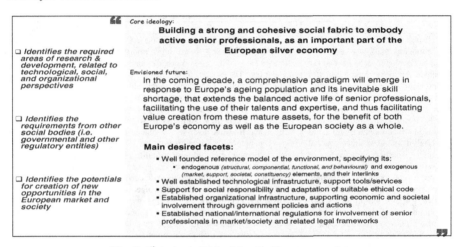

Fig. 5. 1st desired ePAL vision for European society

Below first each such element of this vision is defined and then they are integrated to form the "1st vision statement for the ePAL environment for Active Ageing Society", as shown in Fig. 5. The vision elements are presented in Table below.

Main element	Sub-elements and descriptions
Core Ideology	*(1) Core Values:* Active senior professionals, as an important part of the European silver economy,
	(2) Core Purpose: Building a strong and cohesive social fabric.
Envisioned Future	(1) *Long-term Audacious Goal:* In the coming decade, a comprehensive paradigm will emerge in response to Europe's ageing population and its inevitable skill shortage, that extends the balanced active life of senior professionals, facilitating the use of their talents and expertise, and thus facilitating value creation from these senior professionals, for the benefit of both Europe's economy as well as the European society as a whole,
	(2) *Vivid description:* (a) Well founded reference model of the environment, specifying its endogenous (structural, componental, functional, and behavioural), and exogenous (market, support, societal, constituency) elements, and their interlinks, (b) Well established technological infrastructure, support tools/services, (c) Support for social responsibility and adaptation of suitable ethical code, (d) Established organizational structure (*collaborative network*), supporting economic and societal involvement through government policies and actions, and (e) Established national/international regulations for involvement of senior professionals in market/society and related legal frameworks

Further to the core ideology and the envisioned future, represented inside the quotes, within the definition of vision for ePAL environment, on the left side of the Fig. 5 the three *main outcomes of the vision* are also listed, namely: (i) *identifying required areas for R&D*, (ii) *identifying the requirements from other social bodies such as governmental and other regulatory entities that requires their attention,* and (iii) *Identifying the potentials for creation of new opportunities.*

Instantiation of the vision into multi-disciplines. We base on multi-perspective concepts to instantiate the formulated vision into the three identified perspectives in order to capture fundamental societal and economical activities that senior professionals shall be involved in daily manner. We also base on the visioning approach that

Table 2. Instantiation of the ePAL vision into the three perspectives

Vision instantiation statement		
Technological	**Social**	**Organizational**
In the coming decade, the ICT collaboration platforms and tools will be developed as an easy to use enabler of new approaches for continuation of the active involvement of elderly people in the socio-economic system. As such novel infrastructures and intelligent functionalities will act as a catalyst of new organizational forms, supporting effective management of geographically disperse communities of retired professionals, and facilitating the active participation in the socio-economic activities, as an extension of the human capabilities towards fitted participation.	In the coming decade, extending active professional life will be a high priority strategy in addressing Europe's aging population. The social infrastructure will mature to accommodate demographic shifts through the creation of mechanisms to support active involvement of elderly people in the silver economy. Attitudes in society will evolve towards positive acceptance of elderly people as a value-creating pool of talent, thereby creating opportunities to support and promote active aging. Both senior and young professionals will derive greater benefit from the exchange of knowledge and experience. As the social environment evolves, new support mechanisms will arise to sustain an aging but more active and inclusive population.	In the coming decade, the primary stakeholders e.g. government, intermediate, business, – will adopt positive and proactive policies and approaches that enable senior professionals to continue their active life and generate income that compensates for pension shortfalls and facilitates a valuable contribution to Europe's economy.
Main desired facets		
Technological	**Social**	**Organizational**
▪ Advanced collaboration support services, including (virtual) teams formation and management. ▪ Support for user-generated knowledge content. ▪ "Configure yourself "based philosophy infrastructure. ▪ Easily adaptable and customizable user interfaces. ▪ Affective computing and context aware enriched environments. ▪ Tools supporting the process of value creation. ▪ Novel contractual and cooperation agreements, including negotiation support. ▪ Advanced marketing and brokerage services. ▪ New networking models for elderly communities' involvement with the socio-economic system.	▪ New mechanisms to enhance positive understanding and perception in the society regarding the value of abilities, skills and experience of senior professionals in the economy. ▪ Motivation tools for senior professionals to join elderly associations. ▪ Mechanisms to support for cross-cultural interactions among senior professionals as well as to the active labor force. ▪ Mechanisms to support a balanced economical benefits sharing among the entire society including senior professionals.	▪ Employment and retirement policies will change to provide greater flexibility for seniors to continue as economic actors. ▪ Global regulations and polices will change to encourage the participation of businesses in collaboration with senior professionals. ▪ The knowledge and skills of seniors will be harnessed to generate wealth and stimulate innovation amongst European businesses. ▪ New forms of intermediate organizations will provide highly efficient brokerage that will help seniors engage with businesses in Europe. ▪ There will be significant long-term funding – from both public and private sectors - and the political drive to support new forms of senior associations and other intermediate brokers. ▪ New organizational cultures will positively embrace relationships between senior professionals and pre-retired (active) professionals.

was introduced in the VOmap project regarding the "instantiation of the vision statement" to its main focus areas or perspectives [2]. As such, the vision development mechanism applied in ePAL *instantiates its vision statement* for three main contributing areas, namely: the technological, social, and organizational perspectives. Table 2 summarizes instantiation statements and the main desired facets for each perspective to support realization of the proposed vision.

5 Conclusion

In this paper, we have emphasized the need for systematically formulating a vision for the ePAL while involving all stakeholders in different activities. Applying the proposed approach, a 1st vision statement for ePAL is presented. Furthermore we have shown the main focuses related to technological, social and organizational perspectives that need further attentions. For the proposed vision to be realized there is a need for looking into user friendly collaborative ICT services and infrastructures to facilitate both their usage by seniors as well as the interactions between seniors and other stakeholders. Socially, there is a need to enhance the positive perception of the society towards elder people to view them not as a social and economical burden but as wells of knowledge and experience needed in the society. Organizationally, there is a need for reformulating regulations and organizational models to provide opportunities to senior professionals as other actors in the market.

As future work in relation to development of the **desired vision for the ePAL environment** the following steps can be mentioned: (1) Further refinement and tuning of the 1st ePAL vision, (2) Dissemination and discussion of the ePAL vision, and (3) Achieving the final vision specification for the ePAL environment. Another fundamental aspect that will be addressed by our research is related to the refinement of the areas of R&D related to the three perspectives of the vision.

Acknowledgement. This work was supported in part by the ePAL project funded by the European Commission. The authors acknowledge contributions from partners in ePAL.

References

1. Camarinha-Matos, L.M., Afsarmanesh, H.: A comprehensive modeling framework for collaborative networked organizations. The Journal of Intelligent Manufacturing 18(5), 527–615 (2007)
2. Camarinha-Matos, L.M., Afsarmanesh, H.: A roadmap for strategic research on virtual organizations. In: Proceedings of PRO-VE 2003 - Processes and Foundations for Virtual Organizations. Kluwer Academic Publishers, Dordrecht (2003)
3. Collins, J.C., Porras, J.I.: Organizational vision and visionary organizations. In: Leading organizations – Perspectives for a new era, pp. 234–249. SAGE, Thousand Oaks (1998)
4. Cummings, T.G.: Organization Development and Change. Thomson South-Western (2005)
5. Donald, E.H.: Building leadership vision. Eleven strategic challenges for higher education. The EDUCAUSE review, 25–34 (2003)

6. Hinrichsen, D., Robey, B.: Population and the Environment: The Global Challenge (08/2008),
   http://www.actionbioscience.org/environment/
   hinrichsen_robey.html#primer
7. Kakabadse, N., Kakabadse, A., Lee-Davies, L.: Visioning the pathway: A leadership process model. European Management Journal 23(2), 237–246 (2005)
8. Laubacher, R.J., Malone, T.W.: Two scenarios for 21st century organizations: shifting networks of small firms or all-encompassing "virtual countries"? A working paper, MIT, USA (1997)
9. Senge, P., Kleiner, A., Roberts, C., Ross, R., Smit, B.: The Fifth Discipline Fieldbook - Strategies and Tools for Building A Learning Organization. Doubleday Publishing (1994)
10. Stranges, M.: Immigration As a Remedy for Population Decline? An Overview of the European Countries. European papers on the new welfare, Special issue on the counter ageing society, paper no. 8 (2008)

Exploring the Gap for Effective Extension of Professional Active Life in Europe

Will Leonard[1], Hamideh Afsarmanesh[2], Simon S. Msanjila[2], and Jim Playfoot[1]

[1] White loop Ltd, 54 Poland Street, London W1F 7NJ, UK
{will,jim}@whiteloop.com
[2] Informatics Institute, University of Amsterdam, Science Park 107,
1098 XG, Amsterdam, The Netherlands
{h.afsarmanesh,s.s.msanjila}@uva.nl

Abstract. Extending Professional Active Life (ePAL [2]) of elder people in Europe is affected by a number of factors in the market and society, which have the potential to either positively and negatively influence it. Current practices indicate that the European society, while started to act on this subject, is still slow to recognize the rationale behind and importance of fully supporting the extension of active professional life of seniors. Similarly, the capacity of the service sector to fully support the involvement of seniors in economical activities is at present limited, given the huge number of these seniors in different countries who need to be mobilized. This paper seeks to highlight the identified gaps related to effective mechanisms by which Europe can support its willing senior professionals to remain active. The study on gap identification addresses relevant technological, social, and organizational factors and external influences which have the potential to impact successful future life of elderly population. It also presents the methodology that is applied in our study to identify and analyze the gaps between the current practices in this area, the so-called baseline [2], and the desired future for this area as inspired in the ePAL vision [1] addressed in other research.

Keywords: Gap analysis, professional active life, vision statement.

1 Introduction

Past research has shown that senior professionals (i.e. retired or retiring professionals according to the regulations in respective countries [2]) in Europe view their involvement in some sort of professional activities as a fundamental element of wellness and personal fulfillment [6]. Many of these seniors resent the fact that they were forced to retire at a certain age and they would rather prefer to have the choice to continue working for as long as they wish [8]. ePAL's envisioned future is of an EU (European Union) in which active senior professionals are supported in their work towards filling the emerging skill gaps in European society. This envisioned future is also dependent on governments in different EU countries having recognized the growing trend of an aging workforce and seeing the logic of creating a legal infrastructure to facilitate seniors in extending their active role in society.

L.M. Camarinha-Matos et al. (Eds.): PRO-VE 2009, IFIP AICT 307, pp. 695–706, 2009.

A number of studies have highlighted that regardless of the fact that younger workers will become an increasingly scarce resource, many employers in Europe still attach negative stigmas to senior workers and demonstrate a reluctance to employ or work with them [3]. Thus fundamental societal changes must take place and these changes should follow the guidelines provided by a well-conceived vision for the desired future in this area. At the same time, supporting ICT technology-based tools need to be developed in a senior-friendly manner, which means developing tools that adapt to their needs. Therefore, the creation of new IT tools and systems are required for professionals, having the particular needs of seniors in mind [5]. Currently, there are also concerns that the needed technological, social and organizational changes, necessary to support the ePAL vision, will not take place before the problem of an aging Europe becomes even more critical.

It is therefore essential to analyze the advances in technological and organizational models in relation to their market potential and social function, in supporting the involvement of seniors in daily economic activities. In this sense, those who build these supporting tools must be aware of a growing silver economy, involving seniors and their support organizations as their principal consumers.

The research presented in this paper looks to create a critical analysis of the "gap" between the baseline and the desired vision of the ePAL. In so doing, it is intended to provide guidelines for experts, observing how difficult or easy it is to achieve every facet of the ePAL vision. Within the analysis presented in this paper, first positive and negative factors affecting the global ePAL vision are identified, and then categorized as *strengths, weaknesses* (the capabilities within the EU), *opportunities, and threats* (those influences not directly controlled by the EU).

2   Baseline on Active Senior Professionals in EU

Challenges related to the ageing population of the EU have been well studied by various researchers focusing on different aspects regarding senior professionals [4]. In order to support senior professionals in counteracting these challenges through continuing their active role in the socio-economic system of the EU, a coordinated vision of a positive support environment is needed. A growing awareness of challenges means that this process has already begun so it is necessary to understand the difference between where we are now and where we want to be.

In the private sector, much of these limitations are the consequence of a lack of awareness of senior professionals as potential clients. Though there are some notable exceptions, groups such as Age Concern (http://www.ageconcern.org.uk/) have highlighted the negative connotations and image which still exists concerning the older worker. Employment agencies are aware that employers have this negative image of seniors and therefore focus on jobseekers of a younger age even though they have less experience. There are also issues around quantifying the skills and experience which seniors offer, when they look to effect a career change in later life.

In the current associations of senior professionals, the scale of operations is limited. The low level of membership for these associations in the EU in relation to the percentage of elder people in Europe indicates that these associations are not well equipped to attract all potential members. The social capital and capacity of such associations need to be enhanced to attract more seniors. For example, the Confederation of European Senior Expert Services (CESES –www.ceses.org) represents 25 associations of senior professionals from the member states of the European Union but only offers the skills and life-time experience of around 24,000 Senior Experts. The CESES, which is the main coordinating body in the Europe, sees its role as: "to contribute to raising standards of living in developing economies through voluntary assistance to small and medium-size, financially weak, enterprises and institutions" (www.ceses.org). This though admirable aim, represents a brain drain of the skills of senior professionals working outside of Europe. However, it was observed that there is a lack of demand for services provided by senior professionals. In other words, senior professionals would have a much wider potential than the limited number of opportunities they are involved in today. Thus, there is a clear need for an improved brokerage function to identify the market needs and match them with the skills base available in these associations.

We define the "ePAL gap" as the differences which emerge between the current practice in the area and a desired future support environment for senior professionals, achieving the aims of the ePAL vision. The ePAL gap addresses and covers the three perspectives of social, organizational, and technological. The **Social Perspective** analyses the wider EU's recognition of the rationale behind fully supporting the extension of active professional life. The capacity of the service sector to fully support these activities and the provision of a regulatory and fiscal policy environment which can complement and support this sector is considered within the **Organizational Perspective.** The development of adequate ICT support by which the specific needs of senior professionals constitute part of their design process is considered and addressed in the **Technological Perspective**. Table below presents a summary of the baseline findings for the three perspectives.

Technological baseline	In the technological sector, it is clear that many of the present advances in ICT are not aimed at Senior Professionals as a target user [5]. This is perhaps because those that design the software by and large do not come from a senior generation and do not have a proper understanding of the needs of seniors which they can input into their design. This leads to a vicious circle whereby software and applications are designed for a younger user who then becomes its chief consumers and market, influencing its future development. Even if this trend cannot be broken, fully adaptable interfaces can help seniors overcome this lack of understanding through allowing them to adapt ICT tools to their needs.
Social baseline	The above trend is no more evident than in social networks which are phenomena amongst younger generations, who connect with them in vast numbers and are designed and built around applications with this sector of society very much in mind. Facebook, Bebo and Youtube have made ICT a very important force in mobilizing the social capital of a younger generation, who both relate to this field of communication and are savvy enough to adapt it to their own user generated content. Networks and interconnections are continuously expanded and enriched by this new content. Since this environment is very much designed with the younger user in mind, seniors are wary of and feel excluded from its use. These networks provide a level of adaptability which is aimed largely at a younger generation and while successful, do not help develop online cultures among seniors.
Organizational baseline	From an organizational perspective there is a chronic shortage of models which can effectively leverage the usage of the skills of seniors. At present there is still a lack of communication between employers/customers and seniors concerning the skills and experience they can effectively bring to the marketplace. While some positive examples illustrate how SMEs and start-ups can benefit from support offered by seniors, the demand has remained quite residual. Effective new brokers are needed to ensure that such issues do not slow down the rate of adaptation of recruitment and employment practices to the new demographic realities of the EU.

3   Methodology for Gap Analysis in ePAL

The purpose of the gap analysis is to *identify the gap between the current baseline and the desired vision*. Putting the baseline and the vision statement side by side will allow making both a conceptual as well as a "visual" comparison and therefore better identification and characterization of the gap. For this purpose the following 3 steps are adopted and applied in this paper:

Step 0: Synthesis of the baseline's findings: This step focuses on elaborating a synthesis of the findings regarding the baseline and follow up activities that are currently conducted in other studies [2], and based on the 3 perspectives of technological, organizational and social, addressed by the vision of desired future for this area addressed in other research [1], as intended to be exemplified in Fig. 1. An "*aspect*" in the baseline is one component of the "universe of analysis". For instance, in the technological perspective we could have an aspect referring to architectures for collaborative networks (CN). A "*desired facet*" in the vision usually corresponds to an aspect, characterized with certain aimed value, to support the vision. For instance, a desired facet for the technological vision instantiation, associated to the above facet may refer to novel architectures for CNs.

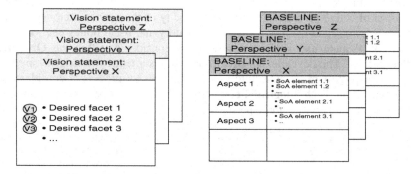

Fig. 1. Synthesis of baseline

Step 1: Elaboration of a macro-gap analysis: In this step a macroscopic analysis is elaborated regarding the global vision statement. For this purpose a SWOT (Strengths, Weaknesses, Opportunities and Threats) analysis method is used as shown in Fig. 2.

The "internal context" shall be the European Union which covers the identification of the Strengths and Weaknesses at the European level regarding the potential to

	Helpful To achieving the vision	Harmful To achieving the vision
Internally originated European union level	**Strengths** • Strength 1 • Strength 2 •	**Weaknesses** • Weakness 1 • Weakness 2 • ....
Externally originated Surrounding environment	**Opportunities** • Opportunity 1 • Opportunity 2 •	**Threats** • Threats 1 • Threats 2 • ....

Fig. 2. SWOT analysis

achieve the vision. The "surrounding environment" refers to both the European socio-economic context and the regions outside Europe. It is split between opportunities that can be exploited and threats to the main actors of the ePAL Vision.

Step 2: Elaboration of a detailed gap analysis: At this stage a detailed gap analysis is performed considering the three perspectives under which the vision shall be instantiated. This step focuses on two lines of analysis: Strengths and Weaknesses / Limitations as shown in Fig. 3 to identify the relevant elements facilitating or constraining the elaboration of a plan of actions related to the vision.

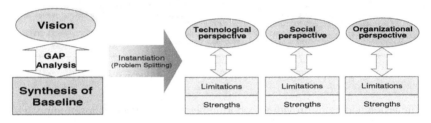

Fig. 3. Gap analysis

For this analysis, the detailed facets considered under each perspective shall define the granularity of the analysis. To determine the gaps, the desired facets in the vision statement are compared with the state of the art elements in the corresponding aspects of the baseline (Fig. 4).

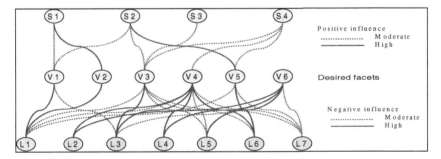

Fig. 4. Influence map – another representation

The identified gaps can be expressed through the generation of a set of three "Influence maps" to represent both the positive and negative influences of the baseline on the achievement of the vision. As shown in Fig. 4, the influence maps developed for the three perspectives provide qualitative analysis of the state of potentials and barriers on the road to reach the vision.

4   Macro Gap Analysis for ePAL Environment

The vision statement introduced in [1], provides a clear direction where the European society shall strive to follow, in order to achieve a balanced life for senior professionals who either need or desire to remain active in the society/market (Fig. 5).

Fig. 5. 1st vision statement for ePAL in European society [1]

The vision addresses providing opportunities and support for those seniors who are willing to get involved in socio-economic activities. It suggests the main areas needing attention from other social bodies and responsible organs, in order to reach this desired state. Clearly enough, the creation of a desired vision for ePAL for the coming decade is not a one shot action rather it is a live and interactive process.

Based on the vision statement and its respective facets as well as the baseline findings, an examination of the strengths, weaknesses, opportunities and threats was performed by applying a SWOT analysis to the ePAL environment in European society. Below are some example results of the SWOT analysis. More detailed results are presented in the project website at www.epal.eu.com.

Strengths
1. **Motivation and awareness of seniors.** Seniors across Europe want to work, have the desire to continue engaging in meaningful activity and are increasingly aware of their political power and economic potential.
2. **Promotion of initiatives, laws and policies across Europe that support active ageing.** There are many initiatives, both at EU level and at national level, that are aimed at addressing issues around seniors continued active participation in society. These include issues around employment policies, pensions, and support for lifelong learning.
3. **ICT infrastructures exist across Europe to provide the technology building blocks that will be needed to implement the ePAL vision.** The strength of the ICT infrastructure facilitates interaction across geographical boundaries, and provides the basis for achieving the ePAL vision. The infrastructure is inducing high levels of engagement in tools that facilitate communication, collaboration, content creation and management, document management etc.

Weaknesses
1. **Lack of effective role for governmental bodies within the EU.** There is a lack of funding opportunities for the activities of senior professionals. More government regulations are also needed for Associations of Senior Professionals e.g. labor systems, IPR, liability. At present, there is also too much regulation in terms of the presently overly restrictive retirement laws imposed by many EU governments.
2. **Weaknesses of Associations of Senior Professionals.** At present there is a lack of new organizational, operational and business models for these associations. Many associations display a low level of marketing ability evidenced by their low membership rate. Another common flaw among many such associations is a lack of sufficient mechanisms for identifying funding opportunities within the EU.

3. **Lack of Support Services for Senior Professionals.** There is, in comparison with other sectors of society, a low level of social networking and trust building among senior professionals. Seniors also need an educational sector which offer more options for higher and further education training opportunities. This should be coupled with more research into the job market opportunities for senior professionals.

Opportunities

1. **People are becoming more community minded thanks to the web.** Recent years have seen the emergence of new organizational forms and ways to work together on the web e.g. Virtual Communities and Virtual Organizations. This means trust creation is becoming easier to achieve, thanks to the use of the web in the sense that people are getting more used to trusting others remotely. These new avenues create more opportunities to cement trust amongst seniors and enable them to collaborate better.
2. **The increasing scarcity of younger workers.** The EU has an aging population which will mean the emergence of skill shortages and lead to a scarcity of younger workers. Thus employers will increasingly need to employ seniors to plug the skill gaps and occupy the positions that the lower number of younger workers will not be able to fill.
3. **Improvements in modern medical science.** People are living longer and modern medical support and healthcare provision means seniors professionals are able to remain actively involved in the socio-economic system of the EU for longer.

Threats

1. **Society does not react to change.** Major stakeholders in society – unions, media, politicians, businesses - fail to reach social consensus that leads to a timely restructuring of society in order to effectively accommodate the new realities of an older population.
2. **Slow pace of adaptation.** The pace of adaptation in society in terms of technology, business models, ways of working etc – leads to higher levels of exclusion amongst older people.
3. **New technology brings privacy/ethical issues.** The development of specialized technologies to facilitate human capabilities and emotional interaction increases the risk of intrusions of privacy and complications around ethical issues.

5 Map of Influence Analysis

In the map of influence analysis, the positive and negative factors established in the macro analysis are further detailed according to level of direct influence upon the individual facets of the ePAL Vision. In so doing, these factors have been divided amongst the three main perspectives for the vision of social, organizational and technological which help to define the extent of the challenge involved in achieving each facet of the vision as well as isolating areas of particular concern. Below we present maps of influences for some example strengths and weaknesses.

Map of influence for social perspective

Strengths	Limitations
S1 The increasing scarcity of younger workers, leading companies to start changing their view of older workers	L1 Negative and outdated assumptions regarding the abilities of senior professionals persist
S2 Improvements in modern medical science, increasing the duration of healthy senior life	L2 There is still evidence of discrimination against seniors in the workplace
S3 Increased competitiveness in the EU Marketplace as a result of globalization, which may open new opportunities for highly experienced professionals	L3 Lack of understanding of the specific needs of senior professionals
S4 Cross Cultural Understanding in Business means improved collaboration	L4 Education in the EU lacks flexibility, with more emphasis needed on life-long learning and retraining opportunities for seniors

As shown in Table 1 the identified strengths and limitations are mapped with the following vision facets related to the social perspective:

V1: New mechanisms to enhance positive understanding and perception in society regarding the value of the abilities, skills and experience of senior professionals in the economy

V2: Motivating mechanisms for senior professionals to join associations of seniors

V3: Mechanisms to support cross-cultural interactions among senior professionals as well as to the active labor force

V4: Mechanisms to support a balanced economic benefits sharing among the entire society including senior professionals.

Table 1. Influence map for social perspective

	V1	V2	V3	V4			
S1	■						Positive Influence
S2		▦				■	High
S3	▦		■			▦	Moderate
S4			■				
							Negative Influence
L1	▦					■	High
L2	▦					▦	Moderate
L3							
L4	▦						

Map of influence for organizational perspective

Strengths	**Limitations**
S1 Some organizational approaches have manifested in practice, focused on the use of the experience and knowledge of senior professionals.	**L1** Lack of common EU-level policies among European countries and the EU itself on the enhancement of active life of senior professionals.
S2 Changes have emerged in ways of working, such as freelancing and service based contracts, which are more suitable for senior professionals.	**L2** Lack of proper organizational/operational models to support the establishment and management of associations of senior professionals effectively involved in socio-economic activities.
S3 There are some new initiatives, laws and policies across Europe oriented towards supporting active ageing for senior professionals.	**L3** Lack of committed organizations and their related business models to act as brokers for senior professionals and to build trust between senior professionals and their potential clients.
S4 New conceptual frameworks and organizational forms, e.g. the collaborative networks paradigm, as well as the implementation of pilot cases, demonstrate new ways of supporting seniors to remain active.	**L4** Lack of comprehensive policies, regulations, and laws which favor the involvement of senior professionals in the silver economy, in particular, related to formal positions, payments, and access to opportunities.

As shown in Table 2, the identified strengths and limitations are mapped with the following vision facets relayed to the organizational perspective:

V1: Employment and retirement policies will change to provide greater flexibility for seniors as economic actors

V2: Global regulations and policies will change to encourage the participation of businesses in collaboration with senior professionals

V3: The knowledge and skills of seniors will be harnessed to generate wealth and stimulate innovation amongst European businesses

V4: New forms of intermediate organization will provide highly efficient brokerage that will help seniors engage with businesses in Europe.

Table 2. Influence map for organizational perspective

	V1	V2	V3	V4		
S1						Positive Influence
S2						High
S3						Moderate
S4						
L1						
L2						Negative Influence
L3						High
L4						Moderate

Map of influence for technological perspective

Strengths	Limitations
S1 Good progress in conceptual models for collaborative networks (although mostly focused on industry)	**L1** Lack of consolidated theoretical base in areas such as reference modeling for active ageing support systems
S2 There is already an understanding of the needed management functionalities for VO breeding environments / professional virtual communities	**L2** Lack of effective and integrated ICT support for collaboration (till large fragmentation of functionalities)
S3 Various partial models and advanced prototypes (e.g. negotiation, trust, value systems) have been developed to support collaborative environments	**L3** ICT research in this area too much focused on the "last phases of life", reducing the needed attention to active ageing support
S4 ICT infrastructures exist across Europe to provide the communication building blocks that is needed to implement the ePAL vision	**L4** Fast proliferation of new tools and functionalities without a holistic approach, an obstacle for adoption by seniors

As shown in Table 3, the identified strengths and limitations are mapped with the following vision facets related to the technological perspective:

V1 Advanced collaboration support services, including teams' formation and management

V2 Development of collaboration ontology supporting variety of stakeholders

V3 Support for user-generated knowledge content

V4 "Configure yourself" based philosophy infrastructure.

Table 3. Influence map for technological perspective

	V1	V2	V3	V4		
S1						
S2						Positive Influence
S3						High
S4						Moderate
L1						
L2						Negative Influence
L3						High
L4						Moderate

6 Summaries of Gap Analysis Findings

Social perspective: The social perspective of the ePAL vision is perhaps the most difficult to achieve as it requires a mass mobilization of a large number of actors. Social cohesion and a change in attitudes towards older professionals is a difficult task. The traditional view that those reaching retirement age are about to make the transition to passive actors must become largely redundant due to the pan European demographic changes of an aging EU. The recognition of this new role is vital for EU governments and older workers themselves. Social cohesion is an important area of consideration as the rise of the senior workers will not happen in isolation. As an ever increasing percentage of EU society, seniors' contribution to their society needs to grow. To ensure that the potential of this contribution is properly coordinated new mechanisms which gather consensus and outline the role of seniors in EU will need to be created. It is important that such mobilization should not lead to the ghettoisation of seniors and become a source of division within EU society.

Seniors and those just starting employment will have to learn to work together and effectively communicate. As part of this there will have to be a greater understanding of the new needs this will create and new forms of leveraging the capabilities of seniors. At the same time "seniority" (position in a company) within a business environment will no longer be so closely linked to age. Maureen Minehan, as early as 1997 noted a trend that while older workers will have to accept that pay in later life will become more linked to performance rather than "seniority", human resource departments are increasingly excepting that new forms of health and other benefits will come into place to attract senior workers [7]. Recent studies show that many older workers still consider themselves to be discriminated in the workplace and some employers are prejudiced by stigmas of inadaptability and lack of learning ability when they apply for jobs [3]. Mechanisms to support cross generational interaction between seniors and younger citizens; fomenting inter-generational solidarity and understanding within the EU would have the knock on effect of improving employment systems and creating a healthy employment balance.

Organizational perspective: The organizational perspective of ePAL can be divided into two main strands. The first is employment policies and regulations which will facilitate the rise of the active senior professional and the second is mechanisms which will harness the potential of these actors and provide increased support and structure to their contribution to the EU economy. As mentioned earlier, there is a need for a full understanding of what seniors, in a non traditional role as active professionals, can bring to society. This requires in part a mobilization of senior social capital by seniors themselves supported through relevant mechanisms.

A full understanding of the needs and issues around active senior professionals can provide the basis for strategic investment into more efficient and specific forms of brokerage and support services tailored to the realities of the silver economy. Such brokerage should also take into account ways of mitigating against problems with cross generational communication and what are the most efficient forms of work for seniors as compared to other types of professionals. It seems increasingly likely that the extension of active life will go hand in hand with a change in the average person's career trajectory. Labor systems have attracted a lot of interest and the reduced labor rigidity and indeed rights such systems bring would have a significant impact on the way people work in the future. Of most relevance to ePAL is the effect such labor law changes would have on the traditional divisions between pre and post retirement life. Fewer EU citizens are working long term for one employer and are incentivized to retrain themselves throughout their lives and consequently take more control of financial provision for their retirement. An accent on life long learning implies that many people will have to take time out of their active professional lives at several stages of their career, with retirement planning forming part of a more sophisticated concept of career and financial planning. Brokerage for senior professionals will need to develop a wider knowledge of how it fits into this equation. Financial services specifically aimed at seniors will have to do the same. However, a pool of senior talent which is used to remarketing itself would in theory, make the role of brokers in leveraging this talent to diverse sources easier. Such career fluidity would also have a consequential effect on the concept of a senior worker itself.

Technological perspective: There are a number of new ICT technologies and advances which show the potential to facilitate the extension of professional active life amongst seniors, but their scope at present is not clearly defined and there is a real need for their advancement to be steered towards the needs of senior professionals.

In order for advances in ICT brokerage systems to have the desired effect they should be developed with a proper understanding of the needs of those who will be using them. This may seem an obvious point, but it would appear important that the technological aspects of ePAL advance in line with organisational models. In a highly competitive industry which develops at a lightning pace with a constantly updated line of services in which new advances quickly become redundant this would mean too much of a barrier to its normal development. One solution to this problem, which is very much in line with present technological trends, is to offer a high degree of built in adaptability to new technology. Advances in "configure yourself" technology and support systems for user generated knowledge content along with easily customizable interfaces are crucial to allow brokers and senior professionals themselves to react to changes in a non static marketplace. Where seniors are working with younger professionals' adaptable technology would have to be compatible and not virtually alienate seniors from their co-workers. The issue of stigma could become a problem within the context of seniors working within a professional environment – if a senior uses an adaptive technology in order to interact with others, this may be seen as a sign of weakness to effectively do the job.

The introduction of new working patterns, relying for instance on remote collaboration of teams of senior professionals interacting with brokerage entities and customers, also introduces the need for new infrastructure functionalities and tools supporting e.g. trust building, value systems alignment, performance assessment in collaborative environments and distributed negotiation mechanisms, etc.

7 Conclusion

The conclusion to be drawn from the results of the performed gap analysis study is that in parallel with the needed development of new supporting technologies, there is a need for a change in culture and attitudes towards older workers. This cultural change is something which must pervade both the public and private sector. From a public sector point of view this problem manifests itself in such things as policies which consider the +55s as a homogeneous group and see healthcare technologies as serving the same group of citizens as leveraging the skills of senior workers. In the private sector, there seems to be a set of persisting overarching negative assumptions about a very diverse sector of society. Furthermore, there is a real lack of recognition of senior professionals as a potential customer base for new ICT tools, which is needed to drive forward change and development of network technologies as well as support systems for an increasingly growing but unexploited marketplace, one which is vital for the economic and social prosperity of the EU. It is arguable that were these cultural changes to take place and a greater appreciation of the active senior professional to emerge, there would be a knock on effect in terms of organizational and technological development. An increased demand for active senior professionals would create new markets for improved support infrastructures. Equally, the creation of organizational models which make the leveraging of professional senior talent efficiently available would serve to counteract negative preconceptions of older workers and in turn increase demand for their services.

One of the key purposes of the gap analysis presented in this paper is to highlight areas of difficulty within the ePAL vision. Difficulties in the context of the vision do not reflect upon the validity or value of the various facets presented, but rather how realistic they would be to achieve or pointing to how much effort they would require given the current political and socio-economic situation in the EU and beyond.

Acknowledgement. This work was supported in part by the ePAL project funded by the European Commission. The authors thank for contributions from partners in the ePAL consortium.

References

1. Afsarmanesh, H., Camarinha-Matos, L.M., Msanjila, S.: A well-conceived vision for extending professional life of seniors. In: Proceedings of PRO-VE 2009 conference (September 2009) (to appear)
2. Camarinha-Matos, L.M., Afsarmanesh, H.: The need for a strategic R&D roadmap for active ageing. In: The proceedings of PRO-VE 2009 conf. (September 2009) (to appear)
3. Canziani, P., Petrongolo, B.: Firing costs and stigma: A theoretical analysis and evidence from microdata. European Econ. Review 45(10), 1877–1906 (2001)
4. DHSSPS: Equality and Inequalities in Health and Social Care: A Statistical Overview, Inequalities and Unfair Access Issues Emerging from the DHSSPS (2004)
5. Hernandez-Encuentra, E., Pousada, M., Gomez-Zuniga, B.: ICT and Older People: Beyond Usability. In Educational Gerontology. Special issue on Adult Education and Lifelong Learning 35(3), 226–245 (2009)
6. Kang, M., Russ, R., Ryu, J.S.: Wellness for Older Adults in Daily Life. Oklahoma Cooperative Extension Fact Sheets, T-2237 (2008), http://osufacts.okstate.edu
7. Minehan, M.: The aging baby boomers - impact of post-retirement employment on companies HR Magazine(1997), http://www.hrmagazine.co.uk/
8. Munnell, A.H.: Policies to promote labor force participation of older people – working paper. Opportunities for Older Americans Series (2006)

Part 22

Collaborative Networks for Active Ageing - II

New Organizational Forms to Extend the Professional Active Life

Antonio del Cura[1], Luis M. Camarinha-Matos[2], Filipa Ferrada[2],
and Patricia del Cura[1]

[1] SKILL Estrategia srl, Spain
{adelcura,pdelcura}@skill.es
[2] New University of Lisbon & Uninova, Portugal
{cam,faf}@uninova.pt

Abstract. A major challenge in effective active ageing support is to iden-
tify/design new organizational structures, approaches, and mechanisms so that
on one hand older people do not feel excluded, and on the other hand they have
the chance to make valued contributions to the communities where they live.
Collaborative networks involving a variety of stakeholders, e.g. senior professionals, intermediary entities, and beneficiaries have the potential of inducing
more effective integration of seniors in the socio-economic system. It is particularly relevant to characterize the various stakeholders to be involved in this
process as well as their roles and inter-relationships. Departing from the analysis of current and emerging organizational forms, this paper identifies the challenges and suggests new directions for active ageing.

Keywords: Active ageing, collaborative organizational forms.

1 Introduction

An effective transformation of the current situation regarding retirement and the barriers to active ageing in Europe requires the introduction of new approaches and ways
to create actively contributing senior professional communities in society, which
support the elderly citizens with a framework for leveraging their talents and expertise
and creating value for the benefit of the Europe's economy. Many elderly citizens,
following retirement, quickly become marginalized and considered as a cost burden
rather than a resource, capable of "value creation" in the society. This feeling of exclusion and isolation creates a vacuum in the life of the elderly citizens which in turn
affects their health and well being. However, with the improvement of health conditions, many senior citizens could continue giving their contribution to the society after
retirement age. Furthermore, it is also becoming clear that seniors' knowledge and
expertise is essential for the younger workers who have to learn quicker in order to fill
the skills gaps that are already noticeable in European society.

The problem that arises when seniors wish to continue contributing to the society is
the lack of proper organizational models capable to support and integrate them adequately. The proposed solution requires the interaction of a range of stakeholders that,
carrying out different roles, facilitate the bringing together of these professionals and

L.M. Camarinha-Matos et al. (Eds.): PRO-VE 2009, IFIP AICT 307, pp. 709–720, 2009.
© IFIP International Federation for Information Processing 2009

the beneficiaries of the services they can provide. Clearly, the approach for active ageing has to rely on contributions from multiple actors – researchers from different fields, decision makers, research policy makers, social care institutions, regional development agencies, etc., and, of course, retired and retiring people themselves, namely through emerging associations of senior professionals. At the same time, in order to guarantee this bringing together, the different stakeholders must develop a whole series of business and behavioral models of varied structure, composition and characteristics to allow a variety of alternatives for the integration of senior professionals. Given the relative newness of the emphasis on keeping retired and retiring people integrated into the socio-economic system and bearing in mind the global tendencies in relation to social security systems, pensions and demography, it is foreseeable that modifications will be necessary with respect to:

- Achieving greater integration of retired and retiring people into economic and social life as a formula for complementing, on one hand the decreasing pension levels, and on the other hand to cope with the greater life expectancy.
- A greater complexity in the relationships that exist between the traditional and new groups of stakeholders involved in or interested in carrying out mediation between retired and retiring people and the possible beneficiaries.

For this purpose, this paper presents a study of the current organizational models and focus on emerging and future collaborative organizational models. This work has been developed within the ePAL project [1] which is developing a strategic research roadmap focused on innovative collaborative solutions and ensuring a balanced post-retirement life-style.

2   Identification of Current Practices

In addition to the traditional initiatives focused only on socialization and entertainment activities for elderly, a number of other organizational forms and mechanisms already exist or are emerging, focused on providing ways to help seniors remaining professionally active after retirement.

Currently, associations of retired professionals represent an important organizational structure supporting active ageing. Therefore, ePAL conducted a survey on 29 of those associations in Europe and outside Europe in order to get a consolidated view of these practices (Fig.1). The main conclusion is that these organizational forms exist due to the fact that retired people refuse to accept the retirement as the end of a professional life, claiming instead for remaining professionally active. The aim of these associations is essentially to provide assistance to organizations, people and companies that cannot afford to pay remunerated services and organizations located in developing countries offering basically business consultancy and mentoring services. The majority work on a voluntary basis sustaining themselves through membership fees and/or private or public funding and sponsorship. In terms of ICT, the majority of organizations use old fashioned tools; nevertheless they are willing to use new and modern tools to help in the daily activities.

These associations are mostly composed of a "professional elite" (people with a high education and that had high positions in the socio-economic system before retirement). In most cases, these people have reasonable pensions (although varying from region to region) and therefore can afford to do voluntary (unpaid) activities. However, the number of people involved in such mechanisms is not very high.

On the other hand, considering the current difficulties of the social security systems all over Europe, most governments are trying to implement new formula for pensions' calculation which in practice means a reduction of the pensions. In such context, it is foreseeable that more and more people will have fewer resources than needed to satisfy their standards of life.

In addition to these associations of senior professionals, various other mechanisms and practices towards active ageing can be found, including free-lancing, keeping some links with former employer (as the case of jubilee professors), etc. [2], [3]. A number of people also join organizations involved in voluntary social work or clubs that promote socialization activities for elderly, such as time banks [4], [5].

The "individualism" approach, such as free-lancing, corresponds perhaps to the most common approach nowadays, but it presents some barriers [6]. Either when pursuing economic benefits (free lancing) or simple voluntary activities, this approach requires a spirit of initiative (even entrepreneurship skills) that many people do not have or are not willing to exercise at this stage of their lives. Working alone also brings risks, namely related to health conditions. Furthermore, this approach lacks the "socialization" part to compensate for the breaking of social links that were present at the working place before retirement.

AGIRabcd (FR)
APCS (PT)
ASECAT (CO)
ASEP (AT)
BSC-I (BE)
COGAMA (ES)
CONFEMAC (ES)
CONJUPES (ES)
ECTI (FR)
EGEE (FR)
FRAE (ES)
ISES (IT)
JUBIQUE (ES)
KOS (PL)
NESTOR (FI)
OTECI (FR)
PUM (NL)
REACH (UK)
RSVP (UK)
SECOT (ES)
SEN@ER (ES)
SENA (BE)
SENIORES (IT)
SES (DE)
SFPA (SI)
SHARE (PT)
SWB (DK)
UDP (ES)
VISVITALIS (PL)

Fig. 1. Analyzed associations

As a consequence of the current situation, it can be concluded that some kind of organizational models is needed in order to support the current, emerging and future trends in extending the retired and retiring professional active life. For that it is extremely important to integrate all relevant stakeholders and characterize them accordingly within the scope of active ageing and silver economy.

Analysis Method. A method for analyzing the organizational forms was adopted including on one hand an evaluation of actual stakeholders and their inter-relationships and on the other hand identifying and characterizing emerging and possible future organizational models.

Fig. 2. Generic steps of the method

As illustrated in Fig. 2, the method is composed of four steps:

1. *Characterization of single stakeholders* - Defining the important stakeholders and characterizing each one of them according to a set of variables.
2. *Analysis of the inter-organizational structures of stakeholders* - Analysis of the different relationships that exist between the different organizational forms,

paying attention to the way they are inter-organized, their way of working and their characteristics interaction with their surrounding environment.

3. _Elaboration of a meta-portfolio of potentials and expectations_ - Analysis of potentials, expectations, and constraints of the different kinds of stakeholders.

4. _Identification and characterization of potential future organizational models_ - An "integrated" organizational model with all stakeholders shall be devised according to the ePAL's vision and some promising future scenarios.

The following sections summarize the results of these steps.

3 Characterization of Stakeholders

This section briefly introduces the classification and characterization of stakeholders as well as the relationships that stakeholders currently have among them and points out some future requirements especially concerning ICT. Considering the ePAL baseline and vision, the following main stakeholders are considered:

Senior Professionals, which are retired, early retired professionals or people in the process of retiring who wish to continue to participate actively in society by offering their experience or transferring their professional knowledge. Various subcategories can be defined based on the form under which they supply their services:

- **Single Senior Professionals (SP)**, which offer their services individually or through intermediaries or associations of senior professionals. Some examples are: freelancers, as well as the associations of senior professionals where each member provides his/her services in an individual manner to clients or beneficiaries.
- **Teams of senior professionals (TSP)**, temporary teams of senior professionals specialized in various fields and jointly providing a combined/complex service to a recipient. This type of organization, not very common yet, is usually supported by an association of senior professionals.
- **Communities of Active Seniors Professionals (CASP)** constitute associations of retired people or those in the process of retiring, who are interested in providing a service to the market. These associations are composed of heterogeneous groups of senior professionals who are independent and geographically dispersed sharing the common objective of being able to contribute to the socio-economic system. When mainly supported by computer networks to facilitate their operation as a community, they constitute a virtual community.

Intermediaries are organizations or people whose principal function is to form a point of contact and act as facilitator of interaction between senior professionals and the market and society. There are two categories depending on their objectives:

- **Brokers** - organizations or people whose principal objective is to provide opportunities for senior professionals to contribute with their services (experience and knowledge) to the market and society. This type of intermediary can include, among others, the associations of senior professionals, government organizations such as regional development agencies, time banks, or even large companies.
- **Supporters** - organizations that establish conditions to support senior professionals providing a range of services that allow them to offer a service in a more structured manner. Three main types of supporters were identified:

- **Financial supporters**, namely banks, investment firms and government.
- **Service supporters**, organizations providing education, facilities, methodologies, advice, assessment, etc. These intermediaries are formed of 3rd Age Universities, Non-Governmental Organizations, Societal Organs, Consulting companies, Regulatory Bodies, etc.
- **Service providers**, organizations providing the technology and ICT tools that ease and improve the quality of life for elderly. Included in this group are the service and production industry and ICT companies.

Recipients are people or organizations that need the services and experience that senior professionals own, either individually or through teams or associations of senior professionals. Depending on their internal characteristics these entities may be further subdivided into:

- **Clients**, including government, large companies, company associations and universities, i.e. any organizations or people that are in the position of being able to pay for services from senior professionals.
- **Beneficiaries,** those people or organizations with low incomes which do not have the necessary revenues to pay for services such as assessment and mentoring/coaching. In this group we would include young entrepreneurs, small startups, SMEs, students, NGOs, etc.

A summary of the characterization of the different stakeholders giving a global view of each stakeholder's role, product and services and how they are able to support the ePAL vision is illustrated in Fig. 3.

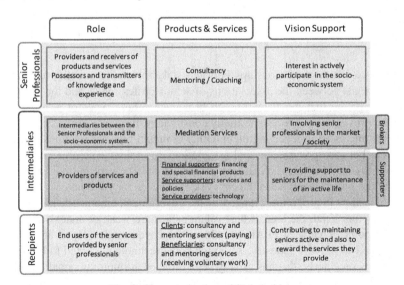

Fig. 3. Characterization of Stakeholders

Current relationships. As shown in Table 1, even though some relationships among these stakeholders may be wide-ranging and strong, there is still sufficient space for the development of a whole range of future models based both on currently defined activities as well as on new activities for senior professionals.

Table 1. Relationship between stakeholders

Entities	Senior Professional association	Government	Societal Organs	Financial Entities	University	Non professional senior association	ICT Industry	Recipients
	- Receiving advice	- Participating in programs		- Collaborating in social programs			- Techno-logical programs	
Advising & mentoring	- Participating in events - Being part of a Network	- Advising - -Participating in programs - Receiving financial support	- Advising	- Advising	- Advising Collaborating in programs	- Participating in events - Being part of a Network	- Techno-logical programs	- Advising & mentoring - Training
Involving entities in programs	- Collaboration in programs - Giving financial	- Participating in events - Collaborating in programs - Being part of a network	- Collaborating in :programs, events, creating new policies			- Participating in events - Giving financial support		- Putting in contact SP and clients
	- Receiving advise - Collaborating in events	- Participating in events - Collaborating in programs - Being part of a network	- Collaborating in: events, studies, creating new policies.			- Collaborating in events		
Collaborating in social programs	- Receiving advice					- Collaborating in social programs and events		- Giving financial support
	- Receiving advice - Involving seniors in mentoring programs							- Creating programs. - Putting in contact students and entrepreneurs with SP
	- Participating in events - Being part of a network	- Participating in events - Receiving financial support	- Collaborating in events	- Collaborating in social programs and events		- Being part of a network - Collaborating in programs and events	- Techno-logical programs	- Developing programs and social events for elders
- Giving technological programs	- Giving technological programs					- Giving technological programs	- Collaborating in developing new technology	- Giving technological programs
	- Receiving advise and mentoring	- Participating in programs - Receiving financial support		- Receiving financial support - Giving special products - Participating in programs (elders)	Participating in programs (entrepreneurs, students)	- Participating in programs and events	- Techno-logical programs	

The most common relationships between stakeholders, as mentioned before, are those that exist between the associations of senior professionals and the recipients of their services, be that direct or through brokerage. These types of relationships involve the provision of services, normally consultancy, by senior professionals to those recipients interested in receiving them. Other common types of relationship are those that occur between government and associations of seniors. The objectives for these relationships may be varied: financing seniors' activities, carrying out brokerage activity by the government, consultancy work by seniors for government or the participation of seniors in programs arranged by the government, among others.

On the other hand, the areas where relationships are weak or nonexistent and that, from the point of view of ePAL, should be improved or developed are principally those related to the ICT industry. Although some technology started to be developed with a focus on elderly, this has usually been directed at improving quality of life, not at extending the working life. Currently only a few elderly associations use some IT programs, normally with very limited functionality, in carrying out their activities. It is necessary to develop new technology that considers the needs of senior professionals and that supports the development of new flexible ways of working.

4 Organizational Forms

New organizational structures are needed in order to address the challenges of the ePAL vision. In this way, departing from the analysis of existing models, some emerging and future forms are suggesting new directions for active ageing.

Existing Models. In order to better understand the current state and potential possibilities, an analysis of the existing organizational models was conducted. Some of the most typical cases are:

Simple Model: In this example the recipient makes direct contact with the senior with the aim of receiving services for a specific project. The professional expert provides the support and consultancy that the recipient needs (1) and the recipient in turn pays for the received

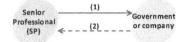

Fig. 4. Existing simple model

services. (2). It is a typical case with free-lancers. This model is not scalable and does not cover the socialization needs, being the elderly "left alone".

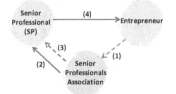

Fig. 5. Existing intermediation model 1

Intermediation Model 1: In this case the entrepreneur typically needs consultancy services in order to get a company project off the ground. The entrepreneur decides to opt for external professional assistance (1), for which it approaches a senior professionals association, given that it does not have the resources to acquire these services at market rates. The association selects the senior that best fits the needs of the entrepreneur from among its members (2). Finally the senior professional provides the required mentoring and consultancy services to the entrepreneur (4). Besides reimbursement of expenses, the senior professional does not receive remuneration from the entrepreneur although he/she might benefit from the association in other ways (3) (e.g. prestige, experience with new methods, infrastructures, etc.).

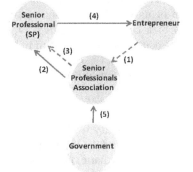

Fig. 6. Existing intermediation model 2

Intermediation Model 2: Similarly to the previous case, the entrepreneur asks for consultancy services from the senior professionals association (1). The association offers the possibility to provide the service to available members (2) who fit the requirements of the entrepreneur, offering them in compensation the methodological approach and infrastructure necessary to carry out the activity (3). The chosen SP provides support and consultancy to the entrepreneur (4). Different from the previous model, in this case the association receives some financial support from the government in addition to that raised from its membership fees.

716   A. del Cura et al.

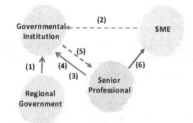

Fig. 7. Existing intermediation model 3

Intermediation Model 3: In this case it is assumed that the Governmental Institution has created a consultancy service to micro companies using senior professionals, financed and supported by Regional Government (1). Interested companies approach the Governmental Institution to solicit consultancy services (2). The Governmental Institution, which has contracted the seniors (3) to carry out the task (4), chooses the senior that better fits the needs of the SME soliciting the service. The chosen senior carries out the mentoring and consultancy task (6), for which he/she receives some monetary remuneration (5) from the Institution.

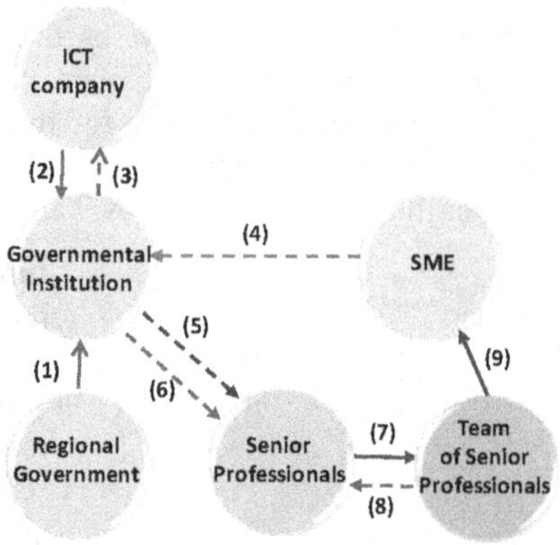

Complex case: As in the previous model, it is assumed that the Governmental Institution created a consultancy program for SMEs, with financial support from the Regional Government (1). Different from the previous case, the consultancy services are provided through a virtual team supported by an ICT platform, which has been provided by an ICT company (2, 3). The Institution carries out the project in collaboration with the senior professional's association (5); for this collaboration the association receives some

Fig. 8. Existing complex model

monetary remuneration (6). The association is in charge of assigning the work to a team of its members (7) and putting them in contact with the recipient in order to offer their consultancy services (9). In order to offer the SME a high quality service, the association creates a Team of Senior Professionals (TSP) specialized in different areas (marketing, finance, management strategy, etc.) which jointly provide integrated mentoring and consultancy services. Senior professionals receive some reward (8).

ICT in the simple models. From the point of view of ePAL, if senior professionals are to be effectively integrated into the socio-economic system with the help of ICT, it would be necessary for them to act through some kind of intermediary organization. In the simple models, those in which senior professionals offer their services directly (without intermediaries) to the recipient, at this moment advanced ICT platforms are not really used due to the existence of a range of limitations, among which the following stand out: (i) Cost - normally a senior cannot individually shoulder the cost of acquiring new technologies; (ii) Training - the majority of seniors is not used to using new technologies and is often reticent to learn how to use new tools and applications; new training courses are necessary, through which the use of new ICT technologies would be encouraged; (iii) Maintenance – there is a need for some organization that would provide maintenance services for the technological platforms.

Despite the existing limitations, there is a high degree of consensus that technology can be of great help. The principal functions that technology could perform in these models are: (i) To facilitate communication between the senior professional and the recipient. Naturally basic communication is guaranteed by simple email systems, but higher levels of professional interaction which require additional tools (e.g. distributed coordination and project management, access to recipient's information system) are not available; (ii) Promote flexibility; through ICT seniors could provide their services from any place and at any time.

ICT in intermediate and complex models. In the cases where various kind of stakeholders are involved, with different characteristics and functions, ICT starts to be used as a way to facilitate coordination and communication among the individuals and/or organizations involved in the model, contributing to make such tasks more efficient. The main improvements that ICT can bring to these cases are: (i) Coordination, organization and communication among the different types of stakeholders, through the creation of collaborative networks; (ii) Communication between the different members of an organization, e.g. between the members of a senior professional's organization; (iii) Greater flexibility, giving the possibility to provide services from any location and at any time; (iv) Allowing the use of common methodological approaches and tools for the provision of mentoring and consultancy; (v) Providing the possibility of continuing an active working life to those members with physical limitations.

Additionally, in those models where seniors form teams in order to offer their services to recipients, technology could help to: (i) Offer an integral consultancy service to recipients. Through the development of virtual teams, various seniors from one association could work together for the same recipient; (ii) Ease transfer of knowledge and documentation between members of the team of seniors. Nevertheless existing tools / platforms are quite limited in what concerns support for team's collaboration.

In summary, from the analyzed cases it can be concluded that: (i) Existing organizational models exist for the integration of SP in the socio-economic system. (ii) Current collaboration models are not adequately developed and do not take advantage of the potential offered by new technologies and new demographic needs. (iii) These models are not integrated into the social and economic structures of the majority of stakeholders. (iv) The models developed for SPs do not address all their necessities and potential opportunities. (v) Current models, even in their most complex form, are still ad-hoc in nature.

Emerging and future models. From the analysis of existing experiences of extending the professional life and also taking into account the current barriers, it becomes evident that the most promising approach should be based on some form of *tri-partite collaborative network*. Such networks should involve senior professionals, recipients of their services, and intermediary entities. Furthermore, besides the individual entities of each of the 3 types of stakeholders, it is also necessary to consider the organizational forms existing within each type.

More effectively organized associations of senior professionals – Communities of Active Senior Professionals (CASP) – will constitute a kind of specialized breeding environment for the dynamic formation of teams of senior professionals (TSP) to respond to market opportunities. Past approaches have been focused on offering services to be performed by seniors working alone. The formation of teams, possibly combining different expertise, will lead to a great improvement in terms of the complexity of the problems/projects that can be addressed as well as the quality of the rendered services. Furthermore, CASPs will provide a socializing environment to help elderly keep and re-enforce social links compensating those broken with the retirement. The organization of training actions and cultural activities is also part of the goals of CASPs.

Start-ups and SMEs are amongst the entities that currently receive the greatest amount of support from senior professionals, both directly (understood as the direct provision of services) as well as indirectly through various intermediary mechanisms. Typical organizations of these recipients include SME associations and incubators that can be used as facilitators in the process of putting together the two communities.

The involvement of intermediaries, i.e. organizations that offer different types of support is necessary in order to achieve the effective involvement of senior professionals into the socio-economic system. In fact, even the most dynamic associations of senior professionals have limited brokerage capabilities and face a number of difficulties in finding recipients to their services, even when those services result from voluntary work. On the other hand, many young entrepreneurs and SMEs could greatly benefit from some form of coaching/mentoring that they cannot afford to contract from market providers. The effective delivery of services to these recipients requires not only the kind of guidance/advice that can be obtained from senior professionals, but also some field work and problem formulation that retired people are no longer willing to do. Thus, intermediary entities can help here.

Putting these three types of entities together will lead to new collaborative contexts which can benefit all participants and the society in general, materializing a new form of silver economy (Fig. 9). In the implementation of such tri-partite collaborative networks a number of interaction channels can be identified:

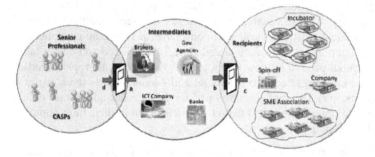

Fig. 9. Model of intermediaries

- *Between intermediaries and senior professionals:* (i) The provision of consultancy services for a wide range of subjects in which the seniors have a great depth of knowledge acquired throughout their professional career. (ii) The provision of mentoring and coaching services on subjects related to company management. (iii) Integration of seniors into the business world in different ways: associations of emeritus of large companies, participation in mentoring programs for young workers, reduced or flexible working days. (iv) Availability of equipment/infrastructure that allows seniors to conduct their activities. (v) Financing the activity carried out by seniors or their organizations. (vi) Training.

- *Between intermediaries and recipients*: (i) Brokerage; normally supporters are responsible for putting companies that need services in contact with the seniors interested in providing these services. (ii) Incentives; providing the financing (normally in the form of subsidies) necessary for the acquisition of consultancy services. (iii) Marketing.
- The increase in the number of intermediaries (brokers and supporters) is a key step for the effective extension of active working lives of senior professionals. The current situation of lack of demand for the services of senior professionals and their associations can only be resolved through an adequate level of involvement of brokers.

The survival of CASPs will increasingly be linked to their ability to effectively fulfill their commitments to recipients. The demand for continuous work of high quality is clearly increasing. For this reason, commitment between seniors or teams of seniors and the client or recipient should increasingly become subject to regulation of procedures and behavior that is imposed and developed by the CASPs in order to better guarantee such commitment. Work in teams is a mean to adequately balance the desire of the senior to maintain a limited active professional life with the needs of the client or recipient who needs timely coverage of their needs. The demand for higher levels of commitment from seniors must be accompanied by the establishment of a clear rewarding system that should be known and accepted by the seniors before they join the CASP and start carrying out their activities. The incorporation of systems for monetary and non-monetary remuneration will make new types of CASPs possible and allow a greater number of senior professionals to extend their active working lives. Future CASPs will thus require a number of improvements both regarding their interaction with the socio-economic system and their internal operation (Table 2).

Table 2. Needed improvements

External order:
• Develop a system of agreements and commitments with brokers such that they guarantee an adequate level of demand for their services, through the creation of specific products and services for each type of broker.
• Define and maintain an adequate level of agreements and commitments with supporters, that guarantee necessary resourcing, not exclusively monetary, in order to reward seniors even in cases where no charge is made to the recipient.
• Establish agreements between CASPs and different levels of European governments that allow for the encouragement, appearance and development of a greater number and type of brokers and supporters that in turn permits the extension of the ePAL philosophy and that a greater number of senior professionals are able to maintain an active working life.
• The need to incorporate new types of service and technology into the CASP's ways of working will mean the development of special relationships between the CASPs and the suppliers of ICT services.
Internal order:
• Establishment of clear, continuing & strong relationships with senior professionals in order to guarantee an adequate, effective and efficient supply of services to clients or recipients.
• Development of new management systems for communities that allow adequate creation of teams of increasing sophistication, new professional rules and regulations as well as adequate systems for monitoring the coverage of work by senior professionals.
• Integration of new ICT platforms and systems.
• Development of training systems to allow an adequate level of up-to-date competencies of the senior professionals incorporated into CASPs.

Having this in mind and as a preliminary assessment of the proposed collaborative models it can be foreseen that they will have a positive impact at seniors, society and economic levels. Nevertheless at this stage of development it is still early to discuss them in detail. In what concerns limitations they pass through the EU legal systems, social security systems and ICT. Without improvements in these areas it will naturally be quite difficult to implement the proposed models.

5 Conclusions

There is a great need both on the part of the EU and seniors to continue employed beyond traditional retirement age. It is important however, to recognize firstly the specific, distinct needs of different groups. The EU, due to significant changes in its demographic make-up, needs seniors to continue to contribute to economic growth by filling skills gaps and generating wealth. Many seniors also do not have the financial means to live a comfortable retirement beyond traditional retirement age without a higher further income than pension systems will struggle to provide.

Collaborative networks can play an important role in the establishment of new organizational forms, involving various stakeholders – senior professionals, intermediaries, and recipients of services – as a way to support active ageing and silver economy.

Acknowledgments. This work was supported in part by the ePAL project funded by the 7th FP of the European Commission.

References

1. Camarinha-Matos, L.M., Afsarmanesh, H.: Collaborative mechanisms for a new perspective on active ageing. In: Proceedings of DEST 2009 - 3rd IEEE International Conference on Digital Ecosystems and Technologies, Istanbul, Turkey (2009)
2. Cheng, J.Y.S., Mujin, Z., Zhiyuan, W.: A Proactive Strategy for the Aging Population That Capitalizes on the Talents of Older Adults in China. Journal of Applied Gerontology 26(5), 454–471 (2007)
3. Potter, N., Leighton, P.: Cooperative Active AGE Support Trust (2005),
   http://ec.europa.eu/information_society/events/ict_bio_2006/docs/concert-meet-projects/cast-w.pdf
4. Collom (ed.): Engagement of the Elderly in Time Banking: The Potential for Social Capital Generation in an Aging Society. Paper presented at the annual meeting of the American Sociological Association, Philadelphia, PA (2005)
5. Camarinha-Matos, L.M., Ferrada, F.: Supporting a Virtual Community for the Elderly. In: Dasgupta, S. (ed.) Encyclopedia of Virtual Communities and Technologies, pp. 428–433. Idea Group Reference (2006)
6. Your Encore – Accelerating innovation through proven experience,
   http://www.yourencore.com/

Towards Modeling a Collaborative Environment for Extension of Professional Active Life

Hamideh Afsarmanesh[1] and Luis Camarinha-Matos[2]

[1] Informatics Institute, University of Amsterdam, Science Park 107,
1098 XG Amsterdam, The Netherlands
h.afsarmanesh@uva.nl
[2] Faculty of Sciences and Technology, New University of Lisbon,
Quinta da Torre, 2829-516, Monte Capatica, Portugal
cam@uninova.pt

Abstract. Progress on computer networks is offering new conditions for individuals to remain active after their retirement. Furthermore, the scarcity of human resources and the increasing percentage of elder professionals in Europe have catalyzed the formation of a new type of collaborative community referred to as community of active senior professionals (CASP). These new networks aim to support retired professionals with their participation in socio-economic activities and thus remaining professionally active. As such, identification of their specificities as well as developing a descriptive model of CASPs is challenging. This paper characterizes the CASP environments and performs a first attempt towards identifying and modeling their constituent elements.

Keywords: Modeling associations of seniors, professional active life.

1 Introduction

Different forms of Collaborative Networks (CN) have been investigated in research and emerged in practice during the last decades [6]. A community of active senior professionals is one type of such network, which has been established in a number of countries aiming to provide the base platform as well as to enhance the preparedness of retired professionals to participate in different activities and in doing so to remain professionally active. However, this type of collaborative networks still lacks sound models for their effective creation and operation. Proper characterization of these environments, namely the Community of Active Senior Professionals (CASP), shall represent and address its stakeholders and their activities, and support the configuration of temporary teams of senior professionals (TSPs) to respond to emerging opportunities. In this paper we introduce the following definitions:

L.M. Camarinha-Matos et al. (Eds.): PRO-VE 2009, IFIP AICT 307, pp. 721–732, 2009.
© IFIP International Federation for Information Processing 2009

CASP constitutes an association of senior professional individuals that are largely autonomous, geographically distributed, and potentially heterogeneous in terms of their: capabilities, offered capacities, culture, system of values, etc., but sharing their main compatible and/or common goals of increasing their active professional life in the society and/or market, through co-working with others in Teams of Senior Professionals supported by computer networks, under the slogan of: "Together Everyone Achieves More!".

TSP is a collaborative network of individuals configured and established within the CASP in response to opportunities in the society and market that are in need of their wisdom and/or knowledge assets that they can offer, which as a consequence supports the retired professionals remaining professionally active.

SP (Senior Professional) is a retired professional who becomes a member of CASP in order to increase his/her chances of staying active and involved in the socio-economic system, and perhaps also through getting involved in potential TSPs established through the CASP.

The paper addresses the modelling of such environments and the results from research work conducted in the ePAL project [5].

2 Related Work on Modeling CNs

As any other scientific discipline or engineering branch, collaborative networks require the development of its models, not only as a help to better understand the area, but also as the basis for the development of methods and tools for better decision making. It is however important to note that modeling is not only necessary for building software systems; in the context of collaborative networks, modeling is fundamental for understanding, managing, simulating or predicting the behavior of the network and its members, and certainly also for software development [2]. A number of models addressing different aspects of collaboration and particularly for virtual organizations and virtual enterprises are developed in research. Some examples of such models follow:

> *SCOR (Supply-Chain Operation Reference-model):* developed as a standard diagnostic tool for supply-chain management in industries by providing guidelines regarding interactions among stakeholders [4].
> *VERAM (Virtual Enterprise Reference Architecture and Methodology):* Aims at providing guideline for increasing preparedness of entities involved in the networks for efficient creation of virtual enterprises. VERAM also facilitates modeling processes through provision of guidelines on how to build the models and how to identify the common characteristics of the virtual enterprise and networks [11].
> *EGA (Enterprise Grid Alliance):* Defines the terminology and glossary of grid computing and identifies various components, interfaces, interactions and data models [8]. It enables interoperability among heterogeneous grid applications and improves integration of grid services.
> *FEA (Federal Enterprise Architecture):* Developed by the US office of Management and Budget (OMB) for the purpose of supporting the identification of opportunities to simplify the processes and unify work across the agencies and within the lines of business of the US Federal government [9].

Some attempts have been made by researchers to develop generic models, frameworks and architectures for collaborative networks. An example of such attempt is

ARCON (<u>A</u> <u>R</u>eference model for <u>C</u>ollaborative <u>N</u>etworks) [1]. ARCON introduces multiple modeling perspectives, including: *environment characteristics, life cycle stages, and modeling intents.*

As a new form of collaborative network for extending active life of senior professionals, CASPs are emerging as a special kind of CNs, primarily aiming to serve as preparedness environments for senior professionals towards remaining professionally active in their society. As such, the entities in these environments and their related interactions, behavior and processes need to be properly addressed by a reference modeling framework such as ARCON. Besides the study of a number of running networks of senior professionals, as addressed in detail in [3], as a pre-step to the ARCON definition of this environment, this paper contributes to provision of general characteristics, a few example scenario definitions, and a first attempt to identification of its constituents and its modeling.

3   Characterizing ePAL Scenario

Scenarios are widely used by organizations of all types, to better understand different ways that future events might unfold. Scenarios are used to characterize an environment for the purpose of identifying its constituent entities, behaviour, processes, life cycle, etc. In relation to the vision for the extension of professional life of elderly, a number of scenarios are developed to support understanding of different future possibilities regarding the enhancement of active life of senior professionals, as well as which events are probable to occur in future. Scenarios are also applied in the ePAL project to identify the stakeholders that will be involved in or impacted by this environment. Developed ePAL environment's scenarios address among others, aspects related to: (i) Technologies that need to be developed or tuned to support involvement of SPs in economical activities, (ii) Policies, rules and regulations that need to be formulated to favour active life of SPs, (iii) Interactions and related motivations among senior professionals and working forces, and (iv) Responsibilities of governments and other regulatory organs in enhancing activeness of SPs.

To enhance the presentation of the main contributions of this paper in regards to the modelling of this environment, namely in section 4, we present below three example scenarios of the ePAL environments. They specifically address: (1) association of SPs, (2) some problems and solutions faced by SPs, (3) provision of services by SPs.

Scenario 1: Senior professionals association

Mario is a senior electrical engineer that used to work for the national energy distributor as a public installations analyst and inspector. Although 65 years old he is a healthy man and felt frustrated for being obliged to retire so soon and at the same time depressed because he was at home with nothing interesting to do; he was feeling that he needed to give his brain some activity. One day, when navigating on the Internet, Mario found a website that attracted his attention – the ActiveSeniors Community. This website supported a community of senior people that was created out of the necessity of people to remain active after retirement through sharing with others their experiences, skills and knowledge. The main objective of ActiveSeniors is providing professional assistance to people, companies or organizations located in developing countries through unpaid/volunteering senior expertise.

Mario felt enthusiastic with the ActiveSeniors Community, especially with the idea of travelling to a new country and of putting his brain in motion again, and registered immediately as a new member. After the registration process Mario received a welcome letter and a collection of information containing the community rules. A couple of months later, Mario was still waiting to be contacted for an assignment and he started to feel anxious with the situation and remembered to start looking for missions. After a couple of days searching he found a small electrical company in Cabinda, Angola, that was passing severe financial problems. Mario contacted both ActiveSeniors and the small Angolan company and after all the arrangements were properly made Mario went to Cabinda. When Mario returned from Angola he was so happy that his relatives realized the importance of keeping retired people active…

In fact, contributing to help a region in need and also having the opportunity to travel was a great reward, specially considering that Mario's pension is enough for his needs. But the lack of opportunities to contribute is something that still worries him … By the way, thinking about the difficulties, he also felt a bit uncomfortable for having to perform his mission alone and having to do some field work in Cabinda to better understand the problem before he actually could contribute to solve it.… As a result his contribution was a bit limited as the resources for the mission ended…

Challenges: A great number of senior/retired communities working on a voluntary basis exist nowadays. Examples can be for instance, Seniors Experts Benevoles – EGEE based in France, or SECOT in Spain. Nevertheless what commonly happens in these communities is that members lose interest due to:
1. The fact that there are not many opportunities to get involved; there are more volunteers than tasks.
2. Communities do not have a good incentive/motivation system for its members; this could be because they cannot evaluate the state of the community and interact adequately.
3. Not being paid for their missions, even if it was a symbolic remuneration it would give them a different motivation.
4. As pensions are getting lower, many potential new members of the associations cannot afford to do much voluntary work as they might need to find some complementary sources of income.
5. Working alone in a mission does not promote socialization and is sometimes risky.
Therefore, some challenges *include:*
(i) Development of new operational models, including more effective brokerage of opportunities.
(ii) Implementation of more effective mechanisms to make the community known.
(iii) Design and development of advanced ICT platforms to better support socialization and team work.
(iv) Find new mechanisms to facilitate interactions between seniors and the receiving entities.
(v) Combine models of voluntary work with other schemes providing some payment or fringe benefits.

Scenario 2: Identifying Problems and providing solutions
Last year Jane was an employee of a hoe manufacturing industry that faced job redundancy. Following a difficult life in the city, six months ago, she decided to go back to her home village in a far remote area. After arriving at the village she learned that there are a number of individuals and small groups of people who are producing traditional hoes manually. Although, these traditional hoes are of relatively less quality as the ones produced by industries but they are cheap and thus affordable by peasants in the village. Jane realized that these craftsmen produce small number of hoes than their capabilities and cannot even sell them as little as they produce. However the craftsmen themselves could not exactly pin-point their problems. She knew from the past that such groups of people can acquire support for knowledge and experience provided through *associations of senior professionals*. Thus the next day she decided to go to the near town to visit one association of senior professionals. At the office of the association she met the administrator, a retired person who used to be district development officer. After explaining to him the purpose of her visit the administrator told her that the members of the association could provide support of knowledge when the problem is clearly defined. She was further told that in past some senior professionals were sent to some areas to solve problems; however they found out that the problems were not in their areas of expertise. Therefore, she needs to workout herself and clearly define what kind of knowledge is needed to those local craftsmen. Lastly Jane was told that at the district office where the administrator used to work there is an office responsible for entrepreneurship. So she was told to try to get support from that office.

Jane left the office of the association and directly went to the *district office* to meet the district community development officer at the entrepreneurship department. At this office she was told that if she can find experts to help her with the task of identifying related inefficiency problems of these craftsmen which need solutions, then the district office will provide necessary funding for the experts. She left the office thinking about how to get the needed experts. Jane decided to call a friend who is a professor in industrial engineering at one university in her previous city of residence to ask for possible approach to help her identify the problems. The professor finds it interesting and promises to send four senior PhD students with different related expertise related to small industries to do the research. But these students need some financial support related to transport and accommodation. Jane confirmed to the professor about the financial support that will be fully compensated by the district office. A week after, the PhD students were sent that under supervision and through mediation of Jane could consult the craftsmen and do some necessary research. After one month, a report was handed by Jane to the district office and the association of senior professionals. The report identified a number of problems, among others; they included lack of steady suppliers of raw materials, lack of capital, lack of needed workers, and poor marketing. The report also suggested some needed specialized training for craftsmen.

The association of senior professionals then used the report to form a few teams of professionals, e.g. for training and providing advice on financial and economical aspects to the village craftsmen, etc., who started their work. One main achievement requested by the district was that the craftsmen should be then capable to produce and sell beyond their village(s) and even in other regions where such traditional technology is lacking. Furthermore, the report motivated the district office and asked Jane to continue collaborating with the association of senior professionals to find possibilities and propose projects that will deliver solutions to existing problems in that village and others in the region. The projects were then be fully funded by the district office. Jane was happy not only because she has found a solution for people in her village but also that she will now have a formal job for a relatively longer period.

Challenges: There is a gap between providers of services (i.e. senior professionals and their associations) and recipients of services (SMEs, and young professionals). This gap needs to be filled with a third party (i.e. intermediaries) in order to smooth the needed interactions. A third party can be a government organization, an NGOs, an individual professor or researcher, or small consulting business, etc., who can support on one hand pinpointing the problem that can be solved by senior professionals and on the other hand mediating it to be solved. There is also a gap in the definition of who is a senior professional. At the moment the term "senior professional" is being defined on the bases of the retirement age. Is Jane who faced redundancy but has not reached retirement age a senior professional? Therefore, some challenges include:

(i) Proper establishment of roles and responsibilities of the three parties, namely: SMEs, the association of senior professionals, and the intermediary elements must be addressed.

(ii) Establishing a clear definition of the term "senior professional" that can be contextually tuned to meet the need of a particular geographical area.

Scenario 3: A service market portal

Manuel just finished his breakfast and while enjoying this lovely morning of early Spring, he is now logging in the ProSolve portal. ProSolve is an electronic market place for innovation and problem solving allowing a community of retired highly skilled professionals to address problems and innovation challenges posted by client companies. A number of mechanisms are implemented in this marketplace, including:

- *Open innovation challenges:* A company looking for new ideas and potential solutions places a "challenge" in the market and indicates the associated monetary value. Members of the pool of experts of ProSolve can offer ideas / solutions (bid) on a confidential basis. The author of the idea / solution picked by the client company will be the one to be paid.

- *Target problem solver:* A company wants to find an expert with the right profile to perform a specific problem solving task. ProSolve helps matching potential experts with the requested expertise and facilitates the negotiation and contractual arrangements as well as other due diligences.

- *Assistance / coaching:* A company needs consultancy / coaching on some best practice. Potential experts are identified by ProSolve (matching mechanisms) and when agreement is reached the task is contracted.

ProSolve plays an important role in all issues related to confidentiality, intellectual property, contractual aspects, and quality monitoring. After browsing over the new opportunities, Manuel found an interesting challenge and started digesting a solution based on his accumulated experience but also considering the pleasure of competing to offer a wining idea.

Two weeks later, Manuel received the great news that his idea was selected. Wow! He had been participating in other challenges before without being selected ... nevertheless he continued just for the pleasure of exercising his knowledge and experience. But now, the 10 000 euros reward for his solution are certainly much welcomed and right on time to plan his summer holidays! While enjoying the news of the day, another idea came to his mind: It would be much more interesting if ProSolve evolved from a marketplace to a real community offering social networking aspects and also mechanisms for teaming up with our experts to work together on a problem instead of being alone ...

Challenges: A number of e-market places along these ideas are in fact emerging lately. Examples are the www.innocentive.com and the www.yourencore.com. While the first one is general purpose, i.e. open to active professionals, the second one is specifically focused on retired professionals. Nevertheless these

initiatives, although showing signs of success, still lack some important features:
(i)   Social networking or virtual community mechanisms are quite limited.
(ii)   Brokerage (opportunity finding) is limited; only the portal management organization acts as a broker. Mechanisms to extend the brokerage potential (and the inclusion of other specialized actors) could increase the number of offers.
(iii) In most cases activities are performed by single individuals, not teams. In some cases the concept is even one of competition. Mechanisms for formation of teams, combining different skills, to better jointly address a problem would improve the quality of the outcomes.

Through the analysis of these three scenarios and many more others (www.epal.eu.com) we have identified the main entities within the ePAL environment that need to be properly modeled. The models will support achieving a thorough understanding of the environment and its constituents. Based on the results of the analysis of a set of scenarios and the comprehensive study of the baseline materials for this environment, in Section 4 we present the modeling of the ePAL environment.

4 Modeling and Characterization of CASPs

With the study of scenarios, as exemplified in Section 3, we have achieved a better understanding of many distinguishing structural, componential, functional and behavioural aspects of the ePAL environment which enable us to address the identification of its constituent elements, and to model its features and components.

4.1 Main Elements of the ePAL Environments

From the lessons learned through the above scenarios, a 1st model of the ePAL environment is developed, to help fully understand this environment. This model addresses the following five elements, as shown in Fig. 1, namely: (A) senior professionals, (B) teams of senior professionals, (C) communities of active senior professionals, (D) intermediaries, and (E) recipients.

A: Senior professionals: These are retired professionals who are willing to provide services in terms of experiences and expertise either directly to the customer as individuals or through TSP configured within CASPs. SPs are encouraged to join CASP in order to increase their chances of getting involved in potential TSPs established within the CASP. The categories for senior professionals include: technicians, knowledge workers, managers, and specialists.

B: Teams of senior professionals: This is another fundament element of ePAL environment which refers to a group of senior professionals temporarily joining their efforts to provide services to a particular recipient. It is a collaborative network of individuals configured and established within the CASP in response to opportunities in the society and market that are in need of their wisdom and/or knowledge assets that they can offer, which as a consequence supports the retired professionals remaining professionally active. Based on how the services are provided and the possible agreements between the recipient and the TSP, we have characterized TSPs into four types, namely TSP operating on: (1) Competitive business activities (market profit), (2) Service business activities (small profit or cost compensation), (3) Voluntary activities (no form of payment) and (4) Voluntary and/or paid involvements (combining the three above possibilities).

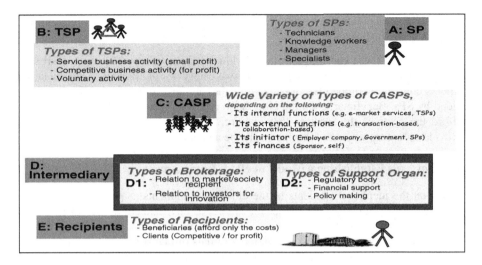

Fig. 1. Main elements of the ePAL environment

C: Communities of senior professionals (CASPs): This is a fundamental element of ePAL environments which constitutes an association of the retiring and retired people who are willing to provide some services to the market/society in response to demands of recipients. Thus a CASP constitutes an association of SPs that are largely autonomous, geographically distributed, and potentially heterogeneous in terms of their: capabilities, offered capacities, culture, system of values, etc., but sharing their main compatible and/or common goals of increasing their active professional life in the society and/or market, through co-working with others in TSPs supported by computer networks. A number of different types of CASPs can be established but they can be distinguished on the basis of the following four characteristics:

1- **Related to its internal functions:** (1.A)   E-market (provision of ready made services) and (1.B) Virtual Organization (team-based new developments).
2- **Related to its external functions:** (2.A)   Transaction-based (sale of products/services)   and   (2.B)   Collaboration-based   (customer   involved   design/development).
3- **Related to how it is initiated:** (3.A)   Employer-initiated (by large / very large organizations), (3.B)   Government-initiated (regional / national initiatives), and (3.C)   Seniors-initiated (brokered by senior professionals).
4- **Related to how it is financed (main source):** (4.A)   Sponsors (government, large companies, etc.), and (4.B)   Self financed - based on commission from profit, subscription fees,…

D: Intermediaries: These are organizations which act as mediators or agents between CASP (or individual SPs) and recipients. Intermediaries are mainly responsible for two fundamental tasks, namely: (D1) *Broker organization*: Brokering of opportunities that can be responded by CASP through configuration of TSPs. The brokered opportunities can also be responded by individual SPs, and (D2) *Support organization*: Establishing conditions that will support CASPs, TSPs and individual SPs to smoothly interact with recipients, such as regulatory bodies, national/international policy making bodies, etc.

E: Recipient: These can range from individual people, groups of people, SMEs, or large organizations. Recipients include the two categories of clients and beneficiaries. Clients constitute competitive organizations that are able to pay for the services provided by SPs. Beneficiaries on the other hand are those recipients that are not able to afford the costs of the services they require, so these recipients seek SPs that can provide voluntary services, for which only the actual costs are paid.

4.2 Towards Establishing a Model of ePAL Environment

Based on the identified elements of the ePAL environments as presented in Section 4.1, we have developed a 1st model for the ePAL environment as shown in Fig. 2. This model can be used as a "reference" for the specification of our ePAL environment vision. The model addresses a variety of kinds of involvements from active SPs, shown as SPs in Fig. 2, in the market and society, thus capturing the structure of both the present involvements as well as future potential involvements.

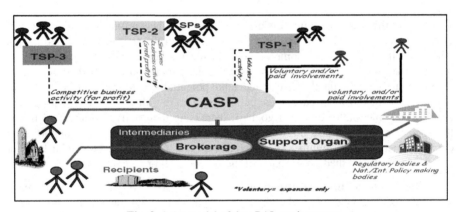

Fig. 2. A 1st model of the ePAL environment

In other words, currently the activities of senior professionals, being voluntary or paid involvement, are concentrated on either: (i) One to one contact with a recipient, as established through simple intermediaries e.g. a regional governmental offices, or (ii) Some regional elderly professional clubs (the early emergence of CASPs) that again connects a senior professional directly with one recipient.

But there are already a few cases in Europe when a team of senior professionals from within an association of senior professionals, and together deliver a service to the market/society. Therefore for the future of the ePAL environment the following structures are foreseen: (1) Team-work type of activities, as specified above by the three kinds of TSPs, (2) Stronger and more pro-active establishment for the CASPs and its administration and involvement in the market/society, and (3) Presence of Brokers and brokerage of senior professional activities as a strong intermediary between the senior professionals and the market/society.

4.3 Modeling Needs for ePAL Environments

A rough summarization of all scenarios studied has revealed a number of areas in need of attention and consideration for the development of the 1st ePAL vision. These areas point to the main lines of related research and development that must be performed in the coming years to support making the desired vision of ePAL a reality. The four main areas in need of great attention within the ePAL vision consist of (see Fig. 3): Reference model, Operational model, Public relation model, and Socialization and trust building model.

Specification of a first model for ePAL environment: A Reference model is a computer science term that describes an abstract framework for understanding significant relationships among the entities of an environment, and for the development of consistent standards or specifications supporting that environment [7, 10]. A reference model is based on a small number of unifying concepts and may be used as a basis for education and explaining standards to a non-specialist. Therefore, reference models are not directly tied to any standards, technologies or other concrete implementation details, but they aim to provide a common semantics that can be used unambiguously across and between different implementations. Research on developing a reference model for ePAL environment shall result:

- *The ePAL environment:* A specification classifying the constituents of the ePAL environment into endogenous and exogenous elements [1]. The endogenous elements include those elements related to the structural, componential, functional and behaviour aspects of the CASPs. The exogenous elements include elements related to the market, support, societal and constituency aspects of CASPs.
- *Specification of inter-relationships between entities of the ePAL environment:* Focuses on defining all entities as well as their roles and responsibilities which guide the nature of their interactions within the CASPs. The inter-relationships / interactions between entities, among others, may include the following: (1) How they operate within the ePAL environment (Operational model), (2) How they relate to the outside environment (public relation), and (3) How they share and exchange information and knowledge (socializing and trust building).

Operational model: An operational model for a business is a schematic element which shows the operating units for the business and the relationships between these operating units. It describes how an organization operates across both business and technology domains. CASPs and TSPs focus on providing services in the market / society e.g. in terms of packages of advice and expertise from SPs. Therefore, an operational model is needed to be researched and developed, for instance for CASPs to on one hand guide the establishment of ICT support and on the other hand to guide the governance and working principles of these associations as shown in Fig. 3.

Public relation model: Public relation is the practice of managing the flow of information between an organization and its public. It facilitates gaining exposure for organizations to their audiences, recipients, partners etc. by addressing public interests that relates to organizational operations as well as the external interactions. A public relation model shall address and provide guidelines on how these aspects can be realized within and between organizations. Particularly, for ePAL environments, such as CASPs, the public relation model shall address: (i) Interaction with senior professionals (socializing,

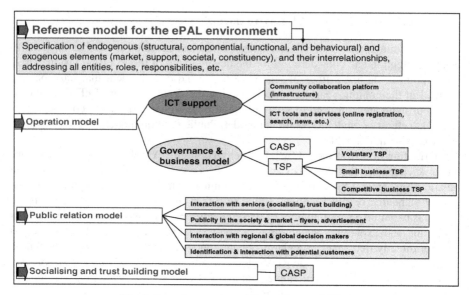

Fig. 3. Some lessons learned related to modelling

trust building), (ii) Publicity in the society and market (flyers, advertisements), (iii) Interaction with regional and global decision makers, and (iv) Identification and interaction with potential customer.

Socialization and trust building model: A fundamental aim of CASPs is to support SPs remain active in their life. One key aspect necessary for SPs to remain active is to continue socializing between each other, as well as with the entire society. An enabler to the needed socializations among SPs is the existence of trust among them. This model shall guide the creation of trust among SPs and from the society towards the SPs and their professional activities.

4.4   The Visioning Related Worlds of ePAL Environment

In order to properly position the ePAL environment within the European society, we need to carefully analyze different kinds of involved organizations and classify them on the basis of their relation to the operation and interaction with CASPs, TSPs, and SPs. Based on the empirical study of existing associations of SPs, extensive requirement analysis for the ePAL environment, identification of the environment trends and drivers, as well as lessons learned from the variety of developed scenarios, we have classified the elements within the general environment of ePAL into three groups, each labelled as one "world" through which the ePAL vision will take us, namely (1) the world of knowledge and talent, (2) the world of mediation and support, and (3) the world of recipients and innovation (Fig. 4):

1. *World of knowledge and talent:* Constitutes individuals such as professional freelancers, group of individuals such as professional virtual communities, organizations such as universities, etc. which act as sources of knowledge that are needed in the market for providing required services. It is in this world from which the SPs originate.

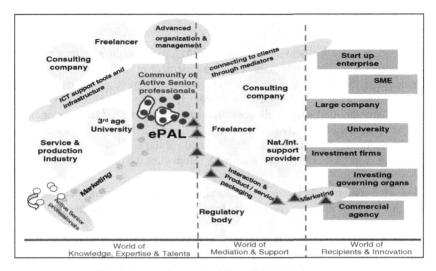

Fig. 4. Lessons learned - vision of ePAL in future

2. *World of mediation and support:* Constitutes the intermediary organs of a wide spectrum from the governmental and decision making bodies to the consulting companies that find/create the market for SPs with the Market and recipients. Therefore, elements in this world support SPs and other collaborating parties, with variety of assistance, e.g. potentially connecting them with recipients, paving the road through establishing needed laws and policies and in delivering required services into the market among many others. Intermediary organs can be consulting companies, freelancers, national and international organizations, regulatory bodies, etc.

3. *World of recipients and innovation:* Constitutes the people and organizations that need the services and expertise which can be provided by the senior professionals either as an individual or through TSPs and CASPs. Recipients may include start-up enterprises, SMEs, large companies, as well as investing firms or government organs that may finance their activities and even support their potential initiatives for innovation. Besides providing packaged services to this world, SPs can establish different forms of co-working and co-development with entities of this world.

Considering these three worlds, we can conceptually design the target for the vision of ePAL environment, visualized as a person walking through these three worlds. First, the vision shall focus on the development of strong communities of retired professionals, supported by advanced organization and management systems, referring to the body and the head of the ePAL vision. Then the strategic plans of each community established to promote active life of SPs, would be to on one hand attract and motivate the active SPs into joining this community, namely the right foot of the ePAL vision, and provide ICT support tools and infrastructure to enable the SPs with contribution of their knowledge and talent, namely the right hand of the ePAL vision. On the other hand absorbing the support and opportunities provided through the mediation and support world, the community can connect to the potential recipients through the mediators, namely the left hand of the ePAL vision, and interact with them, providing products and services, namely the left foot of the ePAL vision.

5 Conclusion

Development of comprehensive models for ePAL environment is an important base for the elaboration of these environments, a base element in the consolidation of existing knowledge in this area, and a base for its consistent progress. As a contribution in this direction, this paper has addressed the characterization of the ePAL environment by: (1) proposing the fundamental elements that must be considered for developing a comprehensive model of the environment, (2) developing a 1st model of the environment and (3) identifying fundamental modelling needs of the environment. As a next step to this research, the ARCON model shall be developed for the ePAL environment.

Acknowledgements. This work was funded in part by the European Commission through the ePAL project. The authors thank the contributions from other partners in the project.

References

1. Afsarmanesh, H., Camarinha-Matos, L.M.: The ARCON modeling framework. In Collaborative networks reference modeling, pp. 67–82. Springer, New York (2008)
2. Afsarmanesh, H., Camarinha-Matos, L.M.: Related work on reference modeling for collaborative networks. In: Collaborative networks: reference modeling, pp. 13–28. Springer, Heidelberg (2008)
3. Camarinha-Matos, L.M., Afsarmanesh, H.: The need for a strategic R&D roadmap for active ageing. In: The proceedings of PRO-VE 2009 conference (September 2009) (to appear)
4. Barnett, M.W., Miller, C.J.: Analysis of the virtual enterprise using distributed supply chain modeling and simulation: An application of e-SCOR. In: Joines, J.A., Barton, R.R., Kang, K., Fishwick, P.A. (eds.) Proceedings of the 2000 Winter Simulation Conference (2000)
5. Camarinha-Matos, L.M., Afsarmanesh, H.: The need for a strategic R&D roadmap for active ageing. In: The proceedings of PRO-VE 2009 conf. (September 2009) (to appear)
6. Camarinha-Matos, L.M., Afsarmanesh, H.: Motivation for a theoretical foundation for collaborative networks. In: Collaborative networks: reference modeling. Springer, Heidelberg (2008)
7. Camarinha-Matos, L.M., Afsarmanesh, H.: Towards a reference model for collaborative networked organizations. In: Information Technology for Balanced Manufacturing Systems, vol. 220, pp. 193–202 (2006) ISBN 978-0-387-36594-7_21
8. EGA. Enterprise Grid Alliance Reference Model (April 13, 2005), http://www.gridalliance.org/en/workgroups/ReferenceModel.asp
9. FEA. FEA Consolidated Reference Model (2003) (May 2005), http://www.whitehouse.gov/omb/egov/documents/CRM.PDF
10. OASISI: Integrated Collaboration Object Model for Interoperable Collaboration Services (2008), http://www.oasis-open.org/committees/icom/charter.php
11. Zwegers, A., Tolle, M., Vesterager, J.: VERAM – Virtual enterprise reference architecture and methodology. In: Proceedings of GLOBEMEN – Global Engineering and Manufacturing in Enterprise Networks, VTT Symposium, vol. 224 (2003)

Methodologies for Active Aging in the Manufacturing Sector

Rosanna Fornasiero[1], Domenica Berdicchia[2], Mario Zambelli[3],
and Giovanni Masino[2]

[1] ITIA-CNR, Via Bassini 15, 20133 Milano, Italy
[2] University of Ferrara, Via Savonarola, 9, 44100 Ferrara, Italy
[3] Politecnico Calzaturiero s.c.a.r.l., Via Venezia, 62, 30100 Vigonza (Pd), Italy
rosanna.fornasiero@itia.cnr.it,
{d.berdicchia,g.masino}@unife.it

Abstract. The research project named "Flexibly Beyond" studied and experimented innovative models for the enhancement of the role of senior workers and prolongation of their working life. The research was based on the application of innovative methods and tools to the ageing society and in particular to the European manufacturing companies represented in the project by apparel and footwear sectors. The project was funded under the Innovative Measures of the art.6 of the European Social Fund (VS/2006/0353) and coordinated by Politecnico Calzaturiero. The real strength of the project was the large network including all the actors of the value chain which allows transferring the theoretical findings to practical level in SMEs manufacturing context.

1 The Issue, the Actors, the Goals

Population aging is one of the most relevant demographic trends in western societies. There are various factors that explain such process: the decrease in fertility, the advances in medical technology, the general improvement of the quality of life, and others. The size and scope of this phenomenon is such that a number of social and economic issues related to the aging of population can now be considered of strategic importance for all western countries ([1]; [2]). In each country, however, there are some peculiar issues that specifically characterize how such a problem is impacting the society and the economic environment. In Italy, for example, the future sustainability of the pension system is a very relevant issue, as well as the economic risk associated with the potential loss of crucial competencies held by senior workers in small and medium enterprises (SMEs), which represent the backbone of the Italian economy. Other countries face similar or slightly different problems, but the common theme is the rapidly increasing magnitude and scope of the aging issue. Recently, the European Commission started to promote activities and studies in order to find ways to turn this problem into an opportunity. In fact, while it is shared that senior citizens and workers do have a lot to offer for the competitiveness of economies and for the improvement of the quality of their own lives and the life of others as well, it is not so clear how to integrate effectively their needs and their skills and abilities within fast-paced, rapidly changing markets and societies.

L.M. Camarinha-Matos et al. (Eds.): PRO-VE 2009, IFIP AICT 307, pp. 733–741, 2009.

The literature on age management offers useful insights about a possible general approach to the problem, one that should coordinate and integrate macro-level institutional actions and policies with micro-level organizational and managerial practices (see for example [3] and [8]). However, concrete successful solutions are hard to observe and implement, since a number of elements seem to increase the complexity of designing actual practices. Conflicting goals, lack of managerial competences and resources, cultural obstacles, insufficient awareness of the urgency and the relevance of the problem, are among the main aspects that seem to create great difficulties when trying to translate a general approach into actual solutions. This is particularly true and relevant where the social and economic context is mostly constituted by (SMEs). Some specific actions have been proposed in other EU projects held under the art.6 of ESF each with its peculiarities of implementation.

In this paper we describe the general methodology and approach developed within the "Flexibly Beyond" project, whose goal was to study and experiment innovative models for the enhancement of the role of senior workers and prolongation of their working life. A number of research activities and experimental actions have been carried out in order to help SMEs to change their approach to the age management problem, with a specific focus on the apparel and footwear industries. The project was funded under the Innovative Measures of the art.6 of the European Social Fund (VS/2006/0353) and Politecnico Calzaturiero coordinated successfully most important stakeholders of the value chain for the definition and implementation of policies for the valorization of senior workers. Education and research institutions, universities, enterprises, industry associations, workers unions and public institutions were part of a multidisciplinary team managed by Politecnico Calzaturiero. The choice to include a variety of points of view and interests has to be considered an important strategy in order to have a holistic approach to the challenge of ageing working population.

Apparel and footwear sectors represent an ideal field for this kind of initiative, for at least two main reasons. First, in many European countries they are very relevant in economic and social terms, as they account for a large share of the overall manufacturing sector, both in terms of employment and all other major economic indicators. Second, in such industries there is a vast majority of SMEs whose competitiveness, both in the short and the long run, is highly dependent on their ability to preserve the core competences and skills mostly held by senior workers. It will be shown that this can be done applying innovative methods and tools integrating new technologies and organizational methods.

The project was carried out thanks to the collaboration of three EU countries (Italy, Germany and Great Britain), in order to propose a general model for designing and implementing those practices in a variety of entrepreneurial contexts. For that goal, the comparison of specific experiences and solutions throughout a number of different countries, cultures, industries and enterprises has played a crucial role.

2 The "Flexibly Beyond" Model

The fundamental background of the project is that no practical solution and experiment could succeed without a strong convergent commitment between all the stakeholders and all the relevant actors' interest.

The first part of the project was based on general analysis of the contexts in which new organizational collaborative solutions and practices could be implemented and tested. In this stage, the points of view of various stakeholders have been considered and analyzed, with a particular focus on senior workers and company's managers and entrepreneurs.

The model is based on the deep desk analysis supported by on-field survey (with company managers, senior workers, public institutions) and aims to propose a system where traditional methods and innovative tools are combined together into an integrated approach to the problem [4].

During the project activities the Flexibly Beyond model was developed and validated by the partners. In fact, the model was proposed for validation to companies other than the project's partners. The model is thought to support companies, and in particular SMEs, willing to face the challenge of losing competences held by senior workers using low cost methods and tools. The model is based on two steps:

1. business process analysis based on guided questionnaires for managers and workers, with dedicated SWOT analysis, Risk Age Management Analysis supported by Senior Age Management, and schemes for dedicated focus groups;
2. experimentation toolbox including methods for improving working time arrangements, new technologies and management support devices, educational and training initiatives, innovative software and others.

The model was conceived on a multi dimensional approach since it includes tools for both senior workers and company management, both at strategic and operative level. This is very important because on the one hand, it shows that a great deal of attention was directed towards the cultural aspects to improve the managers' awareness about the relevance of human resources and, in particular, about how a proper management of senior workers' competences and skills represents a crucial element for the companies' present and future competitiveness. On the other hand, it shows the overall philosophy of the project based on the fact that general problem of age management in SMEs cannot be solved without a shared, strong commitment by all the parties involved. Many senior workers (blue collars) with an operative role in the company have a deep knowledge about the process and the tasks to be performed. This tacit knowledge is very important in sectors where quality of the product and the craftsmanship are crucial. Most of the time such knowledge is not formalized and it is shared with other workers through informal "training on the job" and "learning by doing" practices. But these practices are not enough anymore and need to be formalize with shared paths to create collaborative networks both internally to the company and across the companies.

The toolbox of the Flexibly Beyond project is based on three main areas of action:

- Education: The goal is to help management to define a company Human resources (HR) strategy based on the valorization of competences, to train senior workers to become trainers and educators for junior workers, and to help knowledge transfers within the enterprise. These actions are thought to enhance the importance of such matters both among managers and workers themselves. On one side workers need to understand the importance of their role in the company and at the same time they need to be motivated for the knowledge transfer process which has to be perceived not as a loss but as a gain of knowledge. On the other side SME managers need to acquire aware-ness on the importance of having a clear HR Management policy and in par-ticular of a clear strategy for managing key senior workers holding key core competences.

- Knowledge formalization: The goal is to develop tools in order to support managerial awareness about the age management issues and the available tools to empower and valorize senior workers. Also, the implementation of tools to formalize and codify knowledge in order to facilitate its transmis-sion from seniors to juniors.

- Systems for flexibility: The goal is to support companies with tools of or-ganizational flexibility in order to facilitate the prolonging of seniors' work-ing life, for example by allowing more autonomy in organizing their time between leisure and work.

In the table below the experimentation toolbox is shown by the dimensions of recipi-ents and the proposed tools.

General Goals	Flexibly Beyond: experimental practices to empower and valorize senior workers				
Tools	Education		Knowledge Formalization		Systems for Flexibility
			Innovative Software Applications	Database Applications	
Senior Workers	Education and Training for senior workers: inter-company initiatives	Company Training: coaching, tutoring, training on the job	Software applications for problem solving in operations (CKS-net)	Multimedia tools (video recording, pictures, web based exchange). PDM Software Applications	Time Banks Job Islands Time Flexibility
Managers	Training to HR strategy definition		Human Resource Management Software Applications (Filo d'Arianna)	Enterprise Database (videos, documents, images)	Human Resource Management Policies
Specific Goals	To develop managerial and workers awareness about age management	To help knowledge transfers within the enterprise	To formalize and manage knowledge company wise.	To formalize and codify knowledge in order to facilitate its transmission	To facilitate prolonging of seniors' working life

(Recipients)

Fig. 1. Flexibly Beyond toolbox for experimentation

In the next paragraphs, we will briefly describe some of the actions, and the related outcomes, that have been implemented through the "Flexibly Beyond" toolbox.

3   Analysis of Organizational Structure

In order to make sure that the innovative practices to implement and test were consistent with the specific needs of each company, a number of research and analysis have been carried out. Based on the collaborative network of the consortium, experts and consultants have been selected to help the enterprises' managers to evaluate their organizational and strategic situation, through in depth check-ups and SWOT analysis. In most cases, it was shown that enterprises involved in the project heavily depended on highly skilled senior workers, and that current human resource management practices were not sufficiently developed in order to deal with such a critical situation. In most SMEs, human resource management is considered as a mere administrative field, something that is not worth strategic considerations and investments. Thus, the project's initiative greatly helped the companies to develop their awareness about the limitations implied in such an approach to the general personnel policies, and to age management in particular. Also, the SAM risk analysis (Senior Age Management) helped to focus on specific risks that can identified and measured. Such a technique also allowed to profile each company in terms of what is currently done about the age management issue, what is not being done, and what are the possible consequences. From a comparative point of view, it can be shown that most enterprises, even the ones trying to consciously and carefully deal with the senior workers problem, face a relevant risk of losing crucial skills and competences with the retirement of some key senior workers; replacing or recreating those skills could be a very costly and difficult process.

Those costs and difficulties could be greatly reduced by some well planned-ahead actions. In some cases, it is not hard to imagine that the same practices that could provide to the companies means to prevent those problems and increase their competitiveness, they could also be considered by the senior workers as feasible ways to improve their status, their motivation and their satisfaction in the work place. In fact, several interviews conducted by the Project's staff to senior workers showed a widely shared positive attitude towards knowledge sharing and the extension of their work life, as long as arrangements are made in order to create adequate conditions and incentives, not only financial but also organizational ones. Thus, it seems that a certain convergence of goals and attitudes can be actually pursued and obtained. It is not an easy task, because many obstacles, especially cultural ones, on both sides, have to be overcome. It seems necessary to experiment with a wide variety of practices and changes, while at the same time taking into careful consideration the specific needs of each company.

4   The Implementation of the Model

The results of the first phase of the project have being used to categorize companies and to define specific needs and consequentially specific tools to be implemented. The "Flexibly Beyond" toolbox have been implemented in companies taking into consideration the specific requirements. Implementing the full toolbox in all the companies would have been out of the scope and not necessary. For this reason specific actions have been implemented. A relevant role in the project was played by the education and training initiatives, especially the "Competences Schools" that were created within some of the companies involved in the project. The goal was to establish and reinforce the role of senior workers as trainers and educators for the development of young workers' skills and abilities. While efforts of "training on the job" through unstructured means are commonly found, it has to be emphasized that a more structured approach is certainly necessary for different reasons:

- First, a formally structured approach to training process serves as way to promote throughout the company a culture of knowledge sharing, empowerment and responsibility for senior and junior workers.
- Second, it is also a way to reinforce and stress the relevance of a systematic, planned approach to human resource management.
- Third, a structured approach to education and training is better suited to create synergies with other kinds of tools and practices, like information technology tools and others that are described below.

A systematic approach to training and education, especially when senior workers take on a major role as trainers and educators, cannot, and should not, completely replace informal mechanisms of knowledge transmission. On the contrary, the "Competences Schools" should represent the ideal situation where informal knowledge transfers can be better managed and integrated with the organizational arrangement of the company and with its long term human resources strategy as well. The logic on which the "Competence School" approach is based acknowledges the impossibility of considering the training process just as "the transmission of explicit, abstract knowledge from the head of someone who knows to the head of someone who does not in surrounding that specifically exclude the complexities of practice" (see [5] p. 153). Instead, it affirms that "through experience of imitation and communication with other, [...] internal developmental potentialities are enacted and practiced until they are internalized as an independent development achievement" (see [6], p. 133).

Also, as a final point, the success of "Competences Schools" is strictly dependent on the ability and willingness of senior workers to act as effective trainers and educators. "Competences Schools" have been implemented through both company-specific and cross-company actions. An inter-company course has been implemented in order to motivate senior workers on the need to formalize their know-how. A "training for the trainers" action was implemented involving workers from different companies to create awareness that transfering know-how to other workers is not necessarily a losing strategy.

While it is crucial to improve the companies' ability to transfer and preserve the competences of senior workers, it is also important to provide effective tools for integrating such actions within a broader HRM strategy. The "Flexibly Beyond" model, for that goal, focused towards the development of innovative information technology tools for the management. One relevant example is "Filo d'Arianna", which is an IT tool designed to provide SMEs with a low cost platform for all major needs in terms of HR management. Such integration represents a particularly relevant feature, since it is necessary for companies not only to combine, from a strategic point of view, different aspects of HR management like routine tasks (such as payroll procedures), with non routine activities like career development and assessment, benefits and system for enhancing the role of senior workers. Thus, "Filo d'Arianna" represented a tool to allow managers to integrate HR management policies and activities into a platform that enhances the perception of strategic value of HR without compromising manageability.

Other relevant IT tools and practices have been implemented and tested in other companies. In the apparel sector companies, a tool of the PDM family (Product Data Management) has been customized and implemented in order to codify the procedures of important production activities, the "modeling" and the "prototyping" tasks, typical examples of areas where the experience of senior workers is absolutely crucial for the company. The use of PDM brings a number of advantages, e.g. the valorization of senior workers' know-how and the ability to create a database of well defined procedure that can be easily shared and communicated throughout the company.

Another example of innovative experiment has taken place in a small shoe company, where a Decision Support Application (designed according to the Case Based Reasoning technique) has been implemented in order to help workers to take effective decisions during some crucial stages of the production process, based on criteria of similarity with problems previously solved by senior workers [7]. Finally, a very interesting experience has been developed in other companies where the experience of senior workers was collected, stored and shared through multimedia techniques and procedures (video recording, interviews, etc.) as a simple and easy way to formalize and socialize tacit knowledge.

Generally speaking, technology played a relevant role in the experiments carried out within the "Flexibly Beyond" toolbox. This is not just because technology provides interesting opportunities per se, but also because it is absolutely crucial to disseminate the idea, especially among SMEs in traditional sectors like the clothing and shoe making industries, that technology is not just a way to innovate production processes, but also an effective way to better manage HR and to rethink creatively the organization to promote a cultural change in the overall managerial process of these enterprises. The implementation of such technological solutions was a way to reinforce collaborative networks within the company (increasing the interdependencies between different level workers).

It is worth noting that more traditional (but no less important) organizational changes have been implemented and tested in some of the companies involved in the project. The general goal was to improve the firms' organizational flexibility, so that senior workers could be facilitated and encouraged to extend their working life, to increase their commitment towards the sharing of knowledge and their new role as trainers for younger workers. A number of examples could be mentioned: the "time banks", which is mostly oriented towards the flexibility of working hours; the "work islands", which is an organizational arrangement for increasing of the autonomy of workers; "part-time" arrangements, "job sharing" practices, and other organizational solutions which should facilitate the integration between working time and private time.

5 Conclusion

It is becoming more and more obvious that western societies should carefully consider how to deal with some ongoing dramatic demographic changes, showing that senior citizens and workers are going to play an increasingly relevant role. Such a role does not have to be just a numeric burden on our society, instead it can be used as a positive resource, a new opportunity to improve not just the quality of life of senior citizens, but also to establish a closer knit, a more productive connection between generations, to tighten and strengthen the very fabric of our society as a whole. This might be not just the ethically right way to deal with the problem, but it also might be the only sensible, rational one. In fact, it is becoming clear that social and demographic issues are inextricably connected to economic problems. Many companies, in many different sectors and industries, are seriously threatened by the very real possibility of losing a great deal of their core competencies. The cost of recreating that knowledge might be very high, or even too high, for many of them.

The acceleration of changes (in all realms: social, technological, economic) is making more difficult, and more urgent, to take care of the difficult process of preserving traditional skills and competences and to passing them down to the new generations. In many economic sectors, innovation is not just a process of creating new knowledge, but also a combination of new and old knowledge. In other words, the aging problem in the socio-demographic field is also becoming a real, strategic issue, in the business arena.

The "Flexibly Beyond" project clearly showed that an effective answer to these enormous challenges which SMEs are facing requires a collective, multi-level and multi-disciplinary effort based on the implementation of tools with the support of a collaborative network based on internal relations (managers versus workers and workers themselves) and external relations with all the actors of the value chain (training providers, consultants, trade unions, etc). The support coming from these kind of actors is the basis for improving the performance of the company which is not only linked to productivity but also to quality of life, sustainability of the processes. And social sustainability is one important issue in a sector were human factor is still very strong. The evaluation of performance of the project is based on intangible factors and has indirect effects on production, but it has impact linked to the easen of information retrieving (shorter design process), easen of the knowledge transfer process (shorter learning time), number of workers still in the company after retiring age, etc.

Policy makers and institutions are responsible for adapting laws and regulations to allow industrial companies to face the challenge of active aging. Increasing the flexibility about the retirement timing and modalities probably would allow to design and implement organizational arrangements and innovations that would valorize the role of senior workers and citizens, improve the quality of their life, and facilitate the intergenerational transfer of knowledge, a crucial process for the economic development.

On the other side, the project itself helped companies to take into much higher consideration the problem of age management, and invest in policies, organizational innovation, and tools, specifically designed for that task. Even if one could argue that such a problem seems to concern particularly SMEs in traditional sectors, it is not hard to see that, instead, it should be seriously considered by all companies in every kind of industry. Also, it should taken into careful consideration by SMEs the need to integrate company-level to network-level actions. While the "Flexibly Beyond" project provided tools and methodologies at the company level, it also emphasized that, for various areas (e.g. training and education through Competence Schools) it is absolutely necessary a more collective approach, where collaborative networks between

SMEs could represent the only efficient and effective approach, especially in areas where a critical mass of investments is required and where a district-like economy is present.

Finally, a variety of actions should be taken in order to develop and spread a new culture, a new way of thinking, a new public awareness, both inside the enterprises and in the society as a whole, about how senior citizens and workers should not represent and be considered as a problem, but instead as an opportunity, a positive resource, a chance to make structural changes that can actually benefit all sectors and all actors of the economy and the society. It could be the chance to imagine and implement innovations where the ethical and the rational thing to do will coincide.

Acknowledgments. The authors of this paper would like to acknowledge the project Flexibly Beyond (Flexibly Beyond: tools and methods to manage prolungation of the working life official n.VS/2006/0353), funded by the European Commission under the Innovative Measures of the art.6 of the European Social Fund. We would like to thank in particular Politecnico Calzaturiero, coordinator of the project, all project partners and consultants participating to the definition of the model and implementation of the actions during the year 2008.

References

1. EU Commission: Aumentare il tasso d'occupazione dei lavoratori anziani e differire l'uscita dal mercato del lavoro, Comunicazione della Commissione al Consiglio, al Parlamento europeo, al Comitato economico e sociale europeo e al Comitato delle regioni, COM 146, Bruxelles (2004)
2. EU Commission (Comunicazione della): Il futuro demografico dell'Europa, trasformare una sfida in un'opportunità, COM 571, Bruxelles (2006)
3. Farinelli, D., Gubitta, P.: Il lavoro in età matura: come è fatto, come si può gestire, Franco Angeli, Milano (2007)
4. Berdicchia, D., Fornasiero, R., Masino, G., Zambelli, M.: Soluzioni organizzative per il prolungamento della vita lavorativa. Il lavoratore seniore nell'impresa e nella società. La Press, Venezia (2008)
5. Brown, J., Duguid, P.: Organizational Learning and Communities of Practice: Toward a unified view of working, learning, and innovation. In: Lesser, E.L., Fontaine, M.A., Jason, A. (eds.) Knowledge and Communities. Butterworth-Heinemann, Boston (1991)
6. Kolb, D.A.: Experiential learning: experience as the source of learning and development. Prentice-Hall, Inc., Englewood Cliffs (1984)
7. Bandini, S., Manzoni, S., Sartori, F.: Modelling Stories in the Knowledge Management Context to Improve Learning Within Organizations. In: Bramer, M. (ed.) Artificial Intelligence in Theory and Practice II. Springer, Heidelberg (2008)
8. Masino, G.: Le imprese oltre il fordismo. Retorica, illusioni, realtà, Carocci, Roma (2005)

Part 23

Collaborative Networks for Active Ageing - III

Memory Support in Ambient Assisted Living

Ricardo Costa[1], Paulo Novais[2], Ângelo Costa[2], and José Neves[2]

[1] CIICESI, College of Management and Technology, Polytechnic of Porto,
Felgueiras, Portugal
rcosta@estgf.ipp.pt
[2] CCTC, Departamento de Informática, Universidade do Minho, Braga, Portugal
{pjon,jneves}@di.uminho.pt, angelogoncalocosta@gmail.com

Abstract. Human collective set of experiences makes us who we are and help us delineate a path for our ongoing life. Ageing, however, progressively limits our ability to save, in our internal memory, these same experiences, or, at least, limits our capability to remember them. The capability to remember, intrinsic to our memory, is a very important one to us, as a human been, being this what deferent's us from several other species. In this paper we present a memory assistant sub module of a bigger project, the VirtualECare, which ability will be to remember us, not our past experiences, but our routine day-to-day tasks and activities, in a somehow proactive manner, thus, allowing us to have some relaxation about them, and focus the remaining of our ability in most important facts.

Keywords: e-Health, Memory Assistant, Ambient Assisted Living, Scheduling.

1 Introduction

The human memory, or its collective set of memories, is what makes us who we are. These memories are the combining set of experiences of our ongoing life. They provide us with the sense of self, allow us the sensation of comfort with familiar people and surroundings, connect our past with our present and provide us data to idealize our future. Memory is no more than the concept that refers to the process of remembering [1]. Aging, especially if associated with chronic diseases, affects our ability to remember, thus affects our memory. This is something intrinsic to the human being which cannot be reversed but, with the use of the commonly named new technologies, can be minimized.

1.1 Population Ageing Phenomena

According to the United Nations [2], population ageing is unprecedented, without parallel in human history, and it will keep growing thru the twenty-first century, rapidly than it did in the century just past. We will not return to the young populations that our ancestors knew.

This population ageing phenomena has profound implications in many facets of the human life. One of these facets is that with ageing, memory loss becomes more and more frequent [3].

L.M. Camarinha-Matos et al. (Eds.): PRO-VE 2009, IFIP AICT 307, pp. 745–752, 2009.
© IFIP International Federation for Information Processing 2009

1.2 Memory Assistant Software

With the recent advances in the, so called, Information Society, computational systems, specially embedded ones, are becoming, in a natural way, part or our day-to-day activities. This fact, associated with the decrease in size and cost of devices in general, allows the use of the already available new technologies in new areas where before where impossible. One of these areas is in the aid of our memory. Some memory assistant projects and software already exist [4-9] for several years, but the FP7 Hermes [7] and the SenseCam [8] seem to be the only ones with recent activity.

HERMES is aimed to provide cognitive care. Developed in collaboration between CURE - Center for Usability Research and Engineering, INGEMA Foundation, IBM Haifa Research Lab, University of Bradford, Athens Information Technology and TXT e-Solutions. Each of these companies is located in different countries, such as Austria, Spain, UK, Greece and Italy. The project is supported by the EU under the Framework Programme 7. It tries to provide an independent living and social participation, by boosting the self-efficacy of the user (patient). The main objective is to develop a system, software and hardware, which will reduce the negative impact of declining cognitive capabilities, particularly memory. An important feature of the this project is the implementation of a monitoring system which should be able to record every action, and associated choices, of one user in order to build a associations "map" of the different events and, based on that "map", create a pattern that emulates the human memory mechanisms. Despite its ambitious goals, HERMES is still in a very early stage of development and, as so, the idealized and developed hardware/software combinations are, yet, very simple, with low effectiveness. For instance, the speech recording has to be in certain, limited, parameters in order to be converted to text and the system still needs to be, manually, trained for each user.

SenseCam developed by Microsoft, it is a wearable camera that takes photographs, passively, without the intervention of its user (patient). The objective is to report, in images, the user's day activities and what places he has been. The hardware contains some degree of automation, e.g.: light-intensity and light-color sensors, body heat detector and motion sensors. Suited to be used on a cord around the neck, it will also be possible to clip it in pockets or belts, or attach directly in clothing. Saving the images into its internal memory, the visioning of them can be as a time lapse video of the user all-day activities. Although the Microsoft Research Center admits it is memory assistant software for elderly, in fact it has no significant, on-the-fly, abilities of remembering its users of events and/or tasks. It is merely, a so called time machine, like a video camera used to record what the user has done. However it serves the purpose of remembering the user what he has done, in a determined day. It doesn't have any kind of intelligence associated and it serves merely users with total memory loss, like Alzheimer's.

1.3 VirtualECare

The VirtualECare project [10] is an intelligent multi-agent system able, not only to monitor, but also to interact with its users (patients and/or relatives). It can, and should, be interconnected with other computing systems running in different health care institutions, leisure centers, training facilities and/or shops. It is composed by several components/modules, interconnected through a network (e.g., LAN, MAN, WAN), having each one a specific role (Fig. 1) [11].

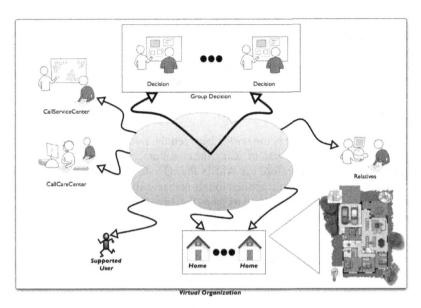

Fig. 1. VirtualECare Project

2   iGenda

The iGenda is one of the base software's in the Home and Relatives modules of the above presented project in conjunction with the monitoring one [12]. Its main objective consists in provide an intelligent organizer and/or scheduler and/or reminder to all the other modules of the VirtualECare project (e.g., GroupDecision, CallCareCenter) in order to allow them to manage the day-to-day diet, medication, activities, tasks and free time of the monitored users [12]. This way, he/she will always know, in real time even if changes are inflicted by one of the several modules, what will be the next "task" to perform.

The major goal is to create a product that will help its users to remember important information, events or tasks, or, in other words, to provide in-the-fly memory assistant. It can help, specially, people with memory loss (partial or total), by keeping his, all day, events and warn when the time to execute them as arrived, providing an increase in the quality of life and also a greater independence to the user. This module will also be able to receive information delivered by the remaining VirtualECare platform modules and organize it the most convenient way, given predefined standards. This way the user will not have to be worried about planning or scheduling events and tasks. The iGenda intends to be easy to operate by its users and will play an important role in his day-to-day life, being responsible for planning it (or week, or month). As an example, if the Group Decision module decides that the user must visit a medical center the iGenda is prepared to receive the respective information and conveniently process it, according to its level of criticism, and reorganize the user schedule in a short period of time. In order to be fully integrated in the VirtualECare architecture the iGenda archetype has to respects its standards protocols of communication [13]. Moreover, it is expected that the user is always in communication with the system, in order that any event of extreme importance could be, at any time, added in its agenda [14]. This system is organized in a hierarchy of states and events intended to deal with the information received (Fig. 2). To fulfill all the work mentioned, four sub-modules will be created: Agenda Manager, Free Time Manager, Conflicts Manager and Interface Manager.

2.1   Agenda Manager

The Agenda Manager (AM) is the bridge between the remaining VirtualECare system modules and the scheduling system, using the communication infrastructure to receive and send information. Therefore the AM is the iGenda starting point. The AM consists in a two stage sub-module application. It manages the incoming, to be scheduled, events and programs the time that triggers the Free Time Manager (FTM). It also supports the receiving of multiple events in the same message in order to increase the overall system performance. When a new task/event is received, the AM parses in order to be processed by the Conflicts Manager (CM). After being transformed, the data is delivered to the CM to be continuously assimilated and processed. The FTM is activated by the AM. The AM contains an internal clock that is configured for each user. It is defined a period of execution for the FTM, and when that period is reached the AM orders its execution. There will also be a set of rules, implemented in Prolog Language, which will be used in the CM, assuring that the new arrived events will be correctly inserted in the user agenda. When a level 1 (high priority) hierarchy conflict is detected, the system will return a message to its sender containing a high priority events overlapping warning, in order to allow the sender to reschedule it to another time. This module is also capable to communicate in with the remaining modules of VirtualECare platform, in order to report possible detected incoherence's during the processing phase of the received messages.

2.2   Free Time Manager

The Free Time Manager (FTM) will schedule recreational activities, according with the user health condition, in the free spaces of its calendar, in order to keep him occupied, increasing his well-being. These activities may be a very important step in order to allow an active ageing, aiming to create social and cultural dynamism, physical and educational activities, thus obtaining conviviality with others. These recreational activities are meticulously planned for each individual user based in his needs and preferences. To achieve these results, the FTM has a database which contains user's information, as, for instance, the user's favorite activities, previously approved by the Decision Group module, thus, allowing him to have, according to its eventual limitations, the best choice of physical and psychological activities at each time.

Initially we where seduced to use Scheduling Techniques (ST) to obtain the best possible arrangement of all the activities. However, we reached to the conclusion that it was not the best way of engaging the problem. We realized that implementing the user preferences system (presented above), in which the user chooses from a Decision Group module approved list, his favorites activities, it is useless to use any ST because we already have a hierarchy list and once we do not have a equal timed scheduling. We

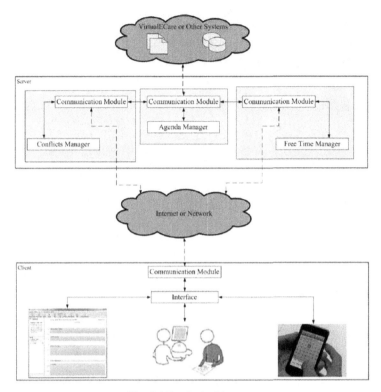

Fig. 2. iGenda Architecture

then verified that using a more simple arithmetic solution: pattern matching, was much more efficient. We simply have to match the gaps available with the time consumed by the activities from the hierarchy, pre-defined, list.

2.3 Conflicts Manager

The Conflicts Manager (CM) main task is to make sure that there are not any over-lapping activities. This module schedules or reorganizes events that are received from the AM, always verifying they are in accordance with other, already scheduled, events. If there a collision is detected, of different hierarchic events, it can be simple decided by methods of intelligent conflicts management (the most important activities overcomes all the other ones), however, in case of overlapping events with the same priority level, the error must be reported to the GDSS (Group Decision module) in order decide how to resolve that, specific, collision.

2.4 Interface Manager

The IGenda sub-module interface must be, above all, intuitive and easy to use. In the implementation phase a technician should introduce the user preferences in the system, which will then be carefully analyzed by a panel of medical specialists (in the

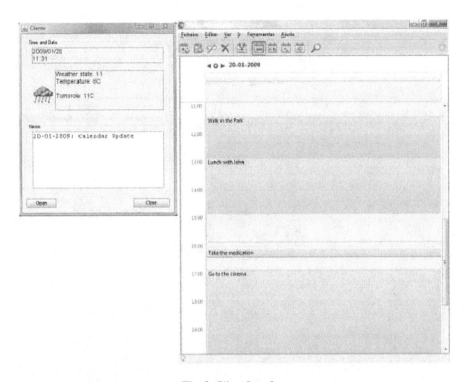

Fig. 3. Client Interface

Decision Group module) according to the user state of health (Fig. 3). The Interface consists of a main window which contains the weather and time information, and a warning notifier. This warning notifier gives the user important information about schedule updates, like new activities/events and/or important information sent directly to him (e.g., a critical warning from the GroupDecision or the CallCareCenter modules). It has also a calendar window, which is meant to be opened by the, already present in the operating system, default calendar software. The compatibility with this software is guaranteed by the using of the standard iCalendar Calendar Data (ICS) format. Is has also been developed a variable warning system responsibly to, properly, warn the user of a specific event. This warning system can be configured in two different states: always active or selective mode. In the first state, the user will always be notified in the beginning, or in the previously time it has been configured, of a specific event. Otherwise, in the selective mode this warning system has some "Intelligence" associated, been able to, through the real time analysis of the available health sensors, decide if the actual activities, not previously scheduled, is more or less important than the schedule one and act in line. For instance, if the user is actually resting, information obtained from the state of the available sensors, and the time for a activity, let say walking, is coming, the warning systems may decide that resting is more important than walking, at the present time.

2.5 Sample Use Scenario

The main goal of the iGenda sub module in the VirtualECare project is to improve end user's quality of life allowing them to better enjoy the so-called active ageing.

To better understand the amplitude of the iGenda sub module, let's consider the following scenario [15]:

"John has a heart condition and wears a smart watch that takes his blood pressure three times a day. He also has a PDA, connected with his watch, which reminds him to take his medications, with the proper dosage, his several events, presents his diet, and presents his, monitored, vital signs statistics. If anything unusual arises, his PDA alerts, both, him and the Group Decision Support System (GDSS) and, at the same time, presents him with a table of possible causes and solutions for the actual condition. The GDSS has, also, access to this table so they can keep it up to date, based on his condition. Currently, John's PDA warns John is time to take 1 pill of his hearth medicament and also detects that his blood pressure is unusually high. The GDSS receives a grade B alert and calls him to check what might be causing his high blood pressure (previous diagnose). At the same time John PDA presents a checklist of possible causes, and possible resolutions, to review. Meanwhile, the GDSS decides John should take 1 additional pill of his high blood pressure medicament and come to an appointment, automatically scheduled in his calendar with high priority. Additionally the GDSS decides that John diet should also be more refined and uploads the new, more refined, diet to his PDA and cancels all the physical exercises activities until the scheduled appointment."

In the above presented scenario, we realize how useful the iGenda sub module may be. It allows John to live his life without been worried if he is going to forget something important, as medication, or its proper dosage. It also allows an enormous proximity between doctor and patient, as, for instance, medicament dosage may be altered in "transit" or the taking of SOS medicaments may be ordered in line with the current condition, cancelation of activities, etc. Additionally it will allow relatives to be kept informed of his current condition.

3 Conclusion

In this paper we discuss the problematic associated with the ageing phenomena, the "normal" memory losses associates with it and we also present the memory assistant module of the VirtualECare project in conjunction with a position of its most recent developments. This is our first approach to human memory assist software, in order to allow a dignified active ageing of the population in general and to the elderly in particular. Our approximation to a possible resolution of this, no new, problematic is very technologically based, which may become an obstacle, especially with the elderly, but we are now starting to conducting several new developments which include the built and day-to-day test of a truly functional (with multiple devices, situations and cases) prototype in order to make the necessary adjustments introduced by real life use. We are also starting to integrate this sub module in our Simulation Environment in order, not only make high volume and adequate tests, but also to experiment odd and unexpected situations, verify the system comportment and make the necessary adjustments.

References

1. Mohs, R.C.: HowStuffWorks "How Human Memory Works (2007),
   http://health.howstuffworks.com/human-memory.htm
2. World Population Ageing: 1950-2050. Population Division, DESA, United Nations (2001)
3. Tucker, G.: Age-Associated Memory Loss: Prevalence and Implications. Journal Watch Psychiatry (1995)
4. Lamming, M., Flynn, M.: Forget-me-not: Intimate computing in support of human memory. In: Proceedings of FRIEND21, vol. 94, pp. 2–4 (1994)
5. Rhodes, B.J.: The wearable remembrance agent: A system for augmented memory. Personal and Ubiquitous Computing 1, 218–224 (1997)
6. Kim, H.J., Burke, D.T., Dowds, M.M., George, J.: Utility of a microcomputer as an external memory aid for a memory-impaired head injury patient during in-patient rehabilitation. Brain Injury 13, 147–150 (1999)
7. Jiang, J., Geven, A., Zhang, S.: HERMES: A FP7 Funded Project towards Computer-Aided Memory Management Via Intelligent Computations. In: 3rd Symposium of Ubiquitous Computing and Ambient Intelligence 2008, p. 249. Springer, Heidelberg (2008)
8. Hodges, S., Williams, L., Berry, E., Izadi, S., Srinivasan, J., Butler, A., Smyth, G., Kapur, N., Wood, K.: SenseCam: A retrospective memory aid. In: Dourish, P., Friday, A. (eds.) UbiComp 2006. LNCS, vol. 4206, pp. 177–193. Springer, Heidelberg (2006)
9. Giraldo, C., Helal, S., Mann, W.: mPCA–A mobile patient care-giving assistant for Alzheimer patients. In: Workshop Ubiquitous Computing for Cognitive Aids, UbiCog 2002 (2002)
10. Costa, R., Novais, P., Lima, L., Carneiro, D., Samico, D., Oliveira, J., Machado, J., Neves, J.: VirtualECare: Intelligent Assisted Living. In: Electronic Healthcare, vol. 1, pp. 138–144. Springer, Heidelberg (2009)
11. Costa, R., Novais, P., Machado, J., Alberto, C., Neves, J.: Inter-organization Cooperation for Care of the Elderly. In: Integration and Innovation Orient to E-Society, vol. 252, pp. 200–208. Springer, Boston (2008)
12. Carneiro, D., Costa, R., Novais, P., Neves, J., Machado, J., Neves, J.: Simulating and Monitoring Ambient Assisted Living. In: Bertelle, C., Ayesh, A. (eds.) ESM 2008, Le Havre, France, pp. 175–182 (2008)
13. Novais, P., Costa, R., Carneiro, D., Machado, J., Lima, L., Neves, J.: Group Support in Collaborative Networks Organizations for Ambient Assisted Living. Towards Sustainable Society on Ubiquitous Networks, 353–362 (2008)
14. Nehmer, J., Becker, M., Karshmer, A., Lamm, R.: Living assistance systems: an ambient intelligence approach. In: Proceedings of the 28th international conference on Software engineering, pp. 43–50. ACM, Shanghai (2006)
15. Björklind, A., Holmlid, S.: Ambient Intelligence to Go. Santa Anna IT Research Institute AB (2003)

Practices and Services for Enabling the Independent Living of Elderly Population

Apostolos Vontas[1], Nikolaos Protogeros[2], and Vasiliki Moumtzi[3]

[1] ALTEC Research Division, 6 M. Kalou Str., 546 29 Thessaloniki, Greece
avo@altec.gr
[2] Department of Accounting and Finance, University of Macedonia, 156 Egnatia Str., 540 06 Thessaloniki, Greece
proto@uom.gr
[3] Faculty of Computing, Information Systems & Mathematics, Kingston University, London UK
vasmoumtzi@gmail.com

Abstract. This paper presents the outcome of the evaluation of existing practices and services that assist the independent living of elderly population. In the context of this investigation we examined already existing practices and services and promote the ones that have the greatest impact to their lives and potential for wider commercial exploitation.

Keywords: Assisting living, elderly people, needs, e-services.

1 Introduction

Today, there are more than 70 million people aged 60 and over in the EU, representing just under one in five of the population. The category occupied by the very old, the over-eighties, are more likely to become ill and dependant. This category is growing rapidly.

The ageing population creates a market on its own, where a significant amount of online services are created and provided for them. Online services should consider the special needs of ageing people and thus create designs that will include them in the benefits of the Information Society. This requires thinking beyond the conventional media and creating a better overall experience which can be communicated via TV.

Many old people need support, as a consequence of losing mobility, mainly caused by illness. Physical, as well as, mental routines are getting more difficult which is influencing their whole lives. Society acknowledges these problems and seeks for solutions to meet its responsibility. Although institutions as well as medical facilities are available to them, from now on there will be many efforts helping people to stay at home longer. Technological solutions seem to be the way out of the expanding costs of health, help and support (Fuchsberger,2008).

This paper explores the types of online services that empower the independent living of ageing people and the telecommunication technologies that support online services.

During our investigation, we carried out an analysis on already existing software applications that support online services for elderly people. From the above we understand

L.M. Camarinha-Matos et al. (Eds.): PRO-VE 2009, IFIP AICT 307, pp. 753–758, 2009.
© IFIP International Federation for Information Processing 2009

that there is an increasingly demand for online homecare services such as emergency treatment, autonomy enhancement and comfort (Nehmer,2006). Meanwhile, telecommunication technology and computer science rapid development established internet use through TV via different communication channels like IP TV and devices such as audiovisual and entertainment equipment, health care devices, home automation systems (Vergados,2008). To this end, our research aims to customise and test a platform integrated according to a user-centric approach for co-creative design and validation of IT products and services set to enhance assisting living of elderly people. Our first intention was to investigate the existing practice and services based on characteristics for interface which could help a platform to reach large audiences more quickly.

2 Methodology

Methodology Steps. The steps we followed in our research can be summarized as follows:

   (i) We oriented the research to services that empower the independent living of ageing people.

  (ii) We focused our research solely on already existing software applications that provide online services for people who live independently and for elderly people.

 (iii) We considered relevant information and telecommunication technology approaches and trends that are accessible and acceptable by elderly people.

 (iv) We investigated the final user's needs and we proposed the best practices that empower the independent living of ageing people.

  (v) We validated the proposed online services through a pilot carried out on real users in Greece.

 (vi) We collected the feedback from the final users of the above trial. The kind of feedback given was oriented to human independence living factors. Based on these, a deep analysis on the feedback specified the added value of the services in terms of a user interface that improves the quality of life for elderly people.

Inclusion Criteria. There has been a rapid growth worldwide in mobile telephony, and broadband access has been growing quickly. Digital TV, HDTV, IPTV and mobile TV are all spreading. Nonetheless, there are access problems, especially in emerging countries. There are three main risks to inclusion: availability, accessibility – both in terms of people with disabilities and those lacking in ICT skills – and affordability.

In particular, here are the critical "success factor" keys considered in EICTA ICT "White Paper of Inclusion" [EICTA,2006] as the main risks exclusion:

- **Availability:** People disadvantaged due to lack of geographical coverage
- **Affordability:** People do not have access due to a lack of resources. Either the average income of a potential consumer is too low or it is not profitable to provide service due to actual operating costs.
- **Accessibility:** This has two elements: 1) people with disabilities such as visual, audio, speech, cognitive or mobility related 2) people who are lacking in ICT skills.

3   Technology Description

This research on already existing practices was completed under specific criteria in order to highlight those that facilitate assisting the life of ageing people that cover the following information and telecommunication technology approaches.

Table 1. List of projects investigated on e-services for aging people

	Advantages	Disadvantages
OLDES - 045282 - (Older People's e-services at home)	• User entertainment services, through easy-to-access thematic channels • Special interest forums supported by animators • Health care facilities based on established Internet and tele-care communication standards.	The aren't any e-services for other fields(such as social services)
SOPRANO - 045212 - (Service Oriented PRogrammable smArt nviroNments for Older Europeans)	• Older people at affordable cost • Meeting requirements of users, family and care providers • Significantly extending the time we can live independently at homes when older.	There is not a deep analysis of the devices which users and family will use
SHARE-it- 045088 - (Supported Human Autonomy for Recovery and Enhancement of cognitive and motor abilities using IT)	• Sensor networks • Assisted mobility • Knowledge engineering • Ambient Intelligence	E-services selection is not a part of this research
PERSONA - 045459 - (PERceptive Spaces prOmoting iNdependent Aging)	• AAL system reference architecture • Micro- and nano-electronics • Human Machine Interfaces • Communication • Software, web and network technologies • Biosensors, embedded and distributed sensors • Energy generation and control technologies • Intelligent software. Tools for decision support.	The project doesn't include a research about the e-services that facilitate assisting living. The research is mainly technical oriented
VITAL (Vital Assistance for the Elderly)	• inter-personal communication, • personal advice, • entertainment, • Ability to move safely in the physical environment	The project is centered only to mobile devices
T-Seniority- 224988- (Expanding the benefits of Information Society to Older People through digital TV)	T-Seniority covers: • a diverse range of care needs in a wide range of service situations (home care, tele-assistance, mobile telecom services). • This innovative service provision will use digital TV.	The selected implemented e-services are not analyzed in details
MonAMI - 035147 - (Mainstreaming on Ambient Intelligence)	• Comfort applications: home control, personalised communication interface, activity planning • Health: monitoring, medication • Safety and security: safety at home, visitor validation, activity detection	There is not a deep analysis regarding the devices which users will finally use

Online Services. Many elderly people need support, due to a deterioration of mobility, often caused by illness. This is not only observed in their physical state but also their mental, thus influencing their whole lives. Society acknowledges this and seeks efficient ways of support in order to meet its responsibility. Although institutions and medical facilities are available to them, from now on there will be many efforts helping people to stay at home longer. Technological solutions seem to be the way out of the expanding costs of health, help and support.

The presented case study implements the above kind of services using the following technologies:

Services for public interest:

- Massive broadcast and access to general interest information, being supplied by public administrations or general content providers (meteorological info, public administrations campaigns and advices, public e-Care Services resources availability, etc.)
- A public e-Care Services repository with extensive information on facilities, persons and programmes / resources dealing with Social Care services provision.
- An appointment module with e-Care Services Public Providers.
- A reservation module for reserving or contracting the use of public e-Care Services resources in a concrete timeframe.
- A "Talk with your PA" module to create direct and always-on communication channels among e-Care Services users and its public administration supervisors.
- A procedure management module to access, start and even accept (using digital signatures, certificates and biometric parameters) the enrolment in available public e-Care Services.

Personalized services:

- An elder communication module to be permanently in contact with their environment by using from simple call backs (low interactivity) to Voice and Video over Internet protocol (V&VoIP) (high interactivity) technologies, including audio and video conference services from home with family, friends, carers and people of the Local Council, according to each user needs.
- A module for Requesting Services for an Independent Living, from which the elder (under the accreditation and control of the Administration), using only a TV remote control, is able to request public or personalized services and to select the providers that will serve him, in matters as diverse as: primary care, pharmacies, transport, meals delivery, teleshopping, entertainment, etc. The Elder-Provider easy of use was the key for success for the rollout of the services and the first T-Seniority users have confirmed this assumption. (Medium interactivity).
- A Tele-monitoring Independent Living module (high interactivity), for controlling conditions about:
  - o Emergencies: existent tele-assistance systems, personalized alerts, fall detection, inactivity detection, etc.
  - o Living Environment: temperature, humidity, gas presence, fire and flood detections, etc.
  - o Vital parameters: blood pressure, sugar level, weight body, etc.

Telecommunication Technologies. Today, end users sitting in front of the TV screen, with a remote control in hand, will be able to choose among many different options of public or personalized services: communicate with their relatives, friends and colleagues; ask for shopping, repairs, appointments, on-line banking, etc... Typical TV end-users will not need to worry about what kind of technology is behind their personal services at home (STB (Set Top Box) adapted to DTT-MHP, IPTV, IP-HOMENETWORKING (IPHN), etc., or their interoperability, because these are completely hidden from them. The users have immediate and easy access to everything they can do, for example, talking with their children by just focusing on a photo with the remote TV control and pressing OK, simply using the remote TV control they already know how to manage. They do not need to go through a difficult learning curve. The telecommunication technologies should facilitate the following:

- Services on Mobiles Devices: The internet, computers, even mobile phones, are terms and tools that the elderly are not used to. It is not easy for them to use these and in most cases they create psychological barriers for the access and use of healthcare services.
- Services in Public Kiosks: This kind of terminals (as desktop models, cashier like or adapted for people with disabilities), which are located inside or outside strategic points where people usually gather.
- Services on TV: The TV channel can be an effective mean to include communities of users to the world of interactive services.

4 Expected Results

For special group of users who are typically not familiar with technologies the assistive environments are considered unique.

The likely benefits might include:

- Better quality of e-services that facilitate independent living of aging people tested, and perhaps an easier and more extended development of innovations in the European market.
- Improve quality of life of older people and their families and increase effectiveness of care systems, and facilitate wide implementation by the public authorities innovative, chronic disease management services.
- More tangible benefits to the underlying local communities of stakeholders and citizens.

5 Conclusions

It is obvious to us that there is a high need for substantially prolonging the time that elderly people can live independently at home and manage their day-today activities in a socially integrated manner. In case someone needs help for independent living which e-services are available to use? Taking in mind that he doesn't have high IT skills how he will be trained to access the internet and through which telecommunication channel? Our experiences show that the concept of online services, which can be easily operated by the elderly, can be an extremely beneficial tool for facilitating living. Any sustainable adoption and usage of online services would need a careful requirements analysis in order to determine the form and extent of elderly population needs. With this in mind, the research emphasizes on the technologies and online services which can easily be operated by elderly and disabled people. Providers, suppliers and designers of e-service tools and methods should examine every aspect of elderly peoples' needs as well as the suitability of the technologies before providing access to the tools. By doing this, the future e-service tools will serve a specific function in a specific situation and therefore provide maximum benefit to a particular group of users and developers (rather than random benefits to diffuse and undefined stakeholders).

The authors' experience and evidence from the results of this research have led to believe that situation-specific online services platforms would be greatly beneficial in providing the elderly a universal access to service resources.

References

1. Fuchsberger, M. V.: Ambient assisted living: elderly people's needs and how to face them. In: Proceeding of the 1st ACM international workshop on Semantic ambient media experiences, SAME 2008 (October 2008)
2. Nehmer, J., Becker, M., Karshmer, A., Lamm, R.: Living assistance systems: an ambient intelligence approach. In: Proceedings of the 28th international conference on Software engineering, ICSE 2006 (May 2006)
3. Vergados, D., Alevizos, A., Mariolis, A., Caragiozidis, M.: Intelligent Services for Assisting Independent Living of Elderly People at Home. In: Proceedings of the 1st international conference on PErvasive Technologies Related to Assistive Environments, PETRA 2008 (July 2008)
4. OLDES - 045282 - (Older People's e-services at home)
5. SOPRANO - 045212 - (Service Oriented PRogrammable smArt enviroNments for Older Europeans)
6. SHARE-it- 045088 - (Supported Human Autonomy for Recovery and Enhancement of cognitive and motor abilities using information technologies)
7. ST-2005-2.6.2 Ambient Assisted Living (AAL) in the Ageing Society European Commission, IST 045459
8. VITAL (Vital Assistance for the Elderly) Contract Type: Specific Targeted Research Project
9. MonAMI - 035147 - (Mainstreaming on Ambient Intelligence)
10. EICTA: European Information & Communications Technology Industry Association. i2010: Toward an Inclusive Information Society. ICT industry White Paper on inclusion, Brussels (December 2006)

A Health Collaborative Network Focus on Self-care Processes in Personal Assistant Practice

Mª Victoria de la Fuente and Lorenzo Ros

U.Politécnica de Cartagena, E.T.S.I.I., Campus Muralla del Mar,
30202 Cartagena, Spain
marivi.fuente@upct.es, lorenzo.ros@upct.es

Abstract. Public health is oriented to the management of an adequate health atmosphere which acts directly on health, as well as health education work and the supervision of environmental health threats. The work presented in this paper aims to reduce inequality, and give disabled people the tools to be integrated more effectively, reducing social exclusion, removing obstacles and barriers, and facilitating mobility and the use of technology. The work is planned to design a special healthcare collaborative network as the best solution for addressing the needs of the disabled self-care and health care community through the creation and implementation of an interconnected, electronic information infrastructure and adoption of open data standards.

Keywords: Self-care processes, Healthcare community, collaborative network.

1 Introduction

The European Union has recognized that particular attention needs to be focused on manifold issues concerning the disabled. Today the number of people with disabilities and chronic health conditions represents over 15% of the EU population. Article 26 of the EU Charter of Fundamental Rights, recognizes the right of disabled people to "benefit from measures designed to ensure their independence".

The increase in the life expectancy indicator shows that the EU will suffer a gradual increase in self-care necessities, either independent or with a personal assistant.

The HOMDISCARE Project approach is the implementation of self-care best practices through the establishment of a health care collaborative network (Public Health European Agency grant projects focused on Best Practices definition).

With the HOMDISCARE project and the design of the healthcare collaborative network, several EU members will be able to reduce care costs, through implementing services that are highly cost efficient and give the population the same, or better, care service as they are currently receiving.

If the quality of the service is not adequate it could increase the time that the disabled person will require support from the health care services. People feel safer when they are in a well-known area, experience services of high quality, have assistants that are close to them and have all the care system "looking after" them and their progress; goals that could be better achieved through the healthcare collaborative network. With the collaborative network, access to long-term care and support services are high

L.M. Camarinha-Matos et al. (Eds.): PRO-VE 2009, IFIP AICT 307, pp. 759–766, 2009.

priorities; other factors to consider also include reducing the heavy burden of disease, minimizing its economic and social consequences and health inequality.

The paper is organized as follows. Section 2 presents the challenges and related work to health care systems and medical information and data exchange techniques. Section 3 discusses the objectives, the integration methodology, and the framework for the self-care collaborative network to be developed in the HOMDISCARE project. Section 4 proposes the architectural design and components of the self-care collaborative network. Section 5 presents the principal conclusions, goals, and benefits for mid- and long-term for the HOMDISCARE project.

2   Information Challenges in the Health Sector

These are exciting times in healthcare. This industry is in the midst of a dynamic era in which significant developments in technology can offer innovative opportunities for health or care improvements on a national and global level [2,14].

Current health care systems are structured and optimized to react to crisis and managing illness. However, Health Information exchange programs are in their infancy in most settings [8], and both need to be coordinated to be evolutionary in their own scope and function. In this sense, the medical community wants to develop new and intelligent medical information systems [9], alongside monitoring systems and wireless sensor networks, which permit the application of new technologies for the observation and control of not only illness, but also wellness, of diverse population group [11].

The current systems for collecting, transmitting and exchanging health care data are evolving; however interoperability across sector stakeholders does not exist [8,9,10]. Furthermore, data standards for coding, sharing and structuring health care information are neither fully developed nor implemented. The health sector professionals collect data in a variety of ways, relying on mail or fax capabilities to transmit them.

Without action, health care stakeholders will continue to struggle, with large gaps in the information that is needed at the patient's bedside, in the office, at local and national public health departments; and EU agencies are under the challenge of acting on health detection and monitoring of diseases and health conditions.

New health information systems should be designed within a framework (service-oriented architecture and web services) which allows planning, design, implementation and integration of digital healthcare applications, and these digital healthcare applications must flexible and responsive enough to be able to meet requirement and evolvement.

3   Working towards a Solution for the Delivery of Self-care Processes

In the 90's, the concept of the social model of disability was defined [12,15]. This model regards disability as resulting from the interaction between individuals and their respective environments rather than as something within the individual.

Disabled people themselves say that impairments are relevant to them and that the elimination of impairment is desirable. People with impairments recognise the barriers, however, they do not want to be classified as "the disabled". What disabled people want are their rights, their full entitlement to resources, policies ensuring that the environment facilitates their participation, their autonomy and their emotional life [15].

Alongside these wishes, and in line with the social model of disability, a health platform that offers high quality health care, medical treatment and daily care services to special needs groups (elderly, frail and disabled populations) should be established [16]. The importance of quality of life has originated from the appearance of national and international associations (e.g., the InterRAI [7]), who carry out special collaborative efforts with formal and informal professional carers and health home care users [16].

Health inequalities between regions and countries in the EU [5,16], are mainly due to great differences in national cultures, health care systems, and socio-economic disparities. It must also be taken into account that there are different welfare state regimes and different modes of proposing social inclusion for special population groups, elderly and people with chronic illness and disabilities [5,6]. To close the gap in health care between EU countries the harmonization of long-term care policies in Europe is necessary, coordinating the different Public Health Delivery Systems [10].

As such, many healthcare stakeholders have recognized the need for improved health care systems, with reductions in the cost of the way the care is provided. This is evident in the EU where the initiatives have been approved by parliament, or even the annual call of the Public Health European Agency.

3.1 Self-care Processes in a Personal Assistant Practice Collaboration Network Project

As previously stated, the HOMDISCARE project aims to reduce inequality and give disabled people the tools to be integrated more effectively. To these means, this project starts with the analysis of self-care processes in several European countries and will develop a methodology to integrate those processes into the care system.

Disability policies are, essentially, the responsibility of the EU member states. While respecting this subsidiary principle, the European Commission does have an important role to play in the disability field, strengthening the cooperation between EU member states and other Member States [3].

Ensuring that everyone has access to high-quality health care is an essential element of the European social model. People who need medical or social care should be able to get it, regardless of their income or wealth, and the cost of such care should not cause poverty to the care recipients or their relatives [4].

On page 8 of "Enabling good health for all" [1], we can read: "European Citizens need reliable and user friendly information about how to stay in good health and the effects of lifestyle on health. When they fall ill, they need authoritative information about their condition and treatment options to help them make decisions. Enabling citizens to make the right choices is indispensable". These three principles ensure and encourage the proposal presented, and demonstrate the added value at European level.

The HOMDISCARE project makes an innovative contribution to the processes available to disabled self-care and health care community in Europe. The results of the project should improve the disabled "quality of life" through:

- Reducing the stress suffered by the Disabled and their care providers involved in home care processes.
- Providing specific tools for the care needs of citizen groups in the self care sector.

In conclusion, improving self-care practices through increasing the value of the care providers increases wealth, not only to the target groups but also to the care providers and other citizen groups.

A recent study, ADHOC-Aged in Home Care [16], carried out in a European setting has characterized home care users, and analyzed the effects of service provision. The presented conclusion is oriented to the exchange of information about users of home care services in Europe. In that sense, the HOMDISCARE project proposes the development of an innovative assessment instrument, and the wide application of the data collected from it is an indispensable tool for providing the necessary information for the move towards the harmonization of healthcare systems and policies in Europe.

The Health-Care Collaborative Network will be focused on coordinating operations (processes and services) in order to reach the target of each process: assistance and self-care practices to customers(target groups).

This Operation System model for the health-care collaborative network must be structured in several levels (Department, Organization, and Area levels) in order to enquiry react to the demand of products and services from the target groups, to achieve technical and organizational efficiency and efficient use of assigned resources and customer satisfaction, to improve business environment by means of regulation of life styles, technology, human resources and services, and financing activities and establishment of political priorities for resources allocation.

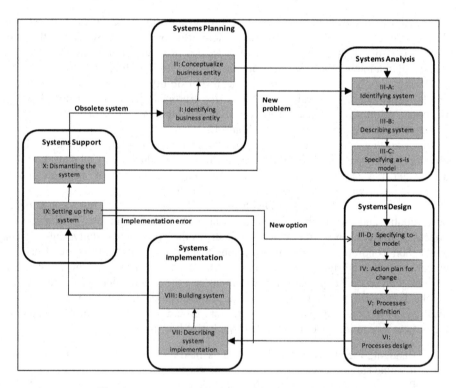

Fig. 1. Phases and stages of the ERE-GIO methodology

For the development of a self-care collaborative network that allows an appropriate paradigm and approach for different healthcare information systems of EU members integration and collaboration, the research team is working with the ERE-GIO methodology [13], based on Integrated Information Architectures, and the experience of the Research team in designing and managing Several Health Care Information systems.

The ERE-GIO methodology (Figure 1) presents a life cycle approach based on the "as-is" model and "to-be" model. This model will be used to develop the methodology for self-care processes in global health care. This double-model methodology will also be used to integrate the methodology and the platform that will support self-care processes, analyzing the performance and constraints of the disabled self-care prototype and further consolidation of the step-by-step HOMDISCARE methodology.

3.2 Developing an Interconnected Self-care Information Infrastructure

There is an obvious necessity to analyse the existing information system in the environment where the development of the collaborative network of self-care is proposed. The fundamental characteristics that the said network proposes are:

- Data come from existing clinical systems and are not stored externally.
- The fact that data are coded and transmitted by using open standards makes critical data sets accessible, efficient and usable by various data consumers.
- Data elements are existing priorities for medical insurers, providers and others.
- Privacy, security and business rule functionality to identify key health events included in design requirements, and processed information will be passed back to the provider at the same time as it is sent to medical insurers.
- Openness to participation: any provider, medical insurer, national or local association that wishes to participate is able to, because the open standards provide a common basis for exchange of information.
- Resulting health information linkages for standards based reporting from clinical information systems is a step on the critical path toward national health information infrastructure.

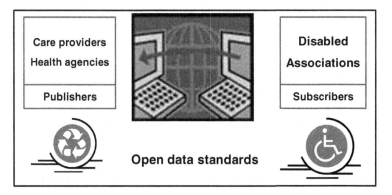

Fig. 2. Interconnected electronic information infrastructure

To summarize, the collaborative network focuses on catalyzing specific actions of the health care organizations (including providers, payers, public health organizations, pharmaceutical companies, information technology suppliers, etc.) with the aim to accelerate the adoption of clinical data standards and to enable the development of an international, interconnected, electronic self-care information infrastructure (Figure 2).

4 The Architectural Design of the Self-care Collaboration Network

The architectural design for this collaborative network is made up of three major components for data transfer and exchange (see Figure 3):

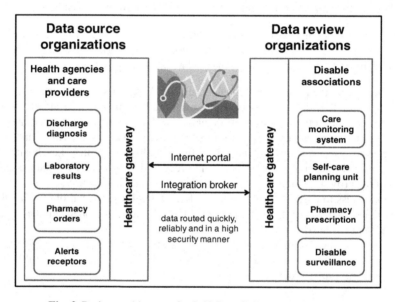

Fig. 3. Project architecture for Self-Care Collaborative Network

- An internet portal, which allows participants to identify and configure the type of clinical information they wish to receive (subscribe) or are willing to provide (publish).
- An integration broker, which transfers messages between publishers to authorized subscribers.
- A gateway, which connects the participant's systems to the network.
- At the participant's site the gateway filters, links, and maps data elements are based on business rules that they establish.

Data are transferred between participants (Publishers and Subscribers) via secure communications channels, with firewall rules at all end points that disallow unrecognized traffic trying to traverse the participant's system infrastructure.

5 Conclusions

Alongside the principal objective of the HOMDISCARE project, design and the start of work of the Healthcare Collaborative Network, the research team is pursuing a longer-term goal that is focused on a wide implementation of the Collaborative Network within the EU countries' healthcare systems. This current initiative focuses on a set of goals that:

- Creates an internet-based information network that enables private and safe-guard transmission of healthcare data.
- Deploys, on a European level, the Self-care Collaborative Network (SCN) methodology to a larger healthcare community.
- Changes the way in which the healthcare system collects, disseminates and ana-lyzes care data.
- Provides a foundation for a rapid response to bio-surveillance, adverse care events and inappropriate care.
- Enables advanced and more efficient interaction between care professionals and self-care patients.

As the Self-care Collaborative Network project finishes, it will hopefully accomplish the following benefits:

- Improve response time for bio-surveillance
- Reduce administration
- Enable rapid ability to aggregate and share data
- Submit clinical data
- Provide a secure environment
- Improve existing applications

If successful, the healthcare industry will have a network that enables not only inter-operability, but more importantly, professional collaboration. This, in turn, will allow stakeholders to achieve the goals of reducing costs and response time to adverse events, of patients located in their own homes, and providing caregivers with the information they need to have a positive impact on the care of individual patients.

References

1. Byrne, D.: Enabling good health for all. A reflection process for a new EU Health Strategy (2004),
   http://ec.europa.eu/health/ph_overview/strategy/
   health_strategy_en.htm
2. CCBH Community Profile – Health Collaborative Network (HCN),
   http://ccbh.ehealthinitiative.org
3. Commission of the European Communities. Situation of disabled people in the European Union: the European Action Plan 2008-2009. Brussels (2007),
   http://ec.europa.eu/social/main

4. Council of the European Union. Joint Report on Social Protection and Social Inclusion 2008, Brussels (2008),
   http://ec.europa.eu/employment_social/spsi/
   health_and_lt_care_en.htm
5. Eikemo, T., Bambra, C., Judge, K., Ringdal, K.: Welfare state regimes and differences in self-perceived health in Europe: multilevel analysis. Social Science & Medicine 66, 2281–2295 (2008)
6. Gannon, B., Nolan, B.: The impact of disability transitions on social inclusion. Social Science & Medicine 64, 1425–1437 (2007)
7. InterRAI Collaborative network, http://www.interrai.org
8. Johnson, K., Gadd, C.: Playing smallball: Approaches to evaluating pilot health information exchange systems. Journal of Biomedical Informatics 26, S21–S26 (2007)
9. Kwon, P., Kim, H., Kim, U.: A study on the web-based intelligent self-diagnosis medical system. Advances in Engineering Software 40, 402–406 (2009)
10. Mays, G., Smith, S., Ingram, R., Racster, L., Lambert, C., Lovely, E.: Public Health Delivery Systems: Evidence, Uncertainty, and Emerging Research Needs. American Journal of Preventive Medicine 36, 256–265 (2009)
11. Milenkovic, A., Otto, C., Jovanov, E.: Wireless sensor networks for personal health monitoring: Issues and implementation. Computer Communications 29, 2521–2533 (2006)
12. Oliver, M.: The politics of disablement. Macmillan, London (1990)
13. Ros, L., de la Fuente, M.V., Ortiz, A.: Enterprise Engineering versus Cyclic Re-engineering Methods. In: Proceedings of the 13th IFAC Symposium on Information Control Problems in Manufacturing, INCOM 2009 (2009)
14. Samaras, G., Horst, R.: A systems engineering perspective on the human-centered design of health information systems. Journal of Biomedical Informatics 38, 61–74 (2005)
15. Shakespeare, T., Watson, N.: The social model of disability: an outdated ideology? Research in Social Science and Disability 2, 9–28 (2001)
16. Sørbye, L., Garms-Homolová, V., Henrard, J., Jónsson, P., Fialová, D., Topinková, E., Gambassi, G.: Shaping home care in Europe: The contribution of the Aged in Home Care project. Maturitas (2009), doi:10.1016/j.maturitas.2008.12.016

Part **24**

Collaborative Educational Networks - I

mEducator: A Best Practice Network for Repurposing and Sharing Medical Educational Multi-type Content

Panagiotis D. Bamidis[1], Eleni Kaldoudi[2], and Costas Pattichis[3]

[1] Medical School, Aristotle University of Thessaloniki,
54124 Thessaloniki, Greece
bamidis@med.auth.gr
[2] Medical School, Democritus University of Thrace,
68100 Alexandroupolis, Greece
kaldoudi@med.duth.gr
[3] Dept. of Computer Science, University of Cyprus, Cyprus
pattichi@ucy.ac.cy

Abstract. Although there is an abundance of medical educational content available in individual EU academic institutions, this is not widely available or easy to discover and retrieve, due to lack of standardized content sharing mechanisms. The mEducator EU project will face this lack by implementing and experimenting between two different sharing mechanisms, namely, one based one mashup technologies, and one based on semantic web services. In addition, the mEducator best practice network will critically evaluate existing standards and reference models in the field of e-learning in order to enable specialized state-of-the-art medical educational content to be discovered, retrieved, shared, repurposed and re-used across European higher academic institutions. Educational content included in mEducator covers and represents the whole range of medical educational content, from traditional instructional teaching to active learning and experiential teaching/studying approaches. It spans the whole range of types, from text to exam sheets, algorithms, teaching files, computer programs (simulators or games) and interactive objects (like virtual patients and electronically traced anatomies), while it covers a variety of topics. In this paper, apart from introducing the relevant project concepts and strategies, emphasis is also placed on the notion of (dynamic) user-generated content, its advantages and peculiarities, as well as, gaps in current research and technology practice upon its embedding into existing standards.

Keywords: User generated content, Web2.0, content sharing, re-purposing, educational networks, collaborative learning, active learning, problem based learning, educational standards, intellectual property rights, creative commons.

1 Introduction

The recently witnessed and technology-driven knowledge explosion in medical practice (ranging from genomics, neuroscience and epidemiology to decision making and

L.M. Camarinha-Matos et al. (Eds.): PRO-VE 2009, IFIP AICT 307, pp. 769–776, 2009.
© IFIP International Federation for Information Processing 2009

medical informatics) constitutes a profound challenge to the mission of medical schools which are often required to alter and enrich their curricula with new courses [1]. To support this, information technology may be employed to develop virtual distributed pools of autonomous, self-described specialized educational modules, but also provide the mechanisms for searching, retrieving, evaluating and rating, adapting and revising educational content in medicine and life sciences.

To support their teaching, academic institutions often use a variety of web-based Learning (Content) Management Systems (LCMS), as well as, educational standards which are developed and adopted to enable the universal description of educational content, namely, IEEE Learning Object Metadata (LOM) [2], and SCORM [3]. Both standards are currently being expanded and adjusted by the MedBiquitous Consortium [4] to address issues specific to healthcare educational content.

Moreover, to implement efficient brokerage mechanisms for educational content sharing "mashup" technologies have recently been used. Web 2.0 applications offer new opportunities for health education since it allows open access to information, sharing of ideas, questions, and opinions etc. But, current e-learning research indicates that access to comprehensive repositories of learning objects and metadata is the crucial factor in the future of e-learning and the vision of interoperability.

However, to effectively enable the sharing of state-of-the-art digital medical educational content among medical educators and students in European higher academic institutions through a standards-based infrastructure one needs to tackle and elaborate on pedagogical, technical, standardization, cultural, social and legal issues towards.

The cultivation of this need was what lead to a newly launched, EU funded best practice network called mEducator[1], aiming to implement and critically evaluate existing standards and reference models in the field of e-learning in order to enable specialized state-of-the-art medical educational content to be discovered, retrieved, shared and re-used across European higher academic institutions.

The following Table attempts a relatively quick overview of mEducator.

Table 1. mEducator "attributes" at a glance

mEducator Attribute	Detailed items
Project Objectives	-identify and collect a critical mass of different types of health educational material -examine to what extend existing standards can address all types of health educational material - recommend extensions -examine to what extend existing standards are adequate to support the packaging and seamless delivery of all educational material types -examine possible extensions of existing ontological schemata, describing the semantics of Los -Liaise with standardization bodies to adopt standards extension /recommendations

---

[1] mEducator is funded by the European Commission under the eContPus2008 programme.

Table 1. (*continued*)

Suggested Solutions	-Solution 1: based on traditional isolated LCMSs, loosely associated via web 2.0 technologies. Partners publish content in their own LCMS. Updates of content in affiliated LCMSs are performed by RSS feed. "Mashup" technology for content sharing (standards based) -Solution 2: based on a federated architecture of LCMSs founded on a reference Semantic Web Service (SWS) architecture "LUISA" [5] for search, interchange and delivery of learning objects.
Expected results	-A metadata scheme for description of all types of medical educational content (standards based) -Recommendations on how to apply and/or extend the medical educational standard Healthcare LOM to address multi- type medical content re-purposing, sharing & exchange -Best practice recommendations for implementing standardized technology; reference models for medical educational content use, re-use and sharing -Multi-type content formally described, re-purposed & delivered (based on standards) in loosely coupled isolated & in federated LCMSs -IPR scheme for educational provided and re-purposed content in academic networks
Target users	-Medical Educators (clinical/non clinical, in academia) -Medical Students (under- and post-graduates) - Residents & Specialized Doctors (continuing medical education)

So, the essence of this paper is to present the notion of educational content within mEducator, provide various snapshots of content types, and discuss the issues of content sharing. Emphasis is placed on user-generated content, its advantages and peculiarities, as well as, gaps in current research and technology practice upon its embedding into existing standards.

2 Medical Educational Content

Content sources and types. Educational content in medicine includes a broad range of learning object types that address both the theoretical as well as the clinical aspects of medical education. Its unique nature lies along with the fact that is produced by both academics and clinical teachers, in a variety of places like hospital wards, healthcare practice units, laboratories, classrooms/lecture theaters, and recently the collaborative web and virtual reality spaces [6].

Another important development in medical educational content is the shift from traditional classroom-based teaching towards adult education [7]. Current approaches focus on situational learning and are active, self-directed and experiential, with a readjustment from process to product. The emerging view is of learning as an active, constructive, social, and self-reflective process with the aim to develop problem-resolving skills, self-directed learning skills and collaboration and group competences. Thus, current medical educational programs increasingly include case-based or problem-based learning and other small group instructional models, collaborative structures/schemas to support student-faculty interactions, and technology-enhanced educational tools.

Under the above considerations, educational content in medicine corresponds to a wide variety of objects. These include:

- conventional educational content types also used in other areas, such as lecture notes, books, lecture presentations, exam questions, practicals, scientific papers, graphs, images/videos, algorithms and simulators;
- educational content types unique in medical education, such as teaching files, virtual patients, evidence based medicine forms, objective standard clinical examinations, clinical guidelines, anatomical atlases, electronic traces of images, etc; and
- alternative educational content types, either reflecting active learning techniques (extensively used in health education) and/or stemming from newly introduced web 2.0 technologies, such as problem/case based learning sessions, serious games (2D/3D), web traces, wikis, blogs/discussion forums, etc., including the notion of medical expert instruction in which ever form this may be presented.

Content item definition. Before going any further, let us define what a medical educational content item is for mEducator. So, a mEducator content item refers to educational material with a registered history of creation, linked with specific educational goals and objectives, as well as, learning outcomes and educational contexts/settings, and is recommended with certain teaching methods and strategies types, while assessed/evaluated by certain means to accomplish the fulfillment of its predefined learning outcomes. To this effect, a content item may be a lecture in Powerpoint slides or podcast/vodcast of any length, or a Virtual Patient of a various size, as long as it is properly accompanied by a clear description (this will be metadata descriptions) of what objectives it meets, what learning outcomes it envisages, how is it supposed to be taught, and how is it assessed (in other words accompanied by its assessment means).

The notion of user generated content in mEducator. An important aspect of mEducator content refers to user-generated content. Its extent and nature varies with the specific content type itself. However, it has to be mentioned that much of the user-generated content in mEducator refers to a specific didactic approach, that is, active learning through the use of problems (problem based learning, PBL) or cases (case based learning, CBL). In typical use of PBL/CBL the problem of case is set, usually ill-posed by the educator to start with, and questions are raised; students/users are then engaged in trying to provide answers to the problem/case questions; it is this user interaction itself that in a way produces and enriches the content. Such content may itself, be it properly described by metadata and standardised, be utilised as a learning material by the instructors, since it provides hints where possible student misconceptions may lie (the instructor may use this to show to current students what previous cohorts have done in attempting to solve the problem/case or where mistakes/ misconceptions occurred, or to reshape the questions or the problem/case). Existing, concrete examples of such user-generated content already available at the mEducator partnership are (Fig. 1):

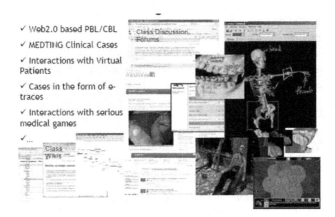

Fig. 1. mEducator starting examples of user-generated content

- Web2.0 based PBL/CBL (e.g. by use wikis, blogs, discussion forums) on specific content and interaction scenaria where this content is user enriched, loosely in-structed and originally ill-posed by the educator [1], [8].
- clinical cases (unsolved) on the MEDTING case repository; user "comments" and "voting" spaces can be utilized to harness opinions from medical educators, medical students or residents [9].
- Interaction with Virtual Patients on Open Labyrinth; a typical user interaction history (where mistakes were done) properly selected by the educator is impor-tant educational material [10].
- Cases in the form of e-traces (web traces of anatomical images); user-generated content relevant for sharing could be the students' image traces that are selected by the educators as being representative of typical misconceptions [11].
- Interactions with serious medical games. Like in the above examples, in game-based learning, the use of user generated content will include game-play-history, accompanied with the appropriate scenario wrappers for adaptation of established training scenarios, simulations and virtual environments [12], [13].

3   Content Sharing

The notion of user generated content in mEducator. Before going any deeper a key elementary question needs to be clarified: "why would people need to standardize and share educational/training content?" The following list provides some arguments towards the efforts for standardizing the process of collaborative sharing. Peers are interesting in the use of metadata that describe the content to be shared so that they are then able to:

- Transfer content into other organizations
- Modularize/re-use content in other courses
- Overcome platform problems /allow for multiple delivery options
- Keep an account of versioning/updating/life-cycle of content
- Relate content to other situations (re-purpose) and
- Add/alter contexts for content (i.e. "where" content might apply; contextualization of content)
- Facilitate easy content localization and discovery
- Share assets, media, competencies related to content (in connection to any learning outcomes attached to content)
- Contribute to economic discourse and the promotion of open-source tools for e-learning
- Allow for gate keeping and content validity
- Aim for audience focusing
- Achieve a tool agnostic process in the long run

Content (sharing) standards. As discussed above, reusability of content and such its (discrete) objects among different organizations requires that they are formally described with standard metadata. Learning objects (LOs), as independent units of educational material targeting to specific training needs, constitute one of the main research topics in the e-learning community. Many research initiatives in the field address the issue of LOs' reusability, via designing standards (official or de facto), specifications and reference architectures. Types of e-learning standards and specifications include among else the following [14]:

- packaging standards, regulating assembly of LOs and complex units of learning, such as IMS Content Packaging/Learning Design, SCORM, and HealthcareS-CORM (extension of SCORM to healthcare).
- metadata standards, addressing attributes used to describe LOs, such as LOM, HealthcareLOM (extension of LOM to healthcare), Ariadne Metadata Specification (which provided input to LOM), Dublin Core, etc.

So, seamless global sharing of medical training/educational content requires a flexible and adaptive metadata scheme for the content description (based on existing standards or the provision of new ones). However, special consideration should be given to issues such as: (a) metadata multiliguality; (b) metadata to address competency/outcomes profile matching; (c) different presentations of the same content, e.g. for users with special needs, for various display devices, etc; (d) contextual learning objects, i.e. originally designed to have a specific meaning and purpose for an intended audience; and (e) mutated learning objects, i.e. re-purposed and/or re-engineered from their original design for a different purpose and/or audience, while attaining an acceptable level of validity.

Sharing and Intellectual Property Rights. Intellectual Property (IP), in general, refers to creations of the mind and Intellectual Property Rights (IPRs), as a term, refers to a bundle of exclusive rights granted to creators' work that are creations of the human intellect. Moreover, copyright, refers to the "right to copy", and is essentially a form of IP applicable to any expressible idea or information that includes creative works [15]. Recently, a new type of licensing framework ideal for the digital economy has emerged, namely, the Creative Commons (CC) licensing platform, recognized as the "ideal" form of "open" licensing for works generally protected by copyright. CC employs both a "Some Rights Reserved" and a "No Rights Reserved" policy scheme, in contrast to the usual/traditional copyright. A division of CC, namely ccLearn, is dedicated to "realizing the full potential of the internet to support open learning and open educational resources" [16]. The four available options/conditions for versioning the CC license account for a good allocation and distribution of any shared material and its accompanying rights. More precisely, the conditions are (i) Attribution, (ii) Non-Commercial, (iii) No Derivative Works, and (iv) Share Alike.

4 mEducator Open Research Issues – Discussion and Outlook

Technology-supported educational interventions are usually successful when specific training requirements are aligned with the learning potential created by and the educational use of technology. Thus, requirements for flexible, adaptive and ubiquitous online content sharing should evoke notions, practices and technologies from respective state-of-the-art evolutions of the Web, but not only. The recent web revolution under the collective term Web 2.0 where the user is considered as a contributor, rather than a passive recipient, together with other artifacts of collaborative educational environments (as outlined in section 2.3), provide multiple facets of what is known as user-generated content. Such educational content is created by participation and collaboration as an emergent product of human education-centred interactions. In the core of research related to the above notion of user-generated content lies an ensemble of standards, protocols, technologies and software development architectures and approaches that enable seamless communication and sharing tools and the creation of communities and networks of services that bring people (medical educators, students, practitioners) together. Are the above mentioned existing ensembles capable of supporting all requirements and resolving all particular issues? Probably not! For example, it is not well defined how current educational standards and metadata might be applied to describe the educational interaction within a PBL Web2.0 scheme facilitated by blogs, wikis and discussion forums. Therefore, the mEducator initiative will have to cluster with standardization bodies and scientific/professional communities to resolve such ambiguities.

Furthermore, central to mEducator is the issue of IPR resolution for the provided content, the newly introduced content (during and after the project) as well as for re-purposed content. The consortium will have to work towards developing a simple IPR procedure to address all these instances of medical content incorporated in a medical educational content sharing network. IPR issues and content description metadata will also be a major factor in determining and deriving content selection rules for content inclusion in the network. Of course, it remains to be seen whether a simple adoptions of ccLearn will be capable of addressing all related mEducator issues or the need for a new standard (or extension of an existing one) might be geared.

It is almost certain that collaboration and content sharing in health education will inevitably alter the overall process of developing and preparing course materials. The formation of task forces and content sharing networks/consortia will ensure that responsibility is not merely vested in just one of the institutions involved. With this in mind, the notion of collaboration goes beyond merely sharing tasks and content across different educators in the EU and not only.

Acknowledgments. The project "mEducator: Multi-type Content Repurposing and Sharing in Medical Education", is supported by the eContentplus 2008 program, Information Society and Media Directorate-General, European Commission (ECP 2008 EDU 418006).

References

1. Kaldoudi, E., Bamidis, P., Papaioakeim, M., Vargemezis, V.: Problem-Based Learning via Web 2.0 Technologies. In: 21st IEEE International Symposium on Computer-Based Medical Systems, pp. 391–396. IEEE Computer Society CPS, USA (2008)
2. IEEE-LOM, Draft Standard for Learning Object Metadata, Learning Technology Standards Committee of the IEEE (2002),
   http://ltsc.ieee.org/wg12/files/
   LOM_1484_12_1_v1_Final_Draft.pdf (last access April 2009)
3. Advanced Distributed Learning. Sharable Content Object Reference Model (2004),
   http://www.adlnet.org/
4. Medbiquitous Consortium, http://www.medbiq.org
5. LUISA, IST- FP6 – 027149, http://www.luisa-project.eu/www/
6. Kaldoudi, E., Bamidis, P., Pattichis, C.: Multi-type content repurposing and sharing in medical education. In: International Association of Technology, Education and Development, Spain (2009)
7. Jones, R., Higgs, R., de Angelis, C., Prideaux, D.: Changing face of medical curricula. Lancet 357(9257), 699–703 (2001)
8. Bamidis, P., Constantinidis, S., Kaldoudi, E., Maglaveras, N., Pappas, C.: The use of Web 2.0 in teaching Medical Informatics to postgraduate medical students: first experiences. J. Med. Internet Res. 10(3), e22 (2008), http://www.jmir.org/2008/3/e22/
9. Cabrer, M.: MDPIXX: The Global Medical Images Repository. J. Med. Internet Res. 10(3), e22 (2008), http://www.jmir.org/2008/3/e22/
10. Ellaway, R., Poulton, T., Fors, U., McGee, J.B., Albright, S.: Building a virtual patient commons. Med. Teach. 30(2), 170–174 (2008)
11. Gorgan, D., Stefanut, T., Gavrea, B.: Pen Based Graphical Annotation in Medical Education. In: 20th IEEE International Symposium on Computer-Based Medical Systems, pp. 681–686. IEEE Computer Society, USA (2007)
12. Hansen, M.M.: Versatile, immersive, creative and dynamic virtual 3-D healthcare learning environments: a review of the literature. J. Med. Internet Res. 10(3), e26 (2008)
13. De Freitas, S., Martin, O.: How can exploratory learning with games and simulations within the curriculum be most effectively evaluated? Computers and Education 46(3), 249–264 (2006)
14. Devedzic, V., Jovanovic, J., Gasevic, D.: The pragmatics of current e-learning standards. IEEE Internet Computing 11(3), 19–27 (2007)
15. Miller, A., Balasubramaniam, C., Poulton, T.: Intellectual Property Issues – coming to an institution near you! The Higher Education Academy (Medicine, Dentistry and Veterinary Medicine), 01.17, 6–7 (2008), http://www.medev.ac.uk
16. Creative Commons Learn, http://learn.creativecommons.org

Semantic Maps Capturing Organization Knowledge in e-Learning

Androklis Mavridis[1], Adamantios Koumpis[1], and Stavros N. Demetriadis[2]

[1] Altec research programmes division, M. Kalou 6 str.
54629 Thessaloniki, Greece
{mavr,akou@}altec.gr
[2] Informatics Department, Aristotle University of Thessaloniki, Greece
sdemetri@csd.auth.gr

Abstract. e-learning, shows much promise in accessibility and opportunity to learn, due to its asynchronous nature and its ability to transmit knowledge fast and effectively. However without a universal standard for online learning and teaching, many systems are proclaimed as "e-learning-compliant", offering nothing more than automated services for delivering courses online, providing no additional enhancement to reusability and learner personalization. Hence, the focus is not on providing reusable and learner-centered content, but on developing the technology aspects of e-learning. This current trend has made it crucial to find a more refined definition of what constitutes knowledge in the e-learning context. We propose an e-learning system architecture that makes use of a knowledge model to facilitate continuous dialogue and inquiry-based knowledge learning, by exploiting the full benefits of the semantic web as a medium capable for supplying the web with formalized knowledge.

Keywords: e-Learning, Semantic Web, Knowledge maps.

1 Introduction

Due to its asynchronous nature, e-learning, shows much promise in accessibility and opportunity to learn. As e-learning can transmit knowledge fast and effectively, it is accepted by many as a means of upgrading themselves and keeping up with the rapid changes that define the Internet.

A literature review [1] unveiled major concerns about its effectiveness and appropriateness. Without a universal standard for online learning and teaching, many organizations proclaiming their systems as "e-learning-compliant", but actually these organizations are only automating their services and delivering their courses online. Except for the elimination of the time and space barrier, the online content provides no additional enhancement to the educational learning experience, and the reusability and learner personalization are not realized, as these organizations are developing e-learning resources to suit their own contexts and using tools that hinder collaboration and reuse.

The focus is not on designing reusable and learner-centred content, as many developers are placing much emphasis on the technology aspects of e-learning [2]. This

L.M. Camarinha-Matos et al. (Eds.): PRO-VE 2009, IFIP AICT 307, pp. 777–784, 2009.

inevitably lead to an unfortunate situation where most content developers are concerned with showcasing their technology-enhanced products, showing little interest in enhancing the "knowledge aspect" of e-learning, which should be at the centre of it. This current trend coupled with the growth in access to ever increasing amounts of information, has made it crucial to find a more refined definition of what constitutes knowledge in the e-learning context. The emphasis should not be placed on the information on the web (as this does not constitute knowledge) but on managing information to transform it into knowledge.

In this paper we focus on these issues and we propose an e-learning system architecture that makes use of a knowledge model to facilitate continuous dialogue and inquiry-based knowledge learning in business environments. This architecture offers a knowledge environment that represents the semantic web version of e-learning, a view clearly reflected in the EU-NSF Strategic Workshop Report 2001, where it is observed that e-learning, even when properly designed and meta-tagged, will not realize full reusability without the full benefits of the semantic web. Aiming to close the gap between knowledge management and e-learning through the integration of different knowledge components, the knowledge map approach is adopted to enable the visualization of knowledge representation, and the personalization of learning experience.

2 Knowledge Personalization

Learning is often described as an ongoing cycle, occurring as a sequence of phases: first, concrete experiences generate an opportunity for observation and reflection; this, in turn, leads to the creation of new concepts and models that are then tested in novel situations; etc.

People need four different types of skills to make their learning cycle effective; more specifically, they have to:

- engage openly and in new experiences,
- reflect and observe their experiences from many perspectives,
- create concepts that integrate observations and,
- use these theories in decision making and problem solving.

In many important learning models, learning starts when the person experiences a practical or a cognitive dissonance. Then routine action breaks down, the learner realizes that active sense-making is needed, and the world needs to be reconstructed. This reconstruction may require reorganization of meaning and also reconfiguration of the material environment. In classroom settings, this process can be simulated by problem-based learning situations, where the student is presented with a specific construction of the world, for example using a textual description, and the dynamics of the world is shown to lead to a contradiction or a problem that needs to be solved. Students may also collaborate in solving the problem, for example, by taking different roles and presenting different interpretations of the situation. Such problem-based learning settings can be enhanced by immersive information environments where the learner can effectively experience cognitive dissonance and where problem-solving resources are readily available. Our architecture specifically addresses the special requirements imposed in these information environments such as business environments, where tacit knowledge, is highly subjective in nature, as it is developed by an individual based on his cognitive and conceptual models of external processes. This organizational tacit knowledge should be defined and structured in a manner enabling further formulation and categorization providing reusability and communication.

However, apart from defining knowledge and its structure, it is important to address knowledge personalization and visualization in any e-learning context. To tackle the problems of knowledge personalization, we follow as a general blueprint the notion of knowledge concept maps in our context referred as knowledge maps. The potential of concept maps as instructional tools and learning personalization via use of concept maps has been proposed previously [3], [4], [5], [6]. Knowledge maps are used as the graphical representations of knowledge to depict both the learning concepts and the relationships between them in a human - oriented approach. Graphically, the knowledge maps consist of nodes and labelled lines that represent some important aspect of a learner's propositional knowledge in a subject domain. In our proposed architecture knowledge maps are technically represented by ontologies. The content is organized in a knowledge base that contains ontologies that define the learning objects semantics and workflows. These ontologies are defined by the tutors with the usage of the design toolkit. The content is stored into the content database, which is a semantic repository that enables semantic queries from the e-learning services.

An ontology is a semantically enriched data model that represents a set of concepts within a domain and the relationships between those concepts [7]. It provides a common vocabulary to refer to the concepts of a domain, specifies relationships using logical statements that describe how the concepts are related and provides also rules for combining concepts and their relations to define extensions to the vocabulary.

The semantic web is an extension of the current web, whereby information is given well-defined meaning, to enable computers and people to work cooperatively [8]. The Web Ontology Language OWL is a semantic markup language for publishing and sharing ontologies on the World Wide Web. It is the most recent development in standard ontology languages, certified by the World Wide Web Consortium (W3C) to promote the Semantic Web vision. OWL is used by applications that need to process the content of information instead of just presenting information to humans. OWL goes beyond the languages XML and RDF in their ability to represent machine interpretable content on the Web, because it has more facilities for expressing meaning and semantics than them [9].

3 Proposed Solution

The design of experiential learning systems requires insights, concepts, technologies, and methodologies from a host of disciplines that often have limited dialogue with one another [10]. This dialogue and collaboration takes time, commitment, and considerable effort, but can ultimately result in a "hybridized theory and practice", capable of addressing problems that no single discipline or cluster of related disciplines can attempt alone.

Prior research in communications theory and the phenomenology of lived and mediated experience provide us with frameworks for understanding how to structure data so as to affect the experiences that human minds create when they encounter these structured data. Assimilating and taking advantage of such data requires recognition of their multimedia nature, the development of semantic models across different media, the representation of complex relationships in the data (such as spatio-temporal, causal, or evolutionary), and finally, the development of paradigms to mediate user-media interactions [11]. To help generate insights from multiple heterogeneous data sources, any environment should allow users apply their senses directly to observe data and manage the information related to a particular event [12].

Our architectural approach contributes towards the proliferation of high quality learning environments, through the establishment of a framework for inquiry-based eLearning, exploiting the emerging paradigm of service-orientated architecture in a semantically web-based environment. In this context, our conceptual platform aims at exploiting the content of personnel education in business environments. This platform facilitates the management of content and the creation of courses and supports a number of additional e-learning services, as shown in Figure 1, which depicts the architecture of the proposed solution.

The platform is operated by three different communities of users, namely:

- the educational content providers that design educational programmes in the form of maps,
- the personnel that participate in the learning environment, accessing maps for their education, and
- the content providers

For the system to support the functionality of these three communities, the platform is divided into three sub systems, which are described below:

- e-learning subsystem: a portal-based e-learning environment that enables the three communities to collaborate through a set of structured learning objects. The learning objects are accessed though a set of e-learning services that wrap semantics and workflows of the information.
- Content and learning objects subsystem: the content is organized in a knowledge base that contains ontologies that define the learning objects semantics and workflows. The ontologies are defined by the tutors with the usage of the design toolkit. The content is stored into the content database, which is a semantic repository that enables semantic queries from the e-learning services; and interoperability services: a set of web services that enable collaboration with external organizations and/or repositories.

The platform network shall function as an integrated, context-sensitive, adaptable and interoperable educational environment, based on the concept of technology-enhanced experiential learning for competency, skills and performance enhancement.

In the core of the proposed pedagogical approach, lies the inquiry-based learning implemented as case-based learning (CBL) methodology in ill-structured domains. The whole learning experience is situated within the context of an "extended" learning community [13], [14]. By "extended" we mean that the community becomes a bridge between learners and the field of practice, motivating field professionals to act as "contributors", that is, providers of "raw" learning material emerging from their experience. This material, after undergoing appropriate didactical transformation, can become learning material in the form of advice-cases and learning scenarios, enabling

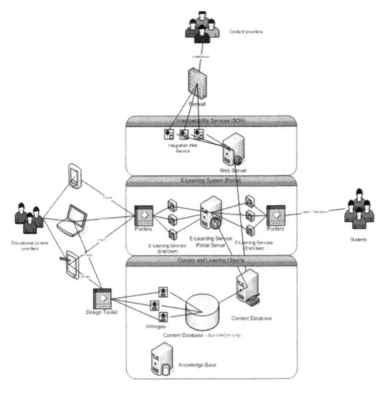

Fig. 1. Proposed architecture

learners to experience the complex and demanding situations encountered in the professional context. From a cognitive point of view our approach emphasizes two critical instructional interventions: "criss-crossing" of the learning material and learner scaffolding.

"Criss-crossing" (a basic tenet of cognitive flexibility theory) refers to guiding the learners through the informational landscape of case-based material, helping them to review relevant information from multiple perspectives. Case-based learning (CBL) is a widely acknowledged pedagogical approach for introducing personnel in the intricacies of ill-structured domains [15]. Cases are narrative structures, which immerse personnel in the context of real-world situations filled with "complexity, uncertainty, instability, uniqueness, and value conflict" [16]. By analyzing case-based material from various perspectives, personnel are expected to develop those flexible cognitive schemata that are necessary for ill-structured problem solving and knowledge transfer. To achieve this, cognitive flexibility theory prescribes that learners should thematically "criss-cross" the domain landscape studying the case material from different conceptual perspectives, in rearranged contexts, and for different purposes [17].

Scaffolds are instructional interventions that aim to help learners develop deeper understandings which might not be within their immediate grasp. Questioning strategies (including learners' self-generated questions) have been reported to significantly improve learning outcomes. In reviewing the literature [18], concludes that questioning strategies help personnel in important cognitive functions, such as focusing attention, stimulating prior knowledge, enhancing comprehension, and facilitating problem-solving processes.

Using the system the contributors may upload and index their material, using a domain specific indexing scheme. Pedagogical content providers ("instructors") can prepare scenarios for learners to work with, construct "paths" to help them criss-cross relevant cases and provide useful cognitive scaffolds (for example, in the form of question prompts) to help them reflect on the material. Learners, finally, can work on assigned scenarios at two levels of expertise (novice or advanced learner), which implies different access privileges and level of difficulty of assigned tasks. Drawing on the above theoretical background, we suggest that four fundamental content organization features in the environment are: the scenario, the learning case, the path and the scripts.

Scenario: In Architecture the learners study by exploring various scenarios. A scenario is the main study unit, presenting to learners a plausible problem-case. Learners are engaged in decision-making process, playing the role of practitioners, who face some open-ended questions (scenario questions) regarding critical decisions of the field experience presented in the scenario.

Advice-cases: In order to successfully deal with the scenario questions, learners need to reflect on decisions taken and practices implemented in other similar situations. Such information is offered to them through criss-crossing of learning advice-cases. These cases present field experiences with some specific outcome (failure or success). Usually it is illustrated how effective or inefficient decisions or actions has resulted to respectively successful or unsuccessful management of the problematic situation. Each advice-case is divided into "case-frames", which are smaller parts of the case presenting some meaningful and self-contained aspect of it. The content of a case-frame refers to the impact of one domain factor (theme) on the specific case, thus enabling the conceptual indexing of the case material. Contributors of the learning material will be able to add conceptual indexing factors depending on their common understanding of the domain, thus collaboratively developing a domain-specific metadata scheme to index the learning material.

Path: Paths are sequences of case-frames from various cases, guiding personnel through past field experiences (advice-cases) and focusing on specific issues. A path, for example, may illustrate how a specific emergency situation was handled (with or without success) in a number of cases. The instructor can flexibly construct a path by assembling any case-frames she likes, depending on the learning objective of the scenario. Each scenario is accompanied by a number of paths guiding learners to criss-cross the material and reviews it from various perspectives (domain factors).

Scaffolding and Scripting: To engage learners in active processing of the material, learner scaffolds (in the form of question prompts) and collaboration scripts will be employed to guide both the learner-content and learner-learner interactions. Regarding the former, a specific questioning scheme will appear each time a case-frame is selected for study. These questions ask learners to: (a) identify concrete events/issues that play important role in the situation, (b) recall other instances, where similar evens/issues were encountered, and (c) state some useful conclusions regarding their expected successful performance (decision taking).

After submitting their answers learners get system feedback in the form of hints that help them self-assess their answers and practices. Regarding the latter (learner-learner interaction), a collaboration script will be used to guide learners on how to collaborate productively. Collaboration scripts [19], are didactic scenarios providing specific instructions for small groups of learners on what activities need to be executed, when they need to be executed, and by whom they need to be executed in order to foster individual knowledge acquisition.

4 Conclusions

In this paper we shed light on these issues of knowledge personalization and visualization in e-learning systems focusing in education in business environments. We argued that the focus should be on transforming the experience held as tacit knowledge into structured formulated and reusable piece of explicit knowledge. For this we propose an architecture presenting the proposed e-learning system. Our system architecture makes use of a knowledge model to facilitate continuous dialogue and inquiry-based knowledge learning in business environments. This architecture offers a knowledge environment that represents the semantic web version of e-learning, aiming to close the gap between knowledge management and e-learning through the employment of graphical representations of knowledge, depicting both the learning concepts and the relationships between them in a human - oriented approach.

References

1. Miltiadis, D.L., Pouloudi, N.: E-learning: Just a waste of time. In: Strong, D., et al. (eds.) Proceedings of the Seventh Americas Conference on Information Systems (AMCIS 2001), Boston, MA, August 3-5, pp. 216–222 (2001)
2. McCalla, G.: The Ecological Approach to the Design of E-Learning Environments: Purpose-based Ca p t u re and Use of Information About Learners. Journal of Interactive Media in Education (2004)
3. Teo, C.B., Gay, K.L.: Concept-based system design to personalize E-learning. WSEAS Trans. Inf. Science Applications 1(5), 1248–1255 (2004b)
4. Teo, C.B., Gay, K.L.: Concept map provision for E-learning. Int. J. Instructional Technology Distance Learning 3(7), 17–32 (2006a)
5. Teo, C.B., Gay, K.L.: Provision of self-directed learning using concept mapping. WSEAS Trans. Advances Eng. Education 3(6), 491–498 (2006b)
6. Teo, C.B., Gay, K.L., Chang, S.C.: Pedagogy considerations for E-learning. Int. J. Instructional Technology Distance Learning 3(5), 3–26 (2006b)
7. Antoniou, G., Van Harmelen, F.: A Semantic Web Primer. MIT Press, Cambridge (2004)
8. Berners-Lee, T., Hendler, J., Lassila, O.: The semantic web. Scientific American (2001)
9. McGuinness, D.L., Van Harmelen, F.: OWL Web Ontology Language Overview. W3C Recommendation. MIT Press, Cambridge (2004)
10. Davis, M.: Theoretical Foundations for Experiential Systems Design. In: Proceedings of ETP 2003, Berkeley, California, USA, pp. 45–52 (2003)

11. Singh, R., Knickmeyer, R., Gupta, P., Jain, R.: Designing Experiential Environments for Management of Personal Multimedia. In: Proceedings of MM 2004, New York, New York, USA, October 10–16, pp. 496–499 (2004)
12. Jain, R.: Experiential Computing. Communications of the ACM 46(7), 48–54 (2003)
13. Demetriadis, S., Barbas, A., Molohides, A., Palaigeorgiou, G., Psillos, D., Vlahavas, I., Tsoukalas, I., Pombortsis, A.: Cultures in Negotiation: Teachers' Acceptance/Resistance Attitudes Considering the Infusion of Technology into Schools. Computers & Education 41(1), 19–37 (2003)
14. Demetriadis, S., Barbas, A., Psillos, D., Pombortsis, A.: Introducing ICT in the Learning Context of Traditional School: what is transformed and why. In: Vrasidas, C., Glass, V.G. (eds.) Current Perspectives on Applied Information Technologies II, pp. 99–116. Information Age Publishing, Charlotte (2004)
15. Jonassen, D.H., Hernandez-Serrano, J.: Case-Based Reasoning and Instructional Design: Using Stories to Support Problem Solving. ETR&D 50(2), 65–77 (2002)
16. Schön, D.A.: The Reflective Practitioner – How Professionals Think in Action. Basic Books, New York (1993)
17. Spiro, R.J., Jehng, J.: Cognitive flexibility and hypertext: Theory and technology for the non-linear and multidimensional traversal of complex subject matter. In: Nix, D., Spiro, R. (eds.) Cognition, Education, and Multimedia. Ehrlbaum, Hillsdale (1990)
18. Ge, X.: Scaffolding personnel' problem-solving processes on an ill-structured task using question prompts and peer interactions. Ph.D. Thesis. Pennsylvania State University, Philadelphia (2001)
19. Weinberger, A., Stegmann, K., Fischer, F., Mandl, H.: Scripting argumentative knowledge construction in computer-supported learning environments. In: Fischer, F., Kollar, I., Mandl, H., Haake, J. (eds.) Scripting computer-supported collaborative learning: Cognitive, computational and educational perspectives, pp. 191–211. Springer, New York (2007)

Thinking Style Diversity and Collaborative Design Learning

Antonio P.Volpentesta[1], Salvatore Ammirato[1], and Francesco Sofo[2]

[1] Department of Electronics, Computer Science and Systems, University of Calabria
via P. Bucci, 42\C, 87036 Rende (CS), Italy
{volpentesta,ammirato}@deis.unical.it
[2] Faculty of Education, University of Canberra ACT 2601
Australia
Francesco.Sofo@canberra.edu.au

Abstract. The paper explores the impact of structured learning experiences that were designed to challenge students' ways of thinking and promote creativity. The aim was to develop the ability of students, coming from different engineering disciplines and characterized by particular thinking style profiles, to collaboratively work on a project-based learning experience in an educational environment. Three project-based learning experiences were structured using critical thinking methods to stimulate creativity. Pre and post-survey data using a specially modified thinking style inventory for 202 design students indicated a thinking style profile of preferences with a focus on exploring and questioning. Statistically significant results showed students successfully developed empathy and openness to multiple perspectives.

Keywords: Thinking style, project-based learning, collaborative design.

1 Introduction

This paper introduces a Project-Based Learning (shortly, PBL) experience approach for collaborative product design learning. It is a methodological aid to develop the ability of students, coming from different engineering disciplines and characterized by different thinking style profiles, to collaboratively work on a PBL experience in an educational environment. The basic idea is that creativity is favored by knowledge spillovers and synergies of many student designers working in a process performed by a virtual group and a team coordinated by a teacher who plays the role of concept design manager. The virtual group works on generating ideas and solutions (in a divergent phase) that are successively evaluated by a team in a collaborative section (in a convergent phase) where a critical thinking method is applied.[1] The outcome of the

---

[1] According to Furst et al. (1999), we define a *group* as a "collection of individuals whose contributions to a product or a process are additive and can be collated and presented by a group manager as the result of group effort. Performance evaluation and accountability for a group will occur at the individual rather than the collective level"; we define a *team* as a "collection of individuals who interact more extensively than group members to produce a deliverable, who are evaluated based on the team outcome, and who are accountable as a team (instead of or in addition to individual accountability) for team outcomes"; we define a *virtual group* (or *virtual team*) as a group (respectively, team) whose members are geographically, temporally, and/or organizationally dispersed and brought together across time and space by way of information and communication technologies to accomplish an organizational task.

L.M. Camarinha-Matos et al. (Eds.): PRO-VE 2009, IFIP AICT 307, pp. 785–796, 2009.
© IFIP International Federation for Information Processing 2009

hypothesis tested and reported in this paper is that project-based learning (PBL) experiences increase the overall diversity of student self-reported thinking style preferences. Much of the literature on style of thinking maintains that styles are relatively fixed and difficult to change. Such variation, apparently in contrast with the literature in the field, is deeper analysed and results are reported and discussed as well.

2 Theoretical Background

It is widely recognized that a collection of differently skilled designers can, in principle, go beyond individual knowledge and reach new concept ideas because design problems are understood from different perspectives (Ivanitskaya et al., 2002; Alves et al., 2006). For this reason, many manufacturing companies are embracing collaborative concept design approaches in the early stages of their product design process that often require participation of individuals from different disciplines, e.g. electronics, software, mechanical, industrial and management engineering, in sharing knowledge, performing design tasks and organizing resources. Collaborative concept design refers to intensive collaboration among designers, who strive for and create a shared understanding of the product concept[2] (Volpentesta and Muzzupappa, 2006).

There exists a body of research literature suggesting that thinking style diversity between individuals involved in a collaborative work is fundamentally responsible for tension leading to conflict but at the same time provides the most effective creative solutions, (Kirton, 2006; Dorthy and Swap, 2005). Under an educational perspective one problem is to establish if and how experiential collaborative learning might affect thinking style (or rather thinking style preferences) diversity between student designers.

Design is both a practice and a way of thinking; experiential design in education gives an opportunity to engage learners in design as an activity and explicitly guide their intellectual process. Moreover, when student designers work collaboratively, not only do they learn technical content but they also develop intellectually in order to communicate their creative ideas and collaboratively apply that content in meaningful ways (Atman et al., 2008).

PBL is one of the more effective ways for students to learn design by experiencing design as active participants; it is a form of experiential learning where design projects are used as vehicles to motivate and integrate learning and it has turned out to be a major innovation in design pedagogy (Kolodner et al, 2005; Luxhol and Hanses, 1996). As a matter of fact, PBL experiences give student designers opportunities to improve their ability to work collaboratively, their communication skills and their

---

[2] In literature (Mamykina et al., 2002; Ulrich and Eppinger, 2003) a *product concept* is defined as a description of the form, function, and features of the product and is usually accompanied by a set of specifications, an analysis of competitive products, and an economic justification of the project; *concept development* is defined as the first phase in the product development process where the needs of the target market are identified, alternative product concepts are generated, and a single concept is selected for further development; *concept design* is defined as the work (task clarification, hypothesis formulation, solution searching,...) done, on a product concept by designers in the concept development phase in order to determine a product concept architecture.

design thinking, that is, how they think and embraces the heart of the design process by highlighting the creation, assessment, selection, and realization of ideas, (Ulrich and Eppinger, 2003; Dym et al., 2005). The attention to style of thinking comes from a keenness to optimize human use of intellectual and creative abilities within many work and life contexts. Adaptability leads to enhanced success so that optimizing performance may result from matching thinking style to the environment. Research findings on thinking styles provide a deeper understanding of the different ways in which people focus to make sense and use of the world. Different variables can have a coercive effect on one's style of thinking including one's family and workplace (Baker, 1968). The result of this is that people may choose to live and work in contexts that suit their style of thinking (Torbit, 1981; Sternberg, 1988). From the literature it is reasonable to conclude that thinking style impacts on performance.

Designers' creativity and diversity play a crucial role in collaborative processes. This is readily apparent when one considers that most creative pursuits in industry involve many individuals with various competencies working together to develop a product concept that cannot be created by a single individual alone (Mamykina et al., 2002) and that using creativity leverages the intelligence of different designers to tackle the complexity and uncertainty of a product concept generation[3]. Many researchers have looked at the issue of diversity as playing a key role in the collaborative development of a new product concept. Types of diversity frequently studied relate to gender, ethnicity, years of experience, technical discipline, Myers-Briggs type, and communication media (Hammond et al., 2005; Agogino et al, 2004; Reilly et al, 2002), but very few studies have specifically regarded thinking style diversity between designers engaged in product concept generation.

Thinking style bridges many domains including cognitive, affective, psychomotor, physiological, psychological and sociological realms. Style of thinking is first and foremost both cognitive and affective in essence. It is cognitive because information is processed; it is affective because one's feelings are involved in one's preferred way of thinking such as welcoming or avoiding various aspects such as authority, conformity, structure, ambiguity, reflectivity and impulsivity. In a more integral sense, style of thinking is 'affective' first and foremost since it refers to preferred thought processes, to the most comfortable ways of thinking. Thinking style has psychomotor and physiological dimensions because one's nervous system and senses are involved in how information is preferred to be perceived and processed. It is psychological because the choice includes preferential interaction of one's personality with the context. To the extent that the context is social, then style is also sociological because it is contingent on preferred crossing points with others. It is therefore evident that style of thinking is a social whole-person preference involving more than the brain alone but also one's creative sense of intuition and feeling. Style of thinking is independent from intelligence and there is some unexplained variation in the theory of intelligence (Sternberg, 1997). Style and ability may be at times confused as people may be thought to be incompetent because of lack of ability where in reality it is an inappropriate use of their ability in their preference for the way of thinking. Only a portion of

---

[3] According Farid-Foad et al. (1993) and Martins et al. (2003) we define creativity is the capacity to produce new and useful ideas, or the combination of existing ideas into new and useful concepts, to satisfy a need in a specified organizational context.

performance is attributed to intelligence, the rest is due to one's preferences for thinking and dealing with information and situations. Contemporary theories of thinking styles have been suggested to explain some of the variation. The theory of reality construction is a general theory that under-emphasizes the principles of societal or mental self-government (Sternberg, 1997) and focuses on dimensions of dependence, inquiry, multiple perspectives, autonomy and imagery (Sofo, 2005). The Thinking Styles Inventory (TSI) emanates from a theory of how people create their reality through their thinking and measures reported preferences for stylistic aspects of intellectual functioning. Inventories based on interviews have been used for comparative analysis in the fields of adult education, cognitive functioning and learning styles since a long time (Zhang and Stenberg, 2006). The name of the theory of reality construction emanates from constructivist theory, the idea that people actively construct their reality from their social interactions which are based on personally preferred ways of thinking. Interpersonal responses or interactions are based on how people like to think about problems. Sofo's (2005) theory of reality construction is a meta-cognitive perspective that underpins 5 styles of thinking. Some of these styles (Exploring, Independent and Creative) may be referred to as divergent thinking reflecting Zhang's (2002) category 1 thinking (Creative) while the Conditional and Inquiring categories are examples of convergent thinking and are similar to Zhang's category 2, concrete thinking. The styles also fit nicely into Zhang and Sternberg's (2005) intellectual styles model. The fives styles refer to how a person likes to accept, make sense of, and react to information, people and tasks. The theory maintains there are at least five mental styles (see Table 1) used in combination as a profile of styles in social interaction and in problem solving within different contexts. The relative response scores on each of the five styles produce a thinking style profile relevant to the particular individual.

Table 1. Summary of the five thinking styles on the TSI (Sofo, 2008)

1.	Conditional	Accepting what others think and say without questioning them
2.	Inquiring	Asking questions to improve understanding of message or information
3.	Exploring	Looking for alternatives and difference
4.	Independent	Allocating priority to one's own thinking
5.	Creative	Thinking in pictures to get a sense of the whole

A person with a particular preference in one circumstance may have a different inclination in another situation which means that people may be flexible and adaptive in their thinking. This also suggests that style of thinking is at least partly socialized because the environment can influence the style that a person prefers to use (Sternberg, 1997). It follows that the key assumption relevant in the development of the measurement of Sofo's theory is that people can be located within a blend of thinking preferences, ranging from conditional to creator, dependent on the characteristic mode in which they solve problems, create or make decisions. All thinking styles are potentially useful. The challenge is to utilize a style that works best for a person in each situation. A situation is dominated by the demands placed there by outside influences such as the law, social expectation, issues of safety and expediency. Other influences may include and demands of a profession, how those in charge of a situation expect subordinates to behave and pressures that individuals may impose on themselves.

De Bono's (1990) six colored hats method is a critical thinking method of organizing thinking patterns so that a person who is thinking can adopt a specific thinking style at any time, instead of having to try to combine all thinking styles at once. Multicolour printing is a useful analogy to explain these six thinking styles. Each color is printed in a separate step and in the final step, all the colors are combined. By analogy every person has the capacity for critical thinking by combining the expert use of all six styles of thinking (Johnson et al., 2007) used this method to design product concepts who reported a comparative study on the results of a competitive design project undertaken simultaneously by two multidisciplinary new product development teams.

3 The PBL Approach

Following the constructivist approach an educational environment is a (virtual and physical) microworld where students and teachers meet to work together, interacting with each other, using a variety of tools and sources of information that allow them to search for learning objectives and activities in order to solve problems. Different studies have shown that the setting-up of an educational environment within a classroom of student designers is the prerequisite for conducting a PBL experience (Dym et al, 2005; His and Agogino, 1994).

The educational environment should be constructed of at least four components (Volpentesta et al, 2008):

1. *Information sources:* Online and offline learning materials (books, encyclopedias, teacher's notes, digital libraries, etc.), lab software reference guides, people analysis documents.
2. *Technological infrastructure:* An integrated set of ICT tools which enables educational modalities, like manipulating and constructing symbols, accessing and searching for information, asynchronous and synchronous interacting with students and teachers, delivering immediate feedback and reports of student or team performance to the teacher.
3. *Simulation:* The implementation of a model of real situations by creating a learning context which drives the student to analyze, integrate, synthesize and apply basic knowledge for solving problems.
4. *Strategy:* A structured set of pedagogical activities that serves as a guide, a feedback sources and promotes learning.

For conducting a PBL experience, the following roles are taken into consideration in the educational environment:

1. *Concept Design Manager* (CDM), played by teacher;
2. *Creative Designer Group* (CDG), formed by some students in the classroom;
3. *Evaluation Designer Team* (EDT), formed by all students in the classroom.

Members of the CDGs, that may be geographically dispersed, are required to work independently on the creative problem solving task. To better carry out their tasks, student designers can use the available ICT tools and information sources. Members of the EDT interact face to face and work together in collaborative sessions to evaluate ideas/solutions developed by CDG members. To better manage and control activities and students performance within the educational environment there should be restricted to 20 students interacting at a time.

The PBL experience comprises a cascade of four stage-gates consisting of defining concept visions, functional schema, functional layouts and construction solutions for a digital mock-up of an innovative product (e.g. a device).

1. The first stage generates product concept visions (cs_i) in response to a request forwarded by the CDM to the student designers.
2. The second stage receives as input cs_i and generate functional schema fs_i related to each of them. The purpose of a functional scheme is to define the functional structure of the product, i.e. macro system components and their interactions.
3. The third stage receives as input fs_i and gives out functional layouts (fl_i) each of which specifies the preliminary layout ,i.e. mutual position of each sub-systems and their possible volumes, and principle solutions for each subsystem.
4. The fourth stage generates some constructive solutions (cs_i) with respect to selected fl_i.

Each stage is composed by five sequential steps developed as follows (see Table 2). In step 1, one or more requests for proposal (ideas or solutions) are transmitted by the CDM to the classroom. Each request contains the specification of the concept vision (for the first stage) or of one of the successful proposals selected by the CDM as output of the previous stage (for the stages after the first).

Table 2. Steps and roles in each stage

Steps in each stage	Roles
1 Launching call for proposals	CDM
2 Generating ideas/solutions	Each designer in a CDG
3 Collecting ideas/solutions	CDM
4 Evaluating ideas/solutions	Designers in the EDT
5 Ranking and selecting ideas/solutions	CDM

In step 2, "generating ideas/solutions" the requests are received by way of input; for each of them a CDG can be formed, thus each CDG consists of the student designers who autonomously choose to work independently on the same request for proposal. The output of this step is the set of original ideas/solutions that can be submitted by each student designer to the CDM. In forming a CDG, teachers neither define the group composition nor select a known leader. This is for two main reasons: first, many students do not possess the experience and skills required to be part of a successful team/group; second, as engineering educators, we are committed to furthering the educational growth of all our students in our course, not just the few talented ones who already possess the skills to succeed. Generating ideas and solutions is a divergent thinking activity aimed to stimulate creativity of independent student designers in order to obtain the larger number of innovative proposals. Such proposals are thus collected by the CDM during the "Collecting ideas/solutions" step 3 and assessed in a collaborative session, "evaluating ideas/solutions", by the EDT. To stimulate convergent thinking during this session, the EDT evaluates proposals collected by the CDM using De Bono's (1990) *six thinking hats method* and to submit such evaluations to the CDM. During the "ranking and selecting ideas/solutions" step 5, the CDM, on the basis of the evaluations of the previous step, ranks the proposals and selects the most suitable ones for successive development (the next stages) or for final teacher-student evaluation.

Each evaluation step consists of a collaboration session performed by the EDTs and is based on the De Bono's "six colored hats" method. In the application of this method we consider six colored sub-sessions. During each of them all members of an EDT metaphorically wear a hat of the same color of the sub-session. These hats indicate the type of thinking being used by EDT members and the type of contribution they are required to give (Volpentesta et al, 2008).

4 The Survey

The paper deals with the following research questions:

1. Can a PBL experience affect the diversity of student self-reported thinking style preferences?
2. Can the students involvement in some design situations induce a variation in some components of the self-reported thinking style preferences?

In order to answer these questions, we conducted a survey research on a sample of 202 students designers attending blending learning classrooms. Such sample was surveyed using a version of the Thinking Style Inventory (Sofo, 2008) specifically tailored to collaborative product design learning, the *CD-TSI*. The purpose of conducting the survey was to analyze the self-report of student designers with regard to changes in their thinking style preferences following the PBL experiences. To do so, pre-delivery and post-delivery data were collected and reported for each student in attendance.

Three PBL experiences where designed according to the proposed PBL approach; each experience consisted of selected activities developed over the course of a week-long intensive course and delivered to blended (virtual and traditional) classrooms of students designers. Surveyed students were all enrolled in engineering degree programs delivered at University of Calabria:

- a classroom of 12 students attending the "Industrial Design" course held in 2007/08. Such experience started from a proposal to generate a concept for "an innovative bookcase for a living room" (Volpentesta et al, 2008);
- a class of 110 students, divided in 6 classrooms of no more than 20 students each, attending the "Computer Aided Design" course held during 2005/06. The experience was based on the design of "a household electrical appliance for differentiated waste disposal" (Volpentesta et al., 2007);
- a class of 80 students, divided in 4 classrooms of 20 students each, attending the "Computer Aided Design" course held during 2004/05. The experience was based on the design of "an innovative vehicle to be used exclusively in shopping centers, airports or campuses". Main characteristics of the methodology and the depicted scenario are presented in Volpentesta and Muzzupappa (2006).

Each classroom has been regarded as an educational environment where product concept design has been developed; the teacher played the role of CDM and concept buyer/user, while students acted as CDG/EDT members.

4.1 The Concept Design – Thinking Style Inventory (CD-TSI)

The fifty items on the CD-TSI require respondents to think about their ways of designing during ten typical design situations (see Appendix 1). The situations proposed to respondents are strictly connected with the stages of a design process (questions 2, 4, 5, 9), with the approach of designers to collaboration (1, 3, 10) and with each personal way of designing (6, 7, 8). Without reflection about their own personal designing processes, subjects would not be able to complete the inventory. In each situation, the meta-thinking process is structured for respondents since they need to reflect in a comparative mode on their ways of designing. Respondents are asked to rank order their preferred ways of designing, pitting five alternative thinking behaviours against each other on each of the ten proposed design situations to determine their overall designing style profile. Each item has five alternatives using a likert-scale from 1 to 5 where 1 signifies designing behaviour that is 'least like me' and 5 signifies 'most like me'. Each of the five alternatives on each of the ten items must be ranked in order of preference. The set of the five sums of values on each column of the inventory (the scores) represents the thinking style profile for each student in the sample. Calculated scores for each individual can be interpreted according to instructions established by Zhang and Sternberg (2006) to identify patterns of thinking styles for individuals and groups. The CD-TSI was indirectly validated by relying on the validity of the Sofo's TSI (Sofo, 2005): a PBL test experience was preliminarily conducted on a classroom of 30 students gathering data with both the CD-TSI and the Sofo's TSI; students' profiles turned out to be similar in both cases.

5 Results and Discussion

In order to address the research hypothesis, pre-experience and post-experience means were calculated for students' thinking style profiles and then statistically analysed through ANOVA techniques and relative standard deviation (shortly RSD, i.e. the standard deviation expressed as a percentage of the mean). The use of such techniques is largely consolidated in scientific literature in the field (Sofo, 2008; Sternberg, 1997).

ANOVA data show no statistically significant differences between the pre-experience and post-experience means on the five thinking styles thus confirming the null hypothesis at 95% confidence level. Table 3 indicates pre-experience and post-experience mean values for each component of the thinking style profile. Standard deviations and range of given values are reported in Table 3 as well. To measure the degree by which data tend to spread from the mean, the RSD is reported as measure of dispersion for each mean value.

The result indicates similar average profiles for both the pre and post-experience data. The thinking style profile of the design students can generally be described as a high preference for seeking multiple perspectives and asking questions (exploring and inquiring preferences had the highest means). The scores on preferences for independence and creativity were also similar while the least preferred thinking style was the conditional style which means that students least prefer to conform to existing models and principles when doing design work.

Table 3. Pre and post experience descriptive statistics for CD-TSI

		Conditional	Inquiring	Exploring	Independent	Creative
Pre-experience	Mean	25.500	33.500	34.333	28.750	27.833
	Standard Deviation	5.962	6.142	3.798	5.101	7.530
	Range	18	21	11	19	25
	RSD (%)	23.38	18.33	11.06	17.74	27.05
Post-experience	Mean	26.750	33.833	32.500	30.000	26.917
	Standard Deviation	8.946	7.791	5.760	6.223	8.372
	Range	25	24	21	19	22
	RSD (%)	33.44	23.03	17.72	20.74	31.1

However overall results of statistical analyses of pre and post-survey data show an increase of diversity of thinking style preferences in terms of relative standard deviation from the mean value of each thinking style in the CD-TSI (this seems to affirmatively answer the first research question).

For what regards the second research question, analyses has been conducted on all items of the CD-TSI in order to reveal possibly changes in the preferences of thinking styles during particular design situations. In this sense, ANOVA tests reveal a change in the preferences of thinking styles reported by students engaged in PBL experiences. Statistically significant differences were found on 5 of the 50 CD-TSI items tested and related to two of the ten proposed situations. The two situations are: "How do you think when clarifying a design task?" and "How do you think when debating and evaluating ideas/solutions?" ANOVA confirms that these differences are significant at $p<0.05$ (see Table 4).

Table 4. Differences in thinking style preferences (pre and post experience)

How do you think when...				
Situation	**Thinking preferences**	**Pre-experience Mean value**	**Post-experience Mean value**	**Sig.**
clarifying a design task?	I define and offer my personal idea on the task (independent)	4.17	2.09	.03
	I accept others' proposals (conditional)	2.01	3.74	.0164
debating and evaluating ideas/solutions?	I offer my personal evaluation (independent)	4.42	1.75	.049
	I ask questions to better understand idea's meanings and others' evaluations on it (exploring)	2.17	3.73	.0248
	I tend to be affected by others' evaluations (conditional)	2.33	3.42	.031

The close clustering of significance in interesting since statistical significance occurs at both ends of the design process, the clarification and evaluation phases. The academic instructors emphasised the critical importance of the beginning and concluding phases of design stressing that they are the critical moments or tipping-point opportunities for significant creativity to occur. In particular De Bono's (1990) six thinking hats strategy was employed consistently during these stages of the simulations to ensure an emphasis on multiple perspectives.

The obtained results don't necessary imply a change in student thinking style profile, but they show that a PBL experience where students act as real designers during a collaborative design project can contribute to increase the awareness in their thinking styles. In this sense, results are not in contrast to what is said in literature ("thinking styles are relatively fixed and difficult to change").

6   Conclusion

In this paper we have investigated the impact of PBL experiences on thinking styles of students engaged in collaborative product design. Results show that a PBL experience can help the meta-cognitive process of highlighting personal thinking styles during design. Our initial exploratory study gives optimism for the education of design students as it points to some success in teaching openness to multiple perspectives and the cultivation of an open mind as the basis for creativity. A future study could evaluate the creativity of the design products of students who have experienced creative simulations with the products of a control group.

Acknowledgements

The authors thank Prof. Maurizio Muzzupappa for his meaningful contribution in designing and conducting the PBL experiences.

References

1. Agogino, A.M., Newman, C., Bauer, M., Mankoff, J.: Perceptions of the Design Process: An Examination of Gendered Aspects of New Product Development. Int. J. Engineering Education 20(3), 452–460 (2004)
2. Alves, J., Marques, M.J., Saur, I., Marques, P.: Building creative ideas for successful new product development. In: Stasiak, M.K., Buijs, J. (eds.) Transformations. Wyzsza Szkola Humanistyczno-Ekonomiczna w Lodzi, pp. 363–383 (2006)
3. Atman, C.J., Kilgore, D., McKenna, A.: Characterizing Design Learning: A Mixed-Methods Study of Engineering Designers' Use of Language. J. of Engineering Education 97(3), 309–326 (2008)
4. Baker, R.: Ecological psychology: concepts and methods for studying the environment of human behavior. Stanford University Press, Stanford (1968)
5. Dorthy, L.B., Swap, W.C.: When Sparks Fly: Harnessing the Power of Group Creativity. Harvard Business School Press (2005)
6. Dym, C.L., Agogino, A.M., Eris, O., Frey, D.D., Leifer, L.J.: Engineering Design Thinking, Teaching, and Learning. J. Engineering Education 94, 103–120 (2005)
7. Furst, S., Blackburn, R., Rosen, B.: Virtual team effectiveness: a proposed research agenda. Inf. Systems J. 9, 249–269 (1999)

8. His, S., Agogino, A.M.: The Impact and Instructional Benefit of Using Multimedia Case Studies to Teach Engineering Design. J. Ed. Hypermedia and Multimedia 3(3-4), 351–376 (1994)
9. Ivanitskaya, L., Clark, D., Montgomery, G., Primeau, R.: Interdisciplinary Learning: Process and Outcomes. Inn. Higher Edu. 27(2), 95–111 (2002)
10. Hammond, J.M., Harvey, C.M., Koubek, R.J., Compton, W.D., Darisipudi, A.: Distributed Collaborative Design Teams: Media Effects on Design Processes. International Journal of Human-Computer Interaction 18(2), 145–165 (2005)
11. Kirton, M.J.: Adaption-Innovation, In the context of diversity and change (Rev. ed.). Routledge, London (2006)
12. Kolodner, J.L., Crismond, D., Fasse, B., Gray, J., Holbrook, J., Puntembakar, S.: Putting a Student-Centered Learning by DesignTM Curriculum into Practice: Lessons Learned. Journal of the Learning Sciences 12(4) (2003)
13. Johnson, P., Griffiths, R., Gill, S.: The 24 hr product: from concept to interactive model in less than a day. Int. J. Design Engineering 1(1), 56–70 (2007)
14. Luxhol, J.T., Hansen, P.H.K.: Engineering Curriculum Reform at Aalborg. Journal of Engineering Education 85(3), 83–84 (1996)
15. Mamykina, L., Candy, L., Edmonds, E.: Collaborative Creativity. Communication of the ACM 45(10), 96–99 (2002)
16. Reilly, R.R., Lynn, G.S., Aronson, Z.L.: The Role of Personality in New Product Development Team Performance. Journal of Engineering & Technology Management 19(1), 39–58 (2002)
17. Sofo, F.: Thinking styles of modern Chinese leaders: independence and exploration in an historically conditional China. Aus. J. Adult Learning 45(3), 304–330 (2005)
18. Sofo, F.: Differences of degree or differences in kind? A comparative analysis of thinking styles. Int. J. Interdisciplinary Social Sc. 3(1), 293–301 (2008)
19. Sternberg, R.: Mental self-government: a theory of intellectual styles and their development. Human Development 31, 197–224 (1988)
20. Sternberg, R.: Thinking styles. Cambridge University Press, Cambridge (1997)
21. Torbit, G.: Counselor learning style: a variable in career choice. Canadian Counselor 15, 193–197 (1981)
22. Ulrich, K.T., Eppinger, S.D.: Product Design and Development. McGraw-Hill, New York (2003)
23. Volpentesta, A.P., Muzzupappa, M., Ammirato, S.: Critical thinking and concept design generation in a collaborative network. In: Camarinha-Matos, L., Picard, W. (eds.) Pervasive Collaborative Networks, vol. 16, pp. 157–164. Springer, Heidelberg (2008)
24. Volpentesta, A.P., Muzzupappa, M., Della Gala, M.: Managing collaborative creativity for product concept design. In: Rapaccini, M., Visintin, F. (eds.) Proceedings of 9th Int. Conf. on MITIP, Florence, Italy, pp. 110–117 (2007)
25. Volpentesta, A.P., Muzzupappa, M.: Identifying partners and organizational logical structures for collaborative conceptual design. In: Camarinha-Matos, L., Afsarmanesh, H., Ollus, M. (eds.) Network-Centric Collaboration and Supporting Frameworks, vol. 224, pp. 397–406. Springer, Boston (2006)
26. Zhang, L.F., Sternberg, R.J.: A threefold model of intellectual styles. Educational Psychology Review 17(1), 1–53 (2005)
27. Zhang, L.F., Sternberg, R.J.: The nature of intellectual styles. Routledge (2006)
28. Zhang, L.F.: Thinking styles and cognitive development. The Journal of Genetic Psychology 163(2), 179–195 (2002)

Appendix: Concept Design Thinking Style Inventory (CD-TSI)

Situation: "How do you think when…"	1	2	3	4	5
1 formulating a design problem?	I prefer to apply known and proven principles and models	I need to follow a question- driven approach	I consider many options in formulating	I likes to be different, I prefer my own approach	I prefer a heuristic approach rather than an algorithmic one
2 searching for a concept vision?	More likely to build on ideas of others, less interest in being original or inventive	I focalize on questions about objectives and requirements of the product	I enjoy dealing with several ideas at once, I divide attention between competing visions	I prefer to search a concept vision alone, less consulting with others on views	I value originality, I likes to play with ideas and to be imaginative
3 clarifying a design task?	I tend to reveal "facts" rather than possibilities that can be created form them	I ask questions about task's objectives, constraints and limitations	I like to investigate all possibilities already on the table	I define and offer my personal ideas on the task rather than to be affected by others' view	I need to visualize possible task's output through sketches and preliminary drawings
4 designing product functionality?	I prefer to work on well defined and well understood product functionality	I inquire into main functional aspects of the product design	I look for functionality with respect to many different use contexts	I rely on my intuition and my problem solving skill	I look for original and unusual product functionality
5 designing product shape and geometry?	I focus on past experience relying on similarities with known artefacts	I ask "what if?" questions to come up with design proposals	I feel comfortable raising alternative shapes and geometries	I tend to minimize distractions to cope with difficulties in designing	I look for original and unusual shapes and geometries
6 retrieving knowledge for a design task?	I rely on other designers' knowledge to complement mine	I inquire into which and where useful knowledge can be	I consider multiple reservoirs of expertise that can be tapped	I rely on knowledge "inside my box" which can be accessed by myself	I am challenged to reject the use of routine knowledge and what is obvious
7 looking for perspectives or use contexts?	I value views and opinions of others, I rely on others' contributions	I question proposals and assumptions other designers rest on	I prefer to explore many ideas to depict different use scenarios	I focus on creating a personal perspective on the base of some usage scenarios	I broaden my thought process, even if it could be more easily distractible
8 searching for product experience/emotions?	more focused on others' emotional/experiential issues	I inquire which feelings strongly influence our perceptions	I investigate various emotional reactions influenced by the product	less interested in dealing with others' emotional/experiential issues	I value unusual emotional reactions
9 searching for a solution to assemble product components?	More likely to change my solutions to suit different situations proposed by others	I ask questions correlated with performance in obtaining design solutions	I try to explore many different solutions in designing components interfaces	Less likely to change or adapt my solutions to situations proposed by others	I follow side thoughts and I increase the tolerance for minor difficulties in designing interfaces
10 debating and evaluating ideas/solutions :	I tend to readily accept the first plausible option	I feel comfortable when all objections and questions are answered	I prefer to consider the full range of options	I look for good reasons to defend my position and possibly persuade others	I like to imagine ideas/solutions within future use context

Part **25**

Collaborative Educational Networks - II

Collaborative Networking for the Development of Quality in Education at University Level

Anni Rytkönen[1] and Taina Kaivola[2]

[1] University of Helsinki, Educational Centre for ICT, P.O. Box 53, FIN-00014
University of Helsinki, Finland
[2] University of Helsinki, Faculty of Science, P.O. Box 68, FIN-00014
University of Helsinki, Finland
{Anni.Rytkonen,Taina.Kaivola}@Helsinki.FI

Abstract. At the University of Helsinki there are two collaborative networks of expertise leading and supporting the development of teaching: the senior lecturers in university pedagogy and the e-learning specialist network. Both networks are based on the guidelines in the university Programme for the development of teaching and studies for the strategy period 2007-2009. The strategic goals, organization and working methods of these two networks are described as examples of overall quality improvement through competence development of the teaching personnel. The paper contributes also to the evaluation of actual, perceived development at the end of the strategy period. The best practices of these networks are summarized as ideal structures supporting the continuous educational development work at universities.

Keywords: Educational Development, Higher Education, E-learning, University Pedagogy, Collaboration, Collaborative Networking, Peer Networking.

1 Introduction and Strategic Grounds

During the last years, emphasis of quality in teaching, learning outcomes and student achievement in higher education has increased. This is due to several reasons, of which meeting the needs of trends and phenomena of the modern information society is among the most important ones. At the University of Helsinki, the strong emphasis on teaching and support of development of pedagogical skills of the academic teaching personnel raises from strategic grounds [3,6]. One of the most visible decisions of this emphasis is the establishment of a network of pedagogical senior lecturers, which form the core of personnel developers at the university. As team members with the senior lecturers there are e-learning specialists, who similarly with the senior lecturers form their own university-wide network of expertise.

University of Helsinki is a research-based university, among the biggest multidisciplinary universities in Northern Europe. The university concentrates on high quality research covering a wide range of academic fields [2]. The 11 faculties at the University of Helsinki are located on four campus areas in the city and suburban area of Helsinki. Both senior lecturers in university pedagogy and e-learning specialists are located distributed on all campuses, which makes networking and collaboration challenging at the

L.M. Camarinha-Matos et al. (Eds.): PRO-VE 2009, IFIP AICT 307, pp. 799–805, 2009.

university level. To find out the needs, methods and partners for collaboration in a peer network of expertise, a survey on the e-learning specialist work was conducted.

The quality of teaching and learning has a significant role at the University of Helsinki. For example, the university enhances the personnel's pedagogical skills by providing personnel training in university pedagogy. In practice, the responsibility of this task rests predominantly on the two specialist networks.

"The pool of university lectureships in higher education will be restructured so that each faculty will be allocated one professorship from this pool to support the development of teaching. The Academic Affairs Committee will prepare a procedure whereby the pool resources and the competence of the post holders can be used for supporting the development of teaching as efficiently and permanently as possible."

"Faculties and departments will work as teams to plan the production processes of online teaching. The faculties will implement online teaching more efficiently, and their educational technology advisors will support and participate in cooperation across faculty and university boundaries." [3, pages 93 and 96]

In this paper, possibilities and ideals in structures and methods for organised and goal-oriented collaboration through coordinated networking are discussed. First, working methods and duties of both specialist networks are explained. Structures and methods for goal-oriented collaboration, based on survey material, are presented, and finally, some future perspectives concerning the development of the structures for collaboration in and between these kinds of specialized networks are discussed.

2   Networks Supporting Educational Development

2.1   The E-Learning Specialist Network

The e-learning specialist network consists of specialists in subfields of educational technology and e-learning. They are located on the campuses in the faculties and departments, in both full-time and part-time positions with duties concerning pedagogical cases of the use of web-based tools and educational technology.

Because further information on tasks, needs and work loads of the network members was needed, a survey by means of a web-based questionnaire was conducted. With the survey results, the overall situation on e-learning support at the university level could also be evaluated. Based on the survey, the e-learning specialists at the University of Helsinki can be profiled into two main types: 1) full-time support, planning and development, typically at the faculty level, collaborating in the same team with other educational developers and 2) support at the departments, provided full- or part-time.

The results of the survey emphasize the importance of having e-learning specialists at the faculty level, and the role of knowledge development through networking for all e-learning specialists. The main duties of the e-learning specialists include planning and developmental duties. They use time also for own knowledge development, studies and personnel training, peer activities, such as networking. Own research is non-typical for both faculty and departmental specialists. Tasks more typical to e-learning specialists in faculties than at departments include pedagogical personal counselling for teachers and offering personnel training, while the work load of the part-time specialists at the departments include tasks through their main duties, such as teaching. There are also tasks that have small roles in the whole work load but do not promote the development of (web-based) teaching either – e.g. IT support.

Both types of support personnel, the developers at the faculties and the departmental contact persons, are needed to ensure both the e-learning viewpoint in the systematic development of teaching and learning, and the instant support in daily teaching routines. At the moment, the faculties at the University of Helsinki provide one of these two types of support: the network members are mostly one per faculty or one per department.

The group activities of the network have been formed during the current strategy period. The developmental needs and interests are worked out in brainstorms twice a year, after which the coordinator analyses the results and makes a proposition for the following period. The proposition is discussed with the members and published on the web-based working areas. The needs become concrete in group meetings and personnel training, and subjects for further development. The work is an ongoing, iterative process with academic term cycles, constant interaction between the coordinator and the network, using collaborative working methods. This activity of the network is coordinated at the Educational Centre for ICT, who is responsible for the training and support services in the use of ICT in teaching and for coordinating the development of online teaching at the University of Helsinki [3, page 94].

2.2 The Network of Senior Lecturers in University Pedagogy

Each of the faculties has one senior lecturer in university pedagogy. The members of the network are responsible for the systematic development of teaching and learning methods in their faculties. Also, their tasks include conducting research related to the field of university pedagogy. The senior lecturers provide courses in university pedagogy, and cooperate in various subject courses in their faculties. They form a network of expertise, discussing topical developmental challenges in education at the university level.

The Helsinki University Centre for Research and Development of Higher Education [7], a unit concentrating on the university pedagogical matters, acts in the co-operation with the senior lecturers in university pedagogy in matters of educational development. The centre is in charge of the degree programme of the studies in university pedagogy provided for the personnel and PhD students. The elementary course is organized regularly not only in the Centre but also on every campus area. These science-based university pedagogy courses offer the personnel an opportunity to identify and foster awareness and understanding of the special features of teaching and instruction approaches of the faculty disciplines.

In their faculties, the lecturers are also in charge of the curriculum development at a degree level, organizing and supporting study guidance. They participate in faculty strategic planning and implementing the strategy of the university in the disciplines of the departments. In some of the faculties, the senior lecturers in university pedagogy are heads of the research and development unit in higher education in their faculty, and all of them are leading pedagogical advisers and experts in their home faculties.

The university has acted upon the recommendation from external evaluations by establishing and funding senior lecturers in pedagogy and encouraging the development of a particular centre for research and development of higher education. The present outcome of this development was highly appreciated by the panellists evaluating the leadership and management of education last year [5].

The university strategy focuses on the learner-centred approach [1]. This principle has been expanded to a teaching evaluation matrix, which is available university-wide. At the moment, an increasing number of academic teaching personnel has pedagogic training.

According to the recent international evaluators, the decision to locate senior lecturers in university pedagogy at the faculties is an excellent example of good practice at the university level [5].

3 Structures and Methods for Organized and Goal-Oriented Collaboration

3.1 Organizational Support

Many e-learning specialist network members named their educational development team and especially the senior lecturer in university pedagogy as the most important collaboration partners in the survey. In fact, those e-learning specialists, who work in faculties, work in teams and collaborate, and those who work at departments, do not have teams. In feedback discussions, the senior lecturers shared the same positive opinions of peer collaboration as the e-learning specialists. They emphasised the need for colleagues in everyday work in faculties not yet having a unit of pedagogical support. Most lecturers indicated that the peer network provides a valuable collegial environment enhancing further development.

In faculties with educational development teams, the collaboration between the specialists in e-learning and the senior lecturers in university pedagogy forms an essential part of the daily activities. For example, improving and developing the student feedback systems is one of the constant fields of collaboration of the specialists. Motivating the teaching personnel to modern working methods including web-based environments needs both effort and knowledge from the two collaborating experts. In many faculties the specialist in e-learning is co-operating with the lecturer in organising and teaching during the basic course in university pedagogy. Teacher cafés and other regular gatherings of the personnel are often organized by a group of these faculty experts.

"Campuses and faculties may establish their own units for developing and supporting teaching. The University will consolidate its common, centrally funded services in the long term, which will allow the faculties to create their own services and thus supplement the University-wide services as they wish.",
"Faculties and departments will work as teams to plan the production processes of online teaching. The faculties will implement online teaching more efficiently [...]"
and
"The University will coordinate the provision of centralised support services for teaching on the campuses based on the faculties' target programmes and user needs."
[3, pages 93–95]

Most faculties at the University of Helsinki have the described team structure for the continuous and systematic educational development, but not all of them have built-in organisational units. We recommend, that the organisational structure is official with own budgeting, being positioned at the faculty office under the dean or vice dean responsible for educational matters, like presented in Figure 1. The team includes the senior lecturer as head and the e-learning specialist and teaching planning officers as members building a meaningful combination. Furthermore, we suggest that the departments have their part-time e-learning contact persons who collaborate with the faculty educational development team and especially with the e-learning specialist.

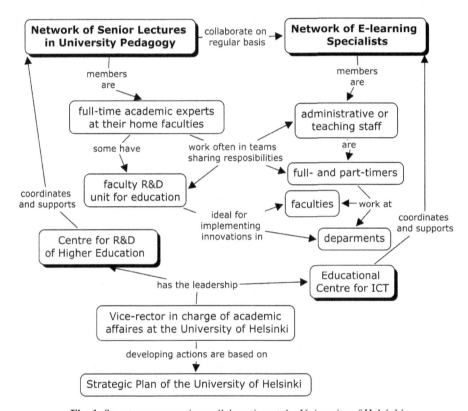

Fig. 1. Structures supporting collaboration at the University of Helsinki

3.2 Peer Networking across the Organizational Structure

The strength of both the e-learning specialist network and the senior lecturer network is considered being in networking to peers. The e-learning specialist network is considered active and the coordinator listens to the needs of the network. The activities support both the members' duties and professional development. Mailing lists, blog entries, micro blogging and instant messaging are actively used as information and discussion channels, the tool being selected based on the information contents and required audience. The information also reaches the designed audience. The network has used a wiki space for collaborative document processing.

The contact networks, including both official cooperation partners and personal contacts, inside the university are available for and used by the specialists when needed. Interest for further contacts was mentioned to other national actors, such as corresponding support networks in other universities. Actually, this kind of supporting structure is quite unique in Finland. There is a national network, which consists of one contact person per university, but there has been almost no activity for some years now.

Since the field of educational technology is under constant development and there is a constant pressure for development of competences and awareness of peer competences, the role of the e-learning specialist network in peer support, learning and development is emphasized. The network is compared to a real-world safety net and the members to trapeze artists balancing on the wire; you can always count on the net, so you dare to try things that you otherwise would not dare. The e-learning specialist network members described the meaning of the peer collaboration in four different ways:

1) Backup; thank you for being there!
2) Increasing awareness on peer knowledge and skills, and contextual information about the university
3) knowledge and skills exchange in concrete support tasks and training
4) Peer discussion support in problematic situations, coping.

To make the increase in awareness, knowledge and skills possible, activities and discussions must be regular. To ensure both regularity and a meaningful goal-oriented scope in the activity, the networks must be coordinated. The coordinator listens to the network and, based on the needs, selects the topics and plans the contents for advanced and specified personnel training, using meaningful web-based collaboration tools for goal-oriented knowledge development of the network members. This coordination must be funded by university central means.

3.3 Knowledge Transfer through Networking

The knowledge gained through the peer network of expertise is transferred to the home organisations of the network members as best practices and ideas for (online) teaching. The information channels are either public like the blog or free for anyone to register to, like Skype and Yammer. Via the public, web-based knowledge repositories the knowledge of the members of the network is turned to knowledge of the whole network.

"[... The] educational technology advisors will support and participate in cooperation across faculty and university boundaries." and

"Cooperation in the provision of support services for the use of ICT in teaching will be intensified between the providers of centralised support services and faculties and other parties. The support service processes will be defined, and responsibilities and roles will be specified." [3, pages 95–96]

The e-learning specialists are central actors in their communities dominating and sharing knowledge on e-learning and educational technology [4]. To enhance the possibilities for the e-learning specialists to work across the university, we suggest that there are commonly agreed duties for the network members, like there are for the senior lecturers, and this university-wide collaboration is included in them. The e-learning specialists are at the moment employed by the faculties and departments, which naturally targets the duties to the organisation in question, while the senior lecturer salaries are paid by the university central administration though they work at the faculties.

4 Future Perspectives

The two collaborative networks of expertise, the e-learning specialists and the senior lecturers in university pedagogy, are examples of best practices for the development of teaching at university level, when they work at best. The continuous development processes have to be supported both vertically with organizational structures and horizontally with coordination of knowledge development in peer networks. The overall situation at the University of Helsinki at the end of the strategy period 2007-2009 is good but not systematically implemented through the structures with faculties and departments. The recommended structures are already there in most faculties, but not all.

The best practices of one of the networks could be implemented also in the other one. The e-learning specialists are coordinated for professional development and awareness increase and web-based environments supporting collaboration in the physically distributed network are actively in use. The senior lecturers are centrally funded and have commonly agreed duties including university-wide participation in the development of education.

As research is multidisciplinary, the university strategy aims at enhancing multidisciplinary collaboration also in teaching (Strategic plan of University of Helsinki, 2006). The two networks working with development of education are the key persons in making this strategic goal reality.

References

1. Biggs, J., Tang, C.: Teaching for Quality Learning at University, 3rd edn. The Society for Research into Higher Education. Open University Press, London (2007)
2. University of Helsinki in Brief. Helsinki, Helsinki University Print (2008),
   http://www.helsinki.fi/inbrief/inbrief.html (retrieved 2.4.2009)
3. Programme for the development of teaching and studies 2007-2009. Helsinki, Helsinki University Print, In English, pp. 71–102 (2006),
   http://www.helsinki.fi/opetus/materiaali/
   Opetuksen%20ja%20opintojen%20kehitt_ohjelma%202007-2009.pdf
   (retrieved 9.2.2009)
4. Ryymin, E.: Teachers' Intelligent Networks. Study on Relationship-based Professional Development Supported by Collaborative Learning Technologies. PhD Thesis, Acta Electronica Universitatis Tamperensis 751 (2008),
   http://acta.uta.fi/haekokoversio.php?id=11101 (retrieved 3.4.2009)
5. Saari, S., Frimodig, M. (eds.): Leadership and Management of Education. Evaluation of Education at the University of Helsinki 2007-2008. Administrative Publications 58, Evaluations. Helsinki University Print, Helsinki (2008)
6. Strategic Plan of the University of Helsinki 2007–2009. Helsinki University Print, In English, pp. 57–80 (2006),
   http://www.helsinki.fi/tutkinnonuudistus/materiaalit/
   strategia2007-2009.pdf (retrieved 3.4.2009).
7. The Helsinki University Centre for Research and Development of Higher Education (2009),
   http://www.helsinki.fi/ktl/yty/english/index.htm (retrieved 10.6.2009)

Provision of Training for the IT Industry:
The ELEVATE Project

Iraklis Paraskakis[1,4], Andreas Konstantinidis[1], Thanassis Bouras[2], Kostas Perakis[2],
Stelios Pantelopoulos[3], and Thanos Hatziapostolou[4]

[1] South East European Research Centre (SEERC), Research Centre of the
University of Sheffield and CITY College,
24 Pr. Koromila Str, 54622 Thessaloniki, Greece
[2] UBITECH Research,
429 Messogion Ave., Ag. Paraskevi Square, 15343 Athens, Greece
[3] SingularLogic, S.A
Al. Panagouli & Siniosoglou, N. Ionia 142 34 Athens, Greece
[4] Department of Computer Science, CITY College, International Faculty of the
University of Sheffield,
13 Tsimiski Str, 54622 Thessaloniki, Greece
{iparaskakis,ankonstantinidis}@seerc.org,
{bouras,kperakis}@ubitech.eu, spantelopoulos@singularlogic.eu,
a.hatziapostolou@city.acdemic.gr

Abstract. This paper will present ELEVATE that aims to deliver an innovative training, educational and certification environment integrating the application software to be taught with the training procedure. ELEVATE aspires to address the training needs of software development SMEs and the solution proposed is based on three basic notions: to provide competence training that is tailored to the needs of the individual trainee, to allow the trainee to carry out authentic activities as well as problem based learning that draws from real life scenarios and finally to allow for the assessment and certification of the skills and competences acquired. In order to achieve the desired results the ELEVATE architecture utilises an *Interactive Interoperability Layer, an Intelligent Personalization Trainer as well as the Training, Evaluation & Certification* component. As an end product, the ELEVATE project The ELEVATE pedagogical model is based on blended learning, the e-Training component (an intelligent system that provides tailored training) and Learning 2.0.

Keywords: Competence training, blended learning, authentic learning, problem based learning, pedagogical methodology and model for training.

1 Introduction

There are currently some 22 million SMEs across Europe employing almost 120 million people and contributing 57 per cent of pan-European gross domestic product. However, the European enterprises suffer particularly from personnel provided with updated technological skills and are poorly informed and/or interested in professional

L.M. Camarinha-Matos et al. (Eds.): PRO-VE 2009, IFIP AICT 307, pp. 806–815, 2009.

training opportunities with which they could increase their know-how assets. In addition, the professional training programs that both SMEs and professionals resort to are not always the most suitable.

Moreover, the introduction of multi-oriented, separate application software (e.g. ERP and CRM) and vendor-driven solutions, which increases the complexity of systems installation, customization, administration and use, making the support of these systems a challenging task, extends the IT gap across the enlarged Europe, consisting of both a competence gap in the existing workforce as well as a shortage of available certified professionals.

The ELEVATE environment aspires to be a hybrid training and certification environment, which integrates the application software to be taught in a pedagogical-documented educational process, allowing the software development SMEs to deliver innovative e-training services and to address the needs of their business partners and customers. Moreover, ELEVATE anticipates to deliver technology know-how in the fields of e-learning, educational content aggregation and material creation, learning management system and application software integration, and pedagogic standards and models.

In the following sections, we present the background knowledge and rationale on which the proposition of the ELEVATE environment is to be based. Following that we elaborate upon the project objectives, as well as aspects of the expected results. Finally, we discuss the current state of the project and conclude by indicating future steps and work.

2   ELEAVATE's Rationale and Objectives

In this section, we justify the conceptualization of the ELEVATE project by presenting the background information which was studied and considered prior to its conception. Through this discussion, we rationalize the necessity of such a project and present the vision and end goals of the project members.

2.1   Provision of Training in the IT Sector: Background

The rapid structural changes in the software industry, comprising mostly of software development SMEs, that deliver and introduce new technologies and application software in the workplace, produce a shift of employment realities. These realities, in turn, require updated application software competencies and technological skills. The same circumstances result in the need for people to recognise that they cannot rely on earning their living in a particular occupation throughout their life, and must increasingly take responsibility for acquiring updated, and often quite different, application software skills as their career progresses.

Training in application software tools and systems has gained from the outset a central position in e-learning activities, particularly in the corporate world, as the software development SMEs who developed these innovative technology applications were the first to realize the use of e-learning and e-training for covering educational needs in their field. Nevertheless, this rather long history in application software training and e-learning has not been fruitful enough, as it has not been accompanied by a corresponding lead at the level of pedagogic quality of this training. What is essentially absent – as the software development SMEs are not capable of providing - from current application software training and e-learning, is the explicit selection of educational approaches which treat the application-to-be-learned as a tool for everyday use, for the learning of which, as has always been the case with human tools, the trainee should sit at the feet of an experienced user of the tool, having the opportunity as an apprentice not just to observe, but mainly to try, interact and participate.

More specifically, the implementation of the application software training is currently based on the simple demonstration of the application to be taught, and on the descriptive analytical presentation of the functionalities of the software application, or on the interaction with a simulation application of the application software to be taught giving the end-user a limited feeling of how the application is used in real life conditions. Besides this weakness, another result is that the learning content integrated with current e-learning systems is costly and static, and, in case of IT software upgrade should be redesigned and recreated.

We claim that e-learning and e-training in application software in conjunction with sophisticated educational approaches and pedagogic models have the potential to become the locomotives in driving growth and creating more and better jobs in Europe. Towards this direction, ELEVATE aspires to introduce a highly innovative combination of services aiming to enable enterprises and organizations to drive productivity through learning content management, knowledge sharing, assessment, rapid authoring, and performance support.

The vision ELEVATE is to leverage e-learning, interoperability and pedagogical know-how into the training services of the software SMEs, in order to elevate the quality of the existing application software products of the software SMEs. Moreover, through the ELEVATE solution software SMEs will be able to provide their clients as well as their business partners and individuals (i.e. professionals and application software users) with a holistic e-learning, educational process monitoring and certification environment adjustable to each application software for training the end-user in realistic conditions.

2.2 ELEVATE's Objectives

To accomplish the vision mentioned above, the ELEVATE project has a three-fold focus that will be achieved through the following research and innovation related activities:

* *Objective I*
  to interactively integrate and fruitfully combine the application software to be taught with the personalised training and educational procedure, providing real-time interoperability and interaction with the e-learning environment in the scope of training process improvement and efficient monitoring of the trainee.

* *Objective II*
  to validate and evaluate the research results by developing proof-of-concept SMEs-specific prototypes, demonstrating the innovative ELEVATE pedagogic approach and educational and certification environment in the training procedure of the application software products of the participating software SMEs.

- *Objective III*
  to facilitate the take-up of the ELEVATE research results by the software development SMEs. That is, there will be formal adoption guidelines for the successful integration and effective deployment of the ELEVATE environment in application software products addressing real-life scenarios. Moreover, there will be a focus on training activities that are aimed at technical and managerial staff of the participating software development SMEs.

3 Eleavate's Pedagogical Methodology

One of the fundamental trends in e-Learning is capturing the attention of the user or student, which is competed by many other media and platforms constantly. Therefore the educational content must be engaging enough to keep the student dedicated to the learning activities. [1] gives a list of study background in capturing the attention of and engaging the learner. Therefore e-learning is not just compiling information and making it available to the learner but rather creating an environment where the learner continuously adds up to his or her knowledge in an effective and permanent fashion.

In addition, the emergence and prominence of the World Wide Web, with its new possibilities of communities, is thus considered the "new pedagogy of learning" [2]. It is therefore imperative that an approach is based on the online learning community principles. Web 2.0, the new approach based on Internet communities, also encourages significantly more interaction between users, a feature that many theorists argue is vital in e-learning. Interaction encourages deeper and more active learning engagement, builds communities of learning [3] and enables feedback from tutors to students. [4] In recent studies, associations have been reported between tutor–student interaction in online learning and raised levels of student motivation. [5], [6]. Finally, growing spectrums of applications are enumerated as several emerging technologies and applications under the Web 2.0 platform [7]. These include RSS, wikis, blogs, and the user comment functionality found in various websites.

Based on the above, as well as other bibliographical research, the ELEVATE environment incorporates principles regarding the theoretical and applied pedagogy, emphasising at the theories of social interactionism, constructivism, and socio-cultural and activity theory. Moreover the pedagogical methodology purported by ELEVATE facilitates the development of specialised e-learning methodology concerning the training in application software skills. This is to be explored through the notion of competences and how these are best taught and acquired for the IT sector. Given the need for competence development, an integral part of this is the assessment and certification of the acquired competences. Thus, it is imperative to create a theoretical underpinning for the evaluation process as well the application software skills certification procedure.

The pedagogical methodology to be explored and used in ELEVATE is based on three basic notions: the notion of blended learning, the notion of Learning 2.0 and finally on the notion that there needs to be an approach that does not fit all but rather tailors the training on the needs of the individual. That is material used for training, is selected in order to suit the learning needs of the specific trainee in the specific circumstances. Moreover it is anticipated that the selected material will further facilitate the learning experience of that individual.

The pedagogic elements (see Fig. 1) comprising the innovative characteristics of the ELEVATE e-learning environment are structurally broken down into three main modules: blended learning, the e-Training and Learning 2.0.

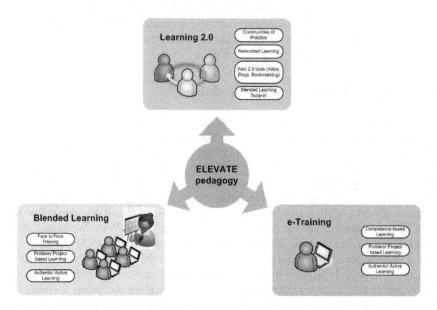

Fig. 1. The proposed ELEVATE Pedagogical Methodology

3.1 Blended Learning

The pedagogical methodology envisioned in ELEVATE incorporates a blended learning cycle, which would include alternating sessions of distance learning and face to face training. In addition, approaches such as problem, competence and authentic/active learning will be explored.

Learning Management Systems (LMSs) are widely used to support blended learning. Learning based on the blending of face-to-face with online training, of formal and informal learning is more acceptable among SMEs than online-training alone. Evidence suggests that the learning experience is better and completion rates are greater where there is tutor support either face to face, on-line or over the telephone.

An LMS is a web-based system used to organise and coordinate the learning material of an educational institution. LMSs also facilitate communication and collaboration of the trainees through the support of communication, collaboration and Web2.0 tools such as forums, blogs, wikis, chat rooms etc.

The blended learning approach of the ELEVATE solution includes the following: (a) face to face training, (b) problem/project based learning, (c) authentic/active learning.

The LMS can be used in a preoperational manner, which is before a face to face class is being held. During this preoperational phase, the trainee may be given some cases studies to consider, some real scenarios to consider and propose solutions and explore them during the face to face session. Some of the advantages of traditional face to face classroom education are: (a) social interaction through personal contact and the exchange of ideas, (b) familiarity, customary method, and (c) an environment which supports multiple communication channels.

Also the LMS can be used in a post operational manner as well. This way, the LMS can be used to further support the learning needs of the learner following the face to face session. Such support can be in the form of further discussion, between the trainer and the trainees, or indeed discussion between the trainees themselves. Particularly the later option gives rise to Learning 2.0.

Moreover, if during the face to face or afterwards, an individual trainee feels that there are aspects of the training session that need further work, this can be achieved via the e-Training module of the ELEVATE pedagogical model.

3.2 e-Training

For the e-Training aspect of the ELEVATE solution we examined the following pedagogical approaches: 1) Authentic Learning, 2) Competence Based Learning, 3) Problem Based Learning, and 4) Project Based Learning, More specifically, for the easier transition of the acquired skills to the real life working environment, an authentic learning approach for the e-Training solution has been proposed. Authentic learning advocates that individuals should engage and interact with authentic activities thus facilitating the transition of the simple application end-user to a trainee. In addition, through competency-based learning environments learners are confronted with authentic, open problems and learning materials which have personal meaning for them and are presented in a variety of formats. For e-Training to operate, the major phases are as follows:

(a) Training Object Generation,
(b) Training and
(c) Evaluation.

During the Training object generation, the trainer/domain expert generates the initial training object by capturing the DOM tree changes caused by his/her activities. During the Training, the trainer provides the necessary metadata enrichment for the enrichment of the training object. The metadata will be used by e-Training to facilitate its tutoring capabilities. Finally, in the evaluation phase, the trainee, is modelled in order to update its profile. The information gathered is used by e-Training system to adopt and personalise the material according to the learning needs of the individual trainee.

3.3 Learning 2.0

Within the scope of Learning 2.0, a pedagogy empowered by digital and network technology, three needs should be satisfied: (a) a learning objects repository (through the implementation of a learning management system), (b) a framework supporting networked learning and the development of communities of practice (through web2.0 tools such as wikis, blogs, social bookmarking etc) and (c) the distance training segment of a blended learning approach (covering distance learning). In Learning 2.0 the trainee is not merely a consumer of the various digital contents but also have the ability to produce content himself/herself as well as create Communities of Practice (CoP) and other networks that best suits the needs of the individual.

Communities of Practice are a set of relations among persons and activities over time and in relation with other tangential and overlapping CoPs [8]. Members of CoPs have a shared set of interests and are motivated to do something about them. In addition, CoPs are self-generating, the membership is self selecting and they are not necessarily co-located.

LMSs can also be utilised to facilitate the creation of online communities. Online communities are a key factor in the development of the Internet based society and business models. In online communities, users interact with each other, share information and cooperate, forming specialized groups either according to common interests or demographic criteria.

3.4 Assessing and Certifying Competences in ELEVATE

It should also be noted that the proposed ELEVATE project supports the integration of advanced, value-added e-training capabilities, based on widely-accepted pedagogic models, into commercial off-the-shelf software products and solutions, embedding the software to be taught into the pedagogical-documented educational procedure. Thus, the ELEVATE environment will enable the acquisition of technological skills and competencies in the application software taught, transferring innovative know-how to the e-training process. More specifically,

- at the technological level, the ELEVATE Training, Educational and Certification Environment enables the complete, interactive integration of the e-learning platforms and tools, utilized for both synchronous and asynchronous e-learning services, with pre-selected software applications products, which constitutes the educational subject, and is supplemented by innovative assisting and training tools, aiming to provide personalized training and educational services;

- at the pedagogical level, the pedagogical-documented ELEVATE Training, Educational and Certification Environment improves the quality of the provided professional e-training services, enables the trainee to become a real end-user of the application software product taught in pragmatic usage scenarios, facilitates the simple application end-user to turn instantly into a trainee, offers mature conditions of apprenticeship development, even with the natural and electronic absence of an experienced application user (or trainer), offers new potentials for interactive e-learning content aggregation, dynamic creation and maintenance, and adopts a widely known and accepted frameworks concerning the monitoring and the evaluation of the e-learning procedure, supporting an automated process regarding the certification of competencies on specific application software products;

4 ELEVATE's Architecture: A Bird's Eye View

The ELEVATE environment constitutes an innovative bridge that represents a critical, added-value element developing an integrated virtual asynchronous e-learning environment prototype, specialized in the training and acquisition of application software competencies. In particular, the ELEVATE environment comprises of three subsystems (presented in Fig. 2, which also presents the involved functional components and subsystems, as well as the communication channels among them):

- *the Interactive Interoperability Layer (IIL)*, which develops the technical preconditions required in order the trainee to be able to use and interact, for training purposes, with the application software (to be taught), instead of using an inflexible and inadequate simulation environment. IIL facilitates the context-sensitive access of the trainee to the components and the functionality of the application software being taught, regarding the learning and training level of the trainee.

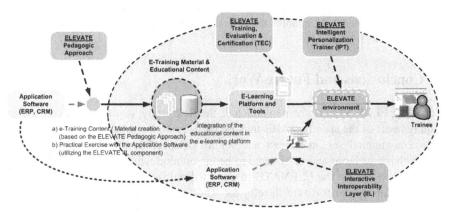

Fig. 2. A bird's eye view of the ELEVATE architecture

- *the Intelligent Personalization Trainer (IPT)* that defines each end-user's access rights to several training areas of the e-learning environment depending on his/her competencies level. IPT ensures intelligent access to the digital learning content, to the appropriate step of the training process and to the suitable components of the application software to be taught. This functionality is provided by bi-directional links and interfaces among the e-learning training and evaluation modules of the e-learning platform and the structural components of the application software.
- *the Training, Evaluation & Certification (TEC)* subsystem that is the support of pedagogic activities regarding the knowledge and competencies evaluation. TEC is a typical system for automatic evaluation including tools for creating queries of several types (e.g. multiple choices), tools for composing tests, an organized exercises repository, test and exercises interfaces, and mechanisms for performance assessment.

Finally, the ELEVATE educational and certification environment supports the usage of introductory evaluation test to assess the initial competency level of the potential trainee regarding a specific application software product. The results of the introductory skills examination provide the information required to the IPT to propose trainee-specific learning paths.

The pedagogic elements comprising the innovative characteristics of the ELEVATE e-learning environment are structurally broken down in three main modules:

- *E-Training Material Creation*:
    integration of various tools that facilitate the dynamic design and creation of e-learning digital content related to the learning environment and the application software being taught,
- *Synchronous E-Learning:*
    Virtual Classroom, comprising both online learning courses and practical training, creating a so-called virtual classroom that is coordinated and guided by a specialized tutor (trainer), and
- *Asynchronous E-Learning and Learning Management System*:
    constituting the "self-paced" mode of the ELEVATE educational environment that enables the trainee to determine his training progression on his own.

5 Conclusions and Future Work

Currently, ELEVATE, is about to conclude the field study, in order to capture the user requirements of the specific SMEs that are partners in the project. During the detailed requirements analyses, interviews and studies of specific software products, certain aspects have surfaced and discovered to be in common while a number of differences were also observed. The ELEVATE solution will utilise an LMS as the basis of training provision by the software developers. The face to face has proved an important aspect of the training session that software companies are keen to maintain, since it provides them a link with their customers and resellers. On the other hand the ELEVATE SME participants are very keen to harness the opportunities offered by ICT in order to streamline the training services that they offer and maximise opportunities. Although the various solutions that are going to be developed within ELEVATE are targeted not only for the SME partners but also for the general European software technology SMEs, it is also a necessity that the final deliverable product should fulfill the requirements of the SME participants in the best way possible.

Therefore, there is a trade-off between complying with the immediate requirements of the specific SMEs and building up a system that is to offer generic solutions to European software technology SMEs with rich innovative methods. ELEVATE will then choose a medium way that should both serve the needs of the SMEs partners but also press innovation at the same time.

Regarding future work the project will strive to develop a pedagogically-documented approach and model that facilitates the specialized and personalized e-training of professionals and end-users in application software products. To accomplish this, related work and pedagogical models will be studies. The main focus will be on competence based learning (CBL). More specifically, CBL is based on the fundamental idea of knowledge space theory that a person's knowledge state in a certain domain can be understood as the set of problems this person is able to solve [9].

In conclusion, according to the above and based on sound pedagogical and psychological principles, we will proceed to propose our ELEVATE pedagogical methodology.

References

1. Conrad, R.M., Donaldson, J.A.: Engaging the Online Learner Activities and Resources for Creative Instruction. John Wiley and Sons, Jossey-Bass, San Francisco (2004)
2. Muske, G., Goetting, M., Vukonick, M.: The World Wide Web: A Training Tool for Family Resource Management Educators. Journal of Extension 39(4) (2001), http://www.joe.org/joe/2001august/a3.html
3. Wenger, E.: Communities of practice social learning systems. Organization 7, 225–256 (2000)
4. Fahy, P.J.: Indicators of support in online interaction. International Review of Research in Open and Distance Learning, 4 (2003), http://www.irrodl.org/index.php/irrodl/article/view/129/600 (accessed December 29, 2006)
5. Shea, P.J., Pickett, A.M., Peltz, W.E.: A follow-up investigation of teaching presence in the SUNY learning network. Journal of Asynchronous Networks 7, 61–80 (2003)
6. Levy, Y.: Comparing dropout and persistence in e-learning courses. Computers and Learning 48, 185–204 (2007)
7. Barsky, E.: Introducing Web 2.0: weblogs and podcasting for health librarians. Journal of Canadian Health Library Association 27, 33–34 (2006)
8. Conrad, R.M., Donaldson, J.A.: Engaging the Online Learner Activities and Resources for Creative Instruction. John Wiley and Sons, Jossey-Bass, San Francisco (2004)
9. Ley, T., Kump, B., Lindstaedt, S.N., Albert, D., Maiden, N.A.M., Jones, S.V.: Competence and Performance in Requirements Engineering: Bringing Learning to the Workplace. In: Proceedings of the Joint International Workshop on Professional Learning, Competence Development and Knowledge Management -LOKMOL and L3NCD Crete, Greece, October 2 (2006)

Building a Collaborative Network for Education and Training in International Trade Facilitation Clusters

John A. Clendenin[1], Nadya N. Petrova[2], and Joshua K. Gill[3]

[1] Instituto de Empressa
Sport@profesor.ie.edu
[2] Supply Chain Center of Regional Excellence
Nadya@ICLogistics.com
[3] Inner Circle Logistics Inc.
jgill@ICLogistics.com

Abstract. The authors present the benefits of collaboration rather than competition in developing educational and training resources for international trade within a geographic region and explore the challenges for business partners, governments and educational institutions. The paper indicates that flexibility in the 21st Century is critical, particularly when striving for virtual implementations of the solution services. It is essential, say the authors, for educators, governments and business executives to focus on performance and the careful orchestration and integration of business, policy and information technology for "Networking" that successfully stimulates inter-governmental cooperation and innovative policies that foster Regional trade facilitation. An innovative way to enhance 21st Century Trade Facilitation is offered with Supply Chain Centers of Regional Excellence (SCcORE).

Keywords: Collaborative Networks for Education, Trade Facilitation, clustering, B2G, B2B, e-infrastructure.

1 Introduction

The benefits of collaboration rather than competition in developing international trade within a geographic region are clear. These benefits include; improved performance among supply chain partners, lower costs, energy conservation and reduced congestion along transportation corridors [1]. However, challenges exist such as the need for training, formal education, and outside consulting services that require careful planning business partners, governments and educational institutions. When developing lifelong learning methodologies in the 21st Century flexibility is crucial, particularly when striving for virtual implementations of the solution services. Both trainees and educational organizations face the challenges of combining time, needs, and resources in a complex system of systems that often have divergent priorities. This complex, interrelated process involving multiple actors was described by Porter as the evolution of economic clusters linked by common technology and skills that are an indelible part of today's knowledge based economy [2].

L.M. Camarinha-Matos et al. (Eds.): PRO-VE 2009, IFIP AICT 307, pp. 816–824, 2009.

2   Collaborative Networks

2.1   General

Collaborative networks in education can lead the way to professional training programs adapted to the needs of the local business community through a virtual exchange of academic competencies. It is essential for educators, governments and business executives to focus on performance and the careful orchestration and integration of business, policy and information technology. The authors address these three pillars: academia, government, business community (chambers of commerce) and the collaboration required for successful "Networking" for education and training which stimulates inter-governmental cooperation and innovative policies that foster Regional trade facilitation.

2.2   Innovation

The evolution of innovation and impact of net-centric tools has been a substantive force in the collaborative capabilities of networks that create economic possibilities that defy traditional molds and allow for the formation of collaborative networks over increasing geographic distance [3], [4]. Successful collaboration, rather than competition, to enhance 21st Century Trade Facilitation is made possible by Supply Chain Centers of Regional Excellence (SCcORE). These "Centers of Excellence" represent an innovative method to stimulate the free movement of knowledge in an effective Regional "Cluster" for increased competence and competitive advantage. SCcORE enables a geographic Region such as Southeastern Europe (SEE) (is SEE not more "accepted" these days?) to compete as a "Trade Cluster" sharing the resources and competitive advantages of collaboration. Today several examples exist of efforts to foster the development of trans-boundary clusters utilizing the connective effects of ICT including Western Europe, the Baltic States, and Central Europe [5], [6], [7].

3   Networks for Trade Facilitation Clusters

3.1   Rapid Change and ICT Infrastructure

Information technology (IT) has become an integral part of our life with new developments occurring at pace never before seen, bringing with it rapid changes in our personal and professional worlds. These changes range from daily interpersonal communication through bio-modified interference to innovative business models that quickly become an indelible part of today's economics and politics. Trade facilitation is a powerful tool for boosting economic growth especially in countries with strategic geographic location. In the past, trade flourished in regions found at geographic "choke points" along trade corridors. An example of this can be found on the Balkan Peninsula, located on trade routes of the Silk Road and an important staging point for trade between Europe and Asia. However, today's prerequisites for the development of global trade are not only geographical resources and geopolitical stability but also efficiency and capabilities in facilitating trade. For example, the importance of utilizing innovative technologies within knowledge networks for trade cluster development has been demonstrated in the Strait of Mallacca. Knowledge transfer was a crucial factor in the emergence of knowledge clusters across four distinct trade clusters: Northwest Malaysian, West Malaysian, North Sumatra, and Singapore-Johore. The use of technology was fundamental in producing innovation, promoting knowledge sharing, and engaging in knowledge transfer to stakeholders through education and training [8]. For example, modern trade facilitation is predicated on building physical infrastructure to facilitate the movement of goods while simultaneously developing an interconnected banking system to facilitate the movement of money. This "developmental mix" to move goods more efficiently along trade corridors is predicated on ICT infrastructure and innovations in net-centric connectivity.

3.2 Facilitating Trade

The efficient and speedy movement of information requires e-infrastructures to facilitate the timely exchange of trade documents among border agencies and trading partners. In an economic environment defined by global trade, the region that is capable of building an e-infrastructure and integrating its transportation and cross-border services into the global supply chain has a distinct competitive advantage. As integrated ICT based trade facilitation continues to be adopted globally, the flow of information and goods will follow the path of least resistance and migrate to the trade corridors that are ICT enabled and offer lower costs, improved shipment visibility, and lower risk [9]. For example, the World Bank consistently ranks Singapore ahead of the Netherlands, Germany, Japan, Hong Kong, and China as a hub for global trade due to its world-class infrastructure and excellent connectivity.

Pervasive in the private sector, ICT is a prerequisite to survive that must be embraced, not only in policy making but also, in educational systems. The benefits of integrating services along an e-enabled trade corridor accrue to participating countries, the business community, and private citizens. The challenge is acquiring the valuable knowledge and skills to become a productive actor in an integrated network of education and life-long learning made up of business, policy and technology with the core philosophy of innovation through collaboration. Core challenges to the creation of such a network is incorporation of the collective learning of multi-disciplinary knowledge for improved business processes, clear understanding of the global marketplace, technical understanding required for continued innovative capacity, adherence to norms valued in a Network Economy and the importance of interaction with and trust of the local community for continued support [10].

A single educational organization is limited in providing knowledge to its individual network but, a system of interconnected universities and educational centers within a region shares an increased capacity as the power of individual networks interact. This System-of-Systems (SoS) focuses on core, common, and unique attributes within the system and its members to ensure mutual exclusivity while being collectively exhaustive [13].

As Kevin Kelly cites Larry Keely in the book New Rules for the New Economies, "No one is as smart as everyone" [11]. Collaborating in a network, they are able to share competencies in a field by sharing best practices, exchanging lectors, bringing academicians together to optimize academic research, exchanging students, and providing academic internships. The collaborative opportunities among educational organizations are abundant as long as the combined competences compliment each other in a field and their sharing increases the value to all. The basic principle of network economic theories includes the concept of an installed base of nodes where "as the number of nodes in a network increases arithmetically, the value of the network increases exponentially" [11]. In the educational concept, collaborating academic institutes and educational centers enjoy exponential growth of opportunities with every single addition of a new collaborating partner as more diverse and customized programs are offered to the pool of current and perspective trainees by an organization within the network. Furthermore, collaborating with partners with complementary competences or specializing in a subject strengthens members within a network as the value of the network increases with network expansion. These results have been shown to hold with continued decreases in the costs of technology that result from the innovative capacity of networks and their ability to disseminate information [13]. The synergistic impact of this approach is further explained in Figure 1.

The Internet provides the opportunity to create a semantic community using net-centric tools to foster collaboration and partnerships where information access is achieved in an integrated environment for informed decision-making based on a multidisciplinary approach [12]. Robust statistical tools and performance metrics are optimized to ensure maximum quality control and service provision for a system of regional training units that allow for the analysis of multiple networks simultaneously in which, there are multiple types of nodes (multi-node) and multiple types of links (multi-plex).

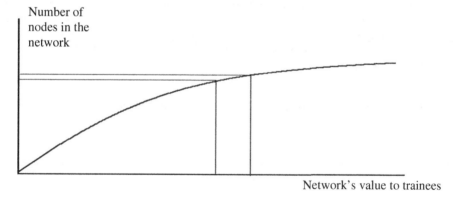

Fig. 1. The Network Effect within a collaborative network

3.3 Collaborative Networks

In collaborative networks for education and lifelong learning, bringing together multiple tiers from institutes of higher education, training centers, and the public and private sector further maximizes network output by providing unprecedented reach and impact to diverse audiences.

3.4 Life-Long Learning

One of the growing components of academic services is the notion of life-long learning and the provision of continuing education to the community. A university can offer a seminar in collaboration with a network participant such as a training center that is practice-oriented rather than theory-oriented and already specializes in the needed field or profession. Collaborating in a network for education in an international environment or a large region, the training center has the capabilities to offer its products and services beyond its existing market. A local partner, as a university located in a new market, is a good channel for information distribution, training promotion, and recruitment as the university gains the capability to offer educational opportunities to an enlarged target group. Combining complimentary competences, the collaborating partners do not deprive each other of applicants for targeting different audiences. The greatest attribute of a collaborative network for education and training is the social organization of its members, integrated and supported by the local community, where the flow of information across a virtually limitless number of areas and interests is encouraged.

3.5 Flexibility

The importance of a collaborative network for education and lifelong learning is not only the co-existence of its constituent parts but also its flexibility in attracting external partners in maximizing the value of networking to all participants. According to Kevin Kelly, "More complex objects and services are capable of permeating far more systems and networks, thus greatly boosting their own value and the plentiful value of all the systems they touch." [11] Supporting economic growth along a trade corridor by transferring competences, a collaborative network for education thrives as the link between policy requirements and business adaptability. In order to contribute to trade facilitation effectively, it must be able to provide up-to-date programs and trainings on at various levels of professional development, as well as to consult government agencies on innovative practices and solutions.

4 Developing and Building a Center of Excellence

4.1 Objectives of a Collaborative Network Program

One of the primary objectives of building a collaborative network for education and training within a cluster is the enhanced understanding of the relationship-building process. Obtaining the ability to identify and analyze a supply chain's functions, processes and activities, both intra-firm and across supply chain partners, that add cost and cost to service trade-offs can be more effectively placed in context with the policy and theory of government and academia. This is an oft missing piece of traditional business training programs. Collaboration helps in developing an understanding of the role of managing supply chain costs and achieving the ability to identify specific customer service needs that will provide a differential advantage in the marketplace. The partnership approach allows for a more thorough understanding of supply chain system components and their complex relationships within individual companies, including cost to service trade-offs, so that a variety of analytical tools, skills and techniques can be used to solve supply chain problems and enhance the profitability of cross border operations. The understanding of the role of supply chain management in both business and government environments also helps the academic community use analytical tools, skills and techniques to solve logistical problems and identify research opportunities. The combination of practical and theoretical research developed in conjunction with government policy makers and business partners enables faculty members to gain the insight to apply innovative technologies and practices to further the research of supply chain optimization. Overall the objective is to position the Center of Excellence with the comprehensive ability to identify and disseminate core knowledge for successful management of global supply chains with the understanding of emerging and world class innovative technologies as they relate to various supply chain components.

4.2   Solution ~ Supply Chain Center of Regional Excellence (SCcORE)

The Supply Chain Center of Regional Excellence (SCcORE) is a non-profit association developed on the "Center of Excellence" model described earlier. With a strong advisory board of business executives, professors and government leaders the SCcORE Centers are partnering with educational institutions, Chambers of Commerce and Trade Associations in the Balkans to optimize the learning and best practices involved in effective cross border trade. Currently, the Center is striving to support the development of Pan-European Trade Corridor X beginning at the Port of Thessaloniki crossing Northern Greece, the Former Yugoslav Republic of Macedonia, and Serbia through Central and Western Europe.

Combining competitive benchmarking through in-depth research in Supply Chain Management, SCcORE provides innovative ideas in Net-Centric trade facilitation. Bringing innovative ideas to policy makers and business associations, its collaborative network enriches with opportunities to provide further trainings to state agencies and businesses for competitiveness and efficiency on the global market [14]. Aiming at regional development through innovation, SCcORE brings together educational organizations (universities, educational centers, etc.) to collaborate with government agencies (ICT agency, Ministry of Transport, Ministry of State Administration, Customs, Phyto-sanitary Agency, Border Police, etc.), and business community (trade associations, chambers of commerce, etc.). Thus, the extended network is able to observe, analyze, and react multi-dimensionally to on-going trade concerns. Figure 2 describes the complex linkages within a SoS that defines the SCcORE approach.

The connection between education and policy making is vital but business communities also need to be exposed to the benefits of the developing technology to stimulate economic growth. Collaborating with business associations, a collaborative network for education and lifelong learning has a better understanding of the business needs. More important than not, it is more flexible in offering trainings and seminars to provide specific professional skills and knowledge than mainstream education. A collaborative network evolves to meet the requirements of the global environment by promoting its most suitable members and bringing value to the system through collective dissemination of competences. In the case of a trans-boundary network, SCcORE becomes vital to the "constructed advantage" through the ability to receive, absorb, and transmit innovative strategies, technological advancement and knowledge over long distances while acting as a repository of this shared knowledge that serves to enhance network value for new entrants [15]. SCcORE's capability to provide linkages addresses several development factors identified in the success of Western European high-tech clusters. Primary among these are the collective learning of multi-disciplinary knowledge for improved business processes, clear understanding of the global marketplace, technical understanding required for continued innovative capacity, adherence to norms valued in a Network Economy and the importance of interaction with and trust of the local community for continued support [4].

This is accomplished by linking the three pillars vital for the sustainability of economic growth: academia, government, and business. Their capability in reacting cohesively to business change and global competition shapes regional competiveness. A big obstacle both to employers and recent graduates in SEE is the incongruence between the demand and supply of labor competences. Bringing equilibrium to the job market is not a two-dimensional equation, however. The third dimension – policy – is as integral a part of the solution matrix. Policy, shaping the educational system and modeling the trade requirements, needs more transparency and ensure access to current and relevant trade statistics in order to evaluate and facilitate the overlapping of academia and business. For example, developing a trade corridor through integration of information systems requires new rules and regulations for cross-border trade but, their effectiveness depends on the way policy makers, business associations, and educational organizations communicate each others' needs in reaching the common goal.

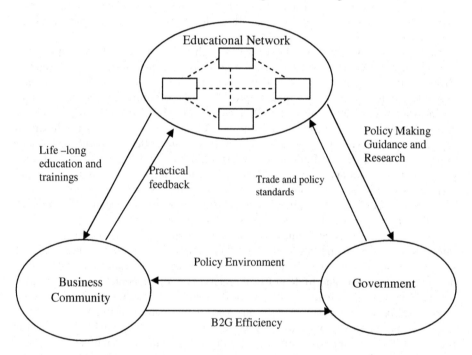

Fig. 2. Collaborative network for education in international trade facilitation: The SCcORE Model

4.3 Knowledge Adaptation Principles

The knowledge flow among the three pillars – government, academia, and business community serves as a generator of ideas where new products, business models, and opportunities proliferate. Differing from an incubator, a collaborative network for education engages a broad spectrum of organizations in achieving an adaptive and agile management and organizational culture for business and governments. The basic framework of a virtual education and training network with the vision of supporting regional competitiveness through trade facilitation provides four main principles for success [16]. The first one is *Be ready for business change and global competition* – in a collaborative environment where optimization of processes and high connectivity among players increases their productivity. The second principle is *Become technically and tactically proficient* - in utilizing Internet and information systems integration and deployment among trading partners and across multiple government agencies to support the sustainability and development of the collaborative network. Real-time exchange of trade documents and data among government agencies and trading partners, timely communication among educational organizations in adapting to the business needs, and a synchronized coordination of activities among the three pillars supported by ICT integration provides a competitive edge in regional trade facilitation. The third principle for success in regional competitiveness is *Benchmark for quality effectiveness* – by adopting recognized benchmarking techniques as a competitive strategy for the development of pan-European trade corridors. Finally, *Balance costs, inventory, and customer service* - to create value by striking the right balance between business productivity and international trading procedures.

4.4 Conclusion

The future holds exciting prospects for partners in collaborative networks for education. A key component for success is the unlimited flow of communication and profound understanding of your partner's capabilities. With clear objectives and the connectivity of the Internet, peer-based networks will be able to do far more than expected with only minimal oversight. "Silicon Valley's greatest 'product' is the social organization of its companies and, most important, the networked architecture of the region itself—the tangled web of former jobs, intimate colleagues, information leakage from one firm to the next, rapid company life cycles, and agile email culture" [11]. This opportunity is especially appropriate for the development of e-enabled trade "clusters." The "21st Century Silk Road" being developed for connectivity between Pan-European Corridors and the global supply chain will bring extraordinary possibilities for the region. One example of innovation that has been demonstrated is a web-based "single-window" that allows for business-to-business (B2B), business-to-government (B2G), and government-to-government (G2G) connectivity through seamless integration of multiple languages, technical formats, and documentation [17].

The collaborative network of education and training that strives to improve abilities, skills, and knowledge along a trade corridor holds an important role for successful development of these "Clusters." A collaborative network for education and lifelong learning cannot be restrained to educational organizations only. The flow of knowledge and proper communication among governmental decision-makers, educators, and traders is essential. The flow of knowledge is part of the movement of information, goods and payments in a global supply chain that facilitates trade. This "Cluster" is dependent on the same e-infrastructure as the three pillars of academia, government, and the business community that can provide the essential knowledge and technology transfer to facilitate competitiveness.

References

1. Bates, W., van Opstal, D.: Five for the Future. Council of Competitiveness (2007)
2. Porter, M.E.: The Competitive Advantage of Nations. Simon and Schuster, New York (1990)
3. Porter, M.E.: Clusters of Innovation: Regional Foundations of U.S. Competitiveness. Council on Competitiveness, Washington (2001)
4. Ketels, C.: The Development of the Cluster Concept – Present Experiences and Further Developments. In: NRW Conference on Clusters, Duisburg, Germany, December 5 (2003)
5. European Biotechnology Science and Industry News. Lyonbiopole and Biowin plan to form a transborder cluster, http://www.eurobiotechnews.eu/western-europe
6. The State Agency of Ukraine for Investments and Innovations: First Transborder Innovation Cluster Founded in Volyn and Rivne Regions, http://www.in.gov.ua
7. European Union Neighbourhood Programme. Riga, Latvia: INTERREG IIIB Baltic Sea Region, http://www.bsrinterreg3a.net
8. Evers, H.-D.: Knowledge hubs and knowledge clusters: Designing a knowledge architecture for development. Center for Development Research (2008)
9. Clendenin, J.A., Gill, J.K.: Increasing SME Competitiveness Using Web-based Technologies for Trade Facilitation. In: COSMO Small Business Conference (2008)
10. Keeble, D., Wilkinson, F.: Collective Learning and Knowledge Development in the Evolution of Regional Clusters of High Technology SMEs in Europe. Reg. Studies 1998 33(4), 295–303 (1998)
11. Kelly, K.: New Rules for the Network Economy, http://www.kk.org
12. Clendenin, J.: Complex Systems and the Science of Net-Centric Supply Chains. Invited Paper, 4th Balkan Conference in Informatics (2009)
13. Clendenin, J.A., Gill, J.K.: Towards an Integrated Southeastern European Trade Facilitation Cluster. Invited Paper, ICEIRD Conference (2009)
14. Clendenin, J.A., Petrova, N.N., Gill, J.K.: Supply Chains Centers for Regional Excellence: Repositories of Knowledge, Tools, and Training. Cosmo Small Business Conference (2008)
15. Cooke, P., Leydesdorff, L.: Regional Development in the Knowledge-Based Economy: The Construction of Advantage. J. of Tech. Transfer 31(1), 5–15 (2006)
16. Clendenin, J.: Supply Chain 101. Harvard Business School (1999)
17. Inner Circle Logistics: Facilitating Regional Competitiveness: The Southeastern Europe Project. USTDA Final Report (2008)

New Vision of Collaborative Networked Study: Fundamentals, Applications and Discipline Formation at CEFET/RJ

Antonio José Cauliraux Pithon

Federal Center of Technological Education CEFET/RJ, Avenida Maracanã, 229,
Bloco E, 5º floor, Brazil
caulliraux@gmail.com

Abstract. Collaborative networks of organizations and/or can be nowadays found in large variety of forms, including virtual organizations, virtual enterprise, extended enterprise, dynamic supply chains, social network, etc. A large body of empiric knowledge related to collaborative networks is already available, but there is an urgent need to consolidated this knowledge and build the foundations for more sustainable development of this area. The establishment of a scientific discipline for collaborative networks is a strong instrument in achieving this purpose. In this context, the article presents the experience developed by Federal Center of Technological Education – CEFET/RJ Brazil that began, in the first semester of 2007, a pilot course on Collaborative Network for students in Master Program in Technology.

Keywords: Collaborative network, Social network, Virtual organization.

1 Introduction

The "term" network is nowadays a central issue in many fields like; social sciences, communications, physics, computer science, virtual organization, virtual enterprise, etc. Among the various types of network, of special relevance are collaborative networks. A collaborative network (CN) is constituted by a variety of entities (e.g., organizations and people) that are largely autonomous in terms of their: operating environment, culture, social capital and goals. Nevertheless these entities collaborate to better achieve common of compatible goals, and whose interactions are supported by computer network (Camarinha-Matos, Afsarmanesh, 2005).

The implementation of collaborative process has accelerated in recent years as a consequence of both new challenges posed to companies and organizations by the fast changing socio-economic conditions and new developments in ICT sector.

In fact during the last three decades the information and communication technologies have been playing a growing role in organizations, namely as an instrument to support integration and flexibility. As a result of these developments, new scientific discipline emerged or where consolidated as in the case of collaborative Network (Camarinha-Matos et al., 2004).

L.M. Camarinha-Matos et al. (Eds.): PRO-VE 2009, IFIP AICT 307, pp. 825–832, 2009.
© IFIP International Federation for Information Processing 2009

Nowadays, several courses in the specific area of Collaborative Network are already being taught or organized at different universities worldwide. For instance, the University of Lisbon (Portugal) offers a 1 semester course on Virtual enterprise to the 5th year students of electrical and Computer engineering since 2002 (Garita, 2004).

Similarly, the Federal University of Santa Catarina (Brazil) offers course of Automation and Systems Engineering and the Costa Rica Institute of Technology [4] started offering Virtual Organization coursers to their students, as well as, on February 2007, Federal Center of Technological Education – CEFET/RJ in Brazil, stared a pilot course.

In the context, the objective of this paper is describe the experience with a pilot initiative of teaching a complete course on Collaborative Network (EDA 3022) at the Federal Center of Technological Education – CEFET/RJ in the Master Technological program in first trimester of 2007 academic year.

The proposal of this course is presented later on.

2 Collaborative Network

The word "net" is very old and it comes from the latin "retis", meaning interlacement of threads with regular openings that form a type of cloth. Starting from interlacement notion, mesh and reticular structures, the word net went winning new meanings along times, passing to be used in different situation.

Leaving of defined concept for (Cândido, et al, 2000.), "nets are organizational systems capable to gather individuals and institutions, of democratic form and share, around similar causes. Flexible structures and established horizon, the work dynamics in net suppose performances collaborative and sustained by the will and likeness of their members, being characterized as a significant organizational resource for the social structuring".

In agreement with, enterprise network are formed initially with objective of reducing uncertainties and risks, organizing economical activities starting from the coordination and cooperation among companies.

Most of the authors study the perspective of nets and her use, as a road to study the organizations, appears to the organizations as social nets and they should be analyzed as such. A social net has there to be with a group of people, organizations, etc., linked through a social relationships group of a specific type. In this perspective, the structure of any organization should be understood and analyzed in terms of multiple nets of internal and external relationships. In that sense, the organizations are nets and the organizational form depends on the characteristics, interests and needs participant companies.

The organizational nets can be considered a consequence of concepts and beginnings of social nets and they can be divided in intra and inter-organization.

We started to detail the several types of formations of nets below:

- Social Network: focus on relationship among social entities, is used widely in the social and behavioural sciences, as well as in economics, marketing, and industrial engineering;
- Virtual Organization: comprising a set of (legally) independent organizations that share resources and skills to achieve its mission/goal, but that is not limited to an

alliance of for profit enterprises. A Virtual Enterprise is therefore, a particular case of Virtual Organization;

- Virtual Enterprise: a temporary alliance of enterprises that come together to share skills or core competencies and resources in order to better respond to business opportunities, and whose cooperation is supported by computer networks;
- Extended Enterprise: a concept typically applied to an organization in which a dominant enterprise "extended" its boundaries to all or some of its suppliers. An Extended Enterprise can be seen as a particular case of Virtual enterprise;
- Agile Enterprise: is the ability of an organization to adapt proficiently in continuously changing, unpredictable business environment;
- Joint Venture: is an entity formed between or more parties to undertake economic activity together. The parties agree to create a new entity by both contributing equity, and they share revenues, expenses, and control of the enterprise;
- Cluster: geographical concentrations of interlinked enterprises that act is a same section of specialized suppliers, providers services and associated institutions, tends in common, besides the location, the contribution for development products of region. They are orientated by beginnings as cooperation, complementarities, community's sense and competition.

In that sense, Collaborative Network course is being implanted, trying to give an approach of concepts mentioned above.

3 Discipline Structure

Collaborative network was included in 2007 as an optical discipline in Master Technological Program at CEFET/RJ and it is part of curricular structure and academic regime. These structure curricula are divided in a cast of obligatory and elective disciplines.

The distribution of those disciplines in curriculum of the course can be seen in Table 1.

The minimum duration for accomplishment of the course is 18 (eighteen) months and the maximum is 24 (twenty for) months. The course is divided in 3 (three) fundamentals steps, to know: obtaining the credits, development of research and defence of the dissertation.

During a period of 12 weeks, each week includes 4h theory, these lectures comprised a presentation of the main concepts, state of the art and supporting technologies, and discussion of major trends and challenges. Although an optional discipline, this attracted 10 students in summer 2007, which is a significant number considering that was the first time that discipline was offered.

Offering this discipline, the Master's degree in Technology of CEFET/RJ answers directly to the student's longings, i.e., offers possibility the same ones know and learn on the emerging organizational concepts that will face in his professional life. The next sections describe in general terms the structure of Collaborative network discipline.

Table 1. Distribution of discipline in Master's degree course

Obligatory Disciplines		
Code	**Denomination**	**Credit**
MAD 3007	Statistical Methods I	3
EDA 3024	Organization	3
EDA 3025	Technology	3
EDA 3300	Seminar for Master dissertation	0
EDA 3301	Research for Master dissertation	0
Elective Disciplines		
EDA 3029	Integrated Analysis of Life Cycle	3
EDA 3302	Study Activity Integrated	0
EDA 3033	Evaluation Projects	3
EDA 3030	Evaluation Technological Projects	3
EDA 3012	Systems Reliability	3
EDA 3013	Structural Reliability	3
EDA 3014	Human Reliability	3
EDA 3022	Corporate Finances	3
EDA 3021	Integration of Administration Systems	3
EDA 3008	Intelligence Computational	3
EDA 3010	Statistical Methods II	3
EDA 3011	Statistical Methods III	3
EDA 3026	Modelling of Phenomena	3
EDA 3022	Collaborative Network	3

4 Structure of Collaborative Network Discipline

Collaborative Network disciplines (EDA 3022) has as presupposition the fact that production of knowledge depends on the relationship among the subject (student) and the teacher. Thus, the discipline provided advanced education in the área of Collaborative Network, including Virtual Enterprises, Virtual Organization, Fractal Enterprise, Contracts in Virtual Organization, Social Network, etc.

The specific contents of the course are described bellow. For each subject the main bibliographic references that may be used.

1. Network
    a) Introduction and concepts [27, 20, 18].
2. Network Models
    a) Social network: definitions, application and examples [27, 2, 19];
    b) Intra-organization Network: definition, application and examples [12];
    c) Inter-organization Network: definition, application and examples [12];
    d) Interpersonal Network: definition, application and examples [12].
3. Virtual Organization [14, 6]
    a) Agile Enterprise [15, 23];
    b) Virtual Enterprise [6, 21, 23];
    c) Extended Enterprise [3];
    d) Fractal Enterprise [25];
    e) Life cycle [10, 28];

f) Contracts in Virtual Organization (legal form) [26];
g) Broker in Virtual Enterprise Formation: [23, 1];
h) Teams in Virtual Enterprise: [23].
4. Cooperative Network
   a) Joint Ventures [22];
   b) Cluster [24];
   c) Scientific Collaborative Network [9].
5) Awareness in Network
   a) Introduction e definitions [13].

5   Objectives of the Course

Collaborative network discipline has how main objectives to do the students are capable of:

- In-depth study of CN paradigm focusing on related information technologies and concrete applications;
- Identify and develop possible subjects for pos-graduation theses/projects;
- Explore the application of CN concepts within a national context;
- Develop in the students basic skills to carry out applied research and publish the corresponding scientific results;
- Aim at the establishment of a research group on CN at the Collaborative Work Nucleus.

6   Discipline Practical Activities

The activity developed at classroom is based in the games as tool that makes possible business existence simulation in their several activities, including from the planning to execution. This technique is very used, mainly in the administration courses, masters degree and MBA's and it portrays, in an informal way and to entertaining, strategies to be adopted by managers in the execution of the tasks, mainly in those that it involves work team, focus of our experiment.

The accomplished experience tried to show the importance of concepts learned at classroom, concerning the structure of a collaborative Network and all their interfaces concerning obtaining of their results. It fits to detach that the exercise happened in real time and attendance, because, it is not very common once the nets operate in virtual way.

The team, composed for team students, a consultant (invited teacher) and the director of enterprise (teacher of the discipline), it was under the consultant's orientation, positioned with the hands given in circle form, halfway some of other ones, in the classroom.

The disposition in circle is due to fact the communication if to give in a lot of directions and his flow is not controlled, just administered, that is, doesn't possess a hierarchy. The consultant distributed numbers written in a piece of paper (from 1 to 10), so that it was put in the ground ahead of the feet of each team member, passing to be this identification numbering of each one. To proceed, the consultant distributed string pieces with approximately 2,5 meters in length, that crossing in diagonal, it tied for the tips each member the other, tends these to tie one of the tips of string in right pulse (Figure 1). In this dispositions and already connected, the consultant explained the game rule that consisted beforehand, in the choice manager on the part of team. Tends the manager been chosen, the consultant request to the same as does the annotations related with what will happen.

At this time, he consultant begins the change of positions of each one in the circle, and in the end of those changes, he grew up a true knot in the string, as seen in the Figure 1. That knots the events that happen the any net type acts, since for beginning, the social nets are not static. The manager's paper was driving the actions that they would be developed by group, in the sense of untying the knot. It was not allowed that in any hypothesis, the string that tied each member of the group was cut and the knot that tied him to the undone pulse. The established time so that the manager drove his task was 5 minutes.

Therefore in beginning, it was noticed that manager didn't stop the control task and nor command of the team, letting his insecurity to appear for the group. With the control loss on the part of manager, the group began showing in a disordered way, random and empiric with objective of undoing knot. Visibly amazed, the team unchained a series of disconnected manifestations that disrupt the search of solution for the problem. The time of five minutes became exhausted and the result was not reached.

Before this problem, the consultant undid the net and it substituted the manager for other member of the group. Starting from this substitution, the group through a disassemble process, got to complete the exercise in the stipulated period of five minutes.

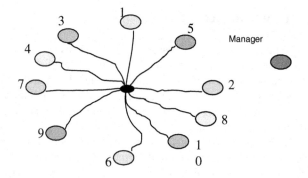

Fig. 1. Teams formation

At the end of the experiment, the teacher of discipline made an analogy with the net concepts, where the collaboration and the trust are fundamental for the development of net.

7 Conclusion

Introduction of Collaborative network discipline in master technological Program at CEFET/RJ, although an optional discipline, is being successful and contributing to preparation of a new generation of engineers and research able to play a major role in the deployment of Collaborative network concept in Brazilian university.

The assertiveness of result this experience is in the number of students that intend to include concepts of collaborative network as theoretical establish (or regarding analysis) in their theme of dissertation research.

As a result, the course is planned to be given again in coming semesters in this program.

Regarding future horizon, the possibility of offering a Virtual Course on Collaborative Network in Spanish (using e-learning techniques) aiming at integration Universities and Institutes of Technology of Latin America and Caribbean countries, can be evaluated.

Finally, it is clear more textbooks in this area are necessary in order to facilitate education tasks.

References

1. Ávila, P., Putnik, G., et al.: Brokerage function in Agile Virtual Enterprise Integration – A Literature Review. In: Camarinha-Matos, L.M. (ed.) Collaborative Business Ecosystems and Virtual Enterprise. Kluwer Academic Publisher, Dordrecht (2002)
2. Burt, R.S., Minor, M.J.: Applied Networks Analysis. Sage, Berverly Hills (1983)
3. Browne, J.: The Extended Enterprise – Manufacturing and the Value chain. In: Afsarmanesh, H. (ed.) Balanced Automation Systems – Architectures and design Methodologies (1995)
4. Camarinha-Matos, L.M., Afsarmanesh, H.: Journal of Intelligent Manufacturing 1(16), 439–452 (2005)
5. Camarinha-Matos, L.M., Cardoso, T.: Education on Virtual Organizations: Na experience at UNL. In: Virtual Enterprise and Collaborative Networks. Kluwer Academic Publisher, Boston (2004)
6. Camarinha-Matos, L.M., Afsarmanesh, H.: The Virtual Enterprise concept. In: Camarina-Matos, L.M., Afsarmanesh, H. (eds.) Infrastructure for Virtual enterprise – Networking Industrial Enterprise, pp. 3–14. Kluwer Academic, Dordrecht (1999)
7. Cândido, G.A., Abreu, A.F.: Os conceitos de redes e as relações inter-organizacionais: um estudo exploratório. In: ENANPAD, Florianópolis, Brasil (2000)
8. Cheng, K.: E-Manufacturing: Fundamentals and Applications (Ed.). WIT Press, London (2005)
9. Dias dos Santos, P.: Redes de Colaboração Científica Interdisciplinares: estudo de caso na Rede Brasileira de Universidades Federais. XXXI Congresso Brasileiro de Ciências da Comunicação – Natal (2008)
10. Fuchs, M.: Design and Implementation of value Systems: The Lifecycle Perspective. Institute for Technology Mabagement, Universty of St. Gallen, Switerland (1999)
11. Garita, C.: A case study of VO education in Costa Rica. In: Virtual enterprise and Collaborative Network. Kluwer Academic Publisher, Boston (2004)
12. Grandori, A., Soda, G.: Inter Firm Networks: Antecedentes, Mechanism and Forms (1995)
13. Gutwin, C., Greenberg, S.: The Importance of Awareness for team Cognition in Distributed Collaboration. In: Salas, E., Fiore, S.M. (eds.) Team Cognition: Understanding the factors that drive Process and Performance, pp. 177–201 (2004)
14. Jägers, H., Jansen, W.: Characteristics of Virtual organization. In: Sieber, P., Griese, J. (eds.) Organization Virtualness, pp. 65–76. Simowa Verlag Bern (1998)

15. Lee, G.H.: Designs of Components and manufacturing Systems for Agile Manufacturing. International Journal of Production Research, 1023–1044 (1998)
16. Leon, M.E.: Uma Análise de Redes de Cooperação das Pequenas e Médias Empresas do Setor de Telecomunicações. Dissertação de Mestrado, Engenharia de Produção da Escola Politécnica da Universidade de São Paulo (1998)
17. Lipnak, J., Stamps, J.: Virtual Teams: People Working Across Boundaries with Technology. John Wiley & Sons, Inc., Chichester (2000)
18. Loiola, E., Moura, S.: Análise de Redes: Uma contribuição aos Estudos Organizacionais. In: Fischer, T. (Org). Gestão Contemporânea: cidades estratégicas e organizações locais, Rio de Janeiro, pp. 53–68 (2007)
19. Martelo, R.M.: Análise das Redes Sociais – aplicação nos estudos de transferência da informação. Revista Ciência e Informação 30(1), 71–81 (2001)
20. Noria, N.: Is a network perspective a useful way of studying organizations? In: Nohria, N., Eccles, R.G. (eds.) Network and Organizations: structure, form and action, pp. 1–22. Harvard Business School Press, Boston (1992)
21. Osório, L., Barata, M., Gibon, P.: Communication Infrastructures Requirements in a Virtual Enterprise. In: Camarinha-Matos, L.M., Afsarmanesh, H. (eds.) Infrastructure for Virtual Enterprises – Networking Industrial Enterprises, pp. 65–76. Kluwer Academic, Dordrecht (1999)
22. Pimenta, E.G.: Joint Ventures – Contratos de Parceria Empresarial no Direito Brasileiro, Juarez de Oliveira Editora (2005)
23. Pithon, A.J.C.: Projeto Organizacional para a Engenharia Concorrente no Âmbito das Empresas Virtuais. Ph.D. Thesis, University of Minho, Guimarães, Portugal (2004)
24. Porter, M.: Clusters and the new economics of competition. Harvard Business Review (1998)
25. Rajan, V.N.: An Agent-Based Fractal model of Agile manufacturing Enterprises: Modeling and Decision-Making Issues. In: Proceedings of the AI and Manufacturing Research Planning Workshop (1996)
26. Teixeira, B.M.: Proposta de um Modelo Contratual para as Empresas Virtuais no Âmbito da Legislação Brasileira. M.Sc Thesis, CEFET/RJ, Rio de Janeiro (2007)
27. Yoguel, G., Kantis, H.: Reestructuración Industrial y Eslabonamientos Productivos: El rol de las pequeñas y Medianas Firmas Subcontratistas. Buenos Aires, CEPAL (1990)
28. Zimmermman, F.: Structural and Managerial Aspects of Virtual Enterprise. University of Bamberg, Business Information Systems (1996)

Author Index

Printed in the United States
By Bookmasters